Films for Anthropological Teaching
8th edition 1995

Special Publications of the American Anthropological Association

29 / *Films for Anthropological Teaching, 8th edition*
Karl G. Heider and Carol Hermer, preparers

28 / *The Tasaday Controversy: Assessing the Evidence*
Thomas N. Headland, ed.

27 / *Training Manual in Applied Medical Anthropology*
Carole E. Hill, ed.

26 / *Surviving Fieldwork: A Report of the Advisory Panel on Health and Safety in Fieldwork*
Nancy Howell

25 / *Culture, Kin, and Cognition in Oceania: Essays in Honor of Ward H. Goodenough*
Mac Marshall and John L. Caughey, eds.

24 / *Anthropology for Tomorrow: Creating Practitioner-Oriented Applied Anthropology Programs*
Robert T. Trotter II, ed.

20 / *Training Manual in Nutritional Anthropology*
Sara A. Quandt and Cheryl Ritenbaugh, eds.

19 / *Training Manual in Policy Ethnography*
John van Willigen and Billie R. DeWalt, eds.

15 / *Culture and Ecology: Eclectic Perspectives*
John G. Kennedy and Robert B. Edgerton, eds.

12 / *Health in the Andes*
Joseph W. Bastien and John M. Donahue, eds.

6 / *The Societies of Borneo: Explorations in the Theory of Cognatic Social Structure*
G. N. Appell, ed.

Films for Anthropological Teaching
8th edition 1995

Prepared by
Karl G. Heider and Carol Hermer

A special publication of the
American Anthropological Association
Number 29

professional series

special publications of the
American Anthropological Association

Published by the
American Anthropological Association
4350 North Fairfax Drive, Suite 640
Arlington, VA 22203-1621
703/528-1902

Library of Congress Cataloging-in-Publication Data

Heider, Karl G., 1935–
  Films for anthropological teaching / prepared by Karl G. Heider and Carol Hermer. — 8th ed.
    p. cm. — (A special publication of the American Anthropological Association ; no. 29)
  Includes indexes.
  ISBN 0-913167-65-7
  1. Anthropology—Study and teaching—Audio-visual aids—Catalogs. I. Hermer, Carol. II. Title.
III. Series.
GN42.3.Z9H44   1995
306′.0208—dc20   94-27936
                                                                                  CIP

Copyright © 1995 by the American Anthropological Association
All rights reserved.
ISBN 0-913167-65-7

Contents

1 / Introduction

4 / Films and Videos by Geographical Area

14 / Films and Videos by Topic

27 / Alphabetical Listing of Films and Videos

291 / Australian Aboriginal Films Warning

292 / Encyclopaedia Cinematographica

294 / Distributors' Codes

299 / Publication Codes

300 / People Index

To the memory of

Timothy Asch

1932–1994

who made so many films for

anthropological teaching

Introduction

This catalog lists and annotates films and videotapes that have been (or would seem to be) useful for teaching anthropology. It has grown through seven earlier editions, which in turn started from a list made up by Robert Gardner. This eighth edition contains some 3,000 titles, which is about double the seventh edition of 1983.

The major work on this edition was finished in the summer of 1993, more than 12 years after the effective closing date (May 1981) of the 1983 edition. Two major technological revolutions have caught up with the catalog in that interval. First, the new material for this edition was first prepared as a computer database, then transferred to a word-processing program to be edited and collated with the seventh edition of *Films for Anthropological Teaching*. Thus, it is now easy to enter new films and notes as they appear, and the next edition should not have to wait another dozen years.

The second major change is the imminent disappearance of film from the teaching scene. Although films are still being shot and edited on celluloid, they are being distributed in videotape form. As older films wear out, they are being replaced by video versions, and new equipment money is going more and more toward video playback equipment, not 16mm projectors. This will have tremendous implications for the ways in which we use these films in our teaching, and we are just beginning to meet this challenge.

The criteria for inclusion in this catalog are nebulous. We have tried to be more inclusive than exclusive. There are some obvious characteristics impelling inclusion: films made by anthropologists, or with anthropologists as consultants; films reviewed by anthropological journals such as the *American Anthropologist, Archaeology, MAN,* or the *Journal of the Association for Physical Anthropology;* films discussed in *Anthropology Today* or the visual anthropology journals (*Visual Anthropology, Visual Anthropology Review, Studies in Visual Communication*). Then, there are the films recommended by anthropologists. And, finally, looking through distributors' fliers, we made guesses about which films might be useful to some anthropologist somewhere.

This brings us to a cry for help. Through all the years and all the editions of *Films for Anthropological Teaching*, almost no anthropologists have sent in any suggestions for films, or notes on how they themselves use films in their own teaching. Once again, we urge contributions: *Anthropologists: Please send in additions and corrections, and especially bibliographic notes and teaching suggestions on films for the next edition.*

Ideally, in addition to credits, distributor information, and description of each film, there is information to help make the film more accessible for teaching: directly relevant bibliography, "focusing question," and "warnings."

The *focusing questions,* or set-up questions, can be used before screening a film to direct the students' viewing. It is relatively less effective to simply screen a film to a cold audience and afterward to ask "How did you like it?" One can always get a response, but it is not likely to be anthropologically insightful because the students have not been looking at the film for its particular anthropological content. The ideal set-up question poses an anthropological problem or riddle, creating tension and attention in the viewers' minds that can only be resolved by close study of the film. Although we would have liked to include set-up questions for each entry, the mass of material made this impossible, so we leave it to the instructors to preview the films and create their own.

Warnings are also intended to be used in preparing a class for a film. These warnings may be concerned with technical problems in the film, or with something in the content that might unintentionally amuse, disgust, or otherwise distract the viewer. Often, by acknowledging and discussing it beforehand, the instructor can defuse the problem and allow the film to be seen more effectively. Of course, these warnings must be used with care—they can backfire if the instructor overdoes the warning and thus raises unnecessary apprehension.

There are several major shortcomings of this catalog. It can never be completely up to date. New films appear; distributors disappear or change their addresses or telephone numbers. Prices change (upward). So, use with care. Again, we beg readers to inform us of any deviations from the text that they may encounter when scheduling films.

Some films listed are no longer available; but since presumably prints still exist, they will be available for anthropological teaching for many years, and so warrant inclusion here.

This catalog is designed for the teacher in the United States. We have not done justice to even Canadian films, not to speak of those from the many other countries that are producing excellent anthropological films. Because our printed scholarship so easily crosses national boundaries, it is always a shock to realize how isolated our film scholarship remains.

The catalog is intended to be an aid to teachers of anthropology. It is based on two major assumptions: First, nearly any film may be of some use to someone in teaching, but the instructor must be familiar with the film. Many instructors have scheduled films "blind" and, viewing for the first time with their students, have been unpleasantly surprised. It is just as desirable to preview a film before selecting it for classroom showing as it is to read a book before assigning it to a class; but, at the very least, the instructor should view the film earlier on the day of class screening in order to prepare students and to tell them what to look for.

Second, no film can stand by itself as a teaching instrument. Films should be backed up by written materials that can be assigned to the class, or at least that can be read by the instructor. Of course, most filmmakers have designed their films as self-sufficient statements, usually by adding a spoken narrative to the visual image. But this is not enough if the films are to be more than classroom entertainment. Students are usually so engaged in the exotic visual impressions that they do not retain the information that has been presented in the narration. And afterward, they should have the sorts of questions that go beyond what could be reasonably communicated by a film alone. As a general rule, the most useful films for anthropological teaching are those with adequate printed materials to supplement the specificity of the visual image.

For example, a film like *The Nuer,* which is primarily a series of visual impressions of Nuer life and land, is tremendously effective when shown in a class that is reading Evans-Pritchard's book, *The Nuer.* The film gives the student a contextual feeling for the people, which then makes even abstract notions of lineage and age set more comprehensible.

In the United States today, film is a medium of aesthetics and entertainment. We are teaching the MTV generation. It is very difficult to overcome such very basic cultural habits. The purpose of this catalog is to facilitate the use of film as a source of information, so we urge filmmakers and anthropologists to work together to produce packages of cinematographic and printed descriptions of cultural behavior. The best model to date for such collaboration is the Balinese project by Linda Connor, Patsy Asch, and Timothy Asch, which includes their book, *Jero Tapakan: Balinese Healer—An Ethnographic Film Monograph* and their five "Jero" films.

Although most of the films herein are more or less documentary nonfiction, the use of fiction films in anthropological teaching has been increasing, and we include a few. Fiction films have been especially useful in courses that talk about Western images of Native Others, such as Native Americans, Pacific Islanders, or Asians. Also, films made locally, for local consumption, can be presented as native texts or people's statements about themselves, especially in area courses. (See, for example, Karl G. Heider's 1991 book on *Indonesian Cinema.*)

Films for Anthropological Teaching is very much a scissors-and-paste job. Most descriptions are lifted straight from distributors' blurbs. It is unlikely that anyone alive has seen all 3,000 films, and it is a fairly noncritical list. We have omitted only the most atrocious films. For critical comments on films, the reader should turn to the reviews in the *American Anthropologist* and the discussions in other anthropological journals.

There are a number of excellent publications that have come out since the last edition of *Films for Anthropological Teaching* that are worth looking at:

A Bibliography of Ethnographic Film, compiled by Rolf Husmann, Ingrid Wellinger, Johannes Ruehl, and Martin Taureg, published in 1992 in Goettingen, is available in the United States through Westview Press, Inc., 5500 Central Avenue, Boulder, CO 80301.

Moving Images of the Pacific Islands. A Catalogue of Films and Videos, edited by Melissa C. Miller, was issued as Occasional Paper 34 by the Center for Pacific Island Studies, University of Hawaii at Manoa, 1890 East-West Road, 215 Moore Hall, Honolulu, HI 96822-1890.

Ethnofilm: Katalog, Beitraege, Interviews, edited by Daniel Dall'Agnolo, Barbara Etterich, and Marc-Olivier Gonseth, was published in 1991 as Ethnologica Helvetica 15 by the Swiss Ethnological Society in Berne.

Videos for Understanding Diversity: A Core Selection and Evaluative Guide, edited by Gregory I. Stevens, was published by the American Library Association, Chicago, in 1993.

And Peter Allen (with the help of Mary Downs and Carole Lazio) is preparing a second edition of his catalog *Archaeology on Film,* to be published by the Archaeological Institute of America in Boston.

In addition to these new catalogs, there has been a tremendous outpouring of new books and journal articles on ethnographic film.

This catalog includes:

(1) *Alphabetical Film Titles.* Films are listed in alphabetical order. Series titles are listed in bold, individual titles in bold italic. For each film, a description, bibliography, prices, and distributor's name are given where possible. The address of the distributor is located in the Distributors' Codes section. The following format is used:

Film Title (date of release) running time. Credits: Director (DI), Producer (PR), Anthropologist (AN), Camera or Photographer (CA), Consultant or Adviser (CON), Writer (WR), Editor (ED), Narrator (NA), Music (MU), Sound Recordist (SR), Research (RE), Filmmaker (FM). *Distributor:* distributors' names have been abbreviated, and the key to abbreviations follows in the Distributors' Codes section. *Order Code Number:* following the distributor's name occasionally will be a number. This is the distributor's order number. If you use it when you order, it will facilitate your order. *Prices:* specified for rental (R) or sale (S), in film version (F) or video (V). *Description:* Film descriptions appear in italics; most are lifted verbatim from promotional fliers, catalogs, and other advertising blurbs or, when noted, reviews. *Bibliographic Entries* following the description list reviews of the film as well as publications that can be used to accompany the film. *Names* following the entry acknowledge individual's contributions to the descriptions, bibliography, or orienting questions of the entry.

(2) *Films by Geographical Area.* This lists all the films relevant to a particular culture area (e.g., Melanesia).

(3) *Films by Topic.* This lists all the films relevant to a particular topic (e.g., archaeology).

(4) *Distributors.* Distributors' codes contain most current names, addresses, and telephone numbers of the distributors.

(5) *People.* The people index lists the people involved in the filmmaking, or in writing about the films.

Acknowledgments

The early editions of *Films for Anthropological Teaching* were subsidized by grants from the Wenner-Gren Foundation for Anthropological Research and were distributed free of charge. The fifth edition was published by the Program in Ethnographic Film (the ancestor of the Society for Visual Anthropology). Since the sixth edition, *Films for Anthropological Teaching* has been published by the American Anthropological Association in its Special Publications series. We would like to thank, particularly, Rick Custer, of the AAA headquarters office, for his patient encouragement; various students who helped type the old and new material onto disks and proofread it: Tracy Steele, Melissa Davis, Caroline Vinel, Melissa Lefko, and Deannie Stevens at the University of South Carolina, and at the University of Washington, Huma Haque and, most of all, Kathy Fowells. James W. Green, at the University of Washington, most generously allowed his new computer to be tied up on this task for months. Don Bartholomew of the Instructional Media Services of the University of Washington was most helpful in tracking down lost distributors. Jonathan Benthall of the Royal Anthropological Institute gave permission to use film reviews from *Anthropology Today,* and Peter Allen allowed us to use his reviews from *Archaeology*. The entire project would have been even further delayed without the enthusiastic support of the Department of Anthropology at the University of Washington in the summer of 1993. Finally, Heider welcomes Hermer on board as coeditor with a great sigh of relief and gratitude.

Karl G. Heider
Department of Anthropology
University of South Carolina
Columbia, South Carolina 29208

Carol Hermer
Department of Anthropology
University of Washington
Seattle, Washington 98195

Films and Videos by Geographical Area

AFRICA *Africa Calls: Its Drums and Musical Instruments; Africa Dances;* Africa Series; *Africa Speaks; Africa: An Introduction; African Soul; L'Afrique et la recherche scientifique (Africa and Scientific Research); Afrique sur Seine (Africa on the Seine); AIDS in Africa; Alger-Le Cap; Alphabetisation des adultes au Mali (Adult Literacy in Mali); Ambara Dama; Anansi the Spider; The Ancient Africans; Atlantic Slave Trade; Babatou, les trois conseils (Babatou, Three Pieces of Advice); Baobab: Portrait of a Tree; The Bible and the Gun* (Africa Series); *Black Women; Bwana Tosh; Camera d'Afrique; Caravans of Gold* (Africa Series); *Different but Equal* (Africa Series); *Faba Tondi; The First Humans; Gentle Winds of Change; Les Gens du Mil (The People of the Millet); Gentle Winds of Change; Goree: Door of No Return; Greystoke: The Legend of Tarzan; Le Griot Badye (Badye, the Storyteller); The Legacy of Lifestyles* (The Africans Series); *Masks and Stones: The Precious Treasures of Black Africa; Mastering a Continent* (Africa Series); *The Nature of a Continent; New Gods* (The Africans Series); *Ouaga; Petit a Petit (Little by Little); Rich Man's Medicine, Poor Man's Medicine; Rise Up and Walk; The Rise of Nationalism* (Africa); *Un lion nomme "L'Americain" (A Lion Named "the American"); Witch Doctor; With These Hands; You Hide Me*

Central Africa *Angola Is Our Country; Bamiki Bandula: Children of the Forest; The Contributions of Zambian Women to Agriculture; Forest People of Central Africa; Garcons et Filles; The Magic Tree; Magicians of the Black Hills (Cameroon); Mbindo Lala: A Hospital in Village Form; People of the Chad; People of the Congo; Regard sur l'Afrique Noire; Rhythm of Africa (Chad); River People of the Chad; Spirits of Defiance: The Mangbetu People of Zaire; A Spiritual Ordering: The Metal Arts of Africa; Stanley and Livingstone; Vessels of the Spirits: Pots and People in North Cameroon; Zebola: Possession and Therapy in Zaire*

East Africa *African Community: The Masai; Angano... Angano... Tales from Madagascar; Arusi ya Mariamu (The Marriage of Mariamu); Aspects of the Behavior of the Sifaka (Propithecus verreauxi verreauxi); The Barabaig; Beyond the Plains; Dandora; Diary of a Maasai Village; Dodoth Morning; Faces of Change; From Sunup; The Gobra;* Hadza (Tanzania); *In Search of Cool Ground: The Kwegu* (Disappearing World Series); *In Search of Cool Ground: The Mursi* (Disappearing World Series); *Iron Smelting* (Tanzania); *Kenya Boran; Kenya Boran; Kwashiorkor; The Leap across the Cattle* (Ethiopia); *The Legacy of L. S. B. Leakey; Lorang's Way* (Kenya Turkana); *Lucy in Disguise;* Making of Mankind; *Man in Ethiopia; Man of the Serengeti; Mandabi; Maragoli; Masai in Tanzania; Masai Manhood; Masai Manhood* (Disappearing World Series); *Masai Women* (Disappearing World Series); *Masat Women; Mau Mau; Memories and Dreams; The Migrants* (Disappearing World Series); *The Mursi; The Mursi* (Disappearing World Series); *The Mursi: Nitha* (Disappearing World Series); *The Mursi: The Land Is Bad* (Disappearing World Series); *Nawi* (Uganda); *Nine Cows and an Ox* (Diary of the Oaasai Village Series); *The Nuer* (Ethiopia); *The Parching Winds of Somalia; People of Many Lands; The Potters of Buur Heybe, Somalia; The Prophet's Family* (Diary of the Maasai Village Series); *The Rendille* (Disappearing World Series); *Rivers of Sand; Sharing Is Unity (Ushirika Ni Umoja); The Shilluk of Southern Sudan; These Hands; The Tree of Iron; To Live with Herds* (Jie); *The Turkana* (From Africa to Asia: Nomads Series); Turkana Conversations Trilogy; *Two Journeys* (Diary of the Maasai Village Series); *Two Mothers* (Diary of the Maasai Village Series); *Two Ways of Justice* (Diary of the Maasai Village Series); *Uganda, Tanzania, Kenya; Under the Men's Tree* (Jie); University of Ife Series; *Voyage au bout de la Piste—un autre Ethiopie; Wedding Camels* (Turkana); *A Wife among Wives; The Women's Olamal: The Organization of a Masai Fertility Ceremony; The Wooden Giraffe* (Barotse, Zambia); *1973 Mgodo wa Mbanguizi; 1973 Mgodo wa Mkandeni; 6000 Years in Suswa*

West Africa *Africa; African Carving: A Dogon Kanaga Mask; African Craftsmen: The Ashanti; African Drought; African Religions and Ritual Dances* (Yoruba); African Village Life Series (Mali: Dogon, Peul, Boso); *Alhaji Bai Konte;* Anufom Series: Bambara of Mali: Dogon of Mali; *Architectes Atorou (The Architects of Atorou); Ashante Market Women* (Disappearing World Series); *Au pays des mages noirs (In the Land of the Black Magic); Baby Ghana; The Bambara Kingdom of Segu; Bataille sur le grand fleuve (Battle on the Great River); Batteries Dogon, elements pour une etude des rythmes ou, tambours de pierre (Dogon Drums, Elements of a Study in Rhythm or, Stone Drums); Becoming a Woman in Okrika; Benin Kinship Rituals; The Blooms of Banjeli: Technology and Gender in African Ironmaking; Bono Medicines; Bono Medicines; Bukoki; Cameroon Brass Casting; Cimetiere dans la falaise (Cemetery in the Cliff); Cocoriro, Monsieur Poulet; The Cows of Dolo Ken Paye* (Kpelle, Liberia); *Dance Like a River; Daouda Sorko; Daybreak in Udi* (Nigeria); *Deep Hearts* (Bororo); *The Devil's Cliff; Djibo: The Zarma Culture of Nigeria; Dokwaza: Last of the African Iron Masters; Dongo Horendi; Dongo Hori; Dongo Yenendi, Gamkalle; A Drum Is Made: A Study in Yoruba Drum Carving; The Dry Season; Duminea; Durs Lapido* (Nigeria); *Embara Death; Emitay* (Senegal); *Eze Nwata: The Small King; A Family of Liberia; Faran Maka fonda (Fara Maka's Path); Fear Woman* (Ghana); *A Festival for the Water Spirits* (East Niger Delta); *Festival a Dakar (Festival at Dakar); Fetes de l'Independence du Niger (Celebrations of the Independence of Niger); Fetes des Gandyi bi a Simiri (Celebration of Gandyi bi at Simiri); Fincho* (Nigeria); *Fulbe of M'Bantou; Gelede: A Yoruba Masquerade; The Glories of Ancient Benin; Hampi; Healers of Aro* (Nigeria); *Hippopota-*

Films and Videos by Geographical Area

mus Hunting (Mali); *In Danaku the Soup Is Sweeter; Initiation a la danse des possedes* (Initiation into Possession Dances); *Jackville; Jaguar; Jean Rouch and His Camera in the Heart of Africa; Kingdom of Bronze; La Chasse a l'hippopotame* (The Hippopotamus Hunt); *La Chasse au lion a l'arc* (The Lion Hunters); *La Goumbe des jeunes noceurs* (The Goumbe of the Young Revellers); *La pyramide humaine* (The Human Pyramid); *La royale Goumbe; Le cocotier* (The Coconut Palm); *Le mil* (Millet); *Le palmier a huile* (Palm Oil); *Le renard pale* (The Pale Fox); *Le retour de i'adventurier; Les ceremonies soixanteraires du Sigui* (The Sixty-Year Cycle of Sigui Ceremonies); *Les Fils de l'eau* (The Sons of the Water); *Les Hommes qui font la pluie: Ou Yenendi, les faiseurs de pluie* (Men Who Make Rain or Yenendi: The Rainmakers); *Les magiciens de Wanzerbe* (The Magicians of Wanzerbe); *Les maitres fous* (Mad Masters); *Les pecheurs de Niger* (The Fishermen of Niger); *Les pierres chantantes d'Ayorou* (The Musical Stones of Ayorou); *The Lion Hunters; Life in The Dust/Fragments of African Voyages; Living Africa: A Village Experience; Madame L'eau; Mammy Water: In Search of the Water Spirits in Nigeria; A Mamprusi Village; Mandabi; Maninka Villages in Transition; The Market's Edge* (Hausa); *Mbambin* (Togo); *Medecines et Medecins* (Medicine and Doctors); *The Mende* (Disappearing World Series); *The Mende of Kpuawala Village; Moi, un Noir* (Me, a Black); *Monsieur Albert, Prophete ou Albert Atcho* (Mr Albert, Prophet: or Albert Atcho); *Moro Naba; Music of Africa* (Nigeria); *Musique et danse des chasseurs Gow* (Music and Dances of the Gow Hunters); *Muslims in Mango; Naked Spaces: Living Is Round; Niger, jeune republique* (Niger, Young Republic); *Pam Kuso Kar (Briser les poteries de pam)* (Breaking Pam's Vases); *Pausse-Pausse* (Cameroon); *A Plague upon the Land; Porto Novo: La danse des reines* (Porto Novo: The Dance of the Queens); *Pousse-Pousse; Reassemblage; River People of the Chad; A Safety Net; Sakpata; Secheresse a Simiri* (Drought at Simiri); *Selbe: One among Many* (As Women See It Series); *Seven Nights and Seven Days; Sigui No. 1: L'enclume de Yougo* (The Anvil of Yougo); *The Singing Fishermen of Ghana; Songs of the Badius; Soro* (Hausa, Nigeria); *Souna Kouma (La nostalgie de Souna)* (Nostalgia of Souna); *Spite: An African Prophet-Healer; Studies in Nigerian Dance* (Tiv, Irgwe, Kambari); *Sur les traces du Renard pale* (Tracking the Pale Fox: Studies on the Dogon); *Tambours et violons des chasseurs Songhay* (The Drums and Violins of Songhay Singers); *Tanda singui (poser le hangar)* (To Fix the Shed); *Taway Nya—La Mere* (Taway Naya—Mother); *The Talking Drums of Nigeria; Three Apprentices* (Nigeria); *Tourou et Bitti, les tambours d'avant* (Tourou and Gitti, the Drums of Yore); *Trade and Markets in West Africa; Trading in Africans: Dutch Outposts in West Africa; Tradition Bearers; Tribal Eye: Behind the Mask; Two West African Fishing Villages; Village Theater Senegal: Queen Ndate and the French Conquest; Water for Tonoumasse; The Ways of Nya are Many; A Week of Sweet Water; Were Ni!* (Nigeria); *Witchcraft among the Azande* (Disappearing World Series); *Women of Niger (Femmes du Niger); Xala; Yenendi de Boukoki* (Rain Dance at Boukoki, Niamey, Niger); *Yenendi de Gamkalle* (Rain Dance at Gamkalle); *Yenendi de Ganghel* (Rain Dance at Ganghel); *Yenendi de Gourbi Beri* (Rain Dance at Gourbi, Niamey, Niger); *Yenendi de Kirkissey* (Rain Dance at Kirkissey); *Yenendi de Kongou* (Rain Dance at Kongou); *Yenendi de Simiri* (Rain Dance at Simiri); *Yenendi de Simiri* (Rain Dance at Simiri); *Yenendi de Simriri accompagne de semailles* (Rain Dance at Simri Accompanied by Seed Planting); *Yenendi de Yantalla* (Rain Dance at Yantalla); *Yenendi: Secheress a Simiri* (Yenendi: Drought at Simiri)

South Africa (San) *An Argument about Marriage; Bitter Melons; Bushmen Series; A Curing Ceremony; The Gods Must Be Crazy; A Group of Women; The Hunters; Journey to Magic Valley; The Kalahari Desert People; !Ko Bushman Series; !Kung Bushman Hunting Equipment; The !Kung San: Resettlement* (The San [Ju/Wasi]: Videos for Elementary and Secondary Use); *The !Kung San: Traditional Life* (The San [Ju/Wasi]: Videos for Elementary and Secondary Use); *Lion Game; The Melon Tossing; N!owa T'ama; N/um Tchai, Pull Ourselves Up or Die Out; Remnants of a Race; San Series;* The San (Ju/Wasi): Videos for Elementary and Secondary Use.

South Africa (Other) *Amazulu; Chopi Africa; Chacma Baboons of Capetown; Change; Come Back Africa; Crossroads/South Africa: The Struggle Continues; Dances of Southern Africa; The Debt Crisis: An African Dilemma; Enthombe; Goldwidows: Women in Lesotho; Heal the Whole Man; Himba Wedding; Katatura; Last Grave at Dimbaza; Liebalala; Lobola; The Long Journey of Clement Zulu; Maids and Madams; Makwayela; Mbira Series; The 1973 Mgodo Series; Ngoma Therapy in an Urban South African Setting; Nyamakuta—The One Who Receives; Phela-Ndaba* (End of the Dialogue); *The Ribbon; Songs of the Adventurers; A South African Farm; The Struggling People; Vimbuza—Chilopa; Waiting for the Caribou; Zulu Dances*

Madagascar *The Bilo; Dance Contest in Esira*

North Africa *Abidjan, port de peche* (Abidjan, Fishing Port); *An African Recovery; Aita* (Morocco, Body and Soul Series); *Ancient Egyptians; Ancient Lives; Ballets of the Atlas; The Bride Market of Imilchil; Carthage: A Mirage of Antiquity; Le circoncision* (Circumcision); *Daughters of the Nile; A Day among the Berbers; Diro and His Talking Musical Bow; Egypt: Cradle of Civilization; Egypt: Quest for Eternity; Egyptian Village; El Moulid: Egyptian Religious Festival; El Sebou': Egyptian Birth Ritual; Falasha: Agony of the Black Jews; For Our Bread; For Those Who Sail to Heaven; Guellala: A Potter's Village in Tunisia; Hadar 75: Field Techniques; Herdsmen of the Sun; Heritage of the Pharaohs; Hombori; Hymns of Praise* (Morocco, Body and Soul Series); *Jews of Djerba; Kabylia; Lost Army; Lutes and Delights* (Morocco, Body and Soul Series); *Master Musicians of Jahjouka; Mauritania: Wealth of Blood* (From Africa to Asia: Nomads Series); *Mudhorse; Mystery of Nefertiti; Nomads on the Savanna; Nuba Wrestling; Permissible Dreams* (As Women See It Series); *Pilgrimage to Ghriba; Places Not Our Own* (Daughters of the Country Series); *Preserving Egypt's Past; Pyramid; Ramparts of Clay* (Tunisia/Algeria); *The Return of the Child; Richard Cardinal: Cry from a Diary of Metis Child; Routes of Exile: A Moroccan Jewish Odyssey; Sad Song of Touha; Sahara; Saints and Spirits* (Disappearing World Series); *Shahira:*

Nomads of the Sahara; Sogow, Bambara Masks; Some Women of Marrakech; The South-East Nuba; Sudan's Pyramids, Azandi's Dream; Suite of Berber Dances; Tanneurs de Marrakesh; Touareg; The Tuareg; The Tuareg (Disappearing World Series); The Tuaregs; Voice of the Whip; Where the Brides Do the Choosing; Wodaabe (Disappearing World Series); Women of the Toubou; Zarda: A Nomadic Tribe's Feast Days

NEAR AND MIDDLE EAST *About the Jews of Yemen: A Vanishing Culture; Adliye: The Ethnography of a Turkish Rural Law Court; Ancient Egypt; Ancient Mesopotamia; Ancient Sardis; The Arab Jews; Arabic X-Ray Film; The Arch Identity; Archaeology in Mesopotamia; Bakhtiari Migration; Be'er Sheva Four; Behind the Veil; The Big Dig; Children of Fire; Communists for a Thousand Years; Crossroads of Civilization Series; Daughters of Abraham: A Fight to Survive?; Demircihukuk; The Dervishes of Kurdistan (The Disappearing World Series); Earliest Writing; The Etruscans; Gaza Ghetto: Portrait of a Palestinian Family; Grass: A Nation's Battle for Life; Howling Dervishes; The Hundred Years War: Personal Notes;* In Search of the Trojan War; *In the Name of Allah; Ispahan: Lettre Persane 1977 (La Mosquee du Chah a Ispahan) (Itpahan: A Persian letter 1977—The Chah Mosque at Isahan); Israel and the Palestinians: The Continuing Conflict; A Journey to Mecca; Kibbutz Series; Land and Water in Iraq; Megiddo—City of Destruction; Megiddo-City of Destruction; Middle East: Mosaic of Peoples; Migrants from Sakaltutan; Mona Lisa of the Galilee; Moulay Idriss; On Our Land; Once in King David's City; Palestinian People Do Have Rights; People of the Wind (Bahktiari); Petra: Crossroad in Stone; Price of Change (Women in the Middle East Series); Royal Archives of Ebla; Saints and Spirits; Sakaltutan: A Time of Change; Samaritans; Search for Herod's Harbor; Sense of Honor; Shahsavan Nomads of Iran; Shibam: Stone Knapping in Modern Turkey; Shoot and Cry; Some Women of Marrakesh; Stones of Eden (Afghanistan); Talking to the Enemy: Voices of Sorrow and Rage; Testament: The Bible and History; Ticket to Tefenni; The Tigris Expedition; Turkey's Sephardim: Five Hundred Years; Veiled Revolution (Women in the Middle East Series); Voices from Gaza; Wedding in a Persian Village;* Women in the Middle East Series; *Women under Siege* (Women in the Middle East Series)

ASIA GENERAL (Including Nepal, Afghanistan, ex-Soviet republics in Asia, Mongolia) *Afghan Exodus* (Disappearing World Series); *Afghanistan; Afghanistan: Threads of Life; Between Time: A Tibetan Village in Nepal; Cowboy in Mongolia; Death Is Afraid of Us; Depending on Heaven: The Desert; Depending on Heaven: The Grasslands; The Dragon Bride; Films Are Dreams that Wander in the Light of Day; Forest of Bliss; Fragile Mountain; Freak Street to Goa: Immigrants on the Rajpath; The Herders of Mongun-Taiga* (Disappearing World Series); *Hinduism and the Song of God; Inner Mongolia—In Search of History* (From Africa to Asia: Nomads Series); *Iron Mountain: Siberian Creation Myth* (see Creation Myth Series); *The Kazakhs of China* (Disappearing World Series); *The Kirghiz of Afghanistan* (Disappearing World Series); *The Living Goddess* (Nepal); *Mongolia: On the Edge of the Gobi* (Disappearing World Series); *Mongolia: The City on the Steppes* (Disappearing World Series); *Mountain People of Central Asia Series; Odyssey in Asia; The Pathans* (Disappearing World Series); *Requiem for a Faith; Rice; Shamans of the Blind Country* (Nepal); *Sherpa High Country; The Sherpas* (Disappearing World Series); *Siberia: After the Shaman; Siberia: Through Siberian Eyes; Sons of Haji Omar; Transition Generation: A Third World Problem* (Afghanistan); *Trekking on Tradition; Village Morning* (Tibet/Ladakh)

South Asia (India, Pakistan, Sri Lanka) *About the Jews in India: Cochin; About the Jews of India: The Shanwar Telis or Bene Israel; Ahimsa, Non-Violence; Ahmedabad: Life of a City in India; Ajuba Dance and Drama Company; Altar of Fire; Amir: An Afghan Refugee Musician's Life in Peshawar, Pakistan; Amra Dujon (Together); "Annapurna Mahila Mandal" An Experience in Grassroots Development for Women; Aparajito; Appointment with the Astrologer: Personal Consultants in Hindu Society; Bake Restudy 1984; Banaras; Banesa's Courtyard; Bangladesh Nationhood: Symbols and Shadows; Being Muslim in India; Benares, the Hindu Heaven; Benares: Steps to Heaven; Bombay: Our City; Calcutta; Chachaji, My Poor Relation; Chang: A Drama of the Wilderness; Changing Rains* (Bhil); *Chittirai Festival; Cinema; Circles-Cycles Kathak Dance; Cochin Jews; Courts and Councils: Dispute Settlement in India; Dadi's Family; Dam at Nagarjunasagar; Day in Shrishnagar; Day Shall Dawn* (Bangladesh); *Devi; Faces of Change; Floating in the Air; Flute and the Arrow* (Muria, India); *Four Families; Four Hindu Sadhus; The Fourth Stage: A Hindu's Quest for Release; Given to a Dance; Gurkha Country; Hajari Bhand of Rajasthan: Jester without Court; Healing Hill; Herding Castes of Central India; Himalayan Farmer; Himalayan Shaman of Northern Nepal; Himalayan Shaman of Southern Nepal; Hindu Loaves and Fishes; Hindu Ritual Sandhya; Hinduism: 330 Million Gods; The Ho: People of the Rice Pot* (Bihar); *Image India; Images of India; In India the Sun Rises in the East; In The Name of God; India and the Infinite; India Cabaret; India's Sacred Cows; India: An Introduction; India: An Introduction; Indian Pilgrimage: Kashi; Indian Pilgrimage: Ramdevra; Indian Worker, Jaco Chondhari (A Tongawallah from Delhi); Inrat Khan Demonstrates the Sitar; Iramudun; The Kalasha—Rites of Spring* (Disappearing World Series); *Kataragama* (Disappearing World Series); *Kataragama* (Sri Lanka); *Kheturni Baya; Khyber* (Disappearing World Series); *The Lion's Roar; Lord of the Dance, Destroyer of Illusion; Lost Tribes; Loving Krishna* (Pleasing God Series); *Maharishi Mahesh; Manifestations of Shiva; Menri Monastery; Modern Brides: Arranged Marriage in South India; Mother Ganges; Mountain Communities of the Himalayas; Munni ('Little Girl'): Childhood and Art in Mithila; The Murga; The Muria; Musical Tradition in Banaras; Nation Uprooted: Afghan Refugees in Pakistan; No Longer Silent; Nomads of Badakshan' North Indian Village; One Hundred Years of Archaeology; Our Asian Neighbors–India Series; Painted Truck; Pather Panchali; Pearl of the East; People of Many Lands* (Sri Lanka); *People of the Rice Pot; Phanton India; Photo Wallahs;* Pleasing God Series; *Principles of Caste; Raj Gonds; Requiem for a Faith; Rhythms of Resis-*

tance; Rivers of Life; Ruju the Guide; Salaam Bombay; Sampuran Singh: A Farmer from Punjab; Song of Ceylon; Sons of Shiva (Pleasing God Series); *Sons of the Moon; Sri Lanka; Sudesha* (As Women See It Series); *Swami Karunananda; The Shanwar Telis or Bene Israel; Tibet in Exile; Tibet: The Bamboo Curtain Falls; Tibet: The Lost Mystery; Tibetan Buddhism: Cycles of Interdependence; Tibetan Buddhism: Preserving the Monastic Tradition; Tibetan Traders; Tragada Bhavai: A Rural Theater Troupe of Gujarat; Tribal Groups of Central India; Two Thousand Years of Freedom and Honor: The Cochin Jews of India; Village Man, City Man; Wages of Action: Religion in a Hindu Village; Wedding of the Goddess: Part I; Women Of Kerala; Work of Gomis* (Sri Lanka); *Working Process of the Potters of India: Massive Terra-Cotta Horse Construction; The World of Apu; A Zenana: Scenes and Recollections; Zoroastrian Ritual: The Yasna*

China and Taiwan *All under Heaven: Life in a Chinese Village* (Long Bow Film Series); *The Ancient Chinese; The Barefoot Doctors of Rural China; Beijing* (The Cities in China Series); *Better Rich than Red* (The Human Face of Hong Kong Series); *Black Market* (Commodities Series); *Buddhism in China; Candles for New Years; Chen and China's Symphony; Children of Soong Ching Ling; China Discovery; China's Only Child; China: A Land Transformed; China: Contemporary Changes in Historical Perspective; China: Hundred Schools to One; China: The Beginnings; China: The Making of a Civilization; Chinese Farm Family: Changes in the Countryside Today; Chinese Popular Religion Series; Chinese X-Ray Films;* Cities in China; *Da Jiu; The Dragon Boat Festival; Dragons in the Sea; Faces of Change; Family Table* (A Taste of China Series); *First Moon: Celebration of a Chinese New Year; From Courtyard House to Block Apartment; Generations: A Chinese Family; Gui Dao—On the Way: A Station of the Yangzi; Han Tomb Find; Historical Relics Unearthed in New China; The Human Face of Hong Kong; Inside China: Living with the Revolution; Inside China: The Newest Revolution* (Disappearing World Series); *Korean and Japanese Dance; Kuan-Yin-Pilgrimage;* Long Bow Film Series; *Love Songs of the Miao in China; Old Treasures from New China; People of Western China; Powerhouse* (Man on the Rim Series); *Return of the Gods and Ancestors: The Five-Year Ceremony; Running from the Ghost* (The Human Face of Hong Kong Series); *Shoot for the Contents; The Silent Army; The Silk Road; Six Hundred Millennia: China's History Unearthed; Small Happiness: Women of a Chinese Village* (Long Bow Film Series); *Some Notes on the Aborignes of Taiwan; Suzhou* (The Cities in China Series); *T'ai Chi Ch'uan; A Taste of China Series; To Taste a Hundred Herbs: Gods, Ancestors and Medicine in a Chinese Village* (Long Bow Film Series); *The Unruly Dragon: The Yellow River; Water Farmers* (A Taste of China Series); *Women in China; Women in China Today; Wuxing People's Commune; Xian* (The Cities in China Series); *Zengbu after Mao; 2100 Year Old Tomb Excavated*

Korea *Birthplace Unknown; An Initiation Kut for a Korean Shaman; A Lone Island; Out There; Two Korean Families; The Working Process of the Korean Folk Potter*

Japan *As Iwata Goes: Is Culture Local; Bwana Toshi; Canoes of the Ainu; Fit Surroundings; Five Faces of Tokyo; Folk Music in Japan; Four Families; From Woman to Women; Frontier Settlement of Japanese from Overseas* (Bolivia); *Future Wave: Japan Design; Gateway to the Gods; Gift of the Dragon; God of Japan; Iyomande* (Ainu); *Japan; Japan* (Asian Insight Series); *Japan They Don't Talk About; Japan: An Interdependent Nation; Japan: The Nation Family;* Japan: Voices of Experience; *Japanese Folk Dance; Japanese Series; Japanese Version; Living of the River Agano (Aga Ni Ikiru); Neighborhood Tokyo; Path; Personality in Culture; Pure and Simple* (Man on the Rim Series); *Rashomon; Raw Fish and Pickle: Traditional Rural and Seafaring Life* (The Human Face of Japan Series); *Ritual; Sam; Seacoast Village of Japan; Shinto: Nature, Gods and Man in Japan; Sons of the Rising Sun; The Rice Ladle: The Changing Roles of Women* (The Human Face of Japan Series); *Uminchu: The Old Man and the East China Sea; Village of Potters of Onda; When Mrs. Hegarty Comes to Japan; 365 Days with Your Baby*

SOUTHEAST ASIA *Hong Kong / Singapore* (Asian Insight Series); *When Invaders Become Colonists*

Indonesia *Anklung Orchestra and Indonesian Dance Class; Art of Indonesia: Tales from the Shadow World; Bali; Bali beyond the Postcard; Bali, Man's Paradise; Bali: Island and Universe; Bali: The Mask of Rangda; A Balinese Family; Balinese Surfer; A Balinese Trance Seance* (Bali Series); *Bathing Babies in Three Cultures; But I'll Always Continue to Write* (The Human Face of Indonesia Series); *Celebration of Origins; Childhood Rivalry in Bali and New Guinea; The Conquest of Indonesia; East Timor: Isle of Fear, Isle of Hope; The Eleven Powers: Balinese Festival; The Goddess and The Computer; Helping the People to Help Themselves* (The Human Face of Indonesia Series); *Horses of Life and Death; The Human Face of Indonesia; Indonesia: A Generation of Change; Indonesia: Time to Grow; Jero on Jero* (Bali Series); *Jero Tapakan: Stories in the Life of a Balinese Healer* (Bali Series); *Journey to a New Life* (The Human Face of Indonesia Series); *Karba's First Years* (Bali); *Kembali: To Return; Ketut di Bali; Learning to Dance in Bali; Lempad of Bali; Light of Many Masks; Mask of Rangda, Island of the Spirits* (Bali); *Master of the Shadows* (The Human Face of Indonesia Series); *The Medium Is the Masseuse* (Bali Series); *Nias and Sumatra; Nini Pantun: Rice Cultivation and Rice Rituals in Bali; Our Asian Neighbors–Indonesia Series; Out of The Shadows* (Indonesia: A Generation of Change Series); *Place in the Sun* (Indonesia: A Generation of Change Series); *Rebels of the Forgotten World; Releasing the Spirits: A Village Cremation in Bali* (Bali Series); *Roti; Sacred Trances in Bali and Java; The Sakuddei of Indonesia* (The Disappearing World Series); *Sanctuary of the Earth Goddess; Spear and Sword: A Payment of Bridewealth on the Island of Roti* (Roti Series); *Taksu: Music in the Life of Bali; Tanah Air—Our Land, Our Water* (Indonesia: A Generation of Change Series); *The Three Worlds of Bali; Tobelo Marriage; Tong Tana: A Journey to the Heart of Borneo;* Traditional Dances of Indonesia; *Trance and Dance in Bali; The Water of Words: A Cultural Ecology of a Small Island in E. Indonesia* (Roti Series); *We Are Nothing without the People* (The

Human Face of Indonesia Series); *Wet Earth and Warm People; The Whale Hunters of Lamalera* (The Disappearing World Series)

Philippines *The Bajao: Seagoing Nomads; Big Problems for Little People; The Cave People of the Philippines; Child of the Philippines; Hanunoo; The Last Tribes of Mindanao; Malnutrition in a Third World Community; Peasant Ecology in the Rural Philippines; People of the Current; Perfumed Nightmare; Philippines* (Asian Insight Series); *Philippines: The Price of Power; Psychic Surgery: A Case History of Shamanic Sleight-of-Hand; Turumba*

Borneo *The Dayak: People of Borneo; The Land Dayaks of Borneo; Rainforest*

Mainland *Angkor: The Lost City; Ao dai (The Tunic Dress); Floating in the Air; Floating Rice; Harvest at Nong Lub; The Hmong Hilltribe People of Laos; How To Behave; Journey from Pha Dong; Karorn—A Southern Village; Ladyboys; Land of the Yao; The Last Performance; Lines of Fire; The Lost Men of Malaya; Magic in the Hills* (Djakut); *Malaysia* (Asian Insight Series); *The Meo* (Disappearing World Series); *Metos Jah Hut (A Jah Hut Myth); Mia Year; Miao Year; Mysteries of the Mekong; Nang Yai; The New Cutting Edge* (Man on the Rim Series); *Nomads of the Jungle; The Opium Trilogy;* Our Asian Neighbors–Thailand Series; *The Rice Cycle in Thailand: Weaving Films; The River Kwai Expedition' Thai Shadow Puppet Drama; Sad Song of Yellow Skin; Samsara; Surname Viet Given Name Nam; Temple of Twenty Pagodas; The Tenth Dancer; Thai: Child of Rural Thailand; Thailand* (Asian Insight Series); *Vietnam: O Mere Paddy!*

EUROPE *100,000 Piece Jigsaw Puzzle* (Viking); *A Bouziques; Across the Tracks—Vlach Gypsies in Hungary* (Disappearing World Series); *The Albanians of Rrogam* (Disappearing World Series); *The Alien's Place* (Netherlands); *Alpine Bread;* The Ancient Romans Series; *The Anthropologist* (Germany); *Asian Heart; Atlantis;* Aubrac Series; *Ausschnitte...* (Romania); *Baby Riazanski* (Russia); *Bandits of Orosolo* (Sardinia); *The Beginning of History, Part III: The Iron Age; Children of Fate: Life and Death in a Sicilian Family; Cronaca* (Ticino Mountain Valley); *Earth in Song* (Czech); *Eternal Song* (Czech); *Four Families; Geel* (Belgium); *Le Grotte de l'Hortus; Gypsies* (Poland); *Gypsy Camp Vanishes into the Blue* (Russia); *The Halperns in Orasac* (Serbia); *The House that Giacomo Built* (Italy); *Hungarian X-Ray Film; In the Shadow of Vesuvius; Inughuit: The People at the Navel of the Earth* (Greenland); *Invisible Enemy* (Disappearing World Series) (Lapps); *Italian Folk Songs; Living North* (Lapp); *Midsummer in Sweden; The Moveable Feast* (Sicily); *Nice Weather, Mr. Pradhan!* (Netherlands); *One Day More* (Yugoslavia); *Paolina's Hairstyle* (Italy); *The Parting* (Yugoslavia); *The Past that Lives* (Netherlands); *People of the River Neretva* (Yugoslavia); *Pompeii: Daily Life of the Ancient Romans; Russian X-Ray Film; Sam's Herders* (Lapp); *Scandinavian Creation Myth* (see Creation Myth Series); *The Shoemaker; Story of the Wasa* (Sweden); *Taiga Nomads: The School and Village* (Russia); *Vikings!; Visit; The World Tree*

Great Britain and Ireland *Anglo-Saxon England; Bath Waters; Bath Waters; The Battle of Culloden* (English-Scottish); *Before the Romans; A Celtic Trilogy; Cracking the Stone Age Code; Decoding Danebury; Granton Trawler* (Scotland); *Gypsies Sing Long Ballads; How the Myth Was Made; Lessons from Gulam: Asian Music in Bradford; The Man of Aran* (Ireland); *The McPeake Family of Ireland; The Mists of Time* (Ireland); *'Oss 'Oss Wee 'Oss; The Shepherds of Bernary (Ciobairean Bhearnaraich); Stonehenge: Mystery in the Plain; Time Stands Still; Treasure in the Deep; Village* (Ireland)

France *Aerea Archaeology in Northern France; The Basques of Santazi* (Disappearing World Series); *Biquefarre; Blow for Blow; Chronique d'une été (Chronicle of a Summer); Family in France: A Story about the Passing of Time; Farrebique; A French Village; Gare du Nord (North Train Station); Gréce et Rome en Provence; Kofi: An African in France; Lascaux; Laurence Wylie in Peyrane, 1983; Learning From the Painters of Lascaux; Punition (The Punishment); Rime and Reason; A Tale of Two Rivers;* Tarap Series

Spain *Carnaval de pueblo; Euskadi: The Stateless Nation; Land without Bread; The Muleteers (Los Arrieros); Pepe's Family; Perico the Bowlmaker; El Pueblo; Romeria: Day of the Virgin; The Shepherd's Family; Terre Sans Pain; Village of Spain; Villagers of the Sierra de Gredos* (Disappearing World Series)

Greece *The Acropolis of Athens; Aegean Sponge Divers; The Anasternaria; Ancient Games; Ancient Moderns: Greek Island Art and Culture: 3,000–2,000 B.C.; Au Fil de L'Aiguille (The Thread of the Needle)* (Rural Greece: Desertion, Migration, Village Life Series); *The Charcoal Makers* (Rural Greece: Desertion, Migration, Village Life Series); *Everyday Is not a Feast Day* (Rural Greece: Desertion, Migration, Village Life Series); *Greece, 478–336 B.C.; Greek Celebrations; A Hard Life* (Rural Greece: Desertion, Migration, Village Life Series); *Heinrich Schliemann: The Rediscovery of Troy; Kalogeros; Kypseli; Let's Get Married* (Rural Greece: Desertion, Migration, Village Life Series); *Life Chances* (Cyprus); *Lord Elgin and Some Stones of No Value; Mt. Athos; My Family and Me* (Rural Greece: Desertion, Migration, Village Life Series); *Passing Shadows; Pericles in America; Rembetika: The Blues of Greece;* Rural Greece: Desertion, Migration, Village Life; *Search for Apollo; Ten Times Empty; Thessaloniki Museum; The Village Watchman; Warriors and Maidens: Gender Relations in a Cretan Mountain Village*

NORTH AMERICA: NATIVE AMERICAN CULTURE (General)
In the White Man's Image (American Experience Series); *Abnaki: The Native People of Maine; Akwesasne: Another Point of View;* American Indian Series; *American Indian Speaks; Annie Mae: Brave Hearted Woman; A Circle of Healing* (Man Alive Series); *Daughters of the Country; Discovering American Indian Music; Doctor, Lawyer, Indian Chief; The Drummaker; The Early Americans; Early Civilizations; The Exiles;* The First Americans Series; *Flaming Arrows* (Man on the Rim Series); *For All People, For All Time; Foster Child; From the Elders; Glooscap;*

Films and Videos by Geographical Area

Haudenosaunee: Way of the Longhouse; Honorable Nations: The Seneca's Land Rights; Ikwe (Daughters of the Country Series); *Incident at Restigouche; Indian Self-Rule: A Problem of History; Kwa' Nu' Te': Micmac and Maliseet Artists; The Legend of Corn;* Legends of Indians; *Lenape: The Original People; The Longest Trail; Man of Lightning; Mohawk Basketmaking: A Cultural Profile; Moowis, Where Are You, Moowis?; Mother of Many Children; The Mystery of the Lost Red Paint People: The Discovery of a Prehistoric North American Sea Culture; Nations within a Nation: Sovereignty and Native American Communities; Native Land: Nomads of the Dawn; No Address; Now that the Buffalo's Gone; Our Lives in Our Hands; The Right to be Mohawk: The Survival of a People and Their Traditions; Sacred Ground; Science or Sacrilege: The Study of Native American Remains; The Search for Ancient Americans; Seeking the First Americans; Shadow Catcher; The Silent Enemy: An Epic of the American Indian; The Spirit Within; Visiting the Indians with George Catlin; The Wake* (Daughters of the Country Series); *Walking in a Sacred Manner; Wilma P. Mankiller: Woman of Power*

Northern Peoples (Inuit, Aleut, Alaskan, Tlingit, etc.)
Angotee; The Annanacks; The Arctic Exiles; At the Times of Whaling; Autumn Winter Camp; Baleen Baskets of the Alaskan Inupiat; Between Two Worlds; Blue: A Tlingit Odyssey (Myth onto Film: A Trilogy from Native Australia, Native America and the Kabbalah Series); *Coppermine; The Drums of Winter (Uksuum Cauyai); Easter in Igloolik; Eskimo Artist Kenojuak; Eskimo Summer* (People of the Seal Series); *Eskimo Winter* (People of the Seal Series); *The Eskimo: Fight for Life; Eskimos of Pond Inlet* (Disappearing World Series); *The Eskimos: A Changing Culture; The Feast in Dream Village;* From the Elders; *From the First People; Hitting Sticks—Healing Hearts; How to Build an Igloo; Hunger Knows No Law; Hunters of the Seal; Huteetl: A Koyukon Memorial Potlatch; Ice People; Inuit Kids; Jenny's Arctic Diary; Kalvak; The Last Days of Okak; The Living Stone; Magic in the Sky; Make Prayers to the Raven; A Matter Of Respect; Migratory Cycle of the Netsilik; Nadlok: Crossing Place of the Deer; Nanook; Nanook Revisited; Netsilik Eskimo; On the Spring Ice; The People of the Seal; People of Tununak; Qaggiq (Gathering Place); Savage Innocents; Songs in Minto Life; Spirit in a Landscape: The People Beyond; Starting Fire with Gunpowder* (As Long as the Rivers Flow Series); *Summer of The Loucheux; Tanana River Rat; Three Stone Blades; Three Stone Blades; A Time to Remember; Tununeremint; Village of No River; Wedding of Paolo; Whaling People; White Dawn; White Justice; Winter Sea Ice Camp; Yesterday, Today: The Netsilik Eskimo; Yesterday, Today*

Canadian (Also see Northwest) As Long as the Rivers Flow; *Attiuk* (Montagnais); *The Ballad of Crowfoot; Cesar's Bark Canoe; Cree Hunters of Mistossini; The Cree of the Paint Hills; Eagles on the Rivers* (Ojbway); *Fires of Spring; Fires of Spring; Flooding Job's Garden* (As Long as the Rivers Flow Series); *The Great Spirit; Grey Owl; Haida Carver; Hunters and Bombers; In Iirgu's Time* (From the Elders Series); *The Indian Speaks: Iyahkimix, The Blackfoot Beaver Ceremony; An Indian View of the Hudson's Bay Company; Joe David: Spirit of the Mask; Kainai: Ka Ke Ki Ku* (Montagnais); *Kamik; Keep the Circle Strong; Land of the Long Day; The Learning Path* (As Long as the Rivers Flow Series); *Like the Trees; Long Day; Longhouse People; The Moontrap; Other Side of the Ledger; The Sacred Circle; The Silent Enemy; Spirit of the Hunt; Spirit Speaking Through; The Spirit that Moves; These Are My People* (Mohawk); *Tikinagan* (As Long as the Rivers Flow Series); *Time Immemorial* (As Long as the Rivers Flow Series); *To Be Indians; The Warrior from Within* (Man Alive Series); *White Fur Clouds; You Are on Indian Land* (Mohawk)

Northwest (Also see Canadian) *...And Women Wove It in a Basket; The Archaeology of Early Man; Blunden Harbor; Box of Treasures; Cooked Beak of Heaven; The Dig; The First Northwesterners; The Fishing People; Full Circle; Haa Shagoon; Haida Carver; Heritage in Cedar; Heritage of the Sea: Makah Indian Treaty Rights; I Will Fight No More Forever; Image Maker and the Indians; In the Land of the War Canoes; Indian Canoes along the Washington Coast; 'Ksan; Kwakuitl; The Land Is the Culture; Little White Salmon Indian Settlement; Loon's Necklace; Lord of the Sky; Makah Indian Treaty Rights; The Marmes Archeological Dig; Northwest Coast Indian Woodworking; Northwest Coast Indian: A Search for the Past; Potlatch; Quillayute Story Skokomish Indian Baskets; Raising the Gilhast Pole; River People: Behind the Case of David Sohappy; The Shadow and the Spirit; Tamanawis Illahee; This Was the Time; Those Born at Masset; Totem Pole* (Kwakuitl); *Totems' Tribal Eye; The Tribe and the Professor; The Tulalip Tribes; Waterborne: Gift of the Indian Canoe; Wooden Box*

California *Acorns; Basketry of the Pomo; Beautiful Tree; Bryan Beavers* (Maidu); *Buckeyes; The Cave Paintings of the Chumash Indians; The Dispossessed* (Pit River); *Dream Dances of the Kashia Pomo; Forty-Seven Cents; Four Butte One: A Lesson in Archaeology* (Maidu); *Game of Staves* (Pomo); *Indian Mainstream;* Indians and Chiefs; *Ishi in Two Worlds; Ishi, the Last Yahi; Kashia Men's Dance; The Many Worlds of Ishi; Modoc; Obsidian Point Making; Of Land and Life: People of the Klamath; Pomo Shaman; Preserving a Way of Life: People of the Klamath; The Probable Passing of Elk Creek; Rock Art Treasures of Ancient America; Watcher of the Winter Sun; The Way of Our Fathers*

Great Basin *American Indian Rock-Shelter* (Nevada); *Broken Treaty at Battle Mountain* (Shoshone); *Pine Nuts; Gatecliff; Montana Indian Children; Washoe*

Plateau *The Price We Paid*

Plains *Before the White Man Came* (Crow); *Calumet, Pipe of Peace; Circle of the Sun* (Blood); *Contrary Warriors: A Film of the Crow Tribe; Crow Dog; Dancing to Give Thanks; The Divided Trail; Falling Star (A Cheyenne Tale); Fort Madison Archaeology; The Great Plains Trilogy; Grey Owl's Little Brother; Is There an American Stonehenge?; Lakota Quillwork: Art and Legend; Land of the Cree; A Man Called Horse; Meet the Sioux Indians; Mighty Warriors; Neshnabek* (Potawatomi); *Neshnabek: The People; Okan* (Blackfoot); *Omaha Tribe; Our Sacred Land; The Pride and the Shame; Red Sunday: The Story of the Battle of the Little Big Horn; The Return of the Sacred Pole; Return to Sovereignty;*

Standing Alone; Tahtonka; To Protect Mother Earth (Broken Treaty II); Tomesha "Ground Afire"; Why Did Gloria Die?; Beadwork

Northeast *The Longhouse People* (Iroquois)

Southeast *Archaeology of the Grand French Battery, Yorktown, Virginia; In Search of Prehistory; Lost in Time; Seminole Indians*

Southwest *An Ancient Gift; The Apache Indian; Arrow to the Sun; Broken Rainbow; The Chaco Legacy; Comrades of the Desert* (Navajo); *Corn Is Life; Daughters of the Anasazi; Dineh; Dinshyin; Emergence; Fonseca: In Search of Coyote; The Forgotten American* (Navajo); *The Four Corners; Gatecliff; Gathering Up Again: Fiesta in Santa Fe; Hopi Songs of the Fourth World; Hopi Songs of the Fourth World; Imagining Indians; Itam Hakim, Hopiit: A Poetic Visualization of Hopi Philosophy and Prophesy; Letter from an Apache; The Long Walk; Los Tejedores; Maria of the Pueblos; Maria's Black Pottery; Maria: Indian Pottery of San Ildefonso; Mystery of the Anasaze; The Navajo; Navajo Canyon Country; Navajo Children; Navajo Code Talkers; Navajo Country; Navajo Film Themselves; The Navajo Indian; The Navajo Indians; The Navajo Indians of the Painted Desert; Navajo Life; Navajo Talking Picture; Navajo Witch; The People; A Pueblo Indian Tale; The Pueblo Presence; Seasons of a Navajo; Separate Visions; Sucking Doctor; The Sun Dagger; The Telltale Tree-Rings; Ten Thousand Beads for Navaho Sam; Thieves of Time; Tule Technology: Northern Paiute Uses of Marsh Resources in Western Nevada; The Water Is so Clear that a Blind Man Could See; A Weave of Time; Weavers of the West; Yaqui Easter Ceremony*

NORTH AMERICA: General and Cultures of European Origin (including Jews, Gypsies, Mennonites, etc.) *Act of Man; Acting Our Age: A Film about Women Growing Old; Adaptation and Aging: Life in a Nursing Home; Add and Mabel's Punkin Center; After Solidarity: Three Polish Families in America; All Hand Work; All My Babies; Almost Heaven; The Amish: Not to Be Modern; America: Everything You've Always Dreamed of; American Boy; American Shoeshine; Arabbin' with the Hucksters of Baltimore; Archaeology; Archaeology of the Grand French Battery, Yorktown, Virginia; Atlantic Slave Trade; Ave Maria: The Story of the Fisherman's Feast; Bar Mitzvah; Bathing Babies in Three Cultures; Being a Joines; Ben's Mill; Between Men; Blue Collar Trap; The Buffalo Crek Flood; But What if the Dream Comes True; Ce pu comme ca anymore; Christ is Risen; Citizen Carney; City of Gold; Coal Miner: Frank Jackson; Coalmining Women; Colonial Williamsburg Series; Coonhound Field Trials; The Cop is in the Middle; A Country Auction: The Paul V. Leitzel Estate Sale; The Country Fiddler; Daisy: The Story of a Facelift; Dialects; Doorway to the Past* (Williamsburg); *Factory; Family Gathering; The Feathered Warrior; The Fight Against Black Monday; Finger Games; Finnish American Lives; Fissura; Four Families; Free Voice of Labor—The Jewish Anarchists; Furnace Brook Site* (New York); *Gefilte Fish; Getting Together; God's Country; Gypsies: The Other Americans; Happy Mother's Day; The Head Men; Heart Broken in Half;* *An Anthropologist Looks at Street Gangs; Hearts and Hands; Hell's Kitchen Chronicle; Hello Columbus; The Hideout; The Holy Ghost People; Home for Life; Hospice; How to Make Sorghum Molasses; The Hutterites; The Immigrant; In Heaven There Is No Beer?; In Her Own Time: Barbara Myerhoff's Final Field Work; In the Shadow of the Law; Included Out; Inheritance; Invisible Walls; Janie's Janie; Jocelyn, Facing Death at 17 with Strong Faith; The Jolo Serpent Handlers; L'An 01 (The Year 01); The Last Pullman Car; Le Regne Du jour; Let the Spirit Move; Luckily I Need Little Sleep; The Mailbox; Man Oh Man—Growing Up Male in America; Marriage and Family in the Bishop Hill Community; Memories in Black and White; Men's Lives; Merchant People: Pride, Power and Belief in Rural America; Mermaids, Frogslegs and Fillets; Metropolitan Avenue; Mrs. Mixon; My Town—Mio Paese; Myths and Moundbuilders; North Georgia Potters; Not So Young Now as Then; Number Our Days; Of Grace and Steel; Over the Hedge; P4W: Prison for Women; Peter, Donald, Willie, Pat; Pittsburgh Police Series; Pizza Pizza Daddy-O; The Plaint of Steve Kreines; Poletown Lives!; The Popovich Brothers of South Chicago; The Quiet in the Land* (Mennonite); *Raananah, A World of Our Own; Ralph Stanley's Bluegrass Festival; A Rather Strange Tribe; Ray Lum, Mule Trader; Religion in Suburbia; Ricky and Rocky; Rights and Reactions; Ritual: Three Portraits; Running Fence; Saint Pascal; Salamanders: A Night at the Phi Delt House; Saugus Iron Works Restoration; Saving and Restoring Historic Communities; Say, Old Man, Can You Play the Fiddle?; The Shakers; The Shakers in America; The Shvitz; Six American Families Series; The Upperville Show; Thoughts on Fox Hunting; Three Apprentices; Total Baby; Two Dollars and a Dream; A Village in Baltimore; The Vinland Mystery; The Visit; Wasyl, An Anecdote; Water from Another Time; Water Witching (Dowsing) in Middle America; We Dig Coal: A Portrait of Three Women; When You Make a Good Crop; Woodrow Cornett, Letcher Country Butcher; Word is Out; Year of the Communes; Young at Heart; Ziveli: Medicine for the Heart*

African-American Cultures *Afro-American Work Songs in a Texas Prison; Always for Pleasure; Atlantic Slave Trade; Black Delta Religion; Black Mother, Black Daughter; The Blues According to Lightnin' Hopkins; Boneshop of the Heart; Capital of the Earth; Celebration: A Caribbean Festival; Chuck Davis, Dancing through West Africa; Clementine Hunter: American Folk Artist; Diary of a Harlem Family; Didn't We Ramble On: The Black Marching Band; Digging for Black Pride; Digging for Black Pride; Dry Wood, Everything Change Up Now; Electric Boogie; Ephesus; Eyes on the Prize: America's Civil Rights Years; Gang Cops; Give My Poor Heart Ease; Gravel Springs Fife and Drum; Hot Pepper; I Shall Moulder before I Shall Be Taken; Iawo; Ida B. Wells: A Passion for Justice; Maroons of Moore Town; Miles of Smiles, Years of Struggle; Moko Jumbie: Traditional Stilt Walkers; Mrs. Mixon; Older, Stronger, Wiser; The Performed Word; Rice and Peas; Sermons and Sacred Pictures; Straight Up Rappin'; The Struggle; Two Black Churches; A View of the South Carolina Sea Islands; Voices of the Gods; Yonder Come Day*

Hispanic-American Cultures *Agueda Martinez; AIDS in the Barrio: Eso no me pasa a mi; Celebracion del matrimonio; Chicano Park; Chulas fronteras; Entre verde y seco; Farmworker's Diary; Forgotten Families; The Heart of Loisaida; Invisible Indians: Mixtec Farmworkers in California; La Acequia; La Musica de la Gente; Living in America: A Hundred Years of Ybor City; Los Que Curan; Los Sures; Los Tejedores; Luisa Torres; Manatic; Maya Fiesta; Maya in Exile; Mi Raza; Norte; Polka; Portrait of a Family; Spanish Influence in the United States; Tierra o muerte: Land or Death; Transnational Fiesta: 1992; Yo soy Chicano; Yo-Yo Man*

Asian-American Cultures *Always There Comes a New Spring; American Chinatown; Becoming American; Between Two Worlds: The Hmong Shaman in America; Blue Collar and Buddha; Children of Change; Chinaman's Choice; Consecration of a Temple; Dance of Tears; The Heavenly Voice of China; House of Spirit: Perspectives on Cambodian Health Care; Mi Raza; Mitsuye and Nellie; Moving Mountains: The Story of the Yiu Mien; A New Year for the Mien; No More Mountains: The Story of the Hmong; Paj Ntaub: Textile Techniques of the Hmong; Peace Has Not Been Made: A Case History of a Hmong Family's Encounter with a Hospital; The Phans of Jersey City; Quiet Passages: The Japanese-American War Bride Experience; Rajvinder: An East Indian Family (Other Lands Series); Rebuilding the Temple: Cambodians in America; Sam; Sewing Woman; Slaying the Dragon; So Far from India; Thanh's War; Two Korean Families; Uprooted! A Japanese American Family's Experience; Who Killed Vincent Chin?*

Mexico *Ancient Footpath; Anselmo; Anselmo and the Women; Artesanos Mexicanos (Mexico's Folk Artists); By Cross and by Sword (A Cruz y a espada); Cajititlan; Changing Town; Civilization in Ancient Chiapas; Corn and the Origins of Settled Life in Meso-America; Cosas de Mi Vida; Cuidad del Nino: A Case Study in Education and Culture; Excavations at La Venta; Fake Fruit; The Feathered Serpent (Man on the Rim Series); Huichol Sacred Pilgrimage to Wirikuta; Huichols; Kiliwa: Hunters and Gatherers of Baja California; The Lacandon Maya Balche Ritual; Land and Water; Magic Windows; Mayordomia: Ritual, Gender, and Cultural Identity in a Zapotec Community; Mexican Heritage Film Series; Miles from the Border; The New Tijuana; Los Oaxaquenos; La Ofrenda: The Days of the Dead; The Peyote Hunt of the Huichols of Mexico; The Ragged Revolution; Rock Paintings of Baja California; A Sacrifice of 10 Dog and Six House; Seeds of Progress; Semana Santa en Nanacatlan; Semanasanta: The Holy Week in Patamban, Purhepacha, Michoacan Mexico; Sentinels of Silence; The Shrine; Slash and Burn; Tarahumara: Racers Against Time; The Tarahumaras; Tarascan Artists; Tepoztian in Transition; Tepoztlan; Time in the Sun; To Find Our Life; To Make the Balance; Touching the Timeless (Millennium: Tribal Wisdom and the Modern World Series); The Tree of Knowledge; Tree of Life (Totonac); Tremors in Guzman; The Turtle People; Via Dolorosa-The Painful Way; We Believe in Nino Fidencial; Weavers in Ahuiran; Yaladog*

Mayan *Appeals to Santiago; Bruji-Shaman; Cakchiquel Maya of San Antonio Palopo (The Disappearing World Series); Caracol, The Lost Maya City; Copan; Daughters of Ischel: Maya Thread of Change; Dawn Ceremony for the House of Xas Koov; El Mirador: A Preclassic City; An Ixil Calendrical Divination; Land of the Eagle; Last of the Mayas; The Living Maya Series; Lost World of the Maya; Maya Land: Where are you Going? (Terre Maya); Maya Lords of the Jungle; Maya through the Ages; Maya: Treasures of an Ancient Civilization; Mayaland; The Mayans: Apocalypse Then; The Mayas; Mystery of the Maya; Ollero Yucateco; Popol Vuh: The Creation Myth of the Maya; Race to Extinction; Sacred Games: Ritual Warfare in a Maya Village; Sentinals of Silence; Shunka's Story; Stairways to the Mayan Gods; The Sun Kingdom of Yucatan; Swidden Horticulture among the Lacandon Maya; Tajimoltik; Tikal; Todos Santos Cuchumatan: Report from a Guatemalan Village; Todos Santos: The Survivors; Twilight of the Mayas; When Mountains Tremble*

MIDDLE AMERICA *Aymara Leadership; Central America: On the Horns of a Dilemma; The Cuna Indians: Island Exiles; Hungry Angels (Guatemala); Of Lives Uprooted; The Spirit of Kuna Yala; Sweat of the Sun (Tribal Eye Series); Zapotecan Village*

CARIBBEAN *Adelaide Village (Bahamas); Before Reggae Hit the Town; Capital of Earth: The Maroons of Moore Town; Carnival T.N.T.; Divine Horsemen; Grenada: Land of Spice; Grenada: Portrait of a Revolution; Grenada: The Future Coming toward Us; Haitian Song (Caribbean Cultures Series); The Harder They Come: Lucia (Cuba); Jamaica Sings; Jojolo (Haiti); Kantik'i Maishi: Songs of Sorghum; Last of the Karaphuna; Legacy of The Spirits (Caribbean Cultures Series); Mangoes under the Tree; Music from Oil Drums; The Oath of Caiman Wood (Le Serment du Bois Caiman); On Borrowed Land; Pocomania (Jamaica); Rastafari Voices; Rastafari: Conversations Concerning Women; Sosua; To Serve The Gods (Caribbean Cultures Series); The Toured: The Other Side of Tourism in Barbados; Voodoo and the Church in Haiti; Voodoo Island (Haiti)*

SOUTH AMERICA *The Brick Makers; Le Chemin des Indiens Morts (The Way of the Dead Indians); The Earth Is Our Mother; The Galapagos: Laboratory for Evolution; Homage to the Yahgans: The Last Indians of Tierra del Fuego and Cape Horn; Inhabitants of the Land of Grace Series; The Mendolin King (Inhabitants of the Land of Grace Series); Prayer to Viracocha; Roads without Wheels (Man on the Rim Series)*

Argentina *Araucanians of Ruca Choroy; Chucalezna; Guri: The Young Gaucho; Imaginero; Las Madres: The Mothers of Plaza de Mayo; The Ora People; Zerda's Children*

Chile *Aspects of Land Tenure*

Bolivia *Aspects of Land Ownership; Blood of the Condor; Bolivian Boy; Campensinos; Changes in Agriculture; Faces of Change Series; Frontier Settlement; Handmade; I Spent My Life in the Mines; Market at La Paz; Simplemente Jenny*

Brazil *Amazon Family; Amazonia: The Road to the End of the Forest; Barren Lives; Black Water; Boy of the Matto Grosso; A Brazilian Family; Carnaval Bahia* (Disappearing World Series); *Caxiri or Manioc Beer* (The Waiapi Indians of Brazil Series); *Contact with a Hostile Tribe; Contact: The Yanomami Indians of Brazil; The Decade of Destruction; Dry Weather Chronicle; The Four Mill House; The Green Puzzle of Altamira; Hail Umbanda; Halting the Fires; Head Men; Iawo; Incident in the Matto Grosso; Jangadieros; Jose Carlos and His Spirits: The Ritual Initiation of Zelador Dos Orixas in a Brazilian Umbanda Center; Journey to Chinale; Jungles of the Amazon; The Kayapo* (Disappearing World Series); *The Land of the Indians; Life at the Source: The Adventures of an Amazon Explorer; The Mehinacu* (Disappearing World Series); *Migracas; Music, Dance, and Festival among the Waiapi Indians of Brazil* (The Waiapi Indians of Brazil Series); *The Myth of Peribo (El mito de Peribo); The Neighborhood of Coehlos; Nomads of the Rainforest; O Pagador de promessa; The Pacification War in Amazonia; The Panare—Scenes from the Frontier; Raoni; The Return of Dr. Fritz: Healing by the Spirits in Brazil; Santa Marta: Two Weeks in the Slums; The Shock of the Other* (Millennium: Tribal Wisdom and the Modern World Series); *The Spirit Possession of Alejandro Mamani; The Tango Is Also a History; This is Not Your Life; Three Apprentices; The Tribe that Hides from Man; Txai Macedo; The Txicao People of Brazil's Matto Grosso; Umbanda The Problem Solver* (Disappearing World Series); *Vision of Juazeiro; Waiapi Body Painting and Ornaments* (The Waiapi Indians of Brazil Series); *The Waiapi Indians of Brazil; Waiapi Instrumental Music* (The Waiapi Indians of Brazil Series); *Waiapi Slash and Burn Cultivation* (The Waiapi Indians of Brazil Series); *War of the Gods* (Disappearing World Series); *We Are Mehinaku; The Xinguana*

Colombia *Bogota: Fragments of a City; Changes in Land Use; Corpus Christi: A Solstice Feast; Embera: The End of The Road* (Disappearing World Series); *Gold: The Sacred Metal; Guambianos; Guelmambi; Guma the Snake; Ika Hands; Improvement and Utilization; The Journey Back: The Earth Is Our Mother II (Rejsen tilbage: Jorden en vores mor 2); The Last of The Cuiva* (Disappearing World Series); *Legend of the Paramo; A Long Hour's Walk; Misa Colombiana; Paredes de piedra; Piraparana; Statement by Enrique Camargo; Statement by Milciades Chavez; Tierra y cultura; Transportation; Villarrica; Virgin Mary (or Holy Sorceress); The Wax and the Feather*

Ecuador Andean Ethnomedicine: Birth and Childhood Illness in Six Ecuadorian Communities; *Evil Wind, Evil Air (Mal viento, mal aire, pasmo); Head Hunters of Ecuador; Icemen of Chimborazo; People of the Barrio; Runa: Guardians of the Forest; Sky Chief; Valley of the Old Ones*

Guyana *Divine Madness: Trance, Dance and Healing in Guyana*

Nicaragua *La casa de mujer—Supporting Women in Nicaragua; Oigame! Oigame!; Sandino, Today and Forever; Thank God and the Revolution; Women in Arms*

Paraguay *Cuarahy Ohecha; Nanduti, A Paraguagan Lace*

Peru *Alpaca Breeders of Chimboya; Amahuaca; Ancient Art of Peru; Ancient Inca Indians; The Ancient Peruvian; Before We Knew Nothing; Carnival in Q'eros; Changing Faces (Jivaro); Choqela: Only Interpretation; Cimarrones; Discovering the Moche; Eduardo the Healer; Fugitive from Fear; In the Footsteps of Taytacha; Inca Royal Architecture in the Cuzco Region; The Incas; The Incas and Their Empire; Lords of the Labyrinth; Martin Chambi and the Heirs of the Incas; Monkey of the Clouds; Mountain Music of Peru; Our God the Condor; Peruvian Archaeology; Peruvian Weaving: A Continuous Warp for 5,000 Years; The Quechua* (Disappearing World Series); *Queros: The Shape Of Survival; So That Men Are Free; Urbanization in the Moche Valley; We Ain't Winning; When The World Turned Dark; Where Land Is Life*

Venezuela *The Ax Fight; A Clearing in the Jungle* (Disappearing World Series); *Curare; Cuyagua; Ebena: Hallucinogenic Ecstasy among the Yanomamo; The Feast; Indians of the Orinoco; Juan Felix Sanchez; La Colonia Tovar; Las Turas; Magical Death; A Man Called "Bee"; Mosori Monika: Yanomamo: A Multi-Disciplinary Study; Peasant Painter* (Inhabitants of the Land of Grace Series); *Reclaiming the Forest; The Warao; Watunna; Yanomamo of the Orinoco: A New Video for Elementary and Secondary Use; Yanomamo Series; Yanomamo: The Sons of Blood; The Yanomamo Tribe in War and Peace*

OCEANIA *Islands of the South Pacific; Life on a Coral Atoll; Marshall Islands—Living with the Bomb* (The Human Face of the Pacific Series)

AUSTRALIA (Some of these films concern secret/sacred matters. See page 291 for restrictions.) Aboriginal Dance Series; *Aborigines of the Sea Coast; At the Canoe Camp; At the Edge of the Old Stone Age; Australia's Twilight of the Dreamtime;* The Australian Institute of Aboriginal Studies Series; *Becoming Aboriginal; Black Man's Houses; Camels and Pitjantjara; Carnarvon' Coniston Muster; Coming of Man; Cycle* (Myth onto Film Series); *Dance of the Buffalo Hunt; Dances at Aurukum; Desert People; Dingari Ceremonies at Papunya; Djalambu; Djungguwan at Gurka'wuy; Duke Tritton, Australian Sheep-Shearer; Emu Ritual at Ruguri; Familiar Places; Fieldwork: Sir Walter Baldwin Spencer (1860–1929)* (Strangers Abroad Series); *The First Invaders* (Triumph of the Nomads Series); *Five Aboriginal Dances from Cape York* (Aboriginal Dance Series); *Goodbye Old Man; The Great Unfenced; Groote Eylandt Series; Gunabibi: An Aboriginal Fertility Cult; The House-Opening; In Memory of Mawalan; The Land of The Lightening Brothers; The Last Tasmanian Series; Larwari and Walkara; Lockhart Festival; Lurugu; Madarrpa Funeral at Gurka'wuy; Making a Bark Canoe; Malbangka Country;* Man on the Rim Series; *Men of the Dream Time; Mourning for Mangatopi; Mulga Seed Ceremony; My Country Djarrakpi; Narritjin at Djarrakpi; Narritjin in Canberra; Ngatjakula; Ngoora; Night Cries: A Rural Tragedy; Not to Lose You My Language; On Sacred Ground; One Man's Response; Pacific Paradox; The Path of Life; The Path of Souls;* People of the Australian Western Desert Series; *People Out of Time; Peppimenarti; Pinturi Revisit Yumari; Primitive People; Reign of the Wanderers*

(Triumph of the Nomads Series); *Roaring Serpect of Arnhem Land; Rock Engravings; Sails of Doom* (Triumph of the Nomads Series); *So They Did Eat; Sons of Namatjira; State Of Shock; A Native People Loses Its Heritage; Takeover; Tent Embassy; Tjurunga; Two Desert Families; Uluru—An Anangu Story; Utu; Waiting for Harry; Walbiri Fire Ceremony; Walbiri Ritual at Gunadjari; Walbiri Ritual at Ngama; Walk-About; We Are the Landowner; We Believe in It; When the Snake Bites the Sun; White Clay and Ochre*

MELANESIA *Angels of War: World War II in Papua New Guinea; Asmat: Cannibal Craftsmen of New Guinea; Bathing Babies in Three Cultures; Bougainville Cooper Project; Cannibal Tours; Character Formation in Different Cultures Series: Death Drums of New Guinea; Child of Papua, New Guinea: The Same Today, the Same Tomorrow; Childhood Rivalry in Bali and New Guinea* (Sepik River); *Expressive Culture in Papua; Ileksen; Kama Wosi: Music in the Trobriand Islands* (Traditional Music of Papua New Guinea Series); *Land Divers of Melanesia; Malagan Labadama: A Tribute to Buk-Buk* (Films from Papua New Guinea Series); *Margaret Mead's New Guinea Journal* (Manus); *Matjemosh* (Asmat, New Guinea); *Me'udana* (Normanby Island); *New Caledonia—A Land in Search of Itself* (The Human Face of the Pacific Series); *People in Change; Primitive Man in Our Society* (Sepik River, New Guinea); *Primitive Man in Our World: Tapa Tidikawa and Freinds; The Red Bowmen* (Films from Papua New Guinea Series); *South Sea Island Life: The Dolphin Hunters* (Solomons); *The Shark Callers of Kontu;* Traditional Music of Papua New Guinea; *Tribal Eye: Man Blong Custom; Trobriand Cricket: An Ingenious Response to Colonialism; The Trobriand Experiment; The Trobriand Islanders of Papua New Guinea* (Disappearing World Series); *Trobriand Islanders; Wow* (Asmat); *Yumi Yet: Independence for Papua New Guinea*

NEW GUINEA HIGHLANDS *Asmat: Cannibal Craftsmen of New Guinea; Axes and Aré: Stone Tools of the Duna; Bathing Babies in Three Cultures; Black Harvest; Dani Houses; Dani Sweet Potatoes; Dani Technology Films; Dani Tribe: Extracting Salt; Dead Birds* (Dani); *First Contact* (Papua New Guinea Series); *First Days in the Life of a New Guinea Baby; Ghosts of the Makihuku; Gourd Men of New Guinea; Her Name Came on Arrows: A Kinship Interview with the Baruya of New Guinea* (A Series on the Baruya); *Joe Leahy's Neighbours* (Papua New Guinea Series); *The Kawelka* (Disappearing World Series); *Kerepe's House* (Maring); *Langda: Polished Stone Adzes in New Guinea; Magical Curing; Man without Pigs* (Films from Papua New Guinea Series); *Maring in Motion;?* The Maring Series; *The Mendi; My Father, My Country; Networking and Systems* (Chimbu); *New Guinea; New Guinea Patrol and Excerpts from Yumi Yet* (People in Change Series); *No Longer Strangers* (Dani); *Ongka's Big Moka;* A Series on the Baruya; *Sinmia; The Sky Above, the Mud below; Songs of a Distant Jungle; Tidikawa and Friends* (Traditional Music of Papua New Guinea Series); *Tidikawa: At the Edge of Heaven; Tighten the Drums: Self-Decoration among the Enga* (Films from Papua New Guinea Series); *To Find Baruya's Story: An Anthropologist at Work with a New Guinea Tribe* (A Series on the Baruya); *Towards Baruya Manhood; Voices in the Forest; A Walk in the Forest; Yeleme: La Hache de Pierre polie en Nouvelle-Guinee*

MICRONESIA *Gogodala: A Cultural Revival?* (Films from Papua New Guinea Series); *Half Life: A Parable for the Nuclear Age; Lamotrek: Heritage of an Island; Micronesia: The Tiny Islands;* Micronesian Series; *Mokil; Pacific Island* (Likiep, Marshalls); *The Navigators: Pathfinders of the Pacific; Samoa i Sisifo*

POLYNESIA *Aku-Aku; American Samoa: Paradise Lost; The Best Kept Secret* (Western Samoa); *Child of New Zealand; Children of Samoa* (Children of the World Series); *Children of the Mist* (Maori); *Coming of Age: Margaret Mead (1901–1978)* (Strangers Abroad Series); *Cry of Nukumanu; Death of an Island Culture* (Nukumanu); *Easter Island; Fa'a Samoa; Fighting Festival; Fiji—Legacies of Empire* (The Human Face of the Pacific Series); *Fiji: The Great Council of Chiefs; Huahine: Land of Discovery; I Am Fijian; In Maori Land; Island Observed* (Easter Island); *Island of the Red Prawn* (Fiji); *Kon Tiki; The Last Horizon* (Man on the Rim Series); *The Lau of Malaita* (Disappearing World Series); *Maori Arts and Culture; A Maori Creation Myth* (Creation Myth Series); *The Maori Today; Margaret Mead and Samoa; Mary Pritchard* (Samoa); *Moana Roa* (Cook Islands); *Niutao-Construction of a Sleeping House; The Other Side of Paradise* (Fiji); *Pacific Island Life Series* (Nuguria); *People of the Free Train* (Fiji); *Place of Power in French Polynesia* (The Human Face of the Pacific Series); *Polynasier* (Nuitai-Ellice-Inseln); *The Primitive Maori; The Punake of Tonga; Puzzle of the Pacific; Rangi and Papa; Samoa I Sisigo; Tabu; Teine Samoa: A Girl of Samoa; Tevia: A Boy Prepares for Manhood; Tonga Royal; Western Samoa—I Can Get Another Wife but I Can't Get Parents* (The Human Face of the Pacific Series); *White Shadows in the South Seas*

Films and Videos by Topic

(Titles in Nonitalic Type Are Series)

FIELDWORK *The Anthropologist; Anthropologists at Work: Careers Making a Difference; Bake Restudy 1984; Familiar Places; Firth on Firth; Gurkha Country; Human Relations Area File; A Man Called "Bee"; Margaret Mead; Margaret Mead's New Guinea Journal; Matjemosh (Asmat, New Guinea); Miss Goodall and the Wild Chimpanzees; Nice Weather, Mr. Pradhan!; Observing Baboons from a Vehicle; Shadow Catcher; Shahira: Nomads of the Sahara; The Spirit of Ethnography;* Strange Beliefs: Sir Edward Evans-Pritchard (1902–1973) (Strangers Abroad Series); *Sur les traces du renard pale* (Tracking the Pale Fox: Studies on the Dogon); To Find the Baruya's Story: An Anthropologist at Work with a New Guinea Tribe (A Series on the Baruya); *Village Morning; Yanamamo: A Multi-Disciplinary Study* (Venezuela)

ETHOLOGY *Adaptation of Female Anubis Baboons to Social System of Hamadryas Baboons; Among Wild Chimpanzees; Analyse cinéradiographique du saut chez un primate: Galago Alleni; Animal War—Animal Peace; Animals in Amboseli; Anthropology on Trial; Ape Vocalization; The Apes of Barbary; Aspects of the Behavior of the Sifaka (Propithecus verreauxi verreauxi); Baboon Behavior; Baboon Development; Baboon Ecology; Baboon Social Organization;* Baboon Social Life; *The Baboon Troop; Baobab; Behavior and Ecology of Vervet Monkeys (Cercopithecus aethiops); Behavior Characteristics of the Rhesus Monkey; Behavior of Free-Ranging Rhesis Monkeys on Cayo Santiago: Mother-Offspring Interactions; Behavior of the Macaques of Japan;* Bleeding Hearts and Bone Crushers; *Carrying of the Young by the Mother; Lesser Mouse Lemur; Cebus Monkeys; Chacma Baboons of Capetown; Cleaning Movements; Climbing I; Red Howler Monkey; Climbing Potto; Climbing Slow Loris;* Cry of the Muriqui; *Defensive Behavior; Greater Sportive Lemur; Dynamics of Male Dominance in a Baboon Troop; Evening Activity; Field Study Sequence; The First Signs of Washoe; Food Preparation. Japanese Macaque; From Conditioned Response to Symbol; The Galapagos: Laboratory for Evolution; Gelada; Gibbon Research in a Designed Environment; Gorilla; Hanuman Langur: Monkey of India; Hominid Evolution I and II; Howler Monkeys of Barro Colorado Island; Ingestion of Food II; Common Tree Shrew; Island of the Moon;* Jane Goodall: Studies of the Chimpanzee; *Locomotion on a Branch; Locomotion on Branches; White-Handed Gibbon; Maternal Behavior; Japanese Macaque; Meshie; Miss Goodall and the Wild Chimpanzees; Monkey into Man; Monkey of the Clouds; Monkey, Apes and Man; The Monkeys of Mysore; Mountain Gorilla;* The Nut-Cracking Chimps of Taï Forest; *Observing Baboons from a Vehicle; Play of the Young. Greater Dwarf Lemur; Play of the Young. Japanese Macaque; Primate;* Primates; *Quadruped Walking; Rhesus Monkey...; Rhesus Monkey in India; A Rhesus Monkey Infant's First Four Month; Search for the Great Apes; Seizing Small Objects. Sacred Baboon; Seizing Small Objects. Woolly Monkey; Social Behavior in the Group. Sacred Baboon; Social Behavior of Rhesus Monkeys;* Sociobiology; Sociobiology: The Human Animal; *Survey of the Primate; Taking Hold of Small Objects; Teaching Sign Language to the Chimpanzee, Washoe; Tree-Top Signaling. Japanese Macaque; Vocalization and Speech in Chimpanzees; Vocalizations of Wild Chimpanzees; Walking Upright. Chimpanzee; Watunna;* Zoo

PHYSICAL ANTHROPOLOGY (Hominid Evolution, Human Origins) *Apemen of Africa; Blood Groups, Skin Color, and Gene Pools; Coming of Man; Dating Game: How Old Are We?; Early Stone Tools;* The Faces of Culture; *First Footsteps* (Man on the Rim Series); *The First Humans; From Homo Erectus to Neanderthal; The Galapagos: Laboratory for Evolution; The Gene Engineers; Genetics: Man the Creator; A Human Way of Life* (The Making of Mankind Series); *Leakey; Lucy in Disguise;* The Making of Mankind; Man on the Rim; *Man on the Rim: The Peopling of the Pacific; Mysteries of Mankind; The Myth of Peribo (El mito de Peribo); Myth onto Film: A Trilogy from Native Australia, Native America and the Kabbala; Prehistoric Humans; Quest for Fire; Salt and Hypertension;* Sociobiology; *Sociobiology: Doing What Comes Naturally; Sociobiology: The Human Animal; A Tale of Two Rivers*

ARCHAEOLOGY *The Acropolis of Athens; American History? It's beneath Your Feet; The Ancient Africans; Ancient Art; The Ancient Chinese; Ancient Egypt; The Ancient Egyptian; Ancient Footpath; Ancient Greece;* Ancient Lives; *The Ancient Mariners; Ancient Moderns: Greek Island Art and Culture: 3,000–2,000 B.C.; The Ancient Peruvian;* Ancient Places (Hidden Places: Where History Lives Series); *The Ancient Romans; Ancient Sardis; Angkor—The Lost City; Anglo-Saxon England; Applied Geoarchaeology; Archaeology; Archaeology: Furnace Brook Site; Archaeology in Mesopotamia; Archaeology of the Grand French Battery, Yorktown, Virginia; Archaeology: Pursuit of Man's Past; Archaeology: Questioning the Past; Archaeology Synthesis; Archaeological Field School; Ascent of Man; Assault on Time; Atlantis; Bath Waters; Be'er Sheva Four; Before the Romans; The Beginning of History, Part Ill: The Iron Age; Black Athena;* Breaking Ground; *Bronze Age Blastoff; Caracol, The Lost Maya City; Carnarvon; Carthage: A Mirage of Antiquity; Cave Dwellers of the Old Stone Age; A Celtic Trilogy; Ceramiques Prehistorique;* The Chaco Legacy; *Civilization in Ancient Chiapas; Civilizations of Ancient America; Colonial Six; Copan; Corn and the Origin of Settled Life in Meso-American; Cracking the Stone Age Code; Decoding Danebury; The Dig; Digging for Black Pride; Digging up the Past: Discovering the Moche (Penn.); Discovery at Sheep Rock; Discovery of Arago Man; Discov-*

ering the Moche; Diving for Roman Plunder; Dr. Leakey and the Dawn of Man; Doorway to the Past; Earliest Writing; The Early Americans; Early Civilizations; Early Man in North America; Earth Lodge People: Excavations at La Venta; The Excavation of Mound 7; The First Americans; The First Family; The First Man and His Environment; The First Northwesterners: The Archaeology of Early Man; Five Foot Square; Fort Madison Archaeology; 4-Butte-l; Glen Canyon Archaeology; Graveyard of the Gulf; The Great Dinosaur Discovery; Greece, 478–336 B.C.; Gripping Beast; Ground Truth: Archaeology in the City; Have You Considered Archaeology; Hedeby: The Salvage of a Viking Ship; Heinrich Schliemann: The Rediscovery of Troy; Heritage of the Pharaohs; History of Archaeology; Huahine: Land of Discovery; The Ice Man; In Search of Grand Canyon's Past; In Search of Prehistory; In Search of the Lost World; In Search of the Magic of Stonehenge; In Search of the Trojan War; *In the Shadow of Vesuvius; The Incas* (Odyssey Series); *Iowa's Ancient Hunters; The Land of the Lightening Brothers* (Australia); *Lascaux; Late Woodland Village; Legacy; Legends of Easter Island; Loot: The Plundered Heritage; Lord Elgin and Some Stones of No Value; The Lost Army; Lucy and the First Family; The Man behind the Mask; The Manhunters; The Marmes Archaeological Dig; Maya Lords of the Jungle; Meadow Croft Rockshelter; Megiddo-City of Destruction; Mill Creek Village People; El Mirador: A Preclassic City* (Mayan); *The Mists of Time; Mona Lisa of the Galilee; The Mystery of Stonehenge; The Mystery of the Lost Red Paint People: The Discovery of a Prehistoric North American Sea Culture; Myths and Moundbuilders; Nadlok: Crossing Place of the Deer; The New Cutting Edge* (Man on the Rim Series); *Northwest Coast Indians; On the Track of the Bog People* (Denmark); *On the Tracks of Abbe Breuit; Once in King David's City; One Hundred Years of Archaeology* (India); *100,000 Piece Jigsaw Puzzle; Oriental Institute;* Out of the Fiery Furnace; *Out of the Past: An Introduction to Archaeology; Petra: Crossroad in Stone; The Plunderers; Pompeii: Daily Life of the Ancient Romans; Prehistoric Cultures; Prehistoric Humans; Prehistoric Images; Prehistoric Man; Prehistoric Man Series; Preserving Egypt's Past; The Riddle of the Dead Sea Scrolls; The Rio Grande's Pueblo Past; The Ritual of the Mounds; River through Time; Rock Art Treasures of Ancient America; Rock Engravings* (Australia); *Science or Sacrilege: The Study of Native American Remains; Search for a Century; Search for a Tropical Arctic; The Search for Alexander the Great; The Search For Ancient Americans; Search for Apollo; Search for Fossil Man; The Search for Herod's Harbor; Secrets of Easter Island; Seeking the First Americans; Sentinels of Silence; Shipwreck: La Trinidad Valencera* (Odyssey Series); *Silent Army* (China); *The Silent Witness: An Investigation into the Shroud of Turin; The Silk Road; Six Hundred Millennia: China's History Unearthed; 6000 Years in Suswa* (East Africa); *Snaketown; Sticks and Stones Will Build Houses; Stonehenge: Mystery in the Plain; Stop Destroying America's Past; Story of the Wasa; The Sun Dagger; Sunken Treasure; A Tale of Two Rivers* (France); *Testament: The Bible and History; Thessaloniki Museum; Thieves of Time* (South-West); *Tikal; Traveller from an Antique Land; Treasure in the Deep* (Great Britain); *The Tribe and the Professor; The Viking Ships of Roskilde* (Denmark); *The Vinland Mystery; Voyage from Antiquity; Watcher of the Winter Sun* (California); *Where Man Lies Buried; White Clay and Ochre; Who Discovered America?; American History? It's Beneath Your Feet; Williamsburg File* (Chronicle Series); *Xian* (The Cities in China Series)

Archaeology: Methods and Techniques *Advance into the Past: Modern Archaeological Methods; Aerial Archaeology in Northern France; The Alchemy of Time; Ancient Projectile Points; Archaeological Dating; Archeologie en laboratoire; The Archaeologist and How He Works; Archaeologists at Work; Archaeology in the Laboratory; Basic Methods in Southeastern Archaeology; Beating the Bellows; The Big Dig; Community Dig; Dating Game: How Old Are We; Demircihukuk; The Dig; The Early Americans; Early Stone Tools; Exploring the Unwritten Past; The Flintworker; The Future of the Past* (Infinite Voyage Series); *Garbage; Gatecliff: American Indian Rock-Shelter; How We Learn about the Past; The Hunters Edge; Langda: Polished Stone Adzes in New Guinea; Made by Hand; Making Primitive Stone Tools; The Marmes Archeological Dig; Nuclear Fingerprinting of Ancient Pottery; Obsidian Point Making; 100,000 Piece Jigsaw Puzzle; Point of Pines; The Shadow of Man; Stone Knapping in Modern Turkey; The Survey; Techniques of Digging and Analysis of Archaeology; To Know the Hurons: An Experiment in Rescue Archaeology; The Tree of Iron; Where Man Lies Buried*

Archaeology: Technology *Ancient Projectile Points; Axes and Are: Stone Tools of the Duna; Blades and Pressure Flaking; Early Stone Tools; The Flintworker; The Hunters' Edge; Obsidian Point-Making; The Shadow of Man*

LIFE CYCLE

Daily Life (including general ethnographic description) (See also Economics) *Au fil de L'aiguille (The Thread of the Needle)* (Greece); *The Bajao: Seagoing Nomads* (Phillipines); *Before We Knew Nothing* (Peru); *Capital of Earth: The Maroons of Moore Town; Le chemin des Indiens morts (The Way of the Dead Indians); Child of Papua, New Guinea: The Same Today, the Same Tomorrow; Children of Samoa* (Children of the World Series); *The Cuna Indians: Island Exiles; Desert People* (Australia); *Easter In Igloolik; Easter Island; Eskimo Fight for Life; Eskimo Summer* (People of the Seal Series); *Eskimo Winter* (People of the Seal Series); *Everyday Is Not a Feast Day* (Rural Greece: Desertion, Migration, Village Life Series); *The Family Table* (A Taste of China Series); *Farm Song* (The Japanese Series); *Les fils de l'eau (The Sons of the Water)* (West Africa); *Four Families; Grass: A Nation's Battle For Life; Guma the Snake* (Colombia); *Haitian Song* (Caribbean Culture Series); *The Herders of Mongun-Taiga* (Disappearing World Series); *Hopi Songs of the Fourth World; How to Behave; I Shall Moulder before I Shall Be Taken* (Guatemala); *Ika Hands* (Colombia); *In Her Own Time: Barbara Myerhoff's Final Field Work; Inside China: Living with the Revolution* (Disappearing World Series); *Into the Deep Freeze* (Man on the Rim Series); *Jenny's Arctic Diary; Ketut di Bali; Living Africa: A Village Experience;* The Living Maya Series; *Luisa Torres; Magic Windows* (Mexico); *Lov-*

ing Krishna (Pleasing God Series); Make Prayers to the Raven; Meet the Sioux Indians; The Mende (Disappearing World Series); The Mende of Kpuawala Village; Mistaken Identity (Millennium: Tribal Wisdom and the Modern World Series); Naked Spaces: Living Is Round (West Africa); Neshnabek: The People; Nomads on the Savanna; El Pueblo (Spain); The Sakuddei of Indonesia (Disappearing World Series); Sharing Is Unity (Ushirika Ni Umoja); Los Sures; Swidden Horticulture among the Lacandon Maya; Ten Times Empty (Greece); Three Stone Blades; Tidikawa and Friends (Traditional Music of Papua New Guinea Series); Todos Santos Cuchumatan: Report from a Guatemalan Village; Women in China Today; Yanomamo of the Orinoco: A New Video for Elementary and Secondary Use; Yesterday, Today: The Netsilik Eskimo

Birth Abuelitas de ombligo (Granny Midwives) (Nicaragua); All My Babies; Angotee; Birth; Chillysmith Farm; Dae (Gypsy Birth); El Sebou': Egyptian Birth Ritual; First Days in the Life of a New Guinea Baby; La Circoncision (Circumcision) (North Africa); Marco; Nyamakuta—The One Who Receives (South Africa); Seven Nights and Seven Days; Small Happiness: Women of a Chinese Village (Long Bow Film Series)

Development of the Child Angotee; A Balinese Family; Bathing Babies in Three Cultures; Big Problems for Little People (Phillipines); Character Formation in Different Cultures Series; Child of Papua, New Guinea: The Same Today, the Same Tomorrow; Child Series; Childhood Rivalry in Bali and New Guinea; Children of Samoa (Children of the World Series); China's Only Child; Coming of Age: Margaret Mead (1901–1978) (Strangers Abroad Series); Cross-Cultural Differences in Newborn Behavior; Development of the Child: A Cross-Cultural Approach to Cognition; Eze Nwata: The Small King; Growth and Development of Children; Kibbutz Series; Life Chances; Montana Indian Children; Rapports Meres-Enfants en Afrique (Rapports between Mothers and Infants in Africa); Richard Cardinal: Cry from a Diary of Metis Child; Rock-A-Bye Baby; Taway Nya—la mere (Taway Nya—Mother) (West Africa); Teine Samoa: A Girl of Samoa (Girl of Series); 365 Days with Your Baby; Total Baby; Les veuves de quinze ans (The Fifteen Year Old Widows)

Initiation Bar Mitzvah; Becoming a Woman in Okrika; Bushman Series; Garcons et Filles (Central Africa); Guri: The Young Gaucho; Initiation; Initiation a la danse des possedes (Initiation into Possession Dances); An Initiation Kut for a Korean Shaman; Masai Manhood (Disappearing World Series); Messing up God's Glory; Moana (Samoa); The Mursi: Nitha (Disappearing World Series); Nias and Sumatra; The Nuer (Ethiopia); Pintubi Revisit Yumari (Australia); The Plaint of Steve Kreines; Rites; Sakpata; Salamanders: A Night at the Phi Delta House; Sinmia; Soro (Hausa, Nigeria); Teiva (Polynesia); Towards Baruya Manhood

Wedding and Marriage Asian Heart; Brides of the Gods; Celebracion del matrimonio; Comalapa: Traditions and Textures; The Bride Market of Imilchil; The Dragon Bride; For Richer for Poorer (The New Pacific Series); Himba Wedding; Island of the Red Prawns; Let's Get Married (Rural Greece: Desertion, Migration, Village Life Series); Liebala; Love Songs of the Miao in China; Modern Brides: Arranged Marriage in South India; The Muria (South Asia); Nine Cows and an Ox (Diary of a Maasai Village Series); Rajvinder: An East Indian Family (Other Lands Series); Spear and Sword: A Payment of Bridewealth on the Island of Roti (Roti Series); Strange Relations (Millennium: Tribal Wisdom and the Modern World Series); Thanh's War; Thread of the Needle (Rural Greece: Desertion, Migration, Village Life Series); Tobelo Marriage; Two Journeys (Diary of a Maasai Village Series); A Village in Baltimore; Wedding Camels; Wedding in a Persian Village; Wedding Song; The Winter Wife; Young at Heart

Aging Acting Our Age: A Film about Women Growing Old; Adaptation and Aging; American Chinatown; Death Is Afraid of Us; Dorothy Molter: Living in the Boundary Waters; Is It Hot in Here? A Film about Menopause; Kicking High . . . in the Golden Years; Life in a Nursing Home; Long Life and Prosperity; New Images of Aging; Nice Weather, Mr. Pradhan!; Night Cries: A Rural Tragedy (Australia); Number Our Days; Sexuality and Aging; The Spirit Possession of Alejandro Mamani (Brazil); Two Worlds to Remember; Water from Another Time

Death and Dying A Country Auction: The Paul V. Leitzel Estate Sale; Asmat: Cannibal Craftsmen of New Guinea; Chillysmith Farm; Death; Goodbye Old Man (Australia); Hitting Sticks—Healing Hearts; Hospice; How Could I Not Be among You; Huteetl: A Koyukon Memorial Potlatch; Jocelyn, Facing Death at 17 with Strong Faith; Madarrpa Funeral at Gurka'wuy; Malagan Labadama: A Tribute to Buk-Buk (Films from Papua New Guinea Series); Pam Kuso Kar (Briser les poteries de pam) (Breaking Pam's Vases); The Parting; To Die Today

Funeral Dead Birds (Dani, New Guinea); Great Tree Has Fallen; Huteetl: A Koyukon Memorial Potlatch; I Shall Moulder before I Shall Be Taken; Madarrpa Funeral at Gurka'wuy; Me'udana (Normanby Island); Passing Shadows. (Greece); Simiri Siddo Kuma; Souna Kouma (La nostalgie de Souna) (Nostalgia of Souna); The Bilo (Madagascar)

LIFE HISTORY Annie Mae: Brave Hearted Woman; Anselmo and the Women (Mexico); Bali beyond the Postcard; But I'll Always Continue to Write (The Human Face of Indonesia Series); Children of Fate: Life and Death in a Sicilian Family; Cine-portrait de Margaret Mead; Colin McPhee: The Lure of Asian Music; Coming of Age: Margaret Mead (1901–1978) (Strangers Abroad Series); Cosas de mi vida; Crow Dog; Dance Masks: The World of Margaret Severn; Discovering Country and Western Music; Dorothy Molter: Living in the Boundary Waters; Dudley Carter; Everything is Relatives: William Rivers (1864–1922) (Strangers Abroad Series); Eze Nwata: The Small King; Family Gathering; Fieldwork: Sir Walter Baldwin Spencer (1860–1929) (Strangers Abroad Series); Finnish American Lives; Firth on Firth; Foster Child; The Fourth Stage: A Hindu's Quest for Release; Foutura: A Lobi Potter Tells Her Story; From The Ashes: Nicaragua Today; From the Elders;

Generations: A Chinese Family; Grey Owl; A Hard Life (Rural Greece: Desertion, Migration, Village Life Series); *Hommage a Marcel Mauss: Germaine Dieterlen (Homage to Marcel Mauss: Germaine Dieterlen); Hommage a Marcel Mauss: Paul Levy (Homage to Marcel Mauss: Paul Levy); Ishi, the Last Yahi; Jero Tapakan: Stories in the Life of a Balinese Healer* (Bali Series); *Joe Sun* (From the Elders Series); *Lempad of Bali; Letter from an Apache; Life at the Source: The Adventures of an Amazon Explorer; Long Journey Home; Longshoremen and Automation: The Changing Face of the Waterfront; Luisa Torres; The Man behind the Mask; The Many Worlds of Ishi; Margaret Mead and Samoa; Margaret Mead: Taking Note; Miles From the Border* (Mexico); *Mother of Many Children; N!ai, The Story of a !Kung Woman; Navajo Talking Picture; Number Our Days; The Past that Lives* (Netherlands); *Sewing Woman; The Shackles of Tradition: Franz Boas (1852–1942)* (Strangers Abroad Series); *Standing Alone* (Plains); *Strange Beliefs: Sir Edward Evans-Pritchard (1902–1973)* (Strangers Abroad Series); *This Is Not Your Life* (Brazil); *Treasured Islands: Robert Louis Stevenson in the Pacific; When Mountains Tremble* (Mayan); *Wilma P. Mankiller: Woman of Power*

WOMEN'S LIVES *Acting Our Age: A Film about Women Growing Old; Angola Is Our Country; "Annapurna Mahila Mandal": An Experience in Grassroots Development for Women; As Women See It; Asante Market Women; Baby Riazanskie* (Russia); *Banesa's Courtyard; Becoming a Woman in Okrika; Behind the Veil* (Middle East); *Behind the Veil: Nuns; The Best Time of My Life; Betty Tells a Story; Black Mother, Black Daughter; Bulimia;* Bushmen Series; *La Casa De Mujer—Supporting Women in Nicaragua; Clotheslines; Coalmining Women; The Contributions of Zambian Women to Agriculture; Dadi's Family;* Daughters of the Country (Native American); *Daughters of the Nile; Diane; Doctor, Lawyer, Indian Chief; The Double Burden; The Double Way; The Emerging Woman; Fake Fruit* (Mexico); *Fear Woman* (Ghana); *A Free Woman; From Sunup* (East Africa); *From The Ashes: Nicaragua Today; From Woman to Women* (Japan); *Goldwidows: Women in Lesotho; Growing up Female; Hearts and Hands; Ida B. Wells: A Passion for Justice; In Danaku the Soup Is Sweeter; India Cabaret; Is It Hot in Here? A Film about Menopause; Joyce at 34; Kheturni Baya; Killing Us Softly, Advertising's Image of Women; Las Madres: The Mothers of Plaza de Mayo; Lucia* (Cuba); *Luckily I Need Little Sleep* (Alberta); *Maids and Madams* (South Africa); *Masai Women* (The Disappearing World Series); *Memories and Dreams* (East Africa); *Messing up God's Glory; Miss ... or Myth?; Mitsuye and Nellie; Mosori Monika* (Venezuela); *Mujer de Milfuegos; No Longer Silent; Older, Stronger, Wiser; P4W: Prison for Women; Permissible Dreams* (As Women See It Series); *The Price of Change* (Women in the Middle East Series); *Quilting Women; Quilts in Women's Lives; Rana* (Our Asian Neighbors–India Series); *Rastafari: Conversations Concerning Women; Reassemblage; The Ribbon* (South Africa); *Rites; Rivers of Sand; Saints and Spirits* (The Disappearing World Series); *Selbe: One among Many* (As Women See It Series); *A Sense of Honor* (Middle East); *Simplemente Jenny; Slaying the Dragon; Small Happiness: Women of a Chinese Village* (Long Bow Film Series); *Sometimes I Wonder Who I Am; Sugar and Spice; Surname Viet Given Name Nam; These Hands* (East Africa); *Thread of the Needle* (Rural Greece: Desertion, Migration, Village Life Series); *Three Lives; A Veiled Revolution; Visa for a Dream* (Mexico); *A Village in Baltimore; Water for Tonoumasse; We Dig Coal: A Portrait of Three Women; Weavers in Ahuiran; Wilma P. Mankiller: Woman of Power; Women in Arms* (Nicaragua); *Women in China; Women in China Today; Women in the Middle East; Women Of Kerala; Women of Niger (Femmes du Niger); Women of the Toubou; Women under Siege* (Women in the Middle East Series); *A Zenana: Scenes and Recollections*

SOCIAL ORGANIZATION AND KINSHIP Anufom Series; *An Argument about Marriage (!Kung Bushmen); At the Threshold* (Millennium: Tribal Wisdom and the Modern World Series); *Better Rich than Red* (The Human Face of Hong Kong Series); *Chachaji, My Poor Relation China's Only Child; A Clearing in the Jungle* (The Disappearing World Series); *Dadi's Family; The Feast* (Venezuela); *Her Name Came on Arrows: A Kinship Interview with the Baruya of New Guinea* (A Series on the Baruya); *Joking Relationship* (San Series); *Lobola* (South Africa); *The Lost Tribes; Marriage and Family in the Bishop Hill Colony; My Family and Me* (Rural Greece: Desertion, Migration, Village Life Series); *North Indian Village; Principles of Caste* (Introduction to Sociology Series); *Strange Relations* (Millennium: Tribal Wisdom and the Modern World Series); *Wuxing People's Commune*

GENDER IDENTITY—SEX ROLES *Adventures in the Gender Trade; Anselmo and the Women* (Mexico); Anufom Series (especially *In Search of Justice); Anything You Want to Be; Balinese Family; Between Men; Black Women; The Blooms of Banjeli: Technology and Gender in African Ironmaking;* Bushmen Series; *Clotheslines; Coalmining Women; Comalapa: Traditions and Textures; Cultural Patterns...; Daughters of The Nile; Dead Birds; Dynamics of Male Dominance in a Baboon Troop;* Faces of Change Series; *Garcons et Filles; Gender: The Enduring Paradox* (Smithsonian World Series); *India Cabaret; A Joking Relationship; Kypseli; Labor More than Once; Ladyboys* (Southeast Asia); *Los Oaxaquenos; Man Oh Man—Growing up Male in America; Mayordomia: Ritual, Gender, and Cultural Identity in a Zapotec Community; Memories and Dreams* (East Africa); *Men's Lives; Miss ... or Myth?; Mosori Monika; N!ai, The Story of a !Kung Woman; Permissible Dreams* (As Women See It Series); *The Pinks and the Blues* (NOVA Series); *Rate It X; The Rice Ladle: The Changing Roles of Women* (The Human Face of Japan Series); *Rights and Reactions; Rivers of Sand; Shunka's Story; Some Women of Marrakech;* A Song of Ceylon Series; *The Women's Olamal: The Organization of a Masai Fertility Ceremony; Warriors and Maidens: Gender Relations in a Cretan Mountain Village; With These Hands* (Africa); *Women of Niger (Femmes du Niger); Women of the Toubou; Word Is Out: Stories of Some of our Lives; Yeleme: La Hache de Pierre polie en Nouvelle-Guinee*

EDUCATION *Alphabetisation des adultes au Mali (Adult Literacy in Mali); Becoming Aboriginal; Beyond the Plains*

(East Africa); Jugs to Be Filled or Candles to Be Lit (The New Pacific Series); *The Learning Path* (As Long as the Rivers Flow Series); *Science on the Cross*

ECONOMICS-ECOLOGY *"Annapurna Mahila Mandal": An Experience in Grassroots Development for Women; Amahuaca: A Tropical Forest Society in Southeastern Peru; Appeals to Santiago* (Mayan); *Asante Market Women* (Disappearing World Series); *Aspects of Land Ownership; Aspects of Land Tenure* (Chile); *Baboon Ecology; Bandits of Orgosolo* (Sardinia); *Barren Lives* (Brazil); *Beautiful Tree; The Best Time of My Life; Black Harvest; Black Market* (Commodities Series); *Bougainville Copper Project; Broken Rainbow; Campesinos and Farming* (Bolivia); *Cane Toads: An Unnatural History; Change* (South Africa); *The Cuna Indians: Island Exiles; The Debt Crisis: An African Dilemma; Fake Fruit* (Mexico); *Fires of Spring* (Central Africa); *Fisher Folk of Lake Patzcuaro* (Mexico); *The Four Corners;* From Africa to Asia: Nomads; *Future Wave: Japan Design; Grass* (Iran); *Himalayan Farmer; Icemen of Chimborazo; If It Fits; In & Out of Africa; In Danaku the Soup Is Sweeter; Japan* (Asian Insight); *The Japan They Don't Talk About; The Kawelka* (Disappearing World Series); *Land and Water* (Mexico); *Land and Water in Iraq; Land without Bread* (Spain); *The Last Pullman Car; Man of Aran* (Ireland); Man on the Rim; *The Maring: Documents of a New Guinea People Series; Market at La Paz; The Market's Edge* (Hausa); *Mokil* (Micronesia); *The Nuer* (Ethiopia); *The Pacific Age* (The New Pacific Series); *Peasant Ecology in the Rural Philippines; Peter Picked a Seal Stick: The Fur Seal Harvest of the Pribilov Islands; A Poor Man Shames Us All* (Millennium: Tribal Wisdom and the Modern World Series); *Selbe: One among Many* (As Women See It Series); *Shadow of the Rising Sun* (The New Pacific Series); *Small Business My Way; Stones of Eden* (Afghanistan); *The Struggling People* (South Africa); *Summer of the Loucheux; Tea Fortunes* (Commodities Series); *A Time to Remember; To Find the Baruya Story: An Anthropologist at Work with a New Guinea Tribe* (A Series on the Baruya); *Tomesha "Ground Afire"; The Turtle People; Turumba* (Phillipines); *Two Dollars and a Dream; The Water of Words: A Cultural Ecology of a Small Island in E. Indonesia* (Roti Series); *Weavers in Ahuiran*

Hunting and Foraging *Acorns: Staple Food of California Indians; Attiuk* (The Caribou); *Au pays des mages noirs (In the Land of the Black Magic); Autumn River Camp* (Netsilik Eskimo); *Bataille sur le grand fleuve (Battle on the Great River); Buckeyes;* Bushmen Series; *Caribou Hunting at the Crossing Place* (Netsilik Eskimo); *La Chasse a l'hippopotame (The Hippopotamus Hunt); La Chasse au lion a l'arc (The Lion Hunters); Les deux chasseurs (The Two Hunters); Eskimo Summer* (People of the Seal Series); *Eskimo Winter* (People of the Seal Series); *Fishing at the Stone Weir* (Netsilik Eskimo); *Food of California Indians; Hadza* (Tanzania); *The Hunters* (!Kung San); *Koli Koli; Un lion nomme "l'Americain" (A Lion Named "the American"); Narritjin at Djarrakpi: Part 1; Narritjin at Djarrakpi: Part 2; Nomads of the Rainforest* (Brazil); *Patterns of Subsistence: Hunter-Gatherers and Pastoralists* (The Faces of Culture Series); *The Panare—Scenes from the Frontier; Spirit of the Hunt*

Fishing *Abidjan, port de peche (Abidjan, Fishing Port); Aegean Sponge Divers; "Anything I Catch . . ." The Handfishing Story; At the Time of Whaling; Baleen Baskets of the Alaskan Inupiat; A Bouziques; Daouda Sorko; Fires of Spring; Fishing in the City; Granton Trawler; Heritage of the Sea: Makah Indian Treaty Rights; Hunger Knows No Law; Jangadieros; Live Lobster* (Maine Lobsterman); *Mammy Water* (West Africa); *The Moontrap; Les pecheurs de Niger (The Fishermen of Niger); Raw Fish and Pickle: Traditional Rural and Seafaring Life* (The Human Face of Japan Series); *The Shark Callers of Kontu; Three Fishermen; Two West African Fishing Villages; Uminchu: The Old Man and the East China Sea; The Water Talks to Me* (United States); *The Whale Hunters of Lamalera* (Disappearing World Series); *Whaling People*

Farming African Village Life Series; *Alpaca Breeders of Chimboya; Biquefarre; Black Harvest* (New Guinea Highlands); *China: A Land Transformed; The Chinampas; Chinese Farm Family: Changes in the Countryside Today; A Connemara Family; The Contributions of Zambian Women to Agriculture; Dani Sweet Potatoes; A Day in Shrishnagar; Depending on Heaven: The Desert; Farmworker's Diary; God's Country; Hanunoo* (Philippines); *India's Sacred Cows; Le mil (Millet); Nini Pantun: Rice Cultivation and Rice Rituals in Bali; On the Cowboy Trail; Le palmier a huile (Palm Oil); Peppimenarti; Rice; Root Hog or Die; Seeds of Progress* (Mexico); *Slash and Burn; A South African Farm; Waiapi Slash and Burn Cultivation* (The Waiapi Indians of Brazil Series); *A Week of Sweet Water* (West Africa); *When You Make a Good Crop; Where Land Is Life* (Peru); *With These Hands* (Africa); *Wuxing People's Commune*

Pastoralism *African Drought; An Ancient Gift; Bakhtiari Migration; The Barabaig* (Tanzania); *Changing Nomadic Cultures; The Cowboy in Mongolia; A Cowhand's Song: Crisis on the Range; Depending on Heaven: The Grasslands; Diary of a Maasai Village; The Gabra; Grass* (Iran); *In Search of Cool Ground: The Kwegu* (Disappearing World Series); *In Search of Cool Ground: The Migrants* (Disappearing World Series); *In Search of Cool Ground: The Mursi* (Disappearing World Series); *Inner Mongolia—In Search of History* (From Africa to Asia: Nomads Series); *Kenya Boran; Longshot; The Muleteers (Los arrieros); Nawi* (Uganda); *Nomads on the Savanna; The Nuer; Patterns of Subsistence: Hunter-Gatherers and Pastoralists* (The Faces of Culture Series); *The Rendille* (Disappearing World Series); *Shahsavan Nomads of Iran; The Shepherd's Family* (Spain); *The Shepherds of Bernary (Ciobairean Bhearnaraich); Siberia: After the Shaman* (From Africa to Asia: Nomads Series); *Sons of Haji Omar; Taiga Nomads: The School and Village; The Tarahumaras; Tempus de Baristas;* Turkana Conversations Trilogy; *Villagers of The Sierra de Gredos* (Disappearing World Series); *Voice of the Whip; The Wodaabe* (Disappearing World Series)

FOOD (See also Technology) *Ave Maria: The Story of the Fisherman's Feast* (United States/Sicily); *Caxiri or Manioc Beer* (The Waiapi Indians of Brazil Series); *Changing the Menu* (Man on the Rim Series); *Le cocotier (The Coconut Palm); Corn Is Life; Dani Sweet Potatoes; Garlic Is* *as Good as Ten Mothers; Grits; Gumbo: The Mysteries of Creole and Cajun Cooking; Hungry Angels; It's Grits; Kwashiorkor; The Moveable Feast* (United States/Sicily); *Manhattan's Greek-Owned Coffee Shops; Rice and Peas; A Safety Net* (West Africa); *The Soul of Rice; The Sugar Film; A Taste of China; The Water of Words: A Cultural Ecology of a Small Island in E. Indonesia* (Roti Series)

TECHNOLOGY—MATERIAL CULTURE (including transportation, mining, manufacturing)(See also Food and Arts and Crafts) *Abidjan, port de peche (Abidjan, Fishing Port); African Village Life Series; Alice Elliott; All Hand Work; Alpine Bread; Ancient Projectile Points; At the Canoe Camp* (Australia); *Axes and Are: Stone Tools of the Duna; Basketry of the Pomo Series; Ben's Mill; Ben's Mill; Biquefarre; Blades and Pressure Flaking; The Blooms of Banjeli: Technology and Gender in African Ironmaking; Bread Making in a Rural Household; Cameroon Brass Casting; Capt'ain Omori; Cesar's Bark Canoe; Chairmaker; Charcoal Makers* (Rural Greece: Desertion, Migration, Village Life Series); *China Discovery; China: A Land Transformed; Colonial Williamsburg Series; Computers in Context: Designing Computers for Workplace Creativity; Dani Houses; Dani Technology Films* (New Guinea); *Dineh Nation: The Navajo Story; Dokwaza: Last of the African Iron Masters; A Drum Is Made: A Study in Yoruba Drum Carving; The Drummaker* (Ojibway); *Earliest Writing; Early Stone Tools; El ojeado (The Evil Eye); The Flour Mill House* (Brazil); *Future Wave: Japan Design; Gui Dao—On the Way: A Station of the Yangzi; Handmade* (Bolivia); *Heritage in Cedar: Northwest Coast Indian Woodworking; Houses of the Arctic and the Tropics; How to Build an Igloo; How to Build an Igloo; How to Make Sorghum Molasses; The Hunter's Edge; I Spent My Life in the Mines* (Bolivia); *Icemen of Chimborazo; If It Fits; In Memory of the Land and the People; Indian Canoes along the Washington Coast; Iron Smelting* (Tanzania); *Japan: The Nation Family; The Jean Richard* (Canada); *Kamik* (Central Africa); *Kathleen Ware, Quiltmaker; Kerepe's House* (Maring, New Guinea); *!Kung Bushmen Hunting Equipment; Lamotrek: Heritage of an Island; The Last Horizon* (Man on the Rim Series); *The Last Pullman Car; Leon "Peck" Clark: Basketmaker;* Longshoremen and Automation: The Changing Face of the Waterfront; *Los tejedores* (weaving); *Magic in the Sky; Magicians of the Black Hills* (Cameroon); *Making a Bark Canoe* (Australia); *Making Primitive Stone Tools; Maria and Julian's Black Pottery; Maria of the Pueblos; Maria's Black Pottery; Mary Pritchard* (Tapa-Samoa); *The Meaders Family: North Georgia Potters; Miles of Smiles, Years of Struggle;* Millennium: Tribal Wisdom and the Modern World; *Morgan Sorghum; Mudhorse; Nanduti, A Paraguayan Lace; Navajo Country; The Navigators: Pathfinders of the Pacific; The New Cutting Edge* (Man on the Rim Series); *New Guinea, Dani Tribe Extracting Salt; The New Tijuana; Niutao: Construction of a Sleeping House; Obsidian Point-Making; Ollero Yucateco* (Mexico); *On Sacred Ground* (Australia); *On the Cowboy Trail; Our Lives in Our Hands* (Near East); *Out of the Fiery Furnace; Painted Truck; Paj Ntaub: Textile Techniques of the Hmong; The Pearl Fisher; Peruvian Weaving: A Continuous Warp for 5,000 Years; Photo Wallahs; Poletown Lives!; The Potters of Buur Heybe, Somalia; The Powerhouse* (Man on the Rim Series); *The Quechua* (Disappearing World Series); *Quilting Woman; Rate it X; Sea of Oil; Sinew Backed Bow; The Skiff of Renald and Thomas; Skokomish Indian Baskets; A Spiritual Ordering: The Metal Arts of Africa; Sticks and Stones Will Build a House; Stone Knapping in Modern Turkey; Tapa; A Taste of China; Tea Fortunes* (Commodities Series); *The Tree of Iron; These Hands* (East Africa); *Tule Technology: Northern Paiute Uses of Marsh Resources in Western Nevada; Turumba* (Phillipines); *Two Dollars and a Dream; The Village Potters of Onda* (Japan); *Water Farmers* (A Taste of China Series); *Water for Tonoumasse; We Believe in It* (Australia); *We Dig Coal: A Portrait of Three Women; Weavers in Ahuiran; Weaving Films; Whaling People; White Fur Clouds; Who Killed Vincent Chin?; Wooden Box; Yeleme: La Hache de Pierre polie en Nouvelle-Guinee*

HOUSING AND ARCHITECTURE *Architectes Atorou (The Architects of Atorou); From Courtyard House to Block Apartment* (China); *Over the Hedge; The Warrior from Within* (Man Alive Series)

ENVIRONMENTAL ISSUES *Act of Man: Incident at Buffalo Creek; African Drought; An African Recovery; Amazonia: The Road to the End of the Forest; Baobab; Black Water* (Brazil); *Bougainville Cooper Project; The Buffalo Creek Flood; Central America: On the Horns of a Dilemma; Children of the Forest* (Central Africa); *Contact: The Yanomami Indians of Brazil; Cry of the Muriqui; The Decade of Destruction; Depending on Heaven: The Grasslands* (Asia); *Dineh Nation: The Navajo Story; An Ecology of the Mind* (Millennium: Tribal Wisdom and the Modern World Series); *Fires of Spring; The Fragile Mountain; The Green Puzzle of Altamira; Halting the Fires* (Brazil); *Himalayan Farmer; Hopi Songs of the Fourth World; Inughuit: The People at the Navel of the Earth; An Invisible Enemy* (Disappearing World Series); *Living of the River Agano (Aga Ni Ikiru); Lord of the Sky; Magic Windows* (Mexico); *The Mursi: The Land Is Bad* (Disappearing World Series); *The Nature of Culture* (The Faces of Culture Series); *Peter Picked a Seal Stick: The Fur Seal Harvest of the Pribilov Islands; Runa: Guardians of the Forest; Secheresse a Simiri (Drought at Simiri); The Spirit of Kuna Yala; The Struggling People; Sudesha* (As Women See It Series); *Tamanawis Illahee; Tanah Air—Our Land, Our Water* (Indonesia: A Generation of Change Series); *The Telltale Tree-Rings; Tong Tana: A Journey to the Heart of Borneo; Toula (The Water Spirit); Walking in a Sacred Manner; Water Farmers* (A Taste of China Series); *Who Killed Lake Erie?*

PSYCHOLOGY/COGNITION (See also Paralinguistics) *Balinese Bathing Babies in Three Cultures; Childhood Rivalry in Bali and New Guinea; Cultural Patterns; Development of the Child: A Cross-Cultural Approach to Cognition; Dream speaker; Everything Is Relatives: William Rivers (1864–1922)* (Strangers Abroad Series); *First Days in the Life of a New Guinea Baby; Geel; Group Concepts...; Karba's First Year; Manatic; Personality in Culture; The Spirit Possession of Alejandro Mamani; 365 Days with Your Baby; Wild Child*

ALTERED STATES OF CONSCIOUSNESS The Anasternaria (Greece); Appeals to Santiago; A Balinese Trance Sequence; Chinese Popular Religious Series; A Curing Ceremony (!Kung Bushmen); Ebena; Eduardo the Healer; Ephesus; Hallucinogenic Ecstasy among the Yanomamo (Venezuela); Floating in the Air; Guma the Snake (Colombia); Hail Umbanda (Brazil); Holy Ghost People (United States); The Howling Dervishes; Hymns of Praise (Morocco, Body and Soul Series); An Indian Pilgrimage: Ramdevra; Jero on Jero (Bali); Jero Tapakan: Stories in the Life of a Balinese Healer (Bali Series); The Lacandon Maya Balche Ritual; Latah: A Culture Specific Elaboration of the Startle Reflex; Ma'Bugi; Les Maitres Fous; N/um Tchai (!Kung Bushmen); Magical Death; The Path; Pocomania (Jamaica); Sacred Trances in Bali and Java; Sons of Shiva (Pleasing God Series); Spirit Possession of Alejandro Mamani; Sucking Doctor; Trance and Dance in Bali; Trance of the Toraja; Vimbuza—Chilopa; Were Ni! He Is a Madman (Yoruba, Nigeria); Zebola: Possession and Therapy in Zaire

RELIGION, MAGIC, WORLDVIEW, CULTS About the Jews in India: Cochin; About the Jews of India: The Shanwar Telis or Bene Israel; About the Jews of Yemen: A Vanishing Culture; Ahimsa, Non-Violence; The Alien's Place (Netherlands); Behind the Veil: Nuns; Being Muslim in India; Benares: Steps to Heaven; Between Two Worlds: The Hmong Shaman in America; Blue Collar and Buddha; Born Again: Life in a Fundamentalist Baptist Church; Brides of the Gods; Buddhism in China; Chichicastenango; Consecration of a Temple; Corn is Life; Corpus Christi: A Solstice Feast; The Dervishes of Kurdistan (The Disappearing World Series); Divine Horsemen (Caribbean); The Drums of Winter (Uksuum Cauyai); Falasha: Agony of the Black Jews; Fifty Ways to Get Enlightened (The New Pacific Series); Forest of Bliss; The Fourth Stage: A Hindu's Quest for Release; The Goddess And the Computer (Indonesia); Heritage: Civilization and the Jews; The Hero's Journey: The World of Joseph Campbell; The Holy Ghost People; In Her Own Time: Barbara Myerhoff's Final Field Work; In The Name of God; India and the Infinite; An Indian Pilgrimage: Kashi; An Indian Pilgrimage: Ramdevra; Islam in America; Island of Saints and Souls; Itam Hakim, Hopiit: A Poetic Visualization of Hopi Philosophy and Prophesy; The Jews of Djerba; Jocelyn, Facing Death at 17 with Strong Faith; The Jolo Serpent Handlers; Jose Carlos and His Spirits: The Ritual Initiation of Zelador Dos Orixas in a Brazilian Umbanda Center; Kataragama (The Disappearing World Series); The Krishna Story; Kuan-Yin-Pilgrimage; Lamotrek: Heritage of an Island; Legacy of the Spirits (Caribbean Culture Series); The Lion's Roar; Lord of the Dance, Destroyer of Illusion; Loving Krishna (Pleasing God Series); Les maitres fous (Mad Masters); Mammy Water: In Search of the Water Spirits in Nigeria; Manifestations of Shiva; Monsieur Albert, Prophete; Ou Albert Atcho (Mr. Albert, Prophet; or Albert Atcho); El Moulid: Egyptian Religious Festival; My Country Djarrakpi; New Gods (The Africans Series); Of Grace and Steel; La Ofrenda: The Days of the Dead; Old Believers; Out of Order; The Performed Word; Pleasing God Series; Powerhouse for God; The Pueblo Presence; Rastafari Voices; Religion in Suburbia; Requiem for a Faith; Rise Up and Walk; Ritual: Three Portraits; Romeria: Day of the Virgin; Saints and Spirits (Disappearing World Series); Santeros: Saintmakers; Science on the Cross; Semanasanta: The Holy Week in Patamban, Purhepacha, Michoacan Mexico; Shinto: Nature, Gods and Man in Japan; The Shrine; Signs of the Times; Sigui No. 1: L'enclume de Yougo (The Anvil of Yougo); Sons of the Moon; The Spirit That Moves; Tanda singui (Poser le hangar) (To Fix the Shed); Thank God and the Revolution (Nicaragua); Three Paths: Hinduism, Buddhism, and Taoism; Tibetan Buddhism: Cycles of Interdependence; Tibetan Buddhism: Preserving the Monastic Tradition; The Traditional World of Islam; Turkey's Sephardim: Five Hundred Years; Two Thousand Years of Freedom and Honor: The Cochin Jews of India; Uluru—An Anangu Story (Australia); Umbanda the Problem Solver (Disappearing World Series); Vision of Juazeiro; Voodoo and the Church in Haiti; The Wages of Action: Religion in a Hindu Village; War of the Gods (Disappearing World Series); The Ways of Nya Are Many; Wedding of the Goddess: Part I; Wedding of the Goddess: Part II; When the Snake Bites the Sun; When the World Turned Dark; The World Between; A Zoroastrian Ritual: The Yasna

RITUAL AND CELEBRATION African Religious and Ritual Dances; African Village Life Series (Dogon); Altar of Fire; Altar of Fire (India); Always for Pleasure; The Apache Indian; Appeals to Santiago; Appeals to Santiago; Ave Maria: The Story of the Fisherman's Feast; Bali: Mask of Rangada; Black Delta Religion; Bukoki; By Cross and by Sword (A cruz y a espada); Carnaval Bahia (Disappearing World Series); Carnaval de pueblo; Carnival in Q'eros; Carnival T.N.T.; Celebration: A Caribbean Festival; A Celebration of Origins; Chichicastenango; Chinese Religion Series; Chittirai Festival; Choqela: Only Interpretation; Christ Is Risen; Corpus Christi: A Solstice Feast; Cuyagua; Da Jiw; Dance for a Chicken: The Cajun Mardi Gras; Dawn Ceremony for the House of Xas Koov; Devi (Indian); Djungguwan at Gurka'wuy; Dongo Hori; Dongo Yenendi, Gamkalle; The Dragon Boat Festival; Dream Dances of the Kashia Pomo; Duminea: A Festival for the Water Spirits (East Niger Delta); El Sebou': Egyptian Birth Ritual; The 11 Powers; Embara Drama; Emu Ritual at Ruguri (Australia); The Feast (Venezuela); The Feast in Dream Village; Fetes des Gandyi bi a Simiri (Celebration of Gandyi bi at Simiri); The Fiesto de Sao Francisco in Caninde: A Brazilian Pilgrimage; First Moon: Celebration of a Chinese New Year; Flight of the Dove; For Those Who Sail to Heaven; Gateway to the Gods (Japan); Gathering up Again: Fiesta in Santa Fe; Gelede; A Gift of the Dragon (Japan); God of Japan; Goodbye Old Man (Australia); Greek Celebrations; Gunabibi: An Aborigine Fertility Cult (Australia); Haa Shagoon; Hail Mother Kali: A Tribute to the Traditions and Healing Arts Brought to Guyana by Indentured Madrasi Labourers; Hail Umbanda; Hello Columbus; Herdsmen of the Sun; The Hindu Ritual Sandhya; Hitting Sticks—Healing Hearts; The Hmong Hilltribe People of Laos; Holy Week in Antigua Guatemala; Horses of Life and Death; Huichol Sacred Pilgrimage to Wirikuta; Iawo (Brazil); Ika Hands; Image India; In Memory of Mawalan; In the Footsteps of Taytacha; In the Name of Allah; An Indian Pilgrimage; An Indian Pilgrimage: Kashi; Initiation; An Initiation Kut for a Korean Shaman; Initiation a la danse des possedes (In-

itiation into Possession Dances); Iramudun; Iyahkimix, the Blackfoot Beaver Bundle Ceremony; Jose Carlos and His Spirits: The Ritual Initiation of Zelador Dos Orixas in a Brazilian Umbanda Center; Kalogeros (Greece); *Kantik'i Maishi: Songs of Sorghum; The Kawelka* (Disappearing World Series); *Kings and Cities* (Africa Series); *Kingship Rituals; !Ksan; Kuan-Yin-Pilgrimage; Kyomande* (Ainu, Japan); *The Lacandon Maya Balche Ritual; The Land of the Eagle* (Guatemala); *Legacy of the Spirits* (Caribbean Cultures Series); *Lord of the Dance, Destroyer of Illusion; Malagan Labadama: A Tribute to Buk-Buk* (Films from Papua New Guinea Series); *Mammy Water: In Search of the Water Spirits in Nigeria; Masai Manhood* (Disappearing World Series); *Mayordomia: Ritual, Gender, and Cultural Identity in a Zapotec Community; The Mehinacu* (Disappearing World Series); *Men of Dream Time* (Australia); *Menri Monastery; Mid-Summer in Sweden; Moko Jumbie: Traditional Stilt Walkers; A Month for the Entertainment of Spirits; Mulga Seed Ceremony* (Australia); *My Town—Mio Paese; Native Cat Ceremonies of Watarka* (Australia); *O Pagador de Promessas* (Brazil); *One Man's Response; Our God The Condor; The Path* (Japan); *The People Who Take up Serpents* (United States); *Place of Power in French Polynesia* (The Human Face of the Pacific Series); *Potlatch; Raj Gonds; The Red Bowmen* (Films from Papua New Guinea Series); *Releasing The Spirits: A Village Cremation in Bali* (Bali Series); *The Return of the Gods and Ancestors: The Five-Year Ceremony; Ritual: Three Portraits; Sacred Games: Ritual Warfare in a Maya Village; Sanctuary of the Earth Goddess; Secheresse a Simiri (Drought at Simiri); Serpent Mother* (Pleasing God Series); *Sinmia* (New Guinea Highlands); *Sons of Shiva* (Pleasing God Series); *The Soul of Rice; This Was the Time* (Haida); *The Three Worlds of Bali; To Find Our Life: The Peyote Hunt of the Huichols of Mexico; To Serve The Gods* (Caribbean Cultures Series); *Tourou et Bitti, les Tambours d'Avant (Tourou and Gitti, the Drums of Yore); Trance and Dance in Bali; Vessels of the Spirits: Pots and People in North Cameroon; Vimbuza—Chilopa* (South Africa); *Voices of the Gods; Walbiri Ritual* (Australia); *Water Witching (Dowsing) in Middle America; We Are Mehinaku; We Believe in Nino Fidencia* (Mexico); *Wedding of the Goddess: Part I; Wedding of the Goddess: Part II; When the World Turned Dark* (Peru); *Witchcraft among the Azande* (Disappearing World Series); *The Xinguana* (Brazil); *A Yoruba Masquerade; Zarda: A Nomadic Tribe's Feast Days*

DIVINATION *African Village Life Series* (Dogon); *An Appointment with the Astrologer: Personal Consultants in Hindu Society; A Balinese Trance Seance* (Bali Series); *The Cows of Dolo Ken Paye* (Kpelle, Liberia); *An Ixil Calendrical Divination* (Maya); *Macumba, Trance and Spirit Healing; Magical Curing* (New Guinea Highlands); *A Month for the Entertainment of Spirits* (Guatemala); *The Prophet's Family* (Diary of a Maasai Village Series); *The Return of Dr. Fritz: Healing by the Spirits in Brazil; Spite: An African Prophet-Healer; Sprout Wings and Fly; Tidikawa and Friends* (Traditional Music of Papua New Guinea Series); *Ngoma Therapy in an Urban South African Setting*

SOCIAL CONFLICT AND RESOLUTION *Animal War-Animal Peace;* Anufom Series; *The Arctic Exiles; An Argument about Marriage* (!Kung Bushmen); *Aymara Leadership; Bandits of Orgosolo* (Sardinia); *Bangladesh Nationhood: Symbols and Shadows; Battle of Culloden* (English/Scottish); *Black Man's Houses* (Australia); *The Brick Makers; Broken Rainbow; Buffalo Creek Revisited; A Circle of Healing* (Man Alive Series); *Come Back Africa; The Cop Is in the Middle; The Cows of Dolo Ken Paye: Resolving Conflict among the Kpelle* (Liberia); *Dead Birds* (Dani, New Guinea); *The Divided Trail; Due Process of Law Denied (Ox Bow Incident); The Earth Is Our Mother; Enthombe; The Feast* (Venezuela); *The Feast in Dream Village; Fiji—Legacies of Empire* (The Human Face of the Pacific Series); *For All People, For All Time* (Near East); *Gare du Nord (North Train Station); Hajari Bhand of Rajasthan: Jester without Court; Heart Broken in Half: An Anthropologist Looks at Street Gangs; The Kalasha—Rites of Spring* (Disappearing World Series); *Last of the Karaphuna* (Caribbean); *The Lau of Malaita* (Disappearing World Series); *Little Injustices: Laura Nader Looks at Law; Maids and Madams* (South Africa); *Malaysia* (Asian Insight Series); *Martin Chambi and the Heirs of the Incas; Matjemosh* (Asmat, New Guinea); *Meat Fight; Mistress Madeleine* (Daughters of the Country Series); *The Mursi; New Caledonia—A Land in Search of Itself* (The Human Face of the Pacific Series); *Man's Response* (Australia); *Peace Has Not Been Made: A Case History of a Hmong Family's Encounter with a Hospital;* Pittsburgh Police Series; *Poletown Lives!; Prayer to Viracocha; The Probable Passing of Elk Creek; Pull Ourselves up or Die Out* (San); *La Pyramide Humaine (The Human Pyramid); The Ragged Revolution* (Mexico); *Rebels of the Forgotten World* (Indonesia); *The Ribbon* (South Africa); *Routes of Exile: A Moroccan Jewish Odyssey; Running from the Ghost* (The Human Face of Hong Kong Series); *Sherea; A South African Farm; Spear and Sword: A Payment of Bridewealth on the Island of Roti* (Roti); *State of Shock; A Native People Loses Its Heritage* (Australia); *Sudesha* (As Women See It Series); *Talking to the Enemy: Voices of Sorrow and Rage* (Middle East); *Tent Embassy* (Australia); *Tierra o Muerte: Land or Death; Time Immemorial* (As Long as the Rivers Flow Series); *To Make the Balance* (Mexico); *The Toured: The Other Side of Tourism in Barbados; The Tree of Knowledge* (Mexico); *Txai Macedo; Uneasy Neighbors; Virgin Mary (or Holy Sorceress)* (Colombia); *The Wake* (Daughters of the Country Series); *When Invaders Become Colonists* (Southeast Asia); *Who Killed Vincent Chin?; The Women's Olamal: The Organization of a Masai Fertility Ceremony; You Are on Indian Land* (Canada)

MEDICINE/CURING/HEALTH/FAMILY PLANNING *Amra Dujon (Together);* Andean Ethnomedicine: Birth and Childhood Illness in Six Ecuadorian Communities; *Arusi Ya Mariamu (The Marriage of Mariamu); Barefoot Doctors of Rural China; Bono Medicines; Brujo-Shaman; Bulimia;* Bushman Series; *Children of Soong Ching Ling; A Curing Ceremony; Dance Therapy: The Power of Movement; Diagnosticos (Diagnoses); Doctora; Doctors All; Eduardo the Healer; Evil Wind, Evil Air (Mal Viento, Mal Aire, Pasmo)* (Ecuador); *Fissura; Free Clinic; Geel* (Belgium); *Hail Mother Kali: A Tribute to the Traditions and Healing Arts Brought to Guyana by Indentured Madrasi Labourers* (The

Human Face of Indonesia Series); *Heal the Whole Man; Healers of Aro; Helping the People to Help Themselves* (Indonesia); *Himalayan Shaman...; Hospital; A Hospital in Village Form; House of Spirit: Perspectives on Cambodian Health Care; Inventing Reality* (Millennium: Tribal Wisdom and the Modern World Series); *Kwashiorkor; Las Que Curan; Latah: A Culture Specific Elaboration of the Startle Reflex; Living of the River Agano (Aga Ni Ikiru); Macumba, Trance and Spirit Healing; Magical Curing* (New Guinea Highlands); *Malnutrition in a Third World Community; Mbindo Lala; Medecines et Medecins* (Medicine and Doctors); *The Medium Is the Masseuse: A Balinese Massage* (Bali Series); *N/um Tchai; Ngoma Therapy in an Urban South African Setting; Nyamakuta—The One Who Receives; A Plague upon the Land* (West Africa); *Pomo Shaman; Psychic Surgery: A Case History of Shamanic Sleight-Of Hand* (Phillipines); *The Return of Dr. Fritz: Healing by the Spirits in Brazil; Rich Man's Medicine, Poor Man's Medicine; Seven Nights and Seven Days; The Spirit Possession of Alejandro Mamani; The Spirit That Moves; Spite: An African Prophet-Healer; Sucking Doctor; That Our Children Will Not Die* (Nigeria); *Ticket to Tefenni; To Care: A Portrait of Three Older Caregivers; To Taste a Hundred Herbs: Gods, Ancestors and Medicine in a Chinese Village* (Long Bow Film Series); *Traditional Healing in Guyana: The Divine Madness of Kali Mai; Traveller from an Antique Land; Valley of the Old Ones; Vimbuza—Chilopa; Water for Tonoumasse; We Are Nothing without the People* (The Human Face of Indonesia Series); *Were Ni! He Is a Madman; Women Of Kerala*

AIDS *Absolutely Positive; AIDS Babies; AIDS in Africa; AIDS in the Barrio: Eso no me pasa a mi*

CHANGE, MODERNIZATION (as a result of technical borrowing and innovation) *Across the Tracks—Vlach Gypsies in Hungary* (Disappearing World Series); *Akwesasne: Another Point of View; All Under Heaven: Life in a Chinese Village* (Long Bow Film Series); *American Samoa: Paradise Lost; The Annanacks; Aunfom Series; The Ballad of Crowfoot; Barren Lives; The Basques of Santazi* (Disappearing World Series); *Before We Knew Nothing* (Peru); *Beyond the Plains; Bougainville Copper Project; Box of Treasures; Bryan Beavers* (Maidu); *Cakchiquel Maya of San Antonio Palopo* (Disappearing World Series); *Camels and the Pitjantjara* (Australia); *A Celebration of Origins* (Indonesia); *Central America: On the Horns of a Dilemma; Changes in Agriculture* (Bolivia); *Changes in Land Use* (Colombia); *Chinese Farm Family: Changes in the Countryside Today; Circle of the Sun; Contact with a Hostile Tribe* (Brazil); *The Cowboy in Mongolia; Cry of Nukumanu; Dam at Nagarjunasagar; Depending on Heaven: The Desert; Entre Verde y Seco; The Eskimos of Pond Inlet* (Disappearing World Series); *A Family in France; Fincho; The Forgotten American* (Navajo); *From Courtyard House to Block Apartment; From the Heart of the World: The Elder Brothers' Warning; Fugitives from Fear* (Peru); *Full Circle; Future Shock; Gefilte Fish; The Great Unfenced* (Australia); *Haudenosaunee: Way of the Longhouse; The Healers Aro* (Nigeria); *In Iirgu's Time* (From the Elders Series); *Incident in the Matto Grosso; The Indian Speaks* (Canada); *An Indian Pilgrimage: Kashi; Inside China: The Newest Revolution* (Disappearing World Series); *Inuit Kids; Ishi in Two Worlds* (California); *Jaguar; The Japanese Version; Joe Leahy's Neighbours* (Papua New Guinea Series); *Jojolo* (Paris/Haiti); *Ka Ke Ki Ku* (Canada); *Kamik; Keep the Circle Strong; The Last of the Cuiva* (Disappearing World Series); *The Last Tribes of Mindanao; The Lost Tribes; Les Maitres Fous; Margaret Mead's New Guinea Journal* (Manus); *A Matter Of Respect; Migrants from Sakaltutan;* Millennium: Tribal Wisdom and the Modern World; *Moana Roa* (Cook Islands); *Mokil* (Micronesia); *Mongolia: On The Edge of The Gobi* (Disappearing World Series); *Mosori Monika* (Venezuela); *My Father, My Country* (New Guinea Highlands); *Narritjin in Canberra; The Nature of Culture* (The Faces of Culture Series); *The Navajo: A Study in Contrast; Navajo Talking Picture; New Lives for Old* (Manus New Guinea); *The New Tijuana; No Longer Strangers* (Dani, New Guinea); *Now That the Buffalo's Gone; O Pagador De Promessas* (Brazil); *The Other Side of Paradise* (Fiji); *Out of the Shadows* (Indonesia: A Generation of Change Series); *People in Change* (Melanesia); *People of the Free Train* (Fiji); *Pull Ourselves up or Die Out; Ramparts of Clay* (Tunisia/Algeria); *Reclaiming the Forest* (Venezuela); *Return to Paradise* (The New Pacific Series); *Return to Sovereignty; Sakaltutan: A Time of Change; Salima in Transition* (Malawi); *Separate Visions; Shahira: Nomads of the Sahara; Sherpas* (Disappearing World Series); *The Shock of the Other* (Millennium: Tribal Wisdom and the Modern World Series); *Sky Chief* (Ecuador); *So That Men Are Free* (Peru); *Songs of the Adventurers* (South Africa); *Sons of Haji Omar; Spirit of the Hunt; A Story about the Passing of Time; Strangers and Kin: A History of the Hillbilly Image; Tahtonka; Tarahumara: Racers against Time; Tepostlan in Transition* (Mexico); *These Are My People* (Canadian Mohawk); *Tidikawa: At the Edge of Heaven; A Time to Remember; The Tribe that Hides from Man* (Brazil); *The Tuareg* (Disappearing World Series); *Turumba* (Phillipines); *Two Thousand Years of Freedom and Honor: The Cochin Jews of India; Village Man, City Man; The Water Talks to Me; The Whale Hunters of Lamalera* (Disappearing World Series); *A Walk in the Forest* (New Guinea); *We Are the Landowner* (Australia); *A Weave of Time; Western Samoa— I Can Get Another Wife but I Can't Get Parents* (The Human Face of the Pacific Series); *Yap... How Did You Know We'd Like TV?; Yesterday, Today: The Netsilik Eskimo; You Are on Indian Land* (Canada); *Zengbu After Mao*

CHANGE THROUGH CULTURE CONTACT: Colonialism, Immigration, Refugees, Tourism *After Solidarity: Three Polish Families in America; Always There Comes a New Spring; Bahia: Africa in the Americas; Becoming American; Between Two Worlds: The Hmong Shaman in America; Birthplace Unknown; Blue Collar and Buddha; The Bride Market of Imilchil; Cannibal Tours; Chicano Park; Children of Change; Cimarrones; Come Back Africa; The Conquest of Indonesia; Consecration of a Temple; Contact: The Yanomami Indians of Brazil; Contrary Warriors: A Film of the Crow Tribe; Coppermine; Crow Dog; Daughters of Abraham: A Fight to Survive?; The Decade of Destruction; The Divided Trail; The Earth Is Our Mother; Embera: The End of the Road* (Disappearing World Series); *Enthombe; The Exiles* (United States); *First Contact* (Papua New Guinea

Films and Videos by Topic

Series); *Flight of the Dove; Flooding Job's Garden* (As Long as the Rivers Flow Series); *Freak Street to Goa: Immigrants on the Rajpath; Gathering up Again: Fiesta in Santa Fe; Gypsies: The Other Americans; Half Life: A Parable for the Nuclear Age* (Micronesia); *The Heavenly Voice of China; House of Spirit: Perspectives on Cambodian Health Care; In the Shadow of the Law; Indian Self-Rule: A Problem of History; The !Kung San: Resettlement* (The San [Ju/Wasi]: Videos for Elementary and Secondary Use); *The Last Days of Okak; The Last Horizon* (Man on the Rim Series); *The Last Performance; Land of Heart's Desire; Living Music for Golden Mountains; Man without Pigs* (Papua New Guinea Series); *Marshall Islands—Living with the Bomb* (The Human Face of the Pacific Series); *Master of the Shadows* (The Human Face of the Pacific Series); *Maya Fiesta; Maya In Exile; Miles from the Border; Mitsuye and Nellie; Mosori Monika* (Venezuela); *Moving Mountains: The Story of the Yiu Mien; A Nation Uprooted: Afghan Refugees in Pakistan; A New Year for the Mien; Nice Weather, Mr. Pradhan!; No More Mountains: The Story of the Hmong; On Our Land* (Middle East); *Palenque: Un Canto* (The African Heritage of a Colombian Village); *The Phans of Jersey City; Peace Has Not Been Made: A Case History of a Hmong Family's Encounter with a Hospital; Pepe's family* (Spain); *Pilgrimage to Ghriba; The Popovich Brothers of South Chicago; Rajvinder: An East Indian Family; Rice and Peas; Sewing Woman; So Far from India; A Song of Ceylon; Songs of the Badius; Sophia's People—Eventful Lives; Sosua* (Caribbean); *The Toured: The Other Side of Tourism in Barbados; Transnational Fiesta: 1992; Trekking on Tradition; Two Korean Families; A Village in Baltimore; Virgin Mary (or Holy Sorceress)* (Colombia); *War of the Gods* (Disappearing World Series); *Wasyl, An Anecdote; We Believe in It* (Australia); *When Invaders Become Colonists; When Mrs. Hegarty Comes to Japan; Where Land Is Life* (Peru); *Who Killed Vincent Chin?; Yumi Yet* (Melanesia); *Ziveli: Medicine for the Heart*

POLITICS: General *Angola Is Our Country; Bangladesh Nationhood: Symbols and Shadows; China: Contemporary Changes in Historical Perspective; Communists for a Thousand Years* (Near East); *Fetes de l'Independence du Niger (Celebrations of the Independence of Niger); Free Voice of Labor—The Jewish Anarchists; Grenada: Portrait of a Revolution; Grenada: The Future Coming toward Us; Ileksen* (Melanesia); *Journey to a New Life* (The Human Face of Indonesia Series); *Kofi: An African in France; Las Madres: The Mothers of Plaza de Mayo; The Long Journey of Clement Zulu; The Magnificent African Cake* (Africa Series); *The Mursi* (Disappearing World Series); *The Palestinian People Do Have Rights; Philippines: The Price of Power; Promises to Keep* (United States); *Raoni* (Brazil); *The Rise of Nationalism* (Africa Series); *The Tightrope of Power* (Millennium: Tribal Wisdom and the Modern World Series); *Tent Embassy* (Australia); *Tibet: The Bamboo Curtain Falls*

POLITICS: American Indian Movements *Abnaki: The Native People of Maine; American Indian Speaks; Ballad of Crowfoot; Broken Treaty at Battle Mountain; Circle of the Sun; The Dispossessed; The Divided Trail; The Exiles; Flooding Job's Garden* (As Long as the Rivers Flow Series); *For All People, For All Time; The Forgotten American; Forty-Seven Cents; Heritage of the Sea: Makah Indian Treaty Rights; Home of the Brave; Hunters and Bombers; Incident at Restigouche; Indian Mainstream; Indian Self-Rule: A Problem of History; The Indian Speaks; Kainai; The Land Is the Culture; Little White Salmon Indian Settlement; A Native American Odyssey; Now That the Buffalo's Gone; Nuhoniyeh: Our Story; The Other Side of the Ledger: An Indian's View of the Hudson's Bay Company; Potlatch; The Price We Paid; The Right to Be Mohawk: The Survival of a People and Their Traditions; River People: Behind the Case of David Sohappy; To Be Indians; The Water Is so Clear That a Blind Man Could See; You Are on Indian Land*

LAW *Adliye: The Ethnography of a Turkish Rural Law Court; Courts and Councils: Dispute Settlement in India; Crimebusters* (Scientific Eye II Series); *Enthombe; Forty-Seven Cents; Gang Cops; The Hideout; Honorable Nations: The Seneca's Land Rights; In Memory of Mawalan; In the Shadow of the Law; Little Injustices: Laura Nader Looks at the Law; Nations within a Nation: Sovereignty and Native American Communities; Of Land and Life: People of the Klamath; On Sacred Ground* (Australia); *Our Sacred Land; P4W: Prison for Women; Return to Sovereignty; The Spirit Within; Time Immemorial* (As Long as the Rivers Flow Series); *To Protect Mother Earth* (Broken Treaty II); *Two Mothers* (Diary of a Maasai Village Series); *Two Ways of Justice* (Diary of a Maasai Village Series); *Tierra o muerte: Land or Death; Uluru—An Anangu Story; White Justice; Witchcraft among the Azande* (The Disappearing World Series)

WAR: Fighting, Revolution *Afghan Exodus* (Disappearing World Series); *Angels of War: World War II in Papua New Guinea; Angola Is Our Country; Between Men; Children of Fire* (Middle East); *Chronique d'une été (Chronicle of a Summer); Daughters of Abraham: A Fight to Survive?; Euskadi: The Stateless Nation; Gaza Ghetto: Portrait of a Palestinian Family; The Hundred Years War: Personal Notes* (Middle East); *Incident at Restigouche; Israel and the Palestinians: The Continuing Conflict; Journey from Pha Dong; Khyber* (Disappearing World Series); *Lines of Fire; Memories in Black and White; Navajo Code Talkers; Of Lives Uprooted; The Past That Lives; The Pathans* (Disappearing World Series); *Radio Bikini; Samsara; Sandino, Today and Forever; Shoot and Cry; Sophia's People—Eventful Lives; Talking to the Enemy: Voices of Sorrow and Rage; The Tenth Dancer; Thanh's War; Thank God and the Revolution* (Nicaragua); *Tibet: The Bamboo Curtain Falls; Tierra Y cultura* (Colombia); *Trobriand Cricket: An Ingenious Response to Colonialism; Todos Santos: The Survivors* (Maya); *Village Theater Senegal: Queen Ndate and the French Conquest; Voices from Gaza; Waiting for the Caribou* (South Africa); *We Are Nothing without the People* (The Human Face of Indonesia Series); *We Ain't Winning* (Peru); *When Mountains Tremble* (Maya); *Women in Arms* (Nicaragua); *Women under Siege* (Women in the Middle East Series)

URBAN PROBLEMS *Chicano Park; Children of Fate: Life and Death in a Sicilian Family; Community Dig; Dandora; The Divided Trail; Down the Project; Electric Boogie; Heart*

Broken in Half: An Anthropologist Looks at Street Gangs; The Heart of Loisaida; Hell's Kitchen Chronicle; Hospice; Inheritance; A Lady Named Baybie; Ladyboys (Southeast Asia); Metropolitan Avenue; Mission Hill and the Miracle of Boston; The Neighborhood of Coehlos; No Address; No Applause, Just Throw Money; Norte; Oigame! Oigame! (Nicaragua); On Borrowed Land; Peter, Donald, Willie, Pat; Places Not Our Own (Daughters of the Country Series); Promises to Keep; Richard Cardinal: Cry from a Diary of Metis Child; Rime and Reason (France); Santa Marta: Two Weeks in the Slums; Straight Up Rappin'; Style Wars; Los Sures; Tremors in Guzman; Uneasy Neighbors; Village Man, City Man; The Wake (Daughters of the Country Series)

HISTORY (including slavery) Africa Series; Babatou, les trois conseils (Babatou, Three Pieces of Advice); The Bambara Kingdom of Segu; The Battle of Carthage: 229 B.C.; The Bible and the Gun (Africa Series); Black Market (Commodities Series); The California Missions; Capital of Earth: The Maroons of Moore Town; Caravans of Gold (Africa Series); China: Contemporary Changes in Historical Perspective; China: The Making of a Civilization; Crossroads of Civilization Series; Different but Equal (Africa Series); Digging for Black Pride; The First Invaders (Triumph of the Nomads Series); Flaming Arrows (Man on the Rim Series); Fort Branch: Preserving a Unique Legacy; The Glories of Ancient Benin; Goree: Door of No Return; Graveyard of the Gulf; Homage to the Yahgans: The Last Indians of Tierra del Fuego and Cape Horn; Hunters and Gatherers (Man on the Rim Series); I Shall Moulder before I Shall Be Taken (Guyana); Iawo; In The White Man's Image (American Experience Series); Man on the Rim; Memories in Black and White; New Guinea Patrol and Excerpts from Yumi Yet (People in Change Series); 90 South: With Scott to the Antarctic; Notman's World; Out of the Fiery Furnace Series; The Parching Winds of Somalia; The Past that Lives; Philippines (Asian Insight Series); Pyramid; The Ragged Revolution (Mexico); The Royal Archives of Ebla; Sails of Doom (Triumph of the Nomads Series); Sermons and Sacred Pictures; The Silent Enemy: An Epic of the American Indian; Stanley and Livingstone; Testament: The Bible and History; Thailand (Asian Insight Series); Trading in Africans: Dutch Outposts in West Africa; Treasure; The Vinland Mystery; Williamsburg File (Chronicle Series); Breaking Ground; By Cross and By Sword (A cruz y a espada); Carthage: A Mirage of Antiquity; Cimarrones (Peru); The Conquest of Indonesia; The Future of the Past (Infinite Voyage Series); Hearts and Hands; Hedeby: The Salvage of a Viking Ship; Ida B. Wells: A Passion for Justice; The Last Days of Okak; Maya Lords of the Jungle; Nanook Revisited; Pilgrimage to Ghriba; The Powerhouse (Man on the Rim Series); Sans Soleil; Search for a Century; The Search for Alexander the Great; The Search for Ancient Americans; Signs of the Times; Story of the Wasa; A Tale of Two Rivers (France); A Weave of Time; Virgin Mary (or Holy Sorceress) (Colombia)

LANGUAGE American Tongues; Arabic X-Ray Film; Birth of Language; Chinese X-Ray Film; Dialects; Documents Sur une Langue Sifflée Pyrennenne; Documents sur une Langue Sifflée Turque; English X-Ray Film; The First Signs of Washoe; Hungarian X-Ray Film; Language (Media Probe Series); Maps and Territories; Not to Lose You My Language (Australia); The Primal Mind; Russian X-Ray Film; Shoot for the Contents (China); Teaching Sign Language to the Chimpanzee, Washoe

NONVERBAL: PARALINGUISTICS, KINESICS, ETC. (See also Dance) Benjamin; Betty Tells a Story; Body Language; Communication: The Nonverbal Agenda, 2nd ed.; A Context Analysis of Family Interviews; Cuidad del Nino: A Case Study in Education and Culture; Dance and History; Espace et comportment; Eye Contact and Proxemics; Gestes; French Gestures: A Preliminary Repertory; Herding Castes of Central India; Hitlerjunge Quex; Home Movie; The Human Voice: Exploring Vocal Paralanguage; The Interpersonal Task; Invisible Walls; Kinesics; Language by Gesture; The Manwatcher; Maring in Motion (New Guinea); Mechanisms of Non-Verbal Communication in the Young Child; Micro-Cultural Incidents in Ten Zoos; Nonverbal Communication; Palm Play; Paralanguage and Proxemics; Step Style; Tales of the Supernatural; Tribal Groups of Central India; Village Morning; A World of Gestures

FOLKLORE/MYTHOLOGY Add and Mabel's Punkin Center; All Hand Work; Anansi the Spider; Angano . . . Angano . . . Tales from Madagascar; Australia's Twilight of the Dreamtime; Bar Yohai (Myth onto Film: A Trilogy from Native Australia, Native America and the Kabbalah Series); Betty Tells a Story; Blue: A Tlingit Odyssey (Myth onto Film: A Trilogy from Native Australia, Native America and the Kabbalah Series); Blunden Harbor; Boneshop of the Heart; Creation Myth Series; Cycle (Myth onto Film: A Trilogy from Native Australia, Native America and the Kabbalah Series); Duke Tritton, Australian Sheep-Shearer; Emergence; Fixin' to Tell about Jack; Foxfire; Glooscap; The Gypsy Camp Vanishes into the Blue (Russia); Harmonize: Folklore in the Lives of Five Families; I Ain't Lying: Folktales from Mississippi; John Jacob Niles; Joseph Campbell and the Power of Myth; Kudzu; Lakota Quillwork: Art and Legend; Lamotrek: Heritage of an Island; The Land of the Lightening Brothers; Legend of the Paramo; Legends of Indians; The Loon's Necklace; Made in Mississippi: Black Folk Art and Crafts; The Magic Tree (Congo); Man of Lightning; The Man, the Snake and the Fox; The Meaders Family: North Georgia Potters; Medoonak the Stormmaker; Medoonak, the Stormmaker (Micmac); Metos jah hut (A Jah Hut Myth); Midsummer in Sweden; Moowis, Where Are You, Moowis?; The Mystery of Stonehenge; Myth onto Film: A Trilogy from Native Australia, Native America and the Kabbala; The Myth of Peribo (El mito de Peribo); Native Land: Nomads of the Dawn; The Northern Lights; The Oath of Caiman Wood (Le serment du Bois Caiman); On the Cowboy Trail; 'Oss 'Oss Wee 'Oss; The Owl Who Married a Goose; The Path of Life; The Path of Souls; Popol Vuh: The Creation Myth of the Maya; Raj Gonds; Le renard pale (The Pale Fox); The Return of the Child; Sogow, Bambara Masks; Stairways to the Mayan Gods; Tales of the Supernatural; They Tell It for the Truth: Ozark Storytelling; Three Stone Blades; The Three Worlds of Bali; Watunna (Venezuela); We Are Mehinaku; The World Between

PLAY AND SPORTS *Alger-Le Cap; The Ancient Games;* Bushmen Series; *Balinese Surfer; The Citizen Carney; Easter in Igloolik; Feathered Warrior; Fighting Festival; Game of Staves; Nuba Wrestling; Pizza Pizza Daddy-O; Thoughts on Fox Hunting; The Tarahumaras* (Mexico); *Trobriand Cricket: An Ingenious Response to Colonialism; Two Ballgames; The Upperville Story; Waterborne: Gift of the Indian Canoe; Yo-Yo Man*

DANCE (See also Nonverbal) Aboriginal Dance; *Africa Dances; African Religious and Ritual Dances; Ajuba Dance and Drama Company; Bake Restudy 1984; Les ballets du Niger (Ballets of the Niger); Bali beyond the Postcard; Circles-Cycles Kathak Dance; Dance and Human History; Dance Contest in Esira; Dance of the Buffalo Hunt; Dance Like a River* (West Africa); *Dance Masks: The World of Margaret Severn; Dance of Tears; Dance Therapy: The Power of Movement; The Drums of Winter* (Uksuum Cauyai); *Electric Boogie; Five Aboriginal Dances from Cape York* (Aboriginal Dance Series); *Full of Life A-Dancin'; Given to a Dance; Grenada: Land of Spice; Horendi; Hymns of Praise* (Morocco, Body and Soul Series); *In Heaven There Is No Beer?; Learning to Dance in Bali; Life in the Dust / Fragments of African Voyages; Light of Many Masks; Lockhart Festival; The Longest Trail; Looking for Me; Mary Wigman: When the Fire Dances between the Two Poles; Moko Jumbie: Traditional Stilt Walkers; Music, Dance, and Festival among the Waiapi Indians of Brazil* (The Waiapi Indians of Brazil Series); *Musique et danse des chasseurs Gow (Music and Dances of the Gow Hunters); New England Dances; Nigerian Dance; No Applause, Just Throw Money; No Maps on My Taps; Palm Play; Polka; Porto Novo: La danse des reines (Porto Novo: The Dance of the Queens); Rhythme de travail (Work Rhythms); Step Style; Studies in Nigerian Dance; The Tango Is also a History* (Brazil); *Tapdancin'; The Tenth Dancer; Three Dances by Gulpilil* (Aboriginal Dance Series); *Traditional Dances of Indonesia; Turlutte*

ART AND CRAFT *African Carving: A Dogon Kanaga Mask; African Craftsmen: The Ashanti; Ancient Art of Peru; Ancient Egypt; Ancient Moderns: Greek Island Art and Culture: 3,000-2,000 B.C.; Ancient Places* (Hidden Places: Where History Lives Series); *. . . And Women Wove It in a Basket; The Art of Living* (Millennium: Tribal Wisdom and the Modern World Series); *Artesanos Mexicanos* (Mexico's Folk Artists); *Asmat: Cannibal Craftsmen of New Guinea; Australia's Twilight of the Dreamtime; Beadwork; Bill Reid* (Haida); *Boneshop of the Heart; Carnarvon* (Australia); *The Cave Painting of the Chumash Indians; Ce Pu Comme ca Anymore; Clementine Hunter: American Folk Artist; Cleto Rojas, Pintor Campesino (Peasant Painter); Daughters of Ischel: Maya Thread of Change; Daughters of the Anasazi; Discovering the Moche; A Drum Is Made: A Study in Yoruba Drum Carving; The Drummakers* (Ojibwa); *Dry Wood* (Black Cajuns); *Eskimo Artist Kenojuak; Eskimo Arts and Crafts; Fonseca: In Search of Coyote; Gogodala: A Cultural Revival?* (Films from Papua New Guinea); *Gripping Beast* (Viking); *Guatemalan Pottery; Guellala: A Potter's Village in Tunisia; Haida Carver; Hampi* (West Africa); *Hand Carved; In & Out of Africa; Indian Art of the Pueblo;* Inhabitants of the Land Grace; *Joe David: Spirit of the Mask; Juan Felix Sanchez* (Venezuela); *Kathputli: The Art of Rajastani Puppeteers; Kwa' Nu' Te': Micmac and Maliseet Artists; Lakota Quillwork: Art and Legend; The Land of the Lightening Brothers* (Australia); *Learning from the Painters of Lascaux; Loon's Necklace; Los Tejedores; Maria: Indian Pottery of San Ildefonso; Masks; Masks and Stones: Matjemosh* (Asmat, New Guinea); *The Meaders Family: North Georgia Potters; Mohawk Basketmaking: A Cultural Profile; Moko Jumbie: Traditional Stilt Walkers; Narritjin at Djarrakpi, Part 1; Narritjin at Djarrakpi, Part 2; Narritjin in Canberra; A Nation Uprooted: Afghan Refugees in Pakistan; The 1973 Mgodo Series; Notman's World; Oaksi; Paj Ntaub: Textile Techniques of the Hmong; Peasant Painter* (Inhabitants of the Land of Grace Series); *Pedro Linares, artesano cartonero (Papier-Mache Artist); Perico the Bowlmaker; Peruvian Weaving: A Continuous Warp for 5,000 Years; Photo Wallahs; Place of Power in French Polynesia* (The Human Face of the Pacific Series); *The Potters of Buur Heybe, Somalia; Pousse-Pousse* (Cameroun); *The Precious Treasure of Black Africa; Prehistoric Images (The First Act of Man); Preserving a Way of Life: People of the Klamath; Primitive Process Pottery; Pure and Simple* (Man on the Rim Series); *Quilts in Women's Lives; Rock Art Treasures of Ancient America; Rock Engravings* (Australia); *Santeros: Saintmakers; Seasons of a Navajo; Separate Visions; The Shadow and the Spirit; Sogow, Bambara Masks; Sons of Namatjira; Spirit Speaking Through; A Spiritual Ordering: The Metal Arts of Africa; Stairways to the Mayan Gods; The Stone Carvers; Style Wars; The Sun Dagger; Totem Pole; Tradition Bearers;* The Traditional World of Islam; University of Ife Series; *Vessels of the Spirits: Pots and People in North Cameroon; Waterborne: Gift of the Indian Canoe; The Wooden Giraffe* (Barotse, Zambia); *The Working Process of the Korean Folk Potter; The Working Process of the Potters of India: Massive Terra-Cotta Horse Construction; Wow* (Asmat); *You Hide Me*

MUSIC *Africa Calls: Its Drums and Musical Instruments; African Soul: Music, Past and Present; Afro-American Worksongs in a Texas Prison; Aita* (Morocco, Body and Soul Series); *Alhaji Bai Konte; Amir: An Afghan Refugee Musician's Life in Peshawar, Pakistan; Angklung Orchestra and Indonesian Dance Class; Anselmo* (Mexico); *Anselmo and the Women; Bake Restudy 1984; Before Reggae Hit the Town; The Blues According to Lightnin' Hopkins; Born for Hard Luck; Buck Dancer; Chen and China's Symphony; Chulas Fronteras; Colin McPhee: The Lure of Asian Music; The Country Fiddle; Delta Blues Singer; Didn't We Ramble On: The Black Marching Band; Diro and His Talking Musical Bow; Discovering American Indian Music; Discovering Country and Western Music; A Drum Is Made—A Study in Yoruba Drum Carving; Dudley Carter; Duke Tritton, Australian Sheep-Shearer; Five String Banjo; Folk Music in Japan; Georgia Sea Island Singers; Grenada: Land of Spice; Le griot Badye (Badye, the Storyteller); Guitar Craft; Gypsies Sing Long Ballads; Gypsy Yodeler; Hajari Bhand of Rajasthan: Jester without Court; The Heavenly Voice of China; Homemade American Music; Hot Pepper; Imaginero* (Argentina); *Imrat Khan Demonstrates the Sitar;* Inhabitants of the Lans Grace; *Italian Folk Songs; Kama Wosi: Music in the Trobriand Islands* (Traditional Music of Papua New Guinea Series); *Kembali: To Return; The Land Where the Blues Began; The Last Performance* (Southeast Asia); *Lessons From Gulam: Asian Music in Bradford; Living Music for Golden Mountains; Love Songs of the Miao in China; Lutes and Delights* (Morocco, Body and Soul Series); *Master Musicians of Jahjouka; The Mendolin King* (Inhabitants of the Land of Grace Series); *Mbira; Morocco, Body and Soul; Morris Family Old Time Music Festival; Mountain Music of Peru; Music, Dance, and Festival among the Waiapi Indians of Brazil* (The Waiapi Indians of Brazil Series); *La musica de la gente; A Musical Tradition in Banaras; Musique et danse des chasseurs Gow (Music and Dances of the Gow Hunters); New England Fiddles; Palenque: Un Canto (The African Heritage of a Colombian Village); Pericles in America; The Popovich Brothers of South Chicago; Pyatachok* (Russia); *Ralph Stanley's Bluegrass Festival; Rembetika: The Blues of Greece; Rhythms of Resistance; Sharing a New Song: An Experiment in Citizen Diplomacy; Le Son des Cajons de la Louisiane Series; Songs in Minto Life; Songs of a Distant Jungle; Songs of the Adventurers* (South Africa); *Songs of the Badius; Sourwood Mountain Dulcimers; Straight Up Rappin'; Studies in Nigerian Dance; Sunny Side of Life; Taksu: Music in the Life of Bali; The Talking Drums of Nigeria; Tough, Pretty or Smart;* Traditional Music of Papua New Guinea; *Waiapi Instrumental Music* (The Waiapi Indians of Brazil Series); *The Wax and the Feather*

THEATRE, FILM, TELEVISION, CULTURAL STUDIES *A j u b a Dance and Drama Company; Art of Indonesia: Tales from the Shadow World; Camera d'Afrique; Cine-Mafia; Cinema; Films Are Dreams that Wander in the Light of Day; How the Myth Was Made* (Great Britain); *Imagining Indians; Ispahan: Lettre Persane 1977 (La Mosquee du Chah a Ispahan) (Itpahan: A Persian letter 1977—The Chah Mosque at Isahan); Jean Rouch and His Camera in the Heart of Africa; Kwagh Hir: Tiv Traditional Theatre* (Nigeria); *Magic in the Sky; Makwayela* (South Africa); *Martin Chambi and the Heirs of the Incas; Nanook Revisited; Nang Yai: Thai Shadow Puppet Drama; Navajo Talking Picture; Ouaga; Perfumed Nightmare* (Phillipines); *Sad Song of Touha; Sans Soleil; Sermons and Sacred Pictures; Shoot for the Contents; Siberia: Through Siberian Eyes; Slaying the Dragon; Strangers and Kin: A History of the Hillbilly Image; Sur les traces du renard pale (Tracking the Pale Fox: Studies on the Dogon); Tragada Bhavai: A Rural Theater Troupe of Gujarat; Village Theater Senegal: Queen Ndate and the French Conquest; Yap . . . How Did You Know We'd Like TV?*

FASHION *Ao Dai (The Tunic Dress); Beauty Knows No Pain; Daisy: The Story of a Facelift; Paolina's Hairstyle* (Italy); *Signatures of the Soul; Tighten the Drums: Self-Decoration among the Enga* (Films from Papua New Guinea); *Waiapi Body Painting and Ornaments* (The Waiapi Indians of Brazil Series)

ANIMATION, ETC. *Anansi the Spider; Arrow to the Sun: A Pueblo Indian Tale;* Creation Myth Series; *Falling Star (A Cheyenne Tale);* The First Americans Series; *Flatland; Gripping Beast; The Loon's Necklace; The Owl Who Married a Goose; A Sacrifice of 10 Dog and Six House*

FICTIONAL, FEATURE, HOLLYWOOD, ETC. *The Anthropologist; Aparajito (The Unvanquished); Archaeology; Baby Riazanski; Battle of Culloden; Before the White Man Came; Black Girl; Blow for Blow; Bwana Toshi; Chang: A Drama of the Wilderness; Day Shall Dawn; Deni (The Goddess); Distant Thunder; Due Process of Law Denied (Ox Bow Incident); Emitay; The Exiles; Fasschuque; The Flute and the Arrow; The Gods Must Be Crazy; Greystoke: The Legend of Tarzan; The Gypsy Camps Vanish into the Blue; The Harder They Come; Hitlerjunge Quex; How the Myth Was Made: A Study of Robert Flaherty's Man of Aran; How Tasty Was My Little Frenchman; Iceman; Ikwe* (Daughters of the Country Series); *The Immigrant; Jaguar; Legend of the Pacamo, The Mailbox; A Man Called Horse; The Man, The Snake and the Fox; Mandabi; O Pagador de Promessas; Pather Panchali; Petit a petit (Little by Little); Pousse-Pousse; La punition (The Punishment); Quest for Fire; The Quiet in the Land; Rampart of Clay; Rashomon; Retour l'adventurier; Salaam Bombay; Salt of the Earth; The Savage Innocents; Spirit of Ethnography; Tahu; Tanana River Rat; Time in the Sun; Utu; Wauw; The Wedding of Palo; The White Dawn; White Shadows in the South Seas; Wild Child; The World of Apu; Xala*

ALPHABETICAL LISTING OF FILMS AND VIDEOS

Abidjan, port de pêche (Abidjan, Fishing Port) (1962) 25 min. Jean Rouch (DI), Centre National de la Recherche Scientifique, Comité du Film Ethnographique (PR). Dist: CFE; DER. *The relationship between industrial and traditional fishing in the Ivory Coast.*

Abnaki: The Native People of Maine (1982) 29 min. Jay Kent and the Tribal Governors, Inc. (FM). Dist: CPI FR$45, FS$425, VS$275. *"Tells the story of the spectacular land claims case of the Passamaquoddies and Penobscots. These tribes ... claimed legal title to about 12.5 million acres of the state of Maine, and ultimately gained an out-of-court settlement of $81.5 million."* [From the review by Harald Prins, AA 90:774–778, 1988. Reviewed by Gifford S. Nickerson, SBF 21:45, 1985.]

Aboriginal Dance (1978) 16 min. Dist: FAA. *This is a compilation video, comprising two films: Three Dances by Gulpilil and Five Aboriginal Dances from Cape York. Aborigines have no written language; the legends and the stories of their past have been kept alive in song and dance. This compilation video provides a beautiful record of aboriginal dance.*

Aborigines of the Sea Coast (1948, revised 1973) 20 min. Dist: AIS FR$5, FS$340. *Aborigines of Arnhem Land, northern Australia.*

About the Jews in India: Cochin (1976) 30 min. Johanna Spector (PR). Dist: SF. [Reviewed by Najwa Adra, AA 90:492, 1988.]

About the Jews of India: The Shanwar Telis or Bene Israel (1978) 40 min. Johanna Spector (PR). Dist: SF. [Reviewed by Najwa Adra, AA 90:492, 1988.]

About the Jews of Yemen: A Vanishing Culture (1986) 77.5 min. Johanna Spector (PR). Dist: SF. [Reviewed by Najwa Adra, AA 90:492, 1988.]

Absolutely Positive (1990) 87 min. Peter Adair (FM). Dist: Larsen, 330 Ritch Street, San Francisco, CA 94107. *Addresses the question of how people handle the news that they are infected with the HIV virus.* [Reviewed by Ralph Bolton, AA 94(3):762–764, 1992]

Abuelitas de ombligo (Granny Midwives) (1983) 30 min. Rachel Field and Jackie Reiter (FM). Dist: WMM VR$50, VS$230. *Focuses on the training and role of midwives in post-Samozan rural Nicaragua.* [Reviewed by Patricia Whelehan, AA 89:250–251, 1987.]

La acequia 10 min. Dist: Blue Sky Productions, P.O. Box 548, Santa Fe, NM 87501 FR$20, FS$175, VS$125. *Documents the annual cleaning of irrigation ditches. This ancient custom continues in northern New Mexico and serves as a binding force in the community.*

Acorns: Staple Food of California Indians (American Indian Series) (1962) 28 min. Samuel Barrett (DI). Dist: UCEMC FR$35, FS$390; PSU (PCR) order #2214K, FR$10.60. *Although at least half of the Indians in the United States used acorns as food, the California Indians made greater use of acorns in their diet than any other people. Acorns became a staple food for three-fourths of the California Indian population. In this film, Pomo tribe members demonstrate the traditional acorn harvesting, storing, and processing methods that have evolved over the generations to a high degree of proficiency. The leaching process shown in this film was used by the aboriginal Indian to remove the poisonous tannic acid from the acorn meal and ultimately accounted for the great quantities of acorn bread, mush, and soup consumed by the California Indians.* [Reviewed by Harold E. Driver, AA 68:596–597, 1966.]

Across the Frontiers (see The Tribal Eye Series)

Across the Tracks—Vlach Gypsies in Hungary (Disappearing World Series) (1988) 52 min. Michael Stewart (AN). Dist: PSU order #51214; FIV VS$198, order #047039. *Set in a village outside the Hungarian town of Gyongyos, this program follows two Gypsy families struggling to maintain their traditions in a modern communist state. At the time of filming, it was government policy to absorb Gypsies into Hungary's 'ruling' working class, but the Gypsies want to maintain their separate identity. Despite the romantic image, Gypsy life is harsh and often brutal. The Gypsies live in semi-slums, and they are forced by law to work, often for very low wages.* [Reviewed by William G. Lockwood, AA 92:554, 1990.]

The Acropolis of Athens (1960) 30 min. Robert Manthoulis (PR, DI). Dist: CF/MH. [Reviewed by Thomas Howe, AA 78:126, 1976.]

Act of Man: Incident at Buffalo Creek (1975) 40 min. Wahler Associates, Jack Wright (PR). Dist: University of Minnesota Film Library. *Stillshots and interviews made following the flooding of Buffalo Creek, West Virginia, in the winter of 1972 as the result of the rupturing of an earthen dam. Local residents are interviewed on the spot, and there are several lengthy statements of the Pittston Coal Company, which operates in the area; statements are also made by members of investigating committees. Content focuses on one major point—the damage done by the flood and the resultant effect upon the community. Cinematic features: Black-and-white still shots of flood damage, slow-paced folk music as background. Printed material focused on the screen often difficult to read. Uses in teaching: Introductory, U.S. cultures. Focusing questions: (1) What effect did the unexpected event have on the established social structure of Buffalo Creek community? (2) What influence does status position have in the development of people's perceptions of the events described? (3) What evidences are there of conflict? How do you explain them? (4) What instances* of social distance and misunderstanding are shown in the film? Related film: *The Buffalo Creek Flood*. [R. Conlin]

Acting Our Age: A Film about Women Growing Old (1987) 58 min. Michal Aviad (FM). Dist: DCL FR$100, FS$895, VS$350. *Presents a look at women and aging in America by focusing on six women, aged 65 to 75. Through their stories of personal struggle and triumph, the film dispels the myths and challenges the stereotypes that define the image of old women in American culture. The film allows the women to speak for themselves with unparalleled candor. Their interviews tackle subjects that are usually considered taboo for older women, including sexuality, being alone, financial difficulties, and dealing with death. Their responses offer insight into the thoughts and lives of older women and reconstruct our expectations about aging. It examines how aging affects women's self-images, their roles in their families, and their relationships to and places in their communities. A source of empowerment for all women and senior citizens, this group of women demonstrates a strength of spirit and dedication to life, which serves as an example for all ages.* [Reviewed by Mary Beth Haralovich and Denise Kervin, *AA* 92(3):835–836, 1990.]

Adaptation and Aging: Life in a Nursing Home (1978) 15 min. Philip Stafford (AN). Dist: IUAVC FR$9.25. *Investigates the adaptations and adjustments of one group of elderly people to life in a nursing home, by intermixing scenes of a typical day with comments by anthropologist Philip Stafford, a participant-observer in the home. Describes the events shown in the context of the residents' cultural adaptations to life in the nursing home. Stresses the importance of observing significant yet somewhat obscure details because "things are not always what they seem."*

Adaptation of Female Anubis Baboons to Social Systems of Hamadryas Baboons (1973) 28 min. Hans Kummer (AN). Dist: PSU FR$24, FS$548. *Records field experiments by Professor Kummer in Ethiopia on adaptive behavior. The first experiment illustrates the "harem" social organization of Hamadryas baboons. The second experiment, in which an anubis female is released into a Hamadryas troop, demonstrates a capacity for rapidly modifying basic social behavior at the species level and for learning a new role.* [Reviewed by Robert B. Eckhardt, *AA* 75:2034, 1973.]

Add and Mabel's Punkin Center 16 min. Richard Kane and Dillon Bustin (FM). Dist: DER FR$30, VR$25, FS$325, VS$175. *A sequel to the highly regarded film* Water from Another Time. *To experience Punkin Center in Southern Indiana is to experience the value of reminiscence. Today, we see a kind of homespun folk museum filled with literally hundreds of thousands of antiques and curios that Add and Mabel Gray have collected since the 1920s. Each item inspires stories about vaudeville acts and organ grinders, Kraft Cheese parties and western swing, Depression days and Amish neighbors. Over the years, Punkin Center grew to become the hub—the true backbone of their Midwestern community, fulfilling a need for isolated rural folk to be in touch with each other and the rest of the world.*

Adelaide Village 15 min. Pierre L'Amare (DI, PR), National Film Board of Canada (PR). Dist: PFI. *Impressionistic picture of a village in the Bahamas.*

Adliye: The Ethnography of a Turkish Rural Law Court (1985) 30 min. June Starr (FM). Dist: Department of Anthropology, SUNY, Stony Brook, NY 11749; (516) 246-6745 VR$25, VS$50. *Shot in a rural Turkish law court [in 1969]. The goal of the production is to give viewers an appreciation of how justice was arrived at in Turkey in the 1960s. Adliye (justice in Turkish) is administered in the civil law tradition, as opposed to the common law tradition with which we are familiar. Study guide included.*

Advance into the Past: Modern Archaeological Methods. 27 min. Jo Muras (DI), H. V. Petrokovits (CON). Dist: Consulates General, Federal Republic of Germany. *Archaeology in the Rhineland.*

Adventures in the Gender Trade (1993) 40 min. Susan Marenco (FM). Dist: Susan Marenco, 1416 15th St., Santa Rosa, CA 95404; (707) 545-9841. *Using transsexual lesbian playwright Kate Bornstein's play* Hidden: A Gender *as a backdrop, this video explores the cultural construction of gender and questions our current bipolar gender system.*

Aegean Sponge Divers 27 min. Bengt Borjeson (FM), H. Russell Bernard (AN). Dist: UCEMC FR$34, FS$380. *An ethnographic documentary on the Greek sponge fishermen of Kalymnos Island in the Dodecanese group. It shows major activities of the islanders, including preparation of the ships, hiring of the crews and advance payment of wages, ceremonial blessing of ships and equipment, festive celebration on the eve of the fleet's departure, and work on board the ships and underwater during the six-month voyage. The film focuses on the divers' lives, showing how their rigid code of masculinity pressures them into ignoring basic safety precautions—overstaying their time underwater and ascending too rapidly, practices that often result in crippling or even fatal cases of the bends. It demonstrates that seemingly irrational, death-defying behavior finds its own logic within the framework of a culture. Underwater cinematography; electronic and local Greek folk music.* [Reviewed by Peter S. Allen, *AA* 74:1584–1585, 1972.] Suggested supplements: H. Russell Bernard, "Kalyminian Sponge Diving." *Human Biology* 39(2):103–130, 1967. H. Russell Bernard and Bengt Borjeson, "The Last of the Sponge Fisherman." *Skin Diver* 17(6):42–43, 1968.

Aerial Archaeology in Northern France (1973) 30 min. Dist: FACSEA FR$16.

Afghan Exodus (Disappearing World Series) (1980) 52 min. Akbar Ahmed and Remy Dor (AN), Andre Singer (PR), David Ash (RE), Granada Television (PR). Dist: PSU order #51244. *When Soviet troops invaded Afghanistan, a million Afghans, including Kirghiz, Hazara, and Pathans, fled over the borders into neighboring countries. But the Pathans were eager to take back their homeland, even if it meant confronting Soviet jets and tanks.* [Reviewed by David H. M. Brooks, *RAIN* 40:3–4, 1980.]

Afghanistan F. Kussmaul, P. Snoy, H. Schlenker (FM). Dist: PSU (Encyclopaedia Cinematographica). *Thirty short* *silent films on Afghanistan, mainly material culture and dance.* [Reviewed by William Trousdale, *AA* 70:656, 1968.]

Afghanistan: Threads of Life (1981) 29 min. Dist: EBEC FR$28, FS$465. *"There was a time when a film like this would have been appreciated as a travelogue.... The film is a generally handsome series of pictures, but it is hardly a useful educational tool. The four-page guide, with summary and questions for discussion, would be useful."* [From the review by Dwight B. Heath, *SBF* 17:98, 1981.]

Africa: An Introduction (1968) 16 min. Dist: IUAVC FR$9.25. *Depicts the life and people of Africa as they adjust to the geographical features of the tropical forests, the wet swamps, the flat grasslands, the high mountains, and the hot deserts. Shows people, dress customs, history, products, resources, and activities of each region of the country. Emphasizes the need for water in farming and factories for new jobs to help the Africans progress from their traditional habits and ways of life.*

Africa Calls: Its Drums and Musical Instruments (1971) 23 min. Dist: PSU FR$14. *African music is an accompaniment to work and worship, and a means of storytelling and emotional expression. Discusses use of animal and snake skins, horns, gourds, clay, discarded metal, trees, or logs. Shows East and West African drums, Equatorial African zanzas (thumb pianos), wooden flutes, bells, xylophones made from gourds, skekere, maracas, Dun-Dun (talking drums), and ogororo (slit-gong signal drums). Demonstrates how drums are made. Magnificent display of African instruments used in other forms by Western cultures.*

Africa Dances (1967) 28 min. United Nations (PR). *Les Ballets Africains performing at the United Nations.* [Reviewed by Joann W. Kealiinonomoku, *AA* 71:800, 1969.]

AFRICA SERIES (1986) RM Arts (PR), Basil Davidson (H). Dist: FIV VS$258. *Reveals the history and present-day life of the continent in breathtaking location photography and rare archival film. There are four tapes and eight programs in the whole series.* See film descriptions under individual titles:

- **Different but Equal**
- **Mastering a Continent**
- **Caravans of Gold**
- **Kings and Cities**
- **The Bible and the Gun**
- **This Magnificent African Cake**
- **The Rise of Nationalism**
- **The Legacy**

Africa Speaks (1920s/1930) 70 min. Dist: FCE FR$85, FS$450.

African Carving: A Dogon Kanaga Mask (1975) 19 min. Eliot Elisofon (CA), Thomas Blakely (WR, ED). Dist: PFI FR$28.50, FS$315. *The Kanaga mask is used in sacred rituals by the Dogon, a people famous for their scriptural arts, living on the Bandiagara escarpment in the Republic of Mali, West Africa. Carving the Kanaga is itself important as ritual. The carver must find a proper Tagoda tree from which to make the mask. A prayer and an offering are given to the tree for allowing the carver to use its sacred wood. In a secluded cave outside the village, the Kanaga is shaped by the carver whose gestures repeat the movements of the dancers who wear the mask. When completed, the Kanaga becomes a visual symbol, rich with complex layers of meaning and purpose. An honored man in the village has died, and the Dogon men perform a ritual dance to release the dead man's spirit. When the dancer wears the Kanaga, he becomes the Creator, symbolically. He touches the ground with his mask and directs the soul to heaven. Although these dances are often performed for the public now, the meaning of the Kanaga is retained by the Dogon, who fear, respect, and depend on the power it signifies.*

African Community: The Masai (1969) 16 min. Dist: BFA FR$42, FS$300; UCEMC FR$23. *Ethnographic portrait of the Masai of northern Tanzania, stressing their adaptation to their environment, their dependence on the land and weather, their eating habits, and the social roles of men and women. Notes that men own the property while women do the physical labor.*

African Craftsmen: The Ashanti 11 min. Frank Garonyi, Clifford Janoff (PR). Dist: BFA FR$29, FS$205.

African Drought: Changing Nomadic Cultures (1974) 26 min. *ABC Broadcast reviewing effects of drought from 1968–74 on nomadic people of the Republic of Niger in the Sahel region of Africa. Focuses on the effects of drought on a complex of nomadic Muslim cultures (Taureg) who once relied entirely on cattle and camels. Having lost their herds, the cultures have relocated their camps near supply outposts where they obtain well over half their food. Illustrates changes the people have and have not made in response to drought conditions, their maintenance of pride and graciousness in spite of conditions, and the role of Muslim fatalism in their dilemma. Reviews and evaluates various foreign aid programs (medical, food, water projects). Focusing questions: What aspects of a culture are most affected by severe environmental change? How has drought affected division of labor, social/political life, religious taboos, etc.? Why do so many nomadic tribes refuse to change (i.e., become sedentary) in spite of impending starvation? What are the effects of short-term relief programs on these cultures? What moral/ethical questions apply to the situation? What adaptation have "refugee" children made to the drought situation?* [Felicia Shinnamon]

An African Recovery (1988) 26 min. Sandra Nichols (DI), United Nations (PR). Dist: FRIF VR$50, VS$190. *During the 1980s, a catastrophic drought ravaged parts of Africa, destroying crops and eroding the landscape of the Sahel. The film focuses on new efforts being made by rural planners and ordinary citizens to minimize the risk of repeating the recent tragedy. Once a flourishing waterway, the Niger River is silted and shallow, bordered by a denuded landscape that can no longer support hunting or farming as overgrazing, forest destruction, and natural disasters force Nigerians to depend heavily on outside emergency aid. But now, community projects among various groups in Niger are* *being explored, examining how local development efforts can help create solutions tailored to local needs.*

African Religions and Ritual Dances (1971) 19 min. Babatunde Olatunji and Dallie (CONS), WCAU-TV (PR). Dist: PSU $13.50. *Dance as an integral part of African life. Reenactment of a Yoruba cult dance, the "Invocation to Igunnu." Ritual fire dance to Shango, the God of Thunder, in which the spirit of Shango seems to enter the dancers' bodies so completely that they can expose themselves to fire without being burned.*

African Soul: Music, Past and Present (1971) 17 min. Babatunde Olatunji and Dallie (CONS), WCAU-TV (PR). Dist: PSU $12.50. *Development of music from primitive origins to present. Blues traced back to the forests and savannas of Africa. Ancient musical art of body percussion. How a simple drumbeat is laid down, improvised upon, and added to.*

AFRICAN VILLAGE LIFE SERIES (1967) International Film Foundation (PR), Hermann Schlenker (CA). Dist: MICH (rental); IFF (sale). *In 1960, the word Mali reappeared on the world maps. Taking its name from the empire that flourished along the Niger River over 500 years ago, the Republic of Mali is one of several recent nations to emerge from French West Africa. The 12 short films concentrate on the essential activities of just three of the many peoples who live along the Niger River in Mali: The Bozo (who are expert fishermen); The Dogon (who are agriculturists); and the Peul, or Fulani (who are nomadic herders). Each group fits into a particular pattern of economic and social life determined by the culture and geography of their individual environments. Each film describes a particular activity of one group.* [Reviewed by Nicholas Hopkins, *AA* 70:843,844, 1968.]

- **Building a Boat** (Bozo) 8 min. FR$26, FS$150.
- **Herding Cattle** (Peul) 7 min. FR$25, FS$135.
- **Onion Farming** (Dogon) 7 min. FR$25, FS$135.
- **Building a House** (Bozo) 7 min. FR$25, FS$135.
- **Hunting Wild Doves** (Dogon) 8 min. FR$25, FS$150.
- **Cotton Growing and Spinning** (Dogon) 6 min. FR$25, FS$125.
- **Daily Life of the Bozo** 16 min. FR$35, FS$280.
- **Fishing on the Niger River** (Bozo) 18 min. FR$35, FS$300.
- **Magic Rites: Divination by Animal Tracks** (Dogon) 7 min. FR$25, FS$135.
- **Magic Rites: Divination by Chicken Sacrifice** (Dogon) 7 min. FR$25, FS$135.
- **Annual Festival of the Dead** (Dogon) 14 min. FR$25, FS$250.
- **Masked Dances** (Dogon) 6 min. FR$25, FS$125.

L'Afrique et la recherche scientifique (Africa and Scientific Research) (1964) 31 min. Jean Rouch (DI), Centre National de la Recherche Scientifique (PR). Dist: CFE; DER.

Afrique sur Seine (Africa on the Seine) (1969) Jean Rouch (DI). Dist: CFE; DER.

Afro-American Worksongs in a Texas Prison (1966) 29 min. (A Folklore Research Film by Peter and Toshi Seeger.) Bruce Jackson and W. D. Alexander (NA), Peter, Toshi, Daniel Seeger (CA). Dist: FIM/RF FR$25, FS$250. *Afro-American work songs survive today in few places outside prison farms. This film records seven of them at the Ellis Unit of the Texas Department of Corrections, near Huntsville. Black prisoners are seen being transported by truck out to the woods and fields early in the morning, then at work singing five tree-chopping songs: "John, O John," "Early in the Morning," "Plumb in the Line," "Julie and the Baby," and "I've Been Working All Day Long" (sung by the man who composed it), and one short hoeing song followed by another, the well-known, "Down by the Riverside."*

After Solidarity: Three Polish Families in America (1987) 58 min. Gaylen Ross (PR). Dist: FL VR$75, VS$445. *"Depicts the assimilation trials and tribulations of three Polish families in America. It does so through the interview question responses by members of each family. Husbands, wives and children present their views of their current situations in their own words. . . . Children are the quickest to adjust, followed by the husbands and then the wives."* [From the review by Kathleen Monk, *AA* 91:525, 1989.]

Agueda Martinez. Our Life, Our Country (1977) 16 min. Moctezuma Esparza (PR). Dist: EMC FR$30, FS$300; MICH. *Now 77, Agueda Martinez is of Navajo-Mexican descent. She lives on her ranch in northern New Mexico. Her roots are in the traditions of her ancestors and in the land that supports her life and occupation as a farmer and weaver. Her life reflects the rhythms of nature and a special harmony with herself and her surroundings. Agueda Martinez explains how "I make my living with my work" and describes her fundamental values: self-sufficiency, family solidarity, religious commitment, and cooperation with the land and nature.*

Ahimsa, Non-Violence (1987) 58 min. Marion Hunt (PR), Michael Tobias (DR). Dist: DCL VR$75, VS$250. *"About modern followers of the Jain religion in India, a small but prosperous group whose central ethical and religious precept of ahimsa (nonviolence) strongly influenced Gandhi."* [From the review by Dennis B. McGilvray, *AA* 91:1094–1095, 1989.]

Ahmedabad: Life of a City in India (1984) 30 min. Howard Spodek (FM). Dist: UW-SAAC FR$25, FS$250. *"Presents an overview of this city of 2.5 million people, showing new arrivals streaming into an already overcrowded area, depicting its Muslim origin in the 15th century and its growth as a unique blend of Hindu and Muslim people and architecture, and describing, visually and in narration, the neighborhoods, handicraft industry, markets, and textile mills."* [From the review by Joan L. Erdman, *AA* 89:251–253, 1987.]

AIDS Babies (1990) 58 min. Monique Oomen (DR). Dist: CG VR$100, VS$350. *"The special problems of pediatric AIDS."* [From the review by Ralph Bolton, *AA* 94(3):762–764, 1992.]

AIDS in Africa 52 min. Roger Pyke Productions with the National Film Board of Canada (PR). Dist: FL VR$75, VS$445. *The health crisis is striking a continent already wracked by civil strife and corruption. There are therefore huge economic and cultural obstacles to prevention efforts. In its investigation, the film takes viewers to remote and previously off-limits locations in Uganda, Zaire, the Ivory Coast, Burundi, Rwanda, South Africa, and several other countries. We hear from both African and foreign public health officials who attest to the magnitude of the problem. The film gives voice to the Africans themselves who, with courage and dignity, face an uncertain future.* [Reviewed by Ralph Bolton, AA 94(3):762–764, 1992; Janet W. McGrath, AJPA 88:255–257, 1992.]

AIDS in the Barrio: Eso no me pasa a mi (1989) 30 min. Dist: CG FR$50, VR$50, FS$425, VS$250. *"For use in HIV prevention efforts in Latino communities.... Depicts the impact of AIDS ... in a Puerto Rican neighborhood in North Philadelphia."* [From the review by Ralph Bolton, AA 94:762, 1992.]

Ain't Scared of Your Jails 1960–61 (see Eyes on the Prize: America's Civil Rights Years Series)

Aita (Morocco, Body and Soul Series) (1987) 26 min. Izza Genini (FM). Dist: FRIF FR$55, FS$470, VS$260. *Fatna bent El Hocine is a "cheika," a female troubadour who travels with dancers and musicians and performs at religious ceremonies, marriages, and circumcisions. She sings of disappointed love and abandoned women in mystical outbursts—the "aita"—which have undertones of nearby Spain. Sometimes a stadium replaces the bedouin tent, and amplifiers allow her a larger audience. Regardless of the setting, when Fatna bent El Hocine throws herself into the "aita," the impact is fantastic.*

Ajuba Dance and Drama Company 20 min. Dist: UW-SAAS FR$20, FS$180. *Introduces a troupe of popular entertainers in North India. Performing in Mango groves and on street corners, they stage a type of theatre known as Nautanki, an amalgam of music, dance, comedy routines, and drama. Nautanki draws as easily from the arts of the royal court as it does from the latest Bombay feature films. Viewers see the performers in their everyday lives; meet Bhaggal, the director; travel with his Ajuba troupe; watch them rehearse their lines and put on their make-up; and finally, under the stars, witness a Nautanki performance itself, with dance, song, color, and romance.*

Aku-Aku, the Secret of Easter Island 84 min. Thor Heyerdahl (FM). Dist: Janus Films, 745 Fifth Avenue, New York, NY 10022. [Reviewed by Alexandra M. Ulana Klymyshyn, AA 78:384–385, 1976.]

Akwesasne: Another Point of View (1981) 21 min. Robert Stiles and John Aki (FM). Dist: FRIF FR$55, FS$500, VS$290. *A portrait of the Mohawk people as they confront two choices: survival or assimilation. The film explores some of the social, political, and legal obstacles faced by Mohawks in recent years in their struggle to retain traditional rights.* [Reviewed by Donald D. Stull, AA 88:775'776, 1986; Samuel Casselberry, SBF 18:214, 1983.]

THE ALASKA NATIVE HERITAGE SERIES (see The Alaskan Eskimo Series)

THE ALASKAN ESKIMO SERIES Dist: DER. See descriptions under titles:
- **On the Spring Ice** FR$60, VR$40, FS$700, VS$400.
- **At the Time of Whaling** FR$60, VR$40, FS$650, VS$400.
- **Tununeremiut: The People of Tununak** FR$50, VR$40, FS$550, VS$400.
- **From the First People** FR$60, VR$40, FS$650, VS$400.

The Albanians of Rrogam (Disappearing World Series) (1991) 52 min. Berit Backer (AN). Dist: FIV VS$198. *Faced with a harsh climate and poor soil, the Rrogamis, inhabitants of a northern Albanian alpine valley, survive now as in the past, by keeping sheep and goats. With the government redistributing land and animals to the peasants, the young taking over village rule, and communities recovering their autonomy, the future of Rrogam is hard to predict.* [Reviewed by Ali Eminov, AA 95:515–517, 1993.]

The Alchemy of Time 26 min. Earl H. Swanson (DI), Idaho State University Museum (PR), Don Crabtree (AN). Dist: IMI FR$30, FS$345. *Explores heat treatment as a means for changing the flaking properties of natural glassy rocks. This is followed by treatment of the ways for producing fluted early spear points, such as the well-known Clovis, Folsom, and Cumberland types. Slow-motion film permits examination of fluting sequences in all three forms. These films are primarily for classroom use and come with teacher's guides.* [Reviewed by Anthony E. Marks, AA 77:914–915, 1975; Susanna R. Katz and Paul R. Katz, ARCH 34(1):60, 1981.]

Alger-Le Cap (1953–54) 102 min. Serge de Poligny (DI), Jean Rouch (consultant). Dist: CFE; DER. *Account of a car rally across the African continent.*

Alhaji Bai Konte (1979) 12 min. Oliver Franklin and Marc Pevar (PR). Dist: Cultural Encounters, Inc., 606 Ridge Avenue, Kennett Square, PA 19348; (215) 444-1157 FR$36, FS$295. *"The life of a Mandinka jali, or professional musician from The Gambia."* [From the review by Roderic Knight, AA 86:239–240, 1984.]

Alice Elliott 11 min. Dist: UCEMC FR$23, FS$160. *The life and work of one of the few remaining Pomo Indian basketmakers.*

The Alien's Place (1979) 87 min. Rudolf van den Berg (FM). Dist: ICF FR$100, FS$1245. *"The personal statement of a 34-year-old Dutch Jew who asks what it means to be a Jew."* [From the review by Riv-Ellen Prell, AA 85:1009–1010, 1983.]

All Hand Work 15 min. Dist: UCEMC FR$26, FS$215. *Portrait of Jenes Cottrell, a well-known 73-year-old "mountain artist" who plays his banjo and sells his homemade whistles, decorative toadstools, billy clubs, bull roarers, and rolling pins at music festivals and crafts fairs throughout West Virginia. Shows Cottrell at home, where he lives with his widowed sister, and in his workshop, where he demonstrates his abilities working on a foot-operated lathe (nei-*

ther his home nor his workshop has electricity). As Cottrell relates how he began doing woodwork, it becomes evident that he is an ingenious character and a skillful manipulator of his own image—an ability that allows him to present himself and the traditions he respects in a manner suited to urban expectations. In conclusion, he performs two pieces of music on his front lawn, explaining between tunes the construction details of his banjo, which uses an automobile transmission housing for a shell and hand-carved walnut for the neck.

All My Babies (1952) George Stoney (PR). Dist: NYU. *An instructional film made for the Georgia Department of Health to train midwives.* [Reviewed by Nancie L. Gonzalez and Stella B. Silverstein, AA 77:173, 1975.]

All under Heaven: Life in a Chinese Village (Long Bow Film Series) (1985) 58 min. Carma Hinton and Richard Gordon (DI). Dist: NDF FR$90, VR$75, FS$800, VS$480. *A penetrating account of change and continuity in a north Chinese village. This film does much to humanize a nation that is viewed by many Westerners through distorting lenses.* [Reviewed by William Graves III, AA 89:253–254, 1987.]

Almost Heaven (1976) 30 min. Peter Griesinger and Carol Griesinger (FM). FR$40, FS$375. *Small-town life in West Virginia.* See also *Small Business My Way.* Available from Griesinger Films, Central West Virginia Media Arts, P.O. Box 1102, 48 E. Main St., Buckhannon, WV 26201; (304) 472-7828. [Reviewed by Linda A. Bennett, AA 86:506–507, 1984.]

Alpaca Breeders of Chimboya (1983) 30 min. Mariane Eyde (FM). Dist: ICF FR$50, FS$495, VS$290. *This film from Peru depicts the life of a small peasant community high in the Andes mountains, which depends on the marketing of alpaca fleece for its survival. The film traces the cycle of the Chimboyan economy, from raising and shearing of the alpacas, to market, to textile production, and to export. The film looks at the structure of the Indian peasant communities, which the alpaca industry supports—middlemen provide credit between marketing seasons, textile exporters ship 85 percent of the Peruvian alpaca each year, but when cash runs low, peasants of different communities must barter among themselves in order to survive.* [Reviewed by William Graves III, AA 89:253–254, 1987; Joanne Rappaport, AA 87:983–985, 1985.]

Alpha noir (Black Alpha) (1965) 10 min. Jean Rouch (DI), Centre National de la Recherche Scientifique, Comité du Film Ethnographique (PR). Dist: CFE; DER.

Alphabétisation des adultes au Mali (Adult Literacy in Mali) (1965) Jean Rouch (DI). Dist: CFE; DER.

Altar of Fire 45 min. Frits Staal (PR), Robert Gardner (DI). Dist: UCEMC FR$45, FS$600. *The world's oldest surviving ritual, the Agnicayana, a Vedic ritual of sacrifice dating back some 3,000 years. It was performed, perhaps for the last time, in April 1975, by Nambudiri Brahmins in Panjal, a village in Kerala, in southwestern India. Through the centuries, this relatively isolated Nambudiri community has remained faithful to its Vedic heritage. The 12-day ritual requires the participation of 17 Nambudiri priests, involves libations of soma juice and oblations of other substances, and is preceded by several months of preparation. After a brief introduction explaining the origin of the Vedas and showing how the oral tradition is passed from father to son and from teacher to pupil, the film presents selected highlights from the ritual itself. The opening shows the construction of several sacrificial altars and sheds, using perishable materials such as clay, wood, and grass. The principal personages are the sacrificer, who throughout the 12 days abstains from most kinds of food, keeps his fists closed like an embryo (for he is about to be reborn), and is not allowed to bathe, shave, or change clothes, and the sacrificer's wife, the only woman allowed in the ritual, who sits behind a parasol. Also prominent are the Hota, who recites from the Rigveda, and the kindler of fires, or Agnidh, who responds to the calls of the main priest. The central feature of the ritual is the construction and consecration of the main altar for Agni, god of fire; the altar is in the shape of a bird and is made of more than 1,000 bricks. On the last day of the ritual, all of the structures are abandoned to fire; the only remnant is the bird-shaped altar.* [Reviewed by Robert A. Paul, AA 80:197–199, 1978.]

Always for Pleasure 58 min. Les Blank (FM). Dist: FF FR$90, FS$890. *New Orleans Mardi Gras.* [Reviewed by Robert Gordon, JAF 92(364):261, 1979.]

Always There Comes a New Spring (1983) 28 min. Donald N. Brown et al. (PR) for Oklahoma Educational Television. Dist: Educational Television Services, Telecommunications Center, Oklahoma State University, Stillwater, OK 74078; (405) 840-1721 VS$90. Rental from the Oklahoma Foundation for the Humanities, 2809 NW Expressway, Suite 500, Oklahoma City, OK 73112; (405) 840-1721. *"Portrays the adjustment of middle-upper class Vietnamese refugees to resettlement in the United States. . . . Claims that . . . the Vietnamese have successfully resumed life in the United States, that they have found spring again. The proof is strong evidence of their commercial success in Oklahoma City and of their resumption of formal religious life through Catholic and Buddhist services conducted by Vietnamese."* [From the review by Marjorie A. Muecke, AA 88:771–772, 1986.]

Amahuaca: A Tropical Forest Society in Southeastern Peru (1974) 25 min. Gertrude Dole (FM, AN). Dist: PSU FR$18.50, FS$385. *Living in isolated family groups, the Amahuaca Indians subsist by hunting wild game and cultivating corn using the slash-burn technique. The film documents their daily activities: grinding corn, preparing corn soup, making a grinding trough and a coil cooking pot. Detailed sequence shows the concentration of bows and arrows and, later, the use of arrows to catch fish. Preparation for the Harvest Festival includes scenes of facial painting, bead adornment, and men's headdresses.*

Amazon Family (1961) 19 min. Francis Thompson (FM), Frank Tan Nenbaum (AN), International Film Foundation (PR). Dist: MICH; IFF FR$35, FS$320. *The pattern of daily life in a remote village of rubber gatherers on the upper Amazon near the common border of Bolivia, Peru, and*

Brazil. [Reviewed by Robert F. Murphy, *AA* 67:603–604, 1965]

Amazonia: The Road to the End of the Forest 96 min. Canadian Broadcasting Corporation (PR). Dist: FL VR$100, VS$495. *This spectacular production provides a comprehensive survey of the global catastrophe escalating in the Amazon basin. The burning of the tropical rain forest is a major contributor to the green house effect. This program explains the failure of a massive resettlement program, which lured millions of migrants to the Amazon. They cleared the forest with the hope of farming, only to discover that the soil was infertile. Despite this, the Brazilian government continued to promote settlement, which threatens many native Amazonian groups, including the Kaiapo Indians and rubber tappers. The film includes one of the last interviews with the late Chico Mendez, leader of the rubber tappers, who was murdered for his outspoken opposition to land clearance. As this program shows, the Western world is both culprit and victim in this tragedy.* [Reviewed by Darna L. Dufour and Paul Shankman, *AJPA* 88:113–115, 1992.]

Amazulu (1979) 24 min. Dist: SU FR$22.50. *Life in a traditional krall (village). Follows the daily routine from early morning with head-boys taking the cattle to graze, to preparation of the common meal, construction of a reed hut, village agriculture, primitive iron smelting, bead making, magic, and spear and shield making. Shows Zulu social structure, duties of each village member, the natural environment, and places the Zulus as a branch of the southern Bantu-speaking people of South Africa.*

Ambara Dama (1974) 60 min. Jean Rouch and Germaine Dieterlen (DI), Centre National de la Recherche Scientifique, Comité du Film Ethnographique (PR). Dist: CFE; DER. *The Sanga Mask Society organizes a grand Dama, a ceremony in which old masks are replaced by new ones.*

America: Everything You've Always Dreamed Of (1973) 26 min. Dist: IUAVC. *A series of four vignettes, scenes from American culture as observed by the camera, rather than acted according to developed script. (1) Honeymoon Hotel—a resort hotel for the newly married. Young couples and owner are interviewed; (2) Risen Indeed—a visit to the training grounds of Campus Crusade for Christ; (3) Best Years of Your Life—a visit to Sun City, Arizona; (4) Muzak—interviews with people who believe efficiency can be increased by the planned and piped-in use of music.* [R. Conlin]

American Boy (1978) 60 min. Martin Scorsese (DI). *Scorsese invites his best friend in for a photo-interview. The first few minutes portray a rough-and-tumble play between the subject of the film and another friend on the scene. Scorsese calms them down and starts the interview. The subject responds to Scorsese's questions about his life, as the son of a military officer who becomes the show manager for rock singer Neil Diamond and a drug addict by his early 20s. The climax of the film is when he graphically describes how he killed a man who was trying to hold him up one night when he was working at an all-night gas station. The film can be viewed as an example of a male pride rap—much emphasis on violent, bizarre experiences. A disturbing film. Cinematic features: Film is primarily close-ups of the subject, with some scenes showing Scorsese in interaction or talking at the camera. Home movies of the subject are woven through the dialogue. Warnings: Scorsese admires his friend—film is likely to provoke very strong emotional reactions about this lifestyle, making it difficult to break through to analysis. Focusing questions to set up viewers: Why is the film titled "American Boy" when its subject is just one young man? What is the role of women for these men, both in terms of what comes out (or doesn't) in the interviews, and the behavior of the women in the background at the filming? Although this "confession" is performed explicitly for purposes of filming, it has its "real life" equivalents. What is the function of this kind of talk for the men?* [Clarice Stasz]

American Chinatown (1982) 30 min. Todd Carrel (FM). Dist: UCEMC FR$40, FS$450, VS$355. *A film about American values in conflict and the efforts of powerless elderly people to retain their dignity. This poignant study documents the plight of America's last rural Chinatown in the northern California community of Locke. An excellent study guide that covers the history of Locke and the history of Chinese in America accompanies the film.* [Reviewed by Paul B. Wiener, *SBF* 18:278, 1983; Karen L. Ito, *AA* 86:786–787, 1984.]

American History? It's beneath Your Feet (1990) 29 min. Robert Starbird and Daniel Rainey (FM). Dist: Rainey, 1200 South Washington Street, #216-E, Alexandria, VA 22314; Media Inc., Box 496, Media, PA 19063-0469; (800) 523-0118. *The purpose of this film is to provide an explanation of historical archaeology in an uban context (specifically in Alexandria, Baltimore, and New York City.) Emphasis is on the difference between historical and prehistoric archaeology, and the ways in which archaeological and historical data can be used together to fill out the historical record.* [From the review by Peter S. Allen, *ARCH* 44(3):56–57, 1991. Reviewed by Stanley South, *AA* 93(2):5113–5114, 1991.]

AMERICAN INDIAN SERIES (1961–65) Samual A. Barrett (AN), Clyde B. Smith, University of California, Berkeley (PR). Dist: UCEMC. [Reviewed by John Adair, *AA* 76:728, 1974; Clement W. Meighan, *AA* 69:271, 1967.] For details, see under individual film title:

- **Acorns: Staple Food of the California Indians**
- **Basketry of the Pomo—Introductory Film**
  - **—Techniques**
  - **—Forms and Ornamentation**
- **Beautiful Tree—Chiskale**
- **Buckeyes: Food of California Indians**
- **Calumet, Pipe of Peace**
- **Dream Dances of the Kashia Pomo**
- **Game of Staves**
- **Kashia Men's Dances: Southwestern Pomo Indians**
- **Obsidian Point-Making**

- Pine Nuts
- Sinew-Backed Bow and Its Arrow
- Totem Pole
- Wooden Box: Made by Steaming and Bending

American Indian Speaks (1973) 23 min. Dist: EBEC; UCEMC FR$27; MICH. *Uses the experiences of the Muskogee Creek, Rosebud Sioux, and Nisqually Indian nations to illustrate various aspects of the struggle for survival the American Indian has waged, and is still waging today.*

American Samoa: Paradise Lost? (1968) 55 min. NET (PR). Dist: IUAVC FR$19.50, S (color $635, B/W $400). *Depicts the influence and challenge United States governing authority is having upon the traditional life of the Polynesians in American Samoa. Discusses both the advantages of American-introduced educational technology, such as educational television, and the potential conflict between Western goals of education and the cultural values of Samoa. Explains that the traditional Samoan values emphasize obedience to family authority, and Western education stresses independence of thought.*

American Shoeshine 29 min. Sparky Greene (PR, DI). Dist: UILL. *Social and economic history of shoeshining.* [Reviewed by John W. Adams, AA 78:961, 1976.]

American Tongues Louis Alvarez and Andrew Holker (FM), Mac 'Dr. John' Rebennack (MU). Dist: CNAMFL VR$85, VS$250; NDF VR$85, VS$285. *Anybody who lives in the United States knows the cliches about how people in various parts of the country handle the English language. This video examines the attitudes Americans have about their speech and how those attitudes reflect larger cultural issues. From Boston Brahmins to black Louisiana teenagers, from Texas cowboys to New York professionals, this film elicits funny, perceptive, sometimes shocking and always telling comments about our diverse society. Part 1 provides a basic overview of American language variety, highlighting differences in pronunciation and vocabulary, as well as illustrating the settlement patterns that helped foster those differences. Part 2 presents the opinions and experiences of a variety of Americans concerning their own and others' dialects.* [Reviewed by Jane Hill, AA 92:553, 1990.]

Amiq: The Aleut People of the Pribilov Islands, a Culture in Transition (1983) 58 min. Susanne Swibold and Helen Corbett (PR). Dist: FTP FS$950, VS$280. *"Depicts life in the Pribilovs today: the Orthodox church as the focus of community solidarity and group and self identity; dependence ... on exploitation of their natural environment reminiscent of the old lifeways. ... Also tells of the war-time relocation under the US government act authorizing relocation and internment of civilians and the Aleut fight for recognition of the wrongs suffered."* [From the review by Lydia Black, AA 88:257–258, 1986.]

Amir: An Afghan Refugee Musician's Life in Peshawar, Pakistan (1985) 52 min. John Baily (FM), Wayne Derrick (CA), Royal Anthropological Institute and the National Film and Television School, UK (PR). Dist: DER FR$50, VS$375. *Between 1973 and 1977, John Baily carried out extensive ethnomusicological fieldwork on the urban music of Afghanistan, particularly in the western city of Herat. In 1985, he traveled to Peshawar to film Afghan refugees, who were musicians, and, again, met his old friend Amir Mohammad, from Herat. The film portrays aspects of Amir's life as a refugee, his living conditions in Peshawar, and his longing to return to Herat. It is also about Amir's life as a professional musician and his relationships with other musicians in Peshawar. Musical performances include resistance songs at a Pakistani wedding.* [Reviewed by Dorothy S. Mull and J. Dennis Mull, AA 91:836–838, 1989.]

Amish: A People of Preservation (1975) 53 min. (28-min. version available). John A. Hostetler (CON, AN), John L. Ruth (PR), Burton Buller (CA). Dist: EBEC 28-min. version FS$380, 53-min. version FS$546. *Shot in Lancaster County, Pennsylvania, 1975. Attempt to show Amish family and community life. Contains brief history of the Amish previous to their migration to North America, shows their adaptations to modern life while attempting to preserve the traditional values of humility, peace, honesty, and hard work. Worldliness and modern technology are carefully controlled in an effort to keep the Amish community free from profane influences. Family farming, religious practices, rearing of children, education, marriage, and relationships with modern society are shown. Focusing questions: (1) What are the basic values of the Amish society? (2) What contrast is there between Amish values and modern American values? (3) How successful are the Amish in controlling technological change in their own communities? (4) What kinds of sanctions are used to protect against unacceptable change? (5) Will it be possible for the Amish to survive as a subculture in modern America? Bibliography: Other films on the Amish: See edited version of this film, running time 28 min. John A. Hostetler, Amish Society. Baltimore: Johns Hopkins Press, 1968. John A. Hostetler, Children in Amish Society: Socialization and Community Education. New York: Holt, Rinehart and Winston, Inc., 1971.* [Reviewed by Calvin Redekop, AA 78:961, 1976; Simon J. Bronner, JAF 92(363):121–123, 1979.] [Lawrence J. Hanson]

The Amish: Not to Be Modern 57 min. Victoria Larimore and Michael Taylor (DI). Dist: FL FR$85, VR$85, FS$850, VS$700. *The Amish do not generally permit photography because of their interpretation of the biblical commandment against the making of graven images. This film is an exclusive portrait of a rarely filmed religious community that separates itself from the world. The filmmakers spent many months living among the Amish, building the rapport necessary to make this important, thought-provoking film. Photographed over the four seasons, the film captures the day-to-day life of a people who have preserved many rural traditions: a father and his sons husking corn, an older woman making quilts, the hustle-bustle of a horse auction. Rather than use a narrator to comment on this unusual lifestyle, the Amish speak for themselves—they tell their own story. Stirring Amish hymns, composed in the 1500s and handed down orally, complete the soundtrack. The film encourages viewers to evaluate their own lifestyle and values, to consider what really determines progress.* [Reviewed by Gertrude E. Huntington, AA 89:775–776, 1987.]

Among Wild Chimpanzees (1984) 48 min. National Geographic Society (PR). Dist: NGSES FS$595, VS$495. *"Appeared on most public television stations in early (1984). . . . Emphasized the personal aspects of Goodall's study."* [From the review by Robert S. O. Harding, *AA* 87:979, 1985.]

Amra Dujon (Together) (1984) 30 min. John Riber (PR), Alamgir Kabir (DI). Dist: DSR, Inc., Box 281, Columbia, MD 21045; (301) 596-0794 FR$50, FS$450, VS$375. *"A depiction of noncoercive decision making on family planning, aimed at Bangladeshi theater audiences."* [From the review by Hugh S. Plunkett, *AA* 89:520, 1987.]

L'An 01 (The Year 01) (1973) Jacques Doillon and Gebe (DI). Dist: CFE; DER. *Includes two sequences directed by Alain Resnais (The Fall of Wall Street) and Jean Rouch (The Subway Museum).*

Analyse Cinéradiographique du Saut Chez un Primate: Galago alleni (1972) 9 min. F. K. Jouffroy, J. P. Gasc, S. Oblin (FM). Dist: Universite Paris, VII, Departement Audio-Visuel, 2, Place Jussieu, Paris-5e, France. *Primate locomotion.* [Reviewed by Farish A. Jenkins, Jr., *AA* 75:2018, 1973.]

Anansi the Spider (African Folklore Series) (1969) 10 min. Gerald McDermott (PR). Dist: PSU FR$10.50. *African folktale concerning the adventures of Anansi, a spider with human qualities and a rascal in the tradition of Br'er Rabbit and Til Eulenspiegel.*

The Anasternaria (1969) 17 min. Peter Haramis (FM). Dist: UCEMC FR$17. *Meeting at the home of the ascetic village elder on the 21st of May in Serres, Macedonia, initiates walk to a ceremonial site where a sacrificial lamb and cow are slaughtered and shared. The village priest blesses the ikons, after which the procession visits each house in the village, then returns to the elder's house for frenzied dancing, culminating in walking without pain or injury across beds of glowing embers, symbolizing the blessed protection of Saint Constantine.* [Reviewed by Peter Allen, *AA* 74:1581–1584, 1972.]

Ancestors: The Last Tasmanian (see The Last Tasmanian Series)

The Ancient Africans (1970) 27 min. Julien Bryan and IFF (PR), Sam Bryan (DI), Richard Ford (AN). Dist: IFF FR$45, FS$450 *A thoughtful, creative look at a variety of African peoples, their civilizations, and their achievements. The viewer is transported back through history to a time before the written word. Civilizations develop, communities grow dynamic, and empires prosper. The life of people is seen through their arts, their trade, their buildings and monuments, and their religion.* [Reviewed by Anne M. Jennings, *AA* 74:1018, 1972.]

Ancient Art of Peru 15 min. Penelope Strouth and Francois Piraud (WR, DI, CA). Dist: FIM/RF FR$20, FS$250. *This film is an introduction to the art of the main cultures of pre-Columbian Peru. Spectacular ruins and choice objects dug out by treasure hunters and archaeologists revive the amazing achievements of 3,000 years of Peruvian civilization.* [Reviewed by Michael E. Mosely, *AA* 78:384, 1976.]

The Ancient Chinese (1974) 24 min. Dist: IFF FR$45, FS$450. *Scenes in Peking's forbidden city, on a silk plantation, and of an artist practicing calligraphy—the ancient art of Chinese writing—help show that China's history and deep-rooted traditions have continued longer than those of any other civilization.* [Reviewed by K. C. Chang, *AA* 78:140, 1976.]

Ancient Egypt (1952) 11 min. Coronet Films (PR), Richard A. Parker (Collab.). Dist: SU. [Reviewed by Thomas Wight Beale, *AA* 78:132, 1976.]

Ancient Egypt 51 min. Brian Blake, Time-Life (PR). Dist: T-L FR$55, FS$600, VFS$150. *The history of Egypt is outlined and illustrated with magnificent art and architecture. Stresses two themes—the sun and the River Nile. We learn of the people who created these monuments, about their gusto for living, their love of sports, their daily lives, and their religion. The film traces the development of "Egyptology."* [Reviewed by Timothy Kendall, *AA* 78:131, 1976.]

The Ancient Egyptian (1963) 27 min. Julien Bryan, Ray Gardner, and Wheaton Galentine (FM), LeRoy Leatherman (WR, DI), John Wilson and Zaki Saad (AN), Julien Bryan (PR). Dist: IFF FR$45, FS$450. *This introduction to the world's first great civilization brings the ancient Egyptians alive through their own art and through Philip Stapp's animation. Tomb paintings, sculpture, and artifacts illustrate their daily lives and pleasures; how they ate and drank; how they hunted and raised food; their values, hopes, and fears; their vision of the hereafter.* [Reviewed by Gus W. Van Beek, *AA* 67:846, 1965.]

Ancient Footpath 20 min. Madeline Tourtelot (FM). Dist: GP FR$25, FS$250. *Documents the migration of the Mixtec Indians in southern Mexico (A.D. 1100–1300) through an Indian boy's dream. Having unearthed an ancient clay idol in the fields, Juan dreams of his forefather's "footpath" through a five-day journey. The people and places are authentically Mixtec, as is the final plume dance performed at the archaeological site, Monte Alban, in Oaxaca.* [Reviewed by Frederick Gorman, *AA* 78:379–380, 1976.]

The Ancient Games (1972) 28 min. Dist: PSU FR$15. *Eric Segal focuses on the events in early olympic games. Olympic champions Rafer Johnson and Bill Toomey recreate the pentathlon, trying out the ancient type javelin, discus, and "halteres." Result is an exercise in experimental archaeology.* [Reviewed by Laura L. Nash, *AA* 78:123, 1976.]

An Ancient Gift (1983) 18 min. Tellens, Inc (PR) for the Museum of Northern Arizona. Dist: UCEMC FR$32, FS$315, VS$240. *"Examines the importance of sheep to the Navajos. . . . Also portrays much about contemporary life in traditional areas. One's attention is focused on learning about the life cycle of sheep, the interdependence of Navajos and their flocks, and the Navajo view that equates sheep with life itself."* [From the review by Charlotte L. Frisbie, *AA* 87:735, 1985. Reviewed by John H. Peterson, Jr., *SBF* 20:40, 1984.]

Ancient Greece (1952) 11 min. Coronet Films (PR), Elmer Louis Kayser (Collab). Dist: SU. [Reviewed by Laura L. Nash, *AA* 78:130, 1976.]

Ancient Inca Indians of South America (1971) 7 min. Dist: IUAVC FR$5.50. *Surveys, with still illustrations, the empire of the Incas with reference to their cities, road systems, religion, farming, and art. Shows the importance of the llama to their way of life. Records the destruction of the Inca civilization by the Spanish.*

ANCIENT LIVES SERIES (1986) 23–29 min. each. John Romer (NA). Dist: FHS FR$65, FS$485, VS$99. *This eight-part series "is ostensibly concerned with illustrating the lives of the artists and craftsmen who quarried and decorated the royal tombs of (primarily) the Ramesside kings of Dynasties 19 and 20. The material is adapted from Romer's book 'Ancient Lives: The Story of the Pharaoh's Tombmakers' (London, 1984), an attempt to bring to life the material and textual remains of Deir el Medina as they reflect the lives of the villagers, seen as ordinary people with very contemporary needs and problems." [From the review by Susan Kane, ARCH 40(2):70–73, 1987.*

The Ancient Mariners (1981) 59 min. Sam Low (FM), George F. Bass (AN). Dist: DER VR$50. *This is a film about underwater archaeology. It highlights three underwater archaeological investigations of shipwrecks undertaken in the eastern Mediterranean Sea by George F. Bass and Michael L. Katzev, of the Institute of Nautical Archaeology, Texas A & M University. The film shows not only the excavations and their ramifications, but also deals with the historical context of the finds. The world renowned authority on maritime history of ancient times, Lionel Casson, is shown addressing this issue.* [Reviewed by Robert L Hohlfelder, *AA* 84:757 8, 1982. Benjamin A. G. Fuller, *ARCH* 34(5):68, 1981.] Bibliography: George F. Bass, *Archaeology Beneath the Sea*. Walker & Co., 1975.

Ancient Mesopotamia (1953) 11 min. Dist: IUAVC FR$6.50; PSU FR$8. *Development of Tigris-Euphrates Valley; occupation of land by Sumerians, Semites, Babylonians, and Assyrians; their contributions such as wheel, code of laws, arch, system of writing, military science, and astronomy.* [Reviewed by Thomas Wight Beale, *AA* 78:137, 1976.]

Ancient Moderns: Greek Island Art and Culture: 3,000–2,000 B.C. (1979) 19 min. Harvey Bellin and Tom Kieffer (FM). Free loan from the Department of Extensions Programs, National Gallery of Art, Washington, DC 20565; (202) 737-4215; EBEC FR$38, FS$380. *The film "is exactly what its title implies—a look at Cycladic art of the third millennium BC from the vantage point of contemporary appreciation for abstract forms."* [From the review by Diana Buitron, *ARCH* 37(1):72, 1984.

The Ancient Peruvian (1968) 27 min. James D. Sage (DI, WR), The International Film Foundation (PR), Sam Bryan (CA), Junius Bird (CON), Thomas Wagner (MU), animation by Gerald McDermott. Dist: IFF FS$450; PSU FR$45. *The Ancient Peruvian was photographed on location in Peru and Bolivia. Many important archaeological sites have been assembled together on film. An original music score incorporates pre-Columbian harmonies based on scales obtained from the tuning of clay and reed flutes. Our story begins with the end . . . the imminent collapse of the Inca empire, and with it, 3,000 years of culture. From this point, we move backward in time, to uncover civilizations far older than the Incas. Live-action footage, intercut with animation, inspired by Indian motifs, portrays the rise and fall of these vanished peoples: where they came from, how they prospered, their religions, their social structure, the physical remnants of their achievements. A major section of the film is devoted to contrasting the art of life of the Ancient Peruvian with scenes of contemporary Peru. The film concludes with a brief description of the Inca world. Machu Picchu becomes a symbol of all the Ancient Peruvians who live out their lives untouched by the sweep and panoply of world history.* [Reviewed by Gordon C. Pollard, *AA* 78:381–382, 1976.]

Ancient Places (Hidden Places: Where History Lives Series) (1982) 30 min. University of Nebraska (PR). Dist: Nebraska Television Network, University of Nebraska, Lincoln, NE 68588; (402) 472-2007 FR$40, VR$30, FS$450, VS$180. *"The film's contextual framework is accurate and reflects current trends in rock art research, and the ugent need to preserve rock art through energetic enforcement of existing laws is clearly stated."* [From the review by Jo Ane Van Tilburg, *ARCH* 38(2):73–80, 1985.]

Ancient Projectile Points 28 min. Earl H. Swanson (DI), Idaho State University Museum (PR), Don E. Crabtree (AN). Dist: IMI FS$355, FR$30. *Focuses on pressure flaking, a technique for detaching flakes by the use of a pointed object pressed against an edge. The film shows techniques for making 8,000- to 10,000-year-old projectile points in North America. The notching of small, late prehistoric projectile points is part of this study of pressure flaking methods. Slow-motion film shows the technique of parallel pressure flaking. These films are primarily for classroom use and come with teachers' guides.* [Reviewed by Anthony E. Marks, *AA* 77:914–915, 1975. Susanna R. Katz and Paul R. Katz, *ARCH* 34(1):60, 1981.]

THE ANCIENT ROMANS SERIES (1985) Joop Kampman (DI), Amedeo T. Zammarano (PR). Dist: EMI FR$75, FS$750, VS$590. *"This series of films, produced in the Netherlands several years ago, has recently been released in the US with an English soundtrack. None of the three films is profound, but they are well made and interesting. All were shot on location, but evidently with little cooperation from the local authorities, since tourists wander through sites and sometimes even mug for the camera. No experts appear on camera; there is only a simple, informative narration with some background music."* [From the review by Peter S. Allen, *ARCH* 41(4):69, 1988.]

• **Builders of an Empire** 14 min. FR$30, FS$295, VS$235. *Gives a sense of the extent of the Roman domain as well as some idea of the means by which it was acquired and maintained.*

- **An Urban Lifestyle** 2 min. FR$25, FS$255, VS$195. *Captures some of the flavor of Roman city life by touring Hadrian's villa and the ruins of Pompeii.*
- **People of Leisure** 13 min. FR$30, FS$275, VS$220. *Various ways the Romans amused themselves are examined.*

Ancient Sardis (1967) 30 min. Charles Lyman (FM), George M. A. Hanfman (CON). Dist: VQ. [Reviewed by James R. Wiseman, *AA* 78:125, 1976.]

And So They Live (1940) 24 min. John Ferno and Julian Roffman (DI, WR). Dist: MOMA FR$20.

ANDEAN ETHNOMEDICINE: BIRTH AND CHILDHOOD ILLNESS IN SIX ECUADORIAN COMMUNITIES Lauris McKee (DI), Archaeological Museum of the Central Bank of Ecuador (PR). Dist: Department of Anthropology, Franklin and Marshall College, Lancaster, PA 17604-3003. [Series reviewed by Stephen D. Glazier, *AA* 89:776–778, 1987.]

- **Evil Wind, Evil Air (Mal viento, mal aire, pasmo)** (1985) 22 min. Dist: PSU VR$18, VS$200. *"The viewer learns the origins and symptomatology of illnesses believed to be caused by Evil Air as well as traditional strategies for protecting children against its effects."* [From the review by Stephen D. Glazier.] See additional description under title.
- **Diagnosticos (Diagnoses)** (1984) 20 min. *"Deals primarily with childhood ailments."* [From the review by Stephen D. Glazier.]
- **El ojeado (The Evil Eye)** (1984) 18 min. *"Opens with an ominous-looking old man watching a baby. The old man, the narrator explains, may not intend to give the evil eye, but cannot help it because he likes the way the baby looks. It is believed that the old man had given the child high fever and a bad stomach."* [From the review by Stephen D. Glazier.]
- **Embarazo, parto y puerperio (Pregnancy, Birth and the Post-Partum Period)** (1984) 25 min. *"Deals with the customs and beliefs pertaining to reproduction, with special attention to sex differences believed to be characteristic of fetal ontogeny."* [From the review by Stephen D. Glazier.]
- **El espanto (Magical Fright)** (1984) 19 min. *"The narrator explains that children become spooked when their hearts pump hard or they have an excess of 'nerves.' Curers and mothers discuss many possible causes for this ailment.... In all cases, the treatment is water."* [From the review by Stephen D. Glazier.]

Angano. . . Angano. . . Tales From Madagascar (1989) 64 min. Marie-Clemence Blanc-Paes (PR), Cesar Paes (DI). Dist: CN FR$95, FS$295. *Contemporary storytellers recount for the camera and their listeners the founding myths of Malagasy culture—the creation of man and woman, the origin of rice cultivation, the reason for animal sacrifice. The filmmakers do not dramatize or animate these stories; rather they document storytelling itself placing it in its specific social context. The tales flow into and out of stunning shots of the Malagasy life that gave them birth and which they, in turn, explain—storms, brush fires, herding, the unique practice of exhuming or "turning the dead." First, the myth about the creation of man is recounted. In this myth, man is made through a collaboration of the Earth and the Sky gods. When man dies, they quarrel over his remains, until they strike a compromise; man's body will stay on earth, but his spirit will rise to the sky. Humans are "caught in between"—between birth and death, nature and culture, chaos and meaning. In Malagasy and French with English subtitles.*

Angels of War: World War II in Papua New Guinea 54 min. Andrew Pike, Hank Nelson, and Gavan Daws (FM). Dist: FL FR$80, VR$80, FS$800, VS$650. *Within a decade after the people of Papua New Guinea were first introduced to the 20th century, they found themselves in the middle of a modern war. Americans, Australians, and Japanese stormed across their island. As native people, the Papuans were abused by the invaders, even by their allies, the Australians. The Papuan tradition of storytelling is evident in their vivid recollections of those bloody days. Their stories are intercut with fascinating visuals from the period—newsreel footage, propaganda films, and feature films from Japan, Australia, and the United States.*

Angkor—The Lost City (1965) 10 min. Dist: PSU FR$8. *View of ancient civilization of Cambodia and its art forms, with accompanying musical score; focuses on famous city of Angkor. Stone relief and sculpture in the Temple of Buddha depict citizens' warlike and religious preoccupations, as well as the sacking of a city. The Temple represents a "monument to the grandeur and frailty of civilization."* [Reviewed by Bennet Bronson, *AA* 78:140, 1976.]

Anglo-Saxon England (1971) 22 min. Dist: PSU FR$13.50. *English history from the end of Roman rule to the Norman invasion. Raids and migrations that changed the face of England. Recent excavations at Cadbury, West Stow, and Winchester. Growth of monasteries. Use of archaeological and historical sources to document history of England, especially the connections between it and other parts of Europe during an intensive formative period.*

Angola Is Our Country (1988) 45 min. Jenny Morgan (DI) in cooperation with Organization of Angolan Women. Dist: WMM VR$75, VS$225. *Angolan women are rarely heard describing from their own experience the impact of racist South Africa's 12-year undeclared war against their country. This documentary, filmed with an Angolan TV crew, offers a rare glimpse of a country that emerged from 14 years of armed struggle against Portuguese colonialism to find itself face to face with the South African army. The tape focuses in particular on the contributions women are making to the reconstruction of Angola, and on the problems and successes of women's other war—against the double legacy of colonialism and machismo.*

Angotee 31 min. National Film Board of Canada (PR). Dist: IFB FR$35, FS$525, VS$385; UCEMC FR$21; PSU (PCR) order # 919.8-2, FR$6.90. *Beginning with a scene in an igloo showing the birth of Angotee to Attootoo, wife of the hunter Koonuk, this is an account of an Eskimo's life from infancy to maturity. During infancy, Angotee is secure in the protection of his mother. His childhood is free as he plays games invented out of the skills he will need as a man. During adolescence, he accompanies his father on the hunt* *and enters the company of men, when he shoots his first seal. This classic story ends as Angotee leaves the parental igloo to set up his own abode as a family man and a hunter of the great snow-swept barrens.*

Animal War—Animal Peace (1968) 28 min. McGraw-Hill Text-Films (PR). Dist: PSU order # 31434, FR$ 17.50.

Animals in Amboseli (see Baboon Social Structure Series)

Anklung Orchestra and Indonesian Dance Class (1963) 5 min. (A Folklore Research Film by Peter and Toshi Seeger.) Dist: FIM/RF FR$10, FS$60. *An anklung orchestra in an Indonesian public high school performing music reminiscent of that produced by Swiss bellringers, followed by a dancing class in which several charming young Indonesian girls practice their traditional dances to a musical accompaniment.*

The Annanacks (1962) 60 min. Crawley Films Ltd. (PR) for the Canadian Broadcasting Corporation. Dist: NFBC. *It deals in a sociological manner with the history of a group of Eskimos who have been living in and around the George River District on Hudson's Straits, and with the founding of an Eskimo Cooperative, and in an entertaining and amusing manner, shows the reactions of three Eskimos who come south to Montreal and Ottawa to see how the white men live.*

"Annapurna Mahila Mandal": An Experience in Grassroots Development for Women 12 min. Sakuntala Narasimhan (PR). Dist: UWC VS$25, order #2315. *Short video narrated and produced by an Indian journalist details ways a successful women's cooperative works for the benefit of its Bombay members. How they go about getting start-up money. Excellent example of ways ordinary women can be empowered to improve their lives and lives of their families.*

Annie Mae: Brave Hearted Woman (1989) 79 min. Lan Brooks Ritz (PR). Dist: Brown Bird Productions, 1971 North Curson Avenue, Hollywood, CA 90046; (213) 851-8928 FR$150, FS$1090. *The life of Annie Mae Aquash, a Micmac activist with the American Indian Movement.* [Reviewed by Jean S. Forward, *AA* 93(4):1034–1035, 1991.]

Annual Festival of the Dead (see African Village Life Series)

Anselmo (1967) 4 min. Chick Strand (FM), La Banda Aguascalientes (MU). Dist: CCC. *An experimental documentary in the sense that it is a symbolic reenactment of a real event. "I asked a Mexican Indian friend what he would like most in the world. His answer was 'A double E flat tuba'. I thought it would be easy to find one at the Goodwill very cheap. This was not so, but a sympathetic man in a music store found a cheap, but beautiful brass wraparound tuba. I bought it, smuggled it into Mexico and gave it to my friend in the desert." This film is a poetic interpretation of this event in celebration of wishes and tubas.*

Anselmo and the Women (1986) 35 min. Dist: CCC. *This film is about the life of a Mexican street musician struggling to make a good life for his children. This film focuses on his relationship with his wife Adela and his mistress, Cruz, and theirs with him. In a society where traditional gender roles are separate and sharply defined, the number of children define male identity and keep the women at home and dependent. Poverty makes daily survival a desperate struggle. Both men and women must cooperate, the men to provide food and shelter and the women to raise and care for the large family. However, the cooperation is often superficial, with very little communication in terms of inner emotional needs. Relationships become economic in essence in which both men and women perceive themselves living in an emotional desert. The film is about life in conflict from three points of view as told by the people involved. It explores the division between the real and the ideal.*

The Anthropologist (1992) 50 min. Andrea Gschwendtner (FM). Dist: Andrea Gschwendtner, Esebeckstrasse 17, 80639 Munich, Germany; 89-157-12-45. *This film weaves drama and documentary to raise questions about the use and misuse of anthropological research. When World War II broke out, Rudolph Poch, the first anthropologist of Vienna, continued his studies in the Austro-Hungarian POW camps. The anthropological studies became part of the materials used during the eugenics movement.*

Anthropologists at Work: Careers Making a Difference (1993) Gheri Arnold (PR, DI), Joanne Walker-Ewald (WR). Dist: AAA VS$25 (students, NAPA members), $30 (non-NAPA members, professionals), $35 (organizations, institutions). *This video depicts the diversity of anthropological careers today in the public, private, and nonprofit sphere in all four subfields of anthropology. The concluding section focuses on the specialized skills and knowledge anthropologists need and the personal rewards and social impacts of a career in anthropology.*

Anthropology on Trial Dist: UTA-FL VR$11, order #VCC-1388. *Bias and relativity in Margaret Mead's traditional Western anthropology.* [Reviewed by Robert D. Evans, *SBF* 20:311, 1985.]

Anufom Series Emile van Rouveroy van Nieuwaal (DI, CA), Els van Rouveroy van Nieuwaal (WR), Robert Warning (ED). Dist: Foundation for Film and Science, Documentation Centre, Hengeveldstraat 29, UTRECHT, The Netherlands. *Social documentary films about the Anufom in Togo (West Africa).* Available in Dutch, English, or French versions.

• **Mbambim, A Lineage Head in Ayikpere, North Togo** 23 min. *Filmed portrait of a head of a patrilineage, comprising about 80 people, in a small Anufo village in North Togo. Mbambim's character of an unassuming, timid person, who shrinks from exercising authority over the members of his family, does not fit the role of lineage head, forced upon him as being the eldest man of the lineage. After the death of his first wife, he is unable to cope with problems presented by the behavior of his children, a junior wife, and several kinsmen whose quarrels threaten to disrupt the family. Analysis of his situation by a diviner and an ensuing ceremony performed by the lineage as a whole, help to reestab-*

lish Mbambim's position and to stress the unity of his lineage once more.

- **Muslims in Mango, North Togo** 35 min. *This film deals with some aspects of Islam in N'zara, the capital of the Anufom in North Togo. Some of the items treated are: the migration of the Anufom from Ano in Ivory Coast to Northern Togo at the end of the 18th century, teaching the Quran at schools, divination and preparation of amulets and the mourning prayers; the Friday prayer has been attended in- and outside the mosque in the men's and women's section.*

- **Sherea, Dispute Settlement at the Court of the Paramount Chief in N'zara, North Togo** 23 min. *The Paramount Chief is the highest traditional authority of Anufom society. Settlement of disputes is one of the main tasks of the Chief. He hears and judges cases together with ward heads of N'zara and some lineage heads of important lineages. This film shows a settlement of a dispute between a man and his wife. The husband, a poor fisherman, accuses his wife of having a love affair with a driver working for the post services. The woman, however, reproaches her husband that he cannot maintain her properly. The driver denies everything and asks the Court: "What must I, husband of four wives, do with the wife of another?" This is a lie. The Court knows this all too well, but since some of them—including the Paramount Chief himself—are closely related to the driver, this fact is disguised. After a severe drubbing, the Court tries everything possible to effect a reconciliation between the fisherman and his wife. A lasting reconciliation, however, seems rather doubtful when the woman suddenly shouts: "Ask my husband by whom I am pregnant!"*

- **A Toad in the Courtyard** (1979) 25 min. *The unhappy position of a Chief in a West African society (the Anufom in northern Togo), being a servant of two masters: the central government and his own tribal community.* Relevant anthropological literature: J. F. Holleman, *Chief Council and Commissioner.* Assen, Holland, 1969. E. A. B. van Rouveroy van Nieuwaal, "Chieftancy in Northern Togo." In: *Verfassung und Recht,* 2 quartal, 1980, p. 115.

- **Bekoidintu—Any House Is Better Than Mine** (1980) 32 min. *Kolani, an old lineage head, is engaged in a bitter conflict about his third and youngest wife. She has run away to her lover, while leaving her son Bekoidintu with her husband. He cannot properly bring up the child, and in any case, he views the bringing up of young children, especially in their first few years, as a mother's job. Nor are his other two wives in any position to care for or bring the child up. An implicit, but important factor in Kolani's wish to have his wife back, is his age: he is now rather old, and his health is failing. He is not likely to live much longer, and the norms of Kolani's society permit a widow to remarry only after the funeral ceremonies for her deceased husband have been completed. Such ceremonies are often rather costly, and a prospective new husband is required to pay a part of these expenses. Since Kolani's runaway wife is still young, it is almost certain that she will remarry soon after his death. This makes it very important to Kolani that she return to him, because his funeral ceremonies will then take place soon after his death, and his soul will be able to rest in peace in its rightful place among his ancestors. The film also raises questions about the value of the local judiciary: is it in many instances competent to deal adequately with the severed relations between parties—that is to say, in accordance with the wishes and desires of all those concerned, and in this case, to repair the broken marriage relationship? This question is important, because the problem is not limited to the effectiveness of the judiciary of a small tribe in north Togo alone, it is also an issue in industrialized societies, where many of the relationships between people are no longer "face to face."* Literature: E. A. B. van Rouveroy van Nieuwaal and E. A. van Rouveroy van Nieuwaal Baerends, "To Claim or Not to Claim, Changing Views about the Restitution of Marital Payments among the Anufom, North Togo." In: *African Law Studies,* 1975, no. 12, pp. 98–118, or in: *New Directions in Family Law in Africa,* S. A. Roberts, ed. 1977, Mouton, the Hague. From the same authors: *Ti Anufo, un coup d'oeil sur la societe des Anufom au Nord-Togo,* 1976.

- **In Search of Justice** (1981) 52 min. *Film about the sociolegal position of the women in the rapidly changing society of the Anufom in the north of Togo. Influences from outside support the women in their opposition against the system of exchange of women between different (patri)lineages. In her search for the most acceptable settlement, she uses the traditional chief, as well as his modern counterpart, the justice of the peace. But both judicial authorities have differing viewpoints concerning the exchange of women, divorce, and the restitution of marriage prestations. These differences may be attributable to their different cultural backgrounds, their educations, and the positions of the justice of the peace and the traditional chief. The first represents "modern" and mostly western law (which in official and educated circles is also regarded as "progressive"), while the chiefs represent traditional rules and values. There is a tension between both judiciary, the chieftancy, and the justice of the peace, and they are more or less competitive with each other. Since both are available to men and women who are looking for a favorable disposition of their disputes, there is an excellent opportunity for many a litigant, especially for the women, to pay off these institutions against each other.* Anthropological literature: E. A. B van Rouveroy van Nieuwaal, *A la recherche de la justice, quelques aspects du droit matrimonial et de la justice coutumiere chez les Anufom au Nord-Togo.* Leiden, 1977.

"Anything I Catch..." The Handfishing Story (1990) 27.30 min. Pat Mire, Charles Bush (FM). Dist: Attakapas Productions, P.O. Box 821, Eunice, LA 70535; (318) 457-8214 VS$150. *This program examines the thrilling regional phenomenon of Cajons who wade in murky bayou waters to catch huge catfish and turtles by reaching into hollow logs and stumps with their bare hands.*

Anything You Want to Be 3 min. Liane Brandon (FM). Dist: NDF. *Socialization of women in America.* [Reviewed by Louise Lamphere, *AA* 79:203, 1977.] See other films by Brandon.

Ao dai (The Tunic Dress) (1991) 13 min. Le Trac (DI). Dist: FRIF VR$35, VS$160. *Examines the traditional Vietnamese tunic dress, looking at its social role through the eyes* *of a teenage schoolgirl who helps her mother sell vegetables in Ben Thanh market during the holidays.*

Aparajito (The Unvanquished) (from the Apu Trilogy) (1958) 108 min. Satyajit Ray (WR, DI), Ravi Shankar (MU). Dist: AB FR$85. *Life in Benares.* Suggested supplement: Robin Wood, *The Apu Trilogy.* Praeger, 1971 (Praeger Film Library paper).

Apartheid (1992) 120 min. Jean-Michel Meurice and Loelle Chesselet (DI). Dist: Doxa Productions, 10 Camp Street, Gardens, Cape Town; (021) 246791. *The unbanning of political organizations and the release of Nelson Mandela saw the ending of an era in South African history. It was at this time that this program was produced. It takes us from the emergence of the apartheid ideology through to the referendum in March 1992. The result is a visual history pieced together from archive material, much of which has never been seen by South Africans.*

Ape Vocalization: From Conditioned Response to Symbol 96 min. Dist: PSU VR$14.50, VS$160, order #90229. *Documents research conducted in the nature of language acquisition through the study of symbolic and syntactical skills in Chimpanzees.*

Apemen of Africa (1972) 20 min. E. G. Marshall (NA). Dist: FI FR$19, FS$260. *Adapted from the MGM Documentary Television Special "The Man Hunters." Australopithecines and the contention surrounding man's ancestry is explored. The film further discusses the Taung child, the public's initial reactions, and later reactions.*

Apes of Barbary (1978) 30 min. Dist: PSU FR$17. *A general description of the social behavior and ecology of Barbary macaques living in the Middle Atlas Mountains of Morocco. The view is led through a yearly cycle starting with autumn (the mating season), through a snowing winter, to spring and summer (the birth and infant-rearing seasons). Well filmed, clearly narrated.* [Reviewed by David Agee Horr, *AA* 75:2006, 1973.]

Appalachian Genesis (1971) 29 min. Bill Richardson, Dave Adams, and Ben Zickafoose (FM). Dist: APPAL FR$45, FS$425. *This film presents a sampling of the issues facing young Appalachians in the early seventies: coal mining, the educational system, job opportunities, health facilities, and politics.*

The Appalshop Show (1977) 90 min. Bill Richardson and Herb E. Smith (FM). Dist: APPAL FR$135, FS$1350. *Excerpts of 12 Appalshop films are compiled into a story of the rich culture and social issues of the Appalachian Region. Includes a look at the unique film workshop and art center. A PBS special for the Documentary Showcase series broadcast January 1977.*

Appeals to Santiago (1969) 28 min. Arnold Baskin (Dl), Carter Wilson (WR), Duane Metzger and Robert Ravicz (AN). Dist: UCEMC FR$45, VS$195. *The film documents an eight-day Maya Indian festival in Chiapas, Mexico. Follows two men as they perform their expensive and exhausting duties (called cargo ceremonies) for one of the town's patron saints. In contrast to Cancian's economic analysis of a similar, neighboring institution, this film presents the native view of the events.* [Reviewed by John Collier, Jr., *AA* 70:1050–1051, 1968.] Suggested supplement: Frank Cancian, *Economics and Prestige in a Maya Community: The Religious Cargo System in Zinacantan.* Stanford, 1965.

Applied Geoarchaeology (1989) 20 min. Chuck Pratt and Brooks Ellwood (PR). Dist: Center for Geoarchaeological Studies, Box 19049, The University of Texas at Arlington, Arlington, TX VS$55. *This film "is aimed at developers, real estate brokers, and those in the general public who are afraid that archaeological surveys and salvage operations, mandated by federal and state laws, will slow down and disrupt their projects."* [From the review by Peter S. Allen, *ARCH* 46(2):70, 1993.] Study guide and set of overheads for classroom use available.

An Appointment with the Astrologer: Personal Consultants in Hindu Society (1985) 40 min. Paul Kuepferle (WR, PR), David Thompson (DI), Edward Bastian and Joseph Elder (EP). Dist: UW-SAAS FR$30, FS$295. *This film shows four highly regarded astrologers in Varanasi (Banaras) practicing a discipline in which they have all received extensive academic training. The film also presents some of the people who come to these astrologers for personal consultations: a woman whose husband has been missing for over a year, an actor confronting a major lawsuit, a young woman whose marriage arrangements have been broken off three times because of her horoscope, the Maharaja of Banaras who needs to know auspicious times to sign important documents, a politician trying to determine whether or not to stand in a forthcoming election, a young man who wants a second opinion on his arranged marriage, and a rickshaw driver who wants to cure his suicide-prone son. Through observing the astrologers' responses to their clients' needs, one sees present-day applications of classical astrological training.*

The Arab Identity: Who Are the Arabs? (1975) 26 min. Dist: IUAVC FR$14. *Documents a pilgrimage to Mecca by millions of Arabs from all over the Middle East and Africa to emphasize the pervasiveness of Islam in their lives. Shows the variety of Arab peoples, diverse in both ethnic characteristics and in the degree of modernization and Westernization. Discusses the political conflicts that have developed between Arab nations and with other non-Arab countries.*

The Arab Jews (1976) 28 min. Mark Dolgoy (Dl), Verite Film Productions (PR). Dist: PFI FR$40, FS$395. *About the Jewish refugees from Moslem Arab countries. The Arab Jews have never been "visible refugees," but have instead been absorbed into their new homelands, obscuring their problems, and leaving their story unnoticed. Jewish refugees from Moslem Arab countries make up the majority of the population of the State of Israel. This film is an attempt to document at least a part of the long history of these people and to bring their story to the world.*

Arabbin' with the Hucksters of Baltimore 25 min. Jay Kent (FM). Dist: Brainstorm Films, 2 Central Green, Winchester, MA 10890 FR$35. *For centuries, tinkers, tradesmen, and travelers used horse-drawn wagons to hawk their* *wares up and down the cities' streets. At a certain time each day, the neighborhood could expect the rolling shopkeeper. Scarcely two generations have passed since the iceman, milkman, and fishmonger hauled their goods with one horsepower. Now in only one American city is this horse-drawn entrepreneur a common sight. The street hucksters of Baltimore are called Arabbers. Each with a distinctive holler, each with an independent spirit, "AY-rabbers" carry on a tradition passed from generation to generation.* [Reviewed by Charles Camp, *JAF* 92(364):255–257, 1979.]

Arabic X-Ray Film (1962) 15 min. Haskins Lab (PR). Dist: PSU Ser. Chg. $5.50. *Standard colloquial Damascan, the ordinary conversational speech of educated male Muslims, is used. Material selected to illustrate contrast between plain and "emphatic" or pharyngealized consonant positions, as far as possible by means of minimal pairs. X-ray techniques show the articulatory process and acoustic output of native speakers. Prepared scripts consisting mainly of short, meaningful utterances illustrate selected phonetic features. Informants were chosen for linguistic suitability and lack of physical characteristics that might interfere with X-ray quality.*

Araucanians of Ruca Choroy (1974) 50 min. Jorge Preloran (PR, Dl). Dist: PFI FR$55, FS$650. *Jorge Preloran documents a man's memoirs of his parents' settling in Argentina, and his own life in their valley of Ruca Choroy. Reminiscent of our own history, old photos comment on the Araucanian Indians' flight through the Andes from the Spaniards. After the fighting was over, they returned to learn to say "yes sir" and "no sir," and the peace was preserved. We explore the modern-day life of their descendants in the Ruca Choroy valley, a life of poverty, shepherding, baking, sowing, dancing, and exquisite weaving. We listen to the unrehearsed dialogue among the villagers on their hopes, destiny, death, myths, complaints, and questions. Throughout we witness the extraordinary landscape in its seasons. An unproductive terrain to man, yet its variety of vista and texture and the intensity of its colors are unbelievable.* [Reviewed by Gertrude Dole, *AA* 75:594, 1973.]

Archaeological Dating: Retracing Time (1976) 18 min. Dist: EBEC; UCEMC FR$23. *Examines a number of dating methods used to study past civilizations, including pottery typology, stratigraphy, tree-ring dating (dendrochronology), archaeomagnetic dating, obsidian hydration dating, and radiocarbon dating.*

The Archaeological History of the British Isles (1982) Janice B. Klein (FM). Dist: RLI FS$39.95. *"This set of three filmstrips (Part 1: 27 minutes, Part 2: 30 minutes, Part 3: 27 minutes) presents a survey of British archaeology from the earliest evidence of human occupation around 250,000 years ago to the Norman Invasion of A.D. 1066."* [From the review by Peter S. Wells, *ARCH* 36(5):64, 1983.]

ARCHAEOLOGICAL SLIDE SETS: AEGEAN SERIES Dist: POR. See reviews in *ARCH* 39(5):69–80, 1986.

• **Delphi** Set of 60 slides, $90. Photographs and text by Karelisa V. Hartigan.

• **Hagia Triada** Set of 61 slides, $93. Photographs, text, and introduction by Joan Aruz.

• **Knossos** Set of 89 slides, $120. Text and photographs by Karelisa V. Hartigan.

• **Mycenae** Set of 59 slides, $120. Text and photographs by Karelisa V. Hartigan.

• **Phaistos** Set of 69 slides, $100. Photographs and text by Joan Aruz.

Archaeologial Slide Sets: Mesoamerican Survey I Dist: POR. Set of 100 slides, $140. See review by Diane Z. Chase and Arlen F. Chase, *ARCH* 40(3):67–68, 1987.

ARCHAEOLOGICAL SLIDE SETS: MEXICAN SERIES Dist: POR. See review by Diane Z. Chase and Arlen F. Chase, *ARCH* 40(3):67–68, 1987.

• **The Aztecs** Set of 68 slides, $97.

• **Monte Alban** Set of 79 slides, $109.

• **The Olmecs** Set of 75 slides, $105.

• **El Tajin** Set of 76 slides, $106.

• **Teotihuacan** Set of 96 slides, $139.

• **Tula** Set of 60 slides, $88.

• **Xochicalco** Set of 50 slides, $77.

ARCHAEOLOGICAL SLIDE SETS: NEAR EASTERN SERIES Dist: POR. See reviews in *ARCH* 39(5):68–69, 1986.

• **Hazor** Set of 90 slides, $125.

• **Jerash** Set of 71 slides, $100. Introduction and annotations by Jerome Schaefer.

• **Jericho I** Set of 56 slides, $80.

• **The Mosaics of Jordan** Set of 84 slides, $114. Text and most photographs by Bastiaan Van Elderen.

• **Pella of the Decapolis** Set of 72 slides, $102. Photographs and text by Robert H. Smith.

• **Petra** Set of 85 slides, $130. Introduction and annotations by Philip C. Hammond.

• **Tel Dan** Set of 80 slides, $115. Text and some photographs by Avraham Biran.

ARCHAEOLOGICAL SLIDE SETS: NORTH AMERICAN SERIES Dist: POR. See reviews in *ARCH* 39(4):70–73, 1986.

• **The Art of the Taino** Set of 55 slides, $85.

• **Canyon de Chelly** Set of 78 slides, $110. Introduction and annotations by Don Morris.

• **Chaco Canyon** Set of 65 slides, $93.

• **Early Caddoan Cultures** Set of 78 slides, $108. Annotations and introduction by Clarence H. Webb.

• **Fort Center** Set of 50 slides, $85. Annotations and introduction by Jerald T. Milanich and Donna Ruhl.

• **Gulf of Georgia** Set of 80 slides, $105. Introduction and annotations by Donald F. Mitchell.

• **Koster** Set of 77 slides, $104. Annotations and introduction by Thomas Genn Cook and Michael D. Wiant.

- **Late Caddoan Cultures** Set of 70 slides, $100. Annotations and introduction by Frank F. Schambach and Ann M. Early.
- **Marksville** Set of 64 slides, $90. Text and photographs by Alan Toth.
- **Mesa Verde** Set of 86 slides, $120.
- **The Mississippian Cultures** Set of 85 slides, $134.
- **Native American Rock Art** Set of 52 slides, $82. Text and photographs by Deborah Marcus and John Noxon.
- **Ohio Mounds** Set of 68 slides, $97.
- **Ozette** Set of 58 slides, $82. Text and photographs by Deborah Marcus and John Noxon.
- **Poverty Point** Set of 63 slides, $95. Annotations and introduction by Clarence H. Webb.
- **Spiro Mounds** Set of 80 slides, $115. Introduction and annotations by Don G. Wyckoff.
- **Stone Sculpture of the Fraser River** Set of 50 slides, $80. Introduction and annotations by Donald H. Mitchell.
- **Weeden Island Culture** Set of 70 slides, $100. Annotations, introduction, and most photographs by Jerald T. Milanich and Donna Ruhl.

Archeologie en laboratoire 26 min. Dist: Pitt. Demonstrates the degree of interaction among the ancillary sciences, both biological and physical, on which archaeological investigation is dependent. The paleoenvironment of Nice, France, is reconstructed by utilizing lithic artifacts and occupational debitage recovered from the excavation. A superficial explanation of the theories and mechanics concerning these methods accompany the visual presentation.

The Archaeologist and How He Works 19 min. International Film Bureau (PR). Dist: IFB FR$19.75, FS$275, VS$210; UCEMC order # 7048. *The painstaking and complex field of archaeology is outlined in this documentary, which observes the planning and carrying out of an expedition to the Middle East by an American university. Concentrating on the discipline of archaeology and its methodology, rather than upon the importance of this particular excavation and its findings, the film shows the full development of the expedition from the inception of its preplanning research to the final postexpedition division of its findings for further study in the university museum. Arriving in the selected area, the scientists make a preliminary survey with student workers, collecting and labeling surface artifacts and mapping the finds. Senior archaeologists analyze this information in choosing the excavation site. A tent village is set up, and equipment, supplies, and provisions are brought in to support the staff and local workers. Since it is presumed that the site—an early agrarian settlement in the Tigris and Euphrates Valley—is one of the world's first settled communities, life scientists (both agronomists and zoologists) are important members of the expedition, for their findings will complement the work of the surveyors and archaeologists. Their work confirms that the valley's rich, arable land could have sustained ancient grain and barley and that animals could have grazed on nearby hills. They collect grain specimens and modern animal bones to compare with similar finds from the excavation. This general overview of how the archaeologist works uses as its illustration the Joint Prehistoric Project of the Department of Prehistory, Istanbul University, and the Oriental Institute, University of Chicago.* [Reviewed by Thomas Wight Beale, *AA* 78:135, 1976.]

Archaeologists at Work (1962) 14 min. Dist: IUAVC FR$7.75. *Describes the work of a group of archaeologists as they study the remnants of an ancient people who once lived in southwestern United States. Describes the careful, systematic practices involved in sifting materials, labeling, making plaster casts, and testing methods. Tree-ring and carbon-14 dating methods are illustrated. Shows that the fragments of knowledge that are gathered are eventually assembled to give an increased understanding of past cultures.* [Reviewed by Thomas R. Hester, *AA* 77:909, 1975.]

Archaeology 14 min. A. Brozowski (Dl), Educational Film Studio, Lodz (PR). Dist: CRM/MH FR$10.50, FS$500. *A fiction film of an archaeological excavation at a site that is finally revealed to be Auschwitz.* [Reviewed by Thomas Wight Beale, *AA* 77:898–899, 1975.]

Archaeology Field School (1975) 28 min. Stephen Church (PR, Dl). Dist: Dept. of Anthropology, University of Minnesota, Minneapolis, MN 55455. FR$20, FS$250.

Archaeology: Furnace Brook Site (1967) 19 min. Robert E. Burdick (PR). Dist: SU FR$9 *The 1966 excavation of the Furnace Brook site, an Onondaga Indian settlement near Syracuse, New York.* [Reviewed by Thomas Wight Beale, *AA* 77:906–907, 1975.]

Archaeology in Mesopotamia 16 min. Dist: EDC FR$20, FS$220, VS$200; PSU (PCR) order #20673, FR$6.40. *The significance of the tells or mounds in Mesopotamia; how the mounds were formed and what they revealed when opened by archaeologists.*

Archaeology in the Laboratory (1969) 27 min. Dist: FACSEA FR$16. [Reviewed by Harvey M. Bricker, *AA* 75:598, 1973.]

Archaeology of the Grand French Battery, Yorktown, Virginia (1977) 16 min. Dist: UCEMC FR$27, FS$230, VS$160. *Records the excavation and reconstruction of two key fortifications occupied in 1781 by America's French allies at the Yorktown battlefield, site of the culminating military engagement of the American Revolution. Shows and explains in detail the stages and procedures in the excavation.*

Archaeology: Pursuit of Man's Past 15 min. Thomas Stanton (PR), James N. Hill (AN). Dist: Stanton Films. *A UCLA excavation of a late prehistoric Chumash site in Ventura County, California.* [Reviewed by Dan D. Fowler, *AA* 74:904, 1975.]

Archaeology: Questioning the Past 25 min. Prof. Betty Goerke (PR). Dist: UCEMC VR$40, VS$250, order #37880. *The film is meant for students of introductory-level archaeology classes. It starts in a classroom with a review of the preparation that students need before they go out on a dig. It includes two sequences of digging, one at an ancient Indian site in northern California and the other at Sand*

Canyon, an Anasazi Pueblo site administered by the Crow Canyon Archaeological Center in Colorado. Students are shown digging, screening, discovering artifacts, and exposing wooden beams, and doing experimental archaeology and flotation. Scenes shift between the classroom, the field, and the laboratory, providing a sense of the full range of archaeological inquiry. Lab scenes include washing and sorting pot sherds, sorting and measuring chipped and ground stone, analysis of shell and bone and obsidian hydration. Of special interest are sequences showing students excavating at the Sand Canyon site. The students speak freely on camera, relating their experiences and commenting on their discoveries. [Reviewed by Peter S. Allen, ARCH 42(5):74, 1989.]

ARCHAEOLOGY SERIES (1992) 22 min. each. Tom Naughton and Nicolas Valcour (PR). Dist: FHS VR$75, VS$149. *This 13-part series has "no unifying theme, no geographical or chronological focus. Nor is there much 'dirt' archaeology. Instead, each episode focuses on a specific issue that has some relevance to archaeology. . . . At one level, this could be characterized as 'sound-byte' archaeology in that the images are often brief and fleeting and there is rarely enough time to do full justice to the issues involved. Nonetheless, there is much valuable material here."* [From the review by Peter S. Allen, ARCH 46(4):67, 1993.]

Archaeology Synthesis (Les temps retrouvés) (1969) 52 min. Dist: FACSEA FR$16.

Architectes atorou (The Architects of Atorou) (1971) 35 min. Jean Rouch (DI), Centre National de la Recherche Scientifique, Comité du Film Ethnographique (PR). Dist: CFE; DER. *For several years, the young people of these villages have constructed a new habitat on the island, appealing to mutual aid; they utilize ancient techiques of "banco" masonry and waterproof coatings, while they are inspired by the architecture of the modern cites.*

The Arctic Exiles 14 min. Dist: CBC VS$69, order #Y8G-8902. *Members of an Inuit band living in Grise Fjord in the high Arctic return to their ancestral home on Hudson's Bay after an absence of 30 years. Although their return was promised when they were taken to Grise Fjord as part of a government experiment, the members of the band make their own way home.*

Arrow to the Sun: A Pueblo Indian Tale 15 min. Gerald McDermott (DI), Charles Hofmann (CON). Dist: Texture Films, Inc., 43 W 16th St., New York, NY 10011. *Animated myth.* [Reviewed by Arthur Einhorn, AA 77:698, 1975.]

Art of Indonesia: Tales from the Shadow World 28 min. Dist: ULFVC VS$29.95, order #SO4385. *Shot on location in Java and Bali, uses exotic landscapes, sculpture, painted scrolls, shadow puppet theatre, architecture, combined with poetic narration incorporating Javanese poetry and other ancient texts. Alternates male and female voices and shows how literary, visual, and performing arts are all intimately interlinked with the basic religions of the area: Hinduism, Buddhism, and remnants of the ancient worship of ancestors. A coproduction of the National Gallery of Art and the Metropolitan Museum of Art.*

The Art of Living (Millennium: Tribal Wisdom and the Modern World Series) (1992) 1 hr. David Maybury-Lewis (H), Hans Zimmer (MU). Dist: PBS VS$49.95, order #MILL 105-RCDC. *While Western society relegates aesthetics to specialists, in tribal cultures, where they have no word for "art" or "artist," views of life and death are traditionally expressed in everyday dances, clothes, sculptures, and paintings. Travel to the Wodaabe tribe of Niger and the Dogon people of Mali to witness the ways they celebrate life and death with acts of beauty and grace. Meet a North American artist who shows us his way of connecting his art to the meaning of life and death.*

Artesanos Mexicanos (Mexico's Folk Artists) (1982) Judith Bronowski (FM). Dist: The Works, 1659 18th Street, Santa Monica, CA 90404; (213) 828-8643. [Series reviewed by John M. Schechter, AA 89:525–532, 1987.]

• **Pedro Linares, artesano cartonero (Papier-Mache Artist)** 22 min. FR$70, FS$425. *"Three generations of cartoneros live in a house near the central market of Mexico City . . . pursuing an art that counts but few remaining practitioners (papier mache)."* [From the review by John M. Schechter.]

• **Manuel Jimenez, artesano en Madera (Woodcarver)** (1977) 22 min. FR$70, FS$425. *"The woodcarving art is shared by the Mexican artist . . . Manuel Jimenez draws artistic inspiration from at least three sources elaborated in this film: his locale . . . religion . . . and his nation's history."* [From the review by John M. Schechter.]

• **Marcelo Ramos, artesano pirotecnico (The Firework Maker's Art)** (1979) 23 min. FR$70, FS$425. *"Marcelo Ramos prepares complex fireworks displays for festivals and fairs. The Ramos family lavish great effort in preparing fire castles."* [From the review by John M. Schechter.]

• **Sabina Sanchez, artesana bordadora (The Art of Embroidery)** (1976) 23 min. FR$70, FS$425. *"Filmed in November 1975, treats a now-deceased Zapotec embroiderer."* [From the review by John M. Schechter.]

Arusi ya Mariamu (The Marriage of Mariamu) 36 min. Nangayoma Ng'oge and Ron Mulvihill (DI), Juma Santos and Munyungo Darryl Jackson (MU). Dist: MF VS$100. *The film centers around the art and science of healing through traditional medicine and is set in contemporary Tanzania. Suffering from a serious illness, Mariamu and those close to her find themselves in conflict with their traditional values. Mariamu's health continues to deteriorate while under treatment at various hospitals. Her illness is complicated by her fear of traditional doctors, which stems from early childhood. Her fears and the hospital's failure to successfully treat her pose problems for her husband Sekondo. He realizes that there is no alternative but to take her to the healer. Through Mariumu's treatment, we discover the causes of her illness and follow her physical, psychological, and spiritual transformation. In Kiswahili, with versions subtitled in English or French.*

As Iwata Goes: Is Culture Local (1993) Hajima Ikela (DI), David W. Plath (WR), Jackson H. Bailey (AN). Dist: UILL-UC, order #9202. *A sketch of activities in two small towns in northeastern Honshu. Tono is nationally famous* for preserving local legends and turning them into a tourist attraction, "everybody's old home town." Towa, a few miles away, strives instead to create new traditions. The 20th century has not been kind to local cultures, and Japan is no exception. People in regional Japan want to have just as special a role in their country's international future as they have in preserving its parochial past. Bibliography: Jackson H. Bailey, *Ordinary People, Extraordinary Lives: Economic and Political Change in a Tohoku Village*. University of Hawaii Press, 1991. Kunie Yanagita, *The Legends of Tono*. Ronald A. Morse, transl. The Japan Foundation, 1975.

AS LONG AS THE RIVERS FLOW (1991) 59 min. James Cullingham and Peter Raymont (PR). Dist: FRIF VR$75, VS$390. *Each of the five documentaries that make up this series lend a unique insight into the epic struggle of Native people in Canada, historically, and in modern times, to regain control over their destinies. Three of the films' directors are Native people, and the series marks the first time that native filmmakers of their stature have collaborated to share visions of their culture.* See descriptions under the individual titles:

- **The Learning Path**
- **Time Immemorial**
- **Flooding Job's Garden**
- **Tikinagan**
- **Starting Fire with Gunpowder**

AS WOMEN SEE IT Faust Films (PR). Dist: WMM. *Most films we see in the United States about the third world are made my men. As Women See It is a rare look, through the women's eyes, at the way they see their own lives. In each, the particular concerns and problems women face are highlighted against the backdrop of everyday life.* See descriptions under the film titles:

- **Selbe: One among Many**
- **Permissible Dreams**
- **Sudesha**

Asante Market Women (Disappearing World Series) 52 min. Granada Television International (PR). Dist: FL VR$75, VS$445. *In the Asante tribe of Ghana, men are polygamous and women are subordinate in all domestic matters. But surprisingly, there is one arena where women reign—the market place. These tough, assertive women have evolved their own power structure. A head woman—the Queen mother—arbitrates all disputes over price and quality. Amidst the noise and color of the Kumasi central market, we perceive the intricacies of the matrilineal society.* [Reviewed by Winifred Lambrecht, *SBF* 19:163, 1984.]

ASCENT OF MAN (1975) 13 episodes, 52 min. each. BBC, Time-Life (PR), Adrian Malone (PR, DI), Jacob Bronowski (WR, AN). Dist: BBC. [Reviewed by Roy Wagner, *AA* 79:993–994, 1977.]

The Ashanti Kingdom 14 min. Dist: FHS VS$89.95, order #DH-3076. *The Ashanti are the best known tribe of Ghana, comprising around 2 million of country's 12 million inhabitants. All of the Ashanti kings, including Ivory Coast's president Felix Houphouet-Boigney, belong to the Oyoko-Dako clan, the clan of chieftains; they are the ones who have created and strengthened the Ashanti nation. This program shows the Ashanti kingdom: it explains the strict hierarchical organization of the village, the importance of the characteristic kente garment, the naming of children, the Ashanti religious beliefs, the importance of traditional values and traditional festivals, and the protocol surrounding the paramount chief of the Ashanti.*

Asian Heart 38 min. Kaerne Film (PR). Dist: FL VR$55, VS$350. *In a reaction against emancipated Western women, some European men are choosing young Asians as "mail order" brides. These women, they believe, will make more accommodating wives. The film follows Danish men as they meet and marry the Philippine girls of their fantasies. Their courtship has been entirely by mail. The human drama unfolds, by turns humorous and poignant. The girls, too, have their hopes and dreams, believing their marriages will lead them to a better life. Some of the marriages work and some don't, but once the woman takes the risk of marrying a foreigner, there is no return. She has no citizenship in her new land and can not return in her native country as a divorced woman.* [Reviewed by Carolyn FluehrLobban, *AA* 92:841–842, 1990.]

ASIAN INSIGHT SERIES (1988) Film Australia (PR). Dist: FIV. *This six-part series introduces the peoples and cultures of the Asian Pacific. Presenting a balanced, objective interpretation of the region's history, Asian Insight illuminates past and present social structures, mores, beliefs, art, and architecture to give viewers a well-rounded look at this newly influential area.* See descriptions under the film titles:

- **Japan**
- **Hong Kong/Singapore**
- **Indonesia**
- **Philippines**
- **Malaysia**
- **Thailand**

Asmat: Cannibal Craftsmen of New Guinea (ca. 1977) 60 min. William Leimbach, Jean-Pierre Dutilleux (FM), Peter VanArsdale (AN). Dist: Mac FR$55, S$600. *The Asmat—"people of the tree"—have ritualized revenge. A warrior killed in battle must be commemorated by an elaborate ceremony. A giant mangrove tree is felled and brought to the village, where the women make a ritual defense against the returning men and the tree. From the tree, a "Bis," or ancestor pole is carved in stylized effigy by skilled craftsmen who take six weeks to complete their work. Then warriors don their warpaint, go out and kill a warrior of the rival village, cut off his head, and eat him. Despite their ferocious makeup and ritualized violence, the Asmat appear as affable, amusing raconteurs. Master carver Agope, for example, explains persuasively the rationale for the revenge ritual, with its headhunting and cannibalism. The intimate daily routine of existence in the village of Otjenep is seen to center about the sago tree, from which they derive an edible pulp, twine for nets, roofing thatch, and basket fibers. Today, with their central ritual banned, the Asmat are left idle, falling* *prey to the tobacco and technology that Western civilization offers in return for the riches in mangrove wood and oil to be found in their ancestral swamps. The carvers' art, and the Asmat themselves, are under the threat of imminent cultural extinction. See also Matjemosh. Related readings: Michael Rockefeller, The Asmat of New Guinea. Adrain Gerbrands, ed. Museum of Primitive Art, New York, 1967. David Eyde, Cultural Correlates of Warfare among the Asmat of South Western New Guinea. University Microfilms, Ann Arbor, 1971. [Reviewed by Robert Mishler, SBF 15:172, 1979.]*

Aspects of Land Ownership and Land Use in the Rural Community of Montero Santa Cruz, Bolivia (1963) 20 min. The Land Tenure Center, University of Wisconsin (PR). Dist: UW. *The film footage was taken near Montero, a small city 40 miles north of Santa Cruz. Shows a new water system being installed through joint labor effort of soldiers and civilians. Discusses Bolivian colonization projects, especially programs to encourage highland Indians to resettle in the east. Discusses agrarian reform and visits the farm of a peasant who received land under the agrarian reform. Also shows changes on large landholdings as a result of the agrarian reforms. [Reviewed by John Murra, AA 69:792, 1967.] Cf. the film, Changes in Agriculture, Population, and Utilization of Resources.*

Aspects of Land Tenure in Chile (1963) 45 min. (in three 15-min. parts). The Land Tenure Center, University of Wisconsin (PR). Dist: UW. *Outlines land tenure problems in the three regions of Chile. Part I visits Chile's central zone. Begins with a view of Santiago, with both its big-city bustle and its rural migrant slums. Visits an intensive grape farm. Discusses the problem of low production and poorly utilized lands on large farms and visits a typical fundo of this type. Illustrates the life of inquilinos or workers of this fundo. Part II studies the northern third of Chile. Visits the Atacama Desert to the far north and discusses its nitrate mines, copper mines, and irrigated lands. In the near north, the film visits the Illapel Valley and shows the lives of inquilinos, minifundistas (small independent farmers) and farmers holding land in a communal arrangement. Part III moves to the southern region—the area south of the Bio Bio River. Studies a Mapuche Indian reservation, problems of sharecroppers, and wheat farming and attendant conservation problems. Includes a visit to the meat and milk economy of the province of Llanquihue and to the sheep country of Tierra del Fuego.*

Aspects of the Behavior of the Sifaka (Propithecus verreauxi verreauxi) 12 min. Thomas T. Struhsaker and Alison Richard (FM). Dist: RUFS FR$15, FS$60. *The island of Madagascar of the Malagasy Republic is one of the most distinctive ecological settings extant. The flora and fauna are so unusual that many species exist nowhere else on earth. Among these are the family Lemuridae, the lemurs, believed by many researchers to be the closest prosimian relatives of humankind. The film depicts the general behavior of the sifaka. [From the review by Norris M. Durham, AJPA 52:601, 1980.]*

Assault on Time (1990) 28 min. Jim Hyde (FM). Dist: NAVC VS$45. *For a good review of looting problems (and some solutions) at sites in U.S. national parks, this film is a valuable resource. [From the review by Peter S. Allen, ARCH 44(3):56–57, 1991.]*

At the Canoe Camp (1981) 41 min. Ian Dunlop (PR), Philip Robertson (DI). Dist: FAA. *The film records the making of two dug-out canoes that Narritjin and his companions are making at a bush camp. We see the lengthy manufacturing process in detail, interspersed between general camp scenes of Narritjin's family. The trees and the land that Narritjin's working on belong to another clan. Through the interclan discussions that have to take place, we learn about the local Aboriginal politics, ownership, and law.*

At the Edge of Conquest: The Voyage of Chief Wai-Wai 28 min. Geoffrey O'Conner (PR). Dist: FL, VR$55, VS$295. *Looks at the situation of the Waiapi Indians, a small, isolated tribe that came into contact with the outside world in the late 1970s. Today, they are threatened by invading gold miners, by the Brazilian government's recent proposal to reduce their land by 10 percent, and the state government's plan to construct a highway directly through their territory. But their strategy for survival has been effective: defend their lands from invasions while their leaders navigate the tricky waters of politics. The film focuses on the charismatic leader, Chief Wai-Wai, as he travels from his remote village to Brazil's capitol, encountering for the first time airplanes, elevators, and skyscrapers. [Reviewed by Charles C. Kolb, SBF 28:86, 1992.]*

At the Edge of the Old Stone Age 25 min. John Greenway (FM, AN). Dist: Anthropology Department, University of Colorado, Boulder, CO 80302 FS$260. *The film shows a day in the life of a small band of the golden-skinned, blond-haired Pitjandjara of the Mann and Musgrave Ranges in west central Australia (with a cursory glimpse of their neighbors, the Ngadadjara and Jangkundjara).*

At the Threshold (Millennium: Tribal Wisdom and the Modern World Series) (1992) 1 hr. David Maybury-Lewis (H), Hans Zimmer (MU). Dist: PBS VS$49.95, order #MILL-110-RCDC. *Has the pursuit of self-interest that has driven our society since the 12th century finally run its course in the 20th century? Explore this possibility in the Millennium series finale. Return to the Xavante tribe in the jungles of Brazil, the Navajo of the American Southwest, and elsewhere, to review the primary wisdoms that tribal people offer to our modernized world. Then travel to central France to explore the most perplexing dilemmas of the Western world—heart vs. mind, body vs. soul, the desires of the individual vs. the needs of society. Visit a rural French family whose lifestyle exhibits the positive influences that Western culture has inherited from its tribal past. Through these intimate views of family life in tribal and Western societies, understand why our survival as a species may now depend on rediscovering the wisdoms of our tribal past.*

At the Time of Whaling 38 min. Leonard Kamerling, Sarah Elder (FM). Dist: DER FR$45, FS$500; UCEMC FR$37. *Gambell, Alaska, is a Yupik-speaking community* on St. Lawrence Island in the Bering Sea. Here, as on the coast, sea mammals are still the major source of food . During their three-week spring migration through the Bering Channel, whales are hunted using a combination of traditional organization and recently introduced technology such as motors and darting guns. An old man recounts the way whaling used to be.

Atlantic Slave Trade 17 min. Dan Shafer, Tom O'Toole (FM). Dist: MINN FS$225. *The 17th-century slave trade is explored from a new viewpoint as it seeks to understand the African input into the trade. The film's thesis is that there is much to be learned about the trade before any mention is made of European ships or traders, and new questions are raised from an African perspective. For example, what part did the trade play in creating or at least continuing internal market systems in Africa? What was indigenous African servitude like and how did the Atlantic slave trade affect it? How did the European presence affect African politics? However, the film never loses sight of the larger issue of the Black Diaspora and the common bond of past suffering and present discrimination shared by Black Americans from Chile to Canada.*

Atlantis (1976) 41 min. Samuel S. Bishop (PR, Dl, WR). Dist: Orpheus Films, Inc., 46 Hollis Ave., Braintree, MA 02184 FR$50, FS$525; UCEMC FR$34. *Detailed consideration of recent archaeological theories and evidence that the island of Santorini (Thera) was the site of Atlantis.* [Reviewed by Peter S. Allen, *ARCH* 280–281, 1977.]

Atoll Life on Kiribati (The Human Face of the Pacific Series) (1987) 56 min. Film Australia (PR). Dist: FIV VS$158. *This film is about one of the most isolated communities in the Pacific, called Kiribati. Kiribati gained its independence in 1979. The film shows how this community has preserved many of its ancient customs.*

Attiuk (The Caribou) (St. Lawrence North Series) 17 min. National Film Board of Canada (PR). Dist: CF/MH FR$15; CRAW. *The Montagnais Indians who live on the north shore of the Gulf of St. Lawrence are caribou hunters who believe that all hunting is accomplished first in dreams, and who still follow their ancient rituals of the hunt.*

AUBRAC SERIES J. D. Lajoux (FM), C. Jest (CON), Centre National de la Recherche Scientifique (PR). Dist: CNRSm Paris. *Six films on an interdisciplinary study of Aubrac, in southern France.* [Reviewed by Andrew Manzardo, *AA* 76:726, 1974.]

Ausschnitte aus den Herbstlichen Totenfest in Desa (Excerpts from the Fall Commemoration of the Dead in Desa) 24 min.; **Sonntaegliche Totenklage in Desa (Sunday Death Lament at Desa)** 16.5 min. A. Amzulescu (FM). Dist: PSU. *Southwest Romanian ritual.* [Reviewed by Gail Kligman, *JAF* 92(363):131–133, 1979.]

Australia's Twilight of the Dreamtime (1988) 60 min. Dist: NGS FS$395, VS$79.95. "*This interesting, well-photographed film is about the Gagudju tribe of Australian aborigines.... Members of the tribe explain their feeling of responsibility for perpetuating their world: they do this by tapping the power of what they call "The Dreamtime," the perpetual moment of creation, now and long ago, conveyed through their artwork.... Undergraduates will like the film, but it really needs to be put into context by the teacher.*" [From the review by John W. Adams, *SBF* 24:305, 1989.] Study guide available.

THE AUSTRALIAN INSTITUTE OF ABORIGINAL STUDIES SERIES
Dist: UCEMC. See individual titles for details:

- **Goodbye Old Man**
- **Camels and the Pitjandjara**
- **Coniston Muster**
- **Emu Ritual at Ruguri**
- **Gunabibi-An Aboriginal Fertility Cult**
- **Larvari and Walkara**
- **Malbangka Country**
- **Mourning for Mangatopi**
- **Mulga Seed Ceremony**
- **Pitubi Revisit Yaru Yaru**
- **Pintubi Revisit Yumari**
- **Walbiri Fire Ceremony**
- **Walbiri Ritual at Gunadjari**
- **Walbiri Ritual at Ngama**

Autumn River Camp, Parts I and II (Netsilik Eskimo Series) (1964) 30 min. each. Doug Wilkinson, Michael Chaloufour, and Quentin Brown (FM), Asen Balikci and Guy Mary Rousseliere (AN), Education Development Center (PR). Dist: EMC FR$33, FS$324; PSU (PCR) part I order #31614, FR$11.10; part II order #31615 FR$11.10. *Part I: People travel in soft snow, build karmaks in river valley— two with snow walls and one with ice walls; man makes jaw-bone toys for child to use with puppy, women gather moss, men go to river to fish, family eats cooked fish in karmak. Part II: Men build igloos and move belongings; then begins whole process of making sled of tent skins, frozen fish, caribou antlers and seal skin thong; concurrently, a woman makes a parka from caribou skins, children play; sled is completed and loaded, family travels down river and toward coast.* [Reviewed by John J. Honigmann, *AA* 72:722–724, 1970.] Cf. the film *Fishing at the Stone Weir*.

Ave Maria: The Story of the Fisherman's Feast (1986) 24 min. Beth Harrington (FM). Dist: UCEMC VR$33, VS$320, order #37423. *This film focuses on the traditions of Italian Americans; it is filmed in the North End of Boston. The focus of the film is the festival of " Madonna del Soccorso." The filmmaker tries to present how through this festival the participants symbolically re-create the community of their origin—a small fishing village in Southwestern Sicily—and connect themselves with their roots.* [Reviewed by Elizabeth Mathias, *AA* 91:268–269, 1989. Reviewed in *VISA* 4:78, 1991.]

Awakenings, 1954–56 (see Eyes on the Prize: America's Civil Rights Years Series)

The Ax Fight (see Yanomamo Series)

Axes and Aré: Stone Tools of the Duna (1977) 41 min. J. Peter White (AN). Dist: UCEMC FR$43, FS$560. *Manufacture of flaked and ground stone tools among the Duna speakers of Horaile, Lake Kopiago, Southern Highland District, Papua New Guinea, demonstrating the use of these tools in the manufacture of bows and arrows. The film is composed of three main parts. The first shows the collection of wood and bamboo for a bow and of stone for small flaked tools (aré) using only a ground stone axe. The materials are returned to a man's house where a skilled craftsman uses them to make a bow and arrow. The second part demonstrates how a ground stone axe, broken while chopping wood for the bow, is removed from its haft and resharpened. The third part shows the collection of materials and the construction of an arrow.* [Reviewed by John Speth, *AA* 81:468, 1979.]

Aymara Leadership (1984) 30 min. Hubert L. Smith (FM). Dist: Kuxtal, Inc., P.O. Box 150, Selma, OR 97538; (503) 597-2142 VR$50, VS$350. *"Most of what we see and hear is natural workaday activity and conversation.... The film helps viewers ... to appreciate the ways in which a young man manages to minimize conflicts, resolve disputes, and generally promote the social welfare in a community where age and experience have traditionally been highly valued."* [From the review by Dwight B. Heath, *AA* 88:1036–1037, 1986.]

Babatou, les trois conseils (Babatou, Three Pieces of Advice) (1975) 90 min. Jean Rouch (DI), Centre National de la Recherche Scientifique, Comite du Film Ethnographique (PR). Dist: CFE; DER. *A cine-history story about the slave wars of Babatou, conqueror of the Songhay from Gurunsiland, during the course of the last century.*

BABOON SOCIAL LIFE SERIES Irven DeVore, S. L. Washburn (AN). [Reviewed by Paul Bohannan, *AA* 75:1977, 1973. Peter Marler, *AA* 75:2000, 1973.] Bibliography: I. DeVore ed., *Primate Behavior* (Articles by DeVore and Hall on Baboon Ecology and Baboon Social Behavior), 1965. Stuart Altmann and Jeanne Altmann, *Baboon Ecology*. 1970. Jane Lancaster, *Primate Behavior and the Emergence of Human Culture*. Holt, Rinehart and Winston, 1975.

- **Baboon Behavior** (1961) 31 min. Dist: UCEMC FR$36, FS$420; PSU (PCR) order #2107K FR$11.60, FS$300. *Many facets of baboon behavior can be observed only in the natural environment. In the wild, baboons live in a highly integrated social unit—the troop. The film emphasizes the many aspects of baboon life, which foster social cohesion between the various ages and sexes that compose the troop. The role of the adult male in predator defense, the attraction of the newborn infant, the social aspect of grooming, and the use of social gestures in maintaining troop organization are among the topics presented. The development of infant behavior is traced from the close association with the mother at birth, through years of play activity in a group of juvenile peers, to the emergence of adult behavior patterns. Sexual behavior is described in connection with such topics as infant care and the relations of the mating pair to the other troop members. Filmed in the Royal Nairobi National Park, Kenya, this film shows baboons together with many other species of animals with which they frequently associate. The availability of plant foods, water, and safe sleeping trees is related to the daily movement and annual range of the baboon troop. Frequent comparison is made between pertinent aspects of baboon behavior and their counterparts in human development and behavior.* Cf. the film, *Animals in Amboseli*. Focusing questions: What are the differences between baboon and human adaptations to the savanna? How can we use this data to understand the behavior of early hominids? What limitations are there to this sort of analogy? Do baboons have culture? How does baboon social organization differ from human social organization? Similarities? What is the significance of the fact that baboon infants are born at a more mature stage of development than human infants? [Randy Pollack]

- **Baboon Ecology** (1962) 21 min. Dist: UCEMC FR$30, FS$300; PSU (PCR) order #2132K FR$7.60, FS$200. *Roaming the broad savannas of East Africa, baboons demonstrate a particular adaptation to life on the grasslands. This film illustrates through the use of live photography and color animation some of the ecological principles at work among the average baboon troop. It is shown through the use of graphic animation that the average baboon troop has a home range of 15 square miles; however, it stays mainly within a three-square-mile core area. Core areas contain food, water sources, and trees for sleeping. Baboon troops maintain an interesting interdependence with many other animal species and are shown grazing with impala, gazelle, hartebeest, bushbuck, and zebra. While grazing, the several species are seen reacting as a unit to potential predators, each species relying upon the alarm signals of others. It is explained that baboons have few successful predators, for while they have been prey of wild dogs, hyenas, jackals, snakes, and eagles, the powerful teeth and fighting ability of the adult male baboon make attack from such smaller carnivores unlikely. Humans have killed more baboons than all other predators combined.* Cf. the film *Animals in Amboseli*.

- **Baboon Social Organization** (1963) 17 min. Dist: UCEMC FR$27, FS$245; PSU (PCR) FR$6.40, FS$160. *A baboon troop is a compact social unit, and its members are highly interdependent. This film analyzes, through live photography and graphic animation, the nature of this interdependence and its close relation to baboon ecology. The troop hierarchy is shown to be established in such a way that the weak are protected at all times. The adult males, key members of the troop, are distinguished by their central and peripheral roles. The large central males, dominant figures in the organization, are shown positioned in the center of the troop near the mothers and infants. They will leave these central positions to confront a troop enemy or to maintain troop order. The peripheral males are shown to take positions on the outside edges of the troop and to alarm the entire unit to action when necessary. Juveniles form play groups within the troop, usually divided according to age. The relative dominance or attractiveness of any one member is demonstrated in the "grooming character." Adult males and mothers with infants are considered prestige members of the troop and the less important members defer to them by grooming their fur. The adult males police the social* system and keep the individual members in line. It is explained that by the time an infant has grown to maturity, his interdependence is assured and he demonstrates no desire to leave the troop. Cf. the film *Animals in Amboseli.*

BABOON SOCIAL STRUCTURE SERIES (1966) Ken Nelson, Michel Chalufour, Quentin Brown (FM), Irven DeVore (AN), Educational Development Center (PR).

• **Animals in Amboseli** 20 min. Dist: EMC FS$240. *This is an introductory film presenting the ecology of a typical region of East Africa, the Masai, Amboseli Game Reserve, particularly with respect to the faunal associations of the open grassland, woodland, and water-hole areas. It is intended to indicate something of the relationship of one species with another and especially to show how baboons coexist with ungulates, carnivores, elephants, and so forth.* Suggested supplements: S. L. Washburn and Irven DeVore, *The Social Life of Baboons.* Scientific American 294:62–72, 1961 (a 10-page introduction to the behavior and ecology of East African baboons, available as Scientific American offprint no. 614). Irven DeVore, ed. *Primate Behavior: Field Studies of Monkeys and Apes,* Holt, Rinehart and Winston, 1965. Sarel Eimerl and Irven DeVore, *The Primates.* Life Nature Library, Time, Inc., 1965.

• **Baboon Development: The Older Infant-Four Months to One Year (Nairobi Park)** 8 min. Dist: EMC FR$11, FS$108. *Infants shown at 4, 8, and 12 months of age, indicating stages of increasing independence, weaning and rejection by the mother, and orientation to adult males and peer groups.*

• **Baboon Development: The Young Infant—Birth to Four Months (Amboseli Reserve)** 10 min. Dist: EMC FS$156. *Behavioral development and relations of the troop to mother and infant. Includes the early development of play, exploration, tasting food items, and riding on the mother's back.*

• **The Baboon Troop (Amboseli Reserve)** 23 min. Dist: EMC FS$276. *Explores a number of aspects of the social relationships of this arboreal primate that spends extended periods of time on the ground; the role of the male as protector and as a central figure around which other troop members orient themselves; the attractive central role of the older females and the young infants; the field evidence of dominance relationships including fighting, displacement, and gestures; the dominance order of the troop as it is revealed by the peculiar problem of maturing males.*

• **Dynamics of Male Dominance in a Baboon Troop** 30 min. Dist: EMC FS$360. *This unit explores in depth the male dominance patterns in one troop of baboons in Nairobi Game Park. The changes in troop hierarchy from those observed in 1959 and 1963 provide a historical perspective for the 1964 filmed data. The film traces a young male's entry into a central dominant position and his subsequent aging and decline. Full identification of individual males brings the raw field data vividly into the classroom as six adult males spar for leadership using characteristic postures of threat and aggression.*

• **Evening Activity (Amboseli Reserve) Field Study Sequence** 5 min. Dist: EMC FS$60. *This is a review unit showing a particularly rich segment of quiet evening social activity. As the events occur in a close approximation to real time, this short unit is a fair simulation of an observation in the field, and an opportunity to observe again relationships learned in more structured films.*

• **Observing Baboons from a Vehicle (Amboseli Reserve)** 5 min. Dist: EMC FS$60. *Designed for the elementary school curriculum, showing the observer leaving camp in a truck, driving up to and observing baboons.*

Baby Ghana (1957) 12 min. Jean Rouch (DI), Centre National de la Recherche Scientifique (PR). Dist: CFE; DER. *The independence of Ghana.*

Baby Riazanskie (The Peasant Women of Riazan) (1927) 70 min. Dist: AB. *Fictional account of rural Russian life.* [Reviewed by Ethel Dunn, AA 80:199–200, 1978.]

Bahia: Africa in the Americas (1988) 58 min. Geovanni and Michael Brewer (DI), Brock Peters (NA). Dist: UCEMC FR$40, VS$395, order #37747. *Located 1,000 miles north of Rio de Janeiro, the Brazilian state of Bahia is "the capital of African culture in the Americas." This documentary examines the African cultural traditions preserved by the people of Bahia in their music, dance, art, food, and, especially, their Candomble religion. The video focuses on the importance of Candomble in Bahia, showing the religion's dramatic ceremonies and allowing its practitioners to explain their beliefs. The ceremony of food preparation and offerings to the Orixas and an important ceremony in which rhythmic music and ritual dancing lead to trances and states of possession are shown. Of special interest is the examination of the intermingling of Candomble and Catholicism.* Teaching notes by Professor Sheila Walker, University of California, Berkeley. [Reviewed by Sidney M. Greenfield, AA 91:530–531, 1989.]

The Bajao: Seagoing Nomads (1983) 18 min. Wayne Mitchell (FM). Dist: BFA FR$55, FS$365, VS$250. *"Captures the lovely tropical environment of the southern Sulu Islands in the Philippines. This short film documents events in the daily routine of a boat-dwelling Bajao family."* [From the review by H. Arlo Nimmo, AA 89:254–255, 1987.]

Bake Restudy (1984) 1 hr. Nazir Ali Jairazbhoy and Amy Ruth Catlin (FM). Dist: AMIE VS$125. *This videotape explores the preservation and transformation of performance in India's southern states of Tamilnadu, Kerala, and Karnataka. It compares Dr. Arnold Adriaan Bake's unique 16mm films, photographs and audio recordings of music, dance, and rituals made in 1938 to the audio-visual documentation collected on a revisit to the same sites by his student and colleague Dr. Nazir Jairazbhoy in 1984 in collaboration with Dr. Amy Catlin. The videotape also shows the background of the Dutch scholar Arnold Bake and the methodologies used in both field trips. The video is accompanied by a newly revised 184-page ethnographic and interpretive monograph that contains a complete script of the video, maps, bibliography, and four-part index.*

Bakhtiari Migration (Edited version) (1974) 27 min. Dist: PSU FR$17, order #32434; FI. *Southwest Iran, seasonal (spring) migration. The film deals with the twice-yearly Bakhtiari transhumance: a migration to fresh pastures. Six geographical obstacles must be surmounted to successfully* *complete the journey. Each of the challenges is described as is the role of leadership.* [Reviewed by Asen Balikci, *AA* 82:229–230, 1980.] Bibliography: L. A. Sweet. *Peoples and Cultures of the Middle East*. Natural History Press, New York, 1970. [Emil R. Liddell]

Baleen Baskets of the Alaskan Inupiat 27 min. North Slope Borough Teleproduction Studio (PR). Dist: MDAI VS$59.95, order #331-04. *The Arctic Bowhead whale has long been the leading natural resource for the Alaskan Inupiat Eskimo. Whales filter plankton through the baleen in their mouths. People have used baleen for many purposes, including buggy whip handles and corset stays. Since the turn of the century, the Inupiat have woven beautiful and distinct baskets from Bowhead baleen.*

Bali beyond the Postcard 60 min. Nancy Dine (PR), Peggy Stern (DI). Dist: FL VR$75, VS$445. *Art and everyday life come together in an intimate story about a Balinese family whose gamelan music and Legong dance tradition spans four generations. The documentary follows an important event in the history of the family—the passing down of the Legong dance legacy to the youngest, a 9-year-old member of the family. From the first rehearsal taught by the mother, to the final debut presided over by the family's 90-year-old patriarch and gamelan master, the filmmakers capture the intensity with which tradition evolves and is passed on in Bali. The result is an intimate view into a dynamic culture steeped in ancient traditions and increasingly exposed to the modern world.*

Bali: Island and Universe 35 min. Hart Spranger (DI), Keith Lorenz (PR), Vishnu Mathur (CM). Dist: VQ. [Reviewed by Philip F. McKean, *AA* 78:724–725, 1976.]

Bali, Man's Paradise (1930s) Dist: FCE FR$85, FS$450. *About Bali as it existed in the 1930s. It contrasts the society of Bali with that of New York in the years of depression and states that Bali is a land without unemployment, without poverty, without crime, and without worry. Among the dances shown are the fire serpent dance, the cowardly lion and the devil, the dance of the garuda bird who is slain by the hero, and the sitting dance.*

BALI SERIES (1986) Linda Connor, Patsy Asch, and Timothy Asch (DI), Australian National University and DER (PR). Dist: DER. *The series focus on a particular Balinese spirit medium named Jero Tapakan—her life and work.* In order to enrich understanding of the films and to enhance their usefulness in teaching, an ethnographic film monograph has been prepared by the filmmakers. The monograph titled *Jero Tapakan: Balinese Healer*, 1986, is available from Cambridge University Press. See descriptions under individual titles:

- A Balinese Trance Seance
- Jero on Jero
- Jero Tapakan
- The Medium Is the Masseuse
- Releasing the Spirits

Bali: The Mask of Rangda 30 min. Dist: HFF FR$45, FS$395, VS$89. *In Bali, the link between man and God . . . conscious and unconscious . . . is acted out frequently in elaborate ceremonies and dramatic performances, such as the self-stabbing trance of Barong-Rangda and the Ketfak trance. Filmed in remote villages of Bali far away from presentations of similar rites, performed for tourists, this film is an authentic picture of a culture, as yet untouched by the West, which has developed this extraordinary means of exorcising violence to preserve "The Spirit of Cooperation."* See also *Mask of Rangda*.

A Balinese Family (Character Formation in Different Cultures series) 1991 (ca. 1951) 20 min. Margaret Mead and Gregory Bateson (AN, FM). Dist: PSU VR$15.50, FS$420, VS$125, order #21793. *A study of a Balinese family showing the way in which father and mother treat the three youngest children—the lap baby, the knee baby, and the child nurse. There are scenes showing the father giving the baby his breast, the behavior of the knee baby during the lap baby's absence, and the difficulties the small child nurse has in caring for the younger baby.* Suggested supplements: Gregory Bateson and Margaret Mead, *Balinese Character*. Special Publications of the New York Academy of Sciences, 2, 1942. Margaret Mead and Frances C. McGregor, *Growth and Culture*. Putman, 1951. For a more complete bibliography on these films, see Margaret Mead, *Continuities in Cultural Evolution*. Yale, 1964 (also a Yale Paperbound Y-154, pp. 349–357.)

Balinese Surfer 50 min. Bill Leimbach (FM). Dist: SFI FS$1500. *Some of the best surfing waves in the world break on the coast of Bali, and this film is about the Balinese boys who have learned to ride them. The Balinese are neither voyagers nor fishermen. They are traditionally suspicious of the sea, and yet the young Balinese surfers have overcome the old fears to master a new sport. The film shows how they have used the new without destroying the old. Through boys like Nyoman and Wayan, the film reveals the deep unity of art and religion in Balinese life, which not only endows the surfers with a natural grace and agility but lets the Balinese people flourish during a period of change that would destroy any other community. We see the boys out on the waves in beautiful slow motion, filmed with underwater cameras to give a view never before seen in surfing. We also watch the boys engaged in the arts and crafts they use in their own lives as well as selling to tourists, and finally we follow them through the dance and worship of their village temple festivals. Their world is changing around them. They are changing with it, but their unique relationship to a traditional lifestyle ensures that the new vision is still totally Balinese.*

A Balinese Trance Seance (Bali Series) (1986) 30 min. Linda Connor (AN), Patsy Asch and Timothy Asch (DI), Australian National University and DER (PR). Dist: DER FR$55, VR$50, FS$550, VS$250. *Jero Tapakan, a spirit medium in a small, central Balinese village, consults with a group of clients in her household shrine. The clients have come to contact the spirit of their dead son, to discover the cause of his death and his wishes for his forthcoming cremation ceremony. Jero enters trance, reciting mantras and lighting incense. She is possessed several times; between each trance, she speaks with her clients, explaining the* meaning of the often ambiguous trance speech. The film offers background on the role of spirit mediums in Bali, and on the life history of Jero Tapakan. Relevant anthropological literature: Jane Belo, *Trance in Bali.* Columbia University Press, 1960. Miguel Covarrubias, *Island of Bali.* Oxford University Press. 1972. Linda Connor, Timothy Asch, and Patsy Asch, *A Balinese Trance Seance: Ethnography for the Film.* (First draft available from DER) 1980. See also the film *Jero on Jero: A Balinese Trance Seance Observed.* [Reviewed by James Dow, *SBF* 18:150–151, 1983. Hildred Geertz, *AA* 86:809–811, 1984. Reviewed in *VISA* 4:68, 1991.]

The Ballad of Crowfoot 10 min. Willie Dunn (FM), National Film Board of Canada (PR). Dist: CRM/MH order #408466, FR$2O, FS$155, VS$120; UCEMC order #7890 FR$8. *This graphic history of the Canadian West was created by a film crew composed of Native Canadians who wish to reflect the traditions, attitudes, and problems of their people. Their training was co-sponsored by the Company of Young Canadians and the National Film Board. Illustrations and photographs are from various private and public archive collections. Words and music of the song that forms the film's commentary are by Willie Dunn, the filmmaker.*

Les Ballets du Niger (Ballets of the Niger) (1961) 25 min. Jean Rouch (DI). Dist: CFE; DER. *A visit by the Nigerian ballet company to the Theatre des Nations in Paris.*

The Bambara Kingdom of Segu 19 min. Dist: FHS VS$99, order #DH-3078. *The history of Bambara can be traced at least as far as the 7th century. In this program, we learn something of their past, and we can imagine more from the extraordinary architecture of their ancient villages, which form a fluid continuum with life in the same region today. A large and flourishing culture, the Bambara lived by collecting enslaved Africans and reselling them to North Africa and the Western Hemisphere; when the slave trade was abolished in Europe, the economic decline of the Bambara followed. As new economic bases were created, a new Bambara civilization emerged, which has retained the artistic vigor of its forebears.*

Bambara of Mali 10 min. Dan Shafer and Tom O'Toole (FM). Dist: MINN FS$1350. *This film reveals some significant insights into Bambara culture, an ethnic group living in nation of Mali. It discusses the difficult question of self-identity and family and ethnic identity. The relationships between population and environment in a society that practices shifting agriculture are examined. Their unusual marriage customs involving extended families are described. The dance of the Tyi Wara and the feast of the well are shown as visible manifestations of old institutions that still exist in a culture that is now starting to break down in the cities.*

Bamiki Bandula: Children of the Forest (1975) 60 min. Kevin Duffy (PR, WR), Colin Turnbull (AN). *Pygmies of the Rain Forest* (edited version, 51 mins., from distributor PSU). *Shot in Ituri Forest. Fine capsule ethnography, in many ways an equivalent film to* The Hunters. *The major focus of the film is on Pygmy ties to the surrounding village farmers (including trade, initiation, and marriage) and Pygmy hunting, especially a climactic elephant hunt. Included, also, are depictions of the environment, forest ecology, child-rearing and family life, women's activities and arts and crafts, band structure, dance and play, ritual ties to the forest, and a brief mention of delocalization. Warnings: Scenes of childbirth and elephant slaughter are graphic, but unlikely to offend viewers. Focusing questions: How does Pygmy treatment of children differ from U.S. child-rearing techniques? Why? What might effects be? In what senses could the Pygmies be termed an affluent society? To what extent is Pygmy technology appropriate and adequate? What are the major contrasts between Pygmy and villager views of their relationship? How do Pygmy rituals contribute to ecological stability? How would you predict that various elements of Pygmy culture will be changed during acculturation?* Bibliography: Colin Turnbull, *The Forest People.* New York: Simon and Schuster, 1961. [Joseph M. O'Neal]

Banaras 22 min. Michael Camerini (FM), Dr. Shyamal Sinha (MU). Dist: UW-SAAS FR$20, FS$175. *The feeling and mood of Banaras rather than a detailed description of any given facet of the city. The film relies on visual images and the original score to evoke the feeling of being in Banaras. It shows the cycle of daily activity, life on the ghats, ties the formal worship in temples to the devotions of pilgrims and the people of the city at the river, and explores the many different types of shrines found in the city. There are many rhythms to the city; the pattern of daily life, the marketplace, the multiple uses of the river and of water, in general, all contribute to the holiness of the city. In exploring these rhythms, the film also gives the viewer a feeling for the people of Banaras: their faces, moods, and activities.*

Bandits of Orgosolo (1961) 79 min. B/W. Vittorio DeSeta (FM, WR, CA). Dist: PATHE. *Set in the area of Orgosolo, Sardinia, this fictional film depicts the relationships between townspeople, shepherds, and bandits; the strong emphasis on family and community versus the alien power of the national government; and the basically fatalistic value system.* [Reviewed by Toni Flores Fratto, *AA* 74:1574, 1575, 1972.] Suggested supplement: Frank Cancian, The Southern Italian Peasant: World View and Political Behavior. *Anthropological Quarterly* 34:1'18, 1961 (a critical discussion of Banfield's study of a Southern Italian community).

Banesa's Courtyard (1990) 58 min. Devitt/Jones Productions (PR). Dist: CRM/F VR$80, VS$295. *This insightful documentary tells the story of the lives of daughters, wives, and mothers in the rural villages of Bangladesh. In their own words, these women describe the traditions that bind them to their families and to the agriculture of the region. Banesa is the matriarch of the extended family studied in this film. Her matter-of-fact descriptions of the household give a rare glimpse into a world of strong cultural and religious mores. As this film shows, an insular society protects people and shelters them from radical changes; what it cannot stop is the process of education that is creating change within Bangladesh today.*

Bangladesh Nationhood: Symbols and Shadows 49 min. Mira Reym Binford and Michael Camerini (FM). Dist: UW-SAAS FR$30, FS$295. *Presents the struggle of a new nation, Bangladesh, to define itself. Filmed one-and-a-half years after Bangladesh's independence, and completed a few months before the assassination of Sheikh Mujib, "Father of the Nation," this film presents a series of interviews with peasants, students, businessmen, and religious and political leaders that reveal those conflicts within Bangladesh society that both defined and limited Sheikh Mujib's years in power. This is a film about the uses of political symbols and about the myths and ideals that shape political processes.* Accompanied by teacher's guides with background information and suggestions for discussions and produced with synchronous sound interviews in Bengali, Hindi, Tamil—with English subtitles.

Baobab: Portrait of a Tree 53 min. Alan Root, Joan Root (PR). DIST: CF/MH. *A holistic ecological description of a major African life form.* [Reviewed by Elizabeth Marshall Thomas, *AA* 78:949, 1976.]

Bar Yohai (Myth onto Film: A Trilogy from Native Australia, Native America and the Kabbalah series) 6 min. Robert Ascher (AR). Dist: CUAV FR$20, FS$110, VS$48. *"Bar Yohai" is about the visions of Shimon Bar Yohai, a 2nd-century mystic who, in popular belief, wrote the "Zohar," or "Book of Splendor," the main Kabbalah text. "Kabbalah" means tradition in Hebrew. The principal painted images—the tree, mirror, and candelabra—and the ten dots with which each is constructed are used in the Zohar to show how the world started with ten emanations and progresses with human participation.* [Reviewed by Stephen Pastner, *AA* 91:523, 1989. Reviewed in *VISA* 3:119, 1990.]

The Barabaig (1979) 39 min. George Klima (FM, AN). Dist: PSU FR$20.50, FS$492. *The Barabaig are a semi-nomadic people who live in northern Tanzania. This film, a visual documentation of George Klima's fieldwork, focuses on the socioeconomic importance of cattle in a tribal society. By virtue of their reliance upon cattle for their subsistence, the Barabaig must devise solutions to protect their herds and to solve social problems arising out of their acquisition and control over domesticated animals. The concept of a "cattle-complex" with its cluster of cultural behavior patterns is illustrated by payment of a cattle fine by men tried and convicted in a women's court, a sacrifice of a bull, a wedding ceremony, and a boy's circumcision ritual.* Suggested supplements: George Klima, *The Barabaig: East African Cattle Herders.* New York: Holt. Rinehart and Winston, 1970.

The Barefoot Doctors of Rural China 52 min. Diane Li (PR, DI), Victor H. Li (Assoc. PR). Dist: CDF FR$80-150, FS$720. *One of few films about China made by Americans of Chinese descent. Presents a unique and intimate view of life in the Chinese countryside. Filmed in the People's Republic of China, the film examines China's innovative efforts to provide adequate health care services for its agrarian population of over 600,000,000 people (at the time). The film focuses on the training and activities of peasant paramedics known as the "barefoot doctors," and their "walk on two legs" policy of combining both Western and Chinese medical techniques. It also discusses the barefoot doctor's role in China's current family planning campaign and the importance of jobs for women to the success of the program.*

Barren Lives (Vidas secas) 115 min. Nelson Pereira dos Santos (FM). *A film of the Sertao, an arid, scarcely populated region of Brazil. After a very long drought, a poor family migrates in search of a fertile plot of land. Their encounters, aspirations, and frustrations are treated with a documentary vision.* [Reviewed by Joan Bamberger, *AA* 75:596–597, 1973.]

Basketmaking in Colonial Virginia (see Colonial Williamsburg Series)

Basketry of the Pomo—Forms and Ornamentation (American Indian Film Series) (1962) 21 min. Dist: UCEMC FR$30, FS$300; PSU (PCR) order #2203K, FR$7.90, FS$200. *Pomo baskets were made in a great variety of shapes and sizes. Of the several basic geometric forms, the most important were the plate-form, the cone, and the spheroid. Some forms are made for ceremonial purposes, others for gifts or the storage of valuables. There were also sitting cradles, the seed beaters, the mortar baskets, and a variety of woven traps for fish and birds. The seven basic design elements of Pomo basketry are shown in the film: the line, triangle, zig-zag, rectangle, rhomboid, diamond, and quail plume. These designs have descriptive names, such as the striped water snake, arrow head, butterfly, crab claw, turtle neck, and deer back. Each basket contained a 'dau,' or door design, believed to let in the special deity of basketry, the spider under whose patronage baskets were made. The finest of all the Pomo baskets were the Sun Baskets—covered entirely with feathers from the red crest of the California woodpecker. These rare and highly prized baskets were used as gifts or as mortuary offerings. The decorative use of feathers from 14 species of birds, as well as other materials, such as clam shell beads and pendants of iridescent shell, are shown in beautiful detail.*

Basketry of the Pomo—Introductory Film (American Indian Film Series) (1962) 30 min. Dist: UCEMC FR$35, FS$410; PSU (PCR) order #2201k, FR$11.10, FS$300. *The Pomo Indians of Northern California were expert basketmakers. They created a great variety of baskets, including many handsome forms with harmonious decorations. Others were more rough and utilitarian, such as the burden baskets, fish and bird traps, and baskets for the sifting and storing of foods. Cooking baskets were woven so tightly they could be used for boiling liquids with hot stones. There were baskets for transport and special baskets such as cradles. This film begins with the gathering of wild plants (the materials that were used in the manufacture of baskets), such as dogwood branches, roots and branches of the white willow, the root stalk of the sedge, black root fiber of the fulrush, and the bark of the redbud. In slow motion close-ups and animation, this film demonstrates the ten basket-making techniques of this tribe, including twining, coiling, and wicker techniques. Baskets ranged in diameter from four feet to a quarter of an inch and had seven basic design* elements. *A most beautiful feature of Pomo basketry was the use of feathers for decoration. Those of the thrush, mallard, meadow lark, quail, oriole, woodpecker, and others were employed.* [Reviewed by John Adair, AA 76:728–730, 1974.]

Basketry of the Pomo—Techniques (American Indian Film Series) (1962) 33 min. Dist: UCEMC FR$38, FS$455; PSU (PCR) order #2202K, FR$12.10, FS$300. *This is a more detailed film on the individual basketry techniques of the Pomo showing precisely how the various weaves were executed, diagonal twining, wrapper-twining (looped binding weave), lattice-twining, three-strand-braiding, wicker, single-rod-coiling, and three-rod-coiling. An Indian basketmaker demonstrates how the various, colorful feathers of the redheaded woodpecker, oriole, mallard, and meadow lark are woven into special decorative patterns, so perfectly that the surface of the basket is almost as smooth as the breast of a bird. A highly significant film for those interested in the precise techniques of Indian basketry.*

The Basques of Santazi (Disappearing World Series) (1987) 51 min. Leslie Woodhead (FM), Sandra Ott (AN). Dist: FIV VS$198, 047001; PSU VR$14, order #51153. *Every summer for hundreds of years, the Basque shepherds of Santazi have brought their sheep to pastures high in the French Pyrenees. Now their traditional way of life is threatened by modern industry. Follows two shepherding families through a year of startling change.* [Reviewed by Steven Ybarrola, AA 90:1045–1046.]

Bataille sur le grand fleuve (Battle on the Great River) (1951–52) 35 min. Jean Rouch (DI), Institut Francais d'Afrique Noir and Centre National du Cinéma (PR). Dist: CFE; DER. *The Sorko hunting the hippopotamus with harpoon on the Niger River.*

Bath Waters Antonia Benedek (PR), for BBC-TV, Barry Cunliffe (AN). (A re-edited version of this was shown in the Odyssey Series, 1981). Dist: FI. *Archaeology of the Roman baths at Bath, England.* Bibliography: Barry Cunliffe, *Roman Bath Discovered.* Routledge and Kegan Paul, 1971. [Reviewed by Miranda C. Marvin, ARCH 34(5):68, 1981.]

Bathing Babies in Three Cultures (Character Formation in Different Cultures Series) (ca. 1954) 9 min. Margaret Mead and Gregory Bateson (AN, FM). Dist: PSU FR$11.50, VR$13, FS$295, VS$75, order #21794; NYU FR$16, FS$135; UCEMC order #8087, FR$7. *A comparative series showing the interplay between mother and child in three different settings—bathing in the Sepik River in New Guinea, in a modern American bathroom, and in a mountain village of Bali in Indonesia.* [Reviewed by Hildred Geertz, AA 78:725–726, 1976.] Cf. the film *A Balinese Family.*

Batteries Dogon, éléments pour une étude des rythmes; ou, tambours de pierre (Dogon Drums, Elements of a Study in Rhythm; or, Stone Drums) (1961) 25 min. Jean Rouch (DI), Centre National de la Recherche Scientifique, Comite du Film Ethnographique (PR), Gilbert Rouget (co-DI). Dist: CFE; DER. *The young goatherders from the cliff of Bandiagara practice on the stone drums of their ancestors. An ethnomusicological film experiment describing the subtle plays of the right and left hand of the Dogon drum players.*

The Battle of Carthage: 229 B.C. (1990) 30 min. Henri de Turenne (PR), Jacques Dupont (DI). Dist: FHS VR$75, VS$149. *"Despites its title, the film spends relatively little time on the actual battle: Instead, it is a rather comprehensive illustrated account of Carthage's history and adversarial relationship with Rome."* [From the review by Peter S. Allen, ARCH 44(5):72–73, 1991.]

Battle of Culloden (1969) 72 min. Peter Watkins (DI), Peter M. Roebeck and Co. (PR). Dist: UCEMC FR$27. *The historic battle in 1746 that ended the cause of Bonnie Prince Charlie, his Jacobite Rebellion, and the Royal House of Stuart. This brilliant objective reenactment, based on authentic documentation and filmed on Culloden Moor, shows in detail the heroics, horror, and stupidity of battle; the slaughter of the ancient highland clans by superior English forces; and the military incompetence of the Scottish Prince. It ends with the ruthless "pacification" of the Highlands by British, Scots, and Hessians—years that scourged Scotland and destroyed the ancient Highland way of life. This outstanding lesson in history gives a depth of historical background and detail in depicting a vivid example of British military success just 35 years before Cornwallis surrendered to end the American Revolution.* Study guide available. Suggested supplement: John Prebble, *Culloden.* Secker, 1960 (Penguin Paperback, 1967).

Beadwork 17 min. Electronic Publishing Institute (PR). Dist: MDAI VS$59.95, order #33201. *Ann Strangeowl Raben shares her Cheyenne Indian heritage through her colorful beadwork. This richly videographed production tells the story of this unique art. Demonstrations give clear instructions of how to produce beadwork creations.*

Beating the Bellows (1982) 25 min. Peter Schmidt and Imogene Lin (FM). Dist: Foundation for the Archaeology of Prehistoric Africa, Department of Anthropology, Brown University, Providence, RI 02912; (401) 863-3251 FR$35, FS$375. *Shows two experimental iron smeltings done at Brown University in 1981 by students imitating techniques used in Bonongo, Tanzania.* [Reviewed by Arthur Steinberg, AA 86:801, 1984.]

Beautiful Tree-Chishkale (American Indian Film Series) (1965) 20 min. Dist: UCEMC FR$29, FS$285; PSU (PCR) order #02204k, FR$7.90, FS$220. *Food made from the acorn was eaten by more than half of the Indian tribes in what is now the United States. This film explains the influence of the acorn on population and settlement patterns, social organization, and to some extent the total way of life of the central California Indians. The Southwestern Pomo, typical of the tribes in this area called the tan oak "Chishkale" (the beautiful tree). The discovery of a technique to remove poisonous tannic acid from acorns by leaching the ground meal made it possible for an entire food economy to be based upon the acorn. The location of many Indian communities was determined by the distribution of the oak trees. From oral traditions and memories of present-day Indians, cooking methods and processing techniques used in making acorn bread have been reconstructed and are* *demonstrated by Pomo Indians. Archaeological findings show evidence for the probable beginning of these processing techniques in precontact times. Though the technology has been modified, acorns are still a significant element in the Indian diet.* [Reviewed by Harold E. Driver, AA 68:596, 1966.]

Beauty Knows No Pain (1988) 25 min. Elliot Erwitt (DI). Dist: ECP. *This film follows a group of Texas co-eds through two weeks of competition as they vie for a chance to join that famous Texas institution, the Kilgore College Rangerettes drill squad. A Texas boot camp for poise and beauty.*

Becoming a Woman in Okrika 27 min. Judith Gleason and Elisa Mereghetti (PR) for Kamel Films. Dist: FL VR$55, VS$295. *This film documents an extraordinary coming-of-age ritual in a village in the Niger Delta. It suggests the conflict third world women face between traditions and the values of the modern world. The rite, called "Iria," consists of elaborately painting the young women's bodies with beautiful designs; subjecting their bodies to public scrutiny by the older women; methodically fattening them; and teaching them the responsibilities of womanhood. After an elaborate celebration, they run a race pursued by young men and their leader, representing a mythological personage who is armed with sticks. By passing through this rite, the women let go of girlish fantasies and prepare for childbearing.* [Reviewed by Pamela Blakely and Thomas Blakely, AA 94(4):1022–1024, 1992.]

Becoming Aboriginal (1978) 10 min. Tom Manefield (PR), David Roberts (DI). Dist: FAA. *This film sets out to explore similarities and differences between education in a formal classroom setting and a traditional Aboriginal one. The children are seen learning European skills and values at school at Bamyili, in the Northern territory. Yet to really become Aboriginal, they must also learn to survive in the bush. This film shows how they learn these skills.*

Becoming American (1982) 58 min. Ken and Ivory Waterworth Levine (DI). Dist: NDF FR$85, FS$800, VS$625. *Hang Sou and his family, preliterate tribal farmers, await resettlement in a refugee camp in Thailand after fleeing their war-consumed native Laos. This film records their odyssey as they travel to and resettle in the United States. As they face nine months of intense culture shock, prejudice, and gradual adaptation to their new home in Seattle, the family provides a rare personal insight into refugee resettlement issues, which are also addressed by teachers, sociologists, anthropologists and refugee workers.*

Be'er Sheva Four 56 min. Ira J. Meistrich (DI), Yohanan Ahroni (CON). Dist: Ira J. Meistrich, 600 West End Ave., New York, NY 10024. *University of Tel Aviv excavations at Beer Sheva in the Negev.* [Reviewed by Ian A. Todd, AA 78:133, 1976.]

Before Reggae Hit the Town (1992) 21 min. Mark Gorney (FM). Dist:UCEMC VR$50, VS$195. *This unusual documentary explores the African roots of music, religion, and dance in Jamaica. It captures several of the principal folk traditions that still survive, including the music of the Maroons; Pocomania, a complex blending of African and Christian traditions; the dancing of the Junkanoo, which is celebrated every Christmas; and the music of the rebellious and persecuted sect of the Nyabinghi. Noted Rasta singer Justin Hinds links these traditions, which predate Jamaican popular music by hundreds of years, with today's reggae.*

Before the Romans (1976) 26.5 min. Terrence Ladlow (PR). Dist: IFB FR$27.50, FS$370. *This film "is apparently intended as an appeal for historic preservation, its approach is that of a travelogue featuring early examples of construction in Britain, which unfortunately produces an almost total lack of organization from an archaeological point of view. The film does show many of the island's best known monuments."* [From the review by Ronald Hicks, ARCH 33(4):60, 1981.]

Before the White Man Came 50 min. Dist: FCE FR$85, FS$450. *This feature was made in the Big Horn Mountains of Montana and Wyoming in the early 1920s. This is the original Crow Country. The cast is made up entirely of Indians, and every effort was made to present life as lived by the Indians in the days before the arrival of the white man.*

Before We Knew Nothing (1989) 62 min. Diane Kitchen (FM). Dist: UCEMC FR$60, VR$60, FS$995, VS$410, order #11367. *This film broke new ground in the ethnographic documentary. It is a brilliant portrait of the life and culture of the Ashaninka (also called the Campa), who inhabit the Amazon rainforest of eastern Peru, as well as a profound reflection of the experience of living and filming among people who continue to resist acculturation into the standards of the modern world. The underlying themes are the loss and transition of culture and the process of cultural change. The program reveals the activities of men and women, the lush tropical environment, and the emotional climate of daily life. An exceptional aspect of the film is its sensitive exploration of the role, activities, and feelings of Ashaninka women. There is footage of childbirth, meal preparations, weaving, grooming, and young girl's play and work.*

The Beginnings of History. Part III: The Iron Age 15 min. British Information Service (PR). Dist: NYU. *1950s film on the Celts.* [Reviewed by Eugene L. Sterud, AA 78:122, 1976.]

Behavior and Ecology of Vervet Monkeys (*Cercopithecus aethiops*) (1971) 40 min. Thomas T. Struhsaker (FM). Dist: RUFS FR$20, FS$400. *"Filmed in the Masai-Amboseli Game Reserve in Kenya, the film focuses on vervet monkeys. Beginning with a firm ecological framework, the film details the various species living with the vervets, such as elephants, antelopes, and gazelles. Grooming, interactions with baboons, reproduction, play, weaning, mother-infant relations, and the famous red, white, and blue display are discussed in excellent detail. It is excellent for upper division undergraduates and beginning graduate students."* [From the review by Norris M. Durham, AJPA 52:602, 1980. Reviewed by Phyllis Dolhinow, AA 75:2006, 1973.]

Behavior Characteristics of the Rhesus Monkey (1947) 11 min. C. R. Carpenter (FM). Dist: PSU. [Reviewed by Barbara Smuts, *AA* 75:2010, 1973.]

Behavior of Free-Ranging Rhesis Monkeys on Cayo Santiago: Mother-Offspring Interactions (1971) 16 min. M. H. Miller and Arthur King (FM). Dist: PSU FR$10, FS$130. *Stressing mother-offspring interactions of the rhesus monkey, this film also depicts male dominance-submission interactions, grooming, infant play, and swimming.*

Behavior of the Macaques of Japan (1969) 28 min. Psychological Cinema Register (PR), C. R. Carpenter (FM, NA). Dist: PSU FR$15, FS$270. *This is a fine film on Macaca fuscata. It compares their social behavior in three colonies: Koshima Island, Takasakiyama, and Chosei Valley. One of the few visual reports of potato-washing, wheat grain-sand separation, and tree-shaking.* [Reviewed by Barbara Smuts, *AA* 75:2010, 1973.]

Behind the Mask (see The Tribal Eye Series)

Behind the Veil 50 min. Eve Arnold (FM). Dist: Impact Films. *Lives of women in the Arab sheikdom of Dubai, on the Arabian peninsula.* [Reviewed by Lois Grant Beck, *AA* 79:196, 1977.]

Behind the Veil: Nuns (1984) 115 min. Signe Johansson (PR), Margaret Wescott (DI). Dist: WFV FR$180, VR$60, FS$1800, VS$600. "*Modern religious women, behind both veil and grating in a cloistered convent in Canada, or behind the sink in a shelter for battered women in Chicago, are the starting point for this . . . production, which seeks . . . to examine critically the history of women in the Christian church of the Western world. . . . The central message the filmmakers want to convey is that women in the Church at one time had considerable power as sacramental ministers and intellectual leaders.*" [From the review by Katherine Murray, *AA* 89:520–522, 1987.]

Beijing (The Cities in China Series) (1981) 45 min. Sue Yung Li and Shirley Sun (PR). Dist: UCEMC FR$55, FS$900, VS$295. *A close look at the texture and flavor of the changing Chinese capital. Highlights include a backstage tour of the Peking Opera, a family reunion of four generations previously dispersed to far-flung outposts, and an interview with the brother of China's last emperor.* [Reviewed by J. Allen Singleton, *SBF* 18:151, 1983.]

Being a Joines: A Life in the Brushy Mountains 55 min. Tom Davenport (FM). Dist: TDF FR$40, FS$400. *John E. "Frail" Joines—a master traditional tale teller—has passed his life in Wilkes County, North Carolina, on the eastern slope of the Blue Ridge. In this film portrait, his tall tales, his comical local anecdotes, his stories of World War II, and his religious narratives mirror changes that have swept away the mountain folk community in a single generation. The tales and other reminiscences by Frail Joines and his wife Blanche show the character and values with which one family met these circumstances—what it has meant, in his time and place, to be a Joines.*

Being Muslim in India 40 min. James Mac Donald and Michael Camerini, Worldview Productions (FM), Joseph Elder (EP). Dist: UW-SAAS FR$30, FS$285. *The film opens in a Muslim neighborhood school, where a religious scholar teaches children the basic tenets of Islam. We enter the home of Qasim, a devout Sunni Muslim and successful businessman, who describes what it is like to be a Muslim, the importance of daily prayer, Islamic education, dietary customs, and the centrality of the Qur'an. They discuss the Muslim teachings concerning social equality and the need to participate actively in worldly responsibilities. Although we do not meet Qasim's first wife, who has been observing seclusion since she was six, we meet his other two wives: Dawn, an Irish convert from Christianity, and Aktar, a teacher until joining Qasim's family. They describe their relationships toward Qasim, each other, and each others' children. A Bismillah ceremony, where a child recites the basic tenets of Islam and begins her formal study of the Qur'an, is also seen.*

Bekoidintu—Any House Is Better Than Mine (see Anuform Series)

Benares: Steps to Heaven 30 min. New Zealand National Film Unit (PR). Dist: WFV FS$595, VS$195. *For 2,500 years, Benares, with its temples, ashrams, and palaces, has been India's most sacred city. In a production of rare visual and spiritual beauty, we discover the city, its people, and the timeless rituals that draw a never-ending stream of pilgrims to the banks of its holy river, the Ganges.* [Reviewed by Joan L. Erdman, *AA* 89:251–253, 1987.]

Benares, the Hindu Heaven (1930s) 10–15 min. Dist: FCE FR$17, FS$95. *Holy men, sacred monkeys, teeming population, and a cremation on the Ganges.*

Benin Kingship Rituals (University of Life Series) 25 min. Dist Pitt. *Examples of various kingship rituals in a southern Nigerian village serve as the basis for this film. Among the complex of rituals presented are the revitalization of divine powers, the placation of evil spirits, and the worship of royal ancestors.*

Benjamin 42 min. Dist: T-L FR$40, VS$$150. *The birth of Benjamin Pile in 1974, and his development for the next six months, were recorded on film and studied by experts. Using slow-motion and frame-by-frame analyses, they discovered that even the youngest babies have an astonishing range of abilities. From birth, Benjamin could move his body in perfect synchronization to words; at eight weeks, he conducted "conversations" with precisely the same patterns as those of an adult.*

Ben's Mill (1981) 59 min. Michael Chalufour and John Karol (FM). Dist: DER VR$50. *A water-powered woodworking mill in Vermont.* [Reviewed by George L. Hicks, *AA* 84:493–494, 1983. Robert K. Evans, *SBF* 18:151, 1983.]

The Best Kept Secret (1976) 16 min. David Tristram, James Wilson (CA, DI), Journal Films (PR). Dist: JF FR$30, FS$275; IFF FR$35, FS$280. *Western Samoa.* "*Tourist aimed . . . Samoans are linked with famous Western personages also enjoying visits to the islands.*" [From the review by Joan Larcom, *AA* 86:814–815, 1984.]

The Best Time of My Life (1987) 58 min. Margaret Pettigrew (PR), for the National Film Board of Canada. Dist: FL FR$85, FS$850, VS$500. "*Portrays women who have started a new business or career after middle age. The women interviewed are articulate and stimulating, in part because several of them are writers.*" [From the review by Benjamin N. Colby, AA 92:1099–1100, 1990. Reviewed by Mary Beth Haralovich and Denise Kervin, AA 92:835–836, 1990.]

Better Rich Than Red (The Human Face of Hong Kong Series) (1988) 47 min. Film Australia (PR). Dist: FIV VS$99. *The film captures the lifestyle of one segment of the rich and powerful stratum of Hong Kong. The men who run the Jockey club are shown to wield immense power. Their lives alternate between managing horse racing, big business—and government.*

Betty Tells Her Story (1973) 20 min. Liane Brandon (FM). Dist: NDF. *Betty narrates twice, differently, an event.* [Reviewed by Louise Lamphere, AA 79:203, 1977.] See other films by Brandon.

Between Men (1979) 57 min. Will Roberts (FM). Dist: United Documentary Films, P.O. Box 315, Franklin Lakes, NJ 07417; (201) 891-8240 FR$75, FS$750. "*A cultural documentary that demonstrates the relationship in America between militarism and masculinity. The film juxtaposes three types of footage: interviews with war veterans and children; narrated sequences taken from everyday civilian and military life; and brief examples of war propaganda coming out of Hollywood.*" [From the review by Stanley Brandes, AA 86:1051–1052, 1984.]

Between Time: A Tibetan Village in Nepal (1984) 20 min. Ken Levine and Ivory Levine (FM). Dist: Iris Film and Video, 720 Blaine St., Seattle, WA 98119; (206) 285-3057 FR$40, FS$325. "*Portrays Tibetan village life on the southern slopes of the Himalaya in northeast Nepal.... Their style of religion, social, and material culture expression is what Himalayanists term Bhotia, referring to a wide variety of Tibetan-like cultures and societies within Nepal's northern border.*" [From the review by Donald A. Messerschmidt, AA 88:517–518, 1986.]

Between Two Worlds (1990) 58 min. Barry Greenwald (DI), Peter Ramont (PR). Dist: FRI FR$125, VR$75, FS$995, VS$390. *Joseph Idlout, an Inuit hunter, attained celebrity status in 1950s Canada as a model eskimo in the "good Indian" mold. The subject of books, the star of films, Idlout symbolized his people to white Canada, a mythical hero akin to Nanook of the North. But for Idlout, his notoriety in their unfamiliar world would ultimately lead to his death. This film documents the human cost of progress. Newsreels trumpet the arrival of southern civilization: teachers, clergy, traders, the Mounted Police, come with canned goods, hospitals, schools, heated houses, all for the sake of civilizing the Inuit. As new pressures intensified, Idlout became unable to cope with his suddenly chaotic world. On June 2, 1968, he was found dead after driving his snowmobile over a cliff. Today the legacy of dependency is frightening. The suicide rate among young Inuit is five times the national average. Unemployment is 50 percent in many communities. The Arctic's past is forgotten; its future is bleak.*

Between Two Worlds: The Hmong Shaman in America 28 min. Taggart Siegel and Dwight Conquergood (PR). Dist: SP VR$40, VS$200. *Many of the more than 60,000 Hmong refugees who have been transplanted from agrarian mountain villages in northern Laos to the United States have resettled in high-rise tenements in Chicago and other cities. With them, they bring their ancient shamanic rituals and ceremonies such as animal sacrifice and trancelike healing. This video captures rare and dramatic footage of the Hmong buying and sacrificing a cow in rural Illinois, a missionary trying to convert a traditional Hmong family, and an unexplained phenomenon (SUNDS) in which young Hmong men die in their sleep. The traditions of this displaced people are in danger of being lost, perhaps forever. The film shows a people caught between two worlds.* [Reviewed by Nancy D. Donnelly, AA 90:1045, 1988.]

Beyond the Plains (1982) 52 min. Dist: VFWW FR$75, FS$735, VS$365. "*This film is a reenactment of a true story. A Masai herdsboy is obliged to leave his rural pastures when he is eight to attend school under a Tanzanian law that requires each family to supply one student for primary education.... This film links ethnography to third world studies of change. Overall, the film's scope and clarity of purpose are good, and the accuracy of information and technical quality are excellent.*" [From the review by Simon D. Messing, SBF 19:301, 1984.]

The Bible and the Gun (Africa Series) (1986) 57 min. RM Arts (PR), Basil Davidson (H). Dist: FIV. *The slave trade decimated the African population and tore the fabric of society. Then new kinds of interlopers came: explorers, missionaries, and entrepeneurs like Cecil Rhodes.*

Bien des mots ont changé... Les Franco Americains de la Nouvelle-Angleterre (1980) 58 min. Daniele Louis (DI), Helene Counture (AD), Jean-Claude La brecque (FM). Dist: PDL FR$75, VR$75, FS$1100, VS$600. *This is a film about Americans of the French Canadian and Acadian ethnicity in New England. The film shows that since the 1860s there has been a constant movement from Quebec and Acadia to New England. Even before then, the Acadians were forced to leave their area of settlement in 1755. During the post–Civil War economic boom, the French-speaking Canadians came to the northeastern United States where they formed a loyal and hardworking labor force; some 600,000 came between 1860 and 1900. We see old shots of Francois Proulx recruiting people from the towns of Quebec to come to New England. A visual tour of the "company towns" a parish, schools run by nuns from Quebec, hospitals, orphanages, and credit unions, sketches the daily milieu in which the French community lived and which they helped build.* [Reviewed by J. Barry Gurdin, AA 83:745–746, 1981.]

The Big Dig (1973) 54 min. Dist: Televisuals, Ltd; UCEMC FR$42. *Shows an important archaeological excavation at the ancient Palestinian mound of Tel Gezer. Explains the principles of modern archaeological methodology in the field and describes the role of the participating an-*

thropologists, historians, geologists, and ceramics experts, as well as the students who have volunteered to work for six-week stints. [Reviewed by Peter S. Allen, *ARCH,* pp. 134–135, 1975. Stanton W. Green, *AA* 79:514, 1977.]

Big Problems for Little People (1975) 23 min. George M. Guthrie and Helen A. Guthrie (AN). Dist: PSU(PCR) FR$14, FS$290. *Relationships between poverty, malnutrition, environment, and sociocultural factors as they relate to human growth development. Documents cases in a rural tropical area of the Philippines.* [Reviewed by James G. Chadney, *AJPA* 55:139, 1981.] Relevant anthropological literature: G. M. Guthrie, Z. Masangkay. and H. A. Guthrie, "Behavior, Malnutrition, and Mental Development." *Journal of Cross-Cultural Psychology* 7(2):169–180, 1976.

Bill Reid 28 min. Jack Long (DI, CA). Dist: NFBC. *Bill Reid is as much a portrait of a people as a portrait of an artist. Set largely in the the Queen Charlotte Islands, the film portrays through rich images and Reid's own narration the story of a man discovering his heritage. As the Haida Indians of Skidegate ceremoniously carry Bill Reid's great totem carving out of its storage shed, the master carver recounts his own development. Born of a Haida mother and a German-Scottish-American father, he became interested in West Coast Indian art when he saw a totem pole from his mother's village, Tanu, on display at the Royal Ontario Museum and gold bracelets his grandmother wore. After attending jewelry classes in Toronto, he went on to design some of the finest jewelry in the West Coast mythical motif, working with gold and silver, as well as argillite. Some of his first major works were commissioned by the University of British Columbia, where he directed the construction of part of a Haida village at what is now known as Totem Park. Out of his desire to acknowledge his Haida roots, he committed all his energy to carving the Skidegate totem pole. While watching Reid carve out the massive cedar log, first roughing it out with chain and electric saws, then using axe, knife, and adze for intricate carving, we cannot help but wonder if he is imposing his own designs or uncovering the spirit within the wood itself. When the pole was finished, the members of the tribe, attired in traditional Haida regalia, bear what many believe represents the soul of their village to its vantage point overlooking the sea. Reid, who feels he may never again embark on a project of such magnitude, watches with pride as the totem created by his Haida heritage is put in place.*

Biquefarre (1984) 90 min. Georges Rouquier (DI). Dist: NYF FR$165, FS$1295. *The theme of technological change and its impact of rural France is at the core of this fictional film. It has close ties to Rouquier's earlier film, Farrebique, named after another farm. This film "returns to the same farm and actor/farmers 38 years later."* [From the review by Deborah Reed-Danahay, *AA* 89:1013–1014, 1987.]

Birth 40 min. Arthur Barron and Even Barron (FM). Dist: FL. *A couple in New York City go through LaMaze classes and prepare for birth.* [Reviewed by Nancie L. Gonzalez et al., *AA* 77:172, 1975.]

Birth of Language (1987) 56 min. Paul Jay (FM). Dist: DCL VR$85, FS$895, VS$350. *Various approaches to the origin of language.* [Reviewed by Philip Lieberman, *AA* 92:264–265.]

Birthplace Unknown 55 min. Karin Junger (DI), Peter Brugman (CA), Leo de Boer (ED), Ruud Monster (PR), Nac Vleeshouwers and Bert Flantua (SR). Dist:ZFL. *Director Karin Junger accompanied her two South Korean adopted sisters when they returned to their native land. A journey back to an unknown past, with hopes of recognition and answers, but without the guarantee of a satisfactory conclusion. The film is a moving report of this journey. The ideas and expectations before departure, the excitement of setting foot on home soil again, visiting places and people from the past. A film about confronting fate and about the importance of having your own roots.*

Bitter Melons (see San Series)

Black Athena (1991) 52 min. Bandung File, Channel 4 (PR). Dist: CN VR$75, VS$195. *Examines Professor Martin Bernal's iconoclastic study of the African origins of Greek civilization and its explosive impact on academic discourse. The film offers a balanced, scholarly introduction to the heated disputes around multiculturalism, "political correctness," and Afrocentric curricula sweeping college campuses today. Bernal charges 19th-century scholars with the construction of a "cult of Greece" as a pure Aryan dawn for Western culture, saying that they have suppressed any connection between Greece and the African cultures. The film scrutinizes the archeological and linguistic evidence underlying Bernal's claim that Bronze Age Greece was rooted in Egyptian civilization. Eminent scholars provide a cross-section of critical commentary on Bernal's work. They suggest that Bernal uses evidence selectively and uncritically to support his own Afrocentric agenda.* [Reviewed by Peter S. Allen, *AA* 94(4):1024–1026, 1992.]

Black Delta Religion 15 min. Bill and Josette Ferris (FM), Judy Peiser (ED). Dist: CSF FR$25, FS$235. *Captures the evolution from traditional rural to sanctified urban religious services in the Mississippi Delta. The film begins with a rural Baptist service at Rose Hill Church where the sermon and unaccompanied singing become so intense that members of the congregation are seized by the Holy Spirit and must be carried outdoors. A baptism follows the church service. New members of the church are led into a pond and immersed in its water by their preacher. Throughout both services, the congregation sings "Dr. Watts Hymns," the oldest form of black religious song. From these traditional rural services, the film moves to a sanctified urban church where guitars and tambourines introduce a powerful rhythmic background for the sermon. One member of the congregation is seized by the Holy Spirit and performs a religious dance during the service. In the final sequences of this film, the Southland Hummingbirds sing gospel music at a rehearsal in their home in Lula Junction, Mississippi. Their fast, rhythmic sound is the modern counterpoint to the slow moaning of Dr. Watts' hymns sung at the beginning of the film.* [Reviewed by Jeff T. Titon, *AA* 77:471–473, 1975. David Evans, *JAF* 90(355):120, 1977.]

Black Girl (La noire de . . .) 60 min. Ousmane Sembene (WR, DI). Dist: NYF. *A fictional film about an African* *woman brought into France as a housemaid.* [Reviewed by Risa Ellovich, *AA* 79:199, 1977.]

Black Girl (The Planning Ahead Series) (1982) 30 min. Dist: UCEMC FR$39, VR$32, FS$470, VS$355. *"This excellently written, directed, and acted film provides a sensitive look at the social and interpersonal issues facing a black matriarchal family and examines their attitudes toward succeeding in a white world."* [From the review by David J. Pratto, *SBF* 18:278, 1983.]

Black Harvest (1991) 90 min. Robin Anderson and Bob Connolly (FM). Dist: DCL. *Joe Leahy, featured in two earlier films* (First Contact *and* Joe Leahy's Neighbors*), goes into partnership with the Ganiga (highlands of Papua New Guinea) in a coffee-growing scheme that does not work out.* [Reviewed by Deborah Gewertz and Frederick Errigton, *AA* 94(4):1026–1027, 1992.]

Black Man's Houses (1992) 58 min. Steve Thomas (FM). Dist: OCL. *In the 1830s, the ill-fated settlement of Wybalenna (Black Man's Houses) was established as a place of internment for the black survivors of the conflict between Europeans and Aborigines on Tasmania. This film documents the reoccupation of this site by Tasmanian Aborigines and explores what Aboriginality means.*

Black Market (Commodities Series) (1986) 28 min. Sue Clayton and Jonathan Curling (PR). Dist: FRIF VR$50, VS$220. *From 1650 onward, the British controlled the seas and, thus, international trade. Opium exports from India to China helped finance the British East India Company's administration of India and paid for the imports of porcelain, silk, and, most importantly, tea, to which the British were heavily addicted. This video illuminates the monopoly trading companies' determination to impose their will on China and to control its markets for their advantage.*

Black Mother, Black Daughter (1989) 29 min. National Film Board of Canada (PR). Dist: IUAVC VR$30, FS$550, VS$250. *Black women in Nova Scotia.* [Reviewed by Colleen Johnson, *AA* 93(3):771–772, 1991.]

Black Water (1990) 28 min. Charlotte Cerf and Allen Moore (FM). Dist: Bahia Film Project, 108 Fitzwater Street, Philadelphia, PA 19147; (215) 755-3756. *Industrial pollution in Bahia, Brazil.* [Reviewed by Dwight B. Heath, *AA* 94(1):253, 1992.]

Black Women 52 min. Tony Brown (PR). Dist: Impact Films. *The situation of black women in Africa.* [Reviewed by Anne M. Jennings, *AA* 79: 206, 1977.]

Blackjack's Family 53 min. William Donker, David Milholland (FM). Dist: G. V. Hood Films, P.O. Box 22213, Milwaukie, OR 97222. *Two years in the life of a Seattle family.* [Reviewed by Beatrice B. Whiting, *AA* 78:953, 1976.]

Blades and Pressure Flaking (1969) 21 min. J. Desmond Clark and Glynn L. Isaac (AN), University of California (PR). Dist: UCEMC FR$30, FS$300. *Francois Bordes, Director of the Laboratory of Prehistory, University of Bordeaux, demonstrates how stone blades were probably made by direct percussion and by the punch technique, and Don Crabtree, an expert in lithic technology, demonstrates various methods of manufacturing tools by pressure-flaking techniques. Chronological implications of various techniques are explained. Pressure-flaking techniques were probably invented as a method of retouching and refining tools formed by percussion flaking; this improvement enabled men to develop delicate and elaborate tools and greatly increased his efficiency not only as a hunter but later as an agriculturalist and artisan. From stone blades, Professor Bordes fashions upper Paleolithic tools such as burins, awls, scrapers, and knives. Mesolithic techniques of fabricating microburins used to make sophisticated hafted tools are shown. He also illustrates the working of Solutrean bifacial foliate points by direct percussion, indicating that laurel leaf points were probably made by percussion flaking, not by pressure flaking as was formerly thought. Professor Bordes demonstrates the initial percussion shaping of a tool, which Don Crabtree then completes by means of pressure flaking. Mr. Crabtree also shows in detail the fluting of Folsom pints and the elegant Valley of Mexico blade technique. Methods of working with flint and obsidian are illustrated, and the uses of many tools are described as their production is shown. In a dramatic conclusion, the film demonstrates that the Valley of Mexico blade, made from obsidian, has the sharpest cutting edge man has ever been able to devise. The film is intended for general use at the high school, college, and adult levels in the study of physical and cultural anthropology, archaeology, and arts and crafts.* [Reviewed by Edwin N. Wilmsen, *AA* 79:970, 1970.]

The Blazing of the Trail (see The Decade of Destruction Series) Bombay: Our City 1985) 82 min. Anand Patwardhan (FM). Dist: ICF FR$125, FS$1195, VS$750. *"Made by an Indian filmmaker, . . . considering the problem: What should be done about Bombay's thousands of shanty-dwellers? . . . Tells the story of the slum-dwellers whose simply constructed housing is demolished by city workers time and time again."* [From the review by Joan L. Erdman, *AA* 89:251–253, 1987.]

Bleeding Hearts and Bone Crushers (1967) 45 min. J. H. Crook (FM). Dist: PSU. *The bleeding heart gelada baboon in Ethiopia.* [Reviewed by Steven Green, *AA* 75:2005, 1973.]

Blind Prophets of Easter Island (Cousteau Odyssey Series) (1979) 24 min. Jacques Cousteau (PR). Dist: WDEM FS$410. *"This is a visually exciting film, and the ideas it presents will lead to interesting classroom discussions."* [From the review by Philip A. Meyers, *SBF* 15:46, 1979.]

The Blind Swordsman (see The Japanese Series)

Blood Groups, Skin Color, and Gene Pools (1960) 30 min. Dist: PSU FR$14. *Dr. Curt Stern explains alleles and hereditary aspects of different genotypic combinations in human blood groups.*

Blood of the Condor (1969) 72 min. Jorge Sanjines (DI), The Ukamau Group (PR). Dist: UNI FR$100. *Sanjines (in exile from his native Bolivia), is a leader among Latin American filmmakers who have set out to create a "cinema of decolonization." He and his group are trying to develop a* *collective method of production—one that seeks the active collaboration of the Indian peoples who are the subjects of the films. Blood of the Condor is a dramatized account of a U.S.-imposed population control program carried out by the Peace Corps in which Quechua Indian women were sterilized without their knowledge or consent. The film also explores the lifestyles, customs, and religious rituals of the Quechua Indians and delineates the relationships of these impoverished people to the members of other social classes in Bolivian society.* Focusing questions: What interests might the United States have in the population control program it is exporting? The portrayal of Americans in the film is very negative. Is it plausible? What American characteristics are depicted and can you identify with them? [Reviewed by Eric Ross, AA 80:203–204, 1978.]

The Blooms of Banjeli: Technology and Gender in African Ironmaking (1986) 29 min. Carlyn Saltman (DI), with Candice Gaucher and Eugenia Herbert. Dist: DER VR$45, VS$275. *Documents research in Banjeli, Togo, on ironsmelting technology and its rituals and sexual prohibitions. It includes rare historical footage from the same village in 1914, providing a unique technological record. It offers a provocative approach to our understanding of the relationship between conceptions of gender and technology in an African society.* [Reviewed by Patrick R. McNaughton, AA 91:1092–1094, 1989.]

Blow for Blow (1972) 89 min. Marin Karmitz (DI). Dist: UNI. *A fictional account of a strike in Rouen, France, based on the events of 1968.* In French with English subtitles. [Reviewed by Rayna Rapp Reiter, AA 79:745, 1977.]

Blue: A Tlingit Odyssey (Myth onto Film: A Trilogy from Native Australia, Native America and the Kabbalah) 6 min. Robert Ascher (PR). Dist: CUAV FR$20, FS$110, VS$49. *A visual rendering of the Tlingit hero myth. The Tlingit are Native Americans who live in southeast Alaska. In their version of the myth, the heroes are four brothers who go in search of blue. The film starts by illustrating the illumination of the world—an event caused by the raven who released the sun from its box. A voice, speaking in Tlingit, accompanies the images and tells how Raven brought daylight to the world. In part one, "The Search," the brothers set out on a journey, encountering marvelous creatures along the way. In the second part, "The Find," the brothers find blue. Having found and taken something so valuable, they are pursued and a storm develops. One of the brothers dies in the storm; the others, with their gift of blue, complete the trip home.* [Reviewed by Paul Stoller, AA 94(2):521–522, 1992.]

Blue Collar and Buddha 57 min. Taggart Siegel and Kati Johnston (PR). Dist: FL VR$75, VS$295, VR$40, VS$200. *This dramatic documentary sensitively explores the dilemma of a community of Laotian refugees, torn between preserving their cultural identity and adapting to their life in America. Resettling in Rockport, Illinois, their adaptation is complicated by the rising tensions with their working-class neighbors who resent their economic gains and view their Buddhism with hostility. With shocking clarity, Rockport's blue-collar workers, many unemployed, voice their hatred of the newcomers, whom they confuse with former enemies in Vietnam. When the Laotians built a Buddhist temple on a small farmstead outside of town, the monks are subject to terrorists attacks. Town officials and clergymen respond to this crisis, some with indifference and some with concern. The Laotians, for their part, feel helpless to assuage the anger they incur since they have no other options but to stay in Rockport, working hard to make a better life for their children.* [Reviewed by Winnie Lambrecht, AA 92:554, 1990.]

Blue Collar Trap (1972) 60 min. Dist: IMS-UW. *Filmed at Ford motor plant in Milpetas, California. Case studies of four 30-and-under workers. Interviews focusing on each worker, wives, and parents. An attempt to capture worker's views about themselves, their jobs, and their future.* Focusing questions: How do the workers' views of work and life differ from those of their parents? Why don't they change jobs? In what way does technology affect their view of work and themselves? How did this come about? How could this situation be changed? By whom? [Dan Early]

The Blues According to Lightin' Hopkins 31 min. Les Blank (FM). Dist: FF. [Reviewed by Roger D. Abrahams, AA 76:206, 1974.]

Blunden Harbor 20 min. William R. Heick and Pierre Jaquemin (FM), Orbit Films and Robert G. Gardner (PR). Dist: UCEMC FR$17. *Pacific Northwest Indian life is seen in this documentary film of one small group of Kwakiutl Indians as they lived in Blunden Harbor in 1950. The film recounts the poetic legend of the Killer Whale becoming a man and also captures the quiet rhythm of the workday life of the Killer Whale's descendants, who gain their sustenance from the sea.*

Boas, Franz (1858–1942) (see *The Shackles of Tradition* in the Strangers Abroad Series)

Body Language (1986) 30 min. Dist: IM VS$129, order #JJ107. *In this clear, fast-paced introduction to kinesics and proxemics, students learn how gestures mirror inner feelings and how posture can reveal opinions and send messages. Emphasizing that much of communication is nonverbal, this still-image program examines the unwritten—but powerfully enforced—rules of eye contact and the concepts of personal and public space, as well as how these concepts differ across cultures.*

Bogotá: Fragments of a City (1979) 15 min. Jan-Henk Klijn (DI, CA), International Film Foundation (PR). Dist: IFF FR$25, FS$250. *A young photographer walks through the plazas and side streets of Colombia's capital, capturing images of life in what he characterizes as a sad and old city. His expressive black-and-white stills of people, and his personal impressions and reactions heard in voice-over, form the focus of the film, which glimpses his wanderings and echoes and amplifies his portraits of a large squatter family clinging to the barrio, an errant street child, a middle-class family headed by a domineering male, and a member of the upper class, born and accustomed to isolating wealth. The young man's reflections on what he sees and learns remind the viewer of the fragmented limitation of his view, yet indicate an acute awareness of the disparate popu-*

lations that comprise the city and the culturally ingrained behavior and outlook of its various citizens.

Boneshop of the Heart (1991) 53 min. Scott Crocker and Toshiaki Ozawa (FM). Dist: UCEMC FR$60, FS$995, VS$295. *Explores a rich vein of visual expression and American individuality through incisive portraits of five contemporary southern folk artists, four of whom are African American. The film reveals art forms so radically different from familiar folk traditions that the artists—"Tin Man" Charlie Lucas, Vollis Simpson, Thortan Dial, Bessie Harvey, and "Sandman" Lonnie Bradley Holley—defy classification. Variously known as "outsider" or "visionary" artists, they create unique aesthetic forms that challenge traditional distinctions between "fine" and "folk" art.*

Bono Medicines (1981) 72 min. J. Scott Dodds, Thomas J. Wallace, and David D. Ohl (FM), D. Michael Warren (AN). Dist: White Pine Films, Box 75, Lone Rock, IA 50559; (515) 295-3962 FR$70, FS$750. *"Filmed in Techiman, the capital of a traditional, Akan-speaking state in Ghana.... We are informed that the Bono see illness as caused by both natural and spiritual forces; in the latter case a spiritual agent causes convulsions.... The second half of the film concerns the integration of traditional and modern medicine in a project under way at the time the film was made."* [From the review by Simon Ottenberg, *AA* 86:802–803, 1984.]

Born Again: Life in a Fundamentalist Baptist Church (1988) 90 (or 55) min. James Ault and Michael Camerini (FM). Dist: James Ault Films, 71 Fifth Avenue, Suite 1100, New York, NY 10003; (212) 799-5052 FR$110, FS$1050, VS$500. *"A portrait of a fundamentalist independent Baptist church in Massachusetts, along with the Christian school it operates."* [From the review by Melinda Bollar Wagner, *AA* 91:1088–1089, 1989.] Study guide available.

Born for Hard Luck: Peg Leg Sam Jackson 29 min. Tom Davenport (FM), Daniel Patterson (AN). Dist: TDF FR$30, FS$275. *Between the Civil War and World War II, many gifted and restless young black musicians found careers in the traveling patent-medicine show, a favorite entertainment in the rural and small-town South. They sang and recited comic routines and danced to attract a crowd for the pitchman and his sales of wonder-cure "snake oil." One of the last and greatest of these medicine-show entertainers is Arthur "Peg Leg Sam" Jackson. Born for Hard Luck includes highlights from Peg Leg Sam's performance at a North Carolina county fair in 1972, the only film record of a live medicine show. It gives excerpts from his comic routines, a mock chanted sermon, "toasts," folktales, three "buck dances," and his brilliant harmonica playing and singing of "Reuben Train," "Greasy Greens," "Hand Me Down," "Who Left My Backdoor Running," and "Froggie Went A-Courting." But the film is a portrait not only of Peg Leg Sam the hobo, living by his wits and talent in the Jim Crow Era, but also of Jackson, the man who left—but has returned to—his roots in a black community of the rural South.*

Bougainville Copper Project (1972) 28 min. Bechtel Corp (PR). Dist: UCEMC FR$26. *An "Industrial Film" made by the company that built the Conzinc Riotinto copper-mining facility. Focuses on the technological achievement.* Suggested supplements: Douglas Oliver, *Bougainville: A Personal History*. Hawaii University Press, 1973. Eugene Ogan, *Cargo, Copper, and Colonialism*. Menlo Park, CA: Cummings.

A Bouziques, une caméra chez vous 27 min. Dist: FACSEA FR$16. *Small fishing village in southern France.* (English)

Box of Treasures 28 min. Chuck Olin (DI), U'mista Cultural Centre (FM). Dist: DER FR$48, VR$35, FS$480, VS$350. *In 1921, the Kwakiutl people of Alert Bay, British Columbia, held their last secret potlatch. Half a century later the splendid masks, blankets and copper heirlooms that had been confiscated by the Canadian government were returned. The Kwakiutl built a cultural center to house these treasures and named it* u'mista, *"something of great value that has come back." This film is eloquent testimony to the persistence and complexity of Kwakiutl society today, to the struggle to redefine cultural identity in one Northwest Coast Native American community.* [Reviewed by Mark S. Fleisher, *AA* 86:1061–1062, 1984.]

A Brazilian Family (1978) 20 min. Vladimir Bibic (DI, CA). Dist: IFF FR$35, FS$350. *The comfortably situated upper-middle-class da Silva family, consisting of a chemical engineer, a social worker, and their two sons, is the focus of this leisurely descriptive overview of Brazilian life. While the da Silvas are admittedly part of a "small but influential minority" of Brazilians, and their modern, well-appointed home is not the norm, the roaming footage and chatty voice-over narration realistically guides the film beyond the confines of this one lifestyle. Additional description of the da Silva's jobs and working conditions, their relatives and close family life, and their holidays and leisure time activities touch on the living conditions of less fortunate farming and industrial families. Economic and geographical highlights, traditional foods, and religious celebrations are presented in an informative way that weighs commentary with observant footage. This film observes the economic disparity caused by rapid urbanization and industrialization, the existing hunger in a nation that gears its rich agricultural yield to export, the pressures that the world energy crisis is placing on Brazil's development, and the emphasis of social services for the educated and professional class, who are felt to make greater contributions to Brazil's development.*

Bread Making in a Rural Household 13 min. Maurice A. Mook (AN), D. P. Duvall and L. P. Greenhill (PR), Encyclopaedia Cinematographica E 1021. Dist: PSU. *Central Pennsylvania.* [Reviewed by Henry Glassie, *AA* 76:725, 1974.]

Breaking Ground (1982) 25 min. Catherine Neukum (FM). Dist: Catherine Neukum, 26 Carmine Street, New York, NY 10017; (212) 581-7100 FR$45, FS$525. *"A short film on historical archaeology in lower Manhattan.... We are taken to excavations at three sites. The most interesting is the Stadt Huys Block, with remains of Dutch houses of the 1640s as well as a later British occupation."* [From the review by Michael D. Coe, *ARCH* 37(3):77, 1984.]

The Brick Makers 42 min. Marta Rodriguez and Jorge Silva (DI). Dist: CG FR$65, VR$65, FS$595, VS$395. *This is a classic anthropological film on the way of life for millions of Latin Americans who live in shantytowns on the outskirts of major cities. These landless peasants have been forced to leave the countryside and migrate to the cities in search of employment where, if they are lucky to find work at all, they become highly exploited and poorly paid laborers at the most undesirable jobs. In detailing the day-to-day existence of a peasant family that produces earthen bricks for a living, the film explores many different aspects of 'the culture of poverty', including interviews with family members on their thoughts about politics, religion, family relations, and relations between owners and workers.* Spanish dialogue with English subtitles.

The Bride Market of Imilchil (1986) 58 min. Christian Pierce and Steffen Pierce (FM). Dist: Pierce Productions, 58 Ridgemont Street, Allston, MA 02134; (607) 254-0281 VR$70, VS$300. *"Along with other tourists, two American travelers attend a Berber festival in a once remote mountain valley now reached by tour buses for the occasion. . . . It is the personal record of an interaction, together with inevitable misunderstandings and projections."* [From the review by Stefania Pandolfo, AA 92(4):1108–109, 1990. Reviewed in *VISA* 4:83, 1991.]

Brides of the Gods (1985) 55 min. William R. Geddes (FM, AN). Dist: OWF FS$850, VS$375. *Examines the ritual of 'divine marriage'.* [Reviewed by Robert Gardner, AA 89:265–267, 1987.]

Brighton Beach (1980) 55 min. Susan Wittenberg and Carol Stein (FM). Dist: AC FR$150, FS$1000. *"An impressionistic portrait of Brighton Beach . . . a little-known neighborhood in Brooklyn. . . . As home to several waves of immigrants, it is one of the more colorful and heterogeneous areas of New York."* [From the review by Faye Ginsburg, AA 87:741–747, 1985.]

Broken Rainbow (1986) 69 min. Mario Floria (WR), Victoria Mudd (WR, DI), Thom Tyson (DI), Martin Sheen, Burgess Meredith, Buffy Sainte-Marie and Semu Huaute (NA), Laura Nyro (MU). Dist: DCL FR$175, FS$995, VS$350. *A moving account of the forced relocation of 12,000 Navajo Indians that is currently taking place in Northern Arizona. The U.S. government claims that by moving the Navajo off the land, it is settling a long-standing territorial dispute between the Navajo and Hopi tribes. To the traditional Navajo and Hopi, there is no dispute. They believe relocation was designed to facilitate energy development. The film captures the majesty of sacred Indian lands and the devastating effect that mining, forced relocation, and stock reduction has had on the land and its people. It speaks for all indigenous people who are struggling to survive as individuals and as distinct cultures in the face of Western technology and values.* [Reviewed by Richard O. Clemmer, AA 89:1014–1015, 1987.]

Broken Treaty at Battle Mountain (1974) 60 min. Joel L. Freedman (DI), Robert Redford (NAR). Dist: UNI FR$150, FS$700. *A documentary film shot from the perspective of a group of Shoshone living in the community of Battle Mountain, Nevada, describing their disagreements with the Bureau of Land Management (BLM) over settlement of a 19th-century land-claim case. Shows events during several meetings with the BLM, representatives of the Indians Claims Commission, and other Shoshone. Describes current conditions in Battle Mountain, contrasts traditional Shoshone harvest of pinon nuts with the BLM uses and abuses of the land for grazing and other purposes.* Focusing questions: What are the differences in the ways Battle Mountain Shoshone use the land and BLM uses? Why do you think there are such differences among the Shoshone over settlement of the claims case? Are there any possibilities for compromise among these different opinions? Why or why not? [Anne Smith Denman]

Brujo—Shaman (1978) 55 min. George Payrastre (CA), Claudine Viallon (SR). Dist: DER FR$65, FS$650. *Brujo, or the cults and shamanism of Mayan Indians in southern Mexico and Guatemala. Through three distinct healing ceremonies, the film illustrates the Indians' uses of their native medicine.*

Bronze Age Blastoff BBC-TV (PR). (Re-edited as *Masters of Metal* for Odyssey Series 1981.) Dist: FI.

Bryan Beavers: A Moving Portrait (1969) 30 min. KVIE, Sacramento, California/Public Television Library (PR). Dist: IUAVC FR$12.50, FS$360. *Bryan Beavers is a Maidu Indian living in a log cabin, which he built by himself, in the wilderness area of Plumas County, California. He is a man who has experienced two distinct cultures, which combined give him a unique personality. As Beavers is talking about his past—Indian Spirits, his ancestral history, and his life—the camera is following him about his daily tasks, such as taking care of his animals, making a snow shoe, and eating.* [Reviewed by John H. Bushnell, AA 71:1235, 1969.]

Buck Dancer (1966/1974) 6 min. Edmund Carpenter, Bess Lomax Hawes, Alan Lomax (FM). Dist: FIM/RF FR$15, FS$75. *When Ed Young of northern Mississippi sets his homemade fife to his lips, he turns into a dark Pan, cocking his instrument at the stars, swaying and stepping in an ancestral dance as he blows one African riff after another. His is the music that was popular at country picnics in Mississippi until a couple of decades ago, and his "buck dance" is a traditional dance of male country blacks of days past. In fact, his may be the only living reminder of the glories of Southern black music in the days before the minstrel shows. He is accompanied in this film by vocals and hand-clapping by the Georgia Sea Island Singers.* [Reviewed by Robert Palmer, *JAF* 90(356):249.]

Buckeyes: Food of California Indians (American Indian Film Series) (1961) 13 min. Dist: UCEMC FR$25, FS$190; PSU (PCR) order #2205K, FR$5.90, SR130. *California buckeyes, or horse chestnuts, were an important article of the California Indians' diet. Although buckeyes are not edible as they come from the tree, centuries ago the Indians of California discovered how to remove the poisons and made an edible meal from these nuts. This film shows how the Nisenan Indians harvested buckeyes and processed them by boiling and leaching. The nuts were then cracked, boiled with hot rocks in cooking baskets, and then mashed.*

A pit was then dug in the gravel on a river bar, lined with sand and large leaves, and used to leach the bitter and poisonous alkaloid from the meal. California Indians ate buckeyes as a heavy mush or as a soup. Buckeyes were second only to acorns in the dietary economy of many California tribes. [Reviewed by Harold E. Driver, *AA* 68:596, 1966.]

Buddhism in China (1983) 30 min. Wan-go Weng (FM) for the China Institute in America. Dist: IUAVC FR$25, FS$360, VS$175. *"A survey of the rise of Chinese Buddhism. . . . Traces the spread of Mahayana Buddhism from India to China, the emergence of different schools of thought, the introduction of Lamaism from Tibet, the three great persecutions, and the final synthesis with the state of Confucian ideology."* [From the review by Kathleen McDermott, *AA* 86:1074, 1984.]

The Buffalo Creek Flood (1975) 40 min. Mimi Pickering (FM). Dist: APPAL FR$50, FS$475. *In 1972 a giant coal waste dam burst, leaving 124 dead, 4,000 homeless, and the Pittston Coal Company calling the disaster "an act of God." A combination of spontaneous filming and postflood interviews give the complete story of the disaster and its aftermath.* Related reading: Kai T. Erikson, *Everything in Its Path: Destruction of Community in the Buffalo Creek Flood.* Simon and Schuster, New York, 1976. See *Buffalo Creek Revisited.*

Buffalo Creek Revisited (1984) 31 min. Mimi Pickering (DI). Dist: APPAL FR$55, FS$500, VS$225. *In 1972, a coal-waste dam at the head of a crowded hollow in southern West Virginia collapsed. A wall of sludge and water slashed through the valley killing 125 people and leaving 4,000 homeless. This film looks at the second disaster of Buffalo Creek, in which the survivors' efforts to rebuild the physical and emotional community shattered by the flood have been thwarted by government insensitivity and a century-old pattern of corporate control of the region's land and resources.* See *The Buffalo Creek Flood.*

Bukoki (1973) 25 min. Jean Rouch (DI), Centre National de la Recherche Scientifique, Comité du Film Ethnographique (PR). Dist: CFE; DER. *A rain ritual in the seventh month of the dry season in a suburb of Niamey. The gods of the sky possess their 'horses' giving rain for the year.*

Bulimia 12 min. ABC (PR), Hugh Downs (NA). Dist: CRM/MH FR$22, FS$215. *This film was originally made for the ABC television program 20/20. "It begins by defining bulimia and its effects; then we are introduced to several young women who discuss their eating problems. . . . It provides a good springboard for classroom discussion of such topics as the relationships that exist between sociocultural contexts and eating habits and disorders, the roles of biological and psychological factors in eating disorders, and gender statuses and roles in the US."* [From the review by Thomas W. Hill, *AJPA* 66:105–106, 1985.]

The Burk Family, Dalton, Georgia (see Six American Families Series)

BUSHMAN SERIES (see The San Film Series)

Bushmen of the Kalahari (1974) 52 min. John Marshall (FM), National Geographic Society (PR). Dist: PSU $22.50. *After a 15-year lapse during which he was unable to enter the area, John Marshall returned to the Kalahari to visit the people he had filmed in* The Hunters. *The film portrays the tremendous changes he found: a fence restricting the movement of men and animals across the political border; some Bushmen restricted to a reservation; and a people who largely have been forced or influenced to give up their old way of life through the loss of their waterholes. Some manage to survive by a marginal existence as workers on white-owned cattle ranches. Others have become herders, keeping flocks of goats, and dependent for survival on the water obtained from deep wells. Many aspects of the traditional Bushman way of life have been lost: their hunting techniques, their music and dance, their waterholes, their freedom of movement, their independence. Uses in teaching: As a follow-up to* The Hunters; *raises questions regarding the desirability of "progress." Do the gains resulting from modernization outweigh the losses?* [Carol G. Goodwin]

Bushmen of the Kalahari 12 min. Tad Danielewski, Blaine Littell, ABC (PR). *Part of a four-hour ABC-TV special on Africa.* [Reviewed by John Marshall, *AA* 73:502, 1971.]

But I'll Always Continue to Write (The Human Face of Indonesia Series) (1987) 30 min. Film Australia (PR). Dist:FIV VS$99. *The film portrays the life and work of a female journalist named Debra Yatim. Debra is a Djakarta newspaper reporter who works under great stress to bring the plight of Djakarta's low-income and poverty groups to her readers.*

But What if the Dream Comes True (1971) 54 min. Dist: CBS FS$271. *An upper-middle-class family has achieved the American dream of "life in the suburbs," but finds that there is a sense of emptiness in spite of material success. Focusing questions: Why did the wife have a problem? What was her problem? Who was at fault? What was the number-one crime in this city? Why? What did the young adults say they could not find? Discuss the interaction between the blacks and whites. Why couldn't the girls accept the blacks on the blacks' terms?*

Bwana Toshi (1965) 115 min. Susumu Hani (DI). Dist: AB FR$80. *In a fiction film shot on location in Africa, Hani compares a compulsive, high-strung specimen of Japanese civilization with a relaxed African people who display their emotions freely and directly. Toshi arrives in rural Africa with a prefabricated house, which he is to erect for a university study group. But the initial contingent of professors become ill and return to Japan, leaving Toshi to build the house by himself in a land where he understands neither the language nor the customs. Although Toshi never fully adjusts to the natives' leisurely, unpretentious mode of life, his warm, often humorous dealings with them teach him something about human values.*

By Cross and by Sword (A cruz y a espada) (1991) 30 min. Juan Francis Urrusti (FM). Dist: Lillia Haugen, San Francisco 1514, Col. del Valle 03100, Mexico, D.F.; (525) 575-4339; fax (525) 575-4335. *An annual event held in the* *state of Zacatecas Mexico, reenacts the battle between the Moors and the Christians of Middle Ages Europe. The epic and performance binds the community together across generations.*

Cajititlán (1966) 41 min. Harry Atwood (FM), Theron A. Nuñez, University of Florida (AN), Harry Atwood and University of Arizona (PR). *Filmed in the summer of 1964 in Cajititlán, Jalisco, Mexico, a highland Mestizo peasant village. Originally intended by the photographer as an "art-travel" film, the collaboration with the anthropologist resulted in a film of some ethnographic interest. It attempts a portrayal of the daily round of life and work in a traditional, though changing, community. Topics covered are landscape, architecture, diet, occupational specialities of the region (farming, fishing, stone-working, mat-making, and so forth), recreation, religion, and culture change.* Suggested supplements: Theron A. Nuñez, Jr., Cultural Discontinuity and Conflict in a Mexican Village. Unpublished Ph.D. dissertation, Berkeley (microfilm), 1963. Theron A. Nuñez, Jr., Tourism, Tradition, and Acculturation: Weekendismo in a Mexican Village. *Ethnology* 2(3):347–352, 1963.

Cakchiquel Maya of San Antonio Palopo (Disappearing World Series) (1991) 52 min. Tracy Bachrach Ehlers (AN). Dist: FIV VS$198. *The Tunecos, mostly Catholics, populate San Antonio Palopo, about three hours drive from Guatemala City. They speak Cakchiquel, one of more than 20 Mayan languages still spoken in Guatemala. As civilization encroaches, the Tunecos must decide whether the loss of their culture is too high a price to pay for incorporation into the world beyond their lakeside village.* [Reviewed by R. Jon McGee, *AA* 95:249–250,1993.]

Calcutta (1968) 97 min. Louis Malle (DI). Dist: Martin Keltz, Campus Programs, EYR, 78 East 56th St., New York, NY. [Reviewed by Susan Seymour, *AA* 73:503, 1971.]

The California Missions (1990) 22 min. Philomene Long (DI), Martin Sheen (NA). Dist: UCEMC FR$45, FS$450, VS$195. *Explores the heritage of the California missions through a beautiful blend of original poetry, mission-era music, and sensitive photography. The film interweaves vintage archival photos with contemporary footage and emphasizes the clash of cultures between the Spanish Franciscan missionaries and the native California Indians.*

Calumet, Pipe of Peace (American Indian Film Series) (1964) 23 min. Dist: UCEMC FR$31, FS$320. *Many legends of the Great Plains Indians ascribe miraculous powers to the calumet peace pipe. The calumet was employed to insure safe conduct, to placate hostile nations, to control the weather, and to conclude lasting peace treaties. Even before the advent of the pipe, tobacco was considered to be a plant of divine origin, and tobacco burning became the principle medium through which the medicine man and priest communicated with the gods and received their inspirations. This film discusses the Indian rituals surrounding pipe and tobacco and shows traditional Indian methods of fashioning, decorating, and consecrating the pipe bowl and stem.* [Reviewed by James H. Howard, *AA* 68:597, 1966.]

Camels and the Pitjantjara (1971) 57 min. Roger Sandall (DI, CA), Australian Institute of Aboriginal Studies (PR). Dist: UCEMC order #8118, FR$51, FS$720. *Documents the way of life that arose when nomadic central Australian Aborigines acquired camels. Shows the hunt for, rounding up of, and nose-pegging of a wild bull camel, as well as the interesting method used by the Pitjantjara to "tranquilize" camels after capture. Illustrates the Westernized life of many "outback" Aborigines now living in government settlements and also the kind of religious ceremony, done in modern dress, that takes place on the settlement outskirts out of sight of the administrative staff. The last part of the film follows activities of a party of men, women, and children on a 90-mile cross-country journey through the Macdonnell Range from one settlement to another. One of the few films ever made showing the life of Aborigines who, though no longer nomadic, still travel widely from one settlement to another; though wearing Western dress, they speak only Pitjantjara among themselves, and despite prolonged missionary contact, they draw most of their spiritual vigor from their old rites and ceremonies.* [Reviewed by J. P. M. Long, *AA* 73:1477–1478, 1971.] Restricted use. This film contains material of a secret/sacred nature and should only be screened for study purposes by appropriate groups.

Camels and the Pitjantjara (short version) (1971) 27 min. The Australian Institute of Aboriginal Studies (PR). Dist: UCEMC order #8089, FR$34, 5$380. *A party of Aboriginal stockmen show how wild camels in the Australian desert used to be rounded up and broken in. Consists of the first 27 minutes of the film described above; useful for teaching purposes because it ends by raising several unanswered questions.*

Camera d'Afrique (1983) 96 min. Ferid Boughedir (DI). Dist: CN. *Offers a historical overview of African cinema from its inception up to 1982. It features clips from 20 years of African filmmaking and interviews with both pioneer and more recent cineastes.*

Cameroon Brass Casting (1950) Paul Gebauer (FM). Dist: Pitt. *The Banum are the focus of this concise illustration of brass casting in the Cameroons. By means of the lost-wax process, these people mold brass masks and figurines to serve both as decorative ornaments and symbols for ritual demonstration.*

Campesinos and Farming on Isla del Sol, Annual Market Days at Casani (Peru-Bolivian Border)—La Paz, Bolivia (1963) 20 min. Dwight Heath (AN), The Land Tenure Center, University of Wisconsin (PR). Dist: UW. *Illustrates the life and farming methods since the agrarian reform of 1953 of Aymara Indians on the Isla del Sol in Bolivia's Lake Titicaca. Shows how campesinos, through a syndicate, now manage and exploit land formerly in a large hacienda. Primitive farming techniques and health problems are discussed. Visits the annual market days and fiesta at Casani on the Peru-Bolivia border. Scenes include the numerous market goods and the dancing and other festival activities.* Cf. the film *Market at La Paz.* See *Changes in Agriculture, Population, and Utilization of Resources.*

Candles for New Years (1992) 28 min. David W. Plath (FM, WR, CA), Jacquetta F. Hill (AN, WR, NA, CA). Dist: Center for Educational Media, Institute for Education on Japan, Earlham College, Richmond, IN 47374; (317) 983-1324 VS$35. *For 200 years, groups of Lahu have been migrating from southwestern China into the highlands of Southeast Asia's "Golden Triangle" region. Though they share much with other migrants in the ethnic patchwork of the region, the Lahu maintain a vigorous sense of themselves as a distinct people, and New Year is their prime time for celebrating what it means to be Lahu. The program follows the cycle of New Year events in a Lahu community that ethnographer Jaquetta Hill has been studying for more than a decade.*

Cane Toads: An Unnatural History (1988) 46 min. Tristram Miall (PR), Mark Lewis (DI). Dist: FRIF FR$95, FS$745, VS$450. *"Focuses on what people, in the multiplicity of their different social classes, genders, and statuses, have to say about a loathsome and rapidly multiplying animal, the cane toad, introduced by science in the 1930s from Hawaii to combat a pest destroying the sugarcane industry."* [From the review by Michael Taussig, *AA* 92(4):1110–1111, 1990.]

Cannibal Tours (1978) 70 min. Dennis O'Rourke (FM). Dist: DCL FR$175, FS$995, VS$350. *When tourists today journey to the farthest reaches of Papua New Guinea, is it the indigenous tribespeople or the white visitors who are the cultural oddity? This documentary explores the differences and the surprising similarities that emerge when the Western and New Guinean people meet within the context of organized "travel adventure tours." This gently ironic film neither condones nor condemns the tourists or the Papua New Guineans. It offers a series of observations that exemplify the quandary of culture clash and the human sameness of peoples everywhere.* [Reviewed by Frederick Errington, *AA* 91:274–275, 1989. Reviewed in *VISR* 6:24, 1990.]

Canoes of the Ainu (1968) 19 min. American Educational Films and The Hokkaido Education Commission (PR). Dist: AEF FR$30 for 3 days, FS$265. [Reviewed by Sister M. Inez Hilger, *AA* 72:1576, 1970.]

Capital of Earth: The Maroons of Moore Town (ca. 1979) 43 min. Jefferson Miller (FM). Dist: PSU VR$23, FS$515, VS$340. *This historical documentary, filmed in Jamaica, focuses on the Maroons, direct descendants of escaped African slaves who formed rebel communities in the Blue Mountains. For almost 100 years, they waged guerrilla warfare against the British forces before finally winning their freedom and political autonomy. Although caught in a rapidly modernizing Jamaica, the Maroons have retained much of their unique and original West African heritage. Capital of Earth illustrates some of their farming and hunting techniques, drumming, dancing, and healing ceremonies. But today, with the migration of young Maroons to the coastal cities in search of work, the traditional cultural boundaries have begun to disappear. New urban social forces and economic pressures are undermining older Maroon beliefs and customs. Through interviews with old and young, the Maroons openly express their feelings of identity and pride as they reflect on the past, present, and future of Moore Town and Jamaica.* [Reviewed by Johnetta B. Cole, *AA* 85:743–744, 1983.]

Capt'ain Omori (1980) Jean Rouch (DI). Dist: CFE; DER. *A portrait of a Japanese merchant marine captain who opened the first commerical line between Japan and South Africa.*

Caracol, The Lost Maya City (1988) 60 min. Robert Schyberg and Leigh Shipley (PR), Robert Charlton (DI). Dist: PyrF VS$150. *"Until now Caracol, a medium-sized site in south-central Belize, has not been considered a major Maya city. But recent excavations have revealed that Caracol once defeated the mighty Maya city of Tikal, and was probably more important than previously thought. This is a film about the discovery and excavation of Caracol, but it is much more than simply a visual site report. The producers use the Caracol excavations to illustrate many fundamental features of Maya culture, while at the same time they comment on the science and practice of archaeology."* [From the review by Peter S. Allen, *ARCH* 41(5):76, 1988.]

Caravans of Gold (Africa Series) (1986) 57 min. RM Arts (PR), Basil Davidson (H). Dist: FIV. *Davidson traces the roots of the medieval gold trade—which reached from Africa to India, China, and Italy—and examines its influence on the African continent.*

Caribou Hunting at the Crossing Place, Parts I and II (Netsilik Eskimo Series) (1970) 30 min. each. Doug Wilkinson, Michel Chalufour, and Quentin Brown (FM), Asen Balikci and Guy Mary-Rousseliere (AN), Educational Development Center (PR). Dist: EMC FS$420 (pt. 1) FS$324 (pt. 2); EDC apply for rental; Part II: PSU (PCR) order #31617, FR$11.10. *Part I: Woman wakes and dresses boy, boy uses sling shot, woman spreads caribou hide to dry, boy picks berries, men return in kayaks with animal, animal is skinned, night falls; in the morning a weasel visits camp, man departs to hunt with bow, woman cleans sinew and spreads it to dry; man repairs arrows, sets snare for gulls, boy stones snared gull to death and plays hunter with antlers, father makes spinning toy for boy. Part II: Two strangers arrive, four men build long array of stone images of men or inukshuit; visitors wait for caribou, chase animals toward inukshuit and then into water, other men pursue in kayaks and kill swimming caribou with spears, hunters beach and skin caribou; boy plays with visitors, woman cooks meat, men eat marrow from bones, men feast on cooked meat.* [Reviewed by John I. Honigmann, *AA* 72:722–724, 1970.] Cf. the film *Fishing at the Stone Weir*.

Carnarvon (Australian Museum Series) (1969) 8 min. Dist: UCEMC FR$17; PSU (PCR) order #10649, FR$12. *Documenting prehistoric art forms of the Australian Aborigines, this film focuses on wall paintings and sculptures found in the Carnarvon Ranges. There, primitive tribal artists painted human beings, weapons, and animals, using natural ochres fixed only with blood or animal fat. The camera shows that the colors have remained fresh to this day, brightly reflecting the way Aborigines lived, hunted, fought, and told stories. Some paintings may have had deep religious significance; others refer to everyday happenings.*

Some show signs of periodic retouching by the artists, as if ritualistically, in order to renew whatever magic the paintings may have symbolized. Mysterious engravings also appear in the soft Carnarvon rock. The camera picks out hands, weapons, animal tracks, and what could be fertility symbols. Under a painting of a woven basket appear engraved kangaroo tracks and emu footprints, dominated by the outline of a stone axe. Stencil painting, found in prehistoric art the world over, is another feature of the Carnarvon caves; in this technique, the artist places his hand or another object against a rock and blows color around it. We are shown the remains of the most remarkable stencil painting in Australia—the complete outline of a man with his arms outstretched. The film closes by pointing out the need for further research and, therefore, for the preservation of the distinctive Aboriginal modes of self-expression.

Carnaval Bahia (Disappearing World Series) (1982) 50 min. Peter Fry (AN). Dist: PSU order #51243; FIV VS$198, order #047035. *The city of Bahia in northern Brazil is a riot of dance, music, and celebration during Carnaval, a pre-Lenten festival that ends on shrove Tuesday. For five days, the poor become the kings of the town, and festival participants divide into groups, each trying to outdo the other in producing spectacular floats, dazzling costumes, and exuberant displays.*

Carnaval De Pueblo (1987) 58 min. Jerome Mintz (DI). Dist: DER FR$85, VR$50, FS$850, VS$400. *Mintz spent extended periods of time in Andalusia, Spain, during the years 1981–85. It was during this period that he filmed carnival events in Cadiz. Carnival composers write songs about local affairs and produce social criticisms of national events. They are filmed performing and practicing at Town Carnival. The film shows that after the carnival a composer is fined for naming a parent of an illegitimate baby. Townspeople discuss the rights of privacy and freedom of speech.* [Reviewed by Jill Dubisch, AA 90:781–782, 1988.]

Carnival in Q'eros (1991) 32 min. John Cohen (DI). Dist: UCEMC FR$50, FS$640, VS$295. *This documentary shows the remarkable Carnival celebrations—never before seen by outsiders—of a remote community of Quechua Indians high in the Peruvian Andes. While providing an extraordinary ethnographic portrait of Indians who refer to themselves as Incas, the film also explores the connections between Andean and jungle cultures and shows the protracted negotiations by which the Indians were compensated for their participation in the project.* [Reviewed by Norman A. Whitters Jr., AA 94(2):522–523, 1992.]

Carnival T.N.T. (1982) 28 min. AB/Energy Productions (PR). Dist: FI FR$50, VR$460. *Documents the bacchanal that is carnival in the island nation of Trinidad and Tobago. Captures and communicates "the sound, movement, and dynamism of carnival. In addition, the film is successful in presenting some of the historical, sociocultural, economic, and political context of the event."* [From the review by George M. Epple, AA 87:979–980, 1985.]

Carrying of the Young by the Mother. Lesser Mouse Lemur 8.5 min. Dist: PSU FR$2.80.

Carthage: A Mirage of Antiquity (1987) 28 min. David Soren (PR, NA), Pamela White and Sally Summer (DI). Dist: American Museum of Natural History, Central Park West at 79th Street, New York, NY 10024-5192; (212) 769-5000 VS$20. *This program "aims to acquaint the viewer with ancient Carthage and its often overlooked role in history. But the film also manages to present modern Tunisia in a very positive light, skillfully integrating images of its past with scenes from the present."* [From the review by Peter S. Allen, ARCH 41(4):68, 1988.]

La Casa De Mujer—Supporting Women in Nicaragua 12 min. Dist: UWC VS$25, order #2321. *Video describes "las casa de mujer" (houses of women) that offer support to women throughout Nicaragua. The houses offer women a place to meet, seek refuge, and organize . They also provide vocational training, sex education, and legal and medical services. The leader, activist and revolutionary, Gladys Baez of Casa de Mujer, is interviewed in Leon, Nicaragua. This video is in English.*

The Case of the Ancient Astronauts 57 min. WGBH (PR). Dist: WGBH FR$65, FS$750, VS$150. *Have astronauts from other worlds already visited us on Earth? Did they help build the pyramids of Egypt and the great statues on Easter Island? Were they the real gods of ancient legends? "Yes," says Erich Von Daniken, author of* Chariots of the Gods. *And millions of people believe him. NOVA takes a hard look at his bold claims.*

Catal Huyuk By James Mellaart. Dist: POR. Set of 91 slides, $140. See review by Peter S. Allen, ARCH 42(5):74–75, 1986.

Catfish Man of the Woods (1974) 27 min. Dist: APPAL FR$40, FS$425. *A portrait of Clarence Gray, a fifth-generation herb doctor whom people call Catfish Man of the Woods. He sells a mixture of roots and herbs called "bitters" for all types of ailments, from rheumatism to heart trouble and which is acclaimed for its ability to make one lose weight. He is outspoken about his philosophy of life and comments freely about sex, religion, and the way of the woods.*

Cave Dwellers of the Old Stone Age (1960) 17 min. Dist: IUAVC FR$9.25. *Recreates from skeletons, tools, weapons, and cave painting, the life led by prehistoric man during the Old Stone Age. Shows how the Neanderthal caveman and the Cro-Magnon family provided themselves with food, clothing, and shelter by dramatizing events in their everyday lives.* [Reviewed by Philip E. L. Smith, AA 77:921, 1975.]

The Cave Paintings of the Chumash Indians 30, 23, 18 min. Steve Penney (FM). Dist: Steve Penney Productions, 206 Vista del Sol, Redondo Beach, CA 90277 FS$395. $320, $245. *The Chumash Indians of southern California left the richest legacy of prehistoric rock paintings in North America. They were a people who believed in a supernatural world that was as real and easily visualized as the natural world, and many of the Chumash paintings were probably depictions of supernatural beings or phenomena. The beautiful polychrome paintings are almost always found in remote mountain areas. It is believed these spectacular* *paintings were connected with the dream or vision quests that played such an important part in the lives of the North American Indians.*

The Cave People of the Philippines (1973) 38 min. Dist: Fl FR$60, FS$565. *A small group of aborigines, the Tasaday, lived undisturbed by civilization for 400 years in the rain forest of Mindanao, the Philippines. These gentle stone-age people existed happily in their subsistence culture oblivious of and unknown to the outside world. In 1971, the 26 Tasadays were discovered. Even though they are being protected by the Philippine government and a foundation, this anthropological documentary may be the last chance to see them before outside contacts and influences unintentionally bring about changes. Focusing questions: What assumptions of our culture are thrown into doubt by the Tasaday culture? What should be the future of the Tasaday? What are the elements of ethnocentrism in the account given of the Tasaday? Bibliography: John Nance, The Gentle Tasaday.* [Pauline Kolenda]

Caxiri or Manioc Beer (The Waiapi Indians of Brazil Series) (1988) 19 min. Victor Fuks (PR). Dist: IUAVC VR$20, VS$105, order #CC3781. *This program discusses manioc, the most important product of Waiapi agriculture, whose several species comprise a substantial part of Waiapi diet. Although the harvested tubers must undergo extensive processing to remove prussic acid and other toxins, the plant is easy to grow, requires little cultivation, is highly resistant to insects, and is quite prolific. The arduous processing results in kwaka flour, which is made into mejus, the pancakes that are eaten with most meals. The mejus are also fermented in large quantities to produce caxiri, the highly esteemed beer that is a crucial accompaniment to Waiapi festivals and musical performances.* [Reviewed in *VISA* 4:91, 1991.]

"Ce pu comme ça anymore" (Le Son des Français de l'Amerique) (1977) 28 min. André Gladu (DI), Michel Brault (CA), Nanouk Films (PR). Dist: Faroun Films, 136A est rue St. Paul, Montreal, Canada PQ H2Y 1G6. [Reviewed by Gerald L. Gold, *AA* 80:760–763, 1978.]

Cebus Monkeys of Barro Colorado Island: Ecology and Behavior (1974) 33 min. John Oppenheimer (AN). Dist: PSU FR$20, FS$425. *Naturalistic behavior of wild Cebus monkeys, Cebus capucinus. Includes descriptions of age and sex classes, locomotion, feeding ecology, vocalizations, and social behavior patterns such as play, grooming, resting, displays, displacement, and agonistic behavior.* Relevant anthropological literature: J. R. Oppenheimer, "Changes in Group Composition and Forehead Patterns of the White-Faced Monkey, Cebus capacinus." In: Recent Advances in Primatology. Carpenter and Hofer, eds. S. Karger, Base, 1969. J. R. Oppenheimer, "Social and Communicatory Behavior in the Cebus monkey." In: Behavioral Regulators of Behavior in Primates. C. R. Carpenter, ed. Bucknell University Press, Lewisburg, 1973. J. R. Oppenheimer and E. C. Oppenheimer, "Preliminary Observations of Cebus nigrivittatus (Primates) on the Venezuelan Llanos." *Folia primat.* 19:409–436, 1973. J. R. Oppenheimer and G. E. Lang, Cebus Monkeys: Effect on Branching of Gustavia trees. *Science* 165:187–188, 1969.

Celebracion del matrimonio 30 min. Margaret Hixon (FM). Dist: UCEMC FR$44, VR$44, FS$530, VS$350, order #11296(f), order #37343(v). *This sensitive portrait of a traditional Hispanic wedding ceremony in northern New Mexico illuminates the rich heritage of Hispanic culture in America and shows the importance of traditional customs and values in contemporary Hispanic life. Available in English- and Spanish-language versions with an accompanying study guide.*

Celebration: A Caribbean Festival 30 min. Karen Kramer (FM). Dist: FL FR$75, VR$55, FS$550, VS$295; KKFL FR$75, VR$55, FS$550, VS$350. *This joyous, upbeat film explodes with the color, music, and pride of Carnival in America's largest Caribbean community. Modeled after the one held "back home" in the islands, this has become an annual event in New York, bringing together Caribbean immigrants from virtually every island in the West Indies. It is filled with striking visual displays of costumed performers, infectious calypso music, steel bands, a mosaic of tropical food, and rocking crowds. The film captures the thoughts and feelings of expatriate West Indians, as they are interviewed during preparations leading up to the Carnival. As we go behind the scenes to watch the step-by-step making of the elaborate and enormous sculpture-like costumes, we learn how the Carnival is a way of maintaining a sense of identity and continuity of cultural tradition.*

A Celebration of Origins (1992) 45 min. Timothy Asch (FM). Dist: DER. *The people of Wai Brama domain, Flores, Indonesia, celebrate the mythic founding of their people with rituals involving the entire community. These rituals do not merely affirm a traditional social order but also provide an arena in which the community may respond to the changing milieu of life in a modern nation state. Thus, the film shows some of the ways in which a remote community attempts to reconcile its tradtions with impinging Catholicism and modernization.*

A Celtic Trilogy (1981) 96 min. Kathleen Dowdey (FM). Dist: FRF FR$165, FS$1300. *Celtic survivals in Ireland, Scotland, Wales, and Brittany.* [Reviewed by Susan Heuck Allen, *AA* 86:511–512, 1984.]

Central America: On the Horns of a Dilemma Billie R. DeWalt (H), University of Kentucky Office of Instructional Resources (PR). Dist: UKOIR VS$99.99. *Addresses the problems associated with deforestation in Central America. Costa Rica is highlighted as one nation that has suffered massive deforestation during the past 30 years and is now attempting revolutionary reforms in land management and production systems in order to remedy the environmental, economic, and social problems associated with the loss of the tropical forest.*

Central Pennsylvania Halloween Customs 12.5 min. Maurice A. Mook (AN), D. P. Duvall, L. P. Greenhill, and C. Conklin (PR). Dist: PSU. [Reviewed by Henry Glassie, *AA* 76:725, 1974.]

Ceramiques Prehistoriques (1979) 25 min. Dist: FACSEA FR$16. (English version)

Les ceremonies soixanteraires du Sigui (The Sixty-Year Cycle of Sigui Ceremonies) (1981) 90 min. Jean Rouch (DI). Dist: CFE; DER. *A synthesis of the seven years of Sigui. See Sigui No. 1 through Sigui No. 7.*

Cesar's Bark Canoe 58 min. National Film Board of Canada (PR). Dist: EDC FR$65, FS$780, VS$585. *On the Manouane Reserve, a little more than 100 miles north of the bustling metropolis of Montreal, Cesar Newashish, a Cree Indian, peels the bark from a birch tree and, with little more than his pocket knife and an axe, builds a canoe, a conveyance unsurpassed in function or beauty of design. The film has no spoken commentary. Each stage of construction, the materials employed and their purposes, are identified by text on the screen in three languages: Cree, French, and English.*

Chachaji, My Poor Relation (1978) 58 min. William Cran (DI), Ved Mehta (WR, NA). Dist: FRIF FR$895, FS$100. *Distinguished writer Ved Mehta brought back from his native India this film about the daily battle for survival in a poor, overcrowded country. Focusing on a relative of Mehta, "Chachaji" serves as a window on Mehta's family, and by extension, all of India's people.*

Chacma Baboons of Cape Town (1967) 14 min. Psychological Cinema Register (PR), C. R. Carpenter (NA). Dist: PSU FR$8. *A fine version of K. R. L. Hall/BBC film of Papio ursinus in South Africa. The complete social organization is discussed, including some experiments with food acceptance.*

The Chaco Legacy (Odyssey Series) (1980) 59 min. Graham Shedd (FM). Dist: DER VR$50, VS$500; PBSV VR$58, VS$135. *"Examines the prehistory of the Chaco Canyon, New Mexico, and the history of archeology in the canyon area. The theme is twofold: the progressive concentration of prehistoric engineering and organizational skills that produced the spectacular archeological record of AD 900–1200; and the progressive complexity of archeological theories about this development, up to (1980)."* [From the review by David P. Brown, *AA* 85:232–233, 1983. Reviewed by Gordon C. Tucker, Jr., *SBF* 18:95, 1982. Peter S. Allen, *ARCH* 33(2):62, 1980.]

Chairmaker (1975) 22 min. Dist: APPAL FR$45, FS$400, VS$175. *Dewey Thompson is an 80-year-old chairmaker who does everything by hand: he even chops down the tree. The film is about his simple lifestyle, getting up at 3 a.m. and whittling on his chairs until 10 p.m. A rough-hewn rocking chair takes form under his experienced hands and well-worn knife during the course of the film.*

Chang: A Drama of the Wilderness (1927) 70 min. Merian C. Cooper and Ernest B. Schoedsack (FM). Dist: MLS VS$39.95, order #MILE006. *Available for the first time in over 45 years, "Chang" is a revelation. Not only is the film the obvious prototype for Cooper and Schoedsack's later masterpiece, King Kong, but it is a terrifically entertaining film in its own right. Shot entirely in Siam, the film tells the story of a farmer and his family who have settled a small patch of land at the edge of the jungle. Their existence is a constant struggle against the many wild animals around them—bears, tigers, leopards, and even . . . changs! The climactic elephant stampede is still one of the most exciting scenes in cinema history.*

Change (1990) 35 min. Hillie Molenaar and Joon van Wijik (FM). Dist: FRIF VR$60, VS$225. *The film centers on a bank in a small Zambian town, where tellers are shown counting out hundreds of thousands, sometimes even millions, of kwachas without thinking twice. The residents are seen carrying suitcases full of money to buy such staples as soap and salt—when they are even available. And the black market for currency is also uncovered. With images that evoke such troubled and depressed economies as post WWI Germany, or the Soviet Union in its last years, Change presents one example of the enormous difficulties that besiege much of the African continent.*

Changes in Agriculture, Population, and Utilization of Resources—Santa Cruz, Bolivia (1963) 20 min. Dwight Heath (AN), Land Tenure Center, University of Wisconsin (PR). Dist: UW. *Shows the Andes mountains and points out the significance of these as a barrier between eastern and western Bolivia. Points out the results of a new highway linking east and west completed in 1954. Visits Santa Cruz, showing both old and new. Discusses general Bolivian economic conditions and what effect these have had on the lowlands. Discusses agriculture around Santa Cruz and visits the experiment station at San Saavedra. Mentions the work of the Bolivian Development Corporation.* Suggested supplements: Dwight B. Heath, Charles J. Erasmus, and Hans C. Buechler, *Land Reform and Social Revolution in Bolivia*. Praeger, 1968 (Heath's chapter on the Oriente amplifies many of the major points made in Heath's films). Dwight B. Heath, "Land Tenure and Social Organization: An Ethnohistorical Study from the Bolivian Oriente." *Inter-American Economic Affairs* 13(4):46–66, 1960. J. Colin Crossley, "Santa Cruz at the Crossroads: A Study of Development Eastern Bolivia." *Tijdschrift voor Economische en Sociale Geographie* 52(8):197–206, 52(9):230–231 (survey of literature on the Oriente, the area treated in the first three films). See also *Campesinos and Farming on Isla del Sol*.

Changes in Land Use and Transportation Problems for Two New Settlements—Tolima, Colombia (1963) 12 min. The Land Tenure Center, University of Wisconsin (PR). Dist: UW. *Considers the problems of carrying out agrarian reform in a highland area with inadequate roads, unequal land distribution, social unrest, and a single-crop agriculture based on coffee. Shows government assistance in providing employment; building homes, roads, and public facilities; providing loans; and redistributing land. The projects viewed are Cafrerias and El Darien near Cunday.*

Changing 18 min. Hubert Smith (FM). Dist: NIMH Drug Abuse Prevention Film Collection, National Audio Visual Center, Washington, DC 20409. *Lifestyle changes in a lower-middle-class Anglo Southern California family.* [Reviewed by Jay Ruby, *AA* 74:1022. 1972.]

Changing Faces 30 min. Lisa Goldberg (FM), Matthew Sheppard (Asst). Dist: VQ. *Achuarä (Jivaro) of the Peru-Ecuador border.* [Reviewed by Eric B. Ross. AA 79:509, 1977.]

The Changing Rains (1968) 20 min. Clark Worswick and Firos Sarkar (FM), Film Study Center, Harvard University (PR). Dist: FSC FR$15, apply for sale. *A poetic evocation of the life of the Bali, a tribal group in the Gujerat of western India.*

Changing the Menu (Man on the Rim Series) 58 min. Dist: LMF VS$295. *The Mongoloids from the north of Asia moved South, virtually swamping the original Australoids, who now occupy an area covering eastern Indonesia, New Guinea, and Australia. The development of horticulture and cultivation of essential food plants advanced the crucial transition from nomadic reliance on hunting and gathering to a settled existence in communities.*

Chantons sous l'occupation (We Sing under Occupation) (1976) Andre Halimi (DI). Dist: CFE; DER. *A montage film with sequences by Jean Rouch.*

CHARACTER FORMATION IN DIFFERENT CULTURES SERIES
Gregory Bateson (FM, AN), Margaret Mead (AN, PR). Dist: NYU. For details, see listings under film titles:

- A Balinese Family
- Bathing Babies in Three Cultures
- Childhood Rivalry in Bali and New Guinea
- First Days in the Life of a New Guinea Baby
- Karba's First Years
- Trance and Dance in Bali (see also: *Learning to Dance in Bali*)

Charcoal Makers (Rural Greece: Desertion, Migration, Village Life Series) (1990) 30 min. Dr. Colette Piault (AN, DI), Susi Arnott (CA), Electra Venaki (ED). Dist: PSA FR$70, VS$320; LFDQ. *We see a strange landscape in the middle of the Greek mountains. The silhouettes of furnaces emerge from the hazy and smoke-dappled light. Charcoal makers, who have come sometimes from distant places with their families, are burning wood to make charcoal. They rent themselves and their work out to contractors during the five or six summer months. This film describes the technical process of charcoal making through its pictures and soundtrack, but more than that, the spectator participates in this difficult and archaic work. Both modern and traditional, the activity of these men and women has a real poetic dimension.* [Reviewed by Paul Sant Cassia, AA 94(2):523–524, 1992.]

La chasse a l'hippopotame (The Hippopotamus Hunt) (1950) 36 min. Jean Rouch (DI). Dist: CFE; DER.

La chasse au lion a l'arc (The Lion Hunters) (1957) 90 min. Jean Rouch (DI), Films de la Pleiade (PR). Dist: CFE; DER. *Follows the technical and religious aspects of lion hunts that took place between 1957 and 1964 in the Yatacala region.*

Le Chemin des Indiens Morts (The Way of the Dead Indians) (1983) 94 min. Michel Perrin and Jean Arlaud (FM). Dist: CNRS. *"The Guahiro Indians live in the high desert of Venezuela and Colombia. . . . This film is a tribute to, and the result of, the way that Isho, a close friend of the anthropologist, his wives, and numerous descendants thaught Perrin about Guahiro life and legend."* [From the review by Steve Dunsky and Jorge Preloran, AA 88:772–773, 1986.]

Chen and China's Symphony (1988) 59 min. Jerry A. Schultz (PR), David M. Kendall (DI). Dist: CEAS-UK VR$90, VS$350. *"This video documents the first major tour of the Central Philharmonic Orchestra outside of China. The theme is a 1987 cultural exchange to promote friendship between China and the United States. Shot mostly during the midwestern segment of the tour, the film is narrated on and off camera by the Central Philharmonic's young conductor, Zuohuang Chen, and punctuated by commentaries from other members of the ensemble."* [From the review by Fred Blake, AA 92:1102–1103, 1990.]

Chicano Park (1989) 60 min. Marilyn Mulford and Mario Barrera (PR). Dist: CG VR$90, FS$795, VS$350. *"This video would be very appropriate for use in college courses in ethnic studies, art, sociocultural change, and community development. It includes almost 100% Mexican-American participation in the production, composition and acting. The video presents the story of a San Diego working class neighborhood . . . from the time of the Mexican Revolution until the 1980s."* [From the review by John H. Chilcott, SBF 28:245, 1992.]

Chichicastenango (1987) 30 min. Claudia Feldmar (PR). Dist: PSU VR$17, VS$185, order #34721. *Recorded during a two-year period in Chicicastenango, this program features Quiche Indians observing a mid-December religious ceremony honoring Santo Tomas, the patron saint of this Guatemalan town. The ceremony was filmed inside the more than four-hundred-year-old church of Santo Tomas, at the Indian Auxiliary Office and at the ancient stone idol Pascual Abaj. The ritual reflects the syncretistic mix of Mayan and folk Catholic elements prevalent in Guatemala.* [Reviewed by Caroline B. Brettell, AA 91:831–834, 1989.]

A Chief in Two Worlds (1993) 52 min. Micah Van der Ryn (PR). Dist: UCEMC VR$65, VS$195, order #38229. *A Samoan resident of Los Angeles makes a dramatic journey to Western Samoa, where he undergoes a formal bestowal ceremony and is invested with the traditional Samoan chieftainship of the Matai system. The video also examines his new role in the Samoan community of Los Angeles, following his return.*

CHILD SERIES (1980) 14 min. each. Dist: SU.

- **Child of Papua New Guinea** FR$14. See description below.
- **Child of Rural Thailand** FR$14.
- **Child of the Philippines** FR$14.
- **Child of Urban Thailand** FR$14.
- **Child of New Zealand** FR$13.

Child of Papua New Guinea: The Same Today, the Same Tomorrow (1980) 14 min. Dist: EBEC FR$16, FS$265. *"This brief film reviews the daily events in the life of the Kewas, a family of the Warena tribe in Papua New Guinea. . . . It is accompanied by an extremely useful guide that contains valuable information and a list of questions for classroom use."* [From the review by Peter S. Allen, *SBF* 17:36, 1981.]

Childhood Rivalry in Bali and New Guinea (Character Formation in Different Cultures Series) (ca. 1952) 17 min. Gregory Bateson and Margaret Mead (FM). Dist: PSU VR$14.50, FS$350, VS$105, order #24638; NYU FR$16, FS$165; UCEMC FR$10. A series of scenes in which children of the same age in the two cultures respond to the mother attending to another baby, the ear piercing of a younger sibling, and the experimental presentation of a doll. Whereas the Balinese mother handles sibling rivalry by theatrical teasing of her own child through conspicuous attention to other babies, the Iatmul mother, even when nursing a newborn infant, makes every effort to keep her own child from feeling jealous. Contrastingly, Balinese children's attention and interest are focused on younger children. Cf. the film *A Balinese Family*.

Children (1970) 34 min. Dist: IUAVC FR$15.75. Compares and contrasts the different styles of childrearing in four cultures—India, Africa, New Guinea, and England. States that all children require love and security and that this is easily provided in the extended families of primitive societies. Points out that in primitive societies children are expected to remain with the family and take care of aging parents; whereas in English families, parents interviewed indicated that they wanted their children to visit but did not expect to be supported.

Children of Change (1983) 26 min. Suzanne Griffin and Giles B. Baker (PR). Dist: IMS-UW VR$12, VS$150. *"The children referred to in the title are teenagers, the youngest refugees from the mountains of Laos who can still remember their homeland, and the critical generation of a preliterate culture that has been suddenly propelled into radical change through resettlement in the United States. Recollections of prewar Hmong life are given to the viewer in effective counterpoint to scenes of Hmong activity in Seattle."* [From the review by Marjorie A. Muecke, *AA* 88:518, 1986.]

Children of Fate: Life and Death in a Sicilian Family (1992) 85 min. Susan Todd, Andrew Young, and Robert Young (FM). Dist: FRIF. *Filmed in 1961 and 1988 in Cortile Cascino, a Palermo slum in Sicily, this film focuses on the life of Angela, featured as a young woman in 1961, who struggles to help her now grown children to survive in the face of economic hardship, marital problems, illness, and death.*

Children of Fire (1990) 50 min. Mai Masri and Jean Chamoun (FM). Dist: Visions Productions Ltd., 23 Grove End Road, London, England NW8 9BL. *Nablus under Israeli occupation.* [Reviewed by Barbara C. Aswad, *AA* 93(4):1040–1042, 1991.]

Children of Samoa (Children of the World Series) (1982) 12 min. Dist: JF FR$30, FS$255. *"This film tries to give an impression of the life in a small village in western Samoa. It follows the lives of a young boy and girl during a typical week. The children do the same kinds of things that children in American society do. . . . The cultural content of their lives, however is different."* [From the review by James Dow, *SBF* 18:287–289, 1983.]

Children of Soong Ching Ling (1985) 30 min. Dist: PyrF FR$65, VR$65, FS$475, VS$395. *"This is an artistic UNICEF production, replete with dancing and singing children. Unfortunately, it does not contribute to an incisive analysis of the problems presented. . . . Soong Ching Ling was better known in the western world as Madame Sun Yat Sen. After World War II she set up health centers and nurseries in Shanghai, then attempted to extend them. . . . The film shows a country that is 80 percent rural, with 350 million children under 15, and it lists China's great problems of overpopulation, lack of safe drinking water, and of preventable childhood diseases."* [From the review by Simon D. Messing, *SBF* 21:172–173, 1986.]

Children of the Forest (1984) 28 min. Kevin Duffy (FM). Dist: PyrF FR$65, FS$475, VS$395. *"About the Mbuti pygmies of the Ituri tropical moist forest in Zaire. . . . The Mbuti see the forest as their parents and themselves as children of the forest."* [From the review by Gilda Morelli, Steve Winn, and Edward Z. Tronick, *AA* 88:773–774, 1986. Reviewed by Carmen H. Owen, *SBF* 21:173, 1986.]

Children of the Mist (ca. 1976) 30 min. New Zealand National Film Unit (PR). Dist: New Zealand Government Tourist Office, 10960 Wilshire Blvd., Suite 1530, Los Angeles, CA 90024. *The film was shot mainly in the Urewera District inland on the northeast portion of New Zealand's North Island and in Auckland, New Zealand, to show the life and problems of a contemporary rural Maori tribe with special regard to rural to urban migration. The beginning of the film deals with a brief history of the Tuhoe Tribe of New Zealand. It then depicts present-day life by focusing of specific individuals and families in the context of school, work, community meetings, and a funeral. The emphasis then leads into some of the problems faced by the tribe regarding future employment, higher education, and increased rural-to-urban migration. The film then focuses on the problems faced by the Tuhoe people who have migrated to Auckland. The final portion of the film deals with the links that still remain lively and connect the urban Maoris to their rural homeland. No easy solutions to the current problems are offered. The film is of primary value in depicting the often confusing choices faced by folk-type societies that still maintain strong ties with the land, community, and family, but, because of demands placed by the desire for better economic and higher education, are often obliged to remove themselves to strange, urban, and often hostile surroundings. Focusing questions: (1) To what degree have the Tuhoe people assimilated into the mainstream of New Zealand life? To what degree have they retained their original culture? (2) What is the importance of the community meeting, funeral, and annual tribal gathering in the life of the people of the Tuhoe tribes? (3) How have the*

Tuhoe tried to retain their tribal and familial ties in urban Auckland? Bibliography: James E. Ritchie, "The Making of a Maori." In: *Polynesia: Readings on a Culture Area*. Alan Howard, ed. Scranton, PA: Chandler Publishing Co., 1971. A. Joan Metge, *The Maoris of New Zealand*. Rev. ed. Boston: Routledge and Kegal Paul, 1976 (especially chapters 4, 5, 6,and 18). Erik Schwimmer, ed., *The Maori People in the Nineteen Sixties*. New York: Humanities Press. [Max E. Stanton]

Chile's Experiments in Agrarian Reform (1976) 39 min. (Part IV: 18 min., Part V: 21 min.) Dist: UW. *Part IV includes visits to three agrarian projects of INPROA, the Catholic Church's experimental reform program. The different approaches used in each of the three projects are examined, as well as the problems experienced by each. Part V shows the present condition of public colonization projects begun as early as 1928. This is followed by visits to the large agrarian reform projects of the Alessandri government near Santiago, and the Mapuche Indian province of Arauco.*

Chillysmith Farm (1981) 55 min. Mark Jury and Dan Jury (FM). Dist: FL FR$75, FS$750, VS$650. *Describes two deaths and a birth.* [Reviewed by Christine Lemieux, *AA* 86:1053–1054, 1984.]

China: A Land Transformed 28 min. National Film Board of Canada (PR). Dist: EDC FR$40, FS$475, VS$355. *For hundreds of years, North China Plain was ravaged by disastrous floods. In the wake of each deluge came soil erosion, famine, and catastrophic loss of life. This film documents the transformation of this devastated landscape into one of the most densely populated agricultural regions in the world. In keeping with the Maoist philosophy, this process was accomplished through the manual labor of hundreds of thousands of people using simple tools and traditional methods. A massive irrigation system was formed by replacing the natural river system with manmade canals, terracing the mountains, and building bridges and viaducts. The torrential summer rains now have been harnessed making the plain fertile and productive. The film contains magnificent footage of the country, documents a remarkable agricultural achievement, and provides insights into both the Chinese people and the transition from a labor-intensive to a technological society.*

China: Contemporary Changes in Historical Perspective 27 min. Vladimir Bibic (FM). Dist: CRM VR$55, VS$295. *This film examines the effects of political and social movements throughout China's long history and illustrates how the stage was set for the dramatic democratic uprising in Tienanmen Square.*

China Discovery (1984) 28 min. Barry Stoner (FM). Dist: Tomwil Films, 5315 Wilkinson Avenue, North Hollywood, CA 96087; (818) 760-4523 VS$175. *An exhibition on Chinese inventions and technology traveled from the People's Republic to several museums in North America a few years ago, and a Seattle television station broadcast this documentary celebrating the exhibition. The producer "shows just enough of the exhibit to tantalize his audience. He devotes most of the film to illustrating the significance of various technological innovations in China and their contributions to the modern world. Thus this documentary is about the nature of technological progress as well as about Chinese discoveries."* [From the review by David W. Goodrich, *ARCH* 39(2):78–79, 1986.]

China: Hundred Schools to One (475 B.C. to 221 B.C.) (1977) 19 min. Wan-go Weng (PR) for the China Institute in America, Inc. Dist: IUAVC FR$15, FS$305, VS$196. *Not long after the death of Confucius in 479 B.C., China entered an era of "Warring States." Every lord called himself a king. States near the border extended outward and gathered large undeveloped areas into the Chinese cultural sphere. This expansion enriched most of the western state in Ch'in, laying the foundation for China's contact with central Asia and the southern state of Ch'u, opening up the vast Yangtze River Valley. The major changes of this period were social, for ability came to count more than birth. Posts were no longer hereditary; men owed no fixed loyalty. Ideas and skill, eloquence and courage, were sufficient to make a man a minister or a general. This climate spurred a "hundred schools of thought," including Militarists, Yang Chu, Confucianists, Taoists, Yin and Yang, and Legalists. The latter called for a disciplined state under an absolute ruler, resolute in war and orderly in peace. The triumph of this school set the stage for the establishment of China's first empire.*

China: Land of My Father (1980) 28 min. Felicia Lowe (FM). Dist: NDF FR$55, FS$450 VS$375. *"A highly personalized film by and of Felicia Lowe, a second-generation Chinese American who tours China with a group of other professional journalists, visiting her father's natal village and meeting her paternal kin."* [From the review by Karen L. Ito, *AA* 86:786–787, 1984.]

China: The Beginnings (1977) 19 min. Wan-go Weng (PR) for the China Institute in America, Inc. Dist: IUAVC FR$15, FS$305, VS$196. *The search for the origin of the Chinese people and their civilization, including Lan-t'ien Man, Peking Man, and the Upper Cave Man. Depicts the emergence about 6,000 years ago of the Yang-shao Neolithic culture characterized by its settlement and burial patterns and the carving or painting of symbols and signs on pottery, which suggest the beginnings of writing. Two other Neolithic cultures, Ch'in-lien-kang and Lung-shan, are also examined. Although there is a possibility that these early cultures had substantial contact with the outside world, distinct Chinese innovations point to an essentially indigenous culture—one that was to evolve into a major civilization with an unmatched continuity. Partly from the Lung-shan culture, the first Chinese historical dynasty, Shang, developed, and with it China entered the Bronze Age. At this time, the basics of writing existed, and great advances were made in technology, architecture, and art.* [Reviewed by Robert Dewar, *ARCH* 33(6):62, 1980.]

China: The Making of a Civilization (1977) 18 min. Wan-go Weng (PR) for the China Institute in America, Inc. Dist IUAVC FR$15, FS$305, VS$196. *A tribe to the west moved into the central Yellow River Valley, conquered the Shang dynasty (taking over Shang's technological and cultural achievements), and ruled as the Chou dynasty, naming their kingdom Chung Kuo, the "Central Kingdom," by* which name China is still known today. They established what was essentially a feudal system, with the king as the absolute ruler. To insulate themselves from invasion, the capital was moved eastward in 770 B.C., dividing the dynasty into the Western Chou and Eastern Chou periods. During the Eastern period, also known as Spring and Autumn, political structure crumbled, causing economic change as well; power gravitated downward to the people; and serfdom yielded to a form of land ownership. Living in an age of uncertainty, thinkers of the period (the foremost of whom was Confucius) searched for a deeper meaning of nature and man. They began to evolve theories for building a better society and tried to influence the rulers to put these ideas into practice. [Reviewed by Robert Dewar, ARCH 33(6):62, 1980.]

China's Only Child (1985) 57 min. Dist: WGBH VR$85, VS$250. *This video shows how China is implementing its population-control policy by limiting families to one child. . . . Avoids taking an ideological stance."* [From the review by David J. Pratto, SBF 22:124–125, 1986.]

Chinaman's Choice (1987) 27 min. Lori Tsang (FM). Dist: Visual Communications, 263 South Los Angeles Street, Room 307, Los Angeles, CA 90012; (213) 680-4462 VR$75. *"Scenes of contemporary lives, punctuated with old photographs, form a backdrop against which this filmmaker's father, Alfred Tsang, seeks to clarify the decisions that destined him for life in the United States."* [From the review by Fred Blake, AA 92:1101–1102, 1990.]

The Chinampas (1990) 31 min. Anne Prutzman (FM). Dist: UCEMC VR$40, VS$250, order #37984. *This important documentary examines an ecologically sustainable system of agriculture that has flourished in Mexico for some 2,000 years. This chinampa zone, which now survives only on the southern edge of Mexico City, is a beautiful area of canals and islands, graceful willow trees, various agricultural crops, and flowers. The video employs graphics, live action, and commentary by chinampa farmers to show how the phenomenally productive chinampa system works. It also shows how the growth and pollution problems of Mexico City threaten the survival of the remaining chinampa farmers.* [Reviewed by Billie R. DeWalt, AA 94(2):524, 1992.]

Chinese Farm Family: Changes in the Countryside Today (1990) 26 min. Dist: CRM/F VR$55, VS$295. *Social changes in modern China have dramatically affected the lives of many farm families, like the An family. An Shiao Min, his wife, Chian, and son, An Dijun, still work in the fields as before. But, today, they are motivated to produce more and better crops for China's burgeoning free-market system. This film shows how typical Chinese extended families are adapting and profiting from sweeping changes in the world's most populous communist state.*

Chinese, Korean and Japanese Dance (1965) 28 min. Clifford Ettinger (DI), Beate Gordon (AN), Board of Education of the City of New York in cooperation with the Asia Society (PR). Dist: BAVI FR$15, FS$250. [Reviewed by I. Eugene and Ji-Ae Knez, AA 68:1328, 1966.]

CHINESE POPULAR RELIGION SERIES Gary Seaman (FM,AN). Dist: FEAV FR$25. *A series of Super 8 format films showing village life in Taiwan, "the folk worldview in China, as opposed to that of the Confucian elite."* Accompanying descriptive material is being prepared.

• **The Rite of Cosmic Renewal** 35 min. FS$250. *Once every 12 years, this community invites the gods to take part in rites of thanksgiving. At the end of seven days of vegetarian fasting, every household sacrifices a pig to the spirits of the hungry ghosts.*

• **The Temple of Lord Kuan** 24 min. FS$250. *This village temple is the center of a spirit-writing cult that worships Kuan Kung, hero of the Romance of the Three Kingdoms. Villagers come to the temple and cast "moonstones" to divine questions of fate. In the night, a spirit-writing seance is held.*

• **Blood, Bones, and Spirits** 36 min. FS$250. *The daughter-in-law of this family is childless. A spirit seance reveals that her barrenness is the result of the curse of an uncle who died with no offspring of his own. The uncle's grave must be renovated, and a grandson of the family must be adopted out to him. This is done under the direction of a shaman, possessed by a god called the Emperor of the Dark Heavens.* [Reviewed by Nancie L. Gonzalez, AA 77:194, 1975.]

• **Weapons** 25 min. FS$250. *The shamans of many Chinese religious cults use ceremonial weapons to inflict wounds on themselves while in trance. These weapons must be ritually purified and initiated before they can be used. This film shows the ritual "blooding" of a new set of weapons.*

• **Feng Shui: Chinese Geomancy** 16 min. FS$150. *Feng Shui concerns the influence of topography on man's fate and is especially important in the placing of graves. This film includes the exhumation of a skeleton, the selection of a new gravesite by a geomancer, the building of a new tomb, and the reinterment of the bones.*

• **The Luck of the Lord of the Land** 15 min. FS$150. *A village neighborhood prepares a feast in honor of the local earth god, called the Lord of the Land. The men consume the feast with gusto, then go to the temple and cast moonstones to select the host for the next feast.*

• **Curing Seance** 15 min. FS$150. *A young girl has an abscessed broken leg. To help in healing it, a special "divining chair" is used to examine the leg. In the course of the seance, a number of geomantical and social relationships are diagnosed as contributing to the girl's illness. The divining chair writes out charms to help correct the condition that afflicts her.*

• **Wedding Feast** 24 min. FS$250. *In the early morning, the groom's family begins to cook the wedding feast. The bridewealth is delivered, then the groom brings home his bride and her dowry. The wedding feast is held at the groom's house, where the bride is formally presented to friends and relatives.*

• **Chinese Funeral Ritual** 24 min. FS$250. *This film is an overview of the standard funeral rites as performed by a group of "Dragon Flower" ritual professionals. The structure and symbolism of funeral rites in peasant households are related to Chinese conceptions of the underworld.*

• **Breaking the Blood Bowl** 18 min. FS$175. *The blood that a Chinese mother spills in childbirth is extremely polluting. She must undergo tortures in hell unless her descendants take this pollution upon themselves. In the course of a woman's funeral rites, a man acting as Buddha leads the mourners into hell, where they symbolically drink the blood of their birth, thus freeing their mother from torment.* [Reviewed by Nancie L. Gonzalez, *AA* 77:193, 1975.]

Chinese X-Ray Film (1962) 22 min. Haskins Lab (PR). Dist: PSU. *Material selected to show various ways that tongue and lips are used to contrast the principal syllable types of Peking Chinese. X-ray techniques show the articulatory process and acoustic output of native speakers. Prepared scripts, consisting mainly of short, meaningful utterances, illustrate selected phonetic features. Informants chosen both for linguistic suitability and lack of physical characteristics that might interfere with X-ray quality.*

The Chittirai Festival Part 1: 25 min., Part II: 35 min. Mira Reym Binford and Michael Camerini (FM). Dist: UW/SAAC FR$14, FS$120 (each). *Occurring annually in the South Indian temple city of Madurai, the festival reenacts the marriage of the city's patron goddess to Lord Shiva and regularly draws half a million people. The Hindu tradition has incorporated many diverse groups, from Brahmans to tribes only recently brought into the caste structure. This festival at once illustrates and unites these diverse "layers" of society. These films provide an unusual opportunity to witness the mosaic aspects of a complex civilization that incorporates different linguistic, religious, ethnic, and artistic components into continually changing patterns. Part I is an exploration of the legends surrounding the founding of the city of Madurai and the temple of Minakshi. Part II makes us participants in the festival that reenacts those legends.* Accompanied by Teachers' Guides with background information and suggestions for discussions. Produced with synchronous sound interviews in Bengali, Hindi, Tamil, with English subtitles.

Chopi Africa (ca. 1965) 53 min. Kevin Duffy (CA), Hugh Tracey (CON). Dist: Maurice A. Machris, 11681 San Vincente Blvd., Los Angeles, CA 90049. [Reviewed by Gordon Gibson, *AA* 70:1249, 1968.]

Choqela: Only Interpretation (1987) 12 min. John Cohen (DI). Dist: CG FR$35, VR$35, FS$195, VS$150. *This documentary acknowledges the dilemma of interpretation as an inherent part of anthropology. The film documents the Choqela ceremony, a ritual of the Aymara Indians of Peru and Bolivia. Invoking good fortune for their crops, they perform the ritual hunt of the vicuna, using animal masks and disguises to become something between spirits and hunters, while the women sing a long song about the hunt. The film offers several different translations of the song and varying anthropological interpretations of the ceremony. Although the ritual continues today, its meaning is obscured by the past and is known only to its participants or, perhaps, only to their ancestors.* [Reviewed by Margot Schevill, *AA* 90:487–488, 1988. Karl G. Heider, *SBF* 24:106–207, 1988.]

Christ Is Risen 13 min. NFBC (PR). Dist: NFB. *Russian Orthodox Easter, Montreal.* [Reviewed by Lydia Fish, *JAF* 94(371):137–138, 1981.]

Chronicle of a Summer (Chronique d'une été) (1961) 90 min. Jean Rouch, Edgar Morin (FM). Dist: Corinth Films, 410 East 62nd St., New York, NY 10021; (212) 421-4770 FR$150. *Life in Paris during the 1958 summer of the Algerian War. This film, with its explicit self-consciousness and spontaneous scenes, was the stimulus for the subsequent French cinéma vérité.* [Reviewed by Jean-Paul Dumont, *AA* 80:1020–1022, 1978. Reviewed in *VISA* 1:400, 1988.] Bibliography: James Blue, the Films of Jean Rouch. *Film Comment* 4(3)(Fall–Winter):82–86, 1967. Tom Milne, Chronicle of a Summer, *Sight and Sound* 31(3) (Summer):144–145, 1962. Roger Sandall, Chronicle of a Summer, *Film Quarterly* 15(2) (Winter):57–59, 1961–62. Mark Shivas, Chronicle of a Summer, *Movie* 2(September):31, 1962. Jacqueline Veuve, Jean Rouch in Conversation with Jacqueline Veuve, *Film Comment* 4(2–3) (Fall and Winter), 1967.

Chucalezna (1979) 22 min. Jorge Preloran (FM). Dist: PFI FR$32, FS$325. *In the heart of the Humahuaca Canyon, in northwestern Argentina, there is a place known only to its inhabitants. Since remote times, it has been called by its Quechua name: Chucalezna. Thirty families form the small community of shepherds and farmers who cultivate the land inherited from their ancestors. Here, only a small school brings a glimpse of the outside world to the community. The teacher is their guide and tutor, influencing everyone with her warmth and dedication. This is a rural school like so many others: humble, isolated, forgotten. And yet, this school is also unique, because here the children happily paint and create their world.*

Chuck Davis, Dancing through West Africa (1985) 28 min. Gorham Kindem (DI). Dist: FL FR$55, VR$55, FS$525, VS$450. *"The principals are Americans who are on a dance tour of West Africa in order to experience indigenous performance in context. Chuck Davis, Afro-American dancer, choreographer, and artistic director ... has organized dance tours of West Africa since the 1970s.... Davis and his integrated American entourage are followed."* [From the review by Brenda Dixon-Stowell, *AA* 90:239–241, 1988.]

Chulas Fronteras (1976) 58 min. Les Blank (FM), Chris Strachwitz (PR). Dist: EMC FR$150, FS$890. *Examines the Texas-Mexican border music known as musica norteña. The film and its music lyrically reflect the personality of the border region, its people, their work, and their celebrations.* [Reviewed by James S. Griffith, *JAF* 91(361):886–887, 1978.]

Cimarrones (1983) 24 min. Carlos Ferrand (DI). Dist: CG FR$50, VR$50, FS$400, VS$295. *This film explores the little-known situation of African slaves in Latin America in the 19th century. After the Spanish conquistadors decimated the indigenous Inca population in the 16th century, they transported African slaves to countries throughout the Caribbean and Central and South America. The slaves frequently rebelled against their oppressive conditions, and* many runaway slaves (cimarrones) established villages in the mountains. This film, shot in authentic locations in Peru, recreates an attack by cimarrones on a Spanish caravan and portrays, in almost anthropological fashion, life in those slave villages. The musical score, composed and performed by Carlos Hayre, an eminent black Peruvian musicologist, was played on instruments reconstructed according to descriptions left by the first slaves brought from Africa. Spanish dialogue with English subtitles and narration. [Reviewed by Michael Kearney, AA 87:480–481, 1985.]

Cimetière dans la falaise (Cemetery in the Cliff) (1951–52) 20 min. Jean Rouch (DI), Centre National de la Recherche Scientifique and Secretariat d'Etat a la Co-operation (PR), Marcel Griaule and Germaine Dieterlen (commentary). Dist: CFE; DER. *Funeral rituals among the Dogon of Ireli on the cliffs of Bandiagara, Mali.*

Cine-Mafia (1980) 35 min. Jean Rouch and Groupe Cinéma of the University of Leyden (DI). Dist: CFE; DER. *A Cine meeting of Joris Ivens, Henri Storck, and Jean Rouch in a village where, in 1929, Joris Ivens shot his first and unique fiction film* The Breakers.

Cine-portrait de Margaret Mead (1977) 35 min. Jean Rouch (DI), Comité du Film Ethnographique and American Museum of Natural History (PR). Dist: CFE; DER. *Margaret is discovered in her office, the work room of the museum, and asked about her hopes for today's anthropology.*

Cinema 3 min. Sebastian C. Schroeder (FM). Dist: FIM/RF FR$10, FS$75. *In Kabul, Afghanistan, there is an itinerant motion picture exhibitor who built a wonderfully weird, gaily-painted street cinema whose light source is the sun (reflected off a mirror into the projection lens) and which must be cranked by hand. Admission is one cent, and a performance lasts about three minutes. The show usually consists of strips of old American and Russian features and, once in a while, a cigarette ad. As he cranks the film through, the operator delivers running commentary, telling his audience what they are seeing—because they cannot really see anything, considering the age of the film and blurred, flickering images! Nevertheless, he always manages to attract an eager crowd of moviegoers—on sunny days, that is.*

A Circle of Healing (Man Alive Series) 54 min. Dist: CBC VS$109, order #Y8L-8811. *This is a powerful documentary filmed at Alkali Lake, the extraordinary Indian reserve that has overcome alcoholism. Now the community is struggling with an ugly hidden secret, for generations under the alcoholic haze—child abuse. This film follows the process of family healing and reconciliation in this courageous community.*

Circle of the Sun (1960) 30 min. Colin Low (WR), Chief Jim White Bull (CON). Dist: NFBC; UCEMC FR$21. *The Blood Indians, second largest of the three Blackfoot tribes, reside in Canada's largest Indian reserve on the rolling plains within the sight of the Rocky Mountains in southern Alberta. The film attempts to picture Indian life and culture through the eyes of members of the younger generation.*

[Reviewed by John C. Ewers, AA 68:1092–1093, 1966; see also a comment on Ewers' review by Elisabeth Tooker, and Ewers' reply to Tooker, both AA 69:369, 1967.]

Circles-Cycles Kathak Dance (1989) 28 min. Robert S. Gottlieb (FM), Zakir Hussian (NA). Dist: UCEMC FR$50, VR$50, FS$550, VS$400, order #11374. *The traditions of kathak, the classical dance form of northern India, can be traced back more than 1,000 years. It is the only Indian dance form that combines influences of both Hindu and Islamic cultures. This beautifully filmed and edited documentary illustrates numerous aspects of the kathak repertoire as demonstrated by some of its greatest living performers. The film, like so much of India's religious and cultural thinking, focuses on themes of circles and cycles and shows how they appear again and again in the dance and its music.* [Reviewed by Najwa Adra, AA 93(1):252, 1991.]

La circoncision (Circumcision) (1948–49) 15 min. Jean Rouch (DI), Centre National de la Recherche Scientifique and Secrétariat d'Etat a la Co-operation (PR). Dist: CFE; DER. *Circumcision rites of 30 Songhay children from the village of Hombori, Mali.*

THE CITIES IN CHINA SERIES (1981) Sue Yung Li and Shirley Sun (PR). Dist: UCEMC. *This renowned series explores the Chinese urban experience, past and present. It captures to an extraordinary degree the sights and sounds of daily Chinese life. See under individual cities:*

- **Xian**
- **Beijing**
- **Suzhou**

Citizen Carney (1980) 28 min. Walter Thomas and David Nugent (FM). Dist: Walter Thomas, 31 Warren St., New York, NY 10007; (212) 406-4099 FR$35, FS$300. *About carnival life in America, portrayed mainly through the words of a half dozen 'carnies' (itinerant carnival workers).* [Reviewed by George Gmelch, AA 88:258–259, 1986.]

City of Gold 22 min. Wolf Koenig and Colin Low (FM), National Film Board of Canada (PR). Dist: CF/MH. *Dawson City and the Yukon gold rush.* [Reviewed by Thomas M. Kiefer, AA 76:205, 1974.]

Civilizations of Ancient America (1972) 22 min. Howard Campbell (DI). Dist: FI FR$50, FS$380. [Reviewed by Paul F. Healy, AA 78:375–376, 1976.]

Civilization in Ancient Chiapas (1980) 27 min. Roger Snodgrass (DI), Brigham Young University (PR). Dist: BYU VR$13.50 VS$325. *"Pursues the idea that the Mixe-Zoque of the Chiapas highlands of Mexico are both the biological and cultural descendants of the prehistoric civilizations of this region."* [From the review by David P. Brown, AA 85:232–233, 1983.]

Cleaning Movements 3 min. Dist: PSU FR$2.80.

A Clearing in the Jungle (Disappearing World Series) (1970) 39 min. Jean-Paul Dumont (AN). Dist: PSU order #40574. *The Panare live in a clearing of a jungle in Venezuela, only 300 miles from Caracas. They deliberately reject* *outsiders in order to maintain their unique Indian way of life. There is no hierarchy and no system of laws and punishments—the Panare are held together by ties of kinship and have only accepted changes when they can benefit the whole society.*

Clementine Hunter: American Folk Artist (1993) 28 min. Katina Simmons (PR). Dist: UCEMC VR$50, VS$195, order #38237. *This video profiles the life and work of one of America's greatest African-American folk artists. She died at 103, and her vivid paintings are remembrances of a hard but joyous life. Local folk music and historical context help viewers to understand the fabric of plantation life in the early part of the century.*

Cleto Rojas, Pintor Campesino (Peasant Painter) (see the Inhabitants of the Land Grace Series)

Climbing I. Red Howler Monkey 3 min. Dist: PSU FR$2.80.

Climbing Potto 4.5 min. Dist: PSU FR$2.80.

Climbing Slow Loris 3 min. Dist: PSU FR$2.80.

Clotheslines (1982) 32 min. Roberta Cantow (PR) for Buffalo Rose Productions. Dist: NFF FR$75, VR$60, FS$550, VS$250. *"Exploring the unexpected subject of laundry in women's lives. . . . The women speak of their work and their lives; of their relationships to husbands, mothers, and neighbors; and the burden and the beauty of having the responsibility for doing laundry. We see women doing laundry . . . in the United States and in India, Taiwan, and an Eskimo village. We see women washing on rocks, on washboards, by hand and by machine."* [From the review by Alice Reich, *AA* 88:259–260, 1986.]

Coal Miner: Frank Jackson (1971) 12 min. Ben Zickafoose (FM). Dist: APPAL FR$20, FS$175. *Frank Jackson, who became a miner when he was 15 years old, talks about a miner's work today and yesterday and notes mining's hold on men. As he is seen in and around the mines, he tells what it's like to have spent a lifetime working underground.*

Coalmining Women (1982) 40 min. Elizabeth Barret (DI). Dist: APPAL FR$70, FS$650, VS$300. *Interviewed at home and on the job, women coal miners tell of the social conditions and economic pressures that led them to seek employment in this traditionally male-dominated industry—and the problems they encountered, once hired. Watching these women bolt mine roofs, shovel beltlines, haul rock dust, and build ventilation barriers with 75-pound blocks leaves little doubt that they can do the work. Proud of their accomplishments, the women also seem to bring a special understanding to the problems all miners face in the country's most hazardous occupation. We see them participating in union affairs, organizing among themselves, and leading the fight for mine health and safety. This film traces women's significant contributions to coalfield struggles and the importance of their new position as working miners.* [Reviewed by Roger B. Trent, *SBF* 18:279, 1983.]

The Cochin Jews 30 min. Johanna Spector (FM). Dist: JMS FR$75, FS$1,000. [Reviewed by Elise Barnett, *Asian Music* 11:144–147.]

Cocoriro, Monsieur Poulet (1974) 90 min. Jean Rouch (DI). Dist: CFE; DER. *The adventures of three friends conducting their business in the Nigerien bush with their old automobile. An attempt at collective improvisation of a Nigerien fable.*

Le cocotier (The Coconut Palm) (1962) 21 min. Jean Rouch (DI), Centre National de la Recherche Scientifique, Comité du Film Ethnographique (PR). Dist: CFE; DER. *Agricultural research of coconut palms in the Ivory Coast.*

Colin McPhee: The Lure of Asian Music (1985) 58 min. Dist: Michael Blackwood Productions, Inc., 251 West 57th Street, New York, NY 10019; (212) 247-4710 FR$110, FS$795. *"Colin McPhee, a talented young Canadian composer . . . left for Bali in 1931, and was to live and study music there until 1938. . . . The film attempts to be simultaneously a biography of a struggling western artist . . . and an account of the meeting of Eastern and Western music."* [From the review by Toby Alice Volkman, *AA* 89:778–779, 1987.]

La colonia Tovar (1976) 13 min. Dist: UCEMC FR$25, FS$190. *Examines the process and effects of change in a small village in the coastal mountains of Venezuela. Settled more than 100 years by a group of immigrants from the Baden area of southern Germany, the colony had few contacts with the outside world at first, and cultural change was slow. The film shows the kinds of adaptation—principally economic and religious—made by the settlers, stressing the continuity of their cultural heritage until about 1940, when they lost political autonomy and a new road linking the village with Caracas was constructed. Now a center for tourists attracted by its old-world charm, the village is changing rapidly. The inhabitants express their views about recent developments. The old people are particularly bewildered; they remember having to share dry bread, but they wonder if the young, who now have plenty of bread, will ever have enough to share.*

Colonial Six (1966) 25 min. James Deetz (AN), Plymouth Plantation (PR). Dist: Pitt. *Follows the excavation and analysis of the 17th-century Colonial site in Plymouth, Massachusetts.* [Reviewed by Joel I. Klein, *AA* 77:905, 1975.]

COLONIAL WILLIAMSBURG SERIES Arthur L. Smith (PR), Gene Bjerke (CA). Dist: CWF. [Reviewed by Michael Gramly, *AA* 77:913, 1975.]

• **The Cooper's Craft** (1967) 39 min.

• **Basketmaking in Colonial Virginia** (1968) 28 min.

• **Gunsmith of Williamsburg** (1969) 58 min.

• **Silversmith of Williamsburg** (1971) 44 min.

• **Hammerman of Williamsburg** 37 min. [Reviewed by Marley Brown III, *AA* 77:912, 1975.]

The Colonists (see Decade of Destruction Series)

Comalapa: Traditions and Textures (1987) 26 min. Claudia Feldmar (PR). Dist: PSU VR$16.50, VS$170, order #34722. *Comalapa is one of Guatemala's "purest" Indian villages, a town whose ancient rites and customs have* *remained relatively unchanged over the centuries. This program highlights several cultural traditions—a Cackcique Indian courtship and a wedding ceremony and the work of local painters and weavers. Also featured are the now-disappearing cofradias, ritual brotherhoods organized in honor of a particular saint, once considered an indispensable part of manhood and the only legitimate route to community status.* [Reviewed by Caroline B. Brettell, *AA* 91:831–834, 1989.]

Come Back Africa (1960) 83 min. Lionol Rogosin (FM), Lewis N'kosi, Bloke Modisane, and Lionol Rogosin (WR), Emic Knebel and Ernst Artaria (CA), Walter Wetter (SR), Carl Lerner (ED). Dist: MOMA. *This story of a Zulu family is a composite of events that reflect the reality of 20th-century apartheid society in South Africa. Enacted by Africans whose experiences were not unlike the story's events, it expresses the brutalizing effects of the life Africans were forced to lead in their own country, subject to an official policy of segregation and political and economic discrimination. Rogosin's crew worked in secret, disguised as a commercial film unit making a musical, and in constant fear of confiscation and deportation. Without the knowledge of South African authorities, they shot on location in the streets of Johannesburg and Sophiatown.*

Coming of Age: Margaret Mead (1901–1978) (Strangers Abroad Series) 52 min. Dist: FHS FR$75, VS$159, order #XD-2545. *The most widely read, the best known, and arguably the most controversial anthropologist is probably Margaret Mead, an American who, at the age of 23, went to study adolescence in the South Sea Islands. In the United States, Bali, and New Guinea, she examined child development, sex, and temperament to see what role society plays in making people what they are. She emphasized that humans arrange their social worlds in many different ways, and that qualitative judgments cannot be made between them.*

Coming of Man (1987) Robert Raymond (PR) for Opus Film. Dist: Sony Video Software Co., 1700 Broadway, New York, NY 10019; (212) 757-4990 VS$19.95. *"Australia is rarely mentioned in discussions of world prehistory, it being assumed that humans arrived late on the continent and thus are of little interest. This excellent video reviews the latest archaeological evidence for the earliest human presence in Australia and arrives at some remarkable conclusions. It features on-site footage of several important digs, as well as the testimony of prominent archaeogogists and prehistorians."* [From the review by Peter S. Allen, *ARCH* 41(6):78, 1988.]

COMMODITIES SERIES (1986) Sue Clayton and Jonathan Curling (PR). Dist: FRIF. See descriptions under individual titles:

- **Black Market** 28 min.
- **Tea Fortunes** 52 min.

Communication: The Nonverbal Agenda, 2nd Ed. (1988) 20 min. Dist: CRM/F VS$625. *This edition examines the fascinating subject of nonverbal communication from a 1980s perspective. Modeled on input from purchasers of the original version, the script refocuses on the elements of nonverbal communication that most often come into play in today's business environment.*

Communists for a Thousand Years (1973) 43 min. Gordon Troeller and Marie Claude Deffarge (FM). Dist: FRIF FR$85, FS$695, VS$375. *The Carmathians of Yemen are the original Arab people who can claim kinship with scientific Marxism.*

Community Dig (1984) 18 min. Patricia Streeten (FM). Dist: Patricia Streeten, 39 John Street (3rd floor), New York, NY 10038; (212) 619-7945 FR$50, FS$350. *This program "is one of the most enjoyable films about archaeology around, but it is scarcely among the most informative.... It documents a volunteer, community-based salvage excavation that took place before the construction of a public garden of Sheridan Square in Greenwhich Village, the central theme is the neighborhood spirit and good will generated by the archaeology."* [From the review by Peter Thorbahn, *ARCH* 39(3):74–75, 1986.]

Computers in Context: Designing Computers for Workplace Creativity (1987) 30 min. Dist: CN VR$60, VS$295. *Comparing computerization in Scandinavia and the United States.*

Comrades of the Desert 10 min. Dist: FCE FR$17, FS$95. *Desert life with the Navahos of the Southwest.*

A Connemara Family (1982) 55 min. Melissa Llewelyn-Davies (DI), BBC (PR). Dist: FI FR$90, VR$90, VS$480. *A film about small farmers in the west of Ireland.* [Reviewed by Robert N. Lynch, *AA* 88:518–519, 1986.]

Coniston Muster (1976) Australian Institute of Aboriginal Studies (PR), Roger Sandall (DI, CA, ED), Laurie Fitzgerald (SR). Dist: UCEMC FR$35, FS$400. *A vivid collection of scenes from the life of an Aboriginal stockman on a ranch in central Australia. Coniston Johnny, a 60-year old "cowboy" provides an anecdotal commentary as he and his fellow stockmen are shown carrying out the annual muster, or roundup. The film shows the typical activities of the stockmen, including separating, or "cutting out," steers from cows and calves, branding and "cutting" (castrating) calves, catching a runaway steer, and breaking in a young horse—this last task accomplished by a skillful mixture of physical force and humorous verbal persuasion. Effectively captured are the pride of the Aborigines in their rugged and often dangerous work. The film is also about Aboriginal customs, race relations in contemporary Australia, and the problems of land and property ownership in a frontier area remote from urban centers of power and law.*

The Conquest of Indonesia 50 min. Dist: FHS VS$149, order #DH2636. *This program recounts the turbulent efforts of the United Dutch East India Company to establish a monopoly in pepper and other spices. The program includes the first voyage to Indonesia in 1594 and the many subsequent ones: the heroic efforts of some explorers and traders and the corruption and treachery of many others; the incredible dangers from the sea, the weather, the jungle, and from peoples who had earlier laid claim to the area—not to mention the native populations; and the ultimate Dutch* *colonization by brute force of the entire Indonesian archipelago.*

Consecration of a Temple 25 min. Dist: UW-SAAS FR$20, FS$200. *Documents the final stages in the dedication of a new Hindu temple to Shri Venkateshvara on a hillside near Pittsburgh, Pennsylvania. The film tells two stories: (1) It shows the intricate Vedic rituals whereby the temple, its shrines, and its statues are converted into a sacred devotional center. (2) It presents a portrait of the American immigrant community from India that raised the funds to build and consecrate the temple. Through interviews with members of the Indian community, the film captures their hopes that the temple may help preserve and transmit their Indian languages and traditions to their children.*

CONSUMING HUNGER SERIES Dist: MWV VS$14.95 (each), $39.95 (set). *Our thoughts and feelings about famine and its victims have been completely shaped by television images. Television belatedly brought us the story of Ethiopia's starvation in 1984–85. Television has become the principal instrument we use to respond to Ethiopia or almost any tragedy, linking millions of people in the developed world through events like the Live Aid concert. Analyzes how such television images have become our reality.*

- **Getting the Story** 29 min. *News events from the Third World face a tough fight for Western television airtime. Competing with stories from Washington and Moscow, by the time the images of grieving mothers holding tiny skeletal children reach our living rooms, those babies may be already dead. The dramatic pictures from Ethiopia launched a major relief effort. Yet those pictures almost did not get aired. This film shows how the tragedy in Ethiopia went from "just another famine" to the most newsworthy story of the decade. It explores the rules of television news and our own attitudes toward the peoples of poor nations.*

- **Shaping the Image** 29 min. *Tragedy in our world can move quickly these days from news story to entertainment. Pictures of starving children become rallying images of fund raisers, movies, and commercials. This video raises questions about the African image created by coverage of the Ethiopian famine, and the images projected by other suffering peoples. And what of our response? Was Live Aid a display of generosity or a celebration of rock and roll? Do we need celebrities to inform us about social problems? Can we listen to the Africans tell their own story?*

- **Selling the Feeling** 29 min. *How much have we learned from the Ethiopian famine? The death of thousands there made people in this country more aware of the plight of their own starving and homeless. The famine also gave birth the relief tool of Live Aid, which inspired similar activities for other important causes. This video examines Madison Avenue's treatment of poverty and the conscious decisions of organizers to avoid political aspects of the problems. Does North America now treat her poor any differently?*

Contact: The Yanomami Indians of Brazil 28 min. Napoleon Chagnon (AN), Geoffrey O'Conner (PR). Dist: FL FR$75, VR$55, FS$595, VS$295. *This film, shot in one of the most remote corners of the Brazilian Amazon, graphically depicts the devastating impact of contact with the outside world on an isolated indigenous tribe, the Yanomami Indians. Since 1987, as the result of the incursion of Brazilian gold miners, an estimated 15 percent of the Yanomami have died of malaria and related diseases to which they have little resistance. Further, the mining operations have polluted rivers and scared away game animals, thereby destroying the Yanomami traditional ecosystem. Although the Brazilian government is ostensibly trying to protect the Indians, such efforts are undermined by the fact that their mineral-rich ancestral land is coveted by mining interests.* [Reviewed by Napoleon A. Chagnon, *AA* 93(1):252–254, 1991. Darna L. Dufour and Paul Shankman, *AJPA* 88:113–115, 1992.]

A Context Analysis of Family Interviews: Part I (1973) 28 min. Dist: PSU FR$18.50, FS$385. *Natural-history method of context analysis developed by Birdwhistell and Scheflen. Concerned with visible and audible behaviors (gestures, voice tone, posture, movement, topic) as they relate to one another in a pattern. Analysis of a family interview.* [Reviewed by Frederick Erickson, *AA* 76:731–732, 1974.] Suggested supplement: Albert E. Scheflen, *Communication Structure: Analysis of a Psychotherapy Transaction.* Indiana, 1973.

Contrary Warriors: A Film of the Crow Tribe (1986) 60 min. Connie Poten, Pamela Roberts, and Beth Ferris (WR), Rattlesnake Productions (PR), Peter Coyote (NA). Dist: DCL FR$85, FS$895, VS$250. *Conveys the impact of the century-long struggle for survival on a native people. It convincingly weaves the story of the Crow tribe's turbulent past into accounts of the lives of contemporary Crows through the experiences of Robert Yellowtail, a 97-year-old leader who is one of the main reasons for the survival of the Crow. Poverty and isolation combine with outside pressures to undermine the Crow, but they resist defeat. The story of the Crow is the story of all Native Americans: the efforts to reconcile two cultures and to gain the fundamental legal and human rights of the U.S. Constitution. Intimate ceremonies demonstrate the spiritual strength and ties to the land that sustain the Crow people.* [Reviewed by Harald Prince, *AA* 90:774, 1988.]

The Contributions of Zambian Women to Agriculture 10 min. Rita Mudenda Mwampole (PR). Dist: UWC VS$25, order #2317. *Video filmed in Zambia of Lozi women with script written by a Zambian senior extension agent. Shows women helping prepare the soil, weeding, fertilizing, rice harvesting, processing grains, and preparing family food. Women's work is recognized, and women receive encouragement to raise cash crops and do income-generating projects. Problems suggested, but positive images predominate. Excellent follow-up audiovisual for a "women in development" presentation on Africa or used with Women in Work in Africa South of Sahara. Questions for review and discussion are included in the guide with selected bibliography.*

Coonhound Field Trials 19 min. Bob Olodort (FM). Dist: UCEMC FR$29, FS$165. *A fascinating ethnographic document of a weekend of coonhound field trials held by a group of rural Californians who have transplanted this tradition* *from the southern United States. It focuses on their customs and interpersonal relationships as they gather to race their dogs after raccoons and to have a good time, the race itself being a secondary theme of the film. There is no commentary; the people speak for themselves. Some scenes that especially convey the convivial atmosphere of the gatherings are parts of the field trials, a dog auction, a couple enthusiastically discussing real and mythical dogs, and country music and dancing in a lively bar.*

The Cooper's Craft (see Colonial Williamsburg Series)

The Cop Is in the Middle (1969) 59 min. P. J. O'Connell, R. A. Lefande, WPSX-TV (Penn State U) (PR). Dist: PSU. *Police in Pittsburgh, Pennsylvania.* [Reviewed by Michael J. Lowy, *AA* 78:956, 1976.]

Copan (1985) 15 min. William Uricchio (PR). Dist: PSU FR$15, VR$14, FS$250, VS$145, order #23495. *Documents the procedures and theories involved in the excavation of this major urban center of Mayan culture, located in Western Honduras.* [Reviewed by Marshall Joseph Becker, *ARCH* 40(6):70, 1987.]

Coppermine 56 min. Ray Harper (DI). Dist: NFB FR$80, FS$775, VS$250. *The Copper Inuit lived in Canada's central arctic, untouched by "modern civilization" until the early 1900s when southern Canadians, Americans, and British moved into the area—the mouth of the Coppermine River. For thousands of years, the nomadic Inuit came here to fish. The whites came for different reasons: mining exploitation, the fur trade, law enforcement, scientific research, even adventure. Missionaries came to spread the word of God and to compete for the souls of the Inuit. This film is about a tragedy that took place during the first part of the 20th century, as these two different cultures met, but it is a story whose sequel continues to be told around the world.*

Corn Is Life (1982) 19 min. Tellens, Inc. (PR) for the Museum of Northern Arizona. Dist: UCEMC FR$33, FS$330, VS$250. *"Because corn is 'mother' in this matrilineal society, the importance of corn to the Hopi cannot be overestimated. Hopi world view encompasses corn and its concommitant, moisture, as major Hopi themes, expressed in thought, word, and deed."* [From the review by Joann W. Kealiinohomoku, *AA* 88:519–520, 1986. Reviewed by Jonathan E. Reyman, *SBF* 20:40, 1984.]

Corn and the Origins of Settled Life in Mesoamerica (1964) 40 min. Michael Coe, Richard MacNeish, and Paul Mangelsdorf (AN), Education Development Center (PR). Dist: EDC FR$45, FS$560 VS$450; UCEMC FR$18; PSU(PCR) part I (archaeological #20671, 19 min.) FR$12, part II (botanical #20672, 21 min.) FR$12. *Explores the role of the domestication of corn in the origin of civilization through excavations made in Tehuacan Valley, Mexico.* [Reviewed by J. Charles Kelly, *AA* 68:841–842, 1966.] Suggested supplement: Richard S. MacNeish, "The Origins of New World Civilization." *Scientific American* 211(I):29–37, 1964. (Available as *Scientific American* offprint no. 625.)

Corpus Christi: A Solstice Feast 25 min. Alejo Santa Maria and Cristina Echavarria (FM). Dist: ETNOS. *Every year around the summer solstice, in a small village of the Sierra Nevada de Santa Marta (Colombia), the devotees of the Holy Sacrament celebrate the Corpus Christi Fiesta. From a historical, geographical, and cultural perspective, the documentary shows the preparation of the devotees and the celebration of this colorful event. In a religious framework inherited from the Spaniards, the dancing devils confront the Holy Sacrament, while black African chants mix with American Indian dances; a fusion of religions that shows how the missionary Church integrated other religious practices with the object of drawing Indians and Africans closer to Christianity.*

Cosas de mi vida (1976) 25 min. Dist: CCC. *Expressive documentary in an ethnographic approach about Anselmo, a Mexican Indian who has struggled for survival. Orphaned at age 7, he supported himself and his baby sister, who eventually starved and died in his arms. The film continues with Anselmo's struggle to live and to do something with his life other than a docile acceptance of poverty. Totally uneducated in a formal way, he taught himself how to play a horn and started his own street band. The film was started in 1965 and finished in 1975. The viewers see change in Anselmo's life in terms of things he could buy to make his family, at first, able to survive, and during the last years, to make them more comfortable.*

Counterpoint of the Agrarian Reform, Chile 1973 (Contrapunto de la reforma agraria, Chile 1973) 42 min. Chile Communications Project, FAO (UNO) and Land Tenure Center and Dept. of Agricultural Journalism, University of Wisconsin (PR). Dist: UW FS$300, FR$20. *In a period of less than eight years, the archaic system of latifundios, which had dominated Chilean agriculture for more than three centuries, was virtually eliminated. How did this change affect the lives of rural people and relationships between diverse social groups in the countryside? This film centers on the social dynamics of the reform process, the repeated confrontations of ideas and social forces competing for land and power. This struggle is vividly recounted by the protagonists themselves. Visual impressions of the change are enhanced by scenes filmed on the same locations in 1965 and 1973.* English and Spanish versions available.

A Country Auction: The Paul V. Leitzel Estate Sale (1984) 58 min. Robert Aibel, Ben Levin, Chris Musello, and Jay Ruby (FM). Dist: PSU (PCR) FR$32, VR$20.50, FS$760, VS$280, order #50688(f), #MVCV-1741(v). *Documents an American rural tradition, the estate auction. The film reveals the personal, social, and economic processes involved when a family dissolves its homestead in a rural Pennsylvania community.* [Reviewed by Michael E. Bell, *AA* 89:779–780, 1987.]

The Country Fiddle (1957) 28 min. (A Folklore Research Film by Peter and Toshi Seeger.) Dist: FIM/RF FR$25, FS$250. *Fiddlers at the National Folk Festival in Oklahoma City. A 92-year-old Illinois fiddler and a French-Canadian wizard of the fiddle are some of the musicians seen and heard in this valuable film in which Pete Seeger examines and records on film the techniques of these superb U.S. and Canadian country fiddlers.*

Courts and Councils: Dispute Settlement in India 30 min. Dist: UW-SAAS FR$30, FS$250. *This film observes: (1) A nyaya panchayat council, recently legislated, taking two farmers' evidence regarding their dispute. (2) A nandiwalla (bulltender) caste panchayat council, colorfully turbaned, that shuns formal courts and assigns fines and other penalties according to its own traditions and group consensus. (3) Formal court tribunals, requiring trained, black-robed lawyers and judges reflecting the British legacy of "adversarial justice." The film contrasts Gandhi's and Ambedkar's views of formal courts and concludes with an Indian Supreme Court justice describing needed judicial reforms.* [Reviewed by Eva Friedlander, AA 86:1070–1071, 1984.]

The Cowboy in Mongolia (1989) 51 min. Andy Duncan and Dave King (FM). Dist: FRIF VR$75, VS$390. *After centuries of unchecked grazing by herders' animals, the grasslands of Inner Mongolia are turning to desert, threatening an old way of life. In 1967, a young marine named Dennis Sheehy almost lost an arm in Vietnam. Recovering from his wounds, Sheehy developed a keen interest in Asian culture. He learned Chinese, later studied rangelands management, and in 1985, returned to fight yet another battle in Asia. Sheehy is now working with the Chinese government, trying to teach the Mongolian herders modern methods that will stop the ecological destruction. He must convince the traditional Mongols that the grasslands' future depends on sharing knowledge—and trust—between cultures from opposite ends of the earth. It is in the context of this ecological effort that the video presents a unique cross-cultural experience.*

A Cowhand's Song: Crisis on the Range (1982) 28 min. Gwendolyn Clancy and Nancy Kelly (FM). Dist: NFF FR$55, VR$45, FS$500, VS$375. *"Communicates to the viewer a vivid sense of the way of life of family cattle ranching operators on the northern California/Nevada border and an appreciation for the strong appeal this traditional life has for people who engage in it."* [From the review by Elizabeth A. Lawrence, AA 86:1058–1059, 1984. Reviewed by John H. Peterson Jr., SBF 18:79, 1983.]

The Cows of Dolo Ken Paye: Resolving Conflict among the Kpelle (1970) 32 min. Marvin Silverman (CA, PR), James L. Gibbs Jr. (AN, PR). Dist: BFA FR$82, FS$585; PSU(PCR) order # 31610, FR$25; UCEMC FR$25. *The wounding of a crop-eating cow by a Kpelle farmer starts a dispute that is followed to its conclusion in a hot-knife trial by ordeal. Photographed in Fokwele, Liberia, in 1968, the film shows the conflict as it actually unfolded. Events filmed before the wounding of a cow indicate that the outburst was not random, but rooted in the ways in which cattle are used and in the complex relationships of the prosperous, cattle-owning chiefs and the ordinary farmers who are their constituents. Flashbacks of actual events provide historical depth. The actions of the ordeal operator invite the viewer to consider how supernatural beliefs, physiological processes, and applications of psychology all contribute to the working of the ordeal.* [Reviewed by Harold Schneider, AA 73:983–984, 1971.] Suggested supplements: John H. Gay and Michael Cole, *The New Mathematics and the Old Culture: A Study of Learning among the Kpelle of Liberia.* Holt, Rinehart and Winston, 1967. James L. Gibbs, Jr., "Poro Values and Courtroom Procedures in a Kpelle Chiefdom." *Southwestern Journal of Anthropology* 18(4):341–350, 1962. James L. Gibbs Jr., "The Kpelle Moot: A Therapeutic Model for the Informal Settlement of Disputes." *Africa* 33(1):1–11, 1963. James L. Gibbs, Jr., "Marital Instability among the Kpelle: Towards a Theory of Epainogamy." *AA* 65:552–573, 1963. James L. Gibbs, "The Kpelle of Liberia." In: *Peoples of Africa.* Holt, Rinehart and Winston, 1965.

Cracking the Stone Age Code 52 min. BBC TV (PR). Dist: BBC. *Was Britain 4,000 years ago peopled by a race of geniuses? Did the ancient Britons anticipate the Greek mathematicians and Egyptian astronomers of antiquity by about 1,000 years? This film examines the work of Alexander Thom, the ex-Professor of Engineering Science from Oxford, whose researches and findings into the meaning of the stone circles and great standing stones of Britain threaten to turn prehistory knowledge upside down. Many archaeologists ridicule Thom's suggestion that the Britons of the Late Stone Age (about 200 B.C.) knew about Pythagorean triangles, observed the major standstills of the moon in order to predict eclipses, and developed a perfectly accurate calendar. But the ranks of his supporters are swelling.* [Reviewed by Ruth E. Tringham, AA 78:116–117, 1976. Ronald Hicks, ARCH 33(3):62, 1981.]

CREATION MYTH SERIES Dist: IFF. *Three animated creation myths from different parts of the world.*

• **Rangi and Papa: A Maori Creation Myth** 8 min. FS$180. *This animated version of the creation by Maori artist Robert Jahnke is based on traditional New Zealand designs from ancient wood and stone carvings. The story tells of the gods' struggle to separate themselves from their parents and, once free, to develop their creative powers and shape the universe.*

• **The Iron Mountain: A Siberian Creation Myth** 10 min. FS$190. *This film, done in clay animation, is based on ancient Siberian sculpture and cave drawings. It stars the Great Creator and the Evil One, who constantly fight for world control—a struggle that continues to the present day. An original electronic score underlines the action.*

• **The World Tree: A Scandinavian Creation Myth** 10 min. FS$175. *Based on ancient Scandinavian rock and cave drawings, this animated film shows the activities of the frost giant, ice cow, trolls, and various gods. The world tree was formed as a bridge between the gods and the universe they had created.*

Cree Hunters of Mistassini (1974) 58 min. National Film Board of Canada (Challenge for Change Program) (PR), Tony Ianuzielo, Boyce Richardson (DI). Dist: UCEMC; NFG; DER FR$60, VR$60, FS$775, VS$400. *Ethnographic portrait of the hunting life and culture of the Cree Indians of northern Quebec. Follows three families on a winter hunting trip; shows the building of a log lodge, canoeing, rituals with the remains of killed animals, and teaching hunting methods to boys and the role and duties of women to girls. Concludes with a warning that the Cree way of life* *is threatened by a proposed dam project.* [Reviewed by John A. Price and Adrian Tanner, *AA* 77(3):696–697, 1975.]

The Cree of Paint Hills 57 min. Dist: CBC FR$40, FS$600. *A look at a group of Canada's native people, relatively unspoiled by civilization. The sturdy independence of spirit and strong ties with tradition of the Cree Indians of Paint Hills, on the eastern shore of James Bay, contrasts sharply with the lives led by many other Canadian Indians. A deep bond of affection unites the Paint Hills Cree, and this comes through as the film shows them working together in their daily round of life or as they assemble for the annual "walking out" ceremony, during which two-year-old children walk out of their tepees, unassisted for the first time.* [Reviewed by John A. Price and Adrian Tanner, *AA* 77:696–697, 1975.]

Crimebusters (Scientific Eye II Series) (1989) 20 min. Dist: JF FR$375, VR$275, FS$3700, VS$2700. *"This video describes the role of forensic science in solving a crime.... Technical aspects of the film are good, utilization of an inquiry format is consistent with recommended science education practices.... The video is recommended for junior high school students."* [From the review by Douglas C. Spring, *SBF* 26:64, 1990.]

Cronaca di Prugiasco/Chronik von Prugiasco: Aufzeichnungen Eines Tessiner Bergodorfes (Chronicle of Prugiasco: Sketches of a Ticino Mountain Village) (1978) 115 min. Remo Legnazzi (FM). Dist: Remo Legnazzi, Filmschaffedder, Altenbergstrasse 14, CH-3013 Bern, Switzerland. [Reviewed by Gene Muehlbauer, *AA* 81:740, 1979.]

The Crooked Beak of Heaven (see Tribal Eye Series)

Cross Cultural Differences in Newborn Behavior (1980) 12 min. Daniel G. Freedman (PR). Dist: PSU FR$9, FS$100. *This film demonstrates some of the research results obtained from the application of the Cambridge Behavioral and Neurological Assessment Scales to normal newborns in hospital nurseries. Striking differences in behavior among ethnic groups—Caucasian, Navajo, Aborigine, African—show up in babies who are only a few days old. Tests include the Moro startle response, the defense reaction (when the baby's nose is covered with a cloth to inhibit breathing), the newborn's walking response, and the ability of the infant to control its head and neck muscles.* Related reading: D. B. Freedman, "Ethnic Differences in Babies." *Human Nature* January:36–43, 1979. D. G. Freedman, *Human Sociobiology.* Free Press, 1979.

Crossroads/South Africa. The Struggle Continues (1980) 50 min. Jonathan Wachs (WR,DI), Jerry Weissman (CA). Dist: CN FR$75, FS$685. *Powerful economic analysis of life of blacks in South Africa.*

CROSSROADS OF CIVILIZATION SERIES (1977) 60 min. each. Anthony Meyer (DI), Anthony Meyer and David Frost (EP). Dist: Document Associates, Inc., 211 East 43rd Street, New York, NY 10017 FR$60, FS$600. *"A series of seven films that presents the history of Iran from the founding of the first Persian Empire more than 2,000 years ago to the present. The first three in the series (listed below) cover the period from the Achaemenians (559–330 B.C.) to the Sasanians (A.D. 208–651). The films were shot almost entirely on location in Iran. They concentrate on both the ancient sites and their environmental setting, emphasizing the close connection between environment and culture."* [From the review by Andrew Moore, *ARCH* 36(2):70–71, 1983.]

- **Origins and Evidence**
- **Heroes or History**
- **Guardians of the Sacred Flame**

Crow Dog (1979) 57 min. Mike Cuesta, David Baxter (DI). Dist: UNI FR$100, FS$750. *Follows Sioux medicine man Leonard Crow Dog, the spiritual leader of 89 American Indian tribes and the spokesman for the traditionalists, those who wish to retain the beliefs and way of life of their forefathers. As a young man, Crow Dog was hidden from missionary schools and social workers and brought up in the ancient ways of his people so that he could continue, like his father and grandfather before him, as the "keeper of all things sacred." Today he is the last living link to an almost vanished culture. The film includes fascinating scenes of sacred Indian ceremonies such as the Vision Quest, the Sweat Lodge, the Ghost Dance, and the Sun Dance. The film also records the late 1960s renaissance of Indian pride marked by a return to their own language and culture, the birth of the American Indian Movement (AIM), its protest activities, including the siege at Wounded Knee, and the U.S. government's campaign of repression against Crow Dog. Crow Dog is not only an informative documentary on the politics, protest, and spiritual power of the American Indian Movement, but also a moving and sympathetic portrait of a people caught between two cultures.* [Reviewed by Gifford S. Nickerson, *SBF* 16:99, 1980.]

Cruz Quinal: El rey del Bandolin (King of the Bandolin) (see the Inhabitants of the Land Grace Series)

Cry of Nukumanu (1972) 52 min. Dist: FI FR$65, FS$690. *Balance of life altered as Polynesians meet Europeans.*

Cry of the Muriqui (1982) 28 min. Andrew Young (DI), World Wildlife Fund (PR). Dist: World Wildlife Fund-US Primate Program, 1601 Connecticut Ave., NW, Washington, DC 20009; (202) 387-0800 FS$300. *"Illustrates the plight of South American monkeys in danger of extinction. ... This film focuses on the muriqui, the woolly spider monkey, the largest monkey in South America and the largest mammal in Brazil. The film's purpose is to educate viewers about conservation."* [From the review by Meredith F. Small, *AA* 87:980–982, 1985.]

Cuarahy Ohecha (1980) D. Dubosc (FM). Dist: PSU(PCR) order # 2223, FR$14.50, FS$265. *Documents a day in the life of a typical Paraguayan peasant family, with emphasis on nonverbal behavior. Shows domestic and agricultural tasks, children's play, and the family sharing a hot midday meal in the field some distance from the house.*

Cuidad del Niño: A Case Study in Education and Culture (1972) 40 min. Dist: LAC FR$35, FS$400. *Filmed in Tijuana, Mexico, at a parochial school for boys. The study* *probes the internal dynamics of the structure of education in a border town school. Shot in a cinema verité style with several long classroom sequences excellent for analysis of behavior. Suggested for use by educators seeking research material for analyzing classroom dynamics.*

Cultural Patterns of Infant Regulations (1958) 30 min. NET (PR). Dist: IU AVC FR$9.50. *Uses dance routines and originally scored music to demonstrate cultural differences in early training of infants. Compares families of southern urban Negroes, the Manus of the Admiralty Islands, and the Hopi Indians of northern Arizona. Describes group objectives of early training, its impact upon the child's personality, and the end result of childhood training.*

Cultural Patterns of Marital Sanction (1958) 30 min. NET (PR). Dist: IU AVC FR$9.50. *Employs dance routines and originally scored music to portray differences in marriage rituals of three societies. Emphasizes the basic motive behind the selection of marriage partners, the rituals that join them, and the values that guide their relationships. Compares Americans, African Bantu speakers, and the Muria of India.*

La culture du mil (Millet Culture) (1951–52) Jean Rouch (DI). Dist: CFE; DER.

The Cumana Devil (see *El Diablo de Cumana* in Inhabitants of the Land of Grace Series) (1984) 28 min. John Dickinson (FM). Dist: DER FR$45, VR$35, FS$480, VS$350. *This film is about a local artist named Luis del Valle Hurtado who regularly transforms himself into a drumming, dancing "black satan" in a festival fusion of Indian, Spanish, and African symbols. His particular satan is based on the popular image of St. Michael killing Lucifer.*

The Cuna Indians: Island Exiles (1983) 22 min. Dist: PFI FR$68, VR$68, FS$450, VS$275. *"This film focuses on the daily life and economy of the colorfully costumed Cuna Indians, who have occupied the islands off the mainland strip of the San Blas Archipelago of Panama at least since the conquest.... In this sanitized version of the Cuna world, the complexities of the culture ... as well as the harsh political realities faced by all traditional Indians in Central and South America have been conspicuously forgotten."* [From the review by Jeffrey Ehrenreich, *SBF* 20:165, 1985.]

Curare: Hunting Poison Preparation among the Sanema-Yanoama (1970) 10 min. Barbara Braendli (PR). [Reviewed by Richard Evans Schultes, *AA* 77:700, 1975.]

Cuyagua (1987) 108 min. Paul Henley (FM). Dist: RAI FS$3720, VS$168. *"Shows us two New World, Afro-Catholic rituals now practiced by people on Venezuela's Carribbean coast. Part 1, 'Devil Dancers' is about a male-centered celebration of Corpus Christi; part 2, 'The Saint with Two Faces' concerns a female-centered Feast of St. John, which follows the devil dancing of Corpus Christi by some two to three weeks."* [From the review by Daniel Segal, *AA* 92:842, 1990.]

Cycle (Myth onto Film: A Trilogy from Native Australia, Native America and the Kabbahah Series) (1986) 4 min. Robert Ascher (AR). Dist: CUAV FR$20, VR$20, FS$110, VS$46. *Drawing on theories of myth, film, and dream, Cycle offers an opportunity to step outside the analytic mode and experience another culture's mythology directly through sound and animated images. The inspiration is the mythology of the Wulamba, a native people of northeastern Australia. The soundtrack is a Wulamba secular poem. The dreamlike images take place on the claypan, where people collect lotus, the roots of which become evening star. It is here that a being—rejecting mortality—changes to moon whose light drops to the sea to become a nautilus shell and eventually returns to the sky and becomes the moon again. This never-ending cycle symbolically relates the people, the spiritual world, and the natural environment.* Study guide available. [Reviewed by Fred Myers, *AA* 90:245–246, 1988. Reviewed in *VISA* 3:119, 1990, and *SBF* 22:245–246, 1987.]

Da jiu Cantonese ritual. [Reviewed by Stephen Feuchtwang, *RAIN* 32:6–7, 1977.]

Dadi's Family (1981) 59 min. James MacDonald, Rina Gill, and Michael Camerini (DI), Michael Ambrosino (EP), Joseph Elder, Doranne Jacobson (AN). Dist: DER FR$60.00, FS$600.00; UTA-FL VR$14.50, VCC-1313; UW-SAAS FR$30.00, FS$295.00. *Dadi is the grandmother and mother-in-law, or as she explains, the "manager" of an extended family. In the Haryana region of Northern India, women leave their natal villages and come as strangers to the households of their husbands' mothers. This film exposes the family and its problems, particularly through the women of Dadi's family. The women speak about inherent tensions created by the authority of Dadi, the loneliness of veiled daughters-in-law who always remain outsiders, and husbands' expectations that wives will labor in the fields as well as taking all the responsibility for running the household. Beyond the internal conflicts and tensions, the film also addresses the issue of how the changes in the larger political and economic life of the village threaten the stability and cohesion of the family.* [Reviewed by Eva Friedlander, *AA* 85:228–229, 1983. Edward O. Henry, *SBF* 18:214, 1983.]

Dae (Gypsy Birth) (1979) 16 min. Stole Popov (FM). Dist: FL. FR$35.00, FS$300.00. *About a Gypsy clan celebrating a new life.* [Reviewed by George Gmelch, *AA* 87:232, 1985.]

Daisy: The Story of a Facelift (1983) 57 min. Michael Rubbo (FM), Giles Walker (PR). Dist: FL FR$80.00, FS$800.00. *"The story of a face lift. Two, in fact, and several breast implants, and nasal reconstructions.... The central figure in the film is a successful, middle-aged woman.... Daisy wansts to feel better about herself; she wrestles with the decision to have a face lift as a difficult one."* [From the review by Alice Reich, *AA* 88:260–261, 1986.]

Dam at Nagarjunasagar (1972) 9 min. Ossie Davis (NR), Gene Searchlinger (CA). Carousel Films, University of California. *Shot in the early 1970s at the site of the construction of the Nagarjunasagar Dam astride the Krishna River in Central India. Documents the quantity of human labor expended in a day's work in the construction of the most massive masonry dam ever built. Depicts a swarm labor force of 30,000 men, women, and children involved in the construction of a dam which took 14 years* to complete. *After laborers are seen toiling up precipitous ramps, close-ups focus in on men transporting giant boulders while women and children carry mortar on their heads. Ironic ending notes the dam will make it possible to feed no more than the number of people born during its construction.* Focusing questions: What type of mobilization and organization of human construction were employed at the dam? How are dams constructed in the United States? Why? What social patterns are evident? What motivates people to work at such a site? Bibliography: T. S. Epstein, *Economic Development and Social Change in South India.* Manchester University Press, 1962. Subramanian Swamy, *Economic Development in China and India, 1952–1970: "A Comparative Appraisal." Economic Development and Cultural Change,* XXI, no. 4, pt. 2, July 1973, 1–84. [Robert D. Lind]

Dance and Human History (1976) 40 min. Alan Lomax (AN). Dist: UCEMC FR$42, FS$540, VS$380. *Introduction to the work of Alan Lomax and his colleagues in developing choreometrics, a cross-cultural method of studying the relationships of dance style to social structure. Lomax, known for his contributions to the study of folk songs and ethnography, teamed with Irmgard Barte Nieff and Forrestine Paulay, both dance specialists, to found the new field. Analyzing dance films from all over the world, the group "came upon certain principles that show the intimate links between movement style and human evolution and between dance style and the role of women in a culture." Demonstrates how dance can be measured using a small number of scales: the human geometry of the movement, the classification of the movements according to one-, two-, or three-dimensionality, and the handling of the torso as a single or multi-unit. The film substantiates Lomax's contention that the principal symbolic function of the arts is to reinforce social adaptive patterns.* [Reviewed by Karl G. Heider, *AA* 79:745–746, 1977. Reed D. Rines, *JAF* 93(368):241–245, 1980.] Warnings: Film gives overload of information, visually and orally. Beginning students get lost and confused, advanced students are put off by rapid-fire dogmatism. Focusing questions: Best to rehearse arguments in advance—explain trunk and arm movements. Can you see the features claimed in each shot? How does the film account for movement style areas? Does this film prove its argument? Why? Why not? What would constitute proof? Are there alternatives to the materialistic explanation? Can you use these categories to judge movement in the next (ethnographic) film you see? What does the notion of one-unit and two-unit trunk suggest about dances like waltz, twist, disco? Bibliography: Alan Lomax, *Folk Song Style and Culture.* Washington, DC, 1968. See related films *Step Style, Palm Play.* Also the film *Maring in Motion,* by Alison and Marek Jablonko, which uses choreometric analysis on a New Guinea group.

Dance Contest in Esira (1936) 11 min. Paul Fejos (DI), R. Frederiksen (CA). Dist: MOMA FR$15.

Dance for a Chicken: The Cajun Mardi Gras (1993) 57 min. Pat Mire (FM). Dist: Attakapas Productions, P.O. Box 821, Eunice, LA 70535; (318)457-8214 VS$150. *Cajun filmmaker Pat Mire gives us an entertaining inside look at the colorful and exotic rural Cajun Mardi Gras. The unruly participants in this ancient tradition play as beggars, fools, and thieves as they raid farmsteads and perform in exchange for charity or, in other words, "dance for a chicken."* Winner of several awards.

Dance Like a River (1985) 45 min. Barry Dornfeld and Tom Rankin (PR), Yacub Addy (AD). Dist: IUAVC FR$35.00, VR$35.00, FS$595.00, VS$170.00, order #RC1278,16 (film), #RC1278,VH (video). *This film documents several of the dance styles, goals, and performances of Odadaa! a remarkable dance troupe from Ghana, West Africa, and introduces viewers to the variations in theme and execution of traditional dances among the Ga and other West African peoples. The performances are explained primarily by Yacub Addy, while individual members of the company offer background information and personal insights into their roles. Portions of several dances are performed in full, resplendent regalia. Yacub Addy also explains the drums, bells, and other instruments used by the group, elaborating on their origins, the contexts in which they are used, and their complex rhythmic relationships.* [Reviewed by Brenda Dixon-Stowell, *AA* 90:238–239, 1988.]

Dance Masks: The World of Margaret Severn (1982) 33 min. Peter Lipskis (FM). Dist: UCEMC FR$40.00, FS$500.00, VS$325.00. *Documents the life of British dancer Margaret Severn.* [Reviewed by Anya Peterson Royce and Fran Snygg, *AA* 87:487–488, 1985.]

Dance Therapy: The Power of Movement (1982) 30 min. Norris Brock (FM), American Dance Therapy Association (PR). Dist: UCEMC FR$39.00, FS$470.00, VS$355.00. *"Emphasizes the primacy of body movement as a medium of communication and uses this as a way for individuals to explore themselves, their relationship to space, and their relationship to other people. . . . Dance therapist Joan Chodorow works with a young woman who is interested in using movement as a way to recover repressed experiences. . . . Dance therapist Barbara Estrin uses movement to provide three men in the prison wing of a psychiatric hospital with a safe means of self-expression."* [From the review by Anya Peterson Royce and Fran Snygg, *AA* 87:485–486, 1985.]

Dance of Tears Swiss TV and the National Council for Traditional Arts (PR). Dist: NCTA. *The escape of the Khmer Classical Dance Troupe from Cambodia in 1979, and their reformation in the United States is the subject of this beautiful film.*

Dance of the Buffalo Hunt 5 min. Dist: AIS FR$1.50, FS$85. *Australian Aborigines recreate buffalo hunt dance.*

Dances at Aurukun, Cape York (1962) 28 min. Ian Dunlop (DI), E. Cranstone (CA), Frank White (SR), Film Australia (PR). Dist: AIAS. *Footage shot at Aurukun mission, a Presbyterian mission near the mouth of the Archer and Holroyd rivers, Cape York Peninsula, northern Queensland, Australia. A series of totemic dances have been recreated for the filmmakers (although the narration provides no hint of this. Also, the narration fails to mention that these peoples have been missionized for several decades.) Brief opening* *scenes show the preparation of ritual gear (principally wooden effigies of ancestral beings) and body painting. There follows a series of excerpts from sacred ceremonies. Context control is unusually poor; the sections presented have no relation to one another. A clumsy ethnographic reconstruction.* [Reviewed by John Greenway AA 69:791–792, 1967.] Focusing questions: What does the film show about traditional Australian aboriginal music and dance? What are the most distinctive features of the body movements in these dances? What does this suggest about native dance esthetics? [Donald Crim]

Dances of Bali: Baris Katekok Jago and Kebyar Duduk (see Traditional Dances of Indonesia Series)

Dances of Bali: Barong (see Traditional Dances of Indonesia Series)

Dances of Bali: Legong Kraton (see Traditional Dances of Indonesia Series)

Dances of Jogjakarta, Central Java: Bekasan Menak (see Traditional Dances of Indonesia Series)

Dances of Jogjakarta, Central Java: Langen Mandra Wanara (see Traditional Dances of Indonesia Series)

Dances of Jogjakarta, Central Java: Lawung Ageng (see Traditional Dances of Indonesia Series)

Dances of Southern Africa (1973) 55 min. Gei Zantzinger (DI), Andrew Tracey (CON). Dist: PSU FR$28, FS$710. *Large numbers of men from many tribes take work contracts at South African mines. The film presents the recreational dances performed by these groups. The typical South African emphasis on stamping movements is compared with the more individual step-dances of the northern Mashona tribes. Dances are performed at the mines and in the Tribal Trust Lands. Working with ethnochoreologist Nadia Chilkovsky, the filmmakers have kept the dance sequences intact and close-ups are avoided so that the dances can be analyzed by choreologists.* Related reading: N. C. Nahumch, *An Introduction to Dance Literacy*. International Library of African Music, Roodepoort, South Africa, 1978. Examples of labanotation used in this book are based on the film *Dances of South Africa*. H. Tracey, African Dances of the Witwatersrand Gold Mines. International Library of African Music, Roodepoort, South Africa, 1952.

Dances of Surakarta, Central Java: Bedoyo Elo Elo (see Traditional Dances of Indonesia Series)

Dances of Surakarta, Central Java: Bedoyo Pangkur (see Traditional Dances of Indonesia Series)

Dances of Surakarta, Central Java: Menak Konchar (see Traditional Dances of Indonesia Series)

Dances of Surakarta, Central Java: Srimpi Anglir Mendung (see Traditional Dances of Indonesia Series)

Dances of Surakarta, Central Java: Srimpi Gondokusomo (see Traditional Dances of Indonesia Series)

Dances of West Sumatra: Tari Piring and Tari Alang (see Traditional Dances of Indonesia Series)

Dancing to Give Thanks (1988) 29 min. Nebraska ETV (PR), Robin Riddington (AN). Dist: NAPBC. *Contemporary Omaha pow-wow.* [Reviewed by Bea Medicine, AA 93(3):76–89, 1991.]

Dandora 20 min. Dist: WBP VS$29.95, order #30917. *With technical assistance from the government, slum-dwelling families near Nairobi, Kenya, build their own houses, learn new skills, and create their own community. The film portrays the experiences of a family that receives a plot of land as part of a successful urban development project. It also shows the development of small-scale businesses, schools, day care centers, and a crafts workshop.*

Dani Houses (1974) 16 min. Karl G. Heider (FM, AN). Dist: UCEMC FR$27, FS$230; PSU. *Shows the house-construction techniques of the Grand Valley Dani, a Papuan culture in the central highlands of the Indonesian province of Irian Jaya (West New Guinea). Filmed when the Dani were in transition from stone axes to steel tools, it follows the building of both round and rectangular houses, demonstrating how the ground is cleared, how walls are made from boards and poles lashed together with vines, and how thatch grass is put on.* See suggested supplements under *Dead Birds*.

Dani Recess (1970) 20 min. Karl G. Heider (FM, AN). *Shot at the Indonesian school at Wakawaka in the Grand Valley of Balim, ca. 10 kilometers north of Dugum Neighborhood, in 1970. Attempt to capture all of the events in some play activities during a mid-morning recess. Shows children about 6–16, mainly girls, playing hit-the-stick, a game introduced from Java within the past year, but already transformed into Dani play.* Cinematic features: Shot in 1/2" videotape. Printed on to 16mm sound film. B/W, sync sound, scan lines, and occasional vertical slips. Long takes and fairly wide angle throughout. Warnings: Low resolution of video image very evident. Focusing questions: What are the rules of the game? What is essential to the game? What is just noise? How many games are going on at once? What is the relation of the rules (culture) to actual play (behavior)? What is variation? What is error (cheating)? What can you infer about the Dani culture from the way the children play? What aspects of nonverbal behavior emerge from a frame-by-frame analysis of the footage? Bibliography: See other films about the Dani (*Dead Birds, Dani Sweet Potatoes, Dani Houses*); see Koch's film on similar game played in Gilbert Islands (PSU). Karl G. Heider, "From Javanese to Dani: The Translation of a Game." In: *Studies in the Anthropology of Play*. Phillips Stevens, Jr., ed. West Point, NY: Leisure Press, 1978, pp. 72–80. Karl G. Heider, *The Grand Valley Dani: Peaceful Warriors*. New York: Holt, Rinehart and Winston, 1991, 2nd ed.

Dani Sweet Potatoes (1974) 19 min. Karl G. Heider (FM, AN). Dist: UCEMC FR$29, FS$270. *Follows the highly sophisticated process of sweet potato horticulture developed by the Grand Valley Dani. The film traces the steps of horticulture, beginning with the clearing and burning of fallow brush, scooping fertile mud from the drainage/irrigation ditches; sweet potatoes are cooked in the steam bun-*

dle. It shows many of the individuals who appear in Dead Birds *made two years earlier in the same area.* See suggested supplements under *Dead Birds*. [Reviewed in *VISA* 1:19, 1987.]

Dani Technology Films 8mm color cartridge loops. Approx. 3 min. each. Karl G. Heider (AN, FM), Education Development Center, Inc, (PR, ED). *Some details of Dani stone age technology.* The footage was shot at 24fps on 16mm; the loops, which required special projectors, are shown at 16fps on 8mm. Films include: (1) *A Tool to Make a Tool;* (2) *Digging Sticks;* (3) *Chopping and Splitting;* (4) *Fire Making.* Cf. the film, *Dead Birds.*

Danses Zaghawa (1963) 27 min. Dist: FACSEA FR$16. French only.

Daouda Sorko (1967) 20 min. Jean Rouch (DI), Centre National de la Recherche Scientifique, Comite du Film Ethnographique (PR). Dist: CFE; DER. *Daouda, a fisherman and high priest in Niger, recounts the myth of the origin of the seven Torou spirits, the principal deities of Songhay mythology.*

Darshen 30 min. Florence Davey (FM). Dist: Satyam Shivam Sundaram, 425 Alexander St., Princeton, NJ 08540. [Reviewed by H. Daniel Smith, *AA* 76:704, 1974.]

Dating Game: How Old Are We? 29 min. Dist: UCEMC FR$35, FS$400, VS$280. *Documents the work of Jeff Bada, a young scientist whose development of an archaeological dating technique based on the reaction of amino acids in an organism after its death enables researchers to penetrate prehistory beyond the 40,000-year limit of the established radiocarbon dating method. Review the scientific and archaeological controversies aroused by his discovery, especially by his dating of North American human skeletal remains at 48,000 years—which would place human arrival in the Western Hemisphere thousands of years earlier than is currently accepted.*

Daughters of Abraham: A Fight to Survive? (1988) 30 min. Beata Lipman (DI), Richard Traylor-Smith (PR). Dist: LMF VR$55.00, VS$250.00. *Contrasts scenes of Tamar, an officer in the Israeli army and Zoa, a Palestinian woman.* "*A subtle propaganda piece clearly designed for American audiences. . . . This is a useful film to illustrate how skillful editing can tilt viewers toward one point of view while superficially mantaining an impression of balance.*" [From the review by Herbert L. Bodman, Jr., *AA* 92:843–844, 1990.]

Daughters of the Anasazi (1990) 28 min. John Anthony (FM). Dist: Interpark, 1540 East MacArthur, Cortex, CO 81321; (303) 565-7453 VS$24.95. *The film documents virtually all the steps in the manufacture of decorated pottery of the Anasazi tradition, which began in the Chaco Canyon in the American southwest.* [Reviewed by Peter S. Allen, *ARCH* 44(3):56–57, 1991.]

DAUGHTERS OF THE COUNTRY SERIES Norma Bailey (PR). Dist: NFB. *Winner of numerous awards for hard-hitting documentaries, this series of historical dramas focuses on four women of Native American heritage who are the victims of social discrimination.* See descriptions under titles:

- **Ikwe**
- **Mistress Madeleine**
- **Places Not Our Own**
- **The Wake**

Daughters of Ischel: Maya Thread of Change (1993) 29 min. Kathryn Lipke Vigesaa and John McKay (FM). Dist: UCEMC VR$50.00, VS$195.00, order #38239. *A beautiful documentary exploring the lives of Maya women weavers, portraying their ancient weaving techniques and examining the economic, political, and cultural forces that are affecting them.*

Daughters of the Nile 46 min. Joop Van Wijk and Hillie Molenaar (PR). Dist: FL VR$65.00, VS$395.00. *This beautifully photographed, revealing film about Egyptian women captures their separate and subordinate life under the Islamic code. Filmed in villages and in the countryside, men and women speak about their traditions, expectations, and patterns of life. We meet lively and articulate women who have had little schooling and whose lives are centered on child bearing and hard physical labor. They acknowledge that their choices in life are limited. Their husbands are selected by their fathers. Often, at puberty, they are taken out of school. They unquestioningly accept circumcision, arranged marriages, huge families, and polygamous husbands. But sometimes they find themselves divorced. Then the need to survive propels them toward independence, with learning to read and write as their first step. Although everyone is familiar with the restrictions on women in an Islamic culture, seeing these practices accepted so matter of factly has a special impact.*

A Day among the Berbers (1947) 14 min. B/W. Dist: FIM. *This picture gives a comprehensive view of commerce, industry, and agriculture among the Berbers of North Africa who live today as they have for a thousand years. We follow a salt merchant, who brings his wares by mule out of the mountains into the town. He bargains with bidders, and purchases various items from great distances. After siesta, our merchant explores the products of the pastry cook and the coffeehouse, the shoemaker, the jeweler, the gunsmith, and the ironworker, and a visit to a North African nightclub where dancing girls entertain.*

A Day in Shrishnagar 15 min. Dist: WBP VS$25.95, order #30916. *This film tells of an extension program in India that trains farmers to use new agricultural methods while helping to preserve traditional culture and values. The film depicts daily life in Shrishnagar, a small village in West Bengal, and the relationship between a government extension agent and two farmers—one who experiments with new techniques and one who continues to use traditional methods.*

Day Shall Dawn (1959) 100 min. Aaejay Karday (DI), Walter Lassally (CA). *A joint British-Pakistani commercial film shot in the fishing village of Saithol, on the Maghna River 30 miles south of Dacca, East Bengal. Excellent dramatization of Bengal village life with a good eye for the* material details. The story involves the clash between rich and poor, traditional and modern patterns.

Daybreak in Udi (1948) 42 min. Central Office of Information, Crown Film Unit (PR). Dist: IUAVC. *Colonial policy in Nigeria.* [Reviewed by David Giltrow, AA 81:736–737, 1979.]

Dead Birds (1968) 83 min. Robert Gardner (FM), Robert Gardner, Karl G. Heider, and Jan Broekhuyse (AN), Film Study Center, Peabody Museum, Harvard University (PR). Dist: CRM/F VR$80.00, VS$295.00; UTA-FL, VR$12.50, order #VCC1322; PSU(PCR) order #80001 FR$40.50; UCEMC FR$45. *A cinematographic interpretation of the life of a group of Grand Valley Dani, who are mountain Papuans in West New Guinea (Irian Barat, Indonesia), studied by the Harvard-Peabody Expedition (1961–63). This film was made by Gardner in 1961, before the area was pacified by the Dutch government. The film focuses on Weyak, the farmer and warrior, and on Pua, the young swine-herd, following them through the events of Dani life: sweet potato horticulture, pig keeping, salt winning, battles, raids, and ceremonies.* [Reviewed by James B. Watson, AA 67:1358–1359, 1965. Peter Loizos, MAN 3(1):166, 1968. Reviewed in VISA 1:19, 1987.] Suggested supplements: Karl G. Heider, *Grand Valley Dani.* Holt, Rinehart and Winston, 1979. Peter Matthiessen, *Under the Mountain Wall.* Viking, 1963 (paperback edition Ballentine Walden 345.01755.125, 1969) (an interpretive description by a novelist and natural historian of the same events shown in *Dead Birds*).

Death 40 min. Arthur Barron and Eve Barron (FM). Dist: FL. [Reviewed by Antoine Seronde, AA 77:189, 1975.]

Death Drums of New Guinea (1930s) 45 min. Dist: FCE FR$85. FS$375.

Death Is Afraid of Us (1980) 26 min. Granada Television and Novosti (PR). Dist: FL FR$50.00, FS$425.00. *"This film's major focus is on dolgozhivtsy (the long living ones) of the Abkhasians of the Caucasus in the Soviet Union. Extravagant claims have been made for these picturesque horsemen: ages ranging anywhere from 110 to 150 years or more, coupled with the claim that their mental and physical capacities remain unimpaired. They are said to participate in the daily labor of their communities, hunt, ride horses, and continue sexual activity well into their seventies."* [From the review by Lydia Black, AA 86:1070, 1984.]

Death of an Island Culture 28 min. Australian Island Films, Inc. (PR). Dist: FI. *Nukumanu, a Polynesian outlier.* [Reviewed by James J. Fox, AA 76:714, 1974.]

THE DECADE OF DESTRUCTION SERIES (1984) 55 min. each. Adrian Cowell (PR). Dist: NFL VR$250.00 VS$990.00 (series); VR$90.00, VS$450.00 (each). *An extraordinary vision of the emergent 'world system'. Cowell has tracked that system to the Brazilian frontier in the Amazon Basin. This documentary "explores the inner mechanism of this sytem, how and why it expands into previously uncharted territory, how it devours populations and whole ecosystems in its path, how it subjugates the world to its rule. Simultaneously, Cowell shows the effects of this devastation, what we will have lost, what consequences that loss might have."* [From the review by Greg Urban, AA 87:735–739, 1985.]

• **Part 1: The Search for the Kidnappers** *"Follows a Brazilian Indian Agency 'pacification' team . . . on the trail of 'kidnappers'—the uncontracted Ure-eu-wau-wau Indians—who had recently abducted a seven year old boy named Fabio."*

• **Part 2: The Blazing of the Trail** *"Framed by haunting images of destruction, flames devouring the once towering rain forest, as settlers slash and burn the area for farms. . . . Just three kilometers beyond . . . we see Uru-eu-wau-wau plantations. This isolated tribe is on the fringe of the world system, and it is destined to be pulled in and transformed by it."*

• **Part 3: In the Ashes of the Forest** *"Explores the colonization process."*

• **Part 4i: The Mechanics of the Forest** *Endeavors to "assess the ecological impact of the devastation of Amazonia. . . . The focus is on scientific research. . . A team of biological researchers has engaged in a two year study of the effects of deforestation."*

• **Part 4ii: The Storms of the Amazon** *Endeavors to "assess the ecological impact of the devastation of Amazonia. . . . We begin to see some of the global climatic consequences of the destruction of Amazonia."*

DECADE OF DESTRUCTION SERIES (1991) Dist: BF VR$25.00, VS$350.00 (for 6 programs, $150 each.) [Reviewed by Thomas J. Maloney, SBF 28:182, 1992.]

• **The Colonists** 12 min.

• **The Development Road** 12 min.

• **The Indians** 17 min.

• **The Politicians** 19 min.

The Debt Crisis: An African Dilemma (1988) 20 min. Steve Whitehouse (DI), United Nations (PR). Dist: FRIF VR$45.00, VS$175.00. *Focusing on the devastation of Zambia's economy due to the collapse of the copper market in the mid 1970s, the video demonstrates the impact of African nations' economic crises. Among the most urbanized of African countries, 75 percent of Zambia's public buses sit idle because the government cannot afford spare parts. Disagreements with the international banking community led Zambia to break off negotiations with the International Monetary Fund and the World Bank. But Zambia is attempting to resolve its disputes with the banks and to restructure its economy to take advantage of such resources as agriculture and tourism. Although full recovery is still distant, the program presents an example of one African nation's efforts to adapt to the ever changing global economy.*

Decoding Danebury (1986) 50 min. BBC (PR). Dist: PSU VR$21.50, VS$198.00, order #50795. *Excavation and analysis of artifacts of a 2,500-year-old Celtic hill fort. Provides answers on social structure, patterns of the farming economy, religious practices, and political structures.* [Reviewed by Pam J. Crabtree, ARCH 40(1):76–77, 1987.]

Deep Hearts (1980) 53 min. Robert Gardner (FM), Robert Fulton (CA, ED). Dist: PFI FR$75, FS$695; UCEMC FR$50. *About the Bororo Fulani of the Niger Republic in Africa. The Bororo are a nomadic people who move with their beloved cattle across the infelicitous Sahel. The film was made during the few weeks that they gather in large numbers during the rains to celebrate their just pride in themselves as independent and beautiful people. At the gathering, they hold a ritual series of dances known as "berewol" in which the younger men compete in a contest of beauty. Deep Hearts is their description of how they must live. For them it is necessary to hide the feelings of envy, which they all experience, and they do this by cultivating a deep and secret heart. They are afraid of being deprived of their beauty, and they are afraid of their own feelings—of wanting to be the most beautiful themselves. The film is solely concerned with the ritual that expresses these concerns and, by implication, what it may mean to be a hostage to culture.* [Reviewed by Michael Leiber, AA 82:224–225, 1980.]

Defensive Behavior. Greater Sportive Lemur 3 min. Dist: PSU FR$2.80.

Delta Blues Singer: James "Sonny Ford" Thomas 45 min. Bill and Josette Ferris (FM). Dist: CSF FR$35, FS$350. *Focuses on the life of blues musician James Thomas, who plays Delta "gut bucket" blues in the tradition of Robert Johnson and Elmore James. The film records Thomas playing his "bottleneck" style in local juke joints near his home of Leland, Mississippi, sculpting unusual skulls, faces, and animals from Delta buckshot clay, and talking about his family and his work.*

Demircihuyuk (1988) 35 min. Institut fur den Wissenschaftlichen Film (PR). Dist: PSU VR$18.00, VS$195.00, order #40467. *Highlights the methodology employed in excavation of an early Bronze Age settlement, located on the Anatolian Plateau (Turkey). Archaeologists prepare grid system (also detailed in scale model), remove and clean artifacts, and examine plant and animal remains. Current life in neighboring village compared with life in prehistoric times.* [Reviewed by Peter S. Allen, ARCH 42(6):78–79, 1989.]

Depending on Heaven: The Desert (1989) 28 min. Peter Entell (FM). Dist: FRIF FR$55.00, FS$530.00, VS$280.00. *Focuses on a different group living on the edge of the spreading Mongolian desert. The peasant farmers featured in this film are applying modern agricultural techniques to combat the continuing erosion and to reclaim their land.* [Reviewed by William Jankowiak, AA 92:845–846, 1990.]

Depending on Heaven: The Grasslands (1987) 28 min. Peter Entell (FM). Dist: FRIF FR$60.00, FS$530.00, VS$280.00. *Follows a nomadic Mongolian family and its ponies, cattle, and goats across the austere but spectacular grasslands of northern China. Sensitive to every nuance of the region's harsh natural forces, this film is a look at a way of life in harmony with its environment.* [Reviewed by Charlotte Ikels, AA 91:838, 1989.]

The Dervishes of Kurdistan (Disappearing World Series) 52 min. Granada Television International (PR). Dist: FL VR$75.00, VS$445.00. *With the Kurdish refugees capturing world attention, this documentary takes on an added interest. It captures on film for the first time the incredible faith and spiritual power among villagers on the stormy mountainous frontier of Iran and Iraq. The Dervishes' religious faith allows them to thrust skewers in their cheeks, plunge daggers in their sides, eat glass, and lick white-hot spoons.*

Desert People (1966) 51 min. Ian Dunlop (DI), Robert Tonkinson (AN). Dist: FAA; CRM/MH FR$39, FS$575. B/W. *Documents the daily life of two families of the Australian Western Desert. Djagamara and his family are camped by a rare pool of clean water in an otherwise dry creek bed. Djagamara flakes stones for tools; his wives and children collect woolybutt grass seed. Back in the camp they grind the seed into flour and cook seed cake. The film then looks at Mima and his family as they travel, hunt lizards and bandicoot, and collect vegetable food. At the end of the day, they make a new camp and cook the day's catch. They sleep behind a wind brake, with a small fire between each person for warmth. This film is made up from materials from parts 1, 2, and 4 of the People of the Australian Western Desert film Series. Warning: Scenes of the hunting and casual killing of lizards may traumatize introductory students. Focusing Questions: What sorts of knowledge are required in order to find food in this harsh environment? What does the film show about family organization, age, and sex roles? What aspects of traditional technology are shown? How do these people regard flies? Bibliography: Robert Tonkinson, The Mardudjara Aborigines: Living the Dream in Australia's Desert. Winston, NY: Holt, Rinehart and Winston, 1978.* [Reviewed by Norman B. Tindale, AA 70:437, 1968.] [Donald Crim]

Les Deux Chasseurs (The Two Hunters) (1981) Jean Rouch (DI). Dist: CFE; DER.

Development of the Child: A Cross-Cultural Approach to Cognition (1975) 20 min. Jerome Kagan (CON). Dist: PSU order #21756, FR$16.50. *Underlying theme of the effects of environment, particularly modernization, on the rate of psychological development. Focus on perceptual inference, memory for objects and locations, performance of memory, growth of reflectivity, and appearance of concrete operational thinking. Compares villages in Japan, Guatemala, and Kenya.*

The Development Road (see Decade of Destruction Series)

Devi (The Goddess) (1960) 90 min. Satyajii Ray (FM, WR), Ali Akbar Khan (MU). Dist: AB FR$75. *The story takes place in present day India where a father dreams that his 17-year-old daughter-in-law is a reincarnation of the goddess Kali. He proclaims his vision and places the naive girl on an altar outside his home. Because of a "miracle," the peasants and the girl come to believe in her divinity, but their blind faith results in a series of tragedies for the family.* [Reviewed by Serena Nanda and Joan Gregg, AA 79:213, 1977.]

The Devil's Cliff (1978) 40 min. Attax Films (PR), Jacques Dumas (DI). Dist: Mac FR$45.00, FS$450.00. *Depicts some aspects of life among the Dogon of Mali.* [Reviewed in *SBF* 15:109–110, 1979.]

El Diablo de Cumana (Cumana Devil) (see Inhabitants of the Land Grace Series)

Diagnosticos (Diagnoses) (see the Andean Ethnomedicine: Birth and childhood illness in Six Ecuadorian Communities Series)

Dialects (see Language and Linguistics Series) (1957) 30 min. NET (PR). Dist: PSU order #32559 FR$12.50. *Analyzes the dialects of five speakers of American English; points out regional differences.*

Diane 26 min. Mary Feldhaus-Weber (DI). Dist: Odeon Films, Inc. *A woman moves from South Dakota to New York to become an actress.* [Reviewed by Mary Mackey, *AA* 79:202, 1977.]

Diary of a Harlem Family (1968) 20 min. Gordon Parks (DI). *Harlem day-by-day description of life of lower-class American family. Depicts turmoil of the lives of each member, focusing on the mother. Not an ethnographic film in the strictest sense. The intent is to describe the consequences of poverty on the lives of one family. There is no in-depth information, but issues on education, health, the welfare system, drugs, housing, and interpersonal violence are raised. Cinematic features: The film is composed of still shots while author reads narration as in a diary. Warnings: A very powerful film; previewing is a must. Focusing questions: What does social class mean in terms of the life chances of members of a class? How do SES and race intersect? How do generalizations and rationalizations about poverty compare to events in this film?* [J. Kelly]

DIARY OF A MAASAI VILLAGE SERIES (1985) 250 min. Melissa Llelewyn-Davies (DI), BBC (PR). Dist: DER VR$200.00, VS$1500.00, FR$50.00, VS$350.00 (each); FIV. *This series of five films looks at daily life among the Masai. This films are presented as a diary of a 7-week visit to a single village. The structure is episodic and the content dependent on various events or stories, some of which are developed through more than one film. The tapes can be used independently or together, to give an in-depth sense of Maasai life.* [Reviewed in *VISR* 8:125, 1992.]

- **Part 1: The Prophet's Family** *Examines the problem of maintaining enough cattle to supply milk and meat versus selling off cattle to raise money for maize, antibiotics, and pesticides; cash is also needed for legal fees for Rerenko, the Laibon's son.*

- **Part 2: Two Ways of Justice** *Young men are ritually prohibited from eating grain. Several of them steal one of the Laibon's goats and then must make reparations.*

- **Part 3: Two Mothers** *Focuses on gender relationships. The principal events for the women are a "coming out ox" ritual and the birth of a child; for the men, the birth of a calf is the central theme.*

- **Part 4: Two Journeys** *Contrasts the journey of Miisia's new wife back to his village with that of Tipaia's to sell cattle for Rerenko's legal fees.*

- **Part 5: Nine Cows and an Ox** *This final segment depicts the ceremony known as the "ox of ilbaa," from which Miisia emerges, acknowledged as a man.*

Didn't We Ramble On: The Black Marching Band (1992) 14 min. Billy Jackson (PR). Dist: FL VR$50.00, FS$400.00, VS$195.00. *"This very short piece . . . attempts to show that black marching bands and fife-and-drum bands are the direct descendants of Yoruba and other African musical processions that are 700 years old. . . . Though direct connections between American black music and the African world are undeniable, the limited scope of this work does not give us more than a general overview of the diaspora."* [From the review by Winnie Lambrecht, *SBF* 28:150, 1992.]

Different but Equal (Africa Series) (1986) 57 min. RM Arts (PR), Basil Davidson (H). Dist: FIV. *For centuries, Africa was ravished by the slave trade, which has distorted our view of its people. Davidson shows that Africa gave rise to some of the world's greatest civilizations.*

The Dig (1970) 20 min. Astrida R. Onat (DI), Seattle Community College (PR), Al Fisk (CA). Dist: Sterling Educational Films. *Excavation of a Puget Sound shell midden.* [Reviewed by Thomas Wight Beale, *AA* 77:907, 1975.]

The Dig (1990) 22 min. George Johnson (PR), David Curnick (DI) for the National Film Board of Canada. Dist: IUAVC FR$30.00, VR$30.00, FS$410.00, VS$150.00. *A brief tribute to a remarkable seventh-grade teacher, Richard Edwardson, who has prepared a series of archaeological "sites" by "salting" the earth with "artifacts" manufactured by himself. Then after careful and lengthy preparation in the classroom, students head to the field, where they excavate these manufactured sites.* [From the review by Peter S. Allen, *ARCH* 44(4):68, 1991. Reviewed by Clement W. Meighan, *AA* 93(4):1035, 1991.]

Digging for Black Pride (1971) 19 min. WNET/13 (PR). Dist: IUAVC FR$7.75, FS$210. *Children in Brooklyn's Bedford-Stuyvesant section are finding artifacts linking them with their 19th-century ancestors and, in classroom activities, learning about their African heritage. Under "Project Weeksville," black children are piecing together the history of the self-sufficient black community of Weeksville that existed during the early 1800s. They are studying the sophisticated organization of the community and how the early Bedford-Stuyvesant residents held off white raiders during the Draft Riot of 1863.* [Reviewed by Elizabeth A. Crowell, *ARCH* 34(2):66, 1981.]

Digging Up the Past (1964) 23 min. Robert Greengo and Richard D. Daugherty (AN), Northern Films (PR). Dist: NF; PSU(PCR) order #30867, FR$14.10, FS$376. [Reviewed by Jay Ruby, *AA* 69:563, 1967.]

Dineh Nation: The Navajo Story 26 min. Russell Richards (PR). Dist:FL VR$55.00, VS$195.00. *This powerful film with its haunting music, was photographed in the sovereign Dineh Indian Reservation, which stretches* through parts of Arizona, New Mexico, and Utah. Here the Navajo people have lived on vast deposits of oil, coal, and uranium. Their religion considers Mother Earth sacred and forbids them from exploiting her resources. But outside forces are at work, strip-mining the coal and polluting the water. The sweet wells on Dineh land are drying up. This land has also suffered a uranium spill larger than that of Three Mile Island. Tens of thousands of Dineh were relocated to untenable locations. Others were fenced off from the land they worship. The film emphasizes the spiritual essence of the Dineh, with their unique art forms and original lifestyle. Native American music is used to produce a rhythmic, deeply moving film.

Dineh: The People (A Portrait of the Navajo) (1974–76) 77 min. Jonathan R. Reinis (PR, WR). Dist: Western World Productions P.O. Box 3594, San Francisco, CA 94119. *Legal battles over Navajo rights.* [Reviewed by David F. Aberle, AA 79:508, 1977.]

Dingari Ceremonies at Papunya—June 1972 15 min. Dist: UCEMC FR$26, FS$215. *Records three sacred dingari (secret) ceremonies performed by Pintubi tribesmen of central Australia: the reenacting of the exploits of two men credited with the creation of numerous plants and animals; the string-cross ritual, intended to placate the powerful dingari spirit; and a mock vengeance in which an evil sorcerer is ostensibly killed.*

Dinshyin 22 min. Robert Fuller (FM). Dist: UCEMC FR$31, FS$310. *An ethnographic chronicle of the many peoples who have lived in and around the Canyon de Chelly and Mesa Verde in northeastern Arizona. It focuses on the Navajo, who came to the area about 700 years ago, after the Pueblo Indians, builders of the great cliff houses, had mysteriously abandoned it. The film traces the Navajo's struggle, first against the Spanish, and then against the "Anglos," to keep their land and their culture intact, and it relates the aftermath of their defeat at the hands of Kit Carson: the killing winter march in 1864 to a concentration camp–reservation in New Mexico. The film shows that the Navajo returned over the years to their native land and now live there much as they always did. Excellent use of Indian art to illustrate the myths and legends that are an integral part of the canyon's history.*

Diro and His Talking Musical Bow (1980) 13 min. Jim Roselini (FM). Dist: AFF FR$25.00, VR$15.00, FS$228.00, VS$228.00. *This is a film about the people of Upper Volta. Diro is a Lobi musician in the southwestern part of the country. He is shown preparing a musical bow and playing it in a traditional hide-and-seek game in which children are given "hot/cold" cues by musical phrases following the tone patterns of speech. About two-thirds of the film concerns preparing the bow, beginning with wood selection, and the remainder shows three turns of the game. The latter was shifted from the usual night setting to daylight for ease of filming. The voice-over narration is good but would be enhanced if a sentence or two were added to say how it is that music can convey speech.* [Reviewed by Gregory A. Finnegan, AA 83:746, 1981.]

DISAPPEARING WORLD SERIES Granada Television (PR). Dist:FIV; PSU; FL. *The Disappearing World Series provides a record of the social structures, beliefs, and practices of societies confronting change and, in some cases, facing extinction by the pressures of our expanding technocratic civilization. Traveling to remote corners of five continents, film crews worked in close association with anthropologists who have done extensive fieldwork living with societies concerned. The academic strengths of this series are heightened by the stature of the anthropologists involved, many of whom hold senior positions at top universities in the United States. The result is a series of accurate, enlightening portraits in which the people, their values, and their behavior are allowed to speak for themselves.* (Discounts are available for purchasing a quantity of films in the Disappearing World Series.) [The entire series appraised by Peter Loizos, AA 82:573–594, 1980.] See film descriptions under individual tititles:

- **War of the Gods** (1971)
- **The Mehinacu** (1974)
- **The Dervishes of Kurdistan** (1973)
- **Kataranga—A God for All Seasons** (1973)
- **The Meo** (1972)
- **The Tuareg** (1972)
- **A Clearing in the Jungle** (1970)
- **The Last of the Cuiva** (1971)
- **Embera—The End of the Road** (1971)
- **The Mursi** (1974)
- **Masai Women** (1974)
- **The Quechua** (1974)
- **The Kawelka: Ongka's Big Moka** (1974)
- **The Sakuddei** (1974)
- **The Eskimos of Pond Inlet: The People's Land** (1975)
- **The Shilluk** (1975)
- **On the Edge of the Gobi** (1975)
- **A City on the Steppes** (1975)
- **The Kirghiz of Afganistan** (1975)
- **The Rendille** (1976)
- **Some Women of Marrakech** (1976)
- **The Sherpas** (1977)
- **Umbanda** (1977)

And since 1977:
- **Afghan Exodus**
- **Across the Tracks—Vlach Gypsies in Hungary**
- **The Albanians of Rrogam**
- **Asante Market Women**
- **The Basques of Santazi**
- **Carnaval Bahia**
- **Cakchiquel Maya of San Antonio Palopo**
- **The Herders of Mongun-Taiga**
- **Inside China: Living with the Revolution**

- Inside China: The Newest Revolution
- The Invisible Enemy
- The Kalasha—Rites of Spring
- The Kayapo: Out of the Forest
- The Kazakhs of China
- Khyber
- The Kwegu
- The Last of the Cuiva
- Masai Manhood
- The Lau of Malaita
- The Mende
- The Migrants
- Mongolia: On the Edge of the Gobi
- Mongolia: The City on the Steppes
- The Mursi: Nitha
- The Mursi: The Land Is Bad
- The Pathans
- Saints and Spirits
- The Trobriand Islanders of Papua New Guinea
- Villagers of the Sierra de Gredos
- The Whale Hunters of Lamalera
- Witchcraft among the Azande
- The Wodaabe

Discovering American Indian Music (1971) 24 min. Baily Film Associates (PR). Dist: Baily Film Associates, 11559 Santa Monica Blvd., Los Angeles, CA 90025. *Film deals with the songs and dances of various North American tribes as performed by contemporary Indians. Authentic dress and traditional instruments are featured. An examination of the social and ceremonial significance of music and dance in Native American culture. Film closes with a contemporary percussion ensemble using native instruments illustrating the variety and complexity of sound that can be produced.* [Robert B. Moorman]

Discovering Country and Western Music (1977) 24 min. Bernard Wilets (PR). Dist: BFA FR$46.00, FS$460.00. *"Asa Martin . . . relates his own life story from a handsaw and bow player as a child, to a family musician and ultimately to a nationally known recording star. He also narrates the story of others including Patsy Montana of the National Barn Dance and Johnny Barnes of the Melody Ranch Show with Gene Autry."* [From the review by Melanie L. Sovine, AA 89:522–525, 1987.]

Discovering the Moche (1979) 25 min. Christopher B. Donnan, Richard Cowan, William B. Lee (FM). Dist: UCEMC FR$30, FS$340, VS$240. *An introduction to the art and culture of the Moche, who flourished between 100 B.C. and A.D. 700 in the arid river valleys of Peru's northern coastal plain. Shows how the study of Moche art, in conjunction with archaeological evidence, ethnographical analogy to present-day Peruvian Indians, and careful reading of early Spanish accounts, can be employed to reconstruct this ancient culture and interpret it in its own terms. Moche had no writing, but they left extensive ethnographic material in the form of fine-line painting and bold sculpture expressed mainly in ceramic vessels.* [Reviewed by Wendy Ashmore AA 84:993–994, 1982. Richard L. Burger, ARCH 38(4):66–67, 1985.]

Discovery at Sheep Rock (1966) 29 min. Dist: PSU FR$14.50, FS$265. *Archaeological excavation at the dry rock shelter at Sheep Rock, Raystown Dam, Pennsylvania. Discovery in 1957 of human remains and artifacts belonging to primitive Indians 8,000 years ago. Excavation procedure. Cataloging of material; sociological implications of the finds. Focuses primarily on the experience of students working at the site during the 1966 summer field school.* [Reviewed by Melburn D. Thurman, AA 77:908–909, 1975.]

Discovery of Arago Man (1969) 17 min. Dist: FACSEA FR$16. [Reviewed by Harvey M. Bricker, AA 77:918, 1975. Ivan G. Pawson, AA 80:509–510, 1978.]

The Dispossessed (1970) 33 min. George Ballis, Maia Sorotor, Judy Whalley, Peter Rand (PR). Dist: UNI FR$45-60, FS$450. *In early June of 1970, a group of Pit River Indians occupied a campground along the Pit River in northern California that was controlled by the Pacific Gas and Electric Company. The Indians were reoccupying a small part of ancestral lands that they claimed had been stolen from their tribe. They were trespassing, said PG&E. Documents the ensuing mass arrests by police and federal marshals and also features discussions with the Pit River Indians about their land and rivers, their poverty, and their rights. The film also analyzes the corporate interlocks that control Indian land and shows how the struggle of the Pit River Indians to regain their land is related to farmworkers, urban blacks, ecology, and foreign wars.* [Reviewed by Shelton H. Davis, AA 74:1576, 1972.]

Distant Thunder Satyajit Ray (DI). *A fictional account of a Bengali Village in 1943.* [Reviewed by Michael Yorke, RAIN 9:6, 1975.]

The Divided Trail. A Native American Odyssey (1978) 33 min. Jerry Aronson (FM), Michael Goldman (DI). Dist: PFI FR$42.50, FS$460, VS$315. *An intense emotional journey through the lives of two Chippewa Indians, Michael Chosa and his sister Betty Chosa Jack, who, along with their friend, Carol Warrington, migrate from their northern Wisconsin reservations to the slums of Chicago. Filmed over an eight-year period, this documentary follows their struggle to overcome the near disintegration of their individual and tribal identities under the enormous pressures of contemporary urban living. Thrust into an unfamiliar urban context, without adequate preparations and assistance from the federal government which encouraged them to leave the reservation in the first place, these Native Americans are forced to fend for themselves against poverty and discrimination in housing, education, and employment. Betty Chosa has fought a successful battle against alcoholism. Now she is a trained counselor, helping Indians cope with the realities of their existence. Her brother, Michael, has also found a sense of purpose and self-worth as he developed from an angry militant into a skillful liaison between his people and the government. He has recently received over $600,000 in* *federal grants for various programs. Carol Warrington was the organizer of the 1970 Chicago Indian Rights Movement. After much struggling, she has managed successfully to work out the conflict between her political activities and personal needs.* [Reviewed by Dwight B. Heath in *AA* 83(3):741–742, 1981, and in *SBF* 15:232, 1980.]

Divine Horsemen (1982) 54 min. Cherel Ito and Teiji Ito (ED), Maya Deren (DI). Dist: WMM FR$130.00, VR$90.00, VS$395.00; Cherel Ito, 106 Bedford Street #4E, New York, NY 10014 FR$100.00, FS$775.00. *This film is about the Vousoun rituals in Haiti. It begins with a general introduction to the voodoo system of beliefs and practices and then goes on to focus and elaborate on the ritual practices of the cults of Rada, Congo, and Petro. Major Voodoo divine spirits focused upon by the filmmakers are: Damballah, Agwe, Ogun, Ghede, and Erzulie.* [Reviewed by George M. Epple, *AA* 84:979–980, 1982.]

Divine Madness: Trance, Dance and Healing in Guyana (1978) 60 min. Philip Singer (FM). Dist: Singer-Sharrette Productions, 336 Main Street, P.O. Box 68, Rochester, MI 48063; (313) 731-5199 FR$73.00. *A ritual healing sequence at a Kali Hundu temple in Albion, Guyana.* [Reviewed by Judith Johnson, *AA* 87:480–481, 1985.]

Diving for Roman Plunder (1978) 24 min. Andrew Solt (PR). Dist: WDEM FS$495.00. *"Cousteau travels to the waters off the Greek island of Antikythera, where Greek sponge divers discovered a Roman shipwreck in 1900 and recovered many art treasures. The film says little about this early recovery, but the original discovery and its circumstances are exciting, intriguing and worth retelling."* [From the review by Robert L. Hohlfelder, *ARCH* 36(1):62–64, 1983.]

Djibo: The Zarma Culture of Niger (1978) 52 min. Jean Pierre Beaurenaut (DI). Dist: Mac FR$50, FS$625. *Illuminates the problem of how to retain traditional African tribal values in a modernization process involving a foreign language and culture. A dialogue between two lifestyles: the quiet existence of a shepherd with close family and Islamic ties, and the dangerous, exciting appeal of Westernized Niamey. Records the conflict in the charming boy Djibo, who is followed from the timeless world of his nomadic ancestors to the seductive riches of the city. Djibo's spontaneously taped reactions serve as a counterpoint to the descriptive sequences, while the director's commentary establishes a dialogue between the voices of Africa and Europe. The means by which boys such as Djibo are being prepared for life in Niamey is an innovative educational program initiated on an experimental basis in 30 isolated villages. A closed-circuit television set turns a native hut into an electronic classroom, while itinerant teachers follow up with tutorial supervision. The result is a revolution involving not only Djibo, but whole generations of children and adults trying to become Modern Africans without losing the beauty and harmony of their former lives.* Bernard Surgue, Contributions à l'étude de la musique sacreezarmas songhay. Centre Nigerian de Recherche en Sciences Humaines. Naimey, Nigeria, 1972.

Djungguwan at Gurka'wuy (1989) 4 hours. Ian Dunlop (FM), Howard Murphy (AN). Dist: FAA. *The djungguwan rituals of the Yolngu-speaking people in northeastern Arnhem Land, Australia.* [Reviewed by Fred R. Myers, *AA* 95(1):250–252, 1993.] Related reading: W. Lloyd Warner, *A Black Civilization*. Harper and Row, 1937.

Doctor, Lawyer, Indian Chief 29 min. Carol Geddes (DI). Dist:NFB FR$60.00, VR$60.00, FS$550.00, VS$250.00. *This inspiring documentary focuses on five successful Native American women. Of varied ages and backgrounds, they have achieved fulfilling careers in their chosen fields: as government minister, employment counselor, band chief, crew member on a fishing boat, and lawyer. Each talks about her personal difficulties in her getting to where she is today and about her life experiences. The women share a profound appreciation of the values of their culture, and for several of them it was the rediscovery of their roots that enabled them to change the course of their lives.*

Dr. Leakey and the Dawn of Man (1967) 26 min. National Geographic Society (PR). Dist: NGS FS$599, VS$545; UCEMC FR$24; PSU(PCR) order #31288, FR$9.60; FI FR$16, FS$327.50. *Photographed in East Africa's Olduvai Gorge, this film shows how some of the most dramatic anthropological discoveries in this century were made after years of searching. It was in this rich fossil depository, between the Ngorongoro Crater and the Serengeti National Park in Tanzania, that Dr. Louis Leakey and his wife Mary proved Leakey's contention that man's origins were in Africa—not in Asia, as was commonly surmised. After 40 fruitless years, Leakey's untiring search was rewarded when he discovered fossil remnants predating all previous evidence of man's existence. Two important discoveries—Zinjanthropus in 1959 and Homo habilis in 1961—indicate that at least two different kinds of manlike creatures roamed Africa almost two million years ago. Dr. Leakey explains and demonstrates his anthropological methods and shows how he conducted his exploration in the gorge. His discoveries again prove that there is still a wealth of unknown knowledge surrounding man and his world.* [Reviewed by Elwyn L. Simmons, *AA* 71:577–578, 1969. C. Loring Brace, *AA* 80:506–507, 1978.]

Doctora (1984) 52 min. Linda Post and Eugene Rosow (FM). Dist: Natazumi Productions, c/o Cultural Research and Communication, Inc., 434 Sycamore Rd., Santa Monica, CA 90402; (213) 459-9448 FR$85.00, FS$800.00. *"A documentary about a remarkable woman who conquers poverty and isolation in order to reach her patients in their community. The film is also about a definition of health and health care that challenges the dominant view of disease as an individual occurence, and cure coming from the physicians's black bag.... Defines health as well being—physically, emotionally, and spiritually. Health care has more to do with empowering a community, supporting self-reliance, and eliminating poverty than in administering pills."* [From the review by David Andrews and Kathleen McDermott, *AA* 88:520–521, 1986.]

Doctors All (1958) 30 min. NET(PR). Dist: IU AVC FR$9.50. *Uses dance routines and originally scored music* to portray reactions to human illness. Describes methods of detection/treatment and acceptance of treatment. Compares Americans, the Ojibway Indians of Canada, and the Djuka Bush Negroes of Dutch Guiana.

Documents sur une langue sifflée Pyrénéenne (Documents on a Pyrenean Whistled Language) 19 min. Dist: FACSEA FR$16. French only.

Documents sur une sangue sifflée Turque (Documents on a Turkish Whistled Language) 12 min. Dist: FACSEA FR$16. French only.

Dodoth Morning (1976) 16 min. Timothy Asch (FM). Dist: UCEMC FR$27, FS$230. *Ethnographic study of a tribe in northern Uganda. Although they are a pastoral people, the Dodoth grow a variety of crops, of which millet is a staple. Using a slice-of-life style with sparse narration, the film focuses on a series of family interactions one morning during harvest time, illustrating a great many aspects of Dodoth life, including social roles and division of labor between the sexes, marital customs, relationships between parents and children, village organization, and religious and mythological beliefs. Though simple in story line, the film is richly detailed and well observed; each scene is filled with valuable and spontaneous data on a people's daily life.*

Dogon of Mali: Cliff Dwellers of Bandiagara 10 min. Dan Shafer, Tom O'Toole (FM). Dist: MINN FS$130. *This film is the result of a visit to the villages of Sanga and Songo in Mali. It shows the two main reasons why the Dogon have come to live on the cliffs in this rather arid land inside the northernmost bend of the Niger River. Some of the religious and political background of this people is woven into the film in a consideration of caves as graves, storage places for masks, and other religious paraphernalia, as well as the sites of initiation ceremonies. This element is again noted in the dance sequence at the end of the film. The social and economic life of the Dogon is discussed.*

Dokwaza: Last of the African Iron Masters (1988) 50 min. D. Paul Morris, Nicholas David, and Yves Le Bleis (FM). Dist: UOC VR$60.00, VS$325.00. "*A visual study of iron manufacturing among the Mafa of northern Cameroon and Nigeria, and it is particularly welcome because the smelting furnaces used were elaborate combinations of art and technology, and the smiths employed a process of secondary ore refinement that is here well documented. This production documents the smelting, refining, and forging of iron.*" [From the review by Patrick R. McNaughton, *AA* 92(4):1109–1110, 1990.]

Dongo Horendi (1966) 30 min. Jean Rouch (DI), Centre National de la Recherche Scientifique, Comite du Film Ethnographique (PR). Dist: CFE; DER. *The beginning of a possession dance by a new Dongo 'horse' (a thunder spirit).*

Dongo Hori (1973) 20 min. Jean Rouch (DI), Centre National de la Recherche Scientifique, Comité du Film Ethnographique (PR). Dist: CFE; DER. *In a new section of the aviation route to Niamey, an old Zima (priestess and medium) 'horse' of the thunder spirit, organizes a celebration to thank the rain master of the sky who has already given and he asks for more.*

Dongo Yenendi, Gamkalle (1966) 10 min. Jean Rouch (DI), Centre National de la Recherche Scientifique, Comite du Film Ethnographique (PR). Dist: CFE; DER. *Ritual ceremony in the village of Gamkalle to obtain rain.*

Doorway to the Past 28 min. Ivor Noel Hume (WR, DI). Dist: Colonial Williamsburg Foundation, Audiovisual Distribution Section, Box C, Williamsburg, VA 23185. *Historical archaeology.* [Reviewed by Barbara Liggett, *AA* 78:363, 1976. Elizabeth A. Crowell, *ARCH* 34(2):66, 1981.]

Dorothy Molter: Living in the Boundary Waters (1986) 42 min. Judith Hadel and Wade Black (FM). Dist: DCL FR$85.00, FS$850.00, VS$250.00. "*Attempts to dispel the stereotypes of older women (as withered hags, helpless creatures, or kindly grandmothers) by allowing Dorothy Molter to talk about her life. . . . Living alone deep in the wilderness, she has been self-sufficient for 40 years.*" [From the review by Mary Beth Haralovich and Denise Kervin, *AA* 92:835–836, 1990.]

The Double Burden (1992) 60 min. Marlene Booth (DI). Dist: NDF VR$75.00, VS$250.00. *The film presents the lives of three families (African American, Eastern European, and Hispanic), each with three generations of women who worked outside the home while also raising the families. Their stories tell of human strength, pride, accomplishment, and sadness, while providing insights into the issues of class, ethnicity, and gender surrounding the tasks of employment and childrearing.*

The Double Way (1975) 53 min. International Women's Film Project (PR), Helena Soldberg-Ladd (DI). Dist: UNI. *The situation of Latin American women.* [Reviewed by Helen I. Safa, *AA* 79:745–747.]

Down the Project (1982) 60 min. Richard Broadman (FM). Dist: CRA FR$96.00, FS$850.00. *Boston public housing problems.* [Reviewed by Sally Engle Merry, *AA* 85:1013–1014, 1983.]

The Dragon Boat Festival (1992) 30 min. Zhuang Kongshao (FM). Dist: UWP VR$60.00, VS$175.00, ISBN 0-295-73051-X. *During the Dragon Boat Festival, which is celebrated all over China in late spring, boat races commemorate the unsuccessful attempt to rescue the 4th-century B.C. poet Qu Yuan from suicide by drowning. It is an occasion for ritual visits and for special family meals. It is also a time when noisy and colorful processions honor the deities enshrined in local temples everywhere. This documentary records the celebration of the Festival in June 1989 in the village of Gutian alongside the Min River. (The following year, the site was flooded to create a hydroelectric plant.) The viewer sees family rituals performed in conjunction with the holiday; the village teams preparing and racing their boats; and the religious procession of the gods, whose images are carried from the temple around the village accompanied by bands, firecrackers and excited villagers.*

The Dragon Bride (1993) 55 min. Joanna Head (FM). Dist: BBC. *The marriage of a teenage girl to four brothers aged eight to sixteen is not unusual among the Nyinba people of the Nepalese Himalayas. This unique form of marriage is essential to their survival in such a harsh and* *rugged environment, but it also has its more subtle costs. As preparations for the lavish wedding begin, the young bride faces the prospects of life with four husbands.*

Dragons in the Sea (The World about Us Series) Hugh Gibb (FM), BBC-TV (PR). *The boat people of Hong Kong.* [Reviewed by Stephen Feuchtwang, *RAIN* 6:9, 1975.]

Dream Dances of the Kashia Pomo (The American Indian Film Series) (1964) 30 min. Dist: UCEMC FR$35, FS$410; PCU(PCR) order #2207K, FR$11.10, FS$300. *Pomo women dance the Bole-Maru of today, expressing contemporary native beliefs nearly a century after the Bole-Maru first evolved, blending the native Kuksu cult with the Maru, or dream religion. The five dances reflect recent influences, including Christianity and World War II: the Hand Power Dance, Star Hoop Dance, Feast Dance, Marriage Dance, and War Flag Dance. Each is danced in elaborate costumes around a fire within a brush enclosure. The singers use rattles, and the dancers blow whistles. As prophet and keeper of tribal customs, the Dreamer (Shaman) expresses the Bole-Maru ideology through her powers to dream, designs paraphernalia, and directs the dancing. Ceremonial activities, the flag raising, preparation of the symbolic dream designs, and ceremony termination feast are interwoven between the dances. Religious belief is expressed in the Dreamer's own words and ethnological commentary is occasionally expressed for elaboration. An authentic document recorded with synchronous sound near Stewart's Point, California.* [Reviewed by Clement W. Meighan, *AA* 69:271–272, 1967.]

Dream Speaker 75 min. Dist: CBC VS$109.00, order #WKJ-7603. *The value and morality of conventional treatment of emotionally disturbed children is questioned in this sensitive story of a boy who escapes from an institution. "Adopted" by an old Indian shaman, the boy discovers he is capable of learning and begins to counteract his violence and fear.*

A Drum Is Made. A Study in Yoruba Drum Carving (University of Ife Series) 24 min. Darius L. Thieme, Mary S. Thieme (PR). Dist: IFB FR$25, FS$335. *A Nigerian artisan carves an iyaalu dundun, "mother" drum of the famous talking drums of Africa. As the narrator explains the construction of the drum, we watch a master drummaker as he selects and cuts a tree, carves and hollows the log, and prepares the goatskins for the drum heads. When all is ready, the master drummer shows how the drum imitates the sounds of the Yoruba language.* [Reviewed by Edward O. Henry, *SBF* 15:232, 1980.]

The Drummaker (Part of the Folklife Studies Monograph/Film Series) 38 min. Smithsonian Institution Office of Folklife Programs (PR). Dist: SU FR$18.50, FS$375, VS$245. *Although many Native American singers today use the white man's marching band drum to accompany their songs, a few Indians still are constructing drums according to traditional practices. The Drummaker presents an Ojibwa Indian, William Bineshi Baker, Jr., on the Lac Court Oreilles Reservation in northern Wisconsin, one of the last individuals among his people to continue the art of drummaking. Step-by-step he constructs a dance drum, dehairing the hides for drumheads, utilizing wooden staves for a frame, and making elaborate decorations for the drum from cloth, fur, beadwork, and ribbon. In his narration, the craftsman expresses his beliefs about tradition, as well as his frustration with others who will not take the time to follow it. A monograph,* The Ojibwa Dance Drum: Its History and Construction, *by Thomas Vennum, Jr., is being prepared for publication by the Smithsonian Institution.*

The Drums of Winter (Uksuum Cauyai) (1988) 90 min. Sarah Elder and Leonard Kramerling (FM). Dist: DER FR$130.00, VR$80.00, FS$1300.00, VS$600.00; Kmlr FR$150.00, VR$75.00, FS$1200.00, VS$175.00. *Explores the traditional dance, music, and spiritual world of the Yup'ik Eskimo people of Emmonak, a remote village at the mouth of the Yukon River on the Bering Sea coast. The people of Emmonak tell us through actualities and interviews how their history, social values, and spiritual beliefs are woven around the songs and dances that have been handed down to them through the generations. Not only are the old songs important; new songs and dance movements are created to reflect modern life. Archival photographs and film footage accompany the words of early missionaries who brought Christianity to the area, providing a historical context and giving a sense of the resilience of Yup'ik culture, having survived despite a century of missionary suppression. The film was collaboratively produced with the people of Emmonak, a community-based approach in which the film's subjects play a central role in determining the themes and direction of the production.* [Reviewed by Richard H. Jordan, *AA* 92:551–553,1990.]

The Dry Season 20 min. Alexander Alland, Jr. (FM, AN), Georg Stanford Brown (NA). *The dry season comes to the Abron people of east central Africa every year in November, when scorching winds from the Sahara overcome those from the Atlantic and dessicate the land. The intense heat of the day drives the villagers into the shade, where they make tools and utensils, weave cloth and baskets, and harvest and store cash crops. In addition to seeing village activities, the viewer sees how hunting is carried out during the dry season by the use of fire, an ever-present danger that the natives turn to advantage by controlling it in order to drive out game. The wind shifts and the fire, grown suddenly out of control, devastates a village. But here again, age-old traditions guide the Abron, as people from surrounding villages come to aid in the cleaning and rebuilding. Life goes on and human life and creation are renewed, just as surely as natural life is with the coming of the rains that end the dry season.* Suggested supplement: Alexander Alland, Jr., *When the Spider Danced: Notes from an African Village.* Anchor, 1976.

Dry Weather Chronicle: The Txicao People of Brazil's Mato Grosso (1978) 70 min. Yves Billon, Patric Menget, Jean Francois Schiano (FM). Dist: Mac FR$65, FS$850. *The Txicaos are a forest people whose youthful appearance and easy smile belie their history of violent forays against neighboring tribes who "made witchcraft" against them. These depredations ended in 1967 when the Villas Boas brothers persuaded them to move from the Jatoba River to a native part of the Mato Grosso, where they receive techni-*

cal and medical assistance from the National Indian Foundation. Shows the unique and significant activities of the April-to-September dry season. An extensive hunting and fishing expedition stocks the vast community lodge for the prolonged festivities. Puberty rites recount the history and origins of the tribe, and ascertain that the young have mastered the skills of maturity: fishing for the boys, and preparation of the basic food—manioc root and maize beer—for the girls. The tattooing ceremony is accompanied by a complex dance for white-faced initiates and sponsors, dressed in toucan and macaw feathers to the beat of ingenious instruments. Offers a unique encounter with the Txicao in interviews that reveal the cadences of their language and the fierce independence of their culture. Natives reflect good naturedly on their former life but remind the interviewers that they have not forgotten how to fight. The Txicao realize their growing dependence on the outside world and question how long they will continue to celebrate the rituals of the dry season.

Dry Wood 37 min. Les Blank (FM). Dist: FF. *Music of black Cajuns of southwestern Louisiana.* [Reviewed by David Evans, *JAF* 90(355):107. Nina Swidler, *AA* 77:475, 1975.]

Dudley Carter (1982) 59 min. Abby Sher (FM). Dist: Sher Film Library, Transit Media Library, P.O. Box 315, 779 Susquehanna, Franklin Lakes, NJ 07417; (201) 891-8240 FR$75.00, FS$750.00 . *"Adopts three historical traditions: life history, ethno-history, and art history. The life and work of Dudley Carter, a 90 year old ax sculptor, is the topical focus."* [From the review by Linda A. Bennett, *AA* 86:1056–1057, 1984.]

Due Process of Law Denied (1943) 35 min. (excerpt from film *Ox Bow Incident,* starring Henry Fonda, Anthony Quinn, Dana Andrews, Henry Morgan). Dist: 20CF; MINN. *The excerpt deals with the posse organized to catch three cattle thieves and the manner in which the group deals with the men when caught. A study in group dynamics, leadership, father-son conflict, perception, authority. A view of the old west and its approaches to problems of justice. Focusing questions: Explain the value system of the posse and the logic of this system given the culture in which it operates. Note the significance of sign and symbol in the film as well as the varied uses of authority. Discuss the importance of these to the characters involved. What personality and cultural stereotypes are presented? How do you explain them?* [R. Colin]

Duke Tritton, Australian Sheep-Shearer (1963) 10 min. A Folklore Research Film by Peter and Toshi Seeger. Dist: FIM/RF FR$15, FS$100. *Duke Tritton has a reputation among folk musicologists that extends beyond his native Australia. This genial sandy-haired old sheep-shearer recounts for Pete Seeger some anecdotes about his life and work shearing sheep on the Western Plains in the years 1905–20. Unaccompanied, he sings one of the songs he orginated, "Shearing in a Bar," to a melody he adapted from a familiar Irish song.* [Reviewed by John Greenway, *JAF* 89(345):521, 1976.]

Duminea (see University of Ife Series)

Duro Ladipo 30 min. Henry Dore (FM), NET(PR). Dist: UIAVC. *The Duro Ladipo Travelling Theater Company of Oshogbo, Nigeria.* [Reviewed by Thomas Keifer, *AA* 76:693.]

Dynamics of Male Dominance in a Baboon Troop (see Baboon Social Structure Series)

Eagles on the River (1976) 28 min. G. E. Mortimore (WR, DI, NA), R. Pollard (CA). Dist: Office of Audio Visual Services, University of Guelph, Guelph, ON, NlG 2W1, Canada. *Dokis Reserve Ojibway (Ontario).* [Reviewed by Edward S. Rogers, *AA* 80:765, 1978.]

Earliest Writing 11 min. Dist: EDS FR$20, FS$150, VS$135. *Shows how the Protoliterate writing of the Sumerians was scribed on wet clay tablets and explores the representational character of the symbols.* [Reviewed by Philip L. Kohl, *AA* 78:136, 1976.]

The Early Americans 41 min. Shell Oil Company (PR). Dist: Shell Film Library, 1433 Sadlier Circle, W., Indianapolis, IN 46239, free loan. *In conjunction with archaeological surveys accompanying construction of the Alaska oil pipeline. Outlines North American archaeology by detailed looks at selected excavations and sites. Shows archaeologists in action. Uses stills of drawings and maps to show distribution of cultures. Shows artifacts being excavated and "experimental" archaeology using or making the artifact via simulation. Also shows important data techniques, C-14 and dendrochronology, in use. A wall chart and user's guide accompany the film. Guide includes study questions and suggested readings.* [Reviewed by Payson Sheets, *ARCH* 33(3):63, 1981. L. J. Zimmerman, *Newsletter of the South Dakota Archaeological Society* 7(2):5, 1977.] Related readings: Kenneth MacGowan and Joseph A. Hester, Jr., *Early Man in the New World.* Garden City, NJ: Doubleday, 1962. Robert Silverberg, *The Mound Builders of Ancient America.* New York: New York Graphic Society, Ltd., 1968. [Charles Van Middlesworth and Larry J. Zimmerman]

Early Civilizations (1979) 20–30 min. Wayne Mitchell (PR). Dist: BFA FR$42.00, FS$350.00. *"This is a well narrated, text-like film on the early civilizations of the Old World."* [From the review by James Dow, *SBF* 16:99, 1980.]

Early Man in North America (1972) 12 min. Howard Campbell (DI). Dist. FI FR$40, FS$235. [Reviewed by Paul F. Healy, *AA* 78:365–366, 1976.]

Early Stone Tools (1967) 20 min. Dist: UCEMC FR$20.00, FS$260.00.; PSU(PCR) order #20783, FR$12. *Some of the percussion flaking techniques, which early man and his predecessors may have used to produce a variety of tools are demonstrated by Professor Francois Bordes, Director of the Laboratory of Prehistory at the University of Bordeaux in France. These tools range from simple pebble choppers and flake tools through finely worked hand axes, to the more sophisticated Neanderthal scrapers, points, and other forms made from flakes struck off disc cores. In addition to Professor Bordes's expert reproductions, actual prehistoric tools from such sites as Olduvai Gorge, Clacton by the Sea, and various Neanderthal sites are shown. Through animation, the development of these tools is clearly shown* to parallel the evolution of man himself from his Australopithecine forebears to Homo sapiens—modern man. The major emphasis on percussion flaking tool techniques comes to a close with the emergence of Homo sapiens. In conclusion, the film suggests that Homo sapiens's skill as a tool maker has led to a technology that has enabled him virtually to reshape his world. [Reviewed by F. Clark Howell, AA 70:436–437, 1968. Susanna R. Katz and Paul R. Katz, ARCH 34(1):60, 1981.]

The Earth Is Our Mother 50 min. Peter Elsass (DI). Dist: FL VR$75.00, VS$445.00. *A Study of two Indian tribes of Colombia and Venezuela by Elsass, who is a psychiatrist and anthropologist. His interest has been in the survival of these tribespeople in the face of encroaching white civilization. The Motilon Indians living in the lowland of Venezuela have become spiritually and economically impoverished. They have given up their traditional ways and have become dependent on the missionaries. In contrast, the Arhuaco Indians, living in the mountains, have a well-organized, hierarchical society. In a dramatic move, they threw out the Catholic missionaries and established their own independent education system. By taking a stand against foreign influences, they are maintaining their cultural identity.*

Earth Lodge People 20 min. Marshall McKusic (FM). Dist: UIOWA order #40121, FR$16.70, FS$350. [Reviewed by William A. Turnbaugh, AA 78:369–370, 1976.]

East Timor: Isle of Fear, Isle of Hope (1976) 17 min. Boubaker Adjali (DI). Dist: UNI FR$25-35. *A documentary report on the "unknown" war being waged in Southeast Asia between the U.S.-backed Indonesian military regime and the Revolutionary Front for an Independent East Timor (FRETILIN). Reveals the reasons for the mass support for FRETILIN, including its health clinics, literacy classes, and agricultural cooperatives.*

Easter in Igloolik (1987) 24 min. Dist: BF FR$50.00, VR$50.00, FS$495.00, VS$350.00. *"Nicely filmed are the games, the hunts, the competitions, and the ceremonies that celebrate the return of summer to the Arctic."* [From the review by George H. Odell, SBF 24:107, 1988.]

Easter Island (1934) 25 min. John Ferno (FM), Henry Lavachery (AN). Dist: IFB FR$22.50, FS$225, VS$185; MOMA FR$25. *The film grew out of the Franco-Belgian Expedition to Easter Island under taken jointly by the Trocadero Museum, Paris, and the Musée Royale of Brussels. . . . A record not only of the work of the expedition but also of the present-day life of the inhabitants. . . . Anthropological information is the burden of the commentary; the visuals and music combine to create an impressionistic picture of relapse and decay, which finds culminating poignance in the sequence depicting the island leper colony. Contains a sequence that makes the film unsuitable for exhibition to an audience that has not been prepared for it in advance. Commentary in French, no English titles.*

Easter Island: Puzzle of the Pacific (1970) 28 min. William Mulloy, Peter Jennings (NA). Dist: Macmillian; UCEMC FR$27. *Shows the culture and art of Easter Island's mysterious ancient people, speculates on their disappearance, and probes the secret of the huge stone statues, some over 30 feet tall and weighing 80 tons, which they erected without metal tools or the wheel.* [Reviewed by Alexandra M. Ulana Klymyshyn, AA 78:384–385, 1976.]

Easter Island Statues By Jo Anne Van Tilburg and David Ochsner. Dist: POR. Set of 50 slides, $85.00. See review by Peter S. Allen, ARCH 42(5):74–75, 1986.

Ebena: Hallucinogenic Ecstasy among the Yanoama (1970) 18 min. Inga S. Goetz (PR), Peter Furst (NA). Dist: LAC FR$20, FS$200. *This film documents the ritual preparation and use of the hallucinogenic snuff, ebena, by Waika-Yanoama Indian men. The drug is compounded by bark fibers of two distinct plants and seeds of the Acacia Anadenanthera peregrina. The effect of the drug is a trance state, in which the men and especially the shaman feel larger than life and as if possessed of great strength. Most importantly, the drug enables them to enter into communication with the hecura, the spirits of animals and plants, whose voices and counsel they hear while in the trance. The shaman in this film exercises his powers while under the influence of ebena in ritual healing.* [Reviewed by Eric R. Wolf, AA 74:196–198, 1972.]

Echoes of War (The New Pacific Series) (1987) 60 min. BBC/ NVC (PR). Dist: FIV VS$79.00. *As the prosperity of the Pacific increases, so does its strategic importance to the world's major powers. The film addresses the prospects and consequences of this international interest in the region.*

An Ecology of the Mind (Millennium: Tribal Wisdom and the Modern World Series) (1992) 1 hour. David Maybury-Lewis (H), Hans Zimmer (MU). Dist: PBS VS$49.95, order #MILL-104-RCDC. *All societies survive by manipulating nature. But while tribal cultures seek harmony with nature, Western societies try to control it, often with devastating consequences. Learn how the Makuna of Colombia pass their sophisticated ecological awareness from generation to generation through complex myths and rituals. And understand how tribal peoples' views contrast with the evolutionary ideas handed down to the modern world from the Bible and from 19th-century Darwinian theory. Then meet a gardener who exemplifies the new attitudes Western cultures will need to ensure humanity's survival on the Earth.*

Eduardo the Healer (1978) 55 min. Richard Cowan (FM), Douglas Sharon (AN). Dist: Serious Business Co., 1145 Mandana Blvd., Oakland, CA 94610; UCEMC FR$43; LAC FR$75, FS$580; PSU FR$23.50, FS$580; PCR FR$29.00, VR$19.00, FS$615.00, VS$245.00, order #50469. *Eduardo Calderon is a fisherman by trade, a sculptor by avocation, and a shaman by profound conviction, who uses hallucinogenic drugs to practice his healing art. Eduardo is a curandero, or healer, who uses a hallucinogen derived from the San Pedro cactus, which has been in continuous use for more than 2,000 years in Peruvian shamanism. When he drinks the San Pedro mixture, Eduardo can see directly into the ailment and removes it.* Bibliography: Douglas Sharon, *Wizard of the Four Winds: A Shaman's Story.* Free Press, 1978. [Reviewed by Irvin Press, AA 82:225–226, 1980.]

Egypt: Cradle of Civilization (1962) 11 min. Dist: IUAVC FR$6.50. *Pictures the people of the upper Nile Valley and describes how they have depended upon the river for food, water, and transportation for centuries. Relates how the primitive tribes of Egypt organized into a united group under one ruler. Depicts the city of Thebes as a great center of learning in ancient Egypt and describes the role of religion throughout the centuries of Egyptian life. Highlights many artifacts that were entombed with the Pharaohs and indicates their effects upon modern art and architecture.* [Reviewed by Edward J. Brovarski, *AA* 78:131, 1976.]

Egypt: Quest for Eternity (1982) 59 min. National Geographic Society (PR). Dist: NGS FS$595.00, VS$545.00; Karol FR$40.00. *"Offers the general audience a rich tapestry of Egyptian sights and sounds, all adroitly interwoven. It touches briefly on such diverse subjects as the religious and funerary concepts of the ancient Egyptians New Year's Festival, the rescue of Abu Simbel from the rising waters of Lake Nasser, and the Aswan Dam."* [From the review by Timothy Kendell, *ARCH* 36(6):72–73, 1983.]

An Egyptian Village (Gueziret Eldahab) (1960) 19 min. Dist: IUAVC FR$8.25. *Pictures the daily activities of the people living in a small village near Cairo to describe the way of the life of the fellah, or farmer, in Egypt. Shows the methods of cultivating and irrigating fields, the education now available to the fellah's children, and stresses the tradition-centered life of the fellah. Follows the wedding arrangements for the fellah's daughter and the social and religious ceremonies associated with the wedding.*

The Egyptologists (edited version) (1968) 25 min. Encylopaedia Brittanica Educational Corporation (PR). Dist: PSU(PCR) order #31342, FR$14.50. *Archaeological trip to save the remnants of antiquity at the Aswan Dam. Work of the historians, archaeologists, and other researchers as they plan and execute this trip in their attempt to salvage history.* [Reviewed by Edward J. Brovarski, *AA* 78:131, 1976.]

Electric Boogie (1983) 30 min. Tana Ross (PR), Freke Vuijst (DI). Dist: Green Room Productions, 120 Riverside Dr., New York, NY 10024; (212) 362-3219 FR$60.00, FS$600.00. *"Concerned with four New York City teenagers who have joined together to work as a breakdancing team named 'The Electric Boogie.' Two of the boys are brothers from a Puerto Rican family, the other two are Black. . . . We hear them discuss what it is like to live in one of the poorest and roughest neighborhoods in the country."* [From the review by Nora Groce, *AA* 87:751–752, 1985.]

The 11 Powers: A Balinese Festival 48 min. (1980) Larry Gartenstein (PR), Frank Heimens (DI), Anthony Forge (AN), Orsen Welles (NA). Dist: FL FR$65.00, VR$65.00, FS$650.00, VS$550.00. *The most spectacular sacred ceremony of the century took place in Bali in the spring of 1979. The Eka Dasa Rudra, or festival of the 11 powers, was held by order of the high priests to restore the balance between good and evil in the universe. The entire Balinese population of two million participated in the holy event. Such involvement is not surprising since Balinese religion governs all aspects of life. A complex synthesis of Buddhism, Animism, Sivaism, and Hinduism, its rituals vary from beautifully sophisticated Hindu forms to primitive rites going back to the dawn of time.* [Reviewed by Jack A. Lucas, *SBF* 16:99, 1980.]

11:59 Last Minute to Choose (1971) 25 min. Dan Zavin (PR). Dist: The Equitable Trust Bank, Public Relations Department, P.O. Box 1556, Baltimore, MD 21203. *Drug use in America.* [Reviewed by Nancie L. Gonzalez, *AA* 77:198, 1975.]

Embara Drama: Enchanting Death 70 min. Jean Rouch and Germaine Dieterlen (FM). Text for the film was adapted from the ethnographic researches of Marcel Griaule. Dist: Centre de Recherche et Documentation Ethnographique, Musee de l'Homme, Palais de Chaillot, 75116, Paris; DER. *In April 1974, Dogon of the Sanga region in the Bandiagara plain celebrated the ceremonies for the lifting of mourning for seven dignitaries who had died in the past year.*

Embarazo, parto y puerperio (Pregnancy, Birth and the Post-partum Period) (see Andean Ethnomedicine: Birth and Childhood Illness in Six Ecuadorian Communities Series)

Embera: The End of the Road (Disappearing World Series) (1971) 51 min. Ariane Deluz (AN). Dist: PSU VR$14.00, order #51148. *Four centuries ago, the Spaniards sought gold in Colombia, tried to enslave the Embera Indians, then massacred them when they fought enslavement. Today, the remaining Embera have been pushed into the headwaters of a remote river, so that in the face of further pressure they have nowhere else to go. An Embera shaman explains, "the road [Pan American Highway] is coming and with it will come all these people—the robbers and bandits, the people who molest us. They are coming to take our land away from us."*

Emergence (1982) 14 min. Barbara Wilk (FM). Dist: POR FR$30.00, FS$235.00. *Portrays a Navajo creation myth.* [Reviewed by Charlotte J. Frisbie, *AA* 87:982, 1985.]

The Emerging Woman 40 min. Helena Solberg-Ladd (DI). Dist: FIM/RF. *Feminist history in the United States.* [Reviewed by Janet Kohen, *AA* 79:201, 1977.]

Emitay 102 min. Ousmane Sembene (WR), Sarah Maldror (DI). Dist: NYF. *A fictional picture of the Diola of Sénégal under French rule.* [Reviewed by J. David Sapir, *AA* 76:693, 1974.]

Emu Ritual at Ruguri (Australian Institute of Aboriginal Studies Series) (1966–67) 33 min. Dist: UCEMC FR$38, FS$455; PSU(PCR) order #31626 FR$12.10. *Shows a Walbiri tribe ceremony, which takes place in an elaborately painted cave. Legend has it that two "emu men" once lived in the cave, while another lived at a waterhole nearby. When these residents were visited by a traveling party of emu men they all joined together in a dance. The ritual enacts this legendary meeting. Besides initiation, the ritual is intended to promote the fertility of emus, once an important item in Walbiri diet. Two moieties share the work of performing the rites. One, the "managers," makes a large ground painting (this is the only known record of such an event), builds* *sacred emblems and ornaments, and decorates the "owners"—the men of the other moiety. For their part, the "owners" sing the songs belonging to the site—near the ground painting and within the cave—instruct novices in the meaning of the designs painted on the wall of the cave, perform a drama portraying the travels of the emu men, and perform the dances with which the rites come to an end.* [Reviewed by Nancy D. Munn, *AA* 72:1201–1202, 1970.] Restricted use: This film contains material of a secret/sacred nature and should only be screened for study purposed by appropriate groups.

English X-Ray Film   (1964) Haskins Lab (PR). Dist: PSU order #20157. *Articulatory movements shown by X-ray techniques. Prepared scripts illustrate selected phonetic features in the phonemic contrasts of the language, ending with several sentences to show the features in running speech. Informants picked for linguistic suitability and lack of physical characteristics that could interfere with X-ray quality and sound processing.*

L'enterrement du Hogon (The Burial of Hogon)   (1972) 30 min. Jean Rouch (DI), Centre National de la Recherche Scientifique, Comité du Film Ethnographique (PR). Dist: CFE; DER. *The Hogon of Sanga, Mali, masterful high priest of the community of Ogal, who died during the night, is rituraly interred.*

Enthombe   (1991) 18 min. Guy Spiller (DI). Dist: FRIF VR$40.00, VS$160.00. *About the forced removal of black South Africans from their ancestral lands because, in the eyes of South African law, the land is not theirs. Twelve Enthombe families have lived on the Saathoek farm for countless generations—Christine Vilikazi, a centenarian, remembers watching her father burying the dead during the Boer War. But in 1989, the property was purchased by a farmer who gave the families 6 months notice to be off the land. The Enthombe refused. The heads of the family were tried according to a 1959 Trespass Act that still stands. Convicted, they were sentenced to nine months in jail. But in December 1990, they were still on the land, despite jail, physical assaults, and having their livestock shot and poisoned.*

Entre verde y seco   (1983) 28 min. Rhonda Vlasak and Lesley Poling-Kempes (FM). Dist: OWM FR$70.00, FS$500.00, VS$275.00. *"Many US Hispanics characterize the quality of their daily lives through a singular remark—'entre verde y seco' [between green and dry]. . . . When someone employs this metaphoric response . . . its message is clear and direct—not all in life is well. Things good are balanced by things bad. . . . Symbolizes the rapidly changing style of life in many Spanish-speaking communities in the American Southwest. Conflict invariably arises, of course, when tradition is theatened by change, just as green gives way unwilling to dry. The setting is Abiquiu, a small bilingual community in the mountainous Chama region of northern New Mexico. . . . A portrayal of the clash between community tradition and community change."* [From the review by Michael H. Logan, *AA* 89:1015–1016, 1987.]

Ephesus   18 min. Fred Padula (FM). Dist: AB. *Black Pentecostal church in Berkeley, California.* [Reviewed by Bruce A. Rosenberg, *JAF* 91(359):634–635, 1978.]

Eskimo Artist Kenojuack   (1964) 20 min. John Feeney (FM), Tom Daly (PR) for the National Film Board of Canada. Dist: NFBC. *Here is a strange world where in the deepening Arctic twilight, the snow, the sky, the very air seems to throng with shadows. The thoughts of the Eskimo graphic artist, Kenojuak, are spoken. "Many are the thoughts that rush over me, like the wings of birds out of darkness," and her pictures appear, like winged birds, wavering shadows on the snow. Kenojuak, wife and mother, does her work when she is free of the duties of trail and camp. The sources of her inspiration are poetically manifest, never directly demonstrated. At the Cooperative Art Center of Cape Dorset, the stonecutter Iyola and the printers are discreetly observed making rice paper prints from Kenojuak's design.* [Reviewed by Susan Dwyer-Shick, *Ethnomusicology* 18(3):399–400, 1974.]

The Eskimo: Fight for Life   51 min. Social Studies Curriculum Program of Education Development Center (PR), Asen Balikci (DI, AN). Dist: EDC FR$55.00, FS$660.00, VS$495.00. *No country on earth is harsher to man than the frozen land of the Arctic Circle. In the wilderness north of Hudson Bay, the Netsilik Eskimo ingeniously adapted the material that nature provided and survived for centuries. Just a decade ago, a small band of Netsilik spent a winter on the sea-ice of Pelly Bay for the last time. This film is the record of that winter. Six families trek across the sea-ice and set up their camp near an area that they hope will provide them with good hunting for several weeks. After searching and hunting for the all-important seal, the families build a large ceremonial igloo joining several of the small one-family igloos under one large roof. Here a seal is divided up among the families, and afterward the people relax and play games. There are many scenes of hunting technology as well as of family life in the camp. As winter ends, the families pack up and move on in search of game in another area. Made from one of a series of nine films, directed by Asen Balikci, of the entire annual migratory cycle of the Netsilik Eskimos of Pelly Bay, Canada. The original series was produced by the Social Studies Curriculum Program of Education Development Center under grants from the National Film Board of Canada. The Eskimo: Fight for Life was made for the CBS Television Network and was released with natural sound and a small amount of explanatory narration.*

Eskimo Summer   (People of the Seal Series) 52 min. National Film Board of Canada (PR). Dist: EDC FR$55.00, FS$720.00, VS$540.00. *This film includes all of the Eskimo activities on the land. In the spring, they begin to fish, gather moss and heather, and search for bird eggs. Summer activities include construction of a kayak for use later in caribou hunting. Moving further inland in August, they join other families at their stone weir, constructed across a river where salmon returning up-river are trapped and easily caught. The families also hunt caribou together. In September, the Netsilik begin their return to the sea-ice.*

Eskimo Winter (People of the Seal Series) 52 min. National Film Board of Canada (PR). Dist: EDC FR$55.00, FS$720.00, VS$540.00. *As the sea-ice freezes, the Netsilik move far out into the bay, search for seal holes, and build their igloos near the best seal-hunting spots. The film then concentrates on seal hunting, on which their lives depend. When a seal is caught, it is divided up between the families and every part is put to some use. The communal games and activities follow a successful hunting season, after which the Netsilik begin their annual trek back to the land.*

Eskimos: A Changing Culture (1971) 17 min. Dist: IUAVC FR$9.75. *Studies the Eskimos of Nunivak Island in the Bering Sea to examine the ways technology has affected their family patterns, values, and other elements of culture. Focuses on Eskimo houses and dances, the trading store, and the annual reindeer drive, and shows Eskimos picking wild celery and berries, getting clams, and fishing. Points out that the older children must go to a big city for their high school education because of the lack of facilities in their town.*

The Eskimos of Pond Inlet (Disappearing World Series) (1977) 52 min. Michael Grigsby (DI), Hugh Brody (AN). Dist: PSU order #51219. *The Inuits of Pond Inlet, a new village built by the Canadian government on Baffin Island, are laborers, and their children attend government schools. The Inuits, formerly known as Eskimos, talk about their lives, their land, and the changes forced upon them by the encroaching culture of the "powerful and frightening whites."* [Reviewed by David Riches, *RAIN* 13:7, 1976.]

Espace et comportement (1971) 33 min. Dist: FACSEA FR$16.

El espanto (Magical Fright) (see Andean Ethnomedicine: Birth and Childhood Illness in Six Ecuadorian Communities Series)

Ethno botanique de la région de Dalat 14 min. Dist: FACSEA FR$16. French only.

Ethnoarchaeology of the Kalinga By William A. Longacre. Dist: POR. Set of 80 slides, $110.00. See review by Carol Kramer, *ARCH* 42(3):75, 1989.

The Etruscan Question (1983) 30 min. Thomas A. Fabiano (FM). Dist: RLI FS$39.95. *An 80-frame filmstrip that summarizes topics dealing with Etruscan civilization.* See the review by Natalie Boymel Kampen, *ARCH* 37(6):66–75, 1984.

The Etruscans (1988) 29 min. Luciano Lucignani (FM). Dist: FHS VR$75.00, VS$149.00. *This film is "impressionistic, jumping from site to site and idea to idea."* [From the review by Peter S. Allen, *ARCH* 44(5):71, 1991.]

Euskadi: The Stateless Nation (1984) 97 min. Arthur Mac Craig (FM). Dist: FRIF VR$100.00, VS$590.00. *"Focuses primarily on the history and development of ETA (Euskadi ta Askatasuna, the Basque Land and Freedom) in the Basque region on northern Spain. Next to the Irish Republican Army, ETA is the oldest militant clandestine organization in Europe.... Individuals are presented who discuss why they either support or oppose the actions of ETA."* [From the review by Steven Ybarrola, *AA* 91:834–835, 1989.]

Evans-Pritchard, Sir Edward (1902–1973) (see *Strange Beliefs* in the Strangers Abroad Series)

Everyday Is Not a Feast Day (Rural Greece: Desertion, Migration, Village Life Series) (1981) 120 min. Colette Piault (FM), Philippe Lavalette (CA), Francois Didio and Manon Barbeau (SR), Bernard Favre (ED). Dist: LFDQ FS$1000.00; PSA VR$100.00, VS$450.00. *As in most Mediterranean area villages, a significant decrease in the population of this mountain village in the Epirus region of Greece has occurred. What effect does this situation have upon the lives of the villagers? Although the village appears to be virtually self-sufficient, the truth is that its economic, social, and family life depend on the outer world to a great extent. Using an observational approach and a sequential structure, the film tries to portray the alternation between the monotony of daily life and special celebration days, which mean the return for brief interludes of family members who have left the village for the city or foreign countries. The celebration is anticipated, remembered, and awaited by all. The film records a wide range of village activities, both secular and sacred very well. Cinegraphic features: Most of the footage is candid, but there are several scenes in which subjects are actually interviewed, and others where it is obvious that they are responding to questions or cues. There is no narration, only a live soundtrack with dialogue translated in subtitles.* [Reveiwed by Peter S. Allen, *AA* 84:754, 1982.]

Everything Change Up Now: A View of the South Carolina Sea Islands (1977) 43 min. Gretchen Robinson (FM, CA, ED), Dennis Yussi (CA). Dist: Gretchen Robinson, P.O. Box 671, Greenville, SC 29602 FR$50, FS$450. *The South Carolina Sea Islands are a group of islands along the coast between Georgetown and Beaufort. Their inhabitants are a complex group of people, the oldest being blacks whose ancestors came from Africa via the Caribbean and whites whose ancestry can be traced to the original land grantees of King George. The island people have maintained themselves in close yet somehow distant proximity to the grandness of Charleston. Because of the changes taking place on the islands, the human ecology that has developed with the natural ecology over the years is now in a delicate state of balance. Most of the blacks speak a dialect called Gullah, which exhibits the African and Caribbean influences. No attempt has been made to translate so that the uniqueness and sound quality of the dialect could be given full play. Shows what has happened to the lifestyles of South Carolina sea islanders since slavery through interviews with Gullah basketweavers, netmakers, fishermen, educators, farmers, "witch doctors" in contrast with antebellum, tourist-oriented Charleston and fast-paced commercial development.*

Everything Is Relatives: William Rivers (1864–1922) (Strangers Abroad Series) 52 min. Dist: FHS FR$75.00, VS$159.00, order #XD2543. *William Rivers originally trained as a doctor. On a Cambridge University expedition to the Torres Straits north of Australia, his psychological* tests on the islanders made him realize the unexpected importance of relatives in their society. His subsequent work as a pioneering psychologist in the First World War and his research into the workings of the nervous system and the action of drugs on the human body, enabled Rivers to bring something new to anthropology: a scientific approach.

Evening Activity (Amboseli Reserve) Field Study Sequence (see Baboon Social Structure Series)

Evil Wind, Evil Air (Mal viento, mal aire, pasmo) (see Andean Ethnomedicine: Birth and Childhood Illness in Six Ecuadorian Communities Series) (1985) 22 min. Lauris McKee (DI), Archaeological Museum of the Central Bank of Ecuador (PR). Dist: PSU/PCR VR$18.00, VS$200.00, order #23956. *This documentary focuses on the supernatural origins, symptoms, and cures of the folk illness, mal aire, especially as it affects children. Set in several rural villages in the Ecuadorian Andes, the tape features scenes of family life and the efforts of mothers and folk healers to protect young children from mal aire. This potentially fatal disease is said to originate from mountain spirits, water spirits, the malignant dead and sinful living. The film features several descriptions and demonstrations of protective strategies and rituals that "clean" the body, ridding it of the evil force. The methods employed by both mothers of endangered children and folk healers include: exposing the child to the strong smells of tobacco, herbs, or alcohol, and rubbing or beating the child's skin. The tape is useful for providing insights into the principles underlying Andean ethnomedical beliefs.* [Reviewed by Stephen D. Glazier, *AA* 89, 1987.]

Evolution and Human Equality (The Faces of Culture Series) 42 min. Stephen Jay Gould (NA). Dist: IM VS$195.00, order #SF68; IV VS$160.00. *Stephen Jay Gould delivers a lecture on the genetic evidence for the equality of the races. Explaining new genetic timing techniques, he describes the pioneering work with mitochondrial DNA and its revelation: that all humans evolved in Africa and that one lineage split in Africa about 100,000 years ago to yield the migrants who colonized the rest of the world.*

Excavations at La Venta (1963) 29 min. Robert F. Heizer (AN). Dist: UCEMC FR$35, FS$400; PSU(PCR) order #3098, FR$15.50. *The archaeological excavation at La Venta helped substantiate the theory that high civilization in Mesoamerica made its earliest appearance in the lowland Gulf Coast region located in the southern part of the State of Veracruz and the northern part of the State of Tabasco. La Venta exhibited the familiar Mesoamerican pattern of pyramids, stone sculpture, and carved jade. However, the singular characteristics of the monolithic flat-topped altars, the sculptured monuments could not be classified as Maya, Zapotec, Toltec, or Aztec. The culture represented by the newly discovered art style was given the name "Olmec." This film reviews, through the use of color still photographs, motion picture film, and detailed animation, the evolution of the large-scale excavation in 1955 of the Olmec site at La Venta, Tabasco, Mexico. Results of earlier investigations in 1942 and 1943 are included. The film summarizes the history of the site from 800 B.C. and shows examples of constructions, sculptures, and small jade and serpentine carvings.* [Reviewed by Michael D. Coe, *AA* 69:127–128, 1967.]

The Excavation of Mound 7—Gran Quivira 43 min. Tom Gray (FM), National Park Service (PR). Dist: Harpers Ferry Historical Association, P.O. Box 147, Harpers Ferry, WV 25425. [Reviewed by Charles Di Peso, *AA* 77:909, 1975.]

The Exiles (1959–61) 72 min. Kent Mackenzie (FM, WR), Erik Daarstad, Robert Kaufman, and John Morrill (CA). Dist: UCEMC FR$40. *Many American Indians have left the tribal reserves to try to find a life in the large cities. There they found themselves caught between two cultures—unwilling to become a part of the dominant pattern they saw around them and yet unable to return to their own way of life, lost in the past. The film shows the story of one anguished but typical night in the lives of three young Indians who have come to live in downtown Los Angeles. The camera follows them through 14 hours of drinking, card playing, picking up girls, and fighting until their frustration finally erupts on a wind-swept hill. There, they beat the drums until dawn, drunkenly trying to swing and dance the old tribal songs. This unusual film of life evolved entirely from the actual lives of protagonists. The young Indians play themselves in their own everyday haunts. They improvised their own dialogue and narration, and the continuity was based on their suggestions.* [Reviewed by Rosalie Wax and Murray Wax, *AA* 67:1079–1080, 1965.]

Exploring the Unwritten Past 22 min. D. C. Chipperfield (PR) for Boulton-Hawker Films Ltd. in cooperation with the British Museum, the Council for British Archaeology, and the University of London. Dist: IFB FR$22.50, FS$310, VS$250. *Archaeologists and geologists are shown using scientific methods to analyze objects for a glimpse of man in Britain prior to the advent of recorded history. Both aerial and ground photography are used to locate prehistoric settlements; stratification and the carbon 14 method are used to date excavated objects; and analysis of organic remains such as bark, pollen, and grain give information on climate and vegetation. The film takes the viewer through significant changes in culture such as the introduction of pottery wheels, looms to make cloth, and coins to replace bartering. A teachers' guide is available.*

Expressive Culture in Papua [Reviewed by Terence E. Hays, *AA* 89:1012, 1987.]

Extinction: The Last Tasmanian (see The Last Tasmanian Series)

Eye Contact and Proxemics (1986) 28 min. Dist: IM VS$129.00, order #JJ109. *This program examines the importance of eye contact and kinesics in nonverbal communication. It illustrates how eye contact can open and close channels of communication, defines the two functions of eye contact (regulatory and expressive), and demonstrates the adverse effects of not maintaining eye contact. The program examines how body movements and gestures—kinesics—are used to send, support, and amplify messages. It defines five types of kinesic movements—emblems, illustrators, af-*

fect displays, regulators, and adaptors—and examines how they affect communication.

EYES ON THE PRIZE: AMERICA'S CIVIL RIGHTS YEARS SERIES (1986) 58 min. each. Henry Hampton (EP). Dist: Blackside, Inc., 486 Shawmut Avenue, Boston, MA 02118; (617) 536-6900 VS$59.95. *Perhaps the finest documentary to date of the civil rights era, covering the historic and tumultuous years of 1954 through 1965.* [Reviewed by Carolyn Fluehr-Lobban, *AA* 92:838–839, 1990.] The episodes include:

- **Awakenings, 1954–56** Deals with the Montgomery bus boycott and features Rosa Parks and Martin Luther King in the birth of the movement.
- **Fighting Back 1957–62** Brown vs. Board of Education *Supreme Court case.*
- **Ain't Scared of Your Jails 1960–61** *Lunchcounter sit-ins and the Freedom rides.*
- **No Easy Walk 1962–66** *March on Washington.*
- **Mississippi, Is This America 1962–64** *Voting rights campaign.*

Eze Nwata: The Small King (1982) 29 min. Georg Jell and Sabine Jell-Bahlsen (FM). Dist: Jell-Bahlsen, 451 Broome St., Apt PHW, New York, NY 10013; (212) 226-7854 FR$60.00, FS$400.00. *Filmed among the Riverain Igbo of the lower Niger region in Nigeria. A narrative of the early life of a young Ibo man, presented through his own eyes.* [Reviewed by Simon Ottenberg, *AA* 86:801–802, 1984.]

Fa'a Samoa. The Samoan Way 17 min. Lowell D. Holmes (AN, CA). Dist: Pitt. *Documents the technological, ceremonial, and social events associated with the construction of a traditional Samoan guest house in a village on the island of Ta'u (the locale of Margaret Mead's famous work, Coming of Age in Samoa). In this study of a small Samoan society cutting copra, fishing, cooking, and ceremonially hosting a party for visiting craftsmen, Holmes has caught the flavor and tempo of a contemporary Polynesian microcosm.* [Reviewed by John Terrell, *AA* 73:1471–1473, 1971.] Suggested supplements: Lowell D. Holmes, *Ta'u: Stability and Change in a Samoan Village.* The Polynesian Society, 1958. Lowell D. Holmes, *Samoan Village.* Holt, Rinehart and Winston, 1974.

Faba Tondi (1976) 20 min. Jean Rouch (DI). Dist: CFE; DER. *At the entrance to the village of Simiri, a buried stone protects the village: Faba Tondi (the stone of protection.)*

FACE VALUES SERIES [Discussed by Ann Hurman, Jean La Fontaine, and Melissa Llewelyn-Davies, *RAIN* 27:6–9, 1978.]

FACES OF CHANGE SERIES American Universities Field Staff (PR). Dist: Wheelock Education Resources, P.O. Box 451, Hanover, NH 03775; (603) 448-3924. *The 27 films focus on people under a variety of ecological conditions and on their aspirations and beliefs. The roles of women, education, social and economic systems, and the effects of modernization on values are themes explored in each of five rural settings—Bolivian highlands, northern Kenya, northern Afghanistan, Taiwan, and the Soko Islands off the China Coast. In the Field Staff's multidisciplinary effort to analyze whole societies, the medium of film has proved a superb ally. The production of a film series that touches on the universals of the human condition reflects the organization's longtime preoccupation with social comparison. Working in tandem, using neither scripts nor professional actors, social scientists and filmmakers have sought to capture a sense of truth that would not only lead to an understanding of unfamiliar cultures, but also cause Western audiences to ask questions about their own society.* A textbook edition, *Faces of Change: Five Rural Societies in Transition,* contains information gathered by the Field Staff's area representatives, including basic documentation, interviews, biographies of key persons in the films, charts, tables, and maps. The materials complement the observational approach used in the filming and help answer questions raised by viewers. [Reviewed by Beatrice Whiting, *AA* 79:751–758, 1977.]

- **KENYA** [Reviewed by Alan Jacobs, *AA* 79:753–754, 1977.]
- **Kenya Boran I and II** 33 min. FR$41 each, FS$340. *A growing town and a new road encroach upon the territory of a once isolated desert people. Two fathers and their sons confront difficulties between old ways and new. The film leads to speculation on the outcome of their choices.*
- **Boran Herdsman** 17 min. FR$22, FS$180. *The Boran of northern Kenya have time-honored solutions for the problems associated with their dependence on cattle for a living. Direct government intervention and the indirect impact of modernization are changing the old patterns. How will the changes be accomplished and what effects will they have?*
- **Harambee (Pull Together)** 19 min. FR$24, FS$200. *Kenya's Independence Day slogan, means "pull together." But the ideal of a united Kenya is still a new concept for formerly isolated peoples in the north. Their accommodation to the Harambee's festivities suggests some of the difficulties of changing long-established beliefs.*
- **Boran Women** 18 min. FR$23, FS$190. *The availability of education and other aspects of modernization are changing Boran women's attitudes even while they maintain their traditional and influential roles in a herding culture.*
- **AFGHANISTAN** [Reviewed by Asen Balikci, *AA* 79:755–756, 1977.]
- **Afghan Village** 45 min. FR$55, FS$460. *A collage of daily life in Aq Kupruk builds from the single voice that calls townspeople to prayer, the brisk exchange of the bazaar, communal labor, and the uninhibited sports and entertainment of rural Afghans.*
- **Naim and Jabar** 50 min. FR$61, FS$510. *The hopes, fears, and aspirations of adolescence expressed in the close friendship of two Afghan boys. With intimate understanding, the filmmakers and their subjects have produced a film rich in fact and themes of universal concern.*
- **Wheat Cycle** 16 min. FR$20, FS$170. *The people and their labor are bound to the land in the cycle of activities from the sowing to the harvesting of wheat. Without narration or subtitles, the film conveys a sense of unity between the people and the land.*
- **Afghan Nomads: The Maldar** 21 min. FR$26, FS$220. *At dawn the caravan descends on Aq Kupruk from the foothills*

of the Hindu Kush. In their camp and in commerce with the townspeople, the Maldar reveal the mixture of faith and distrust that have kept nomads and sedentarists separate yet interdependent over the centuries.

• **Afghan Women** 17 min. FR$22, FS$180. *The words of the women and the rhythm of their lives in seclusion suggest both satisfying and limiting aspects of the women's role in an Afghan rural community.*

• **CHINA COAST** [Reviewed by Judith Strauch, AA 79: 757-758, 1977.]

• **Island in the China Sea** 33 min. FR$41, FS$340. *Tai a Chau is home for both farmers and fishermen, who live aboard small junks and use the island as a permanent harbor. The daily routines of Mr. Wong, a fisherman, and Mr. Ng, a farmer, are representative of their respective problems of survival and hopes for the future.*

• **Hoy Fok and the Island School** 32 min. FR$40, FS$330. *A 14-year-old boy living with his family in a fishing junk near a small island in Hong Kong territory reflects on his visits to an ancient harbor town, on his experience in school, and on his future.*

• **China Coast Fishing** 19 mins. FR$24, FS$200. *The traditional "floating population" who fishes Chinese coastal waters from family-sized junks based in Hong Kong harbor is in competition with salaried fishermen using motorized boats. The combined effect of education and an increased integration with shore life is putting further strain on old ways.*

• **The Island Fishpond** 13 min. FR$17, FS$200. *The need for a new freshwater fishpond focuses the island community, representative of the Hong Kong government, and a single entrepreneur on an effort to increase productivity—and economic well-being—on Tai a Chau.*

• **Three Island Women** 17 min. FR$22, FS$180. *A young, middle-aged, and an old woman all agree that life on a small Chinese island in Hong Kong waters is better for them than in the past. Participating fully in the island's decision-making and economic life, they also share equally with men the rigors of manual labor.*

• **TAIWAN** [Reviewed by Margery Wolf and Arthur P. Wolf, AA 79:756, 1977.]

• **People Are Many, Fields Are Few** 32 min. FR$40, FS$330. *Three farm families, engaged in Taiwan's long summer two-crop rice cycle, compare their lives to those of industrial laborers, expressing both pride and anger concerning present and future conditions of farm life.*

• **They Call Him Ah Kung** 24 min. FR$30, FS$250. *Ah Kung, like most of his schoolmates, will inherit the family farm. Yet he may choose to leave farming, attracted by industry and the urban lifestyle. Ah Kung's personal dilemma symbolizes a national problem affecting Taiwan's ability to continue to feed its population adequately.*

• **Wet Rice Culture** 17 min. FR$22, FS$180. *Taiwan's rice farmers rely less on mechanization than on human labor to produce and harvest two crops during the annual agricultural cycle. Their meticulous cultivation methods achieve the highest average yields per acre in the world.*

• **The Rural Cooperative** 15 min. FR$19, FS$160. *The Tsao Tung Farmers Association typifies rural cooperatives in Taiwan. It is the center of social, leisure, and economic activities for the 9,600 families who own the cooperative and rely on it for services ranging from irrigation, provision of seeds and fertilizers, farm implements, to crop storage and marketing.*

• **A Chinese Farm Wife** 17 min. FR$22, FS$180. *Mrs. Li, whose husband is a salaried factory worker, is a full participant in farming and community activities in addition to her role in supervising the children's education and managing the household.*

• **BOLIVIA** [Reviewed by Paul Doughty, AA 79:752–753, 1977.]

• **Viracocha** 30 min. FR$37, FS$310. *Mestizos and campensinos are linked by an exploitative economic system that heightens their mutual contempt. Market days and fiestas provide opportunities for mestizos, alternately benign and abusive, to assert their social dominance over the Aymara and Quechua.*

• **The Children Know** 33 min. FR$41, FS$340. *The deep division in Andean society between campesinos and mestizos, rural and townspeople, begins at birth, is perpetuated by the schools, and continues through life. Evidence of discrimination's physical effect—the malnourished and diseased children examined by a traveling "doctor"—is not mitigated by the formal Flag Day festivities that bring Indians and mestizos together.*

• **Potato Planters** 19 min. FR$22, FS$180. *An Aymara family plants potatoes, prepares and eats a meal, and discusses the religious and astronomical forces that control their destiny. The stark routine of this typical day contrasts with the complexity of their beliefs, bringing us closer to understanding their life and our own.*

• **Andean Woman** 27 min. FR$24, FS$200. *Aymara women embody a common paradox. The cultural ideal is that women should be subservient to men, and assigned tasks appropriate to their inferior strength and intelligence. In fact, they perform many tasks vital to survival, yet see themselves only as "helpers" in a male-dominated world.*

• **Spirit Possession of Alejandro Mamani** 27 min. FR$13.50. *Film follows old Aymara (Bolivia) man during the last few weeks of his life. Once a wealthy, proud, and respected leader in the Andean community, he has become convinced of his possession by spirits who torment him. The camera documents the gradual erosion of his position in the community and within his family as he searches in vain for a cure. Tense and emotional scenes with Alejandro and members of his family provide most of the information about the drama, in their responses to questions apparently asked by the film crew. Reaches a climax with Alejandro's decision to put his affairs in final order by drawing up a will. This carefully filmed event involving a civil official, Alejandro, and concerned family members is a powerful study of human relations. The film ends with titles indicating that Alejandro took his own life a few weeks later. Warnings: Emotionally powerful document. Viewers who have had close relationships with suicides may respond very strongly. Focusing questions: How does the attitude of*

Alejandro and his family toward his condition change over the course of the film? How can Alejandro's possession be seen as a social as well as personal crisis? To what degree are the social and religious mechanisms of the Aymara successful in dealing with the crisis? Did the film crew influence events? Unravel the syncretism: What is Christian? What is Pagan? [Joel Marrant]

- **Magic and Catholicism** 34 min. FR$42, FS$350. *The people of the Bolivian highlands blend in thought and practice the religion of their ancestors and that of their conquerors. A fatal automobile accident, coincident with the festival of Santiago, provides occasion for unique expressions for both faith and magic in the effort to influence events.*

- **Women in the Changing World** 48 min. FR$59, FS$490. *In the highlands of Bolivia, the cities and towns of Afghanistan, in northern Kenya, and on the China Coast, women are responding to the psychological and technological impact of modernization. In their own words and actions, they speak to issues of universal concern affecting the lives of women everywhere. Traditional women's roles are being challenged by new opportunities created by modern education, family planning, and pressures for economic, social, and political equality.*

FACES OF CULTURE SERIES (1983) 30 min. each. KOCE-TV (PR), Sandra Austin Harden (EP), Ira R. Abrams (WR). Dist: PBS VS$500; Coast Telecourses, Coast Community Colleges, 10231 Slater Ave., Fountain Valley, CA 92708; (714) 926-8861. *An international field trip awaits students who enroll in this introductory cultural anthropology course available from PBS Adult Learning Service. Featuring film footage from around the world, the series explodes many ethnocentric myths and stereotypes and reveals how every society is based on an integrated culture that satisfies human needs and facilitates survival. Of the 26 video programs, 18 are multicultural while eight focus on individual societies such as the Aymara Indians of the Bolivian Andes and the Asmats of New Guinea. Among the concepts explored are: the nature of culture, how cultures are studied, language and communication, marriage and the family, social stratification, religion and magic, culture change, acculturation and child rearing, the arts, patterns of subsistence, and kinship and descent. A student study guide and a cultural anthropology text supplement the series. A faculty guide is also available.* [Reviewed by Karen L. Field, *AA* 87:216–218, 1985.]

A few films in the series are listed under their individual titles:

- **Patterns of Subsistence: Hunter-Gatherers and Pastoralists**

- **The Nature of Culture**

- **Evolution and Human Equality**

Factory (late 1960s) 60 min. Arthur Barron (DI). Dist: EMC FR$18. *Barron's crew goes into a wedding ring factory in Brooklyn, where it studies the activities of the ring makers in contrast to the women packers and the salespeople and executives. It follows ring makers to the bank, where they count out their pay; to home; and to some leisure pursuits. Although the visuals and sound emphasize unrelenting gloom of these men's lives (and their families), the brief shots of the salespeople suggest their lives are only materially better. Much of the power is in the sound of the factory, which drums throughout most of the film. The film takes place during the Vietnam War, which explains some remarks. Cinematic features: Wandering handheld camera, sound synch, b/w. Camera people interview at times, but mostly let natural sound with no distraction dominate. Much nervous camera work: needless zooms, close-ups, pans. Warnings: Obvious bias toward blue-collar men may turn off some. Focusing questions: The packing women in the company obviously have the only comfortable work situation. Why is this? The men offer many reasons for staying with so unsatisfying a job. Do these make sense? What other ones, unnamed, could be operating? What myths about blue-collar men are not supported by the film? What relationships between work and family or leisure or political activities are suggested? Is there a similarity between the way women in the film and the ring makers are treated by management? Bibliography: Jonathon Sennett and Richard Cobb, The Hidden Injuries of Class. Arthur Shostak and William Gomberg, Blue-Collar World. Patricia Sexton, Blue Collars and Hard Hats.* [Clarice Stasz]

Fake Fruit (1986) 22 min. Dist: CCC. *Intimate documentary about young women who make papier-mâché fruit and vegetables in a small factory in Mexico. They have a gringo boss, but the factory is owned by his Mexican wife. The focus of the film is on the color, music, and movement involved, and the gossip that goes on constantly, revealing what the young women think about men.*

Falasha: Agony of the Black Jews (1982) 28 min. Matara Film Productions (FM). Dist: FL FR$50, FS$475, VS$425. *Discusses the plight of the Falashas, the black Jews in Ethiopia. "The Falasha community wants to emigrate to Israel, but neither Haile Selassie, nor the revolutionary government which deposed him, will let them go."* [From the review by Judith Goldstein, *AA* 87:481–482, 1985.]

Falling Star (A Cheyenne Tale) 14 min. Kay Miles and Susan Norton (DI). Dist: VQ. *Animated version of the tale.* [Reviewed by Arthur Einhorn, *AA* 78:954, 1976. Susan Dwyer-Shick, *JAF* 90(355):117.]

Familiar Places (1980) 53 min. Peter Sutton (AN), David MacDougall (DI, CA), Judith MacDougall (SR). Dist: AIAS; UCEMC FR$53. *About the recent movement of Aboriginal people back to their traditional lands after decades of living on missions and in government settlements. It is also a film about an anthropologist working with a community on a matter crucial to their cultural survival. For over a year, a young anthropologist, Peter Sutton, has been mapping sites with Aboriginal families in a remote part of Cape York Peninsula in northern Queensland. As the outstation movement has grown, Aborigines have seen the importance of mapping their traditional country—its campsites, its wells, its sacred places—for their own future use and as an assertion of their rights against possible encroachment by government and mining interests. In the film, an Aboriginal family, the Namponans, return with Sutton to a country* *they are showing their children for the first time. They are joined by an old man, Jack Spear Karntin, who has an intimate knowledge of the country. Together, they visit places familiar to him in an area where they hope someday to resettle their family. Sutton provides a thoughtful and often eloquent commentary on what he has learned about Aboriginal ties to the land while mapping hundreds of individual sites.*

Family 18 min. Hubert Smith (PR). Dist: NIMH Drug Abuse Prevention Film Collection, National Audio Visual Center, Washington, DC 20409. *Upper-middle-class southern California Anglo family.* [Reviewed by Jay Ruby, AA 74:1022, 1973.]

Family Gathering (1988) 30 min. Lise Yasui and Ann Tegnell (PR), Lise Yasui (DI). Dist: NDF FR$60, VR$50, FS$450, VS$325. *"Viewers are asked to consider the roles of home photomedia in the process of documenting and retaining family history. They learn that the search for personal family knowledge is as much about the construction and manipulation of information as it is about learning 'the facts'. . . . The film continues to reveal biographical details of the Yasui family's original settlement in Hood river."* [From the review by Richard Chalfen, AA 91:525–527, 1989.]

A Family in France; A Story about the Passing of Time 40 min. Andre Dryansky (PR). Dist: FL VR$55, VS$295. *This is a portrait of a country family living in a small village, Cassaniouze, in the Auvergne province. Their story typifies how the solid traditions and time-honored ways are slowly fading away in the face of modern life. The village of 700 people has a zero birth rate and most of its inhabitants are retired. The camera picks up with loving detail the routines of a hand hewn life: the home grown food, the slowly simmering cast-iron pot, the leisurely midday meal. Despite the serenity of their surroundings, there is a concern that the village is dying, since the younger members of the community have migrated to the urban centers and come back periodically to visit with their parents. On an anthropological level, this is a film about the disintegration of rural areas in industrialized nations. On another level, it is about the importance of one's roots.*

A Family of Liberia (1970) 17 min. Dist: IUAVC $9.25. *Focuses on the Gbatu family in a Liberian mining town and contrasts their westernized lifestyle with life in less industrialized areas of Liberia. Shows the family's western dress, use of English, and home, which features modern appliances and views the automated mining operation for which John Gbatu works. Contrasts this with a visit to the family's 300-acre farm and a traditional village nearby. Observes the village market day and an initiation ceremony and ends as the children visit their grandfather who still practices old ways.*

The Family Table (see A Taste of China Series) (1984) 29 min. Sue Yung Li (PR). Dist: UCEMC FR$45, FS$580, VS$295. *The contrasting lives of a traditional four-generation rural family in a Sichuan village and a modern, single-child family in urban Hangzhou are viewed through the routines of their daily meals. In the process, we see how the Chinese family has endured and how it is changing.*

Faran Maka Fonda (Fara Maka's Path) (1967) 90 min. Jean Rouch (DI). Dist: CFE; DER. *The path of initiation of the Sorko fisherman from the Niger River.*

Farm Song (see the Japanese Series)

Farmworkers' Diary (1991) 10 min. Paul Shain (FM). Dist: UCEMC FR$25, VS$99. *This thought-provoking documentary provides an inside view of a day in the life of Chicano farmworkers at a farm labor camp in central California. In the farmworkers' own words, it captures their dreams and aspirations, as well as their anxieties, their longing for their families, and their fear of becoming unemployable as farm mechanization increases. An unusual combination of lyricism and social commentary.*

Farrebique (1945–47) 91 min. Georges Rouquier (DI). Dist: AB. *Idealized life on French farm during World War II.* [Reviewed by Laurence Wylie, AA 80:200, 1978.]

Fear Woman 28 min. United Nations (PR), Elspeth McDonald (DI). Dist: CF/MH. *Women in Ghana.* [Reviewed by Filomina Steady, AA 79:197, 1977.]

The Feast (Yanomamo Series) (1970) 29 min. Timothy Asch (FM), Napoleon Chagnon (AN), Center for Documentary Anthropology, Brandeis University and Department of Human Genetics, University of Michigan (PR). Dist: National Audiovisual Center (GSA), Washington, DC 20409 FR$12.50; UCEMC FR$17; PSU(PCR) order #31606, FR$11.10; DER FR$35, FS$275. *Filmed in February 1968, near the headwaters of the Orinoco River,* The Feast *illustrates the feasting practices of the Yanomamo Indians of northern Brazil and southern Venezuela, which provided a means of forming alliances between independent sovereign villages. Attempts to show the type of cinema record that can be made among a primitive people if the anthropologist knows the language and the society well, can predict the basic pattern of social interaction that will occur, and has a conceptual framework in which to organize the action taking place. The film illustrates a chapter of N. Chagnon's ethnography,* The Fierce People, *and also other writings on the subject of alliance, reciprocity economy, and gift exchange. See suggested supplements for the Yanomamo Series.* [Reviewed by Kenneth M. Kensinger, AA 73:500, 1971.]

The Feast in Dream Village (1989) 27 min. Laura Sheerer Whitney and Janet Hoskins (FM). Dist: UCEMC FR$45, FS$530, VS$250. *Documents a ritual feast in a small village on Sumba, the last Indonesian island with a pagan majority. The feast, whose purpose is to revive the fertility of the village's fields and protect the health of its residents, is directed by traditional priests who are hired by the event's sponsor. The film shows the preparations for the feast, the invocations of the spirits, and the performances of numerous sacred rituals. It focuses, however, on the conflict that develops between the head priest and the feast's sponsor over who will control the ceremony. Teaching notes by Prof. Hoskins, USC.*

The Feathered Serpent 58 min. Dist: LMF VS$295. *The Olmec, Toltec, Maya, and Aztec Cultures, which built their huge pyramids and great cities on the dusty plains of Mexico and in steaming jungles of the isthmus, represent the highest achievements of American Indian society. We see the striking skeletons of these complex communities. The Mayan simply vanished. Only the Aztecs maintained their bizarre, sun-struck existence until the outside world, in the form of the Spanish conquistadors, broke in upon them.*

The Feathered Warrior (1973) 12 min. Dist: APPAL FR$20, FS$200. *The illegal sport of game cock fighting is documented in this film in which a fighter explains how he has managed to win over 65 percent of his fights—as he says, "not a very bad record." A slow-motion close-up sequence during a fight shows the sweeping motion of the birds as each attempts to cut to victory.* [Reviewed in *JAF* 87(345):276, 1974.]

Feeding and Food Sharing (see Jane Goodall: Studies on the Chimpanzee Series)

Festival a Dakar (Festival at Dakar) (1963) Jean Rouch (DI), Centre National de la Recherche Scientifique, Comite du Film Ethnographique (PR). Dist: CFE; DER.

Fetes de l'independence du Niger (Celebrations of the Independence of Niger) (1962) 21 min. Jean Rouch (DI), Centre National de la Recherche Scientifique, Comite du Film Ethnographique and Institut Francais d'Afrique Noir (PR). Dist: CFE; DER. *Celebrations of independence in the Republic of Niger in 1961–62.*

Fetes des Gandyi bi a Simiri (Celebration of Gandyi bi at Simiri) (1977) 30 min. Jean Rouch (DI), Centre National de la Recherche Scientifique, Comite du Film Ethnographique (PR). Dist: CFE; DER. *The last ceremony presided over by the Zimba Siddo: the peasants demand protection from the god of the bush against the animal predators. The gods intimate that the Zima Siddo will die that year.*

Fieldwork: Sir Walter Baldwin Spencer (1860–1929) (Strangers Abroad Series) 52 min. Dist: FHS FR$75, VS$159, order #XD2541. *This film shows the work of Sir Walter Baldwin Spencer with the Australian aborigines who had, up until then, been regarded as a step in the evolutionary ladder between neolithic man and the 'civilized' Victorian. Spencer began to work with Frank Gillen, the operator of a telegraph station and an initiated elder of the Aranda tribe. Gillen's special place in aboriginal society enabled both men to witness scenes that no white man had ever seen. The approach that the two men used to study the aborigines came to be known as fieldwork and strongly influenced the way that other cultures have been studied since.*

The Fiesta de Sao Francisco in Caninde: A Brazilian Pilgrimage (1985) 55 min. Sidney M. Greenfield and John Gray (FM). Dist: UWM VR$25, VS$75. *The film has two parts, in the first part the filmmaker lectures about the history of the town of Caninde and the Shrine of Saint Francis there, which is the focus of the film. The second part of the footage shows various scenes from the ten-day festival held at the shrine in 1982. The film tries to capture the emic experience of the festival.* [Reviewed by Stephen D. Glazier *AA* 91:269–270, 1989.]

Fifty Ways to Get Enlightened (The New Pacific Series) (1987) 60 min. BBC/NVC(PR). Dist: FIV VS$79. *Pacific is a region that boasts of numerous religious traditions. Many of the world's major religions are found here—Islam, Buddhism, Hinduism, and Christianity, among other religious systems. The film focuses on the multireligious environment of the region.*

The Fight Against Black Monday 27 min. Marc Siegel (PR, WR). Dist: CRM/MH; CN. *ABC News special on the effect of a U.S. steel plant closing in Youngstown, Ohio, and an attempt by community to take over and operate the plant. Documents the widespread effect on the community of the steel plant closing, led by an ecumenical coalition, as workers and political and community leaders plan and struggle for worker/community ownership and control.* Bibliography: David Moberg, *Shutdown*. Chicago, 1979: In These Times, 1509 N. Milwaukee Ave., Chicago, IL 50622. [Dan Early]

Fighting Back 1957–62 (see Eyes on the Prize: America's Civil Rights Years Series)

Fighting Festival (1985) 30 min. Keiko Ikeda (FM). Dist: UCEMC FR$40, VS$250. *The Fighting Festival is a unique and spectacular Japanese festival rarely seen by outsiders. A kind of cross between a Mardi Gras parade and a citywide football game in the streets, it has for 500 years been the focus of the lives of thousands of villagers along the coast of Japan's inland sea. This acclaimed video shows preparations for and highlights of this colorful event, which remains vital to the villagers' sense of identity in a changing world.* [Reviewed by Theodore C. Bestor, *AA* 88:778–779, 1986. John H. Chilcott, *SBF* 21:231, 1986.]

Fiji—Legacies of Empire (The Human Face of the Pacific Series) (1987) 56 min. Film Australia (PR). Dist: FIV VS$158. *This film looks at the intergroup conflict between the Indian immigrants in Fiji and the the native Fijians. Sugar cane is at the center of this conflict. Indians were brought to Fiji as laborers in colonial times.*

Fiji: The Great Council of Chiefs (1978) 28 min. The Institute for Polynesian Studies, Brigham Young University-Hawaii Campus (PR). Dist: The Institute for Polynesian Studies, BYU-Hawaii Campus; BYU. *Shot in Tubou village, Lakeba, Lau Province, Fiji, in May 1978. This was the first meeting of the Great Council of Chiefs off the main island of Viti Levu in nearly 100 years. The Prime Minister is Tui Naiau, Paramount Chief of the Lau Islands, and he wished to have a film record made of this event. The film documents the events surrounding the gathering of hundreds of people to Lakeba for this event. These include the preparations for the meeting (food preparation, dance practicing, reception of visitors). The formal reception for the Governor-General (the Vunivalu of Bau) is a very elaborate traditional one. Following the opening festivities, the Council meets. Its deliberations and decisions are briefly noted.* Focusing Questions: To what extent do traditional social and political forms seem to function in contemporary Fiji?

How is "culture" defined in the film? What changes in traditional forms are apparent in the film? In content? What is the apparent political and social position of Fijians in Fiji today? What role do the great title bearers play in Fiji's political system today? Bibliography: G. W. Roth, *Fijian Way of Life*. Oxford University Press, 1973. Buell Quain, *Fijian village*. Chicago University Press, 1948. R. A. Derrick, *A History of Fiji*. Fiji Government Press, 1957. Robert Norton, *Race and Politics in Fiji*. Queensland University Press, 1977. [Jerry Loveland and Ishmael Stagner]

Films Are Dreams that Wander in the Light of Day
(1989) 20 min. Sylvia Sensiper (FM). Dist: Sensiper, Department of Urban Planning, UCLA. *"Starts with a mock TV broadcast ... Sylvia Sensiper, a graduate student in visual anthropology at USC, went to Tibet with Lobsang Dakpa ... to make a thesis film. Dakpa is going to see his family and to revisit the scenes of his childhood."* [From the review by Robert Ascher, *AA* 94(2):524–545, 1992.]

FILMS FROM PAPUA NEW GUINEA SERIES Chris Owen (DI), The Institute of Papua New Guinea Studies (PR). Dist: DER. See the individual film descriptions under their titles. A 34-page study guide to three of the films is available from DER.

• **Gogodala: A Cultural Revival?**

• **Malagan Labadama: A Tribute to Buk-Buk**

• **Man without Pigs**

• **The Red Bowmen**

• **Tighten the Drums: Self-Decoration among the Enga**

Au Fil de L'Aiguille (The Thread of the Needle) (1983) 23 min. Colette Piault (FM). Dist: Colette Piault, 5 rue des Sts. Pères 75006, Paris, France; (001) 331-260-2576, FS$125. *Daily life in a northern Greek village.* [Reviewed by by Peter S. Allen, *AA* 86:511–512, 1984.]

Les Fils de l'eau (The Sons of the Water) (1955) 75 min. Jean Rouch (DI), Films de la Pleiade (PR), Suzanne Baron (ED). Dist: CFE; DER. *Life among the Songhay and Dogon during the four seasons.*

Fincho (1958) 76 min. Sam Zebba (FM). Dist: AB FR$40. *About the industrialization and modernization of Nigeria. The locale is a small native village, still tribal and largely under the influence of the local jujuman, or diviner. The only change has come through the efforts of a native school teacher who is constantly rebuffed by the jujuman and the ancient customs and prejudices of the villagers. The first encounter with western civilization occurs as a white man contracts for purchase of lumber on the tribal land. The enterprise begins on a small scale with hand saws, manual labor, and a few of the more adventuresome natives, but grows until the villagers become dependent on the new industry for their livelihood, having largely abandoned their farms. Later, when tractors and power tools are brought in, the villagers "strike," fearing they are to be replaced by automation. The problems are finally resolved as the natives learn to operate and maintain the new equipment, and construct a sawmill, entirely operated by the tribe.*

Finnish American Lives (1983) 46 min. Michael Loukinen (FM). Dist: NMU FR$95, FS$780. *"Documents the lives and thoughts of a three-generation farm family in the remote Upper Peninsula of Michigan.... We are introduced to Erkki Vuorenmaa, who was born in Finland in 1888 ... [and] came to America at 22 in 1910. In 1982, we find him widowed, living with one of his 12 sons, his Finnish born daughter-in-law, and three grandchildren on the farm he cleared."* [From the review by Patricia Slade Lander, *AA* 88:261–263, 1986. Reviewed by Jeffrey Ehrenreich, *SBF* 19:222, 1984.]

Fires of Spring (1980) 33 min. Henry T. Lewis (FM, AN), University of Alberta (PR), Dave Sands (CA). Dist: UAlberta FS$300, VS$125. *Uses filmed interviews of northern Alberta Indian elders and contemporary scenes of controlled burning and related subsistence activities to show ways Slavey Indians used fire to carefully maintain and selectively improve upon habitats of plants, game, and fur-bearing animals. Throughout North America, the Indian customs of burning local habitat was once an integral and dynamic part of hunting and gathering adaptations.* Relevant Anthropological Literature: Henry T. Lewis, "Muskata: The Ecology of Indian Fires in Northern Alberta." *Western Canadian Journal of Anthropology* 7:15–52, 1977. Henry T. Lewis, "Traditional Uses of Fire by Indians in Northern Alberta." *Current Anthropology* 19:401–402, 1978. Henry T. Lewis, "Indian Fires of Spring." *Natural History* 89:76–83, 1980. Henry T. Lewis, *Hunter-Gatherers and Problems for Fire History. Fire History Workshop Symposium Papers*. Tucson: University of Arizona Press, 1981. Henry T. Lewis, "America and Australia." In: *The Regulation of Environmental Resources in Food Collecting Societies*. E. Hann and N. Williams, eds. American Association for the Advancement of Science. [Reviewed by M. A. Baumhoff, *AA* 84:758–759, 1982.]

THE FIRST AMERICAN SERIES

• **Part I: And Their Gods** (1969) 11 min. Philip Stapp (DI). Dist: IFF FR$35. *Animated film dealing with early migration, and with beliefs and customs in Mexico, particularly those of the Aztecs who were flourishing in the highlands when the Spaniards arrived.*

• **Part II: Some Indians of the Southlands** (1976) 17 min. Philip Stapp (DI). Dist: IFF FR$35, FS$300. *Animated film showing the customs and beliefs of certain Indians who lived, and in some cases still live, in what today we call the southern half of the United States. Included are the little-known Natchez Indians, who had a hierarchical class system ruled by an all-powerful chief, the Great Sun; the Natchez's possible ancestors, the "Moundbuilders," whose pyramidal mounds were used for burial grounds and later as bases for temples; and finally the ancient tribes that preceded Pueblo cultures in the southwest, the Hopi, Zuni, and Navajo.*

The First Americans (1969) 53 min. National Broadcasting Company (PR). Dist: FI FR$65, FS$690. *Objectives: To understand the first Americans and their reasons for migrating from Asia; to analyze the scientific methods by which archaeologists reconstruct past cultures; to form a* *hypothesis concerning the first Americans' inability to withstand European migrations.* [Reviewed by Bert Salwen, *AA* 78:359–360, 1976.]

First Contact (Papua New Guinea Series) (1983) 54 min. Bob Connolly and Robin Anderson (FM). Dist: DER FR$85, VR$60, FS$850, VS$400; FL FR$85, VR$60, FS$850, VS$395. *In the 1930s, Australian miners lead by Michael Leahy and his brothers made their first trek into the New Guinea highlands. This was the first contact between white people and highlanders. They captured on film their unexpected confrontation with thousands of native people who had no concept of human life beyond their valleys. Footage of the initial meetings is combined with interviews of the surviving brothers and highlanders who recall the impressions and shock of those long ago events. We see the Papuans 50 years later and hear from many of them their recollections of their first encounter with 20th-century civilization.* [Reviewed by Terence E. Hays, *AA* 86:1076–1077, 1984.]

First Days in the Life of a New Guinea Baby (Character Formation in Different Cultures Series) (ca. 1952) 19 min. Gregory Bateson and Margaret Mead (FM). Dist: NYU FR$16, FS$150; UCEMC FR$10; PSU VR$15.50, FS$315, VS$125, order #24634. *A series of scenes beginning immediately after birth and before the cord is cut, showing the way the newborn child is fed by a wet nurse, bathed, anointed with earth, and carried, with special emphasis on the infant's readiness to respond. Cf. the film, A Balinese Family.*

The First Family (1980) 60 min. Donald Johanson (AN), WVIZ and Cleveland Museum of Natural History (FM). Dist: The Cleveland Museum of Natural History, Wade Oval, University Circle, Cleveland, OH 44106, FR$50, VR$50, FS$450, VS$125. *A film about the first hominids found at the Afar Depression in Ethiopia by Dr. Donald Johanson as the principal investigator. The film is made at two sites, namely the actual site in Ethiopia and the Laboratories in the Cleveland Museum of Natural History.* Bibliography: Donald C. Johanson and Maitland A. Edey, *Lucy: The Beginnings of Humankind.* Simon and Schuster, 1981. [Reviewed by C. Loring Brace *AA* 84:759–761, 1982.]

First Footsteps (Man on the Rim Series) 58 min. Dist: LMF VS$295. *This episode establishes the theme of the series—the concept of the evolving human species spreading out of Asia during and since the last Ice Ages, into all the lands in and around the Pacific Ocean. The human race emerges in Asia, with Peking man and Java man as the two contrasting symbols of our earliest presence in this eastern half of the world. The settlement of two divergent groups in Australia and the Americas points to the great expansion of the human race.*

The First Humans (1983) 11 min. National Film Board of Canada (PR). Dist: Benchmark Films, Inc., 145 Scarborough Road, Briarcliff Manor, NY 10510, FR$30, FS$270. "This animated film suffers from oversimplification and reliance on outdated interpretations. The narration refers to tiny primates inhabiting tropical forests in Africa 20 million years ago, but the animation shows animals that look much like contemporary New World monkeys." [From the review by John H. Peterson, *SBF* 20:311–312, 1985.]

The First Invaders (Triumph of the Nomads Series) 1 hour. Nomad Films International Australia (PR). Dist: WETA $134.95, order #9775-21. *This film explores Australia before European settlement—an Australia still not fully understood, but one with a human history of at least 500 centuries. It demonstrates how the nomadic Aborigines survived and succeeded in a changing environment, often violent and destructive.*

The First Man and His Environment (1974) 43 min. Dist: FACSEA FR$16.

First Moon: Celebration of a Chinese New Year (1987) 37 min. Carma Hinton and Richard Gordon (FM), Kathy Kline (CPR). Dist: NDF2 FR$75, VR$50, FS$500, VS$350. *This film begins with the Kitchen God's return from heaven just before dawn and closes with the lyrical beauty of the Lantern Festival 25 days later. Chinese New Year is like Christmas, Mardi Gras, Thanksgiving, and Easter rolled into one, but also not quite like anything in the West. Out of the brown landscape of late winter, the firecrackers come first, followed by huge adult-size swings, stilt dancing, intricate costumes, floats, pageants, and parades. All are accompanied by the insistent percussion and double-reeded horns of the village band. The film moves with the villagers as the festival widens from the intimacy of family gatherings out into the streets, the neighborhoods, finally encompassing the entire village in a blazing extravaganza of color and sound. First Moon is a celebration of life and hope, of renewal in the earth, and in the lives of the Chinese people who still toil the soil.* [Reviewed by Charlotte Ikels, *AA* 90:1050, 1988.]

The First Northwesterners: The Archaeology of Early Man (1979) 29 min. Louis and Ruth Kirk (PR). Dist: UWP FS$375; IMS-UW FR$35. *The first northwest environment of more than 10,000 years ago and the first humans known to have lived here—a look at the past made possible through the scholarly detective work of archaeologists. Begins by establishing the character of the land as the last ice age closed and gives an idea of the resources available to early man. It then portrays the 1977 discovery at Sequim, Washington, of a mastodon struck by a hunter's bone spear more than 11,000 years ago. Also shown is the recovery of Marmes Man in southeast Washington, an archaeological dig of the late 1960s that produced the oldest human skeletal material in the western hemisphere to be fully documented in place.* [Reviewed by R. Carol Barnes, *ARCH* 36(4):72–73, 1983.] Relevant Anthropological Literature: Ruth Kirk and Richard Daugherty, *Exploring Washington Archaeology*. 1978 (112 pp., 200 photos, 16 color maps. Cloth $12.95; paper $5.95).

The First Signs of Washoe (NOVA Series) (1976) 59 min. Simon Campbell-Jones (PR, WR), Tony Kahn (NR), Boyd Estus (CA). Dist: WGBH; PSU order #60178, FR$24. *Made to review positive evidence for ability of chimpanzees and gorillas to acquire language. Most of the focus is on the work of the Gardners with Washoe. The Gardners explain how they became interested in trying to teach sign language to a* *chimpanzee and the various techniques they used to record and verify the results of their efforts. Washoe is shown (often in clips from the original black-and-white) interacting with and signing to the Gardners and to their research assistants. Rumbaugh's work with the chimpanzee Lana is shown as well. The development of "Yerkish," a linguistic code that allows for only one acceptable string of symbols to convey one idea, is described, and Lana's mastery of this system of communication is demonstrated. Next, Patterson's work with the gorilla infant Koko is shown. The film then mentions ongoing experiments.* Focusing questions: Why did the Gardners choose sign language as a means of communication with Washoe? In what ways can Ameslan be considered a bonafide language? How did the Gardners attempt to insure the objectivity of the experiment? What evidence is there that Washoe understands the concepts behind the signs and can thus generalize the symbol to novel situations? What are the advantages of "Yerkish" over Ameslan? Is there any evidence that any of the apes mastered syntax? Any distinctive features of human language? Bibliography: H. S. Terrace, How Nim Chimpsky Changed My Mind. *Psychology Today* Nov.:65–76, 1979. H. S. Terrace et al., Can an Ape Create a Sentence? *Science* Nov. 23:891–902, 1979. D. M. Rumbaugh, *Language Learning by a Chimpanzee: The Lana Project.* Academic Press, 1977. [John D. Meredith]

Firth on Firth (1993) 49 min. Rolf Husmann (FM), Peter Loizos (AN). Dist: IWF VS$90. *Sir Raymond Firth, a leading figure in British Social Anthropology and one of the grand old men of the field, talks to Peter Loizos about his fieldwork in Tikopia and Malaya, studying under Malinowski and Social Anthropology in the 1930s at the London School of Economics.*

Fishing at the Stone Weir, Parts I and II (Netsilik Eskimo Series) 30 min. each. Doug Wilkinson, Michel Chalufour, and Quentin Brown (FM), Asen Balikci and Guy Mary Rousseliere (AN), Educational Development Center (PR). Dist: EMC FS$324, EDC; PSU(PCR) order #31617, FR$11.10. *Part I includes travel on the tundra, erecting a skin tent, building stone weir in the rapids, woman skinning a duck, braiding her hair, making a balloon for the child, men fishing with three-pronged leister, woman cleaning fish, man using bowdrill to repair leister, family eating raw fish. Part II: Rain on the tundra, many people fishing, children imitating spearing on shore, large hauls coming ashore, men make fire with bowdrill, woman cooks fish in stone pot, men and women eat cooked fish in separate groups, men play with string figures, women clean fish, men build stone caches and fill them.* [Reviewed by Eugene I. Knex, AA 68:1329, 1966.] Suggested supplements: Knud Rasmussen, The Netsilik Eskimos. *Report of the Fifth Thule Expedition*, vol. 8, nos. 1, 2. Copenhagen, 1931. Kaj Birket-Smith, Ethnographic Collections from the Northwest Passage. *Report of the Fifth Thule Expedition*, vol. 6, no. 2. Copenhagen, 1945. Geert van den Steenhoven, *Netsilik Eskimo Legal Concepts.* Department of Northern Affairs and National Resources, Ottawa, 1956. Asen Balikci, Quelques cas de suicide parmi les Esquimaux Netsilik. *Actes du VI Congres International des Sciences Anthropologiques et Ethnologiques*, tome 11 2e vol., pp. 511–516, Paris, 1960. Asen Balikci, Shamanistic Behavior among the Netsilik Eskimos. *Southwestern Journal of Anthropology* 19:380–396, 1963. Asen Balikci, Le Regime matrimonial des Esquimaux Netsilik. *L'Homme.* Septembre–Decembre 1963, 89–101. Asen Balikci, *Development of Basic Socio-Economic Units in Two Eskimo Communities.* National Museum of Canada. Bulletin 202.

Fishing in the City (1991) 28 min. Karen Brodkin Sacks (DI). Dist: UCEMC FR$40, VS$195. *Explores the role of fishing in the social and cultural life of the various ethnic groups that make up the population of Washington, DC. By showing who fishes with whom and what each group does with its catch, this unusual documentary provides a window on some of the social bonds that sustain the city's ethnic communities and on some of the activities that help build bridges across them.*

A Fishing People: The Tulalip Tribes (1980) 17 min. Heather Dew Oaksen (FM) for the Tulalip Tribes of Washington, Kip Anderson, David Altschul (CA). Dist: The Tulalip Tribes, c/o Ray Fryberg, 6700 Totem Beach Rd., Marysville, WA 98270, FR$50, FS$175. *The film traces the historical role of fishing as an integral part of the tribes' cultural and economic heritage. Emphasis is also placed on understanding the contemporary life of community members: their tribal government, socioeconomic status, relationship to the fishing industry. The controversy surrounding the Boldt is viewed from the Indian perspective, without antagonism, with the intention to inform—to dispel misconceptions.*

Fissura 29 min. Mikael Sodersten (FM). Dist: DER FR$50, FS$500, VS$275. *A psychodrama that examines the case of Anna Karin Johansson, who experienced a right hemisphere stroke when she was only 34 years old. This reenactment recounts her experiences of stroke during the first five weeks of her rehabilitation. The camera depicts Anna's inner reality and its collision with the outer environment. Scripting for the film was based on interviews with Anna after her release from the hospital. The period of Anna's illness was chaotic but utterly significant for this young mother's general recovery. The nature of interactions between patient medical providers, family and environment is of utmost importance yet very problematic in such a case where the patient's cognitive capacities are undermined. It provides us with the opportunity to look into the world of the inaccessible, the strange landscape of the shattered mind, and into facts of life yet, to a large extent, unexplainable.*

Fit Surroundings (1993) Hajima Ikela (DI), David W. Plath (WR, CA, AN), Jacquetta F. Hill (AN). Dist: UILL-UC, order #9301. *A modern bias assumes that strenuous labor is only for the youthful. But on the coast of Japan's Shima Peninsula the average of commercial abalone divers is over 50 years—and most of them are female. Local cooperatives control near-shore water as common territory. They regulate access to the water and ban the use of equipment, such as SCUBA, likely to cause over-fishing. By balancing the social ecology of work against the natural ecology of shellfish reproduction, the cooperatives hope to preserve* *surroundings fit to regenerate abalone, and at the same time, to restimulate the competitive enthusiasm of the aging divers.* Bibliography: David W. Plath and Jacquetta F. Hill, "The Reefs of Rivalry: Expertness and Competition among Japanese Shellfish Divers." *Ethnology* 27(3):151–163, 1987. "Fit Surroundings—Japanese Shellfish Divers and the Artisan Option." *Social Behaviour* 3(2):149–159, 1988.

Five Aboriginal Dances from Cape York (Aboriginal Dance Series) (1978) 8 min. John Martin-Jones (PR), Ian Dunlop (DI). Dist: FAA. *Features the performance of five symbolic dances by Australian aborigines at Cape York, Queensland. 1: Atha and Pantji: Three men died and changed into the crow, dove, and geko lizard. 2: Maipaka: The penalty for adultery is death. 3: Ningkushun and Orpul: Orpul, the spirit girl, created the fresh water shark. 4: Pikuwa and Kena: The freshwater and saltwater crocodiles fight. 5: Pipapepe: The courting and mating of curlews. Focuses on topics such as creation, adultery, courting, and mating.*

Five Faces of Tokyo Part I, 24 min.; part II, 29 min. CBS News (PR). Dist: CBS News, 51 W. 52 St., New York, NY 10019. *A documentary that depicts five individuals, ranging from very traditional to less traditional, in their daily lives in Tokyo. Such aspects as family life, home, and religion are included.* [Vivian J. Rohrl]

Five Foot Square 30 min. Petrulis-Fastokas Productions (PR). Dist: Fl FR$55, FS$470. *A filmed report of an archaeological dig from the setting up of tents to the careful cleaning, inspection, and classification of the finds in the laboratory. A group of archaeologists from Canada's Trent University follow up the discovery of ancient artifacts on an island in a small river northeast of Lake Ontario. The film records all the steps in the archaeological study beginning with the laying out of five-foot square plots of ground to carefully locate positions of objects found. They find evidence of an Indian settlement on the site about 2,500 years ago. As tools, bits of pottery, bones of skeletons, and other objects are unearthed, their significance is explained in the narration.* [Reviewed by Steven L. Cox, *AA* 77:904, 1975.]

Fixin' to Tell about Jack (1974) 35 min. Elizabeth Barret (DI, ED). Dist: APPAL FR$45, FS$425, VS$200; UCEMC FR$23 (California only). *Shot in 1973–74 at home of Ray Hicks on Beech Mountain near Banner Elk, NC, and at the Cove Creek Elementary School, Sugar Grove, NC. The Jack Tales are about a young hero named Jack who has various magical adventures. Of British origin, they survive in the southern Appalachians (and one, Jack in the Beanstalk is widely known.) The film shows Ray Hicks, one of the best known storytellers, telling the story "Whikity- Whack, into My Sack." Before and after, scenes of Hicks in his land gathering galax and philosophizing.* Cinematic features: First part of tale told on Hicks' front porch (to camera crew?), second part told to children at school. Warnings: Most audiences have real trouble following Hicks' Watauga County accent. Focusing questions: How does the film conceptualize the folktale? Is there a difference in his performance in two halves of the tale? Analyze tale: structurally, etc. What does galax mean to Hicks? What does Hicks mean when he says, "Anyone could be a Jack?" Bibliography: *North Carolina Folklore Journal*, vol. 26, no. 2, Sept. 1978 (Jack Tales Issue). Richard Chase, *The Jack Tales, Folktales from the Southern Appalachian collected and retold by Richard Chase.* Cambridge, MA: Houghton Mifflin, 1943. George L. Hicks, *Appalachian Valley.* New York: Holt, Rinehart and Winston, 1976.

Flaming Arrows (Man on the Rim Series) 58 min. Dist: LMF VS$295. *More than 20,000 years ago, adventurous Siberian hunters crossed the Bering Strait land bridge into Alaska, bypassed the Canadian ice barrier, and poured into the American prairie. As the copper-colored descendants of the Siberian hunters began to settle down, the "Red Indian" emerged in North America developing an amazing diversity in habitats, cultures, arts and crafts, and technology.*

Flatland 12 min. Eric Martin (DI, Anim), Center for the Visual Arts, Harvard (PR). Dist: CF/MH. *Animated version of the Edwin Abbott story of a two-dimensional world.* [Reviewed by T. O. Beidelman, *AA* 75:589,1973.]

Flight of the Dove 29 minutes. Nancy da Silveira (FM). Dist: UCEMC FR$50, VR$50, FS$595, VS$195, order #11398(f), #37985(v). *A sensitive and perceptive portrait of the Portuguese-American dairy-farming community in the Chino Valley of southern California. The film explores the community's most important annual celebration, the Feast of the Holy Spirit, showing how it preserves community solidarity through its emphasis on shared cultural values. The film traces the evolution of the Feast from its origins in Azores to the contemporary festival in California. The changes in the festival are shown to have helped bridge the gap between immigrants and their children; it now functions to reinforce the identity of its participants as both Portuguese and American. The film focuses on one family and clarifies the difficulties and the rewards of maintaining traditional religious, family, and cultural values while assimilating into mainstream American culture.* [Reviewed by Marie I. Boutte, *AA* 94(1):253–255, 1992.]

The Flintworker 25 min. Earl H. Swanson (DI), Idaho State University Museum (PR), Don E. Crabtree (AN). Dist: IMI FR$30, FS$325. *Treats basic principles of flaking by the use of force (i.e., striking a blow against a suitable rock such as flint or obsidian). Attention is focused upon the production of a cone of force. The control of the cone by the toolmaker allows him to predict shape, size, and direction of a flake he wishes to detach from a piece of stone. The earliest types of flaked stone tools made by the earliest humans are replicated in the film with slow-motion studies (at speeds up to 1,200 frames per second) of selected work. There are drawings to illustrate terms commonly used by flintworkers. These films are primarily for classroom use and come with teacher's guides.* [Reviewed by Anthony E. Marks, *AA* 77:914–915, 1975. Susanna R. Katz and Paul R. Katz, *ARCH* 34(1):60, 1981.]

Floating in the Air, Followed by the Wind (1973) 34 min. Ronald C. Simons (FM, AN), Gunter Pfaff (CA, ED). Dist: IUAVC FR$15.25, FS$450; UCEMC FR$22. *Documents a Hindu religious festival called Thaipusam, which is celebrated each year near Kuala Lumpur, Malaysia. Weeks* *before, devotees gather to prepare themselves spiritually and to construct the Kavadis, highly decorated shoulder poles they will carry at the festival to fulfill their vows. Some worshippers offer the sacrifice of piercing their bodies with long needles and hooks. Those who pierce their bodies do so in groups, led by a guru who is skilled in inducing entranced states. The ecstatic, hypnotic state brought on by rhythmic music, dance, and expectation prevents the worshippers from experiencing pain. The trance is described by worshippers as a state of grace, very pleasurable, "like floating in the air, followed by the wind."* [Reviewed by Paul Hockings, AA 78:722–723, 1976.] Warnings: Many shots of participants piercing their bodies, but all so well contextualized that it should cause no problems to viewers. Focusing question: Why do the people feel no pain?

Floating Rice 14 min. Dist: Sterling.*Thailand Central Plain.* [Reviewed by Steven Piker, AA 78:718, 1976.]

Flooding Job's Garden (As Long as the Rivers Flow Series) (1991) 59 min. Boyce Richardson (DI), James Cullingham and Peter Raymont (PR). Dist: FRIF VR$75, VS$390. *The James Bay and Northern Quebec Agreement of 1975, hailed by governments as a model for future land claims and self government settlements—is considered Canada's first "modern treaty." Fifteen years later, Robert Bourassa's dream of northern hydro-electric power has become a nightmare for the James Bay Cree. Richardson revisits communities he first filmed in the 1970s, before Hydro Quebec began its work, documenting 20 years of massive change. As Bourassa and Hydro Quebec prepare for Phase 2, the Crees are mounting an international campaign to protect the environment and to ensure responsible development.*

The Flour Mill House (1970) 13 min. Geraldo Sarno (DI). Dist: UNI FR$40-55, FS$175. *This documentary depicts the centuries-old process whereby the manioc plant is transformed into flour. This manioc flour is the basic nourishment of the northeastern Brazilian population. Before the arrival of the Europeans on the continent, manioc, an indigenous plant, was already cultivated and processed by the Indians. From them, the colonizers learned the uses of the plant and the methods of its production. Flour mills have existed in Brazil since the beginning of the colonial period. Time and modernization have done little to change them. The farming and processing of manioc are often a family operation. The farmer keeps enough flour for his family and tries to sell the rest of it at the local market. The film portrays the entire process—from the farming and harvesting, to the cooperative work at the mill, to the sale of the flour at the weekly fair.*

The Flute and the Arrow (1958) 78 min. Arne Sucksdorff (WR, FM), Ravi Shankar (MU). Dist: AB FR$65. *About the Muria tribe in India. Portrays the Muria's primitive religious beliefs in pantheistic Gods, guardians, and evil demons in dangerous animals. The flute and the arrow are two things of symbolic importance; the decorated flute stands for tenderness and love, the bow and arrow are the means to defend the tribe against the dangerous jungle animals. The fictional theme of the film describes the villagers' fight against the leopard, and the sacrifice of one man's life to appease the Gods and drive away the animal.*

Folk Music in Japan (1963) 28 min. (A Folklore Research Film by Peter and Toshi Seeger.) Dist: FIM/RF FR$25, FS$250. *Japan is a land of contrast—the very new and the very old mingle in music as well as in other aspects of daily life. This survey begins with a group called "The Wagon Aces," from the Tokyo Grand Ole Opry, playing The Orange Blossom Special and then introduces the traditional shakahachi and other flutes with Mr. Watazumi Tokyo playing ancient Buddhist reed music for the dead. In a Tokyo schoolyard, there are children's songs and games, and on Shikoku Island in southern Japan the rice harvest is reenacted in music and dance from planting the seedlings to harvesting and even to the argument with the tax collector.*

Fonseca: In Search of Coyote (1983) 30 min. Mary Louise King and Fred Aronow (PR). Dist: UCEMC VR$40, VS$295, order #37752. *Noted Native American artist Harry Fonseca illustrates and explains the development of his acclaimed Coyote Series of paintings and drawings in this offbeat, entertaining, and informative documentary. Although Fonseca describes his work as "a sort of funky folk art fling," the film shows how his Coyote grew out of traditional North American Indian art forms and legends surrounding the famous "trickster." Fonseca himself furnishes almost all the commentary for the film. He is seen in his studio working working on and discussing his coyote paintings, as well as at a gallery opening and an Indian market in Santa Fe, NM. Counterpoint is provided by the Indian poetry of Dell Hymes and Peter Blue Cloud, read on the soundtrack by actress and story teller Eda Reiss Merin, with an appropriately witty orchestral score by Arlon Ober.*

Food Preparation (Japanese Macaque) 4 min. Dist: PSU FR$4.30.

Le Foot-Girafe; ou, l'alternative (The Foot Giraffe; or, the Alternative) (1973) Jean Rouch (DI). Dist: CFE; DER. *An advertising film for the Peugeot 403-504.*

For All People, For All Time (1983) 75 min. Mark Jury and Dan Jury (FM). Dist: Valley Filmworks, Inc., 214 E. 31st St., New York, NY 10016; (212) 683-5211, FR$100, FS$950. *"About the residents of the Cuyahoga National Recreation Area betweeen Akron and Cleveland, Ohio, who were forced to move from their homes by the National Park Service between 1979 and 1982. Few films address the crucial topics of the social impacts of federal acquisition of private property for public parks."* [From the review by Lynn Arnold Robbins, AA 88:1040, 1986.]

For Our Own Bread (1988) 26 min. National Film Board of Canada (PR). Dist: IUAVC VR$30, FS$550, VS$160. *Experiences of a development worker in Mali.* [Reviewed by Thomas A. Painter, AA 93:769–770, 1991.]

For Richer for Poorer (The New Pacific Series) (1987) 60 min. BBC/NVC (PR). Dist: FIV VS$79. *Compares weddings in several Pacific nations to reveal their differing social attitudes.*

For Those Who Sail to Heaven (1990) 48 min. Elizabeth Wickett (FM). Dist: FRIF VR$75, VS$375. *At the climax of the annual Opet festival in ancient Luxor, the barques of ancient Theban gods were pulled from Karnak to Luxor and then sailed back on the "waters of inundation." Today, the descendants of Luxor's patron saint, Sheikh Sidi Abu'l Hajjaj, continue this ancient ritual. The families that pull the sheikh's boat describe the many Sufi rites captured in the film including "zikr," the whirling to flutes and drums to achieve the ecstatic state called "malbus," and "mirmah," equestrian games that rekindle the spirit of battles fought long ago. In their eyes, these rites constitute an ancient legacy that they are bound to preserve.*

Forest of Bliss Robert Gardner (FM). Dist: AC FR$150, FS$1500. *This is an unsparing yet redemptive account of the inevitable griefs, religious passions, frequent happinesses that punctuate daily life in Benares, India's most holy city. The film unfolds from one sunrise to the next without commentary, subtitles, or dialogue. It is an attempt to give the viewer a wholly authentic though greatly magnified and concentrated sense of participation in the experiences examined by the film.* [Reviewed by Joanna Kirkpatrick, AA 91:273–274, 1989. Reviewed in VISR 8:125, 1992.]

Forest People of Central Africa 15 min. Department of Anthropology, Harvard University (PR). Dist: FCE FR$17, FS$95. *On the pygmies of Africa.*

The Forgotten American (1968) 28 min. Carousel Films (PR). Dist: PSU(PCR) order #31345, FR$13.25. *Story of the American Navajo Indian and his economic, social, and spiritual plight. His shorter life span, greater number of child deaths, and greater suicide rate indicate the disparity between him and white America. The problem of alienation—the Navajo does not know who he is in the midst of the white middle-class values he is taught. Economic exploitation by the traditional trading posts and efforts being made to locate industry on the reservation to provide work for the Indians.*

Forgotten Families 28 min. Community Health Service, Public Health Service (PR). Dist: National Medical Audiovisual Center, Station K, Atlanta, GA 30324. *Mexican American migrant farm workers in California.* [Reviewed by Nancie L. Gonzalez, AA 77:199, 1975.]

Fort Branch: Preserving a Unique Legacy (1980) 26 min. Randy Lennon (FM). Dist: Underwater Archaeology Unit, North Carolina Divsion of Archives and History, P.O. Box 58, Kure Beach, NC 28449; (919) 458-9042, FS$380, free rental. *Addresses "the destruction of ordinance and supplies on April 10, 1865, by the Confederate commander of Fort Branch before Southern troops withdrew from this fort on the banks of the Roanoke River in North Carolina. The heavy artillery were rolled on their wheeled carriages to the edge of a bluff overlooking the river and pushed over. Supplies of gunpowder, projectiles and small arms were also disposed of in this manner. All came to rest in the deep water of the silty channel. . . . The film depicts the scientific recovery of the artillery by a team of underwater archaeologists."* [From the review by Eugene L. Sterud, ARCH 37(5):70, 1984.]

Fort Madison Archaeology 15 min. Marshall McKusick (FM). Dist: UIOWA order #30241, FR$13.20, FS$235. [Reviewed by David Mayer Gradwohl, AA 78:366–369, 1976.]

Forty-Seven Cents (1973) 25 min. Dist: UCEMC FR$26, FS$220. *Documents how officials of the Bureau of Indian Affairs, the Indian Claims Commission, and a lawyer representing the Pit River Indian Nation of Northern California obtained from the tribe a land settlement that many—and perhaps most—of its members did not want. Traces history of relations between the United States and the Pit River Nation, showing how the United States violated the 1848 Treaty of Guadalupe Hidalgo by taking the Indian land in 1853. Pit River Nation members voted in 1963 to reject the government's offer of 47 cents an acre compensation for the land; but their lawyer, wishing to settle the matter, engineered a second ballot by mail that many tribal members considered highly questionable and that narrowly reversed the vote. When the Indians tried to dismiss the lawyer and hire noted attorney Melvin Belli, the Bureau of Indian Affairs refused to allow the change. Members of the tribe who refused to accept settlement money are interviewed as they repeatedly tried to have the case reopened. Former U.S. Attorney General Ramsey Clark, Senator John Tunney of California, and other officials explain the government's position.* [Reviewed by Mike Moerman, AA 77:695–696, 1975.]

Foster Child 43 min. Gil Cardinal (DI). Dist: NFB FR$70, VR$70, FS$650, VS$300. *This documentary reflects the universal need for cultural identity and roots felt by many foster and adopted children. At age 35, Gill Cardinal began a process of discovery, searching for his Native American family and an understanding of the circumstances that led to his becoming a foster child. Raised happily by a loving white family, he is haunted by the knowledge that although he gained one life, he lost another. We follow his year-long quest for his heritage. In his search, Gil encounters frustrations and loss, but eventually finds his natural family and a renewed sense of his culture.* [Reviewed by Joe Sawchuk, AA 92(4):1096–1097, 1990.]

4-Butte-1: A Lesson in Archaeology (1968) 33 min. Donald Miller (DI, AN), Tony Gorsline (CA), James R. Sackett (AN), University of California EMC and the Archaeological Survey, Department of Anthropology, UCLA (PR). Dist: UCEMC FR$26, FS$380; PSU FR$38, FS$455. *The excavation of a Maidu Indian village in California's Sacramento Valley is the medium through which the main purpose of this film is communicated: to involve the student in the contemporary relationship between archaeology and other disciplines of anthropology. It opens with an impressionistic treatment of the creation of the Maidu world, intercut with shots of an archaeologist reading the legend. The pace is thus set for a past/present orientation that holds through the preliminary research phase, the field reconnaissance (where devastating evidences of the Gold Rush are shown), and the excavation itself. The discovery and analysis of artifacts, an archaeologist explains, is aimed at find-*

ing order in the archaeological record and revealing relationships between man's products and his behavior. Other concepts of modern archaeology are heard in sound montage as students work in the pits. An old newspaper account is read: soldiers have taken the Maidu away to a reservation—but not before the Maidu destroyed their own homes. At this point, we are shown in the pits the charred, blackened housepots of a vanished people. [Reviewed by Jay Ruby, AA 71:380, 1969.]

The Four Corners (1983) 59 min. Christopher McLeod (DI, PR), Glenn Switkes and Randy Hayes (PR). Dist: BF. FR$85, FS$850, VS$450. *"Taking their title from a National Academy of Sciences report that concludes that coal strip-mining could permanently damage the Southwest's semiarid lands, the filmmakers examine the hidden costs of energy development. . . . This film treats strip-mining and then goes on to deal with uranium and oil shale development. It explores the impact of energy development on rural Mormon and Anglo populations as well as on Hopis and Navajos."* [From the review by Louise Lamphere, AA 86:789–790, 1984.]

Four Families (1959) 61 min. Ian MacNeill and Guy Glover (PR), Margaret Mead (AN). Dist: NFB FR$39, FS$495. *Through a comparative look at a typical agrarian family in Japan, India, France, and Canada, this film affords an elementary introduction to the concept of the family and its variation across cultures. It is structured around an in-studio conversation between Mead and Ian MacNeill, who discuss the idea of the family as they look at the footage of typical families.* [Reviewed by Bill Nichols, AA 83:743–744, 1981.]

Four Hindu Sadhus 40 min. Mira Reym Binford and Michael Camerini (FM). Dist: UW-SAAC FR$30, FS$275. *Examines several traditional ways in which a Hindu may renounce the world and yet retain an integral role in society. The film focuses on four different types of sadhus (holy men): the administrator of a Ramakrishna Mission hospital, a traditional guru who heads a monastery, a scholar who is also founder of a national political party, and a recluse with no organizational ties. Although each sadhu has severed his ties with the secular world, each maintains sacredly articulated relationships with the secular world. Interviews with the sadhus and with lay people reveal a wide range of opinions on the role of sadhus in contemporary Hindu society. Focusing questions: Why did these people choose the life of renunciation? How do they relate to the society they have renounced? Accompanied by Teacher's Guides with background information and suggestions for discussions. Produced with synchronous sound interviews in Bengali, Hindu, Tamil, with English subtitles.*

Four Holy Men: Renunciation in Hindu Society (see *Four Hindu Sadhus*)

The Four Seasons in Lenape Indian Life (1983) 58 min. William Sauts Netamuxwe Bock (WR, FM). Dist: Spoken Arts, Inc., 310 North Ave., New Rochelle, NY 10801; (914) 636-5482, FS$129.95. *A sound filmstrip written and illustrated by a Lenape artist. An account of one Woodland people's response to European intrusion.* [Reviewed by Robert S. Grumet, AA 89:1016–1017, 1987.]

4th and 5th Exclusionary Rule (1974) John Marshall (FM). Dist: DER FR$75, FS$875. *Four sequences from the Pittsburgh police series are intercut with a panel discussion moderated by James Vorenberg. Community organizers, police, students, and lawyers discuss the issues raised in the four sequences, including the fourth and fifth amendments, and the exclusionary rule of evidence.*

The Fourth Stage: A Hindu's Quest for Release (1984) 40 min. Paul Kuepferle (WR, PR), David Thompson (DI), Edward Bastian and Joseph Elder (EP). Dist: UW-SAAC FR$30, FS$295. *The film follows a newly retired newspaper editor, E. R. Seturam, as he struggles to decide whether or not to renounce the world, enter the classical Hindu fourth stage of life, and become a sannyasin. Seturam hears his lawyer explain that legally his decision to become a sannyasin would be tantamount to death; he would have to give over all his worldly possessions to his family and renounce any association with them. The film accompanies Seturam as he discusses his possible decision with his colleagues, his family, other sannyasins, and with thoughtful holy men at pilgrimage centers in different parts of India.*

Foutura: A Lobi Potter Tells Her Story (1993) 49 min. Beate Engelbrecht (DI). Dist: IWF VS(DM) 179. *Foutura Sib is a 65-year-old Lobi woman who has been a potter all her life. Today, as an old woman, Foutura produces sacral pots, something that only women who do not menstruate anymore can do. Lobi interpreter, Binaté Kambou, asks Foutura about her life as a potter, the technology and economy of pottery, religion, and future prospects.*

Foxfire 21 min. Dist: CRM/MH FS$355, VS$270. *In 1967, Eliot Wiggenton, a high school English teacher in Rabun Gap, Georgia, started an educational revolution. He set his class, an essentially unmotivated group, to the task of recording the lore, legends, and crafts of their Appalachian folk heritage. What they found was a new direction for themselves and their community. They learned by going into the hills, interviewing rural folk, and publishing their findings in* Foxfire *magazine. This film is their story—told by the people who made it happen. The camera explores the techniques of recording oral history, writing, designing, and running the magazine. The* Foxfire *staff and local residents explain their project, how it works, how it grew, how it changed their lives, and how it spread into a nationwide education movement.*

The Fragile Mountain (1982) 55 min. Sandra Nichols (FM). Dist: Sandra Nichols Productions Ltd., P.O. Box 315, Franklin Lakes, NJ 07417; (201) 891-8240, FR$80, FS$800, VS$600. *"The majestic Himalayan kingdom of Nepal now faces environmental destruction. This ecological disaster not only brings hardship for millions of hill farmers but also threatens to destroy a unique way of life. . . . This film documents the irterrelationships between this human and environmental tragedy."* [From the review by Linda Stone, AA 86:1072, 1984.]

Franz Boas (1858–1942) (see Odyssey Series)

Freak Street to Goa: Immigrants on the Rajpath (1988) 60 min. John Calwell and John L. Pudaite (FM). Dist: FL FR$85, FS$850, VS$445. *A profile of four survivors of the counter-culture of the sixties. Like others of their generation, these rebels migrated to India and Nepal to escape Western materialism. While many Westerners eventually returned, these four chose to live permanently in the East. We meet Jim, a Vietnam vet and AWOL activist who migrated to Nepal and operates a fabric business for tourists. Woody now paints and runs a bakery in Kathmandu, which sells to Westerners. Dick is a Harvard graduate who produces macrobiotic food. Eddy supports himself writing epic poems and novels. The film follows the annual migration of these aging hippies from the mountains of Kathmandu to the beaches of Goa in South India. It captures their lifestyle with all its inherent ironies: idealism that has given way to realism; rebellion that has joined the establishment.* [Reviewed by Linda Stone, *AA* 91:273, 1989.]

Fred's Lounge (see Le Son des Cajuns de la Louisiana Series)

Free Clinic 19 minutes. Paul Deason (FM). Dist: Paul Deason, 2271 Fox Hills Dr., Los Angeles, CA 90064. [Reviewed by Patricia Perrier, *AA* 77:186, 1975.]

Free Voice of Labor—The Jewish Anarchists (1980) 55 min. Joel Sucher and Steven Fischler (FM). Dist: Pacific Street Films Inc., 22 1st Street, Brooklyn, NY 11231. FR$80, FS$800. *"American Jewish anarchism flourished from 1880 to 1914 and its followers were the major source of the unions of New York's 'needle trade.'"* [From the review by Riv-Ellen Prell, *AA* 85:1008–1009, 1983.]

A Free Woman 100 min. Volker Schlorndoff (Dl). Dist: NYF. *Contemporary American women.* [Reviewed by Michelle Z. Rosaldo, *AA* 79:203, 1977.]

French Village (1979) 22 min. James Wilson, David Tristram (CA, Dl). Dist: IFF FR$45, FS$380. *The village of Sainte Alvere, southwestern France.*

FROM AFRICA TO ASIA: NOMADS SERIES (1992) Malone Gill and Freewheel (PR). Dist: FIV. *Nomads live on the fringes, on the social, political, and geographical margins of the modern world. This series of four video programs explores and tries to understand the lives of people who still cherish the freedom to move at will; who through a deep knowledge of their environment and their livestock, manage to live in some of the most remote and harsh regions on Earth. Each program, produced under the guidance of an anthropologist who has lived with the group in question and is fluent in their language, tells a human story illustrating the harsh realities of nomadic life. Titles of the films comprising the series are:*

- **The Turkana**
- **Inner Mongolia—In Search of History**
- **Mauritania: Wealth of Blood**
- **Siberia: After the Shaman**

From Courtyard House to Block Apartment (1987) 23 min. Wynette Yao (WR, PR, NA), Charlie Wu and Kuochiang Chueh (CA), Lian-yuan Su and David Assal (ED). Dist: FRIF VR$50, VS$220; Wynett Yao, 4706 Cedar Avenue, Philadelphia, PA 19143; (215) 726-7706, VR$50, VS$250. *Shot in Taiwan, the film examines how the rapid industrialization of the last two decades has disrupted traditional patterns of living and housing. The traditional Chinese courtyard house offered an arrangement of space and form that was both fixed and yet responsive to the changing needs of large clans living and working in an agricultural society. Today, the most common forms of housing are block apartments based on a Western design adopted in the 1950s. This program explores the transition from an old society to a drastically new one. It captures a glimpse of how life in courtyard houses once was, investigates the reasons why courtyard houses are nearing extinction, and looks into the adjustments the Chinese have made in learning to live in the alien patterns of space presented by block apartments.*

From Homo Erectus to Neanderthal (1972) 18 min. E. G. Marshall (NA). Dist: FI FR$19, FS$230. *Adapted from the MGM Documentary Television Special "The Man Hunters." This film shows various excavation sites of Homo and concerns itself with the evolution of the genus in a chronological sequence through Cro-magnon and Upper Pleistocene man.*

From Sunup (1987) 28 min. Flora M'mbugu (FM). Dist: MWV FR$25, FS$350, VS$50. *A Tanzanian woman has produced a film about Tanzanian women.* [Reviewed by Deborah R. Rubin, *AA* 92:271–272, 1990.]

From the Ashes: Nicaragua Today (1981) 60 min. The International Women's Film Project (PR). Dist: DA2 FR$90, FS$900. *"The Nicaraguan revolution from the perspective of the working-class Chavarria family, and in particular in the view of its four women."* [From the review by John A. Booth, *AA* 86:237–238, 1984.]

FROM THE ELDERS SERIES (1988) Katrina Waters (FM), Sarah Elder and Leonard Kramerling (EP, CC, CA). Dist: DER. *The series is an outgrowth of the earlier films produced by the Alaska Native Heritage Film Project. Each film presents the stories and thoughts of one of three highly regarded Alaska Native Elders. Each of the elders speaks in a different traditional narrative genre. The films reveal ways in which knowledge has traditionally been passed down through generations without the written word and provides a window of understanding into the Eskimo experience. To provide visual context for each story, historical photographs and village scenes are interwoven with footage of the elders talking. See descriptions under the titles:*

- **Joe Sun**
- **In Iirgu's Time**
- **The Reindeer Thief**

From the First People (The Alaskan Eskimo Series) 45 min. Leonard Kamerling, Sarah Felder (FM). Dist: DER FR$50, FS$540. *Change and contemporary life in Shungnak, a village on the Kobuk River in northwestern Alaska,*

75 miles north of the Arctic Circle. Life in this inland community was and still is dominated by the seasons and the river, which freezes up in October and thaws in the spring. Traditional subsistence activities continue, yet much is new: some people use snow machines and packaged foods are common in the kitchen. Eskimos reflect on and express their mixed feelings about the changes they have seen. Relevant Anthropological Literature: Norman A. Chance, *The Eskimo of North Alaska*. Holt, Rinehart, and Winston, 1966. C. C. Hughes, *An Eskimo Village in the Modern World*. Cornell University Press, 1969.

From the Heart of the World: The Elder Brothers' Warning (1991) 88 min. Alan Ereira (PR, DI), BBC (PR). Dist: MFV FR$29.95. *"This is a sort of New Age production that examines a supposedly unknown and unstudied tribe, the Kogi, who live near the city of Santa Marta on the Caribbean coast of northern Colombia.... Their isolation and culture are threatened today by the encroachment of modern civilization and farmers who are settling on Kogi lands. They are also upset by the rampant looting of Tairona tomba around Santa Marta."* [From the review by Peter S. Allen, *ARCH* 46(2):70, 1993.]

From Woman to Women (1993) 58 min. Nanako Kurihara (FM). Dist: Nanako Kurihara, 229 Columbus Ave. #5R, New York, NY 10023; telephone/fax (212) 721-1284. *The director undertakes a personal journey to trace the Japanese women's brand of feminism, called "Woman Lib," to profile five "lib" veterans, and to find her own identity as a Japanese woman in the 1990s.*

La frontera (1982) 28 min. Victoria Schultz (PR). Dist: Hudson River Productions, P.O. Box 315, Franklin Lakes, NJ 07417; (201) 891-8240, VR$50, FS$450, VS$400. *The U.S.-Mexican frontier.* [Reviewed by William Madsen *AA* 86:231–232, 1984.]

Frontier Settlement of Japanese from Overseas, Indians from the Highlands—Santu Cruz, Bolivia (1963) 16 min. The Land Tenure Center, University of Wisconsin (PR), Dwight Heath (AN). Dist: UW. *Covers two colonization projects. One is a colony of Japanese immigrants. Shows progress made by this colony and discusses the social and economic effect of the colony. The second colonization project is on the extreme frontier of new settlement in the lowlands. This is made up primarily of Indians who have moved down from the highlands.* Cf. the film, *Changes in Agriculture, Population and Utilization of Resources.*

Fugitive from Fear 20 min. Kenneth Holmes (FM). Dist: RBMU FR$40. *Made in inland Peru in 1970. Contents: Gospel ministry among the Chayahuita and Quechua Indians of Peru.*

Fulbe of M'Bantou 10 min. Dan Shafer and Tom O'Toole (FM). Dist: MINN FS$130. *The viewer is taken into the daily life of the Fulbe community of M'Bantou, a small village of the Senegal River between Senegal and Mauritania. The pressure of the environment is noted as a key element in the life of the Fulbe. They are nomadic herdsmen who drive their cattle to pasture according to an annual seasonal cycle. Therefore, not all the people remain in the settled village of M'Bantou, which is surrounded by temporary dwellings for migratory Fulbe. The divergence among their three social classes—the nobles, the rimbe, and the neybe—is also made apparent.*

Full Circle (1990) 50 min. Maria Gargiulo and John de Graaf (DI). Dist: UCEMC FR$50, VS$295. *Native Americans in Washington state have been at the forefront of a Native American cultural and economic renaissance. Sparked by legal victories and fueled by a new economic and political power, they are discovering ways to retain their Indian identity while living in contemporary America. This documentary relates this success story by depicting the diverse lives of tribal elders, business leaders, traditional artists, environmental activists, salmon fishermen, and innovative teachers.*

Full Moon Lunch (see The Japanese Series)

Full of Life A-Dancin' (1978) 29 min. Robert Fiore (PR, DI), Richard Nevell (PR). Dist: PFI FR$40, FS$395. *Shows southern mountain folk dancing vigorously.* [Reviewed by Melanie L. Sovine, *AA* 89:522–525, 1987.]

Funérailles à Bongo: Le vieil Anaï (The Funeral at Bongo: The Old Anaï) (1972) 75 min. Jean Rouch and Germaine Dieterlen (DI), Centre National de la Recherche Scientifique, Comité du Film Ethnographique (PR). Dist: CFE; DER. *The oldest member of the village of Bongo, Mali, who died at the age of 122, was the head of the mask society.*

Funérailles de femme à Bongo (Funeral of a Woman from Bongo) (1973) 20 min. Jean Rouch (DI). Dist: CFE; DER.

The Future of the Past (Infinite Voyage Series) (1990) 60 min. Mary Rawson and Marisa Costa (PR). Dist: WQED. *"Many monuments and art treasures around the world are threatened by age, neglect, pollution, earthquakes, and even the well-intended efforts of past conservators.... This informative and well-produced program surveys a fascinating array of projects combatting these and other threats to the world's rich artistic and cultural heritage. It is a captivating chronicle of scientific innovation and of cooperation among art historians, conservators, archaeologists, and scientists."* [From the review by Peter S. Allen, *ARCH* 43(3):70, 1990.]

Future Shock (1972) 42 min. Alex Grosshof (DI), Metromedia Producers Corporation (PR). *This film is based on Alvin Toffler's book* Future Shock. *By depicting the age of technology and the disposability of things and relationships, it declares the death of permanence. Focusing questions: What is future shock? What role does knowledge play? Give examples of disposability.*

Future Wave: Japan Design (1988) 27 min. David Rabinovitch (PR). Dist: UCEMC FR$40, VS$195. *Most of us know Japan primarily through its products—dynamic, seductive consumer goods whose high-tech, high-touch, high-fashion styling has taken the world by storm. Through unprecedented access to top designers and corporate executives in the fields of electronics, furnishings, and fashion, this documentary shows how modern Japanese design has helped create a Japanese consumer lifestyle that is being exported around the world. Discussion guide included.*

The Gabra 60 min. Nancy Archibald (PR), Barbara Moon (WR), Rudolf Kovanic (CA). Dist: CBC FR$45, FS$485. *The Cabra live along the Kenya-Ethiopia border, herding their camels, raising goats and sheep, and waiting for the all-too-short rainy season. They do not till the land, considering this work ritually polluting and must, therefore, follow the rains in search of better conditions. Selling camels and their products, for example, was always considered sacriligious. Yet, droughts within the past few years have forced tribesmen to this practice.*

The Galapagos: Laboratory for Evolution (1971) 36 min. Geo. A. Bartholomew (PR). Dist: Harper and Row Media, 2350 Virginia Avenue, Hagerstown, MD 21740, FR$39.50. *An excellent series of 11 films showing the wonders of the Galapagos. One particular film,* The Experimental Conditions, *is the general introduction to the series and is quite useful in a myriad of courses.* [Reviewed by Norris M. Durham, *AJPA* 48:543, 1978.]

Game of Staves (American Indian Series) (1962) 10 min. Dist: UCEMC FR$22, FS$145; PSU(PCR) order #11221 IK, FR$4.90, FS$100. *Pomo boys are shown playing the game of staves, which was played by most of the Indian tribes throughout North America. A variation of the dice game, using six staves and twelve counters, it is played by both men and women under the supervision of a referee. The film explains the individualized pyrographic ornamentation of the staves and counters.* [Reviewed by John Adair, *AA* 76:728–730, 1974.]

Gang Cops (1987) 30 min. Thomas B. Fleming and Daniel Marks (FM). Dist: OWM FR$90, VR$75, FS$500, VS$250. *This film discusses a very important issue of urban American lifestyle, namely the gang wars. The film captures the conflict between two large, confederated alliances of Los Angeles street gangs. It also shows how the local police handle the conflict and try to maintain some degree of peace.* [Reviewed by R. Lincoln Keiser, *AA* 91:269, 1989.]

Garbage 11 min. King Broadcasting Co. (PR). Dist: BFA. *Life cycle of garbage.* [Reviewed by Thomas Wight Beale, *AA* 77:899, 1975.]

Garçons et Filles (1965) 30 min. Pierre Vidal (CA), Michael Brunet (AN), French Ethnological Film Committee of the Musée de l'Homme (PR). Dist: FSC FR$25, FS$250 (English-language version). *Filmed in 1961 and 1962 in the Bouar-Baboua region of the Central African Republic, near the Yade range. It follows the initiation rites of Cbaya boys and girls. It includes a detailed view of clitoridectomy.*

Gare du Nord (North Train Station) (1966) 20 min. Jean Rouch (DI), Les Films de Losange (PR). Dist: CFE; DER. *The film was shot in real time: a young woman argues with her husband about the sadness in their lives and decides to leave him.*

Garlic Is As Good As Ten Mothers (1980) 56 min. Les Blank (FM). Dist: FF; UNI. *For once music takes a back seat to food in this, Les Blank's first lyrical journey into the delights of the palate. Featuring Alice Waters and her world-renowned restaurant, Chez Panisse in Berkeley, California, and the Cajun music of the Bay Area's own Louisiana Playboys, the film wades through fields of garlic, through the seasoning of suckling pigs from the inside out, through two annual Chez Panisse Garlic Festivals and lingers on the sensuous textures of fine food and its artistic metamorphosis into pleasurable edibles. An education in attitudes toward garlic and good food.*

Gatecliff: American Indian Rock-Shelter (1974) 24 min. David Hurst Thomas (AN), National Geographic Society (PR). Dist: NGS FS$345, VS$315. *Development and testing of hypotheses in archaeology. Nevada rock shelter.* [Reviewed by Frederick Gorman, *AA* 77:901–902, 1975. Reviewed in *ARCH* 33(1):61, 1981.]

Gathering Up Again: Fiesta in Santa Fe (1992) 46 min. Jeanette DeBouzek (FM), Diane Reyna (CA). Dist: QIDR VR$75, VS$275. *A documentary on the representation of history and the performance of ethnicity in one of the country's oldest community celebrations. Following three young people through the entire fiesta cycle from the initial planning and preparation to the highlights of Fiesta weekend itself, the documentary focuses on the formation of ethnic identity in the tricultural city of Santa Fe, New Mexico, on the ongoing impact of the culture of conquest on Native Americans in the region, and on the difficulties involved in creating alternative local histories. While Spanish-American involvement is central to the traditional celebration of Fiesta, the documentary also takes a look at the more recent problem of Anglo-American cultural hegemony. It includes a number of interviews with prominent community leaders, cultural activists, and fiesta participants and observers.*

Gaza Ghetto: Portrait of a Palestinian Family (1984) 82 min. Pea Homquist, Joan Mandell, and Pierre Bjorklund (FM). Dist: Joan Mandell, P.O. Box 445, Cambridge, MA 02140. *"An intimate glimpse into the lives of a refugee family and their friends in the Gaza Strip. . . . Since 1948, the Dimrawi family has resided in Jabalia camp, the largest refugee camp in Gaza with about 50,000 inhabitants. Ordinary events of everyday life . . . take place against the backdrop of occupation and violence."* [From the review by Julie Peteet, *AA* 89:1018–1022, 1987.]

Geel Steven White (FM), Swedish Television, Loela Brothers (PR). Dist: UCEMC. *Mental health in the Belgian town.* [Reviewed by Kathleen Sheehan, *AA* 77:184, 1975.]

Gefilte Fish (1984) 14 min. Karen Silverstein (FM). Dist: FRIF FR$40, FS$295, VS$160. *As the filmmaker's grandmother lectures on the torturous procedure for chopping gefilte fish, her mother prepares to throw the fish into the Cuisinart. More sacrilegious yet is Silverstein's sister, whose thought is to prepare the traditional dish by opening a jar of Manischewitz premade. A light-hearted look at three generations of gefilte fish makers, it reflects on how we preserve tradition and yet remain true to our modern selves.*

Gelada (1980) 18 min. J. H. Crook (AN). Dist: PSU FR$9.50, FS$215. *Depicts the social, agonistic, sexual, and play behavior of the wild Gelada baboon (Theropithecus gelada) in the remote mountains of Ethiopia. It reveals in particular the complex "harem-based" social organization and describes the way in which social structure changes* *when the distribution of food becomes patchy in the dry season.* [Reveiwed by David Agee Horr, *AA* 75:2005, 1973.]

Gelede: A Yoruba Masquerade (1970) 24 min. Peggy Harper (CON), Francis Speed (FM), University of Ife (PR). Dist: CFSLtd FS$240. *A record of the ritual ceremony and entertainment of a gelede festival that culminates in the midnight appearance of the Efe mask in the market place of the Yoruba town of Ijio on the Dahomey border. The film illustrates the role of the masquerade dancer in a festival designed to appease the witches.* Suggested supplement: Peggy Harper, "The Role of Dance in the Gelede Ceremonies of the Village of Ijio." *Odu: A Journal of West African Studies*, New Series, No. 4. Oxford University Press, Ibadan, Nigeria, 1970. (See also University of Ife Series.)

Gender: The Enduring Paradox (Smithsonian World Series) (1991) 60 min. PBS Video (PR). Dist: PBS VR$49.95. *"In the opening discussion, gender is differentiated from biological sexuality per se. Stereotypes and lines that blur masculinity and femininity are explored, along with the importance of gender as an attracting force assuring the next generation of humans. . . . A supplemental reading list helps us toward thinking of gender in a manner that rises above genetics and physical aspects and toward the melding of psychological differences and a more genuine acceptance of personhood as being of utmost importance."* [From the review by Helen S. Gaevert, *SBF* 27:215, 1991.]

The Gene Engineers (NOVA Series) (1977) 58 min. PBS (PR). Dist: PSU(PCR) FR$26, FS$260. *"Using a combination of animation and microphotography, the basic techniques of gene splicing are depicted. The film also deals with the debate about the supposed dangers of uncontrolled experiments with recombinant DNA. . . . This film would enliven any introductory level course that includes a segment on cell biology and basic human genetics."* [From the review by I. G. Pawson, *AJPA* 54:435, 1981.]

Generations: A Chinese Family (1985) 28 min. Richard Gordon, Carma Hinton, and Kathy Kline (FM). Dist: MWV FR$25, VR$15, FS$350, VS$100. *"Dr. Shen Fasheng is a man of considerable prestige and influence. . . . The doctor and his compatriots would assert that the real measure of his success and the essence of his good fortune is his family."* [From the review by William Graves III, *AA* 89:255–256, 1987.]

Genetics: Man the Creator (1971) 22 min. Dist: PSU FR$14. *Human genetic engineering is the major topic of this film. It includes discussion on cloning, genetic surgery, and sperm banks.*

Les gens du mil (The People of the Millet) (1951–52) 20 min. Jean Rouch (DI). Dist: CFE; DER.

Gentle Winds of Change (1961) 33 min. Marshall Segal (FM, WR). Dist: NYU. *Africa*. [Reviewed by Gregory A. Finnegan, *AA* 76:761, 1974.]

The George Family, New York City (see Six American Families Series)

The Georgia Sea Island Singers (1963–74) 12 min. Arthur Goodwin, Edmund Carpenter, Bess Lomax Hawes, Alan Lomax, Stanley Croner, Isidore Mankofsky, Fred Hudson, and William Varney (FM). Dist: FIM/RF FR$20, FS$125. *Cut off by swamp and sea from the mainland of Georgia, St. Simon's Island was, until recent years, a haven for independent black communities with a language and life of their own. Here spirituals can be heard as they were sung perhaps a century or more ago. This film is a record of a performance of some of the traditional religious activities and music of Southern blacks as performed by the Georgia Sea Island Singers. Included are a spiritual, "Moses"; two 'shouts' (religious dances with singing), "Adam in the Garden Picking Up Leaves," and "Down in the Mire"; and one solo dance, "The Buzzard Lope," which comes from Africa.* [Reviewed by David Evans, *JAF* 89(354):516, 1976.]

Gertrude Blom: Guardian of the Rain Forest 55 min. Cinta Productions (PR). Dist: FL VR$75, VS$445. *"Trudi" Blom, the 86-year-old Swiss-born conversationist, has made protecting the rainforests of Southern Mexico and preserving the culture of its native inhabitants her raison d'être. The film tells the story of her life and the unique relationship she has formed with the Lacandon Indians, descendants of the Maya. Trudi Blom is a living legend. She was the first white woman to explore the rainforest. Her haunting photographs of the Indians are world famous. Together with her husband, archaeologist Frans Blom, she has established a research institute and museum in San Christobal, which has attracted anthropologists, conservationists, and filmmakers. Despite her efforts, more than half the rainforests have been cut or burned in the last 50 years. Erosion and flooding have dramatically increased, forcing the extinction of many plants and animals and lessening crop yields.*

Gestes. French Gestures: A Preliminary Repertory Laurence Wylie (FM). Dist: Laurence Wylie, Harvard University. In English.

Getting the Story (see Consuming Hunger Series)

GETTING TOGETHER: A FILM SERIES IN PERSONAL RELATIONSHIPS Gregory Heimer (PR), Hubert Smith (DI). Dist: EB. [Reviewed by Jeanne Guillemin, *AA* 79:509, 1977.]

• **Teenage Relationships: Vanessa and Her Friends** (1973) 19 min.

• **Parental Roles: Don and Mae** (1972–73) 29 min.

• **Adolescent Responsibilities: Craig and Mark** (1972–73) 28 min.

Ghosts of the Makihuku Henry Materna (FM). *New Guinea Highlands, Coroka and Porgera.* [Reviewed in *RAIN* 22:10, 1977.]

Gibbon Research in a Designed Environment (1973) 11 min. C. R. Carpenter, Lori Baldwin, Geza Teleki (FM). Dist: PSU FR$5.50, FS$120. *Filmed on Halls Island, Bermuda, this film details the observation and maintenance facilities, techniques used to record behavioral observations, and the various behavior patterns of the white-handed gibbon, Hylobates lar.*

Give My Poor Heart Ease: Mississippi Delta Bluesmen (1975) 22 min. William Ferris (DI), Dale Lindquist (FM). Dist: CSF FR$30, FS$326. *Featuring performances and comments by B. B. King, this document captures both the sound and sense of the blues experience. A host of Delta bluesmen talk frankly and in moving detail of their trouble with women, poverty, and the law, providing valuable insights into this music's roots. And the music is here, too, in all its rich variety—James Thomas's stirring rendition of "I Want to Ramble" in a crowded juke joint, B. B. King's powerful performance of "The Thrill is Gone" at Yale University, and a backroom jam session where Cleveland Jones keeps time by scraping a broom handle against the floor. A close look at the blues and the men who sing it.* [Reviewed by David Evans, JAF 90(355):113, 1977.]

Given to a Dance (1985) 57 min. Ron Hess (FM). Dist: UW-SAAC. *In Orissa, the province of India south of Bengal, many vivid performances remain intact.... Some forms, however, passed: most notably the singing and dancing of the maharis or devadasis—literally 'servants of God'.... They talk about their early lives, their training, their peformances in the temple. We see them in their 1983 circumstance."* [From the review by Richard Schechner, AA 88:1040–1042, 1986.]

Glen Canyon Archaeology II (1959) 24 min. Jesse D. Jennings (FM, AN), University of Utah (PR). [Reviewed by Nathalie F. S. Woodbury and Richard B. Woodbury, AA 67:209, 1965.]

Glen Canyon Archaeology III (1960) 24 min. See *Glen Canyon Archaeology II.*

Glooscap 26 min. Dist: FH, VS$89.95, order #DH881. *Glooscap, chief of good and of power, came to earth together with his twin, who had been banished from the skies for his misdeeds. Glooscap created the animals, gave them their names and prayed that they would live in peace and harmony; then he created the first Indians. But his wolfheaded brother was jealous and angry because he could not create anything, and breathed suspicion, fear and the threat of famine into the world. Though the world had been created for goodness, evil was here to stay.*

The Glories of Ancient Benin 15 minutes. Dist: FHS VS$89.95, order #DH3077. *Long long ago, three great hunters came upon a termitary from which emerged a nine-headed genie. A city was built on this spot, beside a pond named Abomiressa Adjaga after the god of the hunters. The Portuguese traders who arrived around 1600 called the city Porto-Novo. Teagmani, son of Pokbon, was king at that time, one of a long line of kings whose heritage is preserved in the Museum of Port-Novo. The carved doors of the Royal Palace provide a window into the political, social, economic and cultural life of the kingdom. Its symbols are as applicable today as they were in King Toffa's day, some of the examples being: the snail, to show that the king must guide his people slowly and patiently, the tortoise to symbolize invulnerability of the nation, and the lizard to symbolize unity. The Museum and the Palace contain a wealth of testimonials and memories of Benin's glorious past.*

God of Japan (1973) 26 min. ABC-TV(PR). Dist: Xerox Films, 245 Long Hill Road, Middletown, CT 06457. *Shot on location in Japan among the most famous Buddhist temples and Shinto Shrines. The historical development of the two dominant Japanese religions—Shinto and Buddhism. A somewhat chronological approach with passing contrasts to Judaeo-Christian development. Extremely broad in its scope and probably too general for an anthropology course.* [Arthur Atlas]

The Goddess and the Computer 58 min. J. Stephen Lansing and Andre Singer (DI). Dist: DER VR$60, VS$400. *The film is about an ancient Balinese belief system called "Agama Tritha" (the religion of holy waters). For centuries, rice farmers in the island of Bali have taken great care not to offend Dewi Danu, the water goddess who lives in the crater lake near the peak of Batur volcano. Toward the end of each rainy season, the farmers send representatives to Ulun Danu Batur, the temple on top of the mountains, to make offerings to the goddess. Developmental agencies have always treated it as a wasteful superstition and tried to replace it with more "improved" methods of growing rice and increasing the crop yield. Lansing and Singer have shown in the film that besides placating the goddess, the island's ancient rituals serve to coordinate the irrigation and planting schedules of a hundred scattered villages.*

God's Country (1985) 87 min. Louis Malle (DR). Dist: NYF FR$175, FS$1295. *"French film director Louis Malle has entered the realm of cultural anthropology and produced a rich ethnograhic portrait of rural America . . . the farm community of Glencoe, Minnesota."* [From the review by Charlotte Cerf, AA 92:267–268, 1990.]

The Gods Must Be Crazy (1980) 109 min. Jamie Uys (FM). Dist: 20CF *"This slapstick South African parable of innocence lost opens in the Kalahari Desert, where a group of cheerful Bushmen lead simple lives, foraging and drinking the morning dew.... Harmony is disrupted: a soft drink bottle lands in their midst. At first put to good use, ... the bottle soon stirs unfamiliar emotions: jealousies erupt."* The film includes several clear metaphors: *"The episode replicates in perfect miniature the political reality.... [But] like other ethno-fiction films, the apparently harmless humor of Gods conceals disturbing real-world implications. Apartheid finds legitimation.... The film perpetuates the myth that Bushmen are blissfully simple creatures."* [From the review by Toby Alice Volkman, AA 87:482–483, 1985.]

Gogodala: A Cultural Revival? (Films from Papua New Guinea Series) (1983) 58 min. Chris Owen (DI), The Institute of Papua New Guinea Studies (PR). Dist: DER FR$80, FS$800, VS$400. *Examines the implications of the Australian colonial era for the Gogodala people of the Fly River Delta, Western Papua New Guinea. Excessive missionary zeal, tolerated and encouraged by the government, contributed to the almost total destruction of Gogodala art and culture. More recently, an indirect grant from the Australian government has enabled the people to reconstruct a traditional longhouse, along with a new meaning and function: as a cultural center.* [Reviewed by Terence E. Hays, AA 84:989–990, 1982.]

Gold: The Sacred Metal (1980) 17 min. Lewis W. Bushnell (WR, PR), Jeri Sopanen (CA, DI), Rena Productions (PR). Dist: IFF FR$35, FS$300. *For gold, the conquistadores waged wars and, with their superior weapons, defeated the Latin American Indians. They looted graves and melted many of the golden treasures they found into bullion. Descendents of these Indians, the Koguis, still survive in small villages in Colombia, high in the Sierra Nevadas. Nobody speaks of gold, but twice a year they dance with golden masks, near a holy lake. Today, local treasure seekers called Hauqueros continue to dig for art objects, which they occasionally discover by following almost invisible markings on the ground indicating a grave site. In Colombia, the crafting of gold continues in small workshops where exact reproductions of ancient treasures are made, using the lost wax process. As we study these golden pieces, we learn more of the original craftsmen and of their lost cultures of long ago.*

Goldwidows: Women in Lesotho (1991) 52 min. Don Edkins, Ute Hall, and Mike Schlomer (FM). Dist: FRIF VR$75, VS$390. *"Goldwidows" are women whose husbands work as migrant gold miners in South Africa—often without returning home for five years at a time. It focuses on four Basotho women of Lesotho, a small mountainous country within South Africa, economically dependent on South African industry. Although most Basotho men, and often up to 60 percent at one time, have worked as migrant laborers in South Africa's gold mines, apartheid laws forbid these women and their children to enter South Africa. They live as practical widows, three in a remote mountain village, while the fourth, Sheila Nkueve, has moved to the capital, Maseru, to look for work. Each tells of her life, coping alone, caught in the inhuman web of South Africa's oppressive system.*

Goodbye Old Man (1977) 70 min. David MacDougall (FM), Bryan Butler (SR), Australian Institute of Aboriginal Studies (PR). Dist: UCEMC FR$59, VR$59, FS$800, VS$560, order #10295. *A bereavement ceremony of the Tiwi of Melville Island of the coast of Australia. Among the Tiwi, it was the traditional practice to hold a pukumani ceremony to put to rest the spirit of a recently deceased person and remove the danger and state of imbalance (called pukumani) caused by a death. These ceremonies began to wane in the early and mid-20th century but have seen a remarkable revival in recent years. In 1975 the Mangatopi family of Snake Bay asked that a film be made of the ceremony to be held for the deceased head of their family—an old man who had organized a similar ceremony for his own son (see Mourning for Mangatopi), and who had included the making of a new film in his dying wishes. Goodbye Old Man is the result. It is narrated by one of the participants and it emphasizes the surrounding social and family milieu.* [Reviewed by Robert Mishler, *SBF* 16:278, 1981.] Related reading: C. W. M. Hart and A. R. Pilling, *The Tiwi of northern Australia*, New York, Holt, 1960. J. C. Goodale, "The Tiwi of Northern Australia." In: *Funeral Customs the World Over*, R. W. Habertsen, ed. 1963.

The Good Woman of Bangkok [Reviewed by Martina Reiker, *VISA* 9:116–122, 1993.]

La Goumbe des jeunes noceurs (The Goumbe of the Young Revellers) (1965) 30 min. Jean Rouch (DI), Centre National de la Recherche Scientifique and Films de la Pleiade (PR). Dist: CFE; DER. *La Goumbe is a voluntary association of young people from Upper Volta who work in Abidjan, Ivory Coast.*

Goree: Door of No Return 30 min. Dist: FHS VS$149, order #DH3064. *Goree Islands is where the slave ships anchored, cramming their holds with Africans to be shipped across the Atlantic to work the fields and tend their "owners" throughout the Western Hemisphere; Goree Island is where the enslaved Africans were held until the ships were ready to receive them. This film tells the history of the slave trade: the arrival of the first Europeans, the origin of slavery in the Americas, the development of Goree as a center of the expanding slave trade, the wealthy merchant women who controlled the slave trade on the Island. Today, the Island is a monument to an ignoble past. The program visits the colonial buildings, the homes of the slave traders still standing, the trading warehouse called the house of slaves, and the infamous door of no return, the door through which most of the America's enslaved people passed on their way to the New World.*

Gorilla (1981) 59 min. National Geographic Society (PR). Dist: NGS FS$595, VS$545.

Gourd Men of New Guinea 22 min. Dist: IUAVC FR$10.75. *Dramatizes the habits, culture, and dress of one of the most primitive tribes of New Guinea. Pictures scenes from the dance of the dead. Describes the food and shows eating habits of the natives. Shows the gourd men dressed for warfare with their bows and arrows.* Warning: Several scenes include semi-nude natives, both male and female.

Granton Trawler (1934) 11 min. John Grierson (DI). Dist: AB FR$7.50; MOMA FR$10. *A short study of Scottish fishermen at work with their trawler nets. Grierson doesn't content himself with pictures of men fishing; he used the camera to probe into the social conditions that shape these men and to clarify their role in a larger world.*

Grass (1925) 66 minutes. Silent. B/W. Merian C. Cooper, Marguerite Harrison, and E. Schoedsack (FM). Dist: MFV VS$39.95, order #MILE002; FCE FR$85, FS$475; UCEMC FR$20; MOMA FR$30. *One of the first of the documentary ethnographical films. Cooper and Schoedsack made Chang (about a village in northern Thailand), and the first great primate film, King Kong. The first part of Grass is concerned with the expedition's incidental wanderings in the Near East, looking for a dramatic subject. They finally find it in the yearly migrations (transhumance) of the Bakhtiari tribe of southern Iran. The core of the film shows the trek of the tribe with its herd across a river and over a mountain range in their quest for grass. Twice a year, more than 50,000 people and half a million animals surmount seemingly impossible obstacles, including torrential rivers and 15,000 foot high mountains, to take their herds to pasture.* Selected supplements: Fredrik Barth, *Nomads of South Persia*. Little, Brown, 1961 (200 miles south of Bakhtiari). Carleton S. Coon, *Caravan: The Story of the Middle East* (revised edition). Pp. 218–219, Holt, Rinehart and Winston, 1962 (brief discussion of the Bakhtiari and the film). Merian C. Cooper, *Grass*. Putnam, 1925 (foreword by William Beebe with 64 illustrations from photographs by Ernest B. Schoedsack; the popular account of the making of the film). [Reviewed by Asen Balikci, *AA* 82:229–230, 1980.]

Gravel Springs Fife and Drum   10 min. Bill Ferris (FM), David Evans (SR), Judy Peiser (ED). Dist: CSF FR$20, FS$185. *Gravel Springs Fife and Drum focuses on the northwest Mississippi community of Gravel Springs. Othar Turner, leader of a musical group, works on his farm, makes a cane-fife, and travels to a rural picnic where he and his band play music for their friends. The unusual fife and drum music they perform closely resembles traditional West African music.* [Reviewed by John Greenway, *AA* 75:591–592, 1973. Thornas A. Green, *AA* 77:473, 1975.]

Graveyard of the Gulf   (1975) 35 min. Earl Miller (DI). Dist: Visual Instruction Bureau of the University of Texas at Austin, Drawer W, University Station, Austin, TX 78712, FR$16. *"Presents the early explorations of the Texas Antiquities Committee off Padre Island in 1973. The objects of this search were four Spanish treasure ships blown off course into the Gulf of Mexico during a severe storm in 1554 and presumably wrecked near Padre Island. This film deals with the discovery of one of these ships and the recovery and preservation of artifacts removed from it."* [From the review by Robert L. Hohlfelder, *ARCH* 36(1):62–64, 1983. Reviewed by George F. Bass, *AA* 77:911, 1975.]

The Great Dinosaur Discovery   25 min. John Linton (DI). Dist: BYU FR$38.50, FS$385. *Provides the viewer with a glimpse of some of the fieldwork done at Dry Mesa quarry, high up on the Uncompahgre Plateau in western Colorado. This film captures the mood of excitement surrounding the discovery of two new species of dinosaurs.* [From the review by Wayne I. Anderson, *AJPA* 60:411, 1983.]

THE GREAT PLAINS TRILOGY, PART II. NOMAD AND INDIAN: EARLY MAN ON THE PLAINS   29 min. each. Jack McBride (FM), University of Nebraska (PR). Dist: Instructional Media Center, University Extension Division, University of Nebraska, Lincoln, NB 68508. [Reviewed by John R. Cole, *AA* 76:207, 1974.]

- Man, Animal, Climate and Earth
- Plainsmen of the Past
- The Early Hunters
- The Foragers
- From Nomad to Villager
- The Prehistoric Farmers
- The Dawn of Plains History
- The Rise of the Horsemen Pawnee
- Men of Men
- Tribes of the Eastern Plains
- Displaced Peoples
- Winnebago and Ponca
- The Fighting Cheyennes
- Dakota Wars and Reservation Life

The Great Spirit   27 min. Dist: CBC VS$109, order #Y87-7402. *A rare glimpse of the sacred places, rituals, and ceremonies of Canada's native people as they rediscover their ancient religious heritage and renew their sense of Indian identity.*

Great Tree Has Fallen   (1973) 22 min. Dist: IUAVC FR$10.25, FS$320, VS$195; UCEMC FR$25. *Portrays the grandeur of the eight-day funeral of the King of the Ashanti Nation in Ghana and documents the traditional practices, dances, music, dress, and symbols of position that bind the nation together.*

Grèce et Rome en Provence   40 min. Dist: FACSEA FR$16. *Diggings at St-Blaise and Clanum, 1967.* French only.

GREECE, 478–336 B.C.   (1978) 22 min. BBC (PR). Dist: MG. *"These seven films were developed as part of an interdisciplinary course entitled Greece: 478–336 B.C., first offered in 1979 by the British Open University.... The filmmakers employ such effective didactic techniques as superimposing a drawing of a restored monument upon a view of its foundation, or successively dissolving one amphora profile into another to illustrate the modification of contours over two centuries. The scripts are packed with accurate information and make generous use of ancient testimonia and works of art."* [From the review by Homer Thompson, *ARCH* 35(5):74, 1982.] Films include:

- Games and Festivals
- Acropolis of Athens
- Ships and Seafaring
- The Theatre
- Land and Sea
- The Agora of Athens
- Sculpture: The Human Figure

GREEK CELEBRATIONS SERIES   (1985) Alexandra Anthony and Mary Vouras (FM). Dist: Greek Celebrations, 5 Hastings Square, Cambridge, MA 02139; (617) 492-2247. *"The three films in this series show various annual festivals conducted in several Greek villages during the summer of 1982. Each festival marks a particular saint's commemorative day in the Orthodox calendar."* [From the review by Susan Buck Sutton, *AA* 89:256–257, 1987.]

- **Amarantos** 20 min. VR$35, FS$350. *Shows the festival surrounding the Dormition of the Virgin as carried out in a small, mountain village in northern Greece."* [From the review by Susan Buck.]

- **Agrapha** 30 min. FR$75, FS$500, VS$35. *"Shows another festival devoted to the Virgin in a different but nearby mountain village."* [From the review by Susan Buck.]

- **Aspasia** 30 minutes. FR$75, FS$500, VS$35. *"A musician who plays at such festivals: Aspasia Papadaki, the first woman to play the lyra professionally on the island of Crete."* [From the review by Susan Buck.]

Greek Vases   A series of 200 color slides by William Reid, Jr. Dist: Logos Signum Publications, 19122 Lindsay Land, Huntington Beach, CA 92646. $200. *"There are five sets of* *slides with views of 192 vases from 17 museums in the United States and Europe."* [See the review by Frances Van Keuren, *ARCH* 35(3):74, 1982.]

The Green Puzzle of Altamira (1990) 52 min. Lode Cafmeyer (FM). Dist: Lode Cafmeyer, Berthoutstraat 18, 2600 Berchem, Belgium. *The Kayapo Indians, under the leadership of chief Raoni, mobilize international support to halt the destruction of their homeland, the Brazilian rain forest. With the help of individuals such as pop-star Sting, the Kayapo organize an important meeting in Altamira (Central Brazil) to draw attention to their plight.*

The Greenberg Family, Mill Valley, California (see Six American Families Series)

• **Grenada: Land of Spice** (1982) 17 min. Museum of Modern Art of Latin America (PR). Dist: Museum of Modern Art of Latin America, Organization of American States, 1889 F. St., NW, Washington, DC 20006; (202) 789-6021, FS$170, VS$68. *Presents performances of traditional music and dance from Grenada and Carriacou.* [Reviewed by George M. Epple, *AA* 88:263–264, 1986.]

Grenada: Portrait of a Revolution (1982) 28 min. Joanne Kelley and Skip Sweeney (FM). Dist: Cinewest, 655 4th Ave., Suite 36, San Diego, CA 92101; (619) 238-0066, VR$75 VS$250. *Presents the Peoples Revolutionary Government programs and "a variety of views on the accomplishments and negative impacts of the NJM platform.... A major part of the film is divided into segments focused on specific issues: The Uprising against Gairy's Policies, The Economy, Social Programs, Tourism, Cuban Influence, Elections, and Detention."* [From the review by George M. Epple, *AA* 88:263–264, 1986.]

Grenada: The Future Coming toward Us (1983) 55 min. John Douglas, Carmen Ashhurst, and Samori Marksman (DI), Caribbean Resource Institute and New York Cinema (PR). Dist: CG FR$100, FS$900, VS$750. *"The film was completed just five days before the 'coup' of October (1983). ... Alternates between cuts of interviews with members of the Bishop government of Grenadians who appear to be part of the New Jewel Movement (the political party of the PRG) and scenes of everyday life. Considerable testimony is given to support the claims of progress in a variety of government programs to improve health care, agriculture, education, social conditions, and opportunities for employment. The film is an excellent documentation of the goals, aspirations and acomplishments of the PRG."* [From the review by George M. Epple, *AA* 88:263–264, 1986.]

Grey Owl 56 min. Dist: CBC VS$109, order #X4J-7204. *An account of the major events of the turbulent life of Grey Owl, an Englishman who claimed he was a Canadian Indian. It was not until his death at age 50 that Grey Owl's true identity was revealed, and history has yet to decide whether he was a glory-seeking impostor or a great pioneer naturalist and forerunner of many contemporary attitudes toward environmental preservation.*

Grey Owl's Little Brother 10 min. Dist: FCE FR$17, FS$95. *Grey Owl is an Indian of the Ojibway tribe who reared a young beaver until it was full grown at which time he released it to live and mate in natural life. At the time this film was made, the beaver would respond to a call from Grey Owl and come to the boat.*

Greystoke: The Legend of Tarzan Warner Brothers Motion Pictures (PR). Dist: WHV. *"The rearing of a human hero by wild animals is a theme in mythology which is at least 2,500 years old... The most famous such hero has been Tarzan, the 'ape man' which was the creation of Edgar Rice Burroughs.... This is an innovative addition to the genre of Tarzan films... It is possible to use this film in anthropological teaching, particularly in courses that deal with primate behavior or man's place in nature."* [From the review by Edward E. Hunt, *AJPA* 87:243–244, 1992. Reviewed by Jane Lasswell-Hoff, *AJPA* 66:347–348, 1085.]

Le griot badye (Badye, the Storyteller) (ca. 1970s) 15 min. Jean Rouch (DI), Centre National de la Recherche Scientifique, Comite du Film Ethnographique and Inoussa Ousseini (PR). Dist: CFE; DER. *A traditional singer employing birdsong as a source for the music he uses to accompany his storytelling.*

Gripping Beast 15 min. Holger Phillipsen and Th. Ramskou (PR). Dist: DIO free loan. *An animated film made in Denmark tracing the development of the Viking "Gripping Beast" art motif from its naturalistic beginnings to its late, highly schematic form.*

Grits (1988) 28 min. Stan Woodward (DI). Dist: ECP. *This film travels the South asking the question "Do you eat Grits?" the answer becomes a journey through the hearts, minds, and stomachs of the Southland, collecting a host of bizarre grits recipes along the way, including a frozen "grit sickle," kosher grits in a Mexican restaurant, and a grits souffle whipped up by the* New York Times *Food Editor Craig Claiborne.*

GROOTE EYLANDT SERIES (1969) Alice Moyle (Dl), Don Hauser, Rod Power (CA), Australian Institute of Aboriginal Studies (PR). Dist: AIAS. Relevant anthropological literature available upon request from the Australian Institute of Aboriginal Studies: Explanatory leaflet (including map of area). Report to the Australian Council for the Arts by Alice Moyle and Elphine Allen, includes background of project, details of filming, performers' names, diagrams of dance area and camera placement, notes on the singers, didjeridu players, clapperboard signals, and details of each dance—duration, etc.

• **8.3: Aboriginal Dances** 30 min. *Twelve dances from Groote Eylandt, Northern Territory, were recorded from two camera positions for purposes of music and dance notation. Dances performed by the Wanindilyaugwa group and the Nunggubuyu group from Rose River.*

• **8.4: Five Brolga Dances** 15 min. *Five dances portraying the movements of Brolga birds are performed by Nunggubuyu men from Rose River, eastern Arnhem Land. The dance music consists of related Brolga songs performed by stick-beating singers with didjeridu accompaniment. Recorded from two camera angles for purposes of dance and music study.*

• 8.6: Eight Aboriginal Songs with Didjeridu Accompaniment 20 min. *Songs performed on Groote Eylandt, Northern Territory, recorded for the purpose of music study. Titles of the song items are superimposed on film. No spoken commentary. Dances performed by Nunggubuyu and Wanindilyaugwa groups.*

Le Grotte de l'Hortus (1973) Jean Pierre Baux (Dl), Henry de Lumley (AN), Service du Film de Recherche Scientifique (PR). Dist: SFRS. *Early Wurm environment in the French cave system.* [Reviewed by Harvey M. Bricker, AA 77:917, 1975.]

Ground Truth: Archaeology in the City (1988) 28 min. Richard E. Robinson (FM). Dist: Silverwood Films, P.O. Box 4640, Philadelphia, PA 19127; (215) 482-4992, FR$100, FS$400, VS$85. *"The 'Ground Truth' of this production's title is an archaeological term referring to the confirmation of the written record by archaeological excavation. This tape chronicles a project that began in downtown Philadelphia in 1980 near the corner of 8th and Vine streets when workmen on a city project uncovered human remains."* [From the review by Peter S. Allen, ARCH 43(2):64–67, 1990.]

Group Concepts of Human Birth (1958) 30 min. NET(PR). Dist: IUAVC FR$9.50. *Compares the reactions of Americans, the Manus of the Admiralty Islands, and the Kiriwina of the Trobriand Islands when exposed to the crisis of human birth. Uses dance routines and originally scored music to portray cultural differences in the selection of the birth place, the reactions of husband and wife, and the ways in which a child is delivered.*

Group Patterns of Courtship Behavior (1958) 30 min. NET(PR). Dist: IUAVC FR$9.50. *Uses dance routines and originally scored music to portray differences in personal contact between males and females as sanctioned by three societies. Describes differences in opportunity for courtship, the patterns of association that emerge, and the relationship of these experiences to marriage. Compares Americans, the Bantu-speakers of Africa, and the Muria of central India.*

Group Training in Basic Skills 30 min. NET(PR). Dist: IUAVC FR$9.50. *Uses dance routines and originally scored music to portray cultural differences in training children for group participation. Emphasizes motivating interests, specific skills taught, and the finished product that emerges from the experiences. Shows how the role of the child varies according to the economic level of his society. Compares the cultures of the American, the Tallensi of Africa, and the Balinese.*

Group Ways of Channelizing Aggression 30 min. NET(PR). Dist: IUAVC FR$9.50. *Uses dance routines and originally scored music to portray methods of directing aggression in children. Compares Americans, the Kwoma of Guinea, and the Alorese of the Dutch East Indies. Shows the creation of frustration in children and the direction and utilization of aggressive responses. Explains the types of stimuli that frustrate children.*

Growing Up Female 50 min. Julia Reichart, James Klein (FM). Dist: NDF. *Socialization of American women.* [Reviewed by Nancy Chodorow, AA 79:206, 1977.]

Growth and Development of Children (1961) 28 min. J. M. Tanner, R. H. Whitehouse (PR). Dist: BAVI. [Reviewed by A. F. Roche, AA 80:513–514, 1978.]

Guambianos (1974) 20 min. Ronald R. Duncan and Gloria S. Duncan (FM). Dist: RJD FR$25, FS$200. *This film gives a basic description of the Guambiano Indian group, including family organization, economic patterns, cultural identity, and ceremonies. They occupy a reservation in two high valleys of the Andes in southern Colombia. In the last generation, they have gone through a period of rapid social and economic change that is striking among Colombian small farmers. The film describes them currently and discusses the role of cultural and group identity as a factor in their recent social change experience. The group has severe population pressure on the land within the reservation, and they are involved in continuing efforts to rebuy, reclaim, or invade land that was previously lost.* [Reviewed by Joanne Rappaport, AA 87:983–985, 1985.]

Guardians of the Sacred Flame (see Crossroads of Civilization Series)

Guatemalan Pottery (1987) 60 min. Claudia Feldmar (PR). Dist: PSU VR$17.50, VS$190, order #60638. *This program follows potters through the entire traditional process of pottery making in six different Guatemalan villages: Santa Apolonia (where the potter is the only artisan who still works with pre-Columbian techniques), San Luis Jilotepeque, Chinaulta, Rabinal, Totonicapan, and Antigua. Also documented are the individual styles and techniques of the potter in each town.*

Guellala: A Potter's Village in Tunisia 50 min. Sophie Ferchiou (PR). Dist: FL VR$75, VS$445. *This film documents a lifestyle and craft tradition that dates back to the time of Homer. The potters on this island of Jerba produce a massive array of pottery using the same methods as the ancients did. We watch them mining the clay and preparing it for the potters. Then we see the master craftsmen throwing and handbuilding a variety of classic shapes that are exported all over the Mediterranean. This film documents many other aspects of village life, including farming methods, women's roles, and wedding ceremonies. It also investigates the impact of tourism on the social, cultural, and economic life of the village.* [Reviewed by Gloria London, AA 92:849–850, 1990.]

Guelmambi: A River of Gold (1972) 23 min. Ronald J. Duncan and Nina S. Friedmann (FM). Dist: RJD FR$25, FS$200. *This film describes family organization, residence, and subsistence patterns of isolated Black miners in the tropical rain forest of the Pacific lowlands in Colombia. Corporate family groups are owners of mining rights to river terraces in a unique form of family organization not previously described in the New World. The riverine settlements are organized around those family groups. The film shows the folk-mining process, which includes a mixture of pre-Colombian and colonial mining techniques. Life in the* *riverine settlement is shown in detail. This film is based on five years of anthropological research and analysis by Nina S. Friedmann of the Instituto Colombiano de Antropologiá.*

Gui Dao—On the Way: A Station of the Yangzi 59 min. Georges Dufaux (FM), National Film Board of Canada (PR). Dist: DER FR$60, VR$50, FS$775, VS$400. *A penetrating look at urban life in contemporary China, this film takes us into the rhythms of the great train station in Wuchang, a city of four million in Hubei province, 240 kilometers south of Beijing. We watch long lines of passengers guided and exhorted to be orderly by station employees, who win red flags for their neat rows of travelers. Young and old workers talk about their daily lives, the impact of the revolution, and their jobs. We witness the retirement party of the 60-year-old Lin Pingjie, celebrated with thermoses of tea, drums and cymbals, and resounding speeches. At home, Lin Pingjie, his daughter who will replace him at the station, and others in his family discuss their aspirations.* [Reviewed by Charlotte Ikels, *AA* 87:739–741, 1985.]

Guitar Craft (1977) 19 min. Rob Williams (PR). Dist: Film Fair Communications, Box 1729, 10900 Ventura Boulevard, Studio City, CA 91604; (818) 985-0244, FR$30, FS$350, VS$89. *Narration describes what the viewer sees.* [Reviewed by Melanie L. Sovine, *AA* 89:522–525, 1987.]

Guma the Snake 26 min. Alejo Santa Maria and Cristina Echavarria (FM). Dist: ETNOS. *Beginning with a beautiful myth of origin, this documentary leads into an interesting everyday account, which takes place in a Kogui and Arsario Indian village in the remote mountain valleys of the Sierra Nevada de Santa Marta (North Colombia). Through an unusual construction of a communal house, in which all members participate, it weaves technology, social organization, and philosophy, with a rare recording of the symbolical and practical uses of coca leaves in this indigenous community.*

Gumbo: The Mysteries of Creole and Cajun Cooking 28.5 min. Stephen Duplantier and Marc Porter (FM). Dist: Stephen Duplantier, 1220 N. Gayoso St., New Orleans, LA 70119. [Reviewed by Bruce Lane, *JAF* 94(317):131–137, 1981.]

Gunabibi—An Aboriginal Fertility Cult (1971) 30 min. Australian Institute of Aboriginal Studies (PR). Dist: UCEMC order #8119, FR$35, FS$410. *The most spectacular ceremony of the Arnhem Land tribes, operatic in its scale and the richness of its symbols, myth, and drama, the Gunabibi is a vital living cult today. The events of the last climactic night and the following morning are shown; they take place mainly around a curved pit said to be the womb of the fertility mother Gunabibi. The symbolism is strongly sexual throughout; phallic "Possum dances" are performed and two towering phallic emblems are built. These serpent emblems are finally flung down across the pit; this union of symbols expresses the duality of sexual life. Young men are initiated into the mysteries of the cult and are then said to be "born again"; this is dramatized physically by the men painting themselves with blood to symbolize rebirth.* [Reviewed by L. R. Hiatt, *AA* 74:1023–1024, 1972.] Restricted use. This film contains material of a secret/sacred nature and should only be screened for study purposes by appropriate groups.

Gunsmith of Williamsburg (see Colonial Williamsburg Series)

Guri: The Young Gaucho (1981) 29 min. Eduardo Darino (DR). Dist: IFF FS$450. *"Guri is the recreated story of a gaucho boy's initiation into manhood . . . that captures little of the reality of life on the pampas."* [From the review by Winifred Lambrecht, *SBF* 18:36, 1982.]

Gurkha Country (1967) 19 min. Patricia Hitchcock (CA), John T. Hitchcock (AN), John Hitchcock and Pat Hitchcock (PR). Dist: IFB FR$19.75, FS$275, VS$210; PSU(PCR) order #2176K; UCEMC. *Shot in the Himalayas of central Nepal, the film begins with the problem posed by the fieldwork: comparison between a relatively low and sedentary Magar village where irrigated rice cannot be grown, and a much higher Magar village—too high for rice-growing and much more mobile, because in summertime most of its population moves with livestock to alpine pastures. After showing the search for the second village, the film portrays steps in the fieldwork there: obtaining permission to stay, setting up a school as attempted recompense, taking a census, using still photography to record gestures and material culture, learning the culture while participating in village activities, and so forth. The movement is from fairly easy to more difficult topics of research as the anthropologist and his wife become more familiar to the villagers and more a part of their life.* Suggested supplements: John T. Hitchcock, *The Magars of Banyan Hill.* Holt, Rinehart and Winston, 1966. John T. Hitchcock, "A Nepalese Shamanism and the Classic Inner Asian Tradition." *History of Religions* 7(2):149–158, 1967. John T. Hitchcock, "Fieldwork in Gurkha Country." *Being an Anthropologist,* George Spindler and Louise Spindler, eds. Holt, Rinehart and Winston. John T. Hitchcock, *Sickle and Khukuri.*

Gypsies Sing Long Ballads (1982) 30 min. John Cohen (FM). Dist: Hazardous Films, RD #1, Tompkins Corners, Putnam Valley, NY 10579; (914) 528-6453. *"This film is about ballad singing among Scottish Tinkers or Travellers, a small population living on the fringe of Scottish society who have retained ballads that have long since died out in mainstream Scottish society."* [From the review by George Gmelch, *AA* 88:264–265, 1986.]

Gypsies: The Other Americans (1984) 50 min. Eric Metzgar (DI). Dist:CCC; Triton Films, 516 Orleans Ave., Long Beach, CA 90814; (213) 498-2662, FR$35, FS$520 (26-min. version: FR$20, FS$260) *Celebrated ethnographic film about a tribe of ethnic gypsies (ROM) living in Los Angeles, California. Shows traditional customs and daily activities of this often stereotyped and little understood minority. The wedding of two 13-year-old children, complete with timeless customs, seems to belie any discussion of change, but life is changing for these people: there is less wandering, children are receiving better educations, and men's and women's roles are adapting more and more to American lifestyles. Narrated by a Gypsy man and wife, subtitles are provided when dialogue is in Romanes—the Gypsy language.*

The Gypsy Camp Vanishes into the Blue (Tabor ollhodit webo) (1976) 102 min. Emil Loteanu (Dl). Dist: AB FS$250. *The Moldavian legend of the daring Gypsy horse thief Loiko Zobar and the proud Radda, first written down by Maxim Gorky in his story 'Makar Chudra', is the basis for this feature by the young directors in the multinational Soviet cinema. Old folksongs performed by the singers of the Romen (The Moscow Gypsy Theatre), fill the soundtrack. Gypsy dances punctuate the action, notably the famous "dance of the shoulders," which Loteanu shoots in slow motion, giving a dreamlike quality to the gypsy rhythms. Shot in the green rolling Transcarpathian steppe, it mixes ethnographically fascinating images with a tragic romance of two star-crossed lovers, destroyed by their mutual need for freedom.*

Gypsy Yodeler (1978) 9 min. Ron Taylor (PR). Dist: Ron Taylor, 505 Euclid, Boulder, CO 80302; (303) 444-3340, FR$45, FS$250, VS$175. *"Present[s] the personality and personal history of the folk artist as ethnographic material that stands on its own."* [From the review by Melanie L. Sovine, AA 89:522–5, 1987.]

Haa Shagoon (1983) 29 min. Joseph Kawaky (FM). Dist: UCEMC FR$38, FS$460, VS$345. *"Documents a Chilkoot Tlingit peace ceremony conducted along the Chilkoot River. . . . [T]hey perform the peace ceremony to encourage a positive, mutual relationship with their White neighbors."* [From the review by Mark S. Fleisher, AA 86:1062, 1984. Reviewed by Peter S. Allen, SBF 20:41, 1984.]

Hadar 75: Field Techniques (1976) 32 min. Daniel Cavillon, Michele Cavillon, and Bernard Favre (DI), Centre National de la Recherche Scientifique, France (PR). Dist: French Institute/Alliance Francaise, 22 E. 60th St., New York, NY 10022. *This film "chronicle(s) the field activities of the International Afar research Expedition in the Afar Depression of northern Ethiopia during the field season of 1975."* [From the review by Noel T. Boaz, AA 86:800, 1984.]

The Hadza: The Food Quest of an East African Hunting and Gathering Tribe (1966) 40 min. Sean Hudson (FM), James Woodburn (AN). Dist: James Woodburn, Dept. of Anth., London School of Economics, Univ. of London, Houghton Street, London WC2A 2AE, England, FS$650; Pitt. *The film is about the Eastern Hadza, a small nomadic hunting and gathering tribe living in 1,000 square miles of bush country in the rift valley south of Ngorongoro in Northern Tanzania. With their own distinctive click language and a culture that is unlike that of their agricultural and pastoral neighbors, they remained remarkably independent until 1964, three years after the film was shot, when they were settled by the Tanzanian government. The film was made after the completion of three years of social anthropological field research by James Woodburn. It seeks to give a clear view of the hunting and gathering way of life in this area, which is so important for students of human evolution. The mode of subsistence is shown in some detail and the film emphasizes that in spite of the apparent barrenness of the country, adequate supplies of food can always be obtained without undue effort. Men actually spend more time gambling for arrows than hunting and gathering.* [Reviewed by B. Benedict, Man 2(1):160, 1967. A. M. Hughes, New Scientist 33(532):284, 1967; I. Devore, AA 74:1024–1025, 1972.] Suggested supplements: B. Cooper, "The Kindiga." *Tanganyika Notes and Records* 27:8–15, 1949. L. Kohl-Larsen, *Wildbeuter in Ostafrica, die Tindiga, ein Jager-und Sammlervolk*. Reimer, 1958. M. Sahlins, "The Original Affluent Society." In: *Stone Age Economics*, Aldine, 1972, pp. 1–39. J. C. Woodburn, "The Future of the Tindiga." *Tanganyika Notes and Records* 58159:269–273, 1962. J. C. Woodburn, "An Introduction to Hadza Ecology" and "Stability and Flexibility in Hadza Residential Groupings." In: *Man the Hunter*. R. B. Lee and I. DeVore, eds. Aldine, 1968, pp. 49–55, 103–110. J. C. Woodburn, *Hunters and Gatherers: The Material Culture of the Nomadic Hadza*. The British Museum, 1970. J. C. Woodburn, "Ecology, Nomadic Movement and the Composition of the Local Group among Hunters and Gatherers: An East African Example and Its Implications." *Man, Settlement and Urbanism*. P. J. Ucko et al., eds. Duckworth, 1972, pp. 193–206. J. C. Woodburn, "Minimal Politics: The Political Organization of the Hadza of North Tanzania." *Politics in Leadership*. W. A. Shack and P. S. Cohen, eds. Clarendon Press, 1979, pp. 244–266. J. C. Woodburn, "Hunters and Gatherers Today and Reconstruction of the Past." *Soviet and Western Anthropology*. E. Gellner, ed. Duckworth, 1980, pp. 95–117.

Haida Carver 12 min. National Film Board of Canada (PR). Dist:IFB FR$15, FS$225, VS$195. *The Haida Indians of the Queen Charlotte Islands of Canada's Pacific coast were great carvers of totem poles. Today their rich heritage of folklore and legend is preserved in argillite rather than wood. A young Haida artist travels over a hundred miles to the source of the soft, dark slate. He takes only a small chunk for it hardens quickly. He carves it in the manner his grandfather taught him. This grandson is unusual, for many of his generation shun carving and choose fishing or lumbering as their work. A close examination of several highly polished miniature totems closes this revealing look at a vanishing art form.*

Hail Mother Kali: A Tribute to the Traditions and Healing Arts Brought to Guyana by Indentured Madrasi Labourers (1988) 60 min. Stephanos Stephanides (FM). Dist: Singer-Sharrette Productions, 336 Main Street, P.O. Box 68, Rochester, MI 48063; (313) 731-5199, VS$175. *"This video traces three days and nights of a Hindu puja (healing ceremony) in the canefields of Berbice, Guyana. . . . The ceremony documented is the annual Big Puja at the Blairmont Kali Temple."* [From the review by Judith Johnson, AA 91:531–533, 1989.]

Hail Umbanda (1988) 46 min. Jose Araujo (DI). Dist: UCEMC FR$60, FS$920, VS$385, order #11365. *This unique, insider's view of Umbanda, the fastest-growing religion in Brazil, shows the cult's raucous pageantry and public festivals as well as its more esoteric, exotic, and rarely seen ceremonies. A blending of Catholicism with traditional African and Native American religions, Umbanda is characterized by ritualistic sacrifices and offerings and altered states of consciousness described by devotees as possession by numerous authorities and practitioners, but focuses on* one *Painho* or *Pai de Santo (Father of the Gods), who introduces and explains many different aspects of Umbanda.* [Reviewed by Sidney M. Greenfield, *AA* 91:529–530, 1989.]

Haitian Song   (Caribbean Culture Series) (1982) 52 min. Karen Kramer (FM), Ira Lowenthal (CT). Dist: DER FR$90, FS$900, VR$60, VS$500; KK FR$85, FS$650. *Haitian Song is a lyrical portrait of life in a small village in rural Haiti. The film focuses on the "rituals" that compose the texture of everyday life: getting water from the river; making rope by hand from sisal; cooking rice and beans in an outdoor kitchen; planting and harvesting. The film follows Gustav and Zilmen, a man and a woman, through the cycle of their day and follows the larger community through the cycles of the week: the market on Tuesdays; the cockfight on Saturday; the dance on Sunday. The film is narrated totally in Creole (with English subtitles) by Haitian peasants and interwoven throughout with haunting songs, the film evokes a feeling of rural village life.* [Reviewed by Lois E. Wilcken, *AA* 84:978–979, 1982.]

Hajari Bhand of Rajasthan: Jester without Court   40 min. John and Ulrike Emigh (DI). Dist: DER VR$50, VS$250. *Hajari Bhand of Chittorgarh, Rajasthan, is reknown in the nearby courts, villages, and towns of Mewar for his skill as a "bahurupiya" (a wandering mimic performing mostly comic routines). This videotape highlights Hajari Bhand's assumption of 20 different disguises and his performances of various routines in village settings, interspersed with interview material. Bhands in India perform several functions for their society. Acting as wild cards in an otherwise carefully labeled deck, they entertain, they interpret behavior, and they diffuse tension in conflict situations. The skill and humor of the Bhand's profession is evident in Hajari Bhand's performances and commentary.*

Half Life: A Parable for the Nuclear Age   (1986) 86 min. Dennis O'Rourke (FM). Dist: DCL. "*Beginning where Robert Kiste leaves off. . . a detailed and painful look at the human impacts of above-ground nuclear testing in the Marshall Islands.*" [From the review by Barbara R. Johnston, *AA* 94:764–766, 1992.] Related reading: Robert Kiste, *The Bikinians: A Study in Forced Migration.* Cummings, 1974.

The Halperns in Orasac   (1986) 50 min. Kamenko Katic (FM). Dist: Halpern, Department of Anthropology, University of Massachusetts, Amherst, MA 01003. VR$40, VS$110. "*In 1986 a Belgrade television station made a documentary about the Halperns' three decades as anthropological interpreters of Serbian culture, filming their return to Orasac that summer.*" [From the review by G. James Patterson, *AA* 90:1046–1047, 1988.] Related reading: Joel Halpern, *A Serbian Village in Historical Perspective.* Holt, Rinehart & Winston, 1986.

Halting the Fires   (1990) 53 min. Octavio Bezerra (DI), Channel 4, England (PR). Dist: FL VR$75, VS$445. *Provides a Brazilian view on the crisis in the Amazon. Part 1 (30 min.) describes the destruction wrought by fires in 1987 and 1988, the public outcry that followed, and the formation of IBAMA, the Brazilian agency charged with environmental protection. Part 2 (23 min.) looks at solutions.* [From the review by Darna L. Dufour and Paul Shankman, *AJPA* 88:113–115, 1992. See also *Amazonia: Road to the End of the Rain Forest.*]

Hammerman of Williamsburg   (see Colonial Williamsburg Series)

Hampi   (1960) 25 min. Jean Rouch (DI), Centre National de la Recherche Scientifique, Comite du Film Ethnographique (PR). Dist: CFE;DER. *The display of a ritual vase at the Niamey Museum, Niger.*

Han Tomb Find   28 min. Dist: U.S.-China Peoples Friendship Association, 41 Union Square, New York, NY 10003. [Reviewed by John S. Major, *AA* 78:139, 1976.]

Hand Carved   (1981) 88 min. Herb E. Smith (DI). Dist: APPAL FR$150, FS$1350, VS$600. *The film's succession of grand pictures is about Chester Cornett, who makes chairs with high craft and unbelievable skill. The film's spirit is about a single human who is a hero, a gentle survivor of hard times, bad luck, lost love, and a kitchen that must be the most colossal mess of any place outside the Federal budget office. It is a lovely machine-made tribute to fading handmade craftsmaking.*

Handmade   19 min. Kurt Buser and Ken Schneider (PR). Dist: FL FR$50, VR$50, FS$550, VS$225. *This film takes us to the highlands of Bolivia, a remote region 14,000 feet above sea level. Here thrive the llama and alpaca, treasured for their dense wool. The native people who live in this isolated region are re-learning the traditional process of dyeing yarn with native plants. These ancient methods had been abandoned once the modern world intruded with chemical dyes. The film shows vividly the array of colors available from indigenous plants and flowers.*

Hanuman Langur: Monkey of India   (1980) 30 min. Vishnu Mathur (DI), Canadian Broadcasting Corporation (PR). Dist: CBC VS$125. *A segment of a program in the CBC series,* The Nature of Things. *Its orientation is sociobiological.* "*Records a little bit from the daily lives of six groups of hanuman langurs in a wildlife preserve at Ratambur in Jodhpur and near Mt. Abu proper.*" [From the review by Frances D. Burton, *AA* 87:984–985, 1985. Reviewed by James D. Paterson, *AJPA* 60:125, 1983.]

Hanunoo   (1993 (originally released in 1958) 17 min. Harold Conklin (AN). Dist: PSU VR$13.50. *Domestic and daily life among these mountain agriculturalists in Mindoro, Philippines. Seating styles, food production, household, leisure, and some socioreligious activities. Natural music, no narration. Mimeographed outline available and necessary.* [Reviewed by May Ebihara, *AA* 78:716, 1976.] Suggested supplements: Harold C. Conklin, "Hanunoo Agriculture, a report on an integral system of shifting cultivation in the Philippines." *Food Agr. Organ, U.N. FAO Forest Development Paper, 12, 1957.* Harold C. Conklin, "Hanunoo Color Categories." *Southern Journal of Anthropology* 11:339–344, 1957.

Happy Mother's Day   26 min. Richard Leacock, Joyce Chopra Cole (FM). Dist: D. A. Pennebaker, 562 45th St., New York, NY 10019. *The first month in the lives of the*

Fisher quintuplets of Aberdeen, South Dakota. [Reviewed by Nancie L. Gonzalez, *AA* 74:1572, 1972.]

A Hard Life (Rural Greece: Desertion, Migration, Village Life Series) 55 min. Dr. Colette Piault (AN, DI). Dist: PSA FR$75, VS$300; LFDQ. *Kalliopi Kalogerou has spent her while life in the village where she was born in 1900. Simple witness of the century, she lived through Turkish domination and successive occupations linked to different wars. Most of her family lives elsewhere, in Greece and abroad, and her shattered family world is representative of the Greek diaspora. The film is devoted to her life story, told to a young friend and to her daughter settled in the United States. This film structure is very strict, most shots lasting for ten minutes.*

The Harder They Come 92 min. Perry Henzell (PR, Dl). Dist: New World Pictures, 8831 Sunset Blvd., Los Angeles, CA. *A fictional film about Jamaican life and music.* [Reviewed by Michael Lieber, *AA* 76:199. 1974.]

Harmonize: Folklore in the Lives of Five Families (1981) 21 min. Steve Zeitlin, Paul Wagner (PR). Dist: CSF FR$30, FS$310. *The special traditions families create and observe. Not only are the traditions themselves colorful—like a birthday party for a 100-year-old doll passed down from family to family or the rollicking songs a young couple make up about their adventures together—they're also excellent teaching tools. Mature students will want to consider the functions such traditions serve. Younger students can interview their parents and put together a class treasury of family stories, noting recurring themes and motifs. A unique way of bridging the gap between home and school.*

Harvest at Nong Lub 15 min. *Thai village rice harvest.* [Reviewed by Lucien M. Hanks, *AA* 78:3, 1976.]

The Hasidim 29 min. Vincent R. Tortora (FM). Dist: Vedo Films, 85 Longview Road, Port Washington, NY 11050. *Shot in 1972 in Crown Heights, Brooklyn.* [Reviewed by Barbara Kirschenblatt-Gimblett. *JAF* 90(355):118.]

Haudenosaunee: Way of the Longhouse (1982) 13 min. Robert Stiles and John Akin (FM). Dist: FRIF FR$35, FS$265, VS$160; IF FR$35, VR$35, FS$345, VS$225. *The League of Haudenosaunee, also known as the Six Nation Iroquois Confederacy, was established some 1,000 years ago along the eastern Great Lakes and St. Lawrence waterway and is one of the oldest continuously functioning governments in the Western Hemisphere. The film describes the code of principles and concepts known as the Great Law of Peace, which underlies the traditional Haudenosaunee culture and way of life as it portrays the contemporary Haudenosaunee people—their professions, schools, organizations—a synthesis of the old and new.* [Reviewed by Jeffrey Ehrenreich, *SBF* 18:280, 1983. Reviewed in *AA* 88:774–775, 1986.]

Have You Considered Archaeology? (1968) 15 min. Stuart Scott (PR), Don Blumberg (CA). Dist: Stuart Scott, Department of Anthropology, SUNY Buffalo FR$4, FS$80.99. *A light, humorous, very elementary introduction to archaeology.* [Reviewed by Donald S. Miller, *AA* 72:466–467, 1970.]

Head Hunters of Ecuador 15 min. Dist: FCE FR$17, FS$95. *Remote tribes of head hunters and their jungle life.*

Head Hunters of the Amazon (1930s) 44 min. Dist: FCE FR$85, FS$375.

The Head Men 28 min. B/W. National Film Board of Canada (PR). Dist: NFBC. *In Brazil, the head man may break off a meeting to set an arm or take out an appendix, for there he is both mayor and doctor. In Nigeria, the head man is a dealer in skins and hides, second in authority only to the local king. In Damasck, Saskatchewan, the head man is both mayor and farmer. These three personalities provide an insight into the essential qualities that bring a man to a position of leadership in whatever part of the world he may live.*

Heal the Whole Man 50 min. Paul Robinson (Dl), Jean Comaroff (AN), Stewart Kington (CA). Dist: Chigfield Ltd., 157 Purves Road, London NW10, England, sale only; PFI rental. *Mafeking is the capital village of the Barolong boo Ratshidi, a Tswana tribe. It is part of a South African Bantustan. The film was shot in 1973 by a small team of anthropologists and filmmakers from London. Missionized for nearly 200 years, Barolong religion is now an intricate mixture of Christianity and tribal ancestor-worship. Indeed, throughout southern Africa, zionist and apostolic sects are still multiplying, having doubled to around 6,000 since 1950. The film explores in detail three of the 60-odd sects in Mafeking, with their shamanistically inspired prophets, exotic uniforms, and healing rites. It reveals present-day Barolong cosmology through everyday village activities and shows approaches to healing that transcend cultural boundaries. The central figure is Elizabeth Meloesane, a devout Methodist, who is seen undergoing divination and cure by a ngaka (traditional priest-healer, or witchdoctor).*

Healers of Aro 25 min. George Morshoen (PR), Ron Fehrer (Dl). *A mental health care service developed in the village of Aro, a Yoruba town in Nigeria.* [Reviewed by Nancie L. Gonzalez, et al., *AA* 77:183, 1975.]

The Healing Hill 9 min. Margaret Fairlie (FM), Kenneth A. R. Kennedy (AN). Dist: IRC FR$15, FS$75. *Pilgrimage in India.*

Heart Broken in Half: An Anthropologist Looks at Street Gangs 57 min. Dwight Conquergood and Taggart Siegel (PR), Dwight Conquergood (AN). Dist: FL VR$75, VS$445. *Gangs are society's ultimate devil figure. Few filmmakers have dared or been able to get behind the headlines to confront the human reality and complexity of street gangs in urban America. Challenging stereotypes, this documentary gives a voice to the street youths and reveals their underground culture. Here is an intricate web of symbols and passions, territory and brotherhood, honor and, all too often, death. Images of street bravado are counterpointed with scenes inside laundromats where gang members are folding clothes and playing with babies. A former leader of a female gang talks about her dreams for her two young daughters. The violent death and funeral of a Guatemalan street youth stir up the deepest feelings and most haunting* *questions about both the vulnerability and the heroic ethic of gang life.*

The Heart of Loisaida (1979) 29 min. Marci Reaven and Bienvenidas Matias (FM). Dist: CG FR$55, FS$425, VS$425. *An urban documentary in Manhattan's Lower East Side, where the Hispanic community of Loisaida is struggling to survive. This film deals with the issue of housing and tenant organization.* [Reviewed by Joan Turner, AA 87:985–987, 1985.]

Hearts and Hands (1992) 60 min. Pat Ferrero (DI). Dist: NDF FR$100, VR$75, FS$850, VS$250. *This film presents the role played by women and their textiles in the 19th century's great movements: the Civil War, the abolition of slavery, westward expansion, the suffrage and temperance movements. The film explores lives and accomplishments of anonymous women as well as well-known individuals such as Harriet Tubman, Elizabeth Keckley, Frances Willard, and Abigail Scott Duniway.* [Reviewed by Lorre Weidlich, AA 91:830, 1989.]

The Heavenly Voice of China 23 min. Nila Bogue (FM). Dist: CVA-USC VS$35. *Explores the effect of immigration on the traditional Chinese performance art of Peking Opera. Set within a Chinese community in Los Angeles, the weekly rehearsals of an amateur opera club climax in a colorful public performance. As we discover the sounds of unfamiliar instruments and singing styles, we also come to understand the older generation's struggle to maintain Peking Opera in the United States and pass it on to their children. The film combines singing, acting, and dancing to bring historical stories with strong moral themes to life. Using elaborate make-up and ornate costumes, club members change for the final performance into traditional Chinese characters such as Boa Gong, the staunch defender of justice. This documentary educates us about the art, as well as about the context in which it is practiced and performed in America.*

Hedeby: The Salvage of a Viking Ship (1988) 42 min. Institute furden Wissenschaftlichen Film (PR). Dist: PSU VR$18, VS$195, order #40466. *Detailed presentation on the archaeological excavation of a Viking ship from the harbor of the German seaport of Hedeby. Includes information on gaining access to the artifacts, the excavation of the sealed hull, and the salvage and the temporary preservation of the artifacts.* [Reviewed by Peter S. Allen, ARCH 42(6):78–79, 1989.]

Heinrich Schliemann: The Rediscovery of Troy (1990) 26 min. NHK (PR). Dist: FHS VR$75, VS$149. *Serves as a useful guide to some of the places where Schliemann lived and worked: it provides tours of the village where he grew up and the town where he held his first job. Also shown are the magnificent sites he discovered and excavated, and even his tomb at a cemetery in Athens.* [From the review by Peter S. Allen, ARCH 44(4):68, 1991.]

Hello Columbus (1986) 27 min. Frank Zamacona (FM). Dist: UCEMC VR$34, VS$335. *This film covers a Columbus Day celebration in one part of San Francisco. It focuses on one individual of Italian origin throughout the celebration.* [Reviewed by Elizabeth Mathias, AA 91:268–269, 1989.]

Hell's Kitchen Chronicle (1984) 60 min. Maren Erskine and Reed Erskine (FM). Dist: Lightworks Ltd., 361 W. 36th St., New York, NY 10018; (212) 279-1808, FR$100, FS$900. *An urban documentary. "Provides a richly textured account of the once notorious neighborhood of Hell's Kitchen, an area adjacent to Times Square, spreading west to the Hudson River and extending ten blocks north and south of 42nd Street.... Highlighting the changes wrought by 50 years of large-scale developmental pressures."* [From the review by Joan Turner, AA 87:985–987, 1985.]

Helping the People to Help Themselves (The Human Face of Indonesia Series) (1987) 30 min. Film Australia (PR). Dist: FIV VS$99. *This video focuses on the work of Doctors Billy Sinaga and Budi Rahaya, who serve the province of Nusa Tenggara Timur. They face the challenge of administering health care in poor, remote communities.*

Her Name Came on Arrows: A Kinship Interview with the Baruya of New Guinea (A Series on the Baruya) (1982) 26 min. Allison and Marek Jablonko and Stephen Olsson (DI). Dist: DER FR$45, FS$450, VS$275. *In the eastern highlands of Papua New Guinea, French anthropologist Maurice Godelier invites five of his Baruya friends and informants to his house to discuss Baruya kinship and rules of marriage. As Godelier poses questions, the kinship rules that provide the cohesive fabric of Baruya culture are brought to life. Abstract terms are given practical meanings as Godelier investigates the Baruya customs of stealing wives, exchanging sisters for wives, stealing names, and exchanging "food for blood."*

Herding Castes of Central India. The Mathura—The Hatkar Dhangars 25 min. Margaret Fairlie (DI, CA, ED), Kenneth A. R. Kennedy (AN). Dist: IRC FR$40-75, FS$325. *Daily life, ceremonies, and choreometric analysis of dance.* See also *Tribal Groups.*

The Herders of Mongun-Taiga (Disappearing World Series) (1989) 52 min. Caroline Humphrey (AN). Dist: FIV VS$198, order #047041; PSU order #51220. *Mongun-Taiga is one of the bleakest areas of Tuva, which lies on the Siberian-Mongolian border, and was closed to foreigners until 1988. This program captures the lifestyle of the people of this inhospitable land, whose economy depends on nomadic herding of yaks, sheep, horses, and goats.*

Herdsmen of the Sun (1988) 52 min. Werner Herzog (DI), Patrick Sandrin (PR), Thomas Weber (CA). Dist: IVC. *Herzog went into the drought stricken Sahara to film the Woodabe, focusing on one tribal ritual. Once a year, the young men dress up and parade in front of the women. Each woman must then choose and spend the night with the man she finds the most beautiful. Herzog emphasizes the difference between their culture and ours, and in doing so maintains their dignity. In fact, he exalts it.*

HERITAGE: CIVILIZATION AND THE JEWS (1984) 60 min. each. WNET-TV (PR), Abba Eban (NA). Dist: FI FR$100, FS$800, VS$198 (each); FS$6120, VS$1605 (for the nine-part series). *"The saga of the Jews, which has been unfolding for the past 3,500 to 4,000 years, is brilliantly highlighted against the background of their native and* *foreign cultures in this series of nine one-hour films."* [From the review by Steven Bowman, *ARCH* 40(5):78–82, 1987.] Study guide available.

Heritage in Cedar: Northwest Coast Indian Woodworking, Past and Present (1979) 29 min. Louis and Ruth Kirk (PR). Dist: UWP FS$425. *Wood was the great medium of expression for Northwest Coast Indians and of all the woods they used, western red cedar was the greatest. Through a broad geographic and conceptual approach, Heritage in Cedar brings alive the richness of the Northwest Coast Indian legacy by going to abandoned and living villages, to archaeological digs and to museums. Visits are shown to the Queen Charlotte Islands of British Columbia, the new anthropology museum on the University of British Columbia campus, and Ozette, Ksan, and Hoh Village.* Relevant anthropological literature: Ruth Kirk and Richard Daugherty, *Exploring Washington Archaeology,* 1978, 112 pp., 200 photos, 16 in color, maps.

Heritage of the Pharaohs (1984) 50 min. Teresa Odden (PR). Dist: International Adventure Video, 400 Webster, Palo Alto, CA 94301; (415) 321-9943. *"The producer has developed a video cassette/film with the aim of providing home video viewers who want more than just movies with an alternative in which they can take a trip to the major sites of ancient Egypt.... From a scholarly point of view this video/slide presentation contains serious flaws and misinformation. While it is excusable in certain points of academic theory, it is necessary to provide accurate reasons for adopting a point of view."* [From the review by Eugene Cruz-Uribe, *ARCH* 39(1):66–67, 1986.]

Heritage of the Sea: Makah Indian Treaty Rights, Part I and Part II (1979–80) 29 min. each. Louis and Ruth Kirk (PR). Dist: UWP FS$425. *In the viewpoint of Makah Indians, fishing is an ancient and fundamental way of life guaranteed them in perpetuity by the 1855 treaty agreement with the U.S. Government. Part I gives background information by Makahs including their reminiscences about the past and comments on the future of their tribal salmon management programs. Part II builds on Part I, representing comments by Makah fishermen and elders, and discussions by Seattle lawyer Alvin Ziontz, Professor Alan Hart, and Dr. Richard Daugherty. Artifacts dealing with fishing found at Hoko River and Ozette are discussed.*

Heroes or History (see Crossroads of Civilization Series)

The Hero's Journey: The World of Joseph Campbell (1987) 57 min. William Free (PR). Dist: FI VS$30. *"Portrays Campbell's approach to the universal hero myth, especially as reflected in major world religions, and as filmmakers personify it in Campbell's own life."* [From the review by Muriel Crespi, *AA* 92:1103–1105, 1990.]

The Hideout (1981) 83 min. Brian Patrick (FM). Dist: Beacher Films, 219 Edison St., Salt Lake City, UT 84111; (801) 581-8677. *"A select group of Utah State prisoners, mainly in what appear to be unstructured on-camera interviews."* [From the review by Sam Beck, *AA* 85:1006–1007, 1983.]

Hierarchy and the Alpha Male (see Jane Goodall: Studies of the Chimpanzee Series)

High Lonesome Sound (1963) 30 min. Dist: IUAVC FR$9.50; PSU FR$12.50. *Folk music and spirituals are sung by the mountain people of Eastern Kentucky to preserve tradition and dignity despite worn-out land and the replacement of men by machines in coal mines. Music, an integral part of life, is sung by unemployed workers, coal miners, a church congregation, and a miner's family at home.* [Reviewed by Keith K. Cunningham, *JAF* 90(356):250–251, 1977.]

Los hijos de Sandino (1980) 42 min. Fred Barney and Kimberly Safford (FM). Dist: Third World Newsreel, 160 Fifth Ave., Suite 911, New York, NY 10010; (212) 243-2310, FR$65, FS$525. *The Sandanista revolution in Nicaragua.* [Reviewed by John A. Booth, *AA* 86:237–238, 1984.]

Himalayan Farmer (1967) 16 min. Patricia Hitchcock (CA, PR), John T. Hitchcock (AN, PR). Dist: IFB FR$17.50, FS$240, VS$195; PSU(PCR) order # 2175K. *The film was shot on a Himalayan mountainside near the Dhaulagiri massif. It was made to portray a form of ecological adaptation that also is a "cultural trap" or cul de sac. The question raised for discussion is what is the way out? During the course of the film, whose focus is an exacting daily task, a Magar farmer reveals much about himself, his family and his village.* Cf. the film *Gurkha Country.*

Himalayan Shaman of Northern Nepal (1967) 15 min. Patricia Hitchcock (CA, PR), John T. Hitchcock (AN, PR). Dist IFB FR$17.50, FS$230, VS$190; PSU(PCR) order # 2177K, FR$11.50; UUEMC FR$7. *The film was shot in an Himalayan valley near the Dhaulagiri massif. It shows a shaman whose costume and procedures make connection with the classic Inner Asian tradition. After becoming possessed in order to bring a troubled family into helpful contact with the Other World, he sucks out intrusive objects that were shot into his clients by evil spirits, then purifies his mouth with fire. The film provides visual basis for stress on the psychological benefits of shamanism in a region without doctors or psychiatrists.* Cf. the film *Gurkha Country.*

Himalayan Shaman of Southern Nepal (1967) 14 min. Patricia Hitchcock (CA, PR), John T. Hitchcock (AN, PR). Dist: IFB FR$15, FS$215, VS$190; PSU(PCR) order #2178K, FR$11.50; UUEMC FR$7. *Shot in the lower Himalaya, in a village adjoining Banyan Hill, and mostly around the shaman's farmstead, this film portrays shamanism as a time-consuming but part-time specialty, and one often transmitted in this region from father to son. Since this Magar shaman who uses trance to help his clients also depends on medicines, some of which are Ayurvedic, the film shows that traditional Hindu medical ideas are compatible with the complex. Despite the fact that the practitioner is an ex-Gurkha soldier with many years service in the British Gurkha Brigade, he does not use western medical ideas.* Cf. the film, *Gurkha Country.*

Himba Wedding (1969) 35 min. Gordon D. Gibson (FM, AN); Smithsonian Institution (PR). *Made in South West*

Africa in 1961 to record important rituals not easily described in words. Depicts certain events in the marriage ceremony of the Himba, a cattle-keeping Bantu-speaking people. Cattle sacrifice, feasting, dancing, and mockfighting compose the background against which the bride and groom carry out the solemn acts that establish their new relationship. Details of social organization, religion, and daily life acquire significance in the context of the wedding ceremony. Suggested supplement: Carlos Estermann (C.S.Sp.), "Etnografia do Sudoeste de Angola," O. Grupo Etnico Herero, 3. Lisbon, 1961.

Hindu Loaves and Fishes (1985) 20 min. Philip Singer (FM). Dist: Traditional Healing Films/Earth Research, P.O. Box 68, 336 Main Street, Rochester, MI 48063; (313) 656-0030, FR$65, VR$45, FS$575,VS$250. *"An ethnographic study of middle-level Hindu shamanism centering on trance-linked materialization of objects, this film is a true workshop view of a Hindu holy man-cum-magician."* [From the review by Agehananda Bharati, AA 88:1042–1043, 1986.]

The Hindu Ritual Sandhya 19 min. Doris Srinivasan (PR). Dist: CMC [Reviewed by Paul Hockings, AA 76:218, 1974.]

Hinduism and the Song of God 30 min. Dist: HFF FR$45, FS$395, VS$89. *The physical beauty of India is the backdrop for this award winner on Hinduism. Discusses the law of Karma, the four yogas, and other concepts in the Bhagavad Gita, the Hindu Bible.*

Hinduism: 330 Million Gods (Long Search Series) (1977) 60 min. Ronald Eyre (NA), John Else (FM). Dist: T-L. *A quest (by the narrator) for answers to questions about beginning and ending... philosophical. Seen through one man's eyes (a Londoner). The narrator is a theatre director who is not an authority on Hinduism, just a "searcher." He seeks out people who might have some answers to his many questions about ultimate reality, about the meaning of Hinduism in daily life of Indians, etc. He talks to holy men, to a very British, highly educated ex-Indian who returns with the narrator to his native village in N. India. Focusing questions: How is Western\Eastern philosophy portrayed? How believable is the narration? Note the proxemic behavior between Indians. How do Indians approach or react to crowding behavior? Through whose eyes are most of the comments on Hinduism made? What class of society is represented? What class is ignored?* [Donald A. Messerschmidt]

Hippopotamus Hunting (Autour de l'hippopotame) 52 min. Yves Billon, Djingarey Maiga, Jean-Francois Schiano (FM). Dist: FDV. *A traditional hippopotamus hunt is organized in the bend of the Niger, in Mali. The animal is harpooned with spears attached to floats, as was done fairly regularly a few years ago. The hippopotamus weighs 3 or 4 tons and can supply meat for a village for almost a year, so that for the inhabitants of Ouatagouna, all hopes are concentrated around this animal. For the hunt, there is Abdoula, chief of the Sorko fishermen; Ayouba, chief of the Haoussa fishermen from Nigeria; and Halidou, the oldest fisherman in the area. There is also the master of the river, who has inherited powers capable of killing an animal or of throwing anyone into its jaws. Today, there is also Bouba, who represents the Wood and Forests Administration, whose fiscal and repressive powers are a threat that nobody can ignore. Djingary Maiga, who was born in this village, tells us about the changes in this hunt. During his story, several hippopotamuses are harpooned and pulled out onto the banks to be cut up by the village inhabitants. By taking part in this hunt, the Haoussa, wandering tradespeople, and fishermen, cause complete confusion.*

Historical Relics Unearthed in New China 60 min. Dist: GP FR$75, FS$850. *Over the past two decades, China's archaeologists have undertaken large-scale excavations that have uncovered a remarkable number of priceless historical relics dating from prehistoric times through the 14th century. This film shows these extraordinary relics that form the core of the acclaimed Chinese Art exhibition that has recently toured European capitals and was described by the* Washington Post, *when it went on display at the National Galley in Washington, DC, as representing one of "the major archaeological finds of the century." Shown in detail, these relics are of great value not only as art objects of spectacular beauty and workmanship but also for the study of ancient China's politics, economy, culture, warfare, and contacts with foreign countries during different historical periods.*

History of Archaeology 29 min. Jesse Jennings (AN). Dist: University of Utah Educational Media Center. [Reviewed by Robert K. Evans, AA 77:900, 1975.]

Hitlerjunge Quex (1933) 102 min. Hans Steinhoff (Dl). Dist: MOMA. *This print contains the annotations made by Gregory Bateson. In German, no English titles.*

Hitting Sticks—Healing Hearts (1991) 58 min. Dist: RTP VS$100. *This is a documentary produced at the request of village elders. It provides an in-depth, insiders view of Athabaskan memorial potlatch. It is also about death, grieving, love, community, music and tradition. This particular potlatch in the village of Minto commemorates a young man who had died several years earlier. The memorial potlatch is a family and community ceremony like no other. It provides a cleansing of the spirit and a settlement of all debts. It is a new beginning and an end to grieving. Those who have put on a memorial potlatch say there is nothing that can compare to the relief of completion.*

The Hmong Hilltribe People of Laos (1989) 58 min. David Gilbert (PR). Dist: IMCC VS$100. *This program is an unusual glimpse into the daily life activities, new years ceremonies, and traditional religious rituals of the Hmong people living in the Bon Vinai refugee camp of Thailand. This program is narrated with historical and cultural information, which offers the viewer an inside understanding of the Hmong hilltribe people of Laos. Training manual included.*

The Ho: People of the Rice Pot (1975) 73 min. Michael Yorke (AN, CA), Valerie Yorke (SR), Gregory Harris (ED). Dist: Dr. Michael Yorke, 12 Belsize Park, London NW3 4ES, U.K. *One man and his family throughout one year in* a tribal village of Bihar, India. The film is concerned with their logic and beliefs by looking at the forest and rice cultivating economy, their oral history, marriage, death and illness. It includes two major festivals—the spring Bacchanalia and sweeping out of the evil spirits in summer. It ends on the village's relationship to the outside world and the economy of India, to which it is linked by a nearby iron ore mine. [Reviewed by Hilary Standing, RAIN 9–10, 1975.]

Holy Ghost People (1968) 53 min. Peter Adair (FM), Nathan Gerrard (CON). Dist: UCEMC order #7669, FR$27; CRM/MH order #407920, VR$80, VS$245. A white Pentecostal religious group in Appalachia whose members handle poisonous snakes, drink strychnine, and speak in tongues, following the literal interpretation of the Biblical passage: "In my name they shall speak in new tongues. They shall take up serpents; and if they drink any deadly thing it shall not hurt them." Filmed during a four-hour meeting, the congregation is exhorted by an evangelist, and members tell of revelations they have experienced through communication with the Holy Ghost. As the meeting proceeds, some of the congregation begin to pray, dance, and speak in tongues; several members collapse in trancelike states. At the height of the meeting, boxes of rattlesnakes and copperheads are brought in, and the people pick them up, throw them to one another, and sing. The leader of the group takes a rattlesnake from a box and is bitten. He explains that he has been bitten before and says that if he dies it is God's will. As the meeting continues, we see the man's hand and arm swelling. At this point the film ends. The filmmaker says that the man survived. [Reviewed by Margaret Mead, AA 70:655, 1968. William M. Clements, JAF 90(358):502–556, 1977.] Suggested supplements: Weston La Barre, They Shall Take Up Serpents: Psychology of the Southern Snake-Handling Cult. 1962 (paperback edition, 1969, Schocken SB229). Weston La Barre, "The Snakehandling Cult of the American Southeast." Explorations in Cultural Anthropology. Ward H. Goodenough, ed. McGraw-Hill, 1964, pp. 309–333.

Holy Men of India (1930s) 10–15 minutes. Dist: FCE FR$17, FS$95. Religious festival attracts a million and a half people to the banks of the Ganges. Many Holy Men are shown with their ability to perform difficult feats and to resist pain.

Holy Week in Antigua Guatemala (1987) 26 min. Claudia Feldmar (PR). Dist: PSU VR$16.50, VS$170, order #34725. The residents of Antigua, Guatemala, along with thousands of visitors, participate annually in a Holy Week celebration combining traditional Catholic doctrine with Indian traditions and values. This program highlights the eight hour Nazarene of La Merced Procession and the descent of the cross in the School of Christ. Hundreds of robed men and women carrying the great anda (a 7,000-pound float with an image of Christ bearing the cross) tread across elaborate colored sawdust rugs in front of churches, homes, and in plazas. [Reviewed by Caroline B. Brettell, AA 91:831–834, 1989.]

Homage to the Yahgans: The Last Indians of Tierra del Fuego and Cape Horn (1990) 40 min. Chapman and CNRS-Audiovisuel (FM). Dist: DER VR$40, VS$350. This video's purpose is twofold: the first, to achieve an understanding of certain episodes of western expansion, beginning in the early 17th century, which finally led to the extinction of the Yahgan people; the second, to gain an appreciation of the courage and fortitude of a people who had survived for thousands of years in one of the most inhospitable regions of the planet, but who had been judged by many Europeans as the most degraded human beings in the entire world. The video focuses on the personality and life of a Yahgan called "Jemmy Button" who was taken to England in 1831 by Captain Fitz Roy. He was returned to his homeland two years later, accompanied by Charles Darwin. The video ends with scenes of the four women who still speak Yahgan and who live on Navarino Island in Chile.

Hombori (1948–49) 16 min. Jean Rouch (DI). Dist: CFE; DER. Mali.

Home for Life 58 min. Gerald Tanner (FM). Dist: FI. Old folks' home in Chicago. [Reviewed by Bonnie Holcomb and Stella Silverstein, AA 77:186, 1975.]

Home Movie (1981) 25 min. Ernest Edward Starr, Steve Zeitlin (PR). Dist: CSF FR$35, FS$350. The way we use home movies to create an idealized picture of family life. Scenes of families posed before shiny new cars, on sunny vacations, and romping beneath sprinklers are skillfully combined with their memories of those scenes. The recurrent images raise significant questions about what Americans value and about how we remember and want to be remembered. Students will not only enjoy talking about the film's relationship to their own experiences and home movies but may also wish to show and discuss some of those movies. A valuable teaching aid of special use in values clarification.

Home of the Brave (1985) 53 min. Helena Solberg-Ladd (FM). Dist: CG FR$90, FS$850, VS$595. "A political documentary on native rights.... As a cinematic statement against Euro-American imperialism, this film offers a review of dispossession, exploitation, and repression as international problems that Indian nations throughout the Western Hemisphere hold in common as First Peoples colonized within their own aboriginal lands." [From the review by Harald Prins, AA 90:774–778, 1988.]

Homemade American Music (1980) 30 min. Carrie Aginsky and Yasha Aginsky (PR). Dist: Lawren Productions, Box 666, Mendocino, CA 95460; (707) 937-0536, FR$50, FS$450, VS$360. "Mike Seeger and Alice Gerrard, two urban folk revivalists, begin the film by carefully legitimating their ties with the southern folk music tradition." [From the review by Melanie L. Sovine, AA 89:522–525, 1987.]

Hominid Evolution I and II (1990) 90 min. Anne Zeller (FM, AN). Dist: Director, Audio Visual Center, University of Waterloo, Waterloo, Ontario, N2L 3G1, Canada. [Reviewed by Milford H. Wolpoff, AA 94:525–526, 1992.]

Hommage à Marcel Mauss: Germaine Dieterlen (Homage to Marcel Mauss: Germaine Dieterlen) (1977) 20 min. Jean Rouch (DI), Centre National de la Recherche Scientifique, Comité du Film Ethnographique (PR). Dist:

CFE; DER. *Germaine Dieterlen recalls the facade of the paintings on the Songo sheds, which display the grand myths of the creation of the world among the Dogon. She provokes a discussion on the architectural remains of ancient human establishments.*

Hommage à Marcel Mauss: Paul Levy (Homage to Marcel Mauss: Paul Levy) (1977) 20 min. Jean Rouch (DI), Centre National de la Recherche Scientifique, Comité du Film Ethnographique (PR). Dist: CFE; DER. *At the conclusion of his doctoral thesis at the Sorbonne, Paul Levy discusses his memories of Marcel Mauss.*

Hommage à Marcel Mauss: Taro Okamoto (Homage to Marcel Mauss: Taro Okamoto) (1974) 14 min. Jean Rouch (DI), Centre National de la Recherche Scientifique, Comité du Film Ethnographique (PR). Dist: CFE; DER. *A cine-portrait of an anthropological artist.*

Les Hommes qui font la pluie; ou Yenendi, les faiseurs de pluie (Men Who Make Rain; or Yenendi: The Rainmakers) (1951–52) 27 min. Jean Rouch (DI), Institut Français d'Afrique Noir (PR). Dist: CFE; DER. *Rain rituals with possession dances among the Songhay and Zerma of Simiri, Zermaganda, Niger.*

Hong Kong/Singapore (Asian Insight Series) (1988) 50 min. Film Australia (PR). Dist: FIV VS$158. *This program records the historical events that brought western powers to Asia and compares and contrasts Hong Kong's and Singapore's social structures and ideologies.*

Honorable Nations: The Seneca's Land Rights 54 min. Chana Gazit and David Steward (PR). Dist: FL VR$75, VS$395. *Salamanca is the only city in the United States situated on land owned by Native Americans. For 99 years, the townspeople have rented the land from the Seneca Indians for $1 a year and have gotten used to their right to live and do business on Indian property. On February 19, 1991, the lease expired. The Seneca nation felt it had been exploited and now insisted on a huge rent increase. As one Seneca commented, it was worth more as a cornfield than a city. Townspeople were outraged at higher rents. This film follows the five-year negotiation, as each side heatedly defended their position. Archival footage, historical photographs, and interviews help tell the story of two communities caught in a web of historical injustice. Eventually, an agreement was hammered out. Among its terms is $60 million given by the federal government to the Senecas, the first Native American tribe to receive such reparation.*

Hopi Songs of the Fourth World (1982) 58 min. Pat Ferrero (DI). Dist: Ferrero Films, 908 Rhode Island St., San Francisco, CA 94107; (415) 826-2791, FR$100, FS$850; NDF FR$100, FS$850, VS$600. *This film is a compelling study of the Hopi that captures their deep spirituality and reveals their integration of art and daily life. Amidst beautiful images of Hopi land and life, a variety of Hopi—a farmer, religious elder, grandmother, painter, potter and weaver—speak about the preservation of the Hopi way. Their philosophy of living in balance and harmony with nature is a model to the Western world of an environmental ethic in action.* [Reviewed by Richard O. Clemmer, *AA* 87:223–234, 1985. John W. Adams, *SBF* 20:41, 1984.]

Horendi (1972) 50 min. Jean Rouch (DI), Centre National de la Recherche Scientifique, Comite du Film Ethnographique (PR). Dist: CFE; DER. *An analytic essay about the relationship beteen dance and music at the center of a possession ceremony. Certain sequences are made in synchronous sound and slow-motion.*

Horses of Life and Death (1991) 25 min. Laura Scheerer Whitney (DI). Dist: UCEMC FR$45, FS$500, VS$250. *Explores the concepts of life and death and the role of the horse as a messenger between the human and spirit world on the island of Sumba, the last Indonesian island with a pagan majority. This film follows two major ceremonial events: a large-scale equestrian jousting battle held to celebrate fertility and the harvest, and an elaborate funeral ritual that concludes with a procession led by the dead man's own horse, which carries his soul off to the afterlife.*

Hospice (1979) 26 min. Frank Moynihan (PR). Dist: Billy Budd Films, Inc., 235 East 57th St., New York, NY 10022; (212) 755-3968, FR$35, FS$350, VS$250. *"A demonstration of a hospice in action. Hospice, as the film states, is not a building, but a idea, the idea that a group of trained personnel work together to make the life of a dying person as full and painless as possible."* [From the review by Christine Lemieux, *AA* 86:1054, 1984.]

Hospital 91 min. Frederick Wiseman (Dl, ED). Dist: Zipporah Films, 54 Lewis Wharf, Boston, MA 02210. [Reviewed by Patricia Perrier, *AA* 77:185, 1975.]

Hot Pepper 54 min. Les Blank (FM). Dist: FF. *Music of black Cajuns in southwestern Louisiana.* [Reviewed by David Evans *JAF* 90(255):107, 1977. Nina Swidler, *AA* 77:475, 1975.]

House of Spirit: Perspectives on Cambodian Health Care (1984) 42 min. Ellen Bruno and Ellen Kuras (DI), American Friends Service Committee (PR). Dist: American Friends Service Committee, 15 Rutherford Place, New York, NY 10003; (212) 598-0968, VR$30, VS$100. *"Attempts to summarize both the variety of folk healing traditions currently practiced among the Buddhist Khmer and the historical events since the French colonial rule that have modified those tradtions."* [From the review by Marjorie A. Muecke, *AA* 88:776–778, 1986.]

The House-Opening (1980) 45 min. Judith MacDougall (Dl), David MacDougall (CA). Dist: AIAS. *The willingness of a society to change may be a sign of its strength rather than its weakness. At the Aboriginal community of Aurukum on Australia's Cape York Peninsula, a new ceremony has evolved as a way of dealing with death in the midst of new living patterns. Many of the older people at Aurukun grew up in a nomadic society where, when someone died, camp sites would be vacated and houses burnt to avoid contact with the dead person's spirit. Today, as permanent suburban style housing is constructed, this cannot be done, and the people of Aurukun have responded by creating a new ceremony of ritual purification—the 'house opening'—combining features of traditional Aboriginal mortuary rites* with European and Torres Strait Island elements. This film follows Geraldine Kawangka, the widow of a recently deceased man, as the ceremony is prepared and carried out. In an atmosphere that sometimes seems strangely reminiscent of a European church fete, one can feel the resilience and adaptability of the Aurukun people and the underlying strength of their Aboriginal tradition. Geraldine Kawangka provides an informative and personal commentary.

The House That Giacomo Built (1983) 50 min. Donald S. Pitkin (AN), Bill Anderson (FM). Dist: Donald Pitkin, Department of Anthropology, Amherst College, Amherst, MA 01002; (413) 542-2207, FR$75. *"Focuses on a single family in a small mountain community 50 km south of Rome." The film demonstrates that "industrialization, increased wealth, and increased knowledge of the outside world need not undermine extended family relations."* [From the review by David I. Kertzer, AA 86:1063–1064, 1984.]

Houses of the Arctic and the Tropics (1918) 30 min. Silent. Dist: FCE FR$17, FS$95. *Environment is that combination of nature's gifts that surrounds man where he lives. . . . Eskimos and Fiji.*

How Could I Not Be Among You? (1970) 30 min. Thomas Reichman (FM). Dist: The Eccentric Circle Cinema Workshop, P.O. Box 1481, Evanston, IL 60204. *Death and dying.* [Reviewed by Nancie L. Gonzalez, AA 77:192, 1975.]

How Tasty Was My Little Frenchman 80 min. Nelson Perieras Dos Santos (Dl). Dist: NYF. *A fictional film about a French sailor in 15th-century Brazil.* [Reviewed by James W. Green, AA 77:699, 1975.]

How the Myth Was Made: A Study of Robert Flaherty's Man of Aran (1978) 59 min. George C. Stoney and James Brown (DI), James Brown (CA), Paul Barnes (SR), Trudy Bagdon (ED), P. Barnes and P. Saunders (AED). Dist: MOMA; FI. *This film investigates Robert Flaherty's film Man of Aran (1934). In 1977 George Stoney, himself a pioneer of the social documentary film and whose father was born on Aran, went back to the island. Stoney describes his goal: "We went to record how and why America's greatest film poet, Robert Flaherty, worked as he did, and to see what effects the release of his masterpiece, Man of Aran, had on the people who represented themselves on the screen." They recorded how Flaherty set up his scenes and molded locations and customs to fulfill his vision. Islanders who participated in the original film are interviewed and heatedly argue the "myths" versus the truth in their portrayal more than forty years earlier.* [Reviewed by Paul Hockings, AA 82:227–228, 1980.]

How To Behave (1987) 43 min. Tran Van Thuy (PR). Dist: FRIF VR$75, VS$375. *Originally banned in Vietnam, this is the first "glasnost" documentary from that country. Dying of cancer, the cameraman Dong Xuan Thuyet asks his friends to make a film on the subject of "tu te"—human relations, kindness, fraternity. Thus charged, the filmmakers explore the reality behind the slogans hung on Hanoi's public buildings and reveal troubling scenes of daily Vietnamese life: people laboring as beasts of burden, seamy street vendors, a community that no longer seems able to define humanitarianism—or greed. Children who assume the filmmakers will create yet another idealized portrayal of Vietnam, ask "Aren't you ashamed to show us these false images? Why have the ordinary people disappeared from your films?" This becomes the point of departure for this journey through Vietnamese society.*

How to Build an Igloo 11 min. Douglas Wilkinson (DI). Dist: NFB FR$40, VR$40, FS$275, VS$250. *A skill handed down for generations is still important for survival in the wilderness of the Arctic. We see two Eskimos staying overnight at a trading post to construct an igloo. Using only blocks of snow, a snow knife, and the knowledge developed by their culture, they build an apparently simple but architecturally perfect structure in less than two hours.*

How to Make Sorghum Molasses 20 min. Dist: UCEMC FR$29, FS$285. *Cinema-verite study of farmers in Filmer County, West Virginia, filmed in 1970 as they make sorghum molasses in the traditional way. The cane is cut by hand, the milling equipment is erected, and horses are brought to drive the mill. An unexpected accident enlivens the proceedings when the heavy antique mill falls from its platform; but with help from neighbors, the men are able to lift it back. Afterward, the juice is boiled down until it is ready for bottling. Conveys the personalities of the farmers; as they work together, their jokes and conversations reveal a complex set of values suggestive of an older way of life (though not the pastoral life portrayed by many nostalgic and cliche-ridden visions). A nine-page explanatory essay accompanies the film; it presents the history and context of the molasses-making ritual as seen by the participants, describes the processes and apparatus, and includes a partial transcript of the film's dialogue and a selected bibliography.*

How We Learn about the Past (former title *Men Who Move the Earth*) (1966) 28 min. Edward Chan Sieg (FM), F. J. Clune, Jr. (AN), Anthropology Curriculum Project, UGA (PR). Dist: IFB FR$30, FS$400, VS$325; PSU(PCR) order # 31238. *Basic purpose of the film is twofold: (1) To instruct students in the middle elementary grades in the basic techniques of archaeological methodology. (2) To acquaint the student with a basic knowledge of Southeastern prehistory. To this end, filmed accounts of the excavations and restorations at Etowah—center of the Southern Cult; Ocmulgee National Monument at Macon—where the displays chronicle nearly eight thousand years; and at Dairen—where there are two pre-Ogelthorpe historic sites; Fort Fredrica, fully restored; and Fort King George, now being excavated. Archaeological laboratory work is shown at the facilities of the University of Georgia in Athens.* [Reviewed by Charles H. Fairbanks, AA 71:1007–1008, 1969.]

Howler Monkeys of Barro Colorado Island (1960) 27 min. C.R. Carpenter (FM). Dist: PSU FR$10. *Filmed on Barro Colorado in Panama, this is the only available film to date on Neotropical nonhuman primates. It focuses on the general social behavior of Alouatta palliata.*

Huahine: Land of Discovery (1984) 28 min. Dist: BYU-AVS FS$360, VS$249. *This film "relates the recent archeological discoveries on Huahine, a small island near Tahiti,* to the prehistory, history and current culture of Polynesia, which is a formidable task for a 30-minute film. Unfortunately, the 'travelogue' segments that appear sporadically throughout the film confuse its purpose." [From the review by Sam Casselberry, SBF 21:231, 1986.]

Huichol Sacred Pilgrimage to Wirikuta (1991) 29 min. Larain Boyll (DI). Dist: UCEMC FR$45, VS$250. *This sensitive documentary follows the annual pilgrimage and peyote hunt of the Huichol Indians of western Mexico. It focuses on the sacred sites, the traditional Huichol ceremonies and rituals, and the teachings of the Huichol shamans and elders. Includes the Huichol songs and music that accompany the journey and shows that people now come from around the world to join the pilgrimage and learn from the Indians' ancient sacred traditions.*

Huichols—People of the Peyote 52 min. Steve R. Dreben, Thomas S. Perry (PR), Kalman Muller and Melville See (CA). Dist: Stonedge Productions, 2309 5th St., # 3, Santa Monica, CA 90405; (213) 396-8290, FR$100, FS$675. *The Huichols live in the high pine forests of the Mexican states of Nayarit and Jalisco and speak a language of Uto-Aztecan stock. Living on small, isolated ranches, the Huichols subsist on the barest economy of corn agriculture. Favoring the steep slopes of barrancas, they plant corn, beans, and squash using the primitive digging stick. Because of the uncertainty of attaining a successful corn harvest, the Huichols employ an elaborate ceremonial cycle to enlist the help of the gods. Through the centuries, the Huichols have changed from nomadic hunters, who roamed the dry desert areas of Northern Mexico, to the more settled life of an agricultural society. The dichotomy between hunter and farmer is resolved by the use of hallucinogenic peyote cactus. Through the fantastic visual and spiritual revelations brought about by peyote, the unity of Huichol culture—past and present—is actively perceived.*

THE HUMAN FACE OF HONG KONG (1988) Film Australia (PR). Dist: FIV VS$198. *While Hong Kong is known as a hugely successful manufacturing and trading center and an exotic international stop-over, it is still a British colony. China will regain sovereignty over the area in 1997. This production shows different lifestyles of Hong Kong society—the world of the wealthy and powerful and the world of the working class.* See descriptions under individual titles:

- **Better Rich Than Red**
- **Running from the Ghost**

THE HUMAN FACE OF INDONESIA SERIES (1987) 26 min. each. Film Australia (PR). Dist: FIV VS$99 (each), VS$399 (series). *This remarkable series focuses on the lives of five very different Indonesians. By putting their personal stories into the broader context of modern Indonesia, it presents an enthralling and informative picture of the country's life and culture.*

- **Master of the Shadows** *Bali is the most famous place in Indonesia. Can its traditional culture survive the pressures of tourism? The story of a man whose life is dedicated to nurturing his ancient culture illustrates the conflict between the old and the new.*

- **We Are Nothing without the People** *Brigadier General Dr. Ben Mbio is the governor of Nusa Tenggara Timur. He and his wife discuss their medical work for one of the poorest provinces and talk about the role of the military in Indonesia today.*

- **But I'll Always Continue to Write** *Debra Yatim is a Djakarta newspaper reporter who works under great stress to bring the plight of Djakarta's low income and poverty groups to the notice of her readers.*

- **Helping the People to Help Themselves** *Doctors Billy Sinaga and Budi Rahaya serve the remote province of Nusa Tenggara Timur. They experience the hard work and daily challenges of administering health care in poor, remote communities.*

- **Journey to a New Life** *Overcrowding is a major problem, so the Indonesian government has begun to move people to less populated provinces. This program follows a poor family from their last days in their small village to their new home in East Kalimantan.*

THE HUMAN FACE OF THE PACIFIC SERIES (1987) 28 min. each. Film Australia (PR). Dist: FIV VS$79 (each), VS$470 (series). *The islands of the South Seas have always held an exotic allure for Westerners. This series of video programs looks behind the images of romance and mystery to reveal the islands as they really are—a heterogeneous group of countries and colonies struggling to meet the challenges of the modern world while preserving their cultural identities.*

- **Atoll Life on Kiribati** *Kiribati gained its independence only a decade ago. One of the most isolated communities in the Pacific, it has preserved many of its ancient customs, including canoe building and ceremonial music and dance.*

- **Marshall Islands—Living with the Bomb** *As a result of American testing of nuclear bombs, the native people of this United States Trust Territory were relocated and their culture vanquished.*

- **Place of Power in French Polynesia** *The Polynesian culture of Tahiti was nearly extinguished by years of French rule. However, a recent cultural reemergence has revived traditional arts and rituals.*

- **New Caledonia—A Land in Search of Itself** *New Caledonia is a land divided. This program examines the conflicts between the Kanaks, who want to retain their tribal society, and the Caledonian French, who are concerned with economic progress.*

- **Fiji—Legacies of Empire** *In Fiji, sugar cane is at the center of a severe division between the Indian community, who were brought to Fiji as laborers in colonial times, and the native Fijians, who want to repossess the land taken away from them by British rule.*

- **Western Samoa—I Can Get Another Wife but I Can't Get Parents** *Although Western Samoa is independent, mass emigration to New Zealand continues. This program focuses on a young Samoan couple who must join the exodus and leave their close-knit families.*

Human Relations Area File: A Fund of Knowledge (1970) 15 min. Dist: PSU FR$12.50. *History, uses, and key features of the files, a major data resource and retrieval system for the study of man's behavior, customs, and social life.*

The Human Voice: Exploring Vocal Paralanguage (1993) 30 min. Dane Archer (PR). Dist: UCEMC VR$55, VS$295, order #38242. *This video explores how, every time we speak, our voice reveals our gender, age, geographic background, level of education, native birth, emotional state and our relationship with the person spoken to. There are thousands of ways in which words can be said. This vocal paralanguage contains several clues to facts about ourselves.*

A Human Way of Life (The Making of Mankind Series) (1982) 55 min. BBC/Time-Life (PR). Dist: BBC FR$100, VR$100, FS$850, VS$150; AV. *"While there are several films that describe the physical characteristics of early hominids and how they may have lived, few films demonstrate how this information was learned. 'A Human Way of Life' goes a long way in filling this gap."* [From the review by Nathan Dubowsky, *SBF* 18:215, 1983.]

The Hundred Years War: Personal Notes (1983) 2 parts, 60 min. each. Ilan Ziv (PR). Dist: ICF VR$100, VS$450. This *"production by an Israeli filmmaker presents a profound and jolting critique of Israeli policy and actions toward the Palestinians."* [From the review by Julie Peteet, *AA* 89:1018–1022, 1987.]

Hungarian X-Ray Film (1960) 11 min. Haskins Lab (PR). Dist: PSU. *Articulatory movements shown by X-ray techniques. Prepared scripts illustrate selected phonetic features in the phonemic contrasts of the language, ending with several sentences to show the features in running speech. Informants picked for linguistic suitability and lack of physical characteristics that interfere with X-ray quality and sound processing.*

Hunger Knows No Law 30 min. North Slope Borough Teleproduction Studio (PR). Dist: MDAI VS$59.95, order #331-03. *Whales are a source of food to the North Slope Eskimo. Whales and whaling have been the basis of a culture thousands of years old. Can such a culture exist today?*

Hungry Angels (1961) 20 min. Institute of Nutrition of Central America and Panama (PR). Dist: Association Films, 600 Grand Avenue, Ridgefield, NJ 07657. *Malnutrition in Guatemala.* [Reviewed by John H. Himes, *AA* 80:511–512, 1978.]

The Hunters (1958) 73 min. John Marshall (FM), Study Center, Peabody Museum, Harvard University (PR). Dist: FIV VR$79, FS$845; IUAVC FR$22; NYU FR$22; UCEMC Color FR$29, B/W FR$21; PSU(PCR) B/W order #7003N, FR$14.20, Color order #70010 FR$25.30; CRM/MH FR$50, FS$610. *Life and culture of a group of !Kung San (formerly called Bushmen) in the northern Kalahari Desert, emphasizing the quest for food in the harsh environment. The climax of the film is the 13-day chase after a giraffe is wounded by a poison arrow.* Warning: Although still a magnificent account of San hunting, it represents the 1950s understanding of the San and of foragers in general, exaggerating the role of hunting and neglecting the importance of gathering. [Reviewed by Bill Nichols, *AA* 82:228–229, 1980.] Bibliography: Richard Borshay Lee, *The !Kung San: Men, Women, and the Work in a Foraging Society*. Cambridge: Cambridge University Press, 1979. See other Marshall films listed under San Series.

Hunters and Bombers (1990) 54 min. Nigel Markham and Hugh Brody (FM). Dist: NFB. *"The struggle of the Innu (the Naskapi-Montagnais Indians of Quebec-Labrador) with Canadian federal and provincial authorities over the deployment of NATO low-level fighter-pilot training in Labrador."* [From the review by Stephen Loring., *AA* 94:526–527, 1992.]

Hunters and Gatherers (Man on the Rim Series) 58 min. Dist: LMF VS$295. *This film follows the spread of the first arrivals in the continent of Australia, describing the ingenious ways in which the various tribes adapted to the different regions and their flirtation with agriculture and house building.*

The Hunter's Edge 27 min. Earl H. Swanson (DI), Idaho State University Museum (PR), Don E. Crabtree (AN). Dist: IMI FR$30, FS$355. *A study of blade making, an important prehistoric toolmaking process or series of processes used widely during the last 40,000 years of human prehistory. Blades are remarkable cutting tools associated with widespread prehistoric hunting. The film shows several techniques for making large and small specimens as well as the use of some in composite hunting implements. These films are for classroom use and come with teachers' guides.* [Reviewed by Anthony E. Marks, *AA* 77:914–915, 1975. Susanna R. Katz and Paul R. Katz, *ARCH* 34(1):60, 1981.]

Hunters of the Seal: A Time of Change (1976) 32 min. Dist: T-L FR$40, FS$425, VS$100; IUAVC FR$13.50; SU FR$21. *Discusses the acculturation that has occurred in the traditional lifestyle of the Netsilik Eskimos, the People of the Seal, since the introduction of modern technology by the federal government. Uses historical film footage to show their traditional hunting culture and contrasts this with their new government-built village. Examines other cultural changes and points out the Netsilik's attempt to work with the government while still maintaining their old culture.*

Huteetl: A Koyukon Memorial Potlatch (1983) 55 min. Curt Madison (FM). Dist: Curt Madison, Manley Hot Springs, AK 99756; (907) 672-3262, VS$138; RTP VS$100. *This is a video documenting the final death rites for a young couple who died in a small plane crash in 1981. In the Koyukon Athabaskan tradition, a memorial potlatch was given over a year later. More than 200 people joined the 100 residents of Hughes for the week-long celebration releasing the deceased spirit from a year of wandering.* [Reviewed by Tom Johnston, *AA* 90:1040, 1988.]

The Hutterites (1968) 28 min. B/W. National Film Board of Canada (PR). Dist: Open Circle Cinema, P.O. Box 315, Franklin Lake, NJ 07417, FS$250; PSU (PCR) order

#30546, FR$14; UCEMC FR$13. *The Hutterite way of life. Strong in their rejection of what they regard as the false values of the world, the followers of Jacob Hutter, after four centuries of persecution, finally settled in western Canada where they now live according to their beliefs in prosperous farm colonies. Focusing questions: How are the Hutterites able to achieve a state of cultural pluralism despite pressures toward assimilation? How do the Hutterites differ from current sects and cults? What socialization techniques support the cultural transmission to the younger generation?* Bibliography: John Horsch, *The Hutteritian Brethren 1528–1931*. Gosher, Indiana: The Mennonites Historical Society, 1931. Lee Deets, *The Hutterites: A Study of Social Cohesion*. Gettysberg, PA: Time News Publishing Company, 1939. [James R. Stewart]

The Hutterites: To Care and Not to Care (1984) 58 min. Burton Buller (PR), John L. Ruth (DI). Dist: Buller Films Inc., 1053 N. Main St., Henderson, NE 68371; (402) 723-4737, FR$80, FS$800. *"Scattered over the high plains of North America, from South Dakota to British Columbia, lie the 300 settlements of the Hutterites. For over 400 years, these people . . . have maintained a communal way of life based on Christian teachings. They are descendants of 400 migrants from Russia."* [From the review by George L. Hicks, *AA* 88:1043–1044, 1986.] Study guide included. Suggested supplements: Hostetler and Huntington, *The Hutterites in North America*. Holt, Rinehart & Winston, 1980. John Bennett, *Hutterian Brethren*. Stanford, 1967.

Hymns of Praise (Morocco, Body and Soul Series) (1987) 26 min. Izza Genini (FM). Dist: FRIF FR$55, FS$470, VS$260. *Records the annual pilgrimage to the "moussem," or sanctuary, of Moulay Idriss I, who founded the first Islamic kingdom of Morocco. The festival is inaugurated by several Sufi brotherhoods with a nighttime ceremony called the "Kharma." As they spin to the music of drums and oboes, the Sufi followers reach the ecstatic state of mystical communion with God. For eight days afterward, thousands of pilgrims stream into the moussem, as the houses and cafes fill with the sounds of lutes, violins, and tambourines, beckoning visitors to dance themselves into a trance that will free them from their inner conflicts.*

I Ain't Lying: Folktales from Mississippi (1975) 20 min. William Ferris (DI), Dale Lindquist (FM), Howard Sayre Warner (CON). Dist: CSF FR$30, FS$325. *Tales of gravediggers and rich old ladies, preachers and alligators, and brotherly meetings in hell—all energetically and colorfully told by some of the best storytellers in the region. The film takes you into homes, churches, and juke joints for a gutsy, authentic slice of Southern humor and life. A version for younger students edited for language and content is also available.* [Reviewed by David Evans, *JAF* 90(355):116, 1977.]

I Am Fijian (1980) 26 min. Juniper Films (PR), James Wilson and David Tristram (DI, CA). Dist: IFF FR$45, FS$450. *Fiji has been an independent nation since 1972. The film examines its people in present-day contexts. This leads the viewer to experience the diversities of customs, traditions, and religions. Some, like the Hindu ritual of fire-walking or Fijian Kava ceremony, remain virtually unchanged. Others have been adapted or modified by western influences such as the Polynesian wedding and Fijian funeral service. What does emerge is that the various ethnic groups of Fiji coexist with little cultural borrowing. Traditions and customs are practiced with a fervor that betrays fear that their heritage is being compromised or lost.*

I Shall Moulder before I Shall Be Taken (1978) 58 min. S. Allen Counter and David L. Evans (FM), James Earl Jones (NA). Dist: EDC FR$80, FS$930, VS$695. *The Djuka are descendants of West Africans who were brought to South America in the 1600s as slaves for Dutch plantations. Soon after the slaves arrived, they rebelled, escaping into the jungle and establishing a black tribal society in the New World. Using guerrilla tactics, the Africans defeated European troops and mercenaries sent to subdue them and to return them to slavery. Having won their freedom, the blacks continued to live independently from the white colonial society, preserving the culture they had brought from West Africa. Today, the Djuka remain a remarkably pure example of ancient African culture within the modern world. The film begins with the ritual cleansing of the two Americans as they enter the first Djuka village and receive permission from the headman to remain. It goes on to cover the daily activities of the Djuka, as well as special ceremonies and religious events. The viewer sees women and children tending crops, often farmed many miles from the villages; tribesmen fishing by an ancient method, which involves beating the water with crushed roots that exude a poison, causing the fish to rise to the surface; the special rites preceding the felling of a huge tree destined to become a boat; the obeahman, or medicine man, collecting herbs and plants; ceremonial dances and dramas, performed by the villagers and the Obeahman, reenacting the escape of their ancestors from the plantations and their long and difficult struggle to be free. The highlight of the film is an extraordinary funeral procession, surrounded by elaborate rituals and involving the whole community.*

I Spent My Life in the Mines (1976) 40 min. June Nash, Juan Rojas, and Eduardo Ibanez (DI). Dist: CG FR$65.00, FS$535.00. *"In the late 1800's many peasants left the highlands of Bolivia and the Cochabamba Valley to seek work in the mining towns. The film depicts how they have been incorporated into an industrial labor force while retaining many aspects of their Indian peasant origins."* [From the review by Michael Kearney, *AA* 87:484–485, 1985.]

I Will Fight No More Forever (1975) 106 min. Richard T. Effron (Dl). Dist: AB FR$85. *Dramatization of one of the most tragic of the Indian wars. The 1877 campaign was waged by Army General Oliver Otis Howard against a band of Nez Perce Indians led by Chief Joseph, because the Indians refused to give up their tribal lands in Oregon's Wallawa Valley, as provided for by a treaty with the U.S. Government.*

Iawo (1978) 40 min. Geraldo Sarno (DI). Dist: CG FR$65.00, FS$550.00; UNI FR$65-100, FS$535. *This film examines the cult of the Orisha, Yoruba in origin, which was brought to the new world by black slaves, and which sur-*

vives to this day in several areas of the Americas, specially in Cuba and Brazil. During colonial times, in a society divided into masters and slaves, such religions were the only elements of integration and cultural resistance with which blacks could prevent the total domination of the white man's values. The cult has survived since the times of slavery, despite repression and prejudice, providing patterns of behavior and models of mutual assistance to Brazil's black populace. The initiation of a group of women into a temple serves as a focus of a deeper examination of the religion, its ideology and social meanings. Iawo is the name given to new priestesses.

The Ice Man (1992) 54 min. Katherine Everett (WR, PR). Dist: FHS VR$75.00, VS$90.00. *"This excellent program documents one of the most important archaeological discoveries of the century—the mummified body of a man more than 5,000 years old—an unprecedented bonanza for archaeology and for European prehistory in particular."* [From the review by Peter S. Allen, ARCH 46(3):66, 1993.]

Ice People (1970) 23 min. Dist: Fl FR$22, FS$315. *Over 10,000 years ago, man moved into the Arctic and adapted to its hostile environment. This anthropological study shows that the modern Eskimo must adapt again. These ingenious Arctic people lived with strong family ties, but no real feeling of nationhood. They prized freedom and individuality. Land and game were shared, aggression was abhorred. These admirable qualities are now making life difficult for the Eskimo because they are the antithesis of attitudes that bring success in Western culture. The Arctic people are finding that their old traditions and skills have been subverted. If they are to survive they must create a new lifestyle that bridges the two cultures.*

Iceman 101 min. Panorama Studios (PR). Dist: Swank Motion Pictures Inc., 60 Bethpage Road, Hicksville, NY FR$500.00. *The plot of the film is one for science fiction: time travel. Scientists working in the far north of the American continent find a glacial frament containing biological remains that they thought were from a mammoth but which, on thawing, turned out to be a neanderthal.* [From the review by Robert B. Eckhardt, AJPA 69:413–414, 1986.]

Icemen of Chimborazo (1986) 21 min. Gustavo Guayasamin (FM). Dist: FRIF FR$45.00, FS$400.00, VS$220.00. *"About Ecuadorean Indians who persist in their ancient occupation of carrying ice from the slopes of Mount Chimborazo to sell in local markets. The film traces the icemen's labor, from the braiding of ropes to the chopping of ice on the perilous glaciers of Chimborazo. The integrity, skill, and courage exhibited by the icemen in their traditional occupation contrasts strikingly with the degradation and powerlessness that await them in an urban, industrialized context."* [From the review by Catherine J. Allen, AA 92:1105–1108, 1990.]

Ida B. Wells: A Passion for Justice (1990) 53 min. William Greaves Productions, Inc. (PR). Dist: 230 W. 55th Street, New York, NY 10019 VR$60.00, VS$595.00. *"A worthy addition to any Black, women's or American history media collection."* [From the review by Leigh Marlowe, SBF 27:275, 1991.]

If It Fits (1978) 58 min. John Marshall (FM). Dist: DER FR$65.00, FS$650.00. *This film is set in the town of Haverhill in New England, which was a thriving center of shoe industry in 19th century and has lost its business to countries that offer cheap labor force and production costs. The issues raised in the film, as Sally Engle Merry points out, are extremely important given the global shift of economic centers today, some of these issues are "economic dislocation and its impact on local communities, the powerlessness of local governments in the face of the world economic processes, the competition of foreign producers, and demands for protection of less efficient American industries."* [Reviewed by Sally Engle Merry, AA 84: 986-87, 1982.]

Ifa Films (see University of Ife Series)

Ika Hands (1988) 58 min. Robert Gardner (FM). Dist: MOMA. *This film portrays the life of the Ika, native people of the Sierra Nevadas highlands in northern Colombia, who carry on a pre-Columbian culture. They may be the only surviving members of the once far-flung Mayan civilization. While on an informational level the film records the rounds of daily life, it concentrates on the character of one of the senior members of the group. It is perhaps unique among ethnographic films in that it attempts to understand the interior life of its main character. Gardner achieves this in part through his perceptive use of close-ups of face and hands and sensitive use of sound. His subject is described as a mystic who is part priest, part shaman, and we see him performing magic rituals in lonely and seemingly painful meditation, often accompanied by his own chanting and singing. The wide span of activities covered by the film are introduced by subtitles. Like most works of observational cinema, the film does show difficult to interpret situations.* [Reviewed by Catherine J. Allen, AA 92:1105–1108, 1990.] To assist the viewer, Gardner presents Gerardo Reichel-Dolomatoff, a leading interpreter of Ika life, and we hear his voice-over occasionally explaining some of the more obscure action.

Ikwe (Daughters of the Country Series) 57 min. Norma Bailey (FM). Dist: NFB FR$80.00, VR$80.00, FS$775.00, VS$150.00. *A remote area of North America, 1770. Ikwe, an Indian girl, is given to an ambitious Scot as part of a trade agreement. But the pain of her husband's insensitivity to the ways of her people drives her to leave him. When a small pox epidemic ravages her village, Ikwe puts her hopes in her one surviving child, a daughter, sending her to safety and the future she herself will never see.*

Ileksen (1978) 58 min. Dennis O'Rourke (PR, DI), Gary Kildea (DI). Dist: DCL FR$85.00, FS$895.00, VS$350.00. *Ileksen portrays Papua New Guinea's first general election in 1977. The documentary trails political candidates as they canvass for support and display a variety of approaches to the problem of winning votes. What emerges is a lively portrait of the country's struggle to adapt to a form of democracy that it has imported wholesale.*

IMAGE INDIA: THE HINDU WAY H. David Smith (WR, DI). Dist: Syracuse University Film Rental Center, 1455 E. Colvin St., Syracuse, NY 13210. *An 11-film series on Hindu* *religious rites and celebrations. Photographed on location among the Tengalai Sri-vaisnava Brahmins of Madras, Southern India.* Each film comes with a helpful user's guide. [Reviewed by Paul Hockings, AA 74:1585–1587, 1972.]

- **How a Hindu Worships: At the Home Shrine** 18 min. FS$190.
- **Hindu Temple Rites: Bathing the Image of God** 13 min. FS$140.
- **Hindu Sacraments of Childhood: The First Five Years** 25 min. FS$260.
- **Monthly Ancestral Offerings in Hinduism** 8 min. FS$100.
- **Radha's Day: Hindu Family Life** 17 min. FS$180.
- **Pilgrimage to a Hindu Temple** 14 min. FS$150.
- **Hindu Procession to the Sea** 8 min. FS$100.
- **The Hindu Sacrament of Thread Investiture** 14 min. FS$150.
- **Hindu Devotions at Dawn** 10 min. FS$120.
- **The Hindu Sacrament of Surrender** 8 min. FS$100.
- **A Hindu Family Celebration: 60th Birthday** 9 min. FS$110.

The Image Maker and the Indians (1979/80) 17 min. George Quimby, Bill Holm, David Gerth (PR). Dist: UWP FS$275. *How the famous pioneer cinematographer, Edward S. Curtis, made the first full-length documentary film of native Americans. The 1914 film was edited and restored with Indian soundtrack in 1973 by Quimby, Holm, and Gerth. (See* In the Land of the War Canoes.*) This film is an audiovisual history of Curtis as cinematographer and provides background on how he came to make the film and the methods he used to make it. In addition to previously unpublished photographs and documents, the testimony of Indians who were actors or spectators at the 1914 filming is recorded.* Relevant anthropological literature: Bill Holm and George Irving Quimby, *Edward S. Curtis in the Land of the War Canoes: A Pioneer Cinematographer in the Pacific Northwest,* 1980.

IMAGES OF INDIA SERIES Jerry Bannister and Christina Carver Pratt (WR, NA),George Theisen and Marie O'Brien (FM), R. Rajagopalan (MU). Dist: WCMS VS$100.00 each.

- **Part 1: India—Images from the Cultural Past** 49 min. *Explores cultural themes of traditional India: its archeological antiquity; the 330 million gods of Hinduism, the one god of Islam; the Englightenment of the Buddha; Mughals, Maharajas, and the British Raj.* The videotape utilzes 35mm slide photography put on videotape. Motion is implied through the combination of zooms, pans, and dissoves.
- **Part 2: India—Images of Villages and Cities** 57 min. *Explores contemporary India with its often startling contrasts and continuities between village and city; focuses on religion, family, caste, status of women, poverty, and social needs; urban squatters and appropriate level technology.*

L'Imagination au Pouvoir (The Power of the Imagination) (1969) Jean Rouch (DI). Dist: CFE; DER.

Imaginero 52 min. Jorge Preloran (FM), Robert Gardner. Dist: PFI FR$60, FS$600; UCEMC FR$50. *The story of an Indian folk artist living in the barren country of northwest Argentina. His name is Hermogenes Cayo, a man who has dedicated his life to his art and whose paintings and sculptures express his mystical feelings. With classical simplicity, the filmmaker, himself an artist with the camera, follows Hermogenes in a variety of settings and gradually succeeds in reaching his soul. At the foot of the Andes, at a place where Inca and Spanish traditions meet, a poor peasant has the privilege of experiencing the sentimiento tragico de la vida. This film goes well beyond ethnographic descriptions of the obvious kind. It is essentially a reflection on the universality of the human condition.* [Reviewed by William E. Carter, AA 73:1473–1475, 1971.] English version.

Imagining Indians (1992) 90 min. Victor Masayesva, Jr. (FM). Dist: ISP. *A Hopi filmmaker presents the native perspective on the misrepresentation of Native Americans through American film.*

The Immigrant (1917) 20 min. Charles Chaplin (Dl). Dist: Eastin-Phelan Distributor Corporation, Box 4528, 1235 W. 55 Street, Davenport, IA 52808. *A British-born person's view of aspects of American life is depicted. Two immigrants meet on a boat bringing them to the United States. After adversity, they meet in the new land and unexpectedly encounter a way out of poverty and into happiness. Focusing questions: What signs can be seen to indicate American behavior in contrast to immigrants'? Inasmuch as it is a silent film, one can focus on such signs as clothes and gestures as culturally patterned communication.* [Vivian J. Rohrl]

Improvement and Utilization of Valle Resources—Valle, Colombia (1963) 15 min. The Land Tenure Center, University of Wisconsin (PR). Dist: UW. *The film describes CVC (an agency similar to TVA in the Unites States) in the fertile state of Valle. CVC provides an integrated development program in the state: provides people with land, credit, and education and has built dams and dikes to control floods and to provide for irrigation and electric power. Provides a look at problems of rural people in adjusting to the society of the industrial center of Cali.*

Imrat Khan Demonstrates the Sitar (1963) 12 min. (A Folklore Research Film by Peter and Toshi Seeger.) Dist: FIM/RF FR$15, FS$100. *Imrat Khan is a leading sitar player in India, and he is seen in his home in Calcutta with an accompanist on the tabla (traditional drum) playing and explaining his music to Pete Seeger. Even though the two players perform unrehearsed, they follow each other's rhythm perfectly and build their composition together. For purposes of demonstration, the normal long, slow introduction and gradual build-up of tempo were dispensed with.*

In and Out of Africa (1993) 59 min. Ilisa Barbash and Lucien Taylor (FM). Dist: VAP VR$75.00, VS$295.00; UCEMC VR$75.00, VS$295.00, order #38230. *A highly amusing ethnographic video about the discourses of authenticity and transvaluation of artifacts in the African art market. African art is highly prized and priced in the United States, and the film examines the production of "authentic"* *art pieces and their marketing to a gullible public abroad. The film has won numerous awards.*

In Danaku the Soup Is Sweeter 30 min. Gary Beitel (PR). Dist: FL VR$55.00, VS$295.00. *As in many African villages, life in Danaku in the north of Ghana has been a struggle for subsistence. The women bear the burden of caring for the children, raising food, and trying to make life better for their families. Through a special project of the Canadian International Development Agency, the women were given access to credit for the first time. This film shows how this little bit of financial aid allowed the women to become "entrepreneurs." We follow two women who take advantage of this program, borrowing a little bit of start-up money. We see how hard they work to pay back their loans. One makes butter from arduously pounding vegetables; the other cooks delicious soup from seasonal crops. They each sell their products from door to door and at the market near their village. Eventually, their efforts make small profit that affords their families some more comforts.*

In Heaven There Is No Beer? (1984) 51 min. Les Blank (DI). Dist: CCC FS$100.00. *This is a joyous romp through the dance, food, music, friendship, and even religion of the Polka. The energy and the bursting spirit of the polka subculture is rendered with both warmth and a dedication to scholarship in this journey through Polish-American celebration that takes us from New London, Connecticut's, "polkabration" to the International Polka Association's convention, with a stop along the way for a Polka mass in Milwaukee.*

In Her Own Time: Barbara Myerhoff's Final Field Work (1985) 60 min. Barbara Myerhoff (AN), Lynne Littman (FM), Vikram Jayanti (PR). Dist: DCL FR$100.00, FS$895.00, VS$350.00. *Continuing the important work she began with "Number Our Days," in 1981 anthropologist Barbara Myerhoff began studying the Fairfax neighborhood of Los Angeles. Here, Jews from around the world live together in a "voluntary ghetto." Myerhoff felt that the revitalization of the Fairfax area was due to the growing population of intensely religious Jews, particularly the orthodox Hassidic movement know as Chabad. Fascinated by the way the religion and the neighborhood worked together to create a community, she decided to make a film about this special village in the heart of Los Angeles. Dr. Myerhoff also explored her own evolving relationship to Orthodox Judaism. In doing so, she revealed how religious traditions and practices have meaning for families living active lives in the world today. The final work is a personal, spiritual, and social exploration of Judaism that has meaning for everyone.* [Reviewed by Faye Ginsburg, AA 90:237–238, 1988.]

In Iirgu's Time (From the Elders Series) (1988) 20 min. Katrina Waters (FM), Sarah Elder and Leonard Kramerling (EP, CC, CA). Dist: DER FR$35.00, VR$30.00, FS$390.00, VS$200.00. *Iirgu is an elder from the Siberian Yupik Eskimo village of Gambell on St. Lawrence Island. As two grandchildren listen, Iirgu recounts events in Gambell from the time the first missionaries arrived. His story is known as an ungipamsuk or true historical narrative. With ambivalent feelings, he describes more recent changes—how whaling practices have changed, how life has become easier, but also how younger generations are losing touch with the old ways.* [Reviewed by Richard H. Jordan, AA 92:5313, 1990.]

In India the Sun Rises in the East 14 min. Richard Kaplan Productions (PR). Dist: Richard Kaplan Productions, Inc., London Terrace Towers, 410 West 24th Street, Apt. 8F, New York, NY 10011. *This is a film of uninterrupted views of India. There is no narration, no dialogue—only the natural effects surrounding people and places, and the music native to the country. One sees and hears many things—farmers with their buffaloes and city dwellers with their bikes, chemists, printers, weavers, and potters; politicians, teachers, priests, sailors; transistor radios and the sound of a local language; temples and houses; cities and villages; harvests and celebrations; bazaars and beggars; sunrise and sunset. Seeing and hearing this montage of India, one is made to think, but is not told what to think. It is beautiful to view. It provides a continuity of free-flowing sound and imagery. It raises questions. It allows the fullest exercise of imagination. But the viewer must discover for himself what this film says about India.*

In Maori Land (1930s) 10–15 min. Dist: FCE FR$17, FS$95. *Attention paid to geyser hydrothermal area of New Zealand. Work of the school of carving in particular reference to continuing to make the Maori warrior figures. Reel concludes with dances by the girls and by the men.*

In Memory of Mawalan (1983) 92 min. Ian Dunlop (FM). Dist: FAA. *Malawan was the respected head of the Rirratjingu clan of northeast Arnhem land. He died at Yirrkala mission in 1967. In 1971, his son, Wandjuk Marika, organized a Djangkawu ceremony at Yirrkala, both as a memorial of his father and as a reaffirmation of the Djangkawu Law that Mawalan taught. At Wandjuk's invitation, this film was made. Throughout the ceremony, great importance is given to teaching the Djangkawu Law to the young people. For the Yolngu of Yirrkala, in 1971, the reaffirmation of their law was more important than ever; they had just lost their historic land rights case.*

In Memory of the Land and the People (1982) 50 min. Robert Gates (FM). Dist: Omnificent Systems, 1117 Virginia St., E., Charleston, WV 25301; (304) 342-2624, FR$75.00 FS$650.00. *"This film is effective in accomplishing the intent of its producer 'to provide the viewer with a gut level feeling for what strip mining as it is actually practiced does to the land and the people.'"* [From the review by Elizabeth A. Lawrence, AA 86:1057–1058, 1984.]

In Search of Ancient Astronauts (1972) 52 min. Alan Landsburg (PR), Rod Serling (NA). Dist: UWA. [Reviewed by Thomas Wight Beale, AA 77:899, 1975.]

In Search of Cool Ground: The Kwegu (see *The Kwegu*)

In Search of Cool Ground: The Migrants (see *The Migrants*)

In Search of Cool Ground: The Mursi (see *The Mursi*)

In Search of Grand Canyon's Past (1974) 35 min. Douglas W. Schwartz (DI), National Geographic Society

(PR). Dist: Douglas W. Schwartz, School of American Research, P.O. Box 2188, Santa Fe, NM 87501 FR$75. [Reviewed by David Wilcox and Susan Wilcox, *AA* 78:371–372, 1976.]

In Search of Justice. Dispute Settlement among the Anufom in Northern Togo (see Anufom Series)

In Search of the Magic of Stonehenge 24 min. Alan Landsburg (PR). Dist: PyrF FR$50.00, FS$500.00. *This film "is from the In Search Of television series narrated by Leonard Nimoy. . . . At no point does the narrator come right out and say that the megaliths were built with the aid of ancient astronauts. But this is certainly implied . . . shouldn't be shown to a student audience without knowledgeable critical commentary, and may be most useful as a springboard for discussion of where serious archaeology leaves off and where the lunatic fringe begins."* [From the review by Ronald Hicks, *ARCH* 33(4):60, 1981.]

In Search of Ourselves (1981) 27.5 min. Dist: New Film Company, 331 Newbury St., Boston, MA 02115; (617) 437-1323, FR$40.00, FS$385.00. *Survey of Earthwatch projects.* [Reviewed by by R. Carol Barnes, *AA* 86:504–506, 1984.]

In Search of Prehistory (1983) 30 min. A. M. Karami (FM). Dist: Mobile District Office, US Army Corps of Engineers, P.O. Box 2288, Mobile, AL 36628; (205) 694-4107. *"This film presents a basic view of field archeology as used on the Midden Mound Project on the Tennessee-Tombigbee Waterway in northeastern Mississippi. Field and field laboratory techniques are shown in a straightforward manner, from field survey, through testing and excavation, to processing and cataloging."* [From the review by William Hampton Adams, *AA* 87:226, 1985.]

In Search of the Lost World (1972) 52 min. Howard Campbell (Dl), Michael D. Coe (AN). Dist: Fl FR$65, FS$690. *New World culture history.* [Reviewed by Paul F. Healy, *AA* 78:360–361, 1976.]

IN SEARCH OF THE TROJAN WAR SERIES (1985) 55 min. each. Michael Wood (WR, NA), Bill Lyons (FM) for the BBC. Dist: Station KCET, 4401 Sunset Boulevard, Los Angeles, CA 90027; (213) 666-6500. *This six-part series "is not just a documentary presenting archaeological and literary evidence for a historical, Homeric Troy; the focus is rather on Wood himself and on his adventurous quest, which become ours as we retrace with him the paths of both modern and ancient actors in a drama that is still very much alive."* [From the review by S. Shelby Brown and Jeremy B. Rutter, *ARCH* 39(6):70–71, 1986. Related reading: Michael Wood, *In Search of the Trojan War*, Facts on File Publications, New York, 1985. *The titles in the series are:*

- The Age of Heroes
- The Legend under Siege
- The Singer of Tales
- The Women of Troy
- Empire of the Hittites
- The Fall of Troy

In the Ashes of the Forest (see The Decade of Destruction Series)

In the Footsteps of Taytacha 30 min. Peter Getzels and Harriet Gordon (FM). Dist: DER FR$55.00, VR$35.00, FS$550.00, VS$275.00. *The program follows a groups of Quechua-speaking musicians and dancers as they leave their remote villages high in the Andes Mountains of Peru and join thousands of other highlanders on the annual religious pilgrimage to the most sacred peaks of Qoyllur-Rit'i. Qoyllur-Rit'i, the largest and most important religious ritual in the southern Andes, occurs only five days out of the year and involves walking day and night over 4,400 meters. We learn the different perspectives about the festival from the villagers and the Catholic church. Throughout the festival the villagers explain what the ritual means to them both personally and collectively. By combining interviews with myths and narration, the film introduces us to an image of Andean highlanders and how they position themselves in a predominantly Catholic world.*

In the Good Old Fashioned Way (1973) 29 min. Dist: APPAL FR$45, FS$425. *The Old Regular Baptist Church is the oldest and one of the most unique churches in the mountains. This film shows the spirit and faith of the people of this church and the impact their religion has on their lives. Widespread only among mountain people, this religion is uniquely a product of the Appalachian culture. This film attempts to capture the feeling of the religion by following the people through various services and ceremonies while they explain their church as they see it.* [Reviewed in *JAF* 87(345):276, 1974.]

In the Land of the War Canoes: Kwakiutl Indian Life on the Northwest Coast (1914–74) 47 min. Edward S. Curtis (FM), Bill Holm and George Quimby, Burke Museum, University of Washington (ED, restored). Dist: UWP FS$650; MLS VS$39.95, order #MILE003. *An epic saga of Kwakiutl Indian life on the Northwest Coast of America. It was filmed in the summer of 1914 at Kwakiutl villages on Vancouver Island, Canada, by Edward S. Curtis, famous even then for his still photographs and writings of Indians. Under the old title of* In the Land of the Head Hunters, *the Curtis film was shown in theaters in Seattle and New York City in 1914–15, at which time the motion picture was very favorably reviewed. Then the film lapsed into obscurity and disappeared. In 1967 Professors Bill Holm and George Quimby of the Burke Museum, University of Washington, began a collaboration of research and editing of original Curtis footage owned by the Field Museum of Chicago. This footage had been donated to the Field Museum in 1947 while Professor Quimby was Curator in the Anthropology Department. In 1948, the nitrate film of Curtis was transferred to 16mm safety film, and the flammable original was destroyed. When Professor Quimby moved from the Field Museum to the University of Washington, he brought the film with him. By 1972 Professors Holm and Quimby had decided what to do with the Curtis film but needed technical assistance and thus was added to the project a key figure, David L. Gerth, a graduate of Rice University who had majored in photography and filmmaking at Rice Media Center. Mr. Gerth became Consulting Editor and Sound*

Recordist for the project. Under Holm and Gerth, a complete soundtrack was produced. The spoken parts, singing, and music are all in Kwakiutl and were produced with the aid of 50 Indian consultants, all members of the Kwakiutl Nation. Other sounds, water, fire, etc., were recorded as needed. Next, the Field Museum footage was placed in proper sequence in accord with unpublished evidence known to Holm and Quimby. Then, the 16mm silent film was optically stretched from silent speed to sound speed; the film defects were corrected as much as possible; and finally David Gerth had to mix all the sounds and synchronize them with the expanded film. Suggested supplements: Edward S. Curtis, *In the Land of the Head-Hunters.* World Book Co. (1975 reprint by Tamarack Press). Bill Holm and George Irving Quimby, *Edward S. Curtis in the Land of the War Canoes: A Pioneer Cinematographer in the Pacific Northwest.* Seattle: Washington University Press, 1980. [Reviewed by Ronald P. Rohner, *AA* 78:951, 1976. See *The Image Maker*]

In the Name of Allah (1970) 76 min. Roger Graef (FM), Dai Vaughn (ED), James Mason (NA). Dist: IU FR$18, FS$495. *The culture, vision, history, and scriptures of the religion of Islam are examined by looking closely at all aspects of life in the Muslim community of Fez, Morocco. The Koran, as brought forth by Mohammed, is the guide to all human experience and value. But, like other religions, Islam is suffering contradictions in a modern material world. Captured on film are the events of circumcision, bargaining for a wife, confirmation, and marriage (at which non-Muslims are forbidden), and the ceremonies and rituals surrounding each event.*

In the Name of God (1992) 90 min. Anand Patwardhan (FM). Dist: FRIF. *Hindu fundamentalism is a powerful movement in India. This film focuses on a campaign waged by Bishwa Hindu Parisshad (VHP) to reconstruct a 16th-century mosque where a temple to the Hindu god Ram once stood. It emphasizes the power of symbols in a battle for religious recognition.*

In the Shadow of the Law (1990) 58 min. Paul Espinosa (FM). Dist: UCEMC FR$50.00, VS$295.00. *An outstanding and sensitive portrait of four families who have lived illegally in the United States for many years. This documentary explores the daily lives of the family members, showing their constant fear of apprehension by the INS and their vulnerability to exploitation by those who capitalize on their illegal status. For these families, recent changes in immigration laws represent both hope and apprehension: will they qualify for amnesty and, finally, be able to come out of the shadows?*

In the Shadow of Vesuvius (1987) 59 min. National Geographic Society (PR). Dist: NGS FS$450.00, VS$280.00; Karol FR$50.00. "*The film assesses the impact of living 'in the shadow' of Mount Vesuvius by looking at events—both ancient and modern—that took place in several communities located near what is probably the world's most famous volcano. Only the first half of the film can be said to have archaeological merit; the second half is devoted to more recent eruptions.*" [From the review by Peter S. Allen, *ARCH* 41(3):66, 1988.]

In the White Man's Image (American Experience Series) (1992) 60 min. PBS (FM). Dist: PBS VR$59.95. "*Army officer Richard Henry Pratt wanted to help the Indians.... This is the theme of this illustration of cultural genocide. The film succeeds in showing just what the best of intentions, launched from a springboard of absolute conviction that one's own culture is intrinsically superior, can do to those regarded as inferior.*" [From the review by John A. Broussard, *SBF* 28:245, 1992.]

Inca Royal Architecture in the Cuzco Region By Susan Niles and Anne Paul. Dist: POR. Set of 104 slides, $145.00. See review by Peter S. Allen, *ARCH* 42(5):74–75, 1986.

The Incas (The Odyssey Series) (1980) 59 min. Marian White (DR). Dist: DER FR$50.00, FS$500.00. "*This film deals with current archeological and historical research about the Incas.... [B]eautifully photographed and highly recommended.*" [From the review by Martin K. Nickels, *SBF* 18:36, 1982. Reviewed by Peter S. Allen, *ARCH* 33(2):62, 1980.]

The Incas and Their Empire (1983) 32 min. John Hyslop (FM). Dist: RLI FS$39.95. *This filmstrip briefly explores the historical expansion of the Inca empire from its capital at Cuzco in the southern highland of Peru, setting the story of this great indigenous nation of the Andes in its geographical and chronological contexts.* [See the review by Alan L. Kolata, *ARCH* 40(4):70–71, 1987.]

Incident at Restigouche (1984) 45 min. Alanis Obomsawin (FM). Dist: NFB English Productions, Studio B, P.O. Box 6100, Montreal, Quebec, Canada H3C 3H5; (514) 283-4823. "*Documents the biggest and most violent action against Indians in Canada.... Touching on the question of relative jurisdictional power of Indian Bands vis-a-vis the provincial and federal governments... probes the political setting of native peoples inhabiting Quebec.*" [From the review by Harald Prins, *AA* 90:774–778, 1988.]

Included Out (1973) 2 min. Sharon Neufer Emswiler (PR, Dl). Dist: Mass Media Associated, 2116 North Charles St., Baltimore, MD 21218. *Ethnocentrism.* [Reviewed by Susan Dwyer-Shick, *AA* 77:469, 1975.]

India: An Introduction (1981) 25 min. Michael Camerini, James MacDonald (WR, Dl), Michael Sporn (AN), International Film Foundation (PR). Dist: IFF FR$50.00, FS$500.00. *This introduction to India puts aside images of snake charmers and Maharajas and looks at the more unfamiliar, as it covers India's complex problems. Shows teachers, gurus, farmers, factory workers, and television technicians, as well as artists. The film shows a school in Kerala, Hindus worshipping in Banaras, a movie studio in Bombay, a steel mill near Calcutta, and a cloth mill in Ahmadabad—in the world's seventh most industrialized nation. The film uses animated maps to show the Himalayas and farmlands, the paths of monsoon rains, and population density, as well as highlighting India's many* *alphabets and languages.* [Reviewed by Lina Fruzzetti, *AA* 85:750, 1983. Edward O. Henry, *SBF* 17:22, 1982.]

India and the Infinite 30 min. Huston Smith (NA). Dist: HFF FR$45.00, FS$395.00, VS$89.00. *Dr. Huston Smith guides us through India and her many religions.*

India Cabaret (1986) 60 min. Mira Nair (FM). Dist: FL FR$85.00, FS$850.00, VS$700.00. *"Uses a culturally specific vehicle—the world of cabaret dancers in Bombay—to raise questions about the social contradictions and the double sexual standard in patriarchal societies, especially those societies in which men's honor depends on women's virtue."* [From the review by Serena Nanda, *AA* 90:493, 1988. Reviewed in *VISA* 4:95, 1991.]

India's Sacred Cows (1981) 28 min. Canadian Broadcasting Corp. (PR). Dist: Mac FR$35.00, FS$375.00. *"The importance of cattle in the lives of the people of India, particularly rural, small free-holders and peasant farmers, is well portrayed in this exceedingly professional film."* [From the review by Thomas J. Maloney, *SBF* 17:166, 1982. Study guide available.

Indian Art of the Pueblos (1976) 13 min. Dist: EBEC; UCEMC FR$21. *Shows many of the native arts and crafts of the Pueblo Indians of Arizona and New Mexico and examines their significance in the religious and social life of the tribes.*

Indian Canoes along the Washington Coast (1971) 18 min. Louis and Ruth Kirk for Clover Park School District (PR). Dist: UWP FS$250. *This film demonstrates how, and with what tools, a traditional cedar dugout canoe is carved. Also shown are highly competitive river and saltwater races, the stocking of a king salmon fish hatchery, dancing, and a salmon bake.*

Indian Mainstream 25 min. Vern Korb (FM). Dist: PSU FR$13. *Focuses on the development of an economic base for Native Americans in northern California. Through a unique project at Humboldt State University, called "a walking university of Indian heritage," old skills almost lost to 20th-century technology are being revived and used to support many people who otherwise could not find employment. In addition, the restoration of these skills has sparked a renewed awareness of the meaning of Indian culture among the people involved. The film can be used to demonstrate to minority groups that one's culture need not be sacrificed in order to fit into the 20th century—that, in fact, it can be developed and its continuation can be a source of profit. To illustrate this, the film shows the reconstruction of ancient Hupa and Hurok villages, production of a great red wood dugout canoe, preparation of food in the ancient ways, and traditional basket-weaving, dancing, and beaded costumes.*

An Indian Pilgrimage: Kashi 30 min. Mira Reym Binford and Michael Camerini (FM). Dist: UW-SAAS FR$25.00, FS$225.00. *Follows two Telugu-speaking brahmans and their wives who come from South India to the sacred city of Kashi on the Ganges River to perform classical ancestor rites. They are instructed in the correct performance of these rites by a brahman Telugu-speaking priest who depends for his livelihood on providing services to pilgrims such as these. The pilgrims supplement their orthodox ritual activities with shopping in the bazaars and visiting Kashi's tourist attractions. They explain in their own words their reasons for making the pilgrimage and their pleasure at having finally seen Kashi. Accompanied by teacher's guides with background information and suggestions for discussions. Produced with synchronous sound interviews in Bengali, Hindi, Tamil, with English subtitles.*

An Indian Pilgrimage: Ramdevra 26 min. Mira Reym Binford and Michael Camerini (FM). Dist: UW-SAAS FR$20.00, FS$200.00. *Follows a group of Hindus on a folk pilgrimage to the grave of Ramdev, a medieval martial hero and saint of Rajasthan. In a folk pilgrimage, devotion rather than ritual is emphasized, and pilgrims are free to worship in their own ways with a minimum of priestly intermediaries. At Ramdev's grave, the Bombay pilgrims make their collective offering, including martial flags and a statue of a horse. One of the women goes into a trance as the spirit of Ramdev "enters" her. Outside the shrine, the pilgrims mingle with the crowds of shoppers at the fair, observe other pilgrims, and listen to preachers, hawkers, and devotional singers who throng the Ramdevra festival. Accompanied by teachers' guides with background information and suggestions for discussion. Produced with synchronous sound interviews in Bengali, Hindi, Tamil, with English subtitles.* [Reviewed by Paul Hockings, *AA* 78:958, 1976.]

Indian Self-Rule: A Problem of History 58 min. Selma Thomas (FM), KWSU-TV Seattle (PR). Dist: DER VR$60.00, VS$400.00. *After centuries of struggle, the Indians of North America own less than 2 percent of the land first settled by their ancestors. This video traces the history of white-Indian relations from 19th-century treaties through the present, as tribal leaders, historians, teachers, and other Indians gather at a 1983 conference organized to reevaluate the significance of the Indian Reorganization Act of 1934. The experiences of the Flathead Nation of Montana, the Navajo Nation of the Southwest, and the Quinalt people of the Olympic Peninsula illustrate some of the ways Indians have dealt with shifting demands imposed upon them, from allotment to reorganization to termination and relocation. Particularly eloquent are Indian reflections upon the difficulties of maintaining cultural identities in a changing world and within a larger society that views Indians with ambivalence.* [Reviewed by William Graves III, *AA* 88:265–266, 1986.]

The Indian Speaks 41 min. Dist: NFBC. *Documents the effects of reserve life on the Indians of the Northern Plains of Canada and poses the dilemma faced by them: Shall they live the way of the white man, or cling to what remains of the Indian way?*

Indian Worker: From Village to City (1977) 17 min. Michael Camerini (CA, DI), University of Wisconsin, South Asian Studies (PR). Dist: IFF FR$35, FS$300. *The film depicts the life of an "urban villager" in India. Shripal works at a cloth mill on the outskirts of New Delhi, but his wife and two small children have remained in his village.*

His city friends are from the same area of North India, and they work and live together. Shripal can only rarely visit his family, but when he does, he enjoys village life, and it would be easy for him to adjust to it again.

The Indians (see Decade of Destruction Series)

Indians and Chiefs (1972) 40 min. Judith MacDougall (FM), David MacDougall (CA). Dist: UCEMC FR$28. *This narrationless documentary, in cinema-verite style, shows problems of American Indians trying to maintain their Indian identity while they learn to master the white man's world, on his terms. It focuses on one summer's events at the Los Angeles Indian Center, an Indian-run urban meeting place that provides help for thousands of Indians emigrating from rural reservations. The Indian Center needs funds to survive, so a huge Indian Fair is planned; the mechanics of obtaining permits and publicity, and organizing parking and food concessions becomes, for the commercially inexperienced Indians, an important learning process. The organization's director, Ernie Stevens, producer of the event, and some of his assistants find that they must often act on their own to make speedy decisions, which raises problems because the traditional egalitarian structure of Indian society does not give such authority to leaders. The fair itself combines feathered drummers, Ferris wheels, beauty contests, reservation Indians with their craftwork, Hollywood Indians doing stunts, the mayor accepting an honorary feather bonnet, traditional Indian dancing, and an Indian rock group. It is at times a display of gross commercialism, yet commercial is what it was meant to be. It demonstrates the Indians' newfound ability to manage such a large event, and it shows that the Indians have a saleable product in the white man's world—their own culture.* [Reviewed by Gifford S. Nickerson, *AA* 76:719–720, 1974.]

INDIANS OF THE ORINOCO SERIES International Film Foundation (PR), Hermann Schlenker (CA). Dist: IFF FS$1670 (series). *The Makiritare Indians, of the Caribe family, live in the mountainous jungles of Venezuela and Brazil, near the headwaters of the Orinoco River. Excellent boatsmen and good farmers, their ancestors migrated southward from the West Indies, to southern Venezuela, less than 500 years ago. During a two-month expedition to a typically small Makiritare village, Schlenker filmed many of the Indians' daily activities. The result is a series of eight short color films providing detailed observations on the lives of these people. Today the Makiritare have little contact with the outside world. Its presence is reflected only in some metal pots and tools, bits of cloth, and some beads obtained through trade. They grow and subsist on manioc and bananas, occasionally fishing or hunting monkeys and turkeys. Not having salt, they use chili pepper for seasoning. The village of Kononama, made remote and practically inaccessible by the mountains and dense jungle, consists of 25 people, grouped into several families. There is a chief, his wives, and children, including several young, unmarried girls. Typical of Makiritare villages, one round house shelters most of the people, while a few live in adjacent huts. Some buildings have no walls, as they are used only as workshops and storage sheds. There is a river nearby and the families' fields are within a day's walk.* [Reviewed by Nelly Arvelo-Jimenez, *AA* 74:1588–1589, 1972.]

THE MAKIRITARE (YE'CUANA)

- **Blowgun** 13 min. $230, FR$25.
- **Manioc Bread** 11 min. FS$210, FR$25.
- **Woodwinds and Dance** 10 min. FS$200, FR$25.
- **Craftsmen** 12 min. FS$220, FR$25.
- **Jungle Farming** 10 min. FS$200, FR$25.
- **Village Life** 12 min. FS$220, FR$25.

THE WAIKA AND MAKIRITARE

- **Food Gathering (Snake, Fish, Worms)** 11 min. FS$210, FR$25.
- **Journey to the Makiritare** 9 min. FS$180, FR$25.

Indonesia (Asian Insight Series) (1988) 50 min. Film Australia (PR). Dist: FIV VS$158.00. *Indonesia gained independence from the Netherlands in 1945. Explores the Dutch influence on Indonesian society and the cultural diversity of this region.*

INDONESIA: A GENERATION OF CHANGE (1987) Barbara Barde (DI). Dist: CTC FS$3100.00, VS$1695.00, order #NDSP12. *The first major series of its kind to be produced about this fascinating and rapidly changing part of the Pacific Rim. The world's fifth most populous country is vast both in terms of population, 165 million, and geographic area, which is scattered over an archipelago of almost 14,000 islands. Throughout, the blend of traditional and modern imagery makes this series a rare insight into an important and rapidly evolving country. Titles of the films comprising this series are:*

- **Out of the Shadows**
- **A Place in the Sun**
- **Tanah Air—Our Land, Our Water**
- **To Dream the Possible Dream**
- **Trading Places—Indonesia Meets the West**
- **Legacy of a Javanese Princess**

Indonesia: A Time to Grow 19 min. McGraw-Hill in collaboration with Vision Associates (PR). *The film centers around the trip to market of an Indonesian farmer, Sukanta, and his ten-year-old son, Djuki, who live in a village four miles from the rapidly growing capital city of Djakarta. Farm and village life are seen in reflective scenes. City life is seen through the eyes of Djuki, as he accompanies his older brother Suriana, a scholarship student at the university, on a walking tour of Djakarta. The trip to market and the thoughts of the two brothers suggest the dilemmas posed by the imposition of modern values in a traditional society as Indonesia begins its emergence into the modern world.*

Infant Development (see Jane Goodall: Studies on the Chimpanzee Series)

Ingestion of Food I (Common Tree Shrew) 9.5 min. Dist: PSU FR$2.80.

Ingestion of Food II (Common Tree Shrew) 4.5 min. Dist: PSU FR$2.80.

INHABITANTS OF THE LAND GRACE John Dickinson (FM). Dist: DER. *The series focuses on folk artists of the area around coastal Cumana, close to Trinidad (Eastern Venezuela).* [Reviewed by John M. Schechter, AA 89:525–532, 1987.]

• **Cruz Quinal: El Rey del Bandolin (King of the Bandolin)** (1984) 28 min. FR$45.00, VR$35.00, FS$480.00, VS$350.00. *"Opens with the musician holding a unique musical instrument—a double-fingerboard bandolin."* [From the review by John M. Schechter.]

•**El Diablo de Cumana (Cumana Devil)** (1984) 26 min. FR$40.00, VR$35.00, FS$450.00, VS$350.00. *"Treats 53-year-old Luis del Valle Hurtado, documenting his street theatrical art—that of a 'devilist.' He has adopted Lucifer—black Satan—as his model for regular, heavily attended, peformances at unspecifed religious holidays and at Carnival and New Year's celebrations."* [From the review by John M. Schechter.]

• **Cleto Rojas, Pintor Campesino (Peasant Painter)** (1984) 18 min. FR$30.00, VR$25.00, FS$325.00, VS$250.00. *"Pictured is a modest subsistence farmer, who throughout insists that he loves painting but knows nothing about it. Possessed of a chromatic style, devoted to landscape realism ... with a good admeasure of the fantastic and sensual, the prolific Rojas paints full canvases, enormously detailed, often filled with people."* [From the review by John M. Schechter.]

The Inheritance 60 min. Harold Mayer (Dl), International Ladies Garment Workers Union (PR). Dist: Anti-Defamation League, B'Nai B'Rith; Portland State Media. *Focuses on turn-of-the-century immigrants arriving at New York, conditions of early ethnic neighborhoods, working conditions in sweat shops, acculturation, union organizing and labor struggles through World War II, depression, New Deal, and post–World War II. Cinematic features: B/W, archival photos and film with narration and interviews, excellent folk music score. Focusing questions: What is the relationship between social class and ethnicity? How does each class use the court system? What is The Inheritance?* [Dan Early]

Inheritance (1987) 80 min. Bill Donovan (FM). Dist: Bill Donovan, Inc., 165 Grand Boulevard, Scarsdale, NY 10583; (914) 472-0938 or (212) 757-6300, FS$2000.00, VS$750.00. *The problems of the wealthy in America.* [Reviewed by George E. Marcus AA 92:265–266, 1990.]

Initiation (1975) 45 min. Jean Rouch (DI), Centre National de la Recherche Scientifique, Comité du Film Ethnographique (PR). Dist: CFE; DER. *Ritual initiation to a possession dance of a young women possessed by Kirey, the thunder spirit.*

Initiation à la danse des possédés (Initiation into Possession Dances) (1948–49) 22 min. Jean Rouch (DI), Centre National de la Recherche Scientifique (PR). Dist: CFE; DER. *A woman is initiated into ritual possession dances among the Songhay of Firgoun, Niger.*

An Initiation Kut for a Korean Shaman (1991) 37 min. Laurel Kendall (WR), Diana Lee (FM). Dist: UHP VS$30.00. *Chini, a 32-year-old Korean woman, is convinced that she is a destined shaman and that she will know only hardship and misery until she is successfully initiated. We see her initiation kut and learn of the events leading up to it. At this ritual, Chini must demonstrate her ability to perform like a shaman, shouting out the spirits' oracles. Her teachers coax, scold, and instruct her, revealing their own sense of what it means to become a shaman and to perform a kut. The participants offer their own explanations of Chini's fate and the ritual intended to change her situation. The anthropologist's narration is mingled with the skillfully translated voices of the Korean shamans.*

Inner Mongolia—In Search of History (From Africe to Asia: Nomads) (1992) 60 min. Dr. Margaret Wilson (AN). Dist: FIV VS$198.00. *Today, in the territory once dominated by Genghis Khan, only a few thousand of his descendants are left. The nomads of Bayinhot in inner Mongolia are the last remaining year-round nomads of inner-Asia.*

Inside China: Living with the Revolution (Disappearing World Series) (1983) 52 min. Barbara Hazard (AN). Dist: FIV VS$198.00, order #047036; PSU order #51245. *This program uses firsthand accounts to create a unique portrait of life in China, which is home to a quarter of the world's population. The lives of two families, the Dings and the Zhus, who live near Wuxi in southwest China, are affected daily by the social and political changes that are taking place in their country.*

Inside China: The Newest Revolution (Disappearing World Series) (1983) 52 min. Barbara Hazard (AN). Dist: FIV VS$198.00, order #047037; PSU order #51246. *This program continues the story of the Dings and the Zhus, two families who were first interviewed in "Inside China: Living with the Revolution." Filmed at work and at home, these people show the human side of the political and social changes that have swept China this century.*

THE INTERPERSONAL TASK (1986) 40 min. Dane Archer, Mark Constanzo (PR). Dist UCEMC VR$36.00, VS$370.00. *Shows 30 brief scenes that depict common types of social interaction. Each scene is preceeded by a single question, such as: 'Who is the higher status person?'* [Reviewed by Michael Moerman, AA 90:1041–1042, 1988.]

Into the Deep Freeze (Man on the Rim Series) 58 min. Dist: LMF VS$295.00. *While Ice Age people were moving out of Southeast Asia to Australia and New Guinea, others were pushing north, through northern China to the colder tundra of Siberia and even to the frozen Arctic. Survey the people from Soviet Siberia, Aleutian Islands, and Alaska who have learned to cope with cold.*

Intrepid Shadows (see Navajo Film Themselves Series)

Introduction to Chimpanzee Behavior (see Jane Goodall: Studies on the Chimpanzee Series)

Inughuit: The People at the Navel of the Earth (1987) 85 min. Staffan Julen and Ylva Julen (FM). Dist: AC FR$175.00, FS$1250.00, VS$90.00. *"Documents daily life* *in a village along the northwestern coast of Greenland from the breakup of ice in the spring through summer to the succeeding months of winter darkness. Flashbacks are carefully interwoven to provide a historical perspective on current conditions.... The central theme is cultural survival and the external forces that threaten the future of these people."* [From the review by Richard H. Jordan, *AA* 92:531–533, 1990.]

Inuit Kids (1987) 15 min. Dist: BF FR$35.00, VR$35.00, FS$315.00, VS$245.00. *"Inuit children are portrayed in this program as living within a rich and historic society in which several somewhat incompatible and gradually diverging options are now open to them.... The film can be used to raise issues for class discussion but not without considerable preparation of both the class and instructor."* [From the review by Albert A. Dekin, Jr., *SBF* 24:107, 1988.]

Inventing Reality (Millennium: Tribal Wisdom and the Modern World Series) (1992) David Maybury-Lewis (H), Hans Zimmer (MU). Dist: PBS VS$49.95, order #MILL-108-RCD. *Have our needs for certainty and objectivity in our lives closed off the magical influence of the natural world? Is there, in fact, a balance to strike? Follow Maybury-Lewis to the Huichol Indian villages of central Mexico to witness a Mexican doctor and a tribal shaman battling an epidemic of a rare strain of deadly measles. Then visit a cancer center in Canada. Through these two examples, understand how the certainties of science can combine with natural conceptions of physical disease both in the tribal world of the shaman and in the thinking of modern medical science. Then travel to the wilderness of Australia to ask the question: Is reality something we shape, as the Australian Aborigines believe, or does it shape us?*

An Invisible Enemy (Disappearing World Series) (1987) 52 min. Georg Henriksen (AN). Dist: FIV VS$198.00, order #047038; PSU order #51247. *The radioactive fallout from Chernobyl threatens the economic and cultural survival of the reindeer-breeding Sami of Scandinavia. Radiation has contaminated reindeer meat—up to 133 times the acceptable level—and made it difficult to sell. Sami families are trying to carry on, but Sami youth face a future in which reindeer breeding may have no part.*

Invisible Indians: Mixtec Farmworkers in California (1993) 43 min. Division of Information Technology, UC Davis (PR). Dist: UCEMC VR$50.00, VS$195.00, order #38251. *An interdisciplinary look at the history, culture, and current social economic conditions of the Mixtec people of Oaxaca, Mexico.* Instruction guide included. Available in Spanish.

Invisible Walls (1969) 12 min. Richard A. Cowan and Lucy Turner (AN, FM). Dist: UCEMC FR$12, FS$95; PSU FR$20, FS$105. *Shot mainly in southern California shopping centers with a concealed camera to show peoples' reactions when an actor/actress violates their personal space. Opening and closing sequences composed of many shots showing different uses of space (e.g., Americans have 18-inch bubbles; cultures with higher population density have smaller personal bubbles). Middle section on experiment: confederates, proporting to be interviewing for market study, move in on subject who then takes some evasive action. No systematic concern for subculture variables (i.e., age, sex, etc.).* Warnings: Uses 1950s formulation of "18-inch invisible wall" surrounding "Americans." Deception experiment and at least one sexist shot, which did not seem as bad in the 1960s. Focusing questions: What is your comfortable distance? Is "bubble" a good metaphor for this phenomenon? What factors vary space? Does personal space decrease with increasing population density? What are the ethical considerations in doing this sort of research? Bibliography: Edward T. Hall, *The Silent Language*, 1959 (Doubleday Anchor paperback, 1973) Other works by Hall on Proxemics.

Iowa's Ancient Hunters: An Archaeological Reconstruction of a Prehistoric Site (1978) 28 min. Dist: UIOWA order # 50583, FR$17.50. *Documents the location and excavation of the Cherokee Dig, site of three prehistoric civilizations in northwest Iowa. Emphasizes the need for an interdisciplinary approach—geology, biology, and archaeology—in order to recreate the land forms, weather, plant, animal, and human life that existed in this location over 8,000 years ago. Three deeply buried cultural layers were gradually defined, one on top of another. The deepest lay 26 feet below ground surface. The remains of bison suggested these were hunting camps or places where bison had been trapped and killed a very long time ago. As excitement grew over the discovery scientists from other institutions aided in the investigation. Radiocarbon dates show that the cultural layers dated 6,300, 7,400, and 8,500 years old. An interdisciplinary research team began to work out the complex questions of the climate, terrain, and animal life in the region 8,000 years before Columbus discovered America. The film traces the history of the project from field excavation through laboratory analysis.*

Iramudun (1985) 45 min. Barry Machin (PR). Dist: PCR VR$19.00, VS$245.00, order #50771. *The people of southwestern Sri-Lanka believe that demonic possession causes illness. The first complete record of the ritual conducted to exorcise the demon thought to be responsible for the sickness of a patient that western medicine has failed to cure. The rituals are complex hierarchies of gifts to the demons given in an effort to persuade them to cease afflicting the patient.* [Reviewed by Akos Ostor, *AA* 90:493–494, 1988.]

The Iron Mountain: A Siberian Creation Myth (see Creation Myth Series)

Iron Working in Ufipa National Museum of Tanzania (PR), Kristen L. L. Christensen (CA), P. L. Carter (Dl), Tom Wylie, J. A. R. Wembah-Rashid (AN). Dist: National Museum of Tanzania, P.O. Box 511, Dar es Salaam, Tanzania. B/W. The film is available in three versions: (i) Silent, 50 min. T.shs. 2,400; (ii) Optical English sound, 50 min. T.shs. 2,600; (iii) Optical sound English or Kiswahili, 20 min. T.shs. 1,300. *A demonstration of traditional iron smelting and forging that carries along with it a lot of ritual.* [Reviewed by Arthur Steinberg, *AA* 77:693, 1975.]

Is It Hot in Here? A Film about Menopause (1987) 38 min. John Taylor (PR) for the National Film Board of Canada. Dist: AIMS Media, 6901 Woodley Avenue, Van

Nuys, CA 91406; (800) 367-2467, FR$75.00, FS$545.00, VS$395.00. *"Women, some in a support group setting, talk about the menopausal experience, the psychological and social problems involved, bodily reactions, and the rest. There is a list of symptoms with a discussion of osteoporosis, followed later by an emphasis on exercise as a means of preserving bone mass.... Provides strong arguments against hysterectomies and other medical solutions, emphasizing instead a program of good nutrition and exercise."* [From the review by Benjamin N. Colby, *AA* 92:1099–1100, 1990.]

Is There an American Stonehenge? (1982) 30 min. Harold Mayer (PR), John Eddy (NR). Dist: CRM VR$48.00, FR$48.00, FS$480.00, VS$360.00. *"This no-frills documentary chronicles astronomer John Eddy's interpretation of the great stone Medicine Wheel of Wyoming's Big Horn Mountains. He argues that it was an astronomical observation device which the Plains Indians employed as a means of fixing the date of the summer solstice."* [From the review by Anthony F. Aveni, *ARCH* 37(2):79–81, 1984. Reviewed by Ronald Hicks, *AA* 85:755, 1983.]

Ishi, the Last Yahi (1993) 57 min. Jed Riffe and Pamela Roberts (PR), Anne Makepeace (WR). Dist: UCEMC VR$75.00, FS$1195.00, VS$325.00, order #38245. *The latest contribution about Ishi, the "last wild Indian in North America," has won numerous awards and praise from both critics and anthropologists. It is based on Kroeber's meticulous notes and recordings taken at the time as well as archival film footage and still photographs. It also includes commentary by anthropologists, an 89-year-old man who met Ishi, and Native Americans who discuss the meanings of Ishi's songs and myths and the importance of Ishi's legacy today.*

Ishi in Two Worlds (1960) 19 min. Richard C. Tomkins (WR, FM). Dist: CRM/MH FR$27, FS$325; PSU(PCR) order #Y20769, FR$7.60 *The story of Ishi, the last Yahi Indian, from 1911 when he emerged from his forest refuge in northern California, through his stay with Kroeber in the Museum of Anthropology at the University of California at Berkeley to his death in 1916.* [Reviewed by Arnold R. Pilling, *AA* 70:844, 1968.] Based on the book by Theodora Kroeber. Suggested supplement: Theodora Kroeber, *Ishi in Two Worlds: A Biography of the Last Wild Indian in North America.* University of California Press, 1962.

Islam in America (1992) Dist: Christian Science Monitor Video, P.O. Box 1875, Boston, MA 02117, telephone (800) 775-2775 VS$29.95. *This program provides viewers with the opportunity to learn how the religion is practiced in America today. It includes an introduction to the Five Pillars of Islam, a visit to the first mosque established in America, an explanation of Muslim religious practices, a discussion on the influence of Islam on leaders such as Malcolm X.*

Island of the Moon (1979) 55 min. Dist: CBC VR$59.00, VS$135.00. *An in-depth examination of the lemurs of Madagascar. The cinematography by R. Kovanic is excellent, even outstanding, and since it was shot with synchronized sound, the viewer is presented with a vibrant 'being there' sensory impression. This is heightened by excellent and unobtrusive narration."* [From the review by James D. Paterson, *AJPA* 57:353, 1982.]

Island of Saints and Souls (1991) 29 min. Niel Alexander (DI). Dist: UCEMC FR$45.00, VS$250.00. *This lively and fascinating program shows how the Catholic traditions of numerous immigrant groups have influenced and contributed to the rich cultural texture of New Orleans. The film takes the viewer through a year in the life of the Crescent City, exploring its colorful history, traditions, customs, and feast days.*

Island of the Red Prawns 52 min. William R. Geddes (FM, AN). Dist: UCEMC FR$48, FS$665, VS$465. *Documents the culture of one of the Fiji Islands by recording the traditional wedding of the children of two important chieftains. Interspersed with scenes of the wedding preparations, the ceremony, and the principal figures in the two families, are fascinating sequences showing many local customs. These include the making of a huge ceremonial curtain of tapa cloth; planting, growing, and harvesting food; fishing methods; and ecstatic dancing on burning coals. During the colorful wedding feast, the legend of the red prawns is told in song and dance.* [Reviewed by Winifred Lambrecht, *SBF* 15:172, 1979.]

Island of the Spirits 26 min. Dist: WFV FR$42, FS$420. *Cremation of a Balinese prince.*

Islands of the South Pacific (1959) 15 min. Dist: IUAVC FR$8.25. *Deals briefly with the geologic history, distinctive features, and economic development of the islands of the South Pacific. Locates and identifies the continental islands of Fiji, New Caledonia, New Zealand, Australia, and New Guinea; describes their geologic origins; and pictures the effects of climate on the topographical features and the islands' plant and animal life. Treats some of the oceanic islands and indicates how some were formed on coral reefs. Traces the human habitation of the islands by Melanesian, Polynesian, and Micronesian peoples.*

Ispahan: Lèttre Persane 1977 (La Mosquée du Chah à Ispahan) (Itpahan: A Persian letter 1977—The Chah Mosque at Ispahan) (1977) 35 min. Jean Rouch (DI), Centre National de la Recherche Scientifique, Comité du Film Ethnographique (PR). Dist: CFE; DER. *A Persian cine-portrait shot in Iran where the cineaste, Farrokh Gaffary, discusses with the author the dynamic architecture of the Chah mosque.*

Israel and the Palestinians: The Continuing Conflict 3 5 min. Amram Nowak (DI), Andrea Simon (PR). Dist: Anti-Defamation League of B'nai B'rith, Television, Radio, Film Department, 823 UN Plaza, New York, NY 10017; (212) 490-2525. *Reiterates "arguments to justify Israel's refusal to deal with the PLO and to repatriate the Palestinian refugees. One of the major thrusts of the film is the 1982 Israeli invasion of Lebanon.... Presents an American Zionist view of the conflict."* [From the review by Julie Peteet, *AA* 89:1018–1822, 1987.]

Italian Folk Songs (1964) 10 min. (A Folklore Research Film by Peter and Toshi Seeger.) Dist: FIM/RF FR$ 10,

FS$90. *A holiday gathering of an Italian family at home, with children, parents, grandparents, and friends, is an occasion for some spontaneous, very relaxed, and happy singing of traditional folk songs. The event was recorded on film without embellishment by the Seegers.*

Itam Hakim, Hopiit: A Poetic Visualization of Hopi Philosophy and Prophecy (1984) 58 min. Victor Masayesva, Jr. (FM). Dist: ISP VR$150.00, VS$450.00. *In this unique documentation of a people's legends, myths, histories, and oral traditions, the Hopi producer opens new doors to understanding a people's cultural adaptation to the American Southwest. Macaya, the storyteller, was born in the last decade of the 19th century. The opening reveals Macaya's childhood in Old Oraibi. Next, is the Emergence Story, which contains references to obscure worlds, landscapes, and natural catastrophes in the three worlds past and the emergence here into the present world. He concludes with the Ahl Ceremony. Macaya's account concludes with an admonition that the Hopi people must not adopt Christianity, but remain steadfast in the Hopi religion.* [Reviewed by Robert L. Bee, AA 90:235–237, 1988.]

It's Grits Stan Woodward (FM). Dist: Stan Woodward, P.O. Box 899, Huntsville, AK 35804; (205) 539-1666. *Tongue-in-cheek exploration of an important element in Southern cuisine.*

An Ixil Calendrical Divination (1966) 32 min. Carroll Williams and Joan Williams (FM), Benjamin N. Colby and Lore Colby (AN), Anthropology Film Center (PR). Dist: ZC FR$35, FS$450. *This is a compressed nonlinear synchronous film of a calendrical divining ritual. An Ixil man and his wife are visited by an Ixil priest who arranges beans by calendar count (using the pre-Columbian 260-day ritual calendar) in order to determine whether the family is in danger of divine displeasure. Shot in April 1966 in Nebaj, Department of Quiche, Guatemala.* [Reviewed by Munro S. Edmunson, AA 69:425, 1967.] Suggested supplement: Leonhard Schultzer-Jena, *Die Vuiche von Guatemala.* Gustav Fischer, 1931.

An Ixil Setting Film (1966) 30 min. Carroll and Joan Williams (FM), Benjamin N. Colby and Lore M. Colby (AN), Anthropology Film Center (PR). Dist: ZC FR$35, FS$425. *This is a free-structured film to establish the setting for the research film,* An Ixil Calendrical Divination. *This film shows Ixil activities, particularly religious, in Nebaj in the Cuchumatanes Mountains of Guatemala. Shot in March and April 1966.*

Iyahkimix, the Blackfoot Beaver Bundle Ceremony 5 8 min. University of Alberta, Dept. of Radio and Television (PR). Dist: UAlberta FS$700 (Can.) [Reviewed by Thomas F. Kehoe, AA 77:697–698, 1975.] Suggested supplement: Walter McClintock, "The Blackfoot Beaver Bundle." *The Masterkey* 93(3, 4), 1935.

Iyomande: The Ainu Bear Festival (1930s) 26 min. Neil Gordon Munro (FM). Reedited with sound by Tokyo Olympia Eiga. Dist: UCEMC order #7788, FR$27, FS$235. *Rare and valuable anthropological document of the Ainu people of northern Japan as they existed a generation ago. For these believers in animism, the Bear Festival (Iyomande in the Ainu language) is the most important ceremony of the year, separating the deity of the bear from its visible body so that it can return to its home country. The ceremony is a gift of the Ainu to the bear. In return, they pray to the bear's spirit to bring them more meat and hide. Before the ritual, special food and sake are prepared. Around the altar, dancing and singing. An elder prays for the bear's spirit. A bear cub is shot with decorated arrows, killed, butchered, and cooked. A buoyant feast held in a typical Ainu house concludes the three-day ceremony. Also shows aspects of Ainu daily life—houses, boats, ornate woods, lacquered bowls, religious artifacts, and the elaborately tattooed mouths of the older women.*

Jackville (1965) 20 min. Jean Rouch (DI), Centre National de la Recherche Scientifique, Comité du Film Ethnographique (PR). Dist: CFE; DER. *A Harrist ceremony in Jackville near Abidjan, Ivory Coast.*

Jaguar (1955) 93 min. Jean Rouch (FM). Dist: DER FR$105, FS$1080. *Three young men from the savannah of Niger leave their village to seek wealth and adventure on the coast and in the cities of Ghana. Part fiction, part documentary, and part reflective commentary, the film explores the typical West African pattern of short-term migration from the countryside to the cities. It captures the contrast between the bewildering complexity of urban life, where men strive to become "jaguars" or cityslickers, and the ties to family and other villagers at home on the savannah.* [Reviewed by Thomas O. Beidelman, AA 76:697–698, 1974.] Related readings: J. C. Caldwell, *African Rural-Urban Migration: The Movement to Ghana's Towns.* Columbia University Press, 1969. Cf: Rouch interview, AA 80:1005–1020, 1978.

Jamaica Sings 29.5 min. Crawley Films (PR). Dist: CRAW FS$174.31 *On a "barbecue" on a flagstone terrace in the Blue Mountain home of Louise Bennett, leading Jamaican folksinger, the group of people who know most about their island's folklore sit telling stories and singing songs. They are Philip Sherlock, Vice Chancellor of the University College of the West Indies, Rannie Williams, popular Jamaican comedian, the Frats Quintette, best-known singing group on the island, and of course, Louise herself. They introduce a series of sequences taken in the canefields, in the town and remote village, and in a "Bamboo Club" in Kingston. We catch glimpses of the people singing work songs, the "mentoes" and the spirituals that mean Jamaica wherever they are heard, Louise and Rannie tell amusing "Anansi" stories in the island dialect. The film ends with the whole group, including some neighbors' children who came to listen to the stories, singing the Jamaican Bird song Chi-chi-Bud O.*

JANE GOODALL: STUDIES OF THE CHIMPANZEE (1976–77) 23 min. each. National Geographic Society (PR). Dist: NGSES FS$345.00, VS$315.00; Karol FR$30.00. *"These five films have been pieced together by the National Geographic Society from its vast archive of Hugo van Lawick's footage taken in the late 1960's. Each begins with several minutes of introductory material describing Gombe*

National Park, Tanzania, and Goodall's long term study there." [From the review by Robert S. O. Harding, *AA* 86:1077, 1984.] Teaching guide available.

• **Tool Using** (1976) *How young chimpanzees play with objects and how this play prepares them for making and using tools as adults.*

• **Introduction to Chimpanzee Behavior** (1977) *Overview of Goodall's work.*

• **Infant Development** (1977)

• **Hierarchy and the Alpha Male** (1977)

• **Feeding and Food Sharing** (1976) Dist: IUAVC FR$12.50.

Jangadeiros (1977) 50 min. Bill Leimbach, Harry Zalkowitsch (FM). Dist: SFI FS$1500. *For 2,000 miles, the hazardous waters off the northeast coast of Brazil are fished by the most primitive sea-going craft known to man. These are the Jangada, single-sailed balsa log rafts that have remained unchanged for hundreds of years; and the Jangadeiros who work them use techniques that are found no where else. The film shows us the life of one community. We see the many different kinds of fishing, from inshore trawling to the 'Dormida' when the Jangadeiros stay out on their tiny craft for nights on end. We see the life of the village, the many tasks that are necessary for survival at sea and on land, and the festival, when troubles are forgotten and the Jangadeiros dance to the irresistible rhythm of the Samba. Through Jose, a Jangadeiro of great experience, we are allowed into the lives of these people. We meet his wife Maria and 11 surviving children, we see him building a new Jangada and hear of the sudden and terrifying moods of the sea. Above all, he tells us what the sea means to the Jangadeiros, how they can never leave it, for it is part of them. And yet for all their toughness the Jangadeiros are vanishing. What we are seeing may be the last record of a way of life of courage and endurance and often of great beauty.*

Jangadeiros: Brazilian Fishermen from the North-East 27 min. Yves Billon, Jean Francois Schiano (FM). Dist: FDV. *Jangadeiros are navigators from northeast Brazil. Their boats are a sort of raft with a sail, which they call 'Jangades'. This film, shot in a fishing village of the State of Geara, to the south of Fortaleza, tells of their everyday life and their difficult subsistence. Jangades are small craft, rudimentary, and characteristic of the region. The triangular sail, which allows them to reach the high seas, must be hauled down to fish with a line.*

Janie's Janie (1970–71) 25 min. Geri Ashur, Peter Barton, Marily Milford, Stephanie Palewski (FM). Dist: Odeon Films, P.O. Box 315, Franklin Lakes, NJ 07417. *A white New Jersey welfare mother.* [Reviewed by Betty Reid Mandell, *AA* 79:202, 1977.]

Japan (Asian Insight Series) (1988) 50 min. Film Australia (PR). Dist: FIV VS$158.00. *Though geographically small, Japan is a dominant force in world trade thanks to new manufacturing technology. Here is the history of this complex, paradoxical nation.*

JAPAN SERIES (1988) 60 min. Dist: CFV VS$400 (series), $125 (each). *"This is an entertaining and well-documented analysis of modern Japanese life and culture. The emphasis throughout is on the social psychology of the Japanese, their loyalty to authority figures, their cooperative attitudes, and their emphasis on group achievement.... Unfortunately, the series neglects other socioeconomic factors that have probably been of equal importance in the rise of modern Japan."* [From the review by John A. Broussard, *SBF* 24:305, 1989.] A companion book, free with the series, retails at $22.95.

Japan: An Interdependent Nation (1980) 27 min. Sam Bryan (PR). Dist: IFF FR$45.00, FS$450.00. *"This is an innocuous and disjointed film. Even the point of the title remains obscure since neither the theme of interdependency nor any other theme integrates the potpourri of scenes and commentary."* [From the review by M. Estellie Smith, *SBF* 17:276, 1982.]

The Japan They Don't Talk About (1986) 52 min. NBC News (PR). Dist: FIV VS$79.00. *This acclaimed NBC News White Paper contrasts our popular perception of Japanese manufacturing as a high-tech paradise with more sobering effects about how workers cope with incredibly long workdays, cramped and excruciatingly expensive housing, and other problems.*

Japan: The Nation Family 51 min. Canadian Broadcasting Corporation (PR). Dist: WFV FS$795.00, VS$195.00. *A clue to the remarkable techno-industrial brilliance of contemporary Japan lies in the unique attitudes of its people. A new and arresting examination of a society and its achievements.*

JAPAN: VOICES OF EXPERIENCE (1992) Jackson H. Bailey (Exec.PR), Hajima Ikela (PR), Chet Kincaid and Sharon Wheaton (DI), David W. Plath (CON). Dist: Center for Educational Media, Institute for Education on Japan, Earlham College, Richmond, IN 47374; (317) 983-1324 VS$35. *A series of interviews and conversations with ethnographers who have been studying modern Japan for many years. Produced in the studios of the National Institute of Multimedia Education, Chiba, Japan. Designed by anthropologist David W. Plath, who is host/interviewer for most of the programs. Intended for upper-division and graduate-level college courses.*

• **What's an Anthropologist Doing in Japan?** Order #9216. *David W. Plath talks with five colleagues—Theodore Bestor, Keith Brown, William Kelly, Takio Sugiyama Lebra, and Margaret Lock—about the challenges they have met while using ethnographic techniques to understand a complex modern civilization.*

• **No New Ginzas** Order #9212. *Jackson Bailey and David W. Plath discuss how people in regional Japan are bypassing Tokyo as they reach out directly for a role on the world scene. An examination in broader scope of issues touched upon in the documentary programs,* As Iwata Goes: Is Politics Local? *and* As Iwata Goes: Is Culture Local?

• **Jackson Bailey** Order #9211. *Reflecting upon rice-roots responses to four decades of social change as depicted in his* book, Ordinary People, Extraordinary Lives, *(University of Hawaii Press, 1991.)*

- **Theodore Bestor** Order #9213. *On the field research and sense of problem that led him to write his prize-winning book,* Neighborhood Tokyo.
- **Keith Brown** Order #9215. *Jackson Bailey hosts this discussion of the adaptive vigor of local-level societies, both rural and urban, that Brown has witnessed in regional Japan over the past thirty years.*
- **William Kelly** Order #9217. *On his efforts to track 200 years of agrarian reform and struggles for regional independence on the Shonai Plain of northwestern Honshu.*
- **Takie Sugiyama Lebra** Order #9219. *Describing the evolution of her book* Above the Clouds *(Stanford University Press, 1993), the first report in English on the lives of Japan's former aristocrats.*
- **Margaret Lock** Order #9214. *On middle age and menopause among women in Japan and North America, as examined in her book,* Encounters with Aging *(University of California Press, 1993).*

Japanese Fighting Festival   (see *Fighting Festival*)

Japanese Folk Dances   (1969) 25 min. Clifford Ettinger and Herman Jacobs (DI), Beate Gordon (CON), Board of Education of the City of New York in cooperation with the Asia Society (PR). Dist: BAVI FR$20, FS$260. *Some excerpts and some complete dances culled from the rich folklore heritage of Japan. Some of these dances can be seen only on rare occasions even in Japan, since they are performed at certain festivals in certain regions. The film includes, among others, a mask dance, a drum dance, and a battle dance. The costumes are in striking colors, and the meaning of the various symbols, which are part of the costumes and props, are explained, as are the history and content of the dances themselves. The dancers appearing in the film are the well-known Japan Folk Dance Group, which made its debut in New York City's Kauffman Auditorium in 1969.*

THE JAPANESE SERIES   (1979) 57 min. John Nathan (WR). Dist: Japan Society Films, 333 E 47th St., New York, NY 10017; (212) 832-1155, FR$75, FS$650 (each), FS$1900 (series), VS$300 (series).

- **Full Moon Lunch** *The everyday life of a downtown Tokyo family. The Sugiuras cater elaborate box lunches for memorial services and other formal occasions at nearby Buddhist temples. Eleven adults live and work closely together in their tiny shop in an old, unchanging district of Tokyo. Individually and collectively, the Sugiuras present a wide range of distinctly Japanese relationships. At the same time, they reveal themselves as warm vital human beings, dealing with the universal concerns of maintaining continuity with their unique past while coping with the appeals and stresses of modern urban life.*
- **The Blind Swordsman** *Portrait of superstar Shintaro Katsu. Actor, producer, director, Katsu is the creator of Zato-ichi, the intrepid blind swordsman and most beloved film hero of Japanese of all ages. Flamboyant and unpredictable, impatient, quixotic, and passionately creative, Katsu is a man living on the very brink of life, yet outrageously confident that he is at life's center. Through its turbulent and passionate hero, this film reveals an aspect of Japanese society little known to outsiders. "Lest American audiences suppose all Japanese are essentially mild," explains director John Nathan, "I want to capture high energy, self-assurance, a virulent personality. I had never beheld a man so absolutely in control of his surroundings. Katsu impressed me as a reigning monarch, an Emperor of the Night. His evident hunger for every moment that life can afford him is astonishing, and so is his energy."*
- **Farm Song** *Four generations of a rural Japanese family speak frankly about their backbreaking work, their relationship with each other, and the seasonal celebrations that enliven their world. The film follows the Kato family through a full year, gently probing beneath the familiar rhythms of farm life and ritualized activities to reveal the tensions and the affections that bind the Japanese family.*

The Japanese Version   Louis Alvarez and Andrew Kolker (FM). Dist: CNM. *When we think about Japanese culture, the following things do not usually come to mind: weddings with giant rubber cakes swathed in dry ice; Tokyo businessmen in letter-perfect cowboy outfits humming the theme to "Rawhide"; TV commercials that go to great lengths to recreate the aura of the "Man from UNCLE"; or the institution of the "love hotel," where each room is decorated in a different Western fantasy. Yet, this is mainstream Japan as featured in this film. It is a look at Western influences on contemporary Japanese culture. The Japanese have always taken an omnivorous approach to other cultures, adapting foreign things to their own needs. This film goes beneath the surface wackiness to discern why the Japanese behave this way.*

The Jean Richard   (St. Lawrence North series) (1963) 30 min. each. Dist: CRAW Color FS$210.70, B/W FS$70.38; UCEMC $25. *Follows the building of a goelette (a French Canadian coastal ship) from the winter cutting of the timbers to launching. The people of the St. Lawrence River region take great pride in their craftsmanship as they build these sturdy vessels for their seagoing neighbors. The ship is christened with a family name, and its launching is celebrated with a lively party attended by all those involved in its birth and its future use.*

Jean Rouch and His Camera in the Heart of Africa   74 min. Philo Bregstein (DI). Dist: DER FR$120, VR$70, FS$1300, VS$600. *Provides an in-depth look at the film work of Jean Rouch and his associates from Niger who participated in the production of many of Rouch's Niger-based films; namely, Damoure and Lam. Most of the camera and technical work was accomplished by Niger filmmakers who converse about filmmaking and filmmakers who have had historical influence in the field. Segments from several of Rouch's earlier film works are interspersed with the filming in Niger and with interview.*

Jenny's Arctic Diary   (1988) 52 min. Jenny Gilbertson (FM). Dist: LMF VR$45, VS$295. *"Photographer Jenny Gilbertson (nearer 80 than 70-years-old, as she puts it) spent a year filming the daily lives of the Inuit residents of a* *northeastern Canadian village for this program.... Viewers will not see the hopelessness and despair that characterize similar programs on modern native peoples. Instead this program shows that some solutions are actually forthcoming.... Unfortunately Gilbertson's accent makes some of her observations difficult to understand."* [From the review by Cara E. Richards, *SBF* 25:44, 1989.]

Jero on Jero: A Balinese Trance Seance Observed
(Bali series) (1986) 17 min. Linda Connor, Patsy Asch, and Timothy Asch (DI), Australian National University and DER (PR). Dist: DER FR$35, VR$50, FS$400, VS$250. *In 1980, anthropologist Linda Connor and filmmakers Tim and Patsy Asch returned to Bali with videocassette recordings of* A Balinese Trance Seance. *Jero Tapakan, the spirit medium, was invited to view the footage. The resulting film, presents some of her reactions and comments to Connor as she watched and listened to herself for the first time. Her comments provide insights into how she feels while possessed, her understanding of sorcery, and her humility in the presence of the supernatural world. The film can be most fruitfully used as a companion to* A Balinese Trance Seance, *which could be shown first and followed by a discussion, before screening of* Jero Tapakan's *own responses.* [Reviewed by Hildred Geertz, *AA* 86:809–811, 1984. Reviewed in *VISA* 4:68, 1991.]

Jero Tapakan: Stories in the Life of a Balinese Healer
(Bali series) (1986) 25 min. Linda Connor, Patsy Asch, and Timothy Asch (DI), Australian National University and DER (PR). Dist: DER FR$45, VR$50, FS$600, VS$250. *In Bali, the traditional healer mediates between the human and divine worlds. He or she may become possessed by deities or ancestral spirits who provide clues about the ultimate cause of affliction, the wishes of the deceased or auspicious dates for ceremonies. Many healers, who are also peasant farmers, have additional specialties: the interpretation of palm-leaf manuscripts, midwifery, or divination. In the film, Jero recollects her poverty and despair as a farmer 25 years ago, and how she left her home to wander for months as a peddler in the north Bali countryside. After serious illnesses and mystical visions, she returned to her family, consulted with spirit mediums, and decided to undergo a consecration ceremony as a spirit medium herself. After years of repaying debts, today she sustains a lively practice.* [Reviewed by Hildred Geertz, *AA* 86:809–811, 1984. Reviewed in *VISA* 4:68, 1991.]

The Jesus Freaks 30 min. An Eberlein/Deason Production. Dist: FIM/RF FR$35, FS$350. *From the total immersion baptism in the Pacific Ocean to daily proselytising among the long-haired city street people, these young people, the "Jesus Freaks," as the mass media have labeled them, have dedicated their lives to spreading the gospel. This is fundamentalist gospel religion, and these young people have been compared to 1st-century Christians for their idealism and fervor. There is no mistaking their dedication, for they live on very little money, making no attempt to solicit funds. Their food comes from the spoilage of supermarkets, and they live communally, though strictly segregated by sex. The majority have had drug backgrounds; some have been to college, some to prison; some have run away from home while others never had a home. Whatever their former lives, they now feel they are joined together "in the glory of Jesus." The film depicts the life of one such group of young people. It shows them saving new souls, baptism at a beach crowded with swimmers and surfers, the praying and praising for hours at a time in a specially darkened "prayer room," the ministry on city streets, and the daily life in their house. This film makes no judgments. It is a straightforward presentation without narration, in which the "Jesus Freaks" speak for themselves.* [Reviewed by T. O. Beidelman, *AA* 74:1570–1571, 1972.]

The Jews of Djerba (1977) 26 min. Alain Cohen and Georges Nizan (FM). Dist: JMS FR$100.00. *"Legend has it that Djerba, a tiny island off the southeast coast of Tunisia, received a remnant of the Babylonian captivity in the 6th century BC. Historical records document the persistence of a Jewish enclave on the island over the centuries... Allows us to see and hear the rhythms of work, prayer, and leisure to details of cooking and courtyard sociality.... This group reflects the strong influence of the surrounding Arab culture." This film complements* Pilgrimage to Ghriba. [From the review by Faye Ginsburg, *AA* 87:741–747, 1985.]

Jhaoo Chowdhari (A Tongawallah from Delhi) 28 min. Yavar Abbas (FM). Dist: CMC. [Reviewed by Philip Oldenburg, *AA* 76:706, 1974.]

Jocelyn, Facing Death at 17 with Strong Faith (1981) 28 min. Canadian Broadcasting Corporation (PR). Dist: FL FR$50.00, FS$425.00, VS$375.00. *"Jocelyn is a 17-year-old girl dying of cancer who lives with her parents and brother in Winnipeg, Canada. Most of the film consists of interviews with Jocelyn and her parents.... Touches of religion are scattered through the film."* [From the review by Christine Lemieux, *AA* 86:1052–1053, 1984.]

Joe David: Spirit of the Mask (1982) 24 min. Jennifer Hodge (FM). Dist: Kensington Communications, 104 Bellevue Ave., Toronto, Ontario, Canada M5T 2N9; (416) 968-2697 FR$60.00, FS$525.00, VS$425.00. *"A glimpse into the life of the Nootkan artist, Joe David, which transmits to the viewed the need among Nootkans to retain tenaciously a feeling of closeness with their ancestral past."* [From the review by Mark S. Fleisher, *AA* 86:1061–1062, 1984.]

Joe Leahy's Neighbours (Papua New Guinea series) (1988) 90 min. Bob Connolly and Robin Anderson (FM). Dist: DER FR$200.00, VR$85.00, VS$600.00. *Joe Leahy is the mixed-race son of Australian miner Michael Leahy and a young highland girl. Joe, now in his fifties, is a wealthy coffee plantation owner. He lives in Western-style grandeur amidst his poorer Ganiga neighbors. Joe Leahy's links to his neighbors and their financial and emotional bonds are explored in this film, a follow-up to* First Contact. *The filmmakers lived in the highlands and filmed for 18 months. They built a grass and thatch house on the edge of Joe Leahy's plantation, in the "no man's land" between Joe and the Ganiga. The film poignantly portrays both perspectives without value judgments or resolution for either side.* [Reviewed by Frederick Errington and Deborah Gewertz, *AA* 92:846, 1990.]

Joe Sun (From the Elders series) (1988) 19 min. Katrina Waters (FM), Sarah Elder and Leonard Kramerling (EP, CC, CA). Dist: DER FR$35.00, VR$30.00, FS$390.00, VS$200.00. *Immaluuraq (Joe Sun in English) grew up moving among seasonal camps in the Kobuk River region of Alaska. He now resides in Shungnak. He tells of the legendary Inupiaq prophet, Maniilaq, who was his great uncle. Immaluuraq's talk is known as uqaaqtuaq. Such talks were given by elders to young people who came seeking information and advice.* Subtitled.

John Jacob Niles (1978) 32 min. Bill Richardson, Mimi Pickering, and Ben Zickafoose (FM). Dist: APPAL FR$50, FS$475.

Jojolo 12 min. Herbert Bethune and Don Taylor (FM). Dist: GP FR$10, FS$130. *A subtle study of ambivalent cultural identity in a graceful young woman of Haitian parentage working as a fashion model and film actress in cosmopolitan Paris.*

The Jolo Serpent Handlers (1977) 40 min. Karen Kramer (FM). Dist: KKFL FR$65.00, FS$550.00, VS$400.00. *Focuses on a small snake-handling church in rural West Virginia. The film not only shows two fascinating serpent-handling services, but also answers many of the questions the viewers have about the religion and its followers. The film includes scenes of the rattlesnake hunt through the mountains; the washing of the serpents; the annual outdoor homecoming service; colorful exteriors of the countryside; an all-night vigil held for the victim of a rattlesnake bite. Churchmembers speak of why they handle serpents; what gap it fills in their lives; what it's like to grow up in the religion; the persecutions they have suffered; and the pain of losing a family member to the poisonous snakebite. But it is not all pain and suffering, for the people are linked by deep beliefs, strong family ties, and a wonderful sense of joyous gospel music.* [Reviewed by William M. Clements, JAF 93(363):127–128, 1979.]

Jose Carlos and His Spirits: The Ritual Initiation of Zelador Dos Orixas in a Brazilian Umbanda Center (1989) 85 min. Sidney M. Greenfield (FM). Dist: Sidney M. Greenfield, Department of Anthropology, University of Wisconsin-Milwaukee, P.O. Box 413, Milwaukee, WI 53201; (414) 229-4390 or (414) 332-2244. *Umbanda is a syncretic religion of African, Catholic, shamanistic, American Indian, Kardecian, and other influences.* [Reviewed by Michael Winkelman, AA 93(2):518–519, 1991.]

JOSEPH CAMPBELL AND THE POWER OF MYTH SERIES
Bill Moyers (H). Dist: MFV VS$29.95 (each), $179.70 (set), order code ISET. *Does modern man need myths? In this age of high technology and psychotherapy, of drug abuse, child abuse, and the atomic bomb, is there any room for heroes and villains? Gods and demons? Magic and metaphor? According to the late Joseph Campbell, mythologist, author, scholar, and teacher, the answer is a resounding "yes," for he believes that myths hold the key to human happiness, that they are what enable us to feel "the rapture of being alive." Campbell and Moyers recorded 23 hours of conversation on life, death, marriage, religion, growing up, and growing old. The six shows are culled from those interviews, beautifully illustrated with paintings and film clips, explained and introduced by Moyers.*

• **Sacrifice and Bliss** Order #C104. *Campbell discusses the role of sacrifice in myth, which symbolized the necessity for rebirth. He also talks about the significance of sacrifice—in particular, a mother's sacrifice for her child, and the sacrifice to the relationship in marriage—and stresses the need for every one of us to find our sacred place in the midst of today's fast-paced, technological world.*

• **The Hero's Adventure** Order #C101. *Long before medieval knights charged off to slay dragons, tales of heroic adventures were an integral part of all world cultures. Campbell discusses how the hero's journey is possible even today in everyday life and challenges everyone to see the presence of a heroic journey in his or her own life.*

• **The First Storytellers** Order #C103. *Campbell discusses the importance of accepting death as rebirth as in the myth of the buffalo and the story of Christ, the rite of passage in primitive societies, the role of mystical Shamans, and the decline of ritual in today's society.*

• **The Message of the Myth** Order #C102. *Campbell compares the creation story in Genesis with creation stories from around the world. Because the world changes, religion has to be transformed and new mythologies created. People today are stuck with old metaphors and myths that don't fit their needs.*

• **Masks of Eternity** Order #C106. *Campbell provides challenging insights into the concepts of God, religion, and eternity, as revealed in Christian teachings and the beliefs of Buddhists, Navajo Indians, Schopenhauer, Jung, and others.*

• **Love and the Goddess** Order #C105. *Campbell talks about romantic love, beginning with the 12th-century troubadours, and addresses questions about the image of woman—as goddess, virgin, Mother Earth.*

The Journey Back: The Earth Is Our Mother II (Rejsen Tilbage: Jorden en Vores Mor II) (1992) 52 min. Peter Elsass (FM). Dist: Foreningen Casablanca, St. Kongensgade 108, DK-1264 Copenhagen K, Denmark. *The makers of a film about the Archuaco Indians of Colombia return six years later to show the piece to its subjects and to record their responses. Through the poetic and satirical comments of the Archuaco, combined with inteviews with the descendants of African slaves, government ofiicials, and Catholic missionaries, the conflicts of race and culture are highlighted and redrawn, and the role of filmmaking is questioned.*

Journey from Pha Dong (1967) Dist: CRUA-UM. *Depicts the armed resistance of Hmong tribesman against the Vietnamese and Pathet Lao Communist forces in Laos. The film was obtained from the CIA under the provisions of the Freedom of Information Act of 1983, by a U.S. Air Force officer who was assigned in Laos during 1972–73. It was apparently produced to acknowledge the leadership and bravery of General Vang Pao. It portrays the creation of schools to teach Hmong boys nationalism and literacy, the transport of a select group of children to Thailand to be educated for leadership positions, the training of peasants to use sophisticated weapons, and the economic changes* *brought about by the war. In a post battle scene, letters and strategy notebooks positively identifying the attackers as North Vietnamese are taken from the dead.*

Journey to a New Life (The Human Face of Indonesia Series) (1987) 30 min. Film Australia (PR). Dist: FIV VS$99.00. *Overcrowding is a major problem in Indonesia, so the government has begun to move people to less-populated provinces. This video film captures this process of population movement and relocation.*

Journey to Chinale 25 min. Willard Baldwin (FM). Dist: PSU(PCR) order #31580, FR$10.10 *The story of an Indian family, the only survivors of an epidemic, who leave their village in Brazil and make a voyage through the forest, down an unknown river, to join their kinsmen in Surinam. The film covers many aspects of the life of the Indians, Carib-speaking Oyanas: canoe building, housebuilding, hunting, fishing with bow and arrow, pottery making, weaving, shamanistic chanting, and curing, including comprehensive footage on the feast and ritual ordeal of the Marake in which huge, stinging ants are pressed against the bodies of the initiates. CH/MH distributes a brief ethnographic study guide.*

Journey to Mecca (1942) 16 min. B/W. Marcel Ichac (PR). Dist: FIM/RF FR$15, FS$150. *Actual scenes of the annual journey to the city of Islam, never before recorded by the motion picture camera, were taken for this film by a non-Moslem who daringly penetrated the confines of Mecca. Fifty thousand Moslem pilgrims from Malaya, Turkestan, India, Yugoslavia, and as far away as the Philippines travel to Port Said through the Red Sea and on the Djeddah. Included here is a brief exposition of the historic and ritual significance of the tour that finally leads to the Kaaba, and of the Black Stone that stands in the center of the Great Mosque.*

Joyce at 34 28 min. Joyce Chopra, Claudia Weil (FM). Dist: NDF. [Reviewed by June Nash, *AA* 75:205, 1974.]

Juan Felix Sanchez (1982) 27 min. Calogero Salvo (WR, FM), Dennis Schmeichler (PR). Dist: UCEMC FR$37.00, FS$435.00, VS$330.00. *"Represents the creative life of a multifaceted rural artist of the Venezuelan Andes. The unfiltered perspective is of the traditional artist himself—his words and his art. The unstated theme is the centrality of artistic activity in the life of a high-Andean Venezuelan, and, by extension, the centrality of artistic expression in rural Latin American culture."* [From the review by John M. Schechter, *AA* 89:525–532, 1987.]

Judge Wooten and Coon-on-a-Log (1971) 10 min. Dist: APPAL FR$15, FS$125. *A Fourth of July coon-on-a-log contest serves as the background for this film portrait of Judge George Wooten of Leslie County, Kentucky. His attitude typifies the easygoing mountaineer as he discusses his life in the mountains through subjects ranging from tourism to moonshine.* [Reviewed in *JAF* 87(345):271, 1974.]

Jugs to Be Filled or Candles to Be Lit (The New Pacific Series) (1987) 60 min. BBC/NVC (PR). Dist: FIV VS$79.00. *This tape compares schools and universities in Japan, Korea, California, Samoa, and Papua New Guinea.*

Jungles of the Amazon 15 min. Dist: FCE FR$17, FS$95. *Exploration in the forests of the Amazon.*

Just Black? 57 min. Dist: FL VS$445, VR$75. Francine Winddance Twine, Jonathan F. Warren, Francisco Ferrandiz (PR). *Several articulate young men and women of mixed-race parentage, each with one black parent, share their struggle to establish, acquire, and assert a racial identity. Their experiences lead one to question whether there is room in America for a multiracial identity. Based on the research of Francine Winddance Twine.*

Kabylia (1974) 9 min. B/W. Dist: FIM/RF FR$10, FS$95. *Kabylia is situated between the Sahara Desert and the Mediterranean Sea. The film depicts the Kabyles, or Berbers, cultivating their land in semiprimitive methods, fashioning handicrafts with skill and beauty, their century-old customs and the facts about the Kabyle women held in slavery in their rock-bound tradition. Beside the old Kabylia is the new city. Here the youth apply newly acquired modern knowledge to the forming of new understanding between men and nature.*

Kainai 26 min. Raoul Fox (DI), Colin Low, NFB (PR). Dist: NFB FR$30, FS$430. *On the Blood Indian Reserve, near Cardston, Alberta, a hopeful new development in Indian enterprise. Once rulers of the western plains, the Bloods live on a 500-square mile reserve. Many have lacked gainful employment and now pin their hopes on a prefab factory they have built. Will the production line and work and wages fit into their cultural pattern of life? The film shows how it is working and what the Indians themselves say about their venture.*

Ka Ke Ki Ku (St. Lawrence North Series) B/W. Dist: CRAW FS$75.38. *A poetic insight into the problems of the education of the younger generation of the Montagnais Indians.*

The Kalahari Desert People (1975) 24 min. John Marshall (FM), National Geographic Society (PR). Dist: NGS FS$345, VS315.

The Kalasha—Rites of Spring (Disappearing World Series) (1990) 52 min. Peter Parkes (AN). Dist: FIV VS$198.00, order #047044; PSU order #51221. *The Kalasha live in the high valleys of the Hindu Kush mountains in the North West Frontier Province of Pakistan. Because they mortgaged their land and walnut trees to Chitrali Muslims, their way of life is now threatened. The government is trying to safeguard their existence, but the prospect of living in a tourist park does not appeal to the Kalasha.* [Reviewed by Akos Ostor, *AA* 94(2):527–528, 1992.]

Kalogeros (1969) 12 min. B/W. Dist: Peter Haramis; UCEMC FR$15. *This documentary film captures contemporary observance of the ancient annual Dionysian fertility rites as observed in a village in northern Greece. Kalogeros (the 'Good Old Man') leads a wild, farcical, lewd procession through the village. Despite its coarse humor, the procession has an entirely serious purpose, as a variety of rituals and ceremonies intended to insure that fertile crops are once* *again reenacted.* [Reviewed by Peter Allen, *AA* 74:1581–1584, 1972.]

Kalvak (1970) 18 min. Dist: GPN Films; UCEMC FR$27. *Portrait of an elderly Eskimo artist known to connoisseurs throughout the world for her sensitive and colorful drawings and prints. Shows many of her works and argues against the deterioration of traditional Eskimo art and culture that is resulting from Canadian government policies.*

Kamik 15 min. Elise Swerhone (DI). Dist: NFB FR$40.00, VR$40.00, FS$350.00, VS$200.00. *A traditional skill that has existed for over five thousand years is in danger of extinction. Ulayok Kavlok, a hunter and seamstress, is proud of the fine workmanship she puts into making the seal-skin boots called "kamik." But her skills may soon be lost in the cultural transformation overtaking her community. Dividing her time between the harsh climate of Canada's Arctic and the urbanized South, she, like many Inuits, strives to balance two very different worlds.*

Kantik'i Maishi: Songs of Sorghum (1992) 58 min. Joan Kaufman (PR), Elsio Jansen (PR, NA). Dist: UCEMC VR$60.00, VS$295.00. *This documentary explores the harvest celebrations of Bonaire and Curacao, two islands in the Netherlands Antilles. It demonstrates how industrialization and the rise of a tourist economy have profoundly changed these African-derived folk festivals. Known as Simadan in Bonaire and Seu in Curacao, the festivals celebrate through traditional food, song, and dance the harvesting of sorghum, formerly a staple food. The video highlights the different ways that Simadan and Seu are celebrated and examines the historical roots of these differences. The pace of change in the islands is also documented. While the elders remember the old ways and mourn their loss, the young are forging a new way of life.*

Karba's First Years: A Study of Balinese Childhood (Character Formation in Different Cultures Series) (1991, ca. 1952) 20 min. Gregory Bateson (AN, CM), Margaret Mead, (AN, ED). Dist: PSU VR$15.50, FS$425.00, VS$125.00, order #24637. *A series of scenes in the life of a Balinese child, beginning with a seventh-month birthday ceremonial, showing Karba's relationships to parents, aunts and uncles, child nurse, and other children, as he is suckled, taught to walk and dance, and teased and titillated. The film illustrates that a Balinese child's responsiveness is muted if the parents stimulate him but fail to respond. Cinematic features: Mainly stationary camera-shooting family activity in a Balinese courtyard. No fancy work. B/W. Edited by Mead alone in late 1940s, speeded up from 16 frames per second to 24 fps, narration by Mead. (If projector allows, film can be shown at silent speed with soundtrack on, and narration remains intelligible.) On some prints, the soundtrack is printed many frames off.* Bibliography: Gregory Bateson, "Bali: The Value System of a Steady State." In: *Social Structure: Studies Presented to A. R. Radcliffe-Brown.* Meyer Fortes, ed. Oxford: Clarendon Press, 1949. Gregory Bateson and Margaret Mead, *Balinese Character: A Photographic Analysis.* New York: New York Academy of Sciences, 1942. [Reviewed by Hildred Geertz, *AA* 78:725–726, 1976.]

Karorn—A Southern Village 19 min. *The island of Puket, off the southwest coast of Thailand.* [Reviewed by Jeanne M. Olczyk and Surin Pitsuwan, *AA* 78:719, 1976.]

Kashia Men's Dances: Southwestern Pomo Indians (The American Indian Film Series) (1969) 40 min. Dist: UCEMC FR$42, FS$540; PSU(PCR) order #2210K, FR$15.30, FS$350. *Dancing was a preeminent form of religious expression among American Indians. This film preserves four authentic Pomo dances as they were performed on the Kashia Reservation near Stewart's Point on the northern California coast. Men were the principal participants in many ancient Pomo dances, though women often danced at the side. Certain dances were confined to men only or even a select few. With photographs made before the turn of the century, the history of recent dance development is shown; dancers are seen in their ancient skirts of bark or shredded tule, with very elaborate headdresses. Contemporary Pomo are shown building a brush enclosure for the dance ceremony, as they did in former times. The dancers emerge from the dance house in their elaborate costumes and body paint. They perform a preliminary ceremony and walk to the brush enclosure singing a special song.* [Reviewed by Clement W. Meighan, *AA* 69:271–272, 1967.]

Kataragama (Disappearing World Series) 52 min. Charlie Nairn, Granada Television (PR), Gananath Obeyesekere (AN). *As Sri Lanka (formerly Ceylon) modernizes, her gods change also. Some are fading away, and some are becoming more powerful. The strange story told in this documentary shows a revival of mystical belief in the ancient Hindu god, Kataragama.* [Reviewed by Richard Gombrich, *RAIN* 3:8, 1974. Peter Loizos, *AA* 32:579–580, 1980.]

Katatura 36 min. Ulrich Schweizer (FM). Dist: PFI FR$47.50. *A history and analysis of the plight of blacks in South Africa. The title comes from the word meaning total insecurity.*

Kathleen Ware: Quiltmaker (1979) 33 min. Sharon Sherman (FM). Dist: The Folklore Program, Department of English, University of Oregon, Eugene, OR 97403, FR$35, FS$325. *The folk art of quiltmaking and the personality of an individual folk artist. Located in the coast range of Oregon, the Ware home sits by the side of a well-traveled highway and attracts numerous quilt enthusiasts. The film shows Kathleen Ware's daily life and includes interactions with customers and family members. From the placing of an order to the completion of the last stitch, the film details the entire process of creating a traditional Lone Star quilt. As the quilt grows, so does our knowledge of Ware's vibrant spirit as quiltmaker, wife, mother, and grandmother.*

Kathputli: The Art of Rajastani Puppeteers (1989) 29 min. Smithsonian Institution's Office of Folklife Programs (PR). Dist: PSU(PCR) FR$21.50, VR$13.50, FS$450.00, VS$140.00. *Puppeteers used to be employed in the courts of Rajasthani nobles. The subject of the film is a puppeteer who* *travels with his family to perform.* [Reviewed by Larry Reed, *AA* 92:844, 1990.]

The Kawelka (Disappearing World Series) (1974) 52 min. Andrew Strathern (AN). Dist: PSU VR$14.00, order #51154. *In Papua New Guinea, status is earned by giving things away rather than by acquiring them. This program explores the Moka, a ceremony in which people, sometimes whole tribes, give gifts to members of other tribes. The larger the gift, the greater the victory over the recipient. This program documents the preparations of Ongka, the charismatic 'big man' of the Kawelka tribe.*

The Kayapo (Disappearing World Series) (1987) 52 min. Terry Turner (AN). Dist: PSU order #51222; FIV VS$198.00, order #047011. *The Kayapo are the first tribe to have their own air force. Life changed dramatically for the fiercely independent Kayapo when gold was discovered on their land. In 1982, thousands of Brazilians invaded the Amazonian rain forest to excavate one of the world's largest gold mines. The Kayapo were forced to become "businessmen," or see their traditional way of life destroyed. This is the first of two programs on the Kayapo. See* The Kayapo: Out of the Forest *for the second program.* [Reviewed by William H. Crocker, *AA* 93(2):514–516, 1991. Michael Beckham, *VISA* 2:82, 1982.]

The Kayapo: Out of The Forest (Disappearing World Series) (1989) 53 min. Terry Turner (AN). Dist: PSU VR$14.00, order #51155; FIV VS$198.00, order #047014. *The Kayapo Indians have gained international recognition for their bold political resistance and for the reassertion of their traditional cultural identity. This film looks at the political awakening of the tribe, which has gone hand in hand with an aggressive reassertion of their traditional cultural and social identity. Featured are the campaigning tactics of Chief Ropni and the support of pop star Sting, who has accompanied the chief on his campaign trail.* [Reviewed by William H. Crocker, *AA* 93(2):514–516, 1991.]

The Kazakhs of China (Disappearing World Series) (1983) 53 min. Shirin Akiner (AN). Dist: FIV VS$198.00, order #047006; PSU VR$14.00, order #51158. *The nomadic, fiercely independent Kazakhs live in the mountains between Tibet and Mongolia, away from the Chinese authorities. They adapted to communism and enjoy what they believe to be considerable advantages over their more conventional neighbors.*

Keep the Circle Strong (1990) 28 min. Adobe Foundations (PR). Dist: CG VR$50.00, VS$250.00. *"Keep the Circle Strong is a documentary focusing on the cultural revitalization of Mike Auger, A Canadian Cree, as he contemplates his encounter with white culture, experiences a personal rejuvenation in discovering the value of traditional Cree beliefs, and explores pan-Indianism through his service as a volunteer among the Aymara of Bolivia.... The film successfully introduces the viewer to the contemporary life of two native cultures in a sensitive and compassionate fashion."* [From the review by Samuel E. Casselberry, *SBF* 28:150, 1992.]

Kembali: To Return 46 min. Jim Mayer, Lynn Adler and John Rogen (FM), Ideas in Motion (PR). Dist: FL VR$65.00, FS$395.00; UCEMC VR$60.00, VS$195.00, order #38220. *The music of the Balinese gamelan is one of the world's great musical forms, renowned for its rhythmic sophistication, its tonal range, and quickly shifting tempos. Gamelan music has a critical function in nearly every religious and social event in Bali. Musical activity is as important as religious ceremonies and agricultural work and is supported by the same social structure. Gamelan Sekar Jaya, the most proficient performer of Balinese music in the United States, is an ensemble of 30 American musicians and dancers from Oakland, CA. When they were invited to perform in Bali, they wondered how their performance would be received. They were the first Westerners to perform Balinese music for the Balinese. The group's experience surpassed their wildest dreams. Not only was their musical skill appreciated, but the harmony they found in Bali enhanced their musical performance.*

The Kennedy Family, Albuquerque, New Mexico (see Six American Families Series)

Kenya Boran (Faces of Change Series) (1974) 66 min. James Blue (Dl, SR), David MacDougall (Dl, CA), P. T. W. Baxter (CON), Norman Miller (PR). Dist: WER. *The Boran of northern Kenya are nomadic herders who live in a region of scrub and desert extending to the Ethiopian border. Out of this arid landscape rises a well-watered plateau on which many Boran have settled, attracted by a growing town, education, and agriculture. Recently a road has been built through the once isolated territory. The film is about the irrevocability of change. Two fathers and their sons stand between a familiar but waning mode of life and the uncertain benefits of the modern social order, for which one must pay the price of one's competence in the old society. The film is constructed geometrically out of conversations that pair the major characters in their different interrelationships. The audience is thus afforded an opportunity, through observing the intersection of these lines of behavior, to plot the situation of each against broader social and historical patterns.* [Reviewed by Alan Jacobs, *AA* 79:753–754, 1977. Reviewed in *VISA* 1:400, 1988.] Relevant anthropological literature: Study Guide available in two parts: Part I by Asmarom Legesse; Part II by Norman N. Miller, American Universities Field Staff, 1976. Suggested supplement: Asmarom Legesse, *Cada: Three Approaches to the Study of African Society*. Free Press-Macmillan, 1973.

Kerepe's House—A House Building in New Guinea (1966) 50 min. Alison Jablonko (AN), Marek Jablonko (FM). Dist: PSU order # 50480, FR$25.50, FS$600. *Construction of a house of vines, leaves, and trees from the mountain forest. Interactions of social units involved in house-building among the Fungai. History and social customs discussed. Subjects are aware of the camera crew, who direct much behavior by offscreen cues.* [Reviewed by E. Richard Sorenson, *AA* 70:183–184, 1968.]

Ketut di Bali (1981) 52 min. Serge Raoul (FM). Dist: Serge Raoul, 38 West 76th Street, New York, NY 10023, FR$90.00. *"Ketut is the name given to the fourth child born* *in a Balinese family. By using the birth order name (one of many that a Balinese acquires), the filmmaker has attempted to create a portrait of a Balinese 'everyperson'."* [From the review by Toby Alice Volkman, AA 85:227–228, 1983.]

Kheturni Baya (1982) 19 min. Sharon Wood (FM). Dist: PSU FR$13.00, FS$215.00, VS$145.00. *Women in a household in the Gujerat, India.* [Reviewed by Eva Friedlander, AA 86:240–241, 1984.]

Khyber (Disappearing World Series) (1979) 52 min. Akbar Ahmed and Louis Dupree (AN). Dist: FIV VS$198.00, order #047032; PSU order #51248. *The bloodiest massacre in the history of the British Empire occurred in January 1842 when 17,000 British soldiers, women, and children were massacred by the Pathans in the Khyber pass. The Pakistani army now patrols this region on the border of Pakistan and Afghanistan, but there is constant trouble from Pathans who live in the region.*

KIBBUTZ SERIES L. Joseph Stone, Jeannette G. Stone (FM), Gideon Lewin (Collab). Dist: Campus Films Distributors Corp, 20 E. 46th Street, New York, NY 10017. [Reviewed by A. I. Rabin, AA 78:951. 1976.]

- **Rearing Kibbutz Babies** 29 min.
- **Infant Development in the Kibbutz** 28 min.
- **Day Care for a Kibbutz Toddler** 22 min.

Kicking High... In the Golden Years (1986) 58 min. Grania Gurievitch (FM). Dist: NDF VR$75.00, FS$600.00, VS$325.00. *"[At a] senior center in Queens, New York... six Black participants discuss the meaning of being old."* [From the review by Colleen Johnson. Reviewed by Thomas A. Painter, AA 93(3):769–771, 1991.]

Kiliwa: Hunters and Gatherers of Baja California 14 min. Jacques Albrecht (PR), Ralph C. Michelsen (FM), V. H. Kjonegaard (AN, WR). Dist: UCEMC FR$25, FS$190. *Documents aspects of hunting and gathering food preparation and shelter construction by a group of Baja, California, Indians, as it illustrates the cultural and ecological adaption of the population to the high desert country and the impingement of modern technology on traditional modes of subsistence. The film shows women and children collecting and preparing foodstuffs, including seeds from pamita grass, buds of the biznaga cactus, cholla cactus, and manzanita berries. Men collect honey from feral bees and hunt a traditional source of protein, the wood rat, with bow and arrow. Native tobacco is collected, and a smoking tube is fabricated from an elderberry shoot. The construction of an aboriginal dwelling from site selection and preparation through completion and habitation is shown. The film also illustrates the training of small children in the attitudes and techniques required of a Kiliwa, and it makes important statements about the geography, kinship, funeral practices, and division of labor in small-scale, technologically simple societies, as well as the subtle conservation of cultural traditions. Shot in the early and mid-1960s, the film reflects the close collaboration of more than 20 years' duration between the cinematographer and the principal informant.*

Killing Us Softly: Advertising's Image of Women 30 min. Jean Kilbourne (FM). Dist: CDF FR$46-106, FS$405. *Through years of research, Jean Kilbourne has detected psychological and sexual themes that appear in most ad campaigns, and has edited her findings into a highly visual and exciting commentary on corporate persuasion. With an intriguing mixture of statistics, humor, insight, and outrage, Ms. Kilbourne shows her audience that ads may seem harmless and funny by themselves, but they add up to a powerful form of cultural conditioning—and their message is serious. Using hundreds of ads from magazines, newspapers, album covers, and store front windows, she has produced a concise and important analysis of a $40 billion industry that preys on the fears and insecurities of every consumer in America. Her public-speaking engagements have awakened hundreds of audiences to the distortions and manipulations that advertisers use to peddle billions of dollars' worth of cosmetics, "hygiene products," drugs, and consumer items.*

Kinesics (1964) 73 min. Ray L. Birdwhistell (AN). Dist: PSU order #80036, FR$20.50, FS$440. *Filmed lecture on kinesics, the study of body motion. Communication cues and signals may be given by any and all observable body parts; examples cited by the speaker include the forehead, eyebrows, eyelids, cheeks, shoulders, and abdomen. These communicatory markers are culturally given and may be divisible into a kinesic grammar for each culture.* [Reviewed by Paul Byers, AA 74:192–193, 1972. Samuel E. Casselberry, AA 77:711–712, 1975.] Suggested supplement: Ray L. Birdwhistell, *Kinesics and Context.* University of Pennsylvania Press, 1970.

Kingdom of Bronze (see The Tribal Eye Series)

Kings and Cities (Africa Series) (1986) 57 min. RM Arts (PR), Basil Davidson (H). Dist: FIV. *Kano, Nigeria, is one example of an African kingdom. There, a king still holds court in his 15th-century palace, and ancient rituals continue to command the respect of the people.*

The Kirghiz of Afghanistan (1975) 60 min. Andre Singer (PR), M. Nazif Shahrani (AN), Granada Television (PR). (A re-edited version of this was shown on the Odyssey Series in 1981.) Dist: PSU order #61401; ISHI. *Until recently, Kirghiz tribesmen lived in a remote corner of Afghanistan; their culture had not changed since the middle ages. Survival depended completely on the favor of the Khan, a feudal lord who claimed descent from the legendary Genghis Khan. Since this film was made, the Kirghiz have fled to Pakistan, where they were airlifted to Turkey, thousands of miles to the east.* Bibliography: M. Nazif Shahrani, *The Kirghiz and Wakhi of Afghanistan: Adaptation to Closed Frontiers.* University of Washington Press, 1979.

!KO BUSHMAN SERIES D. Heunemann and J. H. Heinz (FM). Dist: PSU/PCR. *A series of silent films on particular aspects of !Ko Bushmen culture.* [Reviewed by Megan Biesele, AA 80:201–202, 1978.]

- **!Ko Bushmen** 6 min. FR$11.75. Making fire and smoking of tobacco.

- **!Ko Bushmen** 3 min. FR$8.30. *The "lloli" leap frog game of men.*
- **!Ko Bushmen** 4 min. FR$8.30. *Men's game "xhana."*
- **!Ko Bushmen** 11 min. FR$14.75. *Maiden's initiation rites.*

Kon-Tiki (1951) 75 min. Thor Heyerdahl (FM). Dist: Janus Films, 745 Fifth Avenue, New York, NY 10022. [Reviewed by Alexandra M. Ulana Klymyshyn, *AA* 78:384–385, 1976.]

Kofi: An African in France (1993) 58 min. Carlyn Saltman and Beth Epstein (FM). Dist: NFTS. *Kofi Yamgnane wa\s the first African ever to be elected Mayor of a French town. Having left the thatched huts of his native village in Togo, Kofi nevertheless introduces some tribal traditions into the running of the Town Council in the quiet Breton village where he lives with his French wife and all white neighbors.*

Koli Koli (1966) 30 min. Jean Rouch (DI), Centre National de la Recherche Scientifique, Comité du Film Ethnographique (PR). Dist: CFE; DER. *Hunting with dogs by the young people of Gow. Preparation and utilization of guinea fowl traps. Recitation of fakarey (tales) by the young hunters after the conclusion of the hunt.*

'Ksan 27 min. Province of British Columbia (PR). Dist: Canadian Travel Film Library, Suite 915, 111 East Wacker Drive, Chicago, IL 60601. *This film recalls one ancient legend of the Gitksan, the people of the 'Ksan (today called the Skeena), when they lived in the great city of Temlaham that stretched for miles along the banks of the river. The legend is about a proud civilization that came to ruin when people grew careless of the laws of nature and abandoned the ways of their forebears. The city of Temlaham was destroyed; the people scattered to live in five small villages along the 'Ksan; their indigenous culture became submerged in the ways of aliens who came to their land. But the memory of the past glory lived on, from generation to generation. Today the culture of the Gitksan (a division of the Tsimshian) is seeing a rebirth. One of those five Indian villages became the present town of Hazelton, in the mountainous valley of the upper Skeena. That is where the 'Ksan Association was formed to rebuild the ancient village and to establish the Kitanmax School of North West Coast Indian Art. Now people can drive along fine paved highways to the historic tribal site, to walk into the past through restored Indian dwellings and past resplendent new totems that once again evoke the ancestral spirit. Visitors can take with them finely crafted mementoes of Gitksan art and, once a week during summer months, watch 'Ksan dancers in colorful, interpretive ritual.* [Reviewed by John W. Adams, *AA* 79:514, 1977.]

The Krishna Story Rosette Renshaw (DI). *About one thousand years older than the Christian Nativity, the Hindu parallel is found in the revered canonical text, the Bhagavata Purana. It has often been translated from the original Sanskrit. At times, also, its Book X, considered to be Krishna's first biography—a few episodes spill over into Book XI—has been lavishly illustrated. With some three dozen miniature paintings from the Kaviraja set which Jaipur's Maharaja Sawai Man Singh II Museum has graciously made available, the first five chapters of Book X form the basis of the educational television pilot program for this series.*

Ku Klux Klan—The Invisible Empire (1965) 46 min. Dist: IUAVC FR$13.50. *Examines the aims and mentality of the Knights of the Ku Klux Klan from their beginning in Tennessee over a hundred years ago to their still active, prejudicial treatment of Black, Jewish, and Catholic communities. Explores the rituals, meetings, and Klan rallies that have spurred hatred and a reign of terror through the South for the past century. Employs rare film footage of a 1915 Klan ritual and shows many excerpts from actual meetings and secret ceremonies.*

Kuan-Yin-Pilgrimage (1987) 56 min. Chung-fang Yu (DI). Dist: RG VS$125.00. *Filmed in the People's Republic of China in 1987, this film records the religious celebrations connected with Kuan-Yin's birthday, the most important yearly event for this divinity's devotes. The pilgrimage sites shown, Upper Tien-chu Monastery in Hangchow and P'u-t'o Island are two of the most important Kuan-Yin centers in China and have been held sacred by Chinese Buddhists for over a thousand years. Especially featured in the film are the pre-dawn rituals, the singing of devotional songs dedicated to Kuan-Yin, and the devotees' distinctive all-night vigils. Captured here are rare glimpses of religion in contemporary China.*

Kudzu (1988) 16 min. Marjorie Short (DI). Dist: ECP. *This film looks at kudzu, a fast growing vine that Southerners claim can cover up country roads and overtake slow-moving people. President Jimmy Carter and poet James Dickey join others in recounting the folklore and history of this botanical pest.*

!KUNG BUSHMAN SERIES (see San Series)

The !Kung San: Resettlement (The San Series) (JU/WASI): Videos for Elementary and Secondary Use 28 minutes. Dist: DER FR$30.00, VS$150.00. *Using footage from 1978 through 1986, this video shows some of the dramatic changes in lifestyle and subsistence, which the !Kung have undergone since their days of traditional gathering and hunting. No longer relying completely on foods obtained self-sufficiently, we see the !Kung being given handouts of mealie meal, spending earned money from working in the South African Army on alcohol and consumer goods, and living in areas which increase crowding and argument. With a move back to traditional lands and development of cattle herding and planned agriculture, there is a small hope that !Kung can be successful in a mixed economy.*

The !Kung San: Traditional Life 26 min. Dist: DER VS$150.00. *This is an extensive documentary showing aspects of the !Kung lifestyle.* [Reviewed by Dolores B. Allen, *SBF* 24:174, 1989.]

Kwagh Hir: Tiv Traditional Theatre (see University of Ife Series)

The Kwakiutl of British Columbia (1930–73) 55 min. Silent. Franz Boas (PR, AN), Bill Holm (ED). Dist: UWP

FS$500, VS$350. *This unusual documentary film was made during the winter of 1930–31 at Fort Rupert on Vancouver Island, a village important in the history of the Kwakiutl Indians. On this trip, his last to the Pacific Northwest, Boas sought to check and revise his earlier work in the region by recording a wider variety of sources of information on Kwakiutl language and society. Included are scenes depicting traditional Kwakiutl dances, crafts, games, oratory, and the actions of a shaman. This film is believed to be the only documentary Boas prepared.* [Reviewed by Stanley G. Walens, *AA* 80:204–205, 1978.]

Kwa' Nu' Te': Micmac and Maliseet Artists 41 min. Catherine Martin, Kimberlee McTaggart (DI). Dist: NFB FR$70.00, FS$650.00, VS$250.00. *Kwa' Nu' Te' is a peace chant that invokes the power of creation, a way of bringing back and honoring those spirits that share their visions of healing in a wounded world. The eight Native American artists who are portrayed share this spiritual consciousness in varying degrees. Interviews with the artists at work are dissolved into the beautifully lit images of their creations. In linking these native artists to a long native spiritual and artistic tradition, this film explains that art may be considered an emotional response to the issues and concerns of today, but it also transmits a message of hope.*

Kwashiorkor (1968) 32 min. R. G. Whitehead (FM). Dist: PSU(PCR) FR$14.00. *The film focuses on protein-calorie malnutrition (PCM) of infants and young children in Uganda's Province of Buganda during the 1960s and is composed of five major sequences. The first provides general background information; the second shows a young child with a severe case of kwashiorkor; and the third provides an answer as to why malnutrition exists in Buganda. The fourth deals with the diagnostic and therapeutic procedures used for cases of PCM. The final sequence shows a wedding in a village and the foods typically served on such occasions.* [From the review by Thomas W. Hill, *AJPA* 56:203–204, 1981.]

The Kwegu (Disappearing World Series) (Also called *In Search of Cool Ground: The Kwegu.*) (1985) 52 min. David Turton (AN), Andre Singer (PR). Dist: FIV VS$198.00, order #047003; Thomas Howe Associates, Ltd., 1-1226 Homer Street, Vancouver, British Columbia V6B 2Y8 Canada; (604) 687-4215, FR$150.00, VR$60.00, VS$575.00; PSU VR$14.00, order #51149; FL VR$75.00, VS$445.00. *The Kwegu share a remote corner of Ethiopia with the Mursi. This small group of hunters and cultivators provides the Mursi people with a vital service—they make the dugout canoes used to cross the Omo River. In return, the Mursi are patrons and protectors of the Kwegu. We see the ironies of their feudal relationship and explore the ties that bind them.* [Reviewed by William Shack, *AA* 89:780, 1987. Reviewed in *VISR* 8: 117, 1992.]

Kypseli: Women and Men Apart—A Divided Reality (1976) 37 min. Paul Aratow, Richard Cowan, Susannah Hofmann (FM), Susannah Hofmann (AN). Dist: UCEMC FR$42, FS$540. *Depicts how the peasants of Kypseli, a small Greek village in the Cyclades, divide space, time, and activities according to an underlying pattern based on the separation of the sexes and how this division, in turn, determines the village social structure. Shows that the female realm is separate from that of the male, and that life in Kypseli is organized by a principle of male dominance. Utilizes the structuralist methodology of Claude Lévi-Strauss to discover the unconscious assumptions of the people of Kypseli and to reveal how their social structure is related to the prevalent view of women as dangerous and threatening. The women appear to accept their status, but also utilize these fears and fictions for their own benefit. Contrasts the principal activities of the men, (working the fields, crushing grapes, and cooking on feast days), with those of the women, which include the daily cooking, sewing, shopping, and caring for home and children. Examines the nature of marriage in village social life and discusses such related matters as the underlying reasons for the exclusion of women from public roles, the confinement of menstruating women, and the association of women with the occult. Fascinating study of a social structure derived from the cultural heritage shared by all European peoples and, therefore, of relevance to the study of social patterns and traditional sexual roles in America.* [Reviewed by Muriel Dimen-Schein, *AA* 79:94, 1977.] Focusing questions: How do Kypselians divide time according to male-female dichotomy? Space? Possessions? Activities? What assumptions about the nature of male and female are implicit in these divisions? Are the separate "realities" of the two sexes equal? Why not? Why are females considered inferior (i.e., what social-structural features cause their inequality?)? How do women respond to their ambiguous situation? Do you agree that these assumptions about male and female are basic to all western cultures? Can you see similar attitudes in American culture? Give examples. Is there a social-structural basis for such attitudes toward women in American society? Has the women's movement changed any of these attitudes? Bibliography: The pamphlet EMC sent out about the film has a brief ethnography by Hoffman. Ernestine Friedl, *Vasilika*; J. K. Campbell, *Honor, Family, & Contributor.* [Donna Collins]

Labor More Than Once (1983) 52 min. Liz Mursky (FM). Dist: WMM VR$55, VS$350. *"Examines a US lesbian parent's custody dispute with her ex-husband over their son."* [From the review by Patricia Whelehan, *AA* 89:250–251, 1987.]

The Lacandon Maya Balche Ritual 40 min. R. Jon McGee (PR). Dist: UCEMC VR$40, VS$370, order #37738. *Records in detail one of the most important Maya rituals dating back to pre-Columbian times. In the balche ritual, an alcoholic beverage is made, drunk, and offered to the gods in request for a favor or in thanks for favors received. Despite the longstanding prohibition against it by Spanish missionaries, the ritual is still practiced today, nearly 500 years later. The video shows all aspects of the ritual. It begins with the brewing of the balche and continues through the ritual prayers associated with the ceremony, the offering of the balche to the gods, and the ritual drinking of the balche by the Lacandon men who achieve a transcendental state during rituals. The Maya participants watch the video and provide commentary on their actions during the ceremony.* [Reviewed by Dwight B. Heath, *AA* 91:831, 1989.]

A Lady Named Baybie (1980) 60 min. Martha Sandlin (FM). Dist: Martha Sandlin, 227 Dean St., Brooklyn, NY 11217, FR$100, FS$800. *"A blind New York street singer whose favorite haunt is a bit of sidewalk immediately outside Bloomingdale's."* [From the review by Nora Groce, *AA* 86:230–231, 1984.]

Ladyboys (1992) 51 min. Jeremy Marre (FM). Dist: HFL. *Two teenage boys leave their homes in Thailand's countryside to seek fame and fortune as transvestite performers in the glamorous caberets of the urban south. The boys encounter pain, prejudice, and humor as they strive for a new identity.*

Lakota Quillwork: Art and Legend 28 min. Dist: OWM FR$70, VR$70, FS$500, VS$275. *Among the Lakota Sioux, the elders tell the story of Double Woman, who first brought the art of porcupine quillwork from the spirit world to the Lakota women. To some she is a crazy woman, to others an enchantress with whom no man is equal. She sings from rocky cliffs, but is never seen except in dreams. Tanned robes taken to her tipi are returned with finely crafted designs made from the quills of porcupines. Those who dream of her, it is said, will become expert quillworkers. From the legend of Double Woman, the film moves to a close-up look at the exquisite, finely crafted work of Flossie Bear Robe and Alice Blue Legs, who demonstrate the quilling styles most common to the Western Sioux. We see the Blue Leggs' family hunting the porcupine, cleaning and dyeing the quills, and crafting dance costumes and jewelry from the gathered quills. This film tells a story of women as creative artists, women as protectors, and women as practitioners of cultural history.*

Lamotrek: Heritage of an Island 27 min. Dist: CCC. *This is a documentary about the Micronesian Island of Lamotrek in the Pacific Ocean. The film explores the relationship between traditional island skills and the spirit world of Lamotrekan mythology. It focuses on the ancient skills of "Rong," which is specialized knowledge of art and magic involved with navigation, warfare, canoe building, fishing, dancing, weather control, weaving, medicine making, and agriculture. As a result of increasing contact with modern influences of the outside world, the spirits of "Rong" and the skills associated with them have been on the decline. Translations of the songs, chants, and dialogues are given in subtitles.*

Land and Water (1961) 25 min. W. T. Sanders and W. G. Mather (FM). Dist: PSU (PCR) order #2128K, FR$18.50, FS$385. *Peasant and plantation agriculture in a Mexican valley. Human ecology examined in relation to crops grown under conditions of drought, erosion, and winter frost.*

Land and Water in Iraq 13 min. Dist: EDC FR$20, FS$180, VS$160. *Aspects of ecology of modern Iraq; aspects of life between the Tigris and Euphrates that have remained unchanged; annual cycle of flooding and drought on the alluvial plains.*

The Land Dayaks of Borneo (1961–66) 38 min. William R. Geddes (FM, AN). Dist: NYU FR$26, FS$480; PSU FR$17.50. *Shot in 1961 in the village of Mentu Tapuh, Southwestern Sarawak. General life of village, oriented to river, with some gardening and gathering. Climaxed by a medium performing in a Harvest Festival.* [Reviewed by Peter Goethals, *AA* 69:127, 1967.]

Land Divers of Melanesia (1973) 30 min. Kal Muller (FM). Dist: PFI FR$35; PSU FR$15. *The story of the annual ritual when some Pentecost Islanders, anchored by vines tied to their feet, dive from a wooden tower over 100 feet high. The dive takes an appropriate place among many other ceremonies and rituals.*

The Land Is the Culture (1976) 30 min. Fred Cawsey (WR, DI), Gundar Lipsbergs (CA), Union of BC Indian Chiefs (PR). Dist: PCP FR$35, FS$500. *The land-claims story is a complex one. It's not just a story about land, or money; it's about the fate of a culture that is based on a special relationship with the land. In traditional Indian culture, the planet was The Mother, Mother Earth. The deer, the fish, the trees . . . all living things were the spiritual Brothers and Sisters of Indian people. Life itself was sacred. Indians did not cut down trees for firewood. They used dead wood. If they took a standing tree for a house, they did so with great care and feeling, because the life of a tree was important to them. All of Indian culture is based on this relationship with life and the land. This film looks at these values and compares them with the real estate values of the white culture that has dominated North America for 200 years. Specifically, it deals with the promises that were made to Indians in British Columbia and broken by successive generations of politicians. We see what has happened to Indians' hunting and fishing rights as land was taken in British Columbia without treaties. We hear stories of suffering and humiliation endured by generations of BC Indians as their language was beaten out of the children and the potlatch was outlawed. We see the incredible beauty of the land; the relationships Indians still have with the land; spear fishing in Cowichan; and hunting for moose north of Fort St. John.*

Land of Heart's Desire 29 min. Edward Cullen Productions. Dist: CPI FR$45, FS$400, VS$275. *"About an Irish-American couple considering return migration to Ireland. . . . The film switches between images of life in Flushing (New York) and images of life in slow-paced agrarian Ireland."* [From the review by George Gmelch, *AA* 87:223, 1985.]

Land of Jacques Cartier (St. Lawrence North Series) B/W Dist: CRAW FS$75.38. *The bleak, windswept North Shore of the St. Lawrence River is portrayed still much as it was in the days of its first explorer. History seems to reveal itself before the camera, with a commentary that weaves together the original "Relations" of Cartier with a contemporary narrative.*

The Land of the Cree 10 min. Dist: FCE FR$17, FS$95. *Life of the Indians near Hudson Bay in Canada.*

Land of the Lightning Brothers (1987) 26 min. Janet Bell (PR), David Roberts (DI). Dist: FIV VS$129; FAA. *In the sandstone country southwest of Katherine in the Northern territory lies a spectacular concentration of Aboriginal rock art. The Lightning Brothers, Yagjadbula and Jabaringi,* *with wide dark eyes and dramatically striped bodies, are ancestral beings who in the dream time helped shape the traditional land of the Wardaman Aboriginal people. They are also associated with the coming of rain in this part of the country. This film shows how the Wardaman people see the Lightning Brothers as part of their living culture. They perform traditional songs and ceremonies associated with the special dream time places where the art is found. Many rock art sites are extremely vulnerable, and the film looks at the way these valuable sites are being protected. It features the music of the Aboriginal group "Gondwanaland."*

The Land of the Firewalker 9 min. Dist: FCE FR$17, FS$95. *Customs of the Fiji Islands.*

The Land of the Indians (1978) 102 min. Zelito Viana (Dl). Dist: UNI. *Traces the history of the Indian people of Brazil and then focuses on the contemporary situation of the remaining Indian populations that are struggling to preserve their culture and what little land has been left to them. The film is divided into three parts. Part I, "I Was Born and Raised Here," deals with the Indians on the Nonoai reservation in southern Brazil where over 2,000 white families had settled, pushing the Indians into an area only 10 percent the size of their original reservation. The film shows the successful efforts of the Indians to regain by force those lands expropriated from them. Part II, "The Indian as a Business Deal," portrays the exploitation by large corporations and the government on some Indian reservations. It also features a discussion of the government's proposed policy of "Emancipation," which some critics see as a final attempt to eliminate the remaining Indian populations in Brazil. Part III, "Our Identification Card is Tradition," deals with the cultural resistance of the Indians, including the revival of traditional festivals and rituals. Featured is rare footage of a Cajabi Indian festival being celebrated for the first time in ten years. The film's concluding sequence features two remarkable interviews that vividly characterize the plight of Indian peoples in contemporary Brazil—an encounter with Weran, a Suia warrior with less than ten years of contact with white people; and a meeting with Maria Rosa, the last surviving member of the Of aie-Xavante tribe, who is unable to communicate with anyone because no one else alive knows her language.*

Land of the Long Day 37 min. National Film Board of Canada (PR). Dist: NFBC; UCEMC FR$28. *Baffin Island.*

The Land Where the Blues Began (1982) 58 min. Alan Lomax (FM). Dist: PFI FR$75, FS$750. *History and current status of the Blues musical tradition in rural Mississippi.* [Reviewed by by Nora Groce, *AA* 86:509–510, 1984.]

Land without Bread (1932) 28 min. Luis Bunuel (FM). Dist: MOMA FR$25; CF/MH order #1140459-3, FR$25, FS$240. *A social and anthropological document on the unique district of Las Hurdes near the Portuguese border of Spain. . . . Subsisting on the produce of an exhausted soil, its inhabitants have been undernourished for centuries.* Suggested supplements: J. F. Aranda, *Palabra en el Tiempo*. Editorial Lumen, Barcelona, 1969. Vincent Barrantes, *Las Hurde y sus Leyendas*. Establecimiento Tipogràfico de Fortanet, Madrid, 1893. Freddy Bauche, *Luis Bunuel*. Editions L'Age D'Homme S. A., Lausanne, 1970. Raymond Durgnat, *Luis Bunuel*. University of California Press, Berkeley, 1968. Ado Kyrou, *Luis Bunuel*. Editions Seghers, Paris, 1970. Maurice Legendre *Las Jurdes: Etude de Géographie Humaine*. Feret et Fils, Editeurs, Paris, 1927. Carlos Rebolledo, *Luis Bunuel*. Editions Universitaires, Paris, 1964. Las Hurdes. In: *Encyclopedia Universal Illustrada*, vol. 28, p. 742, Editorial Espasa, Barcelona, 1925.

Langda: Polished Stone Adzes in New Guinea 26 min. Bruno Thery, Pierre Pétrequin, Anne Marie Pétrequin (DIM), Etienne Lemaire (PR). Dist: JVP. *A few agriculturalist groups of New Guinea Highlands still produce and use polished stone adzes. A complex and specialized sequence of splitting by fire, flaking with a hammerstone, and polishing, can change rough basalt into an efficient tool for forest clearing. One of the only records we have of a major import stage in human history, when stone axes were essential for the reproduction of farming societies.* French and English versions.

Language (Media Probe Series, Mind Series) (1982) 30 min. Dist: BBC FR$50, FS$500; PBS. "*Language is a delightful film that is designed to introduce persons who have never thought about the functions of language to some basic linguistic concepts.*" [From the review by Ronald C. Simons, *SBF* 18:152, 1983.]

LANGUAGE AND LINGUISTICS SERIES (See *Dialects*)

Larwari and Walkara (1977) 45 min. Stephen Wild (AN). Dist: UCEMC FR$45, FS$600. *Australia: Walbiri, of Northern Territory. Film expresses oppositions in ceremony: male-female; owners-managers; one patrimoiety-the other patrimoiety; Walbiri-Kurintji; (Larrpa)-(Tarrpa); Dreamtime-Present time; lines-circles; Kumaka-danceground; Mamantapari-dingoes; create-destroy. Focusing questions: Discuss the differences between a clean text and a messy performance.* [Reviewed by Robert A. Paul, *AA* 81(1):204–206, 1979.] Restricted use: This film contains material of a secret/sacred nature and should only be screened for study purposes by appropriate groups.

Lascaux: Cradle of Man's Art 17 min. William Chapman (Dl). Dist: IFB FR$19.75, FS$275, VS$195; UCEMC; PSU(PCR) order # 571-2. *The prehistoric Lascaux Cave paintings, discovered in the Dordogne region of France in 1940, are the subject of this exciting film. The film opens by recreating the circumstances of the discovery. Two small boys chasing a rabbit with their dog fall through the ground into caverns whose walls to their amazement were covered with the forms of animals. These are photographed at length, and the result is one of the best art films.* [Reviewed by L. G. Freeman, *AA* 77:919–920, 1975.]

The Last Days of Okak 24 min. Anne Budgell and Nigel Markham (DI). Dist: NFB FR$50, VR$50, FS$500, VS$225. *Today, only grass-covered ruins remain of the once-thriving Inuit town of Okak. Once, within living memory, brass bands would welcome the arrival of Moravian mission ships that docked there twice a year with supplies. But in November 1918, celebration quickly turned to sorrow, for the ship* had also brought Spanish influenza. It was the beginning of the end for Okak. Archival photos, excerpts from missionaries' diaries and interviews with survivors recount the tragedy of Okak when these two cultures met. The film shows what happens to a community when a disaster that overwhelms its people also largely destroys the values by which they lived. This powerful film transforms an incident of local history into a universal account of human suffering and endurance.

Last Grave at Dimbaza (1974) 55 min. Nana Mahomo (PR). Dist: CN FR$50; UNI. *Filmed illegally in South Africa to show inhuman consequences of apartheid policies. This film contrasts the high standard of living enjoyed by South African whites with the poverty and suffering of blacks. Whites are shown living in the midst of material affluence while blacks are shown as grossly underpaid and exploited house servants and laborers. The resettlement of blacks in so-called "homelands" is exposed as resulting in the separation of families, inadequate housing, lack of food resources, and mass starvation of young children. The presence of multinational corporations, their profit-seeking behavior, and the policies of U.S. and European governments are linked to maintenance of the apartheid system. Cinematic features: Quotes taken from the policy statements of government officials accompany visual evidence of the consequences of their policies. Much factual information regarding wages, profits, mortality rates, etc., are provided in the narrative. Focusing questions: Discussion should be set up to channel the emotional energy of the viewer into constructive ways of thinking about and dealing with the problem. One would want to consider the worldwide economic context in which the problem exists as well as its particular sociohistorical context. Bibliography: Colin Legum, Vorster's Gamble for Africa. Rex Collings, London, 1976. Pierre van den Berghe, South Africa: A Study in Conflict. Berkeley, U.S. Press, 1967. The African Resistance Group, Race to Power: The Struggle for Southern Africa. Anchor Books, Garden City, NY, 1974. Donald Wiedner, A History of Africa: South of the Sahara. Vintage, NY, 1962.* [John A. Young]

The Last Horizon (Man on the Rim Series) 58 min. Dist: LMF VS$295. *The epic voyages of the Polynesians using fast but frail outrigger canoes settled island groups as far apart as Hawaii, Tahiti, New Zealand, and Easter Island. From Asia, man explored and colonized the entire Pacific basin. Centuries later, sails appeared over the horizon, and Europe broke into the isolation of the Pacific. The cultures of the East would lie impotent beneath the weight of superior western technology. Today, the vast Asian reservoir of human energy and resource begins to churn and ferment, as the center of dominance swings from the western hemisphere to the East.*

The Last of the Cuiva (Disappearing World Series) (1971) 65 min. Brian Moser (FM), Bernard Arcand (AN), Granada (PR). Dist: PSU order #51222; ISHI FR$85, FS$875. *The last of the Cuiva live in north east Colombia, surrounded by settlers' ranches. Only a few retain their traditional nomadic lifestyle, and many work as day laborers for white ranchers. Canadian anthropologist Jean-Paul Dumont says the Cuiva are being "killed culturally." This powerful and moving program reveals the truth of his statement.* [Reviewed by Pia Maybury-Lewis and David Maybury-Lewis, *AA* 76:487–489, 1974. Cf. Peter Loizos, *AA* 82:577–578, 1980.]

Last of the Karaphuna (1984) 50 min. Philip Thorneycroft Teuscher (DI), Gregory Pettys (PR). Dist: CG FR$85, FS$795, VS$595. *The theme of the film is the resistance of the approximately 2,800 Caribs of Dominica (the Karaphuna) to cultural domination in the 1980s.* [Reviewed by Trevor W. Purcell, *AA* 87:987–989, 1985.]

Last of the Mayas (1981) 27 min. Wilhelm Helmer (PR). Dist: HAN FR$42, VR$42, FS$420, VS$420. *"From the initial shot of exploding volcanoes to the final fade out over the God House, this film is a beautifully photographed monument to a waste of money, materials, and people's time. ... There is no excuse today for a film with so many points of misinformation and racist undercurrents."* [From the review by Karen O. Bruhns, *SBF* 18:37, 1982.]

The Last Performance National Council for Traditional Arts (PR). Dist: NCTA. *This excellent film documents a group of traditional Laotian court and village musicians, and their resettlement in the United States.*

The Last Pullman Car (1983) 56 min. Kartemquin Films (PR). Dist: NDF FR$75, FS$700. *"It is 1980 and the Pullman plant in Illinios, the last American manufacturer of subway and railroad cars, is shutting down. Intended to show the confrontation between Pullman workers fighting to save their jobs and the modern Pullman conglomerate created by the 'merger mania' of the 1970's and 1980's. ... Raises the question of how the American labor movement will survive this era of corporate takeovers and plant closings."* [From the review by Nora Groce, *AA* 87:989–991, 1985.]

THE LAST TASMANIAN SERIES (1980) Artis Film (PR). *The genocide of an entire indigenous people, the Tasmanian Aborigines. Isolated from the rest of the world for some 12,000 years, this distinct race was completely exterminated within a lifetime by British colonists. Australian production.*

• **Ancestors: The Last Tasmanian** 12 min. Dist: CRM/MH FR$20, FS$180, VS$135; UCEMC FR$23. *Covers the geographical origin of Tasmania, its physical separation from Australia, and the resulting isolation of the Tasmanian Aborigines.*

• **Extinction: The Last Tasmanian** 60 min. Dist: CRM/MH FR$90, FS$900, VS$675; UCEMC FR$60. *Relates the colonization of the islands by the British and the ultimate fate of the Tasmanian people.*

The Last Tribes of Mindanao 52 min. National Geographical Society (PR). Dist: NGS FS$595, VS$545; PSU FR$25.50. *Beyond the clattering blades of the helicopter, the nearly naked figures emerged from the forest—and stepped out of the Stone Age into the year A.D. 1971. They were members of the Tasaday tribe of Mindanao Island's interior—a people unknown to the outside world until the arrival of the airborne party of Manuel Elizalde, Jr., of the*

Philippine Government. When first contacted, the Tasadays knew nothing of a nation called the Philippines. A far venturing trapper stumbled on them in 1966. Five years passed before he arranged a meeting between the shy forest-folk and Elizalde. What do the Tasadays themselves think of all this? They seem to be torn between entering the 20th century and melting back into their own shadowed world. [Reviewed by Thomas M. Kiefer, *AA* 78:716, 1976.]

Latah: A Culture Specific Elaboration of the Startle Reflex (1983) 39 min. Ronald C. Simons (PR, DI, AN), Gunter Pfaff (FM). Dist: IUAVC FR$30, FS$495, VS$160; Ronald C. Simons, Department of Psychiatry, Michigan State University, East Lansing, MI 48824-1316, FS$495, VS$385. *Everyone gets startled. In Malaysia, people who startle readily and strongly are repetitively started by others until they reach a highly flustered state in which they may say things that are normally taboo, may match the movements others around them, and may obey forcefully directed commands. These hyperstartling people are called "latahs," and the condition of being a latah exists as a well-defined role in Malay society. In the film, a latah tells how her hyperstartling began and how she became a latah. Other villagers tell how a latah is played with and teased. Villagers say that latahs are not responsible for their actions in the flustered state that follows a startle (one man was found innocent of murder by virtue of having been in a latah state). The film shows men and women latahs in and out of latah states. It demonstrates how biological, psychological and cultural factors interact to shape behavioral events.* [Reviewed by Robert Jay, *AA* 86:1075–1076, 1984.]

Late Woodland Village 22 min. Marshall McKusick (FM). Dist: UIOWA order #40151, FR$14.80, FS$275. [Reviewed by David Mayer Gradwohl, *AA* 78:366–369, 1976.]

The Lau of Malaita (Disappearing World Series) (1987) 51 min. Pierre Maranda (AN). Dist: FIV VS$198, order #047005; GTI VS$500; PSU VR$14, order #51156. *The Lau have established an extraordinary way of life on their man-made coral islands in a South Pacific lagoon. At first sight, their life seems idyllic, with abundant food and no need for money. But now their "life of custom" is threatened by the spread of Christianity and ideas from the outside world, and the Lau people are fighting back in an attempt to maintain their traditional way of life.* [Reviewed by Bradd Shore, *AA* 91:275–276, 1989. Reviewed in *VISA* 1:484, 1988.]

Laurence Wylie in Peyrane (1983) 30 min. Bernard Petit (FM). Dist: Dr. Bernard Petit, Department of Foreign Languages, SUNY College, Brockport, NY 14420; (716) 395-2269, VS$90. *Laurence Wylie's book,* Village in the Vaucluse, *has become a staple of French civilization courses. This program looks at the author's life. "Wylie reminisces about the year he and his family lived in the village.... This production is also about how the community has changed in the interim."* [From the review by Susan Carol Rogers, *AA* 87:747–748, 1985.]

Laurette 19 min. Barrie Howells (PR), Pierre Lasry (DI). Dist: National Film Board of Canada. *A single mother.* [Reviewed by Roslyn L. Feldberg, *AA* 79:208, 1977.]

Laying a Scent Trail 3 min. Dist: PSU FR$2.80.

Leakey (1983) 23 min. National Geographic Society (PR) Dist: NGSES FS$400, VS$360; Karol FR$30. *"Narrative of Louis S. B. Leakey's search for early hominidae in eastern Africa."* [From the review by Russell H. Tuttle, *AA* 86:799–800, 1984.]

The Leap across the Cattle (1979) 45 min. Ivo Strecker (FM). Dist: Institut fuer den wissenschaftlichen Film, 34, Goettingen. Nonnensteig 72. West Germany. *The film, which is set in southern Ethiopia, follows a single Hamar youth through a series of initiation rites at the climax of which he leaps across a row of cattle. Rituals are always full of mystery, even, or perhaps especially, for those who enact them. The commentary of the film, which consists of a description of the rituals by Baldambe (Aike Berinas), an older brother of the initiate Berhane, retains this essential mystery while providing information about such details as the passage of time and the nature of relations between actors. Relevant anthropological literature: Jean Lydall and Ivo Strecker,* The Hamar of Southern Ethiopia, *vols. I–III. Klaus Renner Verlag, 1979. D-8021 Hohenschaeftlarn, Am Sonnenhang 8, West Germany. Ivo Strecker,* The Music of the Hamar. *A double album of music and speech and sound from Hamar. Musikethnologische Abteilung, 1979. Museum fur Volkerkunde, D-1000 BerlineDahlem, West Germany. Serje Tornay,* Etudes Ethiopiennes: Deux Visages de l'Ethnographie. *L'Homme, avril-juin 1980, XX(2), pp. 99–118. Judith Ennew, "Wrapping Up Reality: The Ethnographic Package."* Cambridge Anthropology *6(3), 1981.*

Learning from the Painters of Lascaux Dist: FACSEA FR$16.

The Learning Path (As Long as the Rivers Flow Series) (1991) 59 min. Loretta Todd (DI), James Cullingham and Peter Raymont (PR). Dist: FRIF VR$75, VS$390. *Native control of education is explored in this film, which features Edmonton elders Ann Anderson, Eva Cardinal, and Olive Dickason, remarkable educators who are working with younger natives. They recount harrowing experiences at reservation schools, memories that fueled their determination to preserve their language and identities. Using a unique blend of documentary footage, dramatic reenactments, and archival film, Todd weaves together the life stories of three unsung heroines who are making education relevant in today's native communities.*

Learning to Dance in Bali 1980 (ca. 1930s) 13 min. Margaret Mead and Gregory Bateson (AN, FM). Dist: PSU VR$14.50, FS$270, VS$105, order #24635; NYU FR$20, FS$225. *Among the Balinese, learning is usually dependent on teaching methods that are visual and kinesthetic, rather than verbal. The student, positioned in front of the teacher, is made to perform the correct movements under the guidance of the teacher, who holds the student's torso and limbs, adjusting posture and movement continuously during the dance. At other times in the lessons, the student, positioned behind the teacher, imitates the movements. This film traces the beginning of a Balinese infant's awareness of dance movement by imitation, encouraged by his father, then* records a dance lesson by the master teacher, I Mario, the most celebrated of all Balinese dancers, as he teaches a young student physically by guiding his movements. After the lesson, for amusement, I Mario and a visiting Indian dancer (Nataraj) exchange dance demonstrations, following each other's movements by imitating them. In another sequence, the Gong Pangkung gamelan orchestra of Tababab, Bali, attempts to accompany the unfamiliar movements of the visiting Indian dancer, and, finally, I Mario performs the intricate and difficult Kebiar dance, which he created and which has become essential to traditional Balinese dance repertoire. These sequences demonstrate how students learn passively from dance lessons and acquire separate awareness in different parts of their bodies. Using footage taken by Dr. Gregory Bateson in the late 1930s as part of the fieldwork he and Margaret Mead did together in Bali, the film was edited and completed in 1978 at the request of Dr. Mead. The narration for the film, which was extemporaneous, was the last audio recording made by Dr. Mead several months before her death. [Reviewed by Toby Alice Volkman, AA 85:226–227, 1983.]

The Legacy (Africa Series) (1986) 57 min. RM Arts (PR), Basil Davidson (H). Dist: FIV. *Davidson looks at Africa in the aftermath of colonial rule. Interviews with political leaders illuminate the problems and successes of Africa today.*

LEGACY SERIES (1991) 6 hours. Peter Spry-Leverton (PR), Michael Wood (NR). Dist: Ambrose. *A series of six one-hour videos on six ancient civilizations.* [Reviewed by Robert Wenke, AA 95:252–253, 1993.]

The Legacy of L. S. B. Leakey (1977) 59 min. National Geographic Society (PR). Dist: NGS FS$595, VS$545. *Family, friends, and colleagues Jane Goodall and Dianne Fossey recount Leakey's story.* [Reviewed by Jane E. Phillips-Conroy, ARCH 35(6):62, 1982.]

The Legacy of Lifestyles (The Africans Series) (1986) 60 min. Dist: ACPB VR$100, VS$198. "*This is the second program from The Africans series written and narrated by Ali A. Mazrui. With excellent footage from many parts of Africa, the program attempts to depict a generalized African value system. . . . Mazrui has set himself an impossible task, and the result is a confusing amalgam of random fact and idiosyncratic opinion.*" [From the review by Ronald C. Simons, SBF 23:113, 1987.]

Legacy of The Spirits (Caribbean Culture Series) (1985) 52 min. Karen Kramer (FM). Dist: DER FR$90, VS$500; KKFL FR$90, FS$750, VS$500; Erzulie Films, 22 Leroy Street, New York, NY 10014; (212) 691-3470, FR$90, FS$750, VS$650. *This documentary film shows how Vodou is a valid and serious belief system. The film interweaves Vodou ceremonies, scholarly information, music, and images of colorful ritual objects, to show the beauty behind what has been one of the world's most misunderstood religions. It explains the theology of religion, the meaning of the rituals, the pantheon of spirits, possession, the sacred drawings, the Catholic influence, the history of persecution and more. The film traces the religion from Africa to Haiti to New York City. It is filmed in the Caribbean communities of New York City.* [Reviewed by Elliott Leib, AA 89:257–258, 1987.]

The Legend of Corn (Legends of Indians Series) 26 min. Dist: FHS VS$89.95, order #DH-878. *Zhomin was an excellent fisherman and hunter; killed only for food; valued effort, perseverance, and endurance; and understood that everything in nature is sacred. One day a stranger challenged him to a duel. Zhomin painted his face with the sign meaning he would utter no sound if hurt. He was the victor, and from the stranger's grave a plant grew. The stranger had given his life and was reborn as corn for the good of the people, and as a reward for obedience.*

The Legend of Lake Titicaca (1971) 22 min. Jacques Cousteau (PR). Dist: ChF FR$40, FS$380. "*The viewer is treated to a typical Cousteau adventure set in the high Andes during an underwater search for the legends of the Incas in the world's highest navigable body of water. . . . They take no excavations to test Cousteau's hypothesis that these remains are Inca or even earlier. . . . Any scientific advances resulting from this expedition most certainly are not related to underwater archaeology.*" [From the review by Robert L. Hohlfelder, ARCH 36(1):62–64, 1983.]

Legend of the Paramo (1965) 22 min. Gabriela Samper (WR, PR). Dist: PFI. *A legendary "arriero" (muledriver) in a desolate highland region just below the snowcapped peaks of Caldas, Colombia, is the central figure in the fantasy of the 12-year-old hero. This dramatized fantasy is filmed in the misty mountains of Paramo, whose other-world beauty is the result of a volcanic and glacial past. The young "sangrero" (apprentice muledriver) is part of a muletrain bound for the Upper Paramo. Fear of the cold and desolate mountain regions, combined with the tales of heroes and ghosts the boy has heard, compel his fantasized trip. Such men as the "arrieros" were the real pioneers of the interior of Colombia. The "arriero" is a legendary figure symbolizing courage and daring, as is the Western cowboy in the United States. In Colombia, one often hears of the great "arriero" who never died but has remained to guard the mountain passes still traveled by the dwindling bands of mule drivers. It was initially this legend that inspired the film. The Legend of the Paramo probably represents—more truly than the most factually accurate, educational travelogue—the cultural identity of a people of South America.*

Legends of Easter Island (1989) 58 min. John Lynch and Bettina Lerner (PR). Dist: CFV FS$250. "*Easter Island has been shrouded in mystery ever since the Europeans first discovered it covered with hundreds of gigantic stone statues with haunting visages in the South Pacific in 1722. This program meticulously documents the enormous amount of research that has been done on Easter Island and its people and shows footage of archaeological excavations.*" [From the review by Peter Allen, ARCH 44(2):54–55, 1991.] See also *Secrets of Easter Island*.

LEGENDS OF INDIANS SERIES 26 min. each. Dist: FHS VS$675 (series). *These are authentic stories from various Indian tribes, told by Native Americans in order to rehearse and remember who they are and what they believe. The* *stories are acted out by the tribespeople themselves.* See descriptions under individual titles:

- The Legend of Corn
- The Return of the Child
- The Winter Wife
- Moowis, Where are you Moowis?
- Glooscap
- The Path of Souls
- The World Between
- The Path of Life

Lempad of Bali (1980) 60 min. John Darling (FM), Lorne Blair (DI). Dist: Australian Film Commission, 9229 Sunset Blvd., Los Angeles, CA 90069; (213) 275-7074, FR$150, VR$75, FS$900. *A "biographical film of an artist who lived for more than a century in Bali, Indonesia.... Gusti Nyoman Lempad created sculpture, drawings, temple compounds, carvings, and paintings."* [From the review by Philip F. McKean, *AA* 89: 532, 1987.]

Lenape: The Original People (1985) 22 min. Thomas Agnello (FM). Dist: Agnello Films, P.O. Box 68173, Indianapolis, IN 46268; (317) 299-5300, FR$45, FS$425. *"A wide range of historic stills and recent motion picture footage of the Lenape people [Delaware] are presented. Much of the footage focuses on interviews of Lenape traditionalists."* [From the review by Robert S. Grumet, *AA* 89:1017, 1987. Reviewed by Gifford S. Nickerson, *SBF* 23:47, 1987.]

Leon "Peck" Clark: Basketmaker (1980) 15 min. William Ferris, Judy Peiser (FM). Dist: CSF FR$25, FS$235. *A day in the life of Leon and Ada Clark. The film follows the patient development of a white oak basket from tree to finished product. Detailed scenes of basketmaking blend with the couple's fond reminiscences of their long life together. Basketmaking is a lonely craft nowadays, and Clark notes that there is, "nobody interested in it. Nobody but me." But he works on, for he feels, "If I once sit down and do nothing, I'll be just worn out."*

Lessons from Gulam: Asian Music in Bradford (1986) 49 min. John Baily (FM), Andy Jillings (CA), Royal Anthropological Institute and the National Film and Television School, UK (PR). Dist: DER FR$50, VS$375. *Bradford is a mill town in the north of England with a population of around 60,000 Muslims from South Asia. Muslim values are strongly maintained. This film studies Asian music within the community and contrasts music education in the schools with the very different kind of music enculturation in the family. Gulam Musa is from Gujrat (India) from a Muslim group whose members are traditionally barbers and musicians. He specializes in singing "qawwali," a genre of Muslim devotional music found in India and Pakistan. He runs his own "qawwali" group and takes part in Asian music workshops in the Bradford schools.* Study guide available. [Reviewed by Dorothy S. Mull and J. Dennis Mull, *AA* 91:836–838, 1989.]

Let the Spirit Move 25 min. Bill Gray (FM). Dist: Salem Films, P.O. Box 10749, Salem Station, Winston-Salem, NC 27108. *Erstwhile Prophet Grover Lee Moss of North Carolina.* [Reviewed by Keith K. Cunningham, *JAF* 92(363):116–119, 1979.]

Let's Get Married (Rural Greece: Desertion, Migration, Village Life Series) (1985) 35 min. Colette Piault (FM), Graham Johnston (CA, ED), George Nivoix (SR). Dist: LFDQ; PSA VR$65, VS$300. *In August 1983, on holiday in the Greek mountain village of Ano Ravenia, Epirus, Eleni who was living with her aunt Martha's family in Martin (Tennessee, USA) met Demetrios who was living and working with his father in Kato Ravenia. They fall in love and get married. This observational film follows this wedding and could be assimilated to a family film shot by professional filmmakers as a one single day reportage. As part of the family came from the United States, we attend a Greek-American wedding, mixing some traditional Greek aspects with some outside elements.*

Letter from an Apache (1982) 12 min. Barbara Wilk (FM). Dist: POR FR$25, FS$225. *"Based on a letter that Carlos Montezuma (ca. 1866–1923), a well-known Indian advocate for Indian rights, wrote to the Bureau of American Ethnology in reply to a request for a short biography.... The letter forms the basis of the narration of the film, which illustrates the events described ... with a series of photographs, maps, and animated drawings."* [From the review by Philip J. Greenfeld, *AA* 86:1060, 1984.]

Liebalala (1935) 58 min. Margaret Carson Hubbard (FM). Dist: UCEMC FR$34, FS$350. *In 1935, accompanied by a friend and a cameraman, Hubbard journeyed from Johannesburg to Barotseland, a remote, little-known area on the Zambesi River in what is now western Zambia, to film the Lozi. The result is Liebalala (Sweetheart), an important landmark in the history of ethnographic filmmaking in Africa. The original 35mm nitrate silent print, stored for many years in the American Museum of Natural History in New York City, was recently transferred to 16mm to facilitate widespread distribution. A soundtrack was added, containing authentic Lozi music taped by Dr. Hugh Tracey and a narration by Mrs. Hubbard, who describes her experience and provides her insights of then and now. Moments of unconscious Eurocentrism in her 1935 view of Africa show us something of our developing perception of non-European people, and her narrative retains the spirit of that period's European inquiry in Africa. Liebalala is a rare ethnographic document. Native actors depict scenes from their daily lives, portraying all aspects of a courtship and concluding with an actual wedding ritual. Included are the male's initial wooing; his plea for aid from the witch doctor, who uses divination and medicine to ensure a successful marriage; settlement of a dispute between the hero and his rival for the bride; presentation of cattle and money to the bride's father; re-enactment of marriage by capture; cutting of the bride's hair to married woman fashion; and a wedding celebration in which masked Likishi dancers perform on a high wire and bathe in fire. One sequence in which a young man with magical immunity to stings allows scorpions to crawl on his chest is especially impressive, though peripheral to the main story. Other aspects of Lozi culture shown include the mining, smelting, and shaping of iron by miners and craftsmen, the capture of giraffe, and a* *cooperative fish hunt in which several villages take part.* [Reviewed by Max Gluckman, *AA* 77:701–703, 1975.]

Life at the Source: The Adventures of an Amazon Explorer (1989) 47 min. Cathy Frost (DI). Dist: CG FR$75, VS$295. *Recounts the larger-than-life but true story of Arno P. Calderari—professional adventurer, jungle explorer, deep sea diver, treasure hunter and wildlife filmmaker who has been dubbed "Indiana Jones Arno" by the media. Arno came to the Amazon in 1946 from his native Switzerland and has since traveled all over the globe. He has spent his life exploring locales most people only dream about. The film interweaves Arno's reminiscences with rare film footage of his many adventures.*

Life Chances: Four Families in a Changing Cypriot Village (1974) 43 min. Peter Loizos (FM), Gregory Harris (ED). Dist: UCEMC (rental); Peter Loizos & James Woodburn, Department of Anthropology, London School of Economics, Houghton St., London WC2A 2AE, England (sale). *This 16mm black-and-white documentary sound film was made by an experienced filmmaker as a teaching film. It establishes the nature of traditional peasant agriculture in a Greek Cypriot village and then shows the recent transformation of that agriculture through technology and increased participation in the market economy. Then the film traces the achievements of four families, all the descendants of the same married couple. The families reach different positions in both the local village social structure, and in one case, leave that system and enter the national stratification system at a high point. The factors involved are demographic (sex ratio of children and birth order in a set of siblings); cultural; institutional (the school system, and extension of agricultural credit facilities); as well as properties of the individuals themselves. It, thus, shows how the placement of individuals in a stratification system is complex, but concrete. Because of the details of Cypriot marriage arrangement and property settlements (the provision of dowry houses for women), the film is of particular interest for women's studies; it is also of interest to students of social change; economic development; peasant communities; social stratification. Warnings: Must set students up to appreciate the ethnography, and not expect much filmic excitement. Focusing questions: This film raises the question, are some subjects better handled only by printed words? Could the life chances of these Greek Cypriots be made more visual? The film gives one main cause for sudden social differentiation. Might there be other contributing factors? Any evidence for such in the film? Does it make a difference to you to find out that all these people have had to leave their village because of the Greek-Turkish war and are living as refugees? Relevant anthropological literature:* P. Loizos, "Changes in property transfer among Greek Cypriot villagers." *Man* 10:503–523, 1975. P. Loizos, *The Greek Gift: Politics in a Cypriot Village.* Blackwell & St. Martin's Press, 1975. P. Loizos, *The Heart Grown Bitter: A Chronicle of Cypriot War Refugees.* Cambridge University Press, 1981. Bibliography: J. B. Loudon, "Between the Frames." *RAIN* 18:1–6, 1977. (An appreciation of the film.)

Life in the Dust/Fragments of African Voyages (1986) 20 min. Henry Smith (FM). Dist: Solaris, 264 W. 19th Street, New York, NY 10011. VR$50, VS$200. *"Episodes of the Solaris Dance Theatre's three tours to West Africa, juxtaposed with footage of the dance company in their New York City studio performing their impressions of West African culture through the idiom of modern dance."* [From the review by Julie A. Kerr and John Crawford, *AA* 90:1047–1048, 1988.]

Life on a Coral Atoll 20 min. McGraw-Hill (PR), in collaboration with Authentic Pictures. *This film shows the lives of Pacific atoll inhabitants; their adaptations to their environment; their reliance upon the coconut tree for food, drink, building materials, and sale; as well as their daily activities, which include canoe-building, basket weaving, ornament making, and tattooing.*

Light of Many Masks (1983) 30 min. Karen Goodman and Wayne Lockwood (FM). Dist: Karen Goodman, 107 West 70th St., #PH-1, New York, NY 10023; (212) 873-6531, FR$45, FS$450. *Examines the arts of topeng: Balinese masked dance drama.* [Reviewed by Toby Alice Volkman, *AA* 87:748–749, 1985.]

Like the Trees 14.5 min. Kathleen Shannon (FM). Dist: NFBC. *A Metis woman from northern Alberta.* [Reviewed by Nancy Foner, *AA* 79:211, 1977.]

Lines of Fire (1989) 63 min. Brian Beker (PR). Dist: FRIF FR$125, FS$995, VS$390. *As the violence in Burma edges toward a new high, this film sneaks through the lines of fire into the rebel-held territories, where one of the world's largest, oldest, and least known revolutions is on the brink of losing its fight against an iron-fisted military dictatorship. This film offers the first comprehensive look at the 40-year-old war that has ruined the biggest, and once the wealthiest, country of Southeast Asia. It explores the mercenary politics of the area where lumber is ransom for captured student leaders; where heroin trafficking is camouflaged in the green fatigues of rebellion; where a fourth generation of children is entering the ranks of the ragged rebel armies. Filmed entirely in Burma's jungles during unauthorized border crossings in 1989, it also includes smuggled footage of 1988's bloody student uprising, in which thousands of civilians were gunned down by government troops.*

The Lion Hunters (La chasse au lion à l'arc) 68 min. Jean Rouch (FM), Pierre Braunberger, Films de la Pleiade (PR). Dist: DER FR$95, FS$950; UCEMC order #79388, FR$37. *These tribesmen have abandoned their nomadic hunting lifestyle in favor of the easier life of sedentary millet farming. However, a few adult males, much admired by their fellow tribesmen, occasionally revive the old ways when the pastoral Fulani call upon them to slay lions who threaten the lives of cattle or villagers. Then, equipped with their traditional poisoned arrows, the hunters leave their homeland and travel far into the bush to a Fulani village near the Niger river. Their hunt is as much a celebration of manhood and the kinship of man and beast as a practical venture. The film shows the hunters' traditional rituals of preparing poison, divining the outcome of the hunt, and,* *finally, releasing the souls of slain animals. Interwoven among the ancient practices are Western borrowings: transportation by Land Rover, the use of steel traps, and a bottle of French perfume to lure the lions to the traps. This film illustrates the blend of tribal, Muslim, and Western elements in a related series of rituals, and also presents a perceptive view of the universally human fear, pain, pride, and glory that the hunters experience in the unpredictable course of their venture.* [Reviewed by T. O. Beidelman, *AA* 74:1567–1568, 1972.] See also: "Jean Rouch Talks about his Films to John Marshall and John W. Adams," *AA* 80:1005–1022, 1976.

Un lion nomme "L'americain" (A Lion Named "the American") (1968) 20 min. Jean Rouch (DI), Centre National de la Recherche Scientifique, Comite du Film Ethnographique (PR). Dist: CFE; DER. *In the course of projecting a film made about them, the bow lion hunters decide to clear the shame of the lion called "the American," who escaped in 1965.*

The Lion's Roar (1985) 49 min. Mark R. Elliot (DI), Kenneth H. Green (PR). Dist: CPI FR$80, FS$800, VS$375. *"About the reincarnate Karmapa Lama who leads an entire Tibetan sect from his monastic residence in the Himalayas of Sikkim."* [From the review by Donald A. Messerschmidt, *AA* 89:264–265, 1987.]

The Little Indian Weaver 10 min. Dist: FCE FR$17, FS$95. *A little girl wishes to earn money to buy a doll at the trading post; to do this she must learn to weave as her mother does. Made among the Navaho of the Southwest.*

Little Injustices: Laura Nader Looks at the Law (Odyssey Series) (1980) 59 min. Laura Nader (AN), Michael Ambrosino (PR), Terry Rockefeller (PR). Dist: DER FR$50, FS$500. *Principles of law, drawing on Nader's own work in Mexico.* See also *To Make the Balance*. [Reviewed by John W. Adams, *AA* 85:747–748, 1983.]

Little White Salmon Indian Settlement 30 min. Treaty Indians of the Columbia, Inc. (PR), Harry J. Dawson (DI). Dist: Harry Dawson, Jr., Community Eye, P.O. Box 10042, Portland, OR 97210; UNI FR$45-60, FS$425. *Yakima Indians describe their own history.* [Reviewed by Daniel R. Gross and Susan H. Lees, *AA* 76:486, 1974.]

Live Lobster (Maine Lobsterman Series) (1979) 24 min. Peg Dice (FM). Dist: Bodacious FR$25, FS$250. [Reviewed by Paul Durrenberger, *AA* 85:495–496, 1983.]

Living Africa: A Village Experience (1983) 34 min. James Perry and Patrick O'Meara (PR), Jean-Pol LeFebvre (FM). Dist: IUAVC FR$40, FS$450, VS$175, order #GSC-1541. *Portrays the daily experiences and concerns of the people of Wassetake, a small village on the Senegal River in West Africa, emphasizing changes taking place within and outside of the community. For thousands of years, villages like Wassetake have responded to and participated in new ways of living in order to cope with natural, economic, religious, and political changes; and scenes of contemporary life reveal the persistence of these themes. Also available in French.* [Reviewed by David H. Spain, *AA* 88:779–780, 1988. Winifred Lambrecht, *SBF* 20:165, 1985.]

The Living Goddess 30 min. Dist: WFV FR$47.50, FS$475; UCEMC FR$38. *Incarnation of a goddess in Kathmandu, Nepal.*

Living in America: A Hundred Years of Ybor City 53 min. Gayla Jamison (PR). Dist: FL VR$75, VS$445. *Celebrates the long and rich tradition of Latin culture in this country in its vivid portrayal of Ybor City, Florida. This multicultural community was founded in the 1880s, when Cuban, Spanish, and Italian immigrants arrived to work in the thriving cigar factories. It flourished until World War II when the effects of assimilation, urban renewal, and the decline in the cigar industry led to its demise. We meet people who remember playing dominoes over a steaming cup of cafe con leche, socializing on Saturday nights at the dance clubs, and taking pride in making a perfect, hand-rolled cigar. They tell us too of the hard times and the discrimination, which was made easier to bear by the protective community they had to fall back on.*

THE LIVING MAYA SERIES (1985) 58 min. each. Hubert Smith (FM). Dist: UCEMC FR$45, VS$125. *The four-part series documents life in a Yucatan village, focusing on one family over the course of a year. It is available in Maya, Spanish, and English, with English subtitles.* [Reviewed by Winifred Lambrecht, *SBF* 22:125, 1986.]

• **Program 1** *Introduces the village of Chican and the Colli Colli (Coyee) family and examines the structure of Maya agricultural and village life.*

• **Program 2** *Focuses on the Colli Colli family facing financial and emotional challenges caused by an illness in the family group. It does a very good job of showing how the distressed family uses traditional solidarity to muster resources and comfort. The film shows the Colli Colli family going through this hardship during a time when drought threatens the village's crucial corn crop.*

• **Program 3** *Addresses the issue of change. It focuses on the two youngest sons of the Colli Colli family who plead to be placed in school in Merida. They are the first in the family to reject traditional life.*

• **Program 4** *As the Colli Colli resolve their difficulties and the village harvests a mediocre corn crop, viewers are left with an understanding of the underlying rationales of Maya life and with questions about their own assumptions, priorities, and values.*

Living Music for Golden Mountains (1982) 27 min. Arthur Dong and Elizabeth Meyer (FM). Dist: UCEMC VR$37, FS$435, VS$330. *Cantonese Chinese musician and music in California.* [Reviewed by Franklin C. L., *AA* 85:497–498, 1983.]

The Living North 70 min. Dist: FCE FR$150. *A youngster in Lapland relates how his people herd reindeer and how important they are. The tribe follows the animals and when they find food, they build shelters against the weather.*

Living of the River Agano (Aga Ni Ikiru) (1992) 115 min. Satoh Makoto and the Living of the River Agano Committee (FM). Dist: Jay Film Co. Ltd., 101 New Igusa-Haime 3-22-3, Igusa, Suginami-ku Tokyo 167, Japan; telephone 813-3399-0504; fax 813-3399-9478. *Since the Showa Elec-*

tric Company discharged organic mercury into this important riverway, Minamata disease has been a way of life for communities living along the Agano. This documentary was the result of a film collective who lived with the community for four years, and it documents the politicization of the village that fights to receive recognition and compensation for the long-term effects of Minamata disease.

The Living Stone 22 min. National Film Board of Canada (PR). Dist: NYU; UCEMC FR$11. *An evocative picture of a spring and summer among a few Eskimo at Cape Dorset in Canada's eastern Arctic, showing the inspiration, often related to belief in the supernatural, behind their stone, ivory, and bone carvings.* [Reviewed by Hans Guggenheim, AA 73:1478–1480, 1971.]

Lockhart Festival (1974) 30 min. Curtis Levy (DI), Richard Tucker (CA), Australian Institute of Aboriginal Studies (PR). Dist: AIAS. *A dance festival organized by the Aboriginal people of Lockhart River in northern Queensland became an occasion for forging social links among eight Aboriginal groups in Cape York Peninsula and Groote Eylandt. The film records their varied dance styles and the sense of mutual interest and support that the festival created. For the Lockhart people themselves, the event was important as a test of their commitment to their Aboriginal heritage, and for their children, it stimulated a desire to learn and carry on the performance of traditional dancing.*

Locomotion on Branches (White-Handed Gibbon) 7.5 min. Dist: PSU FR$2.80.

Locomotion on a Branch 4.5 min. Dist: PSU FR$2.80.

LONG BOW FILM SERIES Carma Hinton (DI). Dist: NDF FR$90, VR$75, VS$480. *A series comprising three marvelous films that provide pathos, humor, and new insights about the human condition in rural China.* See descriptions under individual titles:

- **All under Heaven**
- **Small Happiness**
- **To Taste a Hundred Herbs**

Long Hour's Walk (1974) 25 min. Sumner Glimcher (FM) .Dist: IFF FR$45, FS$450. *Long Hour's Walk is the length of time it takes for first- and second-graders to walk to school in parts of rural Colombia. The viewer takes another walk: first, a walk through a rural area, then, a walk through the barrios on the outskirts of Bogota. With Father Rene Garcia, a rebel Roman Catholic priest, as a guide, the viewer learns how 85 percent of the population of Colombia lives (when the film was shot in the early 1970s). Peasants earn 24 cents a day and must work three weeks simply to earn enough money to buy a shovel. When the peasant leaves the country for the city, he substitutes one kind of poverty for another. Boys become beggars, and girls become prostitutes to help sustain their families. In the face of poverty, hunger, illness, and premature death, can there still be hope?*

Long Journey Home (1987) 58 min. Elizabeth Barret (DI). Dist: APPAL FR$90, FS$825, VS$400. *This is a documentary about migration and the struggle of people racked by economic imperatives and their desire to maintain a homeplace. The film interweaves personal recollections of several people. The "history tellers" include storyteller Anndrena Belcher, now of Scott County, Virginia, who has returned to the mountains from a childhood in Chicago; Dr William Turner now a University Professor, who came from a black coal mining family in Lynch, Kentucky; and James and Denise Hardin, returning to the mountains with their children after 17 years in Baltimore. From these experiences, emerge a sense of the economic forces that carry into and out of the mountains and of the social, cultural, and geographic features that continue to hold them or pull them back. With this comes a fuller understanding of the more universal notions of home and community and what they mean to all of us.* [Reviewed by Susan Abbott, AA 92:1098, 1990.]

The Long Journey of Clement Zulu (1992) 59 min. Liz Fish (DI), Ingrid Falck (PR), Narendhra Morar (EP) for the BBC, Gcina Mhlope (NA). Dist: 2 Vredehoek Avenue, Oranjezicht 8001, South Africa. *This documentary traces the first year of freedom for three remarkable men released from South Africa's maximum security political prison, Robben Island. From the first euphoria of freedom, through sobering journeys into the disappointing "new South Africa," the three endure a roller coaster of emotion, political and personal disillusionment, and all the hopes and fears of reintegration into a dramatically changed world.*

Long Life and Prosperity 28.5 min. Dist: UGA FR$25, FS$385. *The film shows the traditional birthday party in honor of a family's 82-year-old grandmother. Younger family members who had left their farm home to work in the city attend the reunion. Although they are now members of a 20th-century urban society, they still observe the ancient rites of ancestor worship and honor their obligations of filial piety.*

The Long Walk 60 min. Phillip Greene (Dl), KQED-TV (PR). Dist: Film Wright, Diamond Heights, Box 31348, San Francisco, CA 94131. *The Long Walk of the Navajo.* [Reviewed by Thomas Kiefer and Louise Lamphere, AA 76:722, 1974.]

The Longest Trail 58 min. Alan Lomax and Forrestine Pauley (DI). Dist: UCEMC FR$60, VR$60, FS$865, VS$410, order #11291(f), #37263(v). *Examines one of the world's great dance traditions—that of the American Indians. Beneath the apparent diversity of Indian dance, the film shows the unifying patterns of movement style that link the dances of Native Americans from Alaska to Argentina into a highly unified creative tradition. In addition to introducing dances of some 50 American Indian cultures (as well as scenes of shamanism, drama, ritual, work, and handicrafts), the film also recounts the story of one of the great human adventures: the settlement of the New World by peoples coming at first across the Bering Strait landbridge thousands of years ago. The film will acquaint general audiences with the antiquity, durability, and essential unity of the American Indian dance tradition.*

The Longhouse People 23 min. National Film Board of Canada (PR). Dist: NFBC. *The life and religion of the Longhouse People. We see how the Iroquois of today still* *maintain a link with their proud past. The film shows a rain dance, a healing ceremony, and a celebration in honor of a newly chosen chief.*

LONGSHOREMEN AND AUTOMATION: THE CHANGING FACE OF THE WATERFRONT SERIES (1986) 30 min. Berry Minott (PR), Berry Minott and Doug Weihnacht (DR). Dist: UCEMC VR$35, VS$350. *Oral history of longshoremen in San Francisco.* [Reviewed by Michael Agar, AA 90:1042–1043, 1988.]

Longshot (1981) 60 min. Jane Hunziker (FM). Dist: Jane Hunziker, 2058 North Seminary, Chicago, IL 60614, FR$150, FS$750, VS$650. *"Documents the rapidly disappearing nomadic way of life of a Basque sheepherder in the contemporary American west."* [From the review by Elizabeth A. Lawrence.]

Looking for Me (1970) 29 min. Norris Brock and Virginia Bartlett (WR), American Dance Therapy Association (PR). Dist: UCEMC FR$28, FS$375, VS$265. *"Emphasizes the primacy of body movement as a medium of communication and uses this as a way for individuals to explore themselves, their relationship to space, and their relationship to other people."* Includes, *"sequences showing four- and five-year-olds learning about the different parts of their bodies through self-exploration and by 'painting' the bodies of other children."* [From the review by Anya Peterson Royce and Fran Snygg, AA 87:485–486, 1985.]

The Loon's Necklace 11 min. Crawley Films (PR). Dist: NYU FR$15; UCEMC FR$11; PSU(PCR) order # 970.1-7, FR$4.40. *Recreation of a Salish legend using Northwest Coast masks.* [Reviewed by Hans Guggenheim, AA 73:1478–1480, 1971.] Focusing questions to set up viewers: What are myths and legends and what function do they serve? From what source does Kelura derive his supernatural powers? What is a vision quest? How do we deal with "pattern numbers"? Why do the Northwest Coast Indians use a pattern number? What number? In what significant ways are terms of kinship used? What do they mean? Who uses them? Do you learn anything from the masks and other works of art? What do they tell us about culture? [Arthur Atlas]

Loot: The Plundered Heritage 30 min. Robert Schyberg (PR). Dist: PyrF VS$80. *"This new production on the looting of archaeological sites, fueled by the antiquities trade, deserves a wide audience. It delivers a basic message vital to the archaeological profession and the preservation of archaeological sites—that sites should be protected from unscientific excavation and that the marketing of antiquities encourages illicit digging that destroys valuable evidence about ancient peoples."* [From the review by Peter S. Allen, ARCH 43(4):69, 1990.]

Lorang's Way (Turkana Conversations Trilogy Series) (1980) 70 min. David and Judith MacDougall (FM). Dist: UCEMC FR$65, FS$995, VS$410. *A portrait of Lorang, the head of the homestead, and one of the important senior men of the Turkana (including Lorang's son) see their way of life continuing unchanged into the future. But Lorang thinks otherwise, for he has seen something of the outside world.*

This is a study of a man who has come to see his society as vulnerable and whose traditional role in it is shaped by that realization. In Turkana, with English subtitles. Relevant anthropological literature: P. H. Gulliver, The Family Herds. Routledge and Kegan Paul, 1955. See related film, The Wedding Camels. [Reviewed by Ben G. Blount, AA 86:803–805, 1984. Robert Mishler, SBF 17:99, 1981.]

Lord Elgin and Some Stones of No Value (1987) 58 min. Christopher Miles (FM). Dist: FI VR$90, VS$198. *"The main body of this work consists of a dramatized history of Lord Elgin's preparation and removal of the famous Parthenon sculptures (and other Greek antiquities) and their eventual shipment to England.... What this film adds to the story is not only texture in the form of reenactments but historical and contextual details that are not known to most."* [From the review by Peter S. Allen, ARCH 42(2):72–73, 1989.]

Lord of the Dance, Destroyer of Illusion 108 min. Richard Kohn (DI), Franz-Christoph Giercke (PR), Jorg Jeshel (CA), Barbara Becker (SR). Dist: FRF. *In the secret Tibetan Tantric rituals during a three-week period, monks become gods and battle the malevolent supernatural forces of the universe. "Just as coronation transforms ordinary men into kings, Tantric empowerment transforms men into Gods," according to Kohn's narration. "The god they wish to become is Garwang Tojaychenpo, Lord of the Dance." Before the main rituals begin, the monks prepare quantities of sacramental substances and magic devices, including pills that will provide spiritual nourishment for the thousand villagers who will come to seek empowerment at the end of the festival.* [Reviewed by Margaret Goldberg, AA 90:782–784, 1988.]

Lord of the Sky 13 min. Ludmila, Zeman Spaleny, and Eugen Spaleny (DI). Dist: NFB FR$40, VR$40, FS$350, VS$200. *Based on the legends of the people of Pacific Northwest, this animated film is an artistic unity of form and content. The directors of the film use a dazzling combination of 3-D models, puppets, special effects, and cutout paper animation to render beautiful drawings that reflect the natural environment and cultural heritage of the Pacific Northwest. In this environmental parable, we find a people living in harmony in nature, until carelessness leads to the ravens' revenge. We follow a boy's courageous journey to the spirit world to find the only one who can save his village from the resulting darkness—Lord of the Sky. Reflecting native storytelling techniques, this film speaks strongly of the need for ecological balance in the world.*

Lords of the Labyrinth (1978) 50 min. Michael Andrews (DI), BBC (PR). Dist: FI FR$75, FS$750, VS$375. *"A summary of prehispanic cultural development on the north coast of Peru."* [From the review by Alexandra M. Ulana Klymyshyn, AA 87:230–231, 1985. Reviewed by Izumi Shimada, ARCH 38(4):67–75, 1985.]

The Lost Army 58 min. Ned Johnston and Susan Todd (DI, ED). Dist: FL FR$125, VR$85, FS$895, VS$445. *An ambitious archaeological expedition to Egypt in search of the legendary "Lost Army of Cambyses" turns into a bizarre, comic odyssey. As reported by Herodotus, the Persian army,* about 50,000 strong, vanished in a sandstorm in 525 B.C. Through the years, many have tried to find the remains and have failed. The expedition was the brainchild of Gary Chavetz, who convinced a number of backers, including National Geographic, that the expedition promised findings of the magnitude of King Tut's tomb. Though equipped with state-of-the-art instruments, things started to go wrong from day one. With wry humor, the filmmakers follow an increasingly disillusioned band through the beautiful desert landscape. Month after month of searching uncovered few clues, only growing confusion. As the seasonal dust storms picked up, Chavetz was forced to abandon his quest. [Reviewed by Peter S. Allen, *ARCH* 43(5):76–77, 1990.]

Lost in Time (1985) Maryanne Culpepper and Bruce Kuerten (PR). Dist: Auburn Television, Auburn University, Auburn, AL 36849; (205) 826-4110, VS$40. *"This documentary intertwines two major themes: the origins and precontact development of aboriginal cultures in the Southeastern United States and the techniques utilized by archaeologists in reconstructing prehistoric life ways."* [From the review by John A. Walthall and John M. Weir, *ARCH* 39(3):71, 1986.]

The Lost Tribes (1984) 52 min. Andre Singer (FM). Dist: UNHCR FS$600, free rental. *"Examines the social condition of Afghan refugees in Pakistan's North-West Frontier Province.... We see for example the implications of patrilineal and patriarchal tribal structures for the allocation of scarce resources under conditions of asylum.... The social effects of religion are clearly acknowledged."* [From the review by Marjorie A. Muecke, *AA* 88:780–781, 1986.]

Lost World of the Maya (1972) 36 min. BBC-TV (PR). Dist: T/L FR$45, FS$475, VS$150; SU FR$25. *Dr. Eric Thompson was probably the world's greatest authority on Mayan civilization. He spent 50 years studying the life of this mysterious people, whose great stone cities, built for ceremony, not trade, rise from the thick forest jungles of Central America. Dr. Thompson talks unselfconsciously about "we Mayans," reads their strange hieroglyphics as if they were Pitman shorthand, and describes the Mayan ritual of human sacrifice to the sun. The contemporary villains of this excursion are the looters and the distinguished museum curators who purchase chunks of Mayan carvings on the black market, no questions asked. Discussion guide available.* [Reviewed by Jeremy A. Sabloff, *AA* 78:377, 1976.]

Louisiana Story (1948) 77 min. Robert Flaherty (FM), Richard Leacock (CA). Dist: FI; UCEMC FR$32. *Robert Flaherty's classic documentary of a young Cajun boy's life in the Louisiana bayou country and the changes brought about by the oil exploration there.* [Reviewed by Gerald L. Gold, *AA* 80:760–762, 1978.]

Love Songs of The Miao in China 45 min. NHK (PR). Dist: FL VR$65, VS$350. *This film captures the lifestyle of Miao who live deep in the mountains of Southern China. The Miao preserve the traditions of the past in their daily life, unaffected by the changes of modern China. As a result, their songs and time-honored customs, which mark each phase of life, continue with the same importance. The Miao's courtship rituals are particularly interesting because of the importance placed on love songs. We watch the young men and women woo one another with their soulful songs. Each year there is a regional festival called Pa-po-jeh where the young go in search of marriage partners from another village. The film focuses on a 17-year-old girl who attends the festival, and her family's everyday life within their village.*

Loving Krishna (Pleasing God Series) 40 min. A. Moore and A. Ostor (FM). Dist: CPI FR$60, FS$595, VS$299. *This film looks at the sacred cult of Krishna in one of its local manifestations and displays the continuing link between worship, arts and crafts, bazaar exchanges, and everyday life. Seen are two major festivals: the celebration of Krishna's birth and the great Chariot Festival. Examined are the central concepts of Hindu worship: the ritual offerings to the gods, the role of images in worship, the divine play of the gods, and the meaning of devotion.*

Lucia 160 min. Humberto Solas (DI), Instituto Cubano del Arte e Industria Cinematográficos (PR). Dist: UNI. *Women in Cuba.* [Reviewed by June Nash, *AA* 79:200, 1977.]

Luckily I Need Little Sleep 7.5 min. Kathleen Shannon (FM). Dist: NFBC. *A Greek woman immigrant to Alberta.* [Reviewed by Judith Friedlander, *AA* 79:210, 1977.]

Lucy and the First Family [Reviewed by George Armelagos, *ARCH* 34(5):68, 1981.]

Lucy in Disguise (1980) 58 min. Cleveland Museum of Natural History and David Smeltzer (FM). Dist: Smeltzer Films, 54 Second Street, Athens, OH 45701, FR$75, VR$75, FS$750, VS$350. *This film is about the earliest Hominids known, the first fossil of which was found in Afar in Ethiopia by Dr. Johanson and was named Lucy. The film starts with the scenery in Central Ethiopia, it also features Dr. Johanson and other members of the excavation team who present the findings from Hadar, the importance of these finds and the controversy surrounding these finds.* [Reviewed by C. Loring Brace, *AA* 84:759–761, 1982. Marc R. Feldesman, *AJPA* 61:389–390, 1983. Glenn C. Conroy, *ARCH* 35(6):63, 1982.]

Luisa Torres (1981) 43 min. Jack Parsons (PR), Michael Earney (DI). Dist: CPI FR$50, FS$500, VS$350. *"Luisa Torres is a Hispanic woman almost 80 years old, living with her husband in their home of 62 years in the mountainous valley and meadow country near the village of Guadalupita on the southeastern flanks of the Sangre de Cristo Mountains in northern New Mexico.... The film portrays this aged lady's daily existence.... Rich in ethnographic detail."* [From the review by Marianne L. Stoller, *AA* 87:486–487, 1985.

Lurugu (1974) 59 min. Curtis Levy (Dl), Geoffrey Burton (CA), John von Sturmer (CON), Australian Institute of Aboriginal Studies (PR). Dist: AIAS. *Lurugu means "newly initiated man" on Mornington Island in the Gulf of Carpentaria. But when this film was made, few young men in recent years had passed through the traditional ceremony that signals manhood. The film shows the effort to revive the* *ceremony and the interplay, in both ritual and everyday contexts, of people on the island: the Landil, the Bentinck Islanders, and the Europeans of the mission staff.*

Lutes and Delights (Morocco, Body and Soul Series) (1987) 26 min. Izza Genini (FM). Dist: FRIF FR$55, FS$470, VS$260. *Combining Arab and Moroccan poetry with accents from flamenco, Abdesadek Chekara and his orchestra, famous throughout Morocco, are among the most faithful interpreters of Arab-Andalusian music. The eleven "noubas," or suites, which they perform, came to North Africa when the Muslims and Jews were expelled from Spain, but the music harkens back to a time of tolerance and coexistence, when Christians, Muslims, and Jews shared the land.*

Luther Metke at 94 (1979) 27 min. Jorge Preloran, Steve Raymen (FM). Dist: Northwest Cultural Films, 85895 Lorane Highway, Eugene, OR 97405, FR$30, FS$340. *Shot over a three-year period in the mountains and surrounding communities of central Oregon, the project was undertaken because of the unique opportunity to document the last of a generation that represented a special lifestyle in the cultural history of the Pacific Northwest. The film depicts the lifestyle of 94-year-old Luther Metke, who for the past 72 years had lived in the Cascade Mountains of central Oregon where he came to homestead in 1907. Among other things, Metke was a builder of log cabins in the traditional manner (by his own account he built some 40 to 50 of them) and a major focus of the film is in showing the building of a unique hexagonal log cabin, which he himself had designed. Also shown are a number of other social processes in which Metke engaged—attending a wedding, a VFW function, a family get-together. Tying it all together is Metke's personal philosophy of life as depicted in his conversation and snatches of poetry, which he composed. It is "an example of the folk wisdom, folk artistry, and genuine human warmth of a man living a full life in his nineties." The film is particularly strong in establishing the practice of a traditional folk arts form within a meaningful and appropriate context.* Warnings: At times sound is a bit erratic; careful listening is required. This film comes up short on "how to" aspects of log cabin building. There is some lack of continuity between scenes. Focusing questions: Does Luther Metke fit the stereotype of a "hermit"? In what ways does Luther Metke incorporate elements of modern technology into the practice of a traditional art form? Is the practice of a traditional art form (log cabin building) consistent with other aspects of Luther Metke's personal philosophy and lifestyle depicted in the film? How can one live a full life in retirement? What kind of attitude is required? How does this contrast with Americans' general notion about retirement? What kind of folk wisdom is contained in Metke's poetry? How does it bear upon the life he has lived for 72 years? What features of pioneer lifestyle are represented in log cabin building? Bibliography: Warren E. Robert, "Folk Architecture." In: *Folklore and Folklife*, Richard M. Dorson, ed. Chicago: University of Chicago Press, 1972, pp. 281–293. [Richard E. Meyer and John A. Young]

Ma'Bugi: Trance of the Toraja (1971) 22 min. Eric Crystal (CA, AN), Catherine Nomura Crystal (SR), Lee M. Rhoades, Jr. (ED). Dist: UCEMC FR$30, FS$300; PSU FR$13. *Depicts an unusual trance ritual that functions to restore the balance of well-being to an afflicted village community and clearly portrays the song, dance, and pulsating tension that precede dramatic instances of spirit possession in the Toraja highlands of Sulawesi (Celebes) Island, Indonesia. Narrated by the officiant priest of the indigenous Toraja religion, the film captures the fundamental concern of the villagers for a bountiful harvest and for bodily health—a concern that impels their extraordinary performances in deep states of trance. Designed to augment the growing body of documentation of ritually sanctioned altered states of consciousness, the film communicates both the psychological abandon of the trance state and the often-neglected motivation underlying activities such as the ascent of a ladder of knives and the supernatural curing of the chronically ill.* [Reviewed by James L. Fox, *AA* 78:723–724, 1976.] Cinematic features: Narration by priest is translated; native music and singing, some "wild sound" in trance scenes; broad view of possession scenes with good contextualization; some stills used with explanation. Uses in teaching: courses and topics—religion, South Asia, altered states of consciousness. Warnings: Shots of possessed persons stabbing themselves, some blood, but well contextualized. Focusing questions: Why is the ceremony held, and what functions does it have for the Toraja? Who participates in the ceremony, and what is different about people who become possessed? What restrictions are placed on those who participate in the Ma'Bugi ceremony? How do "possessed" people act? Why don't possessed people feel pain from their wounds? [Anne Smith Denman]

Macumba, Trance and Spirit Healing 43 min. Madeline Richeport (PR). Dist: FL R$65, FS$650, VS$395. *In today's stressful world, millions of people turn to spiritism for help. This film shows the roots and beliefs of Afrospirit religions as practiced by the privileged rich, as well as the illiterate poor. Although shot principally in Rio de Janeiro, these sects are flourishing in the United States as well. Spiritism is based on the belief that man can communicate with the supernatural world through mediums who act as intermediaries. Grouped commonly under the word "voodoo" or "maumba," these forbidden sects were the targets of police raids. Now some of the techniques of trance healing are used by the medical profession to help individuals to achieve personal and social equilibrium.* [Reviewed by Stephen D. Glazier, *AA* 90:489–490, 1988.]

Madame L'eau (1992) 125 min. Jean Rouch (FM). Dist: NFI. *This is the latest film from Jean Rouch and his West African friends, Lam, Damoure, and Tallou.*

Madarrpa Funeral at Gurka'wuy (1979) 88 min. Ian Dunlop (FM), Howard Morphy (AN), Frances Morphy, Ngalawurr Mununggurr (Ling), Film Australia (PR). Dist: AFC; FAA. *The film explores the way that Yolngu cope with death through ties of clan, religion, and land. When a child died unexpectedly at Gurka'wuy, a clan homeland settlement some 120 kilometers south of Yirrkala, the filmmaker was asked to record the funeral rites. This ethnographic classic explains in detail the complex elements of the ritual and its symbols.*

Made by Hand (1989) 10 min. Juan A. Ramirez (FM). Dist: Media Network, 20 Waterside Plaza, New York, NY 10010; (212) 545-7783. *Brief introduction to flint knapping.* [Reviewed by William Longacre, AA 93:516–517, 1991.]

Made in Mississippi: Black Folk Art and Crafts (1975) 20 min. William Ferris (DI), Dale Lindquist (CA). Dist: CSF FR$30, FS$300. *Seven unique folk artists, ranging from a quiltmaker to a clay sculptor, discuss their work and recall how they learned their crafts. The unifying theme is the use of local materials and discards to create something purely personal, yet rooted in tradition. The first film to examine a range of Afro-American material culture.*

Las Madres: The Mothers of Plaza de Mayo (1986) 64 min. Susana Munoz and Lourdes Portillo (FM). Dist: DCL FR$100, FS$945, VS$350. *1977 was the darkest hour of military dictatorship in Argentina. Fourteen ordinary women began to meet in public every Thursday, risking their lives by marching before the presidential palace in Buenos Aires, in the Plaza de Mayo. They demanded to know where their missing children were. These women sparked an international campaign for the release of all politically "disappeared" persons. Over 30,000 people have disappeared in Argentina since the 1970s. In this documentary, the mothers tell of their children's disappearances and the painful search to discover their fates. What emerges is the landscape of recent Argentine history, the stories of the personal tragedies of the mothers and their families, along with an understanding of women's empowerment in a society where women are expected to be silent.*

Magic in the Hills 52 min. Ivan Polunin, BBC-TV (PR). Dist: TL. *The Djakut people of Malaya.* [Reviewed by Antoine Seronde and Kathleen Sheehan AA 77:179, 1975.]

Magic in the Sky 57 min. Peter Raymont (DI). Dist: NFB R$80, FS$775, VS$350. *This documentary investigates the impact of television on the Inuit people of the Canadian Arctic. But it is more than that. It is the story of the spirit and determination of the Inuit Tapirisat of Canada, the Eskimo Brotherhood, to establish the first Inuit-language television network. Perhaps by investigating the impact of television on these Arctic villages, we can better understand how television has changed all of us. The struggle of Inuit people to create their own indigenous television network mirrors the crisis of any culture trying to preserve its unique identity.*

The Magic Tree (1971) 11 minutes. Gerald McDermott (Anim). Dist: PSU FR$10.50. *A Congo tale about an unloved boy, a lonely river, and a magic tree whose leaves become people. The boy finds a secret paradise, but loses it when he reveals its mystery.*

Magic Windows (1981) 58 min. Manuel Araugo, Hugh Johnston and Suzanne Johnston (PR). Dist: Johnston, 16 Valley Road, Princeton, NJ 08540; (609) 924-7505, FR$90, FS$700, VS$475. *"A portrayal of the culture and significant features of everyday life of an indigenous Nahuatl-speaking village in the state of Guerrero, Mexico.... Geographic and cultural features are represented ... with an emphasis on the impact of geography on the adaptive styles and survival strategies of the people.... Scenes of incense burning, people talking under a withering heat, and the cool interior of a place of worship communicate an intensity of life and a release found through ritual and ceremony."* [From the review by Senon Valadez, AA 86:796, 1984.]

Magical Curing 27 min. William E. Mitchell (AN, FM). Dist: WLP VS$31.95. *Filmed during fieldwork with the Wape people of the West Sepic province of Papua New Guinea. The film offers unusual footage of the curing practices of the Wape people. It captures village scenes of demon curing festivals and exorcisms, as well as the introduced practices of western medical patrols. A viewers film guide is included. The film is a accompaniment to The Bamboo Fire, 2nd ed., a book by Dr. Mitchell.* [Reviewed by Marilyn Jean Schlitz, AA 92:848–849, 1990. Reviewed in VISA 4:57–67, 1991.]

Magical Death (see Yanomamo Series) VR$35, VS$275.

Les magiciens de Wanzerbe (The Magicians of Wanzerbe) (1948–49) 30 min. Jean Rouch (DI), Centre National de la Recherche Scientifique and Secretariat d'Etat a la Co-operation (PR). Dist: CFE; DER.

The Magnificent African Cake (Africa Series) (1986) 57 min. RM Arts (PR), Basil Davidson (H). Dist: FIV. *A thirty-year scramble for Africa, begun in the 1880s, dramatically changed the continent. Nearly all of Africa became subject to colonial rule until World War II.*

Maharishi Mahesh 28 min. Dist: Yavar Abbas (PR). Dist: CMC. *A fashionable ashram in Rishikesh on the Ganges.* [Reviewed by Janet Benson, AA 76:707, 1974.]

Maids and Madams (1985) 52 min. Mira Hamermesh (FM). Dist: FL FR$150, VR$75, FS$1200, VS$195. *This film is about the plight of African female domestic servants in contemporary South Africa.* [Reviewed by George E. Marcus, AA 92:556, 1990.]

The Mailbox (1977) 24 min. David K. Jacobs, (FM, WR). Dist: BYU. *This is an adaptation of a short story written by Mrs. Florence Putt, published in Era. It was filmed in late 1966 and early 1977, and was produced to show common treatment in this country of elderly people. The leading lady, Lethe Tatge, has extensive performing experience dating back to the early Chautauqua tours. She lives in a small farming community 30 miles from Provo, and the film was shot in her own home. Nothing was moved or rearranged; a few props were added to the dining-room table. The photographs are of her husband, who died in the late 1950s. She uses his name in the film. Her home was the first brick home in Heber Valley, of hand-molded adobe brick, built around 1868. The outdoor scenes were shot on Jacobs's property in Provo. Mrs. Tatge was 82 when she made the film. "She is a remarkable woman and in contrast to the lady in the film her life is filled to overflowing with activities and people. Her home is open to visitors, family, and the community. She spearheaded a massive historical data-gathering of her valley and community which resulted in a several-volume history book of the area. She taught a Sunday school class for over 40 years in the Mormon Church and also Relief Society classes and is still a visiting teacher who goes to other people's homes every month to check on their well-be-*

ing. Though unable to have children of her own, she partially adopted many children along the way and all love her dearly" (Jacobs, personal correspondence, 1979). Synopsis: 82-year-old widow watches every day for letters from any of her three children. Her neighbors and mailman love and respect her, but her day begins and ends with her trip to the usually empty mailbox. Her children decide (without consulting her) to have her moved to a rest home so she would be "better off," and they finally write to her, to tell her of their decision. She is so excited that, without getting it open, she has a fatal heart attack. Twenty seconds after the film ends, she reappears on the set as herself with a stern injunction to "write to your mother or grandmother today!" Warnings: Anyone who has recently lost an aged parent or grandparent may find the film too moving and may be overcome with guilt at real or perceived neglect. Focusing questions: What responsibilities do we have to aging parents? How can later years be made more productive and satisfying? Which is closer to the real lifestyle of the aged, Lethe the actress or Lethe the character in the film? What implications does this film have for focusing attention on developmental needs for all stages of life? What skills for living need to be taught for productive later years? [Maxine Edwards]

Les maîtres fous (Mad Masters) (1955) 35 min. Jean Rouch (DI), Films de la Pleiade (PR), Damoure Zika (SO), Suzanne Baron (ED). Dist: CFE; DER FR$45, FS$540; UCEMC. *The ceremony of a religious sect, the Hauka, which was widespread in West Africa from the 1920s to the 1950s. Hauka participants were usually rural migrants to the cities such as Accra in Ghana, and in 1954 there were at least 30,000 Hauka in Accra. In the course of the ritual, the Hauka men were possessed by various spirits associated with western or colonial powers (the governor-general, the engineer, the doctor's wife, and others). Through this intense ceremony, for a short time, the possessed Africans play the part of their colonial oppressors. Since the end of the colonial era, the Hauka sect has gradually died out. Relevant anthropological literature:* Cf. Rouch interview, *AA* 80:1006–1010, 1978. [Reviewed by Jean Claude Miller, *AA* 73:1471, 1971.]

MAKE PRAYERS TO THE RAVEN (1987) 30 min. each. Mark O. Badger and Richard K. Nelson (FM). Dist: KUAC-TV, University of Alaska-Fairbanks, 312 Tanana Drive, Fairbanks, AK 99775; (907) 474-7491, VS$125. *"A series of 5 videotapes centered on the lives of nearly 2,000 people living along the banks of the Yukon River in Alaska and its major tributary, the Koyukuk, manage to be both moving and instructive. Concrete facts, such as the number of dog-salmon necessary to satisfy a 24-dog team for the winter, are presented in a natural flow of activities, the details of which capture the rhythm of camp life throughout the seasonal round."* [From the review by Gregory Button and D.W. Murray, *AA* 91:523–525, 1989.]

Making a Bark Canoe (1969) 20 min. Roger Sandall (DI, CA), Nicolas Peterson (SR), Australian Institute of Aboriginal Studies (PR). Dist: Educational Media Australia, 357 Clarendon St., North Melbourne, Victoria 3000, Australia. *A huge sheet of bark cut from a single tree is the basis of a canoe made by Aborigines in one part of Arnhem Land. Each year Magpie geese in their thousands nest in the extensive swamps of the region. To get their eggs for food, the Aborigines traditionally made this light and shallow-draughtered craft, forming the bark with heat and pressure. In the film, two Aboriginal men show how it is done in the swamps west of Blue Mud Bay.*

MAKING OF MANKIND SERIES (1982) 55 min. each. Richard Leakey (AN), BBC(PR), Peter Spry-Leverton (DI). Dist: AV VS$395. *Richard Leakey traces the origin of the species in this seven-part series. From the fossil beds in East Africa, where Leakey himself made breakthrough discoveries, to tool makers who walked upright. The aggression of the killer apes and the sensitivity of the caveman placing flowers beside a grave come together to form the legacy of* Homo sapiens. [Reviewed by David S. Weaver, *AJPA* 66:349–351, 1985. Norris Durham, *ARCH* 36(3):72–80, 1985. Russell H. Tuttle, *AA* 86:796–797, 1984.] The series titles include:

- **In the Beginning**
- **One Small Step. . .**
- **A Human Way of Life**
- **Beyond Africa**
- **A New Era**
- **Settling Down**
- **The Survival of the Species**

Making Primitive Stone Tools (1950) 10 min. Douglas Leechman (FM). Dist: NYU. [Reviewed by Payson D. Sheets, *AA* 77: 916, 1975. Susanna R. Katz and Paul R. Katz, *ARCH* 34(1):60, 1981.]

The Makiritare (see Indians of the Orinoco Series)

Makwayela (1977) 20 min. Jean Rouch (DI), Centre National de la Recherche Scientifique, Comite du Film Ethnographique (PR). Dist: CFE; DER. *This is a teaching film created as an example of a "shot sequence" (an unbroken take edited in camera) with the students from the Institute Cinema in Mozambique.*

Malagan Labadama: A Tribute to Buk-Buk (Films from Papua New Guinea) (1982) 58 min. Chris Owen (DI), The Institute of Papua New Guinea Studies (PR). Dist: DER FR$120, VR$60, VS$400. *For the people of the Mandak region of New Ireland, Papua New Guinea, the most dramatic and complex ceremonial events in their community are those surrounding death. A malagan is a carved, painted representation, given ceremonially in honor of a deceased person as a final mortuary offering; the term may also refer to the spirit represented by the carving, or to the festivities accompanying its presentation. This is the story of the three Kaparau brothers from Pantagin village who organize a malagan labadama for their deceased kinsman Buk-Buk, the paramount lulai (chief) of the Mandak region. Elaborate preparations that last for months, tatanua dancers performances and the slaughtering of pigs are all part of the malagan that is portrayed in this superbly photographed film.* [Reviewed by Roy Wagner, *AA* 85:223–224, 1983.]

Malaysia (Asian Insight Series) (1988) 50 min. Film Australia (PR). Dist: FIV VS$158. *Malaysia is a Muslim state in a Chinese-dominated market. The problems of a multiracial society are examined.*

Malbangka Country (1977) 30 min. Curtis Levy (DI), Australian Institute of Aboriginal Studies (PR). Dist: UCEMC R$38, FS$410, VS$290. *Portrait of an Aboriginal family that has moved back to its homeland (called an outstation) following unsuccessful government attempts at resettlement in small towns with missionary schools. The head of the family tells his reasons for wishing to return to his native territory; he comments on his desire to build a home, a church, and a school.* H. C. Coombs, B. G. Dexter and L. R. Hiatt, "The Outstation Movement in Aboriginal Australia." *AIAS Newsletter*, no. 14, September, 1981.

Malinowski, Bronislaw (1844-1942) (see *Off the Verandah* in the Strangers Abroad Series)

Malnutrition in a Third World Community (1980) 28 min. George M. Guthrie, Helen A. Guthrie (AN). Dist: PSU FR$18.50, FS$385. *Designed to give students and professionals who have not had extensive Third World experience a clearer idea of the ecology of malnutrition. Shot in a rural Philippines community, the film covers infant feeding practices, breastfeeding, and supplements, showing the difficulties a family faces due to poverty, limited home production of food, and inadequate supplies of pure water.* Relevant anthropological literature: G. M. Guthrie, Z. Masangkay, and H. A. Guthrie, "Behavior, Malnutrition and Mental Development." *Journal of Cross-Cultural Psychology* 7(2):169"180, 1976.

Mammy Water (1953-54) 20 min. Jean Rouch (DI), Centre National de la Recherche Scientifique and Films de la Pleiade (PR). Dist: CFE; DER. *Daily life of the Fanti fishermen of Ghana; a ritual for the opening of the fishing season at Shama, Ghana.*

Mammy Water: In Search of the Water Spirits in Nigeria (1991) 59 min. Dr. Sabine Jell-Bahlsen (FM). Dist: UCEMC FR$60, FS$995, VS$350. *Mammy Water is a pidgin English name for a local water goddess worshipped by the Ibibio-, Ijaw-, and Igbo-speaking peoples of southeastern Nigeria. The water goddess traditionally gives wealth and children, compensates for hardships, and is sought in times of illness and need, especially by women. Her various cults are led, predominantly, by priestesses. This insightful film shows numerous rituals and ceremonies associated with Mammy Water, while devotees provide commentary. An important depiction of the strength of traditional religion in contemporary Nigeria.* [Reviewed by Simon Ottenberg, *AA* 93(1):254-255, 1991.]

A Mamprusi Village (1944) 20 min. John Page (DI, CA), Jim Mellor (ED), British Ministry of Information (PR). Dist: IUAVC. *The Voltaic kingdom of Mamprusi in the Northern Territories of the Gold Coast.* [Reviewed by Gregory A. Finnegan, *AA* 79:748-749. 1977.]

MAN, A COURSE OF STUDY SERIES (see Netsilik Eskimo Series)

MAN ALIVE SERIES Dist: CBC. *A unique award-winning series, Man Alive goes behind the headlines to look at controversial moral issues and the pain and triumph behind current events. The series has won wide praise for its sensitive treatment of a diverse range of complex issues. The titles comprising the series are:*

• **A Circle of Healing**

• **The Warrior from Within**

The Man behind the Mask (1982) 50 min. Melissa Llewelyn-Davies (FM) for the BBC. Dist: FI FR$90, VS$198. *"Heinrich Schliemann (1822-1890) is universally regarded as a major figure in the birth of the scholarly discipline of archaeology in general, and as the father of Aegean prehistory in particular. . . . [This program] explores several episodes of Schliemann's life for which his own testimony has been demonstrated to be either suspect or altogether false."* [From the review by S. Shelby Brown and Jeremy B. Rutter, *ARCH* 39(6):71-74, 1986.]

A Man Called "Bee" (see Yanomamo Series) VR$40, VS$350. [Reviewed in *VISA* 4:91, 1991.]

A Man Called Horse 114 min. Elliot Silverstein (DI), Clyde Dollar (AN). Dist: Columbia Pictures, 711 5th Avenue, New York, NY 10021. *Fictional film about Plains Indians.* [Reviewed by John R. Cole, *AA* 78:959, 1976.]

The Man Hunters 52 min. MGM Documentary (PR), Paul Hockings (RE). Dist: PSU FR$19, FS$600. *A fascinating search from France to China, from Mt. Carmel in Palestine through South Africa, for the earliest evidence of man's existence. Leading anthropologists discuss skeleton parts and artifacts discovered across the world and attempt to reconstruct man as he was in the beginning.* [Reviewed by David A. Horr, *AA* 74:187-188, 1972.] Suggested supplements: Bernard G. Campbell, *Humankind Emerging*. Little, Brown, 1976. Paul Hockings, "Filming the Man Hunters." *Human Organization* 35:178, 1976. Clark F. Howell, *Early Man*. General Learning Press, 1973.

Man in Ethiopia 27 min. Robert Citron (PR). Dist: The Independent Film Producers Company, P.O. Box 501, Pasadena, CA, 91102. [Reviewed by Samarom Legesse, *AA* 74:189, 1972.]

Man of Aran (1934) 77 min. Robert Flaherty (FM). Dist: UCEMC; Pitt. *Harsh life of Irish villagers on the Aran Islands, off the west coast of County Clare, Ireland.* Suggested supplements: Conrad M. Arensberg, *The Irish Countryman: An Anthropological Study*. Macmillan, 1937. Conrad M. Arensberg and Solon T. Kimball, *Family and Community in Ireland*. Harvard, 1940 (reprinted by Peter Smith, Gloucester, 1961). Emily Lawless, *Grania*. 1892. John M. Synge, *The Aran Islands*. 1907 (paperback edition, Vintage Press, V-53, 1962). [Reviewed by Solon T. Kimball, *AA* 79:749-751, 1977.]

Man of Aran (Cinematic Eye Series) (1980) 30 min. Benjamin Dunlap (Discussant). Dist: Janus Films, 745 Fifth Avenue, New York, NY 10022. 3/4" videotape only: FR$45, Lease $250. *One of a series of 13 videotape programs produced for educational television. Benjamin Dunlap dis-*

cusses the making and the structure of Flaherty's Man of Aran.

Man of Lightning (1983) 28 min. Gary Moss (WR, DI). Dist: EMC-GSU VR$30, VS$200. *Dramatization of two Cherokee myths told by Ayunini 'Swimmer', to James Mooney between 1887 and 1890. The myths are The Gambler and The Spear Finger.* [Reviewed by Edward B. Sisson, AA 86:790–791, 1984.]

Man of the Serengeti (1972) 52 min. National Geographic Society (PR). Dist: NGS FS$595, VS$545. *A Masai warrior turned park ranger visits his family in northern Tanzania.* [Reviewed by Thomas O. Beidelman, AA 76:700, 1974.]

Man Oh Man—Growing Up Male in America (1987) 19 min. J. Clements (FM). Dist: NDF FR$45, FS$380, VS$230. *"Focuses on what it is like to be a man in contemporary American society, with an emphasis on how difficult it is to live up to the cultural ideals of manhood."* [From the review by Ralph Bolton, AA 92:836–837, 1990.]

MAN ON THE RIM SERIES 11 parts, 1 hour each. Dist: LMF VS$2895. *This captivating 11-part series portrays the history of the Pacific Rim countries and their intriguing life today. This series traces the greatest succession of migrations in the history of man. The historical and cultural background of this remarkable migration is the subject of this engrossing production. The producers have traveled around and across the entire Pacific basin from Tasmania to Tierra del Fuego, from Siberia to Easter Island, to uncover the footprints of a tremendous cavalcade of human evolution, technological as well as biological. Today, the global economic center of gravity is shifting to the Pacific and the people of the Rim are emerging as a major force in world affairs. This series offers a glimpse of the shape of the next momentous period in human history: the Pacific Century.*

Man on the Rim: The Peopling of the Pacific Anthony Bickley (PR), Robert Raymond and Peter DeVries (DI). [Reviewed by Peter S. Allen, ARCH 44(6):64–66, 1991.]

The Man, the Snake and the Fox 12 min. Dist: NFBC. *Dramatization of a traditional Ojibway legend, related by Basil Johnston, of the Royal Ontario Museum Ethnology Department. As the story unfolds, the characters, played by engaging puppets of cloth, wire and plastic, take on real-life personalities. A man, Debossigae ("Far-Reaching Light"), is out walking in the forest. He hears a strange noise he cannot identify. A serpent with the head of a wolf lies trapped in a hole. Debossigae, against his better judgment, frees the serpent only to be attacked by it. A fox hears the uproar and hurries to the man's rescue. The man in his appreciation, asks the fox how he can repay him for saving his life. "Don't make promises you might not be able to keep," says the fox.*

Man without Pigs (Films from Papua New Guinea) (1990) Chris Owen (DI), The Institute of Papua New Guinea Studies (PR). Dist: DER FR$120, VR$60, VS$400. *John Waiko is the first Papua New Guinean to reach the status of professor. After receiving his doctorate from the Australian National University, he traveled back to his home village of Tabara to celebrate the achievement with his own people of the Binandere clan. Although John has a history of long schooling in village culture and has been educated in Port Moresby, London, and Canberra, he had little knowledge of ritual and no customary wealth in the form of pigs and a long list of favors given and alliances established. When John and his family decided to put on a dance-drama to welcome his return and assert his accomplishment, they were met with challenges and skepticism.* [Reviewed by Margaret Willson, AA 94(1):256–257, 1992.]

Manatic (1988) 53 min. Frank Marlowe and Kevin Robinson (FM). Dist: Socio-Behavioral Research Group, University of California, 760 Westwood Plaza, Room 47-438, Los Angeles, CA 90034; (213) 825-5731, VS$100. *"A cinema verite documentary about Ted, an elderly mentally retarded man who suffered brain damage from a car accident at the age of six and was later institutionalized when his mother died of alcoholism. Ted works the late-night shift at a laudromat where he is a local celebrity and benefactor to homeless people and prostitutes. Entirely narrated by Ted, the film gives us unusual access to the experience of being retarded."* [From the review by Mary Howard, AA 92:1100–1101, 1990.]

Mandabi 90 min. Ousmane Sembene (FM). Dist: GP order #363, FR$100, FS$1450. *About a man who receives a money order; tells how this dubious windfall threatens to destroy the traditional fabric of his life. Sembene's film is unique not only because it marks the arrival of the first truly African filmmaker of international standing; it is also a deeply moving, witty, masterful portrayal of an ancient civilization in the throes of change, a warm, subtle comedy with a series of visual revelations about a world unknown to us. In Wolof with English subtitles.*

Mangoes under the Tree (1990) 55 min. David Parry (DI). Dist: MOMA. *An ethnographic film of a 70-year-old West Indian lime-maker that includes his island's transition to independent nationhood and western values. Rebecca Bailey in* The Valley News *wrote, "A documentary film isn't just about a subject. It's also about the filmmaker's relationship to the subject. In many of Parry's films, that relationship is about as close as you can get."*

Manifestations of Shiva (1985) 58 min. Asia Society (PR), Muriel Peters (EP), Malcolm Leigh (DI, CA, WR). Dist: MOMA; MAAS. *This film was shot largely in Southern India and, apart from a brief introductory statement, has no narration. It is the purpose of the film to demonstrate that the worship of Shiva is not only an act of religious faith but is also integral to all aspects of Hindu life. The film achieves this by showing how the god is worshipped through religious rituals, dance, art, and music. Through images alone, the film depicts the many ways that people in India worship Shiva—the Hindu god and lord of the universe whose role is four fold: lover, ascetic, creator, destroyer. The film shows that worship can take the form of a simple flower offering, ablutions, elaborate powder paintings that are made and destroyed in one day, and highly stylized dances whose practitioners begin at age six or seven to dedicate* *their lives to ancient dance dramas honoring Shiva.* [Reviewed by Linda Stone *AA* 84:988–989, 1982.]

Maninka Villages in Transition   15 min. Dan Shafer, Tom O'Toole (FM). Dist: MINN FS$195. *The film was made during a week of village living in the nations of Senegal and Mali, located in the grasslands of West Africa. It takes the viewer into the life of a smaller villager called Dionkoro in the orchard brush of eastern Senegal where the sequences show farmers plowing and planting with aid of the young people of the village; then to a compound dwelling of a single extended family, with its separate houses for the various members of the polygamous family. The first sequence features a blacksmith of an exogamous clan. It shows him working at the forge and explains how his ritual and social status differs from other villagers. The second sequence portrays both the change from subsistence to market economy and the resilience and flexibility of an ethnic group called the Maninka.*

Man's Biological Heritage   (1987)   77 min.   Dist: Ed.Video, 1401 19th Street, Huntsville, TX 77340. VS$160. *"The history of evolutionary thought, primate systematics, and early hominid fossils, and a view of the emergence of Homo sapiens."* [From the review by B. J. Williams, *AA* 94:255–256, 1992.]

Manuel Jimenez, artesano en madera (Woodcarver) (see the Artesanos Mexicanos (Mexico's Folk Artists) Series)

The Manwatcher   (1980) 52 min. Desmond Morris (AN), BBC (PR). Dist: T-L VS$150. *Hand gestures (emblems). Filmed in Malta and Naples.*

The Many Worlds of Ishi   17 min. George F. Hafer Production (PR). Dist: MDAI VS$59.95, order #327-03. *Ishi was the last member of a tribe of Indians who lived in what is now northern California. While Ishi made his own peace with white civilization, the demise of his tribe was a result of the coming of that civilization. The story is told through beautiful photography of northern California.*

The Maori Today   16 min. New Zealand National Film Unit (PR). Dist: IUAVC FR$8.50. *Depicts the progress made in the integration of the Maori natives into New Zealand society over the past 100 years. Also shows progress made in training Maori to take a place in the industrial development of New Zealand. Indicates the migration of Maori to the cities and the subsequent problems in providing housing and training. Portrays many areas in which Maori have made a contribution and depicts efforts to preserve the Maori culture and traditions while having them become fully integrated into modern New Zealand society.*

Maps and Territories   (1958) 30 min. Dist: IUAVC FR$9.50. *Discusses the power and limitations of symbols, especially words. Describes the significance of the communications network in which humans live. Defines words as "maps" giving directions to "territories" of human experience. Stresses the point that words can be manipulated independently of the experiences they represent. Explains other pitfalls of communication related to word usage.*

Maragoli   (1977) 58 min. Sandra Nichols (FM), Joseph Ssennyonga (AN), Ivan Strasburg (CA), Mike McDuffie (SR). Dist: UCEMC FS$505, FR$32. *The very complex problem of overpopulation in western Kenya. At the Institute of Development Studies, Sussex, England, Professor T. Scarlett Epstein had a project on "Cross-Cultural Study of Population Growth and Rural Poverty." Joseph Ssennyonga, a Ugandan, was doing his Ph.D. research on the Maragoli of Kenya. During the later stages of his fieldwork, Nichols and her crew spent five weeks filming with Ssennyonga.* Warnings: Not a neat story line, but complex treatment of complex subject. Focusing questions: Does it make a difference that the anthropologist is an African? Bibliography: Sandra Nichols, "The Making of Maragoli." *Populi* 5(1):28–38, 1978. [Reviewed by Ruth H. Munroe and Robert L. Munroe, *AA* 81:733–734, 1979. Peter Loizos, *RAIN* 23:6, 1977.]

Marcelo Ramos, artesano pirotécnico (The Firework Maker's Art) (see the Artesanos Mexicanos (Mexico's Folk Artists) Series)

Marco   (1970) Vaile Scott, Louis Marrone (PR). Dist: FIM/RF. *Childbirth in America.* [Reviewed by Nancie L. Gonzalez, *AA* 74:1573, 1972.]

Margaret Mead   27 min. BBC-TV (PR). *The world-renowned anthropologist covers a wide range of topics in a warm, revealing interview.*

Margaret Mead and Samoa   (1988) 51 min. Frank Heimans (FM). Dist: WFV VR$60, VS$150. *Discusses the "Mead-Freeman controversy" and portrays anthropologists at odds with each other.* [Reviewed by Terrence E. Hays, *AA* 92:558–559, 1990. Angela Gilliam, *VISA* 9:105–115, 1993.]

Margaret Mead: Taking Note   (1981) 59 min. Ann Peck (FM, WR), Michael Ambrosino (PR). Dist: DER FR$50, FS$500. *A film biography.* [Reviewed by Emilie de Brigard, *AA* 85:494–495, 1983.]

Margaret Mead's New Guinea Journal   (1968) 90 min. Craig Gilbert (WR, FM). Dist: IU R(B/W $21, Color $27), S(B/W $540, Color $770); PSU(PCR) order #90012, Color FR$30.30; UCEMC order # 8034, FR$30. *Describes Margaret Mead's return to Peri Village, Manus, in 1967, with flashbacks using footage and photographs from her earlier expeditions and wartime newsreels.* Suggested supplements: R. F. Fortune, *Manus Religion: An Ethnological Study of Manus Natives of the Admiralty Islands.* American Philosophical Society, 1935 (paperback edition, University of Nebraska Bison Book BB 303). Margaret Mead, *Growing up in New Guinea: A Comparative Study of Primitive Education.* Morrow, 1930. Margaret Mead, *New Lives for Old: Cultural Transformation—Manus 1928–1953.* Morrow, 1930. Theodore Schwartz, "The Paliau Movement in the Admiralties 1946–1954." *American Museum of Natural History,* 49(2), 1962.

Maria and Julian's Black Pottery   (1938/1978) Silent. 11 min. Arthur A. Baggs, Jr. (FM). Dist: PSU FR$10.50, FS$150. *A classic 1938 documentary on the famed Maria Martinez and her husband Julian creating their black-on-*

black pottery. The film illustrates the step-by-step process from coiling the clay to the final firing and polishing of the pottery developed at San Ildefonso Pueblo in New Mexico.

Maria: Indian Pottery of San Ildefonso (1984) 25 min. National Park Service (PR). Dist: Educational Video Network, Inc., 1401 19th Street, Huntsville, TX 77340; (409) 295-5767. [Reviewed by Richard A. Krause, *AA* 94(3):768–770, 1992.]

Maria of the Pueblos (1971) 15 min. J. Donald McIntyre (AN). *San Ildefonso Pueblo in New Mexico. Focuses on Maria Martinez, showing step-by-step her technique of forming, polishing, decorating, and firing her unique pottery. Also gives background of culture, especially art, and economic conditions of Pueblo Indians.* Focusing questions: What is the significance of art to the Martinez family and to Indians, in general? Why are pots with flaws destroyed? Is there a spiritual process at work here? Bibliography: Alice Lee Marriott, *Maria: The Potter of San Ildefonso.* University of Oklahoma Press, 1948, 1965. Susan Peterson, *Maria Martinez: Five Generations of Potters.* Smithsonian Institute, 1978, for sale by Supt. of Documents, U.S. Printing Office, Washington, DC. [William L. Green]

THE MARING: DOCUMENTS OF A NEW GUINEA PEOPLE SERIES *An eight-part series on the Maring made for Italian television by Allison and Marek Jablonko, K069 Tuoro sul Trasimeno, Perugia, Italy. The visual version of Roy Rappaport,* Pigs for the Ancestors.

Maring in Motion: A Choreometric Analysis of Movement Among a New Guinea People (1968) 18 min. Alison Jablonko (FM, AN). Dist: PSU FR$13, FS$215; NYU FR$19. *A visual presentation of the movement style used by the Maring, swidden horticulturalists living on the slopes of the Bismark Mountains. The movement style is analyzed in terms of how people use their bodies, how they use the space around themselves, and how they use time. . . . By allowing observation of the details of bodily movement, as well as of the more macroscopic patterns of group formation and land use, the film shows how Maring dance utilizes and emphasizes movement patterns that occur in work and that play activities frequently echo dance patterns. Two major characteristics of Maring style become apparent: the Maring impose little arbitrary rhythmic structure upon the natural passage of time, and they impose little rigid spatial structure upon their physical environment. . . . A visual summary of "Dance and Daily Activities among the Maring People of New Guinea: A Cinematographic Analysis of Body Movement Style," a doctoral dissertation by Alison Jablonko in the Department of Anthropology, Columbia University.* Suggested supplement: Roy A. Rappaport, *Pigs for the Ancestors: Ritual in the Ecology of a New Guinea People.* Yale University Press, 1967. A. Jablonko, *Dance and Daily Activities among the Maring People of New Guinea.* Ph.D. dissertation, Columbia University, New York, 1978. T. K. Pitcairn and M. Schleidt, "Dance and Decision: An Analysis of a Courtship Dance of the Medlpa, New Guinea." *Behavior* 58:298–315, 1976. A. Lomax, "Choreometrics and Ethnographic Filmmaking." *Filmmakers Newsletter* 4:27–38, 1971.

Maritime Trade in the Ancient World (1975) 29 min. Lionel Casson (FM). Dist: RLI FS$39.95. *"This filmstrip provides a good synthetic summary of the important role played by maritime trade in antiquity."* [From the review by Faith Hentschel, *ARCH* 37(1):74–75, 1984.]

Market at La Paz, Patterns of Living and Land Use at Vilaque and Near Lake Titicaca—La Paz, Bolivia (1963) 22 min. The Land Tenure Center, University of Wisconsin (PR), Dwight Heath (AN). Dist: UW. *This film footage was shot in the Departamento of La Paz. Shows an open market in the city of La Paz and general farming patterns in the highlands. Discusses Bolivian schooling. Shows intensive cropping in valleys around La Paz and Lake Titicaca. Shows the potential of lowland agriculture. Discusses some results of agrarian reform in Bolivia.* [Reviewed by John Murra, *AA* 69:742, 1967.] Suggested supplements: William C. Carter, "Aymara Communities and Agrarian Reform in Bolivia." *University of Florida Monograph in Social Science,* 24, 1965 (detailed discussion of Aymara Indians, emphasizing continuity). Harold Osborne, *Indians of the Andes.* Harvard, 1952 (general discussion of highland Indians).

The Market's Edge: Glimpses of the Hausa World (1971) 28 min. H. K. Davis and C. E. Hopen (FM). Dist: PSU/PCR FR$22.50. *Economic and auxiliary social functions of markets, as revealed by the Hausa markets in Nigeria. Sequences of traditional craftsmen preparing goods, market dancing, and spirit-possession rituals.* [Reviewed by James L. Gibbs, Jr., *AA* 74:193, 1972.]

The Marmes Archeological Dig (1972) 18 min. Louis and Ruth Kirk for Clover Park School District (PR). Dist: FS$250; PSU FR$11.50. *This film presents the oldest fully documented discovery of early man in the Western Hemisphere—the remains "Marmes Man" found in the hot, dry scablands of southeast Washington. The techniques used by scientists to reconstruct man's past and the nature of his early environment are vividly shown.* [Reviewed in *ARCH* 33(1):61, 1981.]

Marriage and the Family in the Bishop Hill Colony (1978) 28.5 min. Carolyn Wilson (AN), Mary Ann Lamanna (CON). Dist: Audio Visual Dept., University of Nebraska at Omaha, 68182, FR$35, FS$145. *Shot in the studios of Channel 26, Omaha, Nebraska as no. 9 in the series Communes and Utopias. Family life, kinship organization, marriage forms, and their relation to community and religion and patterns of migration in the 19th-century Swedish commune of Bishop Hill, Illinois, are discussed. Research is based on documents, photographs, and interviews. Comment compares kinship in Bishop Hill with kinship in the Kibbutz.* Focusing questions: How did kinship influence the patterns of migration from Sweden to Illinois? What was the principal marriage form in Bishop Hill? The principal household form? How did kinship organization influence economic and power relationships in the Bishop Hill Colony? What comparisons can be made between Bishop Hill Colony and the contemporary kibbutz with respect to kinship and family? Bibliography: Michael A. Mikkelsen *The Bishop Hill Colony.* Philadelphia, Porcupine, 1892[1972].

Paul Elmen, *Wheat Flour Messiah*. Carbondale, Southern Illinois University, 1976. [Wayne Wheeler]

Married Life (1970) 52 min. Dist: IUAVC FR$17. *Compares five different marriages in five different societies to point out that marriage takes many forms and is, in many respects, dependent upon where one lives. Shows a wife with three husbands in the Himalayas, a couple in an affluent English community, a man with three wives in New Guinea, a man with two wives in Botswana, and a young couple in Lancashire, England. Interviews the married couples and discusses the roles assigned to men and women in each society.*

Marshall Islands—Living with the Bomb (The Human Face of the Pacific) (1987) 56 min. Film Australia (PR) Dist: FIV VS$158. *Marshall Islands comprise United States Trust Territory. As a result of American testing of nuclear bombs, the native people of this area were relocated. As a consequence of this relocation, their culture vanquished. This relocation and extinction of the community's culture is the subject of this film.*

Martin Chambi and the Heirs of the Incas (1987) 50 min. Paul Yule and Andy Harries (FM). Dist: CG FR$85, FS$795, VS$495. *"Martin Chambi was a rural mestizo who became a truly great documentary photographer of Cuzco in the 1920s and 1930s. He was also a central figure in the indigenista movement, a pan-Latin American, pro-Indian movement of the 1930s. This cinemantic exploration of Chambi's photographs is sensititve and complex, beautifully bringing out Chambi's clarity of vision and masterful play of light and shadow."* [From the review by Catherine J. Allen, *AA* 92:1105–1108, 1990. [Reviewed in *VISA* 3:492, 1990.]

Mary Pritchard (1971) 30 min. KVZK, Pago Pago (American Samoa) Public Television Library (PR), Charles Moore (Dl). Dist: IU FR$12.50. *Mary Pritchard is struggling to preserve a traditional Polynesian art—the creation of tapa, a cloth material made from the bark of mulberry trees. Filmed on location at the island of Tutuila, American Samoa, she is shown searching for materials and making and designing the tapa. Mary Pritchard also teaches others this art in order that it might be preserved as 20th-century progress threatens to destroy many of the older cultural traditions of Polynesia.*

Mary Wigman: When the Fire Dances between the Two Poles (1983) 43 min. Allegra Fuller Snyder and Annette MacDonald (PR). Dist: UCEMC FR$50, FS$565, VS$325. *"The footage, documenting Wigman's performing career [dance] between 1923 and 1942. . . . The oriental gestures and movements in this suite of dances remind the viewer of the tremendous influence of oriental style and chinoiserie on dance . . . during this period . . . Wigman's feelings about the use of masks are expressed in the narration."* [From the review by Anya Peterson Royce and Fran Snygg, *AA* 87:487–488, 1985.]

Masai in Tanzania (1969) 13 min. Films, Inc. (PR). Dist: PSU(PCR) order #21233, FR$11.50. *Famed warrior tribe, noted for height and lack of Negroid features. Life of shepherd of Masai's most prized possession, their cattle, blood of which is their chief nourishment. Masai in modern market place, a bit uncomfortable with different ways of barter.*

Masai Manhood (Disappearing World Series) (1975) 52 min. Chris Curling (PR), Melissa Llewellyn-Davies (AN). Dist: PSU order #51215. *Masai warriors live in the forest on the fringes of society. They are not allowed to marry and are excluded from decision making. Masai Manhood focuses on the lives of these young warriors and culminates, in Eunoto, a dramatic, four-day ceremony that marks their transition from warrior to elder.* [Reviewed by Thomas O. Beidelman, *AA* 78:958, 1976. British versions reviewed by Paul Spencer, *RAIN* 6:10,1975. Jean La Fontaine, *RAIN* 9:6, 1975.]

Masai Women (Disappearing World Series) (1974) 52 min. Melissa Llewellyn-Davis (AN), Chris Curling (PR). Dist: PSU VR$14, order #51152; ISHI FR$95, FS$875. *The Masai are animal herders in the East African Rift valley. This program looks at the women of the tribe—from childhood through marriage to old age—and their role in a completely male-dominated society.* [Reviewed by Thomas O. Beidelman, *AA* 78:958, 1976.]

Mask of Rangda. Sacred Trances in Bali and Java 2 8 min. Harvey Bellin (PR). Dist: Hartley Productions, Cat Rock Road, Cos Cob, CT 06807. [Reviewed by John W. Adams, *AA* 78:961, 1976.] See also *Bali: The Mask of Rangda*.

Masks (1962) 12 min. Dist: PSU FR$11.50. *Presents primitive and modern masks from North America (Iroquois, Northwest Coast Indians, and Eskimo), Mexico (Olmec), Africa, and Greece. Discusses role of masks in cultural and artistic life of the peoples who make them and explains how they are used in rituals and in dramatizing myths and legends.*

Masks and Stones: The Precious Treasures of Black Africa 60 min. Alfred Ehrhardt (Dl, CA), E. Leuzinger, J. Swernemann, E. Fischer, W. Lohse (AN). Dist: Sterling Educational Films. [Reviewed by Daniel P. Biebuyck, *AA* 76:702, 1974.]

Master Musicans of Jahjouka (1983) 60 min. Michael Mendizza (FM). Dist: Mendizza and Associates, 2502 Petaluma, Long Beach, CA 90815; (213) 598-3177, FR$100, FS$725, VS$525. *"Music in Morocco is popularly considered to be a craft rather than art, and Jahjouka sensitively portrays how this craft is exercised today by a group of professional musicans in a village of northwest Morocco."* [From the review by Dale F. Eickelman, *AA* 86:1069–1070, 1984.]

Master of the Shadows (The Human Face of Indonesia Series) (1987) 30 min. Film Australia (PR). Dist: FIV VS$99. *Bali is the most famous place in Indonesia. Can its traditional culture survive the pressures of tourism? This film explores the conflict between the new and the old.*

Mastering a Continent (Africa Series) (1986) 57 min. RM Arts (PR), Basil Davidson (H). Dist: FIV. *Looking closely at three different communities, Davidson examines the way*

African peoples carve out an existence in an often hostile environment.

Masters of Metal [Reviewed by Tamara Stech, *ARCH* 34(6):75, 1981.]

Maternal Behavior (Japanese Macaque) 4 min. Dist: PSU FR$4.30.

Matjemosh 27 min. Adrian A. Gerbrands (AN), Stichting Film Wetenschap, Universitaire Film, Utrecht (PR). Dist: UCEMC FR$53. *A woodcarver from the village of Amanamkai-Asmat Tribe on the southwest coast of New Guinea. The skilled carver, Matjemosh, carves ancestor figures. First-person narration of carver. A quarrel between two groups erupts. They carve bamboo horn—occasionally ancestral figures, usually purely for decoration. To make drums they go into jungle for wood (long house organization), sharpen digging stick in shell, dig out heart of wood block, open sago tree for grubs—eat raw or in "sage sausage"—essential for feasts, dry drum wood, use fire to enlarge hole, then thin from outside with axe and chisel, and design with magic marker on paper. Aesthetics—praying mantis-headhunter cult. The anthropologist is associated with an Asmater who died and went to heaven to get goods.* [Reviewed by Thomas M. Kiefer, *AA* 68:300, 1966.] Suggested supplements: A. A. Gerbrands, "Symbolism in the Art of Amanamkai, Asmat, New Guinea." In: *The Wonder of Man's Ingenuity.* Mededeligen van het Rijksmuseum voor Volkenkunde, Leiden, 37-41, Brill, 1962. A. A. Gerbrands, *Wow-Ipits: Eight Asmat Woodcarvers of New Guinea.* Asmat Papuans, S.W. New Guinea. The Hague: Mouton, 1966, A. A. Gerbrands, *Asmat. The New Guinea Journal of Michael Clark Rockefeller.* New York Graphic Society, 1968.

A Matter of Respect (1992) 30 min. Ellen Frankenstein and Sharon Gmelch (DI). Dist: NDF VR$55, VS$215. *Portrays a diverse group of people, each expressing their own sense of what it is to be Tlingit in today's world. For some, this is best done through the arts—dancing, carving, and weaving. For others, meaning comes from teaching children to speak Tlingit or to respect nature. For others, this is done by harvesting and preparing foods in traditional ways or restoring community cemeteries. A Matter of Respect is about the the meaning of tradition and change, finding balance, and the passage of culture and identity from one generation to the next.*

Mau Mau 52 min. Anthony-David Productions (PR). Dist: FI. [Reviewed by Thomas O. Beidelman, *AA* 78:950, 1976.]

Mauritania: Wealth of Blood (From Africa to Asia: Nomads Series) (1992) 60 min. Diana Stone (AN). Dist: FIV VS$198. *Archetypal camel nomads, the Moors of Mauritania maintain a traditional lifestyle with enthusiastic support from their government—unusual for nomadic peoples.*

Maya Fiesta (1988) 24 min. Allan F. Burns and Alan Saperstein (FM, AN). Dist: Corn Maya, P.O. Box 147, Indiantown, FL 34956; (904) 392-0299, VS$45. *"The second in a two-part series that represents the first visual anthropological inquiry into the lives of native Guatemalans living as refugees in South Florida."* [From the review by Duncan M. Earle, *AA* 93(1):255–256, 1991.] See also *Maya in Exile.*

Maya in Exile (1985) 28 min. Allan Burns and Alan Saperstein (PR). Dist: Corn Maya, P.O. Box 977, Indiantown, FL 33456; (904) 392-2031, VS$65. *A portrayal of the plight of Guatemalan refugees in South Florida.* [Reviewed by Lauris McKee, *AA* 90:240–241, 1988.] See also *Maya Fiesta.*

Maya Land: Where Are You Going? (Terre Maya) (1992) 55 min. Sami Sarkis and Lucia Montanaro (FM). Dist: EVA. *This video documents the struggle of the Mayans of Guatemala, who although the majority of the population, are nevertheless politically marginalized.*

Maya Lords of the Jungle (Odyssey Series, second season) (1981) 59 min. John Angier (FM). Dist: PBSV VR$70, VS$200; DER VR$50, VS$500. *"The continuity of Maya life from ancient to contemporary times is illustrated.... A brief historical section on pre-20th century investigations begins exploring the first of the major themes: subsistence. ... Another theme, the focus of Maya ritual, is introduced by Chris Jones at Tikal.... The third theme, trade, begins by looking at sites in northwestern Yucatan that have inadequate agrarian foundations to support themselves."* [From the review by Payson D. Sheets, *AA* 85:235–236, 1983. Reviewed by Clemency Coggins, *ARCH* 34(6):76, 1981.]

Maya through the Ages (1949) 45 min. Giles Healey (FM), Willard Pictures (PR). Dist: Willard Pictures; UCEMC FR$29. *The brilliant achievements of the ancient Maya civilization of southern Mexico, Guatemala, and Honduras are reviewed in contrast to the state of its modern descendants, including an almost extinct tribe, the Lacandons, who in 1946 were discovered living in the jungle under very primitive conditions by photographer-anthropologist Giles Healey. After Healey had filmed their agriculture, huntings, and worship, a Lacandon offered to lead him to a lost Mayan City of Bonampak in Mexico's southernmost state of Chiapas. Here, Healey found the magnificent and now-famous frescoes of the Mayan temples, where some of the Lacandons still returned to worship. The next year, an expedition was formed, and the film reveals its remarkable findings, including the detailed transfers and copies the anthropologists made of life-sized frescoes. These Bonampak frescoes reveal in full color the solemnity and mystery of ancient Mayan pageantry processions, priests, prisoners, torture, and battle scenes during the classic Maya empire (A.D. 317–889). Maps and live photography at the start of the film briefly review the great Mayan areas of Tulum.* [Reviewed by Jeremy A. Sabloff, *AA* 78:378–379, 1976.]

Maya: Treasures of an Ancient Civilization (1984) 27.5 min. Charles R. Barnett (PR). Dist: The Albuquerque Museum Foundation, P.O. Box 7006, Albuquerque, NM 87194; (505) 766-7878, FR$40, FS$400, VS$29.95. *"Designed to accompany the outstanding museum exhibit of the same title that opened in the spring of 1985 at the American Museum of Natural History in New York City. The film's objective is to provide audiences with a visual feel for the ancient lowland Maya centers and the larger rain-forest* *setting from which the exhibited artifacts originated."* [From the review by Elsa Redmond, *ARCH* 40(1):75–76, 1987.]

Mayaland: The Classic Maya Federation Reconsidered (1978) 40 min. Dennis J. Cipnic (FM), E. Wyllys Andrews, William R. Coe (AN). Dist: Mac FR$450. *The Maya is a fascinating but mysterious culture, originating over 2,000 years ago and developing into a federation of over two million people concentrated in city-states connected by an extraordinary network of paved roads. The massive Mayan limestone constructions are remarkable for a culture lacking beasts of burden, metal tools, or the wheel. The abrupt termination of the Mayan civilization around the ninth century, at the height of its power and influence, is one of the classic mysteries of archaeology. Tikal, in present-day Yucatan, is a cluster of massive buildings arranged with beautiful symmetry around a plaza designed for ritual ceremonies. A honeycomb of secret stairs and passages connecting multiple-purpose buildings reveals a complex and expanding bureaucracy of ruling classes and monks, served by slaves. Funeral vessels characterize the culture as an hereditary elite, based on trade in luxury goods to nations as far as hundreds of miles away. Copan, in present day Honduras, was an intellectual aristocracy whose remarkable achievement was the most accurate calendar devised up to that time. Its calculations based on the star Venus (which was worshipped), the calendar's "scientific" control over planting and harvesting times not only created a successful agricultural society, but also elevated its discoverers to the level of gods. Palenque, located in southern Mexico, is an architectural marvel resembling a small Versailles, built for a young king and his advisors—the priests who shared his power and wealth. This seafaring people built their city on a river and plied the trade routes of the Gulf of Mexico with their commerce based on cacao. The stone messages, carved in a combination of phonetic and ideographic symbols, record all the dates of key events in Mayan history.*

The Mayans: Apocalypse Then (1988) 26 min. Dist: CPI VR$50, VS$365. *This video "is simply not educationally valuable. There are too many inaccuracies, misleading generalizations, and inappropriately used terms to warrant its recommendation."* [From the review by Samuel E. Casselberry, *SBF* 25:45, 1989.]

The Mayas (1957) 11 min. Coronet Films (PR), I James Quillen (AN). Dist: SU. [Reviewed by Frederick Gorman, *AA* 78:379, 1976.]

Mayordomia: Ritual, Gender, and Cultural Identity in a Zapotec Community 21 min. Lynn Stephen (PR, WR). Dist: UTP VS$100. *Based on extensive research in Mexico, this film focuses on the Gonzalez family and their sponsorship of a saint's day fiesta. Conversations with family members, including two children who now live in Los Angeles but returned home for the celebration, and other members of the Zapotec community reveal much about indigenous religion, the gendered division of labor, migration, and cultural identity.*

Mbambim, A Lineage Head in Ayikpere, North Togo (see Anufom Series)

Mbindo Lala: A Hospital in Village Form (1976) 52 min. Gilles Bibeau (RES), Institute of Scientific Research and the National Board of Educational and Cultural Production of the Republic of Zaire. Dist: International Development Research Center, Box 8500, Ottawa, ON, KIG 3H9 Canada. French only. [Reviewed by John W. Adams, *AA* 80:766, 1978.]

THE MBIRA SERIES Gei Zantzinger, Andrew Tracey, Les Blank (FM). Dist: PSU. *The use of the traditional African mbira in the cultural life of the Shona people of Zimbabwe.*

• **Mbira: The Technique of the Mbira dza Vadzimu** (1978) 19 min. FR$12.50, FS$250. *This first film provides an introduction to the musical technique and sound of the Mbira dza Vadzimu as played by Ephat Mujuru, a leading mbira player. Using animation and freeze-frame techniques, some of the rhythmic and harmonic elements of the music are demonstrated. Various traditional songs illustrate the use of improvisation, different styles of playing, and the combination of two mbiras in duet.*

• **Mbira dza Vadzimu: Religion at the Family Level with Gwanzura Gwenzi** (1977) 66 min. FR$31, FS$805. *This film establishes a religious background for further films in the series by examining the life of Gwanzura Gwenzi, a man in his mid-forties. He is seen in Harare, Zimbabwe, where he works as the head of the messengers pool at Anglo-American. His weekdays in a western urban setting are contrasted with his weekends at home in the Tribal Trust Lands. Joining various members of his family at his country home, he hosts an all-night bira or spirit seance, the main expression of Shona religious ritual. Guests include his sister, who is the family medium; his grandfather's spirit who possesses her; members of his family, past and present; and several neighbors.*

• **Mbira dza vadzimu: Dambatsoko, an Old Cult Centre with Muchatera and Ephat Mujuru** (1977) 51 min. FR$30, FS$650. *The late Muchatera Mujuru was the leader of one of the few remaining traditional cult centers in Shona country. He was a spiritual man, yet concerned with his waning authority in Zimbabwe. Various aspects of his life and the life of his adherents at Dambatsoko are portrayed in this film. Ceremonies include spirit possession at the big banya ritual house; prayers at the mutoro hut, at the rushanga shrine, and at a blood sacrifice.*

• **Mbira: Matepe dza Mhondoro—A Healing Party** (1976) 20 min. FR$13, FS$265. *This re-enactment of a healing ceremony provides the setting for the performance of two complete songs on another type of mbira, the Matepe dza Mhondoro—"the deep notes of the lion spirits." The famous matepe player, Saini Murira, leads a group of four players. Two mediums dance to the music of mbiras, rattles, drums, and singers before and after attending the woman patient.*

• **Mbira: Njari, Karanga Songs in Christian Ceremonies with Simon Mashoko** (1979) 24 min. FR$14.50, FS$310. *Magwenyambira Simon Mashoko is a rural Catholic catechist and Mbira Njari player. Prior to his conversion to Christianity, he played the traditional mbira songs for the Shave spirits. Now, he has adapted the mbira successfully for use in the Catholic Church. He is seen participating in* *recreational beer and dance parties and also in catechism classes and a Sunday church service held at his home.*

• **Mbira dza Vadzimu: Urban and Rural Ceremonies with Hakurotwi Mude** (1979) 45 min. FR$25, FS$560. *The film presents a portrait of Hakurotwi Mude, singer and leader of a professional group of mbira players, and one of the best known Shona musicians of the area. An intense and religious man, he is shown in various kinds of performances—at an informal urban Friday night bira or nhandaro, at a sacrifice, and at a funeral.* L. A. Baldwin, "Producing Ethnographic Films: An Interview With Filmmaker Gei Zantzinger." *Perspectives in Film* 2:10–15, 1979. P. Berliner, *The Soul of Mbira.* University of California Press, Berkeley, 1979. M. L. Daneel, *The God of the Matapo Hills.* Mouton Press, The Hague, 1970. M. W. Murphree, *Christianity and the Shona.* Athlone Press, London, 1969. P. Berliner, *The Soul of Mbira: An Ethnography of the Mbira among the Shona People of Rhodesia.* Berkeley: University of California Press, 1979. P. Berliner, *The Soul of the Mbira.* L. P. Record. None such Records, Washington, DC. M. Bourdillon, *The Shona Peoples.* Mambo Press, Gwelo, Rhodesia, 1976. E. E. Evans-Pritchard, *Witchcraft, Oracles and Magic among the Azande.* Clarendon Press, Oxford, 1937. P. Fry, *Spirits of Protest.* Cambridge University Press, Cambridge, 1976. M. Gelfand, *Shona Ritual.* Juta & Co., Cape Town, 1959. J. F. Holleman, "Accommodating the Spirit Amongst Some Northeastern Shona Tribes." *Rhodes-Livingstone Paper,* 22, Cape Town, 1935. R. M. Ncube, "The True Story re Chaminuka and Lobengula." *Native Affairs Department Annual.* Salisbury, 39:59–67, 1962. A. Tracey, *How to Play the Mbira dza Vadzimu.* International Library of African Music, 1970. P.O. Box 138, Roodepoort 1725, South Africa.

Mead, Margaret (1901–1978) (see *Coming of Age* in the Strangers Abroad Series)

The Meaders Family: North Georgia Potters 31 min. Smithsonian Institution Office of Folklife Programs (PR). Dist: PSU R$17, FS$340, VS$225. *A study of American folklife, this documentary depicts the Meaders family as they work at the family kiln site in Cleveland, Georgia, and tell about their traditional approach to making pottery. After visiting more than 15 Southern potteries, the Smithsonian staff filmed the Meaders, recognizing the unique extent to which style and technology had remained intact from the time the pottery was established in 1893. In the film, Cheever Meaders, his sons Lanier and Edwin, and his wife Arie carry out every step in the complex process from digging clay and grinding it in a mule-powered mill to throwing, glazing, and firing the large crocks and pitchers. They discuss each step of the process while reflecting the feelings and attitudes of folk potter "holdouts" toward such practices as piecing, brick kilns, homemade tools, clay mixtures, and glazes.* This film is part of the Smithsonian Folklife Studies Monograph/Film series. A monograph is now in press on the Meaders Family by Ralph Rinzler and Robert Sayers. Two unedited elapsed-time silent sequences focusing on Cheever and Lanier Meaders, respectively, also are planned for distribution. *In these films, each potter throws, centers, shapes, and finishes a pitcher and a churn on the treadle-operated wheel.*

Meadowcroft Rockshelter: A Question of Questions 30 min. J. Stephen Fairchild (FM), James Adovasio, J. D. Gunn (AN). Dist: Communication Center, G-20 Hilman Library, University of Pittsburgh, Pittsburgh, PA 15260, FR$25, FS$390. *This southwestern Pennsylvania site has documented man's earliest known migrations into the eastern United States. There are indications that people have been using this rockshelter for at least 19,000 years. Meadowcroft represents the longest known sequence of continuous human occupation in the Western Hemisphere. This documentary explores the archaeological techniques used at the site. Laboratory procedures such as radiocarbon and amino acid dating, geological analysis, and computerized cultural research are also explained. Locations include the Geophysical Laboratory of the Carnegie Institution, the Radiation Biology Laboratory of the Smithsonian Institution, and the electron microscopy lab of Queens College. Meadowcroft Rockshelter geologists and archaeologists explain what they are doing and, perhaps more importantly, why they are engaged in the search for man's past.* Suggested supplements: J. M. Adovasio, "Excavations at Meadowcroft Rockshelter, 1973–1974: A Progress Report." *Pennsylvania Archaeologist* 45:1–30, 1975. J. M. Adovasio, "Excavations at Meadowcroft Rockshelter, 1973–1975: A Progress Report." *Proceedings of the XIIth Pacific Science Congress.* University of Alberta Press, 1976. J. M. Adovasio, "Meadowcroft Rockshelter: A 16,000 Year Chronicle." *Transactions of the New York Academy of Science,* 1976. J. M. Adovasio et al., "Meadowcroft Rockshelter: Retrospect." *Pennsylvania Archaeologist,* 1976. [Reviewed by Leland Ferguson, *AA* 80:202, 1978. Reviewed in *ARCH* 33(1):61, 1981.]

The Mechanics of the Forest (see the Decade of Destruction Series)

Mechanisms of Non-Verbal Communication in the Young Child (1976) 40 min. Dist: FACSEA FR$16.

The McPeake Family in Ireland (1964) 12 min. (A Folklore Research Film by Peter and Toshi Seeger.) Dist: FIM/RF FR$10, FS$100. *Gathered in the living room of their small Belfast home, the family of Francis McPeake sings Jug O'Punch and plays Irish harps and Uilean pipes, the traditional Irish bagpipes into which air is pumped from a bellows held under the player's right arm.*

Medecines et medecins (Medicine and Doctors) (1976) 15 min. Jean Rouch (DI), Centre National de la Recherche Scientifique, Comite du Film Ethnographique and Institut de Recherches en Sciences Humaines de Niamey (PR). Dist: CFE; DER. *Retired Niger nurses practice surgery in marketplaces and call on local healers for postoperative care.*

The Medium Is the Masseuse: A Balinese Massage (Bali Series) (1986) 30 min. Linda Connor, Patsy Asch, and Timothy Asch (DI), Australian National University and DER (PR). Dist: DER FR$55, VR$50, FS$650, VS$250. *Unlike many spirit mediums, Jero Tapakan practices as a* *masseuse once every three days, when possession is not auspicious. This film focuses on Jero's treatment of Ida Bagus, a member of the nobility from a neighboring town. Jero has been treating her client for sterility and seizures. She begins work this day with religious preparations and the assembling of traditional medicines. Treatment includes a thorough massage, administration of eye drops, an infusion, and a special paste for the chest. The subtitled dialogue includes a discussion between Linda Connor, Ida Bagus, and Jero, about the nature and treatment of the illness. In an interview, Ida Bagus and his wife speak about the ten-year history of his illness and a variety of diagnoses. A broad view of Jero's practice is given in the film's conclusion, which shows excerpts from the treatments of other patients. [Reviewed by Hildred Geertz, AA 86:809–811, 1984. Reviewed in VISA 4:68, 1991.]*

Medoonak the Stormmaker (1975) 13 min. National Film Board of Canada (PR). Dist: IFB R$17.50, FS$250, VS$210. *A colorful micmac Indian legend illustrating balance in nature. Medoonak is a mighty bird whose wings create terrible storms that drive the fish into deeper waters. The people are soon near starvation since they can spear fish only in shallow waters. A clever brave tricks Medoonak and the storms cease. Unfortunately, algae forms an opaque film on the water, and the fish cannot be seen. This compromise restores harmony: Medoonak will be released if he promises to rest between storms. Interpreted in mime and dance with the narration by the Mermaid Puppet Theater of Wolfville, Nova Scotia.*

Meet the Sioux Indians 11 min. Dist: IFB R$15, FS$195, VS$195. *This film details the ways the Sioux utilized the buffalo for food, clothing, and shelter. Shows how they preserved meat, turnips, corn, and pumpkins.*

Megiddo—City of Destruction (1977) 29 min. Shevat Film Productions, Ltd., Israel (PR), Shira Lindsay (DI). Dist: IUAVC FR$25, FS$400. *A guided view of excavations at Megiddo, Israel, conducted by archaeologist and historian Yigael Yadin of Hebrew University. Megiddo is mentioned in the Bible as the location where the battle of Armageddon was fought. It is also the site where excavations have revealed the ruins of 20 successive cities, one assigned to the time of King David and another to the time of King Solomon. While his colleagues are shown working at the dig uncovering architectural remains and salvaging artifacts, Yadin describes the methodology and theory guiding their research. Yadin explains and shows the architectural and cultural clues that tie together the excavated cities of Megiddo, Hazor, and Gezer as parts of Solomon's kingdom (a finding guided by Yadin's interpretation of I Kings 9:15–19 in the Old Testament.) [Reviewed by Harold Juli, AA 88:266–267, 1986. William G. Dever, ARCH:67–72, 1986.]*

The Mehinacu of Brazil (Disappearing World Series) (1974) 52 min. Thomas Gregor (AN), Carlos Pasini, Granada (PR). Dist: PSU order #51224; ISHI. *The Mehinacu live in a small village near the river Xingu in the central Brazilian rain forest. The focus of this program is their annual, month-long Piqui celebration designed to ensure a good fruit harvest. Now, a peaceful Mehinacu way of life is threatened by a planned road through the forest. [Reviewed in VISA 4:91, 1991. Reviewed by Stephen Hugh-Jones, RAIN 6:9, 1975.] Re-edited for Odyssey Series, 1982, as We Are Mehinacu. Bibliography: Thomas Gregor, Mehinacu: The Drama of Daily Life in a Brazilian Indian Village. University of Chicago Press, 1977.*

Memories and Dreams (1992) 92 min. Melissa Llewelyn-Davies (FM). Dist: Melissa Llewelyn-Davies, 3 Richmond Crescent, London N1 OLZ, UK; 4471-609-0570. *The filmmaker has been working and living with the Maasai of the Loita Hills in Kenya for two decades. A follow up to "A Maasai Diary" and "The Womens' Olamal," this piece provides an intimate exploration of the community's changing attitudes about women's roles, sex, love, and marriage during the past 20 years.*

Memories in Black and White (1987) 20 min. Ara Sahiner (FM). Dist: Ara Sahiner, 173 Marlborough St., Boston, MA 02216; (617) 262-0275, FS$375, VS$175. *"A kaleidoscope of Armenian history seen through 19th and early-20th century photographs.... The subject matter is Armenian genocide by the Turks of the Ottoman Empire in the early-20th century and reactions to this history by contemporary New York Armenians." [From the review by Joanna C. Scherer, AA 92:555–556, 1990.]*

The Mende (Disappearing World Series) (1990) 52 min. Mariane Ferme (AN). Dist: FIV VS$198, order #047043; PSU order #51225. *Kpuawala is a village of 260 Mende people in the forest of Sierra Leone. The houses are made of mud-brick and tin. This village portrait shows successful citizens and unlucky ones, clowns and gossips, happy household and divided ones. As they go about their daily routine, the Mende recognize the constant presence of a supernatural world that affects farming, fishing, and family life.*

The Mende of Kpuawala Village (1990) 52 min. Bruce MacDonald (FM), Mariane Ferme (AN). Dist: FI VS$99. *"A Mende village in Sierra Leone. Anthropologist Mariane Ferme returns to the community where she has lived for an extended period of fieldwork." [From the review by Jaques Maquet, AA 94:766–767, 1992.]*

The Mendi 57 min. Dist: CBC FR$45, FS$485. *A once-in-a-lifetime look at the colorful ancient culture of the Mendi, a people whose very existence was unknown to the world in general until 1930 when a stray passing aircraft spotted smoke curling skyward from some grass huts. Later, during World War II—from which they remained aloof—more information about them came to light through Allied and Japanese patrols. Then, in 1950, two Australians walked into the remote territory and found 55,000 people with an ancient culture intact. Now, this CBC documentary records the daily life of fierce warriors who, as a concession to the white man's presence, have turned more to other cultural traditions. Their last big fight was in 1967. The film shows such rites as a Mendi wedding, a funeral, and the phasing out of a cult, a major event to the tribe. In colorful, clamorous scenes, long lines of bedecked warriors march to a foot-stomping rhythm. Pigs are slaughtered by the score for a gargantuan feast. D'Arcy Ryan, "Marriage in Mendi." In:*

Pigs, Pearlshells and Women: Marriage in the New Guinea Highlands. R. M. Glasse and M. J. Meggitt, eds. Englewood Cliffs, NJ: Prentice Hall, 1969, pp. 159–175.

The Mendolin King (Inhabitants of the Land of Grace) (1985) 28 min. John Dickinson (FM). Dist: DER FR$45, VR$35, FS$480, VS$350. *This film is a portrait of Crud Quinal "the mandolin king," who is a folk artist who lives near Cumana in a mountain valley surrounded by sugarcane fields. Perpetuating 16th-century Spanish traditions of guitar making, Crud fashions such musical instruments as cuatros, marimba, escarpandola, and his own creation, a mandolin with two fretboards. He is an accomplished musician as well. In the film, Crud compares himself to a decaying colonial church across the street: revered yet neglected; the village altar stands, paint peeling, under the open sky.*

Menri Monastery (1993) 25 min. Roslyn Dauber (PR). Dist: UCEMC VR$50, VS$195, order #38247. *This film takes a look at the Menri Monastery in Himachel Pradesh, India, home of the indigenous pre-Buddhist Tibetan Bongo and includes scenes of rarely performed ceremonies.*

Men's Lives (1976) 43 min. Josh Hanig and Will Roberts (FM). Dist: NDF FR$65, FS$600. *Shot in Springfield and Dayton, Ohio, by two Antioch College students. Film was made as part of course in Media and Social Change and won an Oscar for best movie produced by amateurs. The film follows males through early playground years, high school football, college mixers, and factory night shifts. The film consists of a series of interviews with men, who are mostly working class, about the meanings of masculinity. The film is critical and offers a glimpse of men trapped in their roles. Focusing questions: Are there any discrepancies between the verbal and nonverbal action in the case of some men (e.g., the high school basketball coach)? The oppressors are oppressed? What are the alternatives? How do these men see women?* Bibliography: Richard Freudenheim, "The Oppressor's Oppression," *Jump Cut* 11:1–6, 1976. [Mike Hoover] [Reviewed by Marcelo M. Suarez-Orozco, *AA* 86:1050–1051, 1984.]

The Meo (Disappearing World Series) (1972) 53 min. Brian Moser, Granada (PR), Jacques Lemoine, Chris Curling (AN). Dist: PSU order #51249. *The Vietnam War devastated the Meo of Indochina. Before the war, the Meo grew maize and opium and lived in villages with their extended families; when the war destroyed their peaceful environment, most males over the age of 14 went to join the fighting, while tens of thousands of Meo fled to refugee camps.* [Reviewed by Andrew Turton, *RAIN* 4:11, 1974.]

Merchant People: Pride, Power and Belief in Rural America (1984) 28 min. Dist: Griesinger Films, P.O. Box 1102, Buckannon, WV 26201, FR$35, VR$35, FS$450, VS$100. *"Hard, sustained work and rugged individualism are the keys to these "merchant people's" success.... The film plays beautifully, with excellent photography, color, music, sound, and editing. An accompanying guide is useful."* [From the review by Patricia A. Gwariney-Gibbs, *SBF* 21:45, 1985.]

Mermaids, Froglegs and Fillets 18 min. Paul Wagner, Steven Zeitlin, Jack Santino (PR). Dist: PSU R$14.50, FS$270, VS$175. *A documentary about a black man, Lincoln Rorie, a white man, Jerry Williams, and the unique way in which they earn a living. The two met at Captain White's boat, one of several seafood-selling boats on a wharf in Washington, DC, where they developed a technique of using rhymes and "cries" to attract customers to their boat. The film delves into their backgrounds: Lincoln's on the city streets and open-air markets of Washington, and Jerry's among the fishing boats and country stores of the rural Eastern Shore of Virginia. Mermaids also emphasizes the importance of each man's father in the development of their fast-talking abilities and their choice of occupation. A strong theme throughout this documentary is the intersection of creative black-and-white cultures in an urban environment.*

Meshie (1938) 20 min. Harry Raven (FM). Dist: PSU. *A chimp raised in a human family.* [Reviewed by Clifford J. Jolly, *AA* 75:2029, 1973.]

Messing Up God's Glory (1992) 13 min. Avril Johnson and Afua Namiley-Viana (FM). Dist: FRIF. *A personal meditation on the practice of female circumcision and its religious justifications as viewed by the filmmaker, a Ghanaian woman.*

Metos Jah Hut (A Jah Hut Myth) (1987) 10 min. Duncan Holaday, Batin Long bin Hok, and Shanthi Ramanujan (FM). Dist: Annenberg School of Communications, University of Pennsylvania, Philadelphia, PA 19174; (215) 898-1553, VR$15, VS$50. *"The Jah Hut are a Senoi aboriginal group of about 2,500 living in the highlands of peninsular Malaysia's Pahang state. On a return visit to their village, anthropologist Duncan Holaday gave a camera and film to his Jah Hut friends. What we see is their creation: a few introductory shots of people in the village performing routine tasks, followed by the telling of a myth."* [From the review by Richard C. Fidler, *AA* 91:533, 1989.]

Metropolitan Avenue (1984) 60 min. Christine Noschese (FM). Dist: NDF FR$100, FS$850, VS$700. *Articulates "the fundamental dialectical process through which society and individuals create each other" by looking at a Brooklyn neighborhood community. "We see the image of urban decay that fits our image of inner-city neighborhoods.... But in this film we also meet and hear the people who struggle not only to maintain, but to build their community, and we see the fruits of their labors in and around them."* [From the review by Alice Reich, *AA* 88:1044–1045, 1986.] This neighborhood is also the subject of Ida Susser's book, *Norman Street: Poverty and Politics in an Urban Neighborhood,* Oxford, 1982.

Me'Udana (Normandy Island): Fest Zum Abschluss Der Trauerzeit (Bwabware) 21 min. E. Schlesier (FM). Dist: PSU(EC) E 534, FR$19.40. Distributed with an 11-page commentary. [Reviewed by Louis J. Luzbetak, *AA* 67:1080–1081, 1965.]

MEXICAN HERITAGE FILM SERIES South Texas Multi Films Ltd. (PR), Charles Mann (AN). Dist: Fl. Cost of entire series in one language (8 films at 10 percent discount) $1647; cost of entire series in both languages (16 films at 15 percent discount) $3111. Each film available in Spanish or English version.

- **Creative Arts and Crafts of Mexico (Artes creativos de Mexico)** 16 min. Order #354-0001 (English), #354-002 (Spanish), FR$45, FS$305. *Shows the creativity of individual artists and craftsmen all over Mexico. See glass blowers at work, weavers at their looms, and the skilled potter, Valente, making the famous black pottery of Dona Rosa's Alfareria in Oaxaca—only to mention a few. Puppets handcrafted in Mexico bring lively action to the narration of Maria de Lourdes Moreno.*

- **Christmas in Oaxaca (La Navidad en Oaxaca)** 14 min. Order #345-0003 (English), #354-0004 (Spanish), FR$40, FS$270. *The viewer becomes a participant in the Christmas celebration in Oaxaca—from the beautiful folkloric dancers in vivid costumes to the many unique customs of the Oaxaca region—the Noche de Rabanos, Calenda, Vela Dance of Tehuantepec, and the Estudiantinas from the University of Oaxaca.*

- **America's First City—Teotihuacan (La primera ciudad de las Americas-Teotihuacan)** 17 min. Order #354-0005 (English), #354-006 (Spanish), FR$45, FS$320. *Visit the world-famous pyramids of Teotihuacan, 25 miles from Mexico City, and with creative visuals as well as live on-location film, see the "Legend of the Fifth Sun" reenacted—including scenes from Cuicuilco, the oldest round structure in the Americas in view of the Olympic Stadium in Mexico City. The Olympic games of 1968 will highlight this part of the story. The film points out the skills and artistry of the early Mexican people who built this great city—the first city in the Americas—almost 2,000 years ago.*

- **Discover Veracruz (Descubrir Veracruz)** 16 min. Order #354-0007 (English), #354-0008 (Spanish), FR$45, FS$305. *The film introduces the viewer to the little-known Gulf Coast of Mexico and the magnificent state of Veracruz. The narrator, Maria de Lourdes Moreno, takes the viewer through the ancient, grisly Fort of San Juan de Ulua where Cortez first landed in North America, now in the present-day city of Veracruz. The viewer sees the ancient sight of the Voladores, the religious ceremony still performed today with the 'flying' Totanac Indians who 'fly' from a high pole in front of the magnificent temple pyramid of El Tajin. The film visits remote mountain villages and waterfalls from the Sierras in lush tropical forest, young Mexicans working in the "mountain grown" coffee plantations, brilliantly costumed dancers dancing their native folkloric dances, and a kaleidoscope of scenes from this Mexican region of the Totonacs, Huastecas, Olmecas—some of the earliest and most talented Indian groups of Mesoamerica.*

- **Monument to the Sun: The Story of the Aztec Calendar Stone (Monumento del Sol: La Historia de la Piedra Del Sol)** 16 min. Order #354-0011 (English), #354-0012 (Spanish), FR$45, FS$305. *A descriptive film telling about the meaning and history of the monumental carving known as "The Aztec Calendar Stone." The remarkable history of this famous sculptured stone is fascinating. Learn how the ancient calendar of the Maya was handed down through the centuries and how the Aztec astrologers and mathematicians devised their calendar from their very ancient ancestors. Brilliant color graphics make this much-sought-after information easily understood. A "must" for all who are interested in the marvels of Mexico's heritage.*

- **The Story of the Aztecs (La historia de las Aztecas)** 19 min. Order #354-0009 (English), #354-0010 (Spanish), FR$45, FS$345. *The film tells the story of the empire builders of Mexico—the Aztecs—with their driving beliefs that they were the chosen people of the sun god. Through vivid graphics and live film from throughout the Aztec "empire," see the fantastic accomplishments of the Aztec people and see how they relate to Mexican people today—both in Mexico City and in the United States—through ancient customs and legends still a part of their present-day culture.*

- **These Were the Maya (Estos fueron Los Mayas!)** 16 min. Order #354-0013 (English), #354-0014 (Spanish), FR$45, FS$345. *The Yucatan peninsula has been a scene of action in the Americas for at least 4,000 years. The film shows the Yucatan of the Maya with the grandeur of Chichen Itza and Uxmal, the recently discovered site of Dzibilchaltun and indescribably beautiful Tulum on the Caribbean Coast. The Maya, who now populate the cities of Yucatan, are a vigorous part of present-day Mexico. The film shows modern agriculture and industry side by side with some of the old customs. Maya dancers will perform ancient folkloric dances in beautiful, native costumes. Yucatan is still the land of the Maya.*

- **The Many Faces of Mexico (Las muchas caras de Mexico)** 16 min. Order #354-0015 (English), #354-0016 (Spanish), FR$45, FS$335. *Mexico is a land of beauty and vitality. This film shows the many facets of the Mexican scene and Mexican people: from coast to coast and ancient to modern; from majestic mountains to desert lowlands, and lush seashores and tropical foliage; from Mexico City—one of the world's large cosmopolitan centers—to picturesque hamlets; from village crafts to vast scientific industry—the many and varied faces of Mexico.*

Mi Raza: Portrait of a Family (1976) 28 min. Susan Stechnij (Dl, AN), Paul Hockings (PR). Dist: FIM/RF. *The film follows the daily life of one Mexican-American family who live in central Chicago. The father is employed at a bottling works, while the mother keeps herself busy with neighborhood political activities and the care of her four children. The religious, economic, political, and educational situation of Mexican-Americans is exemplified by particular scenes, all of them shot in a quiet observational style.* Suggested supplement: *The Chicanos: Mexican American Voices.* Ed Ludwig and James Santibanez, eds. Pelican Books, 1971.

Miao Year 61 min. William R. Geddes (FM, AN). Dist: UCEMC FR$38. *A detailed film ethnography of the Miao, a hill tribe in northern Thailand.* [Reviewed by Asen Balikci, AA 71:8000, 1969.]

Microcultural Incidents in Ten Zoos (1969) 34 min. J. D. Van Vlack (CA), Ray L. Birdwhistell (AN). Dist: PSU FR$20, FS$425. *Based on a lecture given by R. L. Birdwhistell to the American Anthropological Association on* *context control methods for cross-cultural comparisons. Film excerpts show interaction of members of family with each other and with animals during visit to zoo. Cross-cultural behavior of different families in zoos in England, France, Italy, India, Hong Kong, Japan, and United States.* [Reviewed by Catherine M. Bateson, *AA* 74:191–192, 1972.] Suggested supplement: Ray L. Birdwhistell, *Kinesics and Context*. University of Pennsylvania Press, 1970.

Micronesia: The Tiny Islands 11 min. Oceania Productions (PR). Dist: OP FR$15, FS$115. *A general coverage, especially of the Marshalls, Ponape, Truk, Guam, Palaus, and Yap.*

MICRONESIAN SERIES Dist: Media Dynamics, Box 2312, Stanford, CA 94305, FS$150 each.

• **Marshalls** 13 min. *Includes scenic views of the Majuro atoll, reef, and beaches. Features people working near their homes, fishing, drying copra, and making handicrafts. Activity at the dock with field trip ship docking.*

• **Ponape** 14 min. *Includes scenic views of Ponape and Ant atoll, Nan Madol, waterfalls and villages. Features people harvesting rice and pepper, fishing, and at a sakau ceremony. In-water views of shark and porpoise.*

• **Truk** 12 min. *Includes scenic views of Tol, Fefin, Dublon, and Moen. Features people at the district market, on farms, dancing, building, playing baseball, drying copra, fishing, and traveling by boat to their islands.*

• **Marianas** 13 min. *Includes scenic views of Rota, Tinian, Saipan, and the northern islands. Features Taga Stones, landing beaches, World War II relics, Royal Taga hotel, Joeten shopping center, and homes. People working at docks, in gardens, and at a christening party.*

• **Palau** 12 min. *Includes scenic views of Koror, and the Rock Islands, old abai on Babelthuap. Features women planting and gathering swamp taro, men fishing and making monkeymen and story boards.*

• **Yap** 12 min. *Includes views of Yap Islands. Features girls stick dancing, boys building canoes, United Nations day activities, out-islanders visiting Yap, the men's houses, and chewing betelnut.*

The Middle East: Mosaic of Peoples (1979) 27 min. Vladimir Bibic (PR). Dist: Coronet Instructional Media, 65 East South Water Street, Chicago, IL 60601, FS$440. *"This film, by necessity, contains sweeping generalizations about ethnic, religious, economic and social variations in the Middle East."* [Reviewed in *SBF* 16:37–38, 1980.]

Midsummer in Sweden (1930s) 10–15 minutes. Dist: FCE FR$17, FS$95. *Summer festival in Sweden with dances that are related to the early May Pole dances of the Norsemen.*

Mighty Warriors (1964) 30 min. Dist: IUAVC FR$9.50. *Pictures the major encounters between the white man and the plains Indians. Dramatizes the Battle of Little Big Horn, the Sand Creek Massacre, and the Fetterman Massacre. Points out that Americans are indebted to the Indians for a great amount of agricultural, military, and political knowledge.*

Migraçao 57 min. Jean-Pierre Beaurenaut (FM). Dist: FdV. *The way of Migraçao (migration), a document on Brazilian North-East peasants of the old sugarcane fazendas, in the State of Maranhao, between the North-East and Amazonia. After recalling the history of the region, which used to be prosperous because of sugarcane, the film shows the regression following the collapse of sugar rates and the abolition of slavery through the everyday life of a community of black peasants living in the dying fazenda of Arequipa. It is the return to food-producing crops. But here, as well as in all the North and North-East of Brazil, land belongs to a handful of decadent owners, descendants of sugar mill lords. These owners turn into personal profits almost half of the production of manioc, as true feudal masters, condemning their peasants to stagnation. In spite of the efforts of a countryman from Arequipa who manages a local syndicate of rural workers, the young people prefer to emigrate. The end of the film shows the way of the emigration and the life of a small group of young people, who originate from Arequipa, living in favellas of the town of Sao Luis, the capital of Maranhao.*

The Migrants (Disappearing World Series) (Also called *In Search of Cool Ground: The Migrants*) (1985) 52 min. David Turton (AN), Andre Singer (PR). Dist: FIV VS$198, order #047004; Thomas Howe Associates, Ltd., 1-1226 Homer Street, Vancouver, British Columbia V6B 2Y8 Canada; (604) 687-4215, FR$150, VR$60, VS$575; PSU VR$14, order #51150. *Drought has driven many of the Mursi to the "cool grounds" of the highlands. Here, the proximity of Berka, a market village, along with the tsetse flies' decimation of the Mursi's cattle, are having a profound effect on Mursi culture.* [Reviewed by William Shack, *AA* 89:780, 1987. Reviewed in *VISR* 8:106, 1992.]

Migrants from Sakaltutan (1984) 24 min. Roger Penfound (PR) for the BBC Open University. Dist: MG VR$40, VS$198. *"About Sakaltutan, a village in Central Anatolian Turkey. . . . Focus[es] on socioeconomic and cultural change from the subjects' points of view through a series of interviews with present and former villagers. . . . Deals with people who left the village."* [From the review by Paul J. Magnarella, *AA* 88:1046–1047, 1986. [Reviewed by Peter S. Allen, *ARCH* 21:104, 1985.]

THE MIGRATORY CYCLE OF THE NETSILIK SERIES Dist: EDC FR$75, FS$990 (set). *The BBC has edited the full 11-hour Netsilik Film Series produced by EDC and the National Film Board of Canada into two one-hour films that summarize the entire migratory cycle.*

• **People of the Seal: Eskimo Summer** 52 min. R$55, FS$720, VS$540. *The Netsilik have completed their winter hunting for seal on the sea-ice. They then move to land to prepare for warm weather activities: fishing, gathering eggs and plants, and building a kayak to be used later for caribou hunting. Inland they join other family group members in fishing for salmon at their stone weir and later in caribou hunting. Winter comes early in the Arctic and the Netsilik begin their return to the sea-ice in September.*

• **People of the Seal: Eskimo Winter** 52 min. R$55, FS$720, VS$540. *As the sea-ice freezes, the Netsilik move far out into* *the bay, search for seal holes, and build their igloos near the best seal-hunting spots. The rest of the film focuses on the seal hunting upon which their lives depend. When a seal is caught, it is divided between the families, and every part is put to some use. Communal games and activities follow a successful hunting season, after which the Netsilik begin their annual trek back to the land.*

Le mil (Millet) (1963) 27 min. Jean Rouch (DI), Centre National de la Recherche Scientifique, Comite du Film Ethnographique (PR). Dist: CFE; DER. *Traditional millet agriculture in Niger and problems in agronomic research.*

Miles from the Border (1988) 16 min. Ellen Frankenstein (FM). Dist: NDF VR$40, FS$295, VS$195. *"Part of a master's thesis done in three media: a written text, still photographs, and a short film.... The immigration and assimilation process faced by a Mexican family, originally from a village in Zacatecas, who settled in Fillmore, California in the 1960's."* [From the review by Winnie Lambrecht, AA 91:1090–1091, 1989.]

Miles of Smiles, Years of Struggle (1982) 59 min. Paul Wagner (PR). Dist: Benchmark Films, 145 Scarborough Rd., Briarcliff Manor, NY 10510; (914) 762-3838, FR$85, FS$845. *"The history of the men who worked as porters on the Pullman trains. This all-Black work force provided personal service to generations of wealthy Americans who regularly rode the sleeping cars.... By the 1920's, the Pullman Palace Car Company was the largest single employer of Blacks in the United States."* [From the review by Nora Groce, AA 87:989–991, 1985.]

Mill Creek Village People 26 min. Marshall McKusick (FM). Dist: UIOWA order #50263, FR$18.20, FS$380. [Reviewed by William A. Turnbaugh, AA 78:369, 1976.]

MILLENNIUM: TRIBAL WISDOM AND THE MODERN WORLD SERIES (1992) David Maybury-Lewis (H), Hans Zimmer (MU). Dist: PBS VS$350 (set), order #MILL-000-RCDC. *Many of the strengths of modern technology seem to be our undoing: an economy based on infinite needs leaves many of us too poor to afford adequate health care and food; our desire to control nature threatens our survival with world deforestation; and the spirit of individualism that has powered our greatest achievements prevents us from achieving peace and international cooperation. Show students alternative ideologies by letting them see the world through the eyes of real people living in the tribal world. David Maybury-Lewis's interviews help students understand the hopes, beliefs, and customs of contemporary tribal peoples. Each episode of the ten-part series examines fundamental issues of relevance to people everywhere and raise substantive questions that guide the students through explorations of respect for the world's cultures, family relationships, birth and death, the environment, art, spirituality, material wealth, science and technology, government, and survival. Included with the purchase of the complete Millennium Series are: teacher's reference booklet, student activity sheets, action and resource guide, and viewers guide. See descriptions under individual titles:*

- An Ecology of the Mind
- The Art of Living
- At the Threshold
- The Shock of the Other
- Strange Relations
- Mistaken Identity
- Touching the Timeless
- A Poor Man Shames Us All
- Inventing Reality
- The Tightrope of Power

Million Years of Man (1967) [Reviewed by Fred H. Smith, AA 80:504–505, 1978.]

El Mirador: A Preclassic City (1985) 30 min. Ray T. Matheny (FM). Dist: BYU-AVS FS$355, VS$145. *"Some unusual chacteristics of Maya cities found at Mirador have generated considerable archaeological excitement, among them the impressive Preclassic public buildings and the earliest known examples of several architectural traits, such as decorative masks on building facades.... On the whole, this film offers us good history and progress report on the excavations of Mirador, with a useful summary of what has been learned to date."* [From the review by Marshall Joseph Becker, ARCH 40(6):70–71, 1987.]

Misa Colombiana (1977) 20 min. Anne Fischel, Glenn McNatt (FM). Dist: DER FR$30, FS$290. *A squatter settlement in Medellin, Colombia, where some 370 families have made their homes. The community subsists largely on the "leftovers of the rich," foraged from the city dump on the edge of the settlement. Houses are built of tin and tar paper, there is no running water, and there is little obvious reason for hope. But a dedicated dissident priest works with the local people, and in his mass he challenges them not to despair, but to continue their struggle. "How can there be love in Colombia when we know that 100 children die daily of hunger?" asks the priest.* Relevant anthropological literature: L. Peattie, *The View from the Barrio*. University of Michigan Press, 1968.

Miss Goodall and the Wild Chimpanzees 28 min. Dist: UCEMC FR$21; PSU(PCR) order #31269, FR$10.60; UU FR$6.50; NGS (52-minute version) FS$595, VS$545. *Follows a 26-year-old English anthropologist as she observes and lives with wild chimpanzees in the East African jungles. The film reinforces the belief that better understanding of the behavior of chimpanzees will eventually lead to a better understanding of man. Edited from the National Geographic Society presentation produced for television.*

Miss ... Or Myth? (1987) 60 min. Mark Schwartz, Geoffrey Dunn, and Claire Rubach (PR), Mark Schwarts and Georffey Dunn (DI). Dist: CG FR$100, FS$895, VS$595. *"Intercuts interviews with Lisa Davenport, Miss California 1985, and Ann Simenton, feminist activist and organizer of the Myth California 'pageant.' Speaking from opposing positions, each woman presents her personal and political views of beauty pageants."* [From the review by Mary Beth Haralovich and Denise Kervin, AA 92:837–838, 1990.]

Mission Hill and the Miracle of Boston (1982) 60 min. Richard Boradman (FM). Dist: CRA FR$86, FS$720. *"The destruction of a working-class neighborhood through urban renewal, the construction of public housing, and institutional expansion."* [From the review by Sally Engle Merry, AA 85:1013–1014, 1983.]

Mission San Xavier Del Bac, 1968 (1970) 33 min. Dist: UCEMC FR$32. *Documents the restoration and cleaning of a famous American art treasure, the beautiful Spanish mission near Tucson, Arizona. San Xavier is the best example of mission architecture in the United States—a living church established for and still used by the Papago Indians on their reservation. Shows the dust of nearly two centuries being painstakingly brushed away to reveal dramatically the original beauty of statues, murals, and architectural details. Studies this art at close range during cleaning and shows before and after comparisons. Examines the three retablos of San Xavier that represent 18th-century Spanish baroque style as used in central Mexico—frontier examples of pure Spanish ultrabaroque. Narration explains the history of the mission and the art of the altars, statues, and murals.*

Mississippi Delta Blues 18 min. Bill and Josette Ferris (FM), Judy Peiser (ED). Dist: CSF FR$30, FS$280. *A collection of important filmed field research by Bill Ferris from 1968–70. Ferris traveled from farms to jooks to homes to collect music he felt best expressed the richness of Delta blues. The film begins with Louis Dotson playing his "one-strand on the wall." This one-strand is a wire uncoiled from a broom handle and nailed to a house that serves as a resonator. Dotson plucks the wire and slides a bottle along it to change the tone. This produces a sound similar to West African one-stringed instruments. The film moves to Shelby "Poppa Jazz" Brown's "jook joint" in Leland, Mississippi. James "Son" Thomas and "Little Son" Jefferson play classic Delta blues while couples dance the boogie and "slow drag." Wade Walton uses his barber's razor and leather strap to strike the beat as he performs his original "Barber Shop Boogie." Walton's friends include blues piano player, "Pine Top" Johnson who plays "Pine Top Boogie Woogie," a favorite in the Delta. The final scene shows a Clarksdale, Mississippi soul group. The lead singer is named "Soul Singer Number Three" because she bows only to Aretha Franklin and Diana Ross in her musical talent. Soul dances contrast with slower blues steps to show how music and dance is constantly evolving new forms in the Mississippi Delta. Filmed and edited in Super 8.*

Mississippi, Is This America 1962–64 (see Eyes on the Prize: America's Civil Rights Years Series)

Mistaken Identity (Millennium: Tribal Widsom and the Modern World Series) (1992) 1 hour. David Maybury-Lewis (H), Hans Zimmer (MU). Dist: PBS VS$49.95, order #MILL-103-RCDC. *Who are you? Where does your individual identity begin and end? While Western societies strive to answer these questions through a biological view—conception, birth, adolescence, maturity, and death—tribal cultures define identity by the myths and rituals of their society, by the people who rear them, and by an organic continuum to which they belong. Explore these views of life and death through scenes taken from the family life of an abortion counselor in Canada, a boy's initiation into manhood in a Brazilian Xavante tribe, a high school girl's attempted suicide, and an Indonesian Sumbanese tribesman's relationship to his dead relatives.*

Mistress Madeleine (Daughters of the Country Series) 57 min. Norma Bailey (PR), Aaron Kim Johnston (DI). Dist: NFB R$80, FS$775, VS$150. *1850: the fur trade era. As the wife of a Hudson's Bay Company clerk, Madeleine is happy. She is half Native American and, as was the country's custom, lives with McKay in a common law union. When the company offers McKay a promotion providing he enter into a sanctified marriage with a white woman, he deserts Madeleine and their two children. Heartbroken and shamed, she must come to terms with the prejudice that has shattered her world and reestablish her dignity as a person.*

The Mists of Time 15 min. Patrick Carey (FM). Dist: CRM/MH order # 408319, FR$22, FS$290. *A journey into Ireland's past by means of poetic images, the megaliths and dolmens that dot her history and her landscape.*

Mitsuye and Nellie (1981) 58 min. Allie Light (DI), Light-Saraf Productions (PR). Dist: Light-Saraf Productions, 264 Arbor St., San Francisco, CA 94131; (415) 584-3521, FR$75, FS$740. *"About second generation Japanese American and Chinese American daughters.... Mitsuye Yamada and Nellie Wong are poets, writers, and essayists. Their work and lives concern the dual problems of being Asian and female in America. The juxtaposition of their individual lives and the histories of Chinese and Japanese in America also illustrates how the experiences of Chinese Americans and Japanese Americans parallel and yet how these experiences remain unknown and mysterious to the members of both groups."* [From the review by Karen L. Ito, AA 86:787–789, 1984.]

Moana (1926) 66 min. Robert and Frances Flaherty (FM). Dist: AB FR$10; MOMA $30. *Flaherty's great film on Samoa, focusing on the young man Moana as he goes through the tatooing ceremony.* [Reviewed by Lowell D. Holmes, AA 81:734–736, 1979.]

Moana Roa 32 min. New Zealand National Film Unit (PR). Dist: IUAVC FR$9.50. *Presents the inhabitants of the Cook Islands, their customs, and the effects of New Zealand government on their lives. Highlights Captain Cook's voyage in the 18th century to these islands. Native basket weaving, singing, dancing, and fishing are pictured. The influences on the islanders of the Christian church, education, air and radio communication, medicine, and the introduction of commercial orange growing are discussed. The intermixing of modern and traditional ways is emphasized.*

Modern Brides: Arranged Marriage in South India 3 0 min. Happy Luchsinger (DI), Joseph Elder (EP). Dist: UW-SAAS FR$30, FS$250. *This film describes two marriages that occurred in Mysore, South India, in 1983, within middle-class Brahman communities. The parents of Vinuta (a secretary) and Lokesh (a technician in a tire factory) arranged an entirely "traditional" marriage, complete with* *dowry and horoscope matching. The parents of Geetha (a medical student) and Raghu (a fellow doctor) were informed by the two that they wished to marry each other (i.e., to have a "love marriage"). The parents then proceed with the marriage arrangements as though it were a "traditional" marriage. Through interviews with the brides, the grooms, their parents, and other members of their families, one learns the important ingredients of a "good marriage" that include the families' reputations and the willingness of all parties to adjust to the new circumstances.* [Reviewed by Serena Nanda, *AA* 89:259, 1987.]

Modern Methods of Archaeological Excavation 19 min. Dist: FACSEA FR$16. [Reviewed by Harvey M. Bricker, *AA* 77:900, 1975.]

Modoc (1980) 15 min. Peter Winograd (PR). Dist: EMC FR$25, FS$250. *Describes the dramatic events and personalities of the Modoc Indian War of 1873. The film identifies the causes of the war and places them in their historical context. The Modocs were a tribe of individuals led by strong men with different points of view. Caught in a web of historical forces, they chose to fight to maintain their way of life rather than submit. The conflict within the tribe that undermined their war with the U.S. Army is the focus of the film. It was the only Indian War fought in California, 50 warriors against 1,000 soldiers. The commander of the U.S. Army in the West was assassinated by the Modocs, the only General killed in all the Indian Wars. For the first time in history, war correspondents covered this Indian War, leaving behind a wealth of fascinating visual material. These photographs, engravings, and newspapers, combined with actual location footage results in an authentic view of an era and event.*

Mohawk Basketmaking: A Cultural Profile (1980) 28 min. Frank Semmens (FM). Dist: PSU FR$19.50, FS$385. *Examines Native American basketmaking "as it evolved from a primarily utilitarian to an increasingly commercial activity.... Showcases the skills of Mary Adams, a prominent craftsperson who creates baskets for commercial sale.... Records her procedures, from dyeing the black ash splints ... to finishing baskets that combine both traditional and innovative design elements."* [From the review by William A. Turnbaugh and Sarah Peabody Turnbaugh, *AA* 90:234–235, 1988.]

Moi, un noir (Me, a Black) (1957) 80 min. Jean Rouch (DI), Films de la Pleiade (PR). Dist: CFE; DER. *The lives of young Nigerien emigrees in Treichville on the Ivory Coast.*

Mokil (1950) 58 min. Conrad Bentzen (FM) in collaboration with Mel Sloan. Dist: SPF FR$75, FS$600; UCEMC FR$38. *The problems of a growing population in a closed ecological setting. A burgeoning population and growing dependence on a cash economy place tremendous pressures on scarce land resources. In exploring these problems and some tentative solutions to them, the film touches on almost all aspects of Mokilese life, leaving the viewer with a dramatic visual understanding of life on a tiny Micronesian atoll.* [Reviewed by Robert C. Kiste and Paul D. Schaefer, *AA* 76:715–717, 1974.]

Moko Jumbie: Traditional Stilt Walkers 15 min. Karen Kramer (FM). Dist: FL FR$60, VR$50, FS$400, VS$195; KKFL FR$60, VR$40, FS$400, VS$200. *The name means "dancing spirit," and these ten-foot-high stilt walkers appear at street festivals in New York City, at Carnival celebrations in the Caribbean, and during religious ceremonies in West Africa. Wearing special costumes and masks that add to their mystery, the moko jumbie is both feared and revered. Because of their great height, they are seen as all-powerful figures accompanied by joyous music and feelings of awe. This unique film shows the art, craft, dance, and history of the moko jumbie. It gives background into the costume and dance movements, as well as its origins in West Africa. Narrated by two moko jumbies living in NYC, this lively film provides fresh cultural insight.*

Mona Lisa of the Galilee (1989) 42 min. Catherine Mossek (PR), Nissim Mossek (DI). Dist: Consulate General of Israel, 1020 Statler Office Building, Boston, MA 02116; (617) 542-0041, free loan. *"A mosaic floor that came to light at the site of Sepphoris in 1987 and was removed the following year is a central focus of this film. One panel of this otherwise unremarkable mosaic contains the head of a woman, dubbed the 'Mona Lisa' by the excavators owing to her exquisite beauty and enigmatic countenance. Efforts to preserve and restore the mosaic are documented in this tape, although one has the impression that the mosaic is really just a 'hook' for the production and that the real message is an ecumenical one."* [From the review by Peter S. Allen, *ARCH* 43(2):64–67, 1990.]

Mongolia: On the Edge of the Gobi (Disappearing World Series) 52 min. Owen Lattimore (AN). Dist: PSU order #51216. *Mongolia is a country the size of Western Europe with a population of only 1,500,000. On the great plains, ancient skills of the Mongol horsemen contrast with the new methods of the socialist revolution, which brought collective farming to the steppes.*

Mongolia: The City on the Steppes (Disappearing World Series) (1975) 52 min. Owen Lattimore (AN). Dist: PSU order #51217. *Ulan Bator is Mongolia's capital city and the home of a quarter of its population. In this program, the city celebrates the 53rd anniversary of the revolution with parades, festivals, wrestling, and archery contests, and one of the most remarkable horse races in the world.*

Monkey into Man 15 min. Stuart Legg (FM). *Julian Huxley's classic study of ape behavior, provocative, amusing, and beautifully produced comment on evolution.*

Monkey of the Clouds (1984) 18 min. Andrew Young (DI), World Wildlife Fund (PR). Dist: World Wildlife Fund–US Primate Program, 1601 Connecticut Ave., NW, Washington, DC 20009; (202) 387-0800, FS$300. *"Illustrates the plight of South American monkeys in danger of extinction.... Focuses on the yellow-tailed woolly monkey of northern Peru."* [From the review by Meredith F. Small, *AA* 87:980–982, 1985.]

Monkeys, Apes, and Man 52 min. National Geographic Society (PR). Dist: NGS FS$595, VS$545. *For as long as man has observed the behavior of monkeys and apes, he has* *been fascinated and amused and perhaps most often felt uneasy or even self-conscious. For inevitably he has sensed a similarity—in appearance and behavior—a reflection of himself. Today, increasingly, he is learning that the similarity is not simply superficial. Man is a primate, a member of the order that includes monkeys and apes. Bound by evolution, they have much in common—more than most people ever dreamed even a century ago.*

The Monkeys of Mysore (1963) 19 min. Paul E. Simonds (FM, AN), University of California Extension Media Center (PR). Dist: UCEMC FR$29, FS$270. *Discloses the stable, flexible, and delicately balanced social system of the bonnet macaque monkeys—in many ways similar to their fellow primates, both monkey and man. The social unit is a troop of males, females, and young, which remain together in order to survive. The independent monkey—the one that cannot remain within the troop—rarely survives. The daily activity of the troop, shown from sunrise to sunset, reveals a strictly enforced hierarchy, tempered by close social interactions. This authoritarian dominance serves to maintain troop unity and reduce conflict. Dominance and other social relations are revealed by means of subtle and complex signals, both gestures and sounds. The film discusses food, eating habits, mutual grooming, play, fighting among males, and the resolution of their fights, sexual activity, care of infants, and other activities of the young and adult monkeys whose life span may be as long as 30 years.* [Reviewed by Neil Tappen, AA 69:425–426, 1967.]

Monsieur Albert, prophete; ou Albert Atcho (Mr Albert, Prophet; or Albert Atcho) (1966) 27 min. Jean Rouch (DI), Argos Films and Centre National de la Recherche Scientifique (PR). Dist: CFE; DER. *Life in a community of Harrist followers in the village of Bregbo in the Ivory Coast and their prophet Alberto Atcho.*

A Month for the Entertainment of Spirits (1992) 30 min. Kean Gibson (FM). Dist: UCEMC VR$50, VS$250. *Examines the ceremonies of African-Guyanese, who continue the African traditions of making contact with the spirit world. Rituals are performed year round, but they are most frequent in August, the month in which slavery was abolished in 1838. The video begins with a libation ceremony celebrating emancipation, performed to make contact with their ancestors by descendants of slaves. Then it studies four Comfa ceremonies and explores their similarities with other rituals that access the spirit world.*

The Moontrap (Pour la suite du monde) (1963) 84 min. Pierre Perrault, Michel Brault, and Marcel Carriere (FM). Dist: UCEMC FR$32. *There is a place in Canada where the moon is still held to influence the earth and where souls of the dead are thought to help catch white whales. The filmmakers took their cameras to l'Ile-aux-Coudres. They photographed the revival of an old tradition: the catching of a whale by the ancient method of sinking a fence of strong saplings in offshore mud and then waiting for the right tide. The magnificent creature is actually corralled and trucked alive to a New York aquarium. The villagers have a tremendous zest for life and a great store of wisdom. The whole community is caught up in the all but forgotten pursuit, reviving as well other strange customs such as auction sales for the benefit of souls in purgatory. With their warmth and dedication, the proud people of this small island in the St. Lawrence become the focal point of the film.* [Reviewed by Bernard Bernier, Bernard-R. Emond, AA 80:763–765, 1978. Reviewed in VISA 1:19, 1987.]

Moowis, Where Are You, Moowis? 26 min. Dist: FHS VS$89.95, order #DH-880. *This is the story of a young Algonquin warrior and the chief's beautiful daughter who spurns him. Unable to win her and unwilling that anyone else should, he connives with a spirit to turn a snowman into a man so beautiful that the girl falls in love with him. When the snowman melts, Cochis is heartbroken.*

Montana Indian Children (Part IV—Play and Cultural Continuity) 30 min. Sara H. Arnaud and Nancy E. Curry (FM), Department of Child Development and Child Care, University of Pittsburgh (PR). Dist: Campus Film Distributors Corp., 2 Overhill Road, Scarsdale, NY 10583. *A contemporary (1975) presentation of children's cultural and ethnic role-modeling and attitudinal development toward ethnicity through play. Emphasis is on 3 to 6-year-olds' play interaction. Developmental learning is presented by ethnic agency representatives such as Head Start and Native American Reservation personnel. The main tribes presented are the confederated Kootenai/Salish Tribes of the Flathead Reservation in Montana. The clearest development of the film is its presentation of learning through transfer. There is a strong emphasis placed on the combination of cultural integrity and integration of Native American culture within the contexts of white culture. Major segments of the film highlight the oral tradition, the Indian "baby wrap" bead work, dances, songs, and the pow wow. Probably the strongest focus of this film is its intrinsic plea for cultural ethnic identity. It speaks against the acculturation of a minor culture within a dominant environmental culture. Throughout the film, the Native American narrators express strong feelings about their heritage, their present status socially and politically, and their future, especially with regard to their children. They emphasize the importance of the individual, combined with a deep sense of heritage and group sharing. Cinematography techniques are of the "crop and zoom" category. All play is in an "institutional" setting, which distracts somewhat from the natural play environment one would like to see. For viewers unaware of the current reservation-oriented Native American, the film presents the dilemma of the "submerged" culture.* [Ray Weisenborn]

Morgan Sorghum (1974) 12 min. Dist: APPAL FR$20, FS$200. *The film covers three craftsmen that were featured at the Morgan County (Kentucky) Sorghum Festival: a knifemaker, a broommaker, and a woman who spins her own yarn on a spinning wheel. It details their work, then follows them to the fair where their work is displayed.*

Moro Naba (1957) 27 min. Jean Rouch (DI), Centre National de la Recherche Scientifique and Institut Francais d'Afrique Noir (PR), Jean Ravel (ED). Dist: CFE; DER. *Funeral rituals for a traditional leader in Upper Volta; election and presentation of the new leader.*

MOROCCO, BODY AND SOUL SERIES (1987) 26 min. Izza Genini (FM). Dist: FRIF FR$55, FS$470, VS$260. *The three films that comprise the series look at Morocco's traditional music as they reveal the beauty and diverse influences that have shaped the nations customs.* [Reviewed by M. Elaine Combs-Schilling, AA 93(2):517–518, 1991.] See descriptions under individual titles:

- **Aita**
- **Lutes and Delights**
- **Hymns of Praise**

Morris Family Old Time Music Festival (1980) 30 min. Robert Gates (FM). Dist: DER FR$40, FS$450. *Folk performances in West Virginia.* [Reviewed by George L. Hicks, AA 85:492–494, 1983.]

Mosori Monika (1970) 20 min. Chick Strand (DI). Dist: UCEMC; CCC. *An expressive documentary about women in the third world. This is an ethnographic film about two cultures that have encountered one another. The Spanish Franciscan missionaries went to Venezuela in 1945 to "civilize" the Warao Indians living in the swamps on the Orinoco River Delta. Before the missionaries came, the Waraos lived in relative isolation and were barely affected by the outside world. The acculturation is presented from two viewpoints. A nun tells how the Indians lived when the missionaries arrived and what the nuns have done to "improve" conditions, both spiritually and materially. An old Warao Indian woman tells what she feels have been the important experiences in her life. The viewpoints are structured in counterpoint so that the deeper aspects of the juxtaposition of the modern culture over the old becomes apparent through the revelations of the two women.* [Reviewed by Peter Furst, AA 73:1476–1477, 1971.]

Mother Ganges (1930s) 10–15 min. Dist: FCE FR$17, FS$95. *Benares, the city, the people, the holy men, and a very detailed cremation on the banks of the Ganges.*

Mother of Many Children 60 min. Alanis Obomsawin (DI). Dist: NFB R$80, FS$775, VS$350. *Tracing the lives of four Native American women from childhood to old age, this film reveals how their shared belief in the importance of tradition is a source of strength in the face of change. This film portrays a matriarchal society that has been pressured for centuries into adopting different standards and customs. Despite modern demands, these women maintain their heritage by perpetuating ancient crafts and customs.*

Moulay Idriss 11 min. B/W. Dist: FIM/RF FR$10, FS$100. *One week each year, Moslem pilgrims converge on this holy meeting place for here is hallowed ground and the faithful who are unable to travel to Mecca may come and receive exoneration. This is a film record of what transpires during that eight-day period when masses of people, living in makeshift abodes, gather together for prayer. Throughout Holy Week, this serene and silent city in Morocco seethes with colorful processions and festivities.*

El Moulid: Egyptian Religious Festival 40 min. Fadwa El Guindi (AN, FM). Dist: ENR FR$85, FS$940, VS$400. *Seven centuries ago, Sayyid al-Badawy entered Tanta on horseback, his face double veiled. Today he is a legend; more than a million celebrate annually at his tomb. The film dramatically captures the interplay of various levels of religious experience—the scriptural, the mystical, the ritual, the mythical—as they interact with secular traditional life.* Study guide available.

Mountain Community of the Himalayas 11 min. J. Michael Hagopian (FM). Dist: AP FR$5, FS$150. [Reviewed by Gerald D. Berreman, AA 67:847, 1965.]

Mountain Farmer (1971) 9 min. Dist: APPAL FR$15, FS$125. *Lee Banks practices "what I guess you'd call old-timey farming," tilling the soil with his horse and wooden plow, and using methods barely different from his ancestors. The film is a tribute to a true mountaineer—a strong independent man who finds joy in his work and harmony with the land.*

Mountain Gorilla (1959) 16 min. Psychological Cinema Register (PR), G. Schaller (CA), C.R. Carpenter (NA). Dist: PSU FR$11. *One of the classics, the film depicts the social behavior of the highly endangered mountain gorilla. Distribution, ecology, and population density are also discussed.*

Mountain Music of Peru (1984) 60 min. John Cohen (FM). Dist: Hazardous Films, RD #1, Tompkins Corners, Putnam Valley, NY 10579; (914) 528-6453, FR$100, FS$950. *"A profound musical travelogue, comprising a round trip tour from Qeros, a traditional Andean village, to Lima, a modern coastal metropolis.... The film traces the musical heritage of the Indians, which has endured for more than four centuries since the Spanish conquest."* [From the review by Joseph W. Bastien, AA 88:267, 1986.]

Mountain People (1974) 24 min. Granada (PR). Dist: WFV; UCEMC FR$28; PSU FR$14.50. *Warm and sympathetic portrait of the Appalachian poor, stressing their pride and strength in the face of adversity. Excellent depiction of the relationships between social conditions and human values.*

MOUNTAIN PEOPLES OF CENTRAL ASIA SERIES
International Film Foundation (PR), Hermann Schlenker (CA). Dist: IFF FS$2,240 (series). [Reviewed by Asen Balikci, AA 74:1587–1588, 1972.]

<u>The Pushtu Peoples</u>

- **Making Felt** FS$180, FR$25.
- **Men's Dance** 11 min. FS$200, FR$25.
- **Boy's Games** 5 min. FS$100, FR$25.
- **Baking Bread** 10 min. FS$200, FR$25.
- **Weaving Cloth** 9 min. FS$180, FR$25.

<u>The Tajik Peoples</u> *(B/W)*

- **Making Gun Powder** 10 min. FS$150, FR$25.
- **Grinding Wheat** 7 min. FS$110, FR$25.
- **Building a Bridge** 10 min. FS$150, FR$25.
- **Making Bread** 11 min. FS$165, FR$25.
- **Casting Iron Plow Shares** 11 min. FS$165, FR$25.
- **Pottery Making** 15 min. FS$220, FR$25.

- **Shearing Yaks** 9 min. FS$130, FR$25.
- **Threshing Wheat** 9 min. FS$130, FR$25

<u>Combining Many Afghan Tribes</u>
- **Buzkashi** 9 min. FS$160, FR$25. *Describes one of the most dangerous sports in the world. This once-forbidden game on horseback, is played each year by Afghan tribesmen in a festival attended by their king.*

Mourning for Mangatopi (1975) 56 min. Curtis Levy (DI), Australian Institute for Aboriginal Studies (PR). Dist: UCEMC R$51, FS$710, VS$500. *Detailed documentary record of a mortuary ceremony held by the Tiwi of Melville Island—one of the grandest and most colorful Aboriginal ceremonies held for many years. Mangatopi, a leader of the tribe, was killed by his wife. The tragedy of his death and the high status of his family demanded a special Pukamuni ceremony, which was organized by his relatives in the old way.* (see also *Goodbye, Old Man*). Relevant anthropological literature: C. W. M. Hart and A. R. Pilling, *The Tiwi of Northern Australia.* New York: Holt, 1960. J. C. Goodale, "The Tiwi of Northern Australia." In: *Funeral Customs the World Over.* R. W. Habersten, ed. 1963. [Reviewed in *AA* 81(1):204–206, 1979.]

The Moveable Feast (1993) 28 min. Beth Harrington (PR). Dist: UCEMC VR$50, VS$195, order #38221. *This documentary follows a group of Italian-Americans from Boston to their ancestral hometown in Sicily to participate in the Feast of the Madonna del Soccorso, also known as the Fisherman's Feast. This is a companion piece to an earlier film, "Ave Maria: The Story of the Fisherman's Feast."*

Moving Mountains: The Story of the Yiu Mien 58 min. Elaine Velazquez (FM). Dist: FL FR$100, VR$75, FS$895, VS$445. *A look at the Yiu Mien, a group of Southeast Asian refugees who settled in the Pacific Northwest. In their ancient society in the mountains of Laos, this hill tribe had no electricity, cars or any other 20th-century technology. Their involvement with the CIA during the Vietnam War forced the Mien to lose their homeland. Fleeing as refugees to this country, they were catapulted from one century into another. Through the words of the elders and rare archival footage of the Mien in their mountain homeland, their ancient culture is brought to light. Complex realities of their struggle to adapt to American culture is portrayed. Religious rituals are performed in city apartments, women in traditional dress shop at a mall, women farm with babies on their backs beside freeway traffic. This is a vivid portrayal of the Yiu Mien, a people caught between two worlds.* [Reviewed by Malcolm Collier, *AA* 95:253–255, 1993.]

Mrs. Case 14 min. Barrie Howells, George C. Stoney (PR), Pierre Lasry (DI). Dist: NFBC. *A single mother.* [Reviewed by Roslyn L. Feldberg, *AA* 79:208, 1977.]

Mrs. Mixon 58 min. Hubert Smith, Ernest Johnson (DI). Dist: Dept. of Photography and Cinematography, Ohio State University, 156 West 19th Ave., Columbus, OH 43210. *An African-American woman from rural Alabama tries to get therapy in a Midwestern University hospital.* [Reviewed by Robert B. Edgerton, *AA* 73:981, 1971].

Mt. Athos: The First One Thousand Years (1977) 56 min. John Keshishoglou (FM). Dist: School of Communications, Ithaca College, Ithaca, NY 14850. [Reviewed by Peter S. Allen, *AA* 81:474, 1979.]

Mudhorse (1971) 12 min. Attiat El-Abnoudi (FM). Dist: FRIF FR$25, FS$245. *On the banks of the Nile, workers labor in an open-air brick factory, using methods thousands of years old.*

Mujer de milfuegos (Woman of a Thousand Fires) Chick Strand (FM). Dist: CCC FR$25, FS$250. *A kind of hermetic fantasy film. An expressionistic, surrealistic portrait of a Latin American woman. Not a personal portrait so much as an evocation of the consciousness of women in rural parts of such countries as Spain, Greece, and Mexico; women who wear black from the age of 15 and spend their entire lives giving birth, preparing food, and tending to household and farm responsibilities. Mujer de Milfuegos depicts in poetic, almost abstract terms their daily repetitive tasks as a form of obsessive ritual. The film uses dramatic action to express the thoughts and feelings of a woman living within this culture. As she becomes transformed, her isolation and desire, conveyed in symbolic activities, endows her with a universal quality. Through experiences of ecstasy and madness we are shown different aspects of the human personality. The final sequence presents her awareness of another level of knowledge.*

The Muleteers (Los arrieros) (1992) 15 min. Maria Dolores Fernandez Figares (FM). Dist: Centro de Investigaciones, Ethnologicas Angel Ganivet, Area de Cultura-Diputación, Plaza de los Girones 1, 18009 Granada, Spain; fax 345-822-8591. *The filmmaker accompanies some of the last muleteers and their donkeys during a full working day in the streets of Granada, Spain.*

Mulga Seed Ceremony (Australian Institute of Aboriginal Studies Series) (1969) 25 min. Dist: UCEMC FR$32, FS$340; PSU(PCR) order #3163, FR$10.10. *The Mulga Seed Ceremony is meant to promote the fertility of mulga, a desert tree valued for food and fuel. A legendary conflict between the Mulga Seed Men and the Lizard Men is enacted, and blood is ritually spilled. The performers then climb a 1,500-foot ridge to visit a small cave where the sacred boards were once kept, and they continue their ceremony against the spectacular heights of the Petermann Range. The film observes visits to several sacred stones and the accompanying exhortations of the ritual leaders; the use of mixed blood and sand for body ornament; and the symbolic casting of mulga seed to the four winds. At night, the men perform a sedentary dance around a fire. The next morning, they visit a cave before painting themselves for the afternoon's ceremonial conclusion—the vigorous dance of the Mulga Seed Men.* [Reviewed by Richard A. Gould, *AA* 74:189–191, 1972.] Restricted use. This film contains material of a secret/sacred nature and should only be screened for study purposes by appropriate groups.

Mun Blong Custom (see The Tribal Eye Series)

Munni ('Little Girl'): Childhood and Art in Mithila (1983) 29 min. Joe Elder (PR), Raymond Owens, Ron Hess and

Cheryl Graff (DI). Dist: UW-SAAC VR$25, VS$250. *"Munni is a small girl who lives in a village of Bihar. The region, Mithila, is famous for its folk paintings, a craft followed mainly by women.... Shows the beginning of Munni's initiation into what seems to be a matrilineally descending cottage industry, the products of which are sold as far away as New York or Paris."* [From the review by Paul Hockings, AA 86:807–809, 1984.]

Murga 22 min. Yvonne Hannemann (DI). Dist: Washburn Films, 9 East 32nd St., New York, NY 10016. *Hindu ceremony in Sri Lanka.* [Reviewed by Paul Hockings, AA 76:219, 1974.]

The Muria (1982) 50 min. Melissa Llewelyn-Davies (PR) for the BBC Worlds Apart series. Dist: FI FR$100, FS$800, VS$480. *Deals with tribal peoples in India. "The focus of the film is the well-known Muria institution of the 'youth dormitory,' or ghotul, in which adolescent boys and girls sleep, work, and enjoy leisure pursuits.... The central theme of the film is the emotional conflict suffered by young Muria—especially Muria girls—when the time for their marriage arrives and they are forced to leave the ghotul and break off the close relationships they have developed."* [From the review by Sylvia Vatuk, AA 88:271–273, 1986.]

Murray Avenue (1987) 28 min. Sheila Chamovitz (FM). Dist: NDF VR$50, FS$450, VS$270. *"About a once-vibrant Jewish neighborhood in Pittsburgh as its last immigrant businesses, the kosher butcher and bakery, close."* [From the review by Riv-Ellen Prell, AA 93:519–520, 1991.]

The Mursi (Disappearing World Series) (Also called *In Search of Cool Ground: The Mursi*) (1985) 52 min. David Turton (AN). Dist: PSU VR$14, order #51151. *The Mursi of southwestern Ethiopia have no chiefs or leaders. They practice a remarkable form of democracy in which all decisions are reached through tribal debates. Now, drought and famine are driving the Mursi into contact with the outside world.*

The Mursi (Disappearing World Series) (1974) 58 min. David Turton (AN). Dist: PSU order #61402. *A shortage of grazing during a drought forced the Mursi of Ethiopia into conflict with their neighbors, the Bodi. After many Mursi died fighting, they responded to Bodi peace proposals. This film shows the extraordinary democratic process of the Mursi as they came together to make life-and-death decisions.* [Reviewed by Wendy James and Tsehai Berhane Selassic, *RAIN* 16(6), 1976. Peter Loizos, AA 82:584, 1980.]

The Mursi: Nitha (Disappearing World Series) (1991) 51 min. David Turton (AN). Dist: FIV VS$198. *Watch the age set ceremony, as the Nitha bestows adulthood on an entire generation of Mursi men for the first time in 30 years. Witness a rich banquet of images and emotions, sadly overshadowed by the constant threat to Mursi survival from their neighbors, the Bume, who are armed with automatic rifles, and recently massacred 500 Mursi.* [Reviewed by Jon Abbink, AA 94:1027–1028, 1992. Reviewed in *VISR* 8:106, 1992.]

The Mursi: The Land Is Bad (Disappearing World Series) (1991) 52 min. David Turton (AN). Dist: FIV VS$198. *The Mursi, inhabitants of the Omo Valley on the far edge of Southwest Ethiopia, feel that after a series of natural and man-made disasters, the very land they live on is turning against them. Despite this, they remain faithful to old ways and traditions, herding cattle and cultivating sorghum, even as the Omo's flood level drops continuously.* [Reviewed by Jon Abbink, AA 94:1027–1028, 1992.]

Music, Dance, and Festival among the Waiapi Indians of Brazil (The Waiapi Indians of Brazil Series) (1988) 39 min. Victor Fuks (PR). Dist: IUAVC VR$25, VS$160, order #CC3779. *Music and dance are extremely important to Waiapi culture, and much time is spent daily in music- and festival-related activity. Festivals are used to reenact events in their history and mythology, to celebrate certain animal species important to Waiapi life, to transmit their cultural heritage, and to reinforce cultural identity. Five festivals are examined in which viewers are introduced to several pervasive features of Waiapi culture, including the structure of the festivals, the importance of caxiri or manioc beer to the festivals, a variety of musical instruments and songs, and how Waiapi identity and social order are reinforced by these communal celebrations.*

Music from Oil Drums (1956) 15 min. (A Folklore Research Film by Peter and Toshi Seeger.) Dist: FIM/RF FR$20, FS$150. *How many have heard the enchanting music produced by a steel drum band and wondered how and where these musical instruments were created? On a visit to Trinidad, Pete Seeger met the people who make, tune, and play the oil drums, learned just how they do it, and the fascinating history of how it all started. Returning to his home in the United States with some sample drums, we see him and his backyard neighbors beating out some of the infectious calypso tunes themselves.*

Music of Africa (1963) 30 min. Lela Swift (DI), Elenor F. Finkelstein (PR), NET TV/NY State Ed. Dept., WNDT, NY (PR). Dist: IU FR$9.50, FS$250. *Fela Sowande of Nigeria—a leading African musicologist, composer, and organist—with a group of Nigerian musicians shows how contemporary African music has mingled traditional African and Western idioms to create new forms. African music places greater stress on melody than on rhythm, which makes the music closely resemble African dialects in which meaning is expressed by tonal inflection. Because of this relationship, the talking drum can be used for either purely musical functions or the transmitting of messages.*

La música de la gente 28 min. Dist: Blue Sky Productions, P.O. Box 548, Santa Fe, NM 87501, FS$400, VS$250. *Documentary on contemporary New Mexican Spanish music featuring some of New Mexico's most popular musicians like Al Hurricane, Roberto Griego, Miguel Archibeque, and La Chicanita.*

A Musical Tradition in Banaras 40 min. Dist: UW-SAAS FR$30, FS$295. *Joins Panchu Maharaj, a classical drummer and musical instructor at Banaras Hindu University, in his village home to witness the more private aspects of his life. While performing everyday activities, often with other members of his family, Panchu describes his approach to life and musical perfection. He and his sons and nephews conduct a late-night practice session, where music is played in the casual atmosphere in which it is most frequently* heard, and where musical techniques are mastered under the eye of the expert. This film provides an unusually human view of an Indian master musician.

Musique et danse des chasseurs Gow (Music and Dances of the Gow Hunters) (1965) 20 min. Jean Rouch (DI), Centre National de la Recherche Scientifique, Comite du Film Ethnographique (PR). Dist: CFE; DER. *The film brings together different elements of ritual music of the Gow hunters of the Niger.*

Muslims in Mango (Anufom Series) (1974) 35 min. Emile A. B. von Rouveroy van Nieuwaal (Dl, CA). Dist: Phita Stern, Foundation for Film and Science, Hengeveldstraat 29, Utrecht, The Netherlands. *This film deals with two aspects to the Islam in Sansanne-Mango, North Togo. Treated are: the migration of the Anufom from Ano in Ivory Coast to North Togo; teaching the Koran; divination and preparation of amulets and mourning prayers; the Friday prayer has been attended in and outside the mosque, both in the men's and women's section.*

My Country Djarrakpi (1981) 16 min. Ian Dunlop (FM). Dist: FAA. *Paintings form an integral part of the religious life of the Yolngu of northeast Arnhem land. Every painting is owned by a particular clan. Each tells of the creative acts of the Ancestral Beings; each is, in a way, a map of a particular area of clan land, a clan's title deed to that land. These concepts are brought vividly to life. Narritjin discusses in detail the significance of one of his paintings at Djarrakpi. Then on the wind-swept sand dunes of Djarrakpi itself, he explains the significance of the features of the landscape and the relationship between the Yolngu, their art, and their land.*

My Crazy Life [Reviewed in *VISR* 8:125, 1992.]

My Family and Me (Rural Greece: Desertion, Migration, Village Life Series) (1986) 75 min. Dr. Colette Piault (AN, DI), Graham Johnston (CA, ED), Georges Nivoix (SR). Dist: PSA FR$90, VS$375; LFDQ; B.R.F. Inc., Jean-Claude DuBost, 777 14th Street, NW, Suite 747, Washington, DC 20005; (202) 638-1789. *The film shows one specific aspect of migration: family relationships. Thanassakis, a 13-year-old boy, is staying with his grandparents in a Greek village while his parents are staying with his younger brother in Zurich, Switzerland. Shot through three periods, winter in the village, summer in the village (when his parents returned for holiday), and Christmas in Zurich, when Thanassakis goes to visit his family. The film is an attempt to understand the family relationships not through interviews but following and filming moments of daily life, showing their emotional family atmosphere. It may sometimes look like a fiction film, but nothing has been acted nor asked for.* [Reviewed by Jane K. Cowan, *AA* 90:491, 1988.]

My Father, My Country (1990) 1 hour. Meg Taylor (FM), Film Australia (PR). Dist: CRM VR$80, VS$295. *In 1938, three Australian patrol officers including Jim Taylor made an extraordinary journey into the unexplored highlands of New Guinea. Their mission: explain to Stone Age tribes that 20th-century civilization was about to arrive and change their lives. In 1988, Meg Taylor traced her father's footsteps through bush country, nearly trackless jungles and a near vertical 2,000-meter climb over the region's longest mountain range. She discovered the effects of 50 years of civilization upon several tribal villages: men had abandoned their roles as warriors to work in the gold fields; women remained the main providers of the society; children were being educated in contemporary ways. This is a remarkable study of how an indigenous population accepted civilization while still preserving its identity.*

My Town—Mio Paese (1988) 26 min. Katherine Gulla (FM). Dist: UCEMC VR$35, VS$330, order #37735. *Since the early 1900s, a steady flow of immigrants from Palermiti, a picturesque hillside village in Calabria, southern Italy, has been coming to America. This video shows that although these immigrants abandoned their homeland for a better life in the New World, they brought with them strong and lasting family, religion, and cultural traditions. A thriving community from Palermiti now exists in eastern Massachusetts. On-location footage and personal interviews in Palermiti and in Massachusetts demonstrate the enduring links between the two groups of Palermitesi. The most important event in any rural Italian town is the patron saint's feast day, which is central to this story. Celebrated annually, the festas provide spirited scenes of religious processions, dancing, and singing.* [Reviewed by Carole Counihan, *AA* 92:268–270, 1990. Reviewed in *VISA* 4:78, 1991.]

Mysteries of Mankind (1987) 58 min. Barbara Jampel (PR) for the National Geographic Society and WQED/Pittsburg. Dist: NGS FS$395, VS$80; Karol FR$50. *"This impressive National Geographic Society special is quite simply the best treatment of human evolution ever done on film. It is up to date, uncompromising and never condescending.... The program unfolds chronolgically, beginning with evidence for australopithecines, the oldest recognized hominids. There follows a systematic examination of subsequent developments—homo erectus, Neanderthals, and 'modern' humans. Vintage footage and stills are used to document some of the important early discoveries of Raymond Dart, the Leakeys and Jane Goodall."* [From the review by Peter S. Allen, *ARCH* 41(2):68, 1988.]

Mystery Murals of Baja California 29 min. Dist: UCEMC FR$35, FS$400, VS$280. *Documents the work of Harry Crosby, a photographer and amateur archaeologist, in seeking and discovering new information concerning the rock art of Baja, California. Not a scientific film in the strict sense, but rather a story of adventure, of a man driven to explore and record a phenomenon for posterity.*

Mystery of Nefertiti (1975) 46 min. Dist: IUAVC FR$18, FS$540; UCEMC. *Follows the six-year effort of a team of archaeologists, using computers, to reconstruct, on paper, the huge, pillared courtyard and temple of the Egyptian Queen, Nefertiti, as it existed some 35,000 years ago.*

The Mystery of Stonehenge (1964) 58 min. Columbia Broadcasting Company (PR). Dist: CRM VR$80, VS$195; PSU(PCR) order # 50004, FR$20.20, FS$610. *Stonehenge, the great stone monument that has stood on England's Salisbury Plain for 4,000 years, has long been the object of speculation. The film considers many legends that have* *grown up around it, and reenacts the best known—the religious ceremonies of the Druids. The design of the structure, its stones, archways, holes, and tombs (called barrows), are clearly shown and examined. The source of some of the massive stones is traced to distant Wales, that of others to nearby Marlborough Downs. Models demonstrate how the great stones may have been transported and placed in position by an ancient people who did not yet possess the wheel. The major importance of this extraordinary documentary is its application of modern scientific methods and equipment in testing various theories, especially Dr. Gerald Hawkins's claim that the monument was built by primitive man for use as an observatory and an astronomical "computer" that could help predict eclipses of the sun and moon. An astronomer of the Harvard-Smithsonian Astrophysical Observatory, Dr. Hawkins tests his theory at midsummer and midwinter, applying to the problem electronic computers and precision motion picture cameras. Three of his sun alignments are checked and confirmed. Twice in 1974—as "predicted" by the Stonehenge "computer"—an eclipse of the moon occurred, and the films made of these eclipses are seen. Dr. Hawkins's theory has been vigorously challenged by some British archaeologists, and the film samples reactions, pro and con, by presenting the comments and discussion of leading U.S. and British authorities. [Reviewed by Eric Higgs, AA 68:1588, 1966.]*

Mystery of the Anasazi A series of 140 color slides with booklet by M. H. Spieghel. Dist: Logos Signum Publications, 19122 Lindsay Lane, Huntington Beach, CA 92646. [Reviewed by David Braun, ARCH 33(3):62, 1981.] Bibliography: *Anasazi Pueblo and Cliff Dwellers.*

Mystery of the Anasazi (1976) 60 min. BBC NOVA (PR). Dist: SU FR$35. *About 300 years ago, ruins were discovered near the point where Colorado, Utah, Arizona, and New Mexico meet. The people were called "Anasazi" or the builders, and archaeologists have been trying to figure out who they were, where they come from, and what happened to them. By the year A.D. 750, they became gardeners and started to build above ground. Pueblo Bonito (located in Chaco Canyon, NM) represents the high point in Anasazi culture. A planned town that covers three acres and includes 800 rooms was grouped around a double central plaza. In places, rooms were stacked five stories high and revealed architectural techniques that surpassed anything that was being built in northwest Europe at a comparable date. And yet they had no metal tools, no horses, and had not yet heard of the wheel. Film is highlighted throughout by footage of important sites and artifacts.*

The Mystery of the Lost Red Paint People: The Discovery of a Prehistoric North American Sea Culture (1987) 58 min. Ted Timreck (FM), Will Goetzmann (PR, WR). Dist: Ted Timreck, 35 East 30th St., New York, NY 10016; (212) 685-1134; BF FR$90, FS$895, VS$495. *"Deals with one of the oldest 'mysteries' in New World archeology, the significance of the red ochre burials in northeastern North America."* [From the review by David Sanger, AA 90:779–780, 1988. Reviewed by William W. Fitzhugh, ARCH 40(6):71–84, 1987 under the title "Secrets of the Lost Red Paint People."]

Mystery of the Maya 58 min. Hugh Johnson and Suzanna Johnston, WNET/13 (PR). Dist: WNET/13 Media Service, 356 West 58th St., New York, NY 10019. [Reviewed by Mark P. Leone, AA 78:376–377, 1976.]

The Myth of Peribo (El mito de Peribo) (1988) 8 min. Alonso Toro and Maria Christina Diaz Silva (FM). Dist: Center for International Media Research, Mijndensedijk 74, 3631 NS Nieuwersluis, The Netherlands; telephone 312-943-3459. *A Yanomamo origin myth, depicting them as "sons of the moon," comes to life through claymation.*

Myth of the Pharaohs (1971) 13 min. Hungarofilm (PR). Dist: ACI. *Animated.* [Reviewed by Timothy Kendall, AA 78:133, 1976.]

MYTH ONTO FILM: A TRILOGY FROM NATIVE AUSTRALIA, NATIVE AMERICA AND THE KABBALAH Robert Ascher (AR). Dist: CUAV VS$59. *Each film in this trilogy is a cameraless, hand-painted, animated film. Some 7,000 pictures are drawn or scratched directly onto 35mm clear film. The technique is particularly appropriate for representing a myth, wedding the potentially dreamlike characteristics of the cinema experience and the other worldly logic that myths and dreams so often seem to share.* See descriptions under individual titles:

- **Cycle**
- **Blue: A Tlingit Odyssey**
- **Bar Yohai**

Myths and the Moundbuilders (Odyssey Series, second season) (1981) Graham Chedd (WR, FM), John K. White (AN). Dist: DER FR$50, FS$500. [Reviewed by David Braun, ARCH 34(6):74, 1981.]

N!ai, The Story of a !Kung Woman (Odyssey Series, first season) (1980) 58 min. John Marshall (PR, DI), Adrienne Linden (DI), Patricia Draper (AN). Dist: DER FR$65, FS$675. *The film deals with the destruction of "natural economy." The film portrays the biography of N!ai, from early childhood to middle age, but she and her band are not seen in isolation, rather the film shows how N!ai and her band is transformed from being a relatively independent group of foragers to being confined as (semi) dependent squatters on a reservation that is officially known as "Bushmanland," and how this colonial penetration has affected N!ai's life.* [Reviewed by Robert Gordon, AA 83:740–741, 1981. Robert Mishler, SBF 23:113, 1987.]

Nadlok: Crossing Place of the Deer (1987) 30 min. Bryan C. Gordon (DI). Dist: CMOC. *Nadlok is a tiny river island site in the central part of Canada's Northwest Territories, on the edge of the Arctic circle. Here in 1985 and 1986, Bryan Gordon of the Canadian Museum of Civilization excavated and reconstructed two pairs of Inuit winter and summer huts. He was looking for answers to questions like: Who lived here? From where had they come? Where did they go? Why did they leave? Gordon's excavations revealed that between A.D. 1450 and 1700 the site was lived in by a small group of Copper Inuit who apparently had moved from the coast to this Island site to exploit the caribou who cross here in great numbers during their annual migration. This film* offers a step-by-step documentation of the 1986 excavation, with a heavily descriptive narration by Gordon. About halfway through the film, the scene shifts to an office in the Canadian Museum of Civilization, where Gordon and a young woman discuss a tray of artifacts from Nadlok. [Reviewed by Peter S. Allen, ARCH 42(3):74, 1989.]

Naked Spaces: Living Is Round (1985) 135 min. Jean-Paul Bourdier (PR), Trinh T. Minh-ha (DI). Dist: WMM FR$225, FS$1900, VS$495. *Explores the rhythm and ritual of life in the rural environments of six West African countries. The nonlinear structure challenges the traditions of ethnographic filmmaking, while sensuous sights and sounds lead the viewer on a poetic journey to the most inaccessible parts of the African continent, the private interaction of people in their living spaces.* [Reviewed in VISA 4:160, 1991.]

Namekas: Music in Lake Chambri (Traditional Music of Papua New Guinea Series) (1979) 53 min. Les McLaren (DI). Dist: DER FR$90, VR$60, VS$450. *On the southern shores of Lake Chambri live 1,500 Pondo-speaking villagers. A constant dialogue between man and spirits that have individual personalities and powers, is carried on through various communicative media, including invocations, dreams, and music. As this film beautifully reveals, there is a wealth of musical tradition in Lake Chambri: carved wooden drums whose lively vibrations are said to shake loose ripened fruits for harvest; pairs of sacred bamboo flutes used in boys' initiations and concealed from women; orchestras of flutes identified with dogs or turkeys; flutes captured in warfare used with dance masks to invoke fish; and the panpipe with its melodies of mourning.* [Reviewed by Deborah Gewertz, AA 88:521–522, 1986.]

Nanduti, a Paraguayan Lace (1978) 18 min. Annick Sanjurjo, Albert Casciero (Dl). Dist: UNI FR$45.90, FS$350. *A unique lace-making technique. Nanduti means "cobweb" in Guarani, the native language of Paraguay. The basic shape of this Paraguayan lace is a "solar disc"—a circular doily in which cobweb-like threads radiate from a central hub. On these rays are laced patterns that represent a rich diversity of natural and man-made objects. When they are joined together, these doilies form an endless variety of decorative motifs that are used to adorn everything from luxurious shawls and tablecloths to everyday clothing. The film introduces nanduti through one of the many legends that surround its origin. Then, as the camera follows a peasant woman as she goes about her daily chores, the symbolic patterns of nanduti are juxtaposed with the everyday objects these patterns represent. Finally, we watch as a lacemaker creates a typical piece of nanduti.* [Reviewed by John M. Schechter, AA 89:525–532, 1987.]

Nang Yai: Thai Shadow Puppet Drama 20 min. Banchong Kosalwat and Stephanie Krebs (FM). Dist: Stephanie Krebs, 300 Highland St., West Newton, MA 02165. *Nang Yai is a rapidly disappearing form of Thai shadow drama that presents episodes of the Thai Ramayana. The film features a performance by the last Nang Yai troupe in existence, with descriptive narration by the 83-year-old leader of the troupe. Although composed of local farmers, this troupe continues a long tradition of what once was a royally sponsored dramatic art, with a history reaching back to India and the Hinduized culture of Srivijaya in Indonesia. Since the film was made specifically for Thai audiences, it is of particular interest to anthropologists. Most ethnographic films are made about non-Western peoples for Western audiences; in the case of Nang Yai, however, the conceptual categories and cultural assumptions of the film are purely Thai, and English-speakers are only allowed to eavesdrop on this film through short, but loaded subtitles. The film becomes particularly valuable for anthropologists, especially those not familiar with Southeast Asia, for it challenges them to comprehend the conceptual categories and cultural assumptions underlying the brief subtitles. For instance, at one point in the film the narrator (the leader of the troupe) states: My teacher warned: "Put up the screen properly. Since the screen is sacred, fill in the dirt around the poles of the screen with your hands, not feet." Underlying this subtitle are three basic cultural assumptions that represent key values in Thai society: (1) Dance, drama, and their accompanying paraphernalia are highly sacred, (2) the foot is the most profane part of the body, and (3) veneration of teachers and elders is extremely important in this hierarchical society. Skilled teachers of advanced anthropology or area studies courses may also find this film very useful as primary source material through which their students can search for the basic values and norms of the society that created this cultural product.*

Nanook of the North 55 min. Robert Flaherty (FM). Dist: Sound versions; NYU FR$22; PSU(PCR) order #59149N, FR$10.50; MOMA original silent version. *The great one.* [Reviewed by Ian Jarvie, AA 80:196–197, 1978. Reviewed in VISA 1:19, 1987.]

Nanook Revisited 60 min. Dist: FHS VS$149, order #DH-2250. *Robert Flaherty's "Nanook of the North" created the very genre of film documentary, with its documentation of Nanook the Inuit and the Eskimo traditions that were even then being threatened by the influences of whites. This program revisits the sites of Flaherty's filming and learns that he staged much of what he filmed, sired children to whose future he paid no heed, and is himself now part of Inuit myth.*

Narritjin at Djarrakpi: Part 1 (1981) 50 min. Ian Dunlop (FM). Dist: FAA. *Narritjin and his family have recently left Yirrkala and are establishing their own settlement at Djarrakpi, an important Manggalili clan site on the northern headland of Blue Mud Bay. Narritjin now has the opportunity to teach his sons not only the skills of living in the bush but, more importantly, the sacred law of his clan. He and his sons carefully strip huge sheets of bark from stringy bark trees for use both as building material and as a canvas for paintings. Here at Djarrakpi, they live largely off the land and the sea. Oysters, fish, turtle eggs, and wild honey are part of their diet. Much of their time is used in producing bark paintings and carvings. Through paintings, Narritjin teaches his sons about their clan land and its ancestral history, for within each painting is embedded part of the sacred story of the creator ancestral beings who bequeathed to the Manggalili clan its land.*

Narritjin at Djarrakpi: Part 2 (1981) 39 min. Ian Dunlop (FM). Dist: FAA. *Narritjin's community at Djarrakpi has increased with the arrival of two married daughters and their families. One of Narritjin's sons makes a Yidaki (drone-pipe) for the tourist trade. Wild honey is an important delicacy, and everyone makes short work of a wild bee's nest they find. The young men are seen fishing with spear thrower and spear along the shark-infested shores of the Blue Mud Bay. Narritjin continues with his paintings and tells of his feelings about Djarrakpi and of his hopes for the future.*

Narritjin in Canberra (1981) 40 min. Ian Dunlop (FM). Dist: FAA. *In 1978, Narritjin and his son, Banapana, were awarded fellowships as visiting artists at the Australian National University in Canberra. For three months, they and their families worked at the ANU producing a major collection of Manggalili clan art. Narritjin conducts a seminar with anthropology students and explains his technique of bark painting and the religious significance of his designs.*

A Nation Uprooted: Afghan Refugees in Pakistan (1987) 29 min. Judith Mann and Debra Denker (FM). Dist: POU VR$35, VS$295. *This film is set in the Kachagari refugee camp in Pakistan—one of the numerous camps created for Afghan refugees by the Government of Pakistan. The major focus of the film is to see how the traditional Afghan art is being continued and preserved in times of turmoil and difficulty. The film also features interviews school teachers, poets, and common women besides craftspeople.* [Reviewed by Joanna Kirkpatrick, *AA* 91:272–273, 1989.]

Nations within a Nation: Sovereignty and Native American Communities (1986) 59 min. Donald N. Brown and Mark Ringwald (PR). Dist: NAPBC VS$110. "*Explores native rights.... The tribal sovereignty issue in the United States is reviewed by legal scholars.*" [From the review by Harald Prins, *AA* 90:774–778, 1988.]

Native Cat Ceremonies of Watarka 21 min. Australian National Film Board (PR). Dist: IUAVC FR$9.75. *Shows the various phases of the initiation rites of Australian natives of Watarka, including their ceremonial songs and dances. Presents the songs in native dialect, which is interpreted by the narrator. Points out that their dance movements reflect some of their daily activities, such as digging for water, stalking and spearing a kangaroo, waiting for the arrival of the big game from the hunt, and moving into another village site.*

Native Land: Nomads of the Dawn 58 min. Alvin H. Perlmutter (EP), Jamake Highwater (WR, H), John Peaslee (DI). Dist: CG VR$95, VS$495. *A fascinating exploration of the history and culture of the Native Americans who discovered and civilized the Americas. The story concerns a band of Indians, cut off from the rest of humanity after a long migration in search of food, who accidentally 'discovered' America when they walked across a landbridge between northern Asia and Alaska that was formed during the Ice Age. Cut off from the rest of the world, these Indians started to make their way south. It is a story of remarkable achievements, brilliant inventions, fierce political struggles, unique religious ideals, and colorful mythology. The films offers unusual insight into the function of myths in contemporary society. It shows how all people devise a cosmology out of practical and mythic experiences, and how that cosmology becomes the basis upon which people build every aspect of their diverse societies. When a society's mythology changes, the society changes.* [Reviewed by Robert L. Bee, *AA* 90:235–237, 1988. Reviewed by Bro. John S. Wozniak, *SBF* 22:189, 1987.]

The Nature of a Continent (The Africans Series) (1986) 60 min. Ali Mazrui (AN). Dist: ACPB VR$100, VS$198. "*The first program in the series The Africans, effectively portrays the relationship between the geography and history of this region. . . . Not all observers will agree with the narrator's somewhat anticapitalist, anticommercial perspective, but the program is well reasoned and well documented and deserves serious consideration.*" [From the review by George H. Odell, *SBF* 22:319, 1987.]

The Nature of Culture (The Faces of Culture Series) (1983) 30 min. Dist: IM VS$119, order #SF02. *Footage of !Kung hunters of Africa, Txukarrame Indians of the Amazon River Basin, and the Boran of Kenya shows how different cultures balance the needs of individuals and groups. The program examines the learning and sharing of behavior, beliefs, and attitudes in different cultures, using American culture as a basis for comparison. A segment documenting the devastating results of one culture's inability to adapt to a changing environment illustrates the importance of flexibility for survival. The program also explores the concepts of shared culture and learned culture and investigates the role of symbols in a culture.*

Nature's Way (1974) 22 min. Dist: APPAL FR$35, FS$350. *Many mountaineers still care for their own ailments with the help of herbs, home remedies, and Indian folklore; midwives are still in popular demand. This film shows several people as they explain their cures and remedies and covers a midwife as she assists in the delivery of twins.*

The Navajo, Part I (1963) 29 min. NET(PR). Dist: IUAVC FR$9.50. *Presents a visit to the Navajo reservation to discover the values held by this indigenous community. Questions are put to an Indian family to find out each member's duties, responsibilities, and privileges. Compares Navajo and modern medical practices and religious rituals and beliefs. Concludes by discussing the problems of reconciling traditional Navajo ways with modern technology.*

The Navajo, Part II (1963) 29 min. NET (PR). Dist: IUAVC FR$9.50. *Presents a visit to Windowrock, Arizona, to interview members of the Navajo Tribal Council. Discusses the problems of working within the tribal organizational patterns and of the continuing force of tradition. Questions are answered concerning education, agriculture, religion, and the adaptations to be made in light of modern science and new social values.*

Navajo Canyon Country 13 min. Daggett Productions (PR). Dist: IUAVC FR$7.50. *Depicts the way of life of the*

Navajos and provides some of the historical background of Indian life in Arizona and New Mexico. Shows the Navajos' geographic surroundings, sheep herding and farming activities, home construction and arrangement, some recreational activities, ceremonial dances and rituals, and commercial contacts with the white proprietor of a trading post. Shows the remaining evidence of former Indian inhabitants, including the ruins of Pueblo cliff dwellers.

Navajo Children 11 min. Dist: IUAVC FR$5. *Shows the experiences of a Navajo boy and girl of Arizona and New Mexico in moving with their family from their winter quarters to their summer home. Depicts such activities as camping at night, a marksmanship contest for young Navajo boys, repairing the new home, planting crops, caring for the sheep and goats, and weaving rugs.*

Navajo Code Talkers 28 min. Dist: OWM R$70, FS$500, VS$275. *From the earliest days of World War II, Japanese cryptographers displayed an uncanny ability to break American communication codes. The U.S military response was ingenious. A small group of Native Americans, Navajos, were recruited to serve as radio operators. These soldiers, using their native language, developed a code that the Japanese never cracked. The film tells the story of Native American courage and remembers the Navajo contribution to the U.S. victory in World War II.*

Navajo Country 10 min. Dist: IFB FR$17.50, FS$175, VS$175; IUAVC FR$6.25. *Nomadic Navajo raise sheep and goats for food and the wool used in clothing and handwoven rugs and blankets. They expertly craft jewelry of silver and semiprecious stones.*

NAVAHO FILM THEMSELVES Dist: MOMA; NYU. All seven purchased together receive a 10 percent discount. *A series of seven silent films made by Navaho Indians about themselves. Six Navaho bilinguals and one mono-lingual, all of whom had previously been differentially exposed to film, were taught to conceive, photograph, and edit 16mm silent film under the instruction of Sol Worth (Annenberg School of Communication, University of Pennsylvania) and John Adair (San Francisco State College). The purpose of the project was to see if motion picture film, conceived, photographed, and manipulated by a people such as the Navaho, would reveal aspects of cognition and values that may be inhibited, not observable or analyzable when the means of investigation is dependent on verbal exchange and, particularly, when it is done in the language of the investigator.* [Reviewed by John Collier, AA 76:481–486, 1974]. Suggested supplements: John Adair and Sol Worth, "The Navaho as Filmmaker: A Brief Report of Research in the Cross-Cultural Aspects of Communication." AA 69:76–78, 1967. Sol Worth and John Adair, "Navaho Filmmakers." AA 72:9–34, 1970. Sol Worth and John Adair. *Through Navaho Eyes.* Indiana, 1972.

PROGRAM 1

• **A Navaho Weaver** 22 min. Silent. FS$132. *Susie Benally, a young Navaho, depicts her mother weaving at the loom and includes all of the necessary steps prior to the actual weaving.*

• **Second Weaver** 9 min. FS$54. *This film is the result of Susie Benally teaching her mother to use a camera. Similar to the daughter's film in theme, it depicts the daughter weaving a belt.*

• **Old Antelope Lake** 11 min. Silent. FS$66. *This film begins at the source of the lake, then moves around the lake showing the unity between natural things and human beings in the environment. Made by Mike Anderson.*

PROGRAM 2

• **The Navaho Silversmith** 20 min. Silent. FS$120. *Similar to the weaver films in structure, this film traces the creation in silver of some small Yeibachai figures—from the mining of the silver to the finished figure. Made by Johnny Nelson.*

• **The Shallow Well Project** 14 min. Silent FS$84. *This film by Johnny Nelson is very different in style and approach from Navaho Silversmith. It illustrates the building of a shallow well to replace an open pond once used for water supply.*

PROGRAM 3

• **Intrepid Shadows** 18 min. Silent. FS$108. Al Clah (FM). *One of the most complex films and least understood by the other Navaho, it has been called by Margaret Mead "one of the finest examples of animism shown on film." Contrary to the other films, this film deals with subjective rather than objective aspects of Navaho life. In the film, Al Clah attempts to reconcile the Western notion of god with his traditional Navaho notion of gods. Clah was a very acculturated outsider in the community, influenced by French films. Clah wanted to express basic ideas of Navaho oppositions: energy-calm; sun-shadow; direct gaze-averted gaze; and the danger of the spider web. The film searches for peace in the circle. Clah wanted the audience to feel, at first, tense and grotesque, and, finally, relaxed and calm. It is about an intrusion that threatens the calm of the world. Needs to be used with the book by Worth & Adair. Focusing questions: What do the shadows do? Why the Yeibechai mask? What happens with the spider web?* Bibliography: Sol Worth and John Adair, *Through Navaho Eyes.* Bloomington: Indiana University Press, 1972.

• **The Spirit of the Navaho** 21 min. Silent. FS$126. *This film begins with an old medicine man looking for roots to use in a ceremony. He prepares for a sand painting and part of the actual curing ceremony is featured in which the patient appears. Made by Maxine and Maryjane Tsosie.*

The Navajo Indian 11 min. Coronet Films (PR). Dist: IUAVC FR$6.50. *Shows a Navajo in his daily life and depicts his ability as silversmith and weaver. Includes the Navajo's native habitat, customs, and ceremonials.*

Navajo Indians 11 min. Dist: IUAVC FR$5. *Tells the story of Taska and Alnaba, a young Navajo couple who are betrothed. Portrays their native environment and such activities as building a home, tilling the soil, tending sheep, carding the wool, and weaving it into colorful blankets. Also shows barter at a local trading post, the performance of native dances, the wedding ceremony, and the wedding feast.*

Navajo Indians of the Painted Desert 9 min. Dist: IUAVC FR$5. *Pictures the life of the Navajo Indians of the Painted Desert. Includes their homes, clothing, food, customs, crafts, and industries. Tells of the responsibilities of various members of the family.*

Navajo Life (1961) 9 min. Dist: IUAVC FR$6.75, FS$185. *Visits the national monument of Canyon de Chelly in Arizona. Describes the life of the Navajo Indians living in the canyon. Shows the ancient ruins of early Indian cliff dwellers. Tells how the Indians farm, raise sheep, cook, and build their homes. Concludes with scenes of a trading post and Indian rodeo.*

Navaho Night Witch 10 min. Dist: FCE FR$17, FS$95. *The night witch is a great horned owl.*

The Navajo: A Study in Cultural Contrast (1967) 17 min. Dick Girvin (PR), Oswald Werner and Kenneth Bigishe (CON). Dist: IUAVC FR$8.25. *Portrays the culture, social organization, and physical environment of the Navajo Indian. Views the ceremonial purifying sweat baths and religious sand painting. Surveys the economy based on sheep raising, noting the scarcity of water and the enormous acreage required. Questions whether or not the Navajo can remain relatively inviolate in a country where change is of the essence.* [Reviewed by John Adair, *AA* 72:1575–1576, 1970.]

Navajo Talking Picture (1986) 40 min. Arlene Bowman (DI). Dist: WMM FR$125, VR$85, VS$295. *An urban-raised Navajo film student travels to the Reservation to document the traditional ways of her grandmother. The filmmaking persists in spite of her grandmother's forceful objections to this invasion of her privacy. Ultimately, what emerges is a thought-provoking work that abruptly calls into question issues of "insider/outsider" status in a portrait of an assimilated Navajo struggling to use a "white man's" medium to capture the remnants of her cultural past. Excellent for film studies as well as those interested in Native American culture.*

Navajo: The Last Red Indians 35 min. BBC-TV and Time-Life Films (PR). Dist: BBC R$45, FS$500, VS$100. *The Navajo—America's largest and most enduring Indian tribe—have kept their native language. Forty thousand of them still speak no English. And only recently has their language been written, since their culture has been handed down verbally through the elders of the tribe—the medicine men. This film is about their fight for their way of life against the inroads of the white man's culture. And it contains many exclusive and uncensored scenes of Navajo rituals and ceremonies. Among them are centuries-old Navajo methods of diagnosing illnesses by the primitive trance-like state of hand-trembling. Medicine men conducting a ten-day "sing" or healing ceremony. A medicine man school at which white doctors demonstrate hypnosis. And white doctors referring Navajo patients to medicine men. And medicine men holding healing ceremonies in modern hospitals.* Discussion guide available.

The Navigators: Pathfinders of the Pacific (1983) 59 min. Sanford Low (FM, AN). Dist: DER FR$60, VR$40, FS$600, VS$300. *Over 1,000 years ago, the islands of Polynesia were explored and settled by navigators who used only the waves, the stars, and the flights of birds for guidance. In hand-built, double-hulled canoes 60 feet long, the ancestors of today's Polynesians sailed across a vast ocean area. Sanford Low visited Micronesia's remote Caroline Islands to speak with Mau Piailug, the last navigator to be ceremonially initiated on Satawal, and one of the few men who still practices the art of navigation. Mau Piailug sails a replica of a Polynesian canoe 2,500 miles across the ocean without benefit of any Western navigational instruments. This film reveals the subtleties of this sea science of which to master the lore was to attain great status in traditional Micronesian society. Few men remain with Mau's skills, knowledge, or aspirations, and we see how that system is being transformed from vital social action to proud and sometimes wistful memory.* [Reviewed by Richard A. Gould, *ARCH* 37(4):70, 1984. George M. Epple, *SBF* 20:165, 1985.]

Nawi (1970) 22 min. David MacDougall (FM, CA), Judith MacDougall (SR). Dist: UCEMC R$24, FS$350, VS$260; PSU(PCR) order #21377, FR$25; USC; BU. *During the dry season, the Jie of Uganda leave their homesteads and take their cattle to temporary camps, or nawi, where fresh grass is abundant. The film is about this drive and about the life of the Jie at the cattle camp. Without commentary but with subtitles translating the conversation of the people.* Suggested supplements: F. H. Gulliver, *The Family Herds.* Routledge & Kegan Paul, 1955. Nevill Dyson-Hudson, *Karimojong Politics.* Clarendon Press, 1966.

The Neighborhood of Coehlos 28 min. Dist: WBP VS$39.95, order #30920. *In this unforgettable portrayal of the slums of Recife, Brazil, courageous residents work tirelessly with an urban development program to help create jobs, reclaim swampland, provide education, and establish land tenure. Scenes in the film are sometimes unsettling, but the message is hope, not despair.*

Neighborhood Tokyo (1992) Hajima Ikela (DI), Theodore C. Bestor (AN), Koichi Sakuma and David W. Plath (CA). Dist: UILL-UC, order #9203. *A portrait of Miyamoto-oho, a community of mom-and-pop stores and family enterprises located near the center of Tokyo. Competition from supermarkets and shopping plazas threatens the livelihoods of long-term residents. High land prices tempt owners to tear down older homes and replace them with apartment buildings; this is changing the composition of the population. Against this backdrop, residents strive to maintain the close social ties, symbols of local identity, and community rituals that may keep Miyamoto-cho from becoming just another mailing address.* Bibliography: Theodore C. Bestor, *Neighborhood Tokyo.* Stanford University Press. 1989.

Neshnabek: The People (1979) 30 min. Donald Stull (PR), Gene Bernofsky (DI), Floyd Schultz (CA). Dist: UCEMC R$44, FS$530, VS$350, order #11306; UK FR$12, FS$225. *Based on remarkable original footage taken by amateur anthropologist Floyd Schultz between 1927 and 1941, this film celebrates an extraordinary people: the Prairie Band Potawatomi of Kansas. This film documents the tribe's material culture, pastimes, and religious activities.*

In 1979, the original footage was edited and provided with a soundtrack based on interviews with the older members of the tribe. On the soundtrack, the people tell their own story, share their view of the world, and relate the history of their struggle to preserve their culture and sense of identity. [Reviewed by James A. Clifton, *AA* 84:753–754, 1982.]

NETSILIK ESKIMO FILMS Social Studies Curriculum Project of Education Development Center (PR), Asen Balikci, Guy Mary-Roussiliere (AN), Robert Young (CA). [Reviewed in *AA* 79:510, 1977. *AA* 68:1327, 1966.] See entries under individual titles:

- **Yesterday, Today: The Netsilik Eskimos**
- **The Eskimo: Fight for Life**
- **The Migratory Cycle of the Netsilik** Dist: EMC.
- **People of the Seal: Eskimo Summer**
- **People of the Seal: Eskimo Winter**
- **Hunters of the Seal**
- **Man, a Course of Study**
- **Fishing at the Stone Weir**
- **Winter Sea-Ice Camp**
- **Caribou Hunting at the Crossing Place**
- **Autumn River Camp**
- **Spring Sea-Ice Camp**
- **Group Hunting on the Spring Ice**
- **Jigging for Lake Trout**
- **Stalking Seals on the Spring Ice**
- **Building a Kayak**

Network and Systems (1955) 25 min. Dist: Pitt. *Introduces concepts of networks and systems as examples of the new methodological frameworks used by geographers in recent years to supplement traditional tools of analysis. These tools are applied to the Chimbu tribe of New Guinea. The simple society network of a farmer is also shown.*

New Caledonia—A Land in Search of Itself (The Human Face of the Pacific Series) (1987) 56 min. Film Australia (PR). Dist: FIV VS$158. *This film examines the conflicts between the Kanaks, who want to retain their tribal society, and the Caledonian French, who want economic progress.*

The New Cutting Edge (Man on the Rim Series) 58 min. Dist: LMF VS$295. *Recent findings reinforce the relatively new concept of a genuine Asian "Bronze Age," thousands of years earlier than had ever been suspected. Thailand, Vietnam, and other sites across South-East Asia as far as eastern Indonesia reveal an ancient knowledge of metal working.*

New England Dances (1990) 30 min. John Bishop (FM). Dist: Media Generation, 8378 Faust Avenue, West Hills, CA 91304; (818) 704-9538, VS$59.95. *New England folk dances.* [Reviewed by Nicholas Spitzer, *AA* 93(3):773, 1991.]

New England Fiddles 30 min. John Bishop (FM). Dist: DER FR$50, FS$450, VS$250. *Since colonial times, the fiddle has enjoyed a primary place in American traditional music. The fiddler provides the spirit and music for dances that are important elements for community cohesion. New England styles and tunes originate in French and Anglo-Celtic traditions, which have been transformed into the music we hear at fiddle contests and contra dances in the Northeast today. The film presents seven of the finest traditional musicians in the Northeast, including: Joe Cormier, Jerry Robichaud, Ron West, Paddy Cronin, Harold Luce, Ben Guillemette, and Wilfred Guillete. A 20-minute appendix of 11 additional tunes transferred to videotape from the original 16mm negative is included on all video copies and available on video with the purchase of 16mm prints for $25.* [Reviewed by Nicholas Spitzer, *AA* 93:773–775, 1991. Melanie L. Sovine, *AA* 89:522–525, 1987.]

New Gods (The Africans Series) (1986) 60 min. Ali Mazrui (AN). Dist: ACPB VR$100, VS$198. *"Ali Mazrui of Kenya, professor of political science at the University of Michigan, attempts to present a view of how traditional African religions, Christianity and Islam, coexist and influence each other."* [From the review by Simon D. Messing, *SBF* 22:319–320, 1987.]

New Guinea, Dani Tribe: Extracting Salt Robert Gardner (FM), Cambridge Design Group (ED). Super 8mm cartridge loop, silent color. Cf. the film, *Dead Birds*.

New Guinea Patrol and Excerpts from Yumi Yet (People in Change Series) (1989) 59 min. Film Australia (PR). Dist: FIV VS$129. *New Guinea Patrol, filmed in 1958, follows James Sinclair, an Australian patrol officer in the Western Highlands of Papua New Guinea. It provides a vivid record from the period of colonial administration. In dramatic contrast to New Guinea Patrol, Yumi Yet documents Papua New Guinea's independence celebration.*

New Images (see University of Ife Series)

New Images of Aging (1987) 29 min. Neil Steinberg (PR). Dist: Age Wave, 1900 Powell Street, Suite 800, Emoryville, CA 94608; (415) 652-9099, VR$25, VS$150. *"Directed at correcting stereotypes and misperceptions of aging, the film begins with demographics.... Orienting people to problems of the aged seems necessary in many areas, from the traffic engineers who determine what a walk period on traffic signals should be to publishers (small print), clothes designers (difficult buttons), and medicine packagers (bottle tops)."* [From the review by Benjamin N. Colby, *AA* 92:1099–1100, 1990.]

The New Indians (1977) 58 min. Terry Sanders, Frieda Lee Mock (PR), National Geographic Society (PR). *Contemporary Native American life.* [Reviewed by Michael Dorris, *AA* 79:995, 1977.]

New Lives for Old (Horizons of Science) 20 min. Dist: IUAVC FR$9.75; PSU FR$12. *Presents a comparative study by Margaret Mead of the Manus people of the Admiralty Islands in 1921 and after World War II. Dioramas from the American Museum of Natural History are used to show the life of the people in 1928. Live action photography is used to document the people's lives after 1945 following their exposure to technically advanced cultures during World War II. Cf. the film, Margaret Mead's New Guinea Journal.*

THE NEW PACIFIC (1987) BBC/NVC (PR). Dist: FIV VS$630. *The Pacific Basin supports a third of the world's population. No other region contains so great a diversity of race, language, and culture. With the development of trade, tourism, and telecommunications, the people of the Pacific are facing new challenges to their traditional lifestyles. The New Pacific explores the cultural, historical, economic, and political facets of this colorful and influential sphere of the world. See additional description of the videos comprising this eight part series under the titles:*

- **The Pacific Age**
- **Echoes of War**
- **Return to Paradise**
- **Over Rich, Over Sexed and Over Here**
- **Fifty Ways to Get Enlightened**
- **For Richer for Poorer**
- **Jugs to Be Filled or Candles to Be Lit**
- **Shadow of the Rising Sun**

The New Tijuana (1991) 59 min. Paul Espinosa (PR). Dist: UCEMC FR$50, VS$295. *Luis Valdez narrates this eye-opening profile of booming Tijuana, Mexico, the West Coast's second largest city after Los Angeles. As Tijuana struggles between its heritage as a Third World border town with a sordid past and its promise as a modern center of international finance and high technology, it is rapidly emerging as the cutting edge of Mexico's political, social, and economic transformation. Essential viewing for understanding contemporary Mexico.*

A New Year for the Mien (1986) 55 min. Guy Phillips and Lisa Sassi (PR). Dist: Guy Phillips Productions, 109 11th Avenue E., Seattle, WA 98102; (206) 324-8690, VR$50, VS$245. *Mien refugees from Southeast Asia in the United States.* [Reviewed by Nancy D. Donnelly, *AA* 90:1044–1045, 1988.]

Ngoma Therapy in an Urban South African Setting (1984) 29 min. Sue Schuessler and John M. Janzen (PR). Dist: Sue Schuessler, Department of Anthropology, University of Kansas, Lawrence, KS 66045; (913) 864-4103, VR$15, VS$60. *"Ngoma is an indigenous African term that covers a wide range of therapeutic options with techniques varying considerably.... [It] includes the building of social support as an element in healing as well as divination.... Focuses on the initiation of a single patient, his symptoms, and an explanation of the ngoma belief system."* [From the review by Stephen D. Glazier, *AA* 90:489–490, 1988.]

Ngora: A Camping Place (1962) 50 min. T. D. Campbell (DI, ED, WR). *In this film study of the Walbiri Aborigines at Yuendumu in the Northern Territory, the daily life, hunting, gathering of plant foods, and many other activities of the men, women, and children are shown.* [Reviewed by John Greenway, *AA* 65:791–792, 1967.]

Nias and Sumatra (1930s) 10–15 min. Dist: FCE FR$17, FS$95. *Nias is an island not reached by many people and in many ways untouched. The film shows the ceremony of manhood. An 8-foot stone tower must be leaped by the young men. The dance of the hunters is included. Scenes on Sumatra show the contrast of village life in civilization.*

Nice Weather, Mr. Pradhan! (1989) 28 min. Hans Heijnen (FM), Rajendra Pradhan (AN). Dist: FRIF VR$50, VS$190. *Rajendra Pradhan, an anthropologist from Nepal, arrived in Schoonrewoerd, a small town in the Netherlands, to study the care of the aged in Dutch society. What Mr. Pradhan did not expect was to become the object of close scrutiny himself, as his subjects, few of whom had previous exposure to a Nepalese, found his presence in their community rather curious. The film demonstrates how the initial wariness of the Dutch seniors is ultimately broken down and transformed into a peculiar but very real fondness toward the researcher from Nepal. At the farewell assembly gathered for Mr. Pradhan, the point is emphasized that he carries with him the group's blessing when the time comes for him to "tie the knot."*

Niger, jeune république (Niger, Young Republic) (1961) 58 min. Jean Rouch (DI). Dist: CFE; DER. *Made to commemorate the first anniversary of the independence of Niger.*

Nigerian Dance (see University of Ife Series) Nigerian National Dance Troupe (see University of Ife Series)

Night Cries: A Rural Tragedy (1990) 19 min. Tracey Moffatt (DR). Dist: WMM FR$75, VR$60. *By an Australian Aboriginal filmmaker. The story of an old, toothless white woman confined to a wheelchair and her Aboriginal caretaker.* [Reviewed by Jay Ruby, *AA* 94(1):257–259, 1992.]

Nimrod Workman: To Fit My Own Category (1975) 35 min. Dist: APPAL FR$55, FS$800, VS$225. *This film is a portrait of 78-year-old Nimrod Workman, a retired coal miner and singer who writes and performs songs and traditional ballads. Nimrod reminisces about his life as a miner in the film and sings traditional Appalachian songs.* [Reviewed by Melanie L. Sovine, *AA* 89:522–525, 1987.]

Nine Cows and an Ox (see Diary of a Maasai Village Series) (1985) 50 min. BBC (PR). Dist: FIV VS$198. *The new bride meets her mother-in-law and three co-wives, but there is trouble over the size of her expected wedding gift.*

THE 1973 MGODO SERIES Gei Zantzinger, Andrew Tracey (PR). Dist: PSU. *Each film documents a music and dance performance, Mgodo, composed for the chiefs of Chopi villages in southern Mozambique. Dancers are accompanied by large xylophone orchestras in hour-long performances. History, current affairs, and local events are contained in the shouts and songs. Words in the films are subtitled, first in ChiChopi, then in English. The use of large orchestras of instruments tuned in several pitches, the complete text of each song, and the wide-angle view of the dancers, provides data for detailed analysis.* Hugh Tracey, *Chopi Musicians*. Oxford University Press, 1970. A. G. Zantzinger and A. Tracey, *A Companion to the Films*. Audio-Visual Services, PSU, University Park, 1976. [Reviewed by Marcia Herndon, *AA* 89:388, 1976.]

- **The 1973 Mgodo wa Mbanguzi** 53 min. FR$27, FS$675.
- **The 1973 Mgodo wa Mkandeni** 48 min. FR$25, FS$615.

90 South: With Scott to the Antarctic (1933) 72 min. Herbert G. Ponting (FM), British Film Institute (RE). Dist: MLS VS$39.95, order #MILE004. *A chronicle of Captain Robert Scott's heroic and ultimately tragic race for the South Pole. Not only did Amundsen reach the goal first, but Scott and his entire team died on the return trip. The film quotes from Scott's journal, which was discovered with the explorer's frozen body. These brave and eloquent diary entries tell of the heartbreaking last days of the doomed expedition. Ponting's hauntingly beautiful images of ice caves and Antarctic wildlife are timeless masterpieces of cinematography. Today, Ponting's tribute to his fallen companions remains deeply moving.*

Nini Pantun: Rice Cultivation and Rice Rituals in Bali (1991) 54 min. Institut fur den Wissenschafelichen Film, Gottingen, Germany (PR). Dist: UCEMC VR$60, VS$250, order #38252. *Rice is the agricultural basis of life on Bali, and its cultivation is an integral part of all aspects of life, culture, and religion.*

Niutao—Construction of a Sleeping House 51.5 min. G. Koch (FM). Dist: PSU(EC) E 409, FR$20.50. [Reviewed by Saul Riesenberg, AA 67:1357, 1965.]

No Address 56 min. Alanis Obomsawim (DI). Dist: NFB R$80, FS$775, VS$350. *Increasingly today, cities are being confronted by the problem of the homeless—displaced people living outside the accepted structure of the society. The film focuses on young people of Native American heritage who come to cities in search of a better life and wind up homeless. Often naive in their expectations, these young Native Americans view the city as a place of abundance. The harsh realities emerge when they discover that behind this facade the city is a demanding mistress. Prices are high. Housing is expensive. Jobs are few. The issue of the homeless—particularly among Native Americans is hopeless and there is "no fix." The film opens the way to discussion of this very real problem—a problem that reflects on society itself—and the need to solve it that must be faced today by all of us.*

No Applause, Just Throw Money (1987) 28 min. Karen Goodman (FM). Dist: DCL FR$45, VR$25, FS$535, VS$250. *"In a celebration of urban life, this film features the street performers of New York City. 101 men and women dance, sing, juggle, tell jokes, play instruments and mime on the streets, in the parks, or in subway stations. . . . It is an upbeat, entertaining view of city life."* [From the review by Sally Engle Merry, AA 91:527–528, 1989.]

No Easy Walk 1962–66 (see Eyes on the Prize: America's Civil Rights Years Series)

No Longer Silent Dist: IFB FR$75; UTA-FL VR$17.75, order #VCC-1145. *Focuses on the present position of women in India and documents their struggle against injustice. The women featured discuss their continuing fight for equality and independence—a fight for life.*

No Longer Strangers David Martin (FM). Dist: RBMU FR$40. *Account of western Dani life, Irian Barat (west New Guinea), with scenes from early missionary contact, Dani ceremonies, burning of sacred objects, and Christianization of Dani.* Suggested supplements: Russell T. Hitt, *Cannibal Valley.* Harper and Row, 1962. Helen Manning, *To Perish for Their Saving.* Victory Press, London: 1969 (U.S. paperback edition: Bethany Fellowship, 1971). Denise O'Brien and Anton Ploeg, "Acculturation Movements among the Western Dani." AA 66:281–292, 1964.

No Maps on My Taps (1978) 59 min. George T. Nierenberg (FM). Dist: BW FR$100, FS$800. *A film about the history and working of the world of tap dancing. It shows parts of live performances and draws a portrait of Howard Simms, Charles Green, and Bunny Briggs, all three of whom were top dancers in Harlem during the time of Depression and are still in business.* [Reviewed by Nora Groce, AA 84:984–986, 1982.]

No More Mountains: The Story of the Hmong (1981) 58 min. WGBH Television (PR). Dist: PBSV VR$75, VS$325. *Refugees from Laos living in the United States.* [Reviewed by by Winifred Lambrecht, AA 86:513–514, 1984.]

The Nomads of Badakhshan 26 min. Judith and Stanley Hallet (FM). Dist: FIM/RF FR$40, FS$360. *Late in August in Badakhshan, in northern Afghanistan, we watch the nomad caravans on their way home from summer pastures high in the mountains close to the Russian border. They will spend one month on the road and will travel more than 200 miles before reaching their winter homes near Kunduz. Because they travel the same route twice a year, they find it profitable to carry goods to trade with farmers living in the mountains. Some become so successful at trading that they buy land, leave their families behind, and become full-time traders. A small but typical trading group is taking livestock to Kunduz. Their camels carry butter, yogurt, and grain. They are called the Atakchai, an offshoot of the Durrani, one of Afghanistan's important nomadic tribes. Another, much larger Durrani group is on its way home from Lake Shiwa. They are wealthy, with 2,000 sheep, 500 cattle, 50 camels, and 8 horses. They set up their three large tents and camp for several days, breaking their normal migratory pattern, in order to collect money owed them by nearby farmers. One man, son of the tribe's patriarch, invites us into his tent, describes his family and possessions, and tells how one of his daughters will soon command a high bride's price, because she is strong and pretty and expected to work hard. His young sons are already part of the family work force, responsible for herding and guarding their animals. Here, half the children die because smallpox and cholera spread quickly, and the nomads are far from medical facilities. On the dusty, unpaved, but heavily traveled road, the nomads and their herds of livestock are passed by heavy, brightly decorated Russian- and American-built trucks, transporting their goods much faster than the nomads can. In Afghanistan, camel caravans and painted trucks are still the only means of transportation.*

Nomads of the Jungle (Earth and Its People Series) 25 min. Dist: NYU FR$15; UCEMC FR$11; PSU(PCR) order #915.95-1, FR$5.40. *Shows a group of Malayan aborigines in the mountain jungle. Narrated by the "son of the chief." Use of rattan to make evening camp, women gather yams, men drive and net fish, bread from sago palm flour, use of blowguns for hunting, catch an infant monkey, and collect* *bamboo to take to trading post downstream, where they trade for manufactured goods.*

Nomads of the Rainforest (1987) 59 min. Grant Behrman (PR), Adrian Warren (FM). Dist: UCEMC VR$40, VS$410, order #37559. *Records a multidisciplinary expedition to research the Waorani, a fierce and isolated Indian tribe that inhabits the Amazon rainforest. It contains spectacular scenes of the skilled Waorani blowgun hunters in their lush jungle environment. Also examines the daily life and rituals of this egalitarian tribe whose members have no concept of competition or rank and who are completely free of such Western diseases as cancer, strokes, and heart disease.* [Reviewed by Allyn MacLean Stearman, *AA* 88:782–783, 1986.]

Nomads on the Savanna (1989) Barbara J. Michael (AN), Anne M. Kocherhans (FM). Dist: UAB. *Focuses on the Hawazma Baggara, cattle pastoralists in the Sudan. Couched within the framework of doing fieldwork, the film looks into the lives of the Hawazma Baggara during the rainy season, from both social and ecological perspectives. The film gives an intimate picture of a variety of activities: building houses and sun shelters, milking and marketing, animal husbandry, political meetings, feasts, and afternoon socializing.*

Nonverbal Communication (1991) 27 min. Dist: IM VS$159, order #JJ111. *Based on behavioral research and the incorporation of everyday examples, this program examines how nonverbal communication can be beneficial or detrimental to communication. Specific topics covered include proxemics, posture, and gestures.*

El norte (1983) 139 min. Anna Thomas (PR), Gregory Nava (DI). Dist: Cinecom International, 7 W. 36th St., 6th floor, New York, NY 10018; (212) 239-8360, FR$225, FS$1950, VS$1300. *Follows a brother and sister as they flee their village in Guatamala for the uncertain world of Los Angeles.* [Reviewed by James Loucky, *AA* 87:992–994, 1985.]

North Indian Village (1958) 30 min. Patricia Hitchcock (CA, PR), John T. Hitchcock (AN, PR). Dist: IFB FR$30, FS$425, VS$325; UCEMC FR$22. *Filmed in a Rajput village of Saharanpur District, Uttar Pradesh, India, the emphasis is on showing how typically Indian interpersonal relations governed by caste and kinship look. A subsidiary theme is the contrast between continuity of tradition and place (e.g., the village's ancient Hindu rites, Moghul remains) and many evidences of recent changes (e.g., a new school and council house, a home water pump, diesel drive grist mill, and nearby sugar refinery).* Suggested supplements: John T. Hitchcock, "The Idea of the Martial Rajput." *JAF* 71:10–17, 1959. John T. Hitchcock, "Leadership in a North Indian Village." In: *Leadership and Political Institutions in India.* R. L. Park and I. Tinker, eds. Princeton University Press, 1959, pp. 395–414. John T. Hitchcock, "Surat Singh, Head Judge." *The Company of Man.* J. B. Casagrande, ed. Wiley, 1960, pp. 234–272. Leigh Minturn Triandis and John T. Hitchcock. *The Rajputs of Khalapur.* Wiley, 1965.

The Northern Lights 48 min. Alan Booth (DI). Dist: NFB FR$70, FS$710, VS$300. *Since the beginning of time, people have gazed into the polar skies, spellbound by dancing beams of color . . . the northern lights. Though scientists have advanced many theories to explain the aurora borealis and aboriginal people around the northern pole have passed on their beliefs through centuries, mysteries still linger. This film explores the phenomenon of the aurora borealis and illustrates how the legends and tales of the indigenous people of the north have helped us to understand the shimmering of the northern lights.*

Northwest Coast Indians: A Search for the Past (1973) 26 min. Louis and Ruth Kirk for Clover Park School District (PR). Dist: UWP FS$340, VS$200. *Combining aerial and ground photographs of excavations at the Ozette Indian village at Cape Alava, Washington, with rare old photographs of the village around 1900, this film presents a striking archaeological portrayal of a bygone Indian society.*

Northwest Coast Indians: Ozette Archaeology (1979) 21 min. Louis and Ruth Kirk (PR). Dist: UWP FS$25. *This filmstrip "focuses on the Ozette site itself. The Filmstrip Guide provides background material outlining the unique importance of the site, followed by the filmstrip text and a list of seven selected references for further study."* [From the review by R. Carol Barnes, *ARCH* 36(4):72–73, 1983.]

Not so Young Now as Then 18 min. Liane Brandon (FM). Dist: NDF. *A fifteenth high school reunion.* [Reviewed by Louise Lamphere, *AA* 79:203, 1977.]

Not to Lose You My Language (1975) 27 min. Malcolm Otton and Tim Read (PR), Greg Reading (DI). Dist: FAA. *This film looks at a bilingual education program in the Northern Territory. The aim of the program is to help the Aboriginal children see their language and culture as something worthwhile that in turn will develop their self confidence and self-respect. It is more than just a language program, showing many aspects of Aboriginal dance and craft.*

Notman's World 29 min. Albert Kish (DI). Dist: NFB R$60, FS$550, VS$250. *This film recreates the past through archival photographs, but it goes beyond that to question how photographs shape our sense of history. The work of famous 19th-century photographer William Notman depicts people and places in the Victorian era. His photographs offer a fascinating glimpse of the period. They also remind us that our perception of reality can be influenced by the photographer's choice of subject, giving us an image of the past as portrayed by his lens.*

Now That the Buffalo's Gone 7 min. Burton Gershfield (FM). Dist: CFSoc., UILL. [Reviewed by Jay Ruby, *AA* 71:801–802, 1969.]

Nuba Wrestling (1991) 42 min. Rolf Husmann and Werner Sperschneider (FM). Dist: IWF VS$45, order #D 1774. *In the Sudan, Nuba migrants to Khartoum hold wrestling tournaments each Friday. Their sport helps them strengthen their ethnic identity in a hostile urban environment. Nuba wrestling has developed into a unique mixture of traditional culture and modern sport. The film shows* *wrestling sessions, introduces wrestlers and functionaries, and sets Nuba wrestling into the context of the urban migrants everyday life. It centers around a conflict about changes from traditional to a more westernized form of wrestling.* [Reviewed by James C. Faris, *AA* 94(4):1028–1029, 1992.]

Nuclear Fingerprinting of Ancient Pottery 20 min. Jim Halverson (FM). Dist: USAEC Film Library-TlC, P.O. Box 62, Oak Ridge, TN 37830, free loan. [Reviewed by Ruth Tringham, *AA* 74:1591, 1972.]

The Nuer (1970) 75 min. Hillary Harris and George Breidenbach (FM), Robert Gardner and Hillary Harris (PR) for the Film Study Center, Harvard University. Dist: CRM VR$80, VS$295; UCEMC order #8106, FR$34. *A poetic film concentrating on evocative images of life among a group of Nuer living in Ethiopia. Creates a strong and memorable impression of the people, their cattle, their artifacts, and their land. On occasion, English narration is used to give a more anthropological account of events, especially: a brideprice dispute, a ghost marriage, a revitalistic ceremony intended to combat a smallpox epidemic, and the climax of the film, a gar initiation, where two boys receive the forehead incisions of manhood. The film will leave most anthropology classes a bit bewildered unless it is presented in connection with the writings of Evans-Pritchard and Beidelman.* [Reviewed by E. E. Evans-Pritchard, *AA* 74:1028, 1972.] Suggested supplements: E. E. Evans-Pritchard, *The Nuer*. Clarendon Press, 1940; T. O. Beidelman, "The Ox and Nuer Sacrifice." *Man* 1:453–467, 1966; T. O. Beidelman, "Some Nuer Notions of Nakedness, Nudity and Sexuality." *Africa* 38:113–131, 1968.

Nuhoniyeh: Our Story (1992) 56 min. Mary Code, Allan Code (FM). Dist: DER VS$245, VR$60. *The Sayisi Dene have traditionally lived on the tundra in summer and the forests each winter; a seasonal round based on the barren ground caribou. On the basis of a treaty fraudulently obtained in 1910, unsigned and untranslated, the Canadian Government claims to have bought all their land for $5 a year. This video focuses on the Dene's effort to rebuild their lives after being dislocated and to reclaim that which is rightfully theirs.*

Number Our Days (1977) 29 min. Barbara Myerhoff (AN), Lynne Littman (FM). Dist: DCL FR$55, FS$495, VS$250; Hackford/Littman, 6620 Cahuenga Terrace, Los Angeles, CA 90068. *At the end of their lives, a group of gallant Eastern European Jews have banded together to preserve their heritage in the face of tremendous odds. The men and women seen in the film created an original culture made up of ingredients from their common history. This sometimes jumbled mixture includes Yiddishkeit, Zionism, socialism, and fervent American patriotism. They keep alive the traditions and rituals of shtetl life, adapting old ways to meet the demands of modern America. In turn, they are sustained by their shared heritage. For the most part, they are alone without money or close family. They worked in the ghettos of New York and Chicago and retired by the sea in Southern California where they survive in a hostile environment facing poverty and the constant threat of urban violence. This film is a moving tribute to an enduring Jewish culture and the meaning this culture has for the individual members of the Israel Levin Center in Venice, California.* [Reviewed by Eleanor Wachs, *JAF* 94(371):138–139, 1981.]

N/um Tchai (see San Series)

The Nut-Cracking Chimps of Tai Forest (1991) 25 min. Christophe Boesch, Hedwige Boesch-Achermann (PR). Dist: PSU VS$150, VR$16.50. *Amid the noises of hammering and cracking, viewers follow the chimpanzees of the park as they spend hours collecting, opening, and eating coute tree nuts. In this tropical rain forest setting of the Ivory Coast, the nut-cracking activities of the group are examined closely to detail the chimpanzees' relationships, social life, and dominance.*

Nyamakuta—The One Who Receives 28 min. Chris Sheppard (PR). Dist: FL VR$55, VS$295. *Mai Mafuta is a nyamakuta—a traditional midwife—in Zimbabwe. Half of all births in the developing world are attended by women like her, without the help of modern medicine. People seek her out because she is skillful, compassionate, and because her grandmother was also a midwife. Five years ago, Mai Mafuta was unable to save the life of her own daughter who died while giving birth. In an attempt to prevent such deaths, over eighty counties have begun training traditional midwives in modern medical methods. Mai Mafuta enrolled in one such program. She now tries to reconcile what she has learned at the clinic with traditional birth practices. We see her deliver a child on the dirt floor of a hut. Mai Mafuta narrates her own story, giving the audience an intimate view of the lives of Third World women.*

O Mère Paddy! 25 min. Dist: FACSEA FR$16. *Farming of mountain rice on the high plateaux of South Vietnam, 1963.* French only.

Oaksi (1979) 22 min. Anthony Slone (DI). Dist: APPAL FR$45, FS$400, VS$175. *"Present[s] the personality and personal history of the folk artist as ethnographic material that stands on its own."* [From the review by Melanie L. Sovine, *AA* 89:522–525, 1987.]

The Oath of Caiman Wood (Le serment du Bois Caiman) (1992) 30 min. Charles Jajman (FM). Dist: FHS. *"The Oath of Caiman Wood" is the origin myth of Haiti and refers to the events of August 14, 1791, when, according to oral tradition, the gods of Voodoo spoke through the voice of the rebel leader of the African slaves. Through personal narratives and images of art and rituals, this film shows the power Voodoo still has in Haiti.*

Los Oaxaquenos (1975) 28 min. G. Seaman and A. Rowe (FM), Philip A. Dennis (AN). Dist: FEAV FR$25, FS$175. Super 8 only. *The structure of this film emphasizes the sexual division of labor and the daily round of life, from dawn to dusk. The film includes sequences on taking care of animals, work in the fields, tortilla making, child care, and marketing.*

Obsidian Point-Making (American Indian Film Series) (1964) 13 min. Dist: UCEMC FR$25, FS$190; PSU(PCR) order #12213K, FR$10, FS$170. *The California Indians* utilized three known methods of fashioning obsidian arrow points: direct percussion, indirect percussion, and pressure flaking. The most common method, pressure flaking, is demonstrated by a Tolowe Indian of northern California. California Indians set up workshops near quarries and streambeds where the larger obsidian blocks were reduced to blank size with hammerstone. The blanks, now a portable size, were further reduced to finished arrow points with a bone chipper. In addition to the obsidian points, the film considers other types of projectile points and the uses and significance of many obsidian artifacts in aboriginal cultures. [Reviewed by John Adair, AA 76:728–730, 1974. Susanna R. Katz and Paul R. Katz, ARCH 34(1):60, 1981.]

Ocamo Is My Town (see Yanomamo Series)

ODYSSEY SERIES (First season) Dist: DER. *The anthropology films shown on Public Television in 1980, the first season.* See listings under individual titles:
- N!ai, The Story of a !Kung Woman FR$65-130, FS$650.
- Seeking the First Americans FR$45-90, FS$450.
- Franz Boas(1958–42) FR$45-90, FS$450.
- The Incas FR$45-90, FS$450.
- Other People's Garbage FR$45-50, FS$450.
- The Chaco Legacy FR$45-90, FS$450.

ODYSSEY SERIES (Second season) *The anthropology films shown on Public Television in the United States in 1981–82, the second season.* A very useful study guide/magazine covering the entire series is available from *Odyssey* Magazine, P.O. Box 1000, Boston, MA 02118, for $1, minimum order of 5. See listings under individual titles:
- The Ancient Mariners
- Ben's Mill
- Dadi's Family
- Little Injustices: Laura Nader Looks at Law
- Margaret Mead: Taking Note
- Maya Lords of the Jungle
- Myths and the Moundbuilders
- On the Cowboy Trail
- The Three Worlds of Bali
- Lucy and the First Family (see *The First Family*)
- Bath Waters
- The Kirgiz of Afghanistan
- We Are Mehinaku (see *The Mehinacu of Brazil*)
- Some Women of Marrakech

Of Grace and Steel (1984) 20 min. Phyllis Jeroslow (FM). Dist: Real Film and Video, 1433 10th Street #7, Santa Monica, CA 90401; (213) 394-2984, VS$275. *"This sight of young American men and women wearing conspicuous, all white Punjabi-style garments, including tall turbans, is a source of intense curiosity for many Americans.... The all-white bana (the Sikh uniform) was deliberately chosen to distinguish them not only from other Americans but also from their co-religionists, the Indian Sikhs.... [This film is] not only about the Khalsa (self-ascribed name for a Sikh meaning the 'pure one') but from the Khalsa perspective."* [From the review by M. Nazif Shahrani, AA 89:781–782, 1987.]

Of Land and Life: People of the Klamath 28 min. Jim Culp (FM), Ed Asner (NA). Dist: NDF VR$50, VS$250. *Cultural and religious sovereignty issues are raised when a conflict between the Karuk Indians and the U.S. government goes to court over the protection of ceremonial lands. Using the Freedom of Religion provision of the U.S. Constitution, the Indians win a landmark victory, only to see it later reversed by the Supreme Court. However, an environmental victory was still realized, and in the process, the Indians discovered their ability to control their lives and their destiny.* [Reviewed by Muriel Crespi, AA 92:1103–1105, 1990.]

Of Lives Uprooted (1990) 10 min. National Film Board of Canada (PR). Dist: IUAVC VR$25, FS$275, VS$95. *The struggle in El Salvador, seen through drawings by children in refugee camps in Honduras.* [Reviewed by Michael J. Higgins, AA 93(1):256–257, 1991.]

Off the Verandah: Bronislaw Malinowski (1884–1942) (Strangers Abroad Series) 52 min. Dist: FHS FR$75, VS$159, order #XD-2544. *Bronislaw Malinowski was the anthropologist who changed the way that field studies were carried out. A Pole who chose to live in England, he worked on a remote group of Pacific islands—the Trobriands—and lived for long periods among the people he was studying. A brilliant linguist, he quickly learned their language and later published books that brought the islanders to life. The idea that native peoples were primitive savages was altered with Malinowski's insight into their mastery of their world.*

La Ofrenda: The Days of the Dead (1989) 50 min. Lourdes Portillo and Susana Munoz (PR). Dist: DCL FR$85, VR$75, FS$895, VS$250. *The offerings to the dead during All Saints Day and All Souls Day celebrations in Mexico City, Oaxaca, and California.* [Reviewed by Hugo G. Nutini, AA 93(3):772–773, 1991.]

Oigame! Oigame! (1991) 35 min. Tanya L. Coen, John Payne, and Michael L. Higgins (FM). Dist: EMS-UNC VS$25. *"Set in Nicaragua as the Chamuro regime came to power... a poor neighborhood in Managua that was created... after the 1979 revolution."* [From the review by Allan Burns, AA 94(2):529–530, 1992.]

El ojeado (The Evil Eye) (see Andean Ethnomedicine: Birth and Childhood Illness in Six Ecuadorian Communities Series)

Okan, Sun Dance of the Blackfoot (1966) 64 min. Hugh Dempsey (Technical Advisor), Bill Marsden (Dl), Glenbow Foundation (since renamed Glenbow-Alberta Institute) (PR). Dist: GAI. [Reviewed by William K. Powers, AA 69:561–562. 1967.]

Old Believers (1986) 29 min. Margaret Hixon (FM). Dist: UCEMC R$43, FS$520, VS$345, order #11297(f), #37344(v). *The Old Believers of Oregon are descended from religious dissenters who rebelled against reforms in traditional Orthodox Christian rituals in 17th-century Russia.*

The protesters who thought that these changes undermined the true faith came to be known as "Old Believers" because of their adherence to traditional ways. In the 1960s, the Russian Old Believers settled in rural Oregon. They brought a culture rich in religious and folk tradition, whose expression takes form in chants and folksongs, in the calligraphy of ancient liturgical books, in handiwork, in foodways, and in language. Church services are conducted in Church Slavonic, the language of religious texts that children must learn. These elements of an old Russian way of life are now better preserved in Oregon than in most of the former Soviet Union. The continuing way of life stands as a strong testament to the value of cultural diversity in our country. [Reviewed by Stephen P. Dunn and Ethel Dunn, AA 93(1):256–257, 1991.]

Treasures from New China (1976) 53 min. James Earl Jones (NA). Dist: UCEMC FR$50, FS$650; IUAVC FR$21.50. *Relates China's technological and artistic achievements and its contributions to world civilization from primitive times to the Yuan dynasty (13th century). Uses photographs of artifacts unearthed in China that were part of the exhibition that toured the United States in 1975 to tell the story of China's cultural heritage. Interrelates the cultural aspects with social history, showing such artifacts as bronze sculptures of the Shang dynasty, a jade burial suit, a clay chariot procession, the "flying" horses of the Han dynasty, and porcelain from the Sung and Yuan dynasties.*

Older, Stronger, Wiser (1989) 28 min. National Film Board of Canada (PR). Dist: IUAVC VR$30, FS$550, VS$160. *Six successful black women relate their lives.* [Reviewed by Colleen Johnson, AA 93(3):771–772, 1991.]

Ollero Yucateco (Yucatan Potter) (1965) 25 min. Arnold Baskin and Jay Barr (FM), Duane G. Metzger (AN), University of Illinois Motion Picture Service (PR). Dist: U ILL order # 81437, FR$12.50; PSU(PCR) order # 31406, FR$12.50. *Mayan pottery making, filmed at Urbana, Illinois, during a six-month visit of a native Yucatec Mayan potter. The purpose of the film is (1) to document a preindustrial technology, (2) to trace the evolution of this ceramic tradition, and (3) to introduce an experimental project in the realm of cultural anthropology in which archaeologists and ethnographers join forces to improve their research techniques. The film begins with a Mayan potter exhibiting his primitive techniques and artistic skill as he constructs a vessel. This modern-day potter's work is compared with similar pottery from ancient Maya. In addition, the film concerns itself with the collaborative efforts of archaeologists and ethnographers in search of a more vital and fruitful approach to their understanding of the large and complex structure known as culture.* [Reviewed by June Nash, AA 68:1093–1094, 1966.]

Omaha Tribe: The Land, The People, The Family Three 30-minute programs. Dist: NETCHE, Box 83111, Lincoln, NE 68501; (402) 472-3611, VR$35 (each), $105 (series), FS$275 (each), $825 (series); VS$225 (each), $675 (series).

On Borrowed Land (1990) 51 min. Dist: CG VR$90, VS$350. *"This is a dramatic and skillful portrayal of life in a squatter community occupying a landfill area in Manila.*

... Unfortunately, however, there is no hint here of the underlying cause of the squatters' misery, no pointing out how the Aquino government, bowing to the wishes of the Catholic church, which supported the coup, has now abandoned the family-planning program that was making some headway under Ferdinand Marcos." [From the review by John A. Broussard, SBF 27:245–246, 1991.]

On Our Land (1991) 55 min. Antonia Caccia (PR). Dist: ICF FR$100, FS$865, VS$550. *"Seeing and hearing directly through the eyes and voices of the Palestinian residents of Umm el-Fahm, the viewer is taken on an extensive journey into a Palestinian community that came under Israeli occupation in 1948.... The focus of the film is two-pronged—the proletarianization of the remaining Palestinian community in Israel and the policy of containment."* [From the review by Julie Peteet, AA 89:1018–1022, 1987.]

On Sacred Ground (1981) 50 min. Robin Hughes (PR), Oliver Howes (DI). Dist: FAA. *Presented by an Aboriginal University student who returns to his tribal lands to help his people, this film traces the background to the Noonkanbah dispute, the well-publicized Aboriginal struggle to stop mining on their land in the Kimberly region of Western Australia. This film will do much to help students understand the Aboriginals' ties to the land, the importance of sacred sites, and the reasons for the land-rights struggle.*

On the Cowboy Trail (Odyssey Series, second season) (1981) 59 min. Randy Strothman and Barry Head (FM), Margot Liberty (AN). Dist: DER R$50, FS$500; PBSV FS$500, VS$200. *This is a film about problems and pleasures of ranching life in today's world. It is set in the Tongue River Valley of Montana. It follows the life cycle and routine of three ranchers, one of whom is a woman who moved west from east due to her passion for open space and livestock. An important issue raised in the film is that of emerging strip mining interest in the area and ranchers' response to this new situation.* [Reviewed by Elizabeth A. Lawrence, AA 84:987–988, 1982.]

On the Spring Ice (The Alaskan Eskimo Series) 45 min. Leonard Kamerling, Sarah Elder (FM). Dist: DER FR$50, FS$540. *Walruses as well as whales are hunted by the Eskimos of Gambell on St. Lawrence Island. Long ago, an old man recounts, people used to drift away on dangerous moving sea ice. Today, we see, the Coast Guard is called upon to rescue lost walrus hunters. The next day, another walrus hunt is launched in skin boats and successfully completed.* Relevant anthropological literature: Richard K. Nelson, *Hunters of the Northern Ice.* University of Chicago Press, 1969.

On the Tracks of Abbe Breuil 44 min. Dist: FACSEA FR$16.

On the Tracks of the Bog People 35 min. Borge Heste (PR). Dist: Royal Danish Consulate General, 280 Park Avenue, New York, NY 10017, free rental. *Documents Danish experimental archaeology and illustrates the interrelationship of archaeology, ethnohistory, and physical anthropology. The methods Danish archaeologists use in tracing the habits and patterns of daily life of the people of* *the Iron Age. The site is in Lejre where thorough research into the life of ancient people takes place in original and artificial settings. Experiments monitored include Danish Iron Age pottery-making, plowing, house construction, clothing and armament use, and horse saddle form.* [From the review by John R. Cole, *AJPA* 58:461, 1982. Reviewed by Susan Dwyer-Shick, *AA* 78:117–118, 1976.]

The Ona People: Life and Death in Tierra del Fuego (1977) 55 min. Anne Chapman, Ana Montes de Gonzalez (FM). Dist: DER FR$65, FS$650, VR$60, VS$400. *The Ona Indians formerly lived in Tierra del Fuego, a group of islands at the southern tip of the South American mainland. Traditionally, the Ona hunted, gathered, and fished. In the late 19th century, Europeans "discovered" Tierra del Fuego, sought gold there, and established sheep farms. The Ona were quickly decimated by murder and by disease. In the 1970s, only a few survivors of the Ona remained, and on film they recall their past, the changes they have seen, and their feelings about the present. Using old photographs and other documents, the film recreates the painful history of the extermination of an entire people.* Bibliography: *Drama and Power in a Hunting Society: The Selknam of Tierra del Fuego*, Cambridge University Press, 1982. [Reviewed in *AA* 87:188–189, 1985. Reviewed by Jean E. Jackson, *AA* 88:267–268, 1986.]

Once in King David's City (1984) 50 min. Allen Rogers (DI). Dist: Allen Rogers Productions, 315 East 72nd Street, Suite 15K, New York, NY 10021; (212) 831-5355, FR$125, FS$750, VS$200. *"Each year approximately 300 volunteers join in the excavations of Jerusalem's ancient citadel where the 'ground is rich in promises and puzzles.' They come to participate in the excitement of discovering and reconstructing the Judeo-Christian-Islamic past. The film looks at a recent season of work on the west slope of the Kidron Valley."* [From the review by Peter S. Allen, *ARCH* 43(2):64–67, 1990.]

One Day More 10 min. Vlatko Gilic (DI). Dist: CRM/MH FS$185. *Yugoslav peasants have eternally come to the curative mud baths of Bujanovac to rid themselves of serious illnesses. They daub themselves with the healing mud amidst a sea of bodies and clouds of steaming vapor. Looking more like sculptures than men, their faces reflect suffering and anguished faith. They shower communally, washing the mud from their bodies and sharing a spirit of celebration in an apparent resolution to live just one day more.*

100,000 Piece Jigsaw Puzzle 26 min. Laterna Films (PR). Dist: DIO free. *Conservation and reconstruction of Viking ships.* [Reviewed by Bernard Wailes, *AA* 78:118–119, 1976.]

One Hundred Years of Archaeology (In India) (1962) 18 min. Mr. Ezra-Mir (FM), Government of India (PR). Dist: Information Services of India, Washington, DC. [Reviewed by Walter A. Fairservis, Jr., *AA* 67:1627–1628, 1965.]

One Man's Response (1986) 54 min. Ian Dunlop (FM). Dist: FAA. *This film records Narritjin Maymuru's reaction to the unwelcome establishment of the Gove Bauxite mine. In 1971, Narritjin held a mortuary ceremony at Yirrkala mission in memory of several dead relatives. He decided to open his ceremony to the visitors from the mining town. Through this he hoped to raise money so he and his family could leave Yirrkala and set up their own clan settlement at Djarrakpi some 150 kilometers to the south. He hoped to promote a better appreciation of Yolngu culture among the white population. The first part of the film focuses on a concert given by the Yirrkala school children for the community at the new mining town. This contrasts with the second and major part of the film, which covers the ceremony organized by Narritjin. The school concert and the mortuary ceremony highlight the differences between western-style performance and Yolngu ceremonial performance. But the theme of communication or rather noncommunication is central to both events.*

One on Every Corner: Manhattan's Greek-Owned Coffee Shops (1984) 50 min. Doreen Moses and Andrea Hall (FM). Dist: Doree Moses, 2637 Conecticut Ave., NW, Washington, DC 20008; (202) 328-7888, FR$100, FS$900 *"About family-owned 'coffee shops' that serve breakfasts and light lunches, as well as coffee. . . . Several immigrant owners and their families talk about the homeland and the Greek experience in America."* [From the review by G. James Patterson, *AA* 87:749–750, 1985.]

Oneota Longhouse People 14 min. Marshall McKusick (FM). Dist: UIOWA order #30274, FR$14, 30, FS$275. [Reviewed by William A. Turnbaugh, *AA* 78:370–371, 1976.]

Ongka's Big Moka (Disappearing World Series) Charles Nairn (PR), Andrew Strathern (AN). *A New Guinea highlands Big Man.* [Reviewed by Jerry Leach, *RAIN* 7:7, 1975.]

THE OPIUM TRILOGY (1976) Adrian Cowell (PR), Chris Menges (CA), David Feingold (CON). Dist: ISHI. [Reviewed by Elizabeth von Furer-Haimendorf, *RAIN* 5:5, 1974.]

• **The Opium Warlords** 75 min. FR$125, FS$1250. *Filmed for 18 months in guerilla-held territory in the Shan States of Burma. Explores the role of opium in the life of the Shan people and in the politics of the Golden Triangle.*

• **The Politicians** 58 min. FR$95, FS$995. *The policymaking process from the committee rooms of Congress to the Cabinet room of the White House.*

• **The White Powder Opera** 58 min. FR$95, FS$995. *Filmed among street gangs and narcotic agents, takes a devastating look at narcotics addiction and trafficking in Hong Kong.*

Oriental Institute (1952) 11 min. Dist: University of Kansas Audio Visual Center. *The history of the Oriental Institute of Chicago.* [Reviewed by C. C. Lamberg Karlovsky, *AA* 78:134, 1976.]

Origins and Evidence (see Crossroads of Civilization Series)

Origins of Greek Civilization (1975) 32 min. Barbara Bohen (FM). Dist: RLI FS$39.95. *This filmstrip surveys the Greek Palaeolithic through Archaic periods (ca. 70,000–480*

B.C.). [Reviewed by Karen D. Vitelli, *ARCH* 37(1):72–73, 1984.]

Origins of Man (1965) 30 min. Dist: PSU order #31022, FR$11.50. *William Howells, Harvard University, lectures on the origin of man, using museum exhibits and casts of early hominids to illustrate a theory of human evolution.* [Reviewed by Jeffrey H. Schwartz, *AA* 80:508–509, 1978.]

Origins of Roman Civilizaton, Part 1 (1983) 31 min. Stephen L. Dyson (FM). Dist: RLI FS$39.95 *A 78-frame filmstrip that summarizes topics dealing with Roman civilization.* See the review by Natalie Boymel Kampen, *ARCH* 37(6):66–75, 1984.

Origins of Roman Civilizaton, Part 2 (1983) 30 min. Stephen L. Dyson (FM). Dist: RLI FS$39.95. *A 73-frame filmstrip that summarizes topics dealing with Roman civilization.* See the review by Natalie Boymel Kampen, *ARCH* 37(6):66–75, 1984.

The Other Guy Dist: Maryland Blue Cross and Blue Shield, 32 West Rd., Towson, MD 21204. *Alcoholism.* [Reviewed by Nancie L. Gonzalez, *AA* 77:198, 1975.]

Other People's Garbage (Odyssey Series, first season) (1980) 60 min. Ann Peck and Claire Andrade-Watkins (FM). Dist: DER FR$50, FS$500. *"Excavations of a 19th/20th century mining community (Somersville) in northern California, directed by James Deetz; slave quarters excavations at St. Simon's, Georgia, directed by Charles Fairbanks; and site survey in the Boston metropolitan area associated with a cultural resource mnanagement project."* [From the review by Robert Paynter, *AA* 85:753–755, 1983. Reviewed by Peter S. Allen, *ARCH* 33(2):62, 1980.]

The Other Side of the Ledger: An Indian View of the Hudson's Bay Company (1972) 42 min. Martin Defalco, Willie Dunn (Dl), George Pearson (PR). Dist: NFG FR$40, FS$545; UCEMC FR$32. *The Hudson's Bay Company's 300th anniversary celebration was no occasion for joy among the people whose lives were tied to the trading stores. This film, narrated by George Manuel, president of the National Indian Brotherhood, presents the view of spokesmen for Canadian Indian and Metis groups. There is sharp contrast between the official celebrations, with Queen Elizabeth among the guests, and what Indians have to say about their lot in the Company's operations.*

The Other Way 26 min. Jon Mansfield and Peter Goldchild (PR). Dist: TL. *Filmed primarily in England at Schumacher's home and the Intermediate Technology Group Center. Focus on ideas of E. F. Schumacher. He presents his concepts of intermediate technology; how they can be applied with Schumacher, cuts of examples of intermediate technology in underdeveloped countries, development of an intermediate technological tractor, industrial revolution, cities as energy sink, evaluation of coal, nuclear energy, effect of technology on workers, prices of mass production, growth, economics, and inflation. Focusing questions: What are the criteria for an intermediate technology? Why does it differ from technologies in traditional as well as industrial societies? What are its effects on the environment, workers, and consumers? Can you think of examples of intermediate technologies in your community?* Bibliography: E. F. Schumacher, *Small Is Beautiful.* New York: Harper and Row, 1973. Land de Moll and Gigi Coe, eds. *Stepping Stones: Appropriate Technology and Beyond.* New York: Schocken Books, 1978. [Dan Early]

Ouaga (1988) 52 min. Kwate Nee-Owoo and Kwesu Owusu (DI). Dist: CN. *A documentary film on contemporary African cinema featuring clips from recent films and interviews with filmmakers shot during the 1987 festival of Pan-African Cinema in Ouaga-dougou, Burkina Faso.*

OUR ASIAN NEIGHBORS: INDIA SERIES Film Australia (PR). Dist: AIS.

• **Bijan** 14 min. *A personal look at the life of a Calcutta artist—through his paintings, an inside impression of Calcutta.*

• **Anokhi** 20 min. *The story of John and Faith Singh and their work in maintaining the traditional hand-printed clothing 'industry' of the villages around Jaipur.*

• **Puppeteer** 20 min. *Depicts the modified way of life of a traditional puppeteer in Udaipur today. Living in a tent on a street corner, Bansilal works in a superb Maharajah's Palace—now converted to a five-star hotel.*

• **Viney** 17 min. *A film depicting the daily domestic life of Viney Gupta—a young Hindu housewife living in a comfortable section of New Delhi.*

• **Rana** 19 min. *The story of a young Muslim girl student living in a crowded section of Old Delhi. The customary veiling of women (Purdah) and impending marriage by arrangement are examined.*

• **Bombay Movies** 15 min. *Vinod Kharna is one of the most popular Hindi movie stars. The film explores his life and work as a way of gaining insight into the Indian 'pop' culture.*

• **Teacher in the Sky** 16 min. *A film about India's satellite Instructional Television Experiment—an experiment in education where space-age technology is brought to bear on solving the problems of remote villagers.*

• **Padma** 20 min. *A personal look at renowned Madras dancing teacher. As the result of her star pupil getting married and leaving during the filming, there is an opportunity to examine the Indian Guru-disciple relationship.*

• **Swami Shyam** 20 min. *Involves the audience directly in experiencing an Indian Swami. Set in the Kulu Valley within the Himalayas, the film ends with one of the Swami's three-minute lessons in meditation.*

• **Jyoti** 17 min. *A first-hand account of a 12-year-old girl's daily life in a huge industrial complex on the outskirts of Bombay.*

• **Questions** 15 min. *A relaxed talk between the Australian director and a group of 15-year-old school children. Questions and answers—about Australia, about their lives in India.*

OUR ASIAN NEIGHBORS: INDONESIA SERIES Film Australia (PR). Dist: AIS.

- **An Angklung Orchestra** 6 min. *An angklung is a Javanese bamboo musical instrument. The instrument's complexity is demonstrated and a familiar waltz performed.*
- **Azhari Ali—An Achenese University Student** 23.5 min. *Azhari Ali teaches five nights a week so that he may study agriculture at University. He is a devout Moslem, and only late at night can he find the time to study.*
- **A Balinese Gong Orchestra** 11 min. *An introduction to another form of Indonesian music, the Gamelan gong. Each instrument in the gong orchestra is explained and demonstrated.*
- **The Bupati of Subang— A Government Official** 23 min. *The Bupati is a government official who administers a region. His decisions can affect the lives of over a million people. His daily life—long hours with little time for relaxation—and his family, are portrayed.*
- **The Hassans—A Buginese Trading Family** 23 min. *Pak Hasan and his sons operate a fleet of sailing ships on the Java sea. The launching of a new ship, with its risks and opportunities, is an important moment in their lives.*
- **Marvel—A Jakarta Boy** 17 min. *Marvel and his family are migrants seeking a new way of life in the city of Jakarta. He works hard selling rice cakes, so that he may afford his life's goal of being educated. A companion film to* Taram—a Minangkabau Village.
- **Mastri—A Balinese Woman** 19.5 min. *Mastri and her husband Sukit are a young couple whose aspirations are fundamentally similar to young couples around the world. Their village life and religious beliefs contrast the Bali known to the tourists.*
- **Pak Menggung—A Javanese Aristocrat** 20.5 min. *No longer is Java ruled by kings and queens. The aristocrats are today mostly poor. This film is about the daily life of one who now devotes his remaining years to recording the disappearing traditions and ceremonies of the "old way." A comparison film to* The Bupati of Subang.
- **Sinaga's Family—A Batak Village** 18 min. *Sinaga and his family live in a small fishing village on Lake Toba. To earn a living, he is a rice farmer by day and a fisherman by night. His wife weaves to supplement their income.*
- **Taram—A Minangkabau Village** 22 min. *In the village of Taram, the clan inheritance is passed from mother to daughter—a matrilineal society. The husband is considered a guest—a man of high rank. This film shows the traditional life of a village similar to the one left behind by Marvel and his family. See* Marvel—A Jakarta Boy.

OUR ASIAN NEIGHBORS: THAILAND SERIES Film Australia (PR). Dist: AIS.

- **Chiang Mai—Northern Capital** 13 min. *An intimate glimpse of the people of Chiang Mai, their religious beliefs, and their traditional craftsmanship in silk and silver. The fireworks of a Buddhist festival contrast the solemn offerings to a river goddess.*
- **Children of Bangkok** 18 min. *Through the eye of a camera, we experience a typical day in the lives of three Bangkok boys who share the same city yet are worlds apart. An absorbing study of lifestyles in an Asian city.*
- **Floating Rice** 13 min. *The village of Supanburi stands on the rain-swollen canal banks. The floating rice grows and will soon be ready for harvest. We join a typical village family and experience their way of life.*
- **Harvest at Nong Lub** 20 min. *Without intruding, the camera lets us live with a Thai family at harvest time. Their hard work, modest pleasures, and dreams are revealed in a different lifestyle.*
- **Ka Rorn—Southern Village** 18 min. *Life in a small Thai village community, on an island that few villagers will ever leave. Isolated from the 20th century, the population is self-sufficient, supported by farming and fishing.*
- **The Temple of Twenty Pagodas** 21 min. *The beauty and serenity of Buddhist monastery life is sensitively revealed in a moving filmic experience. In a monastery said to be 2,000 years old, the monks play an important role in village life.*

Our God the Condor 30 min. Paul Yule and Andy Harries (PR). Dist: FL FR$110, VR$55, FS$550, VS$295. *This film, shot in the Southern Andes of Peru, documents the "Yawar Fiesta," an annual event representing the Indians' triumph over the Spaniards. The ceremony pits two animals with symbolic significance against each other: a condor and a bull. The condor, considered the mountain spirit of the Andes, is painstakingly captured and then tied to the back of a bull, the symbol of Spain. It is a spectacular event. The two creatures are locked in ritual battle, the wildly flapping condor atop the lurching, spinning bull. Finally, the two are separated, and the condor sours over the mountains, a symbol of freedom of the Andean people.* [Reviewed by Catherine J. Allen, *AA* 92:1105–1108, 1990.]

Our Lives in Our Hands 49 min. Harold Prins and Karen Carter (FM). Dist: DER FR$60, VR$40, FS$600, VS$300. *Examines the traditional Native American craft of split ash basketmaking as a means of economic and cultural survival for Aroostook Micmac Indians of northern Maine. This documentary of rural off-reservation Indian artisans aims at breaking down stereotypical images. Basketmakers are filmed making baskets in their homes, at work on local potato farms, and at business meetings of the Basket Bank, a cooperative formed by the Aroostook Micmac Council. First-person commentaries are augmented by authentic 17th-century Micmac music.* [Reviewed by William A. Turnbaugh and Sarah Peabody Turnbaugh, *AA* 90:254–255, 1988.]

Our Sacred Land (1984) 27 min. Chris Spotted Eagle (PR). Dist: Spotted Eagle Productions, 2524 Hennepin Ave. South, Minneapolis, MN 55404; (612) 377-4212, FR$110, VR$75, FS$495, VS$260. *"The film was designed, in part, as a political tool to generate support in a struggle to regain native jurisdiction over the sacred Black Hills and Bear Butte.... The major issue concerns rights protected by the American Indian Religious Freedom Act of 1978."* [From the review by Harald Prins, *AA* 90:774–778, 1988.]

Out of Order (1983) 89 min. Bruce Jackson (PR), Diane Christian (DI). Dist: Documentary Research, 96 Rumsey Road, Buffalo, NY 14209; (716) 885-9777, FR$150, FS$1500. *Examines the religious life of six nuns "whose personal narratives are the subject of this film.... Does not* *focus primarily on life within the convent, but does offer a valued contribution to our understanding of how religious life affected the lives of six ... women.... The film addresses three aspects of life in religion: the decision to enter; the decision to leave; and the necessary adjustments faced on the outside."* [From the review by Katherine Murray, AA 88:781–782, 1986.]

OUT OF THE FIERY FURNACE SERIES (1986) Robert Raymond (PR). Dist: PBS VS$198 (each), VS$1250 (seven-part series). *"This series describes how the worldwide exploitation of metal resources has influenced human history. The series spans civilization from the Stone Age to the Space Age, highlighting the discovery, mining, metallurgy, and products of utilitarian metals.... [The program] provides a panoramic perspective on events that shaped our use of metals."* [From the review in ARCH 40(4):71, 1987.] The titles are:

- From Stone to Bronze
- From Swords into Plowshares
- Shining Conquests
- The Industrial Revolution
- Into the Machine Age
- From Alchemy to the Atom
- The Age of Metals

OUT OF THE PAST: AN INTRODUCTION TO ARCHAEOLOGY (1993) 8 programs, 60 min. each. William T. Sanders and David L. Webster (DI), WQED/Pittsburgh (PR). Dist: ACPB VS$29.95 (each), VS$215 (set). *This PBS series and television course uses on-site filming to enable students to explore how archaeologists reconstruct ancient societies and explain how and why they evolved. Research at the Classic Maya center of Copan, Honduras, forms the core of the series, but a broadly comparative perspective includes many other civilizations and cultures, past and present. Students will understand how archaeology and anthropology interact. The emphasis is on how people behaved in the past, by reconstructing basic social, political, and economic institutions of their cultures.* The course components include: eight one-hour television programs; a textbook that introduces students to the concepts presented in the television programs; a study guide that integrates material from the programs and the text; and a faculty guide. [Reviewed by Peter S. Allen, ARCH 46(5):82, 1993.]

- **Program 1: New Worlds** *Columbus' dreams of better trade routes were petty ambitions compared to the reality of contracting the New World. The Age of Discovery shook Europe out of its medieval mindset and into modern times. Like a mirror held up before them, the New World reflected back on Europe a range of cultures from the vast empires of Aztecs and Incas to roving bands of hunter-gatherers. This was irrefutable evidence of cultural evolution as a global process, operating independently in the Old and New Worlds.*
- **Program 2: The Hearth** *But do not all societies, simple or complex, provide for the basic functions of home life? In this episode, we see the variety and similarities of homes and families, learning how enculturation and economic cooperation are expressed in cultures of today and long ago. The remains of houses at archaeological sites reveal the physical contexts of ancient family life, permitting archaeologists to reconstruct family size, composition, and function.*
- **Program 3: Artisans and Traders** *A glance at today's newspaper brings home the global importance of producing marketable goods, and the economic processes of production and distribution are among the most ancient linkages between people, between cultures. Occupational specialization has evolved from the first curers, the first people sought out for their sharper arrows and sturdier baskets, to the present welter of industrial and postindustrial jobs, and we see in this episode how archaeologists detect and measure specialization and economic interdependence.*
- **Program 4: Signs and Symbols** *"What makes us human?" is one of those obvious questions that are fascinatingly difficult to answer. Here we examine symbolic communication as the distinguishing hallmark of human cultures. Speech, art, rituals, status symbols, and writing—all are characteristic of cultures and convey detailed information about them. But in few cases do these symbolic systems leave durable remains, and detecting and interpreting symbols is one especially controversial and difficult but revealing area of archaeological reconstruction.*
- **Program 5: Power, Prestige, and Wealth** *Today's politics seem all too often to be a game played by the powerful, charismatic, and wealthy. Some like to think that ancient societies were more idealistic, but archaeologists have found that the evolution of political systems throughout human history is based on motives that seem remarkably contemporary. How do archaeologists measure the power of a long-dead king? This episode reveals the different methods archaeologists use to study how rulers gain and keep power.*
- **Program 6: Realms** *Governments thrive and weaken. Rulers make alliances with each other, and then break them and go to war. Borders move as capitals rise and fall. Detecting the actual borders of ancient kingdoms is often impossible, but archaeologists can reconstruct much about the internal workings of societies and their external relations played out in marriage alliances, trade, and warfare.*
- **Program 7: The Spirit World** *In all cultures, people turn to religion for comfort, for guidance, for an explanation of spiritual continuities beyond life and death. Ritual behavior and sacred spaces and objects give form to religious meanings, and archaeologists are challenged to detect the spiritual significance and interpret it properly. At times, religion and ideology have been used for cynical purposes, and the archaeologist is challenged to detect these uses, as well.*
- **Program 8: Collapse** *The phrase "the fall of civilization" calls forth images of earthquakes and invading hordes shattering classical buildings and scattering the terrified (but civilized) populace. In this episode, we consider various settings of collapse, particularly that of the Maya of Central America. Classic Maya culture disappeared in its heartland a millennium ago. Archaeologists working at Copan have found that the Maya left an important message for other civilizations, one that reveals the consequences of overpopulation and overexploitation of resources. We meet the enemy,*

and the enemy is our own eternally quick-fix solutions for our long-range global problems.

Out of the Shadows (Indonesia: A Generation of Change Series) (1987) 28 min. Barbara Barde (DI). Dist: CTC FS$535, VS$295, order #OUNS12. *Indonesia, with over 165 million people, approaches the 21st century with a combination of enormous social and ecological problems; however, a determination to participate viably in the fields of industry and technology and a burning desire for self-sufficiency, is rapidly taking this relatively unknown nation "out of the shadows".*

Out There, A Lone Island 67 min. Humphrey W. Leynse (FM). Dist: UCEMC order #8124, FR$37. *A semi-documentary impression of life on a remote Korean island in the Sea of Japan where the eastern philosophy of subordination of self to oneness with nature is lived daily. Man persists on Ullung-do, no matter what the hardships, as life changes rhythmically with the seasons. The actors are island residents; the story—presented without narration or subtitles and with only incidental dialogue, accompanied by an original score—is very close to their own lives. One family is featured: the father is dead; the mother worries about providing for her two sons; the grandfather, who now represents the family's stability and tradition, ponders the future and perpetuation of the family name. Suffering and survival are accompanied by pleasures, however: falling in love, getting drunk with one's friends, having one's rabbit to pet. The island men fish for squid by night, tend fields and cattle by day, help the women with the seaweed harvest, and transport cattle to the city for sale, where they briefly enjoy urban pleasures. A beautiful, unusual, and powerful film that captures the intimacy of family interaction, evokes the stark atmosphere of the island and communicates in a purely visual way the universality of mankind's problems and joys. Korean dialogue.* [Reviewed by Edward Norbeck, AA 74:158, 1972.]

Over Rich, Over Sexed and Over Here (The New Pacific Series) (1987) 60 min. BBC/NVC (PR). Dist: FIV VS$79. *The film brings out the fact that the Pacific is a region where the development of tourism has actually strengthened the traditional culture rather than destroying or distorting it.*

Over the Hedge (1993) 10 min. Karen Davis (FM). Dist: UCEMC VR$40, FS$325, VS$160, order #38248. *This acclaimed film provides an insightful and humorous look at an eccentric aspect of suburban America—people who shape their front-yard hedges and plants into fantastic topiary shapes.*

The Owl Who Married a Goose (1974) 7 min. Dist: IUAVC FR$6.50. *Depicts in sand animation an Eskimo legend about an owl who cannot keep up with the goose he loves and, after a series of misadventures, meets with a tragic fate. Uses Eskimo voices imitating the geese and owl noises as the sound.*

Ozidi Tides of the Delta (see University of Ife Series)

P4W: Prison for Women (see under *Prison for Women*)

The Pacific Age (The New Pacific Series) (1987) 60 min. BBC/NVC (PR). Dist: FIV VS$79. *Dynamic economic growth in the countries on the Asian rim of the Pacific has transformed world trade. The film attempts to capture the parameters and impact of this transformation.*

Pacific Island (1949) 18 min. Julien Bryan (PR) for International Film Productions. Dist: NYU FR$15; PSU(PCR) order #919.2, FR$4.10; IUAVC FR$5.50. *Liliep Atoll, Marshall Islands. Account of fishing and copra production. Emphasis on modern democratic institutions.*

PACIFIC ISLAND LIFE SERIES (1977) International Film Foundation (PR), Herman Schlenker (FM). Dist: IFF FR$25, FS$250. *Filmed on the Polynesian Outlier of Nuguria in Melanesia, which is now part of Papua New Guinea. Each records traditional activities that may be rapidly changing: cooking, canoe making, house building, farming and fishing.* [Reviewed by Joan Larcom, AA 86:814, 1984.]

- **The Coconut Tree** 15 min. FR$25, FS$260.
- **Family Life** 16 min. FR$35, FS$280.
- **Fishing** 14 min. FR$25, FS$260.
- **Food from the Sea** 13 min. FR$25, FS$240.
- **Village Life** 15 min. FR$25, FS$260.

Pacific Paradox 14 min. Dist: IUAVC FR$6.75. *Records the primitive pattern of life in Arnhemland in northern Australia as it is seen and studied by explorers whose expedition was sponsored by the Smithsonian Institution, the National Geographic Society of America, and the Commonwealth of Australia. Depicts a variety of customary activities of the people, including boat making, turtle hunting, ceremonies, and rites.*

The Pacification War in Amazonia 52 min. Yves Billon (FM). Dist: FDV. *This report is the last chapter of the history of Indian tribes in Brazil caught in the trap of modern civilization. The Parkana Indians undergo the first contact, which begins the process of their pacification. They are drawn by presents laid out in the forest, then they are settled around the attraction camps. Afterward they will be parked in native reserves before being completely assimilated by western civilization. Pacifications are always carried out for strategic or economic aims. The potential wealth of the Amazonian subsoil is at the origin of the national integration plan and of the construction of the Trans-amazonian highways. The Serra Norte, containing the most important lodes of iron in the world, is exploited by a North American company. The prospection drives away the Xicrins, who had always lived there. In the Island of Bananal, the Carajas are in the last stage of their integration and of the destruction of their culture. The economic plans of the native service imposes an industrial agriculture upon them, whilst a native policy force achieves the destruction of the traditional authority of the Indian chiefs.*

O Pagador de Promessas (The Given Word; The Keeper of Promises) (1962) 98 min. Anselmo Duarte (WR, DI), original play by Oswaldo Massaini. Dist: AB FR$75. *The film adaptation of the famous Brazilian play that shows a* *peasant in Bahia who is caught between the Roman Catholic church and the syncretic Condombie cult.* [Reviewed by Joan Bamberger, *AA* 75:596–597, 1973.] Suggested supplement: Melville J. Herskovits, "African Gods and Catholic Saints in New World Religious Belief." *AA* 39:635–643, 1973.

The Painted Truck 28 min. Judith and Stanley Hallet and Sebastian C. Schroeder (FM). Dist: FIM/RF FR$35, FS$350. *There are only two methods of transportation in Afghanistan—camels and trucks, and the big trucks are taking over. They have to be big and very strong to carry heavy loads of food, goods, animals, and people over the rugged Afghan mountains. The trucks arrive in Kabul, capital of Afghanistan, from America and England, stripped down to only an engine block mounted on a chassis. The Afghans build big wooden boxes on top of the frames and paint them with extravagent colors and designs: Muslim motifs, movie stars (from Pakistani films), and lush mountain scenes are favorites. In this film, we are introduced to "Malik," a truck owner, and watch one of his trucks being painted by a master painter and his assistants. It takes about ten days to do the job and costs the equivalent of four months' salary for a driver. In the Kabul truck yards, the trucks are always "beefed up" with reinforcements to carry loads no one in Detroit ever anticipated. The emergency brake is always removed. There is no choice, according to Afghan logic, since it could not be depended upon to function under such conditions of overloading. In its place an apprentice driver, called "Cleanar," hangs out the back of the truck and throws a wooden wedge, or "danda panj," behind the rear wheel to prevent the truck from rolling backward down the steep mountain slopes. He does all the dirty work on the trip, because the driver only drives. After three years, the apprentice can hope to become a driver, but never an owner. We also get to know the driver, "Motarwan," a good-natured garrulous fellow who has been a driver for 14 years. He tells what it is like to live and work in Afghanistan, unconsciously revealing a great deal about the social structure, traditions, and cultures of his country, as we travel with him from Kabul to Bamian, in the Hindu Kush, by way of the 12,700-foot Hajigak Pass. It is a fascinating trip: they are hauling rice, soap, wheat, wood, melons, and lots of people, including a group of nomadic tribesmen they pick up on the way.*

Paj Ntaub: Textile Techniques of the Hmong 40 min. Joyce Smith (FM). Dist: HLUA VR$40, VS$100. *The Hmong are a non-Chinese, semi-nomadic group of people from southern China and southeast Asia. In spite of centuries of change and migration, they have kept their textile arts, Paj Ntaub, alive. Paj Ntaub are the Hmong words used to describe all of the techniques Hmong women use to make and decorate cloth. "Paj" means flower, and "Ntaub" means cloth. Today there are over 100,000 Hmong living in the United States as political refugees from war in Laos. In this video, four Hmong women artists who now live in Providence, Rhode Island, are presented. They feel that this video will help to keep their traditional textile arts from extinction.*

Palenque: Un Canto (The African Heritage of a Colombian Village) (1992) 48 min. Maria Raquel Bozzi (FM). Dist: Maria Raquel Bozzi, 10515 Tabor St. #1, Los Angeles, CA 90034; (310) 842-4888, fax (310) 836-3795. *The villagers of San Basilio de Palenque, descendants of African rebel slaves, preserve and maintain the culture of their African forebears in their music, dance, and other aspects of their social lives. This film provides both a historical account of their situation and a documentation of their day-to-day struggles, both in rural and urban areas where women commute to sell their produce.*

The Palestinian People Do Have Rights (1979) 48 min. United Nations (PR). Dist: ICF FR$75, FS$645, VS$480. "*Attempts an assessment of the Palestinian people—their history, the loss of their homeland, and the struggle to regain it along with their national dignity.*" [From the review by Julie Peteet, *AA* 89:1018–1022, 1987.]

Palm Play (1980) 30 min. Alan Lomax (AN). Dist: UCEMC FR$38, FS$470, VS$355. *Analyzes palm gestures in various cultures. Margaret Mead's cross-cultural films on child rearing showed women using different kinds of palm contact in handling their babies, and it has long been observed that the palm is an important secondary erogenous zone, especially for women. In fact, there seems to be a strong relationship between the way the feminine palm is displayed or concealed in dance and the codes that regulate feminine behavior in a given culture. Palm Play illustrates six types of palm presentation prevalent in the dances of different cultural traditions: Openly presented palms are shown to be characteristic of "permissive" societies in which women have the most crucial responsibilities in food production; concealed or hidden palms indicate a highly stratified and sexually restrictive society; and the neutral palm is typical of societies dominated by "masculine" values. See related films Dance and Human History, Step Style.* [Reviewed by Malcolm Farmer, *SBF* 17:99, 1981.]

Le Palmier à huile (Palm Oil) (1962) 20 min. Jean Rouch (DI), Centre National de la Recherche Scientifique, Comité du Film Ethnographique and Institut Francais d'Afrique Noir (PR). Dist: CFE; DER. *Agricultural research on the cultivation of palm oil in the Ivory Coast.*

Pam Kuso Kar (Briser les poteries de Pam) (Breaking Pam's Vases) (1974) 10 min. Jean Rouch (DI), Centre National de la Recherche Scientifique, Comite du Film Ethnographique (PR). Dist: CFE; DER. *In 1974, Pam Sambo Zima, the oldest of the priests of possession in Niamey, Niger, died at the age of seventy-plus years. The faithful from the possession cult symbolically break the dead priest's ritual vases and cry for the deceased.*

The Panare—Scenes from the Frontier (1982) 60 min. Melissa Llewelyn-Davies (PR) for the BBC. Dist: FI FR$100, FS$800, VS$480. "*The Panare, a group of semi-nomadic foragers, are depicted as people who have been exposed to white influence for more than a century. Still, in spite of this contact, they have maintained much of their cultural integrity as Amazonians.*" [From the review by Allyn MacLean Stearman, *AA* 88:782–783, 1986.]

Paolina's Hairstyle (1991) 13 min. Etno Museo Monti Lepini (PR), Vincenzo Padiglione (DI), Donatella Occhiuzzi, Antonio Riccio and Ercole Cerilli (CA). Dist: EMML. *Paolina is a 65-year-old peasant who lives in a hill community of Lazio, Italy. Everyday she spends 15 to 20 minutes to arrange the hairstyle in the manner that she has learned from her grandmother. She begins to loosen the hair and combs it. The hair is divided into two strands using a rope that passes through her mouth. Then she starts to prepare one side of the head to form a plait, joining together six parts; and she closes it using hair which remained in the comb. Then she does the same with the other side and after that she fixes both the plaits on the crown in a skilled and accurate manner. During the recording, Paolina tells some stories about her childhood, episodes on women that sometimes fought at the fountain, pulling each other's hair because of love affairs or the order of the queue. She remembers that saying "the man has to be not down at heel, the woman has to have a tidy hairstyle." The intention of this film is to show a mentality by showing a body technique.*

Paredes de piedra (Walls of Stone) (1973) 20 min. Ronald J. Duncan and Gloria S. Duncan (FM). Dist: RJD FR$30, FS$300. *This film describes the life of small farmers in the Caqueza Valley in the central Andes near Bogotá. Family organization and most activities are concentrated on agricultural production and marketing, which is portrayed in the film. When the people in the film saw it, their reaction was, "We did not know that we were so beautiful." Many people see their problems as small farmers as being insoluble, and they leave for the cities. A barrio in Bogotá is shown where some of the people from Caqueza have migrated, and their housing and nutrition problems are described. The migration of these small farmers into Bogotá has created severe shortages of urban services.*

Paralanguage and Proxemics (1986) 28 min. Dist: IM VS$129, order #JJ108. *Examines the importance of nonverbal communication in creating first impressions and conveying the true meaning of a message. This program defines two nonverbal systems—paralanguage and proxemics. It shows how voice quality, rate and volume of speech, word emphasis, inflection, and tone can change the meaning of words. The program also describes the spatial relationships in a communication system, examining the intimate zone, the personal zone, the social zone, and the public zone.*

The Parching Winds of Somalia (1984) 30 min. QED Enterprises and Charles Geshekter (PR). Dist: IUAVC R$25, FS$150, VS$150, order #CC3286; VU. *A historical perspective on the African nation and a portrait of its people, who endure a harsh nomadic existence on parched terrain they regard as blessed land. Known as a nation of poets, Somalia has transmitted its history by oral tradition, and only since 1972 have efforts been made to record the nation's cultural heritage in writing. Scenes show nomads as they transmit historical information around a nighttime campfire, scholars at work transcribing these oral traditions, and radio stations broadcasting this material for education and entertainment. Traces the history of Somalia from its battles for independence under the Muslim leader Sayyid Muhammad Abdille Hasan to the contemporary concerns, such as the challenge to traditional patriarchal customs by Somali women.*

The Parting 16 min. Ziuko Nikolic (FM). Dist: WFV FR$26.50, FS$265. *Funeral in Montenegro, Yugoslavia.*

The Pasciak Family, Chicago (see Six American Families Series)

Passing Shadows (1984) 34 min. Barrie Machin (FM). Dist: Barrie Machin, Department of Anthropology, Nedlands, Western Australia 6009; 011-61-09/380, VS$500, *"About a funeral in a Greek village on the island of Crete. . . . Van Gennep's familiar rites of passage model provides the theoretical framework for the interpretation of these rituals."* [From the review by Loring M. Danforth, AA 88:1045–1056, 1986.]

The Past That Lives 65 min. Philo Bregstein (FM). Dist: DER FR$80, VR$50. *Jacob Presser, the great Dutch historian, was born at the end of the 19th century in the heart of Amsterdam's Jewish quarter. Presser's intensely personal narrative is embedded in the tremendous upheavals of European history in the first half of the 20th century: the growth of the socialist ideology and the optimism it inspired; the terror of Hitler's rise to power; and the devastation of Amsterdam's 100,000 Jews. With wit and sadness, Presser tells of his childhood in the ghetto; his fascination with socialism, Germany, and the Renaissance; and his marriage. In the postwar return to "normalcy," Presser attempted to make sense of his experiences by interviewing countless survivors of the holocaust and writing his masterpiece "Ashes in the Wind: The Destruction of the Dutch Jewry." The filmmaker interweaves this account with extensive Dutch and German archival photos and film, to create a moving portrait of prewar Amsterdam and its transformations.*

The Path (1973) 34 min. Donald Rundstrom, Ronald Rundstrom, Clinton Bergum (AN, FM). Dist: Sumai Film Co., P.O. Box 26481, Los Angeles, CA 90026, FR$35, FS$345. *Shot for a class in ethnographic film at San Francisco State University. The Rundstroms had studied Zen through archery and wanted to film the Zen of the tea ceremony. Mostly filmed in a collapsible tea house set up in a San Francisco apartment. They worked closely with the tea ceremony teacher who does the ceremony in the film and who helped with some of the shooting. The garden shots were made in a formal Japanese garden near San Jose. The film shows a Japanese tea ceremony in real time from the approach of the guests through their appreciation of the setting to the tea preparation, serving, and drinking of the tea. There are two main themes: the yin yang balance—in some shots this balance is encompassed in the frame (e.g., water running between still banks); in others it is achieved through editing (e.g., cutting from a male painting a character in strong male style to a female making tea). Also: management of energy-building to climax, then release (especially in the early shot of drawing the ideograph for "path, way, do" and making the tea). A unique film. It attempts to use the philosophy and aesthetic of the event itself to structure the film. Warnings: It can be unbearably tedious for students who expect lots of action and storyline. Audiences* need to be set up carefully to participate for 34 minutes. Focusing questions: What sorts of oppositions are brought together within shots? In juxtaposed shots? What is the meaning of the anti-intellectual quotes for the tea masters? Does it really violate the spirit of The Way to examine it, and to film it in this way? How can the same culture have tea ceremonies and the Samurai Code of Bushido? Bibliography: Donald Rundstrom, Ronald Rundstrom, and Clinton Bergum, *Japanese Tea: The Ritual, the Aesthetics, the Way.* New York: MSS Information, 1973. [Reviewed by Richard Beardsley, AA 77:463–464, 1975. Jay Ruby, AA 77:4–466, 1975.]

The Path of Life   26 min. Dist: FHS VS$89.95, order #DH-884. *At the festivities for Wabana, Gujek is nearly overcome at seeing her. He can barely return to the land of the living, where he tells all who will listen that there is a time for life and a time for death, that he who weeps too long for the souls of the dead will never find the true path of life.*

The Path of Souls   26 min. Dist: FHS VS$89.95, order #DH-882. *The first part of a three-part story relates how Gujek enters in the path of souls to find his beloved wife, Wabana. After Gujek's lovely young wife dies, he is too heartbroken to return to his regular village life after the prescribed period of mourning. Instead, he seeks to find Wabana, to find the path of souls on which she has entered.*

The Pathans   (Disappearing World Series) (1980) 45 min. Akbar Ahmed (AN). Dist: PSU, order #51250. *Bound by a common language, a common heritage, and the powerful unifying force of Islam, Pathans do not acknowledge the geographical boundary between Afghanistan and Pakistan, which divides their people. Their code of living is based on personal honor and revenge, and they accept no imposed leadership—as the Soviet invaders of Afghanistan discovered.*

Pather Panchalli (The Song of the Road)   (Apu Trilogy) (1954) 112 min. Satyajit Ray (FM), Ravi Shankar (MU). Dist: AB FR$85. *Fiction film about life in rural Bengal.*

Patterns of Subsistence: Hunter-Gatherers and Pastoralists   (The Faces of Culture Series) (1983) 30 min. Dist: IM VS$119, order #SF04. *The relationship of subsistence patterns to cultural patterns and lifestyles is explored in this program which shows how different cultures have adapted to their environments. It identifies the characteristics of hunter-gatherer cultures and pastoral cultures, examining the contributions of each to the development of modern social organization. Striking footage shows the !Kung woman's role as gatherer and the Mbuti pygmy man's role as hunter. The ways in which the Netsilik Eskimos have adapted to a harsh environment and examined, as is the fierce, nomadic lifestyle of the pastoral Nuer tribe of the Sudan. The battle with the environment is investigated through a view of the Iranian Basseri's search for fertile grazing land.*

Au Pays des mages noirs (In the Land of the Black Magic)   (1946–47) 12 min. Jean Rouch (DI), Actualités Françaises (PR). Dist: CFE; DER. *Hippopotamus hunting with a harpoon by the Sorko of Niger.*

Peace Has Not Been Made: A Case History of a Hmong Family's Encounter with a Hospital   (1983) 25 min. John Fink and Doua Yang (PR), Peter O'Neill (DI). Dist: Rhode Island Office of Refugee Resettlement, 600 New London Ave., Cranston, RI 02920; (401) 464-2127, VR$35, VS$75. *"A case study of one hospitalization of a Hmong boy, wrestles . . . with ethical, cross-cultural and communication problems. . . . A documentary of runaway lack of communication between American hospital staff and the parents of a Hmong patient. A medical crisis precipitates a cultural crisis of conflict between American and Hmong belief systems."* [From the review by Marjorie A. Muecke, AA 88:776–778, 1986.]

The Pearl Fisher   28 min. Dillon Bustin (FM). Dist: DER FR$55, VR$35, FS$550, VS$275. *The freshwater pearl industry once flourished along Indiana's inland waterways. The Wabash, flowing south from Lafayette to join the Ohio at Mt. Vernon, bustled with the shallow boats of such fisherman, with about 600 operating around Vincennes alone. This film documents Barnett Bass as he fishes for freshwater mollusks in the White River in southern Indiana, seeking gem-quality pearls and the mother-of-pearl lining the shells. In addition to the fisherman and his wife, the film depicts the local jewelers, a pearl dealer, and a shell exporter. It explores issues of technological innovation, international trade, and resulting stresses on the environment. On a deeper level, it suggests the traditional symbolic meanings of pearls: immortality, purity, virtue, and trust, as well as the role of Romanticism in everyday life.*

Peasant Ecology in the Rural Philippines   (1971) 26 min. George M. Guthrie (FM). Dist: PSU FR$20, FS$425. *Wet rice cultivation from plowing to harvest, vegetable and fruit production, housing, and village industries of a rural tropical area. Poor diets restrict growth and health of children. Complexity of relationships between culture patterns, physical environment, and limited technology is illustrated.*

Peasant Painter   (Inhabitants of the Land of Grace Series) (1984) 18 min. John Dickinson (FM). Dist: DER FR$30, VR$25, FS$325, VS$250. *In this film, Cleto Rojas, a peasant, paints memories of his journey to Caracas, his fantastic visions, scenes inspired by mythology or the local cinema, and the rural around him.*

Les Pêcheurs de Niger (The Fishermen of Niger)   (1962) Jean Rouch (DI), Centre National de la Recherche Scientifique, Comité du Film Ethnographique (PR). Dist: CFE; DER.

Pedro Linares, artesano cartonero (Papier-Mache Artist)   (see Artesanos Mexicanos (Mexico's Folk Artists) Series)

PEOPLE IN CHANGE SERIES   (1989) Film Australia (PR). Dist: FIV VS$475. *What is traditional culture? How and why do cultures change? People In Change is an excellent resource for teaching social studies, language, natural science, art, crafts, music, and dance. The two programs clearly demonstrate the impact of other cultures on the traditional way of life in Papua New Guinea.* Titles of the programs are:

- New Guinea Patrol and Excerpts from Yumi Yet
- Towards Baruya Manhood

PEOPLE OF MANY LANDS SERIES 20 min. each. BBC-TV (PR). *These programs, produced by BBC School Television, were designed to give children a better understanding of other people's ways of life. They show a wide range of people in widely different settings, whose everyday work and life are presented in the context of the geographical background. Discussion guides available.*

- **Uganda: Fishing Village** *This program begins with a visit to Murchison Falls and shows some of the wildlife on the banks of the River Nile, then moves to the village of Wanseko on the shores of Lake Albert. Here we spend a typical day with the fishermen and their families, watch the catch being unloaded, the fish prepared for sale. We visit the village school, listen to prayers, and watch medical inspections and various school lessons. We see something of the villagers' homes, the work of women and children, and end the day as it began, with the fishing fleet.*
- **Tanzania: Life on Kilmanjaro** *In this film, the various processes of coffee cultivation are shown. The plants are sprayed and, when the berries are ripe, harvested by hand. The hard seeds are removed by machine from the fleshy outer part of the berries, then soaked and dried. Sisal cultivation is shown: first the cultivation of the leaves, then the crushing, and finally the drying of the fibers.*
- **Kenya: Mombasa** *We visit both the old harbor and the modern port of Kilindini. We look at the food markets with cassava, maize, bananas, and coconuts for sale. We watch the wood carvers and silversmiths at work and visit a carpet auction.*
- **Sri Lanka: Life in the Hills** *We visit the Ratwatta tea estate in the low foothills between Kandy and Matale, watch the plucking, weighing, and various factory processes and meet some of the Tamil workers. We see how an elephant is employed on the estate, find out how sugary juice is obtained from the bud of the flower of the kitul palm, and also observe the way of life of the Sinhalese in the nearby villages. We visit one of the Buddhist schools, which both their children and the children of the farmers attend.*
- **Sri Lanka: Coastal Villages and Towns** *Fishermen launch their outrigger in a rough sea and later return with the catch. We see the harvesting of the coconut fruit and are shown some of the many uses to which the various parts of the tree are put. We watch part of a puppet play rehearsal and visit the maskmaker and a family who all help in Batik-making. At the end of the day, we join the people of Ambalangoda as they make their purchases in the market.*

PEOPLE OF THE AUSTRALIAN WESTERN DESERT SERIES (1969) John Martin-Jones (PR), Ian Dunlop (WR, Dl). Dist: UCEMC; FAA (These films may not be imported into Australia for any purpose.) *This important series is the product of a 1965 film expedition sponsored by the Australian Institute of Aboriginal Studies into the "Western Desert," a cultural-linguistic region embracing half a million square miles and the ancestral home of the nomadic Aborigines. The purpose of the expedition was to document on film the disappearing Aboriginal culture and community. The result was some 25,000 feet of black-and-white film, which has been edited into ten films totaling some three hours viewing time. These films record the lives of Diagamara and his family, who were met in the desert; Djun, one of the film unit guides who exhibits sacred boards and leads a tour of the ancestral site and of Minma and his family, who were returned from civilization to the desert.* [Reviewed by James C. Pierson, *AA* 88:269–271, 1986.]

- **Part 1: Seed Cake Making and General Camp Activities** 12 min. Order #7685, FR$16, FS$170. *The women of Djagamara's family gather wollybutt grass seed near surface pools and, returning to camp, thresh and pan the seed, grind it into a grey flour on stones, mix the flour in water, and bake it in hot ashes for about ten minutes.*
- **Part 2: Gum Preparation, Stone Flaking: Djagamara Leaves Badjar** 19 min. Order #7687, FR$15, FS$150. *Djagamara sets off into the desert to collect and beat gum from spinifex grass which, back in camp, he melts onto a stick over a barkfire, then turns to making a spear-thrower blade by flaking a discarded fragment of chalcedony with a hammer-stone; finally, Djagamara sets off again in search of his family who have left to look for food.*
- **Part 4: A Family Moving Camp and Gathering Food** 48 min.
- **Part 5: Old Camp Sites at Tika Tika** 12 min. Order #7678, FR$95. *Minma and his family are encamped at an ancestral site at Tika Tika well, amid old or ancient scattered broken artifacts, grindstones, and other remains. Janindu, one of Minma's wives, mends a cracked wooden dish, then prepares and demonstrates a headache potion made from the seeds of the quandong tree.*
- **Part 6: Spear Making, Boys' Spear Fights** 10 min. Order #7690, FR$ 11, FS$80. *Minma makes a spear from the acacia tree, and two sons play with toy spears.*
- **Part 7: Spear Thrower Making, Including Stone Flaking and Gum Preparation** 33 min.
- **Part 8: Fire Making** 7 min.
- **Part 9: Spinning Hair String, Getting Water from a Well, Binding Girl's Hair** 12 min.
- **Part 10: Cooking Kangaroo** 17 min.
- **Part 12: A Few Days in the Life of Three Families** 55 min.
- **Part 13: Stone and Gum Working** 25 min.
- **Part 14: Making a Wooden Digging Dish** 9 min.
- **Part 16: Chasing Evil Spirit out of Camp** 8 min.
- **Part 19: Kangaroo Cooking at Kunapurul** 19 min.
- **Sacred Boards and Ancestral Sites** 8 min. Order #7688, FR$10, FS$65. *At Badjar, a key ancestral site in the desert, the film unit's guide Djun Burungu brings out and displays the sacred boards he keeps hidden here—sacred ancestral links with the Dreamtime of the legendary past that Aboriginal men still carve with mystic symbols and use in ceremonial rites. In the Dreamtime, Badjar was the site of a revenge expedition and of sexual rites, and remains a focus of religious sentiment.*
- **Desert People** 51 min. FR$30. *A summary film, made from parts of the preceding films and intended for a more*

general audience. *The Aborigines of Australia's Western Desert have almost all migrated to federal campgrounds, into the cities, or to large cattle ranches. When this film was made, only a handful held to their traditional way of life, wandering from water source to water source, gathering food on the way. Soon the traditions of the Aborigines will probably disappear altogether, and this film will remain as one of the rare documents of their past. Two family groups are followed as they go through their normal activities. Djagamara and his family are camped by an unusually plentiful water supply, whereas Minma and his family must spend their day traveling from one well to another, gathering food as they go.* [Reviewed by Norman B. Tindale, *AA* 70:437–438, 1968.]

People of the Barrio (1980) Brian and Caroline Moser (PR). *Guayaquil, Ecuador.* [Reviewed by Peter Lloyd, *RAIN* 39:10–11, 1980.]

People of the Chad (1945) 13 min. BIW Dist: FIM/RF FR$10, FS$125. *A record of native life in the interior of French Equatorial Africa. The inhabitants work the natural resources of the region in the most primitive ways, primarily because of a lack of transportation facilities to and from the port cities. The tremendous potential of this area, the film points out, is far from being utilized. Despite difficulties, however, 20th century influences are penetrating the Chad, and we see some of them at work.*

People of the Congo (The Mangbetu) 10 min. Dist: IUAVC FR$5. *Shows the environment, activities, and customs of the Mangbetu people in the Congo region; the sources and nature of their food and its preparation; their primitive household equipment and their division of labor; head binding, facial treatments, and styles of hairdress; the bartering of services; ivory carving, the preparation of paint, designing and painting; the construction of a stringed musical instrument; and the demonstration of a native dance.*

People of the Current (1971) 28 min. Thomas M. Kiefer and George Csisery (FM). Dist: Bee Cross Media, 36 Dogwood Glen, Rochester, NY 14625, FR$10. *A film printout of videotape made among the Tausug of Jolo Island, Sulu Archipelago, Philippines.* [Reviewed by Arlo H. Nimmo, *AA* 78:717–718, 1976.] Suggested supplement: Thomas M. Keifer, *The Tausug.* Holt, Rinehart and Winston, 1970.

People of the Free Train 14 min. Moyer (PR). Dist: IUAVC FR$7.75; PSU FR$11. *Uses the train of a sugar company on which people can ride "free" to tie together sequences showing the history, the people, and agriculture of Fiji. Indicates the background of the major groups making up the populations of Fiji. Pictures native villages, shows the planting of sugar cane, the harvesting and threshing of rice, and indicates the rather backward state of agriculture in Fiji.*

People of the Rice Pot (1975) 90 min. Michael and Valerie Yorke (FM, AN). Dist: Michael Yorke, 12 Belsize Park, London NW3 4ES. *This is an in-depth anthropological film. It is an intimate observation of a man and his family over a year of their lives in a tribal village of Bihar, India. The film gives a detailed understanding of their social and cosmological structure by way of a didactic commentary and voice-over translation of their dialogue and thoughts. Their way of thinking and logic forms a focus of interest throughout the film. The poetry of language and thought involves the viewer in a detailed discussion that is taken up by the commentary, which puts the material into an anthropological framework. Although primarily aimed at a university audience, it is also of interest to a school audience.* [Reviewed by Hilary Standing, *RAIN* 9–10, 1975.]

People of the River Neretva (1966) 18 min. Zagreb Films (PR). Dist: PSU(PCR) order #21190, FR$10; IUAVC FR$5.75. *Day-to-day life of "amphibious" people settled along small Yugoslav river that forms a large delta as it flows into the Adriatic. Daily routine includes hunting, farming.* [Reviewed by Joel Halpern and Barbara Halpern, *AA* 72:1202–1203, 1970.]

THE PEOPLE OF THE SEAL SERIES (1965) 1 hour each. National Film Board of Canada (PR). Dist: EDC. *In 1963–65, an ethnographic film record was made of a Netsilik Eskimo family following the traditional migratory route used for centuries by their ancestors. One of the most famous and important anthropological documents ever filmed. Since then, the Netsilik have abandoned their traditional way of life and have moved into a permanent government village. The BBC has edited the full 11-hour Netsilik Eskimo Film Series into two films that summarize the migratory cycle of the Netsilik Eskimo.* See individual titles:

- **Eskimo Summer**
- **Eskimo Winter**

People of the Tununak 35 min. Norman and Leonard Kamerling (PR, Dl). Dist: VQ. *Made in collaboration with Alaskan Eskimo, for distribution to Alaskan schools.* [Reviewed by John Collier, *AA* 76:717, 1974.]

People of the Western China 11 min. Dist: IUAVC FR$5. *Pictures the influence of habits and customs of past centuries on modern China. Methods of agriculture, irrigation, and use of bamboo are shown. Representative arts and crafts, methods of transportation, and engineering skills are depicted in their traditional setting.*

People of the Wind (1976) 108 min. Anthony Howarth (Dl). Dist: UNI FR$100-200, FS$1100. *The remarkable story of one of the last of the great nomadic tribes—the Bakhtiari of western Iran (Persia). Every spring, hundreds of thousands of Bakhtiari—men, women, and children—undertake an epic journey in search of new pastures for their massive flocks of sheep. They travel on foot and by mule across 200 miles of rugged mountains and icy rivers, along paths worn by their ancestors over the centuries. People of the Wind captures the quality of nomadic life as no other film has done. It follows one of the annual Bakhtiari migrations, concentrating on the experiences of Jafar Qoli (pronounced Kholi), a Bakhtiari Kalantar or Chief, and the people closest to him on the journey. James Mason speaks the part of the Chief, eloquently rendering in English the thoughts and feelings of this colorful leader. Filmed entirely on location in the Zagros Mountains, People of the Wind is* *a spectacular and authentic drama—not one scene in the film was acted or re-enacted.*

The People Who Take Up Serpents (1977) 36 min. Gretchen Robinson (FM). Dist: Gretchen Robinson, Independent Southern Films, Inc., P.O. Box 2602, Greenville, SC 29602, FR$50, FS$400. *Pentecostal snake handling in South Carolina and Tennessee.*

Pepe's Family (1978) 45 min. Jerome Mintz (FM, AN). Dist: IUAVC FR$13.50, FS$355, VS$245; DER FR$65, FS$600. *The rural exodus in Analusia, Spain, and its effect on family life. The film focuses on the family of a migrant laborer who works in Germany. It depicts the relationship of the children to their grandfather and their mother in the absence of the father. The concerns of the father are portrayed during his holiday visits—his social networks, his present foreign experiences, and his plans for the future. Ultimately, the migrant worker must decide whether to move his family to a factory town at the cost of leaving his father behind in the village. Spanish lyrics and their English translations of songs recorded in this film are available upon request.* [Reviewed by Davydd J. Greenwood and Pilar Fernandez-Caliadas de Greenwood, *AA* 82:226–227, 1980. Reviewed in *VISA* 4:69, 1991.]

Peppimenarti (1983) 50 min. Ron Iddon and John Shaw (PR), Ron Iddon (DI). Dist: FAA. *Peppimenarti is a cattle station run by Aborigines with a turn over of $1 million per annum. It is located in the north of Central Australia. This film looks at the role that the Aboriginals have played in the development of the cattle industry in Northern Australia and traces the history of Peppimenarti. The importance of Aboriginal law and their traditional ownership of the land is also examined. The film also gives rare insights into Aboriginal culture by featuring a sacred ceremony.*

The Performed Word (1982) 58 min. Gerald L. Davis (PR), Carlos de Jesus and Earnest Shinagawa (DI). Dist: Center for Southern Folklore, 1216 Peabody, P.O. Box 40105, Memphis, TN 38104; (901) 726-4205, FR$75, FS$750, VS$475. *"A look into the techniques used by Bishop E. E. Cleveland and his daughter, Reverend Ernestine Cleveland Reems, as they preach to and perform with their separate congregations in Berkeley, California.... Captures some of the experience of being in a Black church."* [From the review by Richard Schechner, *AA* 87:747–748, 1985.]

Perfumed Nightmare 91 min. Kidlat Tahimik (DI). Dist: FF. *There is nothing even remotely nightmarish about this film. It is an enchanting experience, a totally original seriocomic creation with an infectious and exuberant energy. It is a semi-autobiographical fable by a young Filipino named Kidlat Tahimik, about his awakening to, and reaction against, American cultural colonialism. This is a bizarre, hallucinatory movie full of dazzling images and outlandish ideas. It is both real and surreal, poetic and political naive and wise, primitive and supremely accomplished. Tahimik is a master of metaphor. There is the metaphor of the bridge that connects his past, present and future with the great world beyond. And there is the metaphor of the film itself: produced single-handedly for $10,000, it is a triumph of cottage industry, a dazzling testament to the liberty of the imagination.*

Pericles in America (1988) 70 min. John Cohen (FM). Dist: FRIF FR$150, FS$1050, VS$600. *"The life and work of Pericles Halkias, arguably the greatest among the surviving masters of the distinctive clarino (clarinet) tradition of the region of Epirus in northwestern Greece."* [From the review by Jane K. Cowan, *AA* 91:1087–1088, 1989.]

Perico the Bowlmaker (1987) 45 min. Jerome Mintz (FM). Dist: DER FR$65, VR$40, FS$650, VS$250. *This film considers the changing role of a traditional Andalusian craftsman and the social and personal factors that shape his occupation. Depicted are the techniques of carving and the problems of marketing the wares as well as the off-season tasks at cork harvest.*

Permissible Dreams (As Women See It Series) 30 min. Attiat El-Abnoudi (DI), Faust Films (PR). Dist: WMM FR$60, VR$50, FS$600, VS$225. *The story of Om Said, a traditional and typical Egyptian woman. Hers is the story of thousands of women living in rural villages throughout Egypt. She married at 15, had eight children, and did not read or write—yet she was the economist, the doctor, and the planner of her family's future. The film is an unforgettable look at the life of Arab women.*

Personality in Culture 29 min. NET(PR). Dist: UU FR$10.25. *Describes the Japanese national character as a paradoxical complex of restraint and passion, arrogance and servility, pride in being Japanese but apologetic for being Japanese. Explains that Japan, more than any other nation, has wavered between contradictory attitudes and qualities. Discusses the concept of face and what it means to the Japanese to be part of a group.*

Peruvian Archaeology (1954) Pan American Union (PR). Dist: SU. [Reviewed by Gordon C. Pollard, *AA* 78:382, 1976.]

Peruvian Weaving: A Continuous Warp for 5,000 Years (1981) 25 min. John Cohen (DI). Dist: POR FR$50, FS$400; CG R$55, FS$400, VS$275. *This film examines warp pattern weaving in Peru, an Andean Indian tradition that has been handed down from woman to woman over the generations. In addition to a detailed demonstration of the warp pattern technique on back-strap and four stake looms by Indian weavers in Peru today, the film features an interview with Dr. Junius Bird of the American Museum of Natural History who has traced the beginnings of this weaving tradition in Peru back to preceramic period. Archival footage of his 1946 archaeological excavation in Huaca Prieta is combined with a demonstration of how the Museum's ancient tapestry patterns, which used the same warp pattern technique, were reconstructed from bits of fabric faded beyond recognition.* [Reviewed by Karen E. Stothert, *AA* 87:488–490, 1985. John W. Rick, *ARCH* 38(1):67, 1985.]

Peter, Donald, Willie, Pat (1988) 48 min. Mike Majoros and Jim Kaufman (PR). Dist: DER VR$40, VS$300. *This film is a portrait of four homeless men who live in a shelter in Boston, MA. The tape follows them through their routine at the shelter and documents their lives on the streets. Peter* *is an ex-hippie who collects trash to sell at the flea markets. Donald served ten years at Leavenworth on a bank robbery charge. Pat was sexually abused as a child and has been in and out of foster homes for the last 13 years. Willie came to the shelter to recover because he lost six of his fingers after spending a night in a snow bank. The film reveals the complexity and diversity of these men's lives; how in some ways they have been victims, yet in other cases they have succeeded in exploiting the system. The film does not judge; it simply shows how these four men have become members of a new class of survivors.* [Reviewed by Sally Engle Merry, AA 91:528–529, 1989.]

Peter Picked a Seal Stick: The Fur Seal Harvest of the Pribilov Islands (1981) 28 min. Susanne Swibold and Helen Corbett (PR). Dist: FTP FS$480, VS$240. *Documents the 1981 seal harvest—the next to last year that such harvest took place under U.S. government management.* [Reviewed by Lydia Black, AA 88:257–258, 1986.]

Petit a Petit (Little by Little) (1969) 90 min. Jean Rouch (DI), Films de la Pleiade and Centre National de la Recherche Scientifique (PR). Dist: CFE; DER. *A fable produced as a sequel of "Jaguar," which relates the curious and singular adventures of Damoure and Lam, two businessmen of Africa, in search of their role model.*

Petra: Crossroad in Stone (1989) 27 min. Gerald Johnson (PR), Evan Johnson (DI). Dist: Ellida Productions, 3108 Polk Street, NE, Minneapolis, MN 55418; (612) 788-8530, VS$29.95. *"Focuses on archaeological investigations at the Nabataean city of Petra, in present day Jordan. . . . The basic information provided is accurate and interesting, and the scenery is wonderful. But it contains nothing innnovative or imaginative with respect to technique or technology."* [From the review by Peter S. Allen, ARCH 43(2):64–67, 1990.]

The Phans of Jersey City (1979) 55 min. Abbie H. Fink (PR), Stephen L. Forman (PR, DI), Dennis Lanson (DI). Dist: FI FR$65, FS$700, VS$420. *"The Phans are a four generation family who escaped from Saigon in April 1975 and arrived in the United States five months later. . . . Portrays their struggles, hopes, and despair in the United States. . . . It portrays the personal trials of being a resettled refugee from a refugee perspective, showing that trials are deep seated even in satisfactory economic circumstances."* [From the review by Marjorie A. Muecke, AA 88:771–772, 1986.]

Phantom India, Indian Odyssey (1971) Seven parts, 50 min. each. Louis Malle (FM). Dist: NYF. [Reviewed by W. D. Merchant and Paul Hockings, AA 81:469, 1979.]

Phela-Ndaba (End of the Dialogue) (1971) 45 min. Pan Africanist Congress (PR). Dist: International Defense and Aid Fund for South Africa, P.O. Box 17, Cambridge, MA 02138. *A documentary on South Africa filmed secretly by five black members of the then banned Pan Africanist Congress. Film is made from the emic perspective. Filmed in 1969–70, it portrays the unrelenting, corrosive oppression of brown Asians and black South Africans. Visual description of conditions in Soweto. Contrasts the white South Africans' lifestyles and that of the others. Cinematic features: Soundtrack uses sad drumming when black life circumstances depicted and up-beat trumpets when whites are shown enjoying resources denied others. Focusing questions: Is it possible to make an* unbiased *film of South Africa? Was the film in any way* overtly *political? Would more straightforward description have been more or less effective?* [Mike Hoover]

Philippines (Asian Insight Series) (1988) 50 min. Film Australia (PR). Dist: FIV VS$158. *The complex social structure of the Spanish and the religious cult of Santo Nino are still found in Filipino life today due to Spanish and American colonization.*

Philippines: The Price of Power (1986) 28 min. Jeffrey Chester and Charles Drucker (PR). Dist: FRIF FR$55, FS$500, VS$280. *Explores the role of the Igorots, traditional Filipino farmers, in the events that led to the "people's power" revolution as they fought a massive dam project that threatened their lands and culture.*

Photo Wallahs (1991) 60 min. David MacDougall and Judith MacDougall (FM). Dist: Fieldwork Films, 12 Meehan Gardens, Griffith ACT 2603, Canberra, Australia; UCEMC VR$75, FS$1195, VS$295, order #38223. *This film explores the many meanings of photography. It focuses on the photographers of Mussoarie, a hill station in the Himalayan foothills of northern India, whose fame has attracted tourists since the 19th century. The film looks at photography as both an art and social artifact.* [Reviewed by Joanne Cohan Scherer, AA 94(4):1029–1030, 1992.] Supplementary reading: Judith Mara Gutman, *Through Indian Eyes.* Oxford, 1982.

Picuris Indians Harold Joe Waldrum (PR, CA), Herbert W. Dick and John J. Bodine (PR), James T. Heese (CA). Dist: WS VS$150. *This videograph is a glimpse of some of the most intimate, unrehearsed moments of the Picuris Indian people at the site of their ancient pueblo hidden in a "Shangri-La" setting in a high mountain valley in the Picuris Mountains of north central New Mexico. The scenes are not the usual dances viewed by tourists. These are dances and drum choruses performed in the vicinity of their sacred ceremonial room, the kiva, when few outsiders are around. In the making of the videograph, the Picuris role was not a passive one as they guided the photographers to capture important aspects of the ceremonies for future generation preservation. Also included is a discussion of the 1776 Picuris adobe church, church construction, and the role of Catholicism by Harold Joe Waldrum, one of the foremost protectors and painters of ancient churches in New Mexico.*

Les Pièrres chantantes d'Ayorou (The Musical Stones of Ayorou) (1968) 10 min. Jean Rouch (DI), Centre National de la Recherche Scientifique, Comite du Film Ethnographique (PR). Dist: CFE; DER. *On the island of Ayorou, Niger, a large clump of rocks with cup-shaped holes is a singing stone.*

Pilgrimage to Ghriba (1977) 28 min. Alain Cohen and Georges Nizan (FM). Dist: JMS FR$100. *"Legend has it that*

Djerba, a tiny island off the southeast coast of Tunisia, received a remnant of the Babylonian captivity in the 6th century B.C. Historical records document the persistence of a Jewish enclave on the island over the centuries." This film addresses tourism, "showing us the broader social context of what might apear to be an isolated group.... The annual pilgrimage to the holy site of Ghriba in Djerba has become popular with French and North African Jewish tourists." [From the review by Faye Ginsburg, AA 87:741–747, 1985. See also *The Jews of Djerba.*

Pine Nuts (American Indian Film Series) (1961) 13 min. Dist: UCEMC FR$25, FS$135; PSU(PCR) order #2200K, FR$5.90, FS$130. *In the Great Basin area, a semi-desert region between the Rocky Mountains and the Sierra Nevada, the Paviotso, Washo, and other Indian tribes of western Nevada developed a hunting and gathering culture. In adapting themselves to this barren region, the Indians came to depend upon the pine nut or Piflon tree as an essential source of food. Members of the Paviotso and Paiute tribe demonstrate the manner in which the pine nuts were harvested and prepared as food. The techniques demonstrated have been in practice since pre-Columbian times.* [Reviewed by Harold E. Driver, AA 68:598, 1966.]

The Pinks and the Blues (NOVA Series) (1981) 57 min. WGBH Boston (PR). Dist: WGBH FR$75, FS$750, VS$150. *"This film provides an excellent overview of the many ways in which the behaviour of female and male children is differentially shaped within our culture."* [From the review by Herbert H. Bell, SBF 17:36, 1981.]

Pintubi Revisit Yaru Yaru 31 min. Roger Sandall (FM). Dist: UCEMC FR$36, FS$420. *Men of the Pintubi tribe of Australian Aborigines celebrate an ancient myth concerning their creation. According to the legend, two women from the west produced some men, as well as some sacred objects from the soil of Tjarapiri cave. The women then disappeared into the earth at nearby Yaru Yaru cave, were recovered by the men, and subsequently continued their journey to the east. The film shows how the men re-create the story, sing and chant in the caves, and use paint to renew the caves' sacred designs. It shows how they divide into worker and owner moieties, and it portrays the role of each group in the ceremonies. As the men return home, they camp for the night and, for entertainment, hold "revenge party" dances portraying surprise attacks on victims caught alone at night. No narration: subtitles provide necessary background information. This film may not be imported into Australia for any purpose. Restricted use. This film contains material of a secret/sacred nature and should only be screened for study purposes by appropriate groups.*

Pintubi Revisit Yumari (1971) 32 min. Jeremy Long and Ken Hansen (AN), Roger Sandall (FM), Australian Institute of Aboriginal Studies (PR). Dist: UCEMC order #8120, FR$38, FS$445. *Shows a remarkable initiation ritual that takes place at sunset, when a dozen tall churinga (sacred boards) are stood on end beside the red rock of Yumari. When "the ancestors," represented by the churinga, are ready, a smoke signal announces that the initiates should be brought to "meet" them. The initiates—young men with spears—then race across the sand and spinifex to press themselves against the emblems of the tribal past. At night, spectacular "revenge party" dances are held for entertainment. On the second day, two wanigi (hair-string totems) are constructed; two dancers are elaborately decorated; and the concluding rites are performed by the people whose daily life is shown in the People of the Australian Desert Series; it supplements the series material. (At the request of the performers, the film should not be seen by uninitiated aboriginal men or aboriginal women of tribal background.) Restricted use: this film contains material of a secret/sacred nature and should only be screened for study purposes by appropriate groups.*

Piraparana (1969) 30 min. Brian Moser (FM). Dist: Pitt. *Shows the daily life and rituals of the Macuma Indians, a tribe of the Piraparana River region of the Amazon in Colombia. Among the ethnographic contributions are the slash-and-burn cultivation of the coco leaf into cocaine, preparation of manioc, canoe building, ritual ceremonials, music, dancing, and shamanistic practices.*

PITTSBURGH POLICE SERIES John Marshall (CA), Chat Gunter, Chris Tillam, and Randy Franken (SR). Dist: DER. *In the summers of 1968 and 1969, 130,000 feet of 16mm, black-and-white film was shot in the street and police stations of Pittsburgh, Pennsylvania. The various roles of the police in cities are illustrated in this collection of documentary sequences. They provide an opportunity to study the social context of police work and to observe aspects of the administration, policy, and values of a police department and the legal constraints within which the police operate and which, on occasion, they ignore.* Suggested supplements: Paul Chevigny, *Police Power.* Vintage, 1969. Arthur Niederhoffer, *Behind the Sheild.* Doubleday, 1967. Jerome H. Skolnick, *Justice without Trial.* Wiley, 1966. James Q. Wilson, *Varieties of Police Behavior.* Harvard University Press, 1968. [Reviewed by Michael J. Lowy, AA 76:200–204, 1974.]

ROLE OF THE POLICE

• **Manifold Controversy** 3.25 min. FR$ 10, FS$60. *A customer feels he has been cheated out of an exhaust system by a garage owner.*

• **Youth and the Man of Property** 6.5 min. FR$15, FS$100. *A suburban couple calls the police to intervene after being harassed by an irrepressible youth.*

• **Vagrant Woman** 8 min. FR$15, FS$120. *An unemployed woman who has been living in her car is questioned by the police and taken to the Salvation Army.*

• **A Forty Dollar Misunderstanding** 7.5 min. FR$15, FS$120. *White policemen intervene when a black woman calls to complain that her boyfriend "stole" 40 dollars.*

• **Two Brothers** 4 min. FR$10, FS$75. *A man has damaged his brother's car. The family tries to resolve the dispute among themselves after the police have been called to intervene.*

• **Three Domestics** 36.5 min. FR$40, FS$450. *The Pittsburgh police are shown intervening in three domestic situations. (1) The police respond to a call from a household in* which a couple have been living in common-law. The woman wants the police to remove the man. They arrange for his arrest on an assault and battery charge. (2) A woman accuses her boyfriend of beating her, and the man accuses her of lying. The police remove the man with some difficulty. (3) A boisterous and drunken father is removed from his house on the insistence of his wife and older son. He is taken away to spend the night in jail. Throughout the sequence, the father is cared for by his younger son. Viewing these as conflict resolution: What happens? Who calls police? Does the procedure help or hinder? Is wrestling on TV meaningful in film? Is this a failure (bureaucratically) or a success? Why doesn't the battered woman just leave? Is this film an invasion of privacy? Even if the people gave their permission? [Reviewed by Carol B. Stack, *AA* 75:590, 1973.]

INVESTIGATION

- **Wrong Kid** 4.5 min. FR$10, FS$75. *The police, in looking for a suspect, question the wrong youth.*

- **The Informant** 23.5 min. FR$30, FS$260. *During the course of questioning, a suspect offers his services as an "undercover" informant if the police will suppress his burglary charge.*

- **Investigation of a Hit and Run** 35 min. FR$35, FS$390. *Two officers in Pittsburgh's station #9 pursue the investigation of a hit and run accident. The film follows the investigation from the initial reports, the questioning of witnesses of the 18-year-old suspect, through his girlfriend's subsequent interrogation and statement. A number of factors complicate the case: the suspect was without a driver's license; he reported the car stolen to cover himself; he could not be persuaded to confess; the girl is pregnant. The police use considerable pressure on the girl and treat her eventual statement as though it were a confession.*

- **A Legal Discussion of a Hit and Run** 28 min. FR$30, FS$325. *Having been shown Investigation of a Hit and Run, a Harvard Law School class, led by Professor James Vorenberg, discusses the salient legal points about police investigation and interrogation, and the rights of witnesses or suspects.*

- **After the Game** 9.5 min. FR$15, FS$130. *The police search a house for drugs after they have arrested a group of boys who have just returned from a basketball game and are having a loud party and sniffing glue.*

POWERS AND DISCRETION

- **You Wasn't Loitering** 14.5 min. FR$20, FS$ 190. *A group of sequences related to the policy and practice of enforcing loitering ordinances. The sequences include warning youths, police administrators discussing loitering enforcement policy, insults to officers, an arrest of several youths for loitering.*

- **Henry Is Drunk** 7 min. FR$15, FS$100. *The police, observing Henry's driving, tell him to get out of his car and to take a cab.*

- **Nothing Hurt but My Pride** 15 min. FR$20, FS$195. *A group of sequences related to arrests after street fights involving policemen and discussions of the incidents by the police in cars and at the station.*

- **Twenty-One Dollars or Twenty-One Days** 7.5 min. FR$15, FS$120. *A man, arrested for resisting arrest and disorderly conduct, tells his story in night court.*

- **Inside Outside Station Nine** 90 min. (2 reels) FR$85, FS$975. *This is not a film about police, in general, nor about the department in which the film was made. It is a film about some policemen, some events in which they are involved, and some of the people they deal with. Beginning with a domestic intervention, the film proceeds through several fights, showing the reaction of one policeman to these fights. Following is the handling of a case of hit-and-run, a variety of approaches to loitering youths on the street, and the consequences of one approach to a number of young men. A shift is made to Magistrate's Court, where a man who has been asked to move on by the police is arrested, charged with drunkenness and convicted of disorderly conduct. At the same session a young man is identified by detectives as a suspect in two burglaries while being arraigned for a third. In his interrogation, the police see Communism and conspiracy in a militant art gallery. Candidates for the police force are shown being interviewed by members of the department. Their reasons for wanting to be policemen and their thoughts about themselves and the policemen's job place the film in the context of the community from which the department draws its personnel. A number of the sequences listed in this section appear in whole or in part in this film.*

Pizza Pizza Daddy-O (1969) 18 min. Bess Lomax Hawes (FM). Dist: UCEMC order #7695, FR$23, FS$160. *Provides anthropological and folkloric record of eight singing games played by fourth-grade African-American girls on the playground of a school in a Los Angeles ghetto: My Boyfriend Gave Me a Box, This-a-way Valerie, When I Was a Baby, Imbileenie, This-a-way Batman, Mighty Mighty Devil, My Mother Died, and Pizza Pizza Daddy-O. All action undirected; the organization of the games is entirely the work of the children themselves, based on the essential structure and characteristics handed down from one generation of school-children to the next. The primary form, the ring, is demonstrated. The other principle play form, parallel lines of players facing each other, is also shown. The major stylistic feature is call and response; almost every phase is echoed both in singing and movement patterns. The body empathy the children share shows that they enjoy group blending to a degree that white society seems to achieve only under the strictest discipline. Study guide including texts of the songs is available.* [Reviewed by David Evans, *JAF* 89(353):389, 1976.]

A Place in the Sun (Indonesia: A Generation of Change Series) (1987) 28 min. Barbara Bare (DI). Dist: CTC FS$535, VS$295, order #PLNS12. *With over 300 different ethnic groups scattered over almost 14,000 islands, will the country be able to achieve its motto of "Unity in Diversity?" This question is explored through the eyes of four distinct cultural groups that represent different ethnic backgrounds, diverse geographical regions, varying religions, political attitudes, and social customs.*

Place of Power in French Polynesia (The Human Face of the Pacific Series) (1987) 56 min. Film Australia (PR). Dist: FIV VS$158. *This film shows the recent reemergence of the traditional Polynesian culture of Tahiti, which is evidenced in contemporary arts and rituals. This cultural tradition had been nearly wiped out by years of French rule over Tahiti.*

Places Not Our Own (Daughters of the Country Series) 57 min. Norma Bailey (PR), Derek Mazur (DI). Dist: NFB R$80, FS$775, VS$150. *It is 1929, the pre-Depression era in North America. Drought has forced the Lesperances to become itinerant. Although they are relegated to live as squatters on a town's outskirts, Rose has high hopes of freeing her children from a dismal socioeconomic situation. But her family is half Native American, part of an undesirable minority. When the promising 14-year-old Flora is refused enrollment in school, the girl acts out her anger. Rose's spirit refuses to be crushed. She will find a place to make a new start.*

A Plague upon the Land 24 min. Dist: WBP VS$35.95, order #30918. *In a tragic paradox, rivers in west Africa bring to villagers not only water, but also the debilitating disease known as "river blindness." The film depicts the economic and social upheaval that occurs when the disease strikes. In one village, 75 percent of the residents are infected; in others, adult men are so incapacitated that they can no longer work, and young boys must shoulder their responsibilities. Experts comment on the results of a massive international program now underway to eradicate the illness.*

The Plaint of Steve Kreines, as Recorded by His Younger Brother Jeff 47 min. Jeff Kreines (FM). Dist: VQ FR$50, FS$350. [Reviewed by John W. Adams, AA 78:962, 1976]

Play of the Young (Greater Dwarf Lemur) 4.5 min. Dist: PSU FR$2.80.

Play of the Young (Japanese Macaque) 3 min. Dist: PSU FR$4.30.

PLEASING GOD SERIES Dist: CPI. *The films in this series are studies of the devotional practices associated with three major deities of the Hindu pantheon. They were made in the small, historic town of Vishnupur, West Bengal. Vishnupur is a town of temples, crafts, and markets, the center of an old kingdom and a place where daily life and worship are closely intertwined.* [Reviewed by Peter J. Bertocci, AA 89:259–262, 1987.] See descriptions under individual titles:

- Loving Krishna
- Sons of Shiva
- Serpent Mother

THE PLUNDERERS: Part 1, Treasure Trail 50 min. Julia Cave (PR). Dist: TLV. *"Covers the problems of looting in Turkey. It begins with a specific example: the discovery and dismemberment of a Roman marble sarcophagus, parts of which later appeared on the art market. The film clearly makes the point that the looting process often begins in the village where poverty drives many to this lucrative business."* [From the review by Trudy S. Kawami, ARCH 35(1):70–71, 1982.]

THE PLUNDERERS: Part 2, The Hot Pot (1975) 50 min. Julia Cave (PR). Dist: TLV. *"Promises to be an expose of the controversy surrounding the acquisition of the Ruphronios krater, a black figure Greek vase purchased by the Metropolitan Museum of art in 1972 for a sum purported to be over a million dollars. The film fails to deliver on this promise.... It does however, give a view of the supposed findspot and some insight into the world of the tombaroli, the Italian looters who specialize in locating and plundering Etruscan tombs."* [From the review by Trudy S. Kawami, ARCH 35(1):70–71, 1982.]

Pocomania ... A Little Madness 22 min. BBC TV (PR). *In this film, the viewer is taken into the closely guarded world of the Pocomaniac who is a member of one of the strongest of the many cult groups in Jamaica. The exact size of this group is impossible to estimate because (1) few Pocomaniacs will admit that they attend ceremonies, (2) their rites are usually conducted at night and in secret, and (3) strangers who want to observe are not welcome. Parts of their ritual are shown in the film: their frenzy, their incredibly hypnotic drumming and tromping, the unreal hubbub as spirits take possession, and their "speaking in tongues." Even a small miracle is observed. Pocomania was named centuries ago by Spaniards who observed the rites and decided that everyone was a little mad. Mad or not, the cult is dynamic and coming very much into its own because it satisfies the emotional life of the people.* [Reviewed by Eric Almquist and Patricia Perrier, AA 77:177, 1975.]

Point of Pines (1955) 22 min. Dist: NYU FR$10, FS$170. *An introduction to archaeological training techniques employed by the University of Arizona Field School. The excavation of a site, establishing a grid, trenching, physical excavation, stratigraphy, dendrochronology, exhumation, and treatment of a human skeleton.* [Reviewed by Emma Lou Davis, AA 77:905–906, 1975.]

Poletown Lives! (1983) 56 min. George Corsetti, Jeanie Wylie, and Richard Wieske (FM). Dist: Information Factory, 3512 Courville, Detroit, MI 48224; (313) 885-4685, FR$95, VR$75, FS$800, VS$400. *"A vision of the clash between the rich and the poor in America. When one of the largest corporations in the world, General Motors, plans to build a new plant on the site of an integrated, working-class neighborhood in Detroit in 1980, the residents mount an intense and moving struggle to avert the destruction of their lifelong community."* [From the review by Sally Engle Merry, AA 86:1054–1056, 1984.]

The Politicians (see Decade of Destruction Series)

Polka (1986) 50 min. Robert Boonzajer Flaes and Martin Rens (FM). Dist: UA-DA. *The conjunto music of South Texan Chicanos developed around the turn of the century. Although conjunto has a unique flavor, both the polka and its main instrument, the diatonic accordion, have Central European origins. There has never been a direct connection between the European original and its Chicano offspring. The film brings this connection into life when Chicano* *accordionists are brought into contact with musical forebears, Austrian polka players. We see how Conjunto polkas are received by flabbergasted Austrian accordionists. In return, these Austrians play some of their own polka standards. The film sheds light on both the musical and the social and emotional life of the Chicano musicians.*

Polynesier (Niutai, Ellice-Inseln)—Bau eines Schlafhauses (1961) 51.5 min. G. Koch (FM). Dist: IWF. [Reviewed by Saul Riesenberg, *AA* 67:1357, 1965.]

Pomo Shaman (1963) 20 min. Dist: UCEMC FR$24, FS$175. *This remarkable documentary presents the essentials of the second and final night of a curing ceremony held by the Kashia group of the Southwestern Pomo Indians. Each night the ceremony lasted no more than an hour. On the first night, May 31, 1963, the pain was located, while the Shaman was in a hypnotic trance, and the germs were removed from the patient's body. She effected this with the spiritual instrument that she possesses in her throat, and finally the pain was removed in the form of a quartz crystal. The Indian doctor is 61-year-old Essie Parrish; native name, Piwoya. She is the only Southwestern Pomo "sucking doctor" still practicing this ancient form of doctoring. A dreamer and a prophet of the Bole Maru religion, she received her doctoring song in a dream around 1914. She is spiritual head of the Kashia community and the leader of its Mormon group. The Shaman was assisted by four singers in this ceremony, three female and one male. The male or head singer is called* cabe *or "the rock." The two bamboo canes, decorated with dream designs and haliotis ornaments, have special powers for the Shaman. This film is a shortened version of the complete research documentary,* Sucking Doctor. [Reviewed by C. W. Meighan, *AA* 69:271–272, 1967. Nancie L. Gonzalez, *AA* 77:177–178, 1975.]

Pompeii: Daily Life of the Ancient Romans (1989) 45 min. Luigi Constantini (FM). Dist: FHS VR$75, VS$149. *"Opens with some impressive aerial views that give a good sense of the scale and scope of the Roman ruins. Later we join two actors on the ground for a tour of the site, complete with sound effects meant to evoke the past."* [From the review by Peter S. Allen, *Archaeology* 44(5):71, 1991.]

A Poor Man Shames Us All (Millennium: Tribal Wisdom and the Modern World Series) (1992) 1 hour. David Maybury-Lewis (H), Hans Zimmer (MU). Dist: PBS VS$49.95, order #MILL-107-RCDC. *Explores the alternative views of wealth and society that are exhibited in the lives of tribal cultures. This program takes viewers from a New York ad agency to the jungles of Indonesia and the plains of Kenya. Learn why our Western views of wealth and economic needs have created a society of strangers in the midst of material riches, while tribal cultures such as the Weyewa of Indonesia and the Gabra of Kenya create economies of dependency on others and measure wealth through people, not possessions. Follow the host as he traces the development of free-market economics and explores how its characteristics contrast with tribal conceptions of wealth.*

Popol Vuh: The Creation Myth of the Maya (1989) 60 min. Patricia Amlin (FM). Dist: UCEMC R$60, FS$995, VS$410, order #11335(f), #37560(v); UTA-FL FR$31.50, order #C-10648 *This film employs authentic imagery from ancient Maya ceramics to create a riveting depiction of the "Popul Vuh," the Maya creation myth and the foundation of most Native American religious, philosophical, and ethical beliefs. The film introduces the Maya and relates the entire tale, beginning with the creation of the world and concluding with the victory of the Hero Twins over the evil lords of the underworld. There are logical stopping places at quarter-hour intervals to facilitate viewing by younger students. Accompanying teacher's guide co-authored by filmmaker Patricia Amlin and Professor James A. Fox, Stanford University.* [Reviewed by Brian Stross, *AA* 93(1):258–259, 1991. Christopher Jones, *AA* 90:780–781, 1988. Peter S. Allen, *ARCH* 43(4):68, 1990. Peter S. Allen, *ARCH* 41(3):1988. Winifred Lambrecht, *SBF* 24:108, 1988.]

The Popovich Brothers of South Chicago (1978) 60 min. Jill Godmilow (FM), Ethel Raim & Martin Koenig (PR). Dist: Balkan Arts Center, P.O. Box 315, Franklin Lakes, NJ 07417, FR$80-150, FS$750. *The Serbian-American community of South Chicago, focusing on the four Popovich Brothers who have been a focus for ethnic identity through their singing and playing in their tamburitza band. Focusing questions: What happened to the Melting Pot? How Serbian are these Serbian Amerians?* [Reviewed by Paul Hockings, *AA* 81:736, 1979.]

Porto Novo: La danse des reines (Porto Novo: The Dance of the Queens) (1971) 30 min. Jean Rouch (DI), Centre National de la Recherche Scientifique, Comite du Film Ethnographique (PR). Dist: CFE; DER. *Ritual dancing of the queens at the royal palace in Porto Novo, Dahomey. The technique of synchronous slow-motion permits a detailed analysis of the relationship between the dance and the music.*

Potlatch: A Strict Law Bids Us Dance (1975) 53 min. Dennis Wheeler (Dl), U'mista Cultural Society (PR). Dist: PCP FR$65, FS$800; PFI FR$60, FS$700. *Kwakiutl view of their potlatch and history of Canadian government opposition and suppression of ceremony.*

The Potters of Buur Heybe, Somalia 25 min. Tara Belkin (PR). Dist: FL VR$55, VS$295. *In Buur Heybe, a small village in Somalia, only the men make pottery, although their legends give credit to a woman for first finding the clay. Skillfully coordinating their hands and feet, the men transform mounds of clay into beautifully proportioned drinking and cooking vessels. But, like their ancestors, it continues to be the women who mine the clay. This program reveals the entire process of turning rough soil into the beautifully decorated pottery. It shows unique outdoor, above-ground firing method and explains the meanings of the designs that embellish the vessels. It also describes the role of pottery in the economy of village life.* [Reviewed by Richard A. Krause, *AA* 94(3):768–770, 1992.]

THE POWER OF MYTH SERIES (see *Joseph Campbell and the Power of Myth*)

Pour la Suite du Monde (see under *The Moontrap*)

Pousse-Pousse (1975) 110 min. Daniel Kamwa (Dl, WR, Actor). Dist: Transafrica Media Organization, B.P. 560

Douala, Cameroun. *A Cameroun comedy.* [Reviewed by John W. Adams, *AA* 79:215, 1977.]

The Powerhouse (Man on the Rim Series) 58 min. Dist: LMF VS$295. *China is emerging as the true powerhouse of Asia. We explore that aspect of China's long history that displays most graphically the superiority in which she formerly excelled over the rest of the world—her inventiveness. Two thousand years ago, imaginative innovations and inventions—silk production, steel making, the box bellows, printing, and gunpowder, to name a few—gave Shan and Han China an unchallenged cultural and technological primacy.*

Powerhouse for God (1989) 58 min. Barry Dornfeld, Tom Rankin, and Jeff Titon (FM). Dist: DER FR$80, VR$50, FS$800, VS$300. *A stunning portrait of an old-fashioned Baptist preacher, his family, and their church in Virginia's northern Blue Ridge Mountains. Audiences who were born and raised among old-time southern Baptists say this film captures the fierce preaching, determined singing, autobiographical witnessing, and stern doctrine that characterizes these religious communities. The film shows the church members articulating and practicing their religious beliefs, but as a documentary film strives for careful representation, the result is understanding, not endorsement or proselytizing.* [Reviewed by Alexander Moore, *AA* 93(1):259–260, 1991.]

Prayer to Viracocha 5 min. Fountain and Sue Shepherd (PR). Dist: FL VR$40, VS$99. *This short animation, painted in brilliant colors, will be a perfect discussion starter for any class or group dealing with the clash between European and indigenous culture in Latin America. Set at the time of the Spanish conquest, it shows the conflict between the Catholicism brought over by the conquistadors and the religion of the native people.*

PREHISTORIC MAN SERIES (1976) 13 min. each. J. P. Baux (PR). French only.
Titles are:

- **The Origins of Man**
- **One Million Years on the Shores of the Mediterranean Sea**
- **Religion and the Origin of Art**
- **Neolithic Revolution**
- **Man at the Limits of the Planet (The Conquest of Oceania)**
- **The First Metallurgists**

Prehistoric Cultures 28 min. Marshall McKusick (FM). Dist: UIOWA order #50292, FR$18.10, FS$380. [Reviewed by David Mayer Gradwohl, *AA* 78:366–369, 1976.]

Prehistoric Humans (1980) 17 min. Peter Matulavich (PR). Dist: BFA FR$46, FS$330; SU FR$16.50. *Using artwork as well as live action re-enactments, the film introduces viewers to the several prehistoric relatives of modern humans. We learn the several characteristics of primates, and then the specific characteristics of Ramapithecus, Australopithecus robustus, Australopithecus africanus, Homo habilis, Homo erectus, Neanderthal, and Cro-Magnon. We learn of their similarities and differences, that some of them lived during the same period, and that they all had some intriguing ways of adapting to their environments.* [Reviewed in *SBF* 16:99–100, 1980.]

Prehistoric Images (The First Art of Man) (1955) 17 min. Thomas L. Rowe, Arcady (Dl), Abbe Breuil and Martin Almagro (CON). Dist: AB FR$17.50, FS$250. *Filmed in prehistoric caves of Lascaux, Pech Merle, Niaux, Trois Freres, and Altamira.*

Prehistoric Man in Europe (1965) 23 min. Dist: PSU FR$14. *Survey of Old World prehistory. Extensive site coverage in western Europe, including Les Elysees, and Le Moustier. Only authentic artifacts shown.* [Reviewed by James R. Sackett, *AA* 72:202, 1970.]

Prehistoric Man in Northern Europe (1961) 13 min. Hallam L. Movius (AN). Dist: PSU FR$8. *Dramatized reconstruction of Northern European prehistory. Original artifacts used in demonstration of particular traditions. Concentration on Danish sites.* [Reviewed by Ruth E. Tringham, *AA* 78:121, 1976.]

The Pre-Inca Civilizations of the Central Andes (1982) 32 min. John Hyslop (FM). Dist: RLI FS$39.95. *This filmstrip embarks on a survey of six seminal civilizations of the ancient Andes: Chavin, Paracas, Nazca, Moche, Huari-Tiwanaku, and Chimu.* See the review by Alan L. Kolata, *ARCH* 40(4):70–71, 1987.

Preserving a Way of Life: People of the Klamath 28 min. Jim Culp (FM), Ed Asner (NA). Dist: NDF VR$50, VS$250. *The history and philosophy of the Karuk Indians of Northern California is shared in this firsthand account of a culture being passed on from one generation to another. When 76-year-old Karuk Indian Lew Wilder was a boy, he was ridiculed for using his native language, and he watched as police entered their homes to silence their drumming. Now Lew teaches a young Karuk, Leaf Hillman, how to make drums and soapstone pipes. While they work, Leaf learns the history and philosophy of his people. This film tells the story of how the artistic elements of culture are handed down and preserved.*

Preserving Egypt's Past (1982) 23 min. National Geographic Society (PR). Dist: NGSES FS$400, VS$330; Karol FR$30. *"Addresses an important and neglected topic: the survival of the pharaonic monuments of Egypt. It offers the viewer a glimpse behind the archaeological scenes, which will interest both adults and students with some knowledge of ancient culture and its remains. The film is full of unusual and striking visual images."* [From the review by Edna R. Russman, *ARCH* 38(1):66–67, 1985.]

The Price of Change (Women in the Middle East Series) (1982) 26 min. Elizabeth Fernea (PR), Marilyn Gaunt (DI). Dist: FRIF VR$55, FS$470, VS$280. *Once considered shameful, nearly 40 percent of Egyptian women work outside the home, contributing to their family's income. The film examines the consequences working has on five women, including a factory worker and an opposition member of Egypt's Parliament, to present a picture of changing atti-*

tudes toward work, family, and women's place in society. [Reviewed by Barbara Aswad, *AA* 87:233–234, 1985.]

The Price We Paid (1977) 30 min. Colville Tribe, Yakima Tribe Filmmakers (PR). *A documentary film presents the Colville Tribe's point of view on the impacts of the Coulee Dam construction on their traditional and contemporary way of life. Includes interviews with older and younger members of the tribe, excerpts from a government film describing the benefts of Coulee Dam construction; scenes from the area around Coulee Dam.* Focusing questions: What effects did the construction of Coulee Dam have on the way of life of the Colvilles? How do the perspectives of government representatives and of the Colville Tribe differ? What solutions can you see to these kinds of conflicts? [Anne Smith Denman]

The Pride and the Shame (ca. 1966) 31 min. Julian Jacottet (PR), Brian Tufano (CA), Freddie Downton and Stanley Morcom (SR), Peter Hill (ED), Desmond Wilcox (NA), Adam Clapham (CON). Dist: UILL; NFBC. *Shot in 1966 near Cherry Creek, South Dakota. British film team was investigating reservation life among the Sioux of the area. Some brief background provided about living conditions on the reservation (unemployment, and so forth). The bulk of the film consists of interviews conducted with individual Sioux; the interviewer elicited their feelings about what it is like to live on a reservation. A courtroom scene shows the way in which the Anglo system of justice deals with those individuals who have been arrested for drunkenness. The film dwells on the poverty and the hopelessness of the reservation Sioux. One interview with the resident VISTA volunteer underlines the inability of some outsiders to understand the situation in terms of what the Native Americans really need.* Warnings: Poor sound; interviewees often unintelligible. Narration sometimes naive or uniformed ("paleface" reference to war dance unchanged since days of Custer). Focusing questions: Why are the people proud to see their young men join the armed forces? What are the problems involved with being Indian and living on a reservation as far as the Indians are concerned? As far as the VISTA volunteer is concerned? Why is she there? Why is there so much drinking on the reservation? Why is a jail sentence not necessarily a bad thing for someone arrested for drunkenness? Would drunkenness be seen differently by Indians and the Anglo legal system? What indigenous institutions do the Sioux have to run their own affairs? Bibliography: Ethel Nurge, *The Modern Sioux.* University of Nebraska Press. S. Levine and N. O. Lurie, *The American Indian Today.* Penguin. [John D. Meredith]

The Primal Mind 58 min. Alvin H. Perlmutter (EP), Jamake Highwater (WR, H), Richard Berman (DI). Dist: CG R$100, FS$895, VS$595. *Identifies the important distinctions between Native American and Western or European people. The film explores the two cultures' contrasting views of nature, time space, art, architecture, and dance. Language itself plays a crucial role in this regard since languages are not simply different words for the same things—they reflect fundamental differences in human perception, differences which for centuries have led to serious misunderstandings.* [Reviewed by Robert L. Bee, *AA* 90:235–237, 1988. John S. Wozniak, *SBF* 20:223, 1985.]

Primate (1974) 105 min. Frederick Wiseman (PR, ED). Dist: Zipporah Films, 54 Lewis Wharf, Boston, MA 02110. [Reviewed by Edward H. Hunt, Jr., *AJPA* 43(1):150, 1975.]

Primates (1967) 25 min. NBC (PR). Dist: PSU FR$22. *The evolution and development of such important primate traits as stereoscopic vision, grasping reflex, and sociality are discussed. Demonstrates how lower primates adapt and cope with their environment.*

Primitive America (1930s) 10–15 min. Dist: FCE FR$17, FS$95. *Mountaineers of the Great Smokies preserve primitive water wheels, methods of shearing, carding, and spinning; methods of cooking, molding candles and pewter spoons.*

Primitive Man in a Modern World 23 min. Moody Institute of Science (PR). Dist: Moody Institute of Science, 12000 East Washington Blvd., Whittier, CA 90606. [Reviewed by Carolyn Buff, Leon Campbell, Katherine Fritts, W. R. Fritts, *AA* 74:1593, 1972.]

Primitive Man in Our World (1960) 12 min. Dist: PSU FR$11.50. *Shows basic pattern of life in the Sepik River region of New Guinea. House construction, river transportation, festivities, cooking, and some religious art.* Intended for secondary school use.

The Primitive Maori (1920s) 10–15 min. Dist: FCE FR$17, FS$95. *This film was made in the early 1920s. Emphasis is on the making of cloth and dye. Use is made of inner bark and leaves of trees and mud from geysers. Work is done with handmade tools of shell and stone. All too brief references are made to Totara, symbols of wood and the religion of these people. The evergreen twig is sacred. The Holy Men bless the fields at time of planting. The importance of the taboo is indicated and the work is shown. Herbs relieve the pain of work. Games of the men are most intricate and are contrived to develop great muscular strength. In particular, the "stick game" is most interesting as also is the children's game "mati mati."*

PRIMITIVE PEOPLE (AUSTRALIAN ABORIGINES) SERIES Dist: UCEMC FR$14 (set); PSU(PSR).

• **The Nomads** 12 min. PSU(PSR) order #919.4-3, FR$3.40. *Filmed in the Gulf of Carp. Wongari, in monsoon mangrove, fire drill; bask shelter; sleeping platforms in smoke. Spear fishing in ocean; dig for turtle eggs; wild yarn, make "bread."*

• **The Hunt** 12 min. PSU(PSR) order #919.4-4, FR$3.40. *Flint spear making; smear clay, imitate wallabies, butcher and share; dance and sing.*

• **Funeral** 7 min. PSU(PSR) order #914.4-5, FR$2.90. *Long dance; painted "spirit pole"; map; redden bones.*

Primitive Process Pottery (1993) 69 min. Woodsmoke Productions (PR). Dist: UCEMC VR$60, VS$150, order #38254. *This unusual video provides an outstanding and comprehensive demonstration of how ceramic pottery was* *made by ancient peoples, especially those in the American Southwest. Features master potter Wayne Brian.*

Principles of Caste (Introduction to Sociology Series) (1983) 24 min. BBC (PR). Dist: MG R$40, FS$445, VS$310. *"This film illustrates how ritual dominates and organizes the Indian social process.... The film is done in the best tradition of anthropological films."* [From the review by Brian C. Aldrick, *SBF* 21:104, 1985.]

P4W: Prison for Women (1981) 81 min. Janis Cole and Holly Dale (FM). Dist: FRF FR$175, FS$1350. *"Takes us inside Canada's only federal penitentiary for women and into the lives of the prisoners there."* [From the review by Alice Reich, *AA* 88:522–523, 1986.]

The Probable Passing of Elk Creek (1982) 60 min. Rob Wilson (FM). Dist: CG FR$90, FS$900, VS$750. *"This film purports to examine the existential issues confronting modern American society.... These themes are explored against the backdrop of a crisis confronting two northern California communities—the small town of Elk Creek and the neighboring Grindstone Creek Rancheria. The state wants to build a dam on Indian land, thus flooding the valley.... The Nomlaki Indians who live on this tiny reservation are legally entitled to decide whether or not the dam will be built."* [From the review by Donald D. Stull, *AA* 88:523–524, 1986.]

Promises to Keep (1988) 57 min. Ginny Durrin (FM). Dist: Durrin Productions, 1748 Kalorama Road, NW, Washington DC 20009; (202) 387-6700, FR$100, FS$895, VS$250. *"Homelessness is clearly one of the striking social issues of the 1980's America.... The film approaches the issue as an unfolding story of homeless advocacy, and chronicles a political struggle in the nation's capital between advocates for a homeless shelter and the federal bureaucracy.... Much of the film focuses on the movement's central figure, Mitch Snyder."* [From the review by Michael O. Robertson, *AA* 92:839, 1990.]

The Prophet's Family (see Diary of a Maasai Village Series) (1985) 50 min. BBC (PR). Dist: FIV VS$198. *Simel, an important Maasai prophet, accepts a gift of 25 cows from a visiting delegation before prophesying for them and giving them charms to take home. Meanwhile, area youths try to collect money to pay Simel for a goat they stole from him.*

Psychic Surgery: A Case History of Shamanic Sleight-of-Hand (1988) 60 min. Philip Singer and Tom Peterson (PR). Dist: Singer-Sharrette Productions, 2810 Indian Lake Road, Oxford, MI 48051; (313) 693-9447, VS$175. *"Thousands of tourists journey to the Philippines in search of cures that Western medicine has failed to provide. The local healers are renowned for their unusual surgical techniques. They reportedly enter the patient's body barehandedly, remove the diseased tissue, and the close the wound without sutures.... [This film] addresses the modus operandi underlying these 'unorthodox' healing practices."* [From the review by Marilyn Jean Schlitz, *AA* 92:847–848, 1990.]

El Pueblo (1983) 24 min. Tristam and Wilson Productions (PR). Dist: Journal Films, Inc., 930 Pitner Ave., Evanston, IL 60202; (312) 328-6700, FR$45, FS$405. *"One in a series of colorful village portraits.... It was shot entirely in the small hamlet of Villaluenga del Rosario in Cadiz Province in Andalusia—the southern region of Spain.... The film is unusual in that it is without narration.... [I]t consists entirely of cinema verite clips of daily life."* [From the review by David Gilmore, *AA* 88:524–525, 1986.]

The Pueblo Presence (1981) 60 min. Hugh Johnston and Suzanne Johnston (PR) for WNET. Dist: Hugh and Suzanne Johnston, 16 Valley Rd., Princeton, NJ 08540; (609) 924-7505, FR$90, FS$700, VS$475. *"Themes that are central to pueblo ethos are demonstrated in this film. They include the harmonious and respectful relationship of pueblo peoples with mother earth, the interface of art with religion, the intimate connection of ceremonies with the mythic past, and sacral pilgrimages that renew the links with the past.... There is a focus on the pragmatics that allow pueblo cultures to make selective adaptations in order to survive and maintain group identities."* [From the review by Joann W. Kealiinohomoku, *AA* 88:525–526, 1986.]

Pull Ourselves Up or Die Out 26 min. John Marshall and Claire Ritchie (AN). Dist: DER VR$20, VS$150. *This video provides visual and factual information on the current situation of the !Kung San people at Tshum !Kwi, in Namibia, where "N!ai the Story of a !Kung Woman" was filmed. The report includes footage shot at and near Tshum!Kwi between the years of 1980 and 1984. Highlighted in the taped report are: problems and issues that affect the !Kung as their economy continues to shift from subsistence to cash-based; scenes and interviews surrounding the possible establishment of a game reserve in Eastern Bushmanland; development of cattle farming and husbandry in !Kung groups; and confrontations with South African Administration officials regarding the rights to install a water pump and the rights of !Kung to use water.*

The Punake of Tonga (1977) 26 min. Eric B. Shumay (FM, AN). Dist: Division of Learning Resources, BYU—Hawaii Campus, Laie, Hawaii 96762 (video only). *The role of the poet (punake) in the preservation of Tongan cultures through the media of poetry, song, and dance. Shot on location in two villages in Tonga in 1975 on the island of Tonga-tapu. Shows the preparations of two highly regarded Tongan poets as they compose their materials, work with the dances, and bring their work to completion involving groups from the entire kingdom. The punake (poet) in Tonga is charged with preserving and interpreting the most urgent social and political imperatives of the people through the medium of the lakalaka, an extended poem that is set to music and carefully choreographed to bring out the full visual, audio, and ideographic impact of the poem. The film deals with the friendly, but intense, rivalry between two punake as they prepare for and finally present their compositions in a natural dance competition. Peni Tutu'ila Malupo, the innovator and iconoclast, shown in contrast to Malukava, the regal and staid traditionalist, is the central theme of the film. Their preparations and final presentations represent the broader context of the story. Cinematic features: Shot in 3/4" color/sound videotape compatible only with 3/4" VCR units. Uses in teaching: Polynesian Socie-*

ties; Introductory Anthropology; Ethnomusicology. Tape only, not available in film. Focusing questions: What is the importance and place of the poet (punake) in Tongan society? As an outsider, does the "rebellion in style" of Peni Tutu'ila strike you as being as drastic as it was perceived to be by the Tongans? What is the day-to-day life of the poet like outside of the realm of poetry and dance composition? Do the actions of the men and women in the performance of the *lakalaka* clearly demonstrate the male-female dichotomy in Tongan life? Bibliography: Eric B. Shumway, "Ko E Fakalangilangi: The Eulogistic Function of the Tongan Poet." In: *Pacific Studies Vol. 1*, No. I (Sept. 1977). Published by Brigham Young University—Hawaii Campus. Adrienne L. Kaeppler, "Preservation and Evolution of Form and Function in Two Types of Tongan Dance." In: *Polynesian Culture History*, Genevieve A. Highland et al., ed. Bernice P. Bishop, Museum Special Publication, 56. Honolulu: Bishop Museum Press, 1967.

La Punition (The Punishment) (1960) 60 min. Jean Rouch (DI), Films de la Pleiade (PR). Dist: CFE; DER. *A Parisian examination of comedia del arte filmed with the techniques of direct cinema. Leaving her Parisan school, Nadine has several encounters.*

Pure and Simple (Man on the Rim Series) 58 min. Dist: LMF VS$295. *For thousands of years, the Japanese have fought with the utmost determination to remain distinctive from the dominance of China. Japan's long struggle to remain independent and to conserve its cultural identity is manifested in the simplicity and severity of ceremony and design: most vividly in aspects of Japanese life as formal gardens, calligraphy, craftsmanship in pottery, wood, paper, fan making, and bamboo.*

Pyramid (1989) 60 min. Larry Klein (FM), Mark Olshaker (PR), David Macaulay (HO). Dist: PBSV2 VS$59.95. *"Uses the story of the construction of the Great Pyramid of Khufu at Giza as a basis for an exposition on ancient Egyptian history and culture. The program opens at Giza, where Macaulay relates the salient points of early Egyptian history with the Great Pyramids as a backdrop."* [From the review by Peter S. Allen, *ARCH* 44(5):71–72, 1991.]

La pyramide humaine (The Human Pyramid) (1958–59) 80 min. Jean Rouch (DI), Films de la Pleiade (PR). Dist: CFE; DER. *The problems of interracial relations in a school in Abidjan, Ivory Coast.*

Qaggiq (Gathering Place) (1989) 58 min. Zacharias Kunuk (FM). Dist: Igloolik Isuma Prod. Inc., Box 223, Iglookik, Northwest Territories, XOA OLO Canada; (819) 934-8809; fax (819) 934-8700. *This experimental video recreates a late winter camp of the Igloolik Inuit in the 1930s Northwest Territories. Presented as a modern technological version of the ancient storytelling tradition, the plot centers on a wedding proposal.*

Qeros: The Shape of Survival 53 min. John Cohen (DI). Dist: CG R$80, FS$795, VS$495. *The Qeros Indians have lived in the high Peruvian Andes for at least 3,000 years. Although they speak the native tongue of the Incas, their culture is far older. Today, the last survivors live in eight small hamlets almost 14,000 above sea level, far from civilization. Their economy is self-sufficient. They have adapted to the best altitude and grazing land for their alpacas (raised for wool) and llamas (beasts of burden) and grow staple crops far down the mountains. The Qeros employ the same agricultural methods, play panpipes and flutes, and weave cloth using the same sophisticated patterns as those described by Spanish chroniclers in the 16th century. Life for these people is simple and harsh. Death often comes because they lack protection from disease, as the film shows in the funeral of a 17-year-old woman whose husband and baby died just before her own death. Life for the Qeros may seem unduly harsh and primitive, but in the towns of modern Peru, the lot of the more assimilated Andean Indians is not to be envied. Landless, reduced to utter poverty, many eke out a meager income carrying heavy loads on their backs like beasts of burden. In their isolated mountain home, the Qeros have chosen a more dignified life: through patterns of the past they have found isolation and pride to be the keys of their survival.*

Quadruped Walking II (Chimpanzee) 2.5 min. Dist: PSU FR$2.80.

Quadruped Walking (Gorilla) 4 min. Dist: PSU FR$2.80.

Quadruped Walking (Orangutan) 3.5 min. Dist: PSU FR$2.80.

Quadruped Walking (Chimpanzee) 2 min. Dist: PSU FR$2.80.

Los que curan (1976) 43 min. Robert T. Trotter III, Juan Antonio Chavira Grupo Cine Labor (FM). Dist: Pan American University/Far East Films. *Shot in the Lower Rio Grande Valley of Texas and Reynosa, Tamaulipas, the film depicts the activities of a well-known local curandero, a folk healer, in south Texas and northern Mexico. Three cases of diagnosis and treatment are presented, one in which diagnosis is made by reading cards and using fire as divination. The second is a treatment of a patient in his home. The third is a spiritual session held for a group of people in south Texas. The film presents folk medicine as a system, with an accompanying emic theoretical structure, rather than a random accumulation of folk beliefs.* Cinematic features: Synchronous sound, some flash frames left in. There is a two-minute lead-in to the actual film using still photographs of a physician telling other physicians that they need not be upset by the positive way curanderismo is presented. Focusing questions: What does the lead-in tell us about the concerns of the medical establishment as opposed to the concerns of the folk healers in the film? Is folk medicine a theoretical system or merely a collection of beliefs? Contrast the patient visit of the curandero with a typical visit to a physician. What elements of Mexican-American folk medicine are similar to the viewers' own experiences? Bibliography: Robert T. Trotter, II, and Juan Antonio Chavira, *El Don: An Ethnography of Mexican American Folk Medicine*. Athens, University of Georgia Press, (in press). Robert T. Trotter, II, and Juan Antonio Chavira, "Curanderismo: An Emic Theoretical Perspective of Mexican American Folk Medicine." *Medical Anthropology*, 4.

The Quechua (Disappearing World Series) (1974) 51 min. Michael Sallnow (AN), Carlos Pasini (Dl). Dist: PSU VR$14, order #51157. *The Quechua live in an isolated region of the Peruvian Andes. Unlike many tribes in remote areas, they desperately want a road to link them with the outside world and its benefits, especially the tourist trade. This program focuses on a young family as they make the daunting trek to the spectacular festival of Qoyllur Rit'i, where they pray for the construction of the road.* [Reviewed by Olivia Harris, *RAIN* 6:11, 1975. Peter Loizos, *AA* 82:581–582, 1980.]

Queros: Shape of Survival (1980) 58 min. Dist: SU FR$55. *Study of the Peruvian Queros Indians who have lived for 3,000 years in the harsh environment of the Andes. In the 14,000 foot altitude, they raise llamas as beasts of burden and alpacas for wool. Diet staples—potatoes and corn—are grown 8,000 feet down the mountain. The 12-hour trip takes them from tropical to tundra zones several times a year, but they remain independent of monetary strictures. The film observes a funeral (young girl) and notes that half of all babies die, because of no medicine; weaving cloth (warp pattern) using methods 3,000 years old; explains how they sleep on kernels to make their body heat sprout them for wine, how they eat coca leaves for gentle stimulation, and many other facets of this remarkable people that live on tenuous borderlines most of their lives.*

Quest for Fire (1982) 83 min. Jean-Jacques Annaud (FM). Dist: 20 CF. *This is an attempt at producing a fictional reconstruction of the stage of Hominid evolution some 80,000 years ago. The film has been severely critiqued for its inadequacies in the fields of phonology as well as archaeological and paleoanthropological research.* [Reviewed by Philip Lieberman *AA* 84:991–992, 1982. C. Owen Lovejoy, *ARCH* 35(4):78, 1982.]

The Quiet in the Land (1971) 72 min. John Hostetler and John Ruth (CON). Dist: PSU FR$19.50. *Documentary-dramatization of issues in the Mennonite community of Montgomery County, Pennsylvania, in the year of the French and Indian war. Provides an historical perspective on Mennonite society.*

Quiet Passages: The Japanese-American War Bride Experience (1990) 26 min. Jerry Schultz (FM.) Dist: CEAS-UK. "*A low-budget, audiovisual production concerned with the experience of Japanese women who came to Kansas between 1947 and 1962 as brides of American servicemen.*" [From the review by Malcolm Collier, *AA* 95(1):253–255, 1993.]

The Quillayute Story (1951) 25 min. Dist: PSU FR$12. *Transition of the Northwest Coast Indians from a reconstructed baseline to a subculture within contemporary U.S. society. Adoption of the Shaker religion. Incidental sequences of smelt fishing, salmon fishing, baking, dancing, sporting activities, and a potlatch.*

Quilting Women (1976) 28 min. Elizabeth Barret (FM). Dist: APPAL FR$40, FS$425. *A warm and joyful celebration of women artists who with gentle modesty create works of art in textile. The film traces the entire process of quilt-making from piecing to the finale of a quilting bee.*

Quilts in Women's Lives 28 min. Pat Ferrero (DI). Dist: NDF FR$50, FS$450. *This film presents a series of portraits of traditional quiltmakers and provides insight into the spirit of these women who are the basis for this continuing tradition of quilt making. Seven women, among them a California Mennonite, a black Mississippian, and a Bulgarian immigrant, talk about their art and the influences on it. They describe the inspirations for their work—family, tradition, the joy of the creative process, the challenge of design—and how it has become a part of their daily lives.*

Raananah, a World of Our Own (1980) 29 min. Marlene Booth (FM). Dist: Booth, 23 Irving Street, Cambridge, MA 02138. FR$50, FS$420. "*An 'intentional community,' Raananah, a 40-year-old summer colony in New York state begun by immigrant Jewish labor Zionists to realize their ideal of collective ownership of land.*" [From the review by Riv-Ellen Prell, *AA* 85:1007–1008, 1983.]

Radio Bikini (1987) 56 min. Robert Stone (FM). Dist: FRIF FR$125, FS$895. *The internationally acclaimed, award-winning documentary about Operation Crossroads, an early U.S. nuclear weapons test conducted at a remote Pacific atoll called Bikini in the summer of 1946.*

The Ragged Revolution (1981) 37 min. Tony Essex (PR). Dist: Document Associates, Inc., 211 East 43rd St., New York, NY 10017, FR$45, FS$550. *The Mexican revolution, using contemporary footage.* [Reviewed by Martin Diskin, *AA* 86:238–239, 1984.]

Raising the Gilhast Pole (1974) 28 min. Sandy Wilson, Provincial Educational Media Centre, British Columbia (PR). Dist: PEMC. [Reviewed by Alice Bee Kasakoff, *AA* 74:994–995, 1977.]

Rain Forest (1960) 30 min. Tom Harrisson (FM). Dist: Granada TV, 36 Golden Square, London W1 England. *Borneo.* [Reviewed by David Agee, *AA* 75:2015, 1973.]

Raj Gonds (1982) 50 min. Melissa Llewelyn-Davies (PR) for the BBC Worlds Apart series. Dist: FI FR$100, FS$800, VS$480. *Deals with tribal peoples in India.* "*The central focus here is on an annual festival—Dandari—of the pre-harvest season. In it the Gonds reenact en masse the central event of their tribal origin myth: the marriage procession of Yetma, daughter of the God of creation, with the Raj Gond culture hero.*" [From the review by Sylvia Vatuk, *AA* 88:271–273, 1986.]

Raju the Guide 28 min. Yavar Abbas (PR). Dist: CMC. *At Rishikesh, on the Ganges.* [Reviewed by Janet Benson, *AA* 76:707, 1974.]

Rajvinder: An East Indian Family (Other Lands Series) (1984) 16 min. Dist: Beacon Films, P.O. Box 575, Norwood, MA 02062, FS$350, VS$325. *This film "shows some of the customs that accompany a marriage in a Sikh community in North America.... The film can be used to introduce acculturation provided that the post-screening discussion is as elaborate as a pre-screening introduction."* [From the review by Rena C. Gropper, *SBF* 20:223, 1985.]

Ralph Stanley's Bluegrass Festival (1982) 15 min. Jim Kent (FM). Dist: Amberola Productions, 259 Broadway, Cambridge, MA 02139; (617) 353-3498, FR$25, FS$250. *Ralph sits in the yard with a microphone clipped to his collar in taped-filmed interview sessions.* [Reviewed by Melanie L. Sovine, AA 89:522–525, 1987.]

Ramparts of Clay (1970) 85 min. Jean-Louis Bertucelli (PR, DI), Jean Duvignaud (WR), acted by Leila Schenna and the villagers of Tehouda in Algeria. Dist: C5 FR$100. *A dramatization of Duvignaud's book that describes an anthropological study of an isolated village in the Tunisian Maghrib, carried out between 1960 and 1966 by students from the university of Tunis. The project was concerned with the problems of development. Apparently, for political reasons, the film, made by Algerians, was filmed in Algeria, not Tunis.* [Reviewed by Irene Gendzier, AA 76:692–693, 1974.] Suggested supplement: *Change at Shebika. Report from a North African Village* (translated from the French by Frances Frenaye), Pantheon Books, 1970. Focusing questions: Why the introductory quote from Franz Fanon? (Who was Fanon?) How is speech used? What are male versus female worlds? What is the chicken blood business about? The real Shebika was an oasis with a pool, and people grew dates, cherries, almonds, peppers, wheat, peas, and beans. Why the dry village of the film? Why the helicopter shot at the end?

Rana (1977) 19 min. Debby Kingsland (DI, ED), Film Australia (PR). Dist: Wombat Productions, Little Lake, Glandale Rd., P.O. Box 70, Ossining, NY 10562, FR$31.59, FS$315; UCEMC FR$30. *Rana, a young woman living in Delhi, very Moslem, describes her life at home and at college, in excellent English.* Focusing questions: How do you reconcile Rana's westernization with her willingness to have an arranged marriage? What is the relationship between Rana and her father? Has the filmmaker (Debby Kingsland, an Australian) intruded too much into the film?

Rangi and Papa: A Maori Creation Myth (see Creation Myth Series)

Raoni (1976) 60 min. Bill Leimbach and Jean Pierre Dutilleux (FM), Marlon Brando (NA). Dist: SFI; JPD. *Made among the Xingu river tribes of Brazil, this is the story of the politicalisation of a tribal leader, Raoni, and how he learned to take on the encroaching world digging into his rainforest. This is the same Raoni, the Indian, who along with Sting, the musician, toured the major nations in 1989 in search of global support for preservation of Xingu habitat.* [Reviewed by Nancy M. Flowers, AA 90:487–489, 1988.] See Daniel R. Gross, "A Shattered Peace." *Geo* 3:10–34, 1981.

Rapports meres-enfants en Afrique (Rapports between Mothers and Infants in Africa) (1971) 20 min. Jean Rouch (DI), ORTE (PR). Dist: CFE; DER.

Rashomon (1950) 87 min. A Kurosawa (DI). Dist: AB. *Feature Film. In ancient Japan, several people tell the truth about an event, as each person saw it. Filmed in Japan, demonstrating such traditional aspects as the samurai, in addition to the main theme regarding the nature of truth.* Focusing questions: What is the "personal equation"? How does it manifest itself in anthropological field work? What does this film illustrate about truth and the observer? Possible supplement: H. Redfield, *Tepotzlan*. O. Lewis, *Tepotzlan Revisited*. [Vivian J. Rohrl]

Rastafari: Conversations Concerning Women (1984) 60 min. Elliott Leib and Renee Romano (FM). Dist: EI FR$60, FS$250. *Broadens "the image of Jamaican women. Concerned that these women have often been stereotyped as 'docile' and 'submissive', they attempt to show their diversity: visually, through imagery and philosophically, by allowing women to speak for themselves."* [From the review by Anita M. Barrow, AA 89:262–263, 1987.]

Rastafari Voices (1979) 58 min. Elliott Leib and Renee Romano (FM). Dist: EI FR$90, VR$60, FS$715, VS$500. *The "Rastafari" of Jamaica have probably become the world's best-known cult. This fame is linked to reggae, the music associated with Rastafari, and to the Rasta sacramental use of marijuana. The film has little voice-over narration, the focus of the filmmakers is on the imagery, pointing their cameras in the right directions and editing their footage skillfully. The film is perfectly evocative of the Rasta experience without being in the least didactic or ponderous.* [Reviewed by Michael Lieber, AA 83:744–775, 1981.]

Rate It X (1986) 95 min. Lynn Campbell and Claudette Charbonneau (PR), Lucy Winer and Paula de Koenigsberg (DR). Dist: INTERAMA R$175, FS$1500, VS$700. *"How men use women to attract consumer attention in order to sell something."* [From the review by Michael Agar, AA 90:1043–1044, 1988.]

A Rather Strange Tribe 10 min. Tim Wilson (FM), Center for Instructional Communications, Syracuse University (PR). Dist: Film Rental Center, 1455 East Colvin Street, Syracuse University, Syracuse, NY 13210, FR$10. *An actor, playing an African anthropologist, pretends to lecture his class on a rather strange tribe (i.e., the Nacirema). A white view of what a black view would be.*

Raw Fish and Pickle: Traditional Rural and Seafaring Life (The Human Face of Japan Series) (1982) 28 min. Dist: LCA R$50, FS$550, VS$425. *"This film focuses on the political, technological, and human problems of life in an 'economic backwater' of Japan.... The title suggests that the film is more about fishing than is the case.... The film ... stresses the Japanese planning and development strategy of close coordination of government, business and industry."* [From the review by George M. Epple, *SBF* 18:280, 1983.]

Ray Lum: Mule Trader 18 min. Bobby Taylor (FM), Bill Ferris (SR), Judy Peiser (ED). Dist: CSF FR$30, FS$280. *The film focuses on Ray Lum, a trader and storyteller. Born in Rocky Springs, Mississippi, on June 21, 1891, he has traded horses, mules, and cattle throughout the United States. With every trade, he has a tale to tell. From the first horse bought at the age of 12 to 80,000 horses in Laplant, South Dakota, "Mr. Ray" recalls his experiences for customers in his saddle shop. The film shows Mr. Ray at home and at his brother's sale barn in Vicksburg, Mississippi. Throu-*

gout the day, Ray sells whips and saddles, inspects horses and mules, auctions livestock, swaps tales, and talks of yesterday and tomorrow.

Reassemblage (1982) 40 min. Trinh T. Minh-ha (DI), Jean-Paul Bourdier (PR). Dist: WMM FR$90, FS$800, VS$395. *Women are the focus but not the object of Trinh T. Minh-ha's first film, a complex visual study of the women of rural Senegal. Through a complicity of interaction between film and spectator, it reflects on documentary filmmaking and the ethnographic representation of cultures.* [Reviewed in *VISA* 4:160, 1991.]

Rebels of the Forgotten World 52 min. Dist: FHS VS$149, order #DH-3054. *The forceful and forcible efforts of the Indonesian government to resettle and westernize the tribal people of Papua New Guinea have met determined resistance from the dispossessed native population, armed only with bows and arrows.*

Rebuilding the Temple: Cambodians in America (1991) 60 min. Claudia Levin and Lawrence Hott (FM). Dist: DCL. [Reviewed by Malcolm Collier, *AA* 95(1):253–255, 1993.]

Reclaiming the Forest (1986) Paul Henley (DI), National Film and Television School and the Royal Anthropological Institute (PR). Dist: RAI. *"Shows us Carib Indians in Venezuela who have already lost their land base and, being dependent on their market economy for their needs, have become wage workers in gold mines near the Guyana border. However, their ethnic identity remains strong, and they are hoping to find land on which to reestablish subsistence agriculture and economic independence."* [From the review by Nancy M. Flowers, *AA* 90:487–489, 1988.]

The Red Bowmen (Films from Papua New Guinea Series) (1983) 58 min. Chris Owen (DI), The Institute of Papua New Guinea Studies (PR). Dist: DER FR$80, VR$60, FS$800, VS$400. *Every year, a ritual known as "ida" is performed by the Umeda people, who inhabit the dense primary forest of the Waina-Sawanda district of West Sepik, Papua New Guinea. Ida, the central social and cultural drama of the Umeda, is a fertility ritual, in which a dominant theme is the metamorphosis of the cassowaries.* Relevant anthropological literature: Alfred Gell, *Metamorphosis of the Cassowaries*. [Reviewed by Gordon C. Tucker, Jr., *SBF* 18:216, 1983.]

Red Sunday: The Story of the Battle of the Little Big Horn (1975) 28 min. Dist: IUAVC FR$13.50; UCEMC FR$34. *Documents the Battle of Little Big Horn, or "Custer's Last Stand," through original drawings, photographs, and paintings by both Indian and white artists. Covers both sides of the battle in great detail as well as including background material on the events leading up to the battle.*

Reel du Pendu (1972) 57 min. Andre Gladu (DI). Dist: NFBC. [Reviewed by Gerald L. Gold, *AA* 80:760–763.]

Le regne du jour (1966) Pierre Perrault (DI), National Film Board of Canada (PR). Dist: Canadian Embassy, Public Affairs Division, 1771 N St., Washington, DC 20036 (free). *Three villagers from Ile-aux-Coudres in the St. Laurence River return to France looking for their ancestors.*

See also *The Moontrap*. [Reviewed by Bernard Bernier and Bernard-R. Emond, *AA* 80:763–765, 1978.]

Reign of the Wanderers (Triumph of the Nomads Series) 1 hour. Nomad Films International Australia (PR). Dist: PBSV VS$134.95, order #9775-21. *This film examines fire as being central to the Aborigines' way of life, their ability to cope when drought or disease struck, their practice of abortion to control their population, their treatment of old people, and their weapons. It also looks at the Aborigines' mastery of nature that ensured that future generations existed in comparative luxury.*

The Reindeer Queen 28 min. Maria Brooks (PR). Dist: FL VR$55, VS$295. *This video documents the life of an Alaskan Eskimo woman whose tenacity and spirit led her to play a significant role in the turbulent history of Alaska's arctic. Combining rare archival footage, stills, and interviews with people who knew her, this unusual film brings to life the Alaskan frontier at the end of the last century. Her story is all the more remarkable in view of the prejudice against Native Americans during the Gold Rush era. When the Department of the Interior decided to transport the Siberian Reindeer to the United States to develop an industry, Sinrock Mary went to Siberia to act as Russian interpreter. She introduced the first reindeer to the territory and later became the owner of the largest herd in the North. As a woman and a Native American, she was constantly subject to harassment by those trying to gain control of her herd. As her fortunes grew, miners wanted to marry her and Yankee traders did business with her.*

Releasing the Spirits: A Village Cremation in Bali (Bali Series) (1986) 43 min. Linda Connor, Patsy Asch, and Timothy Asch (DI), Australian National University and DER (PR). Dist: DER FR$60, VR$40, FS$650, VS$350. *Cremation rites are the most elaborate rites of passage performed by Balinese householders. Poor families may wait years before accumulating enough resources to cremate their dead, who are buried in the meantime. In 1978 many more cremations than usual were carried out because the religious officials recommended that all Balinese cleanse the island by cremating their dead, in order to prepare for the great Besakhi ceremony. Villagers performed group cremations to reduce the cost to individual families. The film is about one such group cremation. It shows the way they approached this task, as well as the cycle of rituals. Most of the narration is provided by four participants, recorded as they were watching videotapes two years later. Each brings a different perspective to the events documented on the film. The three voices of the filmmakers also provide different insights. The cremation is held in Jero Tapakan's hamlet, and she is a central participant.* [Reviewed by Susan Rodgers, *AA* 95(1):255–256, 1993.]

Religion in Suburbia (1982) 28 min. Aron Ranen (FM). Dist: Aron Ranen, 210 Noe St., San Francisco, CA 94114; (415) 863-6727, VR$50, VS$120. *"Explores the relationship of a surburban Jewish temple to its individual members concerns' about God, death, and existence."* Filmed in Newton, Massachusetts. [From the review by Faye Ginsburg, *AA* 87:741–747, 1985.]

Rembetika: The Blues of Greece 50 min. Anthony Quinn (NA), DNM (PR). Dist: WFV FS$795, VS$110. *Deriving out of the slums of Athens and Piraeus, it has come to symbolize the Greek fight against oppression. Featured in "Never on Sunday" and "Zorba the Greek," it has achieved international recognition. Rembetika is compelling music and song; here it also becomes the microcosm of a nation's recent history. Available in a 30-minute version.* [Reviewed by Loring M. Danforth, AA 87:991–992, 1985.]

Remnants of a Frontier Life (1941) 22 min. Dist: PSU order #22490, FR$9.50. *Carolina rural mountain family demonstrates technology and daily routine in the Great Smokies, against a background of local music. Weaving of corn mats and seats, and construction of a ladder-back chair. Valuable as historical material.*

Remnants of a Race (1953) 18 min. Dist: PSU (PCR) order #916.8-6, FR$13. *Life of the !Kung San in the Kalahari desert in Bechuanaland (now Botswana). Unceasing hunt for food, sketches and paintings on ostrich shells, utensils, clicking manner of speech, religious dances.*

Le renard pale (The Pale Fox) (1981) Jean Rouch, Germaine Dieterlen and Luc de Heusch (DI). Dist: CFE; DER. *Cine-myth: the creation of the world according to the Dogon.*

The Rendille (Disappearing World Series) (1977) 53 min. Chris Curling (PR), Anders Grum (AN.) Dist: PSU order #51251. *Camels enable the Rendille to survive in the harsh African desert in which they live. Because these animals are so precious, every Rendille male must serve 14 years as a warrior herdsman before he is allowed to settle down in the village. But long droughts have rapidly decreased the herd, and the herdsman are being lured to big-city life in Nairobi.* [Reviewed by P. T. W. Baxter, RAIN 20:7, 1977.]

Requiem for a Faith 28 min. Irving and Elda Hartley (PR, DI), Huston Smith (WR, NA). Dist: HFF FR$45, FS$395, VS$89. *Apparently filmed partially in Kathmandu, this film is a recreation of traditional life in Tibet, prior to the Chinese conquest of 1951. A visually rich tour of traditional Tibetan culture, emphasizing the sacred aspects, with a narration that goes far beyond the visual material, and marred by some heavy-handed Cold War rhetoric. Includes secular dance, the founding of hand bells, the painting of tonkas, the carving of printed blocks, and various scenes of monastic life including the reading of sacred scriptures, stylized debate of doctrinal issues, and portions of sacred services, including brief footage of the sacred orchestras, including bells, frame drums, gongs, and both short and long trumpets. Also, shows and describes the exotic "split tone" technique of chanting, in which one voice produces a major triad. Commentary emphasizes the traditional Tibetan World View. Warnings: An opening statement (behind a map showing Tibet being devoured by red China) states "Tibet is no more!" Focusing questions: How do traditional Tibetans view human consciousness? How does this view come to be expressed in their traditional musical, dramatic, and visual arts? How does this musical tradition differ from more familiar Euro-American musical styles?* [Donald Crim]

The Restless Earth: Evidence from Ancient Life (1972) 11 min. WNET/13, British Broadcasting Corporation, Sveriges Radio (Sweden), Australian Broadcasting Commission, and Studio Hamburg (West Germany) (PR). Dist: IUAVC FR$6.75, FS$185, VS$110. *Relationships between the evolution of plant and animal life and the history of our changing earth are examined. Plant life on earth may date as far back as 3,400 million years, and some species of worms are known to be 600 million years old. Living things changed considerably when continents last came together into one large mass. Dinosaurs emerged at this time, but became extinct when this supercontinent broke apart. It was during the last ice age that human life emerged.*

Le retour de l'aventurier 39 min. Moustapha Allassane (DI). Dist: CF/MH. *A cowboy film from Niger.* [Reviewed by J. David Sapir, AA 74:1569, 1972.]

The Return of Dr. Fritz: Healing by the Spirits in Brazil 62 min. Sidney Greenfield (AN, PR). Dist: CLA-UWM VR$25, VS$75. *Dr. Adolph Fritz, a German physician, died during WWI, but his spirit, in possession of the body of Dr. Edson Queiroz, a spiritist medium from Brazil, treats patients every Wednesday. People who have waited perhaps months travel hundreds of miles for treatment from the doctor. A session may vary from a simple homily from Dr. Fritz followed by a consultation with one of his assistants, to a surgical procedure performed without anesthetics. The film explores the religious, socioeconomic, and philosophical relationships and factors that have been responsible for the development and acceptance of "channeled" health care. Case histories are presented that include the voices of the spirits, the mediums and the patients, and the opinions of opponents and professional debunkers.* [Reviewed by Michael Winkleman, AA 93(2):518–519, 1991.]

The Return of the Child 26 min. Dist: FHS VS$89.95, order #DH-877. *So that the sorrow of the living will not haunt the spirit of the dead, Indian tradition limits the length of mourning. But Eshkebuc cannot tear himself away from the graveside. His tears awaken his dead son who appears healthy; but the boy does not eat or smile or speak until the sap of the fir tree frees him from the bonds of death.*

The Return of the Gods and Ancestors: The Five-Year Ceremony (1984) 35 min. Dr. Tai-Li Hu (FM). Dist: Jean Tsien, 144-53 76th Road, Flushing, NY 11367; (718) 261-8897. *"Every five years the deities and ancestors of the Paiwan people descend from their home in the high mountains to visit the Paiwan in scattered, intermontane villages of central and south-central Taiwan. The traditional ritual preformed for this occasion is called Maleveq.... This film documents the various rites of the Maleveq."* [From the review by William Graves III, AA 89:263–264, 1987.]

The Return of the Sacred Pole (1990) 28 min. Nebraska ETV (PR), Robin Riddington (AN). Dist: NAPBC. *Return of an Omaha sacred object from a museum.* [Reviewed by Bea Medicine, AA 93(3):768–769, 1991.]

Return to Appalachia (1983) 28 min. Dist: FL FR$50, FS$475, VS$425. *"The title of this film refers to the return of a young woman to a West Virginia Town following her* *college graduation. . . . Although there are some interesting vignettes, the film has no continuity or direction, and no specific ideas or issues are developed."* [From the review by Gifford S. Nickerson, SBF 19:302, 1984.]

Return to Paradise (The New Pacific Series) (1987) 60 min. BBC/NVC (PR). Dist: FIV VS$79. *The film focuses on the issue of how the peoples of the Pacific islands can maintain their traditional values in the face of technological changes.*

Return to Sovereignty (1987) 46 min. Donald Stull (PR), David Kendall (DI). Dist: UCEMC VR$36, VS$385, order #37558. *This film examines how the Indian Self-determination and Education Assistance act of 1975 has been implemented among the Kansas Kickapoo—how it has succeeded and how it has failed. Kickapoo progress toward self-determination in the areas of economic development and education is explored through commentary by tribal administrators and elders, the local BIA superintendent, specialists in Indian law, and anthropologists. It is a valuable resource for native communities and organizations who face a challenge and struggle similar to that of Kickapoo, as well as for use in college courses in the fields of anthropology, Native American studies, sociology, political science, and history.* [Reviewed by Louise Lamphere, AA 86:1059–1060, 1984.]

La révolution poétique: Mai '68 (The Poetic Revolution: May '68) (1968) 40 min. Jean Rouch (DI). Dist: CFE; DER.

Rhesus Monkey in India (1962) 22 min. Psychological Cinema Register (PR), C. H. Southwick (CA), C. R. Carpenter (NA). Dist: PSU FR$14. *An ecological study of the rhesus monkey. This survey covered over 10,000 miles. The film compares numbers and acivities of the animals in villages, bazaars, railroad stations, and temples.* [Reviewed by Barbara Smuts, AA 75:2010, 1973.]

A Rhesus Monkey Infant's First Four Months (1979) Sylvia Howe (FM). Dist: PSU. *The locale of this film is Madingley Rhesus colony at Cambridge University. The film focuses on presenting the first four months of childhood of a single Rhesus infant.* [Reviewed by Patricia Hurley Hays AA 84:995–996, 1982.]

Rhesus Monkeys of the Santiago Island (1966) 33 min. C. Koford (FM). Dist: NAVC. [Reviewed by David Agee Horr, AA 75:2011, 1973.]

Rhythm of Africa (1940) 17 min. B/W. Francois Villiers (DI). Dist: FIM FR$15, FS$165. *The arts, the handicrafts, and, particularly, the exciting, spectacular traditional ceremonial dances of the Chad in French Equatorial Africa. . . . Conceived by Jean Cocteau, the poetic commentary has been translated by Langston Hughes and narrated by Kenneth Spencer.* [Reviewed by David Evans, JAF 89(354):516, 1976.]

Rhythme de travail (Work Rhythms) (1973) 12 min. Jean Rouch (DI), Centre National de la Recherche Scientifique, Comité du Film Ethnographique (PR). Dist: CFE; DER. *Collective improvisation singing while grinding millet; a peasant chant and a profane dance after a failed possession dance.*

Rhythms of Resistance (1978) 50 min. Chris Austin and Jeremy Marre (FM). Dist: HFL. *"About the Black music of South Africa, . . . a rare opportunity to hear the music of the townships and learn something about the manner in which it functions within that social context, the film roams across the whole spectrum of South African musical life. . . . Their note of anger and opposition is captured."* [From the review by Hannah Charlton, AA 88:1046, 1986.]

The Ribbon (1987) 50 min. Hariet Avshon (DI). Dist: FRIF FR$90, FS$795, VS$480. *"A film about a group of women and their cry for justice. Its subject is the anti-conscription campaign of the Black Sash movement in South Africa."* [From the review by Ellen Messer, AA 92:556–558, 1990.]

Rice (1964) 25 min. Willard Van Dyke, Wheaton Valentine (FM), Howard Enders (WR), Rockefeller Foundation (PR). Dist: MOMA FR$15; PSU (PCR) order #30775, FR$5.90. *To the teeming population of the Rice Bowl of Asia, 1,000,000 new souls are added each and every week—yet rice itself, their staple food, is planted, cultivated, harvested, and sold by methods inherited from neolithic times. Trapped by tradition, the eaters of rice still look to the gods, not to the will or the knowledge of men, to narrow the widening gap between supply and demand, a gap that threatens global disaster. The International Rice Research Institute, sponsored by the Rockefeller and Ford Foundations, is attempting to improve the fertility and cultivation of rice by scientific methods in time to reverse the inertia to the millenniums. Shot in the Philippines, Thailand, Nepal, Japan, and Bali.* [Reviewed by Eugene I. Knez, AA 68:1328–1329, 1966.]

Rice and Peas (1990) 12 min. Karen Kramer (FM). Dist: FRIF VR$35, FS$265, VS$160; KKFL FR$60, VR$40, FS$400, VS$200. *Gill's, in Brooklyn, New York, is a modest restaurant specializing in West Indian cuisine. In this film, Gillian Charles, the restaurant's proprietress and chef, prepares her own recipe for the staple of West Indian fare, rice and peas, while reminiscing about her native Trinidad and the adjustments she has made in the United States. In this way, the film provides an example of how one woman has kept her cultural heritage intact by introducing it into her new world.*

The Rice Cycle in Thailand (1978) 30 min. Dist: UIOWA order #40253, FR$15. *Follows the activities of a rice farmer and his family through the full cycle of rice planting and harvesting. Shows in detail the preparation of the rice beds, the preparation of the fields, control and use of water supply, planting, harvesting, milling, and preparation of the rice as food. Also includes the religious ceremonies that follow the harvesting of the rice. Clearly demonstrates the many ways in which rice is essential to the economy and culture of the area.*

The Rice Ladle: The Changing Roles of Women (The Human Face of Japan Series) (1982) 28 min. Dist: LCA R$50, FS$550, VS$425. *"This excellent production . . . illustrates sex role changes and expectations in the contemporary*

Japanese work force ... by focussing on three Japanese women." [From the review by Charles C. Kolb, *SBF* 18:216, 1983.]

Rich Man's Medicine, Poor Man's Medicine (1976) 43 min. Gordan Troeller, Marie Claude Deffarge, and Francois Partant (FM). Dist: FRIF FR$85, FS$695, VS$420. *Filmed in Gabon, Senegal, and Kenya, this film focuses on the realities of medical care in developing countries. It provides a glimpse into the conflict between "modern" technological development patterns and traditional, indigenous approaches.*

Richard Cardinal: Cry from a Diary of Metis Child 29 min. Alanis Obomsawin (DI). Dist: NFB R$60, FS$550, VS$250. *Richard Cardinal was four when he was removed from his alcoholic parents and placed in a foster home outside his Native American culture. At the age of 17, Richard committed suicide. By the time he died, he had lived in 28 foster homes, group homes, and shelters. The film is based on his diary, which reveals not only his profound loneliness but a nightmarish life of neglect and indifference. His story is a tragic reminder of the damage that can be done by a child welfare system that fails to recognize an individual's human needs.* [Reviewed by Joe Sawchuk, *AA* 92(4):1096–1097, 1990.]

Ricky and Rocky 15 min. Jeff Kreines and Tom Palazallo (FM). Dist: VQ FR$25, FS$175 *A surprise bridal shower in a suburban backyard.* [Reviewed by Richard Chalfen, *AA* 77:466–469, 1975.]

The Riddle of the Dead Sea Scrolls (1990) 2 parts, 50 min. each. James R. Mitchell (PR), Richard Cassidy (DI). Dist: CG VR$100, VS$250 (each), $395 (set). *This video "is a visual presentation of the controversial theories of Barbara Thiering, an Australian scholar who is challenging conventional interpretations of the Dead Sea Scrolls and Scripture. Her thesis is that the scrolls refer to events during the time of Christ, not during the years 150's and 140's B.C. as most scholars maintain.... It is an impressive production and a very thorough presentation of Thiering's idea, but it remains unconvincing."* [From the review by Peter S. Allen, *ARCH* 44(1):72, 1993.]

The Rift Valley 44 min. Dist: FHS VS$149, order #DH-2271. *One of the most magnificent teaching guides to the history of the earth is the great valley formed when the land mass that is now the Arabian Peninsula and East Africa was torn apart. This program examines the geological formations, the unique flora and fauna, and the inhabitants of the longest valley of the world, following the course of this extraordinary region from its barren beginnings round the Dead Sea to the abundant life in Ngorongo Crater, where the Leakeys made their great discoveries.*

The Right to Be Mohawk: The Survival of a People and Their Traditions Hornbein, Stanaway, and Rasmussen (FM). Dist: NDF VR$50, VS$250. *A stereotype-breaking look at contemporary people deep rooted in the past—traditionalist Mohawks of Akwesasne in New York State. This film documents their determination not only to survive, but also to grow and build their nation, in spite of continuous and stepped up pressures to assimilate. Insightful conversations with traditional Mohawk leaders and residents of Akwesasne reveals to us a belief system and culture that has already had a powerful influence on our own.* [Reviewed in *SBF* 25:273, 1990.]

Rights and Reactions (1987) 57 min. Phil Zwickler and Jane Lippman (FM). Dist: Tapestry International, 924 Broadway, New York, NY 10010; (212) 677-6007, FR$125, VR$95, FS$895, VS$395. *"In 1986 the New York City Council approved a bill, Intro. 2, to protect gays and lesbians from discrimination in housing, public accommodations, and employment (after suffering repeated defeats over a period of 15 years).... This film dramatically and effectively documents the intense struggle in New York City between the proponents and the opponents of civil rights protections for gays and lesbians during the final stage of this battle."* [From the review by Ralph Bolton, *AA* 92:840–841, 1990.]

Rime and Reason (1992) 52 min. Francis Guibert (FM). Dist: Les Films du Village, 5 passage Montgallet, 75010 Paris, France; telephone 331-46-28-45-90; fax 331-43-44-97-67. *This film presents a thick slice of French Hip-Hop culture. As rap and ragamuffin go global, working-class and immigrant B-boys and B-girls are dropping rhymes in their own tongue against the backdrop of an increasingly multicultural France.*

The Rio Grande's Pueblo Past 75 min. Douglas W. Schwartz (DI). Dist: Douglas W. Schwartz, School of American Research, P.O. Box 2188, Santa Fe, NM 87501.

The Rise of Nationalism (Africa Series) (1986) 57 min. RM Arts (PR), Basil Davidson (H). Dist: FIV. *Davidson charts Africa's struggle for independence, focusing on the final collapse of the white minority in Zimbabwe and on apartheid in South Africa.*

Rise Up and Walk (1982) 55 min. John Ankele (PR). Dist: UCEMC VR$60, VS$295. *Christianity is growing faster in Africa than anywhere else in the world today. This film shows how several independent African Christian churches interpret and live the Christian faith in the context of their own pre-Christian cultural traditions. Discussion guide available.*

Rites 52 min. Penny Dedman (PR). Dist: FL VR$75, VS$445. *This program explores the custom of female circumcision, which has been commonplace through history. Today it is still practiced in many cultures, particularly in Africa. This film shows the efforts of women throughout the world to stop the practice. The film considers three major contexts in which female genital mutilation (FGM) occurs. The first is "cosmetic," and the second is "punitive." Medical historian Dr. Moscurri describes how women in the late 19th century and early 20th century were subject to FGM if they stepped out of line. The third context is as part of the cultural transition to adulthood and initiation to female life. Routine mutilation has been strongly attacked by Western observers, although such attacks have themselves been the subject of accusations of cultural imperialism.*

Ritual (1978) 30 min. Dist: WFV FR$38. *Impressionistic, ethnographic documentary on Tokyo and the Japanese,* *showing how the city consists of many small "villages" clustered together, and how a sense of community and of group destiny—maintained by subtle social rituals—prevail in these villages.*

The Ritual of the Mounds (1984) 29 min. John Meyer (FM) for the Tennessee Department of Conservation. Dist: Educational Resource Center, Tennessee Department of Conservation, 701 Broadway, Nashville, TN 37203; (615) 742-6567, FR$25, FS$250. *"This film records the 1983 season investigation into one of the Pinson group mounds, recently discovered to be a splendid example of the little-known Hopewellian presence in western Tennessee."* [From the review by James A. Brown and Jane E. Buikstra, *AA* 87:480–481, 1985. Reviewed by William H. Marquardt, *AA* 87(6):68–69, 1985.]

Ritual: Three Portraits of Jewish Life (1989) 60 min. Dist: Jewish Theological Seminary of America, 3080 Broadway, New York, NY 10027; (212) 678-8020. *Jewish ritual in America.* *"Shows traditional Jewish ritual to be part of the lives of men and women, young and old, Orthodox and non-Orthodox, and experts and ordinary families."* [From the review by Riv-Ellen Prell, *AA* 93:519–520, 1991.]

Rituals of the Asmat Tribe 30 min. Dist: FHS VS$149, order #DH-2648. *The Asmat tribes of West Irian were—and perhaps still are, when they are not on camera—headhunters; it was in their domain that Michael Rockefeller disappeared. This program attends a number of their rituals and explains a number of their beliefs, showing as straightforwardly as possible a technologically 'primitive' culture that has barely been touched by modern goods and government.*

The River (1937) 32 min. Pare Lorentz (DI), Virgil Thompson (MU). Dist: VFI VS$24.95. *"This is the story of a river; a record of the Mississippi. Where it comes from, where it goes. What it has meant to us, and what it has cost us."* This is a famous U.S. Farm Security Administration documentary.

The River Kwai Expedition (1962) 12 min. Dist: DIO (NY, LA). *The Thai-Danish Expedition's discoveries of prehistoric cave pictures near the River Kwai.*

River People: Behind the Case of David Sohappy 50 min. Michal Conford and Michele Zaccheo (PR). Dist: FL VR$75, VS$395. *David Sohappy is a Native American spiritual leader who has stood up for his right to lead a traditional Indian lifestyle along the banks of the Columbia River. For 20 years, he fished in open defiance of federal and state laws, claiming an ancestral right to fish. Despite his assertion that fishing was an integral part of his people's religion, he was arrested for selling salmon out of season. As a result, he has become a symbol of resistance for Native Americans in their struggle for treaty rights. River People thus tells a timely tale, exploring what it is like to preserve the remnants of the most ancient cultures of our land in the face of modern society. Behind the controversy is the story of a man caught between two cultures and two seemingly irreconcilable ways of looking at the world.*

River People of Chad (1969) 20 min. Films, Inc. (PR). Dist: PSU(PCR) order #21247, FR$14.50. *River village life of the Kotoko tribe; family and group interrelationships. Contrasts this existence with that of the capital city of Fort Lamy, a modern city with hotels, department stores, and airports.*

River through Time 17 min. David McLeod (DI, CA), David Keenlyside, Judy Keenlyside (AN), NFBC (PR). Dist: NFB. *The results of archaeological research undertaken by staff of the National Museum of Man along the shores of the Tracadie River in northeastern New Brunswick. The Tracadie River attracted prehistoric peoples for millenia primarily because of its unusual ecological setting. Draining into the Gulf of Saint Lawrence, the major course of the Tracadie is a tidal estuary. A rich natural resource containing both fresh-water and salt-water marine life, it long ago became readily accessible for man to exploit. Recollections of an old Acadian man led archaeologists to an early historic Indian site. The man recalled that as a boy, nearly 90 years before, he had seen Micmac Indian camps on the shores of the Tracadie close to his home. Through rare early photographs and paintings, the film reveals the ancient Micmac way of life, illustrating the importance of historical documents to archaeologists for reconstructing past cultures. It focuses on the workings of an archaeological dig. The viewer accompanies the archaeologist in the painstaking, yet exciting, process of peeling away the centuries of soil covering a thousand-year-old fishing camp. Unearthed are stone arrow points, knives, axes, and fragments of ceramic vessels. An analysis of stone materials used shows that extensive trade or long-distance voyages took place a long time ago.*

Rivers, William (1864–1922) (see *Everything Is Relatives* in the Strangers Abroad Series)

Rivers of Life 10 min. Dist: WBP VS$19.95, order #30915. *This photo essay on Bangladesh focuses on the 15,000 miles of rivers and waterways that both bring life to the land and its people and wreak havoc during monsoons and seasonal tropical storms. The film shows how, despite poverty and tremendous natural obstacles, the people of Bangladesh are struggling to raise their standard of living.*

Rivers of Sand (1975) 85 min. Robert Gardner (FM, AN). Dist: PFI FR$75; UCEMC FR$75. *"My first choice as a title for* Rivers of Sand *was* Creatures of Pain. *Though it evoked most aptly the central theme of the work, I was persuaded by friends not to use it. They felt, no doubt correctly, that it was too somber, too susceptible to wrong interpretation. But what I heard in those words is what I felt as I made the film: an ordeal and a process by which men and women accommodate to each other, in the midst of tension and conflict caused by their fidelity to traditional social roles. The people portrayed in this film are called Hamar. They dwell in the thorny scrubland of southwestern Ethiopia, about a hundred miles north of Lake Rudolf, Africa's great inland sea. Anthropologists call them a 'Turkana offshoot', since they share many traits of a much larger congeries of people living far to the south. The Hamar are isolated by some distant choice that now limits their movement and defines their condition. At least until recently, it has caused them to retain a highly traditional way of life. Part of that tradition* was the open, even flamboyant, acknowledgment of male supremacy. In their isolation, they seem to have refined this not uncommon principle of social organization—and personal relationship—to a remarkably pure state. Hamar men are masters and their women are servants. The film is an attempt to disclose not only the activities of the Hamar, but also the effect on mood and behavior of a life governed by sexual inequality." [Reviewed by Lionel Bender, AA 79:197, 1977. Lucy Mair, RAIN 4:11, 1974. Responses to Bender by Jean Lydall and Ivo Strecker, AA 80:945–946, 1978, and Bender's reply, AA 80:946, 1978.]

Roads without Wheels (Man on the Rim Series) 58 min. Dist: LMF VS$295. *Isolated from the rest of the world, the South American Indians produced their own remarkable range of food plants, later introduced to the other continents. They invented the wheel but used it only on toys, never for transport. Their dazzling metal working, particularly in gold, silver and platinum, was unique and astonishing in its technique and imagination.*

Rock-A-Bye-Baby (1969) 28 min. Lothar Wolfe (PR). Dist: TL. *Neonatal development.* [Reviewed by Leonard A. Rosenblum, AA 75:2027, 1973.]

Rock Art Treasures of Ancient America (1983) 25 min. Michael Bober (FM), Dr. E. C. Krupp (WR). Dist: Dave Caldwell Productions Inc, 26934 Halifax Place, Hayward, CA 94542; (415) 538-4286, R$75, FS$396. *The subject of the film is the ancient rock carvings, paintings, and desert figures as created by the first Americans. Three major rock art sites located in Southern California are studied: The Shoshone Petroglyphs at the China Lake; The Mojave intaglios along the southern end of the Colorado River; and the Chumash cave paintings in the Santa Barbara area. The film also suggests that the rock art is symbolic of the culture of the Native Americans who lived in the area and illustrates this by connecting the artwork to the tribes' oral myths and legends.* [Reviewed by Frank Bock, ARCH 38(2):72–73, 1985. Jo Anne Van Tilburg, AA 86:792–793, 1984.]

Rock Engravings (Australian Museum Series) (1969) 7 min. Dist: Australian Museum; UCEMC FR$ 16. *Scenes of the western New South Wales desert introduce the study of Aboriginal rock art, which was created thousands of years before white settlers reached Australia. By hammering pictures into hard rock, the early Aborigines left valuable clues concerning their environment and beliefs. Excellent cinematography reproduces vignettes of their everyday life: the animals they hunted or worshipped, the foods they ate, the weapons they used. They pounded out pictures of the emu; of eggs, berries, and fruits; of the hunter and the speared kangaroo; of the hunter with shield and boomerang. Many engravings are thought to have ritualistic connotations. No actual engraving tools have been found, but it is assumed that heavy stone implements must have been used to incise the hard rock. The film shows how an archaeologist from the Australian Museum studies the engravings by means of judicious chalk dusting to delineate the works for scientific measurement and recording, photographing, and detailed drawings made with the aid of a collapsible grid.*

Rock Paintings of Baja California (Revised Edition) 17 min. Clement W. Meighan (FM). Dist: UCEMC FR$27, FS$245. *Examines the rock paintings at a recently discovered site in a remote area of Baja California. The film provides a brief introduction to representative rock paintings—both petroglyphs and pictographs—throughout the world and compares the style of the Baja paintings with those elsewhere. It shows the paintings—bigger than life-size portraits of hunters, animals, and symbolic figures—in great detail and explains how they were painted, their age, and their significance to the Indians who painted them. Extended sequences describing how an expedition locates, records, and dates such paintings are included.* [Reviewed by Karen Nissen, AA 78:373, 1976.]

Romeria: Day of the Virgin (1986) 54 min. Jerome Mintz (DI). Dist: DER FR$85, VR$50, FS$850, VS$400. *The centerpiece of this film is a religious pilgrimage to a local shrine of the virgin near the town of Alcala de los Gazules, Cadiz, Spain. Families make elaborate preparations for the day-long event. Pilgrimage organizers and worshipers discuss the ambiguities of their beliefs and affiliations.* [Reviewed by Jill Dubisch, AA 90:781–782, 1988. Reviewed in VISA 4:69, 1991.]

Root Hog or Die (1978) 59 min. B/W. Rawn Fulton (CA), Newbold Noyes (SR), Dist: DER FR$60, FS$600. *Begun as a documentary detailing the decline of the family farm, the piece, instead, is a visual tribute to life in rural New England. The program was filmed in western Massachusetts and southern Vermont and chronicles the changing seasons of farm life from maple sugaring in the spring, through cultivating, planting, and harvesting, to chopping wood for the winter. Edited in a free-flowing style, the program moves leisurely from season to season, from location to location, stopping occasionally for an anecdote or an observation delivered from the fields, the back porch or the kitchen table. These anecdotes, interwoven like pieces of oral history, were culled from 120 hours of interviews with some 60 families and give a sense of the history, values, and traditions that created this country. They also provide the only narration for the piece.* [Reviewed by George L. Hicks AA 85:493–494, 1985.]

Rose et Landry (Rose and Landry) (1962) Jean Rouch (DI), ONF, Quebec and the Canadian Film Board (PR). Dist: CFE; DER.

ROTI James Fox, Patsy Asch, and Timothy Asch (DI), Australian National University and DER (PR). Dist: DER. *A series of two films that complement James J. Fox's study of lontar utilizations on Roti, "The Harvest of The Palm," as well as his essays on ritual speech in Indonesia. "The Water of Words" is also available in an Indonesian-language version.*

Routes of Exile: A Moroccan Jewish Odyssey (1981) 90 min. Eugene Rosow (FM). Dist: Diaspora Film Project, Cultural Research and Communication, Inc., 1700 Broadway, Room 4201, New York, NY 10019; (212) 265-2140, FR$175, FS$1500. *"A portrait of the Jews of Morocco. Through interviews and archival footage he . . . documents the variety and difficulties of Moroccan Jewish identity."*

[From the review by Lawrence Rosen, AA 87:232–233, 1985.]

The Royal Archives of Ebla (1980) 58 min. Mildred Freed Alberg (DI). Dist: FI R$80, FS$720, VS$430. *"This is a remarkable film . . . [that] thoughtfully balances background material on ancient Near Eastern civilizations with detailed but engaging explanations of ancient history and epigraphy."* [From the review by Harvey Weiss, ARCH 33(5):58, 1981.]

La Royale Goumbe (1958) Jean Rouch (DI), Centre National de la Recherche Scientifique, Comite du Film Ethnographique (PR). Dist: CFE; DER. *Film of a Goumbe, a society formed by migrants in the coastal towns of West Africa.*

Royale Goumbe (1967) 10 min. Jean Rouch (DI). Dist: CFE; DER. *Upon the marriage of a young woman belonging to the Royal Goumbe social and mutual aid society from the Treichville section of Abidjan, to a young man belonging to the Shooting Star Goumbe of the Adjame section, the two societies come together for a jam session.*

Runa: Guardians of the Forest (1990) 28 min. Ellen Speiser and Dominique Irvine (DI). Dist: UCEMC R$45, FS$575, VS$250, order #11397(f), #37975(v). *The profound ecological knowledge of native Amazonian peoples like the Runa—an Indian community in the Ecuadorian rainforest—offers hope for the future preservation of the rainforests. This unusual documentary explores, with commentary by the Runa themselves, their adaptation to life in the rainforest. It also examines their reactions to outside forces that are increasingly impinging on their environment, their traditional lands, and their way of life.* [Reviewed by Harald E.L. Prins, AA 93(4):1035–1036, 1991.]

Running Fence (1978) 70 min. David Maysles, Charlotte Zwerin, Albert Maysles (DI, FM). *Shot in 1976 during Christo's activities in Sonoma County, California, to establish and construct his "Running Fence" art. The Maysles brothers accompany Christo and his wife, an equal partner in the venture, during attempts to convince ranchers, at first recalcitrant, to his idea; at county supervisor meetings; during the actual fence construction, which is highly dramatic in itself and because a court order threatens the project. Shows ranchers' respect for the project and the workers, yet bemusement at 'city-folk' ways of acting. Richly woven segments of action highlight the many conflicting viewpoints in the development of the project. Cinematic features: Handheld, sync sound for the social activities, supplemented by aerial views of the fence and its construction. No narration. Minimal music added. The Maysles go ethnographic—few close-ups. Focusing questions: What are the different definitions of art expressed in the film, and how do these relate to the speakers' social positions? Christo's advocates and adversaries are not always the people one would expect. Chart these and their influence in the conflict, especially in turning the Board of Supervisors. State and local government intrude throughout the process. What functions do they serve? What dramatic film devices possibly distort or make one suspicious of the event as portrayed here?* [Clarice Stasz]

Running from the Ghost (The Human Face of Hong Kong Series) (1988) 47 min. Film Australia (PR). Dist: FIV VS$99. *This film focuses on the "non-elite" population of Hong Kong and the problems they have to face in everyday life. The film shows that the ordinary, hard-working families do not have access to the law or to the government bureaucracy, which exist to maintain Hong Kong's laissez-faire, low-tax "economic miracle."*

RURAL GREECE: DESERTION, MIGRATION, VILLAGE LIFE SERIES Dr. Colette Piault (AN, DI). Dist: PSA. *A series of six films shot by a French anthropologist, Dr. Colette Piault, Research Director at CNRS, Paris, who studied the migration from the point of view of mountain villagers in a Mediterranean area, Epirus. Shot between 1980 and 1990, some films are more focused on mentalities through conversations whilst some observational showing activities and moments of daily life. No commentary, explanations are given by people themselves. All films are in Greek with English subtitles.* Bibliography: "L'absence vecue au village: l'Ici entre l'Ailleurs et l'Autrefois." In *Aspects du changement social dans la campage grecque*, Special issue, NCS R, Athens, 1981. Translated in Greek: in *The Greek Review for Social Research*, Athens, 1987. "Review of Four Films by C. Piault," Susan B. Sutton, in *CVA Review*, 1990. "European Visual Anthropology: Filming in A Greek Village." Dr. C. Piault, in *Anthropological Filmmaking*, edited by Jack Rollwagen, Harwood Academic Pub., 1988. See film descriptions under individual titles:

- My Family and Me
- Everyday Is Not a Feast Day
- Let's Get Married!
- Thread of the Needle
- A Hard Life
- Charcoal-Makers

Russian X-Ray Film (1962) 11 min. Haskins Lab (PR). Dist: PSU. *Standard Russian spoken by three native male speakers. Palatalization and consonant clusters as well as vowel allophones that go with palatalization. X-ray techniques show the articulatory process and acoustic output of native speakers. Prepared scripts, consisting mainly of short meaningful utterances, illustrate selected phonetic features. Speakers chosen both for linguistic suitability and lack of physical characteristics that might interfere with X-ray quality.*

Sabina Sanchez, artesana bordadora (The Art of Embroidery) (see the Artesanos Mexicanos (Mexico's Folk Artists) Series)

The Sacred Circle (1981) 28:50 min. Donald K. Spence (DI, WR), Earle P. Waugh (WR), Doug Cole (CA), University of Alberta, Access Alberta, National Film Board (PR). Dist: University of Alberta FS$350. *The Sacred Circle takes as its source elements of the Sioux, Siksika, Peigan, Blood, Stony, and Cree traditions to construct a cinematic introduction to the spiritual life and beliefs of the people of the plains. Explores the strengths and validity of a people's identity. Tracing the phases and effects of Indian-European interaction in western Canada, the film testifies to the* *tenacity of this worldview, demonstating the multidimensional forms it continues to take in the contemporary world.*

Sacred Games: Ritual Warfare in a Maya Village (1989) 59 min. Thor Anderson (FM). Dist: UCEMC FR$70, FS$995, VS$410. *Every year, in a small village in the highlands of Chiapas, in southern Mexico, thousands of Maya Indians gather to celebrate Carnival. The Chamula people call their Carnival the "festival of games," and it is the most spectacular, popular, and costly festival of their ritual calendar. The pageant is rich in both pre-Columbian imagery and references to numerous military invasions over the past 500 years. It merges Catholicism with ancient Maya rites. This extraordinary film documents the complex, weeklong activities, focusing on one man's experiences as a ritual leader during the nonstop parading, dancing, and feasting. The film beautifully captures the passion and mystery of the event and shows how the Maya's symbolic world is renewed each year in the celebrations.* [Reviewed by Caroline B. Brettell, *AA* 91:831–834, 1989.]

Sacred Ground (1978) 52 min. (in 2 parts). Freewheelin' Films Ltd., Rodney H. Jacobs, (DI, PR). Dist: New Visions, P.O. Box 599, Aspen, CO 81611, FR$30 (each), $55 (set), FS $275 (each), $550 (set). *Film presents the feelings and emotions of American Indians and their relationship to the land. Part 1 (The Indian and the Land) retraces many Indian sites considered sacred, from earthen mounds in southern Illinois to Canyon de Chelly of the Navahos. Part 2 (Indian Origin, Legend, and Spirit) follows the journey of the Pueblo Indians into New Mexico, a Kiowa legend, and the importance of the dreamlife for the Pima, Yuma, and the Maricopa Indians. The origin and meaning of Hopi rock-writing is explained as well.* [Robert B. Moorman]

Sacred Trances in Bali and Java 30 min. Dist: HFF FR$45, FS$395, VS$89. *In the sacred rituals of Bali and Java, invisible spirits are brought down to enter the bodies of trancers who perform supernormal feats, such as walking on fire, piercing cheeks with pins, and rolling on broken glass. Extraordinary examples of altered states of consciousness in animistic, Hindu, and Muslim rites.*

A Sacrifice of 10 Dog and Six House John Pohl (FM). Dist: John Pohl, 476 Landfair, Los Angeles, CA 90024. *Animated episode from Mixtec codex.*

Sad Song of Yellow Skin National Film Board of Canada (PR). Dist: FI. *The Americanization of Vietnam during the war.* [Reviewed by Thomas Kiefer, *AA* 76:714, 1974].

Sad Song of Touha (1971) 12 min. Attiat El-Abnoudi (FM). Dist: FRIF FR$25, FS$245. *In a poor section of Cairo, jugglers, contortionists, and fire eaters perform.*

A Safety Net (1987) 29 min. National Film Board of Canada (PR). Dist: NFB VR$30, FS$550, VS$160. *"Dilemma of food aid in Africa by looking at the case of Ghana."* [From the review by Thomas M. Painter, *AA* 93(3):769–771, 1991.]

Sahara—la caravane du sel (1969) 53 min. Dist: FI FR$40, FS$550. *A Tuareg salt caravan.*

Sails of Doom (Triumph of the Nomads Series) 1 hour. Nomad Films International Australia (PR). Dist: PBSV VS$134.95, order #9775-21. *This film describes many of the finds of the Aborigines, including edible plants, valuable mines that they worked, new medicines and drugs, manufacturing techniques, and many resources. When the British landed on their shores in 1770, bringing with them all the trappings of a different world, it was the start of an invasion that would forever change the island continent of Australia and the lives of its first people.*

ST. LAWRENCE NORTH SERIES   See descriptions under titles:

- **Attiuk (The Caribou)**
- **Ka Ke Ki Ku**
- **The Jean Richard**
- **Land of Jacques Cartier**
- **Soiree at St. Hilarion**
- **Three Seasons**
- **Turlutte**
- **Whalehunters of Anse aux Basques**

Saint Pascal (1973) 20 min. Gerald L. Gold (FM, AN). Dist: UCEMC FR$24. Suggested supplement: Gerald L. Gold, *Saint Pascal: Changing Leadership and Social Organization in a Quebec Town.* Holt, Rinehart and Winston. Toronto, 1975. [Reviewed by Bernard Bernier and Bernard R. Emond, *AA* 80:763–765, 1978.]

Saints and Spirits (Disappearing World Series and Women in the Middle East Series) (1978) 25 min. Melissa Davies (FM), Elizabeth Fernea (AN). Dist: PSU order #36284; FRIF VR$55, FS$470, VS$280. *Examines women's roles in Islam. Women who profess the Islamic faith in the Moroccan city of Marrakech rarely attend mosque and hold their rituals and celebrations at home. Female pilgrims often make the arduous journey to the mountain shrine of Saint Sidhi Chamharoul, and a shawapa, or seer, performs the annual ritual of sacrifice that binds her to the spirit Sidhi Mahmoun. Shot for Granada TV, edited from footage not used in* Some Women of Marrrakech. Bibliography: Elizabeth W. Fernea, *A Street in Marakech.* Anchor Paperback, 1976.

utan: A Time of Change (1984) 24 min. Roger Penfound (PR) for the BBC Open University, Paul Stirling (NA). Dist: MG VR$40, VS$198. *"About Sakaltutan, a village in Central Anatolian Turkey.... Focus[es] on socioeconomic and cultural change from the subjects' points of view through a series of interviews with present and former villagers.... Largely devoted to transformations that have occured in the village itself: the acquisitions of a new road, electricity, tractors, and income from emigrant workers."* [From the review by Paul J. Magnarella, *AA* 88:1046–1047, 1986. Reviewed by Peter S. Allen, *SBF* 21:104, 1985.]

Sakpata (1958) 25 min. Jean Rouch (DI), Centre National de la Recherche Scientifique, Comité du Film Ethnographique (PR). Dist: CFE; DER. *The initiation of three new 'horsemen' in a Vaudoun d'Allada monastery in southern Benin.*

The Sakuddei of Indonesia (Disappearing World Series) (1974) 52 min. John Sheppard (Dl), Reimar Schefold (AN), Granada Television International (PR). Dist: FL VR$75, VS$445. *Off the coast of Sumatra live the Sakuddei, completely cut off from the outside world. Here is an egalitarian society, in near perfect harmony with the environment. There are no leaders, men and women are equal; peace is cherished. We see how this Utopian way of life is threatened by encroaching civilization.* [Reviewed by Barbara E. Ward, *RAIN* 8:10, 1975.]

Salaam Bombay (1988) Mira Nair (FM). Dist: FL. [Reviewed in *VISA* 4:95, 1991.]

Salamanders: A Night at the Phi Delt House (1972) 14 min. George Hornbein, Marie Horbein, Tom Keiter, and Kenneth Thigpen (FM). Dist: FL FR$40, FS$220; Documentary Resource Center, 615 Clay Lane, State College, PA 16801; (814) 237-6462. *"Each year the brotherhood of Phi Delta Theta fraternity celebrate the rites of spring by swallowing live salamanders washed down with draft beer."* [From the review by Peter S. Allen, *AA* 87:221–222, 1985.]

Salima in Transition 28 min. Max Reid (FM). Dist: Mr. Max Reid, 2512 4th St., Santa Monica, CA 90405, FR$50, FS$350; BU; Kent State; US Florida; USC. *A documentary film of an African culture in transition. Set in Malawi, a former British colony in southeast Africa, the film is focused on a secondary school in the town of Salima. A group of English-speaking students is shown in the process of making the transition from their rural backgrounds into the educated class in an emerging nation. Pictured are their school life, home life, shopping in Salima, a school dance, a visit by one of the boys to his village home.*

Salt and Hypertension (1982) 26 min. Frank Lisciandro (FM). Dist: PyrF FR$55, FS$425. *"Traces the links between sodium consumption, high blood pressure, and heart disease and offers concrete suggestions as to what viewers can do to monitor and reduce their sodium consumption."* [From the review by Carole M. Counihan, *AA* 87:222–223, 1985.]

Salt of the Earth (1954) 94 min. Paul Jarrico (PR), Herbert Biberman (DI). Dist: AB. *Fictional film about the role of militant women in a Chicano mineworkers' strike in New Mexico.* [Reviewed by Karen Sacks, *AA* 79:205, 1977.]

Sam (1971) 20 min. Margaret Bach (FM). Dist: IUAVC FR$8; UCEMC FR$20. *Explores the themes of culture and class through the portrayal of a Japanese-American, whose public persona—as the "Japanese gardener" in a white suburb of Los Angeles—contrasts with glimpses of the private man, his past, and his family. Comments by several of Sam's clients reveal a genuine affection for their gardener. Yet their understanding of Sam—the private man—is very incomplete. Sam is shown singing a Japanese chant and recounting the agonizing tale of his World War II experience: his pre–Pearl Harbor induction into the U.S. Army, his detention because of his ancestry, and his protest, subsequent court-martial, and final imprisonment at five years hard labor. During this time, Sam's future wife, Sally, was living in Hiroshima. She tells the horror of that day in August 1945 when the atomic bomb was dropped. Sam and Sally emerged from these bitter experiences to live a life of apparent placidity, but there is a hint of disappointment; Sally says: "He wanted to be a singer . . . but he's a gardener now."* [Reviewed by James Hirabayashi and Clinton Bergum, *AA* 75:592–594, 1973.]

The Samaritans. The People of the Sacred Mountain 30 min. Johanna Spector (FM), Don Wolman (Dl). Dist: SF. [Reviewed by Laurence Loeb, *AA* 77:694–695, 1975.]

Sami Herders (Lapps) (1979) 28 min. Dist: SU FR$32. *Every year the Haette family spends six months in the subarctic wilderness traveling from Finland Plain (Norway) up to the Arctic coast and back again. Their companions are a large herd of reindeer. Wearing traditional Lapp clothes, living in hastily made tents, the camera records their movements over a 12-month period. Scenes show the reindeer boarding a Navy ferryboat to cross a fjord for summer grazing (formerly they had to swim the icy waters).* [Reviewed by David M. Smith, *AA* 88:783–784, 1986.]

Samoa i Sisifo (Western Samoa) (1983) 26 min. Journal Films (PR), Albert Wendt (NA). Dist: JF FR$45, FS$245; IFF. *Looks at Western Samoa and discusses topics ranging from tourism to the tenth anniversary of Independence.* [Reviewed by Joan Larcom, *AA* 86:814–815, 1984.]

Sampuran Singh: A Farmer from Punjab 28 min. Yavar Abbas (PR). Dist: CMC. [Reviewed by Janet Benson, *AA* 76:707, 1974.]

Samsara 29 min. Ellen Bruno (FM). Dist: SFL FR$65, VR$45, FS$495, VS$195; FL FR$55, FS$550, VS$295. *The film documents the struggle of the Cambodian people to rebuild a shattered society in a climate of war and with limited resources. Ancient prophecy, Buddhist teachings, and folklore provide a context for understanding the Cambodian tragedy, bringing a humanistic perspective to a country in deep political turmoil. The film moves at a deliberate, reflective, and sometimes dreamlike pace, inviting the viewers to stand with the Cambodian people as they strive to understand their past—in their religious and philosophical way and rebuild on their own terms. It is a film that prepares the audience to analyze the political forces that shape Cambodia by forcing them to look at death and rebirth through Cambodian eyes.* [Reviewed by Malcolm Collier, *AA* 95(1):253–255, 1993.]

SAN SERIES (formerly called !Kung Bushman Series) Documentary Educational Resources (PR), John Marshall (FM). Dist: DER. In addition to the films listed below, see separate listing for *The Hunters*. [Reviewed by Patricia Draper, *AA* 76:689–691, 1974.] Suggested supplements: N. J. Connor, Chapter 11, *Aspects of the Developmental Ethnology of a Foraging People* in *Ecological Studies of Child Behavior*. Nick Blurton Hones, ed. Cambridge University Press, 1972. *Man the Hunter*. Irven DeVore and Richard Lee, eds. Aldine, 1968. Richard B. Lee, "The Sociology of !Kung Bushman Trance Performances." In: *Trance and Possession States*. Raymond Prince, ed. R. M. Burke Memorial Society, Montreal, 1968. Richard B. Lee and Irven DeVore, *Kalahari Bushman Studies*. Harvard University Press, 1976. John Marshall, "Man as a Hunter." *Natural*

History Magazine, June/July and August/September 1958. Lorna Marshall, "The Kin Terminology System of the !Kung Bushmen." *Africa* 22(1), January 1957. Lorna Marshall, "Marriage Among the !Kung Bushmen." *Africa* 24(4), October 1959. Lorna Marshall, "!Kung Bushman Bands." *Africa* 30(4), October 1960. Lorna Marshall, "Sharing, Talking and Giving: Relief of Social Tension Among !Kung Bushmen." *Africa* 31(3), July 1961. Lorna Marshall, "!Kung Bushman Religious Beliefs." *Africa* 32(3), July 1962. Lorna Marshall, "The !Kung Bushmen of the Kalahari Desert." In: *People of Africa*, James L. Gibbs, ed. Holt, Rinehart and Winston, 1965. Lorna Marshall, "The Medicine Dance of the !Kung Bushman." *Africa* 34(4), October 1969. Lorna Marshall, *The !Kung of Nyae Nyae*. Harvard University Press, 1976. Elizabeth Marshall Thomas, *The Harmless People*. Vintage, 1965.

- **Argument about a Marriage** 19 min. FR$25, FS$270; UCEMC FR$17. *Conflict between two !Kung bands concerning the legitimacy of a marriage. English narration and subtitles.*

- **Baobab Play** 8 min. FR$15, FS$120. *A group of children and teenagers throw toy spears into a tree, trying to make them stick into the bark. Accompanied by eight pages of film notes.*

- **Bitter Melons** 28.5 min. FR$40, FS$430; UCEMC FR$22. *Music of the !Gwikhwe musician and composer, Ukxone, illustrated with documentary material. Animal songs and games are played together with songs of the land that the !Gwi people depend on for their livelihood and social life.* [Reviewed by Alan Lomax, *AA* 74:1018–1020, 1972.]

- **Children Throw Toy Assegais** 4 min. FR$15, FS$75. *A group of young boys throw toy spears into a tree, trying to make them stick into the bark. Accompanied by eight pages of film notes.*

- **A Curing Ceremony** 8 min. FR$15, FS$100. *Shallgai, a young woman about to have a miscarriage, is cured by Ti!Kay, who enters a mild trance without the stimulus of dancing.* [Reviewed by Nancie L. Gonzalez et al., *AA* 77:175, 1975.]

- **Debe's Tantrum** 8.5 min. FR$15, FS$120. *Di!ai has planned to gather sweet berries with her sister and to leave her five-year-old son, Debe, behind with his half sister, !Nai. Debe, looking forward to the trip, strongly resists being left. The predicament becomes hopeless and Di!ai struggles off, bearing Debe on her back.*

- **A Group of Women** 5 min. FR$15, FS$75. *!Kung women resting, talking, and nursing a baby while lying under the shade of a baobab tree.*

- **A Joking Relationship** 12.5 min. FR$20, FS$140. *For the !Kung, the joking relationship provides opportunities for casual intimacy, emotional release, and support. It is an important part of institutionalized kinship behavior. This film depicts a moment of flirtation in a joking relationship between !Nai, the young wife of Gunda, and her great-uncle, Ti!kay.*

- **!Kung Bushman Hunting Equipment** 37 min. FR$45, FS$480.

- **Lion Game** 3.5 min. FR$15, FS$75. *Gunda, a young man, plays a lion and is "hunted" and "killed" by a group of boys.*

- **Men Bathing** 14 min. FR$20, FS$210. *In Nyae Nyae, water often remains in open pans. Sometimes, if the rains have been heavy, water stays in these pans, like small lakes, all year. One morning five !Kung men went to Nama pan. Ti!kay came to wash the clothes he had acquired on his trip to rescue his wives from white farmers. The other men came to bathe. The men use the opportunity to launch sexual jokes at one another.*

- **N!owa T'ama: The Melon Tossing** 14.5 min. FR$25, FS$210. *In a large repertoire of games in Nyae Nyae, the melon tossing game is unique in the complexity and stability of its music and in the frequency with which it is played. The game is simple; women form a semicircle which moves counterclockwise as each woman, in turn, runs to the center of the circle. There she dances several steps and tosses the melon to the next woman at the proper moment in the song. In this film, women and girls from three separate !Kung bands have gathered at a mangetti grove to play a long and intense game in which undertones of social and personal tension become apparent. Gunda joins the game early and dances spectacularly. Finally, he uses a dance step commonly encountered among Kwesan peoples who have had contact with Okavange- and Sotho-speaking peoples. Nlaoka, Ti!kay's wife, becomes overexcited by Gunda's dancing and falls into a trancelike state. The game begins to disintegrate when !Nai, Gunda's wife, taunts and teases Nlaoka.*

- **Playing with Scorpions** 4 min. FR$15, FS$75. *!Kung people, by and large, are not excited by the threat of dangerous encounters with each other or their environment. They do not respect the warrior or admire the struggle against nature, believing such follies are provoked by the senseless. But !Kung children, tempting fate in small ways, sometimes play with scorpions, which cannot sting without striking.*

- **A Right of Passage** 14 min. FR$20, FS$210. *In Nyae Nyae, hunting has a special importance: the people crave meat; they need skins for clothing and sacks, and sinews to make string for bows and nets. Most importantly, a young man discharges a major social obligation by providing his father-in-law with meat, which is distributed to everyone in the village. The importance of hunting is symbolized in a small ceremony that takes place when a boy has killed his first antelope. This film depicts such a ceremony from the time Ti!kay, a young boy, shoots his first wildebeest, through the tracking and finding of the animal, the cooking and eating of the meat, and the symbolic scarification.* [Reviewed by Thomas Beidelman, *AA* 76:691, 1974.]

- **The Meat Fight** 14 min. FR$25, FS$210. *An argument arises between two bands when an antelope killed by a hunter from one band is found and distributed by a man from another band. The Meat Fight illustrates dramatically the social structure of conflict and the role of leaders in !Kung society. Accompanied by a 28-page study guide.*

- **N/um Tchai** 20 min. FR$25, FS$225. *The most passionate activity in Bushman life is the trance of medicine men in the dance. Although its purpose—the warding off of death—is serious, a medicine dance is not altogether pious or solemn.*

The Bushmen take great pleasure in music and dancing. [Reviewed by Antoine Seronde and Nancie L. Gonzalez, *AA* 77:175–176, 1975. Livingston Film Collective, *AA* 74:193–194, 1972.] Cinematic features: First film to use two-part form: heavily narrated summary of the ceremony is followed by longer repetition of same ceremony with wild sound but no narration. Although ceremony usually performed at night, this was done at dawn so that it could be filmed. Uses in teaching: courses and topics: Africa, religion, medical anthropology. Focusing questions: What is the atmosphere of the ceremony? What sort of community support is evident? How is touching important? What are the medical theories of the San? Medical practices? Would it have been better to shoot it with lights at night? Bibliography: Richard Lee, "Trance Cure of the !Kung Bushmen." *Natural History*, 30–37 November 1967. Lorna Marshall and Megan Biesele, *N/um Tchai. A Study Guide*. Sommerville, MA: DER, 1974.

- **Tug of War** 6 min. FR$15, FS$100. *Twelve or more boys, in two teams, wrestle over a length of rubber hose. Accompanied by six pages of film notes.*

- **The Wasp Nest** 20 min. FR$25, FS$290. *Gathering wild foods is the basic subsistence activity in Nyae Nyae and is the responsibility of !Kung women. Men distribute the game they kill and maintain a network of favors and obligations that binds people together. Women provide only for their immediate families. This film follows a group of women and children as they gather sweet, fresh oley berries and sha roots. The younger women, led by !Nai, bait a nest of wasps. As the day wears on, Debe, Di!ai's young son, becomes restless. Di!ai asks !Nai to take Debe home. She refuses and walks off to join the young women.*

THE SAN (JU/WASI): Videos for Elementary and Secondary Use Dist: DER. *Using resources partially provided by the Massachusetts Council on the Arts and Humanities, DER worked with teachers in Massachusetts schools to edit short videotapes for teaching. The !Kung San: Traditional Life and The !Kung San: Resettlement, based on John Marshall's film studies of the !Kung of Namibia, were developed with social studies teachers who needed new visual material.*

Sanctuary of the Earth Goddess (1986) 42 min. Katherine Stenger Frey (FM). Dist: Canadian Filmakers Distribution Centre, 67A Portland Street, Toronto, Ontario M5V 2M9; (416) 593-1808; Keti Production, 3860 Harvard Avenue, Montreal, Quebec H4A 2W5; (514) 483-4876, FR$75, FS$850, VS$350. *This film takes us "to the far southern periphery of Minangkabau culture concerned with the old fertility cult, where even Islam is ecstatic and mystical."* [From the review by Karl G. Heider, *AA* 90:244–245, 1988.] Bibliography: Katherine Stenger Frey, *Journey to the Land of the Earth Goddess*, Jakarta: Pt. Gramedia, 1986.

Sandino, Today and Forever (1981) 55 min. Tercer Cine (PR), Jan Kees de Rooy (DI). Dist: ICF FR$85, FS$795, VS$540. *"The film introduces several peasants who are veterans of the FSLN's northern front struggle against Somoza.... The film conveys something of the objectives, programs, and spirit of the first two years of the Sandinista revolution."* [From the review by John A. Booth, *AA* 86:793–796, 1984.]

Sans Soleil (1982) 100 min. Chris Marker (FM). Dist: NYF FR$250. *"Drunkards and orators, festivals and demonstrations, revolutions succeeding and being betrayed, horror and pornography on TV, beauty and ugliness, are celebrated in a spare esthetic that transforms.... The disparate elements into a sustained meditation on history and memory, the possibility of happiness, peace, and tranquility."* [From the review by Akos Ostor, *AA* 89:1022–1023, 1987.]

Santa Marta: Two Weeks in the Slums (1988) 54 min. Eduardo Coutinho (DI). Dist: CG FR$90, VS$350. *A remarkable look at daily life in a mountaintop slum in Rio de Janeiro. The video consists of extensive interviews with a wide variety of residents who openly voice complaints about police harassment, the lack of educational and employment opportunities, problems of sanitation, violence, drugs and alcohol in the community, and the social and racial discrimination they face from Rio's white, middle-class citizens. These interviews are interspersed with songs, dancing, street theatre presentations, and the beautiful views afforded by their mountaintop locale. Portuguese dialogue with English subtitles.*

Los Santeros 28 min. Dist: OWM FR$85, VR$70, FS$400, VS$250. *Since the Spanish conquest in the 1600s, the woodcarvers of saints, or Santos have played an integral role in the religion and culture of northern New Mexico. Their carvings, fabricated with hand-hewn tools and painted with natural pigments, are part of a native tradition that has developed into an art of great beauty and power. This film contrasts the work of early Santeros with that of contemporary carvers like Luis Tapia, Orlando Romero, and Horacio Valdez, who reflect on the heritage of their craft and talk about the process of learning and individualizing their art.*

Santeros: Saintmakers 33 min. Telles Productions and Latino Consortium (PR). Dist: IUAVC VR$25, VS$150, order #RC1281,VH. *This sensitive portrait of New Mexican santeros, saintmakers, documents the lifestyle and attitudes of five artisans who continue the 300-year-old traditions of the earliest santeros. The quiet pace, religious devotion, and deep commitment to wood sculpture apparent among these artists have characterized the saintmakers throughout history. They draw on many sources of inspiration for a particular carving from the life of the saint to events in the church calendar, often selling the final piece, sometimes giving it away, other times keeping it. The artists regularly credit the environment as a major influence on their art, a point underscored repeatedly through spectacular shots of the New Mexico landscape.*

Saugus Iron Works Restoration (1957) 17 min. American Iron and Steel Foundation (PR). Dist: SU. *Historical archaeology.* [Reviewed by Michael Gramly, *AA* 78:364, 1976.]

The Savage Innocents (1961) 90 min. Maleno Malenotti (PR), Nicholas Ray (DI), Anthony Quinn, Peter O'Toole, Yoko Tani, Anna May Wong (cast). Dist: AB FR$55. *Adven-*

ture drama about life among the Polar Eskimos, a people fighting for survival. The film was shot in the northernmost Arctic region of Canada. When Inuk, the hunter, decides he wants a wife, he goes out and takes one. It is the custom. And when a missionary refuses to enjoy Inuk's new wife when offered, as is also the custom, Inuk kills him in anger. The white man dies, and Inuk is hunted by troopers for murder. Throughout the story, it becomes clear that primitive customs are "savage" only when judged from modern man's cultural distance.

Saving and Restoring Historic Communities (1978) 28.5 min. Wayne Wheeler and Rod Bass (CON), Hiram Wilson (AN). Dist: Audio Visual Department, University of Nebraska at Omaha, Omaha, NE 68182, FR$35, FS$145. *Shot in the studios of Channel 26, Omaha, Nebraska, as #15 in a series Communes and Utopias. The problems concerning the preservation, restoration, and contemporary uses of historic communities are explored as they relate to the 19th-century communitarian societies of Icaria/Corning (Iowa) and the Bishop Hill Colony (Illinois). Included are perspectives on the uses of documents, photographs, tools, woods, models. What problems face scholars in the preservation and reconstruction of historic communities? What solutions to these are suggested in this film? Is it possible or desirable to reconstruct and restore past communities with 20th century techniques and methods? What uses of documents can be made in the reconstruction and restoration of historic communities?* Bibliography: Porcupine, 1972[1892]. Marie Marchand Ross, *Child of Icaria.* Westport, CT, Hyperion, 1976[1939]. [Wayne Wheeler]

Say, Old Man, Can You Play the Fiddle? (1970, 1974) 20 min. Bess Lomax Hawes and Barbara Lapan Rahm (PR, DI), Bruce Ward and Phil Dunn (CA), John Melville Bishop and Robert W. Eberlein (ED). Dist: FIM/RF FR$20, FS$200. *Earl Collins comes from a long line of championship fiddle players. He was born in 1911 in Missouri, raised in Oklahoma, and moved to Los Angeles as a young man during the Depression. He started playing when he was three or four on a cigar box fiddle made by his father, but music was always a sideline, avidly pursued when time permitted. A favorite playing time was about 3:30 Sunday morning: "Boy, could I fiddle then!" Earl recalls and tells of the old days when folks would "fiddle all night and fiddle all day." He and his son Richard perform six favorite old tunes, during which his marvelously facile playing techniques—bowing, wrist movement, and fingering—are clearly revealed.*

Science on the Cross (1982) 32 min. Dist: Humanistisch Verbond Televisie, Box 114, 3500 AC Utrecht, Netherlands, R$50, FS$800, VS$450. *This film "deals with the controversy over teaching creationism as science in public schools. Focusing on one community in Kentucky, this documentary reveals the religious underpinning of the 'scientific' creationist movement better than other documentaries I have seen."* [From the review by Laurie R. Godfrey, *SBF* 18:216, 1983.]

Science or Sacrilege: The Study of Native American Remains (1983) 41 min. Phillip L. Walker (PR). Dist: Instructional Development Television Services, 2130 Kerr Learning Resources Hall, University of California, Santa Barbara, CA 93106; (805) 961-4344, VR$40, VS$100. *"Deals with the timely question of reburying American Indian skeletal remains, which were and are being excavated through archeological activity. Anthropologists around the country appear to be coming under increasing pressure from various segments of the Native American community to turn over human osteological collections to them for whatever burial they deem proper."* [From the review by Charles F. Merbs, *AA* 87:490–491, 1985. Reviewed by Kenneth A. Bennett, *AJPA* 66:105–106, 1985.]

Sea of Oil (1990) 29 min. Mary Katze (FM). Dist: FL FR$100, VR$55, FS$525, VS$295. *"The effects of the aftermath of the Exxon oil spill on the Prince William Sound community of Valdez, Alaska."* [From the review by Gregory Button, *AA* 94(1):259–260, 1992.]

Seacoast Villages of Japan 19 min. Douglas Carr (FM), Atlantic Productions (PR). Dist: AP FR$10, FS$225. [Reviewed by Edward Norbeck, *AA* 67:1081–1082, 1965.]

Search for a Century (1981) 59 min. Arthur L. Smith (PR). Dist: CWF R$35, FS$595, VS$595. *This film "is simply the best film on archaeology.... Its subject is the excavation and interpretation of the early 17th century settlement of Martin's Hundred, lying within Carter's Grove Plantation along the James River in Virginia."* [From the review by Michael D. Coe, *ARCH* 37(3):77, 1984.]

Search for a Tropical Arctic 28 min. Breakthrough Films (PR). Dist: FL VR$55, VS$295. *The unique story of how a team of international experts piece together an astounding picture of the ancient North as it was 45 million years ago. The scientists from Canada, the United States, England, and Australia travel to the top of the world within 600 miles of the North Pole. They discover the remains of alligators, turtles, rare mammals, and redwood trees. This remarkable evidence shows that the ancient Arctic was not only lush and warm, but a cradle of evolution.*

The Search for Alexander the Great (1980) 4 parts, 60 min. each. Peter Sykes (DI). Dist: FOX VR$40 (each), $150 (set), VS$150 (each), $550 (set). *"Alexander the Great has, over the centuries since his death, been a virtually inexhaustible source of fascination. His appeal is particularly immediate just now by virtue of the recent spectacular discoveries in Macedonia.... The broad outline of the movie is a straight forward chronological presentation of Alexander's life.... The subject is a vast and difficult one, and a valiant attempt has been made to deal with it."* [From the review by Stella G. Miller and Stephen G. Miller, *ARCH* 34(3):64, 1981.] Bibliography: *ARCH* 5(1978):33–41.

The Search for Ancient Americans (The Infinite Voyage Series) Dist: WQED. *A journey through time to examine the primitive people and cultures that evolved in the Americas long before Columbus. From the now submerged Beringia land bridge that once connected Siberia and Alaska, to jungle covered Central America pyramids, it is the epic story* *of humanity spreading across new lands. The Mongol ancestors of North and South American Indians crossed the Beringia land bridge and worked their way south. The program puts together carefully crafted and visually stimulating segments to chronicle that journey, to linger with leading scientists at major archaeological sites where early people settled, and to see the high cultures that would develop centuries later as a result of this trek. Transcripts, detailed study guides, and teaching mannuals are available.* [Reviewed by Peter S. Allen, ARCH 42(1):94–95, 1989.]

Search for Apollo (1981) 25 min. David J. McAllister (FM), David Soren (WR), Steve Twitchell (NA). Dist: UOM. *This is a film about the archaeological excavations at the sanctuary of Apollo on the Island of Cyprus. It presents the findings of three seasons of excavations on the site. The film focuses on the artifacts and architecture of the sanctuary and does not pay much attention to the construction of the geographical or chronological context of the site.* [Reviewed by Joseph A. Greene, AA 84:994–995, 1982. Pamela Gaber-Saletan, ARCH 37(1):73–74, 1984.]

Search for Fossil Man (1974) 24 min. National Geographic Society & Education Expeditions International (PR). NGS FS$330; Karol. *Phillip Tobias, comparative anatomist and paleoanthropologist, leads a team of amateur archaeologists to Makapansgat. Examined are the methods of extracting fossil material and the recording of archaeological data. Tobias discusses the historic Taung skull discovered by Raymond Dart in 1924, which started the whole quest for early man in Africa.* [Robert B. Moorman]

The Search for Herod's Harbor (1989) 28 min. Stephen Fairchild (DI), Thatcher Drew (PR). Dist: Drew//Fairchild, 1841 Broadway, Room 1112, New York, NY 10023; (212) 262-5110, VS$84. *"Most of the tape focuses on excavations in the city itself.... There is a good sequence on the harborworks themselves, illustrated with cartoons and reconstructions, some of which are superimposed on modern photographs to give the viewer a true sense of what was there."* [From the review by Peter S. Allen, ARCH 43(2):64–67, 1990.]

Search for the Great Apes (1975) 52 min. National Geographic Society (PR). Dist: NGS FS$595. *Orangutans in Borneo and mountain gorillas in central Africa.*

The Search for the Kidnappers (see The Decade of Destruction Series)

Seasons of a Navajo (1984) 60 min. John Borden (PR). Dist: PBSV VR$95, VS$250. *"Weaving is an image that recurs throughout [the film]. It is also a suggestive metaphor for the film's dominant theme: the fundamental integrity of nature and culture in the Navajo world.... A colorful depiction of the seasonal life cycle of a Navajo family.... A basic orientation to the symbolic dimension of this matrilineal society."* [From the review by William Graves III, AA 88:526–527, 1986.]

El Sebou': Egyptian Birth Ritual 27 min. Fadwa El Guindi (AN, FM). Dist: ENR R$70, FS$570, VS$370. *This film intimately portrays the Egyptian initiation of newborns on their seventh day of life. It links Egyptian birth to gender symbolism, to traditional crafts, to folk beliefs, to strong womanhood, to the importance of the family. The ritual takes us on a journey to the old bazaar in Cairo and the pottery village in Fustat to purchase herbs and spices and to see traditional crafts. Characteristic of the Egyptian ritual depicted in this film is the gender-linked imagery reflected in the ceremonial clay pot and the cosmological symbolism embedded in the numerical value "seven." In this rite-de-passage, the newborns go through the three universal phases crossing the threshold out of gender and status neutrality.* Study guide available. [Reviewed by Richard A. Lobran, Jr., AA 90:242–243, 1988. Reviewed in VISA 1:497, 1988.]

Sècheresse à Simriri (Drought at Simiri) (1973) 30 min. Jean Rouch (DI), Centre National de la Recherche Scientifique, Comité du Film Ethnographique (PR). Dist: CFE; DER. *In spite of the rain rituals at Yenendi during the month of May, the rains are insufficient and during the course of the month of August, Dongo, the thunder spirit, strikes a tree in the middle of the village. The harvest is poor, and the priests attribute the sickness to the abandonment of traditional customs.*

Sècheresse à Simiri (Drought at Simiri) (1975) 10 min. Jean Rouch (DI), Centre National de la Recherche Scientifique, Comité du Film Ethnographique (PR). Dist: CFE; DER. *A continuation of the 1973 film with the same name.*

Secrets of Easter Island (1989) 58 min. John Lynch and Bettina Lerner (PR). Dist: CFV FS$250. *Easter Island has been shrouded in mystery ever since the Europeans first discovered it covered with hundreds of gigantic stone statues with haunting visages in the South Pacific in 1722. This program meticulously documents the enormous amount of research that has been done on Easter Island and its people and shows footage of archaeological excavations.* [From the review by Peter Allen, ARCH 44(2):54–55, 1991.] See also *Legends of Easter Island.*

Secrets of the Lost Red Paint People (see under **The Mystery of the Lost Red Paint People**)

Seeds of Progress 28 min. Dist: WBP VS$39.95, order #30919. *This film examines a program designed to assist eight million poor farm families in Mexico. The poorest farmers work with the Mexican government to increase farm output, to extend access to electricity, and to build roads, schools, and health centers. The government program encourages the farmers to make their own decisions about how resources will be used in their communities.*

Seen through Navajo Eyes (see Navajos Film Themselves Series)

Seeking the First Americans (The Odyssey Series) (1980) 59 min. Graham Chedd (PR). Dist: DER FR$50, FS$500. *"This examination of current issues relating to the antiquity of man in North America is very skillfully executed."* [From the review by Gifford S. Nickerson, SBF 18:37, 1982. Reviewed by Peter S. Allen, ARCH 33(2):62, 1980.]

Seizing Small Objects (Sacred Baboon) 10 min. Dist: PSU FR$7.

Seizing Small Objects (Woolly Monkey) 9 min. Dist: PSU FR$6.50.

Selbe: One among Many (As Women See It Series) 30 min. Safi Faye (DI), Faust Films (PR). Dist: WMM FR$60, VR$50, FS$600, VS$225. *The revealing documentary offers a rare view of daily life in West Africa. Shot in Senegal, Selbe focuses on the social role and economic responsibility of women in African society. Because men often leave their communities to earn money in the city, women are left with sole responsibility for their families. One women's personal struggle reflects the broader issues facing women in many developing countries.*

Selling the Feeling (see Consuming Hunger Series)

Semana Santa en Nanacatlan 45 min. Jaime Riestra, Jose Antonio Guzman. Dist: Institute Nacional Indigenista, Archivo Etnografico Audiovisual, AV Revolucion No 1279, Mexico 20, DF. *Holy Week ceremonies in a totonac town.*

Semanàsanta: The Holy Week in Patamban, Purhepacha, Michoacan Mexico (1991) 130 min. Beate Engelbrecht (WR, SR), Manfred Kruger (CA, ED). Dist: IWF order #E3135. *The Holy Week is one of the most important religious events of Patamban (Michoacan, Mexico). The Holy Week starts on Palm Sunday with the consecration of the palm leaves and rituals are performed throughout the week, ending with the mass of Easter night. Besides the official church activities a passion play is performed. Catholic liturgy and religious folk traditions are interwoven in the celebration of the Holy Week of Patamban. It is a social event which encompasses the whole village.*

Seminole Indians 11 min. Dist: IFB FR$17.50, FS$175, VS$175. *This film profiles the Seminoles of Florida Everglades. They live in open-sided, raised homes. The women make dolls, sweat grass baskets, and beaded belts. The men hunt fish and skin the frogs they will sell.*

A Sense of Honor (1984) 55 min. Vanya Kewley (PR) for the BBC, Nadia Atif (AN). Dist: FIV VR$90, VS$150. *Attempts to dispell Western stereotypes of Arab women both through an "analysis of the meaning of honor" and through an "exploration of the ways in which Islam can be and has been interpreted to inform women's lives."* [From the review by Lila Abu-Lughod, *AA* 89:782–783, 1987.]

Sentinels of Silence (1973) 19 min. Manuel Arango (PR, DI), Orson Welles (NA), Ignacio Bernal (AN). Dist: EBEC; UCEMC FR$24; PSU FR$11. (Spanish-language version also available: *Centinelas del Silencio*, UCEMC FR$20.) *Striking aerial views, shot from helicopter, of pre-Columbian sites in Mexico (with orchestra).* [Reviewed by Jeremy A. Sabloff, *AA* 78:378–379, 1976.]

Separate Visions (1989) 40 min. Peter Blystone and Nancy Tongue (PR). Dist: UCEMC VR$40, VS$295, order #37899. *Profiles four pioneering American Indian artists: Baje Whitethorne, a Navajo painter; Brenda Spencer, a Navajo weaver; John Federicks, a Hopi kachina carver; and Nora Naranjo-Morse, a Santa Clara sculptor. All four work in the most contemporary modes of their media, and all are on the leading edge of change—a fact that invites controversy among critics and collectors, as well as their own people. Their work, however contemporary, includes strong traditional aspects. Theirs is a generation of great change, and that flux is reflected in their art and lives.*

A SERIES ON THE BARUYA Allison and Marek Jablonko and Stephen Olsson (DI). Dist: DER. *These intriguing films portray the work of French anthropologist Maurice Godelier among the Baruya—a tribe famous throughout the eastern highlands of Papua New Guinea as salt makers and traders. Dr. Godelier, one of modern anthropology's most prominent figures, had been living among and studying the Baruya people on various fieldtrips since 1967. A 67-page companion study guide to these films, authored by the filmmakers, is available from DER. The individual film descriptions appear under their titles:*

- **Her Name Came on Arrows**
- **To Find the Baruya Story**

Sermons and Sacred Pictures (1991) 29 min. Lynne Sachs (FM), Center for Southern Folklore (PR). Dist: UCEMC FR$45, FS$595, VS$195. *This multi-award-winning documentary profiles the life and work of Reverend L. O. Taylor, a black Baptist minister from Memphis, Tennessee. In addition to his ministry work, Reverend Taylor was also an inspired filmmaker with an overwhelming interest in preserving a visual and aural record of the social, cultural, and religious fabric of black American life in the 1930s and 1940s. This stylistically innovative work combines Taylor's black-and-white films and audio recordings with color images of comtemporary Memphis neighborhoods and religious gatherings. Commentary by members of the Memphis community forms an intertwined narrative focusing on Reverend Taylor as a pioneering documentarian and social activist. Essential viewing for all courses in African-American history and culture.*

Serpent Mother (Pleasing God Series) 27 min. A. Moore and A. Ostor (FM). Dist: CPI FR$50, FS$495, VS$279. *Relates the myth of the goddess, Manasha, and shows the making of the images to be consecrated in her worship as well as rituals comprising the great annual festival of the snakes, Jhapan, where devotees play with cobras and worship the goddess with offerings and songs.*

Seven Nights and Seven Days 58 min. Maurice Dores (PR). Dist: FL VR$75, VS$445. *This film documents an unusual healing ceremony in Senegal. It shows how a community gathers together to treat and heal one of its members who is suffering from postpartum depression. After giving birth, the young woman refuses to care for her child. Years before her mother and grandmother had been treated for a similar illness by a shaman, Fat Seck. The ceremony, called the Ndepp, is organized by the Lebou people of Senegal to honor their ancestral spirits and to ask them to allow a cure to take place. Performed over seven days and nights, it is a complicated ceremony with a precise set of rules. A large part of the population participates. The healer resolves this family problem. Trances and sacrifices are part of the cure. At the* *end of the week, the young woman is restored to normal behavior, an effective mother and community member.*

Sewing Woman (1982) 14 min. Arthur Dong (FM). Dist: Arthur Dong, 1548 Lombard St., San Francisco, CA 94123; (415) 776-9049, VR$30, VS$225 *"The story of early Japanese and Chinese immigration to the United States is almost an exclusively male one . . . a limited number of wives were allowed into the country." This film is a documentary about one of those wives, Mrs. Dong, whose life history is the core of the film.* [From the review by Karen L. Ito, *AA* 86:787–789, 1984.]

Sexuality and Aging (1987) 59 min. Gary Hochman (DI). Dist: GPN, P.O. Box 80669, Lincoln, NB 68501; (800) 228-4630, VS$50. *"A lengthy film covering many aspects of sex among the elderly: stereotypes, menopause, hormone replacement therapy, sleep tests for penile tumescence, and support groups. The film seems to be a long advertisement for medical solutions and support groups that affirm these solutions."* [From the review by Benjamin N. Colby, *AA* 92:1099–1100, 1990.]

The Shackles of Tradition: Franz Boas (1852–1942) (Strangers Abroad Series) 52 min. Dist: FHS FR$75, VS$159, order #XD-2542. *In 1883, a young German scientist, Franz Boas, arrived in the Canadian Arctic to map the coastline and indulge in his new interest: the study of other cultures. He became so absorbed by the common features that unite humans everywhere that he made the study of culture his life's work, doing fieldwork in both the Arctic and the North West coast of America among the Indian tribes. Boas was the first distinguished social scientist in the United States to challenge the prevailing concept of racial inferiority and actively campaigned on behalf of black people in America in the early part of the 20th century. He is considered the founding father of American anthropology.* [Reviewed by George W. Stocking, Jr., *AA* 85:231, 1983.]

Shadow Catcher (1975) 88 min. T.C. McLuhan (FM). Dist: PFI; UCEMC FR$61. *Documents the life and work of Edward Curtis (1868–52), photographer, filmmaker, and anthropologist, whose monumental study of North American Indians fills 20 volumes. Includes all of Curtis's recoverable film footage, many of his photographs, and readings from his journals by Donald Sutherland.* [Reviewed by Reed D. Riner, *JAF* 91:622–624, 1978. Additional note in *JAF* 92:136, 1979.]

The Shadow and the Spirit 60 min. Dist: CBC VS$225, order # X4K-80-01. *Filmed from the Columbia River to the Gulf of Alaska along the British Columbia coastline, this documentary employs extensive historical reconstruction to re-create the many unique cultures that developed among these islands and inlets centuries ago. The strikingly original art forms that evolved are considered to be some of the finest examples of native art and hang in museums and galleries around the world. After near extinction in the early part of this century, native carvings and paintings are enjoying a spectacular renaissance. One of the leaders of this revival is contemporary Indian carver, Joe David, whose works are featured in this program.*

The Shadow of Man (1969) 28.5 min. Earl H. Swanson (DI), Norm Holve, Idaho State University News Bureau (CA), Idaho State University Museum (PR). Dist: ISU FR$20, FS$350. *The Shadow of Man records quarrying activities at prehistoric obsidian quarries on the high lava desert of eastern Oregon. The film was taken on location while Don Crabtree of the Idaho State University Museum quarried obsidian for his experiments in flintknapping. Included in the film are scenes showing the natural setting, the preparation of replicas of digging tools, and the actual excavation of obsidian. The Shadow of Man is the first in a projected series of films on experiments in flintknapping by Mr. Crabtree. It is not an introduction to the techniques of flintknapping, but rather illustrates the steps involved in quarrying and the associated flintknapping activites of prehistoric man.* [Reviewed by Barbara Voytek and Anne Whitman, *AA* 77:915–916, 1975. Susanna Katz and Paul Katz, *ARCH* 34(1):60, 1981.]

Shadow of the Rising Sun (The New Pacific Series) (1987) 60 min. BBC/NVC (PR). Dist: FIV VS$79. *The prosperity of Pacific rim nations is challenging American economic dominance, and this issue forms the core of this video.*

Shahira: Nomads of the Sahara 52 min. Film Centre and Bishari Films (PR). Dist: FL VR$65, VS$395. *This is an inspirational documentary about a young Muslim woman, trained as an anthropologist, who suffered hardship and professional censure to save a desert tribe from becoming extinct in the harsh Sahara. The Bishari tribe had lived in the Sahara for 5,000 years but were unknown to Egyptian authorities. The Bishari were living in a time warp, their warriors believing they were still the guardians of the ancient Roman gold mines. When the Aswan Dam was constructed, the Bishari's grazing ground became submerged. Anthropologist Shahira Fawzy discovered them by chance, suffering from illness and malnutrition. Going against the wishes of her traditional family, Shahira went to live among the Bishari. She studied their customs, fought the government on their behalf, and helped them develop skills such as irrigation, well digging, and gardening. Her aim was to ensure that the tribe would maintain its unique culture while surviving in the modern world.*

Shahsavan Nomads of Iran (1984) 28 min. Arlene Dallalfar and Fereydoun Safizadeh (FM). Dist: Safi Productions, 1401 Bentley Avenue, Los Angeles, CA 90025; (213) 479-0164, FR$90, FS$500. *"Offers a unique documentary view of one of Iran's many pastoral nomadic, tribally organized, and non-Persian speaking groups. Filmed in 1977–79 in northwest Iran near the Soviet border . . . [it] provides glimpses of Shahsavan life, defined largely in terms of seasonal migrations, activity in encampments, production of crafts, and ceremonies."* [From the review by Lois Beck, *AA* 89:783–784, 1987.]

The Shakers 29 min. Tom Davenport (FM). Dist: TDF FR$35, FS$295. *The Shakers are America's longest and most successful experiment in Christian communal living. A century ago, nearly 6,000 Shaker brothers and sisters lived together in 19 communities scattered from Maine to Kentucky. Their meeting houses resounded with devotional* *songs and ecstatic dancing, and their communal farms and workshops poured out products and inventions that made their name synonymous with quality and ingenuity. This film traces the growth and decline of the remarkable religious sect through the memories and songs of the surviving Shakers themselves.* [Reviewed by Keith K. Cunningham, *JAF* 355:122, 1977.]

The Shakers in America 28 min. Vincent Tortora (FM). Dist: Vedo Films, 85 Longbiew Rd., Port Washington, NY 11050. [Reviewed by Daniel W. Patterson, *JAF* 89(353):384.]

Shamans of the Blind Country (1980) 224 min. Michael Oppitz (FM), Charlotte Bosanquet (AN). Dist: WSK Productions 5, Carmine Street, New York, NY 10014; University of Texas FR$175, VR$70, FS$4000, VS$1500. *A documentary epic on magical healing in the Himalayas. The film pursues the main features of the great Inner Asian tradition of shamanism, as preserved in the secluded society of the northern Magar in central west Nepal. Part 1 focuses on the sumptuous rituals performed by the Magar shamans during their night-long seances. Their methods of diagnosis and treatment are watched, their techniques of possession and their ritual journeys, undertaken to recover fugitive souls of the patients, all encoded in a rich symbolic language of signs and gestures. Part 2 concentrates on the transmission of the shaman's profession. After preliminary signs for the call, a novice must prove his vocation through a prescribed set of tests and initiation rites. Only then can he or she be born, during a lavish three-day ceremony, on a conifer tree, the tree of life. The film follows these successive tests of aptitude, the making and consecration of the paraphernalia, such as a drum, and culminates in the birth of a female shaman. The professional activities of the magical healers are linked with their daily rounds, with hunting, fishing, agricultural tasks and the past—oral cycle of the transhuman migrations. In visual terms, the film begins with short and rather incomprehensible sequences, which find their explanation later on, as the takes get longer and the filming time approaches real time. With this method, the basic ethnographer's experience—gradual discovery of meaning—is transferred into the film. In terms of language used in the film, four levels of speech have been established; mythical speech—the narrator telling stories; ethnographic speech—the narrator explaining symbolic actions; direct speech—subtitles translating the original soundtrack; and headline speech—subtitles giving information in the silent movie fashion. All actions of the Magar healers are codified in a body of mythical songs that glorify the deeds of the first Shaman, Rama Puran Tsan. These epic songs are the core of Magar religious life and determine its ethos, which in essence is epic.* [Reviewed by Linda Stone, *AA* 90:1049–1050, 1988.]

The Shanwar Telis or Bene Israel 30 min. Johanna Spector (FM). Dist: JMS FR$75, FS$1,000. *The Jewish Community in the Bombay Area.* [Reviewed by Elise Barnett, *Asian Music* 1:144–147.]

Shaping the Image (see Consuming Hunger Series)

Sharing a New Song: An Experiment in Citizen Diplomacy (1988) 58 min. Chris Schmidt (PR). Dist: DER FR$95, VR$60, FS$1000, VS$400. *One of the first truly collaborative U.S.-Soviet documentaries dealing with stereotypes and misperceptions. The film is cross-subtitled in Russian and English. American and Soviet high school students are asked to brainstorm in their respective classrooms—responses are both predictable and surprising. Attention turns to the hope-filled story of a special friendship between an American amateur chorus and a Soviet film studio; how members met, developed friendships, and decided to trade artistic disciplines. Russian and American folk music accompanies their moving reunion in Yaroslavl. Poignant interviews with teachers, students, a cosmonaut, cinematographers and a photo-journalist portray the special friendship that the film documents.*

Sharing Is Unity (Ushirika ni umoja) 23 min. Ron Mulvihill (DI). Dist: MF VS$100. *Explores the rural life and feelings of the Iteso people of Kenya. The African sense of community is experienced through their daily activities ranging from farming to storytelling. The film portrays the Iteso's spirit of sharing and reciprocal giving, values that contribute to the unity and survival of communities in Africa. The film is narrated by members of the Iteso community.* Available in Kiswahili and English.

The Shark Callers of Kontu (1986) 54 min. Dennis O'Rourke (FM). Dist: DCL FR$100, FS$895, VS$350. *For centuries the villagers of Kontu, in Papua New Guinea, have gone to sea in frail outrigger canoes to call, trap, and kill sharks by hand. Now, after a hundred years of colonization and intense missionary activity, only a few men still understand the magic rituals of shark calling.*

The Shepherd's Family (1987) 22 min. Jerome Mintz (DI). Dist: DER FR$45, VR$30, FS$400, VS$200. *The film portrays a shepherd's family that has remained tied to its traditional occupation and to its semifeudal role in rural Andalusian society. The children help by guarding the flock and in earning additional wages by gathering snails, picking cotton, and hoeing.*

The Shepherds of Bernary (Ciobairean Bhearnaraich) (1981) 55 min. Jack Shea (PR, DI), Allan Moore (PR). Dist: MOMA FR$75, FS$725. *Filmed on Bernary Isle, off the northwest coast of Scotland. "A captivating and touching film which juxtaposes the harsh reality of a stark natural setting and the warmth and determination of the people who make their living from it." One of the major themes is "the tenacity of the islanders in continuing a way of life filled with uncertainty and hardship."* [From the review by George M. Epple, *AA* 85:225–226, 1983.]

Sherea, Dispute Settlement at the Court of the Paramount Chief in N'zara, North Togo (see Anufom Series) (1975)

Sherpa (1984) 29 min. Robert Godrey (FM). Dist: CPI FR$50, FS$500, VS$275. *"About a young Sherpa man who leads Western trekkers through the Himalayas of Nepal. The story focuses on the life of the sirdar, or trek leader, Nima Tenzing, as he deals with changes in Sherpa lifestyle* *and values."* [From the review by Donald A. Messerschmidt, *AA* 89:264–265, 1987.]

Sherpa High Country (1977) 20 min. Xenia Lisanevich (FM). Dist: UCEMC FR$29, FS$285. *Sherpas of the Solu Khumbu highlands in Nepal, near Mt. Everest. Commences with a Sherpa man turning prayer wheels along a monastery wall in order to gain religious merit. A close-up of the turning prayer wheels serves as an introduction to the film's principal theme: the prevalence of the wheel-of-life motif throughout Sherpa culture, indicating the tremendous influence of Buddhism in the life of Solu Khumbu. After scenes of Sherpa life at the villages of Lukla, Phortse, and Tangboche, the scene shifts to Tangboche monastery, the seat of Sherpa religion, and the three-day Mani-Rimdu ceremony. Shows the people gathered and selling their wares at this November festival, as well as the first day's procession of monks and the blessing ceremony presided over by the abbot. A long sequence depicts the second day's dance drama performed by the monks of Tangboche; the symbolism in the drama is explained in relation to its function of celebrating and reinforcing Buddhist teachings.* [Reviewed by Robert A. Paul, *AA* 82:230–231, 1980.]

Sherpas (Disappearing World Series) (1977) 52 min. Sherry Ortner (AN). Dist: PSU. order #51218. *Sherpa Tenzing came from Thami, a village 12,500 feet up in the Himalayan mountain range of Nepal. In 1953, he and Sir Edmund Hillary were the first men to reach the summit of Mount Everest. Since then, Sherpas have become famous as guides to mountaineers. This program looks at the contrasting lives of three brothers from Thami: a farmer, a Buddhist monk, and an expedition guide.*

Shichi Fukujin (1983) 66 min. Yashuhiro Omori (FM). Dist: Yashuhiro Omori, National Museum of Ethnology, Expo Park Senri Suita, Osaka 565, Japan; 06/876-2151. Documents *"Shichi Fukujin, a kind of New Year's festival featuring the Seven Young Gods who are expected to visit villages at this time of year. The film focuses on how the villagers organize this festival in a traditional Japanese community."* [From the review by Tsuneo Ayabe and Norboru Miyata, *AA* 87:992, 1985.]

The Shilluk (Disappearing World Series) (1976) 53 min. Chris Curling (DI), Paul Howell and Walter Kunijwok (AN). Dist: PSU order #51252. *In the 16th century, a man named Niyakang united the various groups living along the Nile River into one people, called Shilluk. Shilluk life revolves around the "Reth," who is believed to be the divine incarnation of the Shilluk people. But Shilluk territory is now part of the Sudan, and the Reth has been demoted to local magistrate by the central government.* [Reviewed by Lucy Mair, *RAIN* 12:6, 1976.]

Shinto: Nature, Gods and Man in Japan Peter Grilli and David Westphal (FM). Dist: JS FR$50, FS$550, VS$385. *Introduces the fundamental philosophical, ethical, and aesthetic beliefs of the Shinto tradition. As Japan's native religion, Shinto traces its roots far back into Japanese prehistory and has served to integrate all elements of Japanese culture. It has been a source of ethical values and communal unity as well as a focus for political organization. The film takes the viewer on a journey to the heart of Shinto, to Japan's most ancient ritual sites and most sacred shrines, to prehistoric ceremonies still performed today, and to local festivals and seasonal celebrations. It features: the holy island of Okinoshima; the beautiful buildings and ceremonies of the imperial shrines at Ise; ancient rituals at the historic shrines where the inner sanctuaries are rarely seen by laymen; and Shinto images and works of art.*

Shipwreck: La Trinidad Valencera (Odyssey Series) (1979) 59 min. Dist: DER FR$45, FS$450. *"The film does an excellent job of examining and describing the methods and techniques of underwater excavation as well as the preservation of water-soaked artifacts."* [From the review by Peter S. Allen, *ARCH* 33(2):62, 1980.]

The Shock of the Other (Millennium: Tribal Wisdom and the Modern World Series) (1992) 1 hour. David Maybury-Lewis (H), Hans Zimmer (MU). Dist: PBS VS$49.95, order #MILL-101-RCDC. *The Western world's desire to remake other societies into its own image has robbed our modern world of the gifts of other cultures. The series begins with a visit to Maybury-Lewis's Xavante brother in central Brazil where he explains the need to find balance between cultural diversity and our desire to be like one another. They journey into the heart of the Amazon where they seek to unravel the mystery of a small tribe called the Mascho-Piro who remain hidden from the outside world. Through scenes of the decimation of the tropical rain forests, interviews with theatened indigenous peoples, and the narrator's reflections on the discovery of the Americas and other historical events, we discover why so much is at stake when modern industrialism meets the tribal world.*

The Shoemaker (1978) 34 min. Jerome Mintz (FM). Dist: DER FR$60, FS$550; IUAVC FR$11.75, FS$300, VS$210. *The film concerns the effect of the rural exodus in Spain on the life of a poor Andalusian shoemaker. Deeply attached to his network of family and friends, the shoemaker has always assumed that he would spend his last years in his native village. When his children leave to work in a tourist town, the shoemaker is forced into an unexpected dilemma. Although his financial condition initially improves, it soon becomes necessary for him to join his children. He must close his shop and leave the village in which he has lived and worked all his life. When he arrives in his new setting, he is forced to adapt to his isolation in a new environment.* Spanish lyrics and their English translations of songs upon request. [Reviewed by Davydd J. Greenwood and Pilar Fernandez Canadas de Greenwood, *AA* 82:226–227, 1980. Reviewed in *VISA* 4:69, 1991.]

Shoot and Cry (1988) 52 min. Helen Klodawsky and Miguel Merkin (DI), Mark Zannis, Hean-Roch Marcotte, and Barrie Howells (PR), for the National Film Board of Canada. Dist: FRIF FR$125, VR$75, FS$975, VS$400. *This film's "concern lies in the effect of the occupation of the West Bank and Gaza strip on Israeli society, a dilemma cast in the form of a choice between morality, on the one hand, and security and its handmaiden, settlement, on the other."* [From the review by Herbert L. Bodman, Jr. *AA* 92:843–844, 1990.]

Shoot for the Contents (1991) 101 min. Trinh T. Minh-ha (DI). Dist: WMM FR$225, FS$1600, VS$495. *A unique excursion into the maze of allegorical naming and storytelling in China. This film ponders questions of power and change, politics and culture, as refracted by Tienanmen Square events. If offers at the same time an inquiry into the creative process of filmmaking, intricately layering Chinese popular songs and classical music, the sayings of Mao and Confucius, women's voices and the words of artists, philosophers, and other cultural workers. Video images emulate the gestures of calligraphy and contrast with film footage of rural China and stylized interviews. Exploring color rhythm and the changing relationship between ear and eye, this meditative documentary realizes on screen the shifts of interpretation in contemporary Chinese culture and politics.*

The Shrine (1990) 46 min. Bob Paris and Christiane Badgley (DI). Dist: UCEMC VR$50, VS$295, order #37976. *Innovative exploration of the traditions and mysteries that surround El Santuario, a small adobe church in northern New Mexico. This sacred shrine, with its famed healing dirt and its figure of the Christ child that is said to walk in the night, attracts thousands of people each year in this country's largest religious pilgrimage. This documentary traces the history of El Santuario and relates it to New Mexico's Hispanic cultural heritage. Its unusual visual style leads viewers to reflect on the question: What is a sacred place?* [Reviewed by Sylvia Rodriquez, AA 94(3):767, 1992.]

Shuka's Story (1969) 24 min. Stephanie Frebs (FM, AN), Film Study Center, Harvard University (PR). Dist: UCEMC FR$29, FS$285. *The women's side of life in Zinacantan, Chiapas, Mexico.* [Reviewed by Peter T. Furst, AA 74:194–195, 1972.] Suggested supplement: Evon Z. Vogt, *Zinacantan: A Maya Community in the Highlands of Chiapas.* Harvard, 1969.

The Shvitz (1993) 47 min. Jonathan Berman (FM). Dist: AWF. *A visit to the community that patronizes the last traditional steambaths in the United States.*

Siberia: After the Shaman (From Africa to Asia: Nomads Series) (1992) 60 min. Dr. Piers Vitebsky (AN). Dist: FIV VS$198. *The Even are a little known group of Siberian Arctic pastoralists—reindeer herders—whose nomadic traditions are still being fostered today.*

Siberia: Through Siberian Eyes (1993) 50 min. Mark Badger (FM). Dist: KUAC-TV, University of Alaska, Fairbanks, AK 99775. *In 1990, a group of anthropologists went to Siberia and gave a community video cameras so that they could produce and direct their own short pieces. The results are a combination of individual portraits and family stories that represent the first Siberian produced media.*

Signatures of the Soul 59 min. Geoff Stevens (DI). Dist: FL FR$85, VR$85, FS$850, VS$700. *A fascinating look at the history and practice of tattooing. We see the amazing tattoos of: Maori people, who developed the world's most striking tattoo, the full facial mask; Polynesians on Samoa who gave us the word "tatau." They still use the ancient methods seen by the first European explorers of the Pacific; Yakusa, the Japanese gangster class, who have the world's most impressive and extreme tattoos; California artists in San Diego, Los Angeles, and San Francisco who are known for striking individual styles, such as "neo tribal" solid black designs, photo-realist fine-line and multicolored designs that cover the whole body.* [Reviewed by Ronald C. Simons, SBF 20:223, 1985.]

Signs of the Times (1989) 28 min. Leandra Little (PR). Dist: PSU VR$15.50, VS$180. *Presents an overview of the austere and ultraconservative Old School, or Primitive, Baptists who once thrived in the northeastern United Staes, but who have virtually disappeared. The video features Roxbury, located in a rural Catskill region of New York and shows portions of an Old School Baptist service, archival photos, and many shots of the remaining church buildings. The program also examines how the beliefs of the church members derived from their early opposition to the Church of England and its trappings—stained glass, ornamentation, fine robes, educated priests, and central authority. Their rise in popularity coincides directly with the independent ideals of Jeffersonian democracy. However, this independence of mind also has contributed to their splintering and decline. The video evokes a time when life was simpler and religious life was the basis of a deep sense of community.*

Sigui 66: année zero (Sigui 66: Year Zero) (1966) 15 min. Jean Rouch (DI). Dist: CFE; DER. *The head Hogon of Arou, religious chief of all the Dogon of the Bandiagara Cliffs, Mali, announces the beginning of the Sigui Cérémonies for the next year.*

Sigui No. 1: L'enclume de Yougo (The Anvil of Yougo) (1967) 35 min. Jean Rouch, Gilbert Rouget and Germain Dieterlen (DI), Centre National de la Recherche Scientifique, Comité du Film Ethnographique (PR). Dist: CFE; DER. *The first year of the sixty-year cycle ceremony of Sigui among the Dogon of the Bandiagara cliffs. See also Les Cérémonies Soixanteraires du Sigui.*

Sigui No. 2: Les danseurs de Tyogou (The Dancers of Tyogou) (1968) 50 min. Jean Rouch (DI), Centre National de la Recherche Scientifique, Comité du Film Ethnographique (PR). Dist: CFE; DER. *The second year of the sixty-year cycle of Sigui Cérémonies among the Dogon of the Bandiagara cliffs. See also Les Cérémonies Soixanteraires du Sigui.*

Sigui No. 3: La caverne de Bongo (The Bongo Cave) (1969) 40 min. Jean Rouch (DI), Centre National de la Recherche Scientifique, Comité du Film Ethnographique (PR). Dist: CFE; DER. *The third year of the sixty-year Sigui cycle among the Dogon of the Dandiagara cliffs. See also Les Cérémonies Soixanteraires du Sigui.*

Sigui No. 4: Les clameurs d'Amani (The Clamor of Amani) (1970) 50 min. Jean Rouch (DI), Centre National de la Recherche Scientifique, Comité du Film Ethnographique (PR). Dist: CFE; DER. *The fourth year of the sixty-year Sigui cycle among the Dogon of the Dandiagara cliffs. See also Les Cérémonies Soixanteraires du Sigui.*

Sigui No. 5: La dune d'Idyeli (The Dune of Idyeli) (1971) 40 min. Jean Rouch (DI), Centre National de la Recherche Scientifique, Comité du Film Ethnographique (PR). Dist: CFE; DER. *The fifth year of the sixty-year Sigui cycle among the Dogon of the Dandiagara cliffs. See also Les Cérémonies Soixanteraires du Sigui.*

Sigui No. 6: Les pagnes de Yame (The Loincloths of Yame) 1972 40 min. Jean Rouch (DI), Centre National de la Recherche Scientifique, Comité du Film Ethnographique (PR). Dist: CFE; DER. *The sixth year of the sixty-year cycle ceremony of Sigui among the Dogon of the Bandiagara cliffs. See also Les Cérémonies Soixanteraires du Sigui.*

Sigui No. 7: L'auvent de la irconcision (The Circumcision Shelter) (1973) 15 min. Jean Rouch (DI), Centre National de la Recherche Scientifique, Comité du Film Ethnographique (PR). Dist: CFE; DER. *The seventh year of the sixty-year cycle ceremony of Sigui among the Dogon of the Bandiagara cliffs. See also Les Cérémonies Soixanteraires du Sigui.*

Silent Army (1980) 29 min. WTTW, Chicago (PR). Dist: PBSV VR$55, VS$225. "*The 'silent army' refers to the magnificent collection of terracotta soldiers and horses, some 7,000 strong, excavated from a large pit accompanying the unexcavated tumulus of Qin Shi Huangdi, traditionally known as the first emperor of China.... The title and opening sequence are misleading because the film is not about the excavations of the pit near Qin Shi Huangdi's mounded tomb; rather, it describes the installation of this exhibit at the Field Museum of Natural History in Chicago.*" [From the review by Heather Peters, ARCH 38(5):64–77, 1985.]

The Silent Enemy: An Epic of the American Indian (1930) 84 min. H.P. Carver (DI), William Douglas Burden, William Chanler (PR). Dist: MLS VS$39.95, order #MILE007. *This film is a reconstruction of Ojibway Indian life in the time before the white man settled the Hudson Bay region. The "enemy" is hunger that threatens the tribe as it desperately tracks and hunts for food. A thunderous caribou stampede provides an absolutely thrilling finale. Magnificently photographed on location, The Silent Enemy boasts an all-Indian cast and a compelling sound prologue by Chief Yellow Robe. It is based largely on a 72-volume historical record written by the French missionaries of New France between 1610 and 1791. The musical score by Kur Zhene was adapted from some 150 Ojbway melodies. Critics acclaimed the film a masterpiece on its original release, and it remains so today.*

The Silent Witness: An Investigation into the Shroud of Turin (1978) 55 min. David W. Rolfe (DI), Screenpro Films (PR). Dist: PyrF R$75, FS$750, VS$750. "*Addresses the question of the Shroud's authenticity through an examination of the physical and historical evidence.... There is no pretense of objectivity here; not a single person appears in the film who is not totally convinced that the Shroud once held the body of Christ, nor is there any conflicting evidence or testimony given.*" [From the review by Peter S. Allen, ARCH 35(2):80–81, 1982.] Related reading: Ian Wilson, *The Shroud of Turin.* Doubleday and Co., New York, 1978.

THE SILK ROAD (1991) 6 parts, 55 min. each. Isao Tamai (DI), NHK, CCTV (PR). Dist: CPM VS$29.95 (each), $149.95 (series). "*The Silk Road documents the efforts of a joint Japanese/Chinese expedition to trace the eastern half of the Silk Road from Xian to Jiayuguan, one of the last outposts in China more than 1,000 miles away.... The bulk of each program is spent on getting to the site, not on the site itself.*" [From the review by Peter S. Allen, ARCH 46:90, 1993.] The series includes:

- **Glories of Ancient Chang-an**
- **A Thousand Kilometers beyond the Yellow River**
- **The Art Gallery of the Desert** *The caves at Mo-gao.*
- **The Dark Castle** *A fortified site near the Mongolian border.*
- **In Search of the Kingdom of Lou-lan**
- **Across the Taklamakan Desert**

Silversmith of Williamsburg (see Colonial Williamsburg Series)

Simiri Siddo Kuma (1979) 30 min. Jean Rouch (DI), Centre National de la Recherche Scientifique, Comité du Film Ethnographique (PR). Dist: CFE; DER. *Preparations for the funeral of Zima Siddo, who was responsible for the rituals of possession in the Simiri region, Niger.*

Simplemente Jenny (1977) 30 min. Helena Solberg Ladd (DI), Christine Burrill (ED). Dist: Cinema Inc., P.O. Box 315, Franklin Lakes, NJ 07417, FR$45-90, FS$395. *Simplemente Jenny is a film about women in Latin America and the cultural values that shape their lives. It is a film about image and reality, the models of society and the facts of poverty and violence. It focuses on three adolescent girls in a reformatory in Bolivia. Jenny, Marli, and Patricia tell their stories of rape and forced prostitution and their fantasies of wealth, marriage, and happiness in a society that has no place for them. Scenes of urban slums, abandoned children, and broken homes in Argentina, Ecuador, and Mexico are juxtaposed against society's models. Marli, Patricia, and Jenny cannot be helped, laments the reformatory psychiatrist, because their problems stem from conditions that remain unchanged. Jenny speaks of women's suffering and fantasizes about being rich, but ultimately she says, "I just want to be myself, that's all. I want to be simply Jenny."*

Sinew-Backed Bow and Its Arrows (American Indian Film Series) (1961) 24 min. Samuel A. Barrett (AN). Dist: UCEMC FR$32, FS$330. *Follows the construction of a sinew-backed bow—the finest and strongest of bows used by American Indians—by a Yurok craftsman. A yew tree is felled and the wood is selected, sanded, and cured; sinew is applied with glue, and the bow is painted and strung. Special emphasis is given to the unique process of laminating layers of sinew onto the base of the hardwood. Also demonstrates the making of arrows, showing how the arrow shaft, made of mock orange, was rasped until cylindrical and the sanded with equisetum, a native sandpaper; and how the arrow shafts were fitted with stone arrowheads and hawk feathers and painted with special designs to signify their ownership. Significant historical documentation of an* *aboriginal craft.* [Reviewed by T. M. Hamilton, *AA* 68:842–843, 1966.]

The Singing Fishermen of Ghana (1964) 15 min. (A Folklore Research Film by Peter and Toshi Seeger.) Dist: FIM/RF FR$15, FS$150. *In Ghana, when fishermen dip their oars into the water, they do it to music. It is traditional to take along a drummer and a player of a small metal "clinking" instrument when they go out into the Atlantic in their dugout canoes to lay their nets. Their paddling songs are carried from canoe to canoe, and when they land, the villagers are waiting to help beach the canoes and pull in the nets—with everyone singing together as they work.* [Reviewed by David Evans, *JAF* 89(354):517, 1976.]

Sinmia (1991) 43 min. Kumain Nunguia (FM). Dist: Les Ateliers Varan, 6 6 Impasse Mont-Louis, 75011 Paris, France; telephone 331-56-64-04; fax 331-56-29-02. *A Papua New Guinean–produced video about the initiation of the Baruya, an eight-day community ritual marking the entrance to manhood.*

SIX AMERICAN FAMILIES (1976) 6 parts, 59 min. each. Dist: AB; IUAVC R$29. *Six American Families is a series of real-life programs on how U.S. families live, make decisions, and cope with pressures 200 years after the birth of the nation. Explore the joys, sorrows, tensions, courage, and frustrations of real people in real families across the land. The programs are more than random visits to six homes. The unique experiences of representative families (as of 1976) are mirrors in which we can see ourselves as America moves into its third century. Selecting the families and filming the series took more than a year. The families chosen live in suburban San Francisco; Chicago; rural Georgia and Iowa; Albuquerque, New Mexico; New York City. They are affluent and poor; large and small; white collar and blue collar; urban and rural; Protestant, Catholic, and Jewish. Each was chosen after long consultation with the producers because the particular family could contribute to an understanding of the ethical issues that American families encounter and must solve.*

- **The Greenberg Family, Mill Valley, California**
- **The Stephens Family, Villisca, Iowa**
- **The Pasciack Family, Chicago**
- **The Kennedy Family, Albuquerque, New Mexico**
- **The Burk Family, Dalton, Georgia**
- **The George Family, New York City**

Six Hundred Millennia: China's History Unearthed (1976) 89 min. KQED, San Francisco (PR). Dist: PBSV VR$95, VS$300. *"In 1975, an archaeological exhibit from the People's Republic of China visited the US, a significant cultural exchange that symbolized a new era in US-China relations. Almost half of the film is an extremely interesting documentary of San Francisco's preparation for the exhibit. . . . What follows is an object-by-object tour of the show, accompanied by a course in Chinese archaeology strictly from the viewpoint of the People's Republic of China."* [From the review by Heather Peters, *ARCH* 38(5):64–77, 1985.]

6000 Years in Suswa (1980) 12 min. J. Scott Dodds (FM). Dist: IWS. *This is a short film about the archaeology of East Africa, as well as contemporary Masai. The film is amateurishly put together with a soundtrack that at times seems to lead independent life from what is being shown on the screen. The film could be shrugged off as inconsequential if it did not have the potential of misleading naive viewers.* [Reviewed by Francis P. Conant, *AA* 83:746, 1981]

The Skiff of Renald and Thomas (1980) 58 min. Michel Brault (PR), Bernard Gorsselin (DI). Dist: NFBC VR$80, FS$775, VS$450. *"A meticulous visual account of the construction of a small (19-foot) boat on the Ile-aux-Coudres in the St. Lawrence River of Quebec."* [From the review by Bryce Muir and Margaret Muir, *AA* 85:744–745, 1983.]

Skokomish Indian Baskets: Their Materials and Techniques (1977) 28 min. Super 8 mm. Karen James, Gerald Bruce Miller, Beverly Okada, and Lynn Patterson (PR). Dist: UWP FR$15, FS$75. *This film documents the intricate and varied techniques of basket making by the Skokomish Indians from the Puget Sound region of western Washington, from the gathering of grasses and other natural materials to finished baskets. For this film, many parts of that were filmed in 1971, two elderly Skokomish Indian women who learned the basic skills as children from older members of the tribe, show the variety of materials used, including sweet grass, bear grass, cedar bark, and cattails, the steps involved in their processing, and the techniques of weaving. This film also illustrates the ways traditional methods have been adapted by innovations and individual styles in recent times.*

The Sky above, the Mud Below (1961) 92 min. Dist: VFI VS$39.98. *In 1956 a group of explorers set out to cross the uncharted jungles of Dutch New Guinea where they came face-to-face with man's past. 1961 Academy Award for best documentary.*

Sky Chief (1972) 26 min. Scott Robinson and Michael Scott (FM, AN), with the assistance of the Latin American Studies Program, Cornell University and the Department of Anthropology, UCSB. Dist: UCEMC FR$33, FS$365. *Depicts the encounter and subsequent interaction and conflict of three distinct social groups in the jungle along Ecuador's Amazon frontier: immigrant mestizo cultivators who have moved there to escape drought and the dominance of the large estates; oil workers seeking new deposits for an international consortium in which Texaco is a participant; and the indigenous Cofan, scorned by all the new arrivals. No narration is used: the story unfolds in individuals' responses to questions asked of them (subtitles translate their comments). At one point, the Ecuadorian minister of defense arrives to inspect the area—and to insure noninterference with the oil operations. Government troops have already clashed with settlers "encroaching" on the new oil fields. A Cofan man, wearing a green cotton fatigue cap, describes his fear of newcomers. Other Cofan scavenge for metal canisters among the refuse of the new settlement; they have learned to cook with metal pots, and they come to trade feathers, skins, and spears at a trader's store. The excellent cinematography is most dramatic in portraying the unload-*

ing, from airplane and helicopter, of drill bits, pipe, and gasoline; the construction of derricks in the tropical forest; the mushrooming of corrugated iron huts in the jungle clearings; and the rivers awash with pollution from the oil drilling. As the film makes clear, the oil company and the government will dominate in the short run, but the long-term effects of drastic ecological change may make everyone a loser. [Reviewed by Eric R. Wolf, AA 73:1475–1476, 1971.] Suggested supplements: Lewis Cotlon, *Twilight of the Primitive*. Ballantine paper, 1973. Peter Matthiessen, *At Play in the Fields of the Lord*. Random House, 1965. Julian Steward and Louis Faron, *Native Peoples of South America*. McGraw Hill, 1959.

Slash-and-Burn Agriculture (1975) 17 min. James Ward (PR, ED), Brian Weiss (CA, AN). Dist: B&C FR$35, FS$300; UCEMC FR$18. *Uses live action, diagrams, and drawings to document the entire cycle of tropical slash-and-burn agriculture, from the site selection to harvest. Shows the appropriateness of this method of cultivation to the ecosystem of eastern Nicaragua.* [Reviewed by William E. Carter, AA 79:507, 1977.]

Slaying the Dragon (1988) 60 min. Deborah Gee (DI), Asian Women United (PR). Dist: WMM FR$75, VS$225. *A comprehensive look at media stereotypes of Asian and Asian-American women since the silent era. From the racist use of white actors to portray Asians in early Hollywood films, through the success of Anna May Wongs's sinister dragon lady, to Suzie Wong and the 1950s geisha girls, to the Asian-American anchorwoman of today, the fascinating videotape shows how stereotypes of exoticism and docility have affected the perception of Asian-American women.*

Small Business My Way (1982) 28 min. Peter Griesinger and Michael Herschede (FM). Dist: Griesinger Films, Central West Virginia Media Arts, P.O. Box 1102, 48 E. Main St., Buckhannon, WV 26201; (304) 472-7828, FR$50, FS$435, VS$275; CWVR FR$50, FS$435, VS$275. *Small-town life in West Virginia. "Small business in mid-20th century America is a tenacious reminder of the historic forces that shaped the society.... Viewers catch a glimpse of the living past and through it explore avenues for understanding society today."* [From the review by Patrick E. Fontane, SBF 19: 164, 1984. Reviewed by by Linda A. Bennett AA 86:506–507, 1984.] See also *Almost Heaven*.

Small Happiness: Women of a Chinese Village (Long Bow Film Series) (1984) 58 min. Carma Hinton and Richard Gordon (DI). Dist: NDF R$75, FS$800, VS$480; UTA-FL VR$40, order #SRVCC-1244. *"To give birth to a boy is considered a big happiness. To give birth to a girl is a small happiness." Despite profound changes in women's lives, traditional attitudes still persist in the Chinese countryside. Filmed under unprecedented circumstances without any restrictions, women of Long Bow village talk about marriage, birth control, work, and daily life.* [Reviewed by Charlotte Ikels, AA 87:739–741, 1985.]

Snaketown (1969) 40 min. Emil W. Haury and Helga Teiwes (PR), for the Arizona State Museum. Dist: UCEMC FR$42, FS$540. *Important for its archaeological interest as well as its significance to southwestern American history, this study of the Snaketown excavation explores the previously little-known Hohokan Indian culture. It was filmed over the seven-month period of the excavation in 1964 and 1965 at the site, located in the Pima Indian reservation on southern Arizona. Snaketown, buried for 800 years, represents one of the largest known sites of the Hohokam Indian culture. Paying particular attention to archaeological techniques employed in the excavations—the coordination of powered equipment with hand labor, stratigraphic testing using mechanical screens, the flow of recovered materials from field through laboratory—the film chronologically follows the recovery of information and artifacts. It is narrated by Dr. Emil W. Haury, Department of Anthropology, University of Arizona, who directed the excavations. He explains the significance of the findings, showing their relationship to Hohokam society and to surrounding cultures, past and present. Aerial shots present the original layout of the 300-acre site, and artist's recreations depict life in the village. The site was continuously inhabited for 1500 years, from about 300 B.C. into the 12th century A.D., and the artifacts recovered show trends in the craftsmanship of pottery and talismans, as well as rendering much valuable information regarding Hohokam rituals, customs, and social activity. Of particular interest is the unearthing of a ball court nearly the size of a football field, similar to those found in Mexico, and traces of a canal system, which for its time was the most sophisticated in northern America. One of the principal goals in the choice of Snaketown was to see how far back in time irrigated agriculture could be traced as a way of life among the prehistoric Hohokam farmers. The original and oldest irrigation canal was constructed about 300 B.C.* [Reviewed by Donald S. Miller, AA 73:500, 1971.]

So Far from India (1982) 49 min. Mira Nair (FM). Dist: FL FR$75, FS$750, VS$650. *Features Ashok Sheth, a Gujarati immigrant who works at a magazine stand in a New York subway station. It shows his life in New York as well as his visit to India to see his wife and family.* [Reviewed by Paul Hockings, AA 86:807–809, 1984. Reviewed in VISA 4:95, 1991.]

So That Men Are Free (1963) 25 min. Dist:PSU FR$10.50. *CBS documentary of the Cornell Vicos project, Callejon de Huaylas, Peru. Allan Holmberg explains the use of anthropological method and theory in introducing changes in a highland Indian community. The project has been used as a model by many change agencies. Film is subtly biased toward "progress."*

Social Behavior in the Group (Sacred Baboon) 10.5 min. Dist: PSU FR$11.50.

Social Behavior of Rhesus Monkeys (1947) 26 min. C. R. Carpenter (FM). Dist: PSU. [Reviewed by Barbara Smuts, AA 75:2010, 1973.]

Sociobiology (1971) 22 min. Hobel-Leiterman (PR). Dist: DA FR$40, FS$300. *In the fall of 1859, Charles Darwin's work "The Origin of Species" was published. Its theories on the nature and evolution of man took the Victorian world by storm. Today, a group of scientists are developing theories that in many ways rival in impact and importance the original work done by Darwin. The film shows more recent* behavioral research and explores visually the theories and tests that are clarifying this new field of inquiry. We are introduced to the major scientists, their work, and what it means to the human race. Harvard University biologist Robert Trivers speaks about the possibility of sex-determined behavior. Despite the assertions of the women's liberation movement, Dr. Trivers feels that natural selection has been working for centuries to develop emotional dispositions to match the male's natural physical freedom and female's more vulnerable, child-bearing nature. Anthropologist Irven Devore discusses the competitive drive for status among males of any species and more probable survival of the genes of such dominant individuals. Exciting scenes of baboons in their natural state are shown. The research of zoologist Edward O. Wilson, leading authority in the field of sociobiology, is explained and illustrated with scenes of ant activity in the laboratory.

Sociobiology: Doing What Comes Naturally (1976) 24 min. Dist: PSU(PCR) FR$15.50. *"We learn of the deep biological foundations of human behavior reaching back into the distant past as 'man emerged from the Ice Age about one million years ago. . . .' Awful pretty well sums it up."* [From the review by Jeffrey A. Kurland, *AJPA* 61:267–268, 1983.]

Sociobiology: The Human Animal (NOVA Series) (1977) 54 min. Dist: PSU(PCR) FR$27.50. *"Provides a passable portrayal of sociobiological theory as well as a well balanced presentation of its political and ethical implications. The inclusion of commentary by DeVore, Marvin Harris, and Joseph Shepher as well as the presentation of insect, avian, primate, and human varieties of social behavior nicely fills in the sociobiology controversy as of 1976."* [From the review by Jeffrey A. Kurland, *AJPA* 61:507–508, 1983.]

Sogow, Bambara Masks (1983) 55 min. Jean Paul Colleyn (DI), Catherine De Clippel (PR). Dist: FL VR$75, VS$445. *Explores Bambara art and mythology.* [Reviewed by Sidney Littlefield Kasfir, *AA* 86:1066, 1984.]

Soiree at St. Hilarion (St. Lawrence North Series) B/W. *An old-fashioned soiree in a remote mountain village, with the songs and the dancers that have come down through the centuries from France, the ancestral home of the villagers.*

. . . Somebody's Mother . . . [Reviewed by Andris Skreija, *AA* 93:775, 1991.]

Sometimes I Wonder Who I Am (1970) 5 min. Lian Brandon (FM). Dist: NDF. *Role of women.* [Reviewed by Louise Lamphere, *AA* 79:203, 1977.]

Some Notes on Aborigines of Taiwan 28.5 min. Dist: UGA FR$25, FS$385. *The film observes two tribes, the Yami of Orchid Island and the Paiwan of Santimen, their traditions and their process of assimilation. Cultural influence is exerted both ways as the film shows a Chinese Dance theatre that has adapted aboriginal themes to their modern dance creations. A tourist's view of aboriginal culture is whimsically shown by a visit to a village that caters to the curiosity of tourists from around the world. Additional commentary is supplied by Professor Chen Chilu, National Taiwan University and Lin Hwai-min, Cloud Gate Dance Theatre.*

Some Women of Marrakech (Disappearing World Series) (Reedited for the Odyssey Series, 1981) Melissa L. Davies (DI), Elizabeth Fernea (AN). Dist: ISHI. Bibliography: Elizabeth Fernea, *A Street in Marrakech*. Doubleday-Anchor, 1976. [Reviewed by K. L. Brown, *RAIN* 19:7, 1977. Susan Schaefer Davis, *AA* 86:287–288, 1984.] See also *Saints and Spirits*.

LE SON DES CAJUNS DE LA LOUISIANE SERIES (1976) 28 min. each. Andre Gladu (DI), Michel Brault (CA), Nanouk Films (PR). Dist: Faroun Films, 136 A. est rue St. Paul, Montreal, PQ, H2Y IG6, Canada. [Reviewed by Gerald L. Gold, *AA* 80:760–763, 1978. Barcy Jean Ancelet, *JAF* 91(361):885–886, 1978.] Titles in the series are:

- **Fred's Lounge**
- **Ma Chère Tèrre**
- **Les Créoles**
- **La Réveille**

Song of Ceylon (1934) 45 min. B/W. Basil Wright (DI), John Grierson (PR), for the Ceylon Propaganda Tea Board. Dist: MOMA FR$30; UCEMU FR$17. *A poetic evocation of Ceylon in four parts: (1) The Buddha. A pilgrimage to Adam's Peak. (2) The Virgin Island. Pot making; harvesting dry rice; a dancing class. (3) The Voices of Commerce. Train; elephants clearing trees; copra. (4) The Apparel of a God. Worship at a reclining Buddha; the costuming of a dancer.*

A Song of Ceylon (1985) 51 min. Laleen Jayamanne (DI). Dist: WMM FR$395, VR$125. *A formally rigorous, visually stunning study of colonialism, gender, and the body. The title echoes the classic British documentary and evokes a country erased from the world map. The soundtrack enacts a Sri Lankan anthropological text observing a woman's ritual exorcism. Visually, the film brings together theatrical conventions and recreations of classic film stills, presenting the body in striking tableaux. This remarkable film is a provocative treatise on hybridity, hysteria and performance.*

Songs in Minto Life (1986) 30 min. Dist: RTP VS$100. *This film is set in an Athabaskan Indian village of Minto near the Tanana River in Alaska. The subject is music and the way it weaves through every aspect of life. Music here is not entertainment. Each song contributes to the survival of the community. Some songs composed by the animals themselves bring luck to the hunter, others give advice, and new lively dance songs mark contemporary events. Some memorial songs are sung only once—directly to the spirit. A multi-award-winning film.* [Reviewed by Gregory Button and David W. Murray, *AA* 90:778, 1988.]

Songs of a Distant Jungle (1985) 20 min. Robert Charlton (DI). Dist: UCEMC R$40, FS$410, VS$195, order #11248(f), #37189(v). *A joyous and moving celebration of common humanity and the universality of music. This highly lauded film follows Christopher Roberts, a young American musician from the Juilliard School to the jungles of Papua New Guinea. There he ingeniously bridges the vast cultural gap between his own society and that of the natives.*

Setting out to record, document, and preserve music from some of the remotest villages in the country, he introduces his hosts to the music of Bach and Mozart so they will in turn share their own often sacred music with him. [Reviewed by Terence E. Hays, *AA* 89:784–785, 1987. Edward O. Henry, *SBF* 22:320, 1987.]

Songs of the Adventurers (1987) 48 min. Gei Zantzinger (FM). Dist: CSPI FS$575, VS$230. *Migrant workers from Lesotho compose powerful autobiographical poems about their experiences on the mines of South Africa and at home in Lesotho. Their compositions serve to maintain a sense of cultural identity and individual worth amid the dehumanizing experience of labor migrancy. The film presents performances of song-poems called* difela *within the context of the current social and political situation. An analytical section provides insights to the development of the genre.* [Reviewed by Nancy Schmidt, *AA* 90:1048–1049, 1988.]

Songs of the Badius 35 min. Gei Zantzinger (FM). Dist: CSPI FS$225, VS$125. *Until independence in 1975, the Kriolu music of the Cape Verde Islands, off the west African coast, was neglected, persecuted, or forbidden because the Portuguese colonizers of earlier times feared the focus of natural sentiment that it provided. The descendants of runaway African slaves, still called "Badius" continue to perform several genres of Portuguese and African-based music based upon everyday experiences. These performances and thoughts about the music from two musicians are presented.* [Reviewed by Marilyn Halter, *AA* 90:242, 1988.]

Sons of Haji Omar (1978) 58 min. Timothy Asch and Asen Balikci (FM), National Film Board of Canada (PR). Dist: PSU(PCR) FR$28.50, FS$680, VS$245. *"About a family of Lakenkhel (Pashtun) nomads and farmers and their patterns of adjustment to changing political and economic conditions in northeastern Afghanistan."* [From the review by Bahram Tavakokian, *AA* 86:806–807, 1984.]

Sons of Namatjira (1975) 47 min. Curtis Levy (DI), Geoffrey Burton (CA), Australian Institute of Aboriginal Studies (PR). Dist: AISA. *Keith Namatjira and his relatives live on the outskirts of Alice Springs in the Northern Territory, producing landscapes for the local art and tourist market in the style established by their famous kinsman, Albert Namatjira. Although they live in squalid conditions, their work is much sought after—and it becomes the chief weapon in their struggle as dispossessed people to assert themselves in a world not of their choosing. In a sense, this film is a grim comedy about race relations: on the inability of two cultures to communicate except in dollars and cents, and of the frail hopes, frustrations, and hardened maneuvering on both sides.* Relevant anthropological literature: John von Sturmer, "Talking with Aborigines." *AISA Newsletter* no. 15, March 1981.

Sons of Shiva (Pleasing God Series) 27 min. R. Gardner and A. Ostor (FM). Dist: CPI FR$50, FS$495, VS$279. *The fourth day annual Gajan festival of Shiva, the Great Lord and God of destruction, is seen along with the ritual practices as participants rise to a climax of trance and a merging with divinity. The devotees voluntarily renounce everyday life to be "Sons of Shiva," emulating the god's practices and craving his favor. Also recorded is the unique singing of Bauls, an order of ecstatic, wandering monks.*

Sons of the Moon (1984) 25 min. Dierdre LaPin and Francis Speed (DI). Dist: UCEMC FR$45, FS$500, VS$195. *The Ngas, who live in Nigeria's Jos Plateau, believe the moon governs the growth of crops and schedules all important human events, including the symbolic rite of passage of boys into manhood. This unusual film, told from the point of view of an Ngas bard, traces the moon's influence on Ngas work and thought through an entire growing season.* [Reviewed by Stella B. Silverstein, *AA* 88:527–528, 1986. John W. Adams, *SBF* 21:46, 1985.]

Sophia and Her People [Reviewed in *VISA* 4:81, 1991.]

Sophia's People—Eventful Lives (1985) 37 min. Peter Loizos (FM). Dist: Peter Loizos, Anthropology Department, London School of Economics, Houghton Street, London, WC2A 2AE England. *"Sophia and her family are refugees, Greek Cypriots displaced by the turmoil of 1974 when Turkish troops invaded and occupied the northern part of this Mediterranean island.... About the horrors of war—personal tragedies and disruptions whose effects cannot be erased by time or material sucess."* [From the review by Peter S. Allen, *AA* 90:782, 1988.] Includes teaching notes.

Soro (1968) 25 min. H. Davis and C.E. Hoppen (FM). Dist: PSU(PCR). *In the wet season, the nomadic Fulani of Nigeria establish large camps near Sokoto, a Hausa town. Hausa supply musicians and an audience for dancing by both men and women. In "soro," a two-time flogging of the right pectoral muscle, a boy becomes a man by showing his ability to withstand pain. Fulani display of bravery is to be noted not only by their own young girls, but by the Hausa people.* [Reviewed by Michael M. Horowitz, *AA* 72:970–972, 1970.] Suggested supplement: Cyprian Ekwensi, *Burning Grass: A Story of the Fulani of Northern Nigeria.* Heinemann Education Books Ltd., London, 1962.

Sosua (1981) 30 min. Harriet Taub and Harry Kafka (FM). Dist: Sosua-Sol Productions, 84 Booraen Ave., Jersey City, NJ 07307; (201) 963-7859, FR$58, FS$450. *In 1938, "Rafael Trujillo of the Dominican Republic, opened his country to people fleeing Nazi Germany.... Of the Jews he took in, 705 settled on a northern coastal estate.... The settlement has grown into a successful meat and dairy cooperative and hotel. It employs hundreds of Dominicans from the surrounding area and boasts the only union and highest wages in the country."* The film examines this community. [From the review by Faye Ginsburg, *AA* 87:741–747, 1985.]

The Soul of Rice (1983) 55 min. William R. Geddes (FM, AN). Dist: OWF FS$850, VS$375. *"A visual chronicle of the successive ritual activites connected with planting and harvesting a rice crop."* [From the review by Robert Gardner, *AA* 89:265–267, 1987.]

Souna Kouma (La nostalgie de Souna) (Nostalgia of Souna) (1975) 30 min. Jean Rouch (DI), Centre National de la Recherche Scientifique, Comité du Film Ethnographique (PR). Dist: CFE; DER. *A funeral ritual for a priest who died in January 1975 in Niamey, Niger.*

Sound of Rushing Water (1973) 40 min. Dist: UNI; Pitt. *The Shuar people (at one time known as "headhunter" Indians) recount their centuries-long resistance to the armed might of Inca and Spanish empires and tell of their present efforts to maintain their cultural identity and traditional way of life in the face of colonizing influences and pressures for social integration from today's Latin American republics. The Shuar have created a film essay from their own experience. Their purpose is to explain themselves to themselves, and to others, in their own terms, in their own language, through their own life and artistry.* Related reading: Michael J. Harner, *The Jivaro: People of the Sacred Waterfalls*. Garden City, NJ, 1973. "Jivaro Souls." *AA* 64, 1962. [Dorice Tentchoff]

Sourwood Mountain Dulcimers (1976) 28 min. Gene DuBey (PR). Dist: APPAL FR$50, FS$475, VS$225. *I. D. Stamper appears on the film "hamming it up."* [From the review by Melanie L. Sovine, *AA* 89:522–525, 1987.]

A South African Farm 51 min. Paul Laufer (DI). Dist: DER FR$70, VR$40, FS$700, VS$400. *After a five-year absence from South Africa, Paul Laufer returned to his country to film a microcosm of a society in turmoil, a society in which whites are driven by fears of loss of privilege, and blacks are torn between the material benefits of white "protection" and the desire to be free from oppression. In a time of great concern about South Africa, it is especially important to understand the everyday workings of apartheid and the perspectives of blacks and whites caught in the system. We meet and listen to the voices of diverse men and women who reflect upon black/white relations. The black people on the farm express opinions about homelands, dependency, and the quality of life. The overwhelming impression, however, is of wariness and silencing: the power of this film lies in what is not—what cannot be said.*

The South-East Nuba (1982) 60 min. Melissa Llewelyn-Davies (DI), BBC (PR). Dist: FI R$90, VS$475. *"Its purpose is to counter the image of the Nuba presented by Leni Riefenstahl in her various photographic essays. To this end the film places the Nuba in cultural perspective within the greater Sudan, and ... those very cultural features that Riefenstahl found so visually compelling—the body painting, scarification, fighting sports, and dance of the Nuba—are also clearly placed within a larger ethnographic context."* [From the review by Deborah L. Mack, *AA* 88:528–529, 1986.]

South Sea Island Life: The Dolphin Hunters (1970) 19 min. Dist: IUAVC FR$9.75. *Shows various aspects of life in the Solomon Islands, emphasizing the influence of the sea on the life of the Island people. Depicts the making of shell money, cooking with hot stones, selling and bartering at the market, the harvesting of nuts, and various pagan Cérémonies. Records the importance of the dolphin and its meat to the mountain people.*

South Seas (1930s) 67 min. Dist: FCE FR$85, FS$450.

The Southeastern Ceremonial Complex Dist: POR. Set of 86 slides, $135. [Reviewed by Peter S. Allen, *ARCH* 42(5):74–75, 1986. George H. Odell, *SBF* 27:275, 1991.]

Spanish Influence in the United States (Cultural Influences Series) (1948) 10 min. Dist: IUAVC FR$6.50. *Shows the Spanish influence on American dress, language, customs, architecture, and religion by comparing Spanish culture with American culture. A map shows the spread of Spanish settlements to Florida, the Southwest, and California.*

Spear and Sword: A Payment of Bridewealth on the Island of Roti (Roti Series) (1990) 25 min. James J. Fox, Patsy Asch, and Timothy Asch (DI), Australian National University and DER (PR). Dist: DER FR$55, VR$35, FS$550, VS$275. *Focuses on the negotiations between representatives of two families during a payment of bridewealth. The film begins with an excerpt from a traditional chant about the origin of bridewealth when a daughter of the Sun and Moon married the Lord of the Sea, the Hunter of the Ocean. A brief explanation, over slides, follows. The strength of the film lies in the record of the conversation between the negotiating parties, that at times seems to follow prescribed forms and at times seems to be a free arena for participants to express humor and to manipulate one another. Politics, ritual, and personality intermingle. The film ends when a renowned ritual chanter is asked to recount the history of the first payment of bridewealth.* [Reviewed by Alice G. Dewey, *AA* 93(3):775–777, 1991.]

Spencer, Sir Walter Baldwin (1860–1929) (see *Fieldwork* in the Strangers Abroad Series)

Spend It All 41 min. Les Blank (FM). Dist: FF. [Reviewed by Roger Abrahams, *AA* 76:206, 1974. David Evans, *JAF* 89(353):390, 1976.]

Spirit in a Landscape: The People Beyond 56 min. Dist: CBC VS$109, order #X4B-74-03. *The Inuit of the Canadian Arctic are profiled at work and at play.*

Spirit of Ethnography (1974) 18 min. O. Michael Watson (FM, AN). Dist: PSU FR$10.50, FS$140. *A satire on the basic processes of data gathering in cultural anthropology. Chronicles the field research of a fictitious legendary ethnographer embarking on his first field experience. Humorous view of anthropologists making fun of themselves and some of the classic ethnographic films.* [Reviewed by Gregory A. Finnegan, *AA* 78:926, 1976.]

The Spirit of Kuna Yala 59 min. Andrew Young and Susan Todd (DI), Archipelago Films (PR). Dist: FL VR$75, VS$445. *A lively portrait of a native people determined to survive the encroachment of the Western world, this film features the Kuna Indians of Panama's San Blas Islands as they unite to protect their rainforest homeland, Kuna Yala, and the tradition it inspires. Told entirely in the words of the Kunas, the film is a plea to care for the earth from a people who have a deep relationship with the land. A tragic result of the rapid destruction of tropical rainforests has been the extinction of countless indigenous peoples. The Kuna Indians are a striking exception to this scenario. We learn how they reject the lure of westernization and reaffirm their own traditional values. The issues of conservation and cultural survival are complex, with no simple solutions. But this film offers a hopeful message that the timeless wisdom of indigenous peoples has something vital to offer the West-*

ern world. [Reviewed by Joel Sherzer, *AA* 94(1):280–281, 1992.]

Spirit of the Hunt (1982) 29 min. Thomas Howe Associates (PR). Dist: CPI FR$45, FS$425, VS$275. *"Gets to the issue of the persistence of Native American spirituality in the modern industrialized world. The context is a modern wintertime bison hunt in Canada. The hunters are Native Americans . . . seeking not only bison but self and cultural identity. The fate of the bison herds becomes a loose analogy to the fate of the Native Americans of the 19th century."* [From the review by Robert L. Bee, *AA* 90:235–237, 1988. Reviewed by John S. Wozniak, *SBF* 21:46, 1985.]

The Spirit Possession of Alejandro Mamani 30 min. Hubert Smith (DI). Dist: FL R$55, FS$425, VS$375. *The prize-winning documentary on an 81-year-old Aymara Indian has become a classic for cross-cultural studies on aging, psychological disorders, healing, and suicide. As Mamani struggles with the losses that come with aging, he believes himself possessed by evil spirits. Unable to find a cure, he is drawn inexorably to suicide.*

Spirit Speaking Through 57 min. Dist: CBC VS$109, order #X4K-81-01. *Filmed on location, this program introduces seven native artists who form part of a Canadian art phenomenon, the 25-year-old school of woodland art. Primarily self-taught, these artists defied native taboos against depicting private spiritual rituals in their work.*

The Spirit That Moves 27 min. Dist: CBC VS$69, order #Y8L-87-05. *This film focuses on the remarkable story of the native inhabitants of Alkali Lake in B.C. Sixteen years ago, every man, woman, and child over 10 years of age was an alcoholic. The death rate was four times the national average, and the native culture was being destroyed. Now they have practically eradicated alcohol from the community and even made a film,* The Honour of All, *that has helped native people across North America to battle the scourge of alcohol. Excerpts from this film reveal how the population uses traditional ceremonies and the guidance of elders to ensure a healthy, constructive future for Alkali Lake.*

The Spirit Within 51 min. Gil Cardinal and Wil Campbell (DI). Dist: NFB R$80, FS$775, VS$350. *The smell of burning sweet grass and the traditional spirit cleansing ceremonies of the American Indian sweat lodge can now take place in an exercise yard of a penitentiary. But it is only since the late 1970s and early 1980s that Native American inmates have had their spiritual ceremonies recognized within the penal system. The film takes us inside the prison walls to introduce a rehabilitation program that is truly unique. Through the use of spiritual ceremonies and custom, American Indian inmates learn to forgive themselves and to deal with their own guilt—things not on the normal prison agenda. For them, the sweat lodge and the pipe become the tools to break the cycle of poverty, alienation, and violence.*

Spirits of Defiance: The Mangbetu People of Zaire (1989) 59 min. Jeremy Marre (FM). Dist: Enid Schildkrout, Department of Anthropology, American Museum of Natural History, New York, NY 10024; (212) 769-5432. *Part of the BBC Series,* Under the Sun, *to accompany the American Museum of Natural History exhibition,* African Reflections. *"It displays Mangbetu culture and society as largely intact from the precolonial period, and the Mangbetu people as having a self-conscious interest in retaining their cultural forms and identity."* [From the review by Ivan Karp, *AA* 93(2):520–521, 1991.]

A Spiritual Ordering: The Metal Arts of Africa (1983) 20 min. R. F. Thompson (DI), African-American Institute, New York (PR). Dist: IUAVC FR$35, VS$200, order #RVU-1159. *The film introduces examples of major metal artifacts and sculptures from Western and Central Africa. It traces important themes such as the equestrian figure and Zoomorphic representations of the snake. It also illustrates representation of the theme of possession among the Yoruba as shown in a bronze mask from the Lower Niger. Rare footage taken in 1926 by the Swedish missionary Ohrneman, documents iron forging techniques practiced by Congolese craftsmen. It also shows the lost wax process as used by Ebre people of the Ivory Coast.*

Spite: An African Prophet-Healer 54 min. J.P. Colleyn and Catherine De Clippel (PR). Dist: FL VR$75, VS$445. *People from all over the Ivory Coast seek out Prophet-Healers for treatment of their medical and emotional problems. Some of these ailments may be caused by the stress of cultural change. Often Western medicine can not cure them. This film focuses on Sebim Odjo, who draws upon Muslim, Christian, and traditional African beliefs in his healing ceremonies. He moderates disputes, tracks down the sources of illness, and uses his powers to heal. We see a water cure used on a patient ill with spite.* [Reviewed by Constance R. Sutton, *AA* 89:267–268, 1987. Winifred Lambrecht, *SBF* 20:312, 1985.]

Sprout Wings and Fly (1982) 30 min. Les Blank, Cece Conway, and Alice Gerrard (FM). Dist: FF FR$65, FS$500. *This presentation of a music-maker "involve[s] what may be considered personal intimacies. . . . Tommy Jarrell tells of his dream of talking with his best friend who is now dead."* [From the review by Melanie L. Sovine, *AA* 89:522–525, 1987.]

Stairways to the Mayan Gods 28 min. Joseph Campbell (H). Dist: HFF FR$35, FS$395, VS$89. *Professor Joseph Campbell explores the mythology and spectacular cities of the ancient Maya of Mexico and Central America.*

Standing Alone 58 min. Colin Low (DI). Dist: NFB R$80, FS$775, VS$150. *Pete Standing Alone is a Native American caught between the 19th-century horse culture of the Plains Indians and the politics of the modern oil hungry industrial era. As a young man, he was more a part of the white man's culture than his own. However, confronted with the realization that his children knew very little about their origins, he became determined to pass down to them the customs and traditions of his ancestors. Spanning 25 years in Pete's life, this powerful autobiographical study moves from his early days as an oilrig roughneck, rodeo rider and cowboy, to his present concerns with preserving the spiritual heritage of his people.*

Stanley and Livingstone 12 min. Dist: FHS VS$69.95, order #DH-1744. *Dr. David Livingstone, a Scottish explorer and missionary, disappeared on an expedition into deepest Africa. The American journalist, Henry Morton Stanley was sent to Africa to find the famous man and bring back the story of the century. Stanley found Livingstone alive and also found a new career for himself. After Livingstone's death, Stanley continued the explorations into the heart of Africa and was the first white to see the Congo River.*

Starting Fire with Gunpowder (As Long As the Rivers Flow Series) (1991) 59 min. David Poisey and William Hansen (DI), James Cullingham and Peter Raymont (PR). Dist: FRIF VR$75, VS$390. *The control of the media as a means of Native self-determination is the topic explored in this film. The program chronicles the origins and achievements of the Inuit Broadcasting Corporation (IBC), a model for aboriginal broadcasters the world over. Through documentary, drama, animation, and children's programs, the IBC helps keep Inuit culture and language alive. Its directors and producers make compelling television on ever shrinking budgets. Their story is told by Inuk filmmaker Ann Neetijuk Hanson, who "noticed that the first thing that happens in a revolution is the take-over of the radio and television stations." The film examines how Inuit television will play a critical role in the creation of a modern Inuit nation.*

State of Shock: A Native People Loses Its Heritage 55 min. David Bradbury (PR). Dist: FL VR$75, VS$445. *Like the Native Americans, the Australian Aborigines have lost their land, and along with it, their sense of pride. Cut off from their heritage, they turn their anger inward and drift toward alcohol and violence. Alwyn Peters, a 22-year-old Aborigine living on the reservation, stabbed his girlfriend to death in a drunken rage. In the past, such incidents were dismissed as "just another black death," but this murder, by some historical quirk, raised national consciousness. This film makes a universal statement about dispossessed people everywhere.*

Statement by Enrique Camargo, Director of Incora-Colombia (1963) 9 min. The Land Tenure Center, University of Wisconsin (PR). Dist: UW. *Director Camargo explains the role of INCORA in administering government lands, executing Law 200, the colonization of new lands, land reclamation, and supervised credit programs.*

Statement by Milciades Chavez, Then Serving in Incora as Assistant to the Technical Director-Colombia (1963) 8 min. The Land Tenure Center, University of Wisconsin (PR). Dist: UW. *Assistant Director Chavez tells how INCORA makes detailed investigations of people and resources before beginning parcelization projects. He points out some considerations in carrying out such projects.*

The Stephens Family, Villisca, Iowa (see Six American Families Series)

Step Style (1980) 30 min. Alan Lomax (AN). Dist: UCEMC FR$38, FS$470, VS$355. *Audiences react with great excitement to the nimble stepping of dancers and athletes, because their skills represent a triumph in a lifelong and universal problem area for the human biped—maintaining an erect posture on two legs against the constant pull of gravity. Most dances exhibit a special style of step, and many consist almost exclusively of fancy footwork. Step Style demonstrates how each main zone of culture favors a distinctive use of the leg and foot in its dances. For example, ground-hugging, sliding, and digging is most common in black Africa and the tropics, while a controlled and embroidered step is most frequent in the Far East. The various step styles illustrated are related to productive activities, social structure, and so forth. The longitudinal foot-crossing step common in Eurasia, for example, mirrors the heel-to-toe stride of the plowman; dances that emphasize lower leg agility and the pointing of heel and toe are shown to be typical of highly stratified, socially complex cultures, where lower leg activity is crucial in establishing social distance and levels.* See related films *Dance and Human History* and *Palm Play*. [Reviewed by Malcolm Farmer, SBF 17:99, 1981.]

Sticks and Stones Will Build a House (1971) 30 min. Richard Borstadt (DI, PR). Dist: IU FR$12.50, FS$360. *This film traces the development of Indian architecture in southwestern United States. Initially, shelter was in the form of crude pit-houses. Later, builders began using masonry construction, and, finally, during the great Pueblo period, building sophisticated apartment-type complexes housing as many as 2,000 tenants. Early attempts to explore remaining ruins are seen in film footage photographed during archaeological expeditions in the 1920s.* [Reviewed by Susan Wilcox and David Wilcox, AA, 78:372, 1976.]

The Stone Carvers (1984) 28 min. Marjorie Hunt and Paul Wagner (FM). Dist: DCL FR$55, FS$535, VS$150. *An ethnographic record of stone carving. "The viewer is able to get the distinct flavor of the culture of the work of stone carving and the love the traditional carvers held for their craft."* [From the review by Linda Bennett, AA 88:1047–1048, 1986.]

Stone Knapping in Modern Turkey (1974) 12 min. Jaques and Louis Bordaz (PR). Dist: PSU FR$9, FS$100. *Techniques used by modern Turkish flint knappers to obtain blades from a piece of flint. Method of direct percussion applied to the flint nucleus to strike a blade. Local farmers use the flint blades in threshing sledges. A modern ethnographic example of production that will provide insights into past technologies.* [Reviewed by Linda Braidwood, Robert Braidwood, and Jane Macrae, AA 77:693–694, 1975. Susanna R. Katz and Paul R. Katz, ARCH 34(1):60, 1981.]

Stonehenge: Mystery in the Plain (1984) 24 min. Dist: EBEC FR$49, FS$490, VS$390. *"The core of the film is a discussion of the evidence for ancient astronomy at Stonehenge, starting with the slightly inaccurate observation that the Heel Stone marks the 'exact' point of mid-summer sunrise as viewed from the center of the monument and continuing with a fairly detailed description of the conclusions reached by Gerald Hawkins and Alexander Thom concerning other astronomical alignments at the site. This section is marred primarily by an unquestioning acceptance of their analysis, though by the time the film was produced both archaeologists and others involved in archaeoastronomical* *research had pointed out a number of flaws."* [From the review by Ronald Hicks, *ARCH* 40(1):76–77, 1987.]

Stones of Eden 25 min. William A. Furman (FM, WR), Mel Carlson (WR). Dist: CRM/MH order #407427, FR$33, FS$295. *"The poignant story of Hasan, an impoverished wheat farmer living in the Hindu Kush mountains of Afganistan... dissects poverty and bares its parts to the viewer... follows the day-to-day struggle of Hasan and his family to eke out a living. We see the immutability of his predicament as he tries to wrest his family from the grips of poverty. Armed only with tools that harken back to the early Iron Age, Hasan must cope with the vagaries of uncertain weather, the death of one of his oxen, and all the other impediments that keep his family below the subsistence level. And, as a final disappointment, he must see his son's education sacrificed, dashing any hopes he has for his future."* [Reviewed by William Trousdale, *AA* 70:656, 1968.]

Stop Destroying America's Past (1968) 22 min. Al Binford (DI), Stuart Struever (AN). Dist: CRM/MH FR$27, FS$335; IUAVC FR$7.75, FS$210. *A television documentary alerting audiences to the senseless destruction of America's past, the 14,000 year history of man on this continent. The film focuses on a Northwestern University archaeological field party undertaking an emergency excavation in a 1,000-year-old crematory under extreme weather conditions of cold and snow. Working against time, the film portrays the hazards and excitement of life on an archaeological expedition.* [Reviewed by Jeremy Sabloff, *AA* 73:591, 1973.]

The Storms of the Amazon (see The Decade of Destruction Series)

THE STORY OF ENGLISH SERIES Dist: IMS-UW.

- An English Speaking World
- Mother Tongue
- A Muse of Fire
- The Guid Scots Tongue
- Black on White
- Pioneers, O Pioneers!
- The Muvver Tongue
- The Loaded Weapon
- Next Year's Words: A Look into the Future

Story of the Wasa (1981) 25 min. Anders Wahlgren (DI). Dist: Swedish Information Service, 825 Third Avenue, New York, NY 10022; (212) 751-5900, free loan. *"Features a graphic artistic account of the 1627 sinking of a magnificent Swedish warship during its maiden voyage out of Stockholm harbor. Commissioned by King Gustavus II, the 18-foot square-rigged Wasa was to be the flagship of the Swedish fleet. Questions were immediately raised about what caused the disaster, and the Royal Inquiry that followed is reenacted in the film by actors dressed in costumes of the day."* [From the review by Eugene L. Sterud, *ARCH* 37(5):70, 1984.]

Straight Up Rappin' (1992) 28 min. Green Room Productions (PR). Dist: FL VR$55, VS$295. *This film "provides a very good sampling of the content of much of rap. There is even a class or racial clash presented between the families of "Leave It to Beaver" and Malcolm X.... They are highly effective in showing how the content of rap depicts life in black urban America."* [From the review by David J. Pratto, *SBF* 28:275, 1992.]

Strange Beliefs: Sir Edward Evans-Pritchard (1902–1973) (Strangers Abroad Series) 52 min. Dist: FHS FR$75, VS$159, order #XD-2546. *University professor Sir Edward Evans-Pritchard taught that Western ideas have many features in common with other cultures. He was the first trained anthropologist to do work in Africa, where he lived among the Azande and studied their belief in witchcraft; later, he worked with the Nuer tribe in the Sudan. His work on witchcraft found philosophers asking what could be considered rational thinking in any society; his study of tribal organization was intriguing to political theorists; and his attention to the sophisticated religious sentiments of so-called primitive peoples has had a strong influence on theologians.*

Strange Relations (Millennium: Tribal Wisdom and the Modern World Series) (1992) 1 hour. David Maybury-Lewis (H), Hans Zimmer (MU). Dist: PBS VS$49.95, order #MILL-102-RCDC. *How do we balance our personal desires for romance with our societal need for stable marriages? The video explores how marriages in tribal societies from the valleys of Nepal and the plains of Niger challenge Western ideas and sensibilities yet are moral in the tribal world. Through scenes of a Toronto couple's marriage, it explores the uncertainties that characterize marriages in Western societies and shows how Western attitudes toward love and marriage were changed in the Middle Ages. In the end, we understand how individuals can discover a balance between personal desires and social needs in the context of a loving and nurturing family.* [Reviewed by Patricia A. Gwartney-Gibbs, *SBF* 28:213, 1992.]

STRANGERS ABROAD SERIES See descriptions under individual film titles:

- The Shackles of Tradition: Franz Boas (1852–1942)
- Strange Beliefs: Sir Edward Evans-Pritchard (1902–1973)
- Everything Is Relatives: William Rivers (1864–1922)
- Off the Verandah: Bronislaw Malinowski (1884–1942)
- Coming of Age: Margaret Mead (1901–1978)
- Fieldwork: Sir Walter Baldwin Spencer (1860–1929)

Strangers and Kin: A History of the Hillbilly Image (1984) 58 min. Herb E. Smith (DI). Dist: APPAL FR$90, FS$825, VS$400. *Using funny, sometimes poignant examples, this film shows the development and effect of stereotypes in a region where technological change collides with tradition. The film traces the evolution of the "hillbilly" image through Hollywood films, network news and entertainment shows, dramatic renderings of popular literature, and interviews with contemporary Appalachians. These demonstrate how stereotypes are created, reinforced, and often used to rationalize exploitation. Finally, it shows us how a people embrace modernization without becoming "strangers to their kin."*

The Struggle 35 min. Carl Gilfillan (FM). Dist: Learning Inst. of North Carolina, 1006 Lamond Ave., Durham, NC 27701. *An African-American community in North Carolina.* [Reviewed by Charles Keil, *AA* 71:1234, 1969.]

The Struggling People (1987) 30 min. Rachael Lyon (PR), Barbara Pyle (DI). Dist: FI VR$50, VS$69. *"Set in a Zimbabwean village.... The 'people' in this case are predominantly women, who 'struggle' to ensure sufficient land and economic opportunities for the next generation. The struggle is depicted as both ecological ... and demographic."* [From the review by Ellen Messer, *AA* 92:556–558, 1990.]

STUDIES IN NIGERIAN DANCE Frances Speed (FM), Peggy Harper (CON), Universities of Ife and Ibadan (PR). Dist: CFS Ltd. *Dance study film with synchronized sound and no commentary.* Suggested supplement: Peggy Harper, "The Kambari People and their Dances." *Odu: A Journal of West African Studies,* New Series, no. 5. Oxford University Press, Ibadan, Nigeria, 1971. [Reviewed by Charles Keil, *AA* 71:1234, 1969.]

• **Tiv Women: The Tsough Dance** (No. 1) (1966) 11 min. FS$48. *Shows three complete variations of the Tsough dance. This is a team dance traditional to the women of the Southern Tiv, which is performed on important social occasions and is accompanied by an agabande drum ensemble.* Suggested supplement: Peggy Harper, *Tsough, A Tiv Dance. African Notes, Bulletin of the Institute of African Studies,* University of Ibadan, Nigeria 1970.

• **Miango Dance** (No. 2) (1966) 11 min. FS$48. *Five dances of the male dance ensemble of the Irigwe people living in the Miango village area of the Jos Plateau. The dances are performed to drumming and songs, the texts of which indicated the original function of the dances as an integral part of agricultural festivals.* Suggested supplement: Peggy Harper, *Miango Dances.* 1968. (Paper to accompany film).

• **Kambari** (No. 3) (1970) 11 min. FS$96. *The Kambari people of Yauri Emirate show three typical dance styles. The first two sections of the film were shot in a village in the Yelwa area, show dances celebrating a capture-marriage. The following four sections show dance groups performing at a social occasion in the town of Gerbi on the River Niger.*

Style Wars (1983) 69 min. Tony Silver and Henry Chalfant (PR), Tony Silver (DI). Dist: NDF2 FR$125, FS$875, VS$525. *A study of the secret world and work of the New York City graffiti artists. An attempt is made to review the art within a larger cultural framework—every conceivable aspect of the lives of the teenaged artists, who are part of the so-called "hip-hop" street culture—has been touched on. We learn of the history and evolution of the art form, we hear the teenagers themselves discuss the various styles and nuances of the subway graffiti; we are taken through the tunnels and dark stations of the New York underground to view hundred of cars; we are even treated to an art gallery opening in which graffiti done by some of these same young artists on canvas are sold. Dozens of artists are interviewed, telling how they became interested in this form of expression and relating tales of braving arrest and injury. In addition, public officials and New Yorkers who oppose the "vandalism" are interviewed.* [Reviewed by Nora Groce, *AA* 87:751–752, 1985.]

Sucking Doctor (1964) 45 min. William R. Heick and Gordon Mueller (FM). Dist: UCEMC FR$55, VS$295. *A remarkable documentary that presents, in its entirety, the second and final night of a curing ceremony held by the Kashia group of the Southwestern Pomo Indians. On the first night, while the shaman was in a hypnotic trance, the patient's pain was located and the germs removed from his body. The shaman effected this by means of the spiritual instrument she possesses in her throat, and finally the pain was removed, in the form of a quartz crystal. The Indian doctor is Essie Parrish (her native name is Piwoya), the only Southwestern Pomo sucking doctor still practicing this ancient form of medicine. In this ceremony, the shaman is assisted by four singers, three female and one male. This film is the complete research documentary; Pomo Shaman, a shortened version with repetitive elements eliminated, is also available.*

Sudan's Pyramids, Azandi's Dream (1981) 58 min. Horace Jenkins (FM). Dist: New Images VR$95, FS$550, VS$550. *General coverage of past and present Sudan.* [Reviewed by Richard Lobban *AA* 85:490–491, 1983.]

Sudesha (As Women See It Series) 30 min. Deepa Dhanraj (DI), Faust Films (PR). Dist: WMM FR$60, VR$50, FS$600, VS$225. *From India's leading woman director comes this haunting story of an Indian woman and the contradictions that shape her life. Sudesha lives in the foothills of the Himalayas—an area where the forests have been systematically destroyed by timber merchants. Challenging the rules of Indian society, Sudesha and other women of the region play an active role in the "chipko" protest movement founded to protect the trees and their environment.*

The Sugar Film (1981) 57 min. Frank Lisciandro (FM), John Rubenstein (NA). Dist: PyrF FR$75, FS$695. *"Guides viewers through a tour of the cultural, economic, nutritional, and psychological conditions and effects of high sugar consumption."* [From the review by Carole M. Counihan, *AA* 87:222–223, 1985.]

Sugar and Spice (1974) 32 min. R. Eric Breitbart, Vicki Breitbart, Alan Jacobs (FM). Dist: Odeon Film. *Gender typing in America.* [Reviewed by Nancy Chodorow, *AA* 79:209, 1977.]

Summer of the Loucheux (1982) 27 min. Graydon McCrea (DI). Dist: Tamarack Films, P.O. Box 315, Franklin Lakes, NY 07417; (201) 891-8240, R$50, FS$475, VS$375; NDF R$50, FS$490, VS$390. *In this film, four generations of a northern Athabaskan family maintain traditional summer camp skills that have changed little since contact with modern civilization. It explores Native American values and the critical relationship between traditional skills and self worth, an issue relevant to people everywhere. The remarkable beauty of the north and the rich mosaic of Loucheux camp life blend with rare archival photos to create a film that documents the living heritage of northern Native*

Americans. [Reviewed by Margaret Stott, *AA* 87:492, 1985. Simon D. Messing, *SBF* 20:312, 1985.]

The Sun Dagger (1982) 60 min. Anna Sofaer (DI). Dist: Bullfrog Films, Oley, PA 19547; (215) 779-8226, FR$95, FS$850, VS$450. *Chaco Canyon, New Mexico. "Tells the story of an intriguing discovery in southwestern rock art from a highly personal point of view."* [From the review by Evan Hadingham, *AA* 86:232–233, 1984. Reviewed by John B Carlson, *ARCH* 37(2):78–79, 1984.]

The Sun Kingdom of Yucatan (1984) 20 min. Hugh Johnston and Suzanne Johnston (FM). Dist: Hugh and Suzanne Johnston, 16 Valley Rd., Princeton, NJ 08540; (609) 924-7505, FS$395, VS$340. *"A poetic evocation of Yucatan's people, history and geography, a close-up of one of the world's magic places where a cultural heritage of Maya civilization lives on in Indian villages."* (Mrs. Johnston quoted in the Princeton packet, March (1984). *"The twin themes structuring this . . . are contrast and continuity."* [From the review by Wendy Ashmore, *AA* 88:273–274, 1986. Reviewed by Gretchen Anderson Gwynne, *AA* 38(6):68, 1985.]

Sunken Treasure (1972) 22 min. Jacques Cousteau (PR). Dist: ChF FR$40, FS$380. *"Cousteau and his associates seek Spanish treasure ships in the Silver Banks of the Caribbean Sea. Although they make no effort to conceal their intention—the recovery of treasure—a popular audience could easily confuse their expedition, which uses all the equipment of underwater archaeology and has a pseudoscientific veneer, with scientific investigation. . . . Even more bothersome is the glorification of the '20th century treasure hunt.' "* [From the review by Rovert L. Hohlfelder, *ARCH* 36(1):62–64, 1983.]

Sunny Side of Life (1985) 56 min. Scott Faulkner, Anthony Slone, Jack Wright (DI). Dist: APPAL FR$90, FS$845, VS$400. *"We wanted to cut our mark on earth just like our foreparents did,"* says Joe Carter, who has helped his sister Janette revive the musical tradition of the original Carter Family of southwestern Virginia. Their parents, A. P. and Sara Carter, together with Sara's cousin Maybelle, influenced the development of old-time country music perhaps more than anyone else, but until Janette took the old Carter Store in Maces Spring, Virginia, and turned it into a music hall and gathering place, the Carter family legacy was all but gone from the valley. This is a film tribute to this musical legacy, to Janette, Joe, and all the other members of the Carter family, past and present, and their neighbors and friends, who love to make and hear music.

Sur les traces du renard pale (Tracking the Pale Fox: Studies on the Dogon) (1983) 48 min. Luc de Heusch (FM). Dist: Centre Bruxellois de l'Audio-visuel, 18 rue Joseph II 1040 Bruxelles, Belgium, FR$75, FS$450. *"A historical ethnography of Marcel Griaule, Germaine Dieterlen, and Jean Rouch doing ethnography among the Dogon of Mali. . . . Portrays the growth of a style of research as told by members of the tradition, by chronicling their research with the Dogon of Sanga, Mali, from the 1930's through the 1970's."* [From the review by Constance R. Sutton, *AA* 89:267–268, 1987.]

Los Sures (1984) 58 min. Diego Echeverria (FM). Dist: CG FR$100, FS$895, VS$595. *An urban documentary. "One of the poorest neighborhoods in New York City, Los Sures is the Hispanic section of Williamsburg, Brooklyn. . . . Portraits five of its residents, people who face life with remarkable courage and faith despite the grimness of the external reality they confront."* [From the review by Joan Turner, *AA* 87:985–987, 1985.]

Surname Viet Given Name Nam (1989) 108 min. Trinh T. Minh-ha (DI). Dist: WMM FR$225, FS$1500, VS$495. *Vietnamese-born Trinh T. Minh-ha's profoundly personal documentary explores the role of Vietnamese women historically and in contemporary society. Using dance, printed texts, folk poetry, and the words and experiences of Vietnamese women in Vietnam—both from North and South—and the United States, Trinh's film challenges official culture with the voices of women. A theoretically and formally complex work, this film explores the difficulty of translation, and themes of dislocation and exile, critiquing both traditional society and life since the war.* [Reviewed in *VISR* 6:65, 1990.]

The Survey (1973) Astrida R. Onat (DI). Dist: Sterling Educational Films. *Site survey techniques in the Skagit River Delta, Washington State.* [Reviewed by C. W. Clelow, Jr., and R. A. Cowan, *AA* 77:907, 1975.]

Survey of the Primates (1970) 38 min. D. Rumbaugh, A.H. Reisen, R. Lee (FM). Dist: Appleton-Century-Crofts, 440 Park Ave S., New York, NY 10016. [Reviewed by John Fleagle, *AA* 75:1990, 1973.]

Suzhou (The Cities in China Series) (1981) 28 min. Sue Yung Li and Shirley Sun (PR). Dist: UCEMC FR$45, FS$560, VS$295. *Known for centuries as the center of Chinese culture and aesthetics, this Yangzi delta city has often been called the Venice of the East because of its main canals and ridges. This poetic portrait of the city leads the viewer through markets and teahouses, sweet shops and bookstores, rice paddies and fish stalls, and two of Suzhou's exquisite gardens. Whether sensed in one of these fabled gardens, or evoked in the banter of elderly gentlemen taking tea together, a persistent devotion to basic moral values is shown to be intrinsic to Suzhou life.* [Reviewed by Robert Mishler, *SBF* 18:216, 1983.]

Swami Karunananda 28 min. Yavar Abbas (PR). Dist: CMC. *An Ashram in Rishikash on the Ganges.* [Reviewed by Janet Benson, *AA* 76:707, 1974.]

The Sweat of the Sun (see The Tribal Eye Series)

Swidden Horticulture among the Lacandon Maya (1986) 29 min. R. Jon McGee (PR). Dist: UCEMC VR$35, VS$345, order #37398. *Shows the subsistence cycle of the Lacandon Maya, who live in the rainforest of southeastern Chiapas in Mexico. Focusing on one family, the video follows each step of the four-month swidden (slash and burn) cycle through the successive phases of a horticultural season. All work is done by hand, using axes, digging sticks and machetes. The program illustrates the continuing importance of slash and burn horticulture in many parts of the world. It demonstrates the process by which the Lacandon* *provide abundant food supplies for themselves and at the same time maintain a harmony with their jungle environment.* Study guide available. [Reviewed by Jay Sokolovsky, AA 90:1040–1041, 1988.]

Tabu: A Story of the South Seas (1931) 82 min. F. W. Murnau and Robert Flaherty (DI). Dist: MLS VS$39.95, order #MILE005. *Filmed entirely in Tahiti, Tabu represented an unusual collaboration between legendary directors, Murnau and Flaherty. Two lovers are doomed by a tribal edict decreeing that the girl is "tabu" to all men. While the lovers' flight from judgment and the ultimate power of the tabu are reminiscent of Marnau's expressionist films, Tabu is all open air and sunlight—the brilliant tropical light sparkles on the ocean and glistens on the beautiful young bodies of the men and women.* [Reviewed by John W. Adams, AA 81:739–40, 1979.]

Tahtonka—Plains Indian Buffalo Culture (1963–66) 28 min. Nauman Films, Custer, South Dakota (PR). Dist: UILL; MINN. *The purpose of this film is to teach early American history and to stress the fact that the senseless extermination of the buffalo led to hardships in the economy and to the virtual extinction of the Plains Indians culture. Tahtonka is the Sioux Indian word for the bull buffalo. For most of the Indians who lived on the North American continent, the buffalo was an important source of food. For all of the Plains Indian tribes, the buffalo became the center of their culture. Tahtonka is the story of the buffalo period and the Plains Indians' dependence upon the buffalo from the prehorse days to the time of the Wounded Knee tragedy in 1890, an era representing over 300 years in early American history. When the Spanish first saw buffalo on this continent in 1521, they numbered more than 16 million—but by 1890 there were no more than 300 in all of North America. It was the near extinction of a species—killed for their hides, for their meat, for "sport." Buffalo extermination was the unwritten policy in the winning of the West. When the great buffalo herds were gone, the Plains Indians way of life was also gone. In 1889, the Ute Indian named Wovoka had a vision that spread rapidly and developed into a religion known as the Ghost Dance Cult. As a last hope, it was embraced by many Indian tribes. Through a ritual dance, the Indians perceived a new world where their loved ones would return, the white man would be covered up with earth, and the buffalo would roam once again in abundance. Although the Ghost Dance Cult was not militant, an unfortunate incident brought on the ill-fated massacre at Wounded Knee in 1890. For the Indians, this was the end of even their dream that the buffalo—and their former ways of life—would return.* [Reviewed by W. W. Newcomb, AA 70:184, 1968.]

T'ai Chi Ch'uan 8 min. Tom Davenport (FM). Dist: Tom Davenport Films, Pearlstone, Delaplane, VA 22025. [Reviewed by Jerome Halberstadt, AA 74:1590, 1972.]

Taiga Nomads: The School and Village (1991) 50 min. Heimo Lappalainen and Jouko Aaltonen (FM). Dist: Fin Image, Kansakoulukatu 1B, SF 00100 Helsinki, Finland; 358-0-694-3344; fax 358-0-685-1684. *Filmed during the last year of Soviet rule, this film takes a look at the impact of Russian values and beliefs on the Evenki, a nomadic reindeer herding community of Siberia.*

Tajimoltik—Five Days without Name (1978) 30 min. Georges Payrastre (CA), Claudine Viallon (SR), Okexon (PR). Dist: DER FR$35, FS$375. *The Mayan calendar is comprised of 18 months of 20 days each, a total of 360 days. The five remaining days are the days of carnival, Chaikin, or "Five Days without Name." When the Spanish Dominicans came to evangelize the Indians, they inserted the Catholic Holy Week into these five days of transition. Catholic influence is also responsible for the naming of the Indians who are in charge of the organization and cost of the carnival. They are called "Passions" in memory of the Crucifixion of Christ. The film follows the carnival activities and depicts the varied influences which non-native religions have had on Mayan ritual and beliefs. The propensity of the new Mayan year will depend on the success of these "Five Days without Name."*

Takeover (1980) 90 min. David and Judith MacDougall (FM), Francis Yunkaporta (NA), Australian Institute of Aboriginal Studies (PR). Dist: AIAS. *In March 1978, the State of Queensland moved to take over control of the Aurukun Aboriginal Reserve from the mission organization that had administered it since early in the century. Although it claimed church incompetence as the reason for the takeover, the Queensland State Government was widely accused of seeking easier access to the rich bauxite deposits on the Reserve and of attempting to close down the Aurukun outstation movement, through which Aborigines were reasserting their culture and their rights to traditional Aboriginal land. The church and the Aborigines complained bitterly and soon received support from the Federal Government turning the dispute into a major national confrontation. This film is a day-to-day account of the political events that occurred over the ensuing four-week period, as seen from Aurukun.*

Taking Hold of Small Objects (Chimpanzee) 6 min. Dist: PSU FR$2.80.

Taking Hold of Small Objects (Spider-Monkey) 7.5 min. Dist: PSU FR$2.80.

Taksu: Music in the Life of Bali (1991) 24 min. Jann Pasler (DI). Dist: UCEMC FR$40, VS$195. *Balinese music is like Balinese life. It reflects community harmony, cooperation, and balance. It also serves as a readily accessible "window" onto Balinese culture. This thoughtful documentary is an American musician's unique and sensitive portrait of Balinese life, art, and spirituality. Focusing on the concept of Taksu, or the spiritual power found in music, instruments, costumes, and dance. The production captures the vibrant rhythm that permeates all Balinese art and culture.*

A Tale of Two Rivers 40 min. Clyde B. Smith (PR). Dist: UCEMC FR$42, FS$540. *An interdisciplinary approach to the study of the Dordogne and Vezère river valleys in the Perigord region of southwestern France. Although this area has been of immense importance to archaeologists and prehistorians, it is also a fascinating and important area* for historians, medievalists, art historians, and travelers. The Périgord region is not well known to the average American tourist, despite its proximity to Bordeaux, its renowned sites such as Cro-Magnon and Lascaux, and its fame among gourmets for such delicacies as truffles and foie gras. It has escaped the effects of massive tourism. Lyrical cinematography captures the beauty and charm of the clear, highly reflective rivers, the little farming villages, the ancient caves overlooking the river, the Roman and medieval ruins, and a colorful parade celebrating the traditional Languedocian culture that still flourishes there. The narration of the film largely consists of carefully edited interviews with James Sackett, J. Desmond Clark, Phillipe Wolff, and Hershel Chipp. Francois Bordes demonstrates stone tool making techniques. [Reviewed by L. G. Freeman, AA 77:919–920, 1975. Robert W. Ehrich, ARCH 36(5):64–65, 1983.]

Tales of the Supernatural   (1970) 27 min. Sharon Sherman (FM, AN). Dist: Sharon Sherman, The Folklore Program, Department of English, University of Oregon, Eugene, OR 97403, FR$35, FS$325. Tales of the Supernatural *analyzes the ways in which horror stories ("ghost legends") are transmitted, the functions of such stories for members of the group being filmed, and the relationship between transmission and function in the telling of the tales. The film examines the storytelling situation as a unique communicative event, focusing on the kinesics, proxemics, and remarks, reactions, and tensions of the participants. The storytellers, a group of American teenagers, were in no way prompted so that the film could portray the event as it actually unfolded. The narration raises certain hypotheses regarding the nature of storytelling and discusses the role of horror in oral narrative, literature, and mass media. The film is especially useful for folklorists and anthropologists interested in communicative events, the processes of narrating and the functions of legends and beliefs in America.*

The Talking Drums of Nigeria   (1964) 17 min. (A Folklore Research Film by Peter and Toshi Seeger.) Dist: FIM/RF FR$15, FS$150. *The people demonstrate the way they communicate with their drums by imitating the sounds of their Yoruba language. Greetings, announcements, and an invitation to dance (which is happily accepted by several village children) are messages tapped out on their "talking" drums.*

Talking to the Enemy: Voices of Sorrow and Rage   (1987) 55 min. Mira Hamermesh (FM). Dist: FL FR$150, VR$75, VS$445. *"The theme of the film is the difficulty inherent in dialogue betweeen Israelis and Palestinians.... Produced by Israeli peace activists."* [From the review by Herbert L. Bodman, Jr., AA 92:843–844, 1990.]

Tamanawis Illahee   (1983) 58 min. Ron Finne (DI). Dist: CCC. *A film of the Pacific Northwest, the native people, poetry, history, and the forces of change. This film is a study in the contrast of how native people used the land, as opposed to European settlers who gradually took it over. It is experimental in style, combining time-lapse photography, archive footage, classic photographs by documentarist Edward Curtis, museum artifacts, and other image sources. The film is a plea for spiritual reconnection with native forebears and a recognition of their heritage.*

Tambours et violons des chasseurs Songhay (The Drums and Violins of Songhay Singers)   (1965) Jean Rouch (DI). Dist: CFE; DER.

Tanah Air—Our Land, Our Water   (Indonesia: A Generation of Change Series) (1987) 28 min. Barbara Bare (DI). Dist: CTC FS$535, VS$295, order #TANS12. *Indonesia faces incredible environmental problems, including overpopulation, resource depletion, and the destruction of rain forests. This program examines these issues and some possible solutions. The underpopulated eastern islands are contrasted with the island of Java, with a population of 100 million.*

Tanana River Rat   (1989) 57 min. Curt Madison (PR, DI). Dist: RTP VS$100. Dist: RTP FS$75. *This is a vibrant drama of contemporary life in interior Alaska. Brothers separated by the political realities of Alaska after the 1991 Native land claims are forced together on the river when a cousin drowns. The family and village come together as they always have in the times of crisis. But lifestyles and the charges of selfish greed in the city and self-pity in the village threaten to tear the brothers apart. Finally, at the conclusion, a traditional Athabaskan song that has flowed throughout the drama saves one of the brothers from near fatal frustration. The song and the elder uncle who sings it remind the brothers of the source of their strength. The show contains much unspoken spirituality.*

Tanda singui (poser le hangar) (To Fix the Shed)   (1973) 20 min. Jean Rouch (DI), Centre National de la Recherche Scientifique, Comite du Film Ethnographique (PR). Dist: CFE; DER. *The inhabitants of the lower section of Yantalla open a new santuary dedicated to Dongo, the thunder spirit.*

The Tango Is Also a History   (1983) 56 min. Humberto Rios (FM), Gaston Martinez (WR). Dist: ICF FR$100, FS$895, VS$540. *The film presents both the story of the tango's development in Argentina and the history of Argentina as reflected in the tango. Martinez says, "Since the advent of the tango as a song, this genre has become the most faithful chronicle of Buenos Aires' existence, of its social, political and economic problems." The exploration of this idea, combined with the haunting, romantic tango music, makes this not only an appreciation of Argentinean music, but a unique work of political and cultural history as well.*

Les Tanneurs de Marrakesh   (1967) 21 min. Dist: FACSEA FR$16. French only.

Tapa and Tapu   15 min. Emma Lindsay Squier (NA). Dist: FCE FR$17, FS$95. *South Sea Island life.*

Tapa, Life and Work on a South Sea Island (Moce)   (1973) 23 min. Simon Kooijman (FM, AN). Dist: Simon Kooijman, C/-Rijksmuseum voor Volkenkunde, P.O. Box 212, Leiden, The Netherlands. *The film was made on Moce Island, Lau Group, Fiji, in 1973. It shows the complete process of the making and decorating of barkcloth or tapa by Vosa Olinipa, one of the expert tapa workers of the island. The making of colorful stencilled tapas is the local specialization. These tapas play an important part in the tradi-*

tional trade and exchange relations with the inhabitants of the other islands of the Lau Group. Moce Island is also one of the main producing centers of "commercial" tapa, which is offered for sale in Suva, the capital of Fiji, as well as in New Zealand and Australia. Within the island community, tapas are used in feasts and ceremonies such as marriages and burials. A ceremony called vakataraisula, *which marks the end of a 100-day period of mourning after the death of a chief, is presented in the film. Tapas are spectacular attributes of this feast, the acme of which consists of the offering of an impressive rollerlike tapa of great length to the chief of the island.*

Tapdancin' (1980) 58 min. Christian Blackwood (DI). Dist: BW FR$100, FS$775. *This is a film on tap dancing. It shows many aspects of the art—elderly black performers, dancers reviving the art of tap dancing, dancers rehersing in studios and performing in dance concerts and on stage in clubs and theatres in New York and Las Vegas.* [Reviewed by Nora Groce, *AA* 84:984–986, 1982.]

Tarahumara: Racers against Time (1981) 22 min. Barnett Addis (FM). Dist: UCLA Behavioral Sciences Media Laboratory, Neuropsychiatric Institute, 760 Westwood Plaza, Los Angeles, CA 90024; (213) 825-0448, FR$25, FS$250. *"The Tarahumara Indians are a generally healthy and handsome people who live in the spectacular canyons of northwestern Mexico where the rugged terrain, devoid of mineral wealth afforded them relative isolation throughout the colonial period. Today this is no longer true, and this film emphasizes the increasing impact of modernization in recent years."* [From the review by Dwight B. Heath, *AA* 86:1063, 1984.]

The Tarahumaras (1984) 29 min. Dist: EBEC FS$360, VS$249. *"The Tarahumaras live in northwestern Mexico. Their most exceptional cultural trait is long distance running, often in mountainous terrain, while kicking a small wooden ball. They are herders and farmers, and they move twice a year. These distinctive characteristics provide intrinsically interesting material, some of which is captured in this film. For the most part, however, this is an old-fashioned ethnography that renders a typical, Anglo-centered view."* [From the review by George H. Odell, *SBF* 21:231, 1986.]

TARAP SERIES Corneille Jest (FM), Centre Nationale de la Recherche Scientifique (PR). Dist: Corneille Jest, 56 rue de Sèvres, 92100 Boulogne, France. *On northern Nepal.* French only. [Reviewed by Andrew Manzardo, *AA* 76:709, 1974.]

• **Rta-rab: Tarap, la valleé aux chevaux excellents** 20 min.

• **Dbyar-ston: La Fête du milieu de l'été a Tarap** 19 min.

• **Ma-qciq: La mère, peinture d'une than-ka** 19 min.

Tarascan Artisians 40 min. Madeline Tourtelot (FM). Dist: GP FR$35, FS$300. *Two years in the making, this film documents the Tarascan Indians living by their crafts around the beautiful Lake Patzcuaro, Michoacan, Mexico. The crafts produced are brought to the Patzcuaro market by dug-out canoe.*

A TASTE OF CHINA (1984) Sue Yung Li (PR). Dist: UCEMC FR$45 (each), FS$500 (each), $1750 (set), VR$35 (each), VS$375 (each), $1350 (set). *Introduces Western audiences to traditional Chinese culture. The series was filmed on location in three major regions of China: the northern plains of Shandong, near Beijing; the mountain basis of Sichuan, to the west; and the water country of the Yangzi River delta, to the south.* See also *Cities in China Series.* [Reviewed by Eugene Anderson, *AA* 88:1049, 1986.]

• **Masters of the Wok** *Explores the evolution of Chinese cuisine from basic peasant fare to highly refined imperial cooking. Opens in north China, capturing the behind-the-scenes drama as two of China's master chefs prepare an astonishing 28-course banquet, then visits Confucius's birthplace to study robust peasant cooking. Also shows a cooking academy in Sichuan province and concludes at a Chrysanthemum banquet in celebration of autumn.*

• **Food for Body and Spirit** *Investigates the impact of religious influences on Chinese culture and cuisine. At a sacred Taoist retreat, a priestess shows how the contrasting forces of yin and yang are balanced in cooking. A highlight is a visit to an unusual herbal medicine restaurant where the maitre d' "prescribes" meals according to the ailments of each diner. Finally, at two monasteries we discover the role of Buddhism in the development of China's extensive vegetarian cuisine.*

• **The Family Table** *The contrasting lives of a traditional four-generation rural family in a Sichuan village and a modern, single-child family in urban Hangzhou are viewed through the routines of their daily meals. In the process, we see how the Chinese family has endured and how it is changing.*

• **Water Farmers** *The Yangzi River delta region south of Shanghai is known as the water country. Hundreds of miles of canals link towns and villages and serve as "liquid highways" for wedding boats, traveling vendors, and foot-powered rowboats. Here, near the city of Shaoxing, water has completely shaped the local farmers' way of life. In their lives, we witness the traditional harmonious relationship between the Chinese people and their environment.*

Tauw 26.5 min. Ousmane Sembene (WR, DI). Dist: Broadcasting and Film Division, National Council of Churches, 475 Riverside Drive, New York, NY 10027. *A fictional film about a Wolof youth in Dakar.* [Reviewed by J. David Sapir, *AA* 74:1568, 1972.]

Taway Nya—La Mère (Taway Naya—Mother) (1970) 12 min. Jean Rouch (DI), Centre National de la Recherche Scientifique, Comité du Film Ethnographique (PR). Dist: CFE; DER. *The relationship between a mother and her two-year-old child in the village of Liberté.*

Tea Fortunes (Commodities Series) (1986) 52 min. Sue Clayton and Jonathan Curling (PR). Dist: FRIF VR$75, VS$400. *This video documents the history of the tea industry in China, India, Sri Lanka, and East Africa. Profiling Sir Thomas Lipton, it shows how Lipton and his competitors controlled every stage of the tea process, from planting to blending, packaging to retailing. Today India controls its exports of tea, Sri Lanka has nationalized its tea estates,*

Zimbabwe's state-run plantations generate some cash in rural areas, but three British companies still dominate the international tea trade, and in China, some young women work for some of the lowest wages in the world producing black tea "dust" as filler for western blends.

Teaching Sign Language to the Chimpanzee, Washoe (1973) 48 min. Allen and Beatrice Gardner (PR). Dist: PSU FR$26, FS$530, VS$210, order #50481; IUAVC FR$14.50. *Documents on the controversial experimentation in which a chimpanzee named Washoe was taught American Sign Language (ASL). Explains, with the Gardner research team as narrators, the original purpose of ASL, their rationale in using it, and several basic signs and their meanings. Shows Washoe in early childhood signing indivudual words such as "more" and "drink." Follows her to the age of five as her vocabulary increases and phrases emerge from her signing.*

Techniques of Digging and Analysis in Archaeology 32 min. Richard Boivin, Marc Laberge (PR, DI). Dist: La Société d'archéologie préhistorique du Quebec, 417 rue St. Pierre #30, Montreal PQ H2Y 2M4, Canada. [Reviewed by Thomas Wight Beale, *AA* 77:903, 1975.]

Teine Samoa: A Girl of Samoa (Girl of Series) (1982) 26 min. Dist: JF FR$35, FS$345. *This film "is a reminder of places and cultures where traditional attitudes and roles are not yet actively questioned.... The message seems to be that for 2,000 years Samoan culture has placed primary emphasis on love and loyalty to the family. Unfortunately, the film takes a long time to make this point."* [From the review by Patricia C. Armstrong, *SBF* 18:217, 1983.]

Teiva: A Boy Prepares for Manhood 22 min. Dist: IUAVC FR$9.95. *Deals with the pending manhood of a ten-year-old Polynesian boy. Follows his conquest and penetration of an uninhabited island. Depicts the activities of the boy and his family in preparation for the big day.*

Los tejedores 28 min. Dist: OWM FR$85, VR$70, FS$400, VS$250; Blue Sky Productions, P.O. Box 548, Santa Fe, NM 87501, R$30, FS$325, VS$250. *Since the 18th century, Hispanic and Native American weavers have been an important part of the commercial and cultural life of the Rio Grande valley in the American Southwest. Their work, a rich interplay of form, color and texture, has gained them international recognition. The film offers an engaging introduction to the tools and techniques of these Rio Grande Valley weavers, and it lets some of the weavers speak of their work in their own words. Agueda Martinez, who is descended from Navajo weavers, has been weaving at her country ranch since 1921; she talks of being 81, still dancing, and drawing upon memory for the intricate designs in her work. Gus Martinez remembers weaving at his father's loom when he was too short to reach the pedals; he recalls rebuilding that same loom so that he could continue the craft.*

The Telltale Tree-Rings 14 min. George F. Hafer Production (PR). Dist: MDAI VS$59.95, order #327-01. *A study of dendrochronology. Many species of trees develop varied patterns of tree rings in response to the climatic variations of their growing area. By correlating tree-ring patterns, researchers have established a valuable tree-ring calendar for the Southwest dating back to 59 B.C.*

The Temple of Apollo at Bassae (1971) 16 min. Malcolm R. McBride (PR). Dist: IFB. [Reviewed by Thomas Howe, *AA* 78:719, 1976.]

Temple of Twenty Pagodas 15 min. *A temple near Lampang, northern Thailand.* [Reviewed by Charles F. Keyes, *AA* 78:719, 1976.]

Tempus de Baristas (1993) 100 min. David MacDougall (FM). Dist: Instituto Superiore Regionale Etnográfico, Via A. Mereu 56, 08100 Uuoro, Italy; 39-784-35561; fax 39-784-37484. *In the rugged mountains of eastern Sardinia, the future of goatherding is tenuous as it has become increasingly marginalized. A young goatherd, Pietro, 17, uses the experiences of his father and a friend as reference points by which to measure his life and to consider his future.*

Ten Thousand Beads for Navaho Sam (1971) 25 min. Eccentric Circle Cinema Workshop (PR). *Film deals with the problem of individual adjustment in cross-cultural settings. Sam Begay is the focus of the film. A Navaho Indian living in Chicago, he is living in two worlds: one Indian and one Anglo. Uprooted, alienated, and homesick, Sam strives to teach his children the 'ways of the Indians' through beadwork. Some patterns of prejudice and discrimination are presented as well.* [Robert B. Moorman]

Ten Times Empty (1977) 21 min. James Wilson, David Tristram (CA, DI), Juniper Films (PR). Dist: IFF FR$31, FS$310. *The film is a series of images of everyday and festive scenes from village life in the dry island of Symi in Greece. "There are scenes of fishing, mending nets, unloading boats, relaxing in a coffee house, a funeral, and the colorful celebration of the Greek independence day which opens and closes the film. This film paints an overall picture of life in Symi that is necessarily superficial, but there is much of value here. The photography and other technical aspects of this production are first rate and the scenes are rendered accurately."* [From the review by Peter Allen, *AA* 84:756–757, 1982.]

Tent Embassy (1991) 58 min. David Sandy (FM). Dist: ABC Aboriginal Programs Unit, G.P.O Box 9994, Sydney NSW 2001, Australia; (612) 950-4031; fax (612) 950-4020. *In 1972, four Aboriginal men went to Canberra to set up the Aboriginal Tent Embassy on the lawn of Parliament House as a protest against the Federal Government's policy on land rights concerning the Aboriginal people. This video examines the progress that has been made by the group known as the Aboriginal Black Panther movement.*

The Tenth Dancer (1992) 52 min. Sally Ingleton (FM). Dist BBC. *During the Pol Pot regime, hundreds of thousands of Cambodians were killed. Traditional artists and performers were primary targets. This film looks at one of the surviving practitioners of the dance tradition and how she has reintroduced this cultural form to a whole new generation of dancers.*

Tepoztlan (1969) 30 min. L. Earl Griswold (AN). Dist: BFA FR$81, FS$580; UCEMC. *Tepoztlan, a village just 40* miles south of Mexico City, has been intensively studied by anthropologists over the years. Supplementing studies by Robert Redfield and Oscar Lewis, which are regarded as classics in the field, this film documents traditional lifeways in Tepoztlan. The cultivation of maize provides a seasonal structure for a sensitive filming of daily activities of Tepoztecans, from the planting of seed after the first rains to harvest time and the long dry season. Ancient methods are carefully documented; hand crop cultivation, grinding maize on a metate for tortillas, building charcoal kilns, making adobe. The village is placed in historical context as the theme of land rights is developed from the time of the Spanish conquerors through the Mexican Revolution. Cultural survivals, blending Christian and non-Christian customs, are observed as annual fiestas and celebrations are vividly depicted. [Reviewed by David Kaplan, AA 73:982–983, 1971.]

Tepoztlan in Transition (1970) 20 min. L. Earl Griswold (AN). Dist: UCEMC FR$26; BFA FS$280. *An automatic tortilla maker symbolizes the transitions taking place in Tepoztlan as the village emerges from its traditional isolation. A rapid sequence of change is introduced with the building of a road link with Cuernavaca and Mexico City, bringing Tepoztecans into contact with the larger world. The centuries-old land problem assumes a new significance as land is put to different uses. The old maize pattern continues as a base while new markets lead to the large-scale farming of flowers and garden crops through the introduction of modern methods of irrigation and cultivation. A new type of employer-employee relationship is created as skilled labor develops in the village. Other significant factors for village change include the establishment of a modern school and hospital as well as the industry, international art colony, and tourists attracted to evolving Tepoztlan.* [Reviewed by David Kaplan, AA 73:982–983, 1971.]

Terre sans pain (Land without Bread) 31 min. Luis Bunuel (DI). Dist: DER FR$35, FS$325. *Bunuel's third film is a document of poverty in rural Spain shot in 1932 in Extremadura, one of the poorest, most rugged areas in western Spain. The inhabitants of the mountains, the Hurdanos, eked subsistence out of a barren landscape, raising beans and potatoes and eating unripe cherries when other food runs out. Bunuel entered dreary villages and noted that the only luxurious building is the Catholic church. Bunuel's ironic sensibility gives the film a quality of being more than social documentary, but perhaps also a sharp commentary on the viewers' relationship to what they see and on the anthropologists' romantic dreams of discovering a "pristine" people.* Relevant anthropological literature: Ado Kyrou, *Luis Bunuel*. Simon and Schuster, 1963.

TESTAMENT: THE BIBLE AND HISTORY (1988) 7 parts, 52 min. each. John Romer (PR). Dist: FHS VR$75, VS$149 (each), $849 (set). "*Testament is quite simply the best program of this type ever made. Not only is it highly informative, but it is also great entertainment.... John Romer combines knowledge, humor, skepticism, and awe in a compelling performance.*" [From the review by Peter S. Allen, ARCH 42(4):64–65, 1989.] The titles in the series are:

- **As It Was in the Beginning**
- **Chronicles and Kings**
- **Mightier than the Sword**
- **Gospel Truth**
- **Thine Is the Kingdom**
- **The Power and Glory**
- **Paradise Lost**

Thailand (Asian Insight Series) (1988) 50 min. Film Australia (PR). Dist: FIV VS$158. *A history of Thai society. Thailand differs from its Asian neighbors in that the majority of its people are Buddhists, and the country has never known colonial rule.*

Thanh's War (1991) 58 min. Elizabeth Farnsworth (PR). Dist: UCEMC FR$50, VS$195. *Pham Thanh is a Vietnamese-American whose family was killed when he was 12 by a U.S. grenade that also blew his throat apart. Thanh was rescued by U.S. soldiers and taken to America, where he built a new life in the land he had considered his enemy. He lives today in California, where he owns a home, works in a high-tech company, and is a dedicated baseball fan. He also travels as often as he can to his ancestral village in Vietnam, and his traditional marriage there is captured in the film. This documentary tells Thanh's courageous and poignant story as he grapples with the emotional legacy of the war and tries to make his way in two vastly different cultures. A highlight is a dramatic encounter with a former U.S. army officer in which the two men share their wrenching memories of the war. This is a story of loss, recovery, and reconciliation that will educate and inspire students in a wide variety of disciplines.*

Thank God and the Revolution (1981) 50 min. Tercer Cine (PR), Wolf Tirado and Jackie Reiter (DI). Dist: ICF FR$75, FS$725, VS$480. "*A discussion among members of a rural village about their religion and about the revolution; it reveals the mix of evangelical and ideological enthusiasm, patriotism, and nationalism with which many Nicaraguans—both Catholics and Protestants—react to the revolution.*" [From the review by John A. Booth, AA 86:793–796, 1984.]

That Our Children Will Not Die 60 min. Joyce Chopra (FM). Dist: DER VR$60, VS$500. *Three different community-based approaches to health care in distinct regions of Nigeria, Africa's most populous state and one of the most richly endowed in natural resources. Despite this, Nigeria continues to have high infant mortality rates and other preventable yet serious health problems. The film is sponsored by the Ford Foundation and produced by the Institute of Child Health of the University of Lagos.*

These Are My People 14 min. National Film Board of Canada (PR). Dist: NFBC; UCEMC FR$19. *This is the first film by the Challenge for Change Program's Indian film crew, who shot their first footage at the Akwesasne (St. Regis) Mohawk Reserve and have edited it into a sincere homage to the People of the Longhouse. The film presents the Indian's view of Indian religion and culture, the effect* *of the coming of the white man, and the revival of the Longhouse culture.*

These Hands (1992) 45 min. Flora M'mbugu-Schelling (FM). Dist: Flora M'mbugu-Schelling, 4802 Maple Terrace, Chevy Chase, MD 20815; telephone/fax (301) 907-0397. *This film presents a picture of the daily routine at a colossal gravel pit in Tanzania, where groups of self-employed women scrape a living together by smashing up rocks with hammers and amassing the debris into piles of gravel for the urban construction industry.*

Thessaloniki Museum (1987) 37 min. A. Platides (FM). Dist: Classic Video, P.O. Box 17009, Exochai, GR-542 10, Thessaloniki, Greece, VS$399. *"Thessaloniki, Greece's second largest city, is visited far less frequently than Athens and the more popular Aegean islands, and relatively few Americans are aware that the city's archaeological museum boasts an important and diverse collection of statuary, vases, jewelry, and other objects from all periods of antiquity. Among the most outstanding pieces in the museum are the finds from the famous Vergina tomb, believed by many to belong to Philip of Macedon, father of Alexander the Great."* [From the review by Peter S. Allen, *ARCH* 41(3), 1988.]

They Tell It for the Truth: Ozark Storytelling (1981) 59 min. Kaw Valley Films (PR). Dist: Kaw Valley Films, FS$950.

Thieves of Time (1978) 29 min. KAET-TV, Phoenix, AZ (PR). Dist: PTL. *"Reports one aspect of a worldwide problem: the plundering of archaeological sites, paying particular attention to northern Arizona. Opening with scenes of looted mounds, desecrated graves and the plastic trash left behind by the 'pot hunters,' the film shows the destruction that has befallen many sites."* [From the review by Trudy S. Kawami, *ARCH* 35(1):70–71, 1982.]

This Is Not Your Life (1991) 20 min. Jorge Furtado (FM). Dist: FRIF. *Randomly picking an "average" South Brazilian housewife for his subject, Furtado shows, through her recounting her own life that even "ordinary people" have rich and interesting stories to tell.*

This Magnificent African Cake (see Africa Series)

This Was the Time 16 min. Eugene Boyko (DI), William Brind and Eugene Boyko (PR). Dist: NFB R$20, FS$235, VS$175. *When Masset, a Haidu Indian village in the Queen Charlotte Islands, held a potlatch it seemed as if the past grandeur of the people had returned. This is a colorful recreation of Indian life that faded more than two generations ago when the great totems were toppled by the missionaries and the costly potlatch was forbidden by law. The film shows how the quiet, unkempt village lived again the old glory, with singing, dancing, feasting, and the raising of a towering totem as a lasting reminder of what once was.*

This World Is Not My Home 30 min. Dist: APPAL. *This film is a portrait of 78-year-old Nimrod Workman, a retired coal miner and singer who writes and performs traditional ballads. Nimrod reminisces about his life as a miner in the film and also sings traditional Appalachian songs.*

Those Born at Masset: A Haida Stonemoving and Feast (1976) 70 min. Mary Lee Stearns (AN, PR), Eileen Stearns (PR). *Within the limitations of external political control and changing economic conditions, the Haida of British Columbia, Canada, have preserved many traditional practices connected with the observance of life-cycle events. Such continuity of a variety of cultural elements is possible because the people still inhabit their ancestral villages, carrying on many subsistence activities and conducting internal community relations primarily in the idiom of kinship. Recorded here is one such Haida ritual, the modern equivalent of the traditional memorial potlatch, described by the ethnographer M. L. Stearns, Haida narrators, and others. Elements of the ceremony depicted include the procession to the burial site with the headstone (formerly a totem pole), singing a hymn at the grave, greeting guests, and the memorial feast, distribution of gifts, payment for ritual services to the dead, and speeches. The ceremony's historical and cultural significance is emphasized by intercuts of archival photographs and reproduction of museum artifacts. An original and highly effective series of graphic displays interspersed with appropriate animal representations at the beginning of the film provides background information on the traditional matrilineal kinship system that is necessary to an understanding of the elements in the death rites that persist to this day in the memorial feast.*

Thoughts on Fox Hunting 30 min. Tom Davenport (FM). Dist: TDF FR$45, FS$440. *The art of an American huntsman in traditional English-style fox hunting, filmed near Middleburg, Virginia. Based on Lord Peter Beckford's 1781 classic* Thoughts on Hunting *and featuring Melvin Poe, huntsman, and his national championship hounds.*

Thread of the Needle (Rural Greece: Desertion, Migration, Village Life Series) (1982) 23 min. Colette Piault (FM), Philippe Lavalette (CA), Francois Didio (SR), Charlotte Boigeol (ED). Dist: LFDQ FS$125; PSA VR$50, VS$250. *In a village in Epirus, in the Greek mountains, in 1979, where young men leave the village to find work, learn a trade, or serve in the army, a young woman may leave her father's house only to enter that of her husband. The unmarried girls remain in the village among the elderly folk, meeting together to embroider their trousseaus and chat. The film allows the spectator to sit in on one of these casual sewing sessions where the girls speak to each other of their wishes and their problems, most of which revolve around the marriage that will change their lives. Music is provided by chants sung off camera by the girls themselves. Although the images are important, the principal thrust of this film is dialogue. As they embroider, the young women respond to questions posed by an unseen interviewer.* [Reviewed in *AA* 86:511, 1984.]

Three Apprentices (Comparison Series) (1963) 28 min. National Film Board of Canada (PR). *Comparison of three young apprentices from Nigeria, Canada, and Brazil: their work, their homes, and their hopes for the future.*

Three Dances by Gulpilil (Aboriginal Dance Series) (1978) 8 min. Tom Manefield (PR), David Roberts (DI). Dist: FAA. *Gulpilil, one of the best exponents of Aboriginal dance* in Australia, performs three dances: The Emu, The Kangaroo, and The Fish. The first two are solo performances by Gulpilil and are closer to mime than dance. The third is a group dance with some children from Bamyili in the Northern territory where Gulpilil lives.

Three Fishermen (1964) 28 min. Julian Biggs (PR, DI), John Kemeny (DI), Paul Leach (CA). Dist: NFB FR$19, FS$200; UCEMC FR$19. *A Greek hook and line fisherman, a Thai purse seiner, and a Canadian lobsterman are the three fishermen of the title, and a third of the film is devoted to each. They fish in different ways in different parts of the world but are linked by their dependence on the sea and by the combination of luck, skill, and determination that characterize the lives of fisherman everywhere.* [Reviewed by Peter S. Allen and George M. Epple, *AA* 83:742–743, 1981.]

Three Grandmothers (1963) 28 min. National Film Board of Canada (PR). Dist: PSU FR$12.50. *Glimpses into the lives of three grandmothers in widely different parts of the world—in a hill city in Brazil, a rural community in Manitoba, Canada, and a village compound in Lagos, Nigeria.* [Reviewed by Nancy B. Leis, *AA* 79:198, 1977.]

Three Lives 70 min. Kate Millet (DI), Women's Liberation Cinema Co.(PR). Dist: Impact. *Three American women.* [Reviewed in *AA* 74:1571, 1972.]

365 Days with Your Baby (1954) 28 min. Dist: PSU. *Shows a wide variety of activities in the home environment from birth to first birthday of a baby born in a Japanese middle-class family. Includes feeding, bathing, sleeping, reactions to various stimuli, and interactions with other members of family. Child development and acculturation are easy to follow although narration is in Japanese.*

Three of Us (1975) 15 min. Jeff Nye (FM), Mauricio (Ling.). Dist: Nye Films, P.O. Box 11734, Salt Lake City, UT 84147; (801) 582-7548, FR$25, FS$210. *Rufino, an 81-year-old man, Josefina, a 50-year-old woman, and Rorro, a 12-year-old boy, are three of the Paipai and Kiliwa people of Baja, California. Rorro plays and sings like young people play and sing everywhere. His enthusiasm for life is clearly felt. He is also seen helping his grandmother, Josefina, in her work. Josefina, who is making a carrying bag out of a desert plant, quietly reveals a generous portion of her human quality. And Rufino, the wrinkled and wise old storyteller, conveys much about the intelligence and sense of humor of the people.*

Three Paths: Hinduism, Buddhism, and Taoism (1981) 18 min. Dist: HFF FR$35, FS$350. *"A short film on three major religions is a monumental challenge. This production, unfortunately, does not make the subject matter easier to understand.... Given this caveat, if a discussion period with a knowledgeable person focuses on the similarities and explains the differences among these three important religions, this film may be useful."* [From the review by Tetsuden Kashima, *SBF* 18:37–38, 1982.]

Three Seasons (St. Lawrence North Series) B/W. Dist: CRAW FS$75.38. *On the shores of the St. Lawrence, between the Saguenay and Seven Islands, lies the "côte du bois," the coast of wood, where the men cut pulpwood, working and resting in a rhythm dictated by the seasons—fall is for cutting; winter is for hauling; and the spring is for driving. The log drive is shown as a lusty sort of pastoral.*

Three Stone Blades 15.5 min. Dorothy Goldner and Orville Goldner (PR), Valene L. Smith (AN), Ira Latour (CA). Dist: IFB FR$20, FS$275, VS$225. *This film reconstructs aboriginal Eskimo customs and values. When the husband, provider for the family, goes on a hunting trip and fails to return, his family faces starvation. After their stored food is exhausted, the wife goes to her sister-in-law to get food for her two small children. Instead, the woman gives her three stone blades. As the weakened and despairing wife makes her way home, she enters a mysterious dwelling and the spirits within help her. The beautiful but stark backgrounds of the frozen arctic show what these people must cope with in order to survive. Methods of hunting, skinning, preserving food, and providing shelter are shown as the story unfolds. The presentation incorporates traditions concerning family, reciprocal sharing, shamanism, and transmigration of souls.* [Reviewed by James W. VanStone, *AA* 74:1028–1029, 1972. Charles C. Kolb, *SBF* 18:38, 1982. See also Media Review, April 1973.]

The Three Worlds of Bali (1981) 59 min. Ira R. Abrams (DI), Michael Ambrosino (EP). Dist: DER FR$60, FS$600. *In Balinese cosmology, demons are thought to dwell in the watery underworld, gods in the upper world, and human beings in the middle realm between the two. Much of human effort is directed toward maintaining the proper balance between these worlds and between the forces of growth and decay. The pinnacle of such efforts is the ritual "Eka Dasa Rudra," held once every hundred years. This film is a coverage of the "Eka Dasa Rudra" held in 1979. The entire population of the island is mobilized for this event, preparing offerings and streaming from thousands of village temples in processions to the sea. Eleven demons, of which Rudra is the most powerful, must be transformed into beneficent spirits. There is also a political dimension to the film since the 1979 ritual was held upon the urging of the then President Sukarno, before the calendrically proper year and was attended by the President in person.* Bibliography: J. Stephen Lansing, *The Three Worlds of Bali*.

Through Navajo Eyes (see Navajo Film Themselves Series)

Tibet: The Bamboo Curtain Falls (1984) 50 min. BBC (PR). Dist: FIV VS$198. *China always claimed that Tibet was a part of its own territory; in October 1950, the Chinese attacked. With the invasion and occupation, Tibet's unique culture and religion were destroyed. This video chronicles the determination of the Tibetans as they struggled to stave off the inevitable and shows the devastation and suppression found there in 1979.*

Tibet in Exile Ed-Lazar (DI). Dist: VP VR$45, VS$75. *Under the guidance of their spiritual leader, the Dalai Lama, the Tibetan exiled community is struggling to preserve their ancient culture, to maintain their Buddhist values of compassion, and to regain their country. This film follows the story of ten children smuggled out of Tibet by relatives who crossed the Himalayas on foot so that children might live* *more freely. In exile, these children will receive a proper Tibetan education and health care unavailable in their troubled homeland. Along with an intimate portrait of an exiled community, the video includes rare footage of the Dalai Lama's 1959 escape from Tibet and more recent footage of brutal attacks by the Chinese army on Tibetan monks. While providing enlightenment on the dire situation Tibetans face, this film offers a universal lesson of hope and cultural survival.*

Tibet: The Lost Mystery (1984) 51 min. BBC (PR). Dist: FIV VS$198. *Until 1904, no living European had seen the mysterious and forbidden land of Tibet. Photographs, archive film, and firsthand recollections of visitors recreate the earliest journeys into Tibet, revealing a well-ordered, medieval society with a highly developed culture based on Buddhism. A vivid portrait of a remarkable culture.*

Tibetan Buddhism: Cycles of Interdependence (1983) 56 min. Edward W. Bastian (FM). Dist: UW-SAAC FR$45, FS$380. *"A documentary of monastic and lay Buddhist life among Tibetan peoples in India.... Explores the annual round of Buddhist life in a Tibetan settlement of Ladakh.... The theme of the film is interdependence—the interdependence between monks, laity, nature, Buddhist philosophy, and ritual—through the cycle of the seasons."* [From the review by Linda Stone, AA 86:1073, 1984.]

Tibetan Buddhism: Preserving the Monastic Tradition (1983) 29 min. Joseph W. Elder (PR), Edward W. Bastian (DI). Dist: UW-SAAC FR$35, FS$225. *"A documentary of monastic and lay Buddhist life among Tibetan peoples in India.... Takes us inside the scholarly Sera Monastery of Mysore.... Develops a central theme—namely, the great extent to which immigrant monks at Sera have preserved Buddhist teaching and ritual over a span of some 2,000 years and through the upheaval that drove Tibetan Buddhists to India in the late 1950's."* [From the review by Linda Stone, AA 86:1073, 1984.]

Tibetan Traders 22 min. Dist: AP FS$250; USC FR$10; PSU(PCR) order #20053, FR$5.40. [Reviewed by Gerald D. Berreman, AA 67:87, 1965.] Suggested supplement: S. D. Plant, *The Social Economy of the Himalayas*, 1935.

Ticket to Tefenni (1984) 27 min. Elspeth MacDougall (PR). Dist: United Nations, Radio and Visual Services, Department of Public Information, Room 808, New York, NY 10017; (212) 754-6939, FR$24, FS$405. *"Follows a Turkish doctor from his suburban Minneapolis home to Turkey, where he conducts a much needed clinic in his native village of Tefenni and lectures to doctors and medical students at Hacettpe University in Ankara."* [From the review by Paul J. Magnarella, AA 88:1046–1047, 1986.]

Tidikawa and Friends (Traditional Music of Papua New Guinea Series) (1972) 82 min. Les McLaren (DI), Jef and Su Doring (FM). Dist: PSU; UCEMC; DER FR$120. *This film offers a visual exploration of the daily lives of the Bedamini, swidden horticulturalists in the Great Papuan Plateau. The film focuses on a spirit medium, or gesame taso, named Tidikawa. We follow him as he and his friend Haifi spend their time in work and relaxation around two longhouses, as men hunt in the forest, women garden and collect sago, huge timbers are felled with steel axes, a father plays with a baby, tobacco is smoked, a child dies. The funeral is held; the parents mourn. Tidikawa's spirit child speaks at a seance, and eventually an initiation ceremony, Golyage, is held. Wrists bound with rattan, bodies painted, and hair covered with bark wigs, seven boys are initiated into manhood.* [Reviewed by Edward L. Schieffelin and Bambi B. Schieffelin, AA 76:711–714, 1974.]

Tidikawa: At the Edge of Heaven 50 min. Look Film Productions (PR), Susan Cornwell (DI). Dist: FL VR$75, VS$445. *When Susan Cornwell first encountered the Bedamini in 1971, they were aggressive and practiced cannibalism as part of their religion. She was able to befriend them and make a landmark film,* Tidikawa and Friends. *Tidikawa was a powerful religious leader. Now, on Cornwell's return, she finds people in Western dress, wearing t-shirts instead of nose bones. Many have been converted to Christianity, having abandoned their traditional rituals. They perform their tribal dances for money and use calculators to determine the charges. Susan shows them the old film and they respond with excitement to images of their former selves. Tidikawa, now an old man, lives deep in the jungle where he still practices his sorcery. The skillful intercutting of old and new footage gives drama to this westernization of an indigenous people.*

Tierra o muerte: Land or Death (1992) 59 min. Luis Valdez (NR), Carolyn Hales (PR). Dist: UCEMC VR$60, VS$195, order #38249. *This award-winning documentary explores a land rights battle between Chicanos and Anglos that has been raging in northern New Mexico for 150 years.*

Tierra y cultura (1987) 38 min. Magdalena V. and Sigi S. (DI). Dist: CG FR$70, FS$295, VS$495. *Examines the recuperacion movement among the Indian communities in Colombia where a rebel army of about 6,000 Indians is engaged in guerrilla warfare with a counter-insurgency force of 15,000 Colombian Army troops. The present conflict dates back to 1971 when the Regional Indian Council (CRIC) was founded in an attempt to defend Indian communities against the increasingly brutal encroachments by large land-owners, the army, and the government. Spanish dialogue with English subtitles.*

Tighten the Drums: Self-Decoration among the Enga (Films from Papua New Guinea Series) (1983) 58 min. Chris Owen (DI), The Institute of Papua New Guinea Studies (PR). Dist: DER FR$80, VR$60, FS$800, VS$400. *In the Western Highlands of Papua New Guinea, the Enga people have developed the art of body decoration as a visual language. Using earth paints, tree oils, bird plumes, human hair, and a variety of plants, the Enga turn the body into a medium for an expressive and dramatic symbolism. This film shows the diverse forms of body art in both daily life and ritual in Enga village society.* [Reviewed by Terence E. Hays, AA 85:224–225, 1983. Karl G. Heider, SBF 18:281, 1983.]

The Tightrope of Power (Millennium: Tribal Wisdom and the Modern World Series) (1992) 1 hour. David Maybury-Lewis (H), Hans Zimmer (MU). Dist: PBS VS$49.95, order

#MILL-109-RCDC. *How do tribal societies maintain social order and harmony without the vast legal and governmental institutions that we rely on? This program contrasts the Western forms of state to the tribal practice of democracy through consensus. We travel to Canada to witness the struggles of the Objibwa-Cree and Mohawk tribes against the Canadian federal government and learn how their visions of the world can help us refine our definitions of democracy, pluralism, and the state.*

The Tigris Expedition (1979) 59 min. National Geographic Society (PR). Dist: NGS FS$595, VS$545. *Thor Heyerdahl searches for ancient trade centers on Arabian waters.*

Tikal (1961) 22 min. Karl G. Heider (FM, AN), University Museum, University of Pennsylvania (PR). Dist: PSU FR$14.50, FS$270. *Filmed at the Mayan site of Tikal, in the Guatemala jungles. Introduction to classic Mayan civilization through their architecture and carvings; then follows the excavation of a domestic house mound.* [Reviewed by Gordon R. Willey, AA 78:378, 1976.]

Tikinagan (As Long as the Rivers Flow Series) (1991) 59 min. Gil Cardinal (DI), James Cullingham and Peter Raymont (PR). Dist: FRIF VR$75, VS$390. *This is an account of the native child welfare system. Tikinagan, the Cree word for the cradleboards on which native parents once carried their babies, is the name of a revolutionary native child care agency operating out of Sioux Lookout in northwestern Ontario. Tikinagan workers realize that the welfare of children on their reservations is in peril—gas sniffing and alcoholism are major problems—but they must confront the residue of bitterness and distrust left by years of conflict with provincial child welfare agencies.*

Time Immemorial (As Long as the Rivers Flow Series) (1991) 59 min. Hugh Brody (DI), James Cullingham and Peter Raymont (PR). Dist: FRIF VR$75, VS$390. *The Nisga'a tribe of northwestern British Columbia has long led the fight for aboriginal rights in Canada. The film chronicles their struggle as they take their case for land rights all the way to the Supreme Court of Canada. Documentary footage, archival material, and interviews recount the cultural clash over four generations of Nisga'a, which only now is receiving official attention from the provincial government, 119 years after British Columbia became a part of Canada.*

Time in the Sun (1939) 60 min. Marie Seton (PR), Sergei Eisenstein, Grigori Alexandrov (FM). Dist: AB FR$40. *In the early 1930s, Sergei Eisenstein, Grigori Alexandrov, and Edouard Tisse attempted to make a six-part epic on Mexican culture (which Mr. and Mrs. Upton Sinclair agreed to finance). Unfortunately,* Que Viva Mexico! *was taken away from Eisenstein, but* Time in the Sun *attempts to reconstruct each of Eisenstein's six intended episodes, depicting ancient Yucatan before the coming of the Conquistadores, the arrival of Cortez and the Spanish settlers, the ancient matriarchy of Tehuantpec, the brutality of feudal Mexico, the Revolution, and the traditional festival of All Soul's Day.*

Time Stands Still (1992) 10 min. Simon Everson and Urszula Urbaniak (FM). Dist: NFTS. *Throughout Britain in the aftermath of WWII, numerous temporary camps housed some 40,000 Polish nationals, ex-combatants, and their families. This piece focuses on the last remaining camp where the inhabitants lead existences dominated by their pasts.*

A Time to Remember 28 min. North Slope Borough Teleproduction Studio (PR). Dist: MDAI VS$59.95, order #331-01. *Rare footage filmed by Presbyterian missionaries in Barrow in the 1930s shows how the Eskimos (Inupiat) coped with the harsh Arctic environment in a society without money. This strong heritage helps in coping with the fast-paced materialistic problems of today.*

To Be Indian 55 min. Jesse Nishihata (PR), John Max (CA). Dist: CBC FR$35, FS$345. *The producer wanted to focus on the Indians of the West "as they are and as they want to be." He set out on a modern journey of discovery among the Crees of northern Alberta. Nishihata recorded hour upon hour of interviews on audio tape, while Max recorded hundreds of still photographs. A selection of the resulting photographs was combined with the edited tapes of the interviews to produce this unusual film with no narration and only the Indians speaking for themselves. A sad story epitomized by one Indian who described his life as "living day by day with problems." Social and family discrimination hand in hand with a lack of incentive and meaningful work, and only the occasional small sign of improvement.*

To Care: A Portrait of Three Older Caregivers (1987) 28 min. Nicolas J. Kaufman (FM), Joyce Newman (PR). Dist: Nicolas J. Kaufman Productions, 14 Clyde Street, Newtonville, MA 02160; (617) 964-4466, VR$50, VR$295. *"Caregivers for three persons, each with a different physical ailment, are shown in their daily activites and in interviews. Different kinds of stresses for both victim and caregiver are brought out. A common thread is the attempt to maintain some semblance of normality."* [From the review by Benjamin N. Colby, AA 92:1099–1100, 1990.]

To Die Today 50 min. Jeanine Locke (FM). Dist: FL. *Dr. Elizabeth Kubler Ross discusses death.* [Reviewed by Nancie L. Gonzales, Patricia Perrier, Stella Silverstein, AA 77:190, 1975.]

To Find the Baruya Story: An Anthropologist at Work with a New Guinea Tribe (A Series on the Baruya) (1982) 64 min. Allison and Marek Jablonko and Stephen Olsson (DI). Dist: DER FR$80, FS$800, VS$400. *This multifaceted film, photographed in both 1969 and 1982, illustrates an anthropologist's actual fieldwork methods and personal relationships among the Baruya and provides an in-depth view of the Baruya's traditional salt-based economic system. This film follows Dr. Godelier in his attempt to understand the complexities of Baruya culture. He comments: "I have to find and bring together the different pieces of Baruya culture. . . . That's my job, to find the story."*

To Find Our Life: The Peyote Hunt of the Huichols of Mexico (1969) 65 min. Peter T. Furst (FM, AN), Latin American Center, UCLA (PR). Dist: LAC FR$35, FS$550; PSU(PCR) order #60142, FR$22.30; UCEMC. *This is the first film of the peyote pilgrimage of the Huichols of western Mexico to the northcentral desert of San Luis Potosi, first described some 70 years ago by Carl Lumholtz. Furst accompanied 16 Huichols, including three children, from Nayarit to the sacred peyote country, called Wirikuta, and back, and to record the ritual activities of the pilgrimage on film and tape. Principal rituals recorded are the blindfolding of the novice peyote pilgrims at a sacred place near Zacatecas and the subsequent passage through a symbolic gateway ("Where the Clouds Clash Together"); the ceremonies at the desert springs known as "Where Our Mother Lives," curing rituals; the actual hunt of the psychoactive peyote cactus with bow and arrow; the command eating of the peyote; all-night ceremonies and the final ritual dissolving of the bond of peyote hunters following their return to Nayarit. All of the music and sound was recorded on the journey; the narration was adapted from the native text dictated by Ramon Medina Silva, Huichol shaman and artist, who was the leader of the peyote group.* [Reviewed by Weston La Barre, AA 72:120, 1970.] Suggested supplements: Peter T. Furst, "Huichol Conceptions of the Soul." *Folklore Americas* 27(2):39–160, 1967. Peter T. Furst, "The Parching of the Maize: An Essay on the Survivial of the Huichol Ritual." *Acta Ethnographica et linguistica* 14(1):42, 1968. Peter T. Furst, *Ethnographic Filming and the Peyote Hunt of the Huichols of Mexico* (in preparation). Barbara G. Myerhoff, *The Deer-Maize-Peyote Symbol Complex Among the Huichols.* Ph.D. dissertation, UCLA, 1968.

To Know the Hurons: An Experiment in Rescue Archaeology 29 min. Dist: NFBC. *A salvage operation taking place on the Draper Dig near Pickering, Ontario, 25 miles northeast of Toronto. Known to be the site of an ancient Huron Indian village, the excavation and recovery of artifacts was considered to have some urgency because the Draper farm was slated to be destroyed by the proposed new Toronto International Airport. The dig was led by William D. Finlayson, Director of the Museum of Indian Archaeology at the University of Western Ontario, London. It is his on-site, though mostly off-camera, commentary that gives the discovery of each new fragment meaning and relevance. From each shred recovered, each outline of an ancient inhabitation, postmarks of palisades, burials, pottery designs, even plant seeds, it is possible to reconstruct and picture the life, the customs, and the history of the Indians who lived in the part of southern Ontario between 700 and 1575 A.D. Sixty summer archaeology students did the spadework. Their queries, as the work progresses, and William Finlayson's explanations, are edited for the film in such a way as to produce a coherent pattern of discovery, making the film an invaluable reference for the study of archaeology and of this particular period of North American history. This was one of the first times a computer was used to process and interpret data.*

To Live with Herds (1973) 70 min. David MacDougall (PR, DI, CA), Judith MacDougall (SR). Dist: UCEMC FR$55, FS$790, VS$615. *Examines the effects of nation building in pre-Amin Uganda on the seminomadic, pastoral Jie. The film looks at life in a traditional Jie homestead during a harsh dry season. The talk and work of adults and the games of children go on, but there is also hardship and worry, exacerbated by government policies that seem to attack rather than support the values and economic base of Jie society. A mother counts her children; among them is a son she hardly knows who has joined the educated bureaucracy. Later we find him supervising famine relief for his own people in a situation that seems far beyond his control. At the end of the film, Logoth, the protector of the homestead, travels to the west to rejoin his herds in an area of relative plenty; at least for the time being his life seems free from official interference. The film has achieved classic status among ethnographic films owing to its remarkable success in developing a coherent analytical statement about the world as the Jie see and experience it.* In Jie, with English subtitles. [Reviewed by P. H. Gulliver, AA 75:597–598, 1973.] Suggested supplements: P. H. Gulliver, *The Family Herds.* Routledge & Kegan Paul, 1955. Neville Dyson-Hudson, *Karimojong Politics.* Claredon Press, 1966. P.H. Gulliver, "The Jie of Uganda." In: *Peoples of Africa.* Gibbs, Holt, Rinehart and Winston, 1965.

To Make the Balance (1970) 33 min. Laura Nader (AN). Dist: UCEMC order #7698, FR$430, FS$300. *To Make the Balance is the literal translation of a phrase that stands for a unique kind of community government of Oaxaca, Mexico—an unwritten village legal system with few formalities. The system resolves conflict by minimizing the sense of injustice felt by parties in the case; there is no gap between legal professionals and the average man, nor is there any mechanical application of rules. The law is a style of compromise, equality de-escalation at all cost in balance. Candid photography shows the president—a court official elected from the community at large and serving without pay for a term of one year—handling five disputes. The narrator interprets for the audience as the president scolds, gives advice, and offers short discourses on duty, marriage, and property rights. Finally, he attempts to make the delicate balance between the two sides and arrive at a settlement both parties will accept.* [Reviewed by Jane F. Collier, AA 74:1589–1590, 1972.] Suggested supplements: Laura Nader, "Styles of Court Procedure: To Make the Balance." In: *Law in Culture and Society.* Laura Nader, ed. Pp. 69–91, Aldine, 1969.

To Protect Mother Earth (Broken Treaty II) (1989) 59 min. Joel L. Freedman (FM). Dist: Cinnamon Productions, 225 Lafayette Street, New York, NY 10012; (212) 431-4899, VR$125, FS$1295, VS$360. *Follows* Broken Treaty of Battle Mountain—*treaty and land rights of the Western Shoshone.* [Reviewed by Bea Medicine, AA 93(3):768–769, 1991.]

To Serve the Gods (Caribbean Cultures Series) (1982) 33 min. Karen Kramer (FM). Dist: DER FR$55, FS$650, VR$40, VS$350. *About the beliefs, rituals, and performances of a week-long ceremony given by a Haitian family in honor of its ancestral spirits. This ceremony only occurs every 20 to 30 years. This particular service takes place in a rural community in southern Haiti, on family land, where* *relatives have gathered to propitiate gods inherited by their ancestors. The film has scenes of "possession" and shows very well how gods, land, and both alive and dead members of the extended family structures in this rural community are related to each other in a close network of ties. The filmmaker has been a student of Vodou for 20 years and attended ceremonies for the first time in Haiti in 1971. The film is based on the ethnographic research of anthropologist Ira Lowenthal.* [Reviewed by Drexel G. Woodson AA 84:976–978, 1982.]

To Taste a Hundred Herbs: Gods, Ancestors and Medicine in a Chinese Village (Long Bow Film Series) (1986) 58 min. Carma Hinton and Richard Gordon (DI). Dist: NDF FR$90, VR$75, FS$800, VS$480. *Portrait of a traditional Chinese doctor whose Catholic faith shapes his values and gives him a special role in his community. This film captures wonderfully the warmth, closeness, and traditions of family life in China.* [Reviewed by William Graves III, AA 90:243–244, 1988. John C. Hartnett, SBF 23:177, 1988.]

A Toad in the Courtyard (see Anufom Series)

Tobelo Marriage (1990) 106 min. Dirk Nijland (PR). Dist: UCEMC FR$75, VS$395, order #38012. *This dramatic ethnographic documentary chronicles a remarkable marriage ritual on a Moluccan island of eastern Indonesia. The ritual includes a large-scale exchange of valuables that requires highly diplomatic negotiations, numerous ceremonies, and lengthy preparatory activities. But will the unexpected elopement of the bride and groom spoil everything?* [Reviewed by Janet Alison Hoskins, AA 94(1):281–282, 1992.]

Tobias on the Evolution of Man (1975) 17 min. National Geographic Society (PR). Dist: PSU FR$10. *Dr. Phillip Tobias, paleoanthropologist, traces the evolution of man. Discusses and shows the fossil hominid remains—australopithecenes, Taun, Ples, Zinj, and others. Tobias speculates on speciation, extinction, and the origins of man.* [Reviewed by Robert B Eckhardt, AA 80:509, 1978.]

Todos Santos Cuchumatan: Report from a Guatemalan Village (1982) 41 min. Olivia Carrescia (FM). Dist: FRIF FR$85, FS$685, VS$400. *This film provides an intimate look at everyday life in Todos Santos as it was before the violence. Through discussions with men and women as they go about their daily routines, we discover how cash has become increasingly important to the people of this once self-sustained farming community. We also witness the annual sequence of the harvest, the elaborate Fiesta of Todos Santos, and the mass seasonal migration out of the mountain village in search of work on the cotton plantations of Guatemala's lowlands. This is an insightful documentary that ominously illustrates social changes in the lives of Guatemalan Indians that would lead to the political upheaval of the 1980s.* [Reviewed by John J. Attinasi, AA 86:229–230, 1984.]

Todos Santos: The Survivors (1989) 58 min. Olivia Carrescia (FM). Dist: FRIF FR$125, FS$895, VS$450. *Mayan men and women, wearing traditional carved masks, recount the terror of 1982 that culminated in a night when villagers were locked in their church by the military. This film demonstrates how the political turmoil has affected the village today. Farming and seasonal migration patterns are altered. Some families have fled to Guatemala City, while others are refugees in Mexico. Evangelism challenges the power of the Catholic church. The lives of these nonideological people have changed not only economically, socially, and theologically, but also psychically. Villagers who once were open to conversation with outsiders are afraid to talk about their history or their current situation. This film is a haunting look underneath the silence that blankets much of modern day Guatemala. It documents results of a bloody civil war, and the wounds that are unhealed even after the guns have stopped firing.* [Reviewed by Allan Burns AA 94:528–530, 1992.]

Togo (see Anufom Series)

Tomesha "Ground Afire" 15 min. George F. Hafer Production (PR). Dist: MDAI VS$59.95, order #327-02. *The Panamint Tribe of the Shoshone Indians called their home in Death Valley Tomesha. The Indians found this desert to be a land of plenty while white men starved.*

Tomorrow's People (1973) 17 min. Dist: APPAL FR$30, FS$300. *This is a presentation of mountain music—a sight and sound experience of mountain culture without narration. A visual montage of old-time photographs accompanies the dulcimer sequence, while the central portion of the film turns loose to the banjo and fiddle to render "Fox Chase" by Coy Morton. The film ends with a rousing square dance in a one room schoolhouse high on a mountaintop at Carcassone, Kentucky.*

Tong Tana: A Journey to the Heart of Borneo (1990) 88 min. Dist: FRIF FR$150, FS$1250, VS$490. *"A young man from Switzerland fulfills his childhood dream—to live in a jungle. For the past five years, Bruno Manser has become an occupant of the 160 million-year-old rain forest of Borneo.... The film records a visit with Manser, the forest environment, selected scenes of Penan life, and the current and future survival of the forest, which has been subjected to intense logging since the 1970's."* [From the review by Robert Mishler, SBF 27:118, 1991.]

Tonga Royal (1983) 20 min. Journal Films (PR). Dist: JF FR$35, FS$325; IFF FS$290. *Shows the variety of the Tongan Islands.* [Reviewed by Joan Larcom, AA 86:814–815, 1984.]

Tool Using (see Jane Goodall: Studies of the Chimpanzee Series)

Total Baby (1993) 57 min. Kate Davis and Alyson Denny (FM). Dist: Davis/Denny Productions, 412 West End Ave., Apt #3E, New York, NY 10024; telephone/fax (212) 580-0288. *A historical review of major shifts in Western childrearing practices and beliefs since the Middle Ages. This film deconstructs any notions we might entertain of progress in middle-class child raising. What remains consistent is that these philosophies and practices reflect less about the achievement of perfection in childrearing and more about the hopes and fears of each new generation of parents.*

Totem Pole (American Indian Series) (1963) 27 min. Wilson Duff (AN). Dist: UCEMC FR$34, FS$380; PSU(PCR) order #2213K, FR$9.60, FS$270. *The Northwest Pacific coast was inhabited by many Indian tribes with complex social systems and distinctive arts and mythologies. One of their most remarkable achievements was a bizarre and highly sophisticated wood carving art that found its highest expression in the great carved cedar column, the totem pole. The development of the seven types of totem poles and house posts is lyrically presented in this film. Each is discussed in terms of a social system and mythology that laid stress on kinship, rank, and ostentatious displays of wealth. House posts supported the central beams of the massive communal houses; the Mortuary Pole often held a box of cremated remains; and the Memorial Pole was like the modern tombstone. House Frontal Poles—with their oval holes—served as doorways. The famous Heraldic Pole was always beautifully carved and painted to stand as a "family tree." Newly rich commoners, when giving a potlatch, erected what are called "Potlatch Poles" for no other purpose but to mark the generous affair, an occasion for feasting and distrubuting wealth. The Ridicule—or Shame—Pole was carved to downgrade someone of high rank who had failed to meet a debt or obligation. Only through purchase could it be destroyed and the slight rectified. All of these types are shown. The ancient method of erecting a pole is shown in animation. The felling of a great cedar tree and the carving of the pole by Mungo Martin is seen. Through dance and music (traditional Kwakiutl chants), the myth of how Mungo Martin acquired the crest of the great bird, Hohoq, is retold shortly before the death of this famous carver and Chief of the Kwakiutl.* [Reviewed by Helen Codere, AA 68:843–844, 1966.]

Totems 11 min. National Film Board of Canada (PR). Dist: NFBS; PSU(PCR) order #970.1-10, FR$44.40. *British Columbia.* [Reviewed by Arthur Einhorn, AA 76:718, 1974.]

Touching the Timeless (Millennium: Tribal Wisdom and the Modern World Series) (1992) 1 hour. David Maybury-Lewis (H), Hans Zimmer (MU). Dist: PBS VS$49.95, order #MILL-106-RCDC. *What does it mean to find one's place in the cosmos? What are the different ways that Western societies and tribal cultures seek to elevate their lives from the ordinary world into the extraordinary? Accompany the Huichol people of Mexico on their annual pilgrimage to collect peyote, the sacred food of the gods, and visit the house of a Navajo medicine man who invites the spirits into his world through sand painting, chanting, and "walking in beauty." Then follow David Maybury-Lewis into a consideration of why modernization can be viewed as secularization and what the consequences of this means to Western peoples.*

Tough, Pretty or Smart 29 min. Richard Kane and Dillon Bustin (FM). Dist: DER FR$55, VR$40, FS$475, VS$275. *A portrayal of The Patoka Valley Boys, a six-person string band comprising one of America's finest old time and bluegrass musical groups. Through their own words, the "Boys" proclaim their love for their music, which acts in counterpoint to the technologically advanced jobs they hold.* [Reviewed by Melanie L. Sovine, AA 89:522–525, 1987.]

Toula (The Water Spirit) 80 min. Moustapha Alassane and Anna Soehring (DI). Dist: DER FR$120. *Toula is a tale of drought in the West African Sahel, the ecological belt between the savanna grasslands and the Sahara Desert. There are some farmers in this region, the Hausa and the Songhay, but the Sahel is primarily inhabited by nomadic Fulani pastoralists. Survival here is tied to fluctuations in rainfall. In times of drought, the Fulani are forced to retreat, often seeking sustenance with their more sedentary relatives on the savannah.*

The Toured: The Other Side of Tourism in Barbados (1992) 38 min. Julie Pritchard Wright (PR). Dist: UCEMC VR$50, VS$195, order #38226. *Tourism is the second largest industry in the world, and the "tourist encounter" may be the most important contact today between differing cultures. This award-winning documentary portrays the unequal experience of tourism from the point of view of those who "are toured."*

Tourou et Bitti, les tambours d'Avant (Tourou and Gitti, the Drums of Yore) (1971) 10 min. Jean Rouch (DI), Centre National de la Recherche Scientifique, Comité du Film Ethnographique (PR). Dist: CFE; DER. *The most important moment of a possession ritual during the course of which men from the village of Simiri demand the the spirits of the wilderness protect the coming harvests from locusts.*

TOWARDS BARUYA MANHOOD SERIES (1972) 9 parts, 7.75 hours. Maurice Godelier (AN), Ian Dunlop (FM). Dist: FAA; Papua New Guinea Mission to the United Nations, 100 East 42nd St., 10th Floor, New York, NY 10017. *At about 9 years old, the Baruya boys from the highlands of Papua New Guinea are ritually separated from their mothers and the female world and take up residence in the men's house. Over the next 10 years or so, each boy must pass through four stages of initiation until he finally emerges a full warrior and a man ready for marriage. In 1969, French anthropologist Maurice Godelier invited Dunlop to cooperate with him in filming the initiation ceremonies. The first two films give a general account of Baruya life. The remaining seven films form a continuum.* [Reviewed by William E. Mitchell, AA 77:706–709, 1975.] Also cf. *To Find Baruya's Story: Maurice Godelier's Work with a New Guinea Tribe.*

Towards Baruya Manhood (People in Change Series) (1989) 141 min. Film Australia (PR). Dist: FIV VS$387. *This video has three parts that provide unique insights into the life of the Baruya tribe in the Eastern Highlands of Papua New Guinea. It shows traditional Baruya culture, little changed by European contact.*

Trade and Market in West Africa 15 min. Dan Shafer, Tom O'Toole (FM). Dist: MINN FS$195. *This film ties together many of the other single ethnic studies in a historical and geographical overview. Parts of two of the most important indigenous trading systems of West Africa are examined. The working of the trade systems is described in a three-part typology of local, regional, and international trade. Filmed throughout West Africa in the course of three months' travel in the same conveyances that transport African products to market, the film has a sense of immediacy and motion that help students "feel" the vitality of African* *trading systems. Local and regional markets are featured in the latter sequences. The dominant religion of Islam is quite evident.*

Trading in Africans: Dutch Outposts in West Africa 50 min. Dist: FHS VS$149, order #DH-2643. *Salt for the pickling of herrings, wood to repair sea battered ships, fruits to prevent scurvy, and gold to satisfy their greed: these were the original prizes the Dutch sought in West Africa. But after the Dutch conquest of Brazil in 1637, the demand for slaves to work the Brazilian sugar plantations motivated the Dutch to dislodge the Portuguese and gain a foothold on the African mainland. From the moment they conquered Elmina, the Dutch embarked on the slave trade. This program looks at the European view of the Africans in the mid–17th century, at the nature of the slave trade, and at the life of some of the African tribes on whose backs the Dutch built the most profitable of their many profitable businesses—with the result that close to half of the present population of the Western Hemisphere is descended from Africans.*

Tradition (1973) 20 min. Dist: APPAL R$40, FS$375, VS$150. *Moonshining is regarded as one of the strongest traditions in the mountains. Though the number steadily decreases, there are still mountaineers who "had rather make moonshine than go on welfare." In this film, a moonshiner tells what it's like to have been "sent up" four times for making liquor while IRS agents tell tales of tracking down stills and arresting moonshiners.*

Tradition Bearers (1983) 47 min. Michael Loukinen (FM). Dist: UP North Films, 331 Thomas Fine Arts, Northern Michigan University, Marquette, MI 49855; (906) 227-2041, R$95, FS$780, VS$605. *"Looks at the lives and repertoires of four traditional artists: a woodworker and a weaver, [who left Finland in 1903 and 1913 respectively]; and two Finnish-American artisans, a storyteller, and a lumberjack/folk musician."* [From the review by Patricia Slade Lander, *AA* 88:261–263, 1986.]

TRADITIONAL DANCES OF INDONESIA (1976) William Heick (PR). Dist: UCEMC FR$45, VS$195. *This 12-film series forms an important visual record for anyone interested in traditional Indonesian dance and culture. Each film deals with a different dance form and features some of Indonesia's most celebrated performers. The programs were filmed in 1975–76 but not released until 1990. Contact the University of California Extension Media Center for individual film titles and descriptions.*

- **Dances of Bali: Baris Katekok Jago and Kebyar Duduk** 20 min.
- **Dances of Bali: Barong** 32 min.
- **Dances of Bali: Legong Kraton** 20 min.
- **Dances of Jogjakarta, Central Java: Bekasan Menak**
- **Dances of Jogjakarta, Central Java: Langen Mandra Wanara** 40 min.
- **Dances of Jogjakarta, Central Java: Lawung Ageng**
- **Dances of Surakarta, Central Java: Bedoyo Elo Elo** 23 min.
- **Dances of Surakarta, Central Java: Bedoyo Pangkur** 23 min.
- **Dances of Surakarta, Central Java: Menak Konchar** 11 min.
- **Dances of Surakarta, Central Java: Srimpi Anglir Mendung** 19 min.
- **Dances of Surakarta, Central Java: Srimpi Gondokusomo** 19 min.
- **Dances of West Sumatra: Tari Piring and Tari Alang** 20 min.

Traditional Healing on Guyana: The Divine Madness of Kali Mai Functional Therapy 3 parts, 40 min. each. Philip Singer (FM). Dist: Philip Singer, Dept. of Sociology and Anthropology, Oakland University, Rochester, MI 48063. [Reviewed by Martha Foster Breidenbach, *AA* 81:472–473, 1979.]

TRADITIONAL MUSIC OF PAPUA NEW GUINEA Les McLaren (DI). Dist: DER. See film descriptions under individual titles:

- **Kama Wosi: Music in the Trobriand Islands**
- **Namekas: Music in Lake Chambri**
- **Tidikawa and Friends**

THE TRADITIONAL WORLD OF ISLAM SERIES (1978) 6 parts, 30 min. each. Stephen Cross Ltd (PR). Dist: UTA-FL FR$15; Institutional Cinema, Inc., 10 First St., Saugerties, NY 12477; (914) 246-2848. *Depicts the traditional world of Islam. "The focus is on arts (architecture, calligraphy, and miniature painting), the expression of religious belief, and the development of science."* [From the review by Elizabeth Warnock Fernea, *AA* 87:235–237, 1985. Film titles are:

- **Unit**
- **Patterns of Beauty**
- **Nomad and City**
- **Knowledge of the World**
- **Man and Nature**
- **Inner Life**

Tragada Bhavai: A Rural Theater Troupe of Gujarat (1982) 40 min. Roger Sandall and Jayasinhji Jhala (FM). Dist: DER FR$65, VR$40, FS$675, VS$350. *"Bhavai" is the traditional rural theater of Gujarat. Today there are only a few troupes of Bhavai performers in India. This film follows one troupe as it travels throughout the countryside, performing in villages for audiences of the poor Koli caste. Audience and performers are entirely male, and actors impersonate female roles. A typical Bhavai evening includes a miracle play, comic skits, dances and juggling, and, finally, a romantic drama set in medieval times. The films shows "backstage" preparations, negotiations with sponsoring villagers, interviews with actors and the troupe's leader, and the performance itself.* [Reviewed by Richard Schechner, *AA* 87:492–493, 1985.]

Trance and Dance in Bali (1991, c1952) 22 min. Margaret Mead and Gregory Bateson (AN, FM). Dist: PSU VR$15.50, FS$440, VS$125, order #24636; NYU VR$16, VS$210. *A* *performance of the kris dance, a Balinese ceremonial dance drama in which the neverending struggle between the witch and the dragon—the death dealing and life protecting—as it is given in the village of Pagoetan from 1937–39. The dancers go into violent trance seizures and turn their krisses (daggers) against their breasts without injury. Consciousness is restored with incense and holy water. Balinese music is background for Margaret Mead's narration.* [Reviewed by Hildred Geertz, AA 78:725–726, 1976.] See suggested supplements for *A Balinese Family.*

Transition Generation: A Third World Problem (1977) 20 min. Alexander Von Wetter (PR, DI). Dist: IFF FR$35, FS$360. *Through the lives of a few Afghanis, we witness the problem people all over the world have in combining traditional values with those from Western cultures. Rashid, city educated, feels at times out of place in his home village. Daud, wealthy and educated, cannot find a job. Mobuba, by Afghan standards an emacipated woman, still sees her place to be in the home but does appear in public without a veil.*

Transportation and Community Services in Spontaneous and Planned Colonization, Incora's Rule in New Settlements—Caquetta, Colombia (1963) 16 min. The Land Tenure Center, University of Wisconsin (PR). Dist: UW. *Visits three government colonization projects in the newly opened lowland territory of Caquetta. Considers hardships of farming in the lowlands, transportation problems, and the effect of new roads for new colonies. The three settlements are Valparaiso, La Mono, and Maguare in the Amazon basin.*

Transnational Fiesta: 1992 (1993) 61 min. Wilson Martinex and Paul Gelles (PR). Dist: UCEMC VR$75, VS$295, order #38250. *Five hundred years after the Conquest, indigenous peoples are reasserting their identity with renewed vigor. This video illustrates this by exploring the multicultural and transnational experiences of a family of Peruvian Andean immigrants living in Washington, DC, and follows them as they return to their hometown in Peru to sponsor the annual fiesta of the village's patron saint.*

Traveller from an Antique Land 28 min. Dist: CBC FR$40, FS$375. *The body of a man who lived in ancient Egypt helps the medical profession fight modern disease. This program deals with the process and practice of mummification and an unusual autopsy on the mummy of an Egyptian who lived 20 centuries ago. The autopsy, part of a continuing study, is intended to provide information on the diseases of ancient man, which can then be compared with modern diseases. By comparison, modern doctors hope to determine how diseases evolved and the conditions that produced them. As Dr. Robin Barraco of Wayne State University puts it in the program, "before we can realistically eradicate diseases, we have to know something about their evolution." Dr. Barraco's colleague, Dr. George Lynn, appears in the program along with Dr. N. B. Millet, Anthropological Consultant with the Royal Ontario Museum, and Dr. Peter K. Lewin, Medical Consultant, Hospital for Sick Children, Toronto.*

Treasure (1977) 59 min. National Geographic Society (PR). Dist: NGS FR$50, FS$495, VS$395. *"Deals with the efforts of Mel A. Fisher and his salvage company, Treasure Salvors, to locate the Spanish ship Nuestra Senora de Atocha, lost in 1622 off the coast of Florida, and to recover its treasure of gold and silver estimated at hundreds of millions of dollars. As a story of one person's dream to find a fabled treasure, this film is well done."* [From the review by Robert L. Hohlfelder, ARCH 36(1):62—6, 1983.]

Treasure in the Deep (1983) 27 min. Anabel Olivier Wright (PR), Janice Kay (DI). Dist: British Information Service, 845 Third Avenue, New York, NY 10022, free loan; London Television Service, Hercules House, Hercules Road, London SE1 7DU, England; 01-928-2345, FS$500. *"The 1983 recovery of the 'Mary Rose', flagship of King Henry VIII, by archaeologist Margaret Rule and the Mary Rose Trust, stands out as one of the most ambitious and significant achievements in the history of maritime archeology."* [From the review by Mark D. Myers, AA 89:268–269, 1987. Reviewed by Roger C. Smith, ARCH 39(2):79–80, 1986.]

Treasured Islands: Robert Louis Stevenson in the Pacific (1990) 72 min. Lowell D. Holmes (FM, AN). Dist: Poly Concepts, 2948 North Terrace Drive, Wichita, KS 67220, VS$300. [Reviewed by George W. Stocking, AA 93(2):521–522, 1991.]

The Tree of Iron (1988) 57 min. Peter O'Neill, Frank Muhly, Jr., and Peter Schmidt (FM). Dist: CAS-UF VR$65, FS$750, VS$200. *"About the history and technology of Haya iron smelting in Tanzania, featuring the work of archaeologist Peter Schmidt."* [From the review by Patrick R. McNaughton, AA 91:1092–1094, 1989. Reviewed by Peter S. Allen, ARCH 41(6):77–78, 1988.]

The Tree of Knowledge (1983) 26 min. Pacho Lane (FM). Dist: Folklore Media Center, P.O. Box 266, Cerrillos, NM 87010. VR$50, FS$450, VS$350. *Filmed in Huehuetla, a Totonac/Hispanic community in northern Puebla, Mexico. Examines "the pervasive asymmetrical social and power relationships that exist between Indians and Mestizos."* [From the review by Michael Logan, AA 86:235–237, 1984.] See also *The Tree of Life.*

Tree of Life (1974) 20 min. Bruce Pacho Lane (FM). Dist: FF; UNI; UCEMC FR$27. *Documents and interprets the myth behind the Volardor ritual, as performed today by the Totonac Indians of Huehuetla, Mexico. The ritual, in which men "fly" on ropes tethered at the point of a cone-shaped tower, is probably the oldest religious dance in the Western hemisphere, dating back to A.D. 500.* [Reviewed by Joann W. Kealiinohomoku, JAF 90(357):377–378, 1977. Michael Logan, AA 86:235–236, 1984.] Focusing questions: When you watch a film, you are where the camera was. What person or persons might the camera position indicate? Does that change during the film? What is the intended role of the many close-up camera angles? If you have seen this film more than once, what changed in your understanding or response after another viewing? What elements of native Mexican myth and symbolism can you identify in the film? What elements of Catholic Christian symbolism can you identify? Why do you suppose the Catholic Church allowed the performance of what had been a pagan ritual? Do you think the Voladores have decided not to perform after 1973? If you were given the chance would you do a Voladores flight? Discuss the reasons for your answer? What do you think motivates the Voladores to perform? Discuss an interpretation of the poetry and relate the poetry to the Voladores ritual. Are there experiences in your culture, especially in your own life, that have a similar nature or the same function as the Voladores ritual has for the Totonacs? Bibliography: Angel María Garabay Kintana, *Poesia Nahuatl.* Mexico: Universidad Nacional Autonoma de Mexico, 1964–1968. Alain Ichon, *La Religión de los Totonaca de la Sierra.* Mexico: Instituto Nacional Indigenista, 1973. Rosemary Gibson, Los Voladores, "The Flyers of Mexico." *Western Folklore* 30:269–278, 1971. Gertrude Karuth, "Los Arrieros of Acopilco, Mexico." *Western Folklore* 6:232–236, 1947. [J. B. Colson]

Tree-Top Signaling (Japanese Macaque)   4.5 min. Dist: PSU FR$4.30.

Trekking on Tradition   (1993) 45 min. Dist: UCEMC VR$50, VS$225, order #38224. *This production explores the relationship between the mountain tourists (trekkers) and their guides in Nepal. The film illuminates, often humorously, the controversies and ironic nature of cross-cultural encounters engendered by tourism in developing countries.*

Tremors in Guzman   (1988) 30 min. John Hewitt and Sam Wonderly (DI). Dist: UCEMC FR$40, VS$195. *This documentary takes the viewer to the streets of Ciudad Guzman, a small Mexican city south of Guadalajara, to learn what Mexicans think about the state of their country, its economy, and its political leaders. Shows that many of the same problems fueling revolt elsewhere in Central America—corrupt government officials, uncontrolled inflation, economic depression, and high unemployment—also exist in Mexico. Essential viewing for understanding Mexico's growing social and political unrest.*

THE TRIBAL EYE: AN EXPLORATION OF TRIBAL CULTURES 7 films, 52 min. each. David Attenborough (FM), BBC-TV and Warner Bros. (PR). Dist: T/L R$575 (set), $100 (each), FS$5,000 (set), $850 (each), VS$1000 (set). *Many tribal societies have no word for "art." Their artifacts—most often sacred, ceremonial, or everyday objects—which Western man has carried off to his museums, form the very fabric of their lives. To understand these objects—what they represent, why they are made, how they are used—is to understand the people and the cultures that produce them. David Attenborough, trained as an anthropologist and zoologist, wrote and narrated this program that shows how and why tribal arts and life are inextricably woven together. The filmmakers immersed themselves in the tribal societies of 16 countries for 18 months. In Attenborough's words, he personally conducted the search "to see the fascinating solutions other groups have found to common human problems when not faced with 400 years of imported Western European answers."* [Reviewed by Marie Jeanne Adams, *AA* 79:996–997, 1977.] Discussion guides available.

• **The Crooked Beak of Heaven** (No. 1) *With great ceremony, the Haida chief bestows lavish gifts on his tribesmen and then smashes his most valuable possessions in the frenzied atmoshpere of a "potlatch"—a colorful, almost theatrical event staged by northwestern American Indian tribes. We witness these celebrations as the filmmakers visit a "potlatch" and other traditional ceremonies of the Gitskan, Haida, and Kwakiutl Indians who inhabit the magnificent region of what is now the state of Washington and the Canadian province of British Columbia. We become familiar with their customs and time-honored way of life. As they spend their long winters in communal longhouses, they perform magic-filled rituals and manufacture ceremonial objects: masks, rattles, jewelry, and sculpture; objects that proclaim their wealth and power. But the most powerful, most divine object of all is carved and placed outside—the totem pole. These towering carvings, the largest wooden sculptures made by man, are shown in their village setting, in lines along the shore, and grouped before the longhouses. We learn how to read them: as an imaginistic literature of tribal myth and family history, as symbols of property, aristocracy, and divinity: an intimate part of these peoples' daily lives.* [Reviewed by Dale Idiens, *RAIN* 10:7, 1975.]

• **Behind the Mask** (No. 2) *"To walk through the mud hut villages of the Dogon people of Nigeria, perched hundreds of feet high on sandstone cliffs, one would never suspect that their craftsmen are among the finest sculptors in the world. For their carvings are hidden, guarded by the Mother of Masks, and concealed in remote desert shrines known only to wise old men. Attenborough talks with the Dogon and examines some of their artifacts. These carvings are as meaningful to these people as is the Bible to the Western world and are produced only for the most important rituals and splendid Dogon ceremonies. We see a priest drenching sacred sculptures with libations on millet and gruel and sacrificial blood as Attenborough explains how this act ensures the fertility of the fields and the health of the people. We see the creation of one of their beautiful masks. And the dead are placed in the shrine with their bodies touching the sacred sculptures so their spirits will join those of their ancestors."* [From the review by Philip Goldman, *RAIN* 10:6, 1975.]

• **Man Blong Custom** (No.3) *We go on a perilous journey to virtually unknown villages in the jungle-covered mountains of the New Hebrides. There we witness the sacred ceremonies performed in the village cult house, ceremonies usually reserved only for village holy men. In the privacy of the cult house, initiates are educated in the mysteries of the spirit world. In these houses, we see the construction of rambaramps, life-size effigies, the heads of which human skulls fleshed out with clay, to be used as cavorting puppets in funeral ceremonies. Then the BBC cameras move to the neighboring Solomon Islands where Attenborough depicts the contrasting life of a coastal Melanesian people. We see magnificent war canoes, sea spirit dances, and an anthropological phenomenon—Moro. This island mystic awoke from a trance declaring he had spoken to the Gods of the Island who bade the inhabitants revive the old ways and send the foreign Christians back from whence they came. Attenborough explores this cult and Moro's pidgin English* directive to worship the ancients: "Man blong custom." [Reviewed by Raymond Firth, *RAIN* 10:8, 1975.]

- **The Sweat of the Sun** (No. 4) *Little of the golden hoard of the Aztecs and the Incas escaped the brutal pillaging of the Spanish conquistadors. Attenborough examines some of the most important pre-Colombian objects that eluded European smelting furnaces and describes how these objects were used by priests of the Aztec and Inca cultures in practical and ritual fashion, including human sacrifice. The cameras penetrate the jungles to the various sites of pre-Colombian splendor: Santa Cecelia and the Temple of the Jaguar and Eagle Knights. And to the site of legendary El Dorado, a lake near Bogotá where the world's greatest assembly of golden objects still lies buried in its murky depths. We tour these places and learn of the people who once inhabited them and the complex significance of their artifacts.* [Reviewed by G. H. S. Bushnell, *RAIN* 10:7, 1975.]

- **Woven Gardens** (No. 5) *Qashqa'i rugs are a perfect mirror of the nomadic life of this Iranian people. Wool is gathered from their sheep, goats, and camels. Dyes are made from the juices of plants that grow along their annual route of travel. And the jogging of the packed animals, bearing the looms with unfinished rugs, give the weave its beautiful irregularity. But with Qashqa'i rugs, beauty is second to function. They offer protection from the frozen ground. Hung on the walls of the tents, they provide a shield against bitter winds. Their durability also lends them as fabric for saddle bags and grain sacks. And when a girl marries a man from another group, she weaves the patterns her husband expects to see on his rugs, but she also integrates the images from her own tradition, thus creating a new family design. It is this wonderful combination of beauty, function, and tradition that makes the Qashqa'i rugs a masterpiece of tribal art.* [Reviewed by Schuyler Jones, *RAIN* 10:8, 1975.]

- **Kingdom of Bronze** (No. 6) *In 1897, a great cache of bronzes arrived in London and caused a sensation. The elegance, artistic inspiration, and technical mastery of these works was so consummate that many European experts refused to believe that the bronzesmiths of the obscure Nigerian kingdom of Benin could have developed such a sophisticated technique of casting by themselves. The filmmakers trace the background of the ethnocentric controversy and discover that the Beni learned bronze casting from the Yoruba tribe, predating the known Portuguese influence of the 16th century. The beautiful and elegant portrait busts, plaques, and standing figures read as an impressive chronicle of an elaborate court life under the autocratic Obas of Benin. We are also invited to witness Nigerian bronze casting as practiced today, using the ancient Yoruba and Beni "lost wax" process.* [Reviewed by M. D. McLeod, *RAIN* 10:7, 1075.]

- **Across the Frontier** (No. 7) *"It seems to me hopelessly narrowminded and foolishly romantic to ask that more 'primitive' people should remain the same. Why should they?" Thus, in this overview program, Attenborough summarizes his exploration of tribal ways as seen through tribal arts. Tribal societies are dynamic and are subject to the positive and negative influences of outsiders as well as to the vicissitudes of their own internal processes. But a rising consciousness of the loss of tribal customs is breathing new life into some old tribes and is creating a new breed of anthropological hero. In the 'Ksan community of British Columbia, Indians fashion Totem poles, jewelry, and fabrics for themselves—not for the tourists. An American anthropologist solved the old Dogon problem of water storage and gained acceptance for it through his sensitivity to Dogon customs. A Canadian painter revived Eskimo arts—in a new medium. In these ways, Attenborough characterizes the ever-changing tribal world as a restless and dynamic system and the study of anthropology as a never-ending search for new tribal forms.* [Reviewed by J. B. Loudon, *RAIN* 10:8, 1975.]

Tribal Groups of Central India. The Chota Maria Gonds—The Bhils 40 min. Margaret Fairlie (DI, CA, ED), Kenneth A.R. Kennedy (AN). Dist: IRC FR$75, FS$425. *Daily life, ceremonial rites, and dance forms (from choreometric analysis).* See also *Herding Castes*.

The Tribe and the Professor: Ozette Archaeology (Rev. ed. 1978) 44 min. Louis and Ruth Kirk (PR). Dist: UWP FS$495; IMS-UW FR$45. *Depicting the most recent archaeological excavations at the Ozette Indian village at Cape Alava, Washington, this film portrays the Makah Indians' newly awakened awareness of their rich cultural heritage and their active participation in its preservation. Scenes illustrate the scientific processes involved in the restoration and preservation of the more than 30,000 items found during the excavation, describe the Makah's involvement in the establishment of a museum to display the artifacts, and show the elderly tribespeople teaching their children the ancient Makah language, dances, and crafts. Included are interviews with Professor Richard Daugherty, overall director of the excavations, and members of the Makah Indian Tribe.* [Reviewed by R. Carol Barnes, *ARCH* 36(4):72–73, 1983.]

The Tribe That Hides from Man (1973) 62 min. Adrian Cowell (PR), Chris Menger (CA). Dist: ISHI FR$50, FS$750; PSU FR$25; IUAVC FR$21.50, FS$585. *Records efforts of two Brazilian explorers, Orlando and Claudio Villas Boas, searching through Brazil's Amazon jungle for the Kree-Akorre tribe. Their objective is to save the tribe from extinction. Shows their attitudes, conflicts, and emotions about aiding the Indians facing development and acculturation.* [Reviewed by Terence Turner, *AA* 76:489–491, 1974. Reviewed in *VISA* 4:91, 1991.] Bibliography: Adrian Cowell, *The Tribe That Hides from Man*. New York: Stein and Day, 1974.

TRIUMPH OF THE NOMADS 3 parts, 1 hour each. Nomad Films International (PR). Dist: PBSV VS$134.95, order #9775-21. *This video series introduces students to the Aborigine lifestyle and its influence on the development of modern culture. It shows how the Aborigine's lifestyle prospered through their mastery over nature and the art of survival. The series also examines centuries-old attitudes toward education, sports, trade, religion, and art.* The titles of the films comprising this series are:

- **The First Invaders**
- **Reign of the Wanderers**
- **Sails of Doom**

Trobriand Cricket: An Ingenious Response to Colonialism (1976) 54 min. Jerry Leach and Gary Kildea (DI). Dist: IUAVC VR$19; UCEMC FR$65, FS$995, VS$410. *One of the world's most renowned and widely seen ethnographic films, this classic documentary depicts the many modifications made by Trobriand Islanders, in Papua New Guinea, to the traditional British game of cricket. Demonstrates how the islanders have changed the game into an outlet for tribal rivalry, mock warfare, community interchange, sexual innuendo, and an afternoon of riotous fun.* [Reviewed by Annette B. Weiner, *AA* 79:506, 1977. Edmund Leach, *RAIN* 9:6, 1975. Reviewed in *VISR* 8:106, 1992.]

The Trobriand Experiment (1975) Alec Nisbett (PR, WR), John Cooper (CA). Shown as part of the BBC Horizon Series. [Reviewed by H. A. Powell, *RAIN* 13:2, 1976.]

Trobriand Islander 66 min. H. A. Powell (FM, AN), C. Daryll Forde (CON), University College, London (PR). Dist: H. A. Powell; UCEMC FR$23. *Trobriand is one of the islands off the southeast tip of New Guinea. This film shows the native Trobriand Islanders engaged in many of their tribal and family activities; during ceremonies and dancing, crop planting with magic, funeral celebrations and mourning; the killing of pigs and other preparations for feasting, etc. The "kula" is partly shown and described including the carving of great canoes, sailmaking, and the sailing of the overseas fleet. The "milanmala" or harvest is described, the result of the earlier planting. A marriage with feasting and dancing is included. Warning: This film has an optional soundtrack that was recorded at 16 frames per second (or "silent" speed). It can only be shown on a projector that is capable of showing it at silent speed with the sound "on."*

The Trobriand Islanders of Papua New Guinea (Disappearing World Series) (1990) 52 min. Annette B. Weiner (AN). Dist: PSU order #51227; FIV VS$198, order #047042. *The Trobriand islands, regarded as anthropology's most sacred place, lie off the eastern tip of Papua New Guinea. The island society has a complex balance of male authority and female wealth. Magic spells and sorcery pervade everyday life. This program focuses on two important events: the distribution of women's wealth after a death and the "month of play," a time of celebration following the yam harvest.* [Reviewed by Frederick H. Damon, *AA* 93(4):1036–1031991. Reviewed in *VISR* 8:106, 1992.]

The Tuareg (Disappearing World Series) (1972) 60 min. Jeremy Keenan (AN). Dist: PSU order #61403. *The Tuareg live in the heart of the Algerian desert. Life has changed drastically since slavery, the economic basis of their society, was abolished in 1962. The Tuareg carry on their traditions and customs to maintain prestige, but schools are teaching their children about the world outside the desert.* [Reviewed by Robert F. Murphy, *AA* 75:212, 1974.]

The Tuareg (1974) 46 min. Bruce Parsons (FM). Dist: FRIF VR$75, FS$695, VS$490. [Reviewed by Robert F. Murphy et al. *AA* 85:496–497, 1983.]

Tule Technology: Northern Paiute Uses of Marsh Resources in Western Nevada (1981) 42 min. Catherine Fowler, Thomas Vennum and Margaret Wheat (PR). Dist: PSU FR$22.50, FS$420, VS$185. *"Filmed in two sessions of fieldwork in 1964 and 1979, this documentary is valuable for two reasons: it shows us real people making real items of material culture, and it records the seldom considered lacustrine aspect of human adaptation in the Great Basin."* [From the review by Richard O. Clemmer, *AA* 87:225–226, 1985.]

The Tunica Treasure Jeffrey Brain (PR). Dist: POR. Set of 79 slides, $110. [Reviewed by Peter S. Allen, *ARCH* 42(5):74–75, 1986.]

Tununeremiut: The People of Tununak (The Alaskan Eskimo Series) 35 min. Leonard Kamerling, Sarah Elder (FM). Dist: DER FR$40, FS$450. *Four sequences, filmed over a two-onth period, portray aspects of the lives of the people of Tununak, a village on the southwestern coast of Alaska. Villagers leave their homes because of danger of a tidal wave from a nuclear test on Amchitka Island; men travel by snowmobile to place fishtraps under the river ice; a sudden storm blows laundry wildly in the wind; and villagers meet to dance and tell stories in the meeting hall, in an atmosphere of communal warmth and conviviality.*

Las Turas (1979) 16 min. Ana Maria Enriquez (DI). Dist: UNI FR$40-90, FS$300. *Depicts the celebration of Las Turas, an ancient fertility rite still practiced today by Indian peasants in Venezuela. The annual performance of this centuries-old agricultural ritual consists of joyous dancing and music to offer praise and gratitude for Mother Earth's life-giving powers and to invoke the favor of the many spirits who determine the outcome of the harvest. The portrayal of the ritual is complemented by an explanation of its background and meaning, which utilizes the words of the Indians themselves.*

TURKANA CONVERSATIONS TRILOGY David and Judith MacDougall (DI). Dist: UCEMC FS$3000, VS$1140. *These three feature-length documentaries on the Turkana—relatively isolated seminomadic herders who inhabit the dry country of northwestern Kenya—are among the most important and influential ethnographic films of the last 20 years. Made by the renowned filmmaking team of David and Judith MacDougall, these films are essential viewing for anyone interested in ethnography. All three films are in Turkana, with English subtitles.* [Reviewed by Ben G. Blount, *AA* 86:803–805, 1984.]

The Turkana (From Africa to Asia: Nomads Series) (1992) 60 min. Dr J. Terence McCabe (AN). Dist: FIV VS$198. *The East African Turkana cattle herders are some of the toughest and most opportunistic nomadic pastoralists in the rift valley of Northern Kenya.*

Turkey's Sephardim: Five Hundred Years (1989) 60 min. Laurence Salzman (FM). Dist: 500 Year Project, 3607 Baring Street, Philadelphia, PA 19104; (215) 222-2649. *"Communal life of the 22,000 descendants of Spanish Jews still residing in Turkey."* [From the review by Michael E. Meeker, *AA* 93(4):1037–1038, 1991.]

Turlutte (St. Lawrence North Series) Dist: CRAW FS$210.70 Color, $75.38 B/W. *A delightful film built in the form of the Dance song, the Turlutte, interpreting the ways of the people who live in the old farms and villages in the enchanting valley of the Whirepool River.*

The Turning Point 25 min. Lionel Friedberg (DI). Dist: Contemporary Films, Ltd., 55 Greek St., London, England. *Raymond Dart and the Australopithecines.* [Reviewed by James C. Armstrong, *AA* 76:691, 1974.]

The Turtle People (1973) 26 min. Brian Weiss (CA, AN), James Ward (PR, ED). Dist: B&C FR$35, FS$400; PSU FR$14.50; UW. *The Coastal Miskito Indians of eastern Nicaragua have depended on the green sea turtle to sustain them for over 350 years. For the Miskito food is meat, and meat is the sea turtle. This film documents how the Miskito have entered the market economy, pursuing the turtles not for food, but for cash. The ecological and cultural changes that have taken place provide a unique and useful case study in cultural ecology, acculturation, and "development." When "The Company" arrives to buy turtles, the Miskito are eager salesmen. Participation in the "boom-and-bust" economic cycles of Central America has left the Miskito with a desire for cash and only the turtles to sell. With turtles, a commercial commodity rather than a subsistence resource, distant markets rather than local population determine the rate of exploitation. This has resulted in rapid depletion of the turtle population, which now threatens to provide neither subsistence nor cash. Historical circumstances have put the Miskito in the marketplace, and ecological ones threaten to put them out. The interplay of these forces is shown in the ghost towns left by previous "booms," and in the faces of the villagers as they gather to try to get a pound of scarce meat when a turtle is butchered. Speaking in Creole English, turtlemen explain how a turtle sent to the company yields more money than if butchered and sold in the village, so "turtle meat here now is gold." The film presents the dilemmas and decisions being faced as indigenous groups are increasingly incorporated into market economies. It offers a unique perspective on the ecology of economics and the adaptation of a human population.* [Reviewed by Daniel R. Ross, *AA* 76:487, 1974. Joseph A. Mannino, *AJPA* 66:348–349, 1985.] Suggested supplements: Archie Carr, "Great Reptiles." *Audubon* 74:24–35, 1972. Archie Carr, *So Excellent a Fishe: A Natural History of Sea Turtles.* Anchor Press, 1973. Archie Carr and Robert E. Shroeder, "Carribean Green Turtle: Imperiled Gift of the Sea." *National Geographic* 131(6):876–890, 1967. Mary W. Helms, *Asang.* University of Florida Press, 1971. Mary W. Helms, "The Cultural Ecology of a Colonial Tribe." *Ethnology* 8:76–84, 1969. Bernard Q. Nietschmann, *Between Land and Water: The Subsistence Ecology of the Miskito Indians, Eastern Nicaragua.* Seminar Press, 1973. Bernard Q. Nietschmann, "Hunting and Fishing Focus among the Miskito Indians, Eastern Nicaragua." *Journal of Human Ecology* 1(1):41–67, 1972. James I. Parsons, *The Green Turtle and Man.* University of Florida Press, 1962. Bernard Q. Nietschmann, *Carribean Edge,* Bobbs-merrill. Focusing questions: What is happening to Miskito economy? Where do they get their food? Why does a culture let itself get sucked into such a maladaptive pattern? What responsibility do the soup companies have? After seeing the film, would you eat green turtle soup? Bibliography: Brian Weiss, *Selling a Subsistence System: A User's Guide to the film "The Turtle People."* Sherman Oaks, CA: B&C Films, 1975. Bernard Q. Nietschmann, "When the Turtle Collapses, The World Ends." *Natural History* 83(6):34–43, 1974.

Turumba 94 min. Kidlat Tahimik (DI). Dist: FF. *Set in a tiny Philippine village, this film focuses on one family who traditionally made papier-mache animals to sell during the Turumba religious festivities. One year a department store buyer shows up in town and purchases all their stock. When she returns with an order of 500 more, the family's seasonal occupation becomes year round alienated labor. Of course, they are now able to buy electric fans, TV sets, and Beatles records. Increased production, however, creates inflated needs. Soon virtually the entire village has gone to work on a jungle assembly line, turning out papier-mache mascots for the Munich Olympics. Long before the local bands learns to play "Deutschland Uber Alles," the fabric of traditional life has been torn asunder. Ariel Dorfman has written on the equation between childhood and underdevelopment, but Tahimik uses a facade of bland innocence to mask a welter of ironic observations.*

Twilight of the Maya (ca. 1972) 50 min. Steve Hornick and Mark Lester (FM). Dist: GP FR$75, FS$600. *This is the story of the last remaining tribe of Maya Indians, the Lacandones, who still practice the customs and religion of their ancient ancestors. After two years of extensive research and preliminary exploration, a four-man film crew spent six months in the rain forest jungle of southern Mexico in the state of Chiapas recording the life and culture of the Lacandones. The result is one of the most beautiful and humanitarian film portraits of an Indian culture ever made. Twilight of the Maya tells the story of the Lacandones' attempt to live as their ancestors once did as the rudiments of modern civilization force their way into the condition of their lives. This remarkable film trancends its particular subject matter and location to become, instead, not another typical anthropology film, but rather an important and classic study of a primitive people in the midst of inevitable cultural change.*

Two Ballgames 29 min. David Gluck (FM). Dist: James B. Maas, Dept. of Psychology, Cornell University, Ithaca, NY 14853; Association Films, 600 Grand Ave., Ridgefield, NJ 07657. *The film alternates (16 times) between two groups of children between the ages of 8 and 12; one group (all boys) is engaged in a highly competitive, adult-organized Little League baseball game; the other group (boys and girls) is involved in a more casual "sandlot" softball game. Shot in the mid-seventies in two white middle-class neighborhoods of the American midwest. The intent of the film is to create the comparison between two game settings for the purpose of evaluating the contribution of each to the socialization of American children. The almost inescapable conclusion is that Little League baseball is a potent agent of socialization into the dominant values of American society—but stressful for children who are caught up in performing for adults. In contrast, the child-organizing game is relaxed and playful.*

Socialization obviously is taking place here too; leadership, rules and norms, and group problem solving are important to the game. Focusing questions: Where do the kids have the most fun? Are they "playing" in both? What is the nature of competition of each? How are disputes settled? How does each prepare children for the future? If Little League is as stressful and unpleasant as seen in the film, why is it so popular? Bibliography: E. M. Avedon and Sutton-Smith, *The Study of Games*. New York: John Wiley and Sons, 1971. E. C. Devereux, "Backyard versus Little League Baseball: The Impoverishment of Children's Games." In: *Social Problems in Athletics*, D. M. Landers, ed. Pp. 37–56. Urbana: University of Illinois Press, 1976. Thomas M. Kando, "Where Do the Kids Have the Most Fun?" (film review) *Teaching of Psychology*, February:49–50, 1978. "Peewee Football." *Newsweek,* December 4, 1978:129. B. C. Ogilvie and T. A. Tutko, "If You Want to Build Character Try Something Else." *Psychology Today* 5:60–63, 1971. Thomas Tutko and William Bruns, *Winning Is Everything (and Other American Myths)*. New York: MacMillan Co., 1976. [Phil Osborne]

Two Black Churches (1975) 20 min. William Ferris (DI), Dale Lindquist (FM), Produced in association with Howard Sayre Warner. Dist: CSF FR$30, FS$300. *Black religious expression, ranging from an old-time religious Baptist in rural Mississippi to an urban sanctified service in New Haven, Connecticut. The camera moves unnoticed through the congregations, gradually drawing the viewer in, and providing extraordinary footage of inspired preaching, holy dancing, and a climactic healing ceremony in which a young man confined to a wheelchair is temporarily made to walk.* [Reviewed by David Evans, *JAF* (90)355:121, 1977.]

Two Desert Families (1974) 38 min. John Martin-Jones (PR), Ian Dunlop (DI). Dist: FAA. *This program comprises two parts, namely, Djagamara and Mima. These films are a shortened version of* Desert People *for use in primary schools.*

Two Dollars and a Dream (1987) 56 min. Stanley Nelson (FM). Dist: FL VR$85, FS$850, VS$500. *"A joyous film about the accumulation and expenditure of wealth" in America.* [From the review by George E. Marcus.]

Two Journeys (Diary of a Maasai Village Series) (1985) 50 min. BBC (PR). Dist: FIV VS$198. *As preparations begin for a wedding, Tipayia leaves the village for the markets of Ngong in the hope that he will raise enough money to pay Rerenko's lawyer.*

Two Korean Families 59 min. Patricia Lewis Jaffe (DI). Dist: Mac. *The Shim family are recent arrivals who operate a Manhattan food store; the Chung family left Korea 20 years ago and are New York–based performers of Western classical music. The film is structured along conventional documentary lines in which scenes of activity alternate with interpretive interviews. Like earlier immigrants from other nations, the Shims speak warmly of America's freedom and economic opportunity. The viewer experiences evidence of their zeal as the film depicts the Shim brothers working long hours at their grocery store and sharing a three-bedroom apartment with their families. Moving and informative scenes include one in which the father of the Shim family, a restaurant chef, visits his sons and cooks them a traditional Korean meal. The Chung family emigrated from Korea two decades before the Shims, and they were also motivated by a desire to gain independence from previous social and economic deprivations. Myung Wha, the elder sister, is a concert cellist and the wife of an Associate Press correspondent at the United Nations. Myung's younger sister is a violinist, and her brother an orchestra conductor. The film also includes scenes of an English class for Koreans and an insightful interview with the Rev. Jin Kwan Han, pastor of the Korean Church of Queens, New York, who provides the audience with his perspective on the Korean immigrants' motivations and feelings about their minority status in America.*

Two Mothers (Diary of a Maasai Village Series) (1985) 50 min. BBC (PR). Dist: FIV VS$198. *Nariku, mother to Rerenko, receives news of her imprisoned son from Tipayia. Meanwhile, another of Simel's wives discovers her son has also been imprisoned.*

Two Thousand Years of Freedom and Honor: The Cochin Jews of India (1992) 80 min. Johanna Spector (PR). Dist: SF. *The film documents the rich tapestry of life in the Jewish community in Cochin, India, now unfortunately fading as the remaining 26 members hold a final vigil. The community that existed uninterrupted for 2,000 years was to experience an upheaval in the 20th century. Deeply religious generations of Cochini Jews planned to return to Zion, and in 1947 with the establishment of the State of Israel, entire villages emigrated to the Holy Land. Today, only a handful remain in Cochin, and they have difficulty understanding why their children left such a prosperous and pleasant life for an uncertain future. Members of both communities express their feelings on camera. While Cochinis in India regret the decline and the certain disappearance of their age-old culture, Cochinis in Israel look confidently toward their survival as Jews.*

2100 Year Old Tomb Excavated 30 min. Dist: GP FR$40, FS$450. *The body of a woman and a larger number of burial accecsories were found in a remarkable state of preservation inside a 2100-year-old tomb recently unearthed in central China. The tomb has already been hailed as an extremely rare find of considerable importance. Its contents will contribute to the study of history. This film is a record of that discovery and a penetrating insight into the meaning and value of the tomb, the body, and the artifacts uncovered.*

Two Ways of Justice (Diary of a Maasai Village Series) (1985) 50 min. BBC (PR). Dist: FIV VS$198. *Rerenko, one of Simel's sons, is in prison in Nairobi, accused of cattle theft. A second son, Tipayia, awaits news of him. And the younger area men prepare to plead their case with the prophet.*

Two West African Fishing Villages 10 min. Dan Shafer, Tom O'Toole (FM). Dist: MINN FS$130. *The lives of rural Aficans are depicted in two widely separated West African fishing villages, Sussex in Sierra Leone and Ganvie in Dahomey. The film illustrates the line fishing method of the*

Sherbo who live in Sussex and the practice of fish farming in Ganvie, which seeks to conserve Lake Nakoue's resources by alternating the harvest of fish. Both villages are involved in a cash economy as well as wage labor, rather than in strictly subsistence economy. The transition to metal roofs and cement walls is pointed out as a simple indicator of cash economy and economic change.

Two Worlds to Remember (1970) 37 min. Phyllis Johnson (PR). Dist: Film Play, Date Bureau, Inc., 267 West 25th St., New York, NY 10001. *Two elderly women in New York, moving into a hostpital for the aged.* [Reviewed by Nancie L. Gonzalez, AA 77:187, 1975.]

Txai Macedo (1992) 50 min. Marcia Machado and Tal Danai (FM). Dist: FRIF. *Since the assassination of Chico Mendes, Antonio Macedo has carried on the work of leading an alliance of Indian and white rubber tappers against oppressive Rubber Barons, land owners, and drug lords in Brazil's Amazon Rain Forest. This portrait reveals his continuing struggle to preserve human rights and what remains of the Amazon's precious ecosystem.*

Uluru—An Anangu Story 29 min. Don Murray (PR), David Roberts (DI). Dist: FAA. *The story of Uluru is told by the local Mutitjulu community. Stories from the dream time illustrate the relationship with the rock and how it is pivotal to their tribal laws and way of life. Successive encounters with whites eventually interfered with and almost destroyed their traditions. The Anangu wanted their rock back to ensure some continuity with their heritage. The 1976 Land Rights Act gave some hope, but they had to wait until 1985 before the Hawk government handed it back to the community*

Umbanda: The Problem Solver (Disappearing World Series) (1977) 52 min. Jeff Harvey (DI), Peter Fry (AN). Dist: PSU order #51253. *A religious cult, based on a centuries-old African tribal ritual taken to Latin America by slaves, now has more than 20 million followers in Brazil. Umbanda blends elements of Roman Catholic ritual with belief in spirit possession. This film contains graphic footage of a vast, weekend ceremony of worship, ritual dancing, and hypnosis on the beach of Sao Paolo.* [Reviewed by Jean Comaroff, *RAIN* 26:6–7, 1978.]

Undala (1967) Allison and Marek Jablonko (FM), R. T. Rosen (AN). Dist: PSU FR$15.50, FS$342; NYU. *Undala is the name of the hot, windy months that precede the relief of monsoon rains in India. This film portrays the varied movements and rhythms of life in a small Hindu village that borders on the desert in northwest India (Rajasathan) during that season. For the farmer it is a time of leisure and repair, for women endless water-bearing, and for craftsmen little change in their daily routine. The activities shown are pottery making, spinning, leatherwork, rope making, and the all-important task of drawing water. The diffuse lighting of dust laden air and the dynamic patterns of people at work make this film a unique viewing experience. There is no narration, and the original musical score is in the Hindustani classical and folklore styles.* [Reviewed by Alan Beals, AA 71:1007, 1969.] Bibliography: R. T. Rosen, *Changing Land Tenure and Village Polity in Rajastan, India: An Interactional Perspective.* Ph.D. dissertation, University Microfilm, 1969. R. T. Rosen, "Peasant Adaptations as Process in Land Reform: A Case Study." In: *American Studies in the Anthropology of India.* S. Vatuk, ed. Manohar Book Service, 1978.

Uminchu: The Old Man and the East China Sea (1991) 101 min. John Junkerman (FM). Dist: FRIF FR$150, FS$1350, VS$490. *Follows the travails of 82-year-old Shigeru Itokazu, who rows out to sea alone before dawn every morning in quest of marlin. Itokazu and the residents of tiny Yonakuni Island, a volcanic rock near Okinawa, tell stories of their battles with the sea and of their traditional way of life. Itokazu fishes with a harpoon and net, without the benefit of sonar or drift nets, and although he is a tough and skilled fisherman, Junkerman filmed for two years before Itokazu took a marlin. Itokazu's resolve and fierce pride are characteristic of his community. Soon after filming, Itokazu was found drowned, attached to his boat by a harpoon line that had wrapped around his ankle while fishing for a marlin.*

Under the Men's Tree (1974) 15 min. David MacDougall (FM, CA), Judith MacDougall (SR). Dist: UCEMC R$27, FS$250, VS$210. *At Jie cattle camps in Uganda, men often gather under a special tree to make leather and wooden goods and to talk, relax, and sleep. The conversation on this particular afternoon becomes a kind of reverse ethnography, centering on the European's most noticeable possession, the motor vehicle. A uniquely delicate and intimate film, filled with the humor of the Jie and, implicitly, the ironic wit of the filmmakers. In Jie, with English subtitles.* Suggested Supplements: P. H. Gulliver, *The Family Herds.* Routledge & Kegan Paul, 1955. Neville Dyson-Hudson, *Karimojong Politics.* Claredon Press, 1966.

Uneasy Neighbors (1991) 35 min. Paul Espinosa (PR). Dist: UCEMC FR$50, VS$250. *Investigates the growing tensions between residents of migrant worker camps and affluent homeowners in northern San Diego county, one of the wealthiest and fastest-growing areas in the nation. Here, amid half-million dollar homes and lush golf courses, migrant workers live in camps where conditions are worse than in much of the Third World.* [Reviewed by James Diego Vigil, AA 95:519–520, 1993.]

UNIVERSITY OF IFE SERIES Dist: Colour Film Services Ltd., P.O. Box 4BE 22-25, Portman Close Baker Street, London W1A 4BE England.

- **Nigerian Dance No. 1**
- **Nigerian Dance No. 2**
- **Nigerian Dance No. 3**
- **Were Ni! He Is a Madman**
- **Gelede: A Yoruba Masquerade**
- **Benin Kingship Rituals**
- **Duminea** [Reviewed by Alan Harwood, AA 77:703, 1975.]
- **New Images**
- **Ifa Films**
- **Ozidi Tides of the Delta**

- Kwagh Hir: Tiv Traditional Theatre
- A Drum Is Made
- Nigerian National Dance Troupe

The Unruly Dragon: The Yellow River (1990) 45 min. Jim Laurie (DI), Vladimir Bibic (PR) for ABC News. Dist: CRM VR$55, VS$295. *This documentary takes viewers on a 3,300 mile journey down China's Yellow River for a rare view of Chinese culture. Also known as "China's Sorrow," the Yellow River resembles an angry dragon in form and behavior, often flooding or unleashing yellow liquid mud to cause widespread death and devastation. Chinese civilization was born here 5,000 years ago; and today, 120 million Chinese, Tibetans, Muslims, and Mongols depend on the Yellow River for their livelihood. This film reveals the diverse lifestyles and traditions of the Yellow River population, along with spectacular views of wonders such as the 2,000 Longmen caves carved from granite and containing over 100,000 Buddhist statues.*

Uprooted! A Japanese American Family's Experience (1978) 29 min. Don & Sue Rundstrom (FM) in cooperation with the Manzanar Committee, Inc.; family movies by the Nitake Family, Toyoo Nitake (NA), Harry Nitake (CON, ED). *The film uses family album photographs and home movie footage, preserving the original shooting style and providing a visual context for the chronology of events that played a shameful role in U.S. history. The footage contains scenes of the family's prosperous California lifestyle prior to World War II, including their citrus nursery business. During their subsequent internment following Pearl Harbor, film footage was taken of various concentration camp activities providing a rare glimpse of camp life from the perspective of an internee. The film concludes with a view of the return train trip, and the family's destroyed property. An interview with one family member, recorded over 30 years later, provides a reflexive narrative for the visual context and presents an informative and valuable document of the Japanese American incarceration experience.*

The Upperville Show 9 min. Tom Davenport (FM). Dist: TDF FR$20, FS$125. *Pedigreed animals and people at the nation's oldest horse show in Virginia.*

Urbanisme Africain (African Urbanism) (1962) Jean Rouch (DI). Dist: CFE; DER.

Urbanization in the Moche Valley (1978) 30 min. Betsy Paullada (FM). Dist: Department of Anthropology, California State University, Northridge, CA 91330. *Shot at various sites in the Moche Valley of Peru in the summer of 1976. Focusing questions: What is the importance of the movement toward urbanization for human history? What prior factors are necessary for the process of urbanization? What is the role of social stratification in the process of urbanization? Bibliography: Robert McC. Adams, The Evolution of Urban Society. Aldine Publishing Co., Chicago, IL, 1966. Chrisopher Donnaon and Carol Mackey, Ancient Burial Patterns of the Moche Valley, Peru. University of Texas Press, 1978.*

Utu (1984) 104 min. Geoff Murphy (DI). Dist: KI. *A sprawling, spectacular adventure epic Utu recalls the finest works of Akira Kurosawa, Werner Herzog, and John Ford. Infused with insight, bizarre humor, and grand action sequences, Geoff Murphy presents the dazzlingly kaleidoscopic memories of a Maori chieftain. The Maori were the original inhabitants of New Zealand, colonized in the 1880s by the invading European settlers. The film is set late in the century, with the country already "civilized." A Maori village is destroyed, and the people are massacred by colonial troops. The slaughter is discovered by Te Wheke, a warrior now working for the soldiers. The attack is a military blunder, the village was "friendly" and the dead were Te Wheke's own tribesmen. In grief and anger, Te Wheke prepares his revenge. The word "utu" means retribution, revenge, and honor. As prescribed by the Maori rituals, his face is carved and tattooed as the ancient warriors had done before the Europeans arrived. With a growing band of rebels, Te Wheke engages in a hopeless war against the white settlers and colonial army. The violence finally ends in a surprising and moving climax.*

La vallée des Mervèilles (1971) 21 min. Jean-Pierre Baux (DI), Henry de Lumley (AN). Dist: FACSEA. *Petroglyphs in a valley in southeastern France.* [Reviewed by Harvey M. Bricker, AA 78:119–120, 1976.]

Valley of the Old Ones 26 min. Gene Ayres (PR). Dist: T/L FS$350, VS$150. *Miguel Carpio Mendieta is 124 years old. He is one of ten people over 100 years of age that medical researchers recently discovered living in the tiny valley of Vilcabamba, Ecuador. Church birth records verify these findings and reveal the Old Ones of Vilcabamba to be the oldest group of people of confirmed age in the world. Many are old enough to have lived through the American Civil War, numerous local revolutions and wars, the Industrial Revolution, two World Wars, the Atomic Age and the Space Age, with little or no knowledge of the passage of these events. Reports that Vilcabamba was "an island of immunity to heart disease" reached the outside world in the 1950s, and finally in 1969, a team of doctors went in to investigate. They confirmed that this was, indeed, an extraordinary valley with extraordinary inhabitants. This fascinating documentary examines the phenomenon and ponders the future of this people as Western civilization slowly infiltrates their valley. Discussion guide avalible.*

A Veiled Revolution (Women in the Middle East Series) (1982) 26 min. Elizabeth Fernea (PR), Marilyn Gaunt (DI). Dist: FRIF VR$55, FS$470, VS$280. *Egypt was the first Arab country where women marched in political demonstrations (1919), removed their veils publicly (1923), and were offered free secular education (1924). But today the educated granddaughters of those early Arab feminists are returning to Islamic dress. The film considers the possible reasons for this turn back to tradition—the resurgence of Islamic fundamentalism, the rejection of Western values— as Egyptian women speak out.* [Reviewed by Barbara Aswad, AA 87:233–234, 1985.]

Vessels of the Spirits: Pots and People in North Cameroon (1990) 50 min. Nicholas David and Judy Sterner (AN). Dist: UOC VR$60, VS$275, order #6812ve. *This videotape explores the role of pottery in the daily, social, and religious* *life of North Cameroonian peoples. Pots are people and people are pots to the inhabitants of the Mandara Highlands of North Cameroon. This tape documents unusual techniques of manufacture of utilitarian and figurated sacred pottery among the Mafa, Sirak, and Hide and shows how pots are assimilated to people by their decoration and in their capacity to contain spirits, including those of god and the ancestors. Pots are shown being used in economic, social, and ritual contexts, in the latter as tools for communication with the spirit world. Opening and closing sequences of a festival that involves the release, wild run, and recapture of bulls make the point that bulls symbolize the spirits and that the ceremony is the central religious rite precisely because it offers a general formula for human action.* [Reviewed by Richard A. Krause, AA 94(3):768–770, 1992.]

Les veuves de quinze ans (The Fifteen Year Old Widows) (1964) 25 min. Jean Rouch (DI). Dist: CFE; DER. *The problems of adolescents facing the adult world in 1965.*

Via Dolorosa—The Painful Way (1978) 10 min. Georges Payrastre (CA), Claudine Viallon (SR), Okexnon (PR). Dist: DER FR$15, FS$75. *Each year in Antigua, Guatemala, the people celebrate the "Passion of Christ." After decorating the streets with colorful sawdust and flower carpets, they take turns carrying the image of their faith during the entire day along the Via Dolorosa, or painful way.*

Viewing the Supernatural (1958) 30 min. NET (PR). Dist: IUAVC order #NET1478, FR$9.50. *Uses dance routines and originally scored music to portray cultural differences in solving problems through religion. Emphasizes religious motivation, leadership, rituals, and supernatural controls. Stresses the differences in the meaning of religion. Compares experiences of the southern African-American, the voodoo cult of the Haitian peasant, and the polytheism of the Muria of India.*

The Viking Ships of Roskilde 14 min. DIO (NY, LA, CH), free rental. *The film gives an account of the extensive excavation work following the discovery of the sunken ships from the Viking Age in Peberrenden in Roskilde Fjord. The special circumstances under which the work had to be carried out confronted the scientists and technicians with many problems that had to be solved before parts of the wreck could be removed to the final preservation.* [Reviewed by Bernard Wailes, AA 78:118–119, 1976.]

Vikings! (1980) 10 parts, 30 min. each. Dist: PBSV VR$55, VS$175 (each), $1,195 (series). *"This is a fascinating series. Written and narrated by Magnus Magnusson, one of the leading translators of Icelandic sagas and a veteran exponant of the joys of archaeology on BBC television, this series weaves together the multiple strands of archaeology, history, folklore and experimental reconstruction to create a vibrant tapestry of Viking life and times."* [From the review by Kate Gordon, ARCH 34(4):64, 1981.]

The Village (1969) 70 min. Mark McCarty (FM), Paul Hockings (AN), UCLA Ethnographic Film Program (PR). Dist: UCEMC order #7620, FR$49, FS$680. *An intimate study of the slow-paced diurnal round of activity in Dunquin, County Kerry, Ireland, the westernmost village in Europe and one of the last Gaelic-speaking communities. This portrait of a peasant society was made in 1967, at a time when acculturation by urban tourists was beginning; the language, customs, and subsistence techniques of the past are presented for perhaps the last time. The glimpse of two cultures confronting each other is made extraordinarily vivid by the style of the film, which directly portrays, in the manner of cinema verite, without either commentary or narration, the people of the village and the events of a weekend. Through the gradual weaving together of simultaneous events, we come to know key village characters: the postmistress, who dispenses sweets, gossip, and pensions; the pub owner, who is also landlord, grocer, de facto mayor, and traditional yarn-spinner; and also the last few survivors of nearby Blasket Island, whose heroic past now lives only in sheep-herding, rabbit-hunting, and the handling of flimsy canoes. The British tourists are inimitably themselves, though the incalculable destruction their presence wreaks on the fabric of life in Dunquin is tempered by the wry and loving observation of the filmmakers. This film is at times grave and elegaic, as when we see the village depleted by emigration, and the deserted ruins crumbling on the island; at times it becomes boisterous (Saturday night at the pub), triumphant (the annual canoe-race), and a hilarious revelation of Irish character. Since the camera's presence is part of what is observed, this film makes a notable innovation in the use of motion pictures in social studies. Edited without commentary, this film evokes something very like the ethnographer's field experience. Extensive sequences in Gaelic are subtitled.* [Reviewed by John Messenger, AA 74:1557–1581, 1972. William Ferris, JAF 89(353):385, 1976.] Suggested supplements: Conrad M. Arensberg and Peter Smith, *The Irish Countryman*. Natural History Press, 1968[1937]. Conrad M. Arensberg and Solon T. Kimball, *Family and Community in Ireland*. Harvard University Press, 1967. Hugh Brody, *Inishkillane: Change and Decline in the West of Ireland*. Pelican Books, 1973[1974]. Kevin Danaher, *Irish Country People*. Mercier Press, Cork, 1966. Robein Flower, *The Western Island*. Claredon Press, 1944. Paul Hockings, "The Village": An Introduction. University of California Extension Media Center study guide), 1976. Thomas H. Mason, *The Islands of Ireland*. Mercier Press, 1967. Mark McCarty, "McCarty's Law and How To Break It." In: *Principles of Visual Anthropolgy*, Paul Hockings, ed. Pp. 45–51, Aldine, 1975. John Messenger, *Inis Beag, Isle of Ireland*. Holt, Rinehart and Winston, 1969. Tomas O. Crohan, *The Islandman*. Claredon Press, 1951[1934]. Maurice O'Sullivan, *Twenty Years A-Growing*. Oxford University Press, London, 1953[1933]. Peig Sayers, *An Old Woman's Reflections*. Oxford University Press, London, 1962. John Millington Synge, *The Aran Islands and Other Writings*. Vintage Books, 1962.

A Village in Baltimore (1981) 63 min. Doreen Moses (DI). Dist: Doreen Moses, 1730 21st Street, NW, Washington, DC 20009, FR$150, FS$850. *This film is about images and self-images of Greek-American women living in a certain area of Baltimore. The film explores the structures, dynamics, and events surrounding their marriages to decipher various elements and aspects of these women, their expecta-*

tions, the conflicts they face, the resolutions they come up with, and much much more. [Reviewed by Ruth E. Mandel AA 84:982–984, 1982.]

Village Man, City Man 38 min. Mira Reym Binford and Michael Camerini (FM). Dist: UW/SAAC FR$30, FS$245. *Shows the life of a young mill worker in an industrial section of Delhi and follows him on a return visit to his village in Uttar Pradesh. Changes and continuities in his life are documented by his conversations with his friends at the mill and by observations of how he works and spends his leisure time in both city and village. The traditional religious singing in the city and the new land consolidation in the village suggest that dichotomous "modern traditional" models of change do not necessarily apply in the Indian context. The question of whether this mill worker is a village man or city man remains unanswered. Accompanied by Teachers' Guides with background information and suggestions for discussions. Produced with sychronous sound interviews in Bengali, Hindi, Tamil, with English subtitles.* [Reveiwed by Gregory Finnegan, AA 80:202–203, 1978.]

Village Morning 8 min. Steven Schecter, Ragpa Dorjee, Barbara Johnson (FM). Dist: National Research Film Center, Smithsonian Institution, 955 L'Enfant Plaza, Room 3210, Washington, DC 20560. *A research report film from a study of traditional Tibetan civilization in Mathoo village in Ladakh.*

Village of No River (1981) 58 min. Stuart Hersch (FM), Barbara Lipton (WR). Dist: The Newark Museum, P.O. Box 540, 49 Washington Street, Newark, NJ 07101, FR$80, FS$815, VS$310. *"Kwigillingik, the Village of No River, is, its name notwithstanding, a river village ... in southwest Alaska.... The film begins with the Eskimo origin myth that explains how the river came to be ... then takes us on a guided tour of the village."* [From the review by Jean Briggs, AA 85:233–235, 1983.]

Village of Spain 21 min. G. Fritsch (PR). Dist: Churchill Films, UILL. [Reviewed by Peter S. Allen, AA 77:710, 1975.]

Village Potters of Onda (1966) 25 min. Edith Sperry (FM). Dist: PSU(PCR) order #31414, FR$11. *Detailed account of traditional potterymaking techniques of Japanese folk potters in Onda, a remote village in the mountains of north-central Kyushu. Includes description of personalities and attitudes of villagers, and of village social structure.*

Village Theater Senegal: Queen Ndate and the French Conquest (1983) 14 min. James Perry, Patrick O'Meara (PR), Jean-Pol LeFebvre (PR, DI). Dist: IUAVC FR$20, FS$240, VS$140. *Amateur actors, members of a rural youth association in northwestern Senegal, perform in a play about the conquest of their region by the French in the 19th century. Performed in French language with English subtitles and English introduction.* [Reviewed by David H. Spain, AA 88:779–780, 1986.]

A VILLAGE TRILOGY Films set in a small southern village of 1,500 people. This village is one examined thoroughly in the book Caste, Class, and Power by Dr. Andre Beteille.

• **The Village** 16 min. *A composite look at life in the village incorporating dreams and aspirations of many people.*

• **The Village Economy** 15 min. *The film follows the activities of a middle-class landowner and developments in the village rice industry.*

• **Village Family** 16 min. *A film about a young Brahmin girl who teaches Veena, which enables her to support her family and to put her sister through law school. Although educated, Kausalya resists the trend to move to a bigger city.*

The Village Watchman 18 min. Alastair Kenneil (FM). Dist: Carousel Films, 1501 Broadway, Suite 1503, New York, NY 10036. *Village of Samarina in the Pindus mountains of northern Greece.*

Villagers of the Sierra de Gredos (Disappearing World Series) (1989) 52 min. William Kavanagh (AN). Dist: PSU order #51228; FIV VS$198, order #047016. *The cold, dark village of Navalguijo is perched high in the Sierra de Gredos Mountains in central Spain. Every spring, the inhabitants descend with their herds to the sunlit pastures of the valley below, where the cattle graze from February to June. This seasonal migration makes the villagers one of the last transhumant societies of Europe: people who move between two fixed places, rather than nomads who wander with no fixed home.*

Villarrica (1973) 25 min. Ronald J. Duncan, Gloria S. Duncan, and Nona A. Friedmann (FM). Dist: RJD FR$24, FS$200. *This film portrays the black small farmers and sugar cane workers of the Cauca Valley of southern Colombia. It is based on previous anthropological research by Ronald J. Duncan and Nina S. Friedmann, and it includes definitions by the local people of their community and their perceptions of barriers to their well-being. They define the important areas of their life as being work, recreation, family, sanitation, health, education, and future, and the film is organized around those categories. The people of Villarrica were slaves until about 100 years ago when they got freedom and eventually land. They are now losing their land to giant sugar cane companies, and many of the younger people work with the companies, forming a rural proletariat. Some say that they are going back into slavery.*

Vimbuza—Chilopa (1990) 55 min. Rupert and Ulrike Poschl, University Hospital Gottingen (PR). Dist: PSU FR$19, VS$200, order #61295. *The Tumbuka of Malawi attribute illness (vimbuza) to spirit possession. Vimbuza refers to the illness as well as to the associated spirit possession, healing ceremony, and dance. This videotape is the first complete record of a vimbuza-chilopa healing ritual. After nightlong dances at full moon, singing, clapping, and powerful drumming, the patient reaches a state of "altered consciousness." The ceremony culminates in a ritual animal sacrifice (chilopa) at dawn. Because the illness primarily afflicts women, its inception is linked to sociological conflicts stemming from restricted opportunity for personal achievement and frustrations arising from lack of education, low socioeconomic status, and the practice of polygamy. Different healing ceremonies are shown, portraying the interaction between patient, healer, and community that is considered crucial for a successful outcome. An interview* *with a patient, combined with commentary from the filmmakers, leads the viewer to a deeper understanding of the occurrence of vimbuza and its treatment among the Tumbuka.*

The Vinland Mystery (1986) 29 min. Bill Pettigrew (DI), National Film Board of Canada (PR). Dist: FRIF FR$55, FS$530, VS$290. *The story of L'Anse aux Meadows, in Newfoundland, the only known Norse settlement in North America.*

Virgin Mary (or Holy Sorceress) 50 min. Alejo Santa Maria and Cristina Echavarria (FM). Dist: ETNOS. *During the 16th century, the wars for the conquest of America created a legend in the North of Colombia: according to one version, the Virgin intervened miraculously to save the Spaniards from an Indian rebellion in 1576. The documentary contrasts historical facts with opposing local oral traditions, thereby throwing light on Hispanic colonization strategies. People come from far and wide to commemorate the miracle with theatrical representations that date back to colonial days. In gratitude for the favors received from the Virgin, devotees dress as Indians and honor Her with the old Indian dances, in a colorful fiesta that represents the fusion of religions.*

Visa for a Dream (1990) 30 min. Sonia Fritz (FM). Dist: East Village Exchange, 93 First Avenue, Studio 5C, New York, NY 10003; (212) 979-1144, VR$50, VS$200. *Dominican women in Puerto Rico.* [Reviewed by Jorge Duany, *AA* 93(4):1038–1040, 1991.]

Vision of Juazeiro 19 min. Eduardo Escorel (DI). Dist: CG FR$45, FS$375. *This film portrays the transformation of a small town in northeastern Brazil into a religious shrine. Jazeiro de Norte was only a handful of houses in the late 19th century, but it grew and developed under the guidance of Father Cicero, a local religious and political leader. Following his death in 1935, his followers preserved and spread his teachings. During religious festivities today, thousands of pilgrims descend upon the town. The film analyzes the economic and mystical aspects of this phenomenon. It reveals that while for many the pilgrimage is still an essentially religious experience, for some Jazeiro residents, it has become a commercial as well as a political event.* [Reviewed by Caroline B. Brettell, *AA* 91:831–834, 1989.]

The Visit (1967) 28 min. Bernard Devlin, National Film Board of Canada (PR). Dist: CMC. *A Canadian immigrant returns to Calabria.* [Reviewed by Peter S. Allen, *AA* 79:508, 1977.]

Visiting the Indians with George Catlin 24 min. Marshall McKusick (FM). Dist: U. IOWA Publications Order Department, 17 West College Street, Iowa City, IA 52242, order #50236, FR$18.90, FS$425. [Reviewed by David Mayer Gradwohl, *AA* 78:366–369, 1976.]

Vlach Gypsies (see *Across the Tracks—Vlach Gypsies in Hungary*)

Vocalization and Speech in Chimpanzees 12 min. K. Hayes and C. Hayes (PR). Dist: PSU FR$10, FS$110, VS$85, order #11489. *An early attempt to teach chimps to verbalize, serving as a demonstration that vocal responses can be conditioned.*

Vocalizations of Wild Chimpanzees 40 min. Hugo van Lawick (CA), Peter Marler and Jane van Lawick-Goodall (AN). Dist: RUFS FR$20, FS$400. *This film shows various interactive behaviors of chimpanzees, such as body movements, vocalizations, gestures, and postures. It also discusses the evolution of advanced communication.*

Voice of the Whip (1989) 48 min. Ned Johnston and Lou Werner (DI). Dist: MOMA FR$75, VR$40, VS$190. "*A 40-day trek from the desert pastures of Kordofan province to the camel markets of southern Egypt.*" [From the review by William C. Young, *AA* 93:260–261, 1991.]

Voices from Gaza (1987) 50 min. M. Pachachi and A. Cassia (PR). Dist: ICF. "*Shot in 1987, six months into the uprising of the Palestinians against Israel. More than a historical review of an oppressed people, the film dramatizes the fears, frustrations, and motivations of the inhabitants.*" [From the review by Barbara C. Aswad, *AA* 93(4):1040–1042, 1991.]

Voices in the Forest (1981) 50 min. David Parer (PR) for the Australian National Broadcasting Commission. Dist: Program Sales, ABC-TV, GPO Box 9994, Sydney, NSW 2001, Australia. "*Beneath the level of colorful documentary about birds of paradise lies an intriguing ethnographic account of the important place the birds have in the highland societies of Papua New Guinea.... The film focuses on two highland societies—the Huli in the southern highlands and the Melpa in the western highlands.... The film shows how the birds of paradise plumes are woven into the fabric of Huli culture.*" [From the review by Darrell Whiteman, *AA* 86:812–813, 1984.]

Voices of the Gods (1985) 60 min. Al Santana (FM). Dist: Akuaba Productions, P.O. Box 521, Brooklyn, NY 11238; (718) 636-9747, FR$125, FS$850, VS$650. *Depicts* "*Black American movements which enact African ritual forms in contemporary America. The film contains footage on three separate movements: first, a group that is striving for mastery of Yoruba ritual knowledge, another group that identifies itself with Akan tradition, and, third, the village of Oyotunji in South Carolina, which is supposed to replicate a Yoruba village.*" [From the review by Richard T. Curley, *AA* 88:1050–1051, 1986.]

Voodoo and the Church in Haiti (1989) 40 min. Andrea Leland and Bob Richards (PR). Dist: UCEMC FR$45, VS$370. *Despite centuries of vigilant opposition from the Catholic Church, voodoo has flourished in Haiti. This important documentary dispels the sensationalist stereotypes that surround voodoo. It shows that voodoo is a complex system of beliefs that has developed over time from West African origins. This film also serves as an excellent introduction to the culture, history, sociology, and politics of the first black republic in the New World.* [Reviewed by John P. Homialr, *AA* 93(1):260–262, 1991.]

Voyage au Bout de la Piste—Une Autre Ethiopie (1986) 50 min. Jean-Claude Luyat (FM). Dist: JCL. *This film is* about the tribal groups living in the southwestern Ethiopia. The film shows various tribes and their ways of living. The tribes featured include the Mursi, the Tishana and the Surma. [Reviewed by Jon Abbink AA 91:270–272, 1989.]

Voyage from Antiquity (1987) 60 min. Jack Kelley (PR), Robert Dalva (DI). Dist: Devilleir-Donegan Enterprises, 1608 New Hampshire Ave. NW, Washington, DC 20009; (202) 232-8200, FS$750, VS$150. *Chronicles a project of George Bass, the 'dean of underwater archaeologists.' "The site studied in this film lies underwater just off Cape Ulu Burun near Kas, on the southern coast of Turkey. Discovered in 1982 by local sponge divers, an ancient wrecked ship and its contents lie here in water ranging from 130–175 feet—very close to the limits for divers. It is the oldest intact shipwreck ever excavated, dating to some time in the Late Bronze Age around 1350 B.C." [From the review by Peter S. Allen, ARCH 41(5):76–77, 1988.]*

The Wages of Action: Religion in a Hindu Village 47 min. Dist: UW-SAAS FR$30, FS$295. *Focuses on everyday religious practices in the village of Soyepur, near Banaras. This film observes young men praying to Lord Hanuman before a wrestling match, a grandmother offering water to a sacred tulsi plant, a brahmin priest conducting a Satyanarayan puja, low caste ojhas exorcising spirits from the ill, and a Soyepur couple making a one day pilgrimage to a shrine by the Ganges River. The film shows villagers describing ghosts and their placation, a brahmin housewife explaining how she maintains her kitchen's ritual purity, and an itinerant holy man teaching through song the oneness of God and the inevitability of the wages of one's actions.* [Reviewed by Paul Hockings, AA 86:807–809, 1984.]

THE WAIAPI INDIANS OF BRAZIL (1988) Victor Fuks (PR). Dist: IUAVC. *The Waiapi Indians live in the Amazon rain forest in northeastern South America. This series of five programs focuses on the Waiapi who live in the Amapari region near the Tumukumake mountains in northern Brazil. Because music and dance are essential to Waiapi culture, they provide the primary focus of two programs in the series and major components of the remaining three. Contact with the Western world is a relatively recent event in Waiapi history; as a result, these five programs contribute greatly to understanding this little known culture.* [Reviewed by Allison Jablonko AA 91:1091–1092, 1989.] See specific descriptions under titles:

- Music, Dance, and Festival among the Waiapi Indians of Brazil
- Waiapi Slash and Burn Cultivation
- Caxiri or Manioc Beer
- Waiapi Body Painting and Ornaments
- Waiapi Instrumental Music

Waiapi Body Painting and Ornaments (Waiapi Indians of Brazil Series) (1988) 18 min. Victor Fuks (PR). Dist: IUAVC VR$20, VS$105, order #CC3782. *This program documents Waiapi body ornamentation. Much time is devoted to body painting, and the Waiapi use a variety of methods and materials to accomplish it. These include urucu, a red pigment spread without pattern across body surfaces, also used for dying cloth and painting musical instruments; and genipapo, a black pigment meticulously traced onto the face and body in representations of moju, a mythical snake, panan the butterfly, pira kangwera the fish bone, and others. Feathers, glass beads, combs, and flowers are also favored ornamentations, used, like body painting, to adorn as well as to celebrate various aspects of Waiapi culture.* [Reviewed in VISA 4:91, 1991.]

Waiapi Instrumental Music (Waiapi Indians of Brazil Series) (1988) 58 min. Victor Fuks (PR). Dist: IUAVC VR$35, VS$180, order #CC3783. *Examines a variety of Waiapi wind instruments and the contexts in which they are used. Given the culture's emphasis on music and dance, the importance of the instruments is clear. All of the wind instruments examined here were made from natural elements such as reed, wood, and bone. Several flutes are demonstrated including erebo, similar to pan pipes; so'o kangwera, played solo and made from deer bone; and pira ra'anga, played in ensemble and shown accompanying the dance of a fish festival. Several large nhima poku "trumpets" are explained, as are a variety of reed instruments, among them the jawarun ra'anga and tures. As in dance, the Waiapi make clear gender distinctions in musical performances—women can sing, but only the men play the instruments.*

Waiapi Slash and Burn Cultivation (Waiapi Indians of Brazil Series) (1988) 22 min. Victor Fuks (PR). Dist: IUAVC VR$25, VS$150, order #CC3780. *The Waiapi, like rain forest dwellers throughout the world, use slash-and-burn cultivation to grow foods that provide variety and nutritional balance to their diet. All steps in the process must accommodate both mystical and practical considerations. After a forest area is cut and the vegetation is burned, the ashes are spread for fertilizer. The large, charred stumps are left to deter marauding animals and serve as a ready source of coal. Planting and harvesting is typically done by the women, yielding manioc tubers, caju and papaya fruits, corn, cotton, the fish poison kunami, and a host of other edible and utilitarian plants. After two years, the gardens are abandoned for regeneration by the rain forest, sustaining a healthy, balanced relationship with nature.*

Waiting for Harry (1980) 57 min. Les Hiatt (AN), Kim McKenzie (FM). Dist: AIAS; UCEMC FR$55, FS$850. *Made with the Anbarra people of the Blyth River area near Maningrida on the northern Australian coast. In 1978 they conducted the final mortuary rites for a man, Les Angabarabara, who had died several years earlier. The impetus for conducting these rites and for making this film came from Frank Gurrmananamana. He was a classificatory brother of the dead man, as was anthropologist Dr. Les Hiatt, who also attended the rites. Dr. Hiatt has worked with the Anbarra since the late 1950s, and Angabarabara and Gurrmananamana were particularly close advisors and colleagues at that time. The film follows the organization and preparations leading up to the placement of the deceased's remains in an elaborately painted hollow log coffin. It also records interaction between the anthropologist and the people he has studied for so long.* Suggested supplements: L. R. Hiatt and M. Clunies-Ross, "Sand Sculptures at the Gigjingali Burial Rite." In: *Form in Indigenous Art*,

P. J. Ucko, ed. AIAS, 1978. A volume relevant to this film was co-authored by L. R. Hiatt, F. Gurrmananamana, M. Clunies-Ross, B. Meehan, Rhys Jones, and Kim McKenzie. [Reviewed by Jane C. Goodale, AA 86:813–814, 1984.]

Waiting for the Caribou (1991) 30 min. Peter Entell (FM). Dist: FRIF VR$55, VS$190. *The news has stories of emergency supplies being airlifted to disaster victims almost daily. What goes on behind the headlines? Who are the people delivering these relief goods to devastated regions? This film is the story of Tomas Muhuesa, a warehouse worker in Maputo, the capital of Mozambique, who travels for the first time into the war-torn countryside where millions have fled their homes. It is during this relief expedition that Muhuesa and viewers of the program learn of the many exasperating tribulations—faulty equipment, untrained workers, bureaucratic snags, among other things—that often retard these well-intentioned missions of mercy.*

The Wake (Daughters of the Country Series) 57 min. Norma Bailey (FM). Dist: NFB FR$80, VR$80, FS$775, VS$150. *Intelligent and attractive, Joan is a typical single parent of the 1980s. But her people are American Indian, considered inferior by the white townspeople. There are frequent clashes between teenagers of both groups who attend the local high school. When Jim, a young white police officer, shows rare compassion for some of her relatives, Joan is touched. A romance develops that holds promise of future happiness. But a tragic event makes Joan realize that there is a dichotomy between their two worlds.*

Walbiri Fire Ceremony: Ngatjakula (1977) 21 min. Roger Sandall (DI), Australian Institute of Aboriginal Studies (PR). Dist: UCEMC FR$30, FS$300. *Originally shot in 1967, the footage contained in this film was re-examined ten years later by anthropologist Nicolas Peterson, who gives his interpretation of it in the commentary. Ngatjakula is one of the most spectacular Aboriginal ceremonies of central Australia, employing fire to inflict real and symbolic punishment on those acknowledged by the community to have been responsible for a social transgression. The ceremony serves to resolve conflict and, in the process, makes manifest, in ritual form, the underlying structure of Walbiri society.* Relevant anthropological literature: M. Meggitt, *Desert People: A Study of the Albiri Aborigines of Central Australia.* (Syd) Angus and Robertson, 1962. N. Peterson, "Walbiri Kinship and Marriage in the Light of the Fire Ceremony." AIAS Second General Meeting, Canberra, May 1968.

Walbiri Ritual at Gunadjari (Australian Institute of Aboriginal Study Series) (1969) 28 min. Dist: UCEMC FR$35, FS$390; PSU(PCR) order #31625, FR$11.10. *Documents a three-day ceremony at the place where the lands of the Walbiri and Pintubi tribes join. The ceiling of an immense rock shelter is painted with an elaborate design, and sacred emblems of the ritual are built. Plant down is gathered for decoration, colored with red ochre, and attached to the performers' bodies. Sacred songs are sung, then four ritual acts are performed. Most striking is that of a Pintubi in the role of Wadaingula, a hero of legendary sexual prowess. Another shows a mythical bird ornamented with "bones of the dead," represented by a long feathered stem on the headdress. The ceremonial site is "owned" by an aged political leader and renowned warrior whose participation in the ritual gives it a rare solemnity and intensity. This film contains some of the most vivid material in the series.* [Reviewed by W. H. E. Stanner, AA 72:202, 1970.] Restricted use. This film contains material of a secret/sacred nature and should only be screened for study purposes by appropriate groups.

Walbiri Ritual at Ngama (1969) 23 min. Dist: UCEMC FR$31, FS$320; PSU(PCR) order #312640, FR$16.50. *Shows an "increase ceremony" of the Walbiri tribe associated with a large rock painting of a python. The main objects of the ritual are fertility and initiation: on the one hand it promotes the reproduction of pythons and members of the python clan; on the other it serves to instruct novices in tradition and to reveal the secret songs and mythology known by the older men. An initiate is shown the rock painting, and the meaning of the secret designs carved on the* churinga, *or sacred boards, showing the journeys of tribal ancestors in dreamtime (the legendary past), is explained. Songs tell of the dreamtime journeys and camping spots; landscape features referred to in Ngama legends are shown to the novice. Ceremonial emblems are built and sung over to impart the dreaming essence—the vital spirit of the past. The letting of arm blood, and its use as an adhesive as performers are decorated, is shown. Then three ritual dreams—mimetic "acts" or dances—are performed. The first evokes the dreaming, another portrays the "Ngama Woman," a third represents the python painted on the rock.* [Reviewed by Nancy D. Munn, AA 72:1201–1202, 1970.] Restricted use. This film contains material of a secret/sacred nature and should only be screened for study purposes by appropriate groups.

Walkabout (1974) 25 min. C.P. Mountford (FM, AN), Film Australia (PR). Dist: AIS FR$7.50, FS$425. *An edited film, made from and replacing the old* Walkabout *and* Tjurunga. *The film is a journey with a group of Aborigines through central Australia and with C. P. Mountford, the well-known anthropologist, whose personal account of his experiences is recorded with genuine affection for his companions. The story begins in Adelaide, goes to Oodnadatta by rail, thence by truck through miles of rough track to the point where they pick up camels for the next thousand miles of the journey. Among the places visited is Ayers Rock, the enormous monolith 1,100 feet high and covering four square miles, which rises vertically from the flat desert floor. Mount Honra, a group of great pillars in the form of a hollow square rising to 1,400 feet, is another fascinating site. The conditions experienced by Mountford on this expedition into a red, thirsty desert are similar to those of the early explorers who made hazardous expeditions into this inhospitable country. In the final stages of the journey, the 14 people in the party had only one gallon of water, which had to be rationed between them to stay alive.*

Walking in a Sacred Manner 23 min. Stephen Cross (PR). Dist: IFB FR$45, FS$425, VS$340. *This film recreates a physical and imaginative world of the North American Indians. It captures their world during the "last act" before* *the influence of European civilization forever altered these native cultures. It concentrates on the central element of their traditional life, their attitude toward the natural world. The excursion combines the famous sepia-tinted photographs of Indian life taken by Edward S. Curtis between 1896 and 1930, with recent colored footage of the landscapes and wildlife of the north western plains and mountains of the United States. The commentary consists entirely of the words of Native Americans in which they express their understanding of the meaning and value of the natural world; within nature the Indians found spiritual and psychological well-being.*

Walking Upright (Chimpanzee) 2 min. Dist: PSU FR$2.80.

Wanzerbe (1968) 30 min. Jean Rouch (DI), Centre National de la Recherche Scientifique, Comité du Film Ethnographique (PR). Dist: CFE; DER. *A possession dance was organized to ask the gods to designate the successor to the senior magicians from Wanzerbe who have just died.*

War of the Gods (Disappearing World Series) (1971) 66 min. Peter Silverwood-Cope, Stephen and Christine Hugh-Jones (AN). Dist: PSU order #51229; ISHI FR$85, FS$875. *For thousands of years, the Maku and Barasana Indians have lived in the deep forests of northwest Amazonia. Now, the traditions of the past are giving way to the forces of Christianity as Catholic missionaries and American evangelists compete to convert the Indians.* [Reviewed by Benson Saler, AA 76:210, 1974.]

The Warao 57 min. Jorge Preloran (PR). Dist: UCEMC R$51, FS$720, VS$505. *The Warao (the people of the boat) live surrounded by water at the mouth of the Orinoco River delta in eastern Venezuela. Shows men and women at work—making canoes, fishing, weaving baskets, preparing food, making hammocks—and relaxing at a traditional feast. Casual, well-paced narration relates several Warao myths, some of which are quite ironic. Illustrates some activities of the shaman and shows the imaginative methods of conflict resolution that have replaced bloodshed and physical violence.*

The Warrior from Within (Man Alive Series) 30 min. Dist: CBC VS$69, order #Y8L-89-03. *Douglas Cardinal is one of Canada's most celebrated architects, and his latest creation, the National Museum of Civilization, is a triumph. For Cardinal, a Metis from Alberta's backwoods, the success caps a remarkable personal journey. Through the years of struggle against racism, financial ruin, and professional controversy, Cardinal found strength within his own native faith.*

Warriors and Maidens: Gender Relations in a Cretan Mountain Village 51 min. Barrie Machin (FM). Dist: MRW VS$310. *The village of Pallikari is western Crete has always been at the center of resistance to foreign invasion. Cultural codes, which favor masculine defensiveness and female purity, have been influenced by a long history of warfare. The film examines the way history, economics, and religion intertwine to produce enduring codes governing the relationship between men and women. At the same time, the film is a stunning visual portrait of a way of life.* [Reviewed in VISA 4:82, 1991.]

Washoe (1966) 56 min. Veronika Pataky (WR, DI), Western Artists Corporation (PR). *Here in Dresslerville, largest of the Washoe colonies, the film is built around two of the more important ceremonies, the Pine Nut Dance and the Girl's Puberty Dance, both taking place from the sundown to sun-up, all through the night. The ceremonies are embedded in the daily life of the Washoe community with the preparations winding their way in and out of family life, children at play, and the daily doings of the adults. Besides the narration, the language is Washoe, contributing greatly to the impression and understanding of the life within the tribe. The sounds in the film are authentic. Permeating the film is the thinking and philosphy that still marks the Indians. It is everything they are and do; it is in their games, their dancing, their beautiful songs and chants; it is in the language and in their silence. Behind the film lie the close contact and friendship the director of the film, Veronika Pataky, has acheived with the Washoes over a period of ten years. Thus, the film reaches beyond the boundaries of the visual and becomes a complete and profound experience, an encounter with the Washoes in their own world.* [Reviewed by Stanley A. Freed and John A. Price, AA 69:562–563, 1967.]

Wasyl, an Anecdote 11 min. Michael Trend, Steven Church (FM). Dist: Toad Hall Films, 3624 20th Ave. S, Minneapolis, MN 55407. *A Ukranian immigrant in Minneapolis.* [Reviewed by Oksana I. Grabowicz, AA 74:1575, 1972.]

Watcher of the Winter Sun (1983) 11 min. Michael Bober (FM). Dist: Watcher of the Winter Sun, P.O. Box 8374, Universal City Station, North Hollywood, CA 91608; (213) 259-8145, FS$100. *Explores Native American astronomy. "The subject is a small rockshelter, presumably a Kumeyaay site, on the La Rumorosa Plateau in northeastern Baja California, that may have been used for winter solstice sunrise observations. There is a brief discussion of Kumeyaay hunting and gathering behavior, the area covered, and the foods eaten. In this context, skywatching is essential for understanding seasonal changes."* [From the review by Jonathan E. Reyman, AA 87:228, 1985. Reviewed by Anthony F. Aveni, ARCH 38(2):72, 1985.]

The Water Is so Clear That a Blind Man Could See (1970) 30 min. Dist: PSU order #1664, FR$15.50. *New Mexico's Taos Indians believe that all life is sacred—plant and animal—and live without disturbing their environment. Blue Lake area, sacred to these Indians, was owned by them until 1906, but was leased from the government until 1983. At the time the film was made, lumber companies were trying to get permission to lumber the area when the Indians' lease had expired.*

Water Farmers (A Taste of China Series) (1984) 29 min. Sue Yung Li (PR). Dist: UCEMC FR$45, FS$580, VS$295. *The Yangzi River delta region south of Shanghai is known as the water country. Hundred of miles of canals link towns and villages and serve as "liquid highways" for wedding boats, traveling vendors, and foot-powered rowboats. Here,* *near the city of Shaoxing, water has completely shaped the local farmers' way of life. In their lives, we witness the traditional harmonious relationship between the Chinese people and their environment.*

Water for Tonoumasse Gary Beitel (PR). Dist: FL. *During the long, dry season in the south of Togo, in West Africa, a woman's day began at 1:00 a.m. with an eight-hour trek for water. Unbeknownst to her, the water so arduously collected was contaminated, the source of debilitating diseases. The film shows the efforts of a group of villagers to get clean water by drilling a well nearby. It chronicles the success of the project in which women played a key role. To the surprise of the village men, the women were capable of making decisions, handling money, and learning the mechanics of keeping the pump in working order. We share their joy as they celebrate when water pours forth.* [Reviewed by Nancy J. Schmidt, AA 93(1):262–263, 1991.]

Water from Another Time 29 min. Richard Kane and Dillon Bustin (FM). Dist: DER FR$55, VR$40, FS$475, VS$275. *A documentary capturing the flavor of a lifestyle that many of us have either forgotten or never known at all. Those featured in the film live outside the flow of time, shunning modern conveniences in favor of a more traditional way of life. The filmmakers visit three elderly residents of Orange County, Indiana, talk with them, enjoy their artistic creations, and learn something about the dignity and meaning of aging. Lotus Dickey, 70, a retired factory and construction worker who raised eight children by himself, sits by his parents' farmhouse, playing his violin and singing songs he wrote. Elmer Boyd, 80, a shy bachelor who was always considered odd and old-fashioned shows an ingenious water carrying system he built for his parents in 1943 and shares with us his journal of daily entries, dating from 1923. Artist and poet Lois Doane, 87, shows her albums and sketchbook, reads some of her works, and tells of her family being some of the original Quakers in the area.*

The Water of Words: A Cultural Ecology of a Small Island in Eastern Indonesia (1984) 30 min. Timothy Asch and Patsy Asch (FM), James J. Fox (AN). Dist: DER FR$55, FS$550. *This film explores the poetry and ecology of the lontar (borassus) palm on the eastern Indonesian island of Roti. This account of the utilization of lontar, a tree that provides the mainstays of the Rotinese diet, shows techniques of tapping and cooking the palm juice and its transformation into syrup, beer, and gin ("the water of words"). The film integrates striking visual imagery with the clan leader's description, the paired poetic speech of ritual specialists, and myths that recount the origin of the lontar from the sea.* [Reviewed by Fitz John Porter Poole, AA 89:269–270, 1987.] *The film complements James J. Fox's study of lontar utilization on Roti, "The Harvest of the Palm," as well as his essays on ritual speech in Indonesia. The film is also available in an Indonesian language version.*

The Water Talks to Me 30 min. Nancy Cohen (FM), Noah Adams (NA). Dist: DP VR$40, VS$110. *Provides a close look at a traditional fishing community caught in the midst of change. Shot in the fishing port of Gloucester, Massachusetts, and on vessels in the North Atlantic, the documentary explores the impact of declining fish populations on the lives of two offshore fishermen, a father and son. Fisheries scientists and federal managers are included in the interviews. The result is a multilayered analysis of family and economics, environmental issues and politics.*

Water Witching (Dowsing) in Middle America (1987) 20 min. Philip Singer (FM). Dist: Singer-Sharrette Productions, 2810 Indian Lake Road, Oxford, MI 48051; (313) 693-9447, FS$575, VS$175. *"An annual gathering, on a treeless expanse of central Montana plains, of 'friends and neighbors' to share their experiences of dowsing."* [From the review by Frederick Errington, AA 92:266–267, 1990.]

Waterborne: Gift of the Indian Canoe 13 min. Anne Rutledge and David Current (FM). Dist: NDF VR$40, VS$200. *Told entirely by Indian people from the Pacific Northwest,* Waterborne *documents a great revival as hundreds of Northwest tribal members, young and old, participate in the native art of canoe carving and rekindle the excitement of the canoe race.* Waterborne *links the canoe with both past and present, making the vital connection between canoe, water, fish, and cedar, and shows the renewed determination of Indian people to preserve their beliefs, traditions, and natural resources while living fully as contemporary people.*

Watunna (1990) 24 min. Stacey Steers (PR). Dist: UCEMC VR$45, FS$500, VS$295, order #11369(f), #37907(v). *This stunning and universally acclaimed animated film depicts five stories from the creation myths of the Yekuana Indians who inhabit the Venezuelan rainforest. These fascinating, highly metaphorical stories explore the genesis of evil, night, sexuality, fire, and food. This landmark achievement in animation is handpainted with watercolors using metamorphosing designs drawn in part from ancient Yekuana art.* [Reviewed by Jean-Paul Dumont, AA 94(3):770–771, 1992.]

The Wax and the Feather 26 min. Alejo Santa Maria and Cristina Echavarria (FM). Dist: ETNOS. *An interesting ethnomusical documentary about a small mestizo village in the Sierra Nevada de Santa Marta (North Colombia). In its rescue of these disappearing traditions, it shows the construction of unusual musical instruments, as well as colorful handicrafts of pre-Columbian origin. From a historical perspective, beginning with Indian dances, it examines how the mixture of American Indian, African, and Hispanic cultural traditions led to the growth of a myriad of musical expressions. With the passing of time, these gave birth to the Vallenato ballad folk music, very popular in the North of South America and the Caribbean.*

The Way of Our Fathers 33 min. A film by various northern California Indians; Bradley Wright (FM). Dist: UCEMC FR$38, FS$455; PSU FR$17.50, FS$395. *Members of several northern California Indian tribes depict unique elements of a way of life as it flourished before the imposition of a foreign culture. The consequences of becoming a conquered and victimized people in one's own land are explored, such as the destruction of self-concepts and the loss of cultural heritage and identity by conventional white-oriented educational programs. Several Native American* *teachers discuss historical methods of Indian education and ways in which both methods and content might be incorporated in the mainstream of American education to benefit not only Native Americans but all children. Though a total return to the past is not advocated, certain cultural elements—Indian languages, a knowledge of true Indian history, and a sense of closeness with nature—are shown to be essential to the presevation of the Native American's sense of identity and value system. Other examples of traditional learning depicted include older Indians' recalling and teaching tribal songs and dances to the young, a father instructing his children in how to find and use natural foods and products, a medicine woman in training performing a native song and discussing her reasons for not translating the words into English, and two Indian women preparing acorn food. The Native Americans who guided and participated in* The Way of Our Fathers *believe the problems, principles, and recommendations shown are applicable to Indian people everywhere.* [Reviewed by Gifford S. Nickerson, AA 76:720–722, 1974.]

The Ways of Nya Are Many (1988) Marc Auge and Jean-Paul Colleyn (DI). Dist: FL. *This film coincides with publication of the book,* Les Chemins de Nya: Culte de posséssion au Mali. *In Mali, many possession cults still flourish especially amongst the Minyanka. As the supreme God worries little about their daily problems, the Minyanka address themselves to a series of intermediary forces among which the most popular is Nya. Its power resides in handmade objects that require to be regularly nourished with sacrificial blood. By periodically taking over a possessed person, Nya ensures a communication and continuity between the ancestors and the villagers. The film clarifies several of the major themes in African religions: the relationship between knowledge and power and the controversial notions of fetish, sacrifice, witchcraft, and possession. The cases analyzed show that Minyanka possession is neither caused by illness nor is it a form of social protest.* [Reviewed by Mary H. Moran, AA 86:1065–1066, 1984.]

We Ain't Winning 60 min. David Feingold and Shari Robertson (FM). Dist: OFL FR$95, VS$195. *As the Drug War in Peru is eclipsed by a real war, award-winning filmmakers journeyed to the coca-growing mountains of the Huallaga River Valley, the violent slums of Lima, and the policy jungles of Capitol Hill to analyze what could be America's next Vietnam. Peru is the source of more than 60 percent of the world's coca leaf—the raw material for cocaine. America's War on Drugs, the original cornerstone of U.S. policy toward Peru, has ground to a halt. Meanwhile, the most vicious leftist insurgency in the world Sendero Luminoso, or the Shining Path, marches steadily toward its goal—a takeover of Peru. Peru's equally fearsome military, named by the UN as the worst abuser of human rights for the fifth year in a row, is President Alberto Fujimori's only hedge against the Shining Path. The United States is on the brink of a huge policy shift, and Peru is on the brink of disaster.* We Ain't Winning *is a portrait of the changing relationship between a besieged Latin American nation and the most powerful country in the world.*

We Are the Landowner (1985) 48 min. Ian Dunlop (FM). Dist: FAA. *After a general introduction to Yirrkala and the nearby Gove Bauxite mine, the film goes to Baniyala, the homeland settlement of Madarrpa clan, on the northern shores of the Blue Mud Bay. We see Aboriginal people running their own affairs and exploiting Western technology with competence and pride.*

We Are Mehinaku (1981) 59 min. Carlos Pasini and Melanie Wallace (FM). Dist: GTI. *This film, "offers a splendid and coherent view of myth, ritual, and social relations among a group of 80 Indians who make their life near the head waters of the Xingu River in Brazil." The focus of the film is the month-long rituals associated with harvest during which people act out roles of various spirits.* [From the review by Jeffrey Ehrenreich, AA 84:980–982, 1982.]

We Are Nothing without the People (The Human Face of Indonesia Series) *The governor of the province of Nusa Tenggara Timur and his wife discuss their medical work for one of the poorest provinces in the country. They also talk about the role of the army in Indonesia today.*

We Believe in It (1986) 46 min. Ian Dunlop (FM). Dist: FAA. *The film looks at how the Yolngu and their culture survived 40 years of missionary influence followed by the development of a huge Bauxite mine. It gives an impressionistic picture of Yolngu culture 12 years after mining started. We see the funeral ceremony for a senior woman. Yolngu staff teach aspects of their own culture as an integral part of the curriculum at Yirrkala school. At a Christian Youth Fellowship meeting, the relationship between Yolngu faith and Christianity is discussed, so too are the effects of alcohol and the recently introduced Pacific Island drink, Kava. Yolngu culture is shown as a dynamic and dominant force at Yirrkala today.*

We Believe in Niño Fidencia Jon and Natalie Olson (FM). Dist: Jon and Natalie Olson, P.O. Box 14914, Long Beach, CA 90814, FR$40, FS$325. *Shows a pilgrimage center in Mexico dedicated to a folk healer.* Suggested supplements: Barbara June Macklin and N. Ross Crumrine, "Three North Mexican Folk Movements." *Comparative Studies in Society and History* 15:89–105, Cambridge University Press, 1973. Barbara June Macklin and N. Ross Crumrine, "Sacred Ritual vs. the Unconscious: The Efficacy of Symbols and Structure in North Mexican Folk Saints' Cults and General Ceremonialism." In: *The Unconsious in Levi Strauss' Anthropology,* Ino Ross, ed. E. P. Dutton, 1974. Barbara June Macklin, "El Niño Fidencia; Un Estudio del Curanderismo en Nuevo Leon." *Anuario Humanitas,* Centro de Estudios Humanisticos, Universidad de Nuevo Leon, Monterrey, 1967. Barbara June Macklin, "Folk Saints, Curanderismo, and Spiritualist Cults in Mexico: Divine Election and Social Selection." In: *Caribbean Cults: Individual and Social Change,* Donald Hogg and Joan Koss, eds. Institute for Caribbean Studies, 1973. Barbara June Macklin, "Belief, Ritual and Healing: New England Spiritulaism and Mexican-American Spiritism Compared." In: *Contemporary Religious Movements in America,* Mark Leone and Irving Aretsky, eds. Princeton University Press, 1974.

We Dig Coal: A Portrait of Three Women (1983) 58 min. Thomas C. Goodwin, Dorothy McGhee, and Gerardine Wurzburg (PR). Dist: CG FR$100, FS$795, VS$495. *"Discuss[es] the legal battles women fought for the right to mine and the discrimination and harassment they face on the job. . . . Convey[s] the prejudice and superstitions against women in the mines. . . . Portray[s] the health and safety hazards of coal mining as an occupation and the importance of the union to the miners."* Concentrates *"on three women, one of whom was the first woman to die in a deep mine accident in the United States. The women were the only female employees working underground for the Rushton Mining Company in Osceola Mills, Pennsylvania."* [From the review by Alice Reich, AA 88:784–785, 1986.]

A Weave of Time (1987) 60 min. Susan Fanshel (FM), Deborah Gordon (PR), John Adair (PR, AN). Dist: DCL FR$100, FS$895, VS$350. *In 1938, anthropologist John Adair traveled to the Navajo reservation in Pine Springs, Arizona, where he met and filmed the Burnside family, creating a visual record of Navajo life in the 1930s. This historical footage is woven together with contemporary scenes and in-depth interviews of the Burnside family today. The film documents 50 years and four generations of change in one Navajo family. As their story evolves, a clash of past and present surfaces. The daily struggle for family stability, education, and economic survival in contemporary America challenges the existence of traditional identity, including the Navajo religion, language, and arts. This film of the Burnside history becomes a complex microcosm of Navajo culture in transition.* [Reviewed by Margot Schevill, AA 90:486, 1988.]

Weavers in Ahuiran (1990) 55 min. Beate Engelbrecht & Ulrike Keyser (DI), Manfred Kruger (CA), Beate Engelbrecht (SR), Christina Jaekel (ED). Dist: IWF; UCEMC VR$60, VS$225, order #38253. *Since men are increasingly forced to leave the village to earn money, women in Ahuiran have more and more to support their families. All women are taught weaving as children, and they produce servilletas, white cloth used to transport food, and rebozos, bluish black shawls. The rebozo is an indispensable part of the clothing of the women, and for that reason, the shawls have a permanent market within the region. The film documents the weaving techniques, social organization, and economic situation of women weavers in a village in Mexico. It examines the changes in style and materials as well as in work organization caused by the increasingly difficult economic conditions facing the weavers.* [Reviewed by Stacy B. Schaeffer, AA 95(1):256–257, 1993.]

Weavers of the West (1954) 13 min. Dist: IUAVC FR$7.50. *Shows the country in which the Navajos live, their chief occupation of sheep raising, and the steps in the process of making Navajo rugs from the shearing of sheep to the selling of the finished product at a trading post. Depicts the various steps, including washing and drying the wool, carding and spinning it into yarn, and dyeing and weaving. Shows numerous examples of rug designs.*

Weaving Films Encyclopedia Cinematographica (PR). Dist: PSU. *Sixteen films on weaving in north Thailand.* [Reviewed by Marie Jeanne Adams and Joanne Bradford, AA 78:720, 1976.]

The Wedding Camels (Turkana Conversations Trilogy Series) (1978) 108 min. David and Judith MacDougall (DI). Dist: UCEMC FR$95, FS$1350, VS$450. *An account of a wedding among the Turkana, semi-nomadic pastoralists of the dry savanna of northwestern Kenya. Made during a 14-month stay with the Turkana, it records the delicate and sometimes tense bridewealth negotiations leading up to the actual wedding ceremony, as well as the reactions of a number of the participants afterwards. One aim of the filmmakers was to give some sense of first-hand observation to the events as they unfolded, together with the kind of search for information that is characteristic of fieldwork. Another was to present individual Turkana personalities and the bearing of personality upon formalizing social events. Yet another was to set forth the complex nature of livestock obligation, which gives security and cohesion to families scattered over a wide geographical area. In* The Wedding Camels *a girl of the homestead, Akai, is to marry Kongu, an old friend and age-mate of her father, Lorang. Because of the close ties between Lorang and Kongu, everything should go smoothly, but the pressures within the two families are such that the wedding negotiations become increasingly tense. Arranging the number and type of animals to be given as bridewealth demands an intricate balance between psychology and economics: Kongu must offer enough animals to please Lorang and his relatives, but not so many that he appears weak or foolish, or depletes his own family's herds. Negotiations drag on for several days, then threaten to break down completely. The outcome depends not only on traditional patterns of behavior, but also on the influence exerted by Lorang's wives and the manner in which Lorang chooses to resolve the dilemma that confronts him. In Turkana, with English subtitles.* [Reviewed by Ben G. Blount, AA 86:803–805, 1984. Winifred Lambrecht, SBF 17:100, 1981.] Relevant anthropological literature: P. H. Gulliver, *The Family Herds*. Routledge & Kegan Paul, 1955. P. H. Gulliver, "Jie Marriage." In: *Cultures and Societies of Africa*, Ottenberg, ed. Random House, 1960.

Wedding of the Goddess: Part I 36 min. Dist: UW-SAAS FR$30, FS$250. *Provides the historical background for the annual Chittirai festival in the South Indian city of Madurai. With tales from medieval Tamil poems and paintings and sculptures from local temples, the film illustrates how the city, the main temple, and the goddess Minakshi and the god Sundareshvara have evolved and how the reenactment of the marriage of the god and goddess has become the most important annual festival of Madurai. The film illustrates the basic process of exchange between the temple deities and their worshippers and the importance of festivals in reestablishing cosmic order.*

Wedding of the Goddess: Part II 40 min. Dist: UW-SAAS FR$30, FS$275. *Places the viewer in the midst of the annual Chittirai festival, providing an intimate picture of the day and night proceedings of the 19-day festival. The film shows brahmin priests tracing the initial sacred diagram on the temple floor, the colorful reenactment of the goddess's coronation and marriage, the circumambulation of the medieval* *city by deities in giant carts, a neighboring god's journey to Madurai, and a cult initiation and spirit possession, as the festival unites gods and humans from all walks of life. Through interviews with participants, the film gives an unusual glimpse of the continually changing patterns of festival celebration.*

Wedding in a Persian Village (1962) 11 min. Mansour Ali Faridi (FM). Dist: NYU FR$11, FS$170. *Filmed in the villages of Korvaneh and Aghjehharabeh, Iran. Depicts traditional Muslim marriage ceremonies and rituals in remote regions of Iran. The bride is prepared for her journey to the groom's home by her relatives and friends. She makes the journey on horseback and is escorted by her women and men kinfolk. She is followed by her household possessions. On the way, the girls hold mirrors facing the bride for good luck. The bride is veiled. The groom celebrates with his friends and relatives by having his last meal as a single man and receives money, which is pinned on his jacket. The celebration includes dancing by the groom's kinfolk (only men dancing with men), and one little girl dances for further entertainment. This is the first time the bride and groom see each other. The celebration continues for days with dancing and feasting.* Bibliography: Isaac Adams, *Persia by a Persian*. Chicago, 1900. [Reviewed by Peter S. Allen, *AA* 77:710, 1975.] [Gitta Komangi]

The Wedding of Palo (1937) 72 min. F. Dlasheim and Knud Rasmussen (FM), Palladium Films (PR). Dist: MOMA FR$40. *A study of the east Greenland Eskimos of the Angamagssalik district, told in terms of the marriage of an Eskimo boy and girl. This fictional form is used because it provides an adequate medium for presenting the cultural pattern of this remote people. In Eskimo with English titles.* [Reviewed by Thomas M. Kiefer, *AA* 76:209, 1974.]

Wedding Song (1990) 40 min. Susan Slyomovics and Amanda Dargan (FM). Dist: Department of Performance Studies, Tisch School of the Arts, New York University, 721 Broadway, 6th Floor, New York, NY 10003. *"Premarital rituals for the bride among South Asian Muslims in New York City."* [From the review by Ann Grodzins Gold, *AA* 93(4):1042–1043, 1991.]

A Week of Sweet Water 40 min. Peter Adamson (DI), BBC and UNICEF (PR). Dist: DER FR$50, VS$350. *In the Sahel region of West Africa along the southern edge of the Sahara, drought and famine are feared above other things. Drought conditions have brought the world's attention to the plight of those living at the edge of starvation. Even with yearly rains, millions of people struggle to grow enough food to make one harvest stretch to the next. Among them are Minata and Bouremia, a couple from the village of Somiaga in Upper Volta, who re-enact their story in this award-winning film. A Week of Sweet Water touchingly depicts the complex decision-making process that men must endure to provide for their families, which women must face as they decide for the futures of their children, and which the community must consider as they work to develop their land for the greatest benefit.*

A Well-Spent Life 44 min. Les Blank (FM). Dist: FF. [Reviewed by Roger Abrahams, *AA* 76:206, 1974.]

Were Ni! He Is a Madman (1962) 32 min. Francis Speed (FM), Raymond Prince (AN), University of Ibadan, Nigeria (PR). Dist: CFS Ltd. FS$284. *Psychiatric disorder is widespread amongst the Yoruba of Nigeria and the society has a web of well-developed institutions to deal with it. There are two basic types: treatment centers managed by herbalists and diviners with specialist knowledge of traditional psychiatric therapy and cult groups that provide a setting for the expression of otherwise socially unacceptable behavior through "Possession" and "Masquerade" dances. The film shows some aspects of both types of institution. In treatment centers, some of the patients are shackled until they can be trusted not to abscond; a healer prepares and administers his herbal and magical potions or uses incantation; he carries out eleborate admission and discharge rituals, the latter involving the archaic ceremony of washing the patient in the river and sacrifice of pigeons. Islam and Christianity have made considerable penetrations into the Yoruba world bringing with them a retinue of healing techniques; an Islamic Mallam practices sand divination; a Christian prayer healer treats groups of psychotics with oil, water, and prayer.* [Reviewed by Robert G. Armstrong, *AA* 69:426, 1967; Antoine Seronde, *AA* 77:181–182, 1975.] Suggested supplement: *Trance and Possession States*, Raymond Prince, ed. Proceedings, Second Annual Conference, R. M. Bucke Memorial Society, Montreal, 1966. R. B. Edgerton, A Traditional African Psychiatrist. *Southwestern Journal of Anthropology* 27:259–276, 1971. M. Siegler and H. Osmond, Models of Madness. *British Journal of Psychiatry*, 1194–1203, 1966.

Western Samoa—I Can Get Another Wife but I Can't Get Parents (The Human Face of the Pacific Series) (1987) 56 min. Film Australia (PR). Dist: FIV VS$158. *Although Western Samoa is independent, mass emigration to New Zealand continues. This film is about a young couple who must join the exodus and leave behind their close-knit families.*

Wet Earth and Warm People 58 min. Michael Rubbo (DI, ED), National Film Board of Canada (PR). Dist: FI. *Glimpses of Indonesia by a traveling camera crew.* [Reviewed by James J. Fox, *AA* 78:724, 1975.]

The Whale Hunters of Lamalera (Disappearing World Series) (1988) 52 min. Robert Barnes (AN). Dist: FIV VS$198, order #047040; PSU order #51254. *The Lamaholot live in the village of Lamalera on an island in Indonesia. Armed only with forged iron harpoons, they hunt the sperm whale from May to October, ten hours a day, six days a week. But the Lamaholot way of life is being threatened by the scarcity of their prey, and people are leaving the island to seek more profitable work elsewhere.*

Whalehead (St. Lawrence North Series) CRAW FS$210.70 (color), $75.38 (B/W). *A fishing village of the North Shore, cut off from the rest of the world during most of the year except by bush plane, is cut off in summer from its own fishing grounds by the gradual recession of the sea so that, like the birds, it must migrate to the rocky islands of the river.*

Whalehunters of Anse aux Basques (St. Lawrence North Series) B/W. Dist: CRAW FS$75.38. *A glimpse of the life of two brothers who live mainly from hunting white whales in the waters of the Gulf, reveals their inherited love of a life of freedom and the reasons for their decision to not accede to the demands of life in an industrial town nearby.*

Whaling People 30 min. North Slope Borough Teleproduction Studio (PR). Dist: MDAI VS$59.95, order #331-02. *The North Slope of Alaska is the home of the Inupiat Eskimo, people whose culture was built around whaling. The North Slope is also rich in petroleum. Can the whaling culture of the past survive in the face of the energy culture of today?*

When Invaders Become Colonists 50 min. Dist: FHS VS$149, order #DH-2645. *The Spice Islands were a lodestone, irresistible to traders from all over the world. With a combination of skill, armed might, and exceptional cruelty, the Dutch established a monopoly in nutmeg and possession of the Banda Islands, Malacca, Ceylon, and Java, where Batavia became the the center of Dutch power in Asia. This program tells the story of how the Dutch became colonists and how they tried to create homes so far from home, as well as how a small population of Dutch managed for so long to dominate the native population and the immigrants from elsewhere in Asia.*

When Mountains Tremble (1983) 83 min. Peter Kinoy (PR), Pamela Yates and Thomas Sigel (DI). Dist: NYF. *"Weaves the life history of a Mayan woman into the panorama of recent [Guatamalan] events.... Provides unique footage of government military forces as well as of Guatemala's revolutionary movement."* [From the review by James Loucky, AA, 87:992–994, 1985.]

When Mrs. Hegarty Comes to Japan (1992) 60 min. Noriko Sekiguchi (FM). Dist: FRIF. *The Japanese filmmaker brings her Australian "godmother" to visit her family and records the tensions and complexities of the culture contact.*

When the Snake Bites the Sun (1987) 57 min. Michael Edols (FM), Film Australia (PR). Dist: FIV VS$149. *Michael Edols tells the story of aborigine Sam Woolagoodja, the undisputed "bunman" or spiritual custodian of his people's ancient past. This program explores the genesis of the aborigines' nearly obliterated traditions and recounts the odyssey of a young man's commitment to an old man and his world.*

When the World Turned Dark 51 min. Maria Louisa Lobo (PR), Gianfranco Annichini (DI). Dist: AW FS$700, VS$300. *This film focuses on the religious celebrations of the village of Yanque, in which traditional Andean rites continue to be held with Christian rituals that have survived from the colonial era. The filmmakers examine some myths still current in the Colca valley, such as the one arising from the Spanish assassination of of the Inca Atahualpa, "when the world turned dark" and would so remain, until his resurrection restores the old way of life. This myth, centered on death and resurrection, underlines the parallels and fusions that arise between the Andean and Christian rituals. Capturing the poetic form of the magical world of the Andes, the main text is narrated by a Spanish conquistador and a native of the Andes, in a counterpoint between both cultures, with incidental dialogue by present day villagers.* [Reviewed by Caroline B. Brettell, AA 91:831–834, 1989.]

When You Make a Good Crop (1987) 28 min. Louis Guida (FM). Dist: CSF VR$40, FS$400, VS$150. *Italian farmers in the Mississippi delta.* [Reviewed by Carole Counihan, AA 92:268–270, 1990.]

Where Land Is Life 28 min. Dist: MWV VS$19.95. *For the indigenous people of Peru's Altiplano, the rugged land around Lake Titicaca is more than soil. Centuries of conquests and exploitation have forced the Aymara and Quechua people to give up land that has sustained them. To the Aymaras and the Quechuas, land is culture, land is faith, land is their community—land is life. Today they are reclaiming the land of their birthright and, at the same time, rediscovering the traditional methods of agriculture that made this region the breadbasket of Peru. The Quechuas and Aymaras are optimistic about the future. Problems however, like flooding, early frosts, and violence limit their expectations.*

Where Man Lies Buried 38 min. Kenneth A. R. Kennedy (DI), Margret Fairlie (PR). Dist: IRC FR$33, FS$325. *Filmed on location in India, Sri Lanka, England, and North America, this unique film describes (1) the different kinds of geological and archaeological deposits where the bones of ancient man are found, (2) field techniques of excavating mortuary sites, and (3) methods of laboratory analysis and casting processes whereby the respectful study of human skeletal remains provides important data to questions of an extinct population's lifeways, demographic patterns and health status.* [Reviewed by Gloria J. Edynak, AA 77:902, 1975. Robert B. Eckhardt, AJPA 43(1):149–150, 1975.] J. L. Angel, "Treatment of Archaeological Skulls." *Anthropological Briefs*, 3:3.8, 1943. W. M. Bass, *Human Osteology: A Laboratory and Field Manual of the Human Skeleton.* University of Missouri, Columbia, 1971. Dr. Brothwell, *Digging Up Bones: The Excavation, Treatment, and Study of Human Skeletal Remains.* London: British Museum, 1972.

White Clay and Ochre (Australian Museum Series) (1969) 15 min. Dist: Australian Museum; UCEMC FR$21; PSU(PCR) order #21338, FR$6.90. *A report on studies of the Aborigines of western New South Wales, this film highlights the on-location work of an Australian Museum field party. As background, we are shown one of the few remaining areas where the Aborigine still lives as he has for thousands of years. It is a life of constant search for food and water. There are live shots of the terrain and food resources—kangaroos, lizards, fruits, nuts, game, and seeds. At an Aborigine campsite, occupied until 100 years ago, we see a grindstone, abandoned because of its weight. Close by are engravings hammered into rock by Aboriginal artists, depicting the events of their daily lives. The camera brings into view some rocky hills, containing caves in which primitive artists painted a vivid record of their life. The*

Museum party arrives to make a permanent record of the painting, to determine the age by radiocarbon dating, and to study their history and meaning. The techniques of archaeologist, artist, and photographer are intercut with shots of the paintings, which document the hunting, food gathering, warring, and ceremonialism that made up Aboriginal life. A warning note about preservation of such relics closes this comprehensive and detailed film. [Reviewed by Mary Rusco, AA 78:141, 1976.]

The White Dawn (1974) 110 min. Martin Ronsohoff (PR), Phillip Kaufman (DI). Dist: AB FR$125. *Based on James Houston's true story of an Arctic adventure. Relates the story of three sailors who are separated from their ship during an Arctic hunt for polar bear and walrus. Eskimos who live in Baffin Island, just south of the North Pole, save their lives, but one angry sailor brings fear and violence to all. Magnificent location footage and realistic hunting scenes bring a striking documentary flavor to the intense and passionate conflict.*

White Fur Clouds (1989) 30 min. Joyce Smith (FM). Dist: Joyce Smith, 81 Barnes Street, Providence, RI 02906; (401) 272-7055, VR$40, VS$90. *"A unique survival skill of the Canadian subarctic: the making of garments and blankets from the fragile pelt of the snowshoe hare by the Dene peoples of the Northwest Territories."* [From the review by Judith Schmidt, AA 92(4):1096, 1990.]

White Justice (1987) 57 min. Morgane Laliberte and Francoise Wera (DI). Dist: CG VR$95, VS$395. *"Examines the complicated issue of conflicts that have arisen between the practitioners of a legal system imposed by Euro-Canadian society and the Inuit inhbitants of Arctic Quebec. The movie uses a case-study approach to illustrate different perspectives on the rendering of justice."* [From the review by Richard H. Jordan, AA 92:531–533, 1990.]

White Shadows of the South Seas (1928) 85 min. W. S. Van Dyke (DI). Dist: FI. *A fictional film about the Society Islands.*

Who Discovered America? (1972) 14 min. Howard Campbell (DI). Dist: FI FR$17, FS$190. *Independent development versus diffusion.* [Reviewed by Paul F. Healy, AA 78:361–362, 1976.]

Who Killed Lake Erie (1969) 52 min. Frank McGree (NA). Dist: NNBC Film Exchange, Englewood Cliffs, NJ, FS$500. *Peak of American pollution problem—an example of man's indifference and destruction of his environment. This film shows the pollution of Lake Erie in "scenic background" while a narrator discusses conditions, interviews individuals, and examines the problem from various viewpoints to inform the public of the problem of water pollution through commercial television. The scene is the polluted shoreline as the narrator discusses the amount of money spent by the State of Ohio for lakeshore parks. Polluted rivers flow into the lake as he interviews individuals who live nearby. Cities along the lake are examined as the narrator points out laws they have passed against pollution. The irony of this is that the cities themselves are the polluters with city and industrial wastes. The effect of pollution on the fishing industry and on tourism is graphically depicted with special attention being given Niagara Falls. Indviduals from all walks of life on local, state, and national levels discuss the problem as they see it. Warnings: Students have very strong reactions to this film. Some have claimed it made them physically ill. Focusing questions: What is pollution? Who is polluting Lake Erie? Why is the question of pollution so great that everyone in the film uses the term "they"? The diversity of attitudes of individuals toward this type of problem is interesting to observe—from economics to philosophic indifference. A subquestion is really noticeable with the lack of any solution to the problem. Students keep asking, "What is to be done?" The key is to focus on the solution to the problem rather than look for a scapegoat, to ask not who caused the pollution, but how can we clean it up. What can we do? How soon can we start? Every individual can count, can act through groups and through state and federal government to effect the necessary change.* [John V. Eason]

Who Killed Vincent Chin? 82 min. Christine Choy and Renee Tajima (PR). Dist: FL FR$200, VR$95, FS$2000, VS$495. *This is a powerful statement about racism in working-class America. A 27-year-old Chinese American, Chin was celebrating his last days of bachelorhood in a Detroit bar when an argument broke out between him and Ron Ebens, a Chrysler Motors foreman. Ebens shouted ethnic insults and then, before onlookers, bludgeoned Chin to death with a baseball bat. Ebens was let off with a suspended sentence. Outrage filled the Asian American community to the point that they organized an unprecedented civil rights protest and successfully crusaded for a retrial. This tragic story is interwoven with the whole fabric of timely social issues such as the collapse of the automobile industry under pressure from Japanese imports; the souring of the American dream for the blue-collar worker; and the difficult history of Chinese immigrants in this country.*

Why Did Gloria Die? (1973) 27 min. Dist: IUAVC FR$12.50. *Traces the life of Gloria Curtis, a Chippewa Indian who dies of hepatitis at 27, through her transition from life on the reservation to life in Minneapolis. Focuses on the unemployment and welfare conditions, inadequate housing, and poor medical care she encountered. Discusses with two other members of Minneapolis's Indian ghetto how they made the adjustment from reservation to urban life.*

A Wife among Wives (Turkana Conversations Trilogy) (1981) 72 min. David and Judith MacDougall (DI). Dist: UCEMC FR$65, FS$995, VS$410. *The third and final film of David and Judith MacDougall's trilogy of feature-length ethnographic documentaries on the seminomadic Turkana of northern Kenya. This film covers the period before the filming of* The Wedding Camels, *during which the MacDougalls waited through a dry and rainy season, using the time to investigate how the Turkana, and especially Turkana women, view marriage. First, we hear the testimony of three remarkable sisters (one of them being Arwoto, the senoir wife of Lorang, who figures so prominently in the other films). Then we experience the gradual unfolding of plans for a marriage in the neighboring homestead. In the course of these plans, we learn why a woman would want her* *husband to take a second wife and how the system of polygyny can be a source of solidarity among women while at the same time it may brutally disregard the feelings of the individuals. The Turkana speak rationally and with insight about their choices. They are well aware of the contradictory problems associated with individual liberty and communal survival. The film demonstrates how Turkana culture—and, by extension, human culture—is a living thing, shaped by the people who carry it. In Turkana, with English subtitles. [Reviewed by Ben G. Blount, AA 86:803–805, 1984.]*

Wild Child (1970) 90 min. Francois Truffaut (DI). Dist: United Artists FR$125. *Feature-length fiction based on the journal of J. Itard, which describes the socialization of an abandoned child found in the forests of France in 1797. The film traces the socialization of the Wild Child by J. Itard. When the child is first found, he exhibits animal traits (e.g., walking on all fours, sniffing everything, biting those who came near him, etc.) Throughout the film, he begins to take on human traits (e.g., walking upright, learning to communicate, using tools, and understanding the concept of justice.) The film not only explores the socialization process, but also serves as a metaphor for human evolution. Focusing questions: What does it mean to be civilized? What is meant by the phrase "the noble savage?" Is civilization desirable? What is the relationship between language and civilization? What is socialization? How does the process work? Bibliography: Truffaut and Itard, "The Wild Child." Film Heritage 7(3):1–9, Spring 1972.* [Stephan Papson]

Williamsburg File (Chronicle Series) Dist: CWF FR$20, FS$475. *"Most of the footage appearing in Williamsburg File shows how archaeological evidence was utilized in the restoration of Colonial Williamsburg. . . . The film points out the importance in gaining information about standing buildings."* [From the review by Elizabeth A. Crowell, ARCH 34(2):66, 1981.]

Wilma P. Mankiller: Woman of Power (1992) 29 min. Mary Scott (DI). Dist: WMM FR$60, VS$250. *The first part of a documentary series on women in power, this video is a profile of the first female Chief of the Cherokee Nation. The video follows her through one day in her life and shows how she has done groundbreaking work in governance, community development, and furthering the cause of her people. It effectively shows modern tribal life and raises questions about women and leadership. She provides a strong role model for women and Native Americans as she attempts to find the delicate balance of participating in existing white power structures whilst maintaining her own cultural integrity.*

Winter Sea-Ice Camp, Part I, II, III, IV (Netsilik Eskimo Series) 30 min. each. Doug Wilkinson, Michael Chaluofur, and Quentin Brown (FM), Asen Balikci and Guy Mary-Rousseliere (AN), Education Development Center (PR). Dist: EMC FS$420 (pts. I, II, IV), $325 (pt. III). *This film includes sequences of trekking across sea-ice; building a large ceremonial igloo; hunting seal; liver sharing; children's play outdoors and indoors; games for women, men, and children; trials of strength for men; cooking; clothing repair; making a stone pot; seal meat sharing; visiting; storytelling; juggling; and a drum dance.* [Reviewed by John J. Honigmann, AA 72:722–724, 1970.]

The Winter Wife 26 min. Dist: FHS VS$89.95, order #DH-879. *Jibwes wanted riches above all. One winter, he found a beautiful woman inside a wigwam in the forest. Now there was abundance at Jibwes' camp. But when spring came, the girl would not return with him but made him promise to marry no one else. Each winter she returned, and each spring Jibwes returned to the village alone. But Jibwes wanted still more, so he married the chief's daughter. When the winter wife saw that he had broken his promise, she fled.*

The Witch Doctor 35 min. BBC TV (PR). Dist: T-L. *The social and cultural environment in which African diviners, both men and women, practice their profession is examined in this film. The diviners prosper in countries like Nigeria where they outnumber the medical doctor by far. Their fees are high, their treatment secret, and their methods are, at times, crude. They are confident in their opinions—they never fail. Various case histories of "cures" by diviners are shown. The diviner is a dichotomy: on one hand he uses black magic, and on the other, he inadvertently uses accepted medical practices.* [Reviewed by Eric Almquist, AA 77:182, 1975.]

Witchcraft among the Azande (Disappearing World Series) 52 min. Granada Television International (PR). Dist: FL VR$75, VS$445. *To the Azande of Africa, there is no such thing as bad luck. All misfortune results from witchcraft. This tribe depends on oracles to explain events and to predict the future. We sit in on a trial of a couple accused of adultery. They deny the charge, but their fate will be determined by whether a ritually poisoned chicken will live or die. Here is a Christian tribe where the priest must share his influence with the diviner.* [Reviewed by Philip Leis, AA 86:1066–1067, 1984.]

With These Hands (1987) 33 min. Chris Sheppard and Claude Sauvageot (FM). Dist: FL R$55, FS$525, VS$350. *Three women farmers from Kenya, Zimbabwe, and Burkina Faso tell of their struggle to raise enough food to feed their families. They are frustrated by the men in their villages who own the land but do not farm it, considering such work demeaning. Without their wives consent, land may be sold to investors for a quick profit. The film shows how women are beginning to challenge traditional male authority in their fight against famine.* [Reviewed by Ellen Messer, AA 92:556–558, 1990.]

The Wodaabe (Disappearing World Series) (1988) 52 min. Mette Bovin (AN). Dist: PSU order #51226; FIV VS$198, order #047015. *The Wodaabe are among the last nomadic tribes on earth. They follow their herds for hundreds of miles across one of the harshest landscapes in Africa—the drought-ravaged Sahel south of the Sahara. The Wodaabe say their lives are shaped by joy and hardship and, although survival is difficult, they are determined to preserve their way of life.* [Reviewed by Catherine Ver Eecke, AA 91:835–836, 1989.]

Women in Arms (1980) 59 min. Victoria Schultz (FM). Dist: Hudson River Productions, P.O. Box 1315, Franklin Lakes, NJ 07417; (201) 891-8240, FR$100, VR$100, FS$850, VS$800. *"Focuses on the vital yet under recognized role of women in the Nicaraguan insurrection and revolution."* [From the review by John A. Booth, AA 86:793–796, 1984.]

Women in China (1978) 27 min. Betty McAfee, Open Window (PR). Dist: EDC R$30, FS$405, VS$325. *In 1873, Betty McAfee, a teacher and filmmaker, was invited to join the California Federation of Teacher's delegation to the People's Republic of China. The primary focus of the visit was on education, but Ms. McAfee was interested in what was happening to women in China and talked to women about their past and present status and the changing roles of both men and women. The delegation traveled extensively in China visiting schools, factories, homes, communes, day-care centers, and historical sites. At a worker's village in Shanghai, several women speak about their lives in China's old society and about the contemporary improvements in housing, medical care, education, and employment. The film concludes with a rare glimpse of the more traditional lives of women in Chinese Inner Mongolia and an acupuncture operation in Kwangshow, where a woman, attended by female surgeons, delivers a child by Caesarian section.*

Women in China Today (1983) 46 min. Nippon A-V Productions (PR). Dist: Nippon A-V Productions, 6-27-27 Shinjuku, Shinjuku-ku, Tokyo 160, Japan; 03/926-0491. *"Wuxi, 130 km west of Shanghai, is beautifully presented. . . . The film is organized around the life cycle."* [From the review by Charlotte Ikels, AA 87:739–741, 1985.]

WOMEN IN THE MIDDLE EAST (1982) 26 min. Elizabeth Fernea (PR), Marilyn Gaunt (DI). Dist: FRIF VR$55, FS$470, VS$280. *Elizabeth Fernea has produced four films about women in the Middle East.* [Reviewed by Barbara Aswad, AA 86:233–234, 1984.] See descriptions under individual titles:

- A Veiled Revolution
- The Price of Change
- Women under Siege
- Saints and Spirits

Women of Kerala (1988) 27 min. Canadian Broadcasting Corporation (PR). Dist: FIV VS$99. *Since women in the densely populated state of Kerala in India started a program of education and birth control nearly a decade ago, the birth rate has decreased by 40 percent, and the standard of living has improved markedly. The success of these women serves as a model for underdeveloped areas throughout the world.*

Women of Niger (Femmes du Niger) (1993) 30 min. Anne Laure Folly (FM). Dist: Amanou Productions, 60 rue Violet, 75015 Paris, France; telephone 331-45-79-99-94. *In Niger, a traditionally Islamic country, where polygamy is legal, religious fundamentalism and tradition have worked together to exclude women and to undermine their democratic rights. During the recent elections, men voted by proxy for their women, claiming the Koran as their justification, and emancipated women were assaulted and their property destroyed. This video provides women's own testimony to this situation, as well as their struggles for genuine democracy in a land where even God is on the men's side.*

Women of the Toubou 25 min. Anne Balfour-Fraser (FM). Dist: PFI FR$35; UCEMC FR$35. *The nomadic life of a desert people among whom there is a sexual equality. Portrays the environment and lifestyle of the Toubou tribes in the Sahara Desert. Emphasizes the role of women, their contribution in subsistence activities (food and water collecting, tool-making), and in the economic system (marketing). Describes the division of labor for nomadic tribes and their reluctance to settle in spite of the civil war, drought, and starvation. Describes puberty and marriage ceremonies from the male and female point of view. Discusses the role of cattle and camels in subsistence, political life, and social organization. Focusing questions: What are the determining factors of this nomadic division of labor? How can you account for a woman's high position of respect and dignity in this culture? How is female status reflected in cultural institutions (puberty and marriage ceremonies)? Why is it that nomadic tribes refuse to change in spite of social and political pressures and environmental disaster?* [Felicia Shinnamon]

Women under Siege (Women in the Middle East Series) (1982) 26 min. Elizabeth Fernea (PR), Marilyn Gaunt (DI). Dist: FRIF VR$55, FS$470, VS$280. *Rashadiyah, Lebanon, is six miles from Israel. In 1964, 14,000 Palestinians fleeing Israel transformed this peaceful village overnight into a primary target for repeated Israeli military attacks. The film introduces six women who play crucial roles in this besieged Palestinian community. As mothers, teachers, organizers, laborers, and sometimes as fighters, the women of Rashadiyah provide the foundation for their people's ongoing revolution.* [Reviewed by Barbara Aswad, AA 87:233–234, 1985.]

. . . And Women Wove It in a Basket (1989) 70 min. Bushra Azzouz, Marlene Farnum, and Nettie Kuneki (DI). Dist: WMM FR$140, FS$1200, VS$350. *For the Klickitat Indians in Oregon, basketweaving is a way of reclaiming native forms and heritage. This evocative portrayal of basketweaver Nettie Jackson Kuneki and her family explores Klickitat river culture within an investigation of documentary practice and cultural preservation. Capturing native life as experienced by a contemporary Klickitat woman, the film presents her daily activities through seasonal changes, the documentation of her craft and a visual history of Indian tales and legends. Voices of the filmmakers' own quest supplement Kuneki's reflections, creating a unique tapestry of personal memory and cultural collaboration that is invaluable for ethnographic film studies, Native American collections and women's studies.* [Reviewed by Bea Medicine, AA 93(3):768–769, 1991.]

The Women's Olamal: The Organization of a Masai Fertility Ceremony 110 min. Melissa Llewelyn-Davies (DI), BBC (PR). Dist: DER VR$90, VS$800. *The Women's Olamal follows the events that led up to a controversial ceremony in Loita, Kenya to bless the women and to increase their ability* to have children. *This film, which is presented in observational style with limited commentary, depicts some of the tensions between men and women in Masai society, which, in this case, erupt in a violent row between them. Explanations and insights are given in the form of interviews with the women themselves.*

Wood Cutters of the Deep South (1973) 85 min. Lionol Rogosin (FM, CA), Louis Brigante (ED, CA), S. A. Pillay (SR). Dist: MOMA. *Down in the lush backwoods of Mississippi and Alabama, history is being made. Poor black and white working people are trying to overcome the forces of racism among themselves to organize into a cooperative association in order to free themselves from the bonds of their economic captors: the paper and pulpwood companies. Footage of the fertile and quietly spectacular Deep South is interwoven with the dialogue. Interviews with the men directly involved in the formation of this group—Gulf Coast Pulpwood Association—unfold the intricacies of this endeavor. Through the eyes and minds of the workers and organizers who helped the woodcutters get started in this self-help venture, Rogosin's film reveals the basic needs and struggles encountered in the development of social organization of this nature.*

Wooden Box: Made by Steaming and Bending (American Indian Series) (1962) 33 min. Dist: UCEMC order #5903, FR$38, FS$455. *The Indians of the northwest coast developed woodworking to a degree unequaled elsewhere among aboriginal people. One of the specialties of the Kwakiutl was the steaming and bending of a single wood slab to form a four-sided box, using no nails, screws, or glue. The boxes, some of which were elaborately carved, inlaid, and painted, were used for gifts, drums, storage and transport. Follows each stage of making the Kwakiutl box.* [Reviewed by John Adair, *AA* 76:728–730, 1974.]

The Wooden Giraffe (1966) 26 min. Kevin Duffy (FM). Dist: KDP FR$25, FS$652. *Wood carving of the Barotse, southwestern Zambia.* [Reviewed by Barrie Reynolds, *AA* 70:1051, 1968.]

Woodrow Cornett: Letcher County Butcher (1971) 10 min. Dist: AAAL FR$15, FS$125. *The film follows Woodrow Cornett as he goes through the intricate process of butchering a hog. Narrated by Frank Majority, with a harmonica and humor by Ashland Founts, it is a portrait of a man and his work and a look at the mountain custom of hog butchering performed by a master at the craft.*

Word Is Out: Stories of Some of Our Lives (1980) 45 min. or 2 hour, 24 min. version. Mariposa Film Group (PR) Peter Adair, Nancy Adair, Veronica Selver, Andrew Brown, Robert Epstein, Lucy Massie Phenix (FM). Dist: NYF FS$595. *Twenty-six gay men and lesbian women talk about their experiences in America.* [Reviewed by Paul A. Walker, *SBF* 16:278, 1981.]

The Working Process of the Korean Folk Potter (1977) 28 min. Ron du Bois (FM). Dist: Oklahoma State University, Audiovisual Center, Stillwater, OK 74078; telephone (405) 744-7212. [Reviewed by Richard A. Krause, *AA* 94(3):768–770, 1992.]

The Working Process of the Potters of India: Massive Terra-Cotta Horse Construction (1982) 19 min. Ron du Bois (FM). Dist: Oklahoma State University, Audiovisual Center, Stillwater, OK 74078; telephone (405) 744-7212. [Reviewed by Richard A. Krause *AA* 94:768–770, 1992.]

THE WORLD: A TELEVISION HISTORY 3 parts, 26 min. each. Dist: LMF FS$475, VS$400. *The subject of these three films is the entire span of human prehistory, beginning with the initial divergence of apes and humans from their common ancestor some 4,000,000 to 5,000,000 years ago and leading up to the emergence of the earliest civilizations between 5,000 and 2,000 years before the present time."* The films are based on the 1984 edition of The Times Atlas of World History *(Hammond).* [From the review by John Bower, *ARCH* 41(1):78, 1988.] The titles are:

- **Human Origins: 10,000–8,000 B.C.**
- **The Agricultural Revolution: 8,000–5,000 B.C.**
- **The Birth of Civilization: 6,000–2,000 B.C.**

The World of Apu (Apur Sansar) (Apu Trilogy) (1959) 103 min. B/W. Satyajit Ray (DI, WR), Ravi Shankar (MU). Dist: AB FR$85. *Apu's manhood—his life as a writer in Calcutta, his marriage, and his relationship to his son.*

The World Between 26 min. Dist: FHS VS$89.95, order #DH-883. *Gujek travels along the path of souls, which is strewn with temptations and with obstacles to prevent the traveler from reaching the land of the spirits. But only free spirits can enter the world of spirits, and Gujek is still tied to his body. A magic potion enables him to proceed into the transitory world that lies between the land of the living and the dead, where the festivities for Wabana will soon begin.*

A World of Gestures (1991) 28 min. Dane Archer (DI). Dist: UCEMC VR$50, VS$295, order #38112. *This often humorous and always entertaining video explores gestures from cultures worldwide. It shows people from dozens of countries performing gestures that are by turns powerful, provocative, poignant, subtle—and sometimes obscene. Many types of gestures are illustrated, including those for beauty, sexual behavior, suicide, aggression, and love. The video also examines the meaning and function of gestures and studies their origins. Viewers are guaranteed a greatly enhanced appreciation of cultural diversity and richness. Instructor's guide included.*

The World Tree: A Scandinavian Myth (see Creation Myth Series)

The Work of Gomis 46 min. Yvonne Hannemann (DI). Dist: Washburn Films, 9 East 32nd St., New York, NY 10016. *A Buddhist curer in Sri Lanka.* [Reviewed by Paul Hockings, *AA* 76:219, 1974.]

Woven Gardens (see The Tribal Eye Series)

Wow (1976) 85 min. Bill Leimbach, Jean Pierre Dutilleux (DI). Dist: SFI FS$2000. *Headhunting and cannibalism have always been an essential part of Asmat tribal life. Any death and especially that of a man killed in battle has to be revenged by killing an enemy and taking his head. Asmat revenge also requires the carving of an enormous ancestor* *pole, and it is these poles that are some of the finest woodcarving in the primitive world. It is this link between headhunting and sculpture that inspired the making of Wow and takes us on an exciting journey through the jungle swamps of Indonesian New Guinea. Our destination is a remote and renegade village, renowned not only for its spectacular carving, but also for the death of Michael Rockefeller, the son of the American Vice President. Through Agope, the beautiful master carver of the village, we begin to understand how headhunting and cannibalism can make perfect sense. He also introduces us to the intimate daily routines of Asmat tribal life. Kokoi, the village chief, tells us something of the great headhunting raids and of the mysterious disappearance of Michael Rockefeller. The film offers a rare opportunity to enter an unknown world of great natural beauty and harmony and to share with the Asmat the excitement of one of their most important ritual feasts.*

Wuxing People's Commune 59 min. Boyce Richardson and Tony Lanzelo (DI). National Film Board of Canada (PR). Dist: DER R$60, FS$775, VS$400. *Recent changes in Chinese economy and society make this film an especially valuable portrayal of life and labor in the countryside in 1978. The 14,500 peasants on the Wuxing People's Commune in north China produced enough food in that year to satisfy most of their needs on just 3,000 acres. This film documents the organization of work and its dignity, from 63-year-old Yu Lu Tiao who tends his vegetable field at dawn, to chanting kindergarten youngsters, to the thousands of men, women, and children who mobilize for a great wheat harvest in June.* [Reviewed by Charlotte Ikels, *AA* 87:739–741, 1985.]

Xala (1974) 123 min. Ousmane Sembene (DI, WR), George Caristan (FM). Dist: NYF FR$125. *Shot in Africa, based on Sembene's novel of the same name. The film is a powerful piece of social criticism in the genre of satire and was partialy censored by the Senegalese government (the print distributed by New Yorker Films is complete and uncut). The story begins at the height of its hero's career: a successful businessman takes his place in an all-African Chamber of Commerce and marries his third wife—a lovely young girl. Just at this point, he becomes sexually impotent, he frantically races around spending money on native cures for his malady, and his business falls into ruin. Now a disgrace to the upright business community, he is thrown out of the Chamber of Commerce. His impotence is a metaphor for Senegal's (and other new African nations') continued dependence on white technology and its failure to rid herself of marked social class differences.* Focusing questions: What is Sembene's satire directed at? Monitor your responses to the cultural contrasts depicted in the film. What might these tell you about yourself? In what social contexts is Wolof spoken? French? [Dorice Tentchoff]

Xian (The Cities in China Series) (1981) 58 min. Sue Yung Li and Shirley Sun (PR). Dist: UCEMC FR$65, FS$995, VS$410. *Presents a cultural history of the ancient Chinese imperial city, once the greatest capital in the world. Includes extensive footage of one of the world's most spectacular archaeological sites, the tomb of China's first emperor. His immense underground vault is filled with a life-size pottery army numbering 6,000 warriors plus horses, chariots and weapons.* [Reviewed by Ann Nottingham Kelsall, *ARCH* 36(3):73, 1983.]

The Xinguana: Aborigines of South America (1971) 29 min. Vision Associates (PR). Dist: CRM/MH order #657002-9, FR$33, FS$445. *The Kwarup ceremony, an elaborate ancestral memorial culminating in wrestling matches, is one tribal custom depicted in this film. Spear dances, body ornamentation, and puberty rites are other customs exhibited by the Xinguana, a tribe that continued to live untouched by civilization in the vast jungle watershed of the Xingu River in central Brazil.* [Reviewed by Jean E. Jackson, *AA* 77:700, 1975.] Focusing questions: How is the river used by the Xinguana? How do male and female puberty rites differ? How do male and female roles differ with regard to subsistence activities? Ceremonies? The Trans-Amazon highway will eventually cut right through the Xingu Reserve. How might this affect their culture? What is omitted from the film that would have made it more understandable to someone without an ethnographic background? Bibliography: Ellen B. Basso, *The Kalapalo Indians of Central Brazil*. New York: Holt, Rinehart & Winston, 1973. Thomas Gregor, *Mehinaku: The Drama of Daily Life in a Brazilian Indian Village*. Chicago: University of Chicago Press, 1977. [Randy Pollack]

Yalalag: Changing Town (1973) 18 min. John P. Jopling (FM), Carol F. Jopling (AN). Dist: John P. Jopling, 21 George Road, Maynard, MA 01745, FR$25. *An experimental film intended to demonstrate a possible method for salvaging and presenting valuable data. Made with a handheld Bolex from fieldwork slides taken with a Kodak Instamatic. A Zapotecan mountain village is portrayed through constrasts of traditional agriculture, masked dancers, weaving, leather crafts, fiestas, a wedding ceremony and modern transportation, school and commercial activities all accompanied by appropriate on-site recorded sounds of bands, church bells, fireworks, crowd noises.* [Reviewed by John B. Haviland, *AA* 76:723–724, 1974.]

YANOMAMO MYTHOLOGY SERIES Documentary Education Resources (PR), Timothy Asch (FM), Napoleon Chagnon (AN). Dist: DER. *Yanomamo mythology is rich and complex. In this series of films, knowledgable men dramatically recite entire myths that describe the adventures of the first beings. The activities of these beings, half-human half-spirit, account for many of the ritual beliefs of the present day Yanomamo.*

• **Yanomamo Myth of Naro as Told by Kaobawa** 22 min. FR$30, FS$300.

• **Yanomamo Myth of Naro as Told by Dedeheiwa** 22 min. FR$30, FS$300. *Creativity is a distinctive feature of Yanomamo mythology. Different individuals will modify and embellish myths to suit their own imagination. The myth of Naro tells how jealousy and treachery among brothers leads to the creation of Herkura spirits and the origin of harmful magic. In the two films, the viewer sees how two prominent Yanomamo headmen "act out" these important myths in a distinctly individual manner. Both films are in Yanomamo with a voice over English translation. The films* can be used separately as an example of Yanomamo myth, or together to show the individual variations of the same Yanomamo myth.

- **Moonblood: A Yanomamo Creation Myth as Told by Dedeheiwa** 14 min. FR$25, FS$210. *When the ancestor Suhirina shot Moon (Peribo), human beings were created from Moon's blood. This myth not only accounts for the creations of humans, but also for their capacity for violence. Dedeheiwa again demonstrates his ability as a knowledgable and entertaining myth-teller.* The film is in Yanomamo with a voice-over English translation.

- **Jaguar: A Yanomamo Twin Cycle Myth as Told by Daramasiwa. Part I** 22 min. FR$25, FS$300. *Although Yanomamo apparently do not tell myths straight through, people know them. This was a performance requested by the film crew. Daramasiwa tells the story of how the twin ancestors, Omawa and Yoasiwa, outsmart and kill Jaguar.* Focusing questions: What is the status of this performance? Who is Jaguar? Make kinship diagram to account for kin relationships. What are your emotional reactions to this? Why do American audiences laugh where they do?

- **A Man Called "Bee," Studying the Yanomamo** 40 min. FR$45, FS$540. *The Yanomamo call Chagnon chakti or "bee." This is about his fieldwork. Dramatic opening shot—Yanomamo man struts across a courtyard; then as one looks and realizes that he is not moving in a real Yanomamo style, one gradually recognizes that it is the American anthropologist, Napoleon Chagnon.* Focusing questions: Why should a film show the anthropologist at work? What sort of person is Chagnon? How does this effect what we know about the tribe? If we can ask these questions about the fieldwork itself, should we ask the same about Asch and the film? Cf. also the earlier, but less useful film *Studying the Yanomamo. An Interdisciplinary Study.*

- **Magical Death** 29 min. FR$35, FS$375. *A shaman of great renown organizes a magical attack on a group at war. Shamans use a hallucinogenic drug to summon powerful spirits to assist them. Shamans are not only the curers of their people but are also important mediators of intergroup relations.* [Reviewed by Eric Almquist, AA 77:179, 1975. Eric R. Wolf, AA 77:196–198, 1972.] See suggested supplements under Yanomamo Series.

- **Yanomamo: A Multi-Disciplinary Study** (1968) 45 min. FR$45, FS$540. *The field techniques used by a multidisciplinary team of researchers from the University of Michigan in collaboration with their Venezuelan colleagues. The expedition to the Yanomamo Indian area of southern Venezuela included specialists in human genetics, epidemiology, demography, linguistics, and other fields. The film also offers a brief sketch of Yanomamo society and culture in 1968.* [Reviewed by Paul T. Baker, AA 74:195, 1972]

Yanomamo of the Orinoco: A New Video for Elementary and Secondary Use 29 min. Dist: DER VS$150. *Using resources partially provided by the Massachusetts council on the Arts and Humanities, DER has worked with teachers in Massachusetts schools to edit short videotapes for teaching. It was produced with seventh-grade geography teachers in Massachusetts Public Schools. The tape utilizes film footage from the extensive studies of Napoleon Chagnon and Timothy Asch. It was made to show land use in a South American rain forest. It depicts many of the daily activities of the Yanomamo Indians such as slash and burn gardening, body decorating, gathering firewood, bathing in the river, and preparing for a feast.* [Reviewed by Charles C. Kolb, SBF 24:174, 1989.] This program can be used with the Holt, Rinehart Databank Curriculum or tailored to individual teaching.

YANOMAMO SERIES Documentary Education Resources (PR), Timothy Asch (FM), Napoleon Chagnon (AN). Dist: DER; PSU. In addition to the films listed below, see separate listing for *A Man Called "Bee," The Feast, Magical Death.* [Reviewed by Kenneth M. Kensinger, AA 73:400–502, 1971. Richard Blaustein, JAF 92(364):252–254, 1979.] Suggested supplements: Napoleon A. Chagnon, "Yanomamo—The Fierce People." *Natural History Magazine* 76(1):22–31, 1967. Napoleon A. Chagnon, "The Feast." *Natural History Magazine* 77(4):34–41, 1968. Napoleon A. Chagnon, *Yanomamo—The Fierce People.* Holt, Rinehart & Winston, 1968. Napoleon A. Chagnon, "Yanomamo Social Organization and Warfare." In: *War: The Anthropology of Armed Conflict and Aggression,* Morton Fried, Marvin Harris, and Robert Murphy, eds. Natural History Press. Napoleon A. Chagnon, *Studying the Yanomamo.* Holt, Rinehart & Winston, 1974. David R. Harris, "The Ecology of Swidden Cultivation in the Upper Orinoco Rain Forest, Venezuela." *The Geographical Review* 61(4):475–495, 1971.

- **Arrows** 10 min. FR$15, FS$135. *A large group of boys engage in an arrow fight in the village clearing, shooting blunt arrows at each other to learn to dodge and shoot them.*

- **Weeding the Garden** 14 min. FR$20, FS$180. *This is a quiet sensitive film about one aspect of daily life of Dedeheiwa and his family. Dedeheiwa is a renowned shaman and a headman of his village.*

- **A Father Washes His Children** 15 min. FR$25, FS$200. *Dedeheiwa takes nine of his young children to the river and washes them carefully and patiently.*

- **Firewood** 10 min. FR$20, FS$135. *The irksomeness of daily wood collecting is revealed as a woman patiently and strenuously chops a large log for firewood.*

- **A Man and His Wife Weave A Hammock** 12 min. FR$20, FS$175. *A village headman, Moawa, weaves a hammock. His wife and baby watch.*

- **Children's Magical Death** 7 min. FR$15, FS$105; UCEMC FR$10. *A group of young boys imitate their fathers. They pretend to be shamans, blowing ashes into each other's noses and chanting to the hekura spirits.*

- **Climbing the Peach Palm** 9 min. FR$15, FS$120. *Using an ingenious climbing frame, a young man carefully ascends a spiny peach palm tree to harvest the fruit.*

- **The Ax Fight** 30 min. FR$40, FS$450, VR$35, VS$275. *Shot in 1971, on Asch's second trip to the Yanomamo after Chagnon had spent three years studying them, 400 feet (10 minutes) of film was shot on a single 30-minute event. A quickly escalating melee among the residents and visitors in a Yanomamo village (southern Venezuela). More and more people get drawn into the fight, weapons become more serious, until one man is knocked out, and the fight simmers* *down. The major ethnographic approach: to present different ways of looking at a single event. Second: Selective analysis, Chagnon narrating, explaining events, use of slow motion and still frame. Third: Using kinship diagrams to explain relationships of different participants. Fourth: Edited version. In the first section, film stops but we hear voices of Chagnon, Asch, and Johnson discussing the event—Chagnon's first information turns out later to be wrong. Cinematic features: Important model of different styles of presentation. Also, rare inclusion of anthropologists in informal reaction. (First section not quite unedited—sound of ax blows added in lab.) Focusing questions: Is this just a loud swinging riot? Or are there rules and stages of conflict evident? What role do the women play? What sort of nonverbal behavior is important here? What conflict resolution mechanisms are available? What are the differences in the different versions? What slant does the final version present? Are other slants possible? Why was the first explanation of the fight wrong? [Reviewed by Patricia A. Klein & John E. Klein, AA 79:147, 1977.]*

- **Tapir Distribution** 15 min. FR$25, FS$200. *The ax fight (above) disrupted the political stability in Mishimishmabowie-teri. Several days after the fight, Moawa, the most prominent headman in the village, killed a tapir and presented it to his brothers-in-law who comprise an important political bloc in the village. The gift of the animal served to reinforce his now shaken alliance with them. The film shows how the meat is prepared, cooked, and distributed. The choice meat goes to the important men in the village, the scraps and fat go to the women and the children, and finally the dogs move in for the scant leftovers.* This film compares well with the San (Bushmen) film, *The Meat Fight*, and its accompanying study guide.

- **Ocamo Is My Town** 23 min. FR$20, FS$300. *This film describes the attitudes, accomplishments, and objectives of a Salesian missionary who has spent 14 years in a Yanomamo village. Skeptical about the possibility of immediate success in Christianizing the Yanomamo, the priest emphasizes the importance of his attempts to introduce practical measures that will help soften the impact of civilization when it eventually comes to this village.* Focusing questions: What is the attitude of the missionary toward the Yanomamo? How is he introducing Western culture? How effective do you think the missionary is in bringing about change? [Jack Carter]

- **Tug of War** 9 min. FR$20, FS$120. *The playful side of Yanomamo life is shown on a day during the rainy season when the women and children of the village play a game of tug-o-war.*

- **Bride Service** 10 min. FR$20, FS$135. *Dirimiwa, Dedeheiwa's son, returns from hunting with a wild turkey and a basket of wild fruit for his father-in-law. Dedeheiwa shouts across the village to the man, but he is out. So, his senior wife sends the youngest wife, a girl of about 10 years, to fetch the food. The basket is heavy, and she falls down trying to lift it. Finally, she lifts the basket, carries it across the village, and deposits it at her husband's home. The narration gives essential background information before the event is shown.*

YANOMAMO SERIES (Optical prints). Timothy Asch (FM). Dist: DER. *A series of films that are avalible with optical, not magnetic, soundtracks. Asch uses the term "sloptical" for them to indicate that they are not in the usual finished form.*

- **Children's Evening Play at Patanowa-teri** 8 min. *Two- to nine-year-old children play in the village plaza at Patanowa-teri. A mother comes and scolds her child for spilling a can of beans.*

- **A Woman Spins Cotton** 8 min. *A woman spins cotton in her hammock in Patanowa-teri.*

- **Morning Flowers** 20 min. *A quiet, in-depth portrait of the daily activities at Dedeheiwa's and Moawa's (the two most powerful men in the village) houses. The women and children quietly make decorations from brillant yellow blossoms and spin and weave cotton. The kinship and marriage ties between the families will be described and analyzed in the context of their daily activities.*

- **Yanomamo Hekura Spirits** 14 min. *An experimental film, made for a National Institute of Mental Health Conference, comparing and combining eight minutes of* Magical Death *and four minutes of* Children's Magical Death.

- **Sand Play** 19.5 min. *Four- to seven-year-old boys and girls playing with sand in the center of the village at dusk.*

- **Children at Reahumou Play** 6 min. *Children roast meat and bananas in preparation for a small feast.*

- **Mouth Wrestling** 5 min. *Teenagers fight with each other over a wad of tobacco.*

- **Children Grooming for Lice in Front of Dedeheiwa's House** 7 min.

- **Dedehewai Rests in His Garden** 6 min. *Dedeheiwa weeds his manioc, then goes to sleep in his garden. Several children and grandchildren come back from an expedition of hunting for grubs and wake him.*

- **Moawa Burns Felled Timber** 9 min. *Moawa and his wife work in the garden gathering up brush and burning it in preparation for the planting of crops.*

- **The River Mishimishimabowei-teri** 20 min. *The film shows how several groups of people use the small river, which supplies their village with water.*

- **Children of the Hammock** 7 min. *A small group of boys learn the techniques of hammock manufacture as they attempt to make a small hammock of spun cotton.*

- **Kaobawa Trades with the Reyabobowei-teri** 8 min. *Kaobawa and some of his co-villagers make a long trip to the village of Reyabobowei-teri to feast with them, but by the time they arrive, the meat has been eaten by the hosts. A trade follows, but without much enthusiasm because both hosts and guests are annoyed that a proper feast could not be held for lack of meat.*

- **Hunting Crickets** 10 min. *Young boys, between the ages of 7 and 11, shoot insects in the roof of the village with tiny bows and arrows.*

- **Young Shaman** 10 min. *A young shaman, who is still an initiate, gets sick and loses control of himself on the drug, ebene. The film shows practicing shaman at three levels of* *expertise. Novice initiate, fully initiated, and master (Moawa).*

• **Children Playing in the Rain** 10.5 min. *Approximately 80 boys and just a few girls play in the rain.*

Yanomamo: The Sons of Blood (1974) Geoff Dunlop (FM). Shown on BBC2 as part of the World about Us Series. [Reviewed by Peter Loizos, *RAIN* 4:10, 1974.]

The Yanomamo Tribe in War and Peace (1977) 60 min. Yasushi Toyotomi (DI), Junichi Ushiyama (PR). Dist: Nippon A-V Productions (NAV), 1-363-8 Nishi-Okubo, Shinjuku, Tokyo, Japan. [Reviewed by Gregory A. Finnegan, *AA* 81:470–472, 1979.]

Yap ... How Did You Know We'd Like TV? (1987) 54 min. Dennis O'Rourke (FM). Dist: DCL FR$100, FS$895, VS$350. *This documentary features the people of the small Pacific island of Yap in a sharp look at the social and political impact that television has on their way of life. Yapese news reporter Willy Gorongfel advises his audience to "get out of their betel nut, relax in front of the television and enjoy," but many islanders see television as a threat to their fragile culture. The island was given a television station and a steady supply of American programs by the mysterious "Pacific Taping Company of Los Angeles," but some believe that the company is a conspiracy to promote American cultural values in the seemingly insignificant, but strategically important island.*

Yaqui Easter Ceremony (1941–42) 22 min. Edward Spicer (AN), E. Tad Nichols (CA). Dist: University of Arizona FR$5. *Shot at Pascua (Tucson), Arizona, to record the Yaquis' Easter ceremony as part of fieldwork. Unusual in that the Yaquis do not normally allow photography. Beginning with a brief historical background dealing with the Yaqui village of Pascua, the film documents the highlights of the activities, which begin on Ash Wednesday and continue through Easter. The ceremonial groups' activities are explained in terms of their functions and their personnel. Although the holiday around which the ceremonies are organized is Christian, the groups that participate are Yaqui (Chapayekas, Fariseos, Deer Dancer, Pascola Dancers, and so forth). At the conclusion of the Easter ceremony, the village once again settles down to a daily routine. Cinematic features: Original camera work exaggerates people's movements at times due to variability in camera speed. Some ceremonial activity not recorded due to inability to record at night. Focusing questions: What elements appear to be aboriginally Yaqui and what elements have been introduced via Catholicism in this ceremony? What items, groups, and people represent goodness and grace? Which ones symbolize evil? What role might this ceremony play in promoting community solidarity in Pascua?*

Year of the Communes (1972) 52 min. Dist: Association-Sterling Films, P.O. Box 24642, Los Angeles, CA 90024. [Reviewed by George L. Hicks, *AA* 76:724, 1974.]

Yeleme: La Hache de Pièrre polie en Nouvelle-Guinee 26 min. Bruno Thery, Pierre Petrequin, and Anne-Marie Petrequin (FM). Dist: JVP. *Documents the daily life of the Wano, in Papua New Guinea, who still use stone axes as their main tool of cultivation. The film follows the manufacture and use of these axes, which are used in both forests and farms and also details the social organization, the division of labor by sex, the social status of men, and ritual exchange. Available in French or English.*

Yenendi de Boukoki (Rain Dance at Boukoki, Niamey, Niger) (1967) 25 min. Jean Rouch (DI). Dist: CFE; DER.

Yenendi de Gamkalle (Rain Dance at Gamkalle) (1967) 45 min. Jean Rouch (DI). Dist: CFE; DER.

Yenendi de Ganghel (Rain Dance at Ganghel) (1968) 60 min. Jean Rouch (DI), Centre National de la Recherche Scientifique, Comité du Film Ethnographique (PR). Dist: CFE; DER.

Yenendi de Gourbi Beri (Rain Dance at Gourbi, Niamey, Niger) (1967) 10 min. Jean Rouch (DI). Dist: CFE; DER.

Yenendi de Kirkissey (Rain Dance at Kirkissey) (1967) 10 min. Jean Rouch (DI). Dist: CFE; DER.

Yenendi de Kongou (Rain Dance at Kongou) (1967) 10 min. Jean Rouch (DI). Dist: CFE; DER.

Yenendi de Simiri (Rain Dance at Simiri) (1977) Jean Rouch (DI). Dist: CFE; DER.

Yenendi de Simiri (Rain Dance at Simiri) (1971) 30 min. Jean Rouch (DI), Centre National de la Recherche Scientifique, Comité du Film Ethnographique (PR). Dist: CFE; DER. *After three years of drought, the peasants of the Simiri region, Niger, interrogate the deities of the sky responsible for the causes of their misfortune. The deities respond evasively and accuse them of abandoning their old customs.*

Yenendi de Simriri accompagné de semailles (Rain Dance at Simiri Accompanied by Seed Planting) (1979) Jean Rouch (DI). Dist: CFE; DER.

Yenendi de Yantalla (Rain Dance at Yantalla) (1969) 40 min. Jean Rouch (DI), Centre National de la Recherche Scientifique, Comité du Film Ethnographique (PR). Dist: CFE; DER. *In May at Yantalla, the priests call upon Dongo and his brothers to ask them to make more rain and less thunder than in preceding years.*

Yenendi: Secheress à Simiri (Yenendi: Drought at Simiri) (1976) 120 min. Jean Rouch (DI). Dist: CFE; DER.

Yesterday, Today: The Netsilik Eskimo 57 min. National Film Board of Canada (PR). Dist: EDC FR$60, FS$780, VS$585. *Following the final migration recorded in the film* The Eskimo: Fight for Life, *the Netsilik Eskimo moved into government villages. Ten years later, a camera crew from the National FIlm Board of Canada returned to Pelly Bay in order to document their present life. This film focuses on one day in the life of the same family shown in the earlier films. The changed life of the Netsilik brought about by their contact with Western civilization contrasts sharply with that shown in earlier films. The once nomadic Netsilik now hunt from snowmobiles, having left their igloos for rented government housing and cash their family allowance checks at the Co-op store. Their fresh water is delivered, their fuel oil arrives by plane, their children attend school, a doctor* *and dentist provide medical care. The crafts by which they partially support themselves are their only contact with past traditions; the Eskimo wife works on caribou hides while her husband carves a polar bear from a walrus horn. In ten years, the interdependency and specialization of modern life have replaced the self-sufficiency of traditional Eskimo family life. The Netsilik are now a people in transit, almost weaned from thier past, not quite at home in the present.*

Yo soy Chicano (1972) 59 min. Jesus Salvador Trevino (PR, WR), Victor Millan (NA), Barry Nye (DI, ED). Dist: University of Arizona FR$15.25. *Shot in Texas, New Mexico, California, and Colorado to show the economic and social oppression that Chicanos suffer and to document some of their responses to these injustices. The film consists of a series of interviews with Chicano leaders in various parts of the Southwest coupled with periodic historic (and prehistoric) flashbacks intended to portray key events in Mexican history. Beginning with a farmworkers' meeting in California, the film portrays the organizational efforts of various Chicano activists (Reis Lopez Tijerina in New Mexico, Jose Angel Guiterrez in Texas, "Corky" Gonzales in Colorado) in an effort to show that Chicanos have the willingness and spirit to unite politically. Historic flashbacks highlight the pre-Columbian cultures, the struggle for independence from Spain, and the work of the Flores Magon brothers in fomenting the Mexican Revolution. Also included in these flashbacks are brief descriptions of the Chicano's contributions during WWII and in Vietnam. Rather than being an ethnographic film in the strict sense, this film is designed to provide an introduction to Chicanos today. Focusing questions: What percentage of the current U.S. population is Chicano? What does the term "la Raza" refer to? Aztlan? What social and economic problems do the Chicano face? What organizational efforts have been initiated in an attempt to overcome these problems? Why did the farmworkers feel a need to unionize? What prompted the Tierra Amarilla raid? What did Tijerina hope to accomplish? What is the Raza Unida Party? Who formed it? Why? Where? What is the Crusade for Justice? What is it intended to accomplish? How are the efforts of Tijerina, Gutierrez, Chavez, and Gonzales the same? In what ways do their emphases differ? [John Meredith]*

Yonder Come Day 26 min. Milton Fruchtman (Capital Cities Television) (PR), William Warfield (NA). Dist: CRM/MH FS$435, VS$330. *Yonder Come Day takes us from St. Simon, Georgia, to Yale University in pursuit of the old ways and a remarkable woman who is helping to preserve them for new generations. The woman is 72-year-old folk singer Bessie Jones. At home with Bessie in St. Simon, this film explores life on this tiny island whose isolation preserved traditions long forgotten in the mainstream of society. Now this unique legacy is working to bring young people back in touch with their roots. At Yale University, we join Bessie as she lends her special talents to African-American music courses conducted by jazz musician and teacher Willie Ruff. We learn along with Ruff's students as they investigate the music and the culture it embodies. From Yale, the film journeys to preschool and primary grades where students who have worked with Bessie are sharing what they've learned with yet another generation.*

You Are on Indian Land 37 min. National Film Board of Canada (PR). Dist: NFBC; PSU(PCR) order #40156, FR$12.50; UCEMC order #7920, FR$16. *A film report of a protest demonstration by Mohawk Indians of the St. Regis Reserve on the international bridge between Canada and the United States near Cornwall, Ontario. By blocking the bridge, which is on their Reserve, and causing considerable tie-up of motor traffic, the Indians drew public attention to their grievances that they were prohibited by Canadian authorities from duty-free passage of goods across the border—a right established by the Jay Treaty of 1794. The film shows the confrontation with the police and ensuing action.* [Reviewed by Sol Worth, *AA* 74:1029–1031, 1972.]

You Hide Me (1972) 20 min. Kwate Nee-Owoo (DI). Dist: UNI FR$50, FS$250. *The first film on African art to be produced by an African filmmaker. Deals with the cultural aggression waged by European colonial regimes in Africa. It exposes the policy of the European power, which, in establishing their rule, attempted to wipe out all traces of African civilization, religion, language, and art. As two young Africans examine rarely seen African art works hidden away in the basement of the British Museum in London, the narration explains how and why these pieces were stolen from Africa during the colonialist period. While showing many of these works of African art for their first time, the film also puts them in an illuminating historical and political perspective.*

Yo-Yo Man (1978) 12 min. John Melville Bishop (FM). Dist: DER VR$15, FS$175. *Shot in one week in January 1978 at various locations in Los Angeles including a playground, TV Studio at CSUN, and Yo-Yo man's house. A brief glimpse of the Philippine toy, the yo-yo, and Nemo Concepcion, who demonstrated it across the United States for the Duncan Yo-yo Company.* [Reviewed by Aram A. Yengoyan and Michael Cullinane, *AA* 85:748, 1983.]

Young at Heart (1987) 28 min. Sue Marx and Pamela Conn (PR). Dist: New Dimension Films, 85895 Lorane Highway, Eugene, OR 97405; (503) 484-7125, FR$65, FS$545, VS$295. *"Follows an octogenarian artist couple through a series of in situ interviews before their wedding and seeing their exchange of vows in a conventional Jewish ceremony."* [From the review by Benjamin N. Colby, *AA* 92:1099–1100, 1990.]

Yumi Yet (1987) 54 min. Dennis O'Rourke (FM). Dist: DCL FR$100, FS$895, VS$350; Mac FR$55, FS$600. *In Malaysian, Yumi Yet is a rallying cry meaning, "Just us." This extraordinarily beautiful film captures exuberant celebration in Papua New Guinea during the nation's independence festivities. Traditional tribal customs coexist with the paraphernalia of British and Australian colonialism to create a society of surprising juxtapositions.*

Zapotecan Village 20 min. Madeline Tourtelot (FM). Dist: GP FR$25, FS$300. *A documentary on the life of Zapotecan Indians living today as in the past. The agricultural village is Zoogocho, in the mountains north of Oaxaca.*

Candle making, market day, women at the fountain fed by the mountain springs, gun powder grinding for fireworks, a "torrito," all combine into a pleasant insight into a way of life. Accompanied by locally recorded guitar music.

Zarda: A Nomadic Tribe's Feast Days 50 min. Sophie Ferchiou (PR). Dist: FL VR$75, VS$445. *This production captures the sights and sounds of a spectacular event in Southern Tunisia. Every fall the nomads of this area celebrate their ancestral ties. Their caravans roll through the desert loaded with food, tents, and high-spirited families. This is a time for matchmaking, for showing off jewelry, and for competitive horsemanship. It is also a time of religious devotion and paying respect to one's ancestors.* [Reviewed by Laurence Michalak, AA 93(3):777–778, 1991.]

Zebola: Possession and Therapy in Zaire 53 min. Ellen Corn (RE). [Reviewed by John W. Adams, AA 80:766, 1978.]

Zem Spieva (1933) 68 min. Karel Plicka (DI). Dist: MOMA. [Reviewed by Mark Slobin, AA 79:747–748, 1977.]

A Zenana: Scenes and Recollections 36 min. Roger Sandall and Jayasinhji Jhala (DI). Dist: DER FR$55, FS$550, VR$35, VS$300. *In India, the most secluded section of the palace was the Zenana, or women's quarters. Here, until recently, palace women lived behind protective walls and brass doors that shut firmly at night. This film is an account of women's life in the Zenana of Dhrangadra, in northern India, the seat of power of the Jhala Rajputs from the 11th century A.D. until 1947. The film unfolds through songs, dances, and stories of several palace women, including the Maharani (wife of the Maharaja), who is the mother of one of the filmmakers. She and others reflect upon traditional women's roles, the strictness of their former seclusion, and the ideals of women's purity and inner strength.* [Reviewed by Paul Hockings, AA 86:807–809, 1984.]

Zengbu after Mao (1987) 27 min. Thomas Luehrsen (PR, CA, ED) in collaboration with Jack and Sulamith Potter. Dist: CVA-USC. *A portrait of a rural village of 5,000 peasants in the Peoples' Republic of China and the social and economic changes there since the death of Mao Zedong in 1987. It shows villagers attempting to balance Maoist socialism with their new contact to the world economy through Hong Kong and a recent return of traditional culture. Based on a six-year study of Zengbu, a village in Guandong Province.* [Reviewed by Charlotte Ikels AA 92:272–273, 1990.]

Zerda's Children (1978) 56 min. Jorge Preloran (PR, DI), Henry Fonda (NA). Dist: PFI FR$65, FS$650. *Sixto Ramon Zerda is a powerful, intelligent man, who is also a modern day peasant: illiterate, isolated, and forgotten, a serf of the man for whom he works. There are no laws to protect him, no union to represent him, no one to defend his rights. Yet he understands his situation with great clarity and never hesitates to speak his mind. Earning about $300 dollars a year, he axes down trees, day after day, clearing the land, so that someone else's cattle may pasture, he endlessly chops his life away in the vast forests of central Argentina. Today, after 30 years, he has nothing to show for his work and no hopes for the future. But he does hope for his four remaining children, whom he supports on his earnings of $1 a day. Perhaps they will go to school and break the cycle of poverty in which he is trapped. The plight of the Zerdas is common to the vast majority of rural families living in South America, Asia, and Africa. They are among millions of unrepresented people in this world. In Spanish with English narration.*

Ziveli: Medicine for the Heart 51 min. Les Blank (DI), Maureen Gosling (ED). Dist: FF. *This film features the culture and music of the Serbian-American communities of Chicago and California. Made in association with Serbian-American anthropologist Andrei Simic, the film focuses on the vital cultural strengths of these immigrants from Yugoslavia, who helped to form the backbone of industrial America. Music, dancing, the orthodox church and other community activities are highlighted.* [Reviewed by G. James Patterson, AA 90:485–486, 1988. Reviewed in *L.A. Weekly.*]

Zoo (1993) 130 min. Frederick Wiseman (FM). Dist: Zipporah Films, One Richdale Ave. #4, Cambridge, MA 02140; (617) 576-3603; fax (617) 684-8006. *In his masterful observational style, Wiseman captures the drama of everyday life at the Miami Zoo. What unfolds is the interrelatedness of the animal, human, ethical, research, and financial dimensions of the institution.*

A Zoroastrian Ritual: The Yasna (1982) 31 min. James W. Boyd and William R. Darrow (FM). Dist: Colorado State University, Office of Instructional Services, Fort Collins, CO 80523. *"An unadorned performance of the Yasna provided in minute detail with almost no interpretive commentary whatsoever." Shot in Bombay, India.* [From the review by William O. Beeman, AA 85:1011, 1983.]

Zulu Christian Dances: Part I—The Church of Shembe (1969) 17 min. Hugh Tracey (FM). Dist: PSU FR$13. *Glimpses of mat decoration, hair tying and preparation, the church, and service in the township, marketing produce and fish, making metal bracelets and a toy leather shield, thatching a roof. Formal costumed dances provide an interesting contrast to those performed in Zulu Country Dances.*

Zulu Country Dances (1968) 16 min. Hugh Tracey (FM). Dist: PSU FR$11.50. *Glimpses of rural life and crafts in the village of Chief Ntshide precede a mock battle dance by men carrying stick swords and skin shields. Women sing and applaud, play the musical bow. At Chiefs Mnloluthine Zulu and Moinseni Zulu, men and women join in mock battle dances. Bride's dance is performed at Chief Mtubatuba's. Men's and women's mock battle dance at Chief Mathole's involves the use of horses.*

Australian Aboriginal Films Warning

David MacDougall, director of the film unit of the Australian Institute of Aboriginal Studies, has requested that the following note be included:

Certain films concerning Australian Aboriginal ritual contain material of a secret/sacred nature which should not be shown to general audiences and which under no circumstances should be seen by Aboriginal people who would be prohibited from seeing it by traditional Aboriginal law and custom. Films on secret/sacred matters should normally be shown only to advanced-level students of anthropology and related studies in tertiary institutions and to recognized learned and cultural groups. Their showing should be announced only to those groups concerned. It is essential to ensure that they are not screened to mixed audiences containing Aboriginal persons, uninitiated Aboriginal persons, children, or Aboriginal persons who would not within their own culture normally be privy to the material depicted. If any doubt exists about the propriety of showing a film, it should not be shown. In this book films in this category made by the Australian Institute of Aboriginal Studies carry the notice: *Restricted use*.

These films include *Camels and Pitjantjara* (long version), *Emi Ritual at Ruguri, Gunabibi, Larawari & Walkara, Mulga Seed Ceremony, Pintubi Revisit Yaru Yaru, Pintubi Revisit Yumari, Walbiri Ritual at Gunadjari,* and *Walbiri Ritual at Ngama.*

Encyclopaedia Cinematographica

The *Encyclopaedia Cinematographica* is a scientific encyclopedia in film form. It was proposed and established by its present editor, Gotthard Wolf, director of the Institut für den Wissenschaftlichen Film in Göttigen, Germany. It consists of a growing international collection of scientific films that are of considerable value to university teachers and research workers. Each film in the collection depicts a single phenomenon or type of behavior, and the films are so arranged as to facilitate, for example, comparisons of behavior among different species of animals, or comparisons of cultural similarities and differences among a number of primitive tribes.

The kinds of phenomena recorded on film and included in the collection are those which have one or more of the following characteristics:

(1) They cannot be observed by the unaided human eye and therefore demand the use of such film techniques as slow-motion or time-lapse cinephotography.

(2) They need to be compared with other phenomena—for which purpose verbal descriptions alone are inadequate.

(3) They do not occur frequently; they are not readily available for observation by other scientists or students; or they are disappearing from the culture.

The films in the *Encyclopaedia Cinematographica* have been prepared by scientists from a number of countries. The majority of the films are silent, although sound is used in some instances where it is inherent to the subject.

Most of the films are accompanied by a printed document that provides background information as well as technical particulars pertaining to the circumstances under which the film was made. The document is written in the language of its author, provided that this is either German, French, or English—the official languages of the *Encyclopaedia*.

Some examples from the catalog:

E 999T - Central Europe. Tyrol - *Herding Cattle From the Alm Krimmler Tavern.* 1963 (color, sound, 18 min.) W. Rutz, Nuernberg. R$7.30.

E 706 - Nuer (East Africa, Upper Nile) - *Daily Work in the Cattle Yards.* 1963 (color, 10 min.) H. Luz, Tuebingen; W. Herz. R$4.30.

E 653 - Sindhi (West Pakistan, Sindh) - *Sign Language.* 1961 (5 min.) S. Westphal-Hellbusch, Berlin; H. Westphal, Berlin. R$2.80.

E 237 - Bali (Indonesia) - *Cremation and Incineration of a Prince's Widow.* 1926 (16½ min.) W. Mullens, The Hague. R$4.80.

Distribution

The American Archive is at the Pennsylvania State University. Films may be rented, and a complete Index of Films may be obtained from: Audio-Visual Services, The Pennsylvania State University, University Park, PA 16802; telephone (814) 865-6314.

Areas and Societies Represented in the *Encyclopaedia Cinematographica*

Europe

Northern Europe: Norway, Jutland, Funen, Bornholm
Central Europe (Northern Part): Schleswig, Holstein, Freisland, Saxony, Weser Highlands, Westphalia, Rhineland, Upper Hesse, Southern Bavaria, Württemberg, Baden-Württemberg, Baden Moravia
Central Europe (Southern Part): Graubünden, Salzburg, U. Austria, L. Austria, Burgenland, Tyrol, Lombardy
Western Europe: Auvergne

Africa

North Africa: Rif-Berber, Central Atlas, Tuareg, Schaamba, Fellahin
West Africa: Guinea Coast, Fulbe, Bassari, Mende, Kpelle, Baule, Dan, Gere, Guro, Ewe Scha, Afo, Angas, Njedebua, Senufo
Western Sudan: Dogon, Kassena, Nuna, Senufo, Dagari, Kurumba, Mossi, Rimaibe, Songhai, Fulbe
Central Sudan: Bele, Tubu, Unja, Buduma, Arab, Haddad, Djonkor, Kenga, Dangaleat, Bulala, Haussa, Djaya
Eastern Sudan: Katla, Masakin, Nuer
Northeast Africa: Darassa, Sidamo, Sala, Male, Schangama, Dime
Equatorial Africa: Ekonda, Banda, Nzakara, Ewondo
East Africa: Mbunga, Barundi
South Africa: Zulu

Asia

Near East: Hadrami (Hadramaut), Al-Kuwé Ma'dan Arab
West Asia: Anatolia, Hamadan, Pushtun, Afghani, Tadschik, Hesareh
Central Asia: Tibet, Newari, Sikkim
South Asia: Sindh, Chitral, Gilgit, Bhil, Baiga, Toda, Kuttia Kond, Naga, Marma
Southeast Asia: Akha, Black Lahu, Lisu, Miao, Kachin, Thai, Karen, Vietnam, Java, Bali

Arctic

Greenland: Polar Eskimo

America

North America: Pennsylvania
Central America: Zapotec

South America

Venezuela: Ayaman, Criollo, Guarao, Waika, Makiritare
Peru: North Coast, Puna de Moquegua
Argentina: Atacamenos
Uruguay
Brazil: Tukuna, Tukurina, Kashinaua, Erigpactsa
   Xingu Region: Suya, Schukaramai (Kayapo), Waura, Yawalapiti, Kalapalo
   Araguaia Region: Karaja, Javahe
   Tocantin Region: Kraho

Oceania

Melanesia: Sepik, Markham, Wantoat, Asmat, Normanby Island
Micronesia (Gilberts): Nonouti, Onotoa, Tabiteuea
Polynesia (Ellice): Niutao

Distributors' Codes

Addresses and telephone numbers are subject to change. If the distributor is listed at the last known address (LKA), this is noted after the address.

AB *Audio Brandon*, 866 Third Ave., New York, NY 10022; telephone (212) 935-5101 or (212) 935-4244.

AC *Arthur Cantor Films*, 2112 Broadway, Suite 400, New York, NY 10023; telephone (212) 496-5710.

ACI *ACI Films*, 35 West 45th St., New York, NY 10036; telephone (212) 582-1918 (LKA).

ACPB *The Annenberg/CPB Collection*, P.O. Box 2345, South Burlington, VT 05407-2345; telephone (800) 332-7637.

AEF *American Educational Films, Inc.*, 132 Lasky Dr., Beverly Hills, CA 90212 (LKA).

AFC *Australian Film Commission*, City National Bank Building, 9229 Sunset Blvd., Los Angeles, CA 90046 (LKA). Contact AIS for information.

AFF *African Family Films*, P.O. Box 1109, Venice, CA 90291 (LKA).

AIAS *Australian Institute of Aboriginal Studies*, P.O. Box 553, Canberra City, ACT 2601, Australia.

AIS *Australian Information Service*, Eton Road, Lindfield, NSW 2070, Australia; telephone 02 413 8777; fax 02 416 5672.

AP *Atlantis Productions*, 1252 La Granada Dr., Thousand Oaks, CA 91360; telephone (805) 495-2790.

APPAL *Appalshop, Inc.*, P.O. Box 743, Whitesburg, KY 41858; telephone (800) 545-SHOP or (606) 633-0108.

AUFS *American Universities Field Staff*, 3 Lebanon St., Hanover, NH 03755; telephone (603) 643-2110 (LKA).

AV *Ambrose Video Publishing, Inc.*, 1290 Avenue of the Americas, Suite 2245, New York, NY 10104; telephone (212) 265-7272.

AW *Arawak Inc.*, 177 Ocean Lane Drive, #101, Key Biscayne, FL 33149; telephone (305) 447-9854; fax (305) 447-6340.

AWF *All Weather Films*, 396 Third Avenue #2, New York, NY 10016; telephone (212) 885-7166.

BAVI *Bavi Sales and Rental Unit*, 131 Livingston St., Brooklyn, NY 11201.

B&C *B&C Films*, 3971 Murietta Ave., Sherman Oaks, CA 91423.

BBC *BBC Enterprises*, Woodlands, 80 Wood Lane, London W12 0TT, UK; telephone 4481-576-2000; fax 4481-749-0538.

BF *Bullfrog Films*, Oley, PA 19547; telephone (215) 779-8226.

BFA *Phoenix/BFA Films and Video, Inc.*, 468 Park Avenue South, New York, NY 10016; telephone (800) 221-1274.

BU *Krasker Film Library, School of Education, Boston University*, 765 Commonwealth Ave., Boston, MA 02215.

BW *Blackwood Productions*, 251 West 57th Street, New York, NY 10019.

BYU *Brigham Young University*, Media Marketing, W-STAD, Provo, UT 84602.

BYU-AVS *Brigham Young University*, Audio Visual Services, 101 F.B., Provo, UT 84602; telephone (801) 378-4261.

CAS-UF *Center for African Studies*, 470 GRI, University of Florida, Gainesville, FL 32611; telephone (904) 392-2183.

CBC *Canadian Broadcasting Corporation Educational Films*, English Services Division, in Canada: P.O. Box 500, Terminal "A", Toronto, Ontario M5W 1E6, in the United States: 245 Park Ave., 34th Floor, New York, NY 10017.

CBS/FOX *CBS/FOX*, telephone (800) 800-4369.

CCC *Canyon Cinema Cooperative*, 2325 Third Street, Suite 338, San Francisco, CA 94107.

CDF *Cambridge Documentary Films, Inc.*, P.O. Box 385, Cambridge, MA 02139; telephone (617) 354-3677.

CEAS-UK *The Center for East Asian Studies*, Media Services Department, University of Kansas, 105 Lippincott Hall, Lawrence, Kansas 66044-2146; telephone (913) 864-3352.

C5 *Cinema 5*, 595 Madison Ave., New York, NY 10022.

CFE *Comite du Film Ethnographique*, Musee d l'Homme, Palais de Chaillot, Place du Trocadero, 75116 Paris, France.

CFSLtd *Colour Film Services Ltd.*, P.O. Box 4BE, 22 Portman Close, Baker St., London WIH OEP, England.

CFV *Coronet Film and Video*, 108 Wilmot Road, Deerfield, IL 60015; telephone (800) 621-2131.

CG *Cinema Guild*, 1697 Broadway, New York, NY 10019; telephone (800) 723-5522 or (212) 246-5522; fax (212) 246-5525; telex 238790 NYK.

ChF *Churchill Films*, 12210 Nebraska Ave., Los Angeles, CA 90025.

CIM *Coronet Instructional Media*, 65 East South Water Street, Chicago, IL 60601.

CLA-UWM *The Center for Latin America, University of Wisconsin—Milwaukee*, P.O. Box 413, Milwaukee, WI 53201; telephone (414) 229-4401.

CMC *Center for Mass Communication*, Columbia University Press, 562 West 113th St., New York, NY 10025.

CMOC *Canadian Museum of Civilization*, 100 Laurier Street, P.O. Box 3100, Station B, Hull, Quebec, Canada J8X 4H2; telephone (819) 997-8202.

CN *California Newsreel*, 630 Natoma Street, San Francisco, CA 94103.

CNAMFL *CNAM Film Library*, 445 W. Main Street, Wyckoff, NJ 07481; telephone (201) 891-8240.

CNM *Center for New American Media*, 524 Broadway, 2nd Floor, New York, NY 10012; telephone (212) 925-5665.

CNRS *C.N.R.S. Audiovisuel*, 27, rue Paul Bert, 94200 Ivry, France.

CPI *Centre Productions Inc.*, 1800 30th Street, Suite 207, Boulder, CO 80301; (800) 824-1166 or (303) 444-1166.

CPM *Central Park Media*, 301 W. 53rd St., New York, NY 10019; telephone (212) 977-7456.

CRA *Cine Research Associates*, 1126 Boylston St., 2nd Floor, Boston, MA 02215; telephone (617) 442-9756.

CRAW *Crawley Films, Ltd.*, 19 Fairmount Ave., Ottawa, ON, Canada.

CRM/MH *CRM/McGraw-Hill Films*, PO Box 641, Del Mar, CA 92014; telephone (714) 453-5000.

CRM/F *CRM Films*, 2233 Faraday Avenue, Suite F, Carlsbad, CA 92008; telephone (800) 421-0833.

CRUA-UM *Center for Urban and Regional Affairs, University of Minnesota*, 330 Hubert H. Humphrey Centre, 301 19th Ave. S., Minneapolis, MN 55455; telephone (612) 625-1551.

CSF *Center for Southern Folklore*, P.O. Box 40105, 1215 Peabody, Memphis, TN 38104.

CSPI *Constant Spring Productions, Inc.*, P.O. Box 2, Devault, PA 19432.

CTC *Chip Talor Communications*, 15 Spollett Drive, Derry, NH 03038; telephone (603) 434-9262.

CUAV *Cornell University Audio-Visual Center*, 8 Business/Technology Park, Ithaca, NY 14850; telephone (607) 255-2090; fax (607) 255-9946.

CVA-USC *Center for Visual Anthropology, University of Southern California*, Los Angeles, CA 90089-0661; telephone (213) 743-7100.

CWF *Colonial Williamsburg Foundation*, Audiovisual Distribution Section, Box C, Williamsburg, VA 23185; telephone (804) 229-2490.

CWV *Central West Virginia Media Arts*, P.O Box 1102, 48E Main St., Buckhannon, WV 26201.

DA *Document Associates, Inc.*, 880 Third Ave., New York, NY 10222; telephone (212) 593-1647 (LKA).

DA2 *Document Associates, Inc.*, 211 East 43rd St., New York, NY 10017; telephone (212) 246-5522.

DCL *Direct Cinema Limited*, P.O.Box 10003, Santa Monica, CA 90410; telephone (310) 396-4774 or (800) 525-0000.

DER *Documentary Educational Resources*, 101 Morse St., Watertown, MA 02172; telephone (617) 926-0491.

DF *Documentary Films*, 3217 Trout Gulch Rd., Aptos, CA 95003.

DIO *Danish Information Office*, 280 Park Ave., New York, NY 10017 (offices also in Los Angeles and San Francisco).

DP *Diverse Productions*, Box 519, Cambridge, MA 02238.

EBEC *Encyclopaedia Britannica Educational Corp.*, 310 S. Michigan Avenue, Chicago, IL 60604; telephone (312) 321-7105.

ECP *Echo Pictures*, 307 East, 44th Street, Suite 1704, New York, NY 10017; telephone (212) 949-6079.

EDC *Education Development Center*, 39 Chapel St., Newton, MA 02158; telephone (617) 969-7100.

EI *Eye in I Filmworks*, 173 1/2 Mansfield St., New Haven, CT 06511.

EMC *Educational Media Corporation*, 6930 1/2 Tujunga Ave., North Hollywood, CA 91605; telephone (213) 985-3921.

EMC-GSU *Educational Media Center, Georgia State University*, University Plaza, Atlanta, GA 30303; telephone (404) 658-3311.

EMI *Educational Media International*, Box 1288, Elmhurst, IL 60126; telephone (312) 832-3363.

EMML *Etno Museo Munti Lepini*, Pelazo Baronale, Piazza Risorgimento, 4 04010, Roccagurta, Italy; telephone 0773/958947.

EMS-UNC *Educational Materials Service, University of Northern Colorado*, Greeley, CO 80639.

ENR *El Nil Research*, 1147 Beverwil Drive, Los Angeles, CA 90035; telephone (213) 55 EL NIL.

ETNOS *ETNOS Television*, Apartado Aereo 612, Medellin, Colombia, South America; telephone 242 24 35 or 232 90 91.

EVA *Evatel productions*, 41 Bd de Magenta, 75010 Paris, France; telephone 331-420-87964.

FAA *Film Australia*, Eton Road, Linfield, P.O. Box 46, Linfield, NSW 2070 Australia; telephone 467 9777.

FACSEA *French American Cultural Services and Educational Aid*, 972 Fifth Ave., New York, NY 10021; telephone (212) 570-4400.

FCE *Film Classic Exchange*, 1926 South Vermont Ave., Los Angeles, CA 90007; telephone (213) 731-3854 (LKA).

FdV *Les Films du Village*, 10 Allee des Maison Russes, 93440 le Raincy, France.

FEAV *Far Eastern Audio Visuals*, 1010 West 23rd St., Austin, TX 78705; telephone (512) 255-2124.

FF *Flower Films*, 10341 San Pablo Ave., El Cerrito, CA 94530; telephone (415) 525-0942 or (415) 525-1494.

FHS *Films for the Humanities & Sciences*, P.O. Box 2053, Princeton, NJ 08543-2053; telephone (800) 257-5126 or (609) 542-1128; fax (609) 452-1602.

FI *Films Incorporated* (Video), 5547 N. Ravenswood Avenue, Chicago, Illinois 60640-1199; telephone (800) 323-4222, ext. 43, in IL (312) 878-2600, ext. 43; fax (312) 878-0416.

FIM/RF *Film Images* (a division of Radim Films, Inc.), 17 West 60th St., New York, NY 10023; telephone (212) 279-6653. Or: 1034 Lake St., Oak Park,IL 60301; telephone (312) 386-4826 (LKA).

FIV See address for *Films Incorporated* (**FI**).

FL *Filmmakers Library*, 124 East 40th Street, New York, NY 10016; telephone (212) 808-4980; fax (212) 808-4983.

FOX *Fox/Lorimer, CBS/Fox*.

FRF *First Run Features*, 152 Waverly Place, New York, NY 10014; telephone (212) 673-6881 or (212) 673-6882.

FRIF *First Run Icarus Films*, 153 Waverly Place, New York, NY 10014; telephone (212) 727-1711 or (800) 876-1710; fax (212) 989-7649.

FSC *Film Study Center*, Harvard University, Cambridge, MA 02138; telephone (617) 868-1020.

FTP *Flying Tomato Productions*, Box 910 Canmore, Alberta, Canada T0L 0M0; telephone (403) 678-5027.

GAI *Glenblow-Alberta Institute*, 902 11 Ave., S.W. Calgary, AB, Canada.

GP *Grove Press*, Film Division, 841 Broadway, 4th floor, New York, NY 10003; telephone (212) 614-7850.

GSA *National Audiovisual Systems*, Washington, DC 20409 (LKA).

GTI *Grenada Television International,* 1221 Avenue of the Americas, Suite 3468, New York, NY 10020.
HAN *Handel Film Corp.,* 8730 Sunset Blvd, W. Hollywood, CA 90069.
HFF *Hartley Film Foundation,* Cat Rock Rd., Cos Cob, CT 06807; telephone (203) 869-1818.
HFL *Harcourt Films, Ltd.,* 58 Camden Square, London NW1 9XE, UK; telephone 4471-267-0882; fax 4471-267-1064.
HLUA *Hmong-Lao Unity Association,* 12 Princeton Avenue, Providence, RI 02907.
ICF *ICARUS Films,* 200 Park Avenue South, Suite 1319, New York, NY 10003; telephone (212) 674-3375.
IFB *International Film Bureau,* 332 South Michigan Avenue, Chicago, IL 60604-4382; telephone (312) 427-4545.
IFF *International Film Foundation,* 155 W. 72nd Street, New York, NY 10023; (212) 580-1111.
IM *Insight Media,* 121 West 85th Street, New York, NY 10024; telephone (212) 721-6316; fax (212) 799-5309.
IMCC *Insight Multi-Cultural Communication, Inc.,* 122 Princeton Street, Santa Cruz, CA 95060; telephone (408) 458-1628.
IMI *Information Materials, Inc.,* 1615 West Burbank Blvd., Burbank, CA 91506.
Impact *Impact Films,* 144 Bleeker St., New York, NY 10021.
IMS-UW *Instructional Media Services,* Kane Hall, DG-10, University of Washington, Seattle, WA 98195; telephone (206) 543-9906.
IR *Image Resources,* Film Library, 267 West 25th St., New York, NY 10001.
IRC *Instructional Resources Center,* Ithaca College, Ithaca, NY 14850; telephone (607) 274-3150.
ISHI *ISHI Films,* Suite 252, 3401 Market St., Philadelphia, PA 19104; telephone (215) 896-9056 (LKA).
ISP *IS Productions,* c/o ATLATL, 402 W. Roosevelt, Phoenix, AZ 85003; telephone (303) 494-8308 (LKA).
ISU *Idaho State University,* Audio-Visual Center, Bloomington, IN 47401; telephone (208) 236-2112.
IUAVC *Indiana University, Audio-Visual Center,* Bloomington Indiana, 47405-5901; telephone (812) 855-2103. Now offers rentals only but will advise as to where to purchase films.
IV *Insight Video,* 875 Main Street, Cambridge, MA 02139; telephone (617) 354-7493.
IWF *IWF,* Nonnenstieg 72, W-3400 Gottingen, Germany; telephone 0551/2020; fax 0551/202200.
IWS *IMedia Resource Center,* 121 Pearson Hall, Iowa State University, Ames, IA 50011.
Janus *Janus Films,* 745 Fifth Avenue, New York, NY 10022.
JCL *JCL Films,* 58 rue J-J. Rousseau, Paris 75001, France; telephone 011 331-40264827.
JF *Journal Films,* 930 Pitner St., Evanston, Ill, 60202; telephone (800) 323-448.
JMS *Jewish Media Service,* 15 East 26th Street, New York, NY 10027; telephone (212) 532-4949.
JPD *John Pierre Dutilleux,* 76 Market Street, Venice, CA 90291.
JS *Japan Society,* 333 East 47th Street, New York, NY 10017; telephone (212) 832-1155.

JVP *JVP Films,* 6. boulevard Diderot, 25000 Besancon; telephone 81 50 49 54; fax 81 50 24 00.
Karol *Karol Media,* 22 Riverview Drive, Wayne, NJ 07470; telephone (201) 628-9111.
KDP *Kevin Duffy Productions,* 10616 Blyth Ave., Los Angeles, CA 90064; telephone (212) 827-1095.
KI *Kino International Corporation,* 333 West 39th St., Suite 503, New York, NY 10018; telephone (212) 629-6880.
KKFL *Karen Kramer Film Library,* 22-D Hollywood Avenue, Ho-ho-kus, NJ 07423; telephone (201) 891-8243 (LKA).
KK *Karen Kramer,* 22 Leroy Street, New York, NY 10014.
Kmrl *Leonard Kammerling,* Box 81323, Fairbanks, AK 99708; telephone (907) 455-6542.
LAC *Latin American Center,* UCLA, 405 Hilgard Ave., Los Angeles, CA 90064; telephone (213) 825-4321.
LFDQ *Les Films du Quotidien,* 5, Rue des Saints Peres 75006, Paris, France; telephone (1) 260 25 76.
LMF *Land Mark Films,* 3450 Slade Run Drive, Falls Church, VA 22042; telephone (800) 342-4336.
MAAS *Museum of Art and The Asia Society,* 725 Park Avenue, New York, NY 10021.
Mac *MacMillan Films, Inc.,* 34 MacQuesten Parkway South, Mount Vernon, NY 10550; telephone (914) 664-5051.
MDAI *Media Design Associates, Inc.,* Dept. H, P.O. Box 3189, Boulder, CO 80307-3189; telephone (800) 228-8854 or (303) 443-2800.
MF *Mosaic Films,* 17962 Valley Vista Blvd., Encino, CA 91316; telephone (818) 881-8725.
MFV *Mystic Fire Video,* 70 Greenwish Avenue #410, New York, NY., P.O. Box 9323, Dept. RF, Burlington, VT 05402.
MG *Media Guild,* 11526 Sorrento Valley Road, Suite J, San Diego, CA 92121; telephone (619) 755-9191.
MICH *The University of Michigan, Audio-Visual Center,* 416 Fourth St., Ann Arbor, MI 48103; telephone (313) 764-5361.
MINN *University of Minnesota, Audio-Visual Library Service,* Suite 108, 1313 5th St. SE, Minneapolis, MN 55414; telephone (612) 627-4270.
MLA *Modern Learning Aids,* Division of Wards Natural Science Establishment, Inc., P.O. Box 302, Rochester, NY 14603.
MLS *Milestone Film and Video, Inc.,* 275 West 96th Street, Suite 28c, New York, NY 10025; telephone (212)865-7449; fax (212) 222-8952.
MOMA *Museum of Modern Art,* 11 West 53rd St., New York, NY 10019; telephone (212) 708-9400.
MRW *Meriwa Films,* 43, Meriwa Street, Hollywood, Perth.6009, West Australia; telephone (9)3866452.
MWV *Maryknoll World Video,* Media Relations, Gonzaga Building, Maryknoll, NY 10545; telephone (800) 227-8523.
NAPBC *Native American Public Broadcasting Consortium,* 1800 North 33rd Street, Lincoln, NB 68501; telephone (402) 472-3522.
NAVC *National Audiovisual Center,* Customer Services Staff, 8700 Edgeworth Drive, Capitol Heights, MD 20743-3701; telephone (800) 638-1300 or (301) 763-6025.

NBC *NBC Educational Enterprises,* 30 Rockefeller Plaza, NY 10020; telephone (212) 247-8300.

NCTA *National Council for Traditional Arts,* 806 15th Street, NW, Suite 400, Washington, DC 20005.

NDF *New Day Films,* 121 west 27th Street, Suite 902, New York, NY 10001; telephone (212) 645-8210; fax (212) 645-8652.

NDF2 *New Day Films,* 22 Riverview Drive, Wayne, NJ 07470-3191; telephone (201) 633-0212.

NF *Northern Films,* Box 98, Main Office Station, Seattle, WA 98111 (LKA).

NFB *National Film Board of Canada,* 16th Floor, 1251 Ave. of the Americas, New York, NY 10020; telephone (212) 586-5131.

NFI *Netherlands Film Institute,* P.O. Box 515, 1200 AM Hilversum, The Netherlands; telephone 3135-217-645.

NFL *Nomad Films Ltd.,* 46 Anson Rd., London N7 OAB, England; 01-609-1240 or 01-607-2920.

NFF *New Front Films,* 1409 Willow St., Suite 505, Minneapolis, Minn. 55403; telephone (612) 872-0805.

NFTS *National Film and Television School,* Station Road, Beaconsfield, Bucks, HP9 1LG, UK; telephone 44 494-671-234; fax 44 494-674-042.

NGS *National Geographic Society,* Attn: Educational Services, P.O. Box 98019, Washington, DC 20090; telephone (301) 921-1330.

NGSES See **NGS**.

NMU *Northern Michigan University,* 331 Thomas Fine Arts Building, Marquette, MI 49855; (906) 227-2041.

NWMP *Northwest Media Project,* 925 NW 19th Ave., Portland, OR 97209; telephone (503) 223-5335.

NYF *New Yorker Films,* 16 West 61st Street, New York, NY 10023; telephone (212) 247-6110 or (212) 947-5333.

NYU *New York University Film Library,* 26 Washington Place, New York, NY 10003.

OCL *Open Channel Ltd.,* 13 Victoria Street, Fitzroy, Melbourne, Victoria 3065, Australia; telephone 13-419-5111; fax 03-419-1404.

OFL *Ophidian Films Ltd.,* 1530 Locust Street, #80, Philadelphia, PA 19120; telephone (215) 735-6777; fax (212) 242-8561.

OP *Oceania Productions,* 733 Plymouth Rd., Claremont, CA 91711.

OWF *Other World Films,* 176 Hudson Parade, Clareville, N.S.W. 2107, Australia.

OWM *Onewest Media,* P.O. Box 5766, Santa Fe, NM 87502-5766; telephone (505) 983-8685 (LKA).

PBS and **PBSV** *PBS Video,* 1320 Braddock Place, Alexandria, VA 22314-1698; telephone (800) 328-7271.

PCP *Pacific Cinematheque Pacifique,* 1616 West 3rd Ave., Vancouver, Canada V6J 1K2; telephone (604) 732-5322.

PDL *Productions Daniel Louis,* 2497, rue Coursol, Montreal, Quebec H3J 1C9, Canada.

PFI *Phoenix Films, Inc.,* 2349 Chassee Drive, St Louis, MO 63146; telephone (314) 569-0211.

Pitt *University of Pittsburgh Media Distributing Services,* G-20 Hillman Library, Pittsburgh, PA 15260.

POR *Pictures of Record,* 119 Kettle Creek Rd., Weston, CT 06883; (203) 227-3387.

POU *Portland State University,* Continuing Education Publications, P.O. Box 1894, Portland, OR 97207; telephone (800)547-8887, ext. 4891.

PSA *Dr. Peter S. Allen,* 98 Transit Street, Providence, RI 02906; fax (401) 456-8379.

PSU(PCR) *Audio Visual Service, Pennsylvania State University,* Special Services Building, 1127 Fox Hill Road, University Park, PA 16803-1824; telephone (800) 826-0132 or (814) 865-6314.

PTL *Public Television Library,* 475 L'Enfant Plaza, SW, Washington, DC 20024.

PyrF *Pyramid Films, Ltd.,* Box 1048, Santa Monica, CA 90406; telephone (800) 421-2304 or (213) 828-7577

QIDR *Quotidian Independent Documentary Research,* P.O. Box 2623, Santa Fe, NM 87504; telephone (505) 983-9641.

RAI *Royal Anthropological Institute,* 50 Fitzroy Street, London W1P 5HS England; telephone 01 387 0455.

R.G. *R.G. Video,* 21 West 46th St, New York, NY 10036.

RBMU *Regions Beyond MIssionary Union* has discontinued film distribution.

RJD *Ronald J. Duncan, Department of Sociology and Anthropology, Inter-American University,* San German, PR 00753.

RLI *The Reading Laboratory, Inc.,* Content Materials Division, P.O. Box 28, Georgetown, CT 06929; telephone (203) 544-9233.

RTP *River Tracks Productions,* Box 9, Manley Hot Springs, AL 99756; telephone (907) 672-3262.

RUFS *Rockefeller University Film Service,* Box 72, 1230 York Avenue, New York, NY 10021.

SF *Spector Films,* 400 West 119th Street, New York, NY 10027; telephone (212) 666-9461.

SFI *Survival Films International,* 1065 Barrenjoey Road, Palm Beach, NSW 2108, Australia; telephone 919-5580.

SFL *Samsara Film Library,* 22-D Hollywood Avenue, Ho-Ho-Kus, New Jersey 07423; telephone 800-343-5540.

SI *Smithsonian Institution,* Office of Public Affairs, Washington, DC 20560; telephone (202) 618-1810.

SP *Siegel Productions,* P.O. Box 6123, Evanston, IL 60202; telephone(312) 528-6563 or (312) 334-2753.

SPF *Special Purposes Films,* 26740 Latigo Shore Dr., Malibu, CA 90265.

Stanton *Stanton Films,* 7934 Santa Monica Blvd., Los Angeles, CA 90046.

Sterling *Sterling Educational Films,* 2 41 E. 34th Street, New York, NY 10016.

SU *Syracuse University Film Rental Center,* 1455 East Colvin St., Syracuse, NY 13210.

SUNYB *State University of New York at Buffalo,* Instructional Communication Center, 4242 Ridge Lea Rd., Amherst, NY 14226; telephone (716) 831-1141.

TDF *Tom Davenport Films,* Pearstone, Dept., DM, Delaplane, VA 22025; telephone (703) 592-3701.

Televisuals, Ltd, 4224 Ellenita Avenue, Tarzana CA 91856.

T-L *Time-Life Films,* has discontinued film distribution services. Some films can be obtained from Ambrose Video Pubishing Inc, (AV), HBO or directly from the BBC.

TLV *Time Life Video,* see above.

20CF *20th Century Fox, Distribution Center,* 40 West 57th S., New York, NY 10010.

UAB *Department of Anthropology, University of Alabama at Birmingham,* University Station, Birmingham, AL 35294-3350; telephone (205) 934-3508.

UA-DA *University of Amsterdam, Dept. of Anthropology,* Amsterdam, The Netherlands; telephone 20 - 5252626.

UAlberta *University of Alberta,* Department of Radio and Television, CW005 Biological Sciences Center, Edmonton, AB T6G 2E9 Canada.

UCEMC *University of California Extension Media Center,* 2000 Center Street, Fourth Floor, Berkeley, CA 94704; telephone (510) 642-0460.

UEVA *Universal Education and Visual Arts, Inc.,* 100 Universal Education and Visual Arts, Inc., 100 Universal City Plaza, Universal City, CA 91608.

UGA *Film Library, Georgia Center for Continuing Education, University of Georgia,* Athens, GA 30601; telephone (404) 542-1184.

UHP *University of Hawaii Press,* Order Department, 2840 Kolowalu Street, Honolulu, Hawaii 96822.

UIFVC *University of Illinois Film/Video Center,* 1325 S. Oak Street, Champaign, IL 61820; telephone (800) 367-3456.

UILL *University of Illinois, Visual Aids Service,* 1325 South Oak, Champaign, IL 61820; telephone (217) 333-1360.

UILL-UC *University of Illinois Center for Educational Media, Department of Anthropology,* 109 Davenport Hall, 607 South Mathews Avenue, Urbana, IL 61801; telephone (217) 333-3616.

UK *Film Rental Services, University of Kansas,* Lawrence, Kansas 66045.

UKOIR *University of Kentucky, Office of Instructional Resources,* 170 Taylor Bldg., Lexington, KY 40506-0001; telephone (606) 257-5831.

UNI *UNIFILM* (formerly Tricontinental Film Center and Latin American Film Project) 419 Park Ave., South, New York, NY 10016; telephone (212) 686-9890 (LKA).

UOC *Dept. of Commuications Media-MLB 24, The University of Calgary,* 2500 University Drive, NW, Calgary, Alverta Canada T2N 1N4; telephone (403) 220-3709; fax (403) 282-4497; telex UNIV of CGY 03821545.

UOM *University of Missouri,* University Relations, 400 Lewis Hall, University of Missouri, Columbia, MO 65211.

USC *University of Southern California,* Department of Cinema, Film Distribution Divisoin, Los Angeles, CA 90007.

UTA-FL *University of Texas At Austin, Film Library,* P.O. Box W, Austin, Texas 78713-7448; telephone (512) 471-3572.

UTP *University of Texas Press,* P.O. Box 7819, Austin, Texas 78713; telephone (512) 471-4032 or (800) 252-3206.

UUEMC *Educational Media Center,* 107 Bennion Hall, University of Utah, Salt Lake City, UT 84110.

UW *University of Wisconsin,* Bureau of Audio-Visual Instruction, 1312 West Johnson St., Madison, WI 53706; telephone (608) 262-1644.

UWA *University of Washington, Educational Media Collection,* 35 Kane Hall, DG-10, Seattle, WA 98195; telephone (206) 543-9909.

UWC *The Upper Midwest Women's History Center Collection,* Central Community Center, 6300 Walker St., St. Louis Park, MN 55416; telephone (612) 925-3632.

UWM *University of Wisconsin Milwaukee, Center for Latin America,* College of Letters and Science, P.O. Box 413, Milwaukee, WI 53201; telephone (414) 229-4401.

UWP *Audiovisual Department, University of Washington Press,* P.O. Box 50096, Seattle, WA 98145-5096; telephone (206) 543-4050.

UW-SAAC *Distribution Office, South Asian Area Center,* 1242 Van Hise Hall, University of Wisconsin, Madison, Wisconsin 53706; telephone (608) 262-9690.

VAP *Visual Anthropology Productions,* 90 Popular Avenue, Berkeley, CA 94708; telephone (510) 524-4448.

VFI *Viewfinders, Inc.,* P.O. Box 1665, Evanston, IL 60204-1665; telephone (800) 342-3342 or (708) 869-0600; fax (708) 869-1710.

VFWW *Villon Films, Worldwide,* P.O. Box 41 Gays Mills, WI 54631.

VP *The Video Project,* 5332 College Avenue, Suite 101, Oakland CA 94618; telephone (800) 4-planet.

VQ *Vision Quest, Inc.:* Eastern Office: Box 206, Lawrenceville, NJ 08646; telephone (609) 896-1359. Central Office: 7715 North Sheridan Rd., Chicago, IL 60626; telephone (312) 338-1116. Western Office: 389 Ethel Ave., Mill Valley, CA 94941; telephone (415) 388-9094 (LKA).

WBP *World Bank Publications,* P.O. Box 7247-8619, Philadelphia, PA 19170-8619.

WCMS *Media Services, Western Connecticut State University,* Danbury, CT 06810; telephone (203) 797-4348.

WDEM *Walt Disney Educational Media,* 300 S. Buena Vista St., Burbank, CA 91521.

WETA *Weta Educational Activies,* P.O. Box 2626, Washington, DC 20013; telephone (703) 998 2626. See PBSV.

WFV *Wombat Film & Video,* 250 West 57th Street, Suite 916, New York, NY 10019; telephone (212) 315-2502; fax (800) 542-5554.

WGBH *WGBH-TV Boston,* telephone (617) 492-2777.

WHV *Warner Home Video.*

WLP *Waveland Press, Inc.*

WMM *Women Make Movies,* 462 Broadway, Suite 501, New York, NY 10013; telephone (212) 925-0606; fax (212) 925-2052.

WOMBAT *Wombat Productions, Inc.,* Little Lake, Glendale Road, P.O. Box 70, Ossining, NY 10562.

WQED *WQED,* 4802 Fifth Avenue, Pittsburgh, PA 15213; telephone (412) 456-3856.

WS *Waldrum Studios,* Box 549, Ranchos de Taos, NM 87557-0549; telephone (505) 758-7357.

ZC *Zia Cine,* P.O. Box 493, Santa Fe, NM 87501.

ZFL *Zeitgeist Films, Ltd.,* 200 Waverly Place, Suite 1, New York, NY 10014; telephone (212) 727-1989.

Publication Codes

AA *American Anthropologist*
AJPA *American Journal of Physical Anthropology*
ARCH *Archaeology*
SBF *Science Books & Films*
VISA *Visual Anthropology*

VISR *Visual Anthropology Review*
JAF *Journal of American Folklore*
RAIN *Royal Anthropological Instutute Newsletter*
MAN *Man*

People Index

Aaltonen, Jouko 249
Abbas, Y. 14, 164, 218, 228, 248
Abbink, J. 184, 273
Abbott, Susan 160
Aberle, D. F. 86
Abrahams, R. 58, 243, 279
Abrams, Ira R. 99, 255
Abu-Lughod, Lila 233
Adair, John 33, 52, 111, 189, 190, 196, 278, 284
Adair, N. 284
Adair, Peter 27, 125, 284
Adams, D. 40
Adams, J. W. 34, 46, 126, 150, 159, 170, 172, 214, 242, 249, 290
Adams, M. J. 263, 278
Adams, Noah 276
Adams, William Hampton 134
Adamson, Peter 279
Addis, Barnett 251
Addy, Yacub 80
Adjali, B. 92
Adler, Lynn 148
Adovasio, J. 173
Adra, Najwa 27, 72
Agar, Michael 161
Agee, D. 218
Aginsky, Carrie 125
Aginsky, Yasha 125
Agnello, T. 157
Ahmed, Akbar 28, 149
Ahroni, Y. 53
Aibel, Robert 76
Aki, John 31
Akin, John 121
Akiner, Shirin 148
Alberg, Mildred Freed 226
Albrecht, J. 149
Aldrick, B. C. 216
Alexander, Neil 140
Alexander, W. D. 30
Alexandrov, G. 257
Alland, A. 90
Alassane, M. 221, 260
Allen, Catherine J. 131, 170, 200
Allen, D. B. 150
Allen, P. S. 28, 33, 35, 36, 40, 43, 45, 46, 52, 56, 63, 64, 66, 68, 74, 82, 84, 85, 92, 95, 102, 110, 117, 119, 122, 131, 135, 147, 156, 161, 162, 167, 177, 180, 183, 185, 187, 198, 199, 201, 209, 213, 217, 223, 228, 232, 236, 238, 242, 243, 252, 254, 255, 262, 265, 271, 272, 273, 279
Almagro, M. 214
Almquist, E. 212, 282, 286
Altmann, J. 47
Altmann, S. 47
Altschul, D. 104

Alvarez, Louis 34, 143
Ambrosino, Michael 79, 159, 168, 255
Amlin, Patricia 213
Ancelet, B. 241
Anderson, Bill 127
Anderson, Eugene 251
Anderson, Kip 104
Anderson, M. 189
Anderson, Robin 57, 103, 144
Anderson, Thor 227
Anderson, Wayne 115
Andrade-Watkins, C. 199
Andrews, D. 88, 91
Andrews, E. W. 172
Andrews, Michael 161
Angier, J. 171
Ankele, John 223
Annaud, Jean-Jacques 218
Annichini, Gianfranco 280
Anthony, Alexandra 115
Anthony, John 82
Arango, M. 233
Aratow, P. 151
Araugo, Manuel 164
Araujo, Jose 119
Arcand, Bernard 154
Archer, Dane 129, 138, 284
Archibald, N. 111
Arlaud, Jean 67
Armelagos, George 162
Armstrong, J. C. 266
Armstrong, Patricia C. 252
Armstrong, R. G. 279
Arnaud, S. H. 181
Arnold, E. 54
Arnold, G. 38
Arnott, Susi 67
Aronow, Fred 106
Aronson, J. 87
Artaria, Ernst 74
Aruz, J. 41
Arvelo, N. 137
Asch, Patsy 49-50, 144, 173, 220, 225, 243, 276
Asch, Timothy 49-50, 65, 89, 100, 144, 173, 220, 225, 242, 243, 276, 285-288
Ascher, Robert 51, 58, 79, 186
Ashur, G. 142
Ashhurst, Carmen 116
Ashmore, Wendy 87, 248
Asner, Ed 196, 214
Assal, David 109
Aswad, B. C. 68, 215, 269, 272, 283
Atlas, A. 113, 161
Attenborough, David 263
Attinasi, J. 259

People Index

Atwood, H. 62
Auge, Marc 277
Ault, James 59
Austin, Chris 222
Aveni, Anthony F. 140, 275
Aviad, Michal 28
Avshon, Hariet 222
Ayabe, T. 236
Ayres, G. 269
Azzouz, Bushra 283

Bach, M. 228
Backer, Berit 31
Badger, Mark 165, 237
Badgley, Christiane 237
Bagdon, Trudy 127
Baggs, A. A. 168
Bailey, Norma 82, 131, 179, 212
Bailey, Jackson H. 43, 44, 142
Baily, John 34, 157
Baker, Giles B. 68
Baker, P. T. 286
Baldwin, Lori 112
Baldwin, W. 146
Balfour-Fraser, A. 283
Balikci, Asen 46, 49, 63, 94, 104, 176, 183, 191, 242, 282
Ballis, G. 87
Bamberger, J. 51, 203
Bannister, Jerry 132
Barbash, I. 132
Barbeau, Manon 95
Barde, Barbara 137, 202
Bare, Barbara 211, 250
Barnes, Paul 127
Barnes, R. Carol 134, 194, 264
Barnes, Robert 279
Barnett, Charles R. 171
Barnett, E. 73, 235
Barney, Fred 123
Baron, Suzanne 102, 165
Barr, J. 197
Barrera, Mario 67
Barret, Elizabeth 73, 105, 160, 218
Barrett, Samuel 27, 33-34, 238
Barron, A. 56, 83, 99
Barron, E. 56, 83
Barrow, A. M. 219
Bartholomew, Geo. A. 111
Bartlett, Virginia 161
Barton, P. 142
Baskin, A. 40, 197
Bass, G. F. 36, 115
Bass, R. 231
Bastian, Edward 40, 108, 256
Bastien, J. W. 182
Bateson, Gregory 49, 52, 67, 68, 103, 124, 147, 155, 261
Bateston, C. M. 177
Baumhoff, M. A. 102
Baux, J. P. 117, 214, 269
Baxter, David 78
Baxter, P. T. W. 148, 221

Beale, T. W. 35, 36, 42, 85, 111, 133, 252
Beals, A. 268
Beardsley, R. 205
Beaurenaut, J. P. 88, 177
Beck, L. G. 54, 234
Beck, Sam 123
Becker, Barbara 161
Becker, M. J. 76, 178
Beckham, M. 148
Bee, R. L. 141, 188, 215, 244
Beeman, William O. 290
Behrman, Grant 194
Beibuyck, D. P. 170
Beidelman, T. O. 105, 141, 144, 159, 167, 170, 171, 195, 229
Beitel, Gary 133, 276
Beker, Brian 158
Belkin, Tara 213
Bell, H. H. 210
Bell, Janet 152
Bell, M. E. 76
Bellin, Harvey 36, 170
Bellow, Jane 50
Bender, L. 225
Benally, S. 189
Benedek, A. 52
Benedict, B. 119
Bennett, K. A. 231
Bennett, Linda A. 32, 91, 240, 245
Benson, J. 164, 218, 228, 248
Bentzen, C. 180
Bergum, C. 204, 228
Berman, Jonathan 237
Berman, Richard 215
Bernal, I. 233
Bernard, H. R. 28
Bernier, B. 181, 220, 227
Bernofsky, Gene 190
Berreman, G. D. 182, 256
Bertocci, P. J. 212
Bertucelli, J. L. 219
Bestor, T. C. 101, 142, 143, 190
Beteille, A. 271
Bethune, H. 145
Bezerra, Octavio 120
Bharati, A. 124
Bibeau, G. 172
Biberman, H. 228
Bibic, Vladimir 59, 69, 177, 269
Bickley, Anthony 167
Biesele, M. 230
Biggs, Julian 255
Bigishe, K. 190
Billon, Y. 90, 124, 142, 202
Bin Hok, Batin Long 175
Binford, A. 246
Binford, M. R. 51, 71, 108, 136, 271
Biran, A. 41
Bird, J. 36
Birdwhistell, R. 149, 176
Bishop, John Melville 191, 231, 289
Bishop, S. S. 46

Bjorklund, Pierre 111
Black, Lydia 34, 83, 209
Black, Wade 89
Blackwood, Christian 251
Blair, Lorne 157
Blake, B. 35
Blake, Fred 67, 70
Blakely, P. 53
Blakely, T. 29, 53
Blanc-Paes, Marie-Clemence 37
Blank, Les 32, 58, 71, 91, 111, 126, 133, 172, 243, 244, 279, 290
Blaustein, R. 286
Blom, Frans 112
Blount, B. G. 161, 265, 278, 282
Blue, J. 71, 148
Blumberg, D. 121
Blystone, Peter 233
Boas, F. 58, 150, 234
Boaz, N. T. 119
Bober, Michael 225, 275
Bock, Frank 225
Bock, William Sauts Netamuxwe, 108
Bodine, John J. 209
Bodman, H. L. 82, 236, 250
Boesch, C. 195
Boesch-Achermann, H. 195
Bogue, Nila 122
Bohannan, Paul 47
Bohen, Barbara 198
Bolton, Ralph 27, 30, 31, 167, 223
Boigeol, Charlotte 254
Boivin, Richard 252
Boonzajer Flaes, Robert 212
Booth, Alan 194
Booth, John A. 109, 123, 230, 253, 283
Booth, Marlene 89, 218
Bordaz, J. 245
Bordaz, L. 245
Borden, John 232
Bordes, F. 57
Bornstein, Kate 28
Borjeson, B. 28
Borstadt, R. 245
Bosanquet, C. 235
Boughedir, Ferid 62
Bourdier, Jean-Paul 187, 220
Boutte, M. I. 105
Bovin, Mette 282
Bower, J. R. F. 284
Bowman, Arlene 190
Bowman, S. 123
Boyd, James W. 290
Boyko, E. 254
Boyll, Larain 128
Bozzi, M. R. 203
Brace, C. L. 103, 162
Bradbury, David 245
Bradford, J. 278
Braendli, B. 79
Braidwood, L. 245

Braidwood, R. 245
Brain, Jeffrey 265
Brandes, S. 55
Brandon, Liane 39, 55, 194, 241
Brando, Marlon 219
Brault, Michel 65, 181, 239, 241
Braun, David 186
Bregstein, Philo 143, 204
Breidenbach, G. 195
Breidenbach, M. F. 261
Breitbart, R. E. 247
Breitbart, V. 247
Brettell, C. B. 67, 74, 125, 227, 272, 280
Breuil, Abbe 214
Brewer, Geovanni 48
Brewer, Michael 48
Bricker, H. M. 42, 87, 117, 180, 269
Brigante, Louis 284
Briggs, Jean 271
Brind, W. 254
Broadman, Richard 89
Brock, Norris 80, 161
Brody, Hugh 95, 257
Broekhuyse, J. 83
Bronner, S. J. 34
Bronowski, Jacob 44
Bronowski, Judith 43
Bronson, B. 37
Brooks, D. H. M. 28
Brooks, Maria 220
Broussard, J. A. 135, 142, 197
Brovarski, E. J. 93
Brown, A. 284
Brown, David P. 66, 72
Brown, Donald N. 32, 188
Brown, G. S. 90
Brown, James 127
Brown, James A. 224
Brown, K. L. 143, 241
Brown, Q. 46, 48, 63, 104, 282
Brown, S. S. 134, 166
Brown, T. 57
Brozowski, A. 42
Brugman, Peter 56
Bruhns, K. O. 154
Brunet, M. 111
Bruno, Ellen 126, 228
Bryan, Julian 35, 202
Bryan, Sam 35, 142
Budgell, Anne 153
Buff, C. 215
Buikstra, J. E. 224
Buitron, D. 36
Buller, Burton 34, 130
Bunuel, L. 153, 253
Burden, W. D. 238
Burdick, R. E. 42
Burger, Richard L. 87
Burns, Allan 171, 196, 259
Burrill, C. 238
Burton, G. 162, 242

People Index

Burton, Frances D. 120
Buser, Kurt 120
Bush, Charles 39
Bushnell, G. H. S. 264
Bushnell, J. H. 60
Bushnell, L. W. 114
Bustin, Dillon 28, 205, 260, 276
Butler, B. 114
Button, G. 165, 231, 241
Byers, P. 149

Caccia, Antonia 197
Cafmeyer, Lode 116
Calwell, John 109
Camerini, Michael 50, 51, 54, 59, 71, 79, 108, 135, 136, 271
Camp, C. 41
Campbell, H. 72, 91, 134, 281
Campbell, Joseph 123, 145, 244
Campbell, Leon 215
Campbell, Lynn 219
Campbell, T. D. 192
Campbell, Wil 244
Campbell-Jones, S. 103, 264
Cancian, F. 40, 50
Cantow, Roberta 73
Cardinal, Gil 107, 244, 257
Carey, P. 179
Caristan, G. 285
Carlson, John B. 248
Carpenter, C. R. 54, 65, 112, 127, 182, 222, 240
Carpenter, E. 60, 112
Carr, D. 231
Carrel, Todd 33
Carrescia, Olivia 259
Carriere, M. 181
Carter, J. 287
Carter, P. L. 139
Carter, W. E. 132, 240
Carver, H. P. 238
Casciero, A. 187
Casselberry, Samuel 31, 128, 148, 149
Cassia, A. 67, 272
Cassidy, Richard 223
Casson, Lionel 169
Catlin, Amy Ruth 48
Cave, Julia 212
Cavillon, Daniel 119
Cavillon, Michele 119
Cawsey, F. 152
Cerf, Charlotte 57, 113
Cerilli, Ercole 204
Chadney, J. G. 56
Chagnon, Napoleon 75, 100, 285–288
Chalufour, M. 46, 48, 54, 63, 104, 282
Chalfant, Henry 247
Chalfen, R. 100, 223
Chamoun, Jean 68
Chamovitz, Sheila 184
Chang, K. C. 35
Chanler, W. 238
Chaplin, Charles 132

Chapman, W. 153
Chapman, Anne 198
Charbonneau, Claudette 219
Charlton, Hannah 222
Charlton, Robert 63, 241
Chase, A. F. 41
Chase, D. Z. 41
Chedd, Graham 186, 232
Chesselet, L. 40
Chester, Jeffrey 209
Chilcott, J. H. 67
Chipperfield, D. C. 96
Chodorow, N. 117, 247
Chopra, J. 120, 146, 253
Choy, Christine 281
Christensen, K. L. L. 139
Christian, Diane 200
Chueh, Kuo-chiang 109
Church, S. 42, 275
Cipnic, D. 172
Citron, R. 166
Clah, A. 189
Clancy, Gwendolyn 77
Clapham, A. 215
Clarke, J. D. 57
Clayton, Sue 57, 74, 251
Clelow, C. W. 248
Clements, J. 167
Clements, W. M. 125, 145
Clemmer, R. O. 60, 126, 265
Clune, F. J. 127
Code, Allan 195
Code, Mary 195
Codere, H. 260
Coe, M. D. 59, 76, 96, 134, 231
Coe, William R. 172
Coen, Tanya L. 196
Coggins, Clemency 171
Cohen, Alain 144, 209
Cohen, John 64, 71, 118, 182, 208, 217
Cohen, Nancy 276
Colby, Benjamin N. 140, 141, 191, 234, 257, 289
Colby, L. 141
Cole, D. 226
Cole, J. C. (see Chopra)
Cole, John R. 115, 166, 198
Cole, Janis 216
Cole, Johnetta 63
Cole, Michael 77
Colin, R. 91
Colleyn, Jean-Paul 241, 244, 277
Collier, John 40, 189, 207
Collier, J. F. 258
Collier, Malcolm 218, 220, 228
Collins, D. 151
Colson, J. B. 263
Comaroff, J. 121, 268
Combs-Schilling, M. E. 182
Conant, F. P. 239
Conford, Michal 224
Conklin, C. 65

Conklin, H. 120
Conlin, R. 33
Conn, Pamela 289
Connolly, Bob 57, 103, 144
Connor, Linda 49-50, 144, 173, 220
Conquergood, Dwight 55, 121
Conroy, G. C. 162
Constantini, Luigi 213
Constanzo, Mark 138
Conway, Cece 244
Cook, T. G. 41
Cooper, John 265
Cooper, Merian C. 66, 114
Corbett, Helen 34, 209
Corn, E. 290
Cornwell, Susan 256
Corsetti, George 212
Costa, Marisa 110
Counihan, C. 185, 228, 247, 280
Counter, S. Allen 130
Counture, Helene 55
Cousteau, Jacques 57, 156, 248
Coutinho, Eduardo 230
Covarrubias, Miguel 50
Cowan, Jane K. 185, 208
Cowan, Richard 87, 92, 139, 151, 248
Cowell, Adrian 83, 198, 264
Cox, S. L. 105
Coyote, Peter 75
Crabtree, D. 31, 36
Crabtree, Pam J. 83
Cran, William 66
Cranstone, E. 80
Crawford, John 158
Crespi, M. 123, 196
Crim, D. 81, 221
Crocker, Scott 59
Crocker, William H. 148
Croner, S. 112
Crook, J. H. 57, 111
Cross, Stephen 274
Cruz-Uribe, E. 123
Crowell, E. A. 85, 89, 282
Crystal, C. N. 163
Crystal, E. 163
Csisery, G. 207
Cuesta, Mike 78
Cullinane, M. 289
Cullingham, James 44, 106, 155, 245, 257
Culp, Jim 196, 214
Culpepper, Maryanne 162
Cunliffe, B. 52
Cunningham, K. K. 123, 157, 235
Curley, R. T. 272
Curling, C. 170, 175, 221, 236
Curling, Jonathan 57, 74, 251
Curnick, David 85
Current, David 276
Curry, N. E. 181
Curtis, Edward S. 134
Custer, G. A. 220

da Silveira, Nancy 105
Daarstad, E. 96
Dale, Holly 216
Dallalfar, Arlene 234
Dallie 30
Dalva, Robert 273
Damon, F. H. 265
Danai, Tal 268
Danforth, L. M. 204, 221
Danielewski, T. 61
Dargan, Amanda 279
Darino, Eduardo 118
Darling, John 157
Darrow, William R. 290
Dauber, Roslyn 175
Daugherty, R. D. 85, 123
Davenport, T. 54, 59, 234, 249, 254, 269
Davey, F. 82
David, Nicholas 89, 269
Davidson, Basil 29, 55, 63, 85, 149, 156, 164, 170, 223
Davis, E. L. 212
Davis, Gerald L. 208
Davis, H. 242
Davis, H. K. 169
Davis, Karen 202
Davis, Kate 259
Davis, O. 79
Davis, S. H. 87
Davis, Susan S. 241
Daws, Gavan 37
Dawson, H. J. 159
de Boer, Leo 56
De Clippel, Catherine 241, 244
de Graaf, John 110
de Heusch, Luc 248
de Jesus, Carlos 208
de Koenigsberg, Paula 219
de Lumley, Henry 117
de Rooy, Jan Kees 230
de Turenne, Henri 52
Deason, P. 109
DeBouzek, Jeanette 111
de Brigard, E. 168
Dedman, Penny 223
Deetz, J. 73
Defalco, M. 199
Deffarge, Marie Claude 74, 23
Dekin, A. A. 139
Deluz, Ariane 93
Dempsey, H. 196
Denker, Debra 188
Denman, A. S. 60, 163, 215
Dennis, P. A. 195
Denny, Alyson 259
dePoligny, S. 31
Deren, Maya 88
Derrick, Wayne 34
DeSeta, V. 50
Dever, W. G. 174
Devlin, B. 272
DeVore, I. 47, 48, 119

People Index

DeVries, Peter 167
DeWalt, Billie R. 65, 70
Dewar, R. 69, 70
Dewey, A. G. 243
Dhanraj, Deepa 247
Di Peso, Charles 96
Dick, Herbert W. 209
Dickinson, John 79, 138, 175, 205
Didio, Francois 95, 254
Dieterlen, Germaine 33, 93, 110, 125, 237, 248
Dine, Nancy 49
Diskin, Martin 218
Dixon-Stowell, B. 71, 80
Dlasheim, F. 279
Dodds, J. S. 59, 239
Doillon, Jacques 35
Dole, G. 32, 41
Dolgoy, M. 40
Dolhinow, P. 53
Dollar, C. 166
Dong, Arthur 159, 234
Donker, W. 57
Donnan, Christopher B. 87
Donnelly, Nancy 55, 192
Donovan, Bill 138
Dor, Remy 28
Dore, H. 91
Dores, Maurice 233
Doring, J. 256
Doring, S. 256
Dorjee, R. 271
Dornfeld, Barry 80, 214
Dorris, M. 191
Doughty, P. 98
Douglas, John 116
Dow, James 50, 68, 91
Dowdey, Kathleen 65
Downs, Hugh 61
Downton, F. 215
Draper, Patricia 186, 228
Dreben, S. R. 128
Drew, Thatcher 232
Driver, H. E. 27, 53, 61, 210
Drucker, Charles 209
Dryansky, Andre 100
Duany, J. 272
du Bois, Ron 283
Duarte, A. 202
DuBey, Gene 243
Dubisch, Jill 64, 225
Dubosc, D. 78
Dubowsky, N. 129
Dufaux, Georges 118
Duff, W. 260
Dufour, D. L. 33, 75, 120
Duffy, K. 50, 68, 71, 283
Dumas, Jacques 85
Dumont, Jean-Paul 71, 72, 276
Duncan, Andy 77
Duncan, G. S. 117, 204, 271
Duncan, R. J. 117, 204, 271

Duncan, R. R. 117
Dunlap, B. 166
Dunlop, Ian 45, 80, 84, 88, 105, 133, 163, 185, 187, 188, 198, 206, 260, 267, 277
Dunlop, Geoff 288
Dunn, E. 48, 197
Dunn, Geoffrey 178
Dunn, P. 231
Dunn, Stephen P. 197
Dunn, W. 50, 199
Dunsky, S. 67
Duplantier, S. 118
Dupont, Jacques 52
Dupree, Louis 149
Durham, N. M. 45, 165
Durrenberger, P. 159
Durrin, Ginny 216
Dutilleux, Jean Pierre 44, 219, 284
Duvall, D. P. 59, 65
Duvignaud, J. 219
Dwyer-Shick, S. 94, 99, 135, 198
Dyson, Stephen L. 199

Earle, D. M. 171
Early, A. M. 42
Early, D. 58, 101, 138, 199
Earney, Michael 162
Eason, J. V. 281
Eban, Abba 122
Eberlein, Robert W. 231
Ebihara, M. 120
Echavarria, Cristina 76, 118, 272, 276
Echeverria, Diego 248
Eckhardt, R. B. 28, 131, 259, 280
Eddy, John 140
Edgerton, R. B. 183
Edkins, Don 114
Edmunson, M. S. 141
Edols, Michael 280
Edwards, M. 165
Edynak, G. J. 280
Effron, R. T. 130
Ehlers, Tracy Bachrach 62
Ehrenreich, J. 79, 121
Ehrhardt, A. 170
Ehrich, R. W. 250
Eickelman, D. F. 170
Eimerl, S. 48
Einhorn, A. 43, 99, 260
Eisenstein, S. 257
El Guindi, Fadwa 182, 232
El-Abnoudi, Attiat 183, 208, 227
Elder, Joseph W. 40, 79, 108, 179, 183, 256
Elder, Sarah 45, 90, 109, 133, 145, 197, 265
Elisofon, E. 29
Elizalde, M. 154
Elliot, Mark R. 159
Ellovich, R. 57
Ellwood, Brooks 40
Elsass, Peter 92, 145
Else, J. 124

Emigh, John 120
Emigh, Ulrike 120
Eminov, Ali 31
Emond, B.-R. 181, 220, 227
Emswiler, S. N. 135
Enders, H. 222
Engelbrecht, Beate, 108, 233, 278
Enriquez, A. 265
Entell, Peter 84, 274
Epple, George 64, 88, 116, 190, 219, 235, 255
Epstein, Beth 150
Epstein, R. 284
Epstein, T. S. 80
Erdman, J. L. 30, 54, 57
Ereira, Alan 110
Erickson, F. 75
Erikson, Kai 61
Errington, Frederick 57, 63, 144, 276
Erskine, Maren 122
Erskine, Reed 122
Erwitt, Elliot 53
Escorel, Eduardo 272
Esparza, Moctezuma 30
Espinosa, Paul 135, 192, 268
Essex, Tony 218
Estus, B. 103
Ettinger, C. 70, 143
Eugene, I. 70
Evans, David L. 56, 91, 112, 113, 115, 126, 130, 211, 222, 239, 243, 267
Evans, R. D. 38
Evans, R. K. 54, 124
Evans-Pritchard, E. E. 195, 246
Everett, Katherine 131
Everson, Simon 257
Ewers, John C. 72
Eyde, D. 45
Eyde, Mariane 32
Eyre, R. 124
Ezra-Mir 198

Fabiano, Thomas A. 95
Fairbanks, C. H. 127
Fairchild, J. Stephen 173
Fairchild, Stephen 232
Fairlie, M. 121, 122, 264, 280
Fairservis, W. A. 198
Falck, I. 160
Fanshel, Susan 278
Faridi, M. A. 279
Faris, James 195
Farmer, Malcolm 203, 245
Farnsworth, Elizabeth 253
Farnum, Marlene 283
Faulkner, Scott 248
Favre, Bernard 95, 119
Faye, Safi 233
Feeney, J. 94
Fehrer, R. 121
Feingold, David 198, 277
Fejos, P. 80

Feldberg, R. L. 155, 183
Feldesman, M. R. 162
Feldhaus-Weber, M. 85
Feldmar, Claudia 67, 73, 117, 125
Ferchiou, Sophie 117, 290
Ferguson, L. 173
Ferme, Mariane 174
Fernandez Figares, Maria Dolores 183
Fernandez-Canadas de Greenwood, P.
Fernea, Elizabeth 214, 227, 241, 261, 269, 283
Ferno, J. 37, 92
Ferrand, Carlos 71
Ferrandiz, F. 146
Ferrero, Pat 122, 126, 218
Ferris, Beth 75
Ferris, Bill 56, 84, 113, 115, 130, 157, 164, 179, 219, 267, 270
Ferris, J. 56, 84, 179
Feuchtwang, S. 79
Fidler, R. C. 175
Field, Karen L. 99
Field, Rachel 27
File, Bandung
Films, Faust
Films, Juniper
Fink, Abbie H. 209
Fink, John 205
Finkelstein, E. F. 184
Finne, Ron 250
Finnegan, G. A. 86, 112, 166, 243, 271, 288
Fiore, Robert 110
Firth, Raymond 104, 264
Fischel, A.
Fischer, E. 170
Fischler, Steven 109
Fish, L. 71, 160
Fishel, A. 178
Fisk, A. 85
Fitzgerald, L. 74
Fitzhugh, William W. 186
Flaherty, Frances 179
Flaherty, Robert 127, 162, 166, 179, 187, 249
Flantua, Bert 56
Fleagle, J. 248
Fleisher, M. S. 59, 119, 144
Fleming, Thomas B. 111
Floria, Mario 60
Flowers, N. M. 219, 220
Fluer-Lobban, Carolyn 44, 97
Folly, Anne Laure 283
Fonda, H. 91, 290
Foner, N. 158
Fontane, P. E. 240
Ford, R. 35
Forde, C. D. 265
Forge, A. 93
Forman, Stephen L. 209
Forward, J. S. 38
Fossey, D.
Fowler, Catherine 265
Fowler, D. D. 42

People Index

Fox, James A. 213
Fox, James J. 83, 225, 243, 276, 279
Fox, J. L.
Fox, R. 146
Franken, Randy 210
Frankenstein, Ellen 171, 178
Franklin, C. L. 159
Franklin, Oliver 31
Fratto, T. F. 50
Frebs, Stephanie 237
Frederiksen, R. 80
Free, William
Freed, S. A. 275
Freedman, D. G. 78
Freedman, Joel L. 60, 258
Freeman, L. G. 153, 250
Frey, Katherine Stenger 230
Friedberg, L. 266
Friedl, E. 151
Friedlander, Eva 77, 79, 149
Friedlander, J. 162
Friedman,
Friedmann, N. A. 271
Friedmann, Nina S. 117, 118
Frisbie, Charlotte 35, 93
Fritsch, G. 271
Fritts, K. 215
Fritts, W. R. 215
Fritz, Sonia 272
Frost, Cathy 158
Frost, David 78
Fruchtman, M. 289
Fruzzetti, Lena 136
Fry, Peter 64, 268
Fuks, Victor 65, 184, 273
Fuller, B. A. G. 36
Fuller, Robert 86
Fulton, Rawn 225
Fulton, Robert 84
Furman, W. A. 246
Furst, P. 92, 182, 237, 258
Furtado, Jorge 254

Gaber-Saletan, P. 232
Gaevert, H. S. 112
Galentine, W. 35
Gardner, Allen 227, 252
Gardner, Beatrice, 252
Gardner, Ray 35
Gardner, Robert 32, 58, 60, 83, 84, 107, 131, 191, 195, 224, 242
Gargiulo, Maria 110
Garonyi, F. 29
Gartenstein, L. 93
Gasc, J. P. 35
Gates, Robert 133, 182
Gaucher, Candice 58
Gaunt, Marilyn 214, 269, 283
Gay, John H. 77
Gazit, Chana 126
Gebauer, P. 62

Gebe 35
Geddes, Carol 88
Geddes, William R. 60, 140, 152, 176, 242
Gee, Deborah 240
Geertz, H. 50, 52, 144, 147, 174, 262
Gell, Alfred 220
Gelles, Paul 262
Genini, Izza 31, 130, 163, 182
Gerbrands, A. 45, 171
Gerrard, Alice 244
Gerrard, N.
Gershfield, B. 194
Gerth, D. 132
Geshekter, Charles 204
Getzels, Peter 134
Gewertz, D. 57, 144, 187
Gibb, H. 90
Gibbs, J. L. 77, 169
Gibson, G. 71, 123
Gibson, Kean 181
Giercke, Franz-Christoph 161
Gilbert, C. 168
Gilbert, David 124
Gilbertson, Jenny 143
Gilfillin, Carl 247
Gilic, V. 198
Gill, Malone 109
Gill, Rina 79
Gilliam, A. 168
Gilmore, David 216
Giltrow, D. 83
Ginsburg, Faye 60, 133, 144, 210, 220, 242
Girvin, D. 190
Gladu, A. 65, 220, 241
Glassie, H. 59, 65
Glazier, S. D. 37, 96, 101, 163, 192
Gleason, Judith 53
Glimcher, S. 160
Glover, Guy 108
Gluck, D. 266
Gluckman, M. 158
Gmelch, George 72, 79, 118, 152
Gmelch, Sharon 171
Godelier, M. 233, 257, 260
Godfrey, L. R. 231
Godmilow, J. 213
Godrey, R. 235
Goerke, B. 42
Goethals, P. 152
Goetz, I. S. 92
Goetzmann, Will 186
Gold, A. G. 279
Gold, G. L. 65, 220, 227, 241
Goldberg, L. 67
Goldberg, Margaret 161
Goldberg, R.
Goldchild, P. 199
Goldman, M. 87
Goldman, P. 263
Goldner, D. 255
Goldner, O. 255

Goldstein, Judith 99
Gombrich, R. 147
Gonzalez, Nancie L. 32, 56, 71, 93, 107, 121, 127, 168, 199, 213, 229, 230, 257, 268
Goodale, Jane 114, 274
Goodall, J. 35, 141, 178, 272
Goodman, Karen 158, 193
Goodrich, D. W. 69
Goodwin, A. 112
Goodwin, C. G. 61
Goodwin, Thomas C. 278
Gordon, Beate 70, 143
Gordon, Bryan C. 186
Gordon, Deborah 278
Gordon, Harriet 134
Gordon, Kate 270
Gordon, Richard 32, 103, 112, 240, 259
Gordon, Robert 32, 186
Gorman, F. 35, 111, 172
Gorney, Mark 53
Gorsline, T. 107
Gorsselin, Bernard 239
Gosling, Maureen 290
Gottlieb, Robert S. 72
Gould, R. A. 183, 190
Gould, Stephen Jay 96
Grabowicz, O. I. 275
Gradwohl, D. M. 107, 155, 214, 272
Graef, R. 135
Graff, Cheryl 184
Gramly, M. 73, 230
Gray, B. 157
Gray, John 101
Gray, T. 96
Graves, William 32, 112, 136, 221, 232, 259
Green, J. W. 127
Green, Steven 57
Green, Stanton W. 56
Green, William L. 169
Greene, Joseph A. 232
Greene, P. 160
Greene, S. 34
Greenfeld, P. J. 157
Greenfield, Sidney 48, 101, 120, 145, 221
Greengo, R. 85
Greenhill, L. P. 59, 65
Greenwald, Barry 55
Greenway, J. 45, 91, 115, 192
Greenwood, D. J. 208, 236
Gregg, J. 84
Gregor, Thomas 174
Griaule, Marcel 93, 248
Grierson, J. 114, 241
Griesinger, Carol 32
Griesinger, Peter 32, 240
Griffin, Suzanne 68
Griffith, J. S. 71
Grigsby, M. 95
Grilli, Peter 236
Griswold, L. E. 252, 253
Groce, Nora 93, 152, 153, 154, 178, 193, 247, 251

Gropper, R. C. 218
Grosshof, A. 110
Gross, D. R. 159, 219
Grum, Anders 221
Grumet, R. S. 108, 157
Gschwendtner, Andrea 38
Guayasamin, Gustavo 131
Guggenheim, H. 160, 161
Guibert, Francis 223
Guida, Louis 280
Guillemin, J. 112
Gulla, Katherine 185
Gulliver, P. H. 161, 258, 278
Gunn, J. D. 173
Gunter, Chat 210
Gurdin, J. B. 55
Gurievitch, Grania 149
Guthrie, George M. 56, 166, 205
Guthrie, Helen A. 56, 166
Gutman, J. M. 209
Gwariney-Gibbs, P. A. 175
Guzman, J. A. 233
Gwartney-Gibbs, P. A. 246
Gwynne, G. A. 248

Hadel, Judith 89
Hadingham, E. 248
Hagopian, J. M. 182
Halberstadt, J. 249
Hales, Carolyn 256
Halimi, Andre 67
Hall, Andrea 198
Hall, E. T. 139
Hall, Ute 114
Hallet, J. 193, 203
Hallet, S. 193, 203
Halperin, B. 207
Halpern, J. 120, 207
Halter, M. 242
Halverson, J. 195
Hamermesh, Mira 164, 250
Hamilton, T. M. 239
Hammond, P. C. 41
Hampton, Henry 97
Hanfman, G. M.
Hani, S. 61
Hanig, Josh 175
Hanks, L. M. 121
Hannemann, Y. 184, 284
Hansen, K. 210
Hansen, William 245
Hanson, L. J. 34
Haralovich, Mary Beth 28, 54, 89, 178
Haramis, Peter 35, 146
Harden, Sandra Austin 99
Harding, R. S. O. 35, 142
Harner, M. J.
Harper, Peggy 112, 247
Harper, Ray 76
Harries, Andy 170, 200
Harrington, Beth 46, 182

People Index

Harris, G. 124, 158
Harris, H. 195
Harris, O. 218
Harrisson, Tom 218
Harrison, Marguerite 114
Hart, C. W. M. 114
Hartigan, K. V. 41
Hartley, E. 221
Hartley, I. 221
Harvey, Jeff 268
Harwood, A. 268
Haury, E. W. 240
Hauser, D. 116
Haviland, J. B. 285
Hawes, B. L. 60, 112, 211, 231
Hayes, C. 272
Hayes, K. 272
Hayes, Randy 108
Hays, P. H. 222
Hays, T. E. 96, 103, 113, 168, 242, 256
Hazard, Barbara 138
Head, Barry 197
Head, Joanna 89
Healey, G. 171
Healy, P. F. 72, 91, 134, 281
Heath, D. B. 29, 47, 57, 62, 66, 88, 110, 151, 251
Heese, James T. 209
Heick, William 58, 247, 261
Heider, K. G. 71, 80, 81-82, 83, 230, 256, 257
Heijnen, Hans 192
Heimans, F. 93, 168
Heimer, G. 112
Heinz, J. H. 149
Heizer, R. F. 96
Helmer, Wilhelm 154
Henley, Paul 79, 220
Henriksen, Georg 139
Henry, E. O. 79, 90, 242
Hentschel, Faith 169
Henzell, P. 121
Heramis, P.
Herbert, Eugenia 58
Herndon, M. 192
Hersch, Stuart 271
Herschede, Michael 240
Herzog, Werner 122
Hess, Ron 113, 183
Heste, Borge 197
Hester, T. R. 42
Heunemann, D. 149
Hewitt, John 263
Heyerdahl, T. 31, 150, 257
Hiatt, L. R. 118, 273
Hicks, G. L. 54, 105, 130, 182, 225, 288
Hicks, Ronald 53, 134 , 140, 246
Hicks, Ray 105
Higgins, Michael L. 196
Higgs, E. 186
Highwater, Jamake 188, 215
Hilger, M. I. 63
Hill, Jane 34

Hill, Jacquetta F. 63, 104
Hill, J. N. 42
Hill, Peter 215
Hill, Thomas W. 61, 151
Himes, J. H. 129
Hinton, Carma 32, 103, 112, 160, 240, 259
Hirabayashi, James 228
Hitchcock, J. T. 118, 123, 194
Hitchcock, P. 118, 123, 194
Hixon, Margaret 65, 196
Hochman, Gary 234
Hockings, P. 106, 127, 132, 136, 166, 176, 184, 209, 213, 240, 270, 273, 284, 290
Hodge, Jennifer 144
Hoffman, C. 43
Hofmann, S. 151
Hohlfelder, R. L. 36, 88, 115, 156, 248, 262
Holaday, Duncan 175
Holcomb, B. 125
Holker, Andrew 34
Holleman, J. F. 39
Holm, B. 132, 134, 150
Holmberg, A. 240
Holmes, K. 110
Holmes, Lowell D. 97, 179, 262
Holve, N. 234
Homquist, Pea 111
Honigmann, John J. 46, 63, 282
Hooper, J.
Hoover, M. 175
Hoover, P. 209
Hopen, C. E. 169, 242
Hopkins, N. 30
Horbein, Marie 228
Hornbein, George 228
Hornick, S. 266
Horowitz, M. M. 242
Horr, D. A. 40, 112, 166, 222
Hoskins, Janet 100, 259
Hostetler, J. A. 34, 218
Hott, Lawrence 220
Huangdi, Qin Shi 238
Howard, Alan 69
Howard, J. H. 62
Howard, Mary 167
Howarth, A. 207
Howe, Sylvia 222
Howe, T. 27
Howell, F. C. 92
Howell, Paul 236
Howells, Barrie 155, 236
Howells, W. W. 199
Hu, Tai-Li 221
Huaute, Semu 60
Hubbard, M. C. 157
Hudson, F. 112
Hudson, S. 119
Hugh-Jones, Christine 275
Hugh-Jones, Stephen 174, 275
Hughes, A. M. 119
Hughes, Robin 197

Humphrey, Caroline 122
Hunt, Edward 116
Hunt, Marion 30
Hunt, Marjorie 245
Hunter, E. H. 215
Huntington, Gertrude E. 34
Hunziker, Jane 161
Hurman, A. 97
Husmann, Rolf 104, 194
Hussian, Zakir 72
Huxley, J. 180
Hyde, Jim 45
Hyslop, John 135, 214

Ianuzielo, T. 77
Ibanez, Eduardo 130
Ichac, M. 146
Iddon, Ron 208
Idiens, D. 263
Ikeda, Keiko 101
Ikela, Hajima 43, 104, 142, 190
Ikels, C. 103, 118, 240, 283, 285, 290
Ingleton, Sally 252
Irvine, Dominique 226
Isaac, G. L. 57
Itard, J.
Ito, Cherel 88
Ito, Karen L. 33, 69, 179, 234
Ito, Teiji 88

Jablonko, Allison 80, 122, 148, 169, 233, 257, 268
Jablonko, Marek 80, 122, 148, 169, 233, 257, 268
Jackson, Billy 85
Jackson, Bruce 30, 200
Jackson, F.
Jackson, J. E. 198
Jackson, Munyungo Darryl 43
Jackson, P. L.
Jacobs, A. 97, 148, 247
Jacobs, D. K. 164
Jacobs, H. 143
Jacobs, R. H. 227
Jacobson, D. 79
Jacottet, J. 215
Jaekel, C. 278
Jaffe, P. L. 267
Jairazbhoy, Nazir Ali 48
Jajman, Charles 195
James, K. 239
James, W. 184
Jamison, Gayla 159
Jampel, Barbara 185
Janzen, John M. 192
Jaquemin, P. 58
Jarrico, P. 228
Jarvie, I. 187
Jay, Robert 155
Jayamanne, Laleen 241
Jayanti, Vikram 133
Jell, Georg 97
Jell-Bahlsen, Sabine 97, 166

Jenkins, F. A. 35
Jenkins, Horace 247
Jennings, A. M. 35, 57
Jennings, J. D. 113, 124
Jennings, P. 92
Jeroslow, Phyllis 196
Jeshel, Jorg 161
Jest, C. 46, 251
Jhala, Jayasinhji 261, 290
Jillings, Andy 157
Johanson, D. C. 103
Johansson, Signe 54
Johnson, Avril 175
Johnson, B. 120, 271
Johnson, Colleen 57, 197
Johnson, Ernest 183
Johnson, Evan 209
Johnson, Gerald 209
Johnson, Judith 88, 119
Johnson, H.
Johnson, P. 268
Johnson, R.
Johnston, Aaron Kim 179
Johnston, B.
Johnston, Graham 157, 185
Johnston, Hugh 164, 186, 216, 248
Johnston, Kati 58
Johnston, Ned 161, 272
Johnston, Suzanne 164, 186, 216, 248
Johnston, Tom 129
Johson, George 85
Jolly, C. J. 175
Jones, C. 213
Jones, James Earl 130, 197
Jones, S.
Jopking, J. P.
Jopling, C. F. 285
Jopling, J. P. 285
Jordan, R. H. 90, 133, 139, 281
Jouffroy, F. K. 35
Julen, Staffan 138
Julen, Ylva 138
Juli, Harold 174
Junger, Karin 56
Junkerman, John 268
Jury, Dan 69, 106
Jury, Mark 69, 106

Kabir, Alamgir 35
Kafka, Harry 242
Kagan, J. 84
Kahn, T. 103
Kamerling, L. 45, 90, 109, 133, 145, 197, 207, 265
Kamerling, N. 207
Kampen, N. B. 95, 199
Kampman, Joop 36
Kamway, D. 213
Kane, Richard 28, 260, 276
Kane, Susan 36
Kaplan, D. 253
Kaplan, Richard 133

People Index

Karami, A. M. 134
Karday, A. 82
Karmitz, M. 58
Karol, J. 54
Karp, I. 244
Kasakoff, A. B. 218
Kasfir, S. L. 241
Kashima, T. 255
Katic, Kamenko 120
Katz, Susanna 31, 36, 92, 105, 129, 165, 196, 234, 245
Katz, Paul 31, 36, 92, 105, 129, 165, 196, 234, 245
Katze, Mary 231
Kaufman, Jim
Kaufman, Joan 147
Kaufman, Nicolas J. 257
Kaufman, P. 281
Kaufman, R. 96
Kavanagh, William 271
Kawaky, Joseph 119
Kawami, T. S. 212, 254
Kay, Janice 262
Kayser, E. L. 36
Kealiinohomoku, J. W. 29, 76, 216, 262
Kearney, M. 72, 130
Keenan, Jeremy 265
Keenlyside, D.
Keenlyside, J.
Kehoe, T. 141
Keifer, T. M. 91
Keil, C. 247
Keiser, R. L. 111
Keiter, Tom 228
Kelley, Jack 273
Kelley, Joanne 116
Kelly, J. 85
Kelly, Nancy 77
Kelly, William 142, 143
Kelsall, A. N. 285
Keltz, M. 62
Kemeny, John 255
Kendall, David 67, 222
Kendall, Laurel 138
Kendall, T. 35, 186
Kendell, Timothy 93
Kennedy, K. A. R. 121, 264, 280
Kenneil, A. 271
Kensinger, K. M. 100, 286
Kent, Jay 27, 40
Kent, Jim 219
Kerr, J. A. 158
Kertzer, D. 127
Kervin, Denise 28, 55, 89, 178
Keshishoglou, J. 183
Kewley, Vanya 233
Keyes, C. F. 252
Keyser, Ulrike 278
Kiefer, T. M. 36, 72, 155, 160, 171, 207, 227, 279
Kilbourne, J. 149
Kildea, Gary 265
Kimball, S. T. 166
Kincaid, Chet 142

Kindem, Gorham 71
King, Arthur 54
King, Dave 77
King, Mary Louise 106
Kingsland, D. 219
Kington, S. 121
Kinoy, Peter 280
Kirk, Louis 103, 123, 136, 169, 194, 264
Kirk, Ruth 103, 123, 136, 169, 194, 264
Kirkpatrick, Joanna 107, 188
Kirschenblatt-Gimblett, B. 121
Kish, Albert 194
Kiste, R. C. 180
Kitchen, Diane 53
Kjonegaard, V. H. 149
Klein, John E. 287
Klein, J. I. 73
Klein, James 117
Klein, Janice B. 41
Klein, Larry 217
Klein, P. A. 287
Kligman, G. 46
Klijn, Jan-Henk 58
Klijn, I.
Klima, G. 51
Kline, Kathy 103, 112
Klodawsky, Helen 236
Klymyshyn, A. M. U. 31, 92, 150, 161
Knebel, Emic 74
Knez, Eugene I. 222
Knez, J. A. 70
Knight, R. 31
Koch, G. 193
Kocherhans, Anne M. 194
Koenig, M. 213
Koenig, Wolf 72
Koford, C. 222
Kohen, J. 93
Kohl, P. L. 91
Kohn, Richard 161
Kolata, A. L. 135, 214
Kolb, C. C. 45, 223, 255, 286
Kolker, Andrew 143
Komangi, Gitta 279
Kooijman, S. 250
Korb, V. 136
Kosalwat, B. 187
Kovanic, R. 111
Kramer, Karen 65, 120, 145, 156, 180, 222, 258
Krause, R. A. 169, 213, 270, 284
Krebs, S. 187
Kreines, J. 212, 23
Kroeber, T. 140
Kruger, Manfred 233, 278
Krupp, E. C. 225
Kuepferle, Paul 40, 108
Kuerten, Bruce 162
Kummer, Hans 28
Kuneki, Nettie 283
Kunijwok, Walter 236
Kunuk, Zacharias 217

Kuras, Ellen 126
Kurihara, Nanako 110
Kurland, J. A. 241
Kussmaul, F. 28

L'Amare, P. 28
LaBarre, W. 125, 258
Laberge, Marc 252
Labrecque, J.-C. 55
Ladlow, Terrence 53
LaFontaine, J. 97, 170
Lajoux, J. D. 46
Laliberte, Morgane 281
Lamanna, Mary Ann 169
Lamberg-Karlovsky, C. C. 198
Lambrecht, W. 44, 58, 85, 140, 159, 178, 193, 213, 244, 278
Lamphere, L. 39, 55, 108, 160, 194, 222, 241
Lancaster, Jane 47
Lander, P. S. 102, 261
Landsburg, Alan 133, 134
Lane, Bruce Pacho 118, 262
Lansing, J. Stephen 113
Lanson, Dennis 209
Lanzelo, Tony 285
LaPin, Dierdre 242
Lappalainen, Heimo 249
Larcom, Joan 54, 202, 228, 259
Larimore, Victoria 34
Lasry, P. 155, 183
Lassally, W. 82
Lasswell-Hoff, Jane 116
Latour, Ira 255
Lattimore, Owen 180
Laufer, Paul 243
Laurie, Jim 269
Lavachery, H. 92
Lavalette, Philippe 95, 254
Lawrence, E. A. 77, 133, 161, 197
Le Bleis, Yves 89
Le Trac 39
Leach, E. 265
Leach, Jerry 198, 265
Leach, Paul 255
Leacock, R. 120, 162
Leakey, L. S. B. 88, 155, 156
Leakey, Richard 165
Leatherman, L. R. 35
Lebra, T. S. 142, 143
Lee, Diana
Lee, Richard B. 129, 230, 248
Lee, William 87
Lees, S. H. 159
Leechman, D. 165
Lefande, R. A. 76
LeFebvre, Jean-Pol 159, 271
Legesse, S. 166
Legg, S. 180
Legnassi, Remo 78
Leib, Elliott 156, 219
Leiber, M.
Leigh, Malcolm 167

Leimbach, Bill 44, 49, 142, 219, 284
Leis, N. B. 255
Leis, P. 282
Leland, Andrea 272
Lemaire, Etienne 153
Lemieux, C. 69, 126, 144
Lemoine, Jacques 175
Lengozzie, R.
Lennon, Randy 107
Leone, M. P.
Lerner, Bettina 156, 232
Lerner, Carl 74
Lester, M. 266
Leuzinger, E. 170
Levin, Ben 76
Levin, Claudia 220
Levine, Ivory Waterworth 53, 55
Levine, Ken 53, 55
Levy, C. 160, 162, 166, 183, 242
Levy, Paul 126
Lewis, Henry T. 102
Lewis, Mark 63
Leynse, H. W. 202
Li, D. 51
Li, Sue Yung 54, 72, 100, 248, 251, 275, 285
Li, V. H. 51
Liddell, E. R. 49
Lieber, M. 84, 121, 219
Lieberman, P. 56, 218
Liggett, B. 89
Light, Allie 179
Lin, Imogene 52
Lind, R. D. 80
Linden, Adrienne 186
Lindquist, D. 113, 130, 164, 267
Lindsay, Shira 174
Linton, John 115
Lipke, Kathryn
Lipman, Beata 82
Lippman, Jane 223
Lipsbergs, G. 152
Lipskis, Peter 80
Lipton, Barbara 271
Lisanevich, X. 236
Lisciandro, Frank 228, 247
Littell, B.
Little, Leandra 237
Littman, Lynne 133, 195
Llewelyn-Davies, Melissa 74, 85, 97, 166, 170, 174, 184, 203,, 218, 227, 241, 243, 283
Lloyd, P. 207
Lobban, Richard 247
Lobo, M. L. 280
Lobran, R. A. 232
Lock, Margaret 142, 143
Locke, J. 257
Lockwood, Wayne 158
Lockwood, William G. 27
Loeb, L. D. 224
Logan, M. H. 94, 262
Lohse, W. 170

Loizos, Peter 83, 104, 147, 154, 158, 184, 218, 242, 288
Lomax, Alan 60, 80, 112, 153, 160, 169, 203, 229, 245
London, Gloria 117
Long, J. P. M. 62
Long, Jack 56
Long, Jeremy 210
Long, Philomene 62
Longacre, William A. 95, 164
Lorentz, Pare 224
Lorenz, K. 49
Loring, Stephen 129
Loteanu, E. 119
Loucky, J. 194, 280
Loudon, J. B. 264
Louis, Daniele 55
Loukinen, Michael 102, 261
Lovejoy, C. O. 218
Low, Colin 72, 146, 244
Low, S. 36, 190
Lowe, Felicia 69
Lowenthal, Ira 120
Lowy, M. J. 76, 210
Lucas, J. A. 93
Luchsinger, Happy 179
Lucignani, Luciano 95
Luehrsen, Thomas 290
Luyat, Jean-Claude 272
Luzbetak, L. J. 175
Lydall, J. 155, 225
Lyman, C. 37
Lynch, John 156, 232
Lynch, Robert N. 74
Lynn, G.
Lyon, Rachael 247
Lyons, Bill 134

M'mbugu-Schelling, Flora 109, 254
Maas, J. B. 266
Mac Craig, Arthur 95
Mac Donald, James 54
Macaulay, David 217
MacDonald, Annette 170
MacDonald, Bruce 174
MacDonald, James 79, 135
MacDougall, David 99, 114, 126, 137, 148, 161, 190, 209, 249, 252, 258, 265, 268, 278, 281
MacDougall, Elspeth 100, 256
MacDougall, Judith 99, 126, 137, 161, 190, 209, 249, 258, 265, 268, 278, 281
Machado, Marcia 268
Machin, Barry 139, 204, 275
Mack, D. L. 243
Mackenzie, K. 96
Mackey, M. 85
MacNeill, Ian 108
MacNeish, R. 76
Macrae, J. 245
Madison, C. 129, 250
Madsen, W. 110
Magnarella, P. J. 177, 227, 256
Mahomo, N. 154

Maiga, D. 124
Mair, L. 225, 236
Major, J. S. 120
Majoros, Mike 208
Makepeace, Anne 140
Makoto, Satoh 159
Malinowski, Bronislaw 196
Maldror, S. 93
Malenotti, M. 230
Malle, Louis 113, 209
Malone, A. 44
Maloney, T. J. 83, 136
Mandel, Ruth 271
Mandell, Betty Reid 142
Mandell, Joan 111
Manefield, Tom 53, 254
Mangelsdorf, Paul 76
Mankofsky, I. 112
Mann, Charles 175
Mann, Judith 188
Mannino, Joseph A. 266
Mansfield, J. 199
Manthoulis, R. 27
Manzardo, A. 46, 251
Maranda, Pierre 155
Marcotte, Hean-Roch 236
Marcus, D. 42
Marcus, George 138, 164, 267
Marenco, Susan 28
Marker, Chris 230
Markham, Nigel 129, 153
Marks, A. E. 31, 36, 105, 129
Marks, Daniel 111
Marksman, Samori 116
Marler, Peter 47, 272
Marlowe, Frank 167
Marlowe, Leigh 131
Marquardt, W. H. 224
Marrant, J. 99
Marre, Jeremy 152, 222, 244
Marrone, L. 168
Marsden, B. 196
Marshall, E. G. 40, 109
Marshall, John 61, 108, 129, 131, 146, 159, 186, 210, 216, 228-30
Marshall, Lorna 230
Martin, Catherine 151
Martin, D. 193
Martin, E. 105
Martin-Jones, John 105, 206, 267
Martinex, Wilson 262
Martinez, Gaston 250
Marvin, M. C. 52
Marx, Sue 289
Mary-Rousseliere, Guy 46, 63, 104, 191, 282
Masayesva, Victor Jr 132, 141
Mason, J. 135
Masri, Mai 68
Materna, H. 112
Matheny, Ray T. 178
Mather, W. G. 152

Mathias, E. 46
Mathur, Vishnu 49, 120
Matias, Bienvenidas 122
Matulavich, Peter 214
Mauss, Marcel 125
Max, J. 257
Maybury-Lewis, David 43, 45, 92, 139, 154, 178, 179, 213, 236, 246, 256, 260
Maybury-Lewis, Pia 154
Mayer, Harold 138, 140
Mayer, Jim 148
Maysles, A. 226
Maysles, D. 226
Mazrui, Ali 188, 191
Mazur, Derek 212
McAfee, B. 283
McAllister, David J. 232
McBride, J. 115
McBride, M. 252
McCabe, J. Terence 265
McCarty, M. 270
McCrea, Graydon 247
McDermott, G. 35, 36, 43, 164
McDermott, K. 61, 88
McDonald, E.
McDuffie, M. 168
McGee, R. Jon 62, 151, 248
McGhee, Dorothy 278
McGilvray, Dennis B. 30
McGrath, Janet W. 31
McGree, F. 281
McGregor, F. C. 49
McIntyre, J. Donald 169
McKay, John 82
McKean, P. F. 49, 157
McKee, Lauris 37, 96
McKenzie, Kim 273
McKusick, Marshall 92, 107, 155, 178, 198, 214, 272
McLaren, Les 187, 256, 261
McLeod, Christopher 108, 264
McLeod, David 224
McLeod, M. D.
McLuhan, T. C. 234
McNatt, G. 178
McNaughton, P. R. 58, 89, 262
McNeill, I.
McTaggart, Kimberlee 151
Mead, Margaret 38, 49, 52, 67, 68, 72, 74, 97, 103, 125, 147,, 155, 168, 191, 264
Medicine, Bea 81, 221, 258, 283
Meeker, Michael 265
Meggitt, M. 274
Mehta, Ved 66
Meighan, C. W. 85, 90, 147, 213, 225
Meistrich, I. J. 53
Mellaart, James 64
Mellor, J. 166
Mendizza, Michael 170
Menger, Chris 264
Menges, C. 198
Menget, P. 90

Merbs, C. F. 231
Merchant, W. D. 209
Meredith, Burgess 60
Meredith, John D. 104, 215, 289
Mereghetti, Elisa 53
Merkin, Miguel 236
Merry, S. E. 89, 131, 179, 193, 209, 212
Messenger, J. 270
Messer, E. 222, 247, 282
Messerschmidt, D. A. 55, 124, 159, 236
Messing, Simon D. 55, 68, 191, 248
Metge, A. J. 69
Metke, L.
Metzgar, Eric 118
Metzger, Duane 40, 197
Meyer, Anthony 78
Meyer, Elizabeth 159
Meyer, John 224
Meyer, R. E. 163
Meyers, P. A. 57
Meurice, Jean-Michel 40
Miall, Tristram 63
Michael, Barbara J. 194
Michalak, L. 290
Michelsen, R. C. 149
Milanich, J. T. 41, 42
Miles, Christopher 161
Miles, K. 99
Milford, M. 142
Millan, V. 289
Millder, D.
Miller, Donald 107, 121, 240
Miller, Earl 115
Miller, G. B. 239
Miller, J.
Miller, J. C. 165
Miller, Jefferson 63
Miller, M. H. 54
Miller, N. 148
Miller, S. G. 231
Millet, K. 255
Milholland, D. 57
Milne, T. 71
Minh-ha, Trinh T. 187, 220, 237, 248
Minott, Berry 161
Mintz, Jerome 64, 208, 225, 235, 236
Mire, Pat 39, 80
Mishler, R. 45, 114, 161, 186, 248, 259
Mitchell, D. 41, 42
Mitchell, James R. 223
Mitchell, Wayne 48, 91
Mitchell, William E. 164, 260
Miyate, N. 236
Moberg, David 101
Mock, F. L. 191
Modisane, Bloke 74
Moerman, M. 107, 138
Moffatt, Tracey 192
Molenaar, Hillie 66, 82
Monk, K. 30
Monster, Ruud 56

People Index

Montanaro, Lucia 171
MontesdeGonzales, A. 198
Mook, M. A. 59, 65
Moon, B. 111
Moore, A. 233
Moore, Alexander 162, 214
Moore, Allen 57, 235
Moore, Andrew 78
Moore, C. 170
Moorman, R. B. 87, 227, 232, 252
Moran, Mary H. 277
Morar, N. 160
Morcom, S. 215
Morelli, G. 68
Morgan, H. 91
Morgan, Jenny 37
Morin, E. 71
Morphy, F. 163
Morphy, H. 163
Morrill, J. 96
Morris, Desmond 168
Morris, Don 41
Morris, D. Paul 89
Morse, R. A. 44
Morshoen, G. 121
Mortimore, G. E. 91
Mosely, M. E. 35
Moser, B. 154, 175, 207, 210
Moser, C. 207
Moses, Doreen 198, 270
Moss, Gary 167
Mossek, Catherine 180
Mossek, Nissim 180
Mountford, C. P. 274
Movius, H. L. 214
Moyers, Bill 145
Moyle, A. 116
Moynihan, Frank 126
Mudd, Victoria 60
Muecke, M. A. 32, 68, 126, 162, 205, 209
Muehlbauer, G. 78
Mueller, G. 247
Muhly, Frank, Jr. 262
Muir, B. 239
Muir, M. 239
Mulford, Marilyn 67
Mull, D. S. 34, 157
Mull, J. D. 34, 157
Muller, Kalman 128, 152
Mulloy, W. 92
Mulvihill, Ron 43, 235
Munn, N. D. 94, 274
Munoz, Susana 164, 196
Munro, N. G. 141
Munroe, Robert L. 168
Munroe, Ruth 168
Mununggurr, N. 163
Muras, J. 28
Murnau, F. W. 249
Murphy, Geoff 269
Murphy, Howard 88

Murphy, R. F. 33, 265
Murra, J. 45, 169
Murray, D. W. 165, 241
Murray, Don 268
Murray, Katherine 54, 201
Mursky, Liz 151
Musello, Chris 76
Mwampole, Rita Mudenda 75
Myerhoff, Barbara 133, 195
Myers, Fred 79, 88
Myers, Mark D. 262

Nkosi, Lewis
Nader, L. 159, 258
Nainda, S.
Nair, Mira 136, 228, 240
Nairn, C.
Namiley-Viana, Afua 175
Nance, John 65
Nanda, S. 84, 136, 180
Narasimhan, Sakuntala 38
Nash, June 130, 146, 162, 197
Nash, L. L. 35, 36
Nathan, J. 143
Naughton, Tom 43
Nava, Gregory 194
Nee-Owoo, Kwate 199, 289
Nelson, Hank 37
Nelson, J. 189
Nelson, K. 48
Nelson, Richard K. 165
Nelson, Stanley 267
Neukum, Catherine 59
Newcomb, W. W. 249
Newman, Joyce 257
Ng'oge, Nangayoma 43
Nichols, B. 108, 129
Nichols, E. T. 288
Nichols, Sandra 29, 108, 168
Nickerson, G. S. 27, 78, 137, 157, 222, 277
Nierenberg, George T. 193
Nietschmann, B. Q. 266
Nijland, Dirk 259
Nikolic, Z. 204
Niles, J. J. 145
Niles, Susan 135
Nimmo, A. H. 48, 207
Nisbett, A. 265
Nishihata, J. 257
Nissen, K. 225
Nitake, H. 269
Nitake, T. 269
Nivoix, George 157, 185
Nizan, Georges 144, 209
N'kosi, Lewis 74
Noel Hume, I. 89
Norbeck, E. 202, 231
Norton, S. 99
Noschese, Christine 175
Nowak, Amram 140
Noyes, Newbold 225

Noxon, J. 42
Nugent, David 72
Nunez, T. A. 62
Nunguia, Kumain 239
Nutini, H. G. 196
Nye, B. 289
Nye, J. 255
Nyro, Laura 60

O'Brien, Denise 193
O'Brien, Marie 132
O'Connell, P. J. 76
O'Conner, Geoffrey 45, 75
O'Meara, Patrick 159, 271
O'Neal, J. M. 50
O'Neill, Peter 205, 262
O'Rourke, Dennis 63, 120, 131, 235, 288, 289
O'Toole, P. 230
O'Toole, T. 46, 50, 89, 110, 168, 260, 267
Oaksen, H. D. 104
Obeyesekere, G. 147
Oblin, S. 35
Obomsawin, Alanis 182, 193, 223
Occhiuzzi, Donatella 204
Ochsner, David 92
Odden, Teresa 123
Odell, G. H. 92, 188, 243, 251
Ogan, E. 59
Ohl, David D. 59
Okada, B. 239
Okamoto, T. 126
Olatunji, B. 30
Oldenburg, P. 144
Olczyk, J. M. 147
Olin, Chuck 59
Oliver, D. 59
Olodort, Bob 75
Olshaker, Mark 217
Olson, J. 277
Olson, N. 277
Olsson, Stephen 122, 257
Omori, Yashuhiro 236
Onat, A. R. 85, 248
Oomen, Monique 30
Oppenheimer, J. 65
Oppitz, M.
Oppitz, Michael 235
Ortner, Sherry 236
Osborne, P. 267
Ostor, A. 139, 146, 162, 230, 233, 242
Ott, Sandra 52
Ottenberg, Simon 59, 97, 166
Otton, Malcolm 194
Ousseini, Inoussa
Oval, W.
Owen, Carmen H. 68
Owen, Chris 102, 113, 165, 167, 220, 256
Owen, Magdalena V.
Owen, Sigi S.
Owens, Raymond 183
Owusu, Kwesu 199

Ozawa, Toshiaki 59

Pachachi, M. 272
Padiglione, Vincenzo 204
Padula, F. 94
Paes, Cesar 37
Page, J. 166
Painter, T. A. 106, 149, 227
Palazallo, T. 223
Palewski, S. 142
Palmer, R. 60
Pandolfo, S. 60
Papson, S. 282
Parer, David 272
Paris, Bob 237
Parker, R. A. 35
Parkes, Peter 146
Parks, G. 85
Parry, David 167
Parsons, Bruce 265
Parsons, Jack 162
Partant, Francois 223
Pasini, Carlos 174, 218, 277
Pasler, Jann 249
Pastner, S. 51
Pataky, V. 275
Patrick, Brian 123
Patterson, G. James 198, 290
Paterson, J. D. 120, 140
Patterson, D. W. 59, 235
Patterson, L. 239
Patwardhan, Anand 135
Paul, R. A. 32, 153, 236
Paul, Anne 135
Pauley, Forrestine 160
Paullada, B. 269
Pawson, I. G. 112
Payne, John 196
Paynter, R. 199
Payrastre, G. 60 249, 270
Pearson, G. 199
Peaslee, John
Peck, Ann 168, 199
Peiser, J. 56, 115, 157, 179, 219
Penfound, Roger 177, 227
Penney, S. 64
Pereira, N. dos Santos 51, 127
Perieras, N.
Perlmutter, Alvin H. 188, 215
Perrault, P. 181, 220
Perrier, P. 109, 212, 257
Perrin, Michel 67
Perry, James 159, 271
Perry, T. S. 128
Peteet, J. 111, 129, 140, 197, 203
Peters, Brock 48
Peters, Heather 238, 239
Peters, Muriel 167
Peterson, J. H. 35, 77, 103
Peterson, N. 165
Peterson, Tom 216

People Index

Petit, Bernard 155
Petrequin, Anne Marie 153, 288
Petrequin, Pierre 153, 288
Petrokowitz, H. V. 28
Pettigrew, Bill 272
Pettigrew, Margaret 55
Pettys, Gregory 154
Pevar, Marc 31
Pfaff, G. 105, 155
Phenix, L. M. 284
Phillips, Guy 192
Phillips-Conroy, J. E. 156
Phillipsen, H. 116
Piault, Colette 67, 95, 102, 121, 157, 185, 226, 254
Pickering, Mimi 61, 145
Pierce, Christian 60
Pierce, Steffen 60
Pierson, J. C. 206
Pike, Andrew 37
Piker, S. 106
Pillay, S. A. 284
Pilling, A. R. 114, 140
Piraud, F. 35
Pitkin, Donald S. 127
Pitsuwan, S. 147
Plath, David W. 43, 63, 104, 142, 190
Platides, A. 254
Plicka, K. 290
Ploeg, Anton 193
Plunkett, H. S. 35
Pohl, J. 227
Poisey, David 245
Poling-Kempes, Lesley 94
Pollack, R. 47, 285
Pollard, G. C. 36, 208
Pollard, R. 91
Ponting, Herbert G. 193
Popov, Stole 79
Porter, Mark 118
Portillo, Lourdes 164, 196
Poschl, Rupert 271
Poschl, Ulrike 271
Post, Linda 88
Poten, Connie 75
Potter, Jack 290
Potter, Sulamith 290
Polunin, Ivan 164
Powell, H. A. 265
Power, R. 116
Powers, W. K. 196
Pradhan, Rajendra 192
Pratt, Christina Carver 132
Pratt, Chuck 40
Pratto, D. J. 57, 70, 246
Prebble, John 52
Prell, Riv-Ellen 31, 109, 184, 218, 224
Preloran, J. 41, 67, 71, 132, 163, 275, 290
Press, I. 92
Price, J.A. 78, 275
Prince, R. 279
Prins, Harald 27, 75, 125, 135, 188, 200, 226

Prutzman, Anne 70
Pudaite, John 109
Purcell, T. W. 154
Pyle, Barbara 247

Quillen, I. J. 172
Quimby, G. I. 132, 134
Quinn, A. 91, 221, 230

Rabin, A. I. 149
Rabinovitch, David 110
Rahm, B. L. 231
Raim, E. 213
Rainey, Daniel 33
Rajagopalan, R. 132
Ramanujan, Shanthi 175
Ramirez, Juan A. 164
Ramskou, T. 116
Rand, P. 87
Ranen, Aron 220
Rankin, Tom 80, 214
Raoul, Serge 148
Rappaport, Joanne 32, 117
Rasmussen, K. 279
Ravel, Jean 181
Raven, H. 175
Ravicz, R. 40
Rawson, Mary 110
Ray, N. 230
Ray, S. 40, 84, 87, 205, 284
Raymen, S. 163
Raymond, Robert 74, 167, 201
Raymont, Peter 44, 55, 106, 155, 164, 244, 257
Read, Tim 194
Reading, Greg 194
Reaven, Marci 122
Rebennack, Mac "Dr John" 34
Redekop, C. 34
Redfield, R.
Redford, R. 60
Redmond, Elsa 172
Reed, L. 148
Reed-Danahay, D. 56
Reich, Alice 73, 79, 175, 216, 278
Reichart, J. 117
Reichman, T. 127
Reid, B.
Reid, M. 228
Reid, William 115
Reiker, Martina 114
Reinis, J. R. 86
Reisen, A. H. 248
Reistra, J.
Reiter, Jackie 27, 253
Reiter, R. R. 58
Rens, Martin 212
Renshaw, Rosette 150
Reyman, J. E. 76, 275
Reyna, Diane 111
Reynolds, B. 284
Rhoades, L. M. 163

Riber, John 35
Riccio, Antonio 204
Richard, Alison 45
Richards, Bob 272
Richards, Cara 144
Richards, Russell 85
Richardson, Bill 40, 145
Richardson, Boyce 77, 105, 285
Richeport, Madeline 163
Riches, D. 95
Rick, J. W. 208
Riesenberg, S. 193, 213
Riddington, Robin 81, 221
Riestra, J. 233
Riffe, Jed 140
Riner, R. D. 234
Rines, Reed D. 80
Ringwald, Mark
Rinzler, R.
Rios, Humberto 250
Ritchie, Claire 216
Ritchie, James E. 69
Ritz, Lan Brooks 38
Rivers, William 95
Robbins, L. A. 106
Robe, Chief Yellow 238
Roberts, David 53, 152, 254, 268
Roberts, Pamela 75, 140
Roberts, Will 55, 175
Robertson, M. O. 216
Robertson, Philip 45
Robertson, Shari 277
Robinson, G. 95, 208
Robinson, Kevin 167
Robinson, P. 121
Robinson, Richard E. 117
Robinson, S. 239
Roche, A. F.
Rockefeller, M. 45, 171
Rockefeller, Terry 159
Rodgers, Susan 220
Rodriguez, Marta 60
Rodriquez, Sylvia 237
Roebuck, P. M.
Roffman, J. 37
Rogen, John 148
Rogers, Allen 198
Rogers, E. S. 91
Rogers, S. C. 155
Rogosin, Lionol 74, 284
Rohrl, V. J. 105, 132, 219
Rojas, Juan 130
Rolfe, David W. 238
Romano, Renee 219
Romer, John 36, 253
Ronsohoff, M. 281
Root, A. 51
Root, J. 51
Rosaldo, M. Z. 109
Roselini, Jim 86
Rosen, Lawrence 226

Rosen, R. T. 268
Rosenberg, B. A. 94
Rosenblum, L. A. 225
Rosow, Eugene 88, 225
Ross, Daniel R. 266
Ross, Eric 58
Ross, Gaylen 30
Ross, Tana 93
Rouch, Jean 27, 30, 31, 32, 33, 43, 47, 48, 50, 52, 61, 63, 66, 67, 71, 72, 73, 79, 82, 84, 89, 93, 94, 97, 100, 101, 102, 106, 110, 111, 112, 114, 116, 120, 125, 126, 132, 138, 140, 141, 143, 150, 158, 159, 163, 164, 165, 166, 173, 178, 180, 181, 185, 192, 203, 205, 209, 213, 217, 219, 221, 222, 225, 226, 227, 232, 237, 238, 242, 248, 250, 251, 260, 269, 270, 275, 288
Rouget, Gilbert 237
Rouquier, Georges 56, 100
Rowe, A. 195
Rowe, Thomas L. 214
Royce, A. P. 80, 161, 170
Rubach, Claire 178
Rubbo, Michael 79, 279
Rubenstein, John 247
Rubin, D. R. 109
Ruby, Jay 66, 76, 85, 100, 108, 192, 194, 205
Ruhl, D. 41, 42
Rumbaugh, D. M. 248
Rundstrom, D. 204, 269
Rundstrom, R. 204
Rundstrom, S. 269
Rusco, M. 281
Russman, E. R. 214
Ruth, John L. 34, 130, 218
Rutledge, Anne 276
Rutter, J. B. 134, 166

Saad, Z. 35
Sabloff, J. A. 162, 171, 233, 246
Sachs, Lynne 233
Sackett, J. R. 107, 214
Sacks, Karen Brodkin 104, 228
Safa, H. I. 89
Safford, Kimberly 123
Safizadeh, Fereydoun 234
Sage, J. D. 36
Sahiner, Ara 174
Sainte-Marie, Buffy 60
Sakuma, Koichi 190
Saler, B. 275
Sallnow, Michael 218
Saltman, Carlyn 58, 150
Salvo, Calogero 146
Salwen, B. 103
Salzman, Laurence 265
Samper, G. 156
Sandall, Roger 62, 71, 74, 165, 210, 261, 274, 290
Sanders, T. 191
Sanders, William T. 152, 201
Sandlin, Martha 152
Sandrin, Patrick 122
Sands, Dave 102

People Index

Sandy, David 252
Sanger, David 186
Sanjines, J. 57
Sanjurjo, A. 187
Santa Maria, Alejo 76, 118, 272, 276
Santana, Al 272
Santino, J. 175
Santos, Juma 43
Saperstein, Alan 171
Sapir, J. D. 93, 221, 251
Sarkar, F. R. 67
Sarkis, Sami 171
Sarno, Geraldo 106, 130
Sassi, Lisa 192
Saunders, P. 127
Sauts, William
Sauvageot, Claude 282
Sawchuck, Joe 107, 223
Sayers, R.
Schaefer, J. 41
Schaefer, P. D. 180
Schaeffer, S. B. 278
Schaller, G. 182
Schambach, F. F. 42
Schechner, Richard 113, 208, 261
Schechter, J. M. 43, 138, 146, 187
Schecter, S. 271
Scheflen, A. E. 75
Schefold, R. 228
Schenna, L.
Scherer, J. C. 174, 209
Schevill, M. 71, 278
Schiano, J. F. 90, 124, 142
Schieffelin, B. B. 256
Schieffelin, E. L. 256
Schilkrout, E. 244
Schlenker, Herman 28, 137, 182, 202
Schlesier, E. 175
Schlitz, M. J. 164, 216
Schlomer, Mike 114
Schlorndoff, Volker 109
Schmeichler, Dennis 146
Schmidt, Chris 235
Schmidt, Judith 281
Schmidt, Nancy 242, 276
Schmidt, Peter 52, 262
Schneider, Harold 77
Schneider, Ken 120
Schoedsack, Ernest B. 66, 114
Schroeder, S. C. 72, 203
Schuessler, Sue 192
Schultes, R. E. 79
Schultz, F. 190
Schultz, Jerry 67, 218
Schultz, Victoria 110, 283
Schwartz, D. W. 133, 223
Schwartz, J. H. 199
Schwartz, Mark 178
Schweizer, U. 147
Schwimmer, E. 69
Schyberg, Robert 63, 161

Scorsese, Martin 33
Scott, J.
Scott, Mary 282
Scott, Michael 239
Scott, S. 121
Scott, V. 168
Seaman, G. 70, 195
Searchlinger, G. 79
See, M. 128
Seeger, D. 30
Seeger, P. 30, 38, 76, 91, 106, 132, 140, 173, 184, 239, 250
Seeger, T. 30, 38, 76, 91, 106, 132, 140, 173, 184, 239, 250
Segal, Daniel 79
Segal, E.
Segal, M.
Sekiguchi, Noriko 280
Selassic, T. B. 184
Selver, V. 284
Sembene, O. 56, 93, 167, 251, 285
Semmens, Frank 180
Sensiper, Sylvia 102
Serling, R. 133
Seronde, A. 164, 230, 279
Seton, M. 257
Seymour, S. 62
Shack, W. 151, 177
Shafer, D. 46, 50, 89, 110, 168, 260, 267
Shahrani, Nazif 149, 196
Shain, Paul 100
Shankar, R. 40, 205, 284
Shankman, P. 33, 75, 120
Shannon, K. 158, 162
Sharon, D. 92
Shaw, John 208
Shea, Jack 235
Shedd, Graham 66
Sheehan, K. 111, 164
Sheen, Martin 60, 62
Sheets, P. D. 91, 165, 171
Shepherd, Sue 214
Sheppard, Chris 195, 282
Sheppard, John 228
Sheppard, M. 67
Sher, Abby 91
Sherman, S. 147, 250
Sherzer, J. 244
Shimada, Izumi 161
Shinagawa, Earnest 208
Shinnamon, F. 29 283
Shipley, Leigh 63
Shivas, M. 71
Shore, Bradd 155
Short, Marjorie 150
Shumay, E. B. 216
Sieg, E. C. 127
Siegel, M. 101
Siegel, Taggart 55, 58, 121
Sigel, Thomas 280
Silva, Jorge 60
Silva, M. C. D. 186
Silver, Tony 247

Silverman, M. 77
Silverstein, E. 166
Silverstein, Karen 111
Silverstein, S. B. 32, 125, 242, 257
Silverwood-Cope, Peter, 275
Simmons, Elwyn L. 88
Simmons, Katina 73
Simon, Andrea 140
Simonds, P. E. 181
Simons, R. C. 105, 153, 155, 156, 237
Singer, Andre 28, 113, 149, 151, 162, 177
Singer, Philip 88, 124, 216, 261, 276
Singleton, J. A. 54
Sinha, S. 50
Sisson, E. B. 167
Skreija, A. 241
Sloan, M.
Slobin, M. 290
Slone, Anthony 195, 248
Slyomovics, Susan 279
Small, M. F. 78, 180
Smeltzer, David 162
Smith, Arthur L. 73, 231
Smith, Clyde 33, 249
Smith, David M. 228
Smith, F. H. 178
Smith, H. D. 131
Smith, Henry 158
Smith, Herb E. 40, 120, 246
Smith, Hubert 47, 66, 100, 112, 159, 183, 244
Smith, Huston 136, 221
Smith, Joyce 203, 281
Smith, M. E. 142
Smith, P. E. L. 64
Smith, Roger C. 262
Smith, R. H. 41
Smith, V. L. 255
Smuts, B. 54, 222, 240
Snodgrass, Roger 72
Snoy, P. 28
Snyder, Allegra Fuller 170
Snygg, Fran 80, 161, 170
Sodersten, Mikael 104
Soehring, Anna 260
Sofaer, A. 248
Sokolovsky, J. 249
Solas, H. 162
Solberg, H.
Solberg-Ladd, Helena 89, 93, 125, 238
Solt, Andrew 88
Sopanen, J. 114
Soren, David 64, 232
Sorenson, E. R. 148
Sorotor, M. 87
South, Stanley 33
Southwick, C. H. 222
Sovine, Melanie L. 87, 110, 118, 119, 125, 191, 192, 195, 219, 243, 244, 260
Spain, David H. 159, 271
Spaleny, Eugen 161
Spaleny, Ludmila 161

Spaleny, Zeman 161
Spector, Johanna 27, 73, 228, 235, 267
Speed, Francis 112, 242, 247, 279
Speiser, Ellen 226
Spence, D. K. 226
Spencer, P. 170
Spencer, Sir Walter Baldwin 101
Sperry, E. 271
Sperschneider, Werner 194
Speth, J. 47
Spicer, E. 288
Spieghel, M. H. 186
Spiller, Guy 94
Spitzer, N. 191
Spodek, Howard 30
Sporn, M. 135
Spotted Eagle, Chris 200
Spranger, H. 49
Spring, D. C. 78
Spry-Leverton, Peter 156, 165
Squier, E. L. 250
Srinivasan, D. 124
Ssennyonga, J. 168
Staal, F. 32
Stack, C. B. 211
Stafford, P. 28
Standing, H. 125, 207
Stanner, W. H. E. 274
Stanton, M. E. 69
Stanton, T. 42
Stapp, Philip 102
Starbird, Robert 33
Starr, E. E. 125
Starr, June 28
Stasz, C. 33, 226
Steady, F. 100
Stearman, A. M. 194, 203
Stearns, E. 254
Stearns, M. L. 254
Stech, Tamara 171
Stechniji, S. 176
Steers, Stacey 276
Stein, Carol 60
Steinberg, A. 52, 139
Steinberg, Neil 191
Steinhoff, H. 124
Stenger, Katherine
Stephanides, Stephanos 119
Stephen, Lynn 172
Stern, Peggy 49
Sterner, Judy 269
Sterud, E. L. 53, 107, 246
Stevens, Geoff 237
Stevenson, Robert L. 262
Steward, David 126
Stewart, J. R. 130
Stewart, Michael 27
Stiles, Robert 31, 121
Stirling, Paul 227
Stocking, G. W. 234, 262
Stoller, M. L. 162

People Index

Stoller, P. 58
Stone, Diana 171
Stone, J.
Stone, J. G. 149
Stone, L. Joseph 149
Stone, Linda 108, 109, 168, 235, 256
Stone, Robert 218
Stoner, Barry 69
Stoney, George C. 32, 127, 183
Stothert, K. E. 208
Stott, M. 248
Strachwitz, C. 71
Strand, Chick 38, 182, 183
Strasburg, I. 168
Strathern, Andrew 148, 198
Strauch, J. 98
Strecker, I. 155, 225
Streeten, Patricia 74
Streuver, S. 246
Stross, B. 213
Strothman, Randy 197
Strouth, P. 35
Struhsaker, Thomas T. 45, 53
Stull, Donald 31, 190, 216, 222
Su, Lian-yuan 109
Suarez-Orozco, M. M. 175
Sucher, Joel 109
Sucksdorff, A. 106
Summer, Sally 64
Sun, Shirley 54, 72, 285
Surgue, Bernard 88
Sutton, C. R. 244, 248
Sutton, P. 99
Sutton, S. B. 115
Swanson, E. H. 31, 36, 105, 129, 234
Sweeney, Skip 116
Sweet, L. A. 49
Swerhone, Elise 147
Swernemann, J. 170
Swibold, Susanne 34, 209
Swidler, N. 91, 126
Swift, L. 184
Switkes, Glenn 108
Sykes, Peter 231
Szwed, J. F.

Tahimik, Kidlat 208, 266
Tajima, Renee 281
Tamai, Isao 238
Tannenbaum, F. 32
Tanner, A. 78
Tanner, G. 125
Tanner, J. M. 117
Tani, Yoko 230
Tapakan, J.
Tappen, N. 181
Tarzan 116
Taub, Harriet 242
Taussig, M. 63
Tavakokian, B. 242
Taylor, Bobby 219

Taylor, D. 145
Taylor, John 139
Taylor, L. 132
Taylor, Meg 185
Taylor, Michael 34
Taylor, Ron 119
Tegnell, Ann 100
Teiwes, H. 240
Teleki, Geza 112
Tentchoff, D. 243, 285
Terrace, H. S. 104
Terrell, J. 97
Teuscher, Philip Thorneycroft 154
Theisen, George 132
Thery, Bruno 153, 288
Thieme, D. L. 90
Thieme, M. S. 90
Thigpen, Kenneth 228
Thomas, Anna 194
Thomas, D. H. 111
Thomas, E. M. 51
Thomas, Selma 136
Thomas, Steve 57
Thomas, Walter 72
Thompson, David 40, 108
Thompson, F. 32
Thompson, J. E. S. 162
Thompson, Homer 115
Thompson, R. F. 244
Thompson, Virgil 224
Thorbahn, Peter 74
Thurman, M. D. 87
Tillam, Chris 210
Timreck, Ted 186
Tindale, N. B. 84
Tirado, Wolf 253
Titon, Jeff 56, 214
Tobias, Michael 30
Tobias, P. 232, 259
Todd, I. A. 53
Todd, Loretta 155
Todd, Susan 68, 161, 243
Tomkins, R. C. 140
Tongue, Nancy 233
Tonkinson, R. 84
Tooker, E. 72
Toomey, B.
Toro, Alonso 186
Tortora, V. R. 121, 235
Toth, A. 42
Tourtelot, M. 35, 251, 289
Toyotomi, Y. 288
Trac, Le
Tracey, A. 81, 172, 173, 192
Tracey, H. 71, 290
Traylor-Smith, Richard 82
Trend, M. 275
Trent, Roger B. 73
Trevino, J. S. 289
Tringham, R. E. 77, 195, 214
Tristram, D. 54, 109, 130, 252

Troeller, Gordon 74, 223
Tronick, E. Z. 68
Trotter, R. T. 217
Trousdale, W. 29, 246
Truffaut, Francois 282
Tsang, Lori 70
Tsien, Jean 221
Tsosie, M. 189
Tucker, G. C. 66, 220
Tucker, R. 160
Tufano, B. 215
Turnbaugh, S. P. 180, 200
Turnbaugh, W. A. 92, 178, 180, 198, 200
Turnbull, C. 50
Turner, Joan 122, 248
Turner, L. 139
Turner, Terry 148, 264
Turton, A. 175
Turton, David 151, 177, 184
Tuttle, R. H. 155, 165
Twine, F. W. 146
Twitchell, Steve 232
Tyson, Thom 60

Ufland, Harry
Urban, Greg 83
Urbaniak, Urszula 257
Uricchio, William 76
Urrusti, Juan Francis 61
Ushiyama, J. 288
Uys, Jamie 113

Valadez, Senon 164
Valcour, Nicolas 43
Valdez, Luis 256
Valentine, W. 222
Van Beek, G. W. 35
van den Berg, Rudolf 31
Van der Ryn, Micah 67
Van Elderen, B. 41
Van Keuren, Frances 116
van Lawick, Hugo 272
van Lawick-Goodall, Jane
Van Thuy, Tran 127
Van Tilburg, Jo Anne 36, 92, 225
van Wijk, Joop 66, 82
VanArsdale, P. 44
VanBeek, G. W.
VanDyke, W. 222, 281
VanMiddlesworth, C.
van Rouveroy van Nieuwaal, Els 38
van Rouveroy van Nieuwaal, Emile 38, 39, 185
VanStone, J. W. 255
VanVlack, J. D. 176
Varney, W. 112
Vatuk, S. 184, 218
Vaughn, D. 135
Velazquez, Elaine 183
Venaki, Electra 67
Vennum, Thomas 90, 265
Ver Eecke, C. 282

Veuve, J. 71
Viallon, C. 60, 249, 270
Viana, Z. 153
Vidal, P. 111
Vigesaa, Kathryn Lipke 82
Vigel, J. D. 268
Villiers, F. 222
Vitebsky, Piers 237
Vitelli, K. D. 199
Vlasak, Rhonda 94
Vleeshouwers, Nac 56
Vogt, Evon Z. 237
Volkman, T. A. 73, 113, 149, 156, 158
VonFurer-Haimendorff, E. 198
VonSturmer, J. 162, 242
VonWetter, A. 262
Vorenberg, J.
Vouras, Mary 115
Voytek, B. 234
Vuijst, Freke 92

Wachs, E. 195
Wachs, J. 78
Wagner, M. B. 59
Wagner, Paul 121, 175, 178, 245
Wagner, R. 44, 165
Wagner, Thomas 36
Wahlgren, Anders 246
Wailes, B. 198, 270
Waldrum, Harold Joe 209
Walens, S. G. 151
Walker, Giles 79
Walker, Paul A. 284
Walker, P. L. 231
Walker, Sheila 48
Walker-Ewald, Joanne 38
Wallace, Melanie 277
Wallace, Thomas J. 59
Walthall, J. A. 162
Ward, B. E. 228, 231
Ward, J. 240, 266
Ware, K.
Warfield, W. 289
Warner, H. S. 130
Warner, W. Lloyd 88
Warning, R. 38
Warren, Adrian 194
Warren, D. Michael 59
Warren, J. F. 146
Washburn, S. L. 47, 48
Waters, Katrina 109, 133, 145
Watkins, P. 52
Watson, J. B. 83
Watson, O. M. 243
Waugh, E. P. 226
Wax, M. 96
Wax, R. 96
Weaver, D. S. 165
Webb, C. H. 41
Weber, Thomas 122
Webster, David L. 201

People Index

Weidlich, Lorre 122
Weihnacht, Doug 161
Weil, C. 146
Weiner, Annette B. 265
Weir, J. M. 162
Weiss, B. 240, 266
Weiss, Harvey 226
Weissman, J. 78
Welles, O. 93, 233
Wells, Peter S. 41
Wembah-Rashid, J. A. R. 139
Wendt, Albert 228
Wenke, Robert 156
Weng, Wan-go 61, 69
Wera, Francoise 281
Werner, Lou 272
Werner, O. 190
Wescott, Margaret 54
Westphal, David 236
Wetter, Walter 74
Whalley, J. 87
Wheat, Margaret 265
Wheaton, Sharon 142
Wheeler, D. 213
Wheeler, W. 170, 231
Whelehan, Patricia 27, 151
White, F. 80
White, J. K. 186
White, J. P. 47
White, Marian 135
White, Pamela 64
White, Steven 111
Whitebull, J.
Whitehead, R. G. 151
Whitehouse, R. H. 117
Whitehouse, Steve 83
Whiteman, D. 272
Whiting, B. B. 57, 97
Whitman, A. 234
Whitney, Laura Scheerer 100, 126
Whitters, N. A. 64
Wiant, M. D. 41
Wickett, Elizabeth 107
Wiener, Paul B. 33
Wieske, Richard 21
Wilcken, L. E. 120
Wilcox, D. 214, 245
Wilcox, S. 245
Wild, S. 153
Wilets, Bernard 87
Wilk, Barbara 93, 157
Wilkinson, Douglas 46, 63, 104, 127, 282
Willey, G. R. 257
Williams, B. J. 168
Williams, C. 141
Williams, J. 141
Williams, Rob 118
Willson, Margaret 167
Wilmsen, E. N. 57
Wilson, C. 169
Wilson, Carter 40

Wilson, H. 231
Wilson, Ian 238
Wilson, J. 35, 54, 109, 130, 252
Wilson, Margaret 138
Wilson, Rob 216
Wilson, Sandy 218
Wilson, Tim 219
Winer, Lucy 219
Winkelman, Michael 145, 221
Winn, S. 68
Winograd, P. 180
Wiseman, Frederick 126, 215, 290
Wiseman, J. R. 37
Wittenberg, Susan 60
Wolf, A. P. 98
Wolf, E. R. 92, 240, 286
Wolf, L.
Wolf, M. 98
Wolfe, L. 225
Wolff, P.
Wolman, D. 228
Wolpoff, M. H. 125
Wonderly, Sam 263
Wong, A. M. 230
Wood, Michael 134, 156
Wood, R. 40
Wood, Sharon 149
Woodburn, J. 119
Woodbury, N. F. S. 113
Woodbury, R. B. 113
Woodhead, Leslie 52
Woodson, D. G. 259
Woodward, Stan 116, 141
Worswick, C. 67
Worth, S. 189, 289
Wozniak, J. S. 188, 215, 244
Wright, Anabel Olivier 262
Wright, B. 241, 276
Wright, Jack 27, 248
Wright, Julie Pritchard 260
Wu, Charlie 109
Wurzburg, Gerardine 278
Wyckoff, D. G. 42
Wylie, L. 100, 112, 155
Wylie, Jeanie 212
Wylie, Tom 139

Yanagita, K. 44
Yang, Doua 205
Yao, Wynette 109
Yasui, Lise 100
Yates, Pamela 280
Ybarrola, S. 52, 95
Yengoyan, A. A. 289
Yorke, M. 87, 124, 207
Yorke, V. 124, 207
Young, Andrew 68, 78, 180, 243
Young, J. A. 154, 163
Young, Robert 68, 191
Young, William C. 272
Yu, Chung-fang 150

Yule, Paul 170, 200
Yung-Li, Sue
Yunkaporta, F. 249
Yussi, D. 95

Zaccheo, Michele 224
Zalkowitsch, Harry 142
Zamacona, Frank 122
Zammarano, Amedeo T. 36
Zannis, Mark 236
Zantzinger, Gei 81, 172, 173, 192, 242
Zavin, D. 93
Zebba, S. 102

Zeitlin, S. 121, 125, 175
Zeller, Anne 125
Zhene, Kur 238
Zhuang, K-S. 89
Zickafoose, B. 40, 72, 145
Zika, Damoure 165
Zimmer, Hans 43, 45, 92, 139, 178, 179, 213, 236, 246, 256, 260
Zimmerman, L. J. 91
Ziv, Ilan 129
Zwerin, C. 226
Zwickler, Phil 223

What is the Society for Visual Anthropology?

The Society for Visual Anthropology (SVA), a constituent section of the American Anthropological Association, aims to foster and support a broad range of approaches to visual symbols, phenomena, and media in anthropological research, teaching, theory, methodology, and practice. The SVA encourages the use of visual means of description and analysis to study and interpret human or humanly relevant signification, perception, behavior, interaction, and communication in context, including such topics as:

the analysis of visual symbolic forms;
visual theories;
relationships among different channels and modes of communication;
the visible expression (or construction) of emotion;
proxemic and other analysis of space, place, and territory;
kinesic and other systematic study of body motion communication, gesture, or dance;
the structuring of reality as denoted by visual productions and artifacts;
the study of art, artifacts, or performance from social, cultural, historical, folkloristic, semiotic, or aesthetic points of view;
forms of social organization involved in planning, producing, and using visual signs and systems of signs;
writing systems and other visible forms of language;
visual signs interrelated with speech or verbal art;
visual approaches to the ethology of human and other life forms;
a variety of kinds of visual research in archaeology;
visual analyses and methods in the professional practice of anthropology;
the use of media in cultural feedback;
visual means of communication in classrooms, museums, and between anthropology and the public generally;
the anthropological study, production, and use of film, photography, or video.

Society for Visual Anthropology
American Anthropological Association

New Member/Subscriber Enrollment Form
(Existing membership/subscriptions may not be renewed on this form.)

____ I wish to enroll as a new member of the SVA and the AAA. My payment of $100 (____ $60 if a student) is enclosed.[1]

____ I am currently an AAA member and wish to enroll in the SVA, too. My payment of $25 (____ $15 if a student) is enclosed.[2] I understand that my new SVA membership will be up for renewal at the same time as my current AAA membership.

____ I wish to purchase a subscription only (without membership) to the *Visual Anthropology Review,* for $25 per volume, beginning with the current volume.

[1]Dues include subscriptions to the *Anthropology Newsletter* and the *Visual Anthropology Review*.
[2]Dues include a subscription to the *Visual Anthropology Review*.

Name _____

Address _____

_____

_____

Affiliation, if not shown on address _____

VISA/MasterCard   (circle one)   Expiration date_____

Card # _____

Send this form (or a photocopy), with payment (check, money order, or credit card number), to:

American Anthropological Association
4350 North Fairfax Drive, Suite 640
Arlington, VA 22203-1621

Anthropologists at Work:
Careers Making a Difference

This 36-minute VHS color video depicts anthropological careers in all four subfields, focusing on the skills required and the rewards associated with those careers.

The video captures anthropologists working at home and abroad in diverse settings: from government and human services to manufacturing; conducting research; implementing policy; teaching and providing expertise in the areas of health, development, education and the corporate world.

"[Anthropologists at Work] . . . is a remarkable and engaging product. . . . The video should appeal widely—to anthropology departments, college and university career guidance and placement centers, high school students, staff and advising centers, as well as to potential employers of anthropologists."
[from a review in the *WAPA Newsletter* by Willis E. Sibley]

Anthropologists at Work: Careers Making a Difference is now available for purchase:

$25 (students, NAPA members)
$30 (professionals, non-NAPA members)
$35 (organizations, institutions)

Please make checks payable to the American Anthropological Association and send to

**American Anthropological Association
Careers Video
4350 North Fairfax Drive, Suite 640
Arlington, VA 22203-1621
703/528-1902 ext 3032**